CLINICAL HANDBOOK
OF PSYCHOLOGICAL DISORDERS

Clinical Handbook of Psychological Disorders
A Step-by-Step Treatment Manual
SECOND EDITION

Edited by
David H. Barlow
State University of New York at Albany

THE GUILFORD PRESS
New York   London

For Beverly A. Barlow

Last digit is print number: 9 8 7 6

Library of Congress Cataloging-in-Publication Data

Clinical handbook of psychological disorders : a step-by-step
    treatment manual / David H. Barlow, editor. — 2nd ed.
        p.   cm.
    Includes bibliographical references and index.
    ISBN 0-89862-129-1
    1. Behavior therapy.   I. Barlow, David H.
    [DNLM: 1. Mental Disorders—therapy.   2. Behavior Therapy.
  3. Psychotherapy.   WM 420 C6415 1993]
  RC489.B4C584   1993
  616.89'1—dc20
  DNLM/DLC
  for Library of Congress   93-849
                                                              CIP

CONTRIBUTORS

DAVID H. BARLOW, PhD, Department of Psychology, State University of New York at Albany

AARON T. BECK, MD, Center for Cognitive Therapy, University of Pennsylvania, Philadelphia

TIMOTHY A. BROWN, PsyD, Center for Stress and Anxiety Disorders, State University of New York at Albany

KELLY D. BROWNELL, PhD, Department of Psychology, Yale University, New Haven, CT

KAREN S. CALHOUN, PhD, Department of Psychology, University of Georgia, Athens

MICHAEL P. CAREY, PhD, Department of Psychology, Syracuse University, Syracuse, NY

JAMES V. CORDOVA, MS, Department of Psychology, University of Washington, Seattle

MICHELLE G. CRASKE, PhD, Department of Psychology, University of California, Los Angeles

EDNA B. FOA, PhD, Department of Psychiatry, Medical College of Pennsylvania/Eastern Pennsylvania Psychiatric Institute, Philadelphia

RICHARD G. HEIMBERG, PhD, Department of Psychology, State University of New York at Albany

DEBRA A. HOPE, PhD, Department of Psychology, University of Nebraska, Lincoln

NEIL S. JACOBSON, PhD, Department of Psychology, University of Washington, Seattle

CONSTANCE A. KEHRER, MS, Department of Psychology, University of Washington, Seattle

MARSHA M. LINEHAN, PhD, Department of Psychology, University of Washington, Seattle

BARBARA S. McCRADY, PhD, Center of Alcohol Studies, Rutgers University, Piscataway, NJ

ANDREW W. MEISLER, PhD, Department of Psychology, Yale University, New Haven, CT

TRACY A. O'LEARY, BA, Center for Stress and Anxiety Disorders, State University of New York at Albany

PATRICK MAHLEN O'NEIL, PhD, Department of Psychiatry and Behavioral Sciences, Medical University of South Carolina, Charleston

KATHLEEN M. PIKE, PhD, Department of Psychiatry, Columbia University, New York

PATRICIA A. RESICK, PhD, Department of Psychology, University of Missouri, St. Louis

DAVID S. RIGGS, PhD, Department of Psychiatry, Medical College of Pennsylvania/Eastern Pennsylvania Psychiatric Institute, Philadelphia

ARTHUR WEINBERGER, PhD, Wall Street Center for Cognitive Therapy, New York

G. TERENCE WILSON, PhD, Department of Clinical Psychology, Rutgers University, Piscataway, NJ

JOHN P. WINCZE, PhD, Department of Psychiatry and Human Behavior and Department of Psychology, Brown University, Providence, RI

JEFFREY E. YOUNG, PhD, Department of Psychiatry, Columbia University, New York

PREFACE

The second edition of this book continues to represent a distinct departure from any number of similar books reviewing advances in the treatment of psychological disorders. Increasingly, during the decade of the 1980s and continuing into the 1990s, we have developed a technology of behavior change that necessarily differs from disorder to disorder. This technology consists of a variety of techniques or procedures with more or less proven effectiveness for a given disorder. Naturally, we have more evidence of the effectiveness of these treatments for some disorders than for others. It has also become more apparent since the first edition of this book that considerable clinical skill is required to apply this technology most effectively. Therefore, this book, in its second edition, is *not* another review of therapeutic procedures for a given problem with recommendations for further research. Rather, it is a detailed description of actual treatment protocols in which experienced clinicians implement the technology of behavior change in the context of the 12 most frequently encountered disorders.

New to this edition of the book, and reflecting major developments in the past several years, are five original treatment protocols. Chapter 10 on borderline personality disorder, by Marsha M. Linehan and Constance A. Kehrer, illustrates the first approach with proven effectiveness for this extremely difficult condition. Also new are important and exciting chapters on effective treatments for social phobia by Debra A. Hope and Richard G. Heimberg (see Chapter 3); post-traumatic stress disorder for rape victims by Karen S. Calhoun and Patricia A. Resick (see Chapter 2); eating disorders,

including anorexia, bulimia, and binge eating disorders, by G. Terence Wilson and Kathleen M. Pike (see Chapter 7); and a new protocol for generalized anxiety disorder developed at our Center for Stress and Anxiety Disorders in Albany (see Chapter 4). Other chapters in this book have undergone substantial revision, reflecting the most up-to-date developments in established treatment protocols for major problems. These include greatly revised or almost totally new protocols for panic disorder with agoraphobia, depression, obesity, alcoholism, and sexual dysfunction. The chapter on couple distress by James V. Cordova and Neil S. Jacobson (see Chapter 12) represents a radically different approach both conceptually and practically from the corresponding chapter in the first edition of this book.

As with the first edition, this book was motivated by countless clinical psychology graduate students, psychiatric residents, and other mental health professionals either in training or in practice asking, "But how do I do it?" Realizing that there is no single source in which to find step-by-step treatment protocols for use as a guide to practice, this book attempts to fill the void. To accomplish this purpose a number of specific topics are common to most chapters. Each chapter begins with a brief review of our knowledge of the specific disorder, followed by a description of the particular model or mini-theory that guides the technology utilized with the disorder in question. This model, or mini-theory, typically answers the question: What particular facets of the disorder should be assessed and treated? While clinical application always dilutes theoretical models, clinicians will recognize behavioral and systems approaches with some psychodynamic contributions as the predominant theoretical context.

This model is followed by a description of the typical setting in which the treatment is carried out. The setting varies from disorder to disorder, ranging from the more usual office setting to the home environment of the patient. Similar detailed descriptions of the social context of treatment (e.g., the importance of the involvement of family or friends) as well as therapist and client variables that are important within the context of the particular problem are discussed. For example, therapist variables that may be important in implementing techniques for treatment of agoraphobia or couple distress are described. In addition, the implications for treatment of client variables such as dependency and unassertiveness in many agoraphobics are discussed.

A detailed description of the actual step-by-step process of assessment and treatment follows, liberally sprinkled, in many chapters, with transcripts of therapy sessions. Important components of this process are the specifics of the rationale given the pa-

tient before treatment as well as typical problems that arise during the implementation of the technology. Where data exist, information on clinical predictors of success or failure are provided.

In accomplishing the rather ambitious goals described above, I was very fortunate in this edition of the book, as in the last edition, to have leading clinicians and researchers document in some detail how they actually treat their patients. Once again, these authorities reported that the number of details they had to include in order to convey how they actually applied their treatment programs went far beyond their expectations. My hope is that practicing clinicians and clinical students everywhere will benefit from acquaintance with these details.

My deep appreciation to Mary Ann Beals, my administrative assistant, who virtually produced this second edition from beginning to end, and to Marion Schwartz, Amy Bach, Katie Ingman, and Risa Weisberg for compiling a useful index to this book.

David H. Barlow
Nantucket Island

CONTENTS

Chapter 1

PANIC DISORDER AND AGORAPHOBIA

Michelle G. Craske
University of California, Los Angeles
David H. Barlow
State University of New York at Albany

The treatment protocol described in this chapter represents a substantial advance over the treatment protocol for agoraphobia described in the first edition of this book. In the short space of 8 years, psychological approaches to panic disorder with or without agoraphobia have changed dramatically. That these treatments are successful was recently documented in a consensus conference sponsored by the National Institute of Mental Health, where this treatment, along with certain specific drugs, was recommended as the treatment of choice for panic disorder. In this chapter we present the latest version of this treatment protocol developed at our clinic. This protocol unifies new developments in our approach to panic attacks and, for the first time, fully integrates our protocol for panic disorder with our treatment approach to agoraphobic avoidance.—D. H. B.

INTRODUCTION

Major advances have occurred in the conceptualization and treatment of panic disorder (PD) and agoraphobia since the last edition of the book. In brief, PD is now conceptualized as a learned fearfulness of certain bodily sensations associated with panic attacks, and agoraphobia as a behavioral response to the anticipation of such bodily sensations or their crescendo into a full-blown panic attack. Consequently, newer psychosocial treatment techniques target panic attacks directly by addressing fearfulness of bodily sensations and are presumed to affect change by altering cognitive and associative processes. Traditional *in vivo* exposure is still required to address agoraphobic avoidance. This chapter covers the theoretical developments, treatment outcome data, and treatment methods.

Phenomena of Panic and Agoraphobia

Panic attacks are discrete episodes of intense dread or fear, accompanied by physical and cognitive symptoms, as identified in the panic attack criteria of the fourth edition of the *Diagnostic and Statistical Manual of Mental Disorders* (DSM-IV; American Psychiatric Association [APA], 1993)* (see Table 1.1).

The panic attack is discrete by virtue of its suddenness or abruptness, as opposed to gradually building anxious arousal. Sometimes, the discrete episodes occur unexpectedly. The concept of "unexpectedness" re-

*The DSM-IV criteria cited in this chapter are those that were approved as final by the DSM-IV Anxiety Disorders Work Group and the Task Force on DSM-IV (APA, 1993). These criteria may be subject to minor editorial revisions before the publication of DSM-IV.

TABLE 1.1. Proposed DSM-IV Criteria for Panic Attacks

Panic Attack

A discrete period of intense fear or discomfort, in which at least four of the following symptoms developed abruptly and reached a peak within 10 minutes.

(1) palpitations, pounding heart, or accelerated heart rate

(2) sweating

(3) trembling or shaking

(4) sensations of shortness of breath or smothering

(5) feeling of choking

(6) chest pain or discomfort

(7) nausea or abdominal distress

(8) feeling dizzy, unsteady, lightheaded, or faint

(9) derealization (feelings of unreality) or depersonalization (being detached from oneself)

(10) fear of losing control or going crazy

(11) fear of dying

(12) paresthesias (numbness or tingling sensations)

(13) chills or hot flushes

Panic attacks can occur in a variety of Anxiety Disorders (e.g., Panic Disorder, Social Phobia, Simple Phobia, Post-traumatic Stress Disorder). In determining the differential diagnostic significance of a panic attack, it is important to consider the context in which the panic attack occurs. There are two prototypical relationships between the onset of a panic attack and situational triggers: 1) **unexpected (uncued)** panic attacks, in which the onset of the panic attack is not associated with a situational trigger (i.e., occurring "out of the blue"); the occurrence of unexpected panic attacks is required for a diagnosis of Panic Disorder; and 2) **situationally bound (cued)** panic attacks, in which a panic attack almost invariably occurs immediately upon exposure to, or in anticipation of, the situational trigger ("cue"). Situationally bound panic attacks are most characteristic of Social and Specific Phobias. The differential diagnosis of panic attacks is complicated by the fact that an exclusive relationship does not exist between the type of panic attack and the diagnosis. For instance, although Panic Disorder definitionally requires that at least some of the panic attacks are unexpected, individuals with a disturbance meeting the criteria for this disorder frequently have attacks that are cued, particularly later in their course.

Moreover, there are panic attack presentations that do not comform to either of these prototypical relationships. These **situationally predisposed** panic attacks are more likely to occur upon exposure to the situational trigger ("cue") but are not invariably associated with the cue. In addition, the panic attacks may not necessarily occur immediately after the exposure. There is some evidence that situationally predisposed panic attacks are especially frequent in Panic Disorder but may at times occur in Specific Phobia or Social Phobia.

There are limitations in how specific the criteria sets can be in defining the boundaries between disorders in this section. The criteria sets must necessarily emphasize the prototypic presentations of each disorder. The differential diagnosis section of the DSM-IV text for each of these disorders will discuss the diagnostic issues for difficult boundary cases.

Note. From APA (1993). Copyright 1993 by the American Psychiatric Association. Reprinted by permission.

mains somewhat elusive in the diagnostic criteria. However, it refers to occurrences of panic in situations or at times that were not expected.

Consistent with the emotion theories that emphasize the role of basic action tendencies for the different emotions (Barlow, 1991)—with fear being associated with escape action tendencies—panic attacks are most often associated with an urge to escape. Consistent with cognitive–attributional models (Clark et al., 1988), panic attacks are most often associated with perceptions of

danger or threat (e.g., death, loss of control, and embarrassment). Finally, consistent with psychophysiological models (e.g., Ehlers & Margraf, 1989), panic attacks are often associated with accelerated autonomic nervous system activity.

However, the features of urgency to escape, perception of threat, and physiological arousal are not observable in every self-reported occurrence of panic. For example, Margraf, Taylor, Ehlers, Roth, and Agras (1987) found that 40% of self-reported panic attacks were not associated with accelerated heart rate. It is conceivable that fear in the absence of actual arousal reflects anticipatory anxiety versus true panic. In addition, perceptions of threat or danger are occasionally denied, possibly because of lack of subconscious cognitive mechanisms. Finally, the urgency to escape is sometimes weakened by the presence of safety signals (e.g., significant others or medical facilities) or situational demands.

The occurrence of a panic attack is insufficient to describe the phenomena of panic disorder and panic disorder with agoraphobia (PD/PDA). Several independent investigations have shown that approximately 10%–12% of the general population have experienced at least one unexpected panic attack in the last 12 months (e.g., Norton, Dorward, & Cox, 1986; Telch, Lucas, & Nelson, 1989). In contrast, 2%–6% of the population meet criteria for PD/PDA (Myers et al., 1984). Furthermore, panic attacks occur across a variety of anxiety and mood disorders (Barlow, Vermilyea, Blanchard, Vermilyea, & DiNardo, 1985) and are not limited to PD/PDA. Consequently, the defining feature of PD/PDA has been conceptualized as anxiety about the recurrence of panic versus panic per se (Barlow, 1988). For example, consider the following scenario between client (C) and therapist (T).

C: Sometimes I lay awake at night thinking about a million different possibilities. I think about what is going to happen to my daughter if I get sick, who will look after her, and what would happen if my husband died and we didn't have enough money any more, and my daughter couldn't get a good education. Then I think about where we would live and how we would cope. Sometimes I can work myself up so much that my heart suddenly starts to race, my hands get sweaty, and I feel dizzy and scared. So I have to stop myself from thinking about all those things—I usually get up and watch TV to help me go to sleep.

T: Do the feelings of a racing heart, sweating, and dizziness scare you to the degree that you worry about those feelings happening again?

C: No. They're unpleasant, but they are the least of my concerns. I am more worried about my daughter and our future.

This example illustrates the experience of panic which is not the central focus of the person's anxiety. More likely, this woman is suffering from generalized anxiety disorder, which leads her to experience panic on occasion. Similar examples exist for social phobia, obsessive compulsive disorder (OCD), specific phobias, and mood disorders.

Agoraphobic avoidance refers to avoidance or endurance with dread of situations from which escape might be difficult or help unavailable in the event of a panic attack, or in the event of developing symptoms that could be incapacitating and embarrassing, such as loss of bowel control or vomiting. Typical agoraphobic situations include going to shopping malls, waiting in line, going to movie theaters, traveling by car or bus, entering crowded restaurants, and being alone. Agoraphobic avoidance is rated in terms of impairment in functioning, ranging from mild to moderate to severe. Mild agoraphobia is exemplified by the person who hesitates to drive long distances alone but manages to drive to and from work, prefers to sit on the aisle at movie theaters but still goes to movies, and feels uncomfortable in crowded places. Moderate agoraphobia is exemplified by the person who drives within a 5-mile radius of home but only if accompanied, who shops at off-peak times and avoids large supermarkets, and who avoids flying or traveling by train. Severe agoraphobia is experienced by the truly housebound (or nearly housebound) agoraphobic.

For some individuals, the degree to which they fear and avoid agoraphobic situations remains relatively consistent over time. For others, the situational associations are less consistent, as represented by the following client's statement: "All of these situations can be difficult for me, but sometimes I can deal with them without any problem at all—it all depends on how anxious I feel in general on any given day."

Classification

DSM-IV definitions of PD without agoraphobia and PDA have changed in several ways from definitions of the revised third edition of the *Diagnostic and Statistical Manual of Mental Disorders* (DSM-III-R; APA, 1987).

First, the specification of a certain number of panic attacks has been eliminated and the feature of being unexpected or "out of the blue" has been emphasized (see Table 1.2). Second, the cognitive symptoms that are attributions about, or consequences of, the attack have become part of the definition.

Occasionally clients present with classic agoraphobia without ever having experienced a formal unexpected panic attack. However, almost all clients presenting to a clinic will have experienced at least one of the above symptoms, such as vomiting, profuse sweating, or (fear of) loss of bowel or bladder control. These "limited-symptom attacks" seem to serve the same functional purpose as full-blown panic attacks, but because these individuals have never experienced a panic attack as currently defined, they meet criteria for agoraphobia *without* history of PD. This issue seems to have few implications for the psychosocial treatments described in this chapter. In our experience these individuals respond just as well to treatment.

Presenting Features

Treatment for panic and agoraphobia is usually sought around age 34, although the

---

TABLE 1.2. Assessment Profile for Panic Disorder with Agoraphobia

1. Panic topography
   —Sensations: unreality, dizziness, palpitations
   —Frequency: 3 per week on average
   —Duration: 5 minutes on average
   —Apprehension: on her mind 75% of the time
   —Types: mostly cued and expected, but some uncued

2. Antecedents
   —Situational: driving on freeways, crowds of people, being alone . . . specially at night, restaurants, dusk
   —Internal physical: heart fluctuations, lightheaded feelings, hunger feelings, weakness due to lack of food
   —Internal cognitive: thoughts of the "big one" happening, thoughts of not being able to cope with this for much longer
   —Internal emotional: sometimes anger
   —Activities: reading and concentrating for long periods of time, aerobic activity
   —Stimulants: caffeine
   —Stressful life events: arguments with mother about sister

3. Misappraisals
   —Physical: none
   —Mental: never returning to normality, going crazy
   —Social: others will see I'm anxious and think I'm weird

4. Behavioral reactions to panic attacks
   —Escape: pull off to side of road, leave restaurants and other crowded places
   —Help seeking: have called spouse on occasion but rarely now
   —Protection: cool air, carries valium although rarely uses

5. Behavioral reactions to anticipation of panic attacks
   —Situational avoidance: avoids driving long distances alone, unfamiliar roads and freeways, crowded areas
   —Activity avoidance: avoids exercise and doing any one thing for a long period of time
   —Cognitive avoidance: tries not to think about anxiety
   —Safety signals: carries medication, always knows location of husband

6. Consequences
   —Family: husband is concerned and supportive; mother thinks she should pull herself together because its all in her head
   —Work: still works but has cut back number of hours
   —Leisure: travels much less
   —Social: socializes much less

7. General anxiety: some difficulty concentrating, sleep restlessness, headaches, muscular pains and aches

mean age of onset ranges from 23 to 29 (Breier, Charney, & Heninger, 1986; Craske, Miller, Rotunda, & Barlow, 1990; Noyes et al., 1986). Approximately 72% (Craske et al., 1990) report the presence of identifiable stressors around the time of their first panic attack, including interpersonal and somatic-related stressors, such as negative drug experiences, disease, or death in the family. However, the number of stressors does not differ from the number experienced prior to the onset of other types of anxiety disorders (Pollard, Pollard, & Corn, 1989; Rapee, Litwin, & Barlow, 1990; Roy-Byrne, Geraci, & Uhde, 1986). Approximately half report having experienced panicky feelings at some time before their first panic, suggesting that onset may be either insidious or acute (Craske et al., 1990).

Rarely does the diagnosis occur in isolation. Commonly co-occurring Axis I conditions include simple phobia, social phobia, and dysthymia (Sanderson, DiNardo, Rapee, & Barlow, 1990). Several independent investigations have shown that from 25% to 60% meet criteria for a personality disorder. Most often, these are avoidant and dependent personality disorders (Chambless & Renneberg, 1988; Mavissakalian & Hamman, 1986; Reich, Noyes, & Troughton, 1987). However, the nature of the relationship between PD/PDA and personality disorders remains unclear. For example, comorbidity rates are highly dependent on the method used to establish Axis II diagnosis, as well as the co-occurrence of depressed mood (Chambless & Renneberg, 1988; Alnaes & Torgersen, 1990), and some personality disorders remit after successful treatment of PDA (Mavissakalian & Hamman, 1987; Noyes, Reich, Suelzer, & Christiansen, 1991).

History of Psychological Treatment for PDA

It was not until the third edition of *Diagnostic and Statistical Manual of Mental Disorders* (DSM-III; APA, 1980) that PD was recognized as a specific anxiety problem. Until that time, panic attacks were viewed primarily as a form of free-floating anxiety. The psychological treatment approaches were relatively nonspecific. They included relaxation and cognitive restructuring about life events in general (e.g., Barlow, Cohen, et al., 1984). Many presumed that pharmacotherapy was necessary for the control of panic. In contrast, the treatment of agoraphobia was quite specific from the 1970s onward, using primarily exposure-based approaches to target fears of specific situations. However, relatively little consideration was given to panic attacks in either the conceptualization or the treatment of agoraphobia. Several studies have shown that panic attacks are not reliably controlled by situational exposure approaches (e.g., Michelson, Mavissakalian, & Marchione, 1985). Anecdotal evidence suggests that the persistence of panic increases the likelihood of agoraphobic relapse (Arnow, Taylor, Agras, & Telch, 1985; Craske, Street, & Barlow, 1989). The generation of more specific panic-control treatments was dependent on new conceptualizations of panic attacks and PD.

Models of Panic Disorder

Several highly convergent views of panic have been proposed that differ in their emphasis only (Barlow, 1988; Clark et al., 1988; Ehlers & Margraf, 1989). These theories stress the importance of psychological responses to a set of physiological sensations. More specifically, PD is viewed as a fear of certain bodily sensations associated with panic attacks.

The biopsychosocial approach (Barlow, 1988) is receiving increasing empirical support. Here the initial panic attack is conceptualized as a misfiring of the fear system under stressful life circumstances in physiologically and psychologically vulnerable individuals. The nature of the physiological vulnerability is in question. At the very least, it is construed as an overly reactive or labile autonomic nervous system. Physiological vulnerability, which may be determined in part by genetic transmission, is consistent with the higher concordance rates of PD/PDA within first-degree relatives (Crowe, Noyes, Pauls, & Slymen, 1983; Moran & Andrews, 1985; Torgersen, 1983).

Psychological vulnerability is conceptualized as a set of danger-laden beliefs about bodily sensations ("a racing heart could mean a heart attack" or "I'm too weak to control my emotions") and about the world in general ("events are proceeding uncontrollably"). The concepts of uncontrollability (Barlow, 1988) and anxiety sensitivity (Reiss, Peterson, Gursky, & McNally, 1986) seem central to the cognitive schemas of PD/PDA. Life experiences relevant to the development of such schemas might include warnings from significant others about the physical and mental dangers of certain bodily sensations (e.g., overly protective parents), or significant negative life events that are unpredictable and uncontrollable (e.g., loss of a parent).

As described earlier, the stressful life events around the time of the first panic attack are primarily interpersonal and somatic in nature. PD/PDA is believed to emerge from a diathesis between life stressors and psychological and physiological vulnerabilities. Conceivably, stress raises levels of physiological arousal or enhances cognitive schemas of uncontrollability of and apprehension about bodily sensations.

Barlow (1988) and Wolpe and Rowan (1988) emphasize the traumatic nature of the first panic attack and the consequent learning that takes place. The traumatic nature of initial panic attacks is apparent in the relatively high frequency of individuals' seeking emergency medical help due to their misappraisal of the panic attack as impending death. Consequently, fearful associations are likely to develop with the situational context and the physical sensations present at the time of the first panic. The concept of learning fearfulness of bodily sensations is based on Razran's (1961) account of interoceptive conditioning. This is a form of conditioning that is relatively resistant to extinction and "unconscious." That is, interoceptively conditioned fear responses are not dependent on conscious awareness of triggering cues. Accordingly, panic attacks may seem to be uncued or to occur from out of the blue when in fact they are triggered by benign and subtle fluctuations in physical state (Barlow, 1988). For example, a slight change in blood pressure may elicit fearfulness in anticipation of experiencing a panic attack.

Hence, PD is viewed as a phobia of bodily sensations. However, PD differs from other phobias in two essential ways. First, since the internal fear cues (i.e., bodily sensations) may intensify as a function of anxiety and fear, the emotional experience tends to build on itself. Second, internal fear cues tend to be less predictable and less escapable than are external phobic objects or situations. Consequently, internal fear cues can trigger more abrupt, and less predictable fear, which in turn leads to greater anticipatory anxiety about the recurrence of fear (Craske, 1991). Moreover, anxious anticipation of panic increases the likelihood of its occurrence, since anxious arousal increases the availability of arousal sensations that have become conditioned cues for panic, in addition to increasing the degree of attentional vigilance for such cues (Barlow, 1988). In this manner, a maintaining cycle is established between panic and anxious apprehension about panic.

Empirical support for this conceptualization is growing. For example, persons who panic tend to have stronger beliefs and fears of physical and mental harm arising from specific bodily sensations (Chambless, Caputo, Bright, & Gallagher, 1984; Clark et al., 1988; Holt & Andrews, 1989; McNally & Lorenz, 1987; van den Hout, van der Molen, Griez, & Lousberg, 1987). Although the predicted links between specific bodily sensations and specific cognitions are unstable and lead Costello (1992) to question the validity of the cognitive models, there is some evidence for heightened awareness of and ability to detect bodily sensations of arousal (Ehlers & Breuer, 1992; Ehlers & Margraf, 1989), presumably due to attentional vigilance mechanisms. However, Antony et al., (1993) were unable to replicate this finding. Also, persons with PD are fearful of procedures that elicit bodily sensations similar to the ones experienced during panic attacks, including benign cardiovascular, respiratory, and audiovestibular exercises (Zarate, Rapee, Craske, & Barlow, 1988). Similarly, false physiological feedback paradigms elicit more fearfulness in PD/PDAs than in normal controls (Ehlers, Taylor, Margraf, Roth, & Birnbaumer, 1988). Further support derives from studies showing that correction of misappraisals about certain bodily sensations seems to lessen fearfulness. For example, considerably less panic is reported when subjects are informed about the expected physical effects of hyperventilation (Rapee, Mattick, & Murrell, 1986) or are led to believe they can control the administration of carbon dioxide (Sanderson, Rapee, & Barlow, 1989).

The degree to which agoraphobic avoidance develops in the context of PD is highly variable across individuals. Several attempts have been made to identify predictors of agoraphobic disability. Although agoraphobic persons tend to have longer histories of panic, the relationship with chronicity is relatively weak since a significant portion of these people panic for many years without developing agoraphobic limitations (for a review, see Craske & Barlow, 1988). Nor is agoraphobia related to age of onset, types of symptoms experienced during panic, proportions of different types of panic (i.e., situationally cued vs. uncued, or expected vs. unexpected), or frequency of panic (Craske & Barlow, 1988). On the other hand, females increasingly predominate as degree of avoidance becomes more severe (Thyer, Himle, Curtis, Cameron, & Nesse, 1985). Consequently, it is hypothesized that sex-role behaviors and expectations and associated situational demands influence the degree to which agoraphobia emerges as a behavioral style in response to panic anticipation (Craske & Barlow, 1988). In accord, the likelihood of co-occurring dependent or avoidant personality disorders is considerably greater when agoraphobia is present (Re... ... . 1987), suggesting a behavioral avoidance-response style to threat or challenge in general. It is noteworthy that another style of coping which may be more common for males is to confront anticipated situations with the aid of alcohol or drugs (Barlow, 1988). Therefore, panic attacks and agoraphobia are seen as independent yet closely related responses.

The targets of therapeutic intervention derived from this conceptualization are (1) acute fearfulness of bodily sensations; (2) chronic apprehension of panic and bodily sensations, which involves chronic hyperarousal and attentional vigilance; and (3) agoraphobic avoidance.

CONTEXT OF TREATMENT

Aspects of the context and format of the cognitive-behavioral treatment for PD/PDA are described in this section. The next section describes the therapeutic strategies in detail.

Setting

Three different settings have been employed. The first is the outpatient clinic–office setting, which is suited to education, cognitive restructuring, feedback regarding homework assignments, and role-play rehearsals. In addition, certain *in vivo* practices can be conducted in the office setting, such as the interoceptive exposure described later. However, the built-in safety signals of an office setting may limit the generalizability of learning that takes place in that setting. The safety signals include the therapist and the structure, particularly if in a medical center. Bouton (1988) has highlighted the role of context in learning and the later return of fear.

The second setting for conducting *in vivo* exposure practices, either with the aid of the therapist or alone, is the natural environment. Therapist-directed exposure is particularly useful for clients who lack a social network to support *in vivo* exposure assignments. There is some evidence to suggest, however, that therapist-directed exposure is no more effective than self-directed exposure. Ghosh and Marks (1987) and Jannoun, Munby, Catalan, and Gelder (1980) have shown that structured manualized programs with minimal therapist contact are as effective as programs involving intensive therapist contact. On the other hand, Holden, O'Brien, Barlow, Stetson, and Infantino (1983) found that self-directed exposure was not effective for a group of severe housebound agoraphobics. In addition, there can be a high degree of attrition from self-directed exposure (McNamee, O'Sullivan, Lelliot, & Marks, 1989). Therefore, matching the exposure approach to the client's response profile is recommended. Furthermore, therapist-directed exposure should be followed by self-directed exposure to overcome reliance on the therapist.

A third setting is an inpatient facility. This setting is most appropriate when conducting intensive cognitive-behavioral therapy (e.g., daily therapist contact), or for severely disabled persons who can no longer function in the home environment. In addition, certain medical or drug complications may warrant inpatient treatment. The greatest drawback to the inpatient setting is difficulty in generalizing to the home environment. For this reason, transition sessions and booster sessions conducted by the therapist in the client's own home setting are very beneficial.

Interpersonal Context

The interpersonal context has been researched in terms of its role in the development, maintenance, and treatment of agoraphobia. The reason for this research interest is apparent from the following vignettes:

"My husband really doesn't understand. He thinks it's all in my head. He gets angry at me for not being able to cope. He says I'm weak and irresponsible. He resents having to drive me around, and doing things for the kids that I can't do anymore. We argue a lot because he comes home tired and frustrated from work only to be frustrated more by the problems I'm having. But I can't do anything without him. I'm so afraid that I'll collapse into a helpless wreck without him, or that I'd be alone for the rest of my life. As cruel as he can be, I feel safe around him because he always has everything under control. He always knows what to do."

"My boyfriend really tries hard to help me. He's always cautious of my feelings and doesn't push me to do things that I can't do. He phones me from work to check on me. He stays with me and holds my hand when I feel really scared. He never hesitates to leave and go home if I'm having a bad time. Only last week we visited some of his friends, and we had to leave. I feel guilty because we don't do the things we used to enjoy doing together. We don't go to the movies anymore. We used to love going to ball games, but now it's too much for me. I am so thankful for him. I don't know what I would do without him."

It has been proposed that at least some forms of agoraphobia represent a conflict between desire for autonomy and dependency in interpersonal relationships (Goldstein & Chambless, 1978; Fry, 1962); that the preagoraphobic is trapped in a domineering relationship without the skills needed to activate change. However, a review of the literature leads to the conclusion that the concept of a distinct marital system that predisposes to the development of agoraphobia is almost devoid of empirical support. As mentioned earlier, there may be distinct personality features that serve as predispositions, particularly interpersonal sensitivity (Noyes et al., 1986; Thyer et al., 1985). However, the way in which such interpersonal sensitivity affects marital relations is not known. Alternatively, marital discord/dissatisfaction may represent one of several possible stressors that precipitates panic attacks.

Another possibility is that the marital relationship is negatively impacted by the development of agoraphobia (Buglass, Clarke, Henderson, & Presley, 1977), and in turn contributes to its maintenance. For example, an agoraphobic woman who was previously able to grocery shop now relies on her husband to do the shopping. The husband has new demands placed on him, which in turn leads to marital discord. The marital distress adds to background stress, making progress and recovery even more difficult.

Whether marital distress is a cause or a consequence of PDA, poor marital relations have been found to adversely affect response to exposure-based treatments (Milton & Hafner, 1979; Bland & Hallam, 1981; Dewey & Hunsley, 1989). Other studies have failed to support this relationship (Emmelkamp, 1980; Arrindell & Emmelkamp, 1987). Himadi, Cerny, Barlow, Cohen, and O'Brien (1986) similarly failed to establish a relationship between marital status and treatment outcome. However, the majority of the Himadi et al. (1986) study participants received treatment accompanied by their spouse. Involvement of the spouse in every aspect of treatment has been found to override the negative impact of poor marital relations on phobic improvement (Barlow, O'Brien, & Last, 1984; Cerny, Barlow, Craske, & Himadi, 1987). It should be noted, however, that the samples were limited to those whose spouse was willing to be involved in therapy. Finally, Arnow et al. (1985) examined the effectiveness of specific communication training with spouse as compared to relaxation training, after 4 weeks of *in vivo* exposure therapy. Subjects given communication training gained significantly greater reductions on measures of agoraphobia by posttreatment, with some maintenance of superiority over an 8-month follow-up. Together, these studies suggest the value of including the spouse in the treatment for agoraphobia.

The effect of the agoraphobia treatment process on marital relations remains somewhat unclear. Some have noted that treatment can have deleterious effects (Hafner, 1984; Hand & Lamontagne, 1976). Others note that it has no effect or a positive effect on marital functioning (Barlow, O'Brien, Last, & Holden, 1983; Himadi et al., 1986). Barlow et al. (1983) suggest that negative effects may occur if exposure therapy is conducted intensively without the spouse's involvement, since major role changes may occur beyond the spouse's perceived control.

Therapist Variables

Very little attempt has been made to examine therapist variables as they pertain to the cognitive-behavioral treatment approach. Williams and Chambless (1990) found that patients who rated their therapist as being caring/involved and as modeling self-confidence achieved better outcomes on behavioral approach tests. However, an important confound in this study is that client ratings of therapist qualities may have depended on the client's response to treatment.

Several researchers have emphasized the importance of therapist experience, particularly in terms of the efficacy of cognitive approaches (e.g., Michelson et al., 1990). Recently, Welkowitz et al. (1991) found that when the cognitive-behavioral treatment developed by Barlow, Craske, Cerny, and Klosko (1989) was conducted by "novice" therapists in a medical setting, it was somewhat less effective in comparison to the results reported originally by Barlow et al. (1989): 58% of the Welkowitz et al. (1991) sample achieved panic-free status in comparison to 85% of the Barlow et al. (1989)

sample. This result suggests the value of therapist training and experience.

Client Variables

Similarly, relatively little research has examined client variables that are predictive of outcome. In an uncontrolled study, Sokol and Beck (cited by Beck, 1988) found that the presence of Axis II features slowed down the rate of improvement significantly. Nevertheless, subjects with Axis II comorbidity eventually obtained the same success in controlling panic attacks as did subjects without Axis II pathology. In contrast, Arntz and Arntz (1992) reported that Axis II features did not predict treatment response at all. Further investigation on this topic is needed.

Most of the studies to date have relied on select samples of PD/PDA, excluding subjects who suffer additional problems of alcohol or drug abuse/dependence, severe depression, or psychosis. Therefore, the generalizability of the results to less pure samples is unknown. Furthermore, it is conceivable that the co-ocurrence of other pervasive anxiety disorders (such as social phobia or generalized anxiety disorder) results in less favorable treatment outcomes, but no published reports have examined this issue. Similarly, physical complications, such as arrythmias or asthma, may slow improvement rates, given the additional complications of discriminating anxiety symptomatology from disease symptomatology, increased risk of actual danger, and stress of physical disorders. All these issues of generalizability warrant further investigation.

Life circumstances can be viewed as a client variable that may impact treatment progress. Consider the woman who is a mother of two, a full-time account executive, whose husband is on disability due to a back injury; or the full-time student who works an extra 25 hr a week in order to pay his/her way through school. Under these conditions, treatment assignments of daily relaxation practices or daily *in vivo* exposure exercises are much less likely to be completed. Frustration with lack of treatment progress often results. Therapeutic success requires either a change in life-style that allows the cognitive-behavioral treatment to become a priority or termination of therapy until a later time when life circumstances are less demanding.

Finally, the client's understanding of the nature of his/her problem may be important to the success of cognitive-behavioral treatments. Given the somatic nature of PD/PDA, many clients seek medical help first. Beyond that, however, differences in the way the problem is conceptualized could lead to pharmacological treatment approaches or analytical treatment approaches to be perceived as more credible than cognitive-behavioral treatment approaches. For example, individuals who strongly believe their condition is due to "a neurochemical imbalance" are more likely to seek medication and to refute psychological treatments. Similarly, individuals who attribute their condition to "something about my past—it must be unconscious influences" may resist cognitive-behavioral interpretations.

Concurrent Pharmacological Treatment

Even in a select sample of PD/PDA clients who attend a psychology clinic, approximately 50% reportedly use prescription anxiolytic medications (most often a benzodiazepine or tricyclic antidepressant). The results of controlled investigations of agoraphobia suggest that imipramine (tricyclic antidepressant) enhances the efficacy of *in vivo* exposure therapy and vice versa (e.g., Marks et al., 1983; Mavissakalian & Michelson, 1986; Mavissakalian, Michelson, & Dealy, 1983; Zitrin, Klein, & Woerner, 1980; Zitrin, Klein, Woerner, & Ross, 1983; Telch, Agras, Taylor, Roth, & Gallen, 1985). The results from a recent study confirm these findings (Agras, Telch, Taylor, Roth, & Brouillard, in press). Interestingly, Agras et al. present some preliminary evidence to suggest that the facilitatory effect of imipramine is not on panic attacks but rather on phobic avoidance. A large collaborative project is currently under way at four sites, (whose principal investigators are Barlow, Gorman, Shear, and Woods), to investigate the singular and combined effects of imipramine and panic-control treatments for clients with PD who do not suffer severe levels of agoraphobia.

Clinically, it is important to note the potential for interference with cognitive-behavioral treatments. For example, since some medications usually lessen physical symptomatology, behavioral treatments that emphasize exposure to feared physical sensations may be detrimentally impacted. Also, clients may attribute their success to medications. The lack of perceived self-control may increase relapse potential when medication is withdrawn, or contribute to maintenance of a medication regime under the assumption of its necessity in order to function. These points are illustrated in the vignettes below:

"I started to feel much better after about six months. I had been through a program of cognitive-behavioral therapy, but it was really the imipramine that helped. So, my psychiatrist suggested that I taper off the medication. My first reaction was to be very concerned. I had heard horror stories about what people go through when withdrawing. However, he convinced me that if we went slowly, everything would be OK. So, I began to taper. It really wasn't that bad. Well, I had been completely off the medication for about a month, when the problem started all over again. I remember sitting in a restaurant, feeling really good because I was thinking about how much of a problem restaurants used to be for me before, and how easy it seemed now. Then, wammo. I started to feel dizzy and I immediately thought, oh no, here it comes. I had a really bad panic attack. All I could think of was why didn't I stay on the medication."

"I started to lower my dose of Xanax [alprazolam]. I was OK for the first couple of days. . . . I felt really good. Then, when I woke up on Friday morning, I felt strange. My head felt really tight and I worried about having the same old feelings all over again. The last thing I want to do is to go through that again. So I took my usual dose of Xanax and, within an hour or so, I felt pretty good again. I need the medication—I can't manage without it right now."

Medications may interfere with treatment progress in several other ways. The soothing and sometimes sedating effects may lower levels of motivation so that the amount of effort and time devoted to behavioral practices is reduced. Moreover, side effects such as sedation may interfere with processes of learning. State dependency of learning has been cited as another possibility, resulting in more return of fear when medication is withdrawn (Bouton & Swartzentruber, 1991). Finally, the neurochemical basis of certain medications (i.e., propranolol) may interfere with neurochemical changes proposed to underly exposure-based learning (Gray, 1985).

ASSESSMENT

Jane is a 33-year-old Caucasian, mother of two, who lives with her husband of 8 years. For the past 3 years she has been chronically highly anxious. In addition, she reports episodes of acute fearfulness. The acute episodes are described as unbearable and increasing in frequency. The first time that she felt that way was just over 3 years ago, when she was rushing to her grandmother's house before her grandmother died. She was driving alone on the freeway. She remembers feeling as if everything was moving in slow motion, as if the cars were standing still, and things around her seemed unreal. She recalled feeling short of breath and detached. However, it was so important to reach her destination that she did not really think about how she felt until later. After the day was over, she reflected on how lucky she was not to have had an accident. A few weeks later, the same type of feeling happened, again when driving on the freeway. This time it occurred without the pressure of reaching a destination quickly. It scared her because she was unable to explain the feelings. She pulled off to the side of the road and called her husband, who came to meet her. She followed him home, feeling anxious all the way.

Now Jane has these feelings in many situations. She describes her panic attacks as feelings of unreality, detachment, shortness of breath, a racing heart, and a general fear of the unknown. It is the unreality that scares her the most. Consequently, Jane is sensitive to anything that produces "unreal" types of feelings, such as the semiconsciousness that occurs just before falling asleep, the time of the day when daylight fades, bright lights, alcohol or drugs, and being anxious in general. She reports that she is constantly waiting for the next

episode to occur. She avoids the freeways, driving on familiar surface streets only. She limits herself to a 10-mile radius. In general, she prefers to be with her husband or her mother. However, she can do most things within her "safety" region alone.

Jane describes how different she is from the way she used to be: how weak and scared she is now. The only other incident similar to the current panic attacks occurred in her early 20s. Jane recalls a negative drug (marijuana) experience, when she became very scared of the feeling of losing control and she feared that she would never return to reality. She has not taken drugs since then. Otherwise, there is no history of serious medical conditions or any previous psychological treatment. Even though she was shy as a young child, Jane's social comfort improved considerably in her late teens.

In general, Jane's appetite is good, although her sleep is restless. At least once a week she wakes abruptly in the middle of the night, feeling short of breath and scared. Jane's chronic anxiety is almost solely focused on the possibility of having unreal feelings. She worries somewhat about other issues, such as her children and her parents. However, that worry is not excessive. She has some difficulty concentrating, but in general she functions well within her safety regions. For example, Jane works part time as the manager of a business that she and her husband own. In that setting, she is relaxed and very successful.

A functional behavioral analysis involves several steps.

1. An in-depth interview is the first step in establishing diagnostic and cognitive-behavioral profiles. Several semi- and fully structured interviews have been developed over the last few years. The Anxiety Disorders Interview Schedule—Revised (ADIS–R) (DiNardo & Barlow, 1988) assesses anxiety disorders primarily as well as mood disorders and somatoform disorders. Psychotic and drug conditions are screened by this instrument also. The value of structured interviews lies in their contribution to reliable differential diagnosis and systematic assessment of issues important to consider in any functional analysis of a disorder. Interrater agreement ranges from satisfactory to excellent for the various anxiety disorders using the ADIS–R (DiNardo, Moras,

Barlow, Rapee, & Brown, 1993). Similarly, the Schizophrenia and Affective Disorders Schedule—Life Time Version (Anxiety Modified) produces reliable diagnoses for the majority of the anxiety disorders (generalized anxiety disorder and simple phobia being the exceptions) (Manuzza et al., 1989).

Differential diagnosis is sometimes difficult because, as described earlier, panic is a ubiquitous phenomenon (Barlow, 1988) occurring across a wide variety of emotional disorders. It is not uncommon for persons with simple phobia, generalized anxiety disorder, OCD, and post-traumatic stress disorder to report the experience of panic. For Jane, there was a differential diagnostic question regarding social phobia and PDA. Figure 1.1 presents the ADIS–R questions that addressed this differentiation (Jane's answers are shown in italics).

Figure 1.1 shows that Jane experiences panic attacks in social situations and is concerned about negative evaluations if her anxiety is visibly apparent to others. However, since the social discomfort is based primarily on the possibility of panicking, and since she meets the other criteria for PD (i.e., uncued/nonsocial panic attacks and pervasive apprehension about future panic attacks), the social distress seems best subsumed under the domain of PDA. If Jane reported that she experienced panic attacks in social situations only, or that she worried about having future panic attacks in social situations only, a diagnosis of social phobia would have been warranted. If Jane reported uncued panic attacks, as well as being self-conscious about things that she might do or say in social situations regardless of the occurrence of panic, a dual diagnosis of PDA and social phobia might have been warranted. The same types of diagnostic questioning are useful for distinguishing between PDA and claustrophobia. Other differential diagnostic issues can arise with respect to somatoform disorders, real medical conditions, and avoidant or dependent personality disorders. The ADIS–R assists in resolving those issues.

2. A medical evaluation is generally recommended, since several medical conditions should be ruled out before assigning the diagnosis of PD/PDA. These include thyroid conditions, caffeine or amphetamine intoxication, drug withdrawal, or pheochromocytoma (a tumor, usually on the adrenal gland). Furthermore, certain medical conditions can exacerbate PD, although PD is likely to continue even if these conditions are successfully treated. Mitral valve prolapse (MVP), asthma, allergies, and hypoglycemia fall into this category. According to the model described earlier, these medical conditions exacerbate PD/PDA to the extent that they produce the types of physical sensations now feared by the individual. For example, MVP can produce heart murmurs, asthma produces shortness of breath, and hypoglycemia produces dizziness and weak feelings.

3. Self-monitoring is a very important part of assessment and treatment for PD/PDA. Retrospective recall tends to inflate estimates of panic frequency and intensity (Margraf et al., 1987; Rapee, Craske, & Barlow, 1990). Indeed, inflation of past events may contribute to apprehension about future panic. Consequently, self-monitoring is a therapeutic tool. Also, ongoing self-monitoring is believed to contribute to a more objective self-awareness. Objective self-monitoring replaces self-statements such as "I feel horrible—this is the worst it's ever been—my whole body is out of control" with "My anxiety level is six—my symptoms include tremulousness, dizziness, unreal feelings, and shortness of breath—and this episode lasted ten minutes." Finally, self-monitoring provides objective feedback regarding progress and useful material for discussion of cognitive and behavioral principles in treatment sessions.

Panic attack frequency, duration, context, and symptoms are recorded used the Panic Attack Record shown in Figure 1.2. This record is to be completed as soon as possible after a panic attack occurs and therefore is carried on one's person. Daily levels of anxiety, depression, and worry about panic are monitored using the Daily Mood Record shown in Figure 1.3. This record is completed at the end of each day. Finally, activities can be recorded by logging daily excursions in a diary, or by checking off activities completed from an agoraphobic checklist.

A common problem with self-monitoring is noncompliance. Sometimes noncompliance is due to misunderstanding or lack of perceived credibility in self-monitoring. Most often, however, noncompliance is due to anticipation of experiencing more anxi-

Have you had times when you have felt a sudden rush of intense fear or anxiety, or a feeling of impending doom?   *Yes.*

In what situations have you had those feelings?   *Driving, especially on freeways . . . alone at home . . . at parties or in crowds of people.*

Have you ever had those feelings come "from out of the blue", or while you are at home alone, or in situations where you did not expect them to occur?   *Yes.*

How long does it usually take for the rush of anxiety to become intense?   *It varies, sometimes a couple of seconds and at other times it seems to build more slowly.*

How long does the anxiety usually last at its peak level?   *Depends on where I am at the time. If it happens when I'm alone, sometimes it is over within a few seconds and at other times it seems to last for hours. If I'm in a crowd, then it seems to last until I get away.*

In the last month, how much have you worried about, or how fearful have you been about having another attack?

0	1	2	3	4	5	⑥	7	8
No worry no fear		Rarely worried/ mild fear		Occasionally worried/ moderate fear		Frequently worried/ severe fear		Constantly worried/ extreme fear

Social Phobia Section

In social situations, where you might be observed or evaluated by others, do you feel fearful/anxious/nervous?   *Yes.*

Are you overly concerned that you might do and/or say something that might embarrass or humiliate yourself in front of others, or that others may think badly of you?   *Yes.*

What do you anticipate before going into social situations?   *That I will look anxious to others and they will think I'm weird . . . my face turns white and my eyes look strange when I'm panicky. That I'll flip out in front of them and they won't know what to do.*

Do you avoid these situations because you are afraid that you will have a panic attack?-   *Yes* [*either a panic or that I'll feel unreal*].

If you had the physical symptoms while you were alone, would you still be frightened?   *Yes.*

FIGURE 1.1. Questions from the ADIS–R panic disorder section and social phobia section. From Anxiety Disorders Interview Schedule–Revised (ADIS–R) (pp. 2, 3, 30, 31) by P. DiNardo and D. H. Barlow, 1988, Albany, NY: Graywind. Copyright 1988 by Graywind Publications. Reprinted by permission.

ety as a result of monitoring. This is particularly true for individuals whose preferred style of coping is to distract as much as possible and to avoid "quiet" times when thoughts of panic may invade consciousness. A similar complaint about self-monitoring is reflected in the question, "Why should I interrupt my relief from symptoms by asking myself how bad I feel?" In Jane's case, the self-monitoring task was particularly difficult, since explicit reminders of her anxiety elicited strong concerns about losing touch with reality. Continuous prompting and emphasis on the importance of objective versus subjective self-monitoring were necessary. In addition, the cognitive restructuring conducted in the first few sessions of treatment was very helpful.

4. Several standardized self-report inventories provide useful information for treatment planning, as well as being sensitive markers of therapeutic change. The Mobility Inventory (Chambless, Caputo, Gracely, Jasin, & Williams, 1985) lists common agoraphobic situations that are rated in terms of degree avoidance, when alone and when accompanied. This instrument is very useful for establishing *in vivo* exposure hierarchies. The Anxiety Sensitivity Index (Reiss et al., 1986) has received wide acceptance as a trait measure of threatening beliefs about bodily sensations. It has good psychometric properties and tends to discriminate PD/PDA from other types of anxiety disorders (Telch, Sherman, & Lucas, 1989). More specific information about which particular bodily sensations are feared the most, and which misappraisals occur most often, can

Date: _____   Time began: _____   Duration (min): _____

Alone _____   Friend _____   Stranger _____   Family _____

Stressful? Yes/No _____

Expected? Yes/No

Maximum fear: 0   1   2   3   4   5   6   7   8
                None   Mild   Moderate   Strong   Extreme

Underline first symptom and check all symptoms present:

Difficulty breathing	_____	Hot/cold flashes	_____
Racing/pounding heart	_____	Numbness/tingling	_____
Choking sensations	_____	Feelings of unreality	_____
Sweating	_____	Unsteadiness/dizziness/faintness	_____
Trembling/shaking	_____	Fear of dying	_____
Nausea/abdominal upset	_____	Fear of losing control/going crazy	_____
Chest pain/discomfort	_____		

FIGURE 1.2. Panic Attack Record. From *Mastery of Your Anxiety and Panic* (pp. 2–4) by D. H. Barlow and M. G. Craske, 1989, Albany, NY: Graywind. Copyright 1989 by Graywind Publications. Adapted by permission.

         0   1   2   3   4   5   6   7   8
        None   Mild   Moderate   Strong   Extreme

Date	Average anxiety	Average depression	Average anticipation/ worry about panic

FIGURE 1.3. Daily Mood Record. From *Mastery of Your Anxiety and Panic* (pp. 2–8) by D. H. Barlow and M. G. Craske, 1989, Albany, NY: Graywind. Copyright 1989 by Graywind Publications. Adapted by permission.

be obtained from the Body Sensations and Agoraphobia Cognitions Questionnaires (Chambless et al., 1984). Measures of trait anxiety include the State–Trait Anxiety Inventory (Spielberger, Gorsuch, Lushene, Vagg, & Jacobs, 1983) and the Beck Anxiety Inventory (Beck, Epstein, Brown, & Steer, 1988). Finally, measures of interpersonal context include the Dyadic Adjustment Scale (Spanier, 1976), or the Marital Happiness Scale (Azrin, Naster, & Jones, 1973).

5. The behavioral test is a useful measure of degree of avoidance of specific situations. Behavioral approach tests can be standardized or individually tailored. The standardized behavioral test usually involves walking or driving a particular route, such as a 1-mile loop around the clinic setting. Anxiety levels are rated at regular intervals, and actual distance walked/driven is measured. Individually tailored behavioral tests usually entail attempts at three to five situations that the client has identified as being anywhere from somewhat to extremely difficult. These might include driving two exits on freeway, waiting in a bank line, or shopping in a local supermarket for 15 min. Maximum levels of anxiety and degree of approach (i.e., refused task, attempted but escaped from task, or completed task) are measured for each situation. The advantage of standardized behavioral tests is the relative ease with which they can be conducted. The disadvantage is that the specific task may not be relevant to all clients. For some clients, a 1-mile walk may be only mildly anxiety provoking, hence, the value of individually tailored tasks.

Both standardized and individually tailored behavioral tests are susceptible to demand biases. Borkovec, Weerts, and Bernstein (1977) highlighted the implicit demands for fear and avoidance prior to treatment, and for improvement after treatment. On the other hand, behavioral tests are an important supplement to the self-report of agoraphobic avoidance, especially since clients tend to understate their behavioral capabilities (Craske, Rapee, & Barlow, 1988). Rachman and Bichard (1988) and Craske and Barlow (1988) speculate that the expectation of panicking mediates degree of avoidance, and since the persistence of avoidance prevents panic expectancies from being lowered, a maintaining cycle of fear and avoidance is created. Therefore, behavioral tests provide information that differs often from self-reports.

In addition, behavioral tests reveal information of which the individual is not fully aware, yet which is important for treatment planning. For example, the tendency to remain close to supports, such as railings or walls, may not be apparent until observing the client walk through a shopping mall. In Jane's case, the importance of changes from daylight to night was not apparent until she was asked to drive on a section of road as a behavioral test. Her response was that it was too late in the day to drive because dusk made her feel as if things were unreal. Similarly, it was not until Jane completed a behavioral test that the protective value of air conditioning when driving was recognized. Jane believed that the cool air blowing on her face helped her to remain "in touch with reality." Finally, her physical poise while driving was noticed as a factor that contributed to anxiety, since her shoulders were hunched, she leaned toward the wheel, and she held the wheel very tightly.

6. Physiological measures are not very practical tools for clinicians but can provide important information. In particular, the discrepancy described earlier between reports of symptoms and actual physiological arousal can serve as a therapeutic demonstration of the role of attention and cognition in symptom production. Similarly, actual recordings provide disconfirmation of fears such as "my heart feels like it's going so fast that it will explode" or "I'm sure my blood pressure is so high that I could have a stroke at any minute." Finally, since baseline levels of physiological arousal tend to be elevated in anxious individuals, they are sensitive measures of treatment effectiveness.

The various methods of assessment provide the material for a full functional analysis for Jane as shown in Table 1.3.

TREATMENT DESCRIPTION: COMPONENTS

In this section, the components of treatment are described and evidence for their effectiveness are briefly reviewed. They are integrated into a session-by-session treatment program in the next section. At this

TABLE 1.3. Proposed DSM-IV Definitions of Panic Disorder and Panic Disorder with Agoraphobia

Panic Disorder Without Agoraphobia

A. Both (1) and (2):
   (1) recurrent unexpected panic attacks
   (2) at least one of the attacks has been followed by a month (or more) of: (a) persistent concern about having additional attacks; (b) worry about the implications of the attack or its consequences (e.g., losing control, having a heart attack, "going crazy"); or (c) a change in behavior related to the attacks
B. Absence of Agoraphobia (defined below).
C. The panic attacks are not due to a Substance-Induced or Secondary Anxiety Disorder.
D. The anxiety is not better accounted for by another mental disorder, such as Obsessive Compulsive Disorder (e.g., fear of contamination), Post-traumatic Stress Disorder (e.g., in response to stimuli associated with a severe stressor), Separation Anxiety Disorder, Specific Phobia, or Social Phobia (e.g., fear of embarrassment in social situations).

Panic Disorder With Agoraphobia

A. Both (1) and (2):
   (1) recurrent unexpected panic attacks
   (2) at least one of the attacks has been followed by a month (or more) of: (a) persistent concern about having additional attacks; (b) worry about the implications of the attack or its consequences (e.g., losing control, having a heart attack, "going crazy"); or (c) a significant change in behavior related to the attacks
B. The presence of agoraphobia, i.e., anxiety about being in places or situations in which escape might be difficult (or embarrassing) or in which help may not be available in the event of having an unexpected or situationally predisposed panic attack. Agoraphobic fears typically involve characteristic clusters of situations that include being outside the home alone; being in a crowd or standing in a line; being on a bridge; and traveling in a bus, train, or car.
   [Note: Consider the diagnosis of Specific Phobia if limited to one or only a few specific situations or Social Phobia if the avoidance is limited to social situations.]
C. Agoraphobic situations are avoided (e.g., restricts travel), or else endured with marked distress or with anxiety about having a panic attack, or require the presence of a companion.
D. The panic attacks are not due to a Substance-Induced or Secondary Anxiety Disorder.
E. The anxiety or phobic avoidance is not better accounted for by another mental disorder, such as Specific Phobia (e.g., avoidance limited to a single situation like elevators), Separation Anxiety Disorder (e g., avoidance of school), Obsessive Compulsive Disorder (e.g., fear of contamination), Post-traumatic Stress Disorder (e.g., avoidance of stimuli associated with a severe stressor), or Social Phobia (e.g., avoidance limited to social situations because of fear of embarrassment).

Note. From APA (1993). Copyright 1993 by the American Psychiatric Association. Reprinted by permission.

point we should note once again that the major advance since the last edition of this book has been recognition of the importance of treating panic attacks directly and the development of successful psychological treatments to accomplish that goal. Before reviewing new developments in the application of *in vivo* exposure approaches to agoraphobic avoidance, we will first review treatment components targeting panic attacks directly.

Cognitive Restructuring

Cognitive strategies for panic began by extending Beck's cognitive model of depression (Beck, Rush, Shaw, & Emery, 1979) to anxiety and panic. Cognitive treatment focuses on correcting misappraisals of bodily sensations as threatening. The cognitive strategies are conducted in conjunction with behavioral techniques, although the effective mechanism of change is assumed to lie in the cognitive realm. In an uncontrolled study, Sokol and Beck (cited in Beck, 1988) treated 25 patients with cognitive techniques in combination with interoceptive and *in vivo* exposure for an average of 17 individual sessions. Panic attacks were eliminated in the 17 patients who did not have additional diagnoses of personality disorder, at posttreatment and 12-month assessments. Obviously, it is difficult to attribute the outcome specifically to cognitive strategies given their combination with behavioral strategies.

On the other hand, a preliminary report

from Margraf (1989) suggests that cognitive strategies conducted without exposure procedures are highly effective means of controlling panic attacks. Also, Salkovskis, Clark, and Hackmann (1991) reported results from a single-case multiple-baseline replication design that examined the effects of 2 weeks of focused cognitive therapy with antiexposure instructions. Panic attacks reduced or ceased in all but one of the seven patients.

Breathing Retraining

Several researchers have examined the efficacy of breathing retraining, given that 50% to 60% of panickers describe hyperventilatory symptoms as being similar to their panic-attack symptoms. It is noteworthy, however, that recent research has shown that hyperventilatory symptom report does not accurately represent hyperventilatory physiology: Only 50% of PD subjects show actual reductions in end-tidal carbon dioxide values during panic attacks (Hibbert & Pilsbury, 1988; Hornsveld, Garssen, Fiedeldij Dop, & van Spiegel, 1990), and agoraphobics in particular seem to overreport physical state (Holt & Andrews, 1989).

In the conception of panic attacks that emphasizes hyperventilation, panic attacks are viewed as stress-induced, respiratory changes that either provoke fear because they are perceived as frightening or augment fear already elicited by other phobic stimuli (Clark, Salkovskis, & Chalkley, 1985). Kraft and Hoogduin (1984) found that six biweekly sessions of breathing retraining and progressive relaxation reduced frequency of panic attacks from 10 to 4 per week. However, the treatment was no more effective than either repeated hyperventilation and control of symptoms by breathing into a bag or identification of life stressors and problem solving. Two case reports have described the successful application of breathing retraining in the context of cognitively based treatments, where patients are taught to reinterpret sensations as not dangerous (Rapee, 1985; Salkovskis, Warwick, Clark, & Wessels, 1986). Clark et al. (1985) reported a larger-scale, although uncontrolled, study in which 18 clients with PD received two weekly sessions of respiratory control and cognitive reattribution training.

Panic attacks were reduced markedly in that brief period, especially in subjects who were not significantly agoraphobic. Salkovskis et al. (1986) gave nine patients four weekly sessions of forced hyperventilation, corrective information, and breathing retraining, after which *in vivo* exposure to agoraphobic situations was provided if necessary. Panic frequency reduced, on average, from seven to three episodes per week after respiratory control training.

Although these studies demonstrate impressive results from brief therapeutic interventions, there are several concerns. First, subjects are usually selected on the basis of exhibiting hyperventilatory symptoms and, therefore, generalizability to subjects who do not experience hyperventilatory symptoms is unclear. Second, de Ruiter, Rijken, Garssen, and Kraaimaat (1989), using similarly selected subjects, did not replicate the efficacy of a combination of breathing retraining and cognitive restructuring. Similarly, Hibbert and Chan (1989) failed to find differences between breathing control training and a credible placebo. Third, breathing retraining protocols typically include cognitive restructuring and interoceptive exposure, which, as will be described, have been shown to be effective treatments for panic attacks. Therefore, it is difficult to attribute the results primarily to respiratory control. In an extensive review of efficacy and mechanisms of action, Garssen, de Ruiter, and van Dyck (1992) conclude that breathing retraining effects change by providing a distraction and a sense of control.

Relaxation

A form of relaxation known as applied relaxation has shown promising results as a treatment for panic attacks. Applied relaxation entails training in progressive muscle relaxation (PMR) until skilled in the use of cue-control procedures, at which point the relaxation skill is applied to practice of items from a hierarchy of anxiety-provoking tasks. A theoretical basis for the use of relaxation for panic attacks has not been elaborated beyond the provision of a somatic counterresponse to the muscular tension that is likely to occur during anxiety and panic. However, evidence does not support the somatic counterresponse notion (Rupert,

Dobbins, & Mathew, 1981). An alternative suggestion is that fear and anxiety are reduced to the extent that relaxation provides a sense of control or mastery (Bandura, 1977; Rice & Blanchard, 1982). The procedures and mechanisms accountable for therapeutic gains are further clouded in the case of applied forms of PMR, given the involvement of exposure procedures.

Ost (1988) reported favorable results with the implementation of applied PMR for the control of panic attacks. Of an applied PMR group (n = 8), 100% were panic free after 14 sessions, in comparison to 71.7% of a nonapplied PMR group (n = 8). Furthermore, the results of the first group were maintained at follow-up (approximately 19 months after treatment completion), while maintenance occurred for 57% of the second group. All of the applied PMR group were classified as high end state at follow-up, in comparison to 25% of the PMR group. In contrast, Barlow et al. (1989) found that applied PMR was relatively ineffective for the control of panic attacks. Similarly, Clark et al. (1992) found that applied relaxation did not fare as well as a combination of cognitive and behavioral strategies. This discrepancy may be due to different types of tasks to which cue-controlled relaxation was applied. Ost's (1988) applied PMR condition included exposure to interoceptive cues (i.e., feared bodily sensations), whereas Barlow et al. (1989) limited their PMR condition to external situational tasks. More recently, Michelson et al. (1990) combined applied PMR with breathing retraining and cognitive training for 10 panickers. By treatment completion, all subjects were free of "spontaneous" panics, all but one were free of panic attacks altogether, and all met criteria for high end-state functioning. However, the specific contribution of applied PMR to these results is not known.

Interoceptive Exposure

The purpose of interoceptive exposure, as in the case of exposure to external phobic stimuli, is to disrupt or weaken associations between specific bodily cues and panic reactions. The theoretical basis for interoceptive exposure is one of fear extinction, given the conceptualization of panic attacks as "conditioned" or learned alarm reactions to salient bodily cues (Barlow, 1988). Interoceptive exposure is conducted through procedures that induce panic-type sensations reliably, such as cardiovascular exercise, inhalations of carbon dioxide, spinning in a chair, and hyperventilation. The exposure is conducted using a graduated format. In early studies, Bonn, Harrison, and Rees (1971) and Haslam (1974) observed successful reduction in reactivity with repeated infusions of sodium lactate (a drug that produces panic-type bodily sensations, as do other chemical substances such as caffeine and yohimbine). However, panic was not monitored in these investigations. More recently, Griez and van den Hout (1986) compared six sessions of graduated carbon dioxide inhalations with a treatment regimen of propranolol (a beta blocker chosen because it suppresses symptoms that are induced by carbon dioxide inhalations), both conducted over the course of 2 weeks. Such inhalation treatment resulted in a mean reduction from 12 to 4 panic attacks, which was superior to the results with propranolol. In addition, inhalation treatment resulted in significantly greater reductions in reported fear of sensations. A 6-month follow-up assessment suggested maintenance of treatment gains, although panic frequency was not reported.

In the first controlled study of behavioral treatments for PD, Barlow et al. (1989) compared the following four conditions: applied PMR, interoceptive exposure plus breathing retraining and cognitive restructuring, (which is now referred to as panic-control treatment [PCT]; Barlow & Craske, 1989), their combination, and a wait-list control. Interoceptive exposure entailed repeated exposures using induction techniques, such as forced hyperventilation, spinning, and cardiovascular effort. The two conditions involving interoceptive exposure and cognitive restructuring (PCT) were significantly superior to applied PMR and wait-list conditions in terms of panic frequency. Fully 87% of those two PCT groups were free of panic at posttreatment. The results were maintained up to 24 months following treatment completion for the group receiving interoceptive exposure and cognitive restructuring without PMR, while the combined group tended to deteriorate over the follow-up (Craske, Brown, & Barlow, 1991). This study demonstrates the superiority of interoceptive exposure and cognitive procedures in the short and long term for the control of panic attacks. However, PMR was as effective as the exposure and cognitive strategies for general anxiety reduction.

In a subsequent study, Klosko, Barlow, Tassinari, and Cerny (1990) demonstrated that PCT was as good or better on all measures of outcome immediately after treatment than the most popular pharmacological approach, alprazolam (Xanax). Results indicate 87% of the PCT group free of panic compared to 50% on Xanax and 36% and 33% in a placebo control condition and a wait-list condition, respectively. Preliminary analyses of a dismantling study support the efficacy of the combination of cognitive techniques and interoceptive exposure (Brown, Rapee, Antony, & Barlow, 1990). Although not statistically different at posttreatment from a group receiving cognitive therapy alone, the interoceptive treatment was more effective at blocking fear of strong physical sensations produced through carbon dioxide inhalations.

It is noteworthy that panic is effectively controlled using cognitive, somatic, and interoceptive exposure procedures within relatively short durations. The number of treatment sessions averages approximately 10. Moreover, Hackmann, Clark, Salkovskis, Wells, and Gelder (1992) recently reported effective results from minimal therapist contact and self-help manuals over a period of 4 weeks.

The dramatic control of panic attacks is not always matched by rates of high end-state functioning. The term *high end-state functioning* refers to clinical cure, or functioning within a normative range, and is determined from levels of anxiety, fear, and disability in general. Approximately 50%–60% achieved high end state in the Barlow et al. (1989) and the Michelson et al. (1990) study. In contrast, Ost (1988) and Salkovskis et al. (1991) reported high end-state percentages that equaled the rate of panic control. The discrepancy across studies may be because of (1) sample differences, (2) differences in the way high end state is classified, or (3) true differences in the effectiveness of cognitive-behavioral treatments across sites. Close examination of the Barlow et al.

(1989) data revealed that the presence of agoraphobia sometimes accounted for the lower rates of high end state at follow-up (Craske et al., 1991). Therefore, it is conceivable that agoraphobic severity may account for different rates of high end state across studies.

Nevertheless, almost all of the outcome studies described above involved clients with PD with no more than minimal agoraphobic avoidance. An important issue is the extent to which PCTs affect agoraphobia at moderate or severe levels. At the 1992 World Congress of Cognitive Therapy, the results regarding this issue were contradictory: van den Hout and Arntz (1992) reported minimal effects on agoraphobia, while Ost and Westling (1992) reported significant reductions in agoraphobia. Further investigation is needed on the combination of PCTs, and the situational exposure treatments for agoraphobia (described later). Another issue still being investigated is the effectiveness of combining cognitive-behavioral PCTs with pharmacological approaches. (This is being done in a large collaborative study funded by the National Institute of Mental Health at SUNY Albany, Columbia University, the Western Psychiatric Institute, and Yale University by Barlow, Gorman, Shear, and Woods, respectively.)

Situational Exposure

In vivo situational exposure used to treat agoraphobia refers to repeated confrontation with, or approach to, the object or situation that is avoided. Usually these are typical agoraphobic situations such as malls, churches, or other crowded places and public transportation or other situations from which escape might be difficult in case of a panic attack. When dropouts are excluded, from 60% to 70% of agoraphobics show some clinical improvement, which is maintained on average for 4 years or more (for a review, see Jansson & Ost, 1982). However, 30%–40% fail to benefit, and less than half achieve high end-state functioning (Burns, Thorpe, & Cavallaro, 1986; Cohen, Monteiro, & Marks, 1984; Hafner, 1976; Jacobson, Wilson, & Tupper, 1988; Jansson, Jerremalm, & Ost, 1986; Marks, 1971; Munby & Johnston, 1980). Jacobson et al. (1988) concluded from their review that while 50% show statistically reliable improvement, only 25% on average are no longer agoraphobic by the end of treatment. Finally, as many as 50% who have benefited clinically may relapse, although the relapse is transient and usually followed by a return to levels of therapeutic gain (Munby & Johnston, 1980).

Given these qualifications, attempts to improve efficacy through examination of procedural variables have been ongoing. Such procedural variables include massed versus spaced exposure, graduated versus intensive exposure, therapist-directed versus self-directed exposure, endurance versus controlled escape, focus of attention versus distraction during exposure, use of coping strategies, and targeting of panic attacks and panic apprehension.

Massed Versus Spaced Exposure

At its most intensive, exposure therapy may be conducted 3 to 4 hr a day, 5 days a week. Long, continuous sessions are generally considered more effective than shorter or interrupted sessions (Chaplin & Levine, 1981; Marshall, 1985; Stern & Marks, 1973).

The optimal rate for repeating exposure is unclear. Foa, Jameson, Turner, and Payne (1980) compared 10 weekly sessions with 10 daily sessions of *in vivo* exposure therapy for 11 agoraphobics (counterbalanced crossover design). Short-term superior effects were apparent following massed treatment. Nevertheless, Barlow (1988) suggested that spaced exposure is preferred for the following reasons: Dropout rates are generally higher with massed exposures (Emmelkamp & Ultee, 1974; Emmelkamp & Wessels, 1975); relapse rates may be higher following massed exposure (Hafner, 1976; Jansson & Ost, 1982); and rapid changes are more stressful for the family.

Chambless's (1989) results differed from Barlow's (1988) predictions. In Chambless's study, 36 subjects (of whom approximately half were agoraphobic and half were simple phobics) were assigned to massed or spaced exposure. All subjects received 10 sessions of graduated *in vivo* exposure and training in respiratory control, distraction techniques, and paradoxical intention. Spaced exposure was conducted weekly and massed exposure was conducted daily. The two con-

ditions were equally effective in the short term and at the 6-month follow-up. There was no trend for a differential dropout rate or for differential relapse rates over the 6-month follow-up period. However, some subjects were unwilling to accept massed exposure, creating a sample selection bias. In addition, Chambless pointed out that her results may lack generalization, since spaced exposure is usually interspersed with homework assignments, which may increase outcome efficacy. Nevertheless, Chambless concludes by suggesting that the choice for massed versus spaced exposure is the decision of the therapist and the client.

Graduated Versus Intense Exposure

In vivo exposure is conducted typically in a graduated format, progressing from least to most difficult hierarchy items. Recently, Feigenbaum (1988) reported short- and long-term outcomes from intensive versus graduated exposure treatment conditions. All training sessions were conducted in a massed format over the course of 6 to 10 consecutive days. One group received ungraded exposure (n = 25), beginning with the most feared items from avoidance hierarchies. Another group received graded exposure (n = 23), beginning with the least feared hierarchy items. The sample was severely agoraphobic; approximately one third were housebound at initial assessment. At posttreatment and 8 months later, the conditions proved to be equally effective (although, intriguingly, the graded group reported the treatment to be more distressing). However, ungraded exposure was clearly superior at the 5-year follow-up assessment: 76% of the intensive group versus 35% of the graded group reported themselves to be completely free of symptoms. When 104 subjects were added to the intensive exposure format, the same results were obtained. Of the total of 129 subjects, 78% were reportedly completely symptom free 5 years later. This dramatic set of results suggests that an intensive approach can be very beneficial (at least when conducted in a massed format). The extent to which the outcome generalizes to spaced exposure formats is unknown. Unfortunately, subject attrition rates or treatment acceptance rates were not described, and the validity of the outcome measures is somewhat questionable. Nevertheless, these results raise the possibility that although massed and intensive exposure are acceptable to fewer people, for those who do assent, the outcome is likely to be as effective as, if not more so than, spaced or graduated exposure.

Controlled Escape Versus Endurance

A "golden rule" of *in vivo* exposure has been the continuation of an exposure trial until anxiety reduces (Marks, 1978). Similarly, the emotional-processing model, outlined by Foa and Kozak (1986), posits that long-term fear reduction depends on activation of fearful arousal plus within-session fear reduction. In accord, Marshall (1985) observed substantial benefit from longer periods of exposure, in which time was allowed for complete anxiety reduction. In contrast, Emmelkamp (1982) has demonstrated repeatedly the value of exposure treatment in which subjects are instructed to terminate exposure when anxiety reaches "unduly high" levels. Agras, Leitenberg, and Barlow (1968) similarly reported successful results without endurance of high levels of anxiety in feared situations. DeSilva and Rachman (1984) and Rachman, Craske, Tallman, and Solyom (1986) obtained equally effective results whether subjects escaped exposure tasks when anxiety reached 70 on a 0–100-point scale (as long as escape was followed by immediate return to the situation) or were instructed to remain in the situation until anxiety peaked and reduced by at least 50%. Interestingly, the escape group reported more perceived control and less fear during exposure than the no-escape group, suggesting that maximal fear elicitation was not essential for therapeutic benefit.

The model of therapeutic change described by Bandura (1977, 1988) and Williams (1988) emphasizes performance accomplishment or self-efficacy, as opposed to fear reduction or habituation. A mastery approach is taken that emphasizes the way in which exposure is conducted versus mere approach to a stimulus. Unadaptive, defensive behaviors that inhibit the development of self-efficacy, and that result in performance attribution to protective behaviors instead of to personal capabilities, are corrected. For example, subjects are taught to drive in a relaxed position at the wheel and to walk across a bridge without holding the rail. This type of "guided mastery" has been shown to produce more effective results than "stimulus exposure" treatment (Williams, Turner, & Peer, 1985; Williams & Zane, 1989). Moreover, since mastery subjects tended to report the least anxiety during exposure, the results concur with other findings that high levels of fearful arousal are not a prerequisite for fear reduction from exposure.

The safety-signal perspective (Rachman, 1984) similarly deemphasizes level of anxiety aroused during exposure. Rachman suggested that exposure treatment might be facilitated by incorporating safety signals. For example, instead of entering a supermarket while the therapist waits outside, clients might walk toward the therapist (i.e., the safety signal), who is waiting inside the supermarket. Sartory, Masters, and Rachman (1989) compared safety-signal exposure ($n = 9$) to standard exposure ($n = 10$) for the treatment of agoraphobia over the course of four therapist-directed sessions and 2 weeks of self-directed practice. A small advantage was achieved by the safety-signal condition, particularly during the self-directed practice phase. Although the results were preliminary, they concur with evidence outlined earlier suggesting that exposure can proceed effectively without eliciting and then habituating relatively high levels of fearful arousal. Finally, this approach is consistent with our own model of emotional change that emphasizes the acquisition or a sense of control over preceived unpredictable and uncontrollable events along with a change in (escapist) action tendency as central to change (Barlow, 1988).

Distraction

It has been suggested that exposure is most functional when attention is directed fully toward the phobic object and internal and external sources of distraction are minimized (Borkovec, 1976; Foa & Kozak, 1986). Craske et al. (1989) administered therapist-directed and self-directed exposure to agoraphobics in small groups for 11 sessions. In one condition ($n = 16$) subjects were instructed to monitor bodily sensations and thoughts objectively throughout *in vivo* exposures, and to use thought stopping and focusing self-statements to interrupt distraction. In a second condition ($n = 14$), subjects were taught to use specific distraction tasks during *in vivo* exposures (e.g., word rhymes and spelling), and to use thought stopping and distracting self-statements to interrupt focusing of attention on feared bodily sensations and images. The treatment groups did not differ at posttreatment or at follow-up assessment. However, consistent with previous findings from OCD subjects (Grayson, Foa, & Steketee, 1982), the focused exposure group improved significantly from posttreatment to follow-up, in contrast to a slight deterioration in the distracted exposure group. This clinical trial suggested that instructions to focus on or distract from feared sensations and thoughts during *in vivo* exposures may yield comparable short-term results, although a stronger advantage may develop for focused exposure after treatment completion.

TREATMENT DESCRIPTION: PROTOCOL

Overview

The basic aim of the treatment protocol is to influence directly the cognitive–misinterpretational aspect of panic attacks and anxiety, the hyperventilatory response, conditioned reactions to physical cues, and fear and avoidance of situations. This is done first by providing of accurate information as to the nature of the physiological aspects of the fight–flight response. Such information teaches clients that they experience "sensations" and not "panics" and that these sensations are normal and harmless. Second, treatment aims at teaching specific techniques to help modify cognitions, including identifying and challenging aberrant beliefs. Next, specific information concerning the effects of hyperventilation and its role in panic attacks is provided as well as extensive breathing retraining. Then, repeated exposure to feared internal cues is conducted to decondition fear reactions and allow structured application of cognitive and breathing strategies. *In vivo* exposure

to feared and avoided situations is then practiced to weaken associations between certain situational contexts and the experience of anxiety and panic.

Session 1

The goals of Session 1 are to describe anxiety, provide a treatment rationale and treatment description, and emphasize the importance of self-monitoring and homework practices between treatment sessions. Therapy begins with identifying anxiety patterns and the situations in which anxiety and panic attacks are likely to occur. Many clients have difficulty identifying specific antecedents, reporting that anxiety can occur at almost any time. In accord with the typology of panic attacks described earlier, special emphasis is given to internal cues that may trigger anxiety and fear, particularly negative verbal cognitions, catastrophic imagery, and physical sensations. The following interchange took place between Jane (J) and her therapist (T):

T: In what situations are you most likely to panic?

J: Crowded restaurants and when I'm driving on the freeway. But sometimes I am driving along, feeling OK, when all of a sudden it hits. And other times I can be sitting at home feeling quite relaxed and it just hits. That's when I really get scared because I can't explain it.

T: So, when you are driving on the freeway, what is the very first thing you notice that tells you you're about to panic?

J: Well, the other cars on the road look as if they are moving really slowly.

T: And what is the first thing you notice when you're at home?

J: An unreal feeling, like I'm floating.

T: So, it sounds like the panic attacks that seem to occur for no reason are actually tied in with the sensations of unreality or when things look as if they are moving in slow motion.

J: I guess so. I always thought the physical feelings were the panic attack, but maybe they start the panic attack.

The next step is the three-response-systems model for describing and understanding the concept of anxiety and panic. This is believed to contribute to an objective self-awareness. Also, it provides the basis for an alternative conceptual framework for explaining panic and anxiety, which replaces the client's own misassumptions. Clients are asked to describe cognitive, physiological, and behavioral aspects to their responding. Clients are asked to identify the things that they *feel, think,* and *do* when they are anxious and panicky, using the three-response-systems model just described. Differences between the response profiles of anxiety and panic are highlighted. For example, the cognitive component in general anxiety may involve worrying about future events, whereas the cognitive component in panic fear may involve worrying about immediate danger; the behavioral component in general anxiety may consist of agitation and fidgeting, whereas the behavioral component in panic fear may involve escape or avoidance; the physiological component in general anxiety may involve muscular tension whereas the physiological component in panic fear may involve palpitations. After ensuring that the client has grasped the notion of a three-response-systems analysis in which the modalities are partially independent, the interactions among the response systems are described. The client is asked to describe the three components in a recent panic attack and identify ways in which they interacted to produce heightened distress.

T: How would you describe the three components of the panic attack you had at home last week?

J: Well, physically, my head felt really light, and my hands were clammy. I thought that either I would pass out or that I would somehow dissolve into nothingness. My behavior was to lie down and call my husband who was at work.

T: Now, what was the very first thing you noticed?

J: When I stood up my head started to feel really weird . . . as if it was spinning inside.

T: What was your very next reaction to that feeling?

J: I held onto the chair. I thought something was wrong . . . I thought it could get worse and that I'd collapse.

T: So, it began with a physical sensation, and then you had some very specific thoughts about those sensations. What happened next?

J: I felt very anxious.

T: And what happened next?

J: Well, the dizziness seemed to be getting worse and worse. I became really concerned that this was different from any other experience I had ever had. I was convinced that this was "it."

T: So, as you became more anxious, the physical feelings and the thoughts that something bad was going to happen intensified. What did you do next?

J: I called my husband and lay on the bed until he came home. It was horrible.

T: Can you see how one reaction fed off another, creating a cycle. That it began with a sensation, then some scary thoughts, then feeling anxious, then more sensations and more thoughts, and more fear, and so on. Now, if we had interrupted the cycle earlier on by, say, preventing the scary thoughts from coming into your mind, the anxiety and fear would not have developed.

To continue the development of the alternative conceptual model, a brief description of panic onset is provided. Clients are informed that they can benefit from the treatment without understanding the reasons they began to experience panic attacks, since factors involved in onset are not necessarily the same as the factors involved in the maintenance of a problem. Nevertheless, the initial panic attack is viewed as a manifestation of anxiety/stress. The stressors surrounding the time of the first panic attack are explored with the client, particularly in terms of how the stressors may have increased levels of physiological arousal and primed certain danger-laden cognitive schemas.

The first session ends with a full treatment rationale and description. In response to this information, Jane became highly anxious about the possibility of becoming anxious. She felt unable to tolerate either the treatment procedures or her anticipation of them. She became very agitated in the office and reported feelings of unreality. She opened the office door to find her husband who was waiting outside. The therapist helped Jane understand how the cycle of panic had emerged in the current situation, by identifying Jane's cognitive, physiological, and behavioral reactions: (1) the trigger was the description of treatment procedures entailing confrontation with feared sensations and situations; (2) the description was anxiety producing because Jane believed that she could not cope with the treatment demands, that the treatment would cause her so much anxiety that she would "flip out" and lose touch with reality permanently, or that she would never improve because she would never be able to tolerate a treatment program; (3) the current anxiety in the office elicited sensations of unreality and a racing heart; (4) Jane began to worry that she might panic and lose touch with reality permanently within the next few minutes; (5) the more anxious Jane felt, and the stronger her attempts to escape and find safety, the stronger the physical sensations became; and (6) Jane felt some relief on finding her husband because his presence reassures her that she will be safe. The cognitive misattributions were addressed via reassurance that treatment would progress at a pace at which Jane was comfortable, and by preliminary cognitive restructuring of the improbability of permanently losing touch with reality. After a lengthy discussion, Jane became more receptive to the treatment. A team approach to treatment planning and progress was agreed on so that Jane did not feel that she would be forced to do things she did not think she could do.

The homework for this session entails self-monitoring using the forms described earlier to enhance objective self-awareness. Clients are asked to monitor their fear and anxiety, keeping in mind the three response systems described in this session.

Session 2

The goals of this session are to describe the physiology underlying anxiety and panic and the concepts of hypervigilance and interoceptive conditioning. Basically, this session develops the previous session's goals of an objective self-awareness and an alternative conceptual model. Clients are given a detailed handout to read after the session is over (see Figure 1.4), which summarizes the didactic portion of the treatment.

The main concepts covered in this educational handout are (1) the survival value or protective function of anxiety and panic, (2) the physiological basis to the various sensations experienced during panic and anxiety, and the survival function of the underlying physiology, and (3) the role of specific learned and cognitively mediated fears of certain bodily sensations. The model of panic that was described earlier in this chapter is explained. In particular, the concept of interoceptive conditioning accounts for panic attacks that occur in response to subtle internal cues or physical sensations that may occur at any time. This information reduces anxiety about panic attacks, and enhances the credibility of the subsequent treatment procedures.

This session was very important for Jane, since her inability to explain her panic attacks was a significant part of her anxiety. Here are some of the questions she asked in her attempt to understand more fully.

J: So, if I understand you correctly, you're saying that my panic attacks are the same as the fear I experienced the time we found a burglar in our house. It doesn't feel the same at all.

T: Yes, those two emotional states—an unexpected panic attack and fear when confronted with a burglar—are essentially the same. However, in the case of the burglar, where were you focusing your attention—on the burglar or on the way you were feeling?

J: The burglar, of course, although I did notice my heart was going a mile a minute.

T: And when you have a panic attack, where are you focusing your attention—on the people around you or on the way you are feeling?

J: Well, mostly on the way I'm feeling, although it depends on where I am at the time.

T: Alright, now being most concerned about what's going on inside you can

While an actual definition of anxiety that covers all aspects is very difficult to provide (indeed whole books have been written on the subject), everyone knows the feeling we call anxiety. There is not a person who has not experienced some degree of anxiety, whether it is the feeling upon entering a school room just before an exam, or the feeling when one wakes in the middle of the night, certain that he/she heard a strange sound outside. What is less known, however, is that sensations such as extreme dizziness, spots and blurring of the eyes, numbness and tingling, stiff almost paralyzed muscles, and feelings of breathlessness extending to choking or smothering can also be a part of anxiety. When these sensations occur and people do not understand why, anxiety can increase to levels of panic since people imagine that they must have some disease.

Anxiety is a response to danger or threat. Scientifically, immediate- or short-term anxiety is termed the fight-flight response. It is so named because all of its effects are aimed toward either fighting or fleeing the danger. Thus, the number one purpose for anxiety is to protect the organism. When our ancestors lived in caves, it was vital that when faced with some danger, an automatic response would take over causing them to take immediate action (attack or run). Even in today's hectic world this is a necessary mechanism. Just imagine if you were crossing a street when suddenly a car sped toward you blasting its horn. If you experienced absolutely no anxiety, you would be killed. However, more probably, your fight-flight response would take over and you would run out of the way to be safe. The moral of this story is a simple one—the purpose of anxiety is to protect the organism, not to harm it. It would be totally ridiculous for nature to develop a mechanism whose purpose is to protect an organism and yet, in doing so, harms it.

The best way to think of all of the systems of the fight-flight response (anxiety) is to remember that all are aimed at getting the organism prepared for immediate action and that their purpose is to protect the organism.

When some sort of danger is perceived or anticipated, the brain sends messages to a section of your nerves called the autonomic nervous system. The autonomic nervous system has two subsections or branches called the sympathetic nervous system and the parasympathetic nervous system. It is these two branches of the nervous system that are directly involved in controlling the body's energy levels and preparation for action. Very simply put, the sympathetic nervous system is the fight-flight system which releases energy and gets the body "primed" for action, while the parasympathetic nervous system is the restoring system which returns the body to a normal state.

One important point is that the sympathetic nervous system tends to be largely an all-or-none system. That is, when it is activated, all of its parts respond. In other words, either all symptoms are experienced or no symptoms are experienced; it is rare for changes to occur in one part of the body alone. This may explain why most panic attacks involve many symptoms and not just one or two.

One of the major effects of the sympathetic nervous system is that it releases two chemicals, called adrenalin and noradrenalin, from the adrenal glands on the kidneys. These chemicals, in turn, are used as messengers by the sympathetic nervous system to continue activity so that once activity in the sympathetic nervous system begins, it often continues and increases for some time. However, it is very important to note that sympathetic nervous system activity is stopped in two ways. First, the chemical messengers—adrenalin and noradrenalin—are eventually destroyed by other chemicals in the body. Second, the parasympathetic nervous system (which generally has opposing effects to the sympathetic nervous system) becomes activated and restores a relaxed feeling. It is very important to realize that eventually the body will "have enough" of the fight-flight response and will activate the parasympathetic nervous system to restore a relaxed feeling. In other words, anxiety cannot continue forever or spiral to ever-increasing and possibly damaging levels. The parasympathetic nervous system is an built-in protector that stops the sympathetic nervous system from getting carried away. Another important point is that the chemical messengers, adrenalin and noradrenalin, take some time to be destroyed. Thus, even after the danger has passed and your sympathetic nervous system has stopped responding, you are likely to feel keyed up or apprehensive for some time because the chemicals are still floating around in your system. You must remind yourself that this is perfectly natural and harmless. In fact, this is an adaptive function because, in the wilds, danger often has a habit of returning and it is useful for the organism to be prepared to activate the fight-flight response.

(cont.)

FIGURE 1.4. Handout describing the physiology and psychology of fear and anxiety (Session 1).

Activity in the sympathetic nervous system produces on increase in heart rate and the strength of the heartbeat. This is vital to preparation for activity since it helps speed up the blood flow, thus improving delivery of oxygen to the tissues and removal of waste products from the tissues. This is why a racing or pounding heart is typically experienced during periods of high anxiety or panic. In addition to increased activity in the heart, there is also a change in the blood flow. Basically, blood is redirected away from the places where it is not needed (by a tightening of the blood vessels) and toward the places where it is needed more (by an expansion of the blood vessels). For example, blood is taken away from the skin, fingers, and toes. This is useful because if the organism is attacked and cut in some way, it is less likely to bleed to death. Hence, during anxiety the skin looks pale and feels cold and fingers and toes become cold and sometimes experience numbness and tingling. In addition, the blood is moved to the large muscles such as the thighs and biceps, which helps the body prepare for action.

The fight-flight response is associated with an increase in the speed and depth of breathing. This has obvious importance for the defense of the organism since the tissues need to get more oxygen in order to prepare for action. The feelings produced by this increase in breathing, however, can include breathlessness, choking or smothering feelings, and even pains or tightness in the chest. Importantly, a side effect of increased breathing, especially if no actual activity occurs, is that blood supply to the head is actually decreased. While this is only a small amount and is not at all dangerous, it produces a collection of unpleasant (but harmless) symptoms including dizziness, blurred vision, confusion, unreality, and hot flushes.

Activation of the fight-flight response produces an increase in sweating. This has important adaptive functions such as making the skin more slippery so that it is harder for a predator to grab and cooling the body to stop it from overheating.

Activation of the sympathetic nervous system produces a number of other effects, none of which are in any way harmful. For example, the pupils widen to let in more light, which may result in blurred vision, spots in front of the eyes, and so on. There is a decrease in salivation, resulting in a dry mouth. There is decreased activity in the digestive system, which often produces nausea, a heavy feeling in the stomach, and even constipation. Finally, many of the muscle groups tense up in preparation for fight or flight and this results in subjective feelings of tension, sometimes extending to actual aches and pains as well as to trembling and shaking.

Overall, the fight-flight response results in a general activation of the whole bodily metabolism. Thus, one often feels hot and flushed and, because this process takes a lot of energy, afterwards one generally feels tired, drained, and washed out.

As mentioned before, the fight-flight response prepares the body for action–either to attack or to run. Thus, it is no surprise that the overwhelming urges associated with this response are those of aggression and a desire to escape. When this is not possible (due to social constraints), the urges will often be expressed by such behaviors as foot tapping, pacing, or snapping at people. Overall, the feelings produced are those of being trapped and needing to escape.

The number one effect of the fight-flight response is to alert the organism to the possible existence of danger. Thus, there is an immediate and automatic shift in attention to search the surroundings for potential threat. It becomes very difficult to concentrate on daily tasks when one is anxious. People who are anxious often complain that they are easily distracted from daily chores, that they cannot concentrate, and that they have trouble with their memory. Sometimes, an obvious threat cannot be found. Unfortunately, most people cannot accept having no explanation for something. Therefore, in many cases, when people cannot find an explanation for their sensations, they turn their search to themselves. In other words, "if nothing out there is making me feel anxious, there must be something wrong with me." In this case, the brain invents an explanation, such as "I must be dying, losing control, or going crazy." As we have now seen, nothing could be further from the truth since the purpose of the fight-flight response is to protect the organism, not to harm it. Nevertheless, these are understandable thoughts.

Until now, we have looked at the features and components of general anxiety or the fight-flight response. However, you may be wondering how all this applies to panic attacks. After all why should the fight-flight response be activated during panic attacks since there is apparently nothing to frightened of?

(cont.)

Following extensive research, it appears that people with panic attacks are frightened of (i.e., what causes the panic) the actual physical sensations of the fight-flight response. Thus, panic attacks can be seen as a set of unexpected physical symptoms and a response of panic or fear of the symptoms. The second part of this model is easy to understand. As discussed earlier, the fight-flight response (of which the physical symptoms are a part) causes the brain to search for danger. When the brain cannot find any obvious danger, it turns its search inward and invents a danger such as "I am dying, losing control, etc." Since such interpretations of the physical symptoms are very frightening, it is understandable that fear and panic result. In turn, fear and panic produce more physical symptoms, and therefore a cycle of symptoms, fear, symptoms, fear, and so on, is produced. The first part of the model is harder to understand. Why do you experience the physical symptoms of the fight-flight response if you are not frightened to begin with? There are many ways these symptoms can be produced, not just through fear. For example, it may be that you have become generally stressed in your life and this stress results in an increase in the production of adrenalin and other chemicals that, from time to time, produce symptoms. This increased adrenalin could presumably be maintained chemically in the body even after the stressor has long gone. Another possibility is that you tend to breathe a little too fast (subtle hyperventilation) due to a learned habit, and this also can produce symptoms. Because the overbreathing is very slight, you easily become used to this level of breathing and do not notice that you are hyperventilating. A third possibility is that you are experiencing normal changes in your body (which everyone experiences but most don't notice) and, because you are constantly monitoring and keeping a check on your body, you notice these sensations far more than most people do. In addition to the two reasons already described for experiencing physical symptoms (i.e., stress and overbreathing), you might become conscious of these physical symptoms as a result of a process calleld interoceptive conditioning. Since the physical symptoms have been associated with the trauma of panicking, they have become meaningful signals of threat and danger to you (that is, they have become conditioned stimuli). As a result, it is very likely that you are highly sensitive to these symptoms and react fearfully simply because of the past experiences of panic with which they have been associated. As a consequence of this type of conditioned association, it is possible that symptoms produced by regular activities can also lead to your becoming panicky. For example, the breathless and sweaty feelings produced by physical exercise, the jittery feeling produced by drinking coffee, or the heat produced by overcrowded stores may all lead you to feel panicky.

Even if we are not certain why one experiences the initial symptoms, be assured that they are a part of the fight-flight response and therefore are harmless.

Obviously, then, once you truly believe (100%) that the physical sensations are not dangerous, the fear and panic will no longer occur and you will no longer experience panic attacks. Of course, once you have had a number of panic attacks and you have misinterpreted the symptoms many times, this misinterpretation becomes quite automatic and it becomes very difficult to consciously convince yourself during a panic attack that the symptoms are harmless.

In summary, anxiety is scientifically known as the fight-flight response since its primary purpose is to activate the organism and protect it from harm. Associated with this response are a number of physical, behavioral, and mental changes. Importantly, once the danger has gone, many of these changes (especially the physical ones) can continue, almost with a mind of their own, due to learning and other longer-term bodily changes. When the physical symptoms occur in the absence of an obvious explanation, people often misinterpret the normal fight-flight symptoms as indicating a serious physical or mental problem. In this case, the sensations themselves can often become threatening and can begin the whole fight-flight response again. Many people, when they experience the physical symptoms of the fight-flight response, believe they are "going crazy." They are most likely referring to a severe mental disorder known as schizophrenia. Let us look at schizophrenia to see how likely this is.

Schizophrenia is a major disorder characterized by such severe symptoms as disjointed thoughts and speech, sometimes extending to babbling, delusions, or strange beliefs (e.g., that messages are being received from outer space), and hallucinations (e.g., that there are voices in one's head).

(cont.)

FIGURE 1.4. *(continued)*

Furthermore, schizophrenia appears to be largely a genetically based disorder, running strongly in families.

Schizophrenia generally begins very gradually and not suddenly (as during a panic attack). Additionally, because it runs in families, only a certain proportion of people can become schizophrenic and, in other people, no amount of stress will cause the disorder. A third important point is that people who become schizophrenic usually show some mild symptoms for most of their life (e.g., unusual thoughts and flowery speech). Thus, if this has not been noticed in you yet, the chances are you will not become schizophrenic. This is especially true if you are over 25 since schizophrenia generally first appears in the late teens to early 20s. Finally, if you have been through interviews with a psychologist or psychiatrist, you can be fairly certain that they would have known if you were likely to become schizophrenic.

Some people believe they are going to "lose control" when they panic. Presumably, they mean that they will either become totally paralyzed and not be able to move, or that they will not know what they are doing and will run around wildly killing people or yelling out obscenities and embarrassing themselves. Alternatively, they may not know what to expect but may just experience an overwhelming feeling of "impending doom."

From our earlier discussion, we now know where this feeling comes from. During anxiety the entire body is prepared for action and there is an overwhelming desire to escape. However, the fight-flight response is not aimed at hurting other people (who are not a threat) and it will not produce paralysis. Rather, the entire response is simply aimed at getting the organism away. In addition, there has never been a recorded case of someone going wild during a panic attack. Even though the fight-flight response makes you feel somewhat confused, unreal, and distracted, you are still able to think and function normally. Simply think of how often other people even notice that you are having a panic attack.

Many people are frightened about what might happen to them as a result of their symptoms, perhaps because of some belief that their nerves might become exhausted and they may collapse. As discussed earlier, the fight-flight response is produced chiefly through activity in the sympathetic nervous system which is counteracted by the parasympathetic nervous system. The parasympathetic nervous system is, in a sense, a safeguard against the possibility that the sympathetic nervous system may become "worn out." Nerves are not like electrical wires and anxiety cannot wear out, damage, or use up nerves. The absolute worst that could happen during a panic attack is that an individual could pass out, at which point the sympathetic nervous system would stop its activity and the person would regain consciousness within a few seconds. However, actually passing out as a result of the fight-flight response is extremely rare, and if it does occur, it is an adaptive way of stopping the sympathetic nervous system from going out of control.

Many people misinterpret the symptoms of the fight-flight response and believe they must be dying of a heart attack. This is probably because many people do not have enough knowledge about heart attacks. Let us look at the facts of heart disease and see how this differs from panic attacks.

The major symptoms of heart disease are breathlessness and chest pain as well as occasional palpitations and fainting. The symptoms in heart disease are generally directly related to effort. That is, the harder you exercise, the worse the symptoms and the less you exercise, the better. The symptoms will usually go away fairly quickly with rest. This is very different to the symptoms associated with panic attacks, which often occur at rest and seem to have a mind of their own. Certainly, panic symptoms can occur during exercise or can be made worse during exercise, but they are different from the symptoms of a heart attack since they can occur equally often at rest. Of most importance, heart disease will almost always produce major electrical changes in the heart, which are picked up by the electrocardiogram (EKG). In panic attacks, the only change that shows up on the EKG is a slight increase in heart rate. Thus, if you have had an EKG and the doctor has given you the all-clear, you can safely assume you do not have heart disease. Also, if your symptoms occur any time and not only upon exertion, this is additional evidence against a heart attack.

FIGURE 1.4. (*continued*)

lead to a very different type of experience than being concerned about the burglar, even though basically the same physiological response is occurring. For example, remember our description of the way in which fear of sensations can intensify the sensations.

J: But what about the feelings of unreality. How can they be protective or how can feeling unreal help me deal with a danger situation?

T: OK, remember that it's the physiological events that are the protective ones, and the sensations are just the end result of those events. Now, feelings of unreality can be caused by changes in your blood flow to your brain, although not dangerously so, or from overbreathing, or from concentrating too intensely on what's going on inside you. So, the unreality sensation may not be protective, but the changes in blood flow and overbreathing are.

J: I understand how I can create a panic attack by being afraid of my bodily feelings, like my heart racing or feeling unreal. But sometimes it happens so quickly that I don't have time to think.

T: Yes, these reactions can occur very quickly, at times automatically. But remember, we are tuned to react instantaneously to things, including our own bodies, that we think mean danger. Picture yourself walking through a jungle. Let's say that after about half an hour of relaxed walking, you are informed that a lion has been sighted nearby. Now, your attention shifts dramatically to anything that suggests the possibility of a lion attack, such as noises in the bushes, or branches moving. And when the noises are heard or the branches move, your reaction is extraordinarily fast. Well, the same thing happens with panic: But now it's the physical sensations that are the signals instead of the branches and noises in the jungle, and now it's the belief that you'll lose touch with reality permanently that is the danger instead of the lion.

The homework for this session is to continue the development of an alternative conceptual framework and an objective versus subjective self-awareness. This is achieved through self-monitoring of panics, keeping in mind the principles discussed to date, and rereading the handout.

Session 3

The primary goal of the third session is to begin breathing control. Clients are asked to voluntarily hyperventilate by standing and breathing fast and deep, as if blowing up a balloon, for 1½ min. With prompting and encouragement from the therapist, clients can often complete the full 1½ min, after which time they are asked to sit, close their eyes and breathe very slowly, pausing at the end of each breath, until the symptoms have abated. The experience is then discussed in terms of the degree to which it produced symptoms similar to those that occur naturally during anxiety or panic. Approximately 50% to 60% report similarity of the symptoms. Often, however, similarity of the symptoms is confused with similarity of the anxiety. Since the exercise is conducted in a safe environment, and the symptoms have an obvious cause, most clients rate the experience as less anxiety provoking than if the same symptoms had occurred naturally. This distinction is important, since it demonstrates the significance of perceived safety for the degree of anxiety experienced. Jane rated the hyperventilation exercise as very anxiety provoking (6 on a 0–8-point scale), and rated the symptoms as being quite similar to her panic symptoms (5.5 on a 0–8-point scale). She terminated the task after approximately 40 sec, in anticipation of experiencing a full-blown panic attack. This experience was discussed in terms of the three response systems and the role of misappraisals and interoceptive conditioning described in Session 2.

The next phase of breathing retraining is education about the physiological basis of hyperventilation. As before, the goal of the didactic presentation is to allay misinterpretations of the dangers of overbreathing, and to provide a basis of information on which to draw when actively challenging misinterpretations. The educational content is shown in Figure 1.5, in protocol format, al-

The body needs oxygen in order to survive. Whenever a person inhales, oxygen is taken into the lungs where it is picked up by the hemoglobin (the "oxygen-sticky" chemical in blood). The hemoglobin carries the oxygen around the body where it is released for use by the body's cells. The cells use the oxygen in their energy reactions, subsequently producing a by-product of carbon dioxide (CO_2) which is, in turn, released back to the blood, transported to the lungs, and exhaled.

Efficient control of the body's energy reactions depends on the maintenance of a specific balance between oxygen and CO_2. This balance can be maintained chiefly through an appropriate rate and depth of breathing. Obviously, breathing "too much" will have the effect of increasing levels of oxygen (in the blood only) and decreasing levels of CO_2, while breathing too little will have the effect of decreasing levels of oxygen and increasing levels of CO_2. The appropriate rate of breathing, at rest, is usually around 10–14 breaths per minute.

Hyperventilation is defined as a rate and depth of breathing that are too much for the body's needs at a particular point in time. Naturally, if the need for oxygen and the production of CO_2 both increase (such as during exercise), breathing should increase appropriately. Alternately, if the need for oxygen and the production of CO_2 both decrease (such as during relaxation), breathing should decrease appropriately.

While most of the body's mechanisms are controlled by "automatic" chemical and physical means (and breathing is no exception), breathing has an additional property of being able to be put under voluntary control. For example, it is quite easy for us to hold our breath (swimming under water) or speed up our breathing (blowing up a balloon). Therefore, a number of "nonautomatic" factors such as emotion, stress, or habit can cause us to increase our breathing. These factors may be especially important in people who suffer panic attacks causing a tendency to breathe too much.

Interestingly, while most of us consider oxygen to be the determining factor in our breathing, the body actually uses CO_2 as its "marker" for appropriate breathing. The most important effect of hyperventilation, then, is to produce a marked drop in CO_2. This, in turn, produces a drop in the acid content of the blood leading to what is known as alkaline blood. It is these two effects—a decrease in blood CO_2 content and an increase in blood alkalinity—which are responsible for most of the physical changes that occur during hyperventilation.

One of the most important changes produced by hyperventilation is a constriction or narrowing of certain blood vessels around the body. In particular the blood going to the brain is somewhat decreased. Coupled with this tightening of blood vessels is the fact that the hemoglobin increases its "stickiness" for oxygen. Thus, not only does less blood reach certain areas of the body, but the oxygen carried by this blood is less likely to be released to the tissues. Paradoxically, then, while overbreathing means more oxygen is taken in, less oxygen reaches certain areas of our brain and body. This effect results in two broad categories of symptoms: (1) centrally, some symptoms are produced by the slight reduction in oxygen to certain parts of the brain (including, dizziness, lightheadedness, confusion, breathlessness, blurred vision, and unreality); (2) peripherally, some symptoms are produced by the slight reduction in oxygen to certain parts of the body (including an increase in heartbeat to pump more blood around; numbness and tingling in the extremities; cold, clammy hands, and sometimes stiffness of muscles). It is important to remember that the reductions in oxygen are slight and are totally harmless. It is important, too, to note that hyperventilating (possibly through a reduction in oxygen to certain parts of the brain) can produce a feeling of breathlessness, sometimes extending to feelings of choking or smothering, so that it actually feels as if the person is not getting enough air.

Hyperventilation is also responsible for a number of overall effects. First, the act of overbreathing is hard physical work. Hence, the individual may often feel hot, flushed, and sweaty. Second, because it is hard work to overbreathe, prolonged periods of overbreathing will often result in tiredness and exhaustion. Third, people who overbreathe often tend to breathe from their chest rather than their diaphragm. This means that their chest muscles tend to become tired and tense. Thus, they can experience symptoms of chest tightness and even severe chest pains. Finally, many people who overbreathe tend to engage in a habit of repeatedly sighing or yawning. These tics are actually forms of hyperventilation since whenever people yawn or sigh they are "dumping" a large quantity of CO_2

(cont.)

FIGURE 1.5. Handout describing the physiology of overbreathing (Session 3).

very quickly. Therefore, when combatting the problem, it is important to become aware of habitual sighing and yawning and to try and suppress these habits.

One important point to be made about hyperventilation is that it is not necessarily obvious to the observer. In many cases hyperventilation can be very subtle. This is especially true if the individual has been slightly overbreathing for a long time. In this case there can be marked drop in CO_2 but, due to compensation in the body, relatively little change in alkalinity. Thus, symptoms will not be produced. However, because CO_2 levels are kept low, the body loses its ability to cope with changes in CO_2 so that even a slight change in breathing (e.g., through a yawn) can be enough to suddenly trigger symptoms. This may account for the sudden nature of many panic attacks, for example, often during sleep, and is one reason why many sufferers report, "I don't feel as if I'm hyperventilating."

Probably the most important point to be made about hyperventilation is that it is not dangerous. Hyperventilation is an integral part of the fight-flight response and thus its purpose is to protect the body from danger, not to be dangerous. The changes associated with hyperventilation are those that prepare the body for action in order to escape potential harm. Thus, it is an automatic reaction for the brain to immediately expect danger and for the individual to feel the urge to escape. Consequently, it is perfectly understandable, if there is no obvious danger, for the sufferer to believe the danger must be internal. Nevertheless, this is not so. It is important to remember that far from being harmful, hyperventilation is part of a natural, biological response aimed at protecting the body from harm.

FIGURE 1.5. (*continued*)

though it should be tailored to the client's own verbal level.

The next step is to teach breathing control, which begins by relying more on the diaphragm than on chest muscles. In addition, clients are instructed to concentrate on their breathing, by counting on their inhalations and thinking the word *relax* on exhalations. (Slow breathing is introduced in the next session.) Therapists model the suggested breathing patterns and then provide corrective feedback to clients while they practice in the office setting.

Breathing control is a skill that requires considerable practice before it can be successfully used to manage episodes of high anxiety or panic. In addition, initial reactions to the exercise can be negative for clients who are afraid of respiratory sensations (since the exercise entails concentration on breathing), or for clients who are chronic overbreathers and for whom the interruption of habitual breathing patterns initially increases overbreathing symptomatology. In both cases, continued practice is advisable, with reassurance that sensations such as shortness of breath are not harmful.

Finally, the integration of breathing-control techniques and cognitive strategies is emphasized. On occasion, clients mistakenly view breathing control as a way of re-

lieving themselves of terrifying symptoms, thus falling into the trap of fearing dire consequences should they not succeed in changing their breathing. The homework for this session entails continued self-monitoring and practice of diaphragmatic breathing at least two times a day, at least 10 min each time.

Session 4

The goals of this session are to develop breathing control and to begin active cognitive restructuring. Therapists review the client's week of breathing-control practice. Jane was disappointed with her attempts to control her own breathing.

J: I just didn't seem to be able to do it the right way. Sometimes I would start off OK and then the more I tried, the more it felt like I was running out of air, and I'd have to take a big gulp between breaths. At other times, I felt dizzy and the unreal feelings would start, at which point I would stop the breathing and try to do "busy work" to keep my mind occupied.

T: It sounds like quite a few things were going on. First of all, remember that this is a skill, just like learning to ride a bike, and you cannot expect it to be easy from the get go. Second, it sounds like you experienced some uncomfortable physical feelings that worried you. You said it felt like you were running out of air. Based on what we talked about last week, what do you think might have caused that feeling?

J: Well, maybe I wasn't getting enough air into my lungs, because it's really hard for me to use my diaphragm. I felt like I was suffocating myself.

T: Possibly it's just a matter of learning to use the diaphragm muscle, but were you really suffocating or was it an interpretation that you might be suffocating?

J: I don't know . . . I've had the feeling of suffocating before, especially when I'm trapped in a crowded room.

T: So, how do you know you were suffocating?

J: I don't know . . . it just felt that way.

T: So, let's put all of the evidence together. You've had the feelings before and never suffocated. In fact, a lot of people have those feelings and they do not actually suffocate. As we talked about last time, changing your breathing or becoming anxious can sometimes create a sensation of shortness of breath even though you are getting plenty of air. Finally, the exercise was forcing you to concentrate on those feelings. On the basis of all of these facts, can you think of an alternative explanation?

J: Well, maybe I wasn't suffocating, maybe it just felt like that. I hope it doesn't always feel that way.

T: As you relax with the procedure, and realize that the sensations of dizziness or shortness of breath are not going to hurt you, and as you become more skilled at diaphragmatic and slow breathing, it will get easier.

Jane's complaints represent typical concerns that should be addressed. The next step is to slow the rate of breathing until the client can comfortably span a full inhalation and exhalation cycle over 6 sec. Again, the therapist models and then provides corrective feedback as practice is conducted in the session. Clients are instructed to practice slow breathing in "safe" or relaxing environments. They are discouraged from applying slow breathing when anxious or panicking until fully skilled in its application.

Cognitive restructuring is introduced by explaining that errors in thinking occur for everyone when they are anxious, thus helping the client to expect his/her thinking to be distorted, since the state of anxiety means being on extra alert for threat or danger. Therefore, the importance of treating thoughts as hypotheses or guesses rather than facts is stressed. The notions of automatic thinking and discrete predictions are explained also, to emphasize the need to become an astute observer of one's own habitual self-statements in specific situations. Recognition of the thought "I feel terrible—something bad could happen" is insufficient, nontherapeutic, and may serve to intensify anxiety by virtue of its global and nondirective nature. Instead, recognition of the thought "I am afraid that if I get too anxious while driving then I'll lose control of the wheel and drive off the side of the road and die" allows for constructive questioning to challenge the series of misassumptions.

Two main types of errors in cognitions are described. The first is overestimation, or jumping to negative conclusions and treating negative events as probable when in fact they are unlikely to occur. The client is asked to identify overestimations from the anxiety and panic incidents over the past 2 weeks: "Can you think of events that you felt sure were going to happen when you were feeling anxious, only to find out in the end that they did not happen at all." Usually, clients can identify such events easily, but with protestations.

J: Well, several times I thought that I really was going to lose it this time . . . that I would flip out and never return to reality. It never actually happened, *but* it could still happen.

T: Why do you think "it" could still happen?

J: Part of me feels like I've always managed to escape it just in time, either by removing myself from the situation, or by having my husband help me, or by holding on long enough for the feeling to pass. But what if next time I can't hold on.

T: Knowing what we know about our thoughts when we are anxious, can you classify any of the ideas you just expressed, of "just holding on" or "just escaping in time," as overestimations.

J: I suppose you're saying that I can hold on or I can always escape in time.

T: More that you feel the need to hold on and the need to escape because you are overestimating the likelihood of flipping out and never returning to reality.

J: But it really feels like I will.

T: The confusion between what you think will happen and what actually happens is the very problem that we are addressing in this session.

The reasons why overestimations persist despite repeated disconfirmation are explored. Typically, the absence of danger is attributed to external safety signals or behaviors (e.g., "I only made it because I managed to find help in time"; "If I had not taken Xanax last week when I panicked in the store, I'm sure I would have passed out"; or "I wouldn't have made it if I hadn't pull off the road in time"), or to "luck," instead of to the inaccuracy of the original prediction. Similarly, clients assume that the only reason why they are still alive, sane, and so on, is because the "big one" has not happened, but it will. In this case, a direct correlation is made by the client between the intensity of the panic attack and the risk of dying, losing control, and so forth, which is another misinterpretation to be recognized.

The method for countering overestimation errors is to question the evidence for probability judgments. The general format is to treat thoughts as hypotheses or guesses rather than facts and examine the evidence for predictions, while considering alternative, more realistic predictions. This is best done in a socratic style so that clients examine the content of their statements and reach alternatives. Questioning of the client's specific logic (e.g., "How does a racing heart lead to heart attack"), or the bases from which judgments are made (e.g., misinformation from others or unusual sensations) are useful in this regard. Continuing with the previous example from Jane, the questioning took the following course:

T: One of the specific self-statements you have identified is that you will flip out and never return to reality. What specifically leads you to think that that is likely to happen?

J: Well, I guess it really feels like that.

T: Be more specific. What feelings?

J: Well, I feel spacy and unreal, like things around me are different and that I'm not connected.

T: And why do you think those feelings mean that you have actually lost touch with reality?

J: I don't know—it feels as if I have.

T: Well, do you respond if someone asks you a question during those episodes?

J: Well, I respond to you even though I feel that way sometimes in here.

T: OK, and can you walk or write or drive when you feel that way?

J: Yes, but it feels different.

T: But you do perform those functions despite feeling detached. So, what does that tell you?

J: Well, maybe I haven't lost complete touch with reality. But what if I do?

T: How many times have you felt detached?

J: Hundreds and hundreds of times.

T: And how many times have you lost touch with reality permanently?

J: Never. But what if the feelings don't go away, maybe I'll lose it then?

T: So what else tells you that this is a possibility?

J: Well, what about my second cousin. He lost it when he was about twenty-five, and now he's just a mess. He can hardly function at all and he is constantly being admitted to psychiatric hospitals. They have him on a bunch of heavy-duty drugs. I'll never forget the time I saw him totally out of it at his home—he was talking to himself in jibberish.

T: So, do you make a connection between him and yourself?

J: Yes.

T: What are the similarities between the two of you?

J: There are none really. It's just that he is what I think I will become?

T: Did he ever feel the way you feel now?

J: I don't know.

T: And if another one of your cousins had severe back problems, would you be concerned that you would end up with severe back problems?.

J: No.

T: Why not?

J: Because I never think about having back problems.

T: So, you think you'll be like your cousin because he is suffering a condition that you fear but you don't think you would be like another cousin who has back problems because you are not afraid of suffering back problems.

J: I suppose so.

T: So, lets consider all of the evidence, and consider some alternatives. You have felt unreal hundreds of times, and you've never lost touch with reality because you've continued to function in the midst of those feelings, and they have never lasted forever. You are afraid of becoming like your cousin even though there doesn't seem to be reason to assume that what he is experiencing is anything like what you are going through. Also, keep in mind our previous discussion of where feelings of unreality can come from [i.e., anxious arousal and overbreathing]. So, what is the realistic probability that you will lose touch with reality permanently? Use a 0-to-100-point scale, where 0 = no chance at all and 100 = definitely will happen.

J: Well, maybe it is lower than I thought. Maybe 20%.

T: So that would mean that you have actually lost touch with reality in a permanent way once every five times you have felt unreal?

J: When its put like that, I guess not. Maybe it's a very small possibility.

T: Yes, so what is an alternative explanation?

J: Perhaps the feelings of unreality are caused by feeling anxious or over-breathing, and that having those feelings does not mean that I am actually losing touch with reality, and that I am not like my cousin at all.

The homework assignment for this session is to practice breathing control and monitor examples of overestimation and restructure them by questioning the odds and looking at the evidence.

Session 5

The goals of this session are application of breathing control and extension of cognitive restructuring to the second type of cognitive error, which is catastrophizing. Clients are asked to practice breathing control in demanding environments, for example, while sitting at a desk at work or while waiting at a stoplight in the car. They are encouraged to do "mini-practices" often throughout the day.

The second type of cognitive error arises from viewing an event as "dangerous," "insufferable," or "catastrophic" when, in actuality, it is not. Hence, typical kinds of catastrophic errors are, "If I faint people will think that I'm weak and that would be unbearable"; "Panic attacks are the worst thing I can imagine"; and "The whole evening is ruined if I start to feel anxious." Decatastrophizing means to realize that the occurrences are not as "catastrophic" as stated, which is achieved by considering how negative events are managed versus how "bad" they are. For example, it is important for the person who states that negative judgments from others are unbearable to discuss what he/she would do to cope should someone else make an explicit negative judgment. Similarly, for the person who states that the physical symptoms of panic are intolerable, the following type of questioning between therapist (T) and client (C) is helpful:

T: What is so bad about your heart racing and feeling dizzy?

C: It's such a horrible feeling, I hate it. I wish the symptoms would just go away.

T: But what makes it so bad?

C: Because I can't get rid of the symptoms.

T: And what if we were to make it a ruling that you would have a racing heart and dizziness for the rest of your life?

C: I couldn't stand it.

T: What would you do? Let's make it easier. Let's say that you developed a disease that meant that for the rest of your life you would have pain in your left wrist. Now, what would you do to cope with that?

C: Well, I guess that I would try to do the best that I could. Maybe I'd do some exercises to relieve the pain. I'd probably continue to do most things that I do now, but perhaps not as easily.

T: OK, so you would cope. Now, how is that different from a racing heart and feeling dizzy?

C: I feel like I can't do anything when I feel those symptoms.

T: Are you overestimating? What can you not do?

C: You're right . . . it's probably that I just think I can't do things. I mean, even though I feel those symptoms, I still read, talk to people, and drive around. Maybe I could do other things that I've been avoiding because I didn't think I could manage—like playing sports again.

T: Good. Now, when you realize that a racing heart and dizziness are manageable, do you see how the feelings themselves are likely to diminish.

The homework is applied breathing control and identifying and challenging overestimations and catastrophic styles of thinking.

Session 6

The main goal of this session is to begin interoceptive exposure, although initially time is spent reviewing the cognitive restructuring principles, particularly in terms of the client's application of cognitive strategies to anxiety and panic episodes throughout the preceding week. The rationale for interoceptive exposure is very important for facilitating generalization from in-session practices to daily experiences. The therapist reviews the concept of interoceptive conditioning described in the second session. The way in which avoidance of feared sensations serves to maintain fearfulness is explored. Activities that are avoided because of the associated physical sensations may not be immediately obvious to the client. They may include physical exercise, emotional discussions, suspenseful movies, steamy rooms (e.g., shower with doors and windows closed), certain foods, or stimulants. The purpose of interoceptive exposure is to repeatedly induce the sensations that are feared and to weaken the fear response through habituating and learning that no actual danger results. In addition, the repeated inductions allow practice in applying the cognitive strategies and breathing strategies. As a result, fear of physical sensations that occur naturally is significantly reduced.

The procedure begins by assessing the client's response to a series of standardized exercises. The therapist models each exercise first. Then, after the client has completed the exercise, the therapist records the sensations, anxiety level (0–8), sensation intensity (0–8), and similarity to naturally occurring panic sensations (0–8). The exercises are listed in Table 1.4. If none of these exercises produces sensations at least moderately similar to those that occur naturally, other individually tailored exercises are generated. For example, if chest pain is the primary feared sensation, tightness around the chest can be induced by taking a deep breath before hyperventilating. If heat is the main feared sensation, a hot room can be used. If the most feared sensation is choking, possibilities include a tongue depressor, a high-collared sweater, or a necktie.

If clients report little or no fear because they feel safe in the presence of the therapist, they are asked to attempt each exercise alone, while the therapist leaves the office or at home. For a minority of clients, the known cause and course of the sensations override the fear response. For the majority of clients, at least several of the exercises are feared despite knowing the cause of the sensations and their controllability.

The exercises rated as producing at least somewhat similar sensations (at least 3 on the 0–8-point scale) are selected for repeated

TABLE 1.4. Interoceptive Exposure Exercises

Exercise	Duration (sec)	Sensation intensity (0–8)	Anxiety (0–8)	Similarity (0–8)
Shake head from side to side	30			
Place head between legs and then lift	30			
Run on spot	60			
Hold breath	30 or as long as possible			
Complete body muscle tension or hold push up	60 or as long as possible			
Spin in swivel chair	60			
Hyperventilate 60				
Breath through narrow straw	120			
Stare at spot on wall or own mirror image	90			

exposure in the next session. From the selected exercises, a hierarchy is established on the basis of the anxiety ratings. The homework is to continue cognitive monitoring and challenging.

Session 7

The primary goal of this session is to conduct repeated interoceptive exposure. First, however, breathing control is reviewed. Clients are encouraged to apply breathing control at times of anxiety or uncomfortable physical sensations from this point on. Also, hypothesis testing is introduced to facilitate cognitive restructuring. Hypothesis testing involves identifying overestimations or catastrophic predictions about situations that are likely to be encountered in the near future. The likelihood of the prediction's coming true is rated in this session. For example, Jane predicted that it was 60% likely that someone at the business dinner she was attending during the week would comment on how weird she looked. It is important to note that hypothesis testing does not call for the likelihood of Jane's having a panic attack at the business dinner, but rather for the perceived likelihood of the feared event (i.e., "someone commenting

on how weird she looks"). At the next session, the client and therapist examine the evidence that either supports or refutes the predictions that were made the week prior. In this manner, the client obtains more concrete evidence that few if any of his/her dire predictions come true. Hypothesis testing is particularly useful for catastrophic predictions about the effects of anxiety on ability to function.

A graduated approach is used for interoceptive exposure, beginning with the lowest item on the hierarchy established last session. For each trial of exposure, the client is asked to begin the induction, indicate when the sensations are first experienced (e.g., by raising a hand), and continue the induction for at least 30 sec longer in order to break the action tendency to avoid and resist the sensations. After terminating the induction, anxiety is rated and the client is given time to apply cognitive and breathing management strategies. Finally, the therapist reviews the induction experience and the application of management strategies with the client. During this review, the therapist emphasizes the importance of experiencing the sensations fully during the induction, of concentrating objectively on the sensations versus distracting from them, and the importance of identifying specific cognitions and challenging them by considering all of the evidence. In addition, the therapist asks key questions to help the client realize his/her safety (e.g., "What would have happened if you had continued spinning for another 60 seconds"), and to generalize to naturally occurring experiences (e.g., "How is this different from when you feel dizzy at work"). In other words, cognitive challenging extends the cognitive reprocessing already taking place as a result of repeated interoceptive exposure. Furthermore, specific cognitions not previously recognized sometimes become apparent. For example, Jane became more aware of her assumption that she would lose control of her limbs if she felt very spacy or lightheaded. This related to her concern about causing an accident when driving. During repeated hyperventilation exercises and with prompting of "what ifs" from the therapist, the fear of not being able to move her arms or legs in a controlled fashion was discovered. This assumption was then behaviorally challenged by having Jane overbreathe for longer periods of time, followed immediately by walking, picking up objects, and so on.

The trials are repeated enough times until the anxiety level for a given exercise is no greater than 2 (or, mild). Then, the procedure is repeated for the next exercise on the hierarchy.

Occasionally, clients report that since the exercise-induced sensations are predictable and controllable, they are less fear provoking than naturally occurring sensations. This demarcation limits the learning value of the interoceptive exercises. A cognitive approach, illustrated in the following example, is helpful at these times.

J: After spinning and hyperventilating several times, I really do feel much less anxious. I was terrified at the start but now I am mildly anxious only, if at all. But, this is different from what happens to me when I'm on the freeway or at home.

T: How is it different?

J: I don't know when the feelings of dizziness and unreality are going to hit.

T: First of all, from our previous discussions, what accounts for you feeling dizzy or unreal at certain times?

J: I know . . . I have to keep remembering that it could be my breathing, or just feeling anxious, or tired, or a bunch of different things.

T: OK. Now, second of all, why is it so important to know when those feelings will occur?

J: Because I don't want them to be there at all.

T: And why not . . . what are you afraid of?

J: I guess it's the same old thing . . . that I'll lose it somehow?

T: So let's go back to the cognitive restructuring that you have been doing. What specifically are you afraid of? How likely is it to happen? What are the alternatives?

J: I understand.

T: So, now you see that whether the sensations of dizziness or unreality are produced by anxiety, overbreathing, diet, or the exercises we do here, its all the same—they are just uncomfortable physical sensations. The only reason they perturb you more when you are driving or at home is because of the meaning you still give to them in those situations.

Homework practice is very important since safety signals present in the clinical setting or deriving from the therapist per se may again limit generalizability to the natural setting. Clients are instructed to practice the interoceptive items conducted in session on a daily basis.

Session 8

The goals of this session are to continue the hypothesis testing and interoceptive exposure from the preceding session. It is especially important to review the client's daily practice of interoceptive exposure. The possibility of avoidance should be evaluated: either overt failure to practice, or covert avoidance by minimizing the intensity or duration of the sensations induced or limiting practices to the presence of a safety signal (such as a significant other) or to times when the client does not feel at all anxious. The sources of avoidance include continued misinterpretation of the dangers of bodily sensations (i.e., "I don't want to hyperventilate because I'm afraid that I won't be able to stop overbreathing and no one will be there to help me"), or the misperception that anxiety levels will not reduce over repetition of the task. Another concern occurred for Jane, who by this time in therapy was reporting very few panic attacks and considerably fewer physical sensations of anxiety. She practiced interoceptive exposure exercises about half of the days between sessions, but remained cautious for fear that the exercises would cause her to revert to her state of several weeks earlier. That is, she was concerned that the inductions would leave her in a state of persistent symptomatology. All these avoidance motivations must be addressed cognitively, using the principles described in the previous sessions. The homework from this session is to continue proceeding up the interoceptive exposure hierarchy, hypothesis testing, and cognitive restructuring when anxious or panicky.

Session 9

The primary goal of this session is to extend interoceptive exposure to naturalistic tasks. In addition, cognitive restructuring is continued through hypothesis testing and reinforcement of monitoring and challenging as anxiety arises.

Naturalistic interoceptive exposure refers to exposure to daily tasks or activities that have been avoided or endured with dread because of the associated sensations. Typical examples include aerobic exercise or vigorous physical activity, running up flights of stairs, eating foods that create a sensation of fullness or are associated with sensations of choking, standing quickly from a seated position, saunas or steamy showers, driving with the windows rolled up and the heater on, caffeine consumption, and so on. (Of course, these exercises may be modified in the event of actual medical complications, such as asthma or high blood pressure.) From a list of typically feared activities and the generation of items specific to the individual's own experience, a hierarchy is established. Each item is ranked in terms of anxiety ratings. Jane's hierarchy is shown in Table 1.5.

TABLE 1.5. Jane's Naturalistic Interoceptive Exposure Hierarchy

Item	Anxiety level (0–8)
Look out through venetian blinds	3
Watch *The Cuckoo's Nest*	4
Scan labels on supermarket shelf	5
Drive with windows closed and heater on	6
Go to night club with strobe lights	7
Go on rides at Disney Land	8

Clients are instructed to identify maladaptive cognitions and rehearse cognitive restructuring before beginning each activity. In-session rehearsal of the cognitive preparation allows therapists to provide corrective feedback. It is important to identify and remove (gradually, if necessary) safety signals or protective behaviors such as portable phones, lucky charms, and staying in close proximity to medical facilities. Clients are asked to practice two items from their hierarchy at least three times each before the next treatment session.

Session 10

The primary goals of this session are to review the naturalistic exposure exercises over the past week and to begin exposure to feared and avoided situations. As with earlier interoceptive exposure homework assignments, it is important to evaluate and correct tendencies to avoid naturalistic interoceptive exposure tasks.

Situational exposure targets agoraphobic situations in which anxiety and panic are anticipated to occur and from which escape is difficult or help is unavailable. In contrast, naturalistic interoceptive exposure targets activities that produce sensations that are feared and avoided. Situational exposure is introduced at this point since most clients have acquired sufficient control of their panic and anxiety to allow situational exposure to proceed relatively smoothly. However, situational exposure may be introduced earlier in certain cases, for example, for clients who report no fear of standard sensation-induction exercises and who are afraid of sensations only when they occur in the context of agoraphobic situations. Under these conditions, situational exposure can be initiated in Session 7. Also, clients who have controlled their fear of sensations very quickly, would benefit from earlier introduction of situational exposure.

The amount of time devoted to situational exposure depends on the client's agoraphobic profile. Obviously, more time is appropriate for more severely agoraphobic clients. Also, the benefit obtained from involving significant others in the treatment process may depend on the pervasiveness of agoraphobia and the extent to which family roles and interactions have been affected by or contribute to the agoraphobic pattern. Another decision concerns the way in which situational exposure is conducted. A graduated, spaced approach (vs. intense, massed) is used most often. However, as reported earlier, recent research (Feigenbaum, 1988) has shown superior results with more intense and massed approaches. Therefore, choice of approach may be best decided with the client by describing the options and considering their preferred method of coping with challenges.

The first step is to provide a rationale for conducting situational exposure. The rationale is similar to that for interoceptive exposure: to learn through repeated confrontations that feared negative events are unlikely or manageable. The reduction of anxiety and fear after repetitions of a single task is described to provide incentive for continued practice and to allay concerns that the situational tasks will remain difficult. In other words, situational exposure is presented as being manageable to minimize perceptions of helplessness.

Jane and her therapist selected a graduated, spaced approach with the aid of Jane's husband, since he played a significant role in her agoraphobic patterns. Jane disliked the intense approach because she would not feel "in control." By this point in treatment, Jane had not had a panic attack for 4 weeks. Her sensitivity to bodily sensations, particularly feelings of unreality, had declined significantly. However, she retained a mild level of apprehension—"is this going to last," or "what if the panic attacks return"—which accounted for her resistance to intense situational exposure. Some reduction had occurred in her agoraphobic behaviors as a function of the PCT. For example, Jane was now driving further distances on surface streets, although she still avoided the freeways. Also, Jane was spending more time alone than before, although she still preferred the presence of her husband or her mother. She was eager to begin the situational exposure phase and become more independent. Jane's husband, Larry, was very willing to be involved in treatment. While he could have been present from the beginning of treatment, Jane and the therapist chose to include Larry for the situational exposure component.

Session 11

The primary goals of this session are to provide an overview of the treatment conceptualization to the significant other/spouse, describe the method for involving the spouse, establish a hierarchy of situational items, and begin exposure practice. Consequently, Larry attended this session and the remaining four sessions (four sessions were scheduled given Jane's level of agoraphobic avoidance to be overcome). The treatment conceptualization provided to the significant other is exactly the same as that given to the client, hence the benefit of including the significant other from the beginning of treatment. The conceptualization is intended to reduce the spouse's frustration and/or negative attributions about the client's emotional functioning (e.g., "Oh, she's just making it up . . . there's nothing really wrong with her," or "He has been like this since before we were married and he'll never change"). The way in which the agoraphobic problem has disrupted daily routines and distribution of home responsibilities is explored and discussed also. Examples might include social activities, leisure activities, and household chores. It is explained that family activities may be structured around the agoraphobic fear and avoidance in order to help the client function without intense anxiety. At the same time, the reassignment to the spouse of tasks that were previously completed by the client may actually reinforce the agoraphobic pattern of behavior. Consequently, the importance of complying with home-work *in vivo* exposure instructions even though the client may experience some distress initially is emphasized.

The spouse is encouraged to become an active participant by providing his/her perception of the client's behavior and fearfulness and the impact on the home environment. Sometimes spouses provide information of which the client was not fully aware, or does not report, particularly in relation to how the client's behavior affects the spouse's own daily functioning. Larry, for example, described how he feels restricted at home in the evenings; whereas before he occasionally played basketball with his friends at the local gym, now he stays at home because he feels guilty if he leaves Jane alone.

The next step is to describe the role of the significant other in situational exposure tasks. The significant other is viewed as a coach, and the couple are encouraged to approach the tasks as a problem-solving team. This includes deciding exactly where and when to practice hierarchy items. In preparation for practice, the client identifies his/her fears about the task and generates cognitive alternatives. The spouse is encouraged to help the client question his/her own "anxious" thoughts. Role plays of this type of questioning of the client by the spouse can be conducted in session, so the therapist can provide corrective feedback to each partner. Throughout the task, the significant other reminds the client to apply cognitive challenges and/or breathing control. Since the spouse is usually a safety signal, tasks are less anxiety provoking. However, the safety signal must be weaned eventually. Therefore, initial attempts are conducted with the spouse and later trials are conducted alone. Weaning from the spouse may be graduated, as in the case of driving first with the spouse in the car, second with the spouse in a car behind, third meeting the spouse at a destination point, and fourth driving alone.

Very important to the success of this collaboration is style of communication. Spouses are discouraged from magnifying the experience of panic and encouraged to help the client apply coping statements when anxious. On the other hand, spouses are encouraged to be patient given the fact

that progress for the client may be erratic. The client and spouse are instructed to use a 0–8-point rating to communicate with each other about the client's current level of anxiety or distress, as a way of diminishing the awkwardness associated with discussing anxiety, especially in public situations. Clients are warned about the tendency to avoid discussing their feelings with their spouse, because of embarrassment or in an attempt to avoid their anxiety for fear that discussion with their spouse and concentration on anxiety may intensify their distress level. Avoidance of feelings is discouraged since distraction is less beneficial in the long term than is more direct confrontation. Clients are reassured that the initial discomfort and embarrassment will most likely be reduced as the couple become more familiar with discussing anxiety levels and their management. Furthermore, clients' concerns about their spouse being insensitive or too pushy are addressed. For example, a spouse may presume to know the client's level of anxiety and anxious thoughts without confirmation from the client, or the spouse may become angry toward the client for avoiding or escaping from situations or being fearful. All these issues are described as relatively common and understandable patterns of communication, but nevertheless in need of correction. Role playing in session of more adaptive communication styles during episodes of heightened anxiety is a useful learning technique, especially in combination with participant modeling from the therapist for the spouse. On occasion, more specific communications training may be beneficial, especially if the couple frequently argue in their attempts to generate items or methods for conducting *in vivo* exposure.

Since a graduated approach was chosen for Jane, the next step was to generate a hierarchy of situational tasks. The items range from mildly distressing to very distressing (as rated on 0–8-point scales of fear and/or avoidance). Each item is worded very specifically to minimize confusion when conducting practices. Jane's hierarchy is shown in Table 1.6.

Jane and Larry rehearsed their approach to the first task (sitting in the middle row on the aisle of a crowded movie theater) in session, while the therapist provided corrective feedback using the principles of com-

TABLE 1.6. Jane's Situational Exposure Hierarchy

Item	Anxiety level (0–8)
Drive home from work at dusk, alone	3
Sit in middle row, on aisle, crowded movie theater, with husband	3
Sit in middle row, in middle, crowded movie theater, with husband	4
Drive two exits on freeway, with husband in car behind	5
Drive two exits on freeway alone	6
Drive four exits on freeway, with husband waiting at destination	7

munication and coping described above. They were instructed to practice this task at least three times over the next week. On at least one occasion, Jane was to practice the item alone.

Sessions 12–15

Each of the remaining sessions entails review of the situational exposure practices, provision of feedback where appropriate about cognitive restructuring or spouse's coaching, and rehearsal of new tasks for the coming week. Issues commonly covered include specific danger cognitions that have not been identified previously. For example, Jane reported that during her practices at the movie theater, she became afraid of having to leave the theatre and thereby disturb the audience's enjoyment of the movie. This cognition was identified as an overestimation and a catastrophic thinking error. Other issues include controlling the urge to escape at times of heightened anxiety. Retreat from a situation (e.g., going to a rest room for relief from the crowded restaurant situation) is viewed as appropriate if it is used to restructure and is followed by a return to the situation. In the 13th session, Jane stated that she had failed because she had pulled off to the side of the road when practicing driving, and she waited for Larry to catch up to her. The therapist emphasized that difficulty in an exposure task does not represent failure but rather the presence of fear mechanisms in a particular situation. The therapist rehearsed with Jane how to use time-outs from a task to evaluate what had happened, to cognitively restructure, and to prepare for returning to the task. Finally, maintaining an objective awareness of the situational context and reactions is emphasized. Distraction is discouraged. In this way, the interoceptive exposure from earlier sessions is incorporated. That is, clients are encouraged to monitor their own bodily sensations objectively while practicing situational tasks, as opposed to maintaining apprehension about them. Statements such as "I hope I don't get those dizzy feelings when I practice driving on the freeway" represent incomplete exposure.

In this protocol, the last few treatment sessions are scheduled biweekly in order to enhance generalization from the treatment setting. Finally, the last treatment session reviews all of the principles and skills learned and provides the client with a template of coping techniques for potential high-risk situations in the future. Jane finished the program after 15 sessions, by which time she had not panicked in 8 weeks, rarely experienced dizziness or feelings of unreality, and was driving further distances. There were some situations still in need of exposure practices (such as traveling very long distances away from home and freeway driving at dusk). However, Jane and Larry agreed to continue situational exposure practices over the next few months in order to consolidate her learning and to continue her improvement.

CONCLUSION

As noted earlier in the chapter, the cognitive-behavioral treatments for panic and agoraphobia are highly effective and represent one of the success stories of psychotherapeutic development. Between 80% and 100% of patients undergoing these treatments will be panic free at the end of treatment, and these gains are maintained for follow-ups of at least 2 years. Between 50% and 80% of these patients are "cured" and many of the remainder have only residual symptomatology. Nevertheless, we should not be deluded into thinking that we have the answers for PD and can move on to some other problem. Several major difficulties remain.

First, the fact remains that these treatments are not foolproof. As noted above, as many as 50% of the patients suffering from panic disorder or agoraphobia retain some substantial symptomatology despite initial improvement. Further research must determine how treatments can be improved or better individualized to alleviate continued suffering. For example, one of us (D. H. B.) continues to see a client who completed an initial course of treatment 4 years ago. This client was essentially better for approximately 9 months but found himself relapsing during a particularly stressful time at work. A few booster sessions restored his functioning, but he was back in the office 6 months later with reemerging symptomatology. This pattern has essentially continued for 4 years and has been characterized by symptom-free periods followed by (seemingly) stress-related relapses. Furthermore, the reemerging panic disorder will sometimes last from 3 to 6 months before disappearing again, perhaps with the help of the booster sessions.

While this case is somewhat unusual in our experience, there is no easy explanation for this pattern of relapses and remissions. The client, who has a doctorate, understands and accepts the treatment model and fully implements the treatment program. There is also no question that he fully comprehends the nature of anxiety and panic and the intricacies of the therapeutic strategies. While in the office, he can recite chapter and verse on the nature of these emotional states, and the detailed process of his own reaction while in these states. Nevertheless, while away from the office the client finds himself repeatedly hoping that he will not "go over the brink" during a panic despite verbalizing very clearly the irrationality of this concept while in the office. In addition, he continues to attempt to reduce minor physiological symptoms associated with anxiety and panic despite a full rational understanding of the nature of these symptoms, including the fact that they are the same symptoms that he feels during a state of excitement, which he enjoys. He's limited tolerance of these physical sensations is also puzzling in view of his tremendous capacity to endure pain. (He never takes any anesthesia for dental work, for example.)

Any number of factors might account for what seems to be "overvalued ideation" or very strongly held irrational ideas during periods of pain, including the fact that the client has several siblings who have been repeatedly hospitalized for emotional disorders, seemingly mood disorders or schizo-affective disorders. Nevertheless, the fact remains that we do not know why this client does not respond as well as most people.

Other clients, as noted above, seem uninterested in engaging in treatment, preferring to conceptualize their problems as chemical imbalances. Still others have difficulty grasping some of the cognitive strategies and further attempts are necessary to make these treatments more "user friendly."

It also may seem that this structured, protocol-driven treatment is applied in a very standard fashion across individuals. Nothing could be further from the truth. The clinical art involved in this, and all treatments described in this book, requires a careful adaptation of these treatment strategies to the individual case. Many of Jane's symptoms revolved around feelings of unreality (derealization and depersonalization). Emphasizing rational explanations for the productions of these feelings, as well as adapting cognitive and exposure exercises so as to maximize these sensations, is an important part of this treatment program. Although standard interoceptive provocation exercises seemed sufficient to produce relevant symptomatology in Jane's case, we have recently had to develop new procedures to deal with people with severe derealization. Some of these procedures, interestingly, involved staring in a mirror for a while or staring at a dot on the wall. Other innovations in both cognitive and behavioral procedures will be required by individual therapists as they apply these procedures.

Finally, although these new treatments seem highly successful, when applied by trained therapists, treatment is not readily available to individuals suffering from these disorders. In fact, these treatments, while brief and structured, are far more difficult to deliver than, for example, pharmacological treatments (which are also often misapplied). Furthermore, few people are currently skilled in the application of these treatments. What seems to be needed for these, and other successful psychosocial treatments is a new method of disseminating them so that they reach the maximum number of clients. Modification of these treatment protocols into more user-friendly formats as well as brief periods of training for qualified therapists to a point of certification would seem important steps in successfully delivering these treatments. This may be difficult to accomplish.

Finally, it will be crucially important to work out the relationship of these treatments to popular medication approaches. Here, client–treatment matching and investigations into the interactive effects of these treatments, in view of the fact that many people with PD are initially placed on medications, will be important research agendas for the immediate future.

REFERENCES

Agras, W. S., Leitenberg, H., & Barlow, D. H. (1968). Social reinforcement in the modification of agoraphobia. *Archives of General Psychiatry, 19*, 423–427.

Agras, W. S., Telch, M. J., Taylor, C. B., Roth, W. T., & Brouillard, M. (in press). Imipramine and exposure therapy in agoraphobia: The type of exposure may matter. *Behavior Therapy*.

Alneas, R., & Torgersen, S. (1990). DSM-III personality disorders among patients with major depression, anxiety disorders, and mixed conditions. *Journal of Nervous and Mental Disease, 178*, 693–698.

American Psychiatric Association. (1980). *Diagnostic and statistical manual of mental disorders* (3rd ed.). Washington, DC: Author.

American Psychiatric Association (1987). *Diagnostic and statistical manual for mental disorders* (3rd ed., rev.). Washington, DC: Author.

American Psychiatric Association. (1993). *DSM-IV draft criteria as of 3/1/93*. Washington, DC: Author.

Antony, M., Brown, T. A., Craske, M. G., Barlow, D. H., Mitchell, W. B., & Meadows, E. (1993). *Accuracy of heart beat perception in panic disorder, social phobic, and nonanxious subjects*. Manuscript submitted for publication.

Arnow, B. A., Taylor, C. B., Agras, W. S., & Telch, M. J. (1985). Enhancing agoraphobia treatment outcome by changing couple communication patterns. *Behavior Therapy, 16*, 452–467.

Arntz, L., & Arntz, A. (1992, June). *Do personality disorders influence the results of cognitive-behavioral therapies for panic disorder?* Paper presented at World Congress of Cognitive Therapy, Toronto, Canada.

Arrindell, W., & Emmelkamp, P. (1987). Psychological states and traits in female agoraphobics: A controlled study. *Journal of Psychopathology and Behavioral Assessment, 9*, 237–253.

Azrin, N., Naster, B., & Jones, R. (1973). Reciprocity

counselling: A rapid learning-based procedure for marital counselling. *Behaviour Research and Therapy, 11*, 365–382.

Bandura, A. (1977). Self-efficacy: Toward a unifying theory of behavioral change. *Psychological Review, 84*, 191–215.

Bandura, A. (1988). Self-efficacy conception of anxiety. *Anxiety Research, 1*, 77–98.

Barlow, D. H. (1988). *Anxiety and its disorders: The nature and treatment of anxiety and panic*. New York: Guilford Press.

Barlow, D. H. (1991). Disorders of emotion. *Psychological Inquiry, 2*, 58–71.

Barlow, D. H., Cohen, A., Waddell, M., Vermilyea, J., Klosko, J., Blanchard, E., & DiNardo, P. (1984). Panic and generalized anxiety disorders: Nature and treatment. *Behavior Therapy, 15*, 431–449.

Barlow, D. H., & Craske, M. G. (1989). *Mastery of your anxiety and panic*. Albany, NY: Graywind.

Barlow, D. H., Craske, M. G., Cerny, J. A., & Klosko, J. S. (1989). Behavioral treatment of panic disorder. *Behavior Therapy, 20*, 261–282.

Barlow, D. H., O'Brien, G. T., & Last, C. G. (1984). Couples treatment of agoraphobia. *Behavior Therapy, 15*, 41–58.

Barlow, D. H., O'Brien, G. T., Last, C. G., & Holden, A. (1983). Couples treatment of agoraphobia: Initial outcome. In K. D. Craig and R. J. McMahon (Eds.), *Advances in clinical behavior therapy*. New York: Brunner/Mazel.

Barlow, D. H., Vermilyea, J., Blanchard, E., Vermilyea, B., DiNardo, P., & Cerny, J. (1985). Phenomenon of panic. *Journal of Abnormal Psychology, 94*, 320–328.

Beck, A. T. (1988). Cognitive approaches to panic disorder: Theory and therapy. In S. Rachman & J. D. Maser (Eds.), *Panic: Psychological perspectives*. Hillsdale, NJ: Erlbaum.

Beck, A. T., Epstein, N., Brown, G., & Steer, R. (1988). An inventory for measuring clinical anxiety: Psychometric properties. *Journal of Consulting and Clinical Psychology, 56*, 893–897.

Beck, A. T., Rush, A. J., Shaw, B. F., & Emery, G. (1979). *Cognitive therapy of depression*. New York: Guilford Press.

Bland, K., & Hallam, R. (1981). Relationship between response to graded exposure and marital satisfaction in agoraphobics. *Behaviour Research and Therapy, 19*, 335–338.

Bonn, J. A., Harrison, J., & Rees, W. (1971). Lactate-induced anxiety: Therapeutic application. *British Journal of Psychiatry, 119*, 468–470.

Borkovec, T. (1976). Physiological and cognitive processes in the regulation of anxiety. In G. Schwartz & D. Shapiro (Eds.), *Consciousness and self-regulation: Advances in research* (Vol. 1). New York: Plenum Press.

Borkovec, T., Weerts, T., & Bernstein, D. (1977). Assessment of anxiety. In A. Ciminero, K. Calhoun, & H. Adams (Eds.), *Handbook of behavioral assessment*. New York: Wiley.

Bouton, M. (1988). Context and ambiguity in the extinction of emotional learning: Implications for exposure therapy. *Behaviour Research and Therapy, 26*, 137–149.

Bouton, M. & Swartzentruber, D. (1991). Sources of relapse after extinction in pavlovian conditioning and instrumental conditioning. *Behavioral Neuroscience, 104,* 44–55.

Breier, A., Charney, D. S., & Heninger, G. R. (1986). Agoraphobia with panic attacks. *Archives of General Psychiatry, 43,* 1029–1036.

Brown, T. A., Rapee, R. M., Antony, M., & Barlow, D. H. (1990, November). *Patterns of responding to hyperventilation and carbon dioxide inhalation following behavioral treatment of panic disorder.* Paper presented at Association for the Advancement of Behavior Therapy, San Francisco, CA.

Buglass, P., Clarke, J., Henderson, A., & Presley, A. (1977). A study of agoraphobic housewives. *Psychological Medicine, 7,* 73–86.

Burns, L. E., Thorpe, G. L., & Cavallaro, L. A. (1986). Agoraphobia eight years after behavioral treatment: A follow-up study with interview, self-report, and behavioral data. *Behavior Therapy, 17,* 580–591.

Cerny, J. A., Barlow, D. H., Craske, M. G., & Himadi, W. G. (1987). Couples treatment of agoraphobia: A two-year follow-up. *Behavior Therapy, 18,* 401–415.

Chambless, D. L. (1989, November). *Spacing of exposure sessions in the treatment of phobia.* Poster presented at 22nd Annual Association for the Advancement of Behavior Therapy Convention, New York, NY.

Chambless, D. L., Caputo, G., Bright, P., & Gallagher, R. (1984). Assessment of fear in agoraphobics: The Body Sensations Questionnaire and the Agoraphobic Cognitions Questionnaire. *Journal of Consulting and Clinical Psychology, 52,* 1090–1097.

Chambless, D. L., Caputo, G., Gracely, S., Jasin, E., & Williams, C. (1985). The Mobility Inventory for agoraphobia. *Behaviour Research and Therapy, 23,* 35–44.

Chambless, D. L., & Renneberg, B. (1988, September). *Personality disorders of agoraphobics.* Paper presented at World Congress of Behavior Therapy, Edinburgh, Scotland.

Chaplin, E. W., & Levine, B. A. (1981). The effects of total exposure duration and interrupted versus continued exposure in flooding therapy. *Behavior Therapy, 12,* 360–368.

Clark, D., Salkovskis, P., & Chalkley, A. (1985). Respiratory control as a treatment for panic attacks. *Journal of Behavior Therapy and Experimental Psychiatry, 16,* 23–30.

Clark, D. M., Salkovskis, P., Gelder, M., Koehler, C., Martin, M., Anastasiades, P., Hackmann, A., Middleton, H., & Jeavons, A. (1988). Tests of a cognitive theory of panic. In I. Hand & H. Wittchen (Eds.), *Panic and phobias II.* Berlin, Germany: Springer-Verlag.

Clark, D. M., Salkovskis, P. M., Hackmann, A., Middleton, H., Anastasiades, P., & Gelder, M. (1992). *A comparison of cognitive therapy, applied relaxation, and imipramine in the treatment of panic disorder.* Manuscript submitted for publication.

Cohen, S. D., Monteiro, W., & Marks, I. M. (1984). Two-year follow-up of agoraphobics after exposure and imipramine. *British Journal of Psychiatry, 144,* 276–281.

Costello, C. (1992). Problems in recent tests of two cognitive theories of panic. *Behaviour Research and Therapy, 30,* 1–5.

Craske, M. G. (1991). Phobic fear and panic attacks: The same emotional state triggered by different cues? *Clinical Psychology Review, 11,* 599–620.

Craske, M. G., & Barlow, D. H. (1988). A review of the relationship between panic and avoidance. *Clinical Psychology Review, 8,* 667–685.

Craske, M. G., Brown, T. A., & Barlow, D. H. (1991). Behavioral treatment of panic disorder: A two-year follow-up. *Behavior Therapy, 22,* 289–304.

Craske, M. G., Miller, P. P., Rotunda, R., & Barlow, D. H. (1990). A descriptive report of features of initial unexpected panic attacks in minimal and extensive avoiders. *Behaviour Research and Therapy, 28,* 395–400.

Craske, M. G., Rapee, R. M., & Barlow, D. H. (1988). The significance of panic expectancy for individual patterns of avoidance. *Behavior Therapy, 19,* 577–592.

Craske, M. G., Street, L., & Barlow, D. H. (1989). Instructions to focus upon or distract from internal cues during exposure treatment for agoraphobic avoidance. *Behaviour Research and Therapy, 27,* 663–672.

Crowe, R. R., Noyes, R., Pauls, D. L., & Slymen, D. J. (1983). A family study of panic disorder. *Archives of General Psychiatry, 40,* 1065–1069.

de Ruiter, C., Rijken, H., Garssen, B., & Kraaimaat, F. (1989). Breathing retraining, exposure and a combination of both, in the treatment of panic disorder with agoraphobia. *Behaviour Research and Therapy, 27,* 647–656.

DeSilva, P., & Rachman, S. J. (1984). Does escape behavior strengthen agoraphobic avoidance? A preliminary study. *Behaviour Research and Therapy, 22,* 87–91.

Dewey, D., & Hunsley, J. (1989). The effects of marital adjustment and spouse involvement on the behavioral treatment of agoraphobia: A meta-analytic review. *Anxiety Research.*

DiNardo, P., & Barlow, D. H. (1988). *Anxiety Disorders Interview Schedule–Revised (ADIS–R).* Albany, NY: Graywind Publications.

DiNardo, P. A., Moras, K., Barlow, D. H., Rapee, R. M. & Brown, T. (1993). Reliability of DSM-III-R anxiety disorder categories using the Anxiety Disorders Interview Schedule-Revised (ADIS-R). *Archives of General Psychiatry, 50,* 251–256.

Ehlers, A., & Breuer, P. (1992). Increased cardiac awareness in panic disorder. *Journal of Abnormal Psychology, 101,* 371–382.

Ehlers, A., & Margraf, J. (1989). The psychophysiological model of panic attacks. In P. M. G. Emmelkamp (Ed.), *Anxiety disorders: Annual series of European research in behavior therapy.* (Vol. 4). Amsterdam: Swets.

Ehlers, A., Taylor, B., Margraf, J., Roth, W., & Birnbaumer, R. (1988). Anxiety induced by false heart rate feedback in patients with panic disorder. *Behaviour Research and Therapy, 26,* 2–11.

Emmelkamp, P. (1980). Agoraphobic's interpersonal problems. *Archives of General Psychiatry, 37,* 1303–1306.

Emmelkamp, P. (1982). *Phobic and obsessive-compulsive disorders: Theory, research, and practice.* New York: Plenum Press.

Emmelkamp, P. M. G., & Ultee, K. A. (1974). A comparison of "successive approximation" and "self-observation" in the treatment of agoraphobia. *Behavior Therapy, 5,* 606–613.

Emmelkamp, P. M. G., & Wessels, H. (1975). Flooding

in imagination vs. flooding in vivo: A comparison with agoraphobics. *Behaviour Research and Therapy, 13*, 7–15.

Feigenbaum, W. (1988). Long-term efficacy of ungraded versus graded massed exposure in agoraphobics. In I. Hand & H. Wittchen (Eds.), *Panic and phobias: Treatments and variables affecting course and outcome.* Berlin, Germany: Springer-Verlag.

Foa, E. B., Jameson, J. S., Turner, R. M., & Payne, L. L. (1980). Massed vs. spaced exposure sessions in the treatment of agoraphobia. *Behaviour Research and Therapy, 18*, 333–338.

Foa, E. B., & Kozak, M. S. (1986). Emotional processing of fear: Exposure to corrective information. *Psychological Bulletin, 99*, 20–35.

Fry, W. (1962). The marital context of an anxiety syndrome. *Family Process, 1*, 245–252.

Garssen, B., de Ruiter, C., & van Dyck, R. (1992). Breathing retraining: A rational placebo? *Clinical Psychology Review, 12*, 141–153.

Gitlin, B., Martin, M., Shear, K., Frances, A., Ball, G., & Josephson, S. (1985). Behavior therapy for panic disorder. *Journal of Nervous and Mental Disease, 173*, 742–743.

Ghosh, A., & Marks, I. M. (1987). Self-directed exposure for agoraphobia: A controlled trial. *Behavior Therapy, 18*, 3–16.

Goldstein, A., & Chambless, D. (1978). A reanalysis of agoraphobia. *Behavior Therapy, 9*, 47–59.

Gray, J. A. (1985). Issues in the neuropsychology of anxiety. In A. H. Tuma & J. D. Maser (Eds.), *Anxiety and the anxiety disorders.* Hillsdale, NJ: Erlbaum.

Grayson, J. B., Foa, E. B., & Steketee, G. (1982). Habituation during exposure treatment: Distraction versus attention-focusing. *Behaviour Research and Therapy, 20*, 323–328.

Griez, E., & van den Hout, M. A. (1986). CO_2 inhalation in the treatment of panic attacks. *Behaviour Research and Therapy, 24*, 145–150.

Hackmann, A., Clark, D., Salkovskis, P., Wells, A., & Gelder, M. (1992, June). *Making cognitive therapy for panic more efficient: Preliminary results with a four session version of the treatment.* Paper presented at World Congress of Cognitive Therapy, Toronto, Canada.

Hafner, R. J. (1976). Fresh symptom emergence after intensive behavior therapy. *British Journal of Psychiatry, 129*, 378–383.

Hafner, R. J. (1984). Predicting the effects on husbands of behavior therapy for agoraphobia. *Behaviour Research and Therapy, 22*, 217–226.

Hand, I., & Lamontagne, Y. (1976). The exacerbation of interpersonal problems after rapid phobia removal. *Psychotherapy: Theory, Research and Practice, 13*, 405–411.

Haslam, M. T. (1974). The relationship between the effect of lactate infusion on anxiety states and their amelioration by carbon dioxide inhalation. *British Journal of Psychiatry, 125*, 88–90.

Hibbert, G., & Chan, M. (1989). Respiratory control: Its contribution to the treatment of panic attacks. *British Journal of Psychiatry, 154*, 232–236.

Hibbert, G., & Pilsbury, D. (1988). Hyperventilation in panic attacks: Ambulatory monitoring of transcutaneous carbon dioxide. *British Journal of Psychiatry, 153*, 76–80.

Himadi, W., Cerny, J., Barlow, D., Cohen, S., & O'Brien, G. (1986). The relationship of marital adjustment to agoraphobia treatment outcome. *Behaviour Research and Therapy, 24*, 107–115.

Holden, A .E. O., O'Brien, G. T., Barlow, D. H., Stetson, D., & Infantino, A. (1983). Self-help manual for agoraphobia: A preliminary report of effectiveness. *Behavior Therapy, 14*, 545–556.

Holt, P., & Andrews, G. (1989). Hyperventilation and anxiety in panic disorder, agoraphobia, and generalized anxiety disorder. *Behaviour Research and Therapy, 27*, 453–460.

Hornsveld, H., Garssen, B., Fiedeldij Dop, M., & van Spiegel, P. (1990). Symptom reporting during voluntary hyperventilation and mental load: Implications for diagnosing hyperventilation syndrome. *Journal of Psychosomatic Research, 34*, 687–697.

Jacobson, N. S., Wilson, L., & Tupper, C. (1988). The clinical significance of treatment gains resulting from exposure-based interventions for agoraphobia: A re-analysis of outcome data. *Behavior Therapy, 19*, 539–554.

Jannoun, L., Munby, M., Catalan, J., & Gelder, M. (1980). A home-based treatment program for agoraphobia: Replication and controlled evaluation. *Behavior Therapy, 11*, 294–305.

Jansson, L., Jerremalm, A., & Ost, L. G. (1986). Follow-up of agoraphobic patients treated with exposure in vivo or applied relaxation. *British Journal of Psychiatry, 149*, 486–490.

Jansson, L., & Ost, L. G. (1982). Behavioral treatments for agoraphobia: An evaluative review. *Clinical Psychology Review, 2*, 311–336.

Klosko, J. S., Barlow, D. H., Tassinari, R. & Cerny, J. A. (1990). A comparison of alprazolam and behavior therapy in treatment of panic disorder. *Journal of Consulting and Clinical Psychology, 58*, 77–84.

Kraft, A. R., & Hoogduin, C. A. (1984). The hyperventilation syndrome: A pilot study of the effectiveness of treatment. *British Journal of Psychiatry, 145*, 538–542.

Mannuzza, S., Fyer, A. J., Martin, L. Y., Gallops, M. S., Endicott, J., Gorman, J., Liebowitz, M. R., & Klein, D. F. (1989). Reliability of anxiety assessment: 1. Diagnostic agreement. *Archives of General Psychiatry, 46*, 1093–1101.

Margraf, J. (1989, June). *Comparative efficacy of cognitive, exposure, and combined treatments for panic disorder.* Paper presented at the annual meeting of the European Association for Behavior Therapy, Vienna.

Margraf, J., Taylor, C. B., Ehlers, A., Roth, W. T., & Agras, W. S. (1987). Panic attacks in the natural environment. *Journal of Nervous and Mental Disease, 175*, 558–565.

Marks, I. M. (1971). Phobic disorders four years after treatment: A prospective follow-up. *British Journal of Psychiatry, 118*, 683–686.

Marks, I. M. (1978). *Living with fear.* New York: McGraw-Hill.

Marks, I., Grey, S., Cohen, S. D., Hill, R., Mawson, D., Ramm, E., & Stern, R. (1983). Imipramine and brief therapist-aided exposure in agoraphobics having self-exposure homework: A controlled trial. *Archives of General Psychiatry, 40*, 153–162.

Marshall, W. L. (1985). The effects of variable exposure in flooding therapy. *Behavior Therapy, 16* 117–135.

Mavissakalian, M., & Hamman, M. (1986). DSM-III personality disorder in agoraphobia. *Comprehensive Psychiatry, 27*, 471–479.

Mavissakalian, M., & Hamman, M. (1987). DSM-III personality disorder in agoraphobia. II Changes with treatment. *Comprehensive Psychiatry, 28,* 356–361.

Mavissakalian, M., & Michelson, L. (1986). Two-year follow-up of exposure and imipramine treatment of agoraphobia. *American Journal of Psychiatry, 143,* 1106–1112.

Mavissakalian, M., Michelson, L., & Dealy, R. (1983). Pharmacological treatment of agoraphobia: Imipramine versus imipramine with programmed practice. *British Journal of Psychiatry, 143,* 348–355.

McNally, R., & Lorenz, M. (1987). *Journal of Behaviour Therapy and Experimental Psychiatry, 18,* 3–11.

McNamee, G., O'Sullivan, G., Lelliott, P., & Marks, I. M. (1989). Telephone-guided treatment for housebound agoraphobics with panic disorder: Exposure vs. relaxation. *Behavior Therapy, 20,* 491–497.

Michelson, L., Mavassakalian, M., & Marchione, K. (1985). Cognitive and behavioral treatments of agoraphobia: Clinical, behavioral and psychophysiological outcomes. *Journal of Consulting and Clinical Psychology, 53,* 913–925.

Michelson, L., Mavissakalian, M., Marchione, K., Ulrich, R., Marchione, N., & Testa, S. (1990). Psychophysiological outcome of cognitive, behavioral, and psychophysiologically based treatments of agoraphobia. *Behaviour Research and Therapy, 28,* 127–139.

Milton, F., & Hafner, J. (1979). The outcome of behavior therapy for agoraphobia in relation to marital adjustment. *Archives of General Psychiatry, 36,* 807–811.

Moran, C., & Andrews, G. (1985). The familial occurrence of agoraphobia. *British Journal of Psychiatry, 146,* 262–267.

Munby, J., & Johnston, D. W. (1980). Agoraphobia: The long-term follow-up of behavioural treatment. *British Journal of Psychiatry, 137,* 418–427.

Myers, J., Weissman, M., Tischler, C., Holzer, C., Orvaschel, H., Anthony, J., Boyd, J., Burke, J., Kramer, M., & Stoltzman, R. (1984). Six-month prevalence of psychiatric disorders in three communities. *Archives of General Psychiatry, 41,* 959–967.

Norton, G., Dorward, J., & Cox, B. (1986). Factors associated with panic attacks in nonclinical subjects. *Behavior Therapy, 17,* 239–252.

Noyes, R., Crowe, R. R., Harris, E. L., Hamra, B. J., McChesney, C. M., & Chaudhry, D. R. (1986). Relationship between panic disorder and agoraphobia: A family study. *Archives of General Psychiatry, 43,* 227–232.

Noyes, R., Reich, J., Suelzer, M., & Christiansen, J. (1991). Personality traits associated with panic disorder: Change associated with treatment. *Comprehensive Psychiatry, 32,* 282–294.

Ost, L. G. (1988). Applied relaxation vs. progressive relaxation in the treatment of panic disorder. *Behaviour Research and Therapy, 26,* 13–22.

Ost, L. G., & Westling, B. (1992, June). *Applied relaxation versus cognitive therapy in panic disorder: Immediate response versus long-term outcome.* Paper presented at World Congress of Cognitive Therapy, Toronto, Canada.

Pollard, C. A., Pollard, H. J., & Corn, K. J. (1989). Panic onset and major events in the lives of agoraphobics: A test of contiguity. *Journal of Abnormal Psychology, 98,* 318–321.

Rachman, S. J. (1984). Agoraphobia: A safety-signal perspective. *Behaviour Research and Therapy, 22,* 59–70.

Rachman, S. J., & Bichard, S. (1988). The overprediction of fear. *Clinical Psychology Review, 8,* 303–312.

Rachman, S. J., Craske, M. G., Tallman, K., & Solyom, C. (1986). Does escape behavior strengthen agoraphobic avoidance? A replication. *Behaviour Therapy, 17,* 366–384.

Rapee, R. M. (1985). A case of panic disorder treated with breathing retraining. *Behavior Therapy and Experimental Psychiatry, 16,* 63–65.

Rapee, R. M., Craske, M. G., & Barlow, D. H. (1990). Subject described features of panic attacks using a new self-monitoring form. *Journal of Anxiety Disorders, 4,* 171–181.

Rapee, R. M., Litwin, E. M., & Barlow, D. H. (1990). Impact of life events on subjects with panic disorder and on comparison subjects. *American Journal of Psychiatry, 147,* 640–644.

Rapee, R. M., Mattick, R., & Murrell, E. (1986). Cognitive mediation in the affective component of spontaneous panic attacks. *Journal of Behavior Therapy and Experimental Psychiatry, 17,* 245–253.

Rapee, R. M., Craske, M. G., & Barlow, D. H. (1990). Subject described features of panic attacks using a new self-monitoring form. *Journal of Anxiety Disorders, 4,* 171–181.

Razran, G. (1961). The observable unconscious and the inferable conscious in current soviet psychophysiology: Interoceptive conditioning, semantic conditioning, and the orienting reflex. *Psychological Review, 68,* 81–147.

Reich, J., Noyes, R., & Troughton, E. (1987). Dependent personality disorder associated with phobic avoidance in patients with panic disorder. *American Journal of Psychiatry, 144,* 323–326.

Reiss, S., Peterson, R., Gursky, D., & McNally, R. (1986). Anxiety sensitivity, anxiety frequency, and the prediction of fearfulness. *Behaviour Research and Therapy, 24,* 1–8.

Rice, K. M., & Blanchard, E. B. (1982). Biofeedback in the treatment of anxiety disorders. *Clinical Psychology Review, 2,* 557–577.

Roy-Byrne, P. P., Geraci, M., & Uhde, T. W. (1986). Life events and the onset of panic disorder. *American Journal of Psychiatry, 143,* 1424–1427.

Rupert, P. A., Dobbins, K., & Mathew, R. J. (1981). EMG biofeedback and relaxation instructions in the treatment of chronic anxiety. *American Journal of Clinical Biofeedback, 4,* 52–61.

Salkovskis, P., Clark, D., & Hackmann, A. (1991). Treatment of panic attacks using cognitive therapy without exposure or breathing retraining. *Behaviour Research and Therapy, 29,* 161–166.

Salkovskis, P., Warwick, H., Clark, D., & Wessels, D. (1986). A demonstration of acute hyperventilation during naturally occurring panic attacks. *Behaviour Research and Therapy, 24,* 91–94.

Sanderson, W. S., Rapee, R. M., & Barlow, D. H. (1989). The influence of an illusion of control on panic attacks induced via inhalation of 5.5% carbon dioxide enriched air. *Archives of General Psychiatry, 48,* 157–162.

Sanderson, W. C., DiNardo, P. A., Rapee, R. M., & Barlow, D. H. (1990). Syndrome comorbidity in patients diagnosed with a DSM-III-R Anxiety

Disorder. *Journal of Abnormal Psychology, 99*, 308–312.

Sartory, G., Masters, D., & Rachman, S. J. (1989). Safety-signal therapy in agoraphobics: A preliminary test. *Behaviour Research and Therapy, 27*, 205–209.

Spanier, G. (1976). Measuring dyadic adjustment: New scales for assessing the quality of marriage and similar dyads. *Journal of Marriage and the Family, 38*, 15–38.

Spielberger, C., Gorsuch, R., Lushene, R., Vagg, P., & Jacobs, G. (1983). *Manual for the State–Trait Anxiety Inventory.* Palo Alto, CA: Consulting Psychologists Press.

Stern, R. S., & Marks, I. M. (1973). Brief and prolonged flooding: A comparison of agoraphobic patients. *Archives of General Psychiatry, 28*, 270–276.

Telch, M. J., Agras, W. S., Taylor, C. B., Roth, W. T., & Gallen, C. (1985). Combined pharmacological and behavioral treatment for agoraphobia. *Behaviour Research and Therapy, 21*, 505–527.

Telch, M. J., Lucas, J. A., & Nelson, P. (1989). Nonclinical panic in college students: An investigation of prevalence and symptomatology. *Journal of Abnormal Psychology, 98*, 300–306.

Telch, M. J., Sherman, M., & Lucas, J. (1989). Anxiety sensitivity: Unitary personality trait or domain specific appraisals? *Journal of Anxiety Disorders, 3*, 25–32.

Thyer, B. A., Himle, J., Curtis, G. C., Cameron, O. G., & Nesse, R. M. (1985). A comparison of panic disorder and agoraphobia with panic attacks. *Comprehensive Psychiatry, 26*, 208–214.

Torgersen, S. (1983). Genetic factors in anxiety disorders. *Archives of General Psychiatry, 40*, 1085–1089.

van den Hout, M., & Arntz, A. (1992, June). *Cognitive therapy for panic disorders and agoraphobia: Anti-panic effects but no anti-agoraphobic effects. Results from two controlled trials.* Paper presented at World Congress of Cognitive Therapy, Toronto, Canada.

van den Hout, van der Molen, Griez, & Lousberg, G. (1987). Specificity of interoceptive fear to panic disorders. *Journal of Psychopathology and Behavioral Assessment, 9*, 99–109.

Welkowitz, L., Papp, L., Cloitre, M., Liebowitz, M., Martin, L., & Gorman, J. (1991). Cognitive-behavior therapy for panic disorder delivered by psychopharmacologically oriented clinicians. *Journal of Nervous and Mental Disease, 179*, 473–477.

Williams, K. E., & Chambless, D. (1990). The relationship between therapist characteristics and outcome of in vivo exposure treatment for agoraphobia. *Behavior Therapy, 21*, 111–116.

Williams, S. L. (1988). Addressing misconceptions about phobia, anxiety, and self-efficacy: A reply to Marks. *Journal of Anxiety Disorders, 2*, 277–289.

Williams, S. L, Turner, S. M., & Peer, D. F. (1985). Guided mastery and performance desensitization treatments for severe acrophobia. *Journal of Consulting and Clinical Psychology, 53*, 237–247.

Williams, S. L., & Zane, G. (1989). Guided mastery and stimulus exposure treatments for severe performance anxiety in agoraphobics. *Behaviour Research and Therapy, 27*, 237–245.

Wolpe, J., & Rowan, V. (1988). Panic disorder: A product of classical conditioning. *Behaviour Research and Therapy, 26*, 441–450.

Zarate, R., Rapee, R. M., Craske, M. G., & Barlow, D. H. (1988). *Response norms for symptom induction procedures.* Poster presented at 22nd Annual Association for the Advancement of Behavior Therapy Convention, New York, NY.

Zitrin, C. M., Klein, D. F., & Woerner, M. G. (1980). Behavior therapy, supportive psychotherapy, imipramine, and phobias. *Archives of General Psychiatry, 37*, 63–72.

Zitrin, C. M., Klein, D. F., Woerner, M. G., & Ross, D. C. (1983). Treatment of phobias I. Comparison of imipramine hydrochloride and placebo. *Archives of General Psychiatry, 40*, 125–138.

Chapter 2

POST-TRAUMATIC STRESS DISORDER

Karen S. Calhoun
University of Georgia, Athens
Patricia A. Resick
University of Missouri, St. Louis

There are few, if any, more tragic examples of severe psychopathology than rape-induced post-traumatic stress disorder. The occurrence of rape is far more common than we had previously thought and the emotional consequences can be life-long. In this chapter, the case of "Cindy" illustrates the psychopathology associated with post-traumatic stress disorder in all its nuances and provides a very personal and lucid account of the impact of rape trauma. More important, the next generation of treatments for post-traumatic stress disorder, termed *cognitive processing therapy* by the authors, is sufficiently detailed to allow knowledgeable practitioners to incorporate this treatment program into their practice. This comprehensive treatment program takes advantage of the latest developments in our knowledge of the psychopathology of trauma impact by incorporating treatment strategies specifically tailored to overcome trauma-related psychopathology.—D. H. B.

INTRODUCTION

Post-traumatic stress disorder (PTSD) was introduced in the third edition of the *Diagnostic and Statistical Manual of Mental Disorders* (DSM-III; American Psychiatric Association [APA], 1980). Previous editions had referred to stress reactions with terms like *gross stress reaction*, and *transient situational disturbance*, but without empirical support or specific criteria. Classified as a form of anxiety disorder (no longer a neurosis), the DSM-III description of PTSD was based on the existing empirical literature, most of it derived from studies of combat veterans. But it was recognized that exposure to other forms of trauma could lead to similar symptoms. This stimulated a convergence of disparate areas of research on different types of trauma, which is resulting in rapid developments in theory and treatment. It is now commonly accepted that the type of trauma experienced (although each has some unique features) is less important than trauma severity and individual reactions and vulnerabilities. In this chapter we focus on rape-related PTSD.

The criteria for PTSD in the fourth edition of the *Diagnostic and Statistical Manual of Mental Disorders* (DSM-IV; APA, 1993)* (shown in Table 2.1) represent refinements over DSM-III and the revised third edition of the *Diagnostic and Statistical Manual of Mental Disorders* (DSM-III-R; APA, 1987) cri-

---

*The DSM-IV criteria cited in this chapter are those that were approved as final by the DSM-IV Anxiety Disorders Work Group and the Task Force on DSM-IV (APA, 1993). These criteria may be subject to minor editorial revisions before the publication of DSM-IV.

teria based on recent research advances. Major changes include use of the term *traumatic event* and the requirement that the event be threatening to the life or physical integrity of oneself or others, *and* that the response to the event involve intense fear, helplessness, or horror. The inclusion of an individual's reaction to the event resulted from research showing that fear of death or injury is a strong predictor of PTSD symptoms. The three major characteristics of the disorder (reexperiencing, avoidance and numbing, and increased arousal) remain intact, with minor changes. Internal as well as external cues are now recognized as having potential to trigger reexperiencing. Physiological reactivity has been moved from the list of indicators of increased arousal to the reexperiencing list.

The specification of delayed onset is retained in cases where onset of symptoms occurs more than 6 months after the trauma. The acute–chronic distinction, dropped in DSM-III-R, is reintroduced and refined, setting the differentiating duration point at 3 months rather than 6.

Newly introduced in DSM-IV is acute stress disorder, to be applied to immediate short-term (less than 4 weeks), severe reactions to trauma. The criteria focus on two types of symptoms, dissociative and emotional reactions, that occur during or immediately following the traumatic event. It is probable that the majority of rape victims, and many victims of other traumas, will meet criteria for acute stress disorder.

Reexperiencing phenomena such as flashbacks and nightmares are considered the hallmark symptoms of PTSD. Nightmares are often exact replications of the traumatic experience, or of earlier traumas, memories of which are reactivated by a new event. Flashbacks are characterized by extreme emotional and physiological arousal during which the person may feel immobilized and unaware of immediate surroundings. They may be described as "waking nightmares." Almost any stimulus associated with the trauma can trigger flashbacks, even when its connection with the traumatic experience goes unrecognized. For example, a rape victim did not understand why she could not tolerate the odor of roses until she recalled a vase of roses in the room in which she was attacked. She remembered thinking at one

point during the assault how inappropriate their presence seemed. When clients do not understand the origins of their symptoms, which often happens in cases of delayed onset, it increases their perception that the symptoms are both unpredictable and uncontrollable.

Avoidance symptoms, including emotional numbing, are usually viewed as attempts to control or protect against the negative affect and arousal associated with reexperiencing. Avoidance behavior can be extreme, as in the case of a rape victim who became agoraphobic and refused to leave her house for years. Emotional numbing is not well understood. Litz (1992) described emotional numbing as a "complex, multiply determined problem that is best characterized as a selective emotional-processing deficit. This emotional deficit is chiefly manifested during symptomatic states (and is thus episodic in nature) and entails a muting of positively valenced responses and a heightened reactivity to negative events" (p. 429). It may be combined, in some cases, with a fear of losing control, a fear reinforced by the outbursts of extreme anger (increased arousal symptoms) that many victims experience. Such outbursts are more readily seen in male combat veterans than in female sufferers of PTSD. However, they are not at all uncommon among women and are all the more frightening when inconsistent with their pretrauma behavior and self-concept. Emotional numbing presents one of the most difficult treatment challenges and may persist long after other symptoms disappear. Emotional numbing often includes failure to enjoy sex, not only for rape victims but for others as well. Resick (1987) found this effect, for example, among male robbery victims. Feldman-Summers, Gordon, and Meagher (1979) found that rape victims rated their level of sexual satisfaction significantly lower than did control subjects, even though they were equally orgasmic. Thus, some aspects of emotional numbing might be an irreversible effect of trauma.

Studies have shown that PTSD is a very common consequence of rape. Kilpatrick et al. (1987) found that 57% of women in a community sample who had been raped developed PTSD at some point in their life. More recently, a nationwide survey by

TABLE 2.1. Proposed DSM-IV Post-Traumatic Stress Disorder Criteria

A. The person has been exposed to a traumatic event in which both of the following have been present:
   (1) the person has experienced, witnessed, or been confronted with an event or events that involve actual or threatened death or serious injury, or a threat to the physical integrity of oneself or others
   (2) the person's response involved intense fear, helplessness, or horror (in children, disorganized or agitated behavior)

B. The traumatic event is persistently reexperienced in at least one of the following ways:
   (1) recurrent and intrusive distressing recollections of the event, including images, thoughts, or perceptions (In young children, repetitive play may occur in which themes or aspects of the trauma are expressed.)
   (2) recurrent distressing dreams of the event (in children, there may be frightening dreams without recognizable content)
   (3) acting or feeling as if the traumatic event were recurring (includes a sense of reliving the experience, illusions, hallucination, and dissociative [flashback] episodes, including those that occur upon awakening or when intoxicated) (in young children, trauma-specific reenactment may occur)
   (4) intense psychological distress at exposure to internal or external cues that symbolize or resemble an aspect of the traumatic event
   (5) physiologic reactivity upon exposure to internal or external cues that symbolize or resemble an aspect of the traumatic event

C. Persistent avoidance of stimuli associated with the trauma and numbing of general responsiveness (not present before the trauma), as indicated by at least three of the following:
   (1) efforts to avoid thoughts or feelings associated with the trauma
   (2) efforts to avoid activities, places, or people that arouse recollections of the trauma
   (3) inability to recall an important aspect of the trauma
   (4) markedly diminished interest or participation in significant activities
   (5) feeling of detachment or estrangement from others
   (6) restricted range of affect (e.g., unable to have loving feelings)
   (7) sense of a foreshortened future (e.g., does not expect to have a career, marriage, children, or a normal life span)

D. Persistent symptoms of increased arousal (not present before the trauma), as indicated by at least two of the following:
   (1) difficulty falling or staying asleep
   (2) irritability or outbursts of anger
   (3) difficulty concentrating
   (4) hypervigilance
   (5) exaggerated startle response

E. Duration of the disturbance (symptoms in B, C, and D) is at least one month.

F. The disturbance causes marked distress or significant impairment in social or occupational functioning.

Specify if:
Acute: if duration of symptoms is less than three months
Chronic: if duration of symptoms is three months or more

Specify if:
With Delayed Onset: onset of symptoms at least six months after the stressor

Acute Stress Disorder

A. The person has been exposed to a traumatic event in which both of the following have been present:
   (1) the person has experienced, witnessed, or been confronted with an event or events that involve actual or threatened death or injury, or a threat to the physical integrity of oneself or others.
   (2) the person's response involved intense fear, helplessness, or horror

B. Either while experiencing, or immediately after experiencing, the distressing event, the individual has at least four of the following dissociative symptoms:
   (1) stupor, i.e., reduction in spontaneous and responsive activity, appearing to be unaware of one's surroundings
   (2) derealization, i.e., the environment is experienced as unreal or dreamlike
   (3) depersonalization, i.e., an experience of feeling detached, as if one is an outside observer of one's own mental processes or body, or feeling like an automaton
   (4) subjective sense of numbing, absence of emotional responsiveness or a feeling of detachment from others
   (5) amnesia, i.e., inability to recall events associated with the distressing experience

(cont.)

TABLE 2.1. *(cont.)*

C. Either while experiencing, or immediately after experiencing, the distressing event, the individual has at least three of the following anxiety and other symptoms:

(1) sudden experiences of terror, fear, or anxiety
(2) hyperarousal, including difficulty concentrating, hypervigilance, exaggerated startle response
(3) somatic symptoms, including tremor, hyperventilation, tachycardia, palpitations, muscle tension, restlessness, and fatigue
(4) intrusive recollection or preoccupation with memories of the trauma
(5) sleep disturbance, including insomnia, night terrors, and nightmares
(6) anger
(7) psychomotor agitation
(8) despair or hopelessness
(9) social withdrawal

D. The disturbance causes significant impairment or distress as manifested by either of the following:

(1) markedly interferes with social or occupational functioning
(2) prevents the individual from pursuing some necessary task, such as obtaining necessary medical or legal assistance or mobilizing personal resources by telling family members about the traumatic experience

E. An episode of the disturbance lasts less than four weeks. (When the diagnosis must be made without waiting for recovery, it should be qualified as "provisional.")

F. This disturbance is not due to a Substance-Induced Disorder (e.g., Substance Intoxication) or a Secondary Dissociative Disorder, and is not merely an exacerbation of a preexisting Axis I or Axis II disorder.

Note. From APA (1993). Copyright 1993 by the American Psychiatric Association. Reprinted by permission.

the National Victim Center (Kilpatrick, Edmunds, & Seymour, 1992) found that 31% of rape victims developed PTSD at some point, compared to 5% of nonvictims. At the time of the survey, 11% had diagnosable PTSD. The report estimated that based on their rape incidence results, 1.3 million American women currently have rape-related PTSD and approximately 211,000 will develop it each year. Prospective studies report even higher rates. Rothbaum, Foa, Riggs, Murdock, and Walsh (1992) found that 94% of women entering a longitudinal study following rape met criteria for PTSD at approximately 2 weeks postrape and about 50% at 12 weeks.

Given the high incidence of sexual assault, it is probable that female victims make up the single largest group of those suffering from PTSD. For example, in the Kilpatrick et al. (1992) study, 13% of women reported having been victims of at least one completed forcible rape. Of these, 39% had been raped more than once. Men are also victimized by sexual assault (overwhelmingly by other men). However, little is known about the prevalence or consequences. Forman (1982) found that 5.7% of reported rapes involved male victims. This may well be an underestimate since men are assumed to be even more reluctant than women to report sexual assault. Kaufman, Divasto, Jackson, Vorhees, and Christy (1980) found that 10% of victims were male. These were adult samples. If sexual assault of children is included, the percentage of male victims is higher. Burnam et al. (1988) found that 18% of sexual assault victims in the Los Angeles area were male, combining child and adult victims. Men may be less likely than women to disclose a history of sexual assault when seeking treatment, so therapists should be alert to signs of it. Very little research has been done on male victims, but there are indications that they suffer as much as women. Goyer and Eddleman (1984) identified PTSD symptoms in 13 male sexual assault victims who sought treatment at a naval psychiatric center. Kaszniak, Nussbaum, Berren, and Santiago (1988) reported a case of an adult male who had functional retrograde amnesia for all autobiographical information after being sexually assaulted at gunpoint by two men. Male victims have been found to be at higher risk for substance abuse than women (Burnam et al., 1988), although gender did not predict probability of any other disorder.

THEORETICAL MODELS OF PTSD

A large number of theoretical models have been proposed in attempts to organize observed patterns of reactions in PTSD and to explain the development of these patterns. The models vary considerably in their level of comprehensiveness and they tend to overlap a great deal. The major trends in development of theoretical models are outlined here.

Prior to the recognition of PTSD as a syndrome, the majority of theoretical ideas concerning stress reactions were psychodynamic in origin. Freud (1937–1939/1964) in observing traumatized World War I veterans, noted two of the major characteristics now identified with PTSD. These were repetition (reexperiencing) and denial (avoidance). Horowitz (1976) incorporated these ideas into his information processing model of response to trauma. This model has been highly influential. It incorporates not only traditional psychodynamic ideas but ideas from cognitive theories of emotion and information processing. According to this model, adjustment to a traumatic event requires incorporating it into existing cognitive schemas or developing new schemas. Until this process is complete, the trauma remains in active memory. In active memory the information concerning the traumatic event is out of conscious awareness and the mechanisms of denial and emotional numbing are employed to keep the individual from being overwhelmed by it. However, representations of the events stored in active memory tend to be repeated as part of the attempt to process and integrate them. This results in intrusive thoughts and images about the trauma that are accompanied by intense emotions. Horowitz refers to oscillation between periods of intrusive ideas and emotions and periods of denial and numbing. Reexperiencing phenomena such as nightmares and flashbacks are intrusions aimed at facilitating information processing. However, uncontrolled intrusions can lead to retraumatization and out-of-control emotions. Avoidance and numbing are seen as control processes aimed at regulating information processing so the individual is not overwhelmed. However, excessive controls may prevent complete cognitive processing of the event. Horowitz (1986) continued the development of this model and incorporated new ideas. For example, he notes the potential for strong, positive social support to help protect against the development of PTSD. In research on stress, one of the most consistent empirical findings has been the buffering effect of social support. Although Horowitz's model is among the most comprehensive, it fails to address one of the great puzzles in this area: Why do some individuals develop PTSD and others exposed to the same trauma do not? In addition, the clinical procedures suggested by this model are less explicit and testable than those generated by other theoretical models.

Biological models attempt to explain the development of PTSD on an entirely different level. Van der Kolk, Boyd, Krystal, and Greenberg (1984) developed a biological model based on the observation that PTSD shares many similarities with the animal model of inescapable shock. Both involve exposure to severe and uncontrollable stress. Van der Kolk et al. (1984) postulated that PTSD symptoms result from changes in neurotransmitter activity. The hyperamnesia symptoms, exaggerated startle responses, and aggressive outbursts are thought to be associated with noradrenergic overreactivity to trauma-relevant stimuli followed by depletion of these brain biochemicals. Decreases in central nervous system levels of noradrenalin are thought to account for symptoms such as anhedonia, social withdrawal, and affective numbing. Endogenous opiates released during reexposure result in stress-induced analgesia. Subsequent depletion of the endogenous opiates is experienced as aversive, setting up a cycle of behavior in which the victim may seek exposure to stress repeatedly in an attempt to regain the analgesic effects.

Kolb (1987) proposed another model for the pathophysiology of PTSD. Both Kolb (1987) and McGaugh (1990) emphasized the effects of exposure to stressors on the central nervous system. Excessive stimulation experienced in traumatic events may cause damage or alteration of neuronal pathways. Other recent research supports trauma-induced change in brain neurochemical systems as contributing to PTSD symptoms. For example, Charney et al. (Charney, Woods, Krystal, & Heninger, 1990; Charney, Delgado, Price, & Heninger, 1991) found that changes in serotonin function may be associated with anhedonic symptoms.

Although such biological models are intriguing, it should be remembered that they are preliminary in nature and leave many of the puzzles of PTSD unexplained. For example, delayed onset of symptoms, impact of mediating variables, and individual differences in response to trauma have not been addressed by most of these models (Jones & Barlow, 1990).

Two-factor learning theory models of PTSD symptom development were proposed by Keane, Zimering, and Caddell (1985). Kilpatrick, Veronen, and Resick (1979) used similar explanations for rape-related PTSD symptoms. According to this model, any stimulus associated with the traumatic event can become, through the process of classical conditioning, capable of eliciting a conditioned response similar to that associated with the original trauma. Additional stimuli, associated indirectly with the trauma, create similar reactions through stimulus generalization and higher-order conditioning. Avoidance behaviors are learned in order to escape or prevent the conditioned response. Thus, repeated negative reinforcement of avoidance makes it very resistant to extinction. This explains the persistence of anxiety symptoms long after other symptoms decrease significantly. The principles of higher-order conditioning in stimulus generalization are used to explain why symptoms often worsen over time as more and more stimuli elicit traumatic memories and physiological arousal. Keane, Scott, et al. (1985) suggested that delayed onset of PTSD may actually result from symptoms gradually worsening over time until they reach a critical point.

Behavioral models of PTSD development continue to evolve and have begun to incorporate additional variables such as individual characteristics, including social support as well as cognitions. Foy, Osato, Houskamp, and Neumann (1992) proposed a behavioral model in which the maintenance of PTSD symptoms is influenced substantially by buffering factors such as social support and vulnerability factors such as family history of psychopathology.

Information processing models of PTSD are based on Lang's (1977, 1979, 1985) theory of emotion. Lang posited a seman-tic memory network of interconnected points of information including trauma-relevant stimuli, information about response events, and information about the meaning of both stimuli and responses. Foa, Steketee, and Rothbaum (1989) suggested that traumatic events create especially large and complex fear networks that are activated readily because of the large number of interconnections formed through conditioning and generalization. Associations that were once considered neutral or safe may now be connected with fear. This leads to a sense of unpredictability and uncontrollability that is important in the development and maintenance of PTSD. Chemtob, Roitblat, Hamada, Carlson, and Twentyman (1988) have developed a similar information processing model of PTSD. However, it appears to fit combat-related PTSD better than rape or other single-event traumas.

Theoretical models are becoming increasingly sophisticated and comprehensive as our knowledge mounts concerning the effects of trauma. For example, Creamer, Burgess, and Pattison (1992) proposed a cognitive processing model for reactions to trauma that includes a feedback loop among intrusions, avoidance, and symptom levels. Like other cognitive processing models, Creamer et al.'s model views the successful processing or integrating of the trauma as central to successful recovery. This model sees the cognitive processing mechanisms involved in recovery over time as occurring in five stages. Stage 1 is objective exposure. The major factor at this stage is the severity of the traumatic stressor. Stage 2 is network formation. This is determined primarily by subjective perceptions and meaning attached to the experience. Stage 3 is labeled intrusion. During this stage, the memory network is activated in an attempt to process and resolve the trauma-related memories. Stage 4, avoidance, is characterized by the use of escape and avoidance as coping strategies in response to intrusions. During Stage 5, which is labeled outcome, recovery is achieved through network resolution processing. Such factors as pretrauma functioning and biological processes are not incorporated into this model although the authors acknowledge their importance.

In a more comprehensive recent model, Jones and Barlow (1992) proposed that variables important in the etiology and maintenance of other anxiety disorders, along with anxious apprehension, explain the development of PTSD. The role of biological vulnerability is acknowledged in this model and family and twin studies are cited to support this role. Jones and Barlow (1992) postulate that what is inherited may be a predisposition to respond to stress with chronic autonomic overarousal or noradrenal lability. This is consistent with findings that combat veterans with PTSD exhibited higher resting heart rate than did controls (Blanchard, Kolb, Pallmayer, & Gerardi, 1982; Blanchard, Kolb, Gerardi, Ryan, & Pallmayer, 1986). Central to this model is the observation of similarities between PTSD and other anxiety disorders, in particular panic disorder. If an individual with biological and psychological vulnerabilities is exposed to a trauma and develops anxious apprehension, the stage is set for PTSD. Anxious apprehension involves distorted processing of information along with extremely negative affect. The individual perceives the traumatic event and subsequent reexperiencing as unpredictable, uncontrollable aversive events and reacts with chronic overarousal, hyperviligance, and narrowing of attention. This sets up a feedback loop in which hyperarousal, hyperviligance, and narrowing of attentional focus increase intrusive thoughts and reexperiencing.

ASSESSMENT

The first essential step in assessment is to identify sexual assault or other major trauma in the client's history. Many rape victims fail to disclose their trauma history without being specifically asked. This is consistent with their general pattern of avoidance of trauma-related reminders. Even when seeking treatment, trauma victims often fail to recognize that their psychological problems are associated with their assault. Kilpatrick (1983) suggested several other reasons victims might not be forthcoming with this information. They may fear a negative reaction to disclosure, especially if previous disclosure has resulted in disbelief or blame. Additionally, many victims do not recognize or identify their experience as a rape, especially if the assailant was an acquaintance or

a relative. In actuality, the majority of rapes are committed by someone known to the victim.

Resnick, Kilpatrick, and Lipovsky (1991) suggest supportive, nonevaluative questioning of sexual assault history. Saunders, Kilpatrick, Resnick, and Tidwell (1989) developed a 10-question screening interview to detect history of crime victimization including rape. Its use as part of a standard intake at a mental health center resulted in identification of sexual assault in 41.7% of female clients, compared to 13.3% using a standard intake. A self-report instrument that can be used for screening identification of rape and other forms of sexual assault is the Sexual Experiences Survey by Koss and Gidycz (1985). This is a 10-item self-report instrument that assesses types of coercion or force, as well as types of molestation or sexual assault. It was reported to have internal consistency of .74 and a test–retest reliability over a 1-week interval of .93.

There are two major aims in assessment: diagnosis and treatment planning. A third purpose is suggested by the high rates of comorbidity with PTSD. Depression, anxiety disorders, and substance abuse are especially common comorbid disorders. Whether the primary purpose of assessment is diagnosis or treatment planning, a multidimensional, multiaxial approach is necessary. Because a cross-sectional view taken at a single point in time may fail to capture the full range and pattern of symptoms, a longitudinal approach to assessment has been advocated by Denny, Robinowitz, and Penk (1987) and Sutker, Uddo-Crane, and Allain (1991). Certainly for purposes of treatment, ongoing assessment of symptom patterns and treatment effectiveness is essential. We will review some of the most widely used assessment approaches for rape-related PTSD. For a more comprehensive discussion of issues and procedures in assessment of rape related PTSD, the reader is referred to Resnick et al. (1991).

Researchers in combat-related PTSD have led the field in development of assessment procedures (Keane, Malloy, & Fairbank, 1984; Keane Wolfe, & Taylor, 1987; Keane, Caddell, & Taylor, 1988). Several of these procedures have been adapted for use with civilian victims. Keane et al. (1987) report the development of a comprehensive structured assessment battery that is useful not only for diagnostic purposes but for the development of treatment goals and the evaluation of treatment outcome. Although developed for assessment of combat-related PTSD, the principles embodied in this battery are relevant to other forms of trauma as well. The battery includes both objective and subjective data collected through structured interview formats, as well as quantifiable psychological inventories. It assesses past and present functioning in a wide range of cognitive, affective, behavioral, and physiological areas (Wolfe & Keane, 1990).

A note of caution regarding assessment is in order. Suicide risk should always be carefully assessed and monitored. The National Women's Study (Kilpatrick et al., 1992) found that 13% of rape victims had made a suicide attempt. This is compared to 1% of the nonvictims. Additionally, 33% of the rape victims compared to 8% of nonvictims stated that they had seriously considered suicide at some point.

Structured Diagnostic Interviews

For diagnostic purposes the Structured Clinical Interview (SCID) for DSM-III-R is one of the most widely used. The SCID (Spitzer, Wiliams, & Gibbon, 1987) includes assessment of PTSD symptomatology and was developed for use by experienced clinicians. Presumably, a revised version will be published following the adoption of DSM-IV. However, with minor modifications the SCID should continue to be useful. Resnick et al. (1991) recommend modifications for use with rape victims since the PTSD module of the SCID was originally developed for use with combat veterans. These modifications include more sensitive screening questions for history of rape and other major traumatic events. Additionally, assessment of exposure to multiple traumatic events is important for treatment planning purposes.

A second widely used structured interview is the Diagnostic Interview Schedule (DIS; Robbins, Helzer, Croughan, & Ratcliff, 1981). It is a highly structured interview schedule that has the advantage of requiring less training and experience than does the SCID. The PTSD section assesses exposure to civilian trauma but uses the term

rape without any further specification. Thus the modifications suggested by Resnick et al. (1991) are appropriate for this instrument as well.

The Clinician Administered PTSD Scale (CAPS) developed by Blake et al. (1990) is newer, but preliminary reports of psychometric properties are very promising (Nagy et al., 1992; Weathers et al., 1992a, 1992b). The CAPS has several attractive features. It assesses both severity and frequency of symptoms, using specific criteria. Additionally, it gives clear guidelines for assessing changes in behavior following exposure to trauma. Two forms are available. CAPS-1 (current and lifetime diagnostic version) assesses symptoms over a 1-month period. CAPS-2 (1-week status version) measures symptoms over the past week.

The Anxiety Disorders Interview Schedule—Revised (ADIS–R; DiNardo & Barlow, 1988) is the most comprehensive instrument for differential diagnosis of anxiety and related disorders and assessment of comorbid disorders. It includes sections on major depression, substance abuse, and psychoses. Blanchard et al. (1986) reported interrater agreement on PTSD diagnosis of 93%.

Psychometric Instruments

The Impact of Events Scale (IES; Horowitz, Wilner, Alvarez, 1979) is one of the most widely used instruments for measuring trauma impact. It is a 15-item self-report inventory with subscales that measure intrusion and avoidance symptoms.

Derogatis Symptom Checklist 90-R (SCL-90-R; Derogatis, 1977) is another widely used instrument. It is a 90-item self-report measure with nine symptom-related subscales and three global indices of distress. The Global Severity Index has been most widely used in research with rape victims. Kilpatrick, Veronen, and Resick (1982) and Kilpatrick and Veronen (1983) reported that the Global Severity Index was able to discriminate rape victims from matched controls.

The SCL-90-R Crime-Related PTSD scale was developed by Saunders, Mandoki, and Kilpatrick (1990) as a brief screening measure for crime-related PTSD. It includes 28 items from the SCL-90-R that were found to provide the best discrimination between PTSD-positive and -negative groups. It has high internal consistency and good discriminative ability.

The Rape Aftermath Symptom Test (Kilpatrick, 1988) is a 70-item self-report inventory. It combines items from the SCL-90-R and the Modified Fear Survey (Veronen & Kilpatrick, 1980). The items selected were those found to discriminate most highly between rape victims and nonvictims at 3 months postassault. It has good internal consistency and test–retest reliability.

The PTSD Symptom Scale (Foa, Riggs, Dancu, & Rothbaum, 1991) is a brief (17-item) scale with three subscales that measure each of the major symptom areas: reexperiencing, avoidance and numbing, and hyperarousal. Internal consistency of .91 and 1-month test–retest reliability of .74 were reported in a sample of recent rape victims. The test correctly identified PTSD status, as measured by the SCID, in 86% of the sample.

The Ways of Coping Questionnaire (Folkman & Lazarus, 1988) has been used to examine coping strategies in rape victims. It may be useful in treatment planning and evaluation. Gershuny, Dancu, Hembru, and Foa (1992) factor-analyzed responses of victims assessed soon after assault, forcing items into three factors: Wishing Trauma Away, Problem Solving, and Passive Acceptance. Scores on Wishing Trauma Away were significantly related to PTSD symptomatology and severity, as well as to other measures of psychopathology, assessed 1-month later. It contributed significantly to the prediction of PTSD severity beyond that contributed by perceived life threat and guilt.

Psychophysiological Assessment

The ideal assessment would include measurement in multiple response channels, including physiological. However, in clinical settings this might not be feasible because the technology and expertise are not always available. At any rate, research on physiological response patterns in non-combat-related PTSD has not advanced to the point where such measures could be recommended with any confidence for use in clinical settings. Research with combat veterans indicates that such measures may hold promise. In that population, a consistent finding is that psychophysiological measures discriminate well between veterans with and without PTSD (Blanchard et al., 1982; Pitman, Orr, Forgue, de Tong, & Claiborn, 1987). Both resting heart rate and reaction to combat cues have shown this discriminant ability.

Research with rape victims has been less consistent. A few case studies have reported the use of physiological measures (Blanchard & Abel, 1976; Kilpatrick & Amick, 1985), but few group studies have been reported to date. Kilpatrick, Best, Amick, and Veronen (1984) measured heart rate and skin conductance in response to neutral, pleasant, and rape-related imagery. No overall elevations in baseline rates of arousal or changes in response to rape imagery were found. Only a small subgroup of victims (11.5%) responded at a high level on both physiological indices. PTSD diagnoses were not made, so it is possible that the subgroup of responders were those with elevated PTSD symptoms.

Kozak, Foa, Rothbaum, and Murdock (1988) reported preliminary results of heart rate and skin conductance responses to neutral and rape scenes. Twelve women with rape-related PTSD were compared with a matched group of nonvictims. Both physiological measures showed reactivity during rape scenes, as well as a decline in reactivity after several repetitions of the scenes. However, large variations in responsiveness appeared to obscure significant group differences in such a small sample.

Research in this area would be very helpful in determining the usefulness of psychophysiological measures in rape-related PTSD. As Resnick et al. (1991) point out, most of the research in this area has been done with men and may not be generalizable to female trauma victims.

TREATMENT

Very little controlled treatment research has been conducted with victims of rape and other civilian traumas. However, a wide variety of approaches have been described anecdotally or in uncontrolled case reports.

These include psychodynamic psychotherapy, biofeedback, flooding, systematic desensitization, cognitive therapy, and approaches aimed at specific problems such as sexual dysfunctions (for reviews, see Resick & Schnicke, 1990; Solomon, Gerrity, & Muff, 1992).

Stress Inoculation Training

The earliest comprehensive approach described specifically for use with rape victims was stress inoculation training (SIT; Kilpatrick et al., 1982; Kilpatrick & Amick, 1985). Based on Meichenbaum's (1985) approach, it is aimed at giving the client a sense of mastery over her fears by teaching a variety of coping skills. The approach is tailored to the individual problems and needs of each client, so it is flexible and can be used in individual or group settings. SIT is approached in phases. The first phase is preparation for treatment and includes an educational element to provide an explanatory or conceptual framework from which the client can understand the nature and origin of her fear and anxiety and make sense of the assault and its aftermath. In SIT, a social learning theory explanation is used. Along with this, fear and anxiety reactions are explained as occurring along three channels (Lang, 1968): (1) the physical or autonomic channel, (2) the behavioral or motoric channel, and (3) the cognitive channel. Specific examples are given for each and the client identifies her own reactions within each channel. Interrelationships among the three channels are explained and discussed.

The second phase of SIT is the training of coping skills. At least two coping skills (a primary and secondary, or backup, skill) are taught for each of the three channels. The client first selects three target fears she would like to reduce. She is asked to complete an emotion thermometer on which she rates her level of fear and her level of happiness three times a day. In addition, she keeps a daily record of the number of thoughts she has regarding each target fear during each morning, afternoon, and evening.

The general format for training of coping skills is the same for all six skills taught.

It includes, in sequence, a definition of the coping skill, a rationale, an explanation of the mechanism by which the skill works, a demonstration of the skill, application by the client of the skill with a problem area that is unrelated to the target behaviors, a review of how well the skill worked, and, finally, application and practice of the skill with one of the target fears. Skills taught most often for coping with fear in the physical channel are muscle relaxation and breathing control.

Muscle Relaxation

To teach muscle relaxation, the Jacobsonian tension–relaxation contrast method is used most frequently. Total relaxation of all major muscle groups is included during the first training session. In addition, a tape of the relaxation session is provided for the victim to take home and use in practice assignments. Training is continued until proficiency is reached. Women are encouraged to practice their relaxation skills during everyday activities.

Breath Control

Deep diaphragmatic breathing is taught using psychocybernetics exercises. This skill is practiced in session and at home between sessions.

For the behavioral channel, covert modeling and role playing are the coping skills usually taught.

Covert Modeling

The woman is taught to visualize a fear or anxiety-provoking situation and to imagine herself confronting it successfully. This skill is practiced until proficiency is obtained. Because people vary widely in their ability to visualize such situations, the time needed to master this skill is quite variable. The skill is useful in preparing for situations that a woman knows will likely produce fear and anxiety reactions.

Role Playing

The client and therapist act out successful coping in anxiety-producing scenes with which the woman expects to be confronted.

In group situations, other group members may be used in the role playing as well. The woman may then be asked to role play scenes with family members or friends.

Thought Stopping

For the cognitive channel, thought stopping is especially useful in breaking into the ruminative thoughts that characterize many victims' reactions. The client is asked to begin generating thoughts about the feared stimuli and then those thoughts are interrupted, initially by having the therapist yell "Stop!" simultaneously clapping hands together loudly. Then the woman is asked to use the word *stop* subvocally or to devise her own covert thought-stopping term or visualization. She then learns to use thought stopping covertly and to substitute a relaxed state for the anxious state.

Guided Self-Dialogue

The client is taught to focus on her internal dialogue and trained to label negative irrational and maladaptive self-statements. She is then taught to substitute more adaptive self-verbalizations. Self-dialogue is taught in four categories: preparation, confrontation and management, coping with feelings of being overwhelmed, and reinforcement. For each of these categories, a series of questions and/or statements is generated that encourage the client to assess the actual probability of the negative event's happening, to manage the overwhelming fear and avoidance behavior, to control self-criticism and self-devaluation, to engage in the feared behavior, and finally to reinforce herself for making the attempt and following the steps.

For each coping skill, practice assignments are given. Mild everyday stresses are confronted first. When the use of skills in these situations is mastered, the trauma-related target behaviors are confronted. The client confronts each of the target behaviors she has identified in sequence. Following successful coping with the first target behavior, treatment focuses on the second. During this phase the client again completes the emotion ratings on a daily basis. This allows the therapist to check on progress and adjust the treatment as needed.

Veronen and Kilpatrick (1980, 1983) and Kilpatrick and Amick (1985) reported that SIT was effective in reducing fear, anxiety, negative mood, and physiological reactivity in uncontrolled and case studies. Resick, Jordan, Girelli, Hutter, and Marhoefer-Dvorak (1988) compared SIT with assertion training and supportive therapy in a group format, conducted in 12, 2-hour sessions. All three approaches resulted in significant improvements that were maintained at 6-month follow-up. Foa et al. (1991) compared SIT to prolonged exposure, supportive counseling, and a wait-list control group, with clients being seen individually. SIT was the most effective immediately posttreatment in reducing PTSD symptoms, anxiety, and depression. However, at 3½-month follow-up, the exposure approach showed the greatest efficacy.

Prolonged Exposure

Foa and colleagues have developed a cognitive-behavioral treatment approach specifically for rape-related PTSD (Foa et al., 1991; Rothbaum & Foa, 1992). It is based on an elaboration (Foa & Kozak, 1986) of Lang's (1979) model regarding emotional processing of fear, proposing that PTSD results from inadequate processing of the trauma stimuli, responses, and the meaning associated with them. Treatment requires activation of the fear memory and incorporation of new information incompatible with the current fear structure, so that new memories are formed. The memory is activated through exposure techniques similar to those used with victims of other types of trauma (e.g., war veterans) (Fairbank & Keane, 1982). Specifically, the victim is asked to recall the assault in detail and helped to process the memory until it is no longer intensely painful. This is combined with *in vivo* exposure to feared (but objectively safe) stimuli.

The treatment is conducted individually in nine biweekly 90-min sessions. The first two sessions are for information gathering, treatment planning, and explanation of treatment rationale. A hierarchical list is generated of major stimuli that are feared and avoided. In the remaining sessions, the rape scene is relived in imagination and the client is asked to describe it aloud in the present tense. The level of detail is left to the client for the first two sessions, but thereafter she is encouraged to include more and more detail about external cues and internal cues such as thoughts, physiological responses, and feared consequences. Descriptions are repeated several times each session (for 60 min) and tape-recorded. Clients are assigned homework: to listen to the tape and engage in *in vivo* tasks. Tasks are chosen from the hierarchy that match the level of anxiety (subjectively rated) confronted in that session. Care is taken in sessions to ensure that anxiety decreases before the session is terminated, aided by the therapist if necessary. Decision guidelines developed by Litz, Blake, Gerardi, and Keane (1990) for exposure therapy are used in case of complications such as extreme fear or inability to generate images.

This approach was found to be more effective than a wait-list control group (Foa et al., 1991) and more effective than SIT at 3½-month follow-up. It addresses both the unpredictability and uncontrollability of the trauma and could be combined with additional skill training (e.g., assertion training) if necessary in individual cases.

Cognitive Processing Therapy

Cognitive processing therapy (CPT) is a therapy model developed to treat the specific symptoms of post-traumatic stress disorder in victims of sexual assault (Resick & Schnicke, 1992, in press). CPT is a 12-session structured therapy program based on an information processing model of PTSD. A unique feature of CPT is that it combines the main ingredient of exposure-based therapies with the cognitive restructuring components found in most cognitively based therapies. Moreover, the content of the cognitive portion of the therapy challenges specific cognitions that are most likely to have been disrupted as a result of the trauma. Clients are given homework assignments at each session, so much of the therapeutic work is carried out between sessions. What follows is a brief description of CPT. A case illustrating the use of CPT is provided at the end of the chapter. For a more detailed description of CPT procedures, the reader is referred to Ellis, Black, and Resick (1992); Resick (1992); and Resick and Schnicke (1992, in press).

In their discussion of information processing theory in PTSD, Foa, Steketee, and Rothbaum (1989) and Foa and Kozak (1986) described how established fear structures can be dismantled. They proposed that two conditions are necessary for the reduction of fear: (1) the fear memory must be activated and (2) new information must be provided that is incompatible with the current fear structure in order for a new memory to be formed. They suggested that activation can occur through any of the three network elements—information about the stimuli, responses, or meaning. They recommend the use of some type of exposure-based therapy to achieve this goal.

Foa et al. (1989) proposed that systematic exposure to the traumatic memory in a safe environment serves to alter the feared memory such that threat cues are reevaluated and habituated. However, while activation of the network, or schemas, in a safe environment may sufficiently alter perceptions of danger, and hence fear, there may be no change in emotional reactions other than fear without direct confrontation of conflicts, misattributions, or expectations. Victims may still blame themselves and feel shame, disgust, anger, or confusion, all of which could be sufficiently intense to facilitate intrusive memories, arousal, and avoidance reactions.

An approach that elicits memories of the event and then *directly* confronts conflicts and maladaptive beliefs might be more effective than exposure only. Prolonged exposure (PE) activates the memory structure but does not provide direct corrective information regarding misattributions or other maladaptive beliefs. CPT, specifically designed for treatment of PTSD, provides another means for activating the memory structure. This would include conflicting beliefs and meanings attributed to the event and expectations regarding the future that might not be elicited by other forms of exposure therapy. Therefore, it appears more advantageous to implement a therapy that will activate the memories of the event and also provide corrective information for conflicts, faulty attributions, or expectations that interfere with complete processing or cause other symptoms (depression, low self-esteem, fear).

An underlying assumption of CPT is that the symptoms of PTSD are usually caused by conflict between this new information and prior schemas. These conflicts *may* be concerned with danger and safety ("I don't feel safe going out alone"), but they could reflect other conflicts on other themes such as self-esteem, competence, and intimacy (McCann & Pearlman, 1990a). These cognitive conflicts could account for the intrusive, arousal, and avoidance symptoms observed in PTSD. Therefore, while there are modules included to introduce the concept of faulty thinking patterns or assumptions, most of the focus of CPT is on identifying and modifying "stuck points" (i.e., conflicts between prior schemas and this new information).

The exposure component of CPT is quite different than the type usually practiced with PE therapies. In CPT, clients write about the event in detail including sensory memories, thoughts, and feelings during the event. They are encouraged to write at a time and place where they can express their emotions and are instructed to read the account to themselves daily. During the session they read the account aloud and the therapist helps them to label their feelings and identify stuck points. This component of the treatment lasts only two sessions. While it could be argued that only two sessions do not constitute PE, the results obtained thus far do not indicate that more time is needed for single-incident traumas.

Findings regarding CPT are promising. In a first, quasi-experimental study, Resick and Schnicke (1992) compared 19 CPT clients with 20 wait-list comparison subjects. They found that the wait-list group did not change over time, but the CPT group improved significantly on all PTSD and depression measures.

Resick and Schnicke (in press) reported further findings on 45 women who had received either group or individual CPT. The findings reported for the first 19 subjects continued to hold. At posttreatment, 88% of the women who had initially met full criteria for PTSD no longer met the criteria. At the 6-month follow-up, this increased to 92%. At pretreatment, 60% of the women

also met DSM-III-R criteria for depression. At posttreatment, 14% still met criteria for depression and 6 months later 11% were depressed.

Therapist Variables

Gender

Since rape is a highly personal and intimate crime that often leads to distrust of men, the issue of therapist gender is relevant. Frequently, clients prefer or insist on a female therapist. The effectiveness of male therapists has not been studied specifically, but it is felt that they can be quite effective if well trained (Resick et al., 1988). Issues for male therapists are discussed by Silverman (1977) and Koss and Harvey (1991), and include the tendency for men to view rape as more of a sexual crime than a crime of violence (Burt, 1980) and therefore to focus too much on sexual aspects.

Rape Attitudes

Whether the therapist is male or female it is essential that the therapist be knowledgeable about rape and PTSD. This includes the literature on reactions to rape and mediating variables as well as on rape myths and attitudes about rape. Therapists bring their culturally learned perceptions with them, as do clients, and these can interfere with their effectiveness if they follow any of the common misperceptions about rape (e.g., rape is primarily about sex or most rapists are strangers). Rape victims are extremely sensitive to implications that they might have been to blame, for example, and many drop out of treatment when they sense that the therapist might secretly blame them.

Vicarious Traumatization

Working with trauma victims can have negative effects on therapists similar to problems shown by their clients. This has been labeled secondary or vicarious traumatization. McCann and Pearlman (1990b) discussed this impact as disruption of the therapist's own cognitive schemas about self and the world. Hearing clients' traumatic experiences may be shocking and lead to lasting alterations in assumptions and expectations, which in turn impacts therapists' feelings and relationships. Working with trauma victims can challenge therapists' assumptions about personal invulnerability and safety, as well as beliefs that the world is a meaningful, orderly place filled with trustworthy people. According to the model presented by McCann and Pearlman (1990b), an individual therapist's reaction depends on the degree of discrepancy between the traumatic imagery and the therapist's cognitive schemas. For example, if the therapist's own complex experiences have led to the development of safety assumptions (schemas) as central to his/her well-being, working with crime victims can be distressing due to a heightened sense of vulnerability. In addition, the therapist's memory system may be altered to incorporate traumatic imagery that can become intrusive.

To counteract the effects of vicarious traumatization, therapists should be prepared to recognize and acknowledge these effects and take steps to deal with them. McCann and Pearlman recommend the use of one's professional network as a source of support, avoiding isolation. Talking to other professionals who work with victims is especially useful because they can help recognize the effects of vicarious traumatization and normalize these reactions. Other coping strategies suggested by McCann and Pearlman include balancing victim with nonvictim cases, engaging in other professional and personal activities, recognizing one's own limitations, working for social change, and focusing on the positive personal impact of this work and ways it can enrich one's life.

Client Variables

Resistance

Clients with PTSD can be notoriously difficult due to their ambivalence about therapy. They want help but fear confronting their memories. Avoidance behaviors, including avoiding cognitions, are part of the criteria for PTSD. Therefore, no-shows are common at the first session and both subtle and obvious avoidance is seen throughout the beginning stages of therapy.

If possible, treatment should start on the telephone prior to the first session. The no-show rate is likely to drop if the therapist expresses understanding of the client's hesitance to come in and encourages attendance. The therapist should describe avoidance as a symptom of PTSD and an ineffective means of coping. If this is seen only as resistance, it interferes with therapist effectiveness. This and other challenges in working with victims are discussed by Koss and Harvey (1991) and Kilpatrick and Veronen (1983).

Multiple-Trauma Victims

The treatment approaches presented have been shown to produce significant improvement in civilian trauma victims within a brief time. It should be noted, however, that most of the research has been done with single-trauma victims. More complicated cases, especially those with multiple-trauma histories, may take longer. Cognitive-behavioral treatment approaches are flexible and readily adaptable to more complex cases. Victims of child sexual abuse present additional challenges. Their traumatization often interferes with normal development. It usually involves a relative or trusted adult and represents a serious betrayal by someone on whom the child depends for basic safety and protection. Clients with this kind of history may need more time to process and integrate such an experience. They may need more help with skill development as well, especially interpersonal skills. In some cases, sexual dysfunctions must be addressed. This can be added to an individual treatment program or referral to a sex therapy specialist may be made—but only after the treatment for trauma is complete.

Setting Variables

Group Treatment

The decision to use a group or an individual format for treatment is usually made on the basis of clinical judgment and practicality. There is little research comparing the two procedures. Most of the interventions that have been used with trauma victims are adaptable for use in either format. Group treatment may be a useful adjunct to

individual therapy in many cases. Many rape
crisis centers and other public service agencies offer self-help support groups for victims.

Group treatment has several advantages
that make it popular among survivors as well
as among professionals. Koss and Harvey
(1991) discussed a number of these: Group
treatment reduces the sense of isolation felt
by most victims, who withdraw from interactions with others and believe that others
cannot understand their feelings. It provides
social support that is unambiguous and
nonblaming. It helps to validate and normalize feelings and reactions to the trauma.
Group treatment confirms the reality of the
traumatic experience and allows sharing of
coping strategies. It counteracts self-blame
and promotes self-esteem. Because it is
more egalitarian than individual therapy,
group treatment can promote reempower-
ment and decrease dependency. It provides
a safe environment for developing attach-
ment and intimacy and an opportunity for
sharing grief and loss. Finally, group treatment can help victims assign meaning to the
event, promoting cognitive processing.

Group approaches have drawbacks as
well, and care should be taken to screen
clients to assess their readiness for joining
a group. McCann and Pearlman (1990a)
suggest that clients with severe PTSD should
be in individual therapy simultaneously with
group treatment, because groups may elicit
strong affect and memories that can overwhelm an unprepared client. For similar
reasons, Resick and Markaway (1991) warn
against having group members share their
rape experiences during the first few sessions. While important for recovery, the
sharing of "war stories" should be done
later in the group process or in individual
sessions, to avoid frightening other group
members or sensitizing them to other vulnerable situations. Poor candidates for
group treatment, as suggested by Koss and
Harvey (1991) and McCann and Pearlman
(1990a), are suicidal clients, those with heavy
substance abuse problems, self-mutilating or
substance-abusing clients with a borderline
personality disorder diagnosis, clients with
very unstable, disorganized lives, and clients
who have never before spoken about the
trauma or whose memory of it is incomplete.

CASE STUDY

"Cindy" is a 26-year-old client who sought
treatment for a rape that had occurred 10
years earlier. Because she was treated within
an ongoing treatment study, she was assessed
by a psychologist on staff using standardized
interviews and a battery of self-report questionnaires. She was then assigned to the second author (PAR) for treatment using the
standardized format for CPT.

Background

At the time of intake, Cindy was married,
the mother of two young children, and was
not employed outside of the home, although
she had just been hired for a free-lance job
that was scheduled to start during the course
of her therapy. She had a 12th-grade education with some business school classes.

Cindy had become depressed during the
fall of the year (3 months before the intake
interview) following an affair she had had
for 5 weeks. During the affair, she began to
have flashbacks of events that had occurred
a decade earlier. When she realized that this
affair coincided with the exact time of year
she had been raped, she broke it off and
became increasingly depressed and agitated
as more memories surfaced. It was only
now, 10 years later, that she began to label
what had previously occurred as rape. She
had sought therapy before, three different
times, each lasting only one session.

At the initial interview, Cindy reported
that she had been raped repeatedly over a
5-week period by a close friend of the family who was her age and lived across the
street. The boy came from an abusive family and Cindy's family "adopted" him. He
was best friends with her brother so he spent
a great deal of time in their home and her
parents were also quite fond of him. Cindy
had always had a sibling-type relationship
with "Mark." During the initial interview,
Cindy gave only the sketchiest of accounts
and had no eye contact with the interviewer.
The interviewer did not press her for a detailed description of the events but continued to ask standardized questions.

These interview questions revealed that
Cindy had been a virgin prior to the rape
and had trusted the assailant quite a bit

before the assault. She was verbally threatened by him, although no weapons or physical injuries were involved. She was subjected to a range of sex acts, including oral, vaginal, and anal intercourse. During the assaults, her most prominent reactions were feeling detached and numb, guilty, and embarrassed. The incidents were never reported to the police and she received no medical care. At the interview, Cindy reported receiving negative reactions to her disclosure about the rape from those who were closest to her and that presently her social support was poor. She reported no child abuse or incest. During the initial interview Cindy also stated that she smoked marijuana quite a bit. She was defensive about her use of it and said that she did not want to quit. She also stated that a prior therapist had made a big deal about it. When Cindy told the therapist that she felt she was using pot as a crutch, he informed her that the pot was the problem, not a symptom. She disagreed, told the interviewer that she did not want to make it the focus of the therapy, and quit therapy.

Scores on all of the initial assessment measures were very elevated and similar to those of other rape victims entering treatment (Resick & Schnicke, 1992). Cindy scored a total of 34 on the PTSD Symptom Scale, and 35 on the IES Intrusion scale, and 30 on the IES Avoidance scale. She also scored a 36 on the Beck Depression Inventory. In addition to the self-report measures, she was given the PTSD and depression modules from the SCID for DSM-III-R (Spitzer et al., 1987). Cindy was diagnosed as meeting criteria for PTSD and major depression.

Cindy was 45 min late for her first scheduled therapy session. The therapist labeled Cindy's behavior as avoidant and normalized it as a symptom of PTSD. The therapist talked about how avoidance had prevented her from recovering from the rape and that Cindy was going to need to confront her fears head on in order to deal with them in therapy. Cindy admitted that she had been afraid to come to the session and that she could see the storm (emotions and memories) coming. The therapist reminded her that after a storm, the land dries up and the grass grows again. The flood waters don't last forever. Cindy expressed hopeful-

ness about the future and made some positive statements about herself. The "session" lasted 10 min and another session was scheduled.

Session 1

Cindy arrived on time for the next session, which became the first actual therapy session. She remained wrapped and huddled in her jacket the entire time. During the session Cindy admitted that she had smoked marijuana before the session to calm her nerves. The therapist downplayed the marijuana use but labeled it as another form of avoidance and requested that Cindy not use marijuana before sessions or while doing the homework, which would be assigned at every session. Later during the session, while describing areas of functioning that are likely to be affected by rape, the marijuana use was described as an indicator of problems with self-intimacy, the ability to self-soothe without external substances. Cindy agreed to refrain from substance use while working on therapy issues.

The purposes of the first therapy session were to (1) describe the symptoms of PTSD; (2) give the client a framework for understanding why these symptoms developed and why they have not remitted; (3) present an overview of treatment to help the client understand why homework completion and therapy attendance are important, to elicit cooperation, and to explain the progressive nature of the therapy; (4) build rapport between the client and therapist; and (5) give the client an opportunity to talk about the rape or other issues.

The therapist began the session by going over the results of the assessment. At the time of treatment, Cindy was suffering from PTSD and major depression. The symptoms of PTSD and depression were described and an information processing explanation of these symptoms was offered. The therapist described how rape, for most people, is a schema-discrepant event: It does not fit prior beliefs about oneself, others, or the world. In order to incorporate this event into memory, the information becomes altered (assimilated) or beliefs are changed to accommodate the event. Examples of assimilation are distorting the event so that it is not labeled a rape or blaming oneself for its occurrence. Overaccommodation was described as changing beliefs too much as a result of the rape (e.g., no one can be trusted). Areas of beliefs often affected by rape are safety, trust, power, esteem, and intimacy. The therapist described how people have beliefs in these areas regarding oneself and others and that either locus can be affected. The therapist also pointed out that if one had a sheltered environment and positive beliefs prior to the rape, these beliefs are likely to be disrupted by the event. However, if one had negative beliefs prior to the rape on any of these topics, the rape would seemingly confirm these negative beliefs.

Cindy, at this point, described her childhood as a happy one. She described her house as the safe house in the neighborhood where all of the kids could come to play, and where some found refuge when there were problems in their own home. She said her father had been a Vietnam veteran and still has PTSD. She described him as emotionally closed but also spoke fondly of him. She described her mother as a self-help fanatic and said that their house was filled with self-help books. She also stated that she had a close and supportive relationship with her mother. Cindy has one older brother with whom she was close until the rape.

After describing her childhood before the rape, Cindy spent some time describing how drastically things changed after these incidents. Cindy said that she told her mother what had happened and that her mother stopped the abuse. However, upon further questioning by the therapist, what emerged was that Cindy told her mother that Mark had been "coming on" to her, that it had gotten out of control, and that she needed help getting out of the situation. She never told her mother that she had been raped. Therefore, her family did not understand why she changed. After the rape, Cindy withdrew from her normal high school activities and began to hang out with troubled kids. Over the next year she lied a lot and began drinking. She described herself as floating in and out of reality. She and her mother fought a lot. A year later a friend of hers was driving recklessly and crashed

the car in which Cindy was a passenger. Cindy was out of school for 2 months and had a long recovery from a broken back. She became a "total rebel" and dated a "wild guy who was total bad news." She became pregnant by him and didn't know what to do. At that time Cindy let her father take over and arrange for an abortion. Although she might have come to the same decision, Cindy now regretted that she gave up the right to decide. Cindy did not have the confidence to go to college. Her mother talked her into going to a business school for secretarial training. Cindy worked as an executive secretary until the current year. At the time she entered therapy, she had been unemployed for 6 months. She had been married for 5 years and had two children.

The therapist's comment after hearing this account was, "When the rapes happened, it derailed you." Her response was, "Yes, I've been lost." Fortunately, Cindy had "the good sense" to marry a fine man who had been very supportive of her and did not give up on her after the affair. He was very supportive of her efforts to receive therapy.

At this point in the session, the following sequence between Cindy (C) and the therapist (T) occurred:

C: (*Agitated*) It's so bad you don't want to think about it.

T: That's when the avoidance is a two-edged sword. On the one hand it makes you more comfortable at the moment if you push it away, but it doesn't let you get better either.

C: No . . .

T: Our average length of time for someone to come into treatment with us is eight years later.

C: (*Openmouthed with surprise*) I was so embarrassed! I thought I was dredging up the bottom of the barrel.

T: No, you're typical. We get a few early on, but we've had women come in 30 years later.

C: I guess you reach a point where you start becoming in sync with your mind again—where you say this has to be dealt with.

T: It's not going to go away. You've got to get to the point where you say, "Whatever I'm doing, it's not working."

C: You say, "This was my life and it was . . . and I'm . . . here today."

T: What we're going to be doing is very systematic. I'm going to be giving you homework assignments and each thing will build upon the last. The first thing we're going to start with is a writing assignment. Next time we're going to talk about feelings and labeling them, and work on the connection between thoughts and feelings—what you say to yourself, your beliefs, and how you feel. And from there, you'll do some writing about the rape, and not just a police blotter version, but the real . . .

C: Rape.

T: (*Nods*) Yes, and that means feelings, and what you remember, and all the stuff you don't remember—the hard stuff that we'll get into in therapy. That's what you've got to do even if you don't want to.

C: (*Agitated*) Oh, God.

T: It'll get easier after that.

C: (*Covering face*) Oh, no.

T: That is to help you remember. We don't want any more closed doors in your mind. It's time to air out those rooms.

C: It's the hardest thing to open.

T: It is, and there are probably some points in there that are the hardest parts to remember, and that's what we'll have to get into. To get it out here and put it in black and white, talk about it, put it out here in front of you so you can accept it. The feelings get easier over time and that's the one thing I can promise you. When you let yourself feel your feelings about something, it gets easier each time, and then eventually it doesn't bother you after that. On the other hand, if you have these strong feelings, and you stuff them, then every time you think of it you feel the same feelings all over again. We've got to let all the feelings out and let them run their course.

C: It just scares the hell out of me.

T: I know. I know. And we're going to help you brace yourself for it. And my job is to sit here and keep you on track, and not let you avoid. And I'm going to be listening for all those little games that you play with yourself, and saying, "Now what are you skipping here?"

C: I do.

T: So that's what I'm going to be listening for—is there some little stuck point that you're skirting around? Is there some little fragment of a memory that you just can't get past? You know, the place where the record gets . . .

C&T: (*Simultaneously*) stuck.

T: It's better if you're working with me than hiding from me. We need to work together.

The therapist explained that there would be three major goals for the therapy: to remember and accept the rape, to allow Cindy to feel her emotions and let them run their course (extinguish) so the memory could be put away without such strong feelings still attached, and to get beliefs that had been disrupted and distorted back in balance. After describing the therapy, Cindy was given her first assignment, to write about the meaning of the event. This assignment is given to determine the client's interpretation of the rape and to begin to determine what assimilation, accommodation, and overaccommodation have occurred since the assault. Stuck points, places of conflict between the event and prior beliefs, are often identified with this first assignment. The assignment was given as follows:

Please write at least one page on what it means to you that you were raped. Please consider the effects the rape has had on your beliefs about yourself, your beliefs about others, and your beliefs about the world. Also consider the following topics while writing your answer: safety, trust, power/competence, esteem, and intimacy. Bring this with you to the next session.

Session 2

The purposes of the second session were to discuss the meaning of the event and to help the client begin to label emotions, recognize thoughts, and see the connection between what she says to herself and how she feels. Cindy arrived at the session with obvious emotion and cried periodically throughout the session. She stated that she had been feeling quite angry all week. She said she was disgusted with society and particularly politicians and people with money and power. She said they were all greedy and self-righteous. She expressed a great deal of anger over the William Kennedy Smith trial, which occurred just before she started therapy. It became evident to the therapist that Cindy had overgeneralized a great deal of anger and distrust from the rapist, who had gone on to a military academy and an illustrious career, to all people with money and power. She also felt anger at the people in her life who did not recognize what pain she was in.

C: I walked away from a lot of people. I didn't talk to none of them.

T: But you didn't tell them either.

C: No, but there were signs. I gave off signs but they didn't choose to see or ask.

T: Have you been angry all along, or just this week?

C: All along. That's why I think I turned the bitterness inward.

The client went on to say that at the time, she didn't have the courage to tell her family. When asked, Cindy said that she thought her parents would have believed her and would not have blamed her (a perennial problem with teenage rape victims), but that she did not want to break their hearts. They had taken Mark into their home and treated him like a son. They were quite proud of his accomplishments. The therapist attempted to reframe Cindy's decision to remain silent not as cowardly but as protective of her parents and, therefore, courageous. Cindy then moved on to a topic that often emerges early in therapy.

C: Why did this have to happen? Why? Why?

T: Why did the rape have to happen?

C: Yeah. Why did he do that to me? Why should I have to feel this? I'm a product of my environment. I really feel like that.

T: We all are to a certain extent.

C: Yeah. We are.

T: What answer have you given yourself up to this point to that why question? Why did it have to happen? Why do you have to go through this?

C: Because, just, that's my life, that was my past. (*laughs*) That is what happened.

T: But you still keep asking why.

C: I think my why question just stems from, you know, you stupid son-of-a-bitch, you don't take that from people. (*long pause*) You know, it's not why did he take it from me. One thing I get mad at myself is, (*crying*) why did I let him?

T: You didn't let him.

C: I know.

T: Did you? He just did it.

C: It happened. I was fifteen. I was so scared.

T: And confused.

C: Yeah, and alone. I think that's why I'm mad. Because I was so alone and I walked away from so many people. It kind of wiped away all the good memories.

T: It's a scary decision for a 15-year-old to try to reach out to people when she's feeling bad about herself. At times a person in that position is going to pull away because she's so afraid of compounding the trauma by other people rejecting her. It seems almost better to walk away yourself than let other people reject you. So you were rejecting them first.

C: Well, for that year afterward I was really mixed up.

T: Um hmm.

C: I can see how I confused them and that's why I say, you know, I was giving off signs.

T: But you didn't have a label for what happened to you. Did you? You weren't saying, "I have been raped," were you? So even if they had asked, you wouldn't have been able to put it into words to express what you had been through.

C: I didn't consider it rape. I didn't know what to consider it.

T: You knew it was awful but you didn't have a word for it.

C: I was so ashamed of it.

T: When did you start to label it rape?

C: 2 months ago.

T: That recently. Why not before that?

C: I just didn't remember. . . . I think a lot of years I've been angry.

At this point, the therapist asked Cindy to read her homework assignment aloud to the therapist. Clients in individual CPT are always asked to read their homework assignments aloud. If the therapist were to read them, the clients could dissociate or otherwise avoid their own reactions to their material. Cindy had written:

When Mark raped me he also raped and manipulated my mind. I no longer trusted anyone, not even myself. I was bitter and angry at the world. I was also very frightened. I didn't feel safe anywhere, unless I was in the woods. I hated my bedroom. It had always been my safest place. It was where I was raped every time. I've been angry at him for taking that from me. For raping me on my own bed. I had to sleep in the bed for two more years. I took nothing with me when I moved out. All of those years of good memories were shattered. I felt nothing was sacred or special. I walked away from childhood, junior high, high school, college, and work friends. I feel this relates to intimacy. It makes me sad that I turned and walked away from so many people.

The rape created a "hate" toward society, religion, politicians, and especially business people. After the rape I was very lost, hurt, bitter and alone. Society seemed so self-righteous and unbalanced. Before the rape I saw the world that way a little bit, but I had a lot of hope. The majority of people were good. I was going to make a difference. I had a lot of love and compassion to give.

After the rape and during, the world seemed distorted and grotesque. The majority of people are greedy, self-righteous scum. The Kennedy family really reinforces that. Every time I watch the news or read the newspaper it reinforces that idea.

I've turned some of this anger toward myself for letting the rape happen. This inward anger has created a war in my mind. This war took a lot of my self-confidence, esteem, and identity.

It is breaking my heart to look back and see how much was taken. The people, memories, and the feelings I feel for myself. It hurts that someone had the power and wanted to take this from someone else. Mark took this from me.

Her assignment and the first issues she brought into therapy made evident the first stuck points that would have to be challenged. Cindy was assimilating in that she had difficulty labeling the events as rape and that she believed she had let them happen. She had overaccommodated in her distrust of society and had a great deal of generalized anger. She had ambivalent feelings toward the rapist and felt unsupported by her family, even though she had chosen not to tell them what happened. She also expressed self-esteem problems. Although safety did not appear to be a major content issue, trust, power, esteem, and intimacy were all disrupted.

After reading the composition, the therapist asked Cindy what her feelings were. Cindy said, "Lost, sad." From there the therapist described how important it is to be able to label emotions and to begin to identify what she is saying to herself. The therapist and client discussed how different interpretations (self-statements) of events could lead to very different emotional reactions. They generated several examples of how changes in self-statements would result in different reactions. The therapist also pointed out that there are some interpretations and reactions that follow naturally from rape and do not need to be altered. For example, if Cindy says that her rights have been violated and she feels angry, the therapist would not challenge that statement but would encourage her to feel her anger and let it run its course. If she recognized that she had lost something, it would be perfectly natural to feel sad. At this point Cindy said, "My feelings scare me. What do I do with my anger?" The therapist gave her several options: "Feel it, write about it, cry, talk to someone. If you need to expend energy, do it in constructive ways: run, walk, or clean house. Don't do aggressive things." The therapist made sure that Cindy could discriminate anger from aggression and stated that it was her philosophy not to have clients practice aggression as a way of expressing anger (no pounding pillows or bataka bats). The therapist also reminded the client that she had observed that the client appeared to have many good coping skills.

Cindy was given some A-B-C sheets as homework to begin to identify what she was telling herself and what her emotions were. In the first column Cindy was instructed to write down an event under A, "Something Happens." Under the middle column, B, "I tell myself something," she was asked to record her thoughts about the event. Under column C, "I feel and/or do something," she was asked to write down her behavioral and emotional responses to the event. The therapist pointed out that if one says something to oneself a lot, it becomes automatic. After a while, one doesn't need to consciously think the thought but can go straight to the feeling. It is important to stop and recognize automatic thoughts in order to decide whether they make sense or should be changed.

Session 3

Cindy handed the therapist her homework as soon as she arrived. The therapist went over the sheets with Cindy and pointed out that she had done a good job labeling her feelings and recognizing her thoughts. Some of the homework is shown in Figure 2.1.

Because the purpose of the exercise was to identify thoughts and feelings, not to challenge heavily at this point, the therapist noted the self-blame that again emerged but did not argue with the client. The therapist just quietly restated that Cindy did not *let* Mark rape her and pointed out that "the alternative is scary—that you didn't *let* him but that he did it anyway."

The therapist asked Cindy why she focused on Ted Kennedy and not on William Kennedy Smith. Cindy said, "Ted Kennedy is even worse. He's in political power. He killed a girl and got away with it. He defended his nephew." With regard to the thought about mainstream society, the

---

Date: _____   Client #: _____

Activating Event	Belief	Consequence
A ⟶	B ⟶	C
"Something happens"	"I tell myself something"	"I feel and do something"
I was raped.	I let it happen.	I feel ashamed.
My virginity is taken.	I told myself I'm used.	I feel a loss.
I feel the need to destroy Ted Kennedy.	I tell myself he's not worth it. God will deal with him.	I feel relieved and hopeful.
I'm told not all people are bad.	I know what I've seen. They are.	I feel bitter and misunderstood.
My husband is supportive.	I'm proud he's mine.	I feel good.

Does it make sense to tell yourself "B" above? _____

_____

What can you tell yourself on such occasions in the future? _____

_____

FIGURE 2.1. A-B-C sheet.

therapist said that she didn't understand how the self-statement led to the feelings Cindy had recorded. Cindy went on for many minutes about her belief that all people are bad. There is violence and poverty, and people in power make too much money, while others are homeless. She was very agitated as she talked and was teary at times. The therapist asked whether the people who are trying to help the homeless are also bad. Cindy responded that it was not enough. The therapist decided to see how much Cindy would cling to the belief that *all* people are bad. She asked whether Cindy also included the homeless as "bad."

C: No.

T: You said *all*.

C: I don't include them in mainstream society. (*pause*) I know I associate a lot of this in my mind because Mark went on and in society's mind is very successful.

T: And everyone who is in those positions is like Mark.

C: Yes, because they are probably the type to turn away and don't get involved, so they can keep what they have.

T: (*Trying to see if she would budge*) They might or they might not. There are some other kinds of people.

C: (*Pause*) I know they all aren't bad.

Although it might not be evident at first why Cindy kept coming back to her anger at society, it appeared to the therapist that it was probably more than overgeneralization from Mark to everyone who is successful or powerful. Focusing on her generalized anger helped deflect some of her feelings from the issue at hand—*her* rape. By being vague and general, she could avoid talking about the specifics of what happened to her. Because the goal is for the client to challenge and dismantle her own beliefs, the therapist probed but did not pursue the issue too far. And although Cindy did move away from her extreme stance a bit within the session, the therapist was not expecting any dramatic changes. She was focusing mostly on being supportive and building rapport to help the client get through the most difficult sessions which were to come next. The therapist also remained quiet during most of Cindy's diatribe because she didn't want to reinforce avoidance by engaging in a major discussion of society and all its woes.

The therapist did praise the client for her ability to recognize and label thoughts and feelings and said that she wanted Cindy to attend to both during the next assignment— writing about the rape. Cindy asked which rape to write about because it was a series of assaults. The therapist asked which one was the most traumatic for Cindy and she replied that the first one was. The therapist asked her to start with that one. Cindy was asked to write, for homework, a detailed account and to include as many sensory details as possible. She was asked to include her thoughts and feelings during the rape. She was instructed to start as soon as possible and to pick a time and place where she would have privacy and could express her emotions. If she was unable to complete the account in one sitting, she was asked to draw a line where she stopped. (The place where the client stops is often a place in the event where there is a stuck point, where the client gave up fighting, where something particularly heinous occurred, and so on.) Then when she could continue, Cindy was to read what she had already written and then write more. She was told that if there were parts she didn't remember, she should draw a line and continue on at the point she remembers next. She was also instructed to read the account to herself every day until her next session.

Cindy was told that there are several purposes for the assignment: to get the full memory back, to feel her emotions about it, and for the therapist and client to begin to look for stuck points. Cindy was also reassured that although this might be a difficult week for her, it would not continue to be so intense and she would soon be over the hardest part of the therapy.

Session 4

At the beginning of the session, the therapist asked Cindy to read her account. Before starting, Cindy asked the therapist to remind her of the benefit of reading. The therapist reminded Cindy of what they had talked about the previous session and added that the act of reading aloud would help her to access the whole memory and her feelings about it. Cindy read what she had written quietly, crying most of the time.

We were in the front room dancing. We practiced all the time. It was a slow song. We weren't dancing nasty, we were practicing so we could win a contest and also because we both loved to dance. We were dance partners. As we were dancing he kissed me. We kept on dancing and I was enjoying it. He slid his hand on my breast and for a brief moment it felt really good, but I had a boyfriend. I pushed his hand away and gave him a dirty look but continued dancing. We never really stopped dancing. It was like it was part of the dance. When the song finished he was smiling at me. He had a hard-on. I felt very uncomfortable and confused. We never kissed when we danced. Inside I felt threatened. I'm standing there trying to comprehend the situation when he puts his arms around me and starts kissing my neck. I pushed him away but he tightened his arms around me. He whispers that he can tell I like it. This will feel good. Come on he won't tell anyone, especially not my boyfriend. This angered me. It disgusted me. I tried to break free and I was talking hateful. I told him to leave me alone, let me go, and shut up. He tightened his grip more and wrestled me down the hall to my bedroom to the bed. He fell on me. I tried to wiggle free and I couldn't. I could not get away. He had me pinned. His hands were clenched around my wrists and he had his legs locked on top of mine. He put my right forearm under his right armpit and held my left wrist with his hand. With his other hand he pulled my shorts down and then his. He smiled at me while he gently stroked his dick like he was letting it know it was in for something good. I tried to break free again. He put both hands back on my wrists and then pried my legs apart with his legs. I screamed at the top of my lungs when he put himself in me. He shoved my own arm in my mouth. Then he started kissing me gently all over. I just laid there feeling hollow. I was crying but I felt very numb. The sheet was stuck to my cheek. It was all wet. I can feel myself laying there numb, tears rolling down my cheek, my head was turned completely to the side, and my eyes were squeezed shut. I thought about my parents, family, childhood, boyfriend, and friends, as if life was flashing before me. Then he kissed my cheek. He wasn't on me anymore. I opened my eyes and his shorts were up and he was walking out. I heard him go out the front door. It was over. I was laying on my bed in shock. I still didn't feel I could move. Then I felt the pain and the wetness between my legs. I knew what had happened. Crying, I got up. I noticed the cum on my belly and almost puked right then. I ripped the sheets off my bed, took off my shorts, and placed them on the sheets. I went into the bathroom and took a shower. I watched the water wash away the blood on my inner thighs. I scrubbed and scrubbed. Then I was too exhausted to stand. I sat all huddled in the shower sobbing uncontrollably. I was in there for about 30 minutes. Ten of those minutes were after the hot water ran out. It felt good though. It was almost icy. I finally got out and put on my pajamas. It was only 4:30 p.m. I went to bed in my parents room. I didn't know what to think or feel. I didn't want to think about what had happened. I was so exhausted I just wanted to go to sleep. How would I even begin to explain. I wasn't quite sure myself. I knew the facts but it didn't make sense. I just wanted to go to sleep and forget. When my mom came home I told her I was sick. I laid in that dark room all night. I wasn't sleeping yet or dreaming, but I could feel my mind racing. It was as if my mind was thinking in more detail about the things I thought about when I was actually in the process of being raped. It was violent yet gentle. I loved him but hated him. I had been proud of him and now was disgusted. Oh my God, I'm not a virgin anymore. I didn't give it away, I let someone take it, or I lost it, or it was taken from me. I knew for sure though, I didn't give it away and that really hurt me. I wanted my first time to be special. I played around with my boyfriend. I knew it probably would feel good when I was ready, but it would be special with someone special. Hell, I was only 15 years old. I really liked Bob my boyfriend. We had only been dating a month and really liked each other. He was two years older. He was a really good guy. We dated, kissed, and walked in the halls, but didn't even consider sex. I could feel myself transforming that night. I could feel myself changing, my thoughts, fears, and wishes. It was on a totally subconscious level. Consciously, I was laying in my parents bed curled up in blankets sleeping all night.

I don't think I moved a muscle. Yet, I could feel my subconscious working very hard. I knew I would never be the same. The change happened that night. I woke up a different person.

I chose not to tell to save a lot of people from being hurt. I would not be the messenger of that kind of hurt and pain. I knew they all had felt it before just as I did. That is what I chose as the best solution. I put the sheets and shorts in the washer and it was over.

I went to school as usual. I was quiet and distant. Mark passed me in the hall. I remember standing there at my locker glaring at him. Standing there in the hall around so many people, seeing him and remembering, I felt used and ashamed. For the rest of the day I avoided everyone and kept to myself. I stayed after school for softball. I got home around 6:00 p.m. and everyone was home at my house. I went to bed early again. The next day was a little better, but not much. I actually talked. That afternoon Mark said he wanted to talk to me when we got off the bus. I stared out the bus window the whole way home. It was always such a beautiful drive. I thought maybe he wanted to apologize. Even though it was violent, he had been gentle. I would rip him up with my words for what he did to me. Then I would forgive him, or at least try and handle it. But it didn't happen like that.

We sat on the couch and he started talking about what happened. He was sorry it happened like that. It could be a lot better if I wouldn't fight. He knew I liked it. I didn't scream until he stuck himself in me and I didn't tell anyone. I told him he was lying and that he was sick. I told him he violated me. He told me I was lying and that I did like it. I didn't scream or fight throughout the entire rape and didn't tell anyone. He starts talking about my boyfriend. What would he say if he knew. What would my parents think of me if they knew. If they all knew that I liked it. I didn't stop it from happening. He said I knew I was strong enough to stop it and I didn't. He took my hand and led me to the bedroom, pulled down my pants, and started kissing my body and neck. He told me how I was going to like it and that no one will know because I didn't want them to know I liked it. They'd be ashamed. It would be between he and I and we would both really enjoy it. I stood there dead. I can't let him tell anyone what happened two days before. He was going to tell them I wanted it. He was going to

tell people what he did to me and that I liked it. I let him put me on the bed and have sex. It didn't matter anymore. I felt if anyone knew it would destroy me. People would look at me differently. They would treat me like a slut and here I lay with him on top of me. He manipulated me this way for three weeks. I hated myself. I hated him. I didn't care anymore. He would make me do things I knew I didn't like. One time he made me lie on my stomach and he put himself in my anus. I screamed out in pain and then cried, "No more!" He stopped then and left. A few days later he came over again. He was threatening. He will tell everything. The truth was even worse now. It has been four weeks. He became more violent and persistent. I went deeper into a black hole. I came home from school a few incidents later and called my mom. It had to stop, whatever the cost. As I told her I could see her heart breaking so I told her I let it happen but things were out of control and asked her to please make it stop. That next afternoon I went to my mom's work. I sat out back on the bluff. I remember singing "I'm on top of the world looking down on creation." I felt a lot of hope.

Then at school he started threatening me. Hanging it over my head. Whispering that I couldn't get away, even though my parents made arrangements for me to stay with a friend after school. The odd part was that my own home wasn't even safe. His sister told me not to cause any problems. After a while Mark went on and left me alone. He started becoming more involved with studies and sports. I kept it inside and blamed myself for all that happened. I probably was a slut. Nothing mattered anymore. A ten-year war had started in my mind. What he told me was true versus what I knew was true. He raped me. He manipulated me. He tortured and tormented me. He raped my mind and my body. Back then I didn't know what to believe or do so I started lying about who I was, like in a fantasy.

I was terrified at the thought that he might be right. That I wanted it. I couldn't believe it but why didn't I scream, fight, and tell. Maybe I did ask for it. Everyone became my enemy. The people close to me were pushed away so they wouldn't get hurt and everyone else was pushed away so I wouldn't get hurt.

After reading the account, Cindy turned it upside down and set it on the table in the therapy room. The therapist asked her what she was feeling.

C: (*Long pause, shakes head*) Bitter.

T: You have a right to that feeling. He blackmailed you.

C: I know.

T: And made you feel guilty.

C: That's why I've blamed myself for all these years and never considered it rape. After awhile I just started believing it, seeing him go on to . . . (*drifts off*)

T: But it was rape.

C: I know.

T: And part of that rape was making you feel guilty—that somehow you should have responded differently.

C: And I didn't respond because I didn't want to hurt people, even him!

T: You know how most women respond? (*Cindy looks up*) They freeze. They go into emotional shock.

C: Yeah. You can't believe it. You're trying to take in what is happening . . . And then other people all say, "You should have . . ."

At this point, a discussion ensued regarding how hurtful it is to hear other people's general comments about rape. Cindy described how much anger she had and how she turned her anger against society, especially when she heard people say unfair things. From there she went on to describe how difficult the week had been with her husband. They had gotten into several fights and she was angry that her husband had stopped being supportive. The therapist talked about other people's reactions to rape and that sometimes their strong feelings interfere with their ability to be supportive. The therapist offered to have another therapist meet with Cindy's husband to help him process his own reactions. Cindy also expressed disappointment in a friend's reaction. When she told this "friend" how difficult the week had been because of all the memories surfacing, the woman responded by saying, "Get over it." She continued making other unsupportive comments. Cindy said that they had been friends since high school but that it was rather one-sided. She supported her friend and listened to her problems but had never asked for support before. Later in the session the therapist brought the discussion back to the rape and the assignment. She asked Cindy what stuck points she had identified. The following dialogue then occurred:

C: (*Crying*) Over the years, when I thought about it, I put all the blame back on myself. I could never remember what exactly happened the first time.

T: And now you do. Are any pieces missing? . . .

C: (*Interrupts*) (*crying*) No.

T: . . . Or is it the whole thing?

C: (*Very quietly*) (*sobbing*) I *know*. Oh. When I started remembering, I knew it was rape, without a doubt . . . then I started to get angry.

T: The fact that you didn't remember would have been a clue, if you'd known, that it was rape.

C: Yeah.

T: If it wasn't rape you would have remembered.

C: I never could remember the first time.

T: Um hmm.

C: And then, that's why I told myself . . . Maybe somehow, some way I started it.

T: In this case, you were just trying not to remember it. Because it clearly was.

C: (*Picks up writing assignment, puts it away, takes it out again*) Maybe I should look at that. (*looks at assignment silently for a long time*) I don't know where to go from here.

T: You wrote in there about what he said and that you were at war between believing and not believing. Where are you in terms of that now?

C: I know what the truth is.

T: Do you have any self-blame at this point?

C: No, umm, other than that, I think I'll always have doubts . . . the fact that I didn't do anything and . . . I'll always wish that . . .

T: There's a difference between wishing and blaming.

C: Yeah, that's true.

T: But I think we need to work on that because I don't want you saying that you *always* will.

C: (*Interrupts*) I'll always blame myself.

T: Because there's no need for that.

C: And reading back to this, my God!

T: The ironic part to me is that you chose not to tell, not because you liked it, or because you were a coward, or anything else. You chose not to tell because you didn't want to hurt people.

C: (*Cries*)

T: You were doing what you considered the right and noble thing to do and then he twisted it around.

C: He used it against me.

T: And he used it against you.

C: And then, after 4 weeks, then I'm really ... you know ... it's like ... (*makes the sound of an explosion*) It's even worse than the original, you know. Because it must be proof that ... (*moans*) Oh, God. (*looks up with a small smile*) Nobody ever found out.

The therapist's interpretation to Cindy was that Cindy had done the best she could in an impossible situation. The therapist then checked the client's emotional state to make sure she was calmer than she had been and was ready to close the session. She praised Cindy for doing a great job on the writing assignment and said it would be important not to quit now. Cindy's response was, "I'm more determined than ever." The therapist then took the first account and gave the client the homework assignment to write the entire account again. The therapist asked Cindy to add any details she might have left out of the first account and to record any thoughts and feelings she was having now in parentheses along with her thoughts and feelings at the time.

Session 5

Cindy arrived at the next session looking quite animated and cheerful. She reported that she had felt a great deal of energy and had done a lot of housecleaning and 13 loads of laundry. The therapist asked how everything was going between her and her husband. Cindy said that they had talked and he had apologized and had been extrasensitive, supportive, and loving. He didn't feel that he needed counseling at this time and Cindy had been pleased by his responsiveness and her openness during their discussion. Cindy had also talked a lot with her mother during the week and had felt supported. She then went on to talk a bit about her longtime friend and began to realize more clearly that this woman was not a friend to her, but that she had stuck with her out of loyalty and perhaps for some self-destructive reasons. This woman confirmed Cindy's poor view of herself with her vitriolic attacks. Cindy began to suggest that perhaps, as a friend, she was like the battered wife who stays with a spouse who seems to need her, but is also abusive.

The therapist asked Cindy how the writing had gone the second time. Cindy responded that there were no tears. She was a little shaky but not as emotional. The first part of the account was very similar but a bit shorter. Cindy found herself writing more about the later events.

After reading for only a few minutes and getting to the part where she was being dragged down the hall, the therapist interrupted Cindy with the following:

T: You don't have any thoughts and feelings in there that you had at the time. Were you having trouble bringing it to mind or ...

C: No, I, umm, I, I felt numb, I mean I, I feel that way about it right now.

T: Numb or neutral?

C: Neutral.

T: OK. When I think of numb I think of you holding something big back.

C: No, because I think I brought that out in the first one.

T: So you just feel like there's less feeling about it then?

C: Yeah. I know that I experienced a lot of pain and there were a lot of emotions mixed in there and I brought those out, and I guess I did, because ... it's just ... that's what happened, (*laughs*) you know? I feel, I guess neutral is the right word.

T: Um hmm.

C: It doesn't seem like it took . . . I don't know. It doesn't seem as painful. It does, but it doesn't. When I was writing this it was, but when I read it back the first time it was a little bit.

T: But each time you do it, it gets a little less.

C: And then when I was out in the truck a little while ago, I read over it and it was like . . . *(laughs and makes determined gestures)*

T: It happened, didn't it? It happened and there it is.

C: Yeah. You know, because it seems like for months I have been feeling all of the anger and the confusion, just remembering the pain, and here for a couple of weeks, kept dreaming about that person and so I knew this was it. My mind wouldn't let me deny it and I guess now it's, it's not as . . . it's better, you know.

T: Um hmm. OK.

C: I feel that way now.

T: Good. Well, let's just see. If you're not avoiding it, and you can think about it, and it doesn't cause you that much pain, then that probably is what you're looking for. If you have to avoid it, or if it's numb, holding back feelings, then you're not done—so you'll be able to tell the difference.

C: I mean it, it makes me feel uncomfortable. *(laughs)*

T: Um hmm. Yeah, but it will get easier.

At this point Cindy went back to reading and read the remainder softly, quickly, with expression but not overt emotion. Totally new to this account was the following:

On my wedding night he showed up in his Academy uniform. He had apparently asked my brother if he could come. He said yes. He walked up to me with such sadness in his eyes. He asked me to dance. It was the first time we danced together since the rape. In my wedding dress, with everyone so cheerful and happy looking at the bride, I danced with him. It was a slow song. He told me I looked beau-

tiful. The room seemed to be spinning. This white dress, his uniform, everyone smiling, we were dancing, it was my wedding night. "Jim" [husband] drank too much at the reception and passed out at the hotel. I sat up all night. I was remembering bits and pieces. I was angry. I was sad. I had a lot of questions. Why did he want to go to my wedding, for forgiveness? That's not the time or place. Why dance with me? I hadn't seen him in a couple of years. Why now, tonight? Jim didn't know. He was over there talking to him, looking at him with admiration, and thanking him for coming. All the girls kept asking who that guy in the uniform was. Oh, he's so gorgeous, etc.

I kept it inside again. I had bad feelings about my wedding day for about two years. But I blamed it on my in-laws. I couldn't blame it on something that is not there. No one knew. I still wonder why he showed up on my wedding day. The more questions I answer, the more questions I have.

The therapist asked Cindy if the feelings this week were different or just less intense. Cindy responded that there were times she was just tired of thinking about it. She said that there were moments that overwhelmed her, and she let them (the therapist told Cindy that was fine, to allow herself to have feelings), but that mostly she felt good. She was being more positive in her self-statements. The therapist helped Cindy recognize that she didn't have to be so afraid of her emotions anymore and that she was learning that she could tolerate her feelings, even big feelings. Cindy acknowledged that she had noticed that it was getting easier and that when the feelings passed she felt normal again.

After discussing her reactions to her memories, Cindy talked some more about her reactions to other people. At this point she focused on her brother more and described how she had thought her brother had let her down because he didn't see the truth about Mark. She said she needed him to be her big brother. When asked if she ever tried to talk to him about it, Cindy responded that it would be like talking to a brick wall. She was resistant to the possibility of discussing it with him now because he is still friends with Mark and is wrapped up in his own life. After this discussion, the therapist turned to the first of a series of tools used to help challenge assumptions. She said:

T: You've moved through a lot already but I think you're going to need to focus on any places you might have stuck points and start challenging them. So, over the next few sessions we're going work on skills to attack stuck points directly.

C: OK.

T: OK, because remember I said on some of this stuff you are going to have to feel your feelings. Some of those feelings are very legitimate. Now, some examples of stuck points are if you blame yourself, if you say, "I let it happen" or if you say . . .

C: (*Laughs*) Those stuck points I'm bashing with a sledge hammer.

T: The time before that we were talking and you kind of generalized: Everybody who's got power, everybody who's got money is a bad guy. *Everybody*. So that's one we should chip away at.

C: I can't trust anyone.

T: Yeah. All those topics. I can't trust anyone or I can't trust myself. Safety, trust, power, esteem, intimacy. We're going to work on each of those themes. As a way of doing that we're going to go through a couple of different steps. I'm going to give you a more complicated worksheet to help you. Every time you have a stuck point, it helps you work right through it. So you can change what you're saying or at least challenge . . .

C: Kind of like that A-B-C thing . . .

T: Yeah, except it's a little bit more complicated because it actually takes you through the rest of the steps of how to analyze it and if you want to change it, change it, and actually get to the point where it's changed.

C: OK.

T: This is the first step of this (*indicates Challenging Questions list*) [See Session 8 for Challenging Questions list] Let's go over these a little bit together. These are questions you can start asking yourself. So let's say you make a statement, "I let it happen" or "I let it happen for 5 weeks" or whatever. "So there's some-

thing wrong with me, I let it happen." The first question you ask yourself is, "What's the evidence for or against this idea?"

C: That I let it happen.

T: That you *let* it happen. Did you *let* it happen or did it just happen?

C: Yeah.

T: What's the evidence that you let it happen?

C: I'd say, "I don't believe that anymore." (*laughs*)

T: OK. So, but if it's something that you're really stuck on . . . one of the ways I identify when people have a stuck point is that they'll say, "Well, I know it's this way, but I feel . . . the opposite." And I'll say, "No, you've got two sets of beliefs that are contradictory. It's possible to have two contradictory beliefs in your head at the same time."

C: Yeah. (*nods understanding*)

T: So sometimes, when you're in the process of changing, you do have both in your head. You've got one you see as more logical and more fact based, but then you have this gut feeling.

C: Emotional. Yeah, I know.

T: The other thought has all this feeling attached and when the feeling is attached it seems more real.

C: Yeah.

T: Yeah, we'll be looking for those. Maybe we ought to pick one that you're still stuck on.

C: (*Thinks silently for a while*) Well, I don't know. I'm trying to think of something.

T: How about trust? How are you on this?

C: Thanks. That's a really hard one. Yeah, I think that would be a good one.

T: OK. What would the statement be that you would feel like . . . that you can't trust what?

C: But, I don't want to trust too much though.

T: We're looking for balance. Not that you need to trust everybody.

C: I just . . . it's almost like the *idea* of trust—I don't. I guess one of my really stuck points that I need to work on is the lack of confidence I have in my ability to judge who I can trust and who I can't trust.

T: OK.

C: And I think that's why I have problems with trust, because I don't know if my censoring devices are picking up . . . you know . . . is this a bad guy or . . .

T: So the statement you want to make is, "I don't know if I can trust my own judgment . . ."

C: Yeah, regarding trust.

T: So what we have here is a list of questions to start asking yourself. "What's the evidence for or against this?" What is the evidence that you have good judgment about who to trust and who not to trust? What's the evidence against that? How does that weigh out when you look at the facts and not just your feelings?

C: Yeah.

The rest of the session was spent going over the list of questions to make sure Cindy understood them. Although most of the questions focused on the issue of trust, at times other issues were brought in just to illustrate the meaning of the questions. For example, Cindy was asked, "Was the source reliable?" with reference to the rapist's insistence that she liked it (the rape). Cindy also engaged in a lively discussion with the therapist over the following questions: "Are you taking selected examples out of context?" "Are you focusing on irrelevant factors?" The therapist pointed out that perhaps the fact that Mark was popular and went on to the Academy was not relevant to the rape or to whether she could trust people. The more relevant context was that Mark was from a troubled, abusive home and that he was lashing out. Cindy began to accept that she had made a faulty connection between the person who raped her and went on to be successful and everyone else who is successful.

Session 6

Cindy started her new job and worked more than 40 hrs in the first week. She was quite excited by the job and the people she was

meeting. For the first time, Cindy came to a session without having her homework completed. She said that she had looked at it a few times. She then expressed concern about how much she was changing and said that she wanted to figure out what things she didn't want to change. It seemed to the therapist that Cindy was still ambivalent about what it meant to be successful and was fearful that if she changed too much (i.e., became "successful"), she would become one of those people she had always despised. The therapist assured Cindy that it was not her intention to assist Cindy in becoming a person Cindy didn't like. Cindy expressed some dismay that the rape had affected her in so many ways. It is likely that she didn't complete her homework because the thoughts that were bothering her were still vague and unformed. The therapist helped her to pin them down.

T: You are certainly more than a rape victim. You always were. But the rape did affect some of your beliefs.

C: I am still very afraid to trust.

T: This isn't something that's going to change in a couple of sessions.

C: I wanted it to. (*laughs*)

T: The purpose of the therapy is to give you the tools you need to empower you to decide what you want to change and not, and not to just react automatically to the rape, but to have choice . . .

C: . . . and control.

T: The whole idea is to give you different ways of viewing things so you're not stuck anymore in your reactions. So that you're not always in that defensive posture, which is what that total lack of trust is, a defensive stance.

C: Yeah, because you don't let anybody in.

T: And then you can't choose who to trust or not trust, so you don't trust anybody. It's not a matter of exploring and deciding and having choice over it.

C: Even the people that you love dearly . . . that just hurts.

T: That wasn't something you intentionally did, but by not having a label for it you didn't have an option either. For a long time you didn't have the option of recovering because it wasn't labeled a rape, therefore you couldn't get the help that you needed to . . .

C: . . . get over it.

T: Yeah. In looking over the list what comes to mind? You said you looked over it several times. In terms of some of the stuck points we talked about.

C: Trust was a big one. And identity was a big one. I just kept thinking about that.

T: When you looked at the list?

C: Yeah. I couldn't answer. It was like . . . am I?

T: Are you what?

C: Confusing habit with fact? Or am I somebody different or am I the person I thought I was? I was raped and that's affected some part of my life. But I look back and I see that all throughout that time it's always been on my mind, so is it habit or is it fact?

T: The other thing is that if there were certain things that preexisted the rape that you saw as being negative beliefs, those could have been seemingly confirmed by it . . . by that event. I mentioned that at the beginning of therapy but we haven't talked about that much. If you were having identity issues or problems . . .

C: Well, I was 15.

T: So if you're feeling negative about yourself before it happens, which is pretty typical for . . .

C: Well, you don't know at that point.

T: So, some of that stuff can get set off in another direction because of that event . . . because maybe you didn't have a good, solid sense of yourself, being a teenager.

C: Yeah, I was just starting into it.

T: But you described yourself when you read about the rape you said, very clearly, "I changed that night." So that clearly means you changed from what you had been.

C: I did. (*pauses*) I closed, I . . .

T: Then the idea of not being closed is a scary one for you.

C: Yeah.

T: What would it mean to change back again a bit, to find some balance point.

C: I think it would be so healthy. It's just habit.

T: There isn't anything you can label and say, "Here's the scary part, I'll get raped again"?

C: No.

T: Or "I'll be hurt by somebody"?

C: I guess it's "I'll be hurt by somebody." I just, it's just my security to stay closed up. Then nobody can hurt me. No one can take . . .

T: Can't they? Look at the sheet. What's the evidence that if you stay closed up nobody can hurt you?

C: Because they don't know my inner core. They never reach that point.

T: But they still could hurt you in other ways.

C: Yeah.

T: But aren't you hurt when you're that closed up?

C: Yeah.

T: Seems like you're hurting yourself. You're not waiting for anyone else to do it.

C: Yeah, I, well . . . it's like paranoia, it really destroys you. Why should I be closed up? I want to be open and I don't think people are out to hurt me.

T: Let's go through the list in terms of the stuck point: "I'm afraid to be open." What's the evidence that you're going to get hurt if you're open?

C: People are just . . . umm . . . there's no evidence. I don't think I was before.

T: It happened once?

C: Not just once but a few times I did that. A few times I did kind of try to reach out. People, with human nature, reacted . . . (*leans back, makes a closed face*)

T: Could we change the word "will" to "might?" "I might get hurt," not "I will get hurt." It hasn't been uniform; 100% of the people haven't hurt you, have they?

C: No. And some of the time I was hurt because they didn't know how to help me.

T: Because in fact you weren't open.

C: Yeah. They did *not* know what was actually happening to help me.

T: OK. So, in fact, being closed didn't protect you in that sense.

C: No, it didn't.

T: OK. So there's some evidence that being closed doesn't necessarily keep you safe.

C: And that makes me feel alone.

T: Which then hurts. So there's some evidence right there looking back. It's not necessarily that being open is going to get you hurt. Being closed can get you just as hurt but in a different way.

C: Yeah. Inside me.

T: Because people don't understand. They don't know what you're going through.

C: What they see on the surface as opposed to what I see on the inside.

T: Um hmm.

C: And it protects me but yet it hurts me inside.

T: OK. So following up with this statement, "If I'm open, I'll get hurt," what's question number 2 on the list?

C: (*Reads*) "Are you confusing the habit with the fact?" It's a habit. I didn't know I chose it that night but if I'm to carry this or whatever . . . I mean I'm alone. I'm going to walk alone and I'll be strong. Nobody will get inside. Nobody at all.

T: But now it's become a habit.

C: Yeah.

T: That you hadn't, at least until this point in time, questioned.

C: I see my father do it. That's the way he dealt with his problems and still does.

T: And has it worked for him?

C: No. (*both laugh*) I think he's crazy.

T: Well.

C: It's one of those things they say, "You're just like your father." I say, "Don't say that" you know, but I am.

T: So you need to find a different way. If it didn't work for him and it's not working for you, then you've got to find a different path.

C: Well, I see why it doesn't work. It's just . . . people, they do want to help. It's very hard to convince people like me and him because it's OK to hurt. Well, it's not OK to hurt, but in your mind you tell yourself it is, rather than having other . . .

T: You have control over it then.

C: Yeah. Rather than other people hurting you. You can't deal with that but you can deal with . . .

C&T: . . . hurting yourself.

T: Probably for two reasons: One, you have some control over it and, two, that it is more predictable and you know where it's coming from; you're doing it to yourself. On the other hand, look what you're missing: the opportunity for people to come through for you.

C: When you do need them.

T: Yeah.

C: And you want them.

T: Think how good you'd feel if you could open up and they could be there for you. If you'd give them the opportunity.

C: Yeah.

The therapist pointed out the example from the previous week where Cindy opened up with her husband and he responded by being supportive. Cindy agreed that it had worked well. The therapist and Cindy spent a considerable portion of the session going over the questions on the sheet with this particular stuck point in mind. At one point the therapist suggested that they might look at the statement "If I open up, I will get hurt" differently. The therapist asked, "Open up about what? The rape? Other things? Everything?" The therapist pointed out that some topics are probably lower risk than others, like the weather. A place to start with people is with something that is less touchy. The therapist and client also talked about asking for support. The therapist reminded Cindy that people often want to be supportive but that they don't know what to do or what she wants. The therapist and Cindy discussed how to tell people what Cindy wants from them.

After this discussion, the therapist introduced the Faulty Thinking Patterns list (for sample, see Session 8). The list includes seven types of faulty thinking patterns (e.g., oversimplifying, overgeneralizing, and emotional reasoning). The therapist described how one can move from very specific thoughts to examining more general patterns. The client and therapist went through the Faulty Thinking Patterns list and generated examples for each of the patterns. For example, for "Disregarding important aspects of a situation," the therapist pointed out something that Cindy had brought up several times during therapy. Cindy had said that she almost never watched the news because it just showed how violent the world had become and how bad everyone was. The therapist said that what she was disregarding was that this was "news"; that events are announced because they are unusual, bad, and/or important. Broadcasters don't announce how many millions of people weren't crime victims or didn't do something illegal that day.

When they got to the item "overgeneralizing from a single incident," Cindy said that she had noticed that she was beginning to change her thoughts. When she saw someone with a nice car or someone on television in a position of authority, she was beginning to say to herself, "Just because someone accomplishes something, that doesn't necessarily mean they walked over bodies to get there. Maybe they worked hard." The therapist added that people who work hard don't usually make the news. They are quietly getting on with their life, working or studying or raising their family. Cindy was given the assignment to read over the list and note examples of times when she used some of these faulty thinking patterns.

Session 7

Cindy again started the session by talking about her new job. She was quite exhausted from working over 60 hrs during the past week. The therapist asked whether she had been able to complete her homework assignment. She did not write on the form, but Cindy said she had looked at the Faulty Thinking Patterns list frequently and had found herself applying it to her friend. She recognized that she had used a number of

faulty thinking patterns over the years in this friendship and said that she also saw this friend using many of the same patterns. During the week, the friend called Cindy's house. Cindy's husband answered and the woman said a number of insulting things about Cindy. Cindy's husband told the friend that Cindy is a wonderful woman and never to contact them again. Although it had been her husband who broke off the relationship, Cindy was glad he had and would have done so herself very soon. She expressed a sense of relief over finally being extricated from a destructive friendship.

The therapist spent some time going over the sheet while Cindy gave examples of faulty patterns she had experienced in the past. By this point in therapy, the therapist was sitting back and allowing Cindy to challenge her own cognitions. The therapist rarely needed to intervene anymore, but just added information. At this point the therapist introduced the Challenging Beliefs worksheet (for examples, see Session 9):

T: Good. Good. Let's go over some of this new stuff I want to show you.

C: OK.

T: Now this you can't skip. You've got to do this.

C: OK.

T: We're going to add a new form. You know how you did the A-B-C sheets?

C: Yes.

T: (*Pointing to boxes on sheet*) This is A, B, and C. This is the new sheet, and this is to work on stuck points. And even if you feel some of them are resolved, just work through these to make sure you got it.

C: OK. I'm sure there are a few. I'm . . . you know.

T: Well, the issues about trust, who to trust and not trust, and intimacy.

C: Yeah, my own self-judgment, and even still a little bit of the confidence. I think self-esteem.

T: So I want you to pick a couple of the stuck points and start thinking about them. Now, we're going to start talking about safety and see if you have any safety stuck points. And what you're talking about the news could be perceived as a safety stuck point, that the whole world is *so* violent that this is the norm. That was kind of a stuck point because you were perceiving everything as being extreme rather than trying to . . .

C: Yeah, like the whole world was . . . just like the majority of it was rotten. Even the newscasters bringing it to me were rotten for bringing it to me. (*both laugh*)

T: Yeah. This is A, B, and C. so here's the event, thought or belief and here's where you put your feelings. And here's your automatic thought, but this time we want you to actually rate your belief in it. In other words, how much do you believe this? Because you know when you're in transition, at the beginning you say, "Everybody's rotten. I believe that 100%." So as you're in transition you might say, "Well, maybe. I think this mostly." So let's try to specify how much do you actually believe that. See if there are any chinks in the armor.

C: Yeah.

T: Then you put your feelings here. That's the C part. And again, we try to get you to rate them because we're going to have you rate them at the end when you get done with the sheet you can see, "Have I changed?" I'll show you an example in a second. So, you rate how strong is the emotion? Are you feeling 100% or 30% or 50%? And you can have more than one feeling. You might be sad, you might be angry, you might be scared, you might be happy.

C: I still do feel a little anger toward *him*.

T: Um hmm. So this is that part, then these are the questions you ask yourself. Here's the first question on the list: What's the evidence? So whatever your stuck point is, you go through your list and think about what's the evidence and am I thinking in all-or-none terms? Is it taking this out of context or whatever. And here are the faulty thinking patterns: Am I falling into these kinds of things? Am I exaggerating the meaning of it? Am I disregarding the important?

C: Yeah.

T: Am I engaging in emotional reasoning?

C: Oversimplifying. That's as bad or good.

T: Yeah. So then, this is the important one: What else could I say? I mean, given that there's not as much evidence as I thought, or maybe I'm just kind of doing all-or-none stuff. What else could I say to myself? How else could I interpret it? What else could I say? How else could I interpret this event? OK?

C: Kind of pulling the opposite side that almost comes up.

T: Or the more balanced. Sometimes it's not moving something from one extreme to the other, but it's moving it, (*gestures part way*) "Well, okay, *some* people are bad. But that doesn't mean that I'm going to always get attacked, that I'll never be safe, or that there's nobody who can be trusted." Then you try to come up with something to say that's a little healthier to say to yourself.

C: Not everybody from the Academy is bad. (*both laugh*)

T: OK? This little section's kind of fun to play with because sometimes you get the idea if something happens it's totally catastrophic. What's the worst that could ever happen? If somebody betrays you, you could say, "Well, I'll give them another chance, or I'll find somebody else, or, I'll . . . you know. So you have to think about what's the worst that's going to happen and if it did, how will I cope with it? What could I do about it? Because sometimes if you take that extreme view out here and bring it down a little bit, sometimes the catastrophe isn't so . . .

C: And address it too, it's not so overwhelming.

T: And address it directly. Then what you want to do when you get to the end of all this work, then you rerate your belief. Now, having gone through this, and asked yourself these questions, and looked at the pattern, and come up with the alternatives, how much do you really believe this anymore? And what are you feeling now that you've finished the worksheet? So this is an active way of actually working through something on the spot.

C: Like the process your brain goes through, only it's visually . . .

T: We've been doing this all along. I've been giving you other ways of viewing things and saying, "Hold it a second."

C: Yeah.

T: So, we've been doing this together and you've done a lot of it, and now, from here on out, you've got to take it over so you don't slide into some old patterns. The other point of this is that other things may happen in your life.

C: Well, that's what I thought.

T: This is going to give you some tools that you're going to have forever to deal with whatever comes up in your life.

C: I know these did (*indicating Challenging Questions and Faulty Thinking Patterns lists*), because when I had the problem with the friend, I sat down with that and it really made sense. I see a lot that I never . . .

T: Yeah. So I've got a lot of these for you to take home and work on.

C: OK.

T: The other thing I wanted to show you was an example of it. This is the one that another client did and we just use it as an example because sometimes it's hard to see it on an empty sheet. OK, here's her stuck point, "I perceive myself to be damaged in some way, kind of ruined, because I was raped. There's something wrong with me now." OK. So she says to herself the thought that she had that was feeding that stuck point was, "There's something wrong with me that he thought he could rape me in the first place." That sound familiar?

C: Yeah. (*laughs*) Is this mine?

T: No.

The therapist and client went over the example sheet and Cindy was able to follow it quite well. The therapist reminded Cindy that she might find that she isn't using faulty patterns or statements, and in that case, no change in feelings would be expected. She was also cautioned that she shouldn't expect her beliefs and feelings to change completely in the process of doing the sheet. The old thought would need to be dismantled completely and the new thought would need to become more habitual for

her to see a more permanent change. It was suggested that she read the sheets over to herself a number of times to facilitate the process.

The topic of safety was then introduced. Cindy was given the first of five modules (two- to three-page handouts on each of five topics: safety, trust, power, esteem, intimacy) to read and Challenging Beliefs worksheets to use. These modules discuss how beliefs about self and others can be shattered or seemingly confirmed after rape depending on experiences prior to the rape. The modules describe the emotional and behavioral effects of faulty beliefs with each of the topics and suggest alternative self-statements (for modules, see Resick & Schnicke, in press).

Cindy reported that she had always felt safe before the rape and felt that she or her family could protect her. Since the rape, safety had not been as much of a problem as trust, but she did have some issues about it, as evidenced by her avoidance of television news. The therapist suggested that Cindy might want to complete a worksheet on this topic.

Session 8

Cindy arrived at the session with the two homework sheets that she had not completed previously: Challenging Questions and Faulty Thinking Patterns. She had not completed any worksheets on the safety module. On the Challenging Questions list (Figure 2.2), Cindy decided to work on the statement, "If I did come forth and get help when I was raped, I would have been the accused to some." The therapist noted that this statement already reflected some movement from previous statements that were more extreme. She read off the answers shown in Figure 2.2.

After reading and discussing her answers, Cindy read three examples of faulty thinking patterns that she had noticed with regard to the rape. She left the remainder blank. The therapist and Cindy discussed the three items she did complete as shown in Figure 2.3.

The therapist pointed out that sometimes the rape itself, the sex acts, is not as hard to remember as some other defining mo-

Below are a list of questions to be used in helping you challenge your maladaptive or problematic beliefs. Not all questions will be appropriate for the belief you choose to challenge. Answer as many questions as you can for the belief you have chosen to challenge below.

Belief: *If I did come forth and get help when I was raped, I would have become the accused to some.*

1. What is the evidence for and against this idea?
   Although some people would believe, there were people who would think Mark wouldn't do that so I must have wanted it and now I'm trying to hurt him.

2. Are you confusing a habit with a fact?
   This is a fact.

3. Are your interpretations of the situation too far removed from reality to be accurate?
   Yes, I thought the majority of people viewed rape and abuse differently. The general population cares.

4. Are you thinking in all-or-none terms?
   I was. To sit by and let it happen makes you guilty. I believed they (general population) didn't want rape and abuse to happen and when it did they either don't want to get involved or, in some cases, the girl is told, even in court, she asked for it and liked it.

5. Are you using words or phrases that are extreme or exaggerated (i.e., always, forever, never, need, should, must, can't, and every time)?
   Yes.

6. Are you taking selected examples out of context?
   Yes, because I was raped repeatedly, I knew the hell of these other women and children. Keeping my own pain inside, I felt the anger and pain of each rape victim and sexually abused child that was broadcast on TV. My anger was built on the pain of a lot of others when I wouldn't think of my own pain.

7. Are you making excuses (e.g., I'm not afraid. I just don't want to go out; the other people expect me to be perfect; or I don't want to make the call because I don't have time)?
   No, other than they won't hurt me. If they try, I'll hurt them.

8. Is the source of information reliable?
   The TV was my source of information. The source was reliable. I was taking it out of context.

9. Are you thinking in terms of certainties instead of probabilities?
   I was certain if I told anyone it would ruin my life. Everyone would probably believe him.

10. Are you confusing a low probability with a high probability?
    Yes. I believe it would most likely work out for him and not me.

11. Are your judgments based on feelings rather than facts?
    Yes. It was based on feelings. I never gave fact a chance.

12. Are you focusing on irrelevant factors?
    Yes. Just because it did not work for some of the people that I had seen on TV, there were a lot of people that were being helped, but it wasn't a big media event.

FIGURE 2.2. Challenging Questions.

ments. Mark's dragging Cindy down the hall defined the event as a rape, so that was the part of the event that was most schema discrepant, and therefore most subject to distortion (or amnesia). The therapist asked Cindy if she could now think of some examples of the items she had left blank: oversimplifying events as bad or good, emotional reasoning, and mind reading. Cindy responded by saying that she had been over-simplifying in many ways and rattled off a list: "These people are bad"; "The judicial system is wrong"; "I'm bad"; "Because he went to the Academy, he's good." She gave several other examples of emotional reasoning but was a bit stuck on mind reading. The therapist gave the example of how she assumed people would react. Cindy responded, "I didn't give my parents a chance. I didn't give anyone a chance."

Below are listed several types of faulty thinking patterns that people use in different life situations. These patterns often become automatic, habitual thoughts that cause us to engage in self-defeating behavior.

Consider your own stuck points and find examples for each of the patterns. Write in the stuck point under the appropriate pattern and describe how it fits that pattern. Think about how that pattern affects you.

1. Drawing conclusions when evidence is lacking or even contradictory.
   I didn't tell anyone what happened to me but yet I was convinced I would be the accused. I would be shamed. I never came forth so I don't know how people would have reacted. For all I know they might have been supportive.

2. Exaggerating or minimizing the meaning of an event: blowing things way out of proportion or shrinking their importance inappropriately.
   I let it get out of control when I let him kiss me when we were dancing. When he kissed me then I was stimulated. Why didn't I fight more? Because I was in shock. A kiss is OK. Rape is not.

3. Disregarding important aspects of a situation.
   Rape is rape. Blocking out how he dragged me down the hallway.

4. Oversimplifying events or beliefs as good-bad, right-wrong.

5. Overgeneralizing from a single incident: viewing a negative event as a never-ending pattern of defeat, or applying an association of the rapist to a whole group.

6. Mind reading: assuming that people are thinking negatively of you when there is no definite evidence for this.

7. Emotional reasoning: reasoning from how you feel.

FIGURE 2.3. Faulty Thinking Patterns.

Even though she hadn't done the homework on safety, the therapist brought the session around to the topic of safety to explore whether Cindy had any stuck points. Upon probing, Cindy responded that she doesn't feel unsafe when alone with a man, she is vigilant when getting into her car, she frequently makes game plans when she finds herself in a potentially unsafe situation, and she doesn't carry a gun. Generally she felt quite comfortable with her level of precautions and was not overly concerned about the dangerousness of others. She said she had realized when Mark raped her that meant that anyone could. However, she felt she was now more able to protect herself and she believed she would probably fight more if she were ever attacked again. The therapist decided to leave the topic of safety, because Cindy's beliefs were not extreme and she did practice reasonable safety precautions.

They moved on to the topic of trust. Cindy pointed out that the people who are closest to her are the ones who scare her the most. However, she also readily admitted that her experiences prior to the rape were quite positive. The therapist and Cindy went over the trust module and Cindy felt that all of the potential effects that were listed all pertained to her. She reported that she had really been trying to open up with her husband and was saying a lot more and was feeling more. They were communicating better and she felt more relaxed and comfortable.

When the therapist asked her about other relationships, Cindy responded by saying that she didn't have any other close relationships except with her mother. She said that she had had that other friend but that she couldn't trust her. She also added that at her new job, she was forcing herself to go up to people and be friendlier. The therapist asked Cindy whether there were any people on the horizon with whom she could develop friendships. Cindy said yes, there were lots. She also added thoughtfully that if she had met the people at work before therapy, she would have been suspicious and would have judged them to be fake. Now she recognized that they're not. They are sincere and nice. The therapist ended by reminding Cindy that trust does not work with an on-off switch. Trust moves through levels and takes time.

Session 9

Cindy canceled a session due to another 60-hr workweek compounded by a death in her husband's family. At the next session, however, she arrived with a number of completed Challenging Beliefs worksheets. Although Cindy said that she did not currently feel as strongly as she once had, she had decided to complete several worksheets on her

Column A	Column B	Column C	Column D	Column E	Column F
Situation	Automatic thoughts	Challenging your automatic thoughts	Faulty thinking patterns	Alternative thoughts	De-catastro-phizing
Describe the event(s), thought(s), or belief(s) leading to the unpleasant emotion(s).	Write automatic thought(s) preceding emotion(s) in Column A. Rate belief in each automatic thought(s) below from 0–100%.	Use the Challenging Questions sheets to examine your automatic thought(s) from Column B.	Use the Faulty Thinking Patterns sheet to examine your automatic thought(s) from Column B.	What else can I say instead of Column B? How else can I interpret the event instead of Column B? Rate belief in alternative thought(s) from 0–100%.	What's the worst thought could ever *realistically* happen? *To become the accused.*
No one would believe me if I told them. **Emotion(s)** Specify sad, angry, etc., and rate the degree you feel each emotion from 0–100%. *Angry: 85%* *Confused: 5%* *Sad: 10%*	*I would have to prove I'm the victim. I did not have substantial proof.* *75%*	*The way I saw other rape victims that came forward. In most cases, they became the accused.*	*Assuming I would be the accused. Assuming no one would believe me. Drawing conclusions.*	*I did not tell so I can't assume no one would believe me.* *55%* *By not telling a lot of people were saved from a lot of pain. I cared for those people more than I cared about making Mark pay for his crime.* *90%*	Even if that happened, what could I do? *Fight for my honor. Not ever let them get inside of me.* **Outcome** Re-rate belief in automatic thought(s) in Column B from 0–100%. *65%* Specify and rate subsequent emotion(s) from 0–100%. *Angry: 60%* *Confused: 10%* *Sad: 30%*

FIGURE 2.4. Challenging Beliefs Worksheet 1.

perceptions after the rape because they had so strongly affected her level of trust in others. (Two of these sheets are shown in Figures 2.4 and 2.5.)

The therapist praised Cindy for completing the worksheets. She pointed out that on the first worksheet Cindy did not change her belief or feelings very much, but there was a great deal of validity to her statement on the worksheet. She discussed the reality of coming forward with an acquaintance rape now, much less 10 years ago. And given how popular Mark was, it was likely that many people would not be able to comprehend that he could/would commit rape. The important thing to remember is that not *everyone* would disbelieve. Cindy readily agreed and her second sheet evidenced the fact that she was moving away from her generalized distrust. The therapist and Cindy spent longer on the third sheet, shown in Figure 2.6.

T: Why do you want to forgive him?
C: Because I cared about him and I don't want to go through life hating.

T: Do you have to go through life hating to not forgive him?

C: I don't know.

T: I mean forgiving is not the same thing . . .

T&C: . . . as hating.

T: You could let the angry feelings go at some point and still say, "I don't have to forgive him."

C: But still, I want to know why. I want it explained because we were very close.

T: How are you going to feel if you don't get the answer you want?

C: (*Long pause*) I don't know. I guess I'll just go on. In one sense, I feel I'll be just as determined with myself, but I don't want to be a mind reader. I want to hear it come out of his mouth.

Column A	Column B	Column C	Column D	Column E	Column F
Situation	Automatic thoughts	Challenging your automatic thoughts	Faulty thinking patterns	Alternative thoughts	De-catastro-phizing
Describe the event(s), thought(s), or belief(s) leading to the unpleasant emotion(s).	Write automatic thought(s) preceding emotion(s) in Column A. Rate belief in each automatic thought(s) below from 0–100%.	Use the Challenging Questions sheets to examine your automatic thought(s) from Column B.	Use the Faulty Thinking Patterns sheet to examine your automatic thought(s) from Column B.	What else can I say instead of Column B? How else can I interpret the event instead of Column B? Rate belief in alternative thought(s) from 0–100%.	What's the worst thought could ever *realistically* happen? *Being hurt by someone*
Trustworthiness of people close to me.	*Anyone can hurt me. I cannot trust anyone.* *100%*	*It is true anyone can hurt me and I may not be able to trust everyone, but that doesn't mean I have to stop trusting the people I used to trust.*	*Mind reading—I prejudged everyone.* *Exaggerating the meaning—I could not trust some people, but some I could have trusted.*	*It is easier to trust others once I started trusting myself and my judgment.* *I will always be a little skeptical of people in general, but there will be people I trust.*	Even if that happened, what could I do? *Stay focused. I cannot control other people. Hold my head up and stay proud of who I am.*
Emotion(s)					
Specify sad, angry, etc., and rate the degree you feel each emotion from 0–100%. *Sad: 80%* *Angry: 20%*					**Outcome**
					Re-rate belief in automatic thought(s) in Column B from 0–100%. *0%* Specify and rate subsequent emotion(s) from 0–100%. *Sad: 20%* *Angry: 5%* *Happy: 75%*

FIGURE 2.5. Challenging Beliefs Worksheet 2.

T: What answer would be acceptable to you?

C: Anything other than just something manipulative and deceitful.

T: What could he say if he were honest enough . . .

C: I'm sorry.

T: But that doesn't tell you *why* he did it. If he were going to be honest and say,

"You're right. I did it," and then he'd say, "I was confused. I was young. I was angry. There was all this stuff going on at home. I wanted to get my needs met my way. I was wrong." Is that acceptable?

C: Yeah . . . I guess, more or less, I want to tell him, have him realize, how much it affected my life. How much pain it caused. How much I've had to work

Column A	Column B	Column C	Column D	Column E	Column F
Situation	Automatic thoughts	Challenging your automatic thoughts	Faulty thinking patterns	Alternative thoughts	De-catastro-phizing
Describe the event(s), thought(s), or belief(s) leading to the unpleasant emotion(s).	Write automatic thought(s) preceding emotion(s) in Column A. Rate belief in each automatic thought(s) below from 0–100%.	Use the Challenging Questions sheets to examine your automatic thought(s) from Column B.	Use the Faulty Thinking Patterns sheet to examine your automatic thought(s) from Column B.	What else can I say instead of Column B? How else can I interpret the event instead of Column B? Rate belief in alternative thought(s) from 0–100%.	What's the worst thought could ever *realistically* happen? *It could be very disturbing.*
I want him to tell me why. Why did he do that to me?	*I deserve to know.* 100% *I want to forgive him.* 80% *I won't get completely over it until he and I talk about it.* 90%	*I just feel very strong about it. I want the truth to be told.*	*I don't want to mind read or draw conclusions. I want to know the truth from the only person who can give it.*	*I'm scared.* 25%	Even if that happened, what could I do? *Continue to know in my heart the truth. Hold my head up high and go on.*
Emotion(s) Specify sad, angry, etc., and rate the degree you feel each emotion from 0–100%. *Angry: 75%* *Sad: 20%* *Scared: 5%*					**Outcome** Re-rate belief in automatic thought(s) in Column B from 0–100%. *95%* Specify and rate subsequent emotion(s) from 0–100%. *Angry: 75%* *Sad: 15%* *Scared: 10%*

FIGURE 2.6. Challenging Beliefs Worksheet 3.

through . . . I guess more than any-thing, it's not that I want to ask him why, as much as I want to deliver a mes-sage.

T: That's different. That's why I was won-dering how it would help to know why. That wouldn't excuse it.

Cindy responded that she still encounters Mark in social settings occasionally when he comes home for visits and that he is still friendly with her brother. She reiterated her desire to confront him.

T: What would happen if he were in denial? "What are you talking about? I never did any such thing?"

C: I'd remind him that I know the truth and no matter what he says, I still know. That's all that matters to me. I'm not denying it to myself any more. He'd know that I know the truth and nothing could ever change that.

T: (*Nodding*) As long as you're not looking for him to confirm what happened.

C: No. I don't need him to confirm. I know. I'm almost proud of myself for knowing!

T: Good. That's what I wanted to hear from you. (*both laugh*) Sometimes people have the idea of confronting someone to get them to acknowledge, to make it "real."

C: At the beginning, I did want him to.

T: Look at the need you had for 10 years to distort what happened and call it something else. Now if this is what the victim does, can you imagine how much the perpetrator distorts and does not remember?

The therapist asked whether Cindy would feel more comfortable writing a letter than confronting Mark face to face. Cindy said she didn't want to write a letter because Mark might not read it. She wanted to look him right in the face.

T: What would that do to your relationship with your brother?

C: I don't think I'll tell him. . . . And I miss my brother. I haven't talked to him in a month.

T: Because of this? (*waving her arm to indi-cate therapy*)

C: Yeah.

T: What are you going to do about that?

C: That's what my mother keeps asking me. Apparently he's upset and wishes I would call.

T: Do you realize, you've stopped Mark from totally destroying your life. But he's still interfering with your relationship with your brother and you haven't taken that back. Is it because you're afraid your brother will side with Mark?

C: No. It will hurt him.

T: So? He's still your brother and it's hurt-ing him that you're maintaining this dis-tance. Maybe one way to do it is to say something like, "There's something that happened a long time ago and I never told you about it because I was afraid it would hurt you so badly. But on the other hand, I can see what it's doing to our relationship to keep this giant secret between us. I need to know that you can be supportive of me so we can work this relationship out, so we can get close again. So I'm willing to take this risk, but I don't know if you can handle it." It might help him understand a lot of things, like why you changed and why you grew distant from him.

C: And a lot of people.

T: Sure. He is old enough to handle it now.

C: Part of me wants to talk to him and part of me doesn't want to hurt him.

T: You're not allowing him the opportunity to grow closer to you. You're not allow-ing him the opportunity to provide you some support.

C: And I am hurting him, and myself, by not talking to him.

T: You're also protecting him and not al-lowing him to have his own reactions.

C: But I know he'll be upset.

T: That's for *him* to deal with.

C: Because it did happen. It did, to me, and that's something that can't be denied.

T: No. And it's okay to feel sad or hurt if something happened to his sister. Those are legitimate feelings that he should be allowed to have. But don't be surprised if he has a little anger at you because you haven't told him. Because sometimes when you wait a long time before you tell people, you have to preface it and explain *why* you never told them first. Otherwise, they get so caught up in "why didn't you tell me?" that they kind of lose the message and forget to be supportive because they're so busy being hurt themselves that you didn't trust them. So that's why you have to say, "I never told you because I knew you would be hurt. And I knew it would tear you in terms of your allegiances, and [whatever else you need to say]. Now I'm seeing it's done a lot of damage between us and I don't want that to continue."

C: It has. I think that's why I just needed to stop talking to him. It just bothered me so.

T: Well, you can tell him you were working on it in therapy and before it was too painful to talk to him.

C: To talk, yeah. I'm sure once we'd sit down we'd get it all out. Maybe it would even bring us closer.

T: That would be the purpose of doing it. It's also a way of taking back that relationship as one more area of your life that Mark messed up, and now you can take it back.

C: Because I was angry at him for a long time about it, you know.

T: Guilt by association?

C: Why couldn't I talk to him?

T: You could but you couldn't.

C: I couldn't trust him, you know. I didn't know who he would side with. I wasn't sure he would side with me because Mark was also someone very important in his life.

T: Well, and it's hard to tell. He'd have to struggle with that but that's his struggle, not yours.

C: I need to talk to him.

The therapist then asked Cindy about her relationship with her father. In talking about it, it became apparent to the therapist that Cindy was still protecting her father, in this case because he has PTSD

from Vietnam. The therapist suggested to Cindy that rather than parenting her father, it might be time to allow her father to parent her.

At this point, the therapist introduced the module on power/control. They went over the module and the therapist speculated that Cindy had let go of control in the year after the rape. Cindy agreed that everything had seemed out of control then. They also talked about how she had attempted, and was still attempting, to control information as a way to protect people. Cindy was given another homework assignment, this time to complete Challenging Beliefs worksheets on power/control.

Session 10

Cindy began the session by announcing that she had written a letter to her brother that she thought she probably wouldn't send. She read the letter aloud and in it she expressed her concerns that her brother would be hurt and might not believe what had happened. She described the events generally and expressed her feelings about these events.

Cindy stated that she had read the power/control module over and over since the last session and that she started to realize that she is not responsible for her brother's reactions. She said that she felt some relief that she could let go of this burden. She reported a change in her whole outlook. She realized she had been using a lot of "should" words like "I *should* have had control." The therapist and Cindy went over her latest worksheets, shown in Figures 2.7 and 2.8.

Cindy described how her belief in self-betrayal ("I had control, but didn't do anything") led to problems with self-esteem. The same was true of her belief that she was unable to make good decisions—the sense of helplessness that followed the rape. The natural flow in topics between feelings of helplessness and self-evaluation served as a perfect segue to the next topic—esteem. The therapist gave Cindy a list of common assumptions (see Table 2.2) and asked her to put a checkmark by each statement she believed to be true for herself. Fortunately, Cindy marked only a few of the items, in the areas of control and competence. Cindy

Column A	Column B	Column C	Column D	Column E	Column F
Situation	Automatic thoughts	Challenging your automatic thoughts	Faulty thinking patterns	Alternative thoughts	De-catastro-phizing
Describe the event(s), thought(s), or beliefs (s) leading to the unpleasant emotion(s).	Write automatic thought(s) preceding emotion(s) in Column A. Rate belief in each automatic thought(s) below from 0–100%.	Use the Challenging Questions sheets to examine your automatic thought(s) from Column B.	Use the Faulty Thinking Patterns sheet to examine your automatic thought(s) from Column B.	What else can I say instead of Column B? How else can I interpret the event instead of Column B? Rate belief in alternative thought(s) from 0–100%.	What's the worst thought could ever *realistically* happen? *Feeling I betrayed myself.*
Feeling of self-betrayal for being raped.	*I should have had control. I should have gained control and not let it go on for five weeks.* *90%*	*I was not in control. Mark was in control of the rape. I was in control of who I told. I was not in total control of people knowing or not. Mark had the power to tell people and even lie about it.* *I cannot control all events outside of myself, but I do have some control over what happens to me and my reactions to events.*	*Drawing conclusions—I should have been in control.* *Disregarding important aspects—I do not have control over other people. I did have some control by not telling, but I was not in total control, I was in shock.*	*I did not betray myself. Mark betrayed me. I did not let him rape me. With what control I did have over the choices that were available at that time, I did not betray myself. I chose a path that was very painful and lonely, but protected my inner self, perhaps out of a great sense of love for myself.* *95%*	Even if that happened what could I do? *Re-evaluate the situation. Get help, if needed. Remember who I am and where I came from. Read these sheets.*
Emotion(s)					**Outcome**
Specify sad, angry, etc., and rate the degree you feel each emotion from 0–100%. *Angry: 85%* *Sad: 15%*					Re-rate belief in automatic thought(s) in Column B from 0–100%. *5%* Specify and rate subsequent emotion(s) from 0–100%. *Angry: 3%* *Sad. 7%* *Determined: 90%*

FIGURE 2.7. Challenging Beliefs Worksheet 4.

admitted that the "accomplishment thing" became very large in her mind because Mark had gone to the Academy with a full 4-year scholarship while she had only gone on to business school.

After reviewing the esteem module, the therapist asked Cindy to complete Challenging Beliefs worksheets on any of the items from the assumptions sheet on which she felt stuck, as well as any stuck points relating to esteem. She was also given two other assignments: to practice giving and receiving compliments every day and to do one nice thing for herself every day (noncontingently). These assignments were to help her with her self-esteem.

Session 11

Cindy completed a worksheet on self-esteem but said that it was how she used to feel about it rather than how she felt now. She stated that she didn't feel stuck on esteem issues. The therapist and Cindy went over the items she had circled from the assumptions sheet to make sure she was no longer making extreme expectations for herself. Cindy said that she really didn't feel stuck on any of them now. The therapist and

Cindy spent some time talking about her previous assumption that people should be judged as bad if they had money or professional success. She was now able to see that people are much more than just their professional accomplishments. They also have other activities and relationships with their family, friends, and themselves.

The therapist asked about giving and receiving compliments. Cindy replied that it had gone fine. She had to make herself reach out and it felt awkward, but the results

Column A	Column B	Column C	Column D	Column E	Column F
Situation	Automatic thoughts	Challenging your automatic thoughts	Faulty thinking patterns	Alternative thoughts	De-catastrophizing
Describe the event(s), thought(s), or belief(s) leading to the unpleasant emotion(s).	Write automatic thought(s) preceding emotion(s) in Column A. Rate belief in each automatic thought(s) below from 0–100%.	Use the Challenging Questions sheets to examine your automatic thought(s) from Column B.	Use the Faulty Thinking Patterns sheet to examine your automatic thought(s) from Column B.	What else can I say instead of Column B? How else can I interpret the event instead of Column B? Rate belief in alternative thought(s) from 0–100%.	What's the worst thought could ever *realistically* happen? *Make a bad decision or judgement.*
Inability to make decisions. ___ **Emotion(s)** ___ Specify sad, angry, etc., and rate the degree you feel each emotion from 0–100%. *Sad: 75%* *Angry: 25%*	*Look at what I let happen to me in the past.* *85%*	*I made very wise decisions in the past. The outcome of all major decisions I've made have put me where I am today.*	*Disregarding important aspects of the situation— Even while being raped I was making decisions on how to handle the situation. My decisions in the past were well thought out even though I didn't know it at the time.*	*In re-evaluating the choices I've made, it makes me gain a stronger sense of respect for myself and a deep sense of respect in my ability to make sound decisions. This, in turn, makes me feel more secure with my judgments*	Even if that happened, what could I do? *Re-evaluate the situation and learn from it.* ___ **Outcome** ___ Re-rate belief in automatic thought(s) in Column B from 0–100%. *2%* Specify and rate subsequent emotion(s) from 0–100%. *Sad: 0%* *Angry: 0%* *Happy: 75%* *Glad: 25%*

FIGURE 2.8. Challenging Beliefs Worksheet 5.

TABLE 2.2. Identifying Assumptions List

Listed below are beliefs that some people hold. Please circle the number next to the beliefs that are *true for you.*

A. Acceptance
  1. I have to be cared for by someone who loves me.
  2. I need to be understood.
  3. I can't be left alone.
  4. I'm nothing unless I'm loved.
  5. To be rejected is the worst thing in the world.
  6. I can't get others mad at me.
  7. I have to please others.
  8. I can't stand being separated from others.
  9. Criticism means personal rejection.
  10. I can't be alone.

B. Competence
  1. I am what I accomplish.
  2. I have to be somebody.
  3. Success is everything.
  4. There are winners and losers in life.
  5. If I'm not on top, I'm a flop.
  6. If I let up, I'll fail.
  7. I have to be the best at whatever I do.
  8. Others' successes take away from mine.
  9. If I make a mistake, I'll fail.
  10. Failure is the end of the world.

C. Control
  1. I have to be my own boss.
  2. I'm the only one who can solve my problems.
  3. I can't tolerate others telling me what to do.
  4. I can't ask for help.
  5. Others are always trying to control me.
  6. I have to be perfect to have control.
  7. I'm either completely in control or completely out of control.
  8. I can't tolerate being out of control.
  9. Rules and regulations imprison me.
  10. If I let someone get too close, that person will control me.

were good. She said that she normally doesn't talk to people in public, but she made an effort to talk to people in the grocery store. The bagger was so pleased with her attention that in the parking lot, he ran over to her and told her about his comic book collection. She also found that she was able to disarm a usually critical in-law at a family gathering by complimenting her. The therapist asked Cindy whether she had received any compliments. Cindy responded

that she had from her husband. This time she didn't deflect them but listened and thanked her husband for noticing.

The therapist told Cindy that she had asked her to do nice things for herself because women often take care of themselves only after everyone else has been cared for and only if they feel they deserve it, which many never feel they do. Cindy said that she had complied with the assignment and had really enjoyed it. She found it relaxing and noticed that her mood improved. Cindy's list of compliments and activities are shown in Figure 2.9.

After discussing self-esteem, the therapist and client discussed esteem toward others. Cindy readily admitted that this had been a major problem for her prior to therapy. She had been overwhelmed with the belief that people are bad, malicious, or evil. She related a great deal to the content of the esteem module but felt that it was in the past. She had worked on it so much in therapy that she had moved this belief a great deal. Cindy realized how much stereotyping she had done and judging based on first impressions. Because she felt fairly re-

---

Use the worksheets to confront stuck points regarding self- and other-esteem. Make sure you examine the items you checked on the Identifying Assumptions List in order to identify stuck points regarding esteem and competence. Complete worksheets on some of the most troublesome beliefs.

In addition to the worksheets, practice giving and receiving compliments during the week and do at least one nice thing for yourself each day (without having to earn it). Write down on this sheet what you did for yourself and who you complimented.

	Activity	Compliment
Thursday	*2 hr of reading*	*Lady in line at grocery store*
Friday	*Afternoon to myself*	*My mom bought lingerie*
Saturday	*Watched a movie*	*Jim* [husband] *on his helpfulness and charm*
Sunday	_____	*Jim, and cousin who's always very hateful and sarcastic*
Monday	*Watched a movie alone*	*Bag boy at grocery store*

FIGURE 2.9. Homework Assignment 10.

solved on this issue, the therapist moved on to introduce the final module, on intimacy.

T: This, I think, is an interesting one. I mentioned it to you in the beginning because of the marijuana. Self-soothing is the ability to calm yourself when you're feeling strong emotions. It's the ability to regulate without having to do outside things. And that's something small children, babies, can't regulate. You know, you see them and one minute they're screaming and the next minute they're laughing and then they're crying again and their emotions are just . . .

C: Yeah, up and down.

T: And as they grow older they're going to learn to contain their emotions a bit more and modulate them, to have some control over them, to express them or not to express them as the situation arises, and so forth. When emotions happen that are too strong and you don't know what to do with them, you may tend to go to outside things. Or, sometimes people are taught to do outside things. You see this sometimes with overweight people. When they were babies, if every time they cried somebody stuck something in their mouth, they would learn that the way to soothe themselves is to stick something in their mouth. So when they get upset about something they move their chair in front of the refrigerator and just stay there. Or it may be some other kind of external thing like alcohol or going on spending binges. All those things end up being addictions because it's not you that's controlling your own stuff, it's this outside thing that's bringing relief and, of course, it doesn't last very long so then you keep needing more and more.

C: It can put you back, you know, even just . . .

T: Well, and it can cause a whole different set of problems. You can become addicted to alcohol. Now you just don't have an outside crutch, you have an alcohol addiction. So, it ends up being a double whammy and a serious one. You end up in major debt if you go on spending binges. It's hard to make up

for those outside crutches things. I got the impression you were using the marijuana initially that way to a certain extent. That you were needing . . .

C: Yeah, by myself.

T: And it wasn't because it was something you did to enjoy occasionally, it was because you were upset and were trying to calm yourself.

C: (*Nods*)

T: I also got the impression, we haven't talked about it much, that that's sort of dropped out.

C: Yeah. Yeah, it's really toned down. I don't want it in a pacifying sense. When I've got everything done and I'm sitting, relaxing . . . I mean it's kind of like having a glass of wine, or drinking one of those little pony beers and it'll be real nice. But I think that it has toned itself down. I now feel myself wanting to give up cigarettes. You know, thinking about it, I think I wanted to smoke then because nobody else did and it was different, and "I'm not like you, I'm different from you."

T: Were you also using them as a way, when you're anxious, to calm yourself down?

C: Yeah. Oh, yeah.

T: So maybe that's one that you'll still want to focus on. And one of the things to notice is when you are doing it. And is there something else you can do? So before you just automatically do it, is there some other way you can calm yourself, soothe yourself internally, before you do something external? And you are learning. That's what we've been doing here is learning ways to modulate.

C: I think so, yeah.

T: Because you can analyze what's going on. Then when you feel them you know they're not going to just keep getting worse and worse. But by feeling them they do get less.

C: Usually by the time you reach that point you've already peaked off.

T: You just kind of let it go. But the other part of this thing is how to look at things in a way and say, "Okay, hold it a second. What's the evidence for this?"

C: Yeah. That's what I mean. You're at your peak going, "Wait a minute."

T: And then you can find out if it's based on something irrational. Other times the emotions are absolutely, perfectly legitimate. If you are hurt, it's perfectly legitimate to feel sad or angry. If somebody hurts you intentionally, it's okay to feel angry and if it's a loss, to feel sad. You don't want to not feel those feelings because that's part of what the experience is.

C: Yeah.

T: Umm. And I think sometimes that self-soothing stuff comes in when you feel like you're not supposed to feel those feelings. You've got so many bottled up that you start to feel that it's going to overwhelm you.

C: Yeah. Or it already does so I just want to get it out of my mind. I'm tired of thinking about it.

T: So hopefully, once we've finished here you're going to kind of be back to a clean slate. So if you get an emotion, you can feel it and be done with it at the time, so that it doesn't pile up. So that you're not saying "If I feel it, I'm just going to flood."

C: Yeah.

T: And so then you don't need the external stuff so much because it's not something that's overwhelming and enormous. It's a . . .

C: I'm not as anxious.

T: Also, I think having known that you can get through this, that hopefully, when crises come up in the future you can say, "There is something I can do. I can get through this."

C: Well, I really believe that because I . . . this was something just really. . . . It amazes me what an impact it had on my life and my thoughts. How much it really just impacted my life and, you know, I held it for a long time.

The therapist and client went on to discuss intimacy with others, a topic that had been introduced earlier in the context of trust. Although Cindy didn't feel stuck, the therapist stated that her goal for Cindy was for her to begin to open up and take chances with other people, at work, in the neighborhood, and through her children's school activities. The therapist pointed out that these last two modules are long term and the purpose is to identify any remaining stuck points and to set out long-term goals. The homework assignments for the final session were to work on the intimacy module (with worksheets) and to rewrite the meaning of the event assignment that Cindy had written at the first session.

Session 12

As usual, the therapist began by asking how the homework went. Cindy discussed her reactions to the module and how it related to her experience. She talked about attempting to fill empty feelings with "stuff." The therapist asked her whether she had any remaining stuck points and Cindy replied that they were not stuck points but goals to work toward and that she had a clearer idea where she was going now. With regard to intimacy with others, Cindy recognized that it was going to take some time. She observed that at the time she was raped, she had never yet experienced a real intimate relationship. She also added that she thought it was important that she was no longer ashamed that she had been raped.

The therapist talked generally about friendships and reminded Cindy that because it takes two people, it may not always work out. She might need to try again. The therapist also reminded Cindy that the quality of another person is no reflection on her.

The therapist then asked Cindy to read what she had written about the meaning of the event for her. Cindy wrote:

The rape deeply affected me. My views, opinions, thoughts, and feelings were affected. I cannot change this and don't want to. I now realize the need for balance and to put the rape into perspective. It was once part of my life. I am who I am today because of that part of my life. I'm proud of who I am today.

When Mark raped me I was shattered in-

*side. It has taken me 10 years to pick up the
pieces. The puzzle is almost done. The last few
pieces are falling into place. It helps when you
now know what the picture is. It's who I am
and what I'm about and it's beautiful.*

*Because I was 15 years old and still devel-
oping at that time, I lost my sense of self. It
almost feels as if until now I've never had a
sense of who I am. I think that is why I was
so sad and felt so alone inside.*

*I feel very strong and have a very strong
spirit. If I believe in myself I can do anything.
I still have a feeling that I will achieve a lot
of my goals. In fact, it's even stronger. I'm
being called. I don't know where, but I can
feel it. My spiritual side is almost upsetting
sometimes. It scares me. Since I've opened up
inside my spirit has risen. My dreams always
seem to have a point to them, symbolism is
appearing everywhere. I have a great sense of
well-being.*

*A part of all of this is the girl who was
raped, abused, and manipulated. I will never
forget, but I will not let it destroy me. That
girl survived and did a damn good job.*

*I don't know if anything will ever be as
traumatic as being raped was. I hope my view
of life is different. The worst thing that could
possibly happen is to lose my sense of self
again. I don't think I could let that happen.
I never want to go that deep into hell again.*

*I believe Mark raped me. I was not in con-
trol of the situation, Mark was. I was in
shock. I did not let him rape me. I did not let
him abuse me. I have nothing to feel ashamed
about. He was responsible for raping me. I
was not responsible for being raped.*

*I have learned a lot through counseling. In
the beginning, I knew it would help me. I
knew a change needed to be made. I had to
face the demon in my head. The rape emotionally continued for years.*

*I hoped counseling would be cleansing. It
has been. I hoped I would find those missing
pieces and I did.*

*To pull my deepest, darkest inner secret up
has been very hard. It was poisoning me
though. With genuine help, I pulled that secret
demon out and faced him head on. Thank
you. I couldn't do it alone. You helped me
because you were let in. You were the first one
I trusted. You helped me break the ice.*

Cindy was a bit teary as she finished reading. The therapist asked Cindy whether she

remembered what she wrote the first time.
Cindy said no, so the therapist read to her
her first assignment. Cindy laughed at the
line that most people are greedy, self-righteous scum. The therapist pointed out that
Cindy had come a long way and Cindy
agreed. Cindy was also amazed to see her
first A-B-C sheets. The therapist and Cindy
reviewed the whole therapy process, what
they had covered, and the stuck points that
Cindy had challenged. Cindy offered that
the faulty thinking patterns are really easy
to pick out once you get the hang of it. She
ended by talking about her goal of improving her relationship with her brother and
father. She said that the only things her
father knows about her are secondhand,
through her mother. Cindy recognized that
she didn't communicate with him directly.

Follow-up

The week after the therapy ended, Cindy
met with another clinician for her post-
therapy assessment, the results of which are
found in Table 2.3. She no longer met criteria for PTSD or depression on the SCID
and exhibited marked decreases on all of
her scores. Cindy's assessment scores for the
3-month and 6-month follow-up are also
listed in Table 2.3.

Two weeks after completing treatment
Cindy called the therapist with the news that
she had told her brother about the rapes.
As expected, Cindy's brother had difficulty
hearing that his good friend had raped his
sister. Because Cindy had distanced herself
from her brother, he assumed that she
blamed him in some way for the rape, or
because he didn't know. He called back the
next day and they discussed it more. Cindy
was pleased she had told her brother so that
he would understand why she had distanced
herself from him. She also recognized that
her brother's conflict was his own and not
hers. She did, however, ask that he not call
Mark until she decided whether she wanted
to talk with him. Cindy said she was using
worksheets to work through the decision
whether to talk to Mark, what she is anticipating, and what the possible outcomes
might be.

At 3 months posttreatment, Cindy came
in for a follow-up assessment. She was con-

TABLE 2.3. Cindy's Scores Before and After Treatment

Measure	Pretreatment	Posttreatment	3 mo	6 mo
PTSD Symptom Scale	34	02	05	03
Reexperiencing	06	01	02	01
Avoidance	14	01	02	02
Arousal	44	00	01	00
Impact of Events	65	16	18	17
Intrusion	35	13	10	13
Avoidance	30	03	08	04
Beck Depression Inventory	36	00	01	04
SCL-90-R				
Somatization	1.67	.42	.25	.25
Obsessive compulsive	2.40	.70	.20	.10
Interpersonal sensitivity	3.11	.11	.22	.11
Depression	2.31	0	.23	.31
Anxiety	2.40	0	.10	0
Hostility	2.00	0	.17	0
Phobic anxiety	.57	0	0	0
Paranoid ideation	2.33	.33	.33	.50
Psychoticism	2.00	.30	.10	.20
PTSD	2.25	.29	.11	.11

tinuing to do well and continued to score low on all of the PTSD and depression measures. A few weeks after the assessment, the therapist asked Cindy to come in for a follow-up interview for this chapter. Overall, Cindy reported that she was doing very well and that she had a new outlook on life. She feels sad or hurt occasionally when she thinks of Mark and said that it will probably take more time to let go of the feelings completely.

She reported that her relationship with her brother had become somewhat strained because he was pushing her to confront Mark, in the hope they [he?] could resolve it. Cindy had not buckled under his pressure and was still debating whether to talk to Mark, but said that it did not preoccupy her. She wanted to wait until she felt strong and confident enough to handle whatever reactions Mark had. Her job was still going well and Cindy and her husband and children were getting along very well.

Cindy reported that her relationship with her father was slowly improving. Although they didn't talk about the rape, they were spending more time together and talked about her work or other family news. Her friendships at work were also developing and she has made several close friends and they go out together. She reported being

cautious and as yet has not exposed much confidential material, but Cindy described her disclosures and efforts to trust as "dipping my toe in the water." However, she has been pleased with their reactions to her disclosures thus far and felt they were honest and positive. The ex-friend also tried to reestablish contact, but Cindy merely told her that they didn't have much to say to each other and asked the ex-friend to please stay away from her. Cindy expressed relief at having such a negative influence out of her life and was pleased with her handling of the phone call when she didn't rise to baiting.

Finally, the therapist asked about Cindy's reactions to successful or powerful people she encounters or sees on the news. She responded that when she sees others who are greedy, she doesn't take it so much to heart and just shrugs them off with "Boy, they're a real case."

REFERENCES

Amercian Psychiatric Association. (1980). *Diagnostic and statistical manual of mental disorders* (3rd ed.). Washington, DC: Author.

American Psychiatric Association. (1987). *Diagnostic and statistical manual of mental disorders* (3rd ed., rev.). Washington, DC: Author.

American Psychiatric Association. (1993). *DSM-IV draft criteria as of 3/1/93*. Washington, DC: Author.

Blake, D. D., Weathers, F. W., Nagy, L. M., Kaloupek, D. G., Klauminzer, G., Charney, D., & Keane, T. (1990). A clinician rating scale for assessing current and lifetime PTSD: The CAPS-1. *Behavior Therapist, 13,* 137–188.

Blanchard, E. B., & Abel, G. G. (1976). An experimental case study of the biofeedback treatment of a rape induced psychophysiological cardiovascular disorder. *Behavior Therapy, 7,* 113–119.

Blanchard, E. B., Kolb, L. C., Gerardi, R., Ryan, P., & Pallmayer, T. P. (1986). Cardiac response to relevant stimuli as an adjunctive tool for diagnosing post-traumatic stress disorder in combat veterans. *Behavior Therapy, 17,* 592–606.

Blanchard, E. B., Kolb, L. C., Pallmayer, T. P., & Gerardi, R. T. (1982). The development of a psychophysiological assessment procedure for PTSD in Vietnam veterans. *Psychiatric Quarterly, 54,* 220–228.

Burnam, M. A., Stein, J. A., Golding, J. M., Siegel, J. M., Sorenson, S. B., Forsythe, A. B., & Telles, C. A. (1988). Sexual assault and mental disorders in a community population. *Journal of Consulting and Clinical Psychology, 56,* 843–850.

Burt, M. R. (1980). Cultural myths and supports for rape. *Journal of Personality and Social Psychology, 38,* 217–230.

Charney, D. S., Delgado, P. L., Price, L. H., & Heninger, G. R. (1991). The receptor sensitivity hypothesis of antidepressant function. A review of antidepressant effects on serotonin function. In S. Brown & H. van Praag (Eds.), *The role of serotonin in psychiatric disorders* (pp. 27–57). New York: Brunner/Mazel.

Charney, D. S., Woods, S. W., Krystal, J. H., & Heninger, G. R. (1990). Neurobiological mechanisms of human anxiety. In R. Pohl & D. Gershon (Eds.), *Bases of psychiatric treatment* (pp. 242–283). New York: Karger.

Chemtob, C., Roitblat, H., Hamada, R., Carlson, J., & Twentyman, C. (1988). A cognitive action theory of posttraumatic stress disorder. *Journal of Anxiety Disorders, 2,* 253–275.

Creamer, M., Burgess, P., & Pattison, P. (1992). Reaction to trauma: A cognitive processing model. *Journal of Abnormal Psychology, 101,* 453–459.

Denny, N., Robinowitz, R., & Penk, W. (1987). Conducting applied research on Vietnam combat-related post-traumatic stress disorder. *Journal of Clinical Psychology, 43,* 56–66.

Derogatis, L. R. (1977). *SCL-90-R manual*. Baltimore, MD: Johns Hopkins University Press.

DiNardo, P. A., & Barlow, D. H. (1988). *Anxiety Disorders Interview Schedule—Revised (ADIS-R)*. Albany, NY: Graywind Publications.

Ellis, L. F., Black, L. D., & Resick, P. A. (1992). Cognitive-behavioral treatment approaches for victims of crime. In P. A. Keller & S. R. Heyman (Eds.), *Innovations in clinical practice: A sourcebook* (pp. 23–38). Sarasota, FL: Professional Resource Exchange.

Fairbank, J. A., & Keane, T. M. (1982). Flooding for combat-related stress disorders: Assessment of anxiety reduction across traumatic memories. *Behavior Therapy, 13,* 499–510.

Feldman-Summers, S., Gordon, P. E., & Meagher, J. R. (1979). The impact of rape on sexual satisfaction. *Journal of Abnormal Psychology, 88,* 101–105.

Foa, E. B., & Kozak, M. J. (1986). Emotional processing of fear: Exposure to corrective information. *Psychological Bulletin, 99,* 20–35.

Foa, E. B., Riggs, D. S., Dancu, C. V., & Rothbaum, B. O. (1991). Reliability and validity of a brief instrument for assessing post-traumatic stress disorder. *Journal of Traumatic Stress.*

Foa, E. B., Steketee, G. S., & Rothbaum, B. O. (1989). Behavioral/cognitive conceptualizations of post-traumatic stress disorder. *Behavior Therapy, 20,* 155–176.

Folkman, S., & Lazarus, R. S. (1988). *Manual for the Ways of Coping Questionnaire*. Palo Alto, CA: Consulting Psychologists Press.

Forman, B. D. (1982). Reported male rape. *Victimology, 7,* 235–236.

Foy, D. W., Osato, S. S., Houskamp, B. M., & Neumann, D. A. (1992). Etiology of posttraumatic stress disorder. In P. A. Saigh (Ed.), *Posttraumatic stress disorder* (pp. 28–49). New York: Macmillan.

Freud, S. (1964). Moses and monotheism. In J. Strachey (Ed. and Trans.), *The standard edition of the complete psychological works of Sigmund Freud* (Vol. 23, pp. 1–137). London: Hogarth Press. (Original work published 1937–1939)

Gershuny, B. S., Dancu, C. V., Hembru, E. A., & Foa, E. B. (1992, November). *Ways of coping with an assault: Effects on the development and severity of posttraumatic stress disorder*. Paper presented at the Association for the Advancement of Behavior Therapy, Boston, MA.

Goyer, P., & Eddleman, H. (1984). Same-sex rape of nonincarcerated men. *American Journal of Psychiatry, 141,* 576–579.

Horowitz, M. (1976). *Stress response syndromes*. New York: Aronson.

Horowitz, M. (1986). *Stress response syndromes* (2nd ed.). New York: Aronson.

Horowitz, M., Wilner, N., & Alvarez, W. (1979). Impact of Event Scale: A measure of subjective stress. *Psychological Medicine, 4,* 209–218.

Jones, J. C., & Barlow, D. H. (1990). The etiology of posttraumatic stress disorder. *Clinical Psychology Review, 10,* 299–328.

Jones, J. C., & Barlow, D. H. (1992). A new model of posttraumatic stress disorder: Implications for the future. In P. A. Saigh (Ed.), *Posttraumatic stress disorder* (pp. 147–165). New York: Macmillan.

Kaszniak, A. W., Nussbaum, P. D., Berren, M. R., & Santiago, J. (1988). Amnesia as a consequence of male rape: A case report. *Journal of Abnormal Psychology, 97,* 100–104.

Kaufman, A., Divasto, P., Jackson, R., Voorhees, D., & Christy, J. (1980). Male rape victims: Noninstitutionalized assault. *American Journal of Psychiatry, 137,* 221–223.

Keane, T. M., Caddell, J. M., & Taylor, K. L. (1988). The Mississippi Scale for combat-related PTSD: Studies in reliability and validity. *Journal of Consulting and Clinical Psychology, 56,* 85–90.

Keane, T. M., Fairbank, J. A., Caddell, J. M., Zimering, R. T., & Bender, M. E. (1985). A behavioral approach to treating posttraumatic stress disorder in Vietnam veterans. In C. R. Figley (Ed.), *Trauma and its wake* (Vol. 1, pp. 257–294). New York: Brunner/Mazel.

Keane, T. M., Malloy, P. F., & Fairbank, J. A. (1984). The

empirical development of an MMPI-subscale for the assessment of combat-related post-traumatic stress disorders. *Journal of Consulting and Clinical Psychology, 52,* 888–891.

Keane, T. M., Scott, W. O., Chavoya, G. A., Lamparski, D. M., & Fairbank, J. A. (1985). Social support in Vietnam veterans: A comparative analysis. *Journal of Consulting and Clinical Psychology, 53,* 95–102.

Keane, T. M., Wolfe, J., & Taylor, K. L. (1987). Posttraumatic stress disorder: Evidence for diagnostic validity and methods of psychological assessment. *Journal of Clinical Psychology, 43,* 32–43.

Keane, T. M., Zimering, R. T., & Caddell, J. M. (1985). A behavioral formulation of posttraumatic stress disorder in Vietnam veterans. *Behavior Therapist, 8,* 9–12.

Kilpatrick, D. G. (1983). Rape victims: Detection, assessment and treatment. *Clinical Psychologist, 36,* 92–95.

Kilpatrick, D. G. (1988). Rape aftermath symptom test. In M. Hersen & A. S. Bellack (Eds.), *Dictionary of behavioral assessment techniques* (pp. 366–367). New York: Pergamon Press.

Kilpatrick, D. G., & Amick, A. E. (1985). Rape trauma. In M. Hersen & C. Last (Eds.), *Behavior therapy casebook* (pp. 86–103). New York: Springer.

Kilpatrick, D. G., Best, C. L., Amick, A. E., & Veronen, L. J. (1984, November). *Psychophysiological assessment in the treatment of rape-induced anxiety.* Paper presented at the 18th Annual Convention of the Association for Advancement of Behavior Therapy, Philadelphia, PA.

Kilpatrick, D. G., Edmunds, C. N., & Seymour, A. K. (1992). *Rape in America: A report to the nation.* Arlington, VA: National Victim Center.

Kilpatrick, D. G., & Veronen, L. J. (1983). Treatment of rape-related problems: Crisis intervention is not enough. In L. H. Cohen, W. L. Claiborn, & G. A. Specter (Eds.), *Crisis intervention* (pp. 165–185). New York: Human Sciences Press.

Kilpatrick, D. G., Veronen, L. J., & Resick, P. A. (1979). The aftermath of rape: Recent empirical findings. *American Journal of Orthopsychiatry, 49*(4), 658–669.

Kilpatrick, D. G., Veronen, L. J., & Resick, P. A. (1982). Psychological sequelae to rape. In D. M. Doleys, R. L. Meredith, & A. R. Ciminero (Eds.), *Behavioral medicine: Assessment and treatment strategies* (pp. 473–498). New York: Plenum Press.

Kilpatrick, D. G., Veronen, L. J., Saunders, B. E., Best, C. L., Amick-McMullen, A. E., & Paduhovich, J. (1987, March). *The psychological impact of crime: A study of randomly surveyed crime victims* (Final report, Grant No. 84-IF-CX-0039). Washington, DC: National Institute of Justice.

Kolb, L. C. (1987). A neuropsychological hypothesis explaining posttraumatic stress disorder. *American Journal of Psychiatry, 144,* 989–995.

Koss, M. P., & Gidycz, C. A. (1985). Sexual Experiences Survey: Reliability and validity. *Journal of Consulting and Clinical Psychology, 53,* 422–423.

Koss, M. P., & Harvey, M. (1991). *The rape victim: Clinical and community approaches to treatment* (2nd ed.). Lexington, MA: Stephen Greene Press.

Kozak, M. J., Foa, E. B., Rothbaum, B. O., & Murdock, T. (1988, September). *Psychophysiological responses of rape victims during imagery of rape and neutral scenes.* Paper presented at World Congress of Behaviour Therapy, Edinburgh, Scotland.

Lang, P. J. (1968). Fear reduction and fear behavior: Problems in treating a construct. *Research in Psychotherapy, 3,* 9–102.

Lang, P. J. (1977). Imagery in therapy: An information processing analysis of fear. *Behavior Therapy, 8,* 862–886.

Lang, P. J. (1979). A bio-informational theory of emotional imagery. *Psychophysiology, 16,* 495–512.

Lang, P. J. (1985). The cognitive psychophysiology of emotion: Fear and anxiety. In A. H. Tuma & J. D. Maser (Eds.), *Anxiety and the anxiety disorders* (pp. 131–170). Hillsdale, NJ: Erlbaum.

Litz, B. T. (1992). Emotional numbing in combat-related post-traumatic stress disorder: A critical review and reformulation. *Clinical Psychology Review, 12,* 417–432.

Litz, B. T., Blake, D. D., Gerardi, R. G., & Keane, T. M. (1990). Decision-making guidelines for the use of direct therapeutic exposure in the treatment of post-traumatic stress disorder. *Behavior Therapist, 13,* 91–93.

McCann, I. L., & Pearlman, L. A. (1990a). *Psychological trauma and the adult survivor: Theory, therapy and transformation.* New York: Brunner/Mazel.

McCann, I. L., & Pearlman, L. A. (1990b). Vicarious traumatization: A framework for understanding the psychological effects of working with victims. *Journal of Traumatic Stress, 3*(1), 131–149.

McGaugh, J. L. (1990). Significance and remembrance: The role of neuromodulatory systems. *Psychological Science, 1,* 15–25.

Meichenbaum, D. H. (1985). *Stress inoculation training.* New York: Pergamon Press.

Nagy, L. M., Blake, D. D., Dan, E., Riney, S. J., Mangine, W., Southwick, S. M., Gusman, F. D., & Charney, D. S. (1992, October). *Clinician administered PTSD scale—weekly version (CAPS-2): Reliability, validity, and sensitivity to change.* Paper presented at the Eighth Annual Meeting of the International Society for Traumatic Stress Studies, Los Angeles, CA.

Pitman, R. K., Orr, S. P., Forgue, D. F., de Tong, J. B., & Claiborn, J. M. (1987). Psychophysiological assessment of posttraumatic stress disorder imagery in Vietnam combat veterans. *Archives of General Psychiatry, 44,* 970–975.

Resick, P. A. (1987). *Reactions of female and male victims of rape and robbery* (Final report, NIJ Grant No. MH37296). Washington, DC: National Institute of Justice.

Resick, P. A. (1992). Cognitive treatment of crime-related post-traumatic stress disorder. In R. Peters, R. McMahon, & V. Quinsey (Eds.), *Aggression and violence throughout the life span* (pp. 171–191). Newbury Park, CA: Sage.

Resick, P. A., Jordan, C. G., Girelli, S. A., Hutter, C. H., & Marhoefer-Dvorak, S. (1988). A comparative outcome study of behavioral group therapy for sexual assault victims. *Behavior Therapy, 19,* 385–401.

Resick, P. A., & Markaway, B. E. G. (1991). Clinical treatment of adult female victims of sexual assault. In C. R. Hollin & K. Howells (Eds.), *Clinical approaches to sex offenders and their victims* (pp. 261–284). New York: Wiley.

Resick, P. A., & Schnicke, M. K. (1990). Treating symptoms in adult victims of sexual assault. *Journal of Interpersonal Violence, 5,* 488–506.

Resick, P. A., & Schnicke, M. K. (1992). Cognitive processing therapy for sexual assault victims. *Journal of Consulting and Clinical Psychology, 60,* 748–756.

Resick, P. A., & Schnicke, M. K. (in press). *Cognitive processing therapy for rape victim: A treatment manual.* Newbury Park, CA: Sage.

Resnick, H. S., Kilpatrick, D. G., & Lipovsky, J. A. (1991). Assessment of rape-related posttraumatic stress disorder: Stressor and symptom dimensions. *Psychological Assessment, 3,* 561–572.

Robins, L. N., Helzer, J. D., Croughan, J., & Ratcliff, K. S. (1981). The National Institute of Mental Health diagnostic interview schedule: Its history, characteristics, and validity. *Archives of General Psychiatry, 38,* 381–389.

Rothbaum, B. O., & Foa, E. B. (1992). Exposure therapy for rape victims with post-traumatic stress disorder. *Behavior Therapist, 15,* 219–222.

Rothbaum, B. O., Foa, E. B., Riggs, D. S., Murdock, T., & Walsh, W. (1992). A prospective examination of post-traumatic stress disorder in rape victims. *Journal of Traumatic Stress, 5,* 455–475.

Saunders, B. E., Kilpatrick, D. G., Resnick, H. S., & Tidwell, R. P. (1989). Brief screening for lifetime history of criminal victimization at mental health intake. *Journal of Interpersonal Violence, 4,* 267–277.

Saunders, B. E., Mandoki, K. A., & Kilpatrick, D. G. (1990). Development of a crime-related post-traumatic stress disorder scale within the SCL-90-R. *Journal of Traumatic Stress, 3,* 439–448.

Silverman, D. (1977). First do not more harm: Female rape victims and the male counselor. *American Journal of Orthopsychiatry, 47,* 91–96.

Solomon, S. D., Gerrity, E. T., & Muff, A. M. (1992). Efficacy of treatments for posttraumatic stress disorder: An empirical review. *Journal of the American Medical Association, 268,* 633–638.

Spitzer, R. L., Williams, J. B., & Gibbon, M. (1987). *Structured Clinical Interview for DSM-III-R–Non-patient version.* New York: New York State Psychiatric Institute.

Sutker, P. B., Uddo-Crane, M., & Allain, A. N. (1991). Clinical and research assessment of posttraumatic stress disorder: A conceptual overview. *Psychological Assessment, 3,* 520–530.

Van der Kolk, B., Boyd, H., Krystal, J., & Greenberg, M. (1984). Post-traumatic stress disorder as a biologically based disorder: Implications of the animal model of inescapable shock. In B. Van der Kolk (Ed.), *Post-traumatic stress disorder: Psychological and biological sequelae* (pp. 124–134). Washington, DC: American Psychiatric Press.

Veronen, L. J., & Kilpatrick, D. G. (1980). Self-reported fears of rape victims: A preliminary investigation. *Behavior Modification, 4,* 383–396.

Veronen, L. J., & Kilpatrick, D. G. (1983). Stress management for rape victims. In D. Meichenbaum & M. E. Jaremko (Eds.), *Stress reduction and prevention* (pp. 341–374). New York: Plenum Press.

Weathers, F. W., Blake, D. D., Krinsley, K. E., Haddad, W., Huska, J. A., & Keane, T. M. (1992a, October). *The clinician administered PTSD scale–diagnostic version (CAPS-1): Description, use and psychometric properties.* Paper presented at the Eighth Annual Meeting of the International Society for Traumatic Stress Studies, Los Angeles, CA.

Weathers, F. W., Blake, D. D., Krinsley, K. D., Haddad, W. Huska, J. A., & Keane, T. M. (1992b, November). *The clinician administered PTSD scale: Reliability and construct validity.* Paper presented at the 26th Annual Convention of the Association for Advancement of Behavioral Therapy, Boston, MA.

Wolfe, J., & Keane, T. M. (1990). The diagnostic validity of post-traumatic stress disorder. In M. Wolf & A. Mosnaim (Eds.), *Post-traumatic stress disorder: Etiology, phenomenology, and treatment.* Washington, DC: American Psychiatric Press.

Chapter 3

SOCIAL PHOBIA AND SOCIAL ANXIETY

Debra A. Hope
University of Nebraska, Lincoln
Richard G. Heimberg
State University of New York at Albany

M any people are very shy and somewhat inhibited. For this reason, the suffering associated with social phobia is often minimized as a trait common in the population that does not require the heavy artillery of formalized treatment interventions, either drugs or psychological treatments. Nothing could be further from the truth. For the approximately 2% of the population who suffer from debilitating social phobia, the seemingly simple process of interacting with people or forming relationships provokes overwhelming terror and is often avoided. The effect on career and quality of life can be devastating. This chapter examines the latest iteration of what is currently the most powerful psychological treatment for social phobia. As is increasingly true of our new generation of psychological interventions, cognitive-behavioral group therapy has proven to be significantly better than equally credible but less focused psychological interventions, and its effect is increasingly powerful over time. As such, this treatment is among the best of the new generation of psychological treatments characterized by power and specificity. —D. H. B.

INTRODUCTION

Our understanding of the nature and treatment of social phobia has expanded immensely since its inclusion as a separate diagnostic category in the third edition of the *Diagnostic and Statistical Manual of Mental Disorders* (DSM-III; American Psychiatric Association [APA], 1980) over a decade ago. At that time social phobia was considered a special case of simple phobia with fears limited to one or two situations and, except in extreme cases, unlikely to result in more than minimal disruption in role functioning. As we outline below, however, research has revealed that social phobia represents a significant mental health problem that can be incapacitating in its most severe forms. After a brief overview of the epidemiological and psychopathological research, the research on efficacy of combined exposure and cognitive treatments is discussed. Next the chapter highlights two major theoretical models of social phobia and social anxiety. Each model emphasizes a different aspect of social anxiety, so the goal will be to provide a general background to facilitate understanding of the treatment strategies discussed in the remainder of the chapter. The bulk of the chapter centers around a particular therapeutic approach, cognitive-behavioral group therapy (CBGT), including a detailed presentation of a treated case.

Diagnosis, Prevalence, and Comorbidity

Diagnosis

According to the fourth edition of the *Diagnostic and Statistical Manual of Mental Disorders* (DSM-IV; APA, 1993)*, a social phobic is someone who fears a variety of social and performance situations because he/she is concerned about being humiliated or embarrassed by performing inadequately or by displaying visible anxiety symptoms. The possible feared situations range from non-contingent interactions such as public speaking to one-on-one conversations. Social phobics may become anxious in circumstances in which required complex motor behaviors would be visibly disrupted by a fine tremor or lack of concentration (e.g., eating, drinking, typing, or writing in front of others). Traditionally, fear of using public toilets, often referred to as "bashful bladder," has been considered a potential social phobic situation, although data from our laboratory suggest that this situation is unrelated to other situations reported as difficult by social phobics (Holt, Heimberg, Hope, & Liebowitz, 1992). Most social phobics fear, and consequently avoid, two or more of these situations (Holt, Heimberg, Hope, & Leibowitz, 1992; Turner, Beidel, Dancu, & Keys, 1986), with a portion fearing most social contact with others. Persons with these broad-based fears of social contact are classified to the *generalized* subtype of social phobia in the revised third edition of the *Diagnostic and Statistical Manual of Mental Disorders* (DSM-III-R; APA, 1987) and DSM-IV. Feared situations may be avoided or endured despite intense anxiety.

Contrary to DSM-III, social phobics' fear and avoidance typically impair their social and occupational functioning to a significant degree. It is not unusual to find a social phobic who is grossly underemployed, such as one recent client who was employed as a night janitor despite having earned a 4-year college degree. He had recently refused a promotion to supervise two coworkers because he could not face the interpersonal demands of the position. In fact, the vast majority of social phobics believe their career, academic, and/or general social functioning is impaired by their social fears (Liebowitz, Gorman, Fyer, & Klein, 1985; Turner et al., 1986). Sanderson, DiNardo, Rapee, and Barlow (1990) reported that, despite a mean age in the early 30s, half of the social phobics in their sample had never married compared to 36% of individuals with panic disorder with agoraphobia (PDA) and 18% of those with generalized anxiety disorder.

Prevalence and Onset

The 6-month prevalence of social phobia according to the National Institute of Mental Health epidemiological catchment area (ECA) studies is 0.9%–1.7% for men and 1.5%–2.6% for women (Myers et al., 1984). It should be noted that this study utilized DSM-III criteria and included only individuals with specific performance anxiety. The prevalence may be much higher using the DSM-IV criteria which include individuals with more generalized fears. Unlike some of the other anxiety disorders, social phobia is equally common among men and women (Bourdon et al., 1988). Social phobics may represent as many as 18% of those requesting treatment in anxiety disorders clinics (Sanderson et al., 1990). Bourdon et al.'s (1988) analyses of the ECA data revealed a median age of onset of 12 years old with 91% indicating onset before age 25. This likely overestimates the age of onset because individuals who indicated they had been a social phobic their "whole life" were excluded from the analyses.

Comorbidity

Other Axis I Disorders

Social phobics seeking treatment often present with a complicated diagnostic picture that includes other Axis I disorders. Turner, Beidel, Borden, Stanley, and Jacob

*The DSM-IV criteria cited in this chapter are those that were approved as final by the DSM-IV Anxiety Disorders Work Group and the Task Force on DSM-IV (APA, 1993). These criteria may be subject to minor editorial revisions before the publication of DSM-IV.

(1991) reported that 43% of 71 social phobics received an additional Axis I disorder, most commonly generalized anxiety disorder. In a smaller sample of 24 social phobics, nearly 60% of individuals with a primary diagnosis of social phobia met criteria for at least one additional clinical syndrome, including dysthymia (21%), simple phobia (25%), or PDA (17%) (Sanderson et al., 1990). Nearly one fifth of the latter sample used benzodiazepines on a daily basis to control their social anxiety. Studies of alcoholics reveal a high prevalence of social phobia, with evidence that many of these individuals may be drinking to reduce their social anxiety (Chambless, Cherney, Caputo, & Rheinstein, 1987; Mullaney & Trippett, 1979; Smail, Stockwell, Canter, & Hodgson, 1984).

Avoidant Personality Disorder

The inclusion of the generalized subtype of social phobia in DSM-III-R and DSM-IV has highlighted the confusion about the relationship between social phobia and avoidant personality disorder (APD). APD is characterized by a long-standing pattern of avoidance of interpersonal contact, fear of rejection, and fear of blushing or performing inadequately in social encounters. In four recent studies (Herbert, Hope, & Bellack, 1992; Holt, Heimberg, & Hope, 1992; Schneier, Spitzer, Gibbon, Fyer, & Liebowitz, 1991; Turner, Beidel, & Townsley, 1992), 22.1% to 70% of social phobics received an additional diagnosis of APD. Despite lack of agreement regarding the comorbidity of social phobia and APD, all these authors concluded that APD features are common among social phobics, particularly those with more generalized fears. However, the evidence is equivocal with respect to whether social phobia and APD should be classified as separate disorders. For example, generalized social phobics with and without APD reported similar ages of onset for their social fears, but those with APD were more likely to have concurrent depressive disorders (Holt, Heimberg, & Hope, 1992). Perhaps individuals with APD are simply the most severely impaired social phobics, with quantitative but not qualitative distinctions between social phobia with and without APD (Herbert et al., 1992; but see also Holt, Heimberg, & Hope, 1992).

Furthermore, little empirical support exists for the notion that some individuals may meet the criteria for APD without also meeting the criteria for social phobia (Widiger, 1992).

Differential Diagnosis

Although social phobics may sometimes experience panic attacks in social situations and both social phobics and individuals with PDA may avoid similar situations (e.g., restaurants), the two disorders are clearly distinct. Furthermore, differential diagnosis is crucial because different treatments are indicated (see Craske & Barlow, Chapter 1, this volume). Three issues should be addressed in making the differential diagnosis:

1. Is the individual afraid of the symptoms themselves? Individuals with PDA would be concerned about the anxiety symptoms even if no one else could see them, as would be the case when they are alone. Social phobics, in contrast, are most concerned that others will see the symptoms and evaluate them negatively on that basis.
2. Do panic attacks occur in nonsocial situations? The range of situations feared by those with PDA depends on the history or probability of experiencing a panic attack and may include situations in which social evaluation is, at best, extremely unlikely.
3. Is the onset of the disorder more typical of PDA or social phobia? The first panic attack is frequently quite salient to individuals with PDA, even many years later. Social phobics, in contrast, often do not remember a specific onset, stating they have been socially anxious all of their life or since high school.

To further complicate matters, social phobia and PDA are sometimes comorbid. If that is the case, it may be necessary to treat both disorders, with the one that is the most severe (or of the most concern to the client) being addressed first.

Occasionally a potential client will present for treatment with severe social–evaluative anxiety related to a compulsion such as staring at or touching women's breasts or men's genitals. Obviously, if the individual actually engaged in such behavior, there would be social repercussions. Clinical experience suggests such individuals are best conceptualized as experiencing obsessive compulsive disorder and treated accordingly.

Superficially, at least, it would seem difficult to distinguish between severe social phobia and schizoid or paranoid personality disorders. In practice, the need to make this differential diagnosis arises infrequently. Schizoid individuals do not find social interaction reinforcing and are therefore unlikely to seek treatment to increase their comfort in social situations. Social phobics, on the other hand, desire the social contact they desperately fear. The distinction between social phobia and paranoid personality disorder depends largely on the person's ability to consider the possibility that others' intentions may not be malevolent. This judgment call may be difficult to make without extending the assessment period and examining the outcome of two to three role-played social interactions.

Generalization of Fear and Diagnostic Subtypes

Generalization of Fear

Fear of negative evaluation by others is the hallmark of social phobia. In spite of this common thread, the circumstances that evoke this fear vary widely from one social phobic to another. As noted above, some social phobics fear only a few situations, while others may become anxious about almost any interpersonal contact. In a detailed examination of social phobics' feared situations, Holt, Heimberg, Hope, and Liebowitz (1992) clustered situations into four domains (groups of functionally related situations)—formal speaking/interaction, informal speaking/interaction, assertion, and observation of behavior (e.g., writing in public). Formal speaking/interaction was the most commonly feared domain, involving 70% of the sample. Informal speaking/interaction, assertion, and observation of behavior were feared by 46%, 31%, and 22% of the sample, respectively. Most individuals feared multiple domains, but in a hierarchical pattern. If someone feared only one domain, it was most likely formal speaking/interaction. Those who feared informal speaking/interaction were more likely to fear formal speaking/interaction than the other two domains. Similarly, those who feared assertion also tended to fear formal and informal speaking/interaction, but not necessarily observation of behavior. Those who feared observation of behavior also tended to fear the other three domains. Thus one can consider the domains to be arranged hierarchically in the following order: formal speaking/interaction, informal speaking/interaction, assertion, and observation of behavior. If an individual reports fear in a given domain (e.g., assertion), he/she likely also fears those domains that occur earlier in the list (e.g., formal and informal speaking/interaction, but not observation of behavior). This does not imply that social phobia is a progressive disorder in which a particular social phobic's fears would generalize in this manner across his/her lifetime. Rather, it appears that when one considers social phobics as a group, it may be possible to categorize the pervasiveness of their fears in a loosely hierarchical fashion. As will be seen later, this information can be useful in constructing fear and avoidance hierarchies and designing graduated exposures to feared situations.

Diagnostic Subtypes

The heterogeneity of social phobia has been the topic of much discussion for several years. Numerous studies have attempted to subdivide social phobic samples primarily on the type of feared situation or pervasiveness of the fear. As Heimberg, Holt, Schneier, Spitzer, and Liebowitz (in press) reported in their extensive review of the subtyping question, studies often report subtype differences on demographic variables, clinician-rated and self-reported anxiety, avoidance and depression, behavioral measures, and, occasionally, physiological measures and response to treatment. Although several subtyping schemes were considered by the DSM-IV work group, DSM-IV retains the subtyping scheme first seen in DSM-III-R. Clinicians are given the option of specifying a *generalized type* if the person's fears include most social situations. More research is needed to determine whether other subtypes of social phobia could be specified that would differ on important etiological, assessment, or treatment variables.

Efficacy of Cognitive and Exposure Treatment for Social Phobia

Researchers have investigated the efficacy of a broad range of treatments for social phobia including social skills training; cognitive therapy; various forms of relaxation; imaginal, *in vivo*, and role-played exposure; brief Morita therapy; dynamically oriented supportive psychotherapy; and various pharmacotherapies. A thorough analysis of the literature is beyond the scope of this chapter. This review examines studies that have tested the efficacy of combined exposure and a cognitive intervention, the type of treatment on which this chapter focuses. Readers interested in a more extensive discussion should consult Heimberg (1989), Heimberg and Barlow (1991), Levin, Schneier, and Liebowitz (1989), or Hope, Holt, and Heimberg (1993).

Combined cognitive and exposure treatments have been investigated more frequently than any other psychosocial treatments for social phobia. This is not surprising since exposure treatments have been successful for many of the anxiety disorders. The addition of a cognitive component has not always added to the efficacy of exposure alone in the other anxiety disorders. Several researchers (e.g., Butler, 1989) have argued, however, that social phobics' fear of negative evaluation is essentially a cognitive construct and cognitive interventions may be particularly important in this group. In their review of treatments for social phobia, Hope et al. (1993) concluded that the data are inconclusive as to whether exposure plus cognitive therapy is more effective than exposure alone, but cognitive interventions likely play a more important role in the treatment of social phobia than in the other anxiety disorders.

Butler, Cullington, Munby, Amies, and Gelder (1984) compared *in vivo* exposure to *in vivo* exposure plus an anxiety management program comprised of distraction, relaxation, and rational self-talk and a wait-list control. Although anxiety management training was not a purely cognitive intervention, a post hoc analysis indicated that subjects may have found the rational self-talk the most helpful aspect of the package. To control for time spent on the anxiety management program, the exposure-alone condition included a filler treatment that, unfortunately, was not entirely credible to subjects. At posttest, both exposure treatments were more effective than the wait-list control across a variety of measures, with few differences between the active treatments. However, at follow-up, subjects who received the exposure plus anxiety management training fared better than subjects who received exposure alone.

Mattick and colleagues (Mattick & Peters, 1988; Mattick, Peters, & Clarke, 1989) conducted two studies examining the efficacy of a combined package of therapist-assisted and *in vivo* exposure and cognitive restructuring. In the first study (Mattick & Peters, 1988), the combined treatment was compared to exposure alone. Subjects in both groups improved, with somewhat greater improvement in the combined condition, particularly at 3-month follow-up. In the second study, the combined treatment was compared to each component alone and to a wait-list control. All active treatments improved relative to the wait list but the type and pattern of change differed among the treatments. Subjects in all three active treatments reduced phobic avoidance, but subjects receiving cognitive restructuring alone or in combination with exposure also improved on cognitive measures such as irrational beliefs and negative self-evaluation. Compared to the other treatments, the combined condition was most improved on behavioral test measures. Cognitive-restructuring-alone subjects were slowest to improve on the behavioral test but made continued gains during the follow-up period, whereas the exposure-alone subjects deteriorated somewhat. Although it appears that each of the components of the combined package was effective at reducing subjects' social–evaluative fears, the combination of exposure and cognitive therapy might have been superior.

In the first of several studies evaluating CBGT, the treatment described in the case presentation later in the chapter, Heimberg, Becker, Goldfinger, and Vermilyea (1985) treated seven social phobics—five with public speaking fears and two with heterosocial fears—in a multiple-baseline design. This early version of CBGT consisted of imaginal exposure, role-played exposure during group therapy sessions, cognitive restructuring, and homework for *in vivo* exposure. At the end of the 14-week treatment, all subjects improved on a range of behavioral, physiological, and subjective measures. Gains were maintained at 6-month follow-up for six of seven subjects.

Few studies in the social phobia treatment outcome literature employ an attention placebo condition to control for the nonspecific effects of therapy. This is a more rigorous test than a comparison to a wait list because subjects are actively involved in a credible treatment but one that fails to include the specific theoretically effective component(s). Using such a design, Heimberg, Dodge, et al., (1990) evaluated an updated version of CBGT that eliminated the imaginal exposure component and reduced treatment time to 12 weeks. The attention control treatment, called educational supportive group therapy (ES), consisted of education about social phobia and nondirective supportive group therapy. As expected, subjects in both treatments improved significantly on most measures. However, at both posttest and 6-month follow-up, CBGT subjects were more improved on some key measures. In particular, CBGT subjects reported less anxiety during an individualized behavioral test and were more likely to be rated as improved by a clinician. At 6-month follow-up, the internal dialogue of CBGT subjects was characterized by a "positive dialogue," a state thought to be associated with good mental health according to Schwartz and Garamoni's (1989) States of Mind (SOM) model. The internal dialogue of ES subjects, in contrast, represented a "negative monologue," the most pathological state of mind described in the SOM model (Bruch, Heimberg, & Hope, 1991). A 5-year follow-up on a subset of subjects from the original sample indicated that individuals who had received CBGT were more likely to maintain their gains and continued to be more improved than comparable attention control subjects (Heimberg, Salzman, Holt, & Blendell, 1993).

In a component analysis of CBGT, Hope, Heimberg, and Bruch (1990) reported that CBGT and exposure alone were more effective than a wait-list control. At posttest, there was evidence that the exposure-alone condition was more effective than CBGT, but these differences disappeared at 6-month follow-up. However, the authors noted that subjects in both treatment conditions made less progress than anticipated, possibly due to attrition in some of the therapy groups.

Two studies have compared Heimberg's CBGT to pharmacotherapy. In the first, two medications, phenelzine and alprazolam, and pill placebo were contrasted with CBGT (Gelernter et al., 1991). All subjects in the pharmacotherapy and placebo conditions also received encouragement for self-exposure. The design included the withdrawal of medication during the 2-month follow-up period, after 12 weeks of active treatment. In general all subjects, even those receiving placebo, improved with very few differences among the groups. The authors attribute the improvement of placebo subjects to their high rate of self-guided exposure. There was some evidence that alprazolam subjects were more likely to relapse when medication was withdrawn, whereas phenelzine subjects responded better initially and were more likely to maintain their progress without medication. It should be noted that CBGT was conducted somewhat differently in this study than in previous studies. For example, subjects were treated in larger groups than typically used for this treatment package (10 per group as opposed to 6 per group).

Finally, preliminary data are available from a multicenter study conducted by Heimberg and Liebowitz (1992) comparing phenelzine, CBGT, pill placebo, and the same attention control psychotherapy previously developed by Heimberg, Dodge, et al. (1990). Independent assessors blind to treatment condition have classified 77 individuals who completed treatment (excluding 15 who dropped out) as either responders or nonresponders. Eighty percent of subjects receiving CBGT and 71% of those receiving phenelzine were considered responders. These rates did not differ from each other but were significantly higher than those achieved by patients receiving pill placebo (37%) or the attention control treatment (27%).

In summary, it appears that a combined package of exposure and cognitive restructuring such as CBGT represents an effective intervention for social phobia. Whether it is the most effective treatment or more effective than exposure or cognitive therapy alone is more difficult to determine given the limited number of studies and mixed results. However, more important to practitioners is the mounting evidence that three out of four social phobics are likely to make clinically significant changes after a reasonably intensive trial of CBGT or a similar combined exposure and cognitive restructuring package.

Selected Theories of Social Phobia

Numerous theorists have developed models to explain the development and maintenance of social anxiety and social phobia. For the purposes of this chapter, however, only two will be reviewed. Beck and Emery's (1985) cognitive theory and Leary's (1988) self-presentational model offer useful frameworks within which to conceptualize the cognitive-behavioral treatment of social phobia. The former forms the conceptual base for the cognitive restructuring component of CBGT. The latter helps identify situations in which someone might become socially anxious and potential reasons the anxiety may occur. As will be seen later, understanding these reasons helps the clinician identify appropriate treatment strategies and goals. Each of these models is described briefly below.

Beck and Emery's Cognitive Theory of Social Anxiety

Beck and Emery (1985) developed a cognitive model of anxiety and phobias, including social phobia. The *schema*, the basic cognitive structure that guides the processing of information, serves as the core concept in their cognitive model. Schemas are sets of "rules" that classify, prioritize, and interpret incoming information to the person as well as facilitate the retrieval of relevant information from memory. Schemas are grouped into *modes* that create a cognitive set or processing bias that operates across situations. Anxiety-disordered individuals, according to Beck and Emery, typically function in the *vulnerability* mode. That is, the individual sees the world as a dangerous place in which he/she must constantly be vigilant to potential threat. As a result, neutral or mildly positive cues are misinterpreted negatively, while positive or safety cues are discounted or ignored. Memories of past successes or available coping re-

sources are also underestimated or overlooked. Thus, schemas manifest themselves in logical errors in thinking that become apparent when the person reports his/her thoughts about anxiety-provoking stimuli.

The cues to which the hypothesized hypervigilance is "tuned" differ from one anxiety disorder to another. Snake phobics, for example, are hypervigilant to cues that denote the presence of snakes, including long, thin objects that resemble their shape or rustling in tall grass that may foreshadow their arrival. Social phobics are hypervigilant to cues that denote the possibility of negative evaluation by others. These cues may be situational (e.g., an offhand comment by an instructor about upcoming classroom presentations), interpersonal (e.g., a coworker who fails to respond to a greeting), or internal (e.g., increased heart rate or body temperature that signals anxiety that may be visible to others or interfere with performance of required behavior). In fact, social phobics do appear to devote excessive attentional resources to the detection of potential social threat cues (Hope, Rapee, Heimberg, & Dombeck, 1990; Mattia, Heimberg, & Hope, 1993; Smith, Ingram, & Brehm, 1983). By narrowing their attention to the social threat cues, the importance of these cues may then be exaggerated so that a barely noticeable stutter during a conversation is interpreted as incoherence and the refused request for a date portends an isolated and solitary existence.

The goal of CBGT is to modify social phobics' schemas to be more similar to those of nonanxious persons. The rules that govern social phobics' processing of information need to be modified to provide a more balanced view of internal and external stimuli. This modification is thought to occur when the schemas are repeatedly confronted with discrepant information. In practice, this involves repeatedly challenging logical errors in thinking with evidence supporting more rational interpretations until the person's automatic information processing incorporates the more rational information processing strategies. The evidence used in these challenges comes from two primary sources: direct verbal challenges during cognitive restructuring and deliberately focusing the person's attention on experiential evidence derived from role-played exposures and homework assignments. It appears that treatment success is associated with a reallocation of attentional resources as would be expected by the cognitive model (Mattia et al., 1993). However, Mattia et al. reported that effective treatments other than CBGT also affect this change, suggesting that explicit cognitive restructuring may not be essential for the cognitive change described in the model.

Self-Presentational Model of Social Anxiety

The self-presentational model of social anxiety (Schlenker & Leary, 1982) proposed that social anxiety occurs when an individual desires to make a particular impression on others and doubts that he/she will be successful in doing so. Both conditions must be met; how he/she will appear to others must be of importance *and* there must be apprehension about one's ability to engage in sufficient impression management. Later, Leary (summarized in Leary, 1988) refined the model and hypothesized that specific situational and dispositional factors may increase the motivation to engage in impression management and/or decrease one's sense of self-efficacy about doing so successfully.

According to Leary (1988), individuals may be excessively motivated to create a particular impression because of a high need for approval. On the other hand, several factors can affect a person's expectations about meeting impression management goals. These factors include perceived or actual deficits in social skill, low self-esteem, and low outcome expectancies. Low self-esteem may contribute to social anxiety because such individuals likely presume that others will view them as poorly as they regard themselves. Perceived social skills deficits, whether or not they exist by some external criterion, epitomize Bandura's (1977) concept of low efficacy expectations (lack of confidence that one can perform a given behavior). Sometimes a socially anxious person may believe that, even if he/she performs flawlessly, the other person will not form the preferred impression. Bandura (1977) has labeled such a belief a low outcome expectancy, and in this case, Leary suggests that low outcome expectancy may result from low self-esteem or an unchari-

table opinion of impression formation or social interactions. For example, Leary, Kowalski, and Campbell (1988) found that socially anxious individuals believed interaction partners would evaluate them negatively, as one would expect. However, they also expected interaction partners to provide equally unkind evaluations of other people.

One advantage of the self-presentational model is that it provides an excellent framework to predict when a given individual will experience social anxiety. Furthermore, by incorporating related concepts such as the relationship between social skills and social anxiety into the model, Leary has strengthened its explanatory power. The expanded theory acknowledges that individuals are anxious for different reasons and identifies important areas for a clinician to address in assessment. Is the client overly motivated to make a good impression or does the client doubt his/her ability to perform adequately? Has the client developed this doubt because of actual behavioral deficits or does the client hold a distorted image of him/herself, other people, or social interactions? The answers to these questions provide useful fodder for selection of a treatment strategy and direction in cognitive restructuring in the cognitive-behavioral intervention described below.

CBGT FOR SOCIAL PHOBIA

CBGT consists of three primary components—simulated exposures to feared situations, cognitive restructuring, and homework assignments for *in vivo* exposure (Heimberg, 1991). The simulated exposures form the heart of the protocol with the cognitive interventions occurring before, during, and after each exposure. Homework is typically based on the situation developed in the in-session exposure.

General Considerations in CBGT

Group Format

Exposure-based treatments require tremendous commitment and courage on the part of clients. After all, the purpose of exposure is to have individuals face the fears they may have avoided for many years. Although it would seem counterintuitive to treat social phobics in a group format, the group provides a number of advantages over individual treatment that help social phobics face their fears. These advantages include vicarious learning, seeing others with similar problems, making a public commitment to change, the availability of multiple role-play partners, and a range of people to provide evidence to counter distorted thinking (Heimberg, 1991; Sank & Shaffer, 1984). Because of the nature of the disorder, many social phobics have never discussed their fears with anyone and, consequently, often believe that their problems are unique. The group provides a tremendous opportunity for members to discover that others have similar thoughts and feelings and to learn from each others' attempts to overcome their fears, illustrated here in an excerpt between group members (M1, M2, M3) and therapists (T1, T2) from a recent CBGT group:

M1: I was thinking all week about that rational response CD [another group member] was using last week.

T1: The rational response from the exposure we did of having a conversation with a next-door neighbor?

M1: Yes. "I'm only responsible for 50% of the conversation" was what he said. When we were talking about that last week, it was like a light bulb went on. I realized that, just like CD, I always feel a lot of pressure to keep the conversation going. When I tried thinking about only being responsible for 50% of the conversation, I felt a lot more comfortable. If it dies, it isn't necessarily my fault. The other person has to do their part, too.

This group member was able to accept the positive coping statement developed for another member and incorporate it into his own arsenal of strategies to combat anxiety.

One of the difficulties in treating social phobia is to create realistic, yet controllable, exposure situations (Butler, 1989; Hope, 1993). The group format greatly facilitates the design of exposures because the other group members and two therapists are available to serve as role players or audience members as needed. Furthermore, group members can provide more credible feedback on the quality of an individual's performance in an exposure than is available from an individual therapist. During cognitive restructuring, group members often provide evidence to counter a fellow member's distorted thinking, as demonstrated below:

T1: So your automatic thought is, "I don't know how to have a conversation," is that right?

M1: Yeah, I always screw it up.

T1: Alright, let's ask the rest of the group what they think about that. Who has had a conversation with [M1] or noticed her talking with someone else?

M2: Well, there is the role play she did last week when she talked to me.

T2: OK, how about something other than an exposure, something like chatting before group starts . . .

M3: We walked out to our cars together last week and talked in the parking lot for awhile.

[Several other group members listed similar conversations.]

T1: So it sounds like you have had a number of conversations with the rest of the group.

M1: I guess so.

T1: Group, how did she do? How did the conversations go?

M2: It was fine. She was asking me about my car because she has been looking for a new one so we talked mostly about that.

[Other group members provided similar answers.]

T1: Well, [M1], the rest of the group doesn't seem to agree that you don't know how to have conversations.

M1: I guess I have always been so nervous that I never stopped to think that sometimes the conversations go OK.

Size and Composition of Groups

Experience in running groups with four to seven members suggests that six is the ideal group size. With this number, each client can get individual attention every other session. On the other hand, if one or two members are absent or drop out of treatment, there are still an adequate number to constitute a workable group. These six clients plus two therapists should provide a range of gender, age, and experience to cover most needs for role players for the first eight or nine treatment sessions. Later, as described below, other people can serve this function once the options within the group have been exhausted.

As in other group treatments, selecting group members may be the most important decision the therapist makes in CBGT. A number of factors should be considered. First, the group should be balanced for gender, age, and severity of social phobia. If one group member differs dramatically from all the rest, he/she is likely to be uncomfortable and may drop out of the group. As a rule of thumb, each member should have someone with whom he/she can identify (e.g., a second member over 45 years old or a second person who is reasonably high functioning, except in the specific feared situation[s]). Second, individuals who are likely to be disruptive to the group process should be excluded. Typically this includes potential group members with significant features of borderline personality disorder or who are excessively hostile or demanding. Occasionally a social phobic's fears are so intense that he/she has developed an angry response to maintain an adequate distance from others. In such cases the demands of the group may provoke this response and be disruptive. Other treatment options should be considered prior to or instead of CBGT.

Scheduling and Setting

CBGT groups are designed to meet for 12 weekly 2- to 2½-hr sessions. When selecting the meeting time, the therapists should beware of holidays or other activities that would disrupt the regularity of the meetings. An occasional skipped week is unavoidable but more than that severely disrupts the momentum of the group.

The relatively long sessions require a comfortable setting. Living-room-style furniture is ideal as long as group members do not have to sit too close to one another on a sofa. A portion of the furniture should be movable as the role-played exposures frequently require the furniture to be rearranged.

The group room should be equipped with an audiocassette recorder and an easel or a blackboard. Taping sessions allows the therapists to review the group activities with each other or with a supervisor between sessions. This allows continuous feedback on their performance and frees them from note taking during sessions. A large easel with a pad of newsprint and a marking pen or a blackboard with chalk are essential to record thoughts and rational responses elicited during cognitive restructuring. They provide much needed visual cues to group members, whose attention may be limited by their heightened anxiety. The easel and pad are preferable to a blackboard because they allow the group to refer back to previous material. In any case, the pad or blackboard should be portable so it can be set up for easier reference by the target client during simulated exposures.

Therapists

On the surface, CBGT appears to be a straightforward series of structured but individualized activities. In reality, it is a complex process that requires experienced group therapists. At the very least, the therapists need to be intimately familiar with the cognitive-behavioral model of social phobia and CBGT procedures. They also need to have experience with exposure-based treatments and cognitive therapy and, ideally, to have worked previously with social phobics. Ensuring that all group members are adequately involved, managing the session time, and monitoring group members' emotional states while negotiating the intricacies of cognitive work and simulated exposures are simply not feasible for novice therapists.

It is extremely difficult and fatiguing to conduct CBGT with only one therapist, and two are highly recommended. If necessary, one can be somewhat less experienced if he/she receives training, including role playing the procedures, before the group meetings begin. Male–female therapist pairs are ideal. Not only do they bring different perspectives on the social interactions that the clients fear, but this arrangement provides maximum flexibility for therapists to serve as role-play partners. For example, in exposures for dating situations, the appropriate gender for the role player is crucial. Other clients may be too anxious, or their reactions too unpredictable, to participate in role plays, particularly early in treatment.

Appropriate Clients

Five factors should be considered when recommending CBGT for a particular client with social phobia. First, as noted above, clients who are likely to be disruptive to the group process should be excluded. Not only are they likely to derive little benefit, but they will impede others' progress as well. Second, a few social phobics experience such severe anxiety in the group setting itself that they will not be able to tolerate it. Almost all potential group members experience some anxiety, particularly in the first few sessions. However, an occasional person will be too overwhelmed by his/her anxiety to comprehend the concepts taught in the group and will attempt to reduce his/her anxiety by not participating or avoiding sessions. It is unlikely that such individuals will benefit from CBGT. Third, social phobia should be the primary problem for which the individual seeks treatment. This requires a careful diagnostic assessment. In cases in which the social phobia is comorbid with other disorders, the clinician and client should reach a joint decision as to the primary problem. Fourth, in determining appropriateness for CBGT, the client's level of depression should be carefully evaluated. As noted below, elevated depression is a predictor of negative outcome in CBGT (Holt, Heimberg, & Hope, 1989; Klosko, Heimberg, Becker, Dodge, & Kennedy, 1984). The disruption in functioning caused by social fears results in some dysphoria in many social phobics. This is inconsequential and should decrease as their social phobia improves. However, a significantly depressed social phobic, particularly if his/her depression is not secondary to his/her social anxiety, will fare poorly in such a demanding treatment and may adversely impact the group. The clinician should evaluate carefully whether treatment for depression should precede CBGT.

Finally, individuals with severe deficits in interpersonal skills may not derive maximum benefit from CBGT. Unfortunately, assessment of skills deficits among social phobics is difficult. A significant portion, although by no means all, of social phobics perform poorly in their feared situations. However, this poor performance may be attributable to the disruptive effects of anxiety (including negative thinking) or a lack of skill. Hope et al. (1993) proposed a three-part assessment to distinguish between these two possibilities. First it is assumed that if the client can demonstrate appropriate skills under any circumstances, he/she likely possesses the skills. A client who is appropriate for CBGT should be able to demonstrate adequate performance, although not necessarily perfect skills, in one of the following situations: (1) role plays that elicit a minimal amount of anxiety; (2) naturally occurring interactions with the therapist, particularly after they have had some contact and the client is becoming more comfortable; or (3) verbal descriptions of how a third person would behave in representative situations. Individuals whose fears about performing poorly are realistic given their lack of social skill may need social skills training in addition to or instead of CBGT.

Potential Group Members on Anxiolytic Medication

Anxiolytic medication has been prescribed for many social phobics to help control their social anxiety. Ideally, they should withdraw from medication under a physician's supervision before beginning CBGT. After all, if the medication were effective and they wanted to continue taking it, they would not be seeking further treatment. However, the medication may be the only tool they have had for many years and it is not unreasonable for potential group members to resist discontinuing its use. A reasonable compromise is to stabilize the dosage before starting treatment and defer further discussion until later. As the individuals improve in treatment, they may stop taking the medication on their own, or a specific plan for withdrawal can be developed after treatment. Such a plan would include monitoring to avoid possible relapse as the individuals withdraw from medication. Individuals who take the medication on an "as needed" basis should be asked to refrain from taking it before group sessions or exposure homework assignments.

Assessment

In addition to the assessment described below as part of the treatment orientation interview, most clinicians want further assessment data that will serve as a baseline for measurement of treatment progress. Most commonly, this assessment consists of self-report questionnaires and measures derived from a naturalistic or role-played sample of behavior. Selected measures will be mentioned briefly but interested readers should refer to Arnkoff and Glass (1989) and Glass and Arnkoff (1989).

Self-Report Questionnaires

A number of questionnaires are frequently used to assess social anxiety and avoidance. The Social Avoidance and Distress Scale (SADS; Watson & Friend, 1969) and Fear of Negative Evaluation Scale (FNE; Watson & Friend, 1969) have been used for many years. The SADS is a 28-item true–false scale that assesses anxiety in and avoidance of a variety of performance situations and social interactions. The FNE is a 30-item scale that assesses concern about being evaluated negatively by others, a core aspect of social phobia. The original FNE contained numerous redundant items and a brief version that utilizes a Likert-type response format has been developed (Leary, 1983). Turner, McCanna, and Beidel (1987) argued that the SADS and the FNE assess general distress rather than social anxiety because individuals with anxiety disorders other than social phobia also have elevated SADS and FNE scores. However, this may reflect the pervasiveness of social anxiety across the anxiety and mood disorders (Heimberg, Hope, Rapee, & Bruch, 1988).

Unfortunately, the SADS and FNE were developed with college students rather than clinical samples of social phobics, in contrast to four self-report scales developed more recently. The Social Phobia and Anxiety Inventory (SPAI; Turner, Beidel, Dancu, & Stanley, 1989) consists of 45 items (32 on the SPAI Social Phobia scale; 13 on the

SPAI Agoraphobia scale) that assess verbal, behavioral, and physiological responses across a variety of situations. The situational focus of the items can make it a particularly useful measure for treatment planning. Mattick and Clarke (1989) wrote two separate 20-item scales for anxiety in social interactions (Social Interaction Anxiety Scale [SIAS]) and anxiety while being observed (Social Phobia Scale [SPS]). These scales cover a broad range of situations and address the issue of social phobia subtypes not covered by other scales. Heimberg, Mueller, Holt, Hope, and Liebowitz (1992) reported data supporting the use of the SIAS and SPS with social phobics as well as mean scores for two social phobia subtypes and community and college samples. Finally, Marks and Mathews's (1979) Fear Questionnaire (FQ) contains a Social Phobia scale as well as Agoraphobia and Blood–Injury Phobia scales. Clients are asked to rate their level of avoidance for five social phobic situations. This scale makes a useful adjunct if scores on the other two subscales are also of interest to the clinician.

Self-Monitoring

In order to build a better picture of a social phobic's experience of anxiety in his/ her daily life, the client can be asked to self-monitor the occurrence of anxiety and avoidance behavior on a daily basis. Complex self-monitoring reduces compliance, but most clients can easily track anxiety and performance quality ratings for naturally occurring situations on a daily basis. This information may be useful for planning homework assignments during CBGT, so self-monitoring should be continued throughout treatment if possible.

Behavioral Assessment

Research settings typically employ one or more behavioral tests as part of pretreatment assessment. Although these may be more difficult to conduct in nonresearch settings, limited versions are usually feasible. Typically, the client is asked to enact one or more situations that generate moderately high to high anxiety. The clinician asks for anxiety ratings before, at several points during, and after the role play. Other measures, such as asking clients to rate the quality of their performance or to list the thoughts they had during the role play, are also easily incorporated. Affordable ambulatory physiological equipment, particularly pulse monitors, are increasingly available and should be used if possible. Heart rate monitoring is of particular use with public speaking phobics who may demonstrate excessive cardiac arousal (Heimberg, Hope, Dodge, & Becker, 1990). The clinician can choose to test the limits of the client's ability to perform when anxious by asking him/her to remain in the situation for a certain period of time (typically 4–5 min). On the other hand, the clinician may give the client explicit permission to stop when the anxiety is excessive, and latency to escape the situation becomes an additional measure of social phobic avoidance. If the latter strategy is used in assessment, it should be made clear that this will not be the approach taken in treatment when the client will be expected to stay in the situation until instructed otherwise by the therapist(s).

In addition to or in place of structured behavioral tests, the clinician may have numerous opportunities to observe the client interact with others. These include interactions with the therapist, with receptionists or other clerical staff in the office, and later, when treatment has started, with other group members. Usually, *in vivo* observation is far too intrusive for the type of situations social phobics fear, but occasionally it is feasible. For example, a client can make conversation with a salesclerk while purchasing a pack of chewing gum, and the clinician may observe from a discrete distance. The client can provide many of the ratings described above for these situations as well.

Overview of CBGT Activities

Treatment Orientation Interview

Once the clinician has done enough assessment to determine the diagnosis and the potential group member's appropriateness for treatment, as described above, the treatment orientation interview should be completed by one or both of the therapists for the group. This interview has four primary purposes. First, it introduces the therapist(s) and client to each other if this has not already happened and allows the therapist to preview the nature of the group treatment for the client. Second, the therapist teaches the client how to use the Subjective Units of Discomfort Scale (SUDS; Wolpe & Lazarus, 1966). Third, a fear and avoidance hierarchy is constructed. Finally, the therapist(s) and client develop an explicit treatment contract. Each of these is described in turn.

Treatment Preview

CBGT requires substantial energy and commitment on the part of the client and, consequently, potential group members need to be apprised of what treatment will involve. The therapist should outline the cognitive-behavioral model of social phobia in understandable terms and explain how confronting one's fears is essential to overcoming them. Furthermore, the role of cognitive intervention in helping group members benefit from the exposure and cope with their anxiety should be emphasized. At this point, many social phobics say that they have tried exposure on their own and it did not work. Typically, their attempts were not systematic and their distorted cognitive processing prevented them from taking credit for any success they may have had. Many potential group members are alarmed at the prospect of *group* treatment. This can be overcome by outlining the advantages of group treatment described above. Extensive "selling" of the group should be avoided, but the therapist should be enthusiastic and instill some hope that the person will be able to make significant changes as a result of the treatment.

SUDS Training

SUDS ratings are used throughout the course of treatment, so it is worthwhile to spend some time making them more valid and reliable. First, the therapist should explain that SUDS is a 0–100 scale with greater numbers indicating greater distress. Anchor points are developed at 25 (mild anxiety), 50 (moderate anxiety, beginning to have difficulty concentrating), 75 (high anxiety, thoughts of escaping), and 100 (worst anxiety he/she has experienced or can imagine experiencing) by asking the client to report specific situations in which he/she experienced that level of anxiety. Later in treatment if the client's ratings seem to be drifting and/or he/she is only using a portion of the scale, the therapist can refer back to the original anchor points.

Fear and Avoidance Hierarchy

The bulk of the treatment orientation interview is spent developing an individualized fear and avoidance hierarchy. A completed hierarchy (see Table 3.1) will have 10 rank-ordered situations rated for fear, avoidance, and fear of negative evaluation by others. It is easiest first to have the client brainstorm potential hierarchy items and then to rank order and rate them. The hierarchy should contain representative situations that are important to the client and his/her functioning. Often a situation will appear twice on the hierarchy, as in Table 3.1, and differ on some dimension such as the number or familiarity of other people present (for further discussion of this point, see Hope, 1993). The hierarchy is utilized

---

TABLE 3.1. Sample Fear and Avoidance Hierarchy

My worst fear is:
Being on a date with someone I don't know very well—having dinner

My 2nd worst fear is:
Same as my worst fear but at a movie

My 3rd worst fear is:
Talking to a professor

My 4th worst fear is:
Having a casual conversation with an unfamiliar guy

My 5th worst fear is:
Attending a party where I don't know the other guests very well

My 6th worst fear is:
Asking a question in class

My 7th worst fear is:
Having a casual conversation with an unfamiliar woman

My 8th worst fear is:
Answering a question in class

My 9th worst fear is:
Talking to an unfamiliar person on the phone

My 10th worst fear is:
Attending a family gathering at a relative's house

---

throughout treatment as therapists determine the nature and order of therapeutic exposures.

Treatment Contract

As has been repeatedly discussed, social phobics often fear and avoid a variety of situations, usually more than can be realistically addressed in 12 weeks of treatment. Therefore it is important to agree on the two or three situations that will be the primary focus of treatment. The therapist should help pick reasonable goals, but, ultimately, it is the individual's decision about what is important to him/her that determines treatment targets. Fear and avoidance in other situations will likely improve also, particularly if the client makes an effort to apply the skills learned in treatment to those situations as well.

Sessions 1 and 2

The first two sessions of CBGT are devoted to setting the stage for treatment and training clients in the fundamental skills of cognitive restructuring. This allows group members to become more comfortable in the group setting, to develop some group cohesion, and to gain an elementary understanding of cognitive restructuring before engaging in therapeutic exposure. It should be noted that many of the procedures in the first two sessions are derived from Sank and Shaffer (1984) and all therapeutic procedures in CBGT are described in more detail in Heimberg (1991).

All sessions begin with clients completing the Beck Depression Inventory (BDI; Beck, Ward, Mendelson, Mock, & Erbaugh, 1961). This allows the therapists to track each group member's affective state from week to week, particularly when a group member may be too uncomfortable to discuss his/her distress in group. Leary's brief FNE (1983), with rewritten instructions to reflect the past week, can be used in addition to monitor group members' progress on this important construct. After the first week when the questionnaires are explained, they can be made available ahead of time and group members can complete them while waiting for group to start. Therapists should review them briefly before starting group

TABLE 3.2. Outline of CBGT Procedures for Session 1

1. Complete BDI and any other optional questionnaire(s).
2. Make introductions.
3. Review basic ground rules [therapists].
4. Share social fears and goals for treatment [each member].
5. Describe cognitive-behavioral model for social phobia and rationale for treatment [therapists].
6. Provide initial training in cognitive restructuring.
   a. Exercise 1: Therapist relates personal situation.
   b. Exercise 2: Group members share ATs regarding coming to group for the first time.
7. Assign homework.

Note. BDI, Beck Depression Inventory; AT, automatic thought.

and discuss any notable changes, either during the session or individually afterwards.

Session 1

Table 3.2 contains an outline of the tasks for the first session. After explaining and completing questionnaires, the therapists and then each group member briefly introduce themselves, stating their name and one or two things about themselves. The therapists then take turns outlining basic issues related to the importance of attendance, participation, homework completion, and confidentiality. It is helpful to have group members and therapists sign an informal contract asserting that each promises to maintain confidentiality.

After these housekeeping details, each member shares briefly their social fears and goals for treatment. The therapists assist more reticent individuals to speak and draw out similarities between group members (similar feared situations or similar anxiety symptoms). This helps build group cohesion as group members discover others have similar concerns.

The major portion of the first session is devoted to discussing a cognitive-behavioral model for social phobia (Beck & Emery, 1985). This will be a more extended version of what members heard in the treatment orientation interview. The model offers a common understanding and language in which to discuss social phobia and promotes

a rationale for the treatment. Social phobia is described as a learned response with interactive physiological, behavioral (avoidance and performance disruption), and cognitive components. The cognitive components emphasize the role of automatic thoughts (ATs) in heightening and maintaining anxiety. The three primary components of treatment, role-played exposure in the group, cognitive restructuring, and homework for *in vivo* exposure, are described in the context of the model.

The final portion of the first session is devoted to training in cognitive restructuring. Two exercises center on the process of identifying ATs and previewing strategies to confront them that will be taught in the second session. In the first exercise, one of the therapists utilizes a personal situation and lists his/her ATs encountered in that situation on the easel. The therapists provide group members with a list of questions to use in confronting these ATs and encourage them to identify the irrationality in the ATs. The therapists and the group then generate positive rebuttals to the ATs. This exercise allows group members to see how the cognitive techniques work without having to confront the idea that their own ATs may be irrational. In the second exercise, group members report the ATs they had about coming to group while one of the therapists records them on the easel. The session ends with the two therapists gently challenging these ATs: One therapist plays the irrational AT and the other plays a logical, rational point of view.

Homework for Session 1 consists of recording two or three anxiety-provoking situations during the week and listing several ATs for each one. This gives the group members their first opportunity to monitor their ATs on their own.

Session 2

Following completion of the questionnaire(s), the group reviews the previous week's homework (see Table 3.3). Two or three ATs from each group member are recorded on the easel for later exercises. Next, the therapists distribute a list of cognitive distortions based on the work of Burns (1980) and Persons (1989). Each cognitive distortion, or logical error in think-

TABLE 3.3. Outline of CBGT for Session 2

1. Complete BDI and any other optional questionnaire(s).

2. Review homework from previous week.

3. Continue training in cognitive restructuring.
   a. Therapists introduce concept of "cognitive distortion."
   b. Exercise 3: Group identifies distortions in ATs from homework.
   c. Therapists introduce dispute handles and rational responses.
   d. Exercise 4: Imaginal scenario.
   e. Exercise 5: Group challenges ATs from homework and develops rational responses.

4. Assign homework.

Note. BDI, Beck Depression Inventory; AT, automatic thought.

ing, is described briefly. Then the entire group helps identify the distortion in each AT recorded during the review of homework.

The next step in cognitive restructuring is to challenge the ATs and develop rational responses or rebuttals. This is done with the assistance of Sank and Shaffer's (1984) "dispute handles." The dispute handles are generic questions (e.g., "Do I know for certain that _____ will happen?") that can be applied to ATs. The answers to the questions consolidate into one or two rational responses. Before attempting this procedure on their own thoughts from homework, however, the therapists describe a scenario (e.g., being called into the boss's office) in which most people are likely to experience anxiety. ATs generated by the imagined scenario are then listed on the easel. Together the group members identify the cognitive distortion in each AT, question it using the dispute handles, and answer the dispute handle questions to form rational responses. Once group members understand the basic procedure, the group returns to the ATs from homework and challenges them.

Homework for Session 2 involves recording ATs from anxiety-provoking situations as in the previous week, but then identifying the cognitive distortions, questioning the ATs, and developing rational responses. Thus group members enter Session 3 and their first simulated exposures with substan-

tial practice in the logistics of the cognitive techniques.

Sessions 3–11

Sessions 3 through 11 follow a similar format as outlined in Table 3.4. After completion of the questionnaire(s), homework from the previous week is reviewed. For the majority of the session, group members take turns completing role-played exposures. The therapists meet between sessions and plan a role-played exposure for each group member and the order in which they should be completed. If members are unexpectedly absent, plans are in place for someone else. Typically three exposures are completed during each session, allowing an exposure every other session for every participant in a six-member group. Each session ends with homework assignments for the next week. These consist of *in vivo* exposure tasks once the client has completed his/her first in-session exposure. Until then, the client continues the cognitive homework from the second session.

Designing Exposures

The simulated exposures consist of role plays of anxiety-provoking situations. The therapists, other group members, and, later

TABLE 3.4. Outline of CBGT for Sessions 3–11

1. Complete BDI and any other optional questionnaire(s).

2. Review homework from previous week.

3. Complete three in-session exposures.
   a. Select target group member and briefly outline exposure situation.
   b. Elicit ATs.
   c. Pick one or two thoughts to pursue further.
   d. Label cognitive distortion(s) in selected AT(s).
   e. Challenge selected AT(s) using the dispute handles.
   f. Develop one or two rational responses.
   g. Develop details of the exposure situation.
   h. Set a nonperfectionistic, behavioral goal.
   i. Complete role play.
   j. Debrief exposure.
      1. Review goal attainment.
      2. Other activities as appropriate.

4. Assign homework.

Note. BDI, Beck Depression Inventory; AT, automatic thought.

in treatment, outside personnel serve as role-play partners. The exposure situations are individualized and range from having a conversation with an unfamiliar person to giving a presentation at a staff meeting. The first exposure should be of a situation to which the client assigns a SUDS rating of at least 50, with successive exposures moving up the hierarchy as quickly as the client can tolerate. In selecting situations, it is important to consider that each group member will have approximately six in-session exposures over the course of treatment.

The exposures are made as realistic as possible by rearranging furniture, using props, and instructing role-play partners to behave in particular ways. A bit of effort in making the situation more realistic can be the difference between an exposure that elicits significant anxiety and one that is too artificial to be relevant. Commonly used props include food or drink for individuals with fears of eating, drinking, or serving food in front of others and client-prepared notes for presentations. Careful attention should be paid to aspects of the situation that make it more or less anxiety provoking. For example, a public speaking phobic may be more anxious standing, speaking from notes with questions from the audience, compared to sitting, giving an unprepared talk to a silent audience. See the case presentation described later for further considerations when designing exposures.

Integrating Cognitive Restructuring and Exposure

The essence of CBGT is the coordination between the cognitive tasks and the exposure. As is evident in the case presentation and outlined in Table 3.4, this coordination is achieved by interweaving the cognitive and exposure activities as was first practiced in the exercises in Session 2. After selecting the group member for the next exposure, one therapist sketches the situation in three or four sentences. This therapist then elicits ATs regarding the situation from the target group member while the second therapist records the thoughts on the easel. Once the most important thoughts have been identified, the therapist picks one or two thoughts for further attention. The selected AT(s) should contain an obvious

cognitive distortion, be important to the individual's experience of anxiety in the situation, and be reasonably challenged in the time available for discussion and exposure. The entire group helps label the cognitive distortion(s), challenge the thought with the dispute handles, and develop rational responses. Early in treatment the therapists must take primary responsibility for this process, modeling a Socratic approach. However, as treatment progresses, the group members should increasingly be able to confront their own and others' ATs. Once a rational response is developed, it is written on the easel within view of the target client during the simulated exposure.

After the initial cognitive work is done, the details of the exposure are discussed. The target member assists by providing necessary details such as the setting in which the activity would likely take place and the expected behavior of the interaction partners. Next a nonperfectionistic, behavioral goal for the exposure is set. This often requires some negotiation as social phobics tend to desire unrealistic or unmeasurable goals (e.g., "I won't get anxious" or "I won't stumble over my words at all").

During the exposure itself, one of the therapists requests SUDS ratings at 1-min intervals and whenever anxiety appears to decrease. At each SUDS prompt, the target member also reads his or her rational response (written on the easel) aloud. Clients quickly adjust to this disruption, particularly if the role player(s) help reorient them with a verbal cue (e.g., "You were talking about . . ."). The exposure should continue until anxiety has begun to decrease or plateau and the goal has been met, typically 5–10 min.

Debriefing the exposure includes a review of goal attainment, a discussion of the use of the rational response, and identification of any unexpected ATs that should be addressed in the future. It may also be useful to review the pattern SUDS ratings given by the target client or to have group members give their impressions of his/her performance. One primary goal of the debriefing is to identify which thoughts make anxiety increase (irrational thoughts) and decrease (rational thoughts). Finally, the rest of the group congratulates the target member for his/her courage at facing the feared situation and the procedure begins again with the next person.

Session 12

The first half of the last session progresses similarly to the previous nine sessions (see Table 3.4). The second half is devoted to reviewing group members' progress in the group, identifying important rational responses they will want to continue to use, and setting goals for continued work on their own after treatment. The session concludes with a brief social time with refreshments to allow members to say good-bye and to close the group on a pleasant note.

Case Presentation

In order to illustrate more clearly how CBGT is implemented, an example of a typical case is presented. First, some background on the case is given, followed by data from the pretreatment assessment. Then a description of the client's progress through the 12 therapy sessions provides a detailed account of the integration of cognitive restructuring with exposures in session and during homework assignments. Finally, data from the 6-month follow-up assessment and an informal update from 1 year posttreatment are described.

"Kathy" was a 19-year-old woman who was completing her first year of college when she sought treatment for her social phobia. She was the youngest of three children and lived at home with her parents who were in their middle 50s. She reported the onset of her fear at age 15, denying any difficulties socializing in elementary school or junior high. Kathy reported that she rarely consumed alcohol and had never used illegal drugs. She attended a small local college where the majority of students commuted. This made it particularly difficult to make friends as there was little campus social life. It later became evident that she had selected this particular school in part because of the limited social demands.

Kathy's social fears inhibited her life in a number of ways. She had virtually no close friends and would typically spend an entire semester in a class without learning the names of any of her classmates. She had had only two dates, both of which she described as "disastrous" due to her severe fear. Kathy was somewhat more confident in academic situations, occasionally asking and answering questions in class and meeting with instructors individually, although usually with significant distress. She also expressed concern that she would limit her career choices to jobs that required little interpersonal interaction. In fact, she had never found a summer job on her own because she was anxious about interviewing and meeting strangers.

Kathy's treatment group began in late summer when she had a part-time clerical job in a relative's small business. This job offered her primary opportunity for social interaction outside her family during the summer. Once classes resumed in the fall, there were further opportunities to interact with peers.

Pretreatment Assessment

Kathy received treatment as part of a series of ongoing studies evaluating the efficacy of CBGT. As part of the standard pretreatment assessment, Kathy was interviewed with the Anxiety Disorders Interview Schedule—Revised (ADIS–R; DiNardo & Barlow, 1988). The ADIS–R is a semistructured diagnostic interview for DSM-III-R that yields a 0–8 global rating of clinical severity (clinician's severity rating [CSR]) as well as diagnostic information. Kathy received a primary diagnosis of social phobia, generalized subtype with a CSR of 5, indicating that the severity of her symptoms and impairment in functioning were moderate. A severity rating of 4 or greater was required for participation in the treatment study.

During the CBGT treatment orientation interview described above, Kathy completed a fear and avoidance hierarchy with one of her group therapists. (See Table 3.5.) Situations were rank-ordered from the most difficult (being at dinner with a date) to least difficult (attending a family gathering at a relative's house). After developing the hierarchy of situations, Kathy rated each situation on three 0–100 scales (higher numbers indicate greater severity): how fearful she became or would become in the situation, how likely she was to avoid the situation, and how concerned she was about being negatively evaluated by others in the situation (pretreatment ratings appear in Table 3.5). During the interview, Kathy and the therapist agreed that reducing her fear when socializing with peers would be her primary treatment goal.

Kathy also completed a battery of questionnaires and an individualized behavioral test. The questionnaire battery included the BDI (Beck et al., 1961), Watson and Friend's (1969) SADS and FNE and Marks and Mathews's (1979) FQ. The BDI is a commonly used measure of self-reported depression with a possible range of scores from 0 to 63. Kathy's score of 13 on the BDI is typical of social phobics in our treatment pro-

gram (Elting, Hope, & Heimberg, 1992). Kathy scored a 21 on the SADS. Possible scores range from 0 to 28, with social phobics typically scoring around 20 (Elting et al., 1992). Kathy achieved the maximum score of 30 on the FNE, a feat not uncommon among social phobics who average 24.2 on this measure (Elting et al., 1992). In order to understand the severity of Kathy's fears, unscreened samples of college undergraduates typically scored less than 10 on both the FNE ($M = 9.11$, $SD = 8.01$) and SADS ($M = 6.68$, $SD = 5.53$) (Heimberg, 1988).

In the individualized behavioral test, clients are asked to role play an anxiety-pro-

TABLE 3.5. Kathy's Fear and Avoidance Hierarchy at Pretreatment, Posttreatment, and 6-Month Follow-up

Situation	Assessment point	Fear	Avoidance	Evaluation
My worst fear is:	Pretest	80	75	90
Being on a date with someone I don't know	Posttest	90	70	80
very well—having dinner	Follow-up	70	40	70
My 2nd worst fear is:	Pretest	70	70	90
Same as my worst fear but at a movie	Posttest	80	60	70
	Follow-up	50	40	70
My 3rd worst fear is:	Pretest	60	50	70
Talking to a professor	Posttest	50	40	60
	Follow-up	30	25	50
My 4th worst fear is:	Pretest	60	60	70
Having a casual conversation with an	Posttest	50	50	60
unfamiliar guy	Follow-up	30	20	25
My 5th worst fear is:	Pretest	50	50	60
Attending a party where I don't know the	Posttest	50	30	50
other guests very well	Follow-up	30	25	40
My 6th worst fear is:	Pretest	50	60	50
Asking a question in class	Posttest	30	25	40
	Follow-up	25	20	25
My 7th worst fear is:	Pretest	40	30	40
Having a casual conversation with an	Posttest	25	20	25
unfamiliar woman	Follow-up	10	10	20
My 8th worst fear is:	Pretest	30	25	40
Answering a question in class	Posttest	25	20	25
	Follow-up	10	10	20
My 9th worst fear is:	Pretest	30	20	20
Talking to an unfamiliar person on the	Posttest	10	10	20
phone	Follow-up	0	0	10
My 10th worst fear is:	Pretest	25	20	25
Attending a family gathering at a relative's	Posttest	10	10	20
house	Follow-up	10	0	10

Note. Ratings are of fear, avoidance, and fear of negative evaluation by others. All ratings are on 0–100 scales with higher numbers signifying greater fear or more extensive avoidance.

voking situation that they rate as at least a 75 on the 0–100 SUDS. Although clients are made aware of the general nature of the behavioral test as part of informed consent, they are unaware of the specific situation they will enact until the test begins. The particular version of the behavioral test that Kathy completed included three phases, the first two of which are presented here: 3-min anticipatory phase in which clients are asked to imagine themselves in the role-play situation described by the experimenter and a 4-min performance phase in which they enact the role play with a trained research assistant. During each phase, clients are prompted for minute-by-minute SUDS ratings. After the performance phase, they complete several measures about their experience including two 0–100 ratings of peak anxiety experienced during the role play and overall performance quality (higher ratings are associated with more anxiety and better performance).

The situation Kathy enacted for her behavioral test was a conversation with a male student while waiting for one of her college classes to start. The research assistant played the role of someone whom she had seen in class but with whom she had never conversed. Her anxiety started at a moderate level of 45, increased throughout the anticipatory phase and the 1st min of the performance phase, finally leveling off at 80, indicating high anxiety. Kathy became tearful when her anxiety reached 80 and the confederate was forced to carry the bulk of the conversation, with only nods and monosyllabic responses from Kathy. Kathy rated her peak anxiety level during the behavioral test as 80 and the quality of her performance as 30, a relatively poor rating.

Course of Treatment

Sessions 1 and 2

As described above, the first two sessions of CBGT are devoted to laying the groundwork for the group, building group cohesion, educating members about the cognitive-behavioral model of social phobia, and beginning training on the cognitive restructuring skills. Kathy participated in the discussions in response to direct questions but made few spontaneous comments. During the course of the cognitive exercises, it became apparent that Kathy's automatic thoughts were characterized by three primary cognitive distortions (Burns, 1980): fortune telling (e.g., "I won't be able to keep the conversation going"; "I'll get anxious"; "I'll get teary"), mind reading ("They won't like me"; "He'll think I'm weird because I look so anxious") and all-or-nothing thinking ("I don't know how to talk to people [perfectly]." "I'll get so nervous I won't be able to go on"). By the time she had completed the homework assignment for the second session, it was apparent from Kathy's written work that she had a solid basic understanding of the mechanics of the cognitive skills and was able to identify, analyze, and dispute many of her ATs. As with most group members, she remained somewhat skeptical about the utility of the cognitive procedures and had little faith in the veracity of the rational responses to her ATs at this early point in treatment.

Session 3

In the third session, two of Kathy's fellow group members completed their first role-played exposures. Kathy was not selected to be one of the first individuals to engage in an exposure because of her relatively poor performance during the pretreatment behavioral test. It seemed likely that she would become tearful or speak very little and such an experience would heighten the group's anxiety as they saw their worst fears becoming reality. Furthermore, by waiting an extra session, the therapists hoped that Kathy would become more comfortable in the group and thus begin the exposure from a lower baseline anxiety level. Her homework for Session 3 was to continue practicing the cognitive skills by analyzing the ATs generated by a naturally occurring anxiety-provoking situation during the upcoming week.

Session 4

Kathy's first exposure occurred in Session 4. In order to ensure that Kathy's first exposure was a success, the therapists decided that she would enact a conversation with two unfamiliar women. She rated talking with one unfamiliar woman as a 50 on her hierarchy and indicated that talking with two women would be easier because there would be less pressure to talk. One of the therapists and a high-functioning group member who had already completed her first exposure served as role-play partners. The following are excerpts from the cognitive restructuring prior to the exposure between Kathy (K), the therapists (T1, T2) and group members (M1, M2, . . .).

T2: Alright Kathy, now it's your turn for an exposure.

K: (*Sigh*) OK. I was afraid of that.

T2: One of the situations you have described as hard is having conversations, particularly with people you don't know very well.

K: Right.

T2: What we thought we would have you do tonight is have a conversation with two women you don't know very well, maybe a couple of women who work in the office with you or something like that. Is that the kind of thing that would make you anxious?

K: Yes.

T2: OK. What I would like you to do is imagine yourself in that situation. Think about what it would be like if you were to have a conversation with a couple of your coworkers, maybe during a break or before work, sometime when it is OK to stand around and chat a bit. As you think about that situation, what thoughts come into your mind?

K: I worry about not knowing what to say.

T2: That's good. Let's phrase it as a statement so it will be easier to work with. How about, "I won't know what to say"? Does that sound right?

K: Yeah, that's it.

(*T1 writes "I won't know what to say" on the easel.*)

T2: What other automatic thoughts come into your mind as you imagine yourself talking with these two women?

K: I'll get anxious.

T2: That's a good one. (*to T1*) Write that one up there. What else?

K: I worry about crying if the conversation dies and it gets awkward. That might

not be so bad if there are two people though because they will probably just keep talking without me and I could make an excuse and slip away.

T2: What do you think, group? It sounds like there might be a couple of automatic thoughts in there. Can anyone spot them?

M1: She's worried about crying.

T2: Good. So "I'll cry" might be an automatic thought?

(*Several group members nod.*)

T2: What other ATs might be in there? Kathy says she worries about crying if the conversation dies and it gets awkward.

[With assistance, Kathy and the other group members identified two more ATs—"The conversation will die"; "It will be awkward." These thoughts are added to the list on the easel.]

T2: Alright, that looks like a good list. Let's pick one to focus on. "I'll get anxious" is probably true. [The therapists chose to ignore the all-or-nothing thinking inherent in this thought.] That's the whole reason you are here and part of what is supposed to happen in exposures is that you get anxious. It sounds like "I won't know what to say" is the start of a chain. "I won't know what to say so the conversation will die and it will be awkward." Is that what you are thinking, Kathy?

K: Yeah. When I get in these situations I just go blank. I don't know what to talk about.

T2: So it sounds like if we can work on not knowing what to say, that we can help keep this chain of thoughts from getting out of control and making you anxious. Does that make sense?

K: Um hmm.

T2: Let's look at "I won't know what to say." Take out your list of cognitive distortions and let's see where that thought might fit. Group, feel free to help Kathy out on this.

[Group members suggested several possible cognitive distortions including fortune telling and all-or-nothing thinking.]

T2: Now let's look at the dispute handles to see if there is any way to question this thought. Kathy, do you see any that might be helpful?

K: Do I know for certain I won't have anything to say?

T2: Good. How would you answer that question?

K: Well, I'm pretty sure. I usually have trouble in these kind of conversations.

T2: How about the third dispute handle on your list? Try that one.

K: Am I 100% sure I won't have anything to say?

T2: Are you *100%* sure you won't have *anything* to say?

K: Well, I'm pretty sure.

T2: 100%?

K: Probably not 100%. Maybe more like 90%.

T2: So you are 90% sure you won't have *anything* to say, absolutely nothing. You will open your mouth and nothing will come out.

K: Well, no. I can say *something*, it just won't be very good.

T2: Alright. How likely is it that you won't have anything to say, not even something that isn't very good?

K: That's pretty unlikely. I suppose I can almost always say something stupid. Maybe it's about 10%.

T2: So there's at least a 90% chance you can say something, although it might not be exactly perfect?

K: Um hmm.

T2: For right now, let's not worry about you saying something perfect, let's just focus on getting something out. We'll worry about how good it is later. Group, can you help Kathy turn this idea about having something to say into a rational response she can use in the situation?

M3: How about "There's a 90% chance you can say something, even if it's stupid."

T2: That's a good start. Can we make it a little more positive?

K: There's a good chance I can think of something to say.

T2: That sounds good. We'll write that up on the easel to help you remember it. During the exposure when you start worrying about running out of things to say, repeat this rational response to yourself—There's a good chance I can think of something to say. Hopefully, that will help you calm down enough so you can get something out. Remember, we are going to worry about the quality of what you say later. Now just focus on being able to say *something*.

The therapists selected that particular AT for a first exposure because it was straightforward and relatively simple to challenge. At this point, they simply wanted to get Kathy through a relatively quick phase of cognitive restructuring because the longer the exposure was delayed, the more anxious she would get. The next step was to set up the exposure. At this point, the details of the situation were worked out, role players were selected and instructed in their roles, and the necessary seating rearrangement was completed. This interaction proceeded as follows:

T2: Now let's set up the situation for the exposure. Kathy, if you were going to have a conversation with a couple of the women at work, where would that likely happen?

K: Sometimes the people hang out in the room where the coffee machine and refrigerator are. There's a little table where the secretaries usually sit and talk on break.

T2: That's sounds perfect. If we set this up so that a couple of the women were in there talking, you could go up and join them. Would that be fairly realistic?

K: Yes.

T2: Let's use that then. T1, you will be one of the people and (*turning to another group member*) would you help us out and be the other person?

M4: OK. What do I have to do?

T2: T1 and you will be sitting there talking. Since you haven't done this before, you can let T1 take the lead and you can follow her cue. Why don't you both sit on the couch and we'll pull the other chair over for Kathy. Kathy, you would probably be most likely to talk with a couple of the secretaries, right?

K: Um hmm.

T2: So both of you will be secretaries in this office and Kathy will come up and join the conversation. Before we start, however, we have to come up with a goal so we will know if the experience is a success. What do you want to set for a goal, Kathy?

K: I don't want to get anxious.

T2: As we said last week, that's a good goal for the end of treatment. I'm not sure it is reasonable to expect yourself not to get anxious when that is the whole reason you came to group. How about a smaller goal for this time? Maybe something similar to what some of the other folks used last week for their exposures?

K: I am worried about just getting through. Even right now I just want to leave and skip the whole thing.

T2: That sounds like there might be a goal there. How about just staying in the situation until we stop it?

K: I think I can do that.

T2: Let's get going then. Kathy, remember I will be interrupting you periodically and asking for SUDS ratings. When I do that, just give me a number, read your rational response aloud off the easel, and go right back to the conversation. Ready?

The first therapist and the other group member began talking about upcoming weekend plans and after a couple of exchanges, Kathy joined the conversation. Initially, the therapist asked some questions to help Kathy get started and helped carry the conversation because Kathy appeared quite anxious and teary. However, after 3 to 4 min she became less anxious and initiated a couple of questions on her own. The therapists let the exposure continue for 10 min to let Kathy experience several minutes in which she was functioning at a more appropriate level, gaining confidence after a somewhat rocky start.

After the exposure, the therapists explored Kathy's perceptions of her performance, how successful she was at using the rational response, and any ATs that occurred.

T2: So how did you do?

K: Awful. I was really anxious!

T1: Did you meet your goal?

K: No, it was harder than I expected.

T1: What was your goal? Group, do you remember?

M3: To stay in the situation until the end.

T2: Right, did you do that, Kathy? Did you hang in there until the end?

K: (*Grudgingly*) I guess so.

The therapists encourage other group members to give Kathy feedback on achievement of her goal. Several commented that she stayed despite being very anxious, especially at first. Kathy finally conceded that she met her goal.

T2: How about that automatic thought we were working on? Did you worry about having something to say?

K: Yes. Especially at the beginning, I felt like my mind was totally blank.

T2: Did the rational response help at all?

K: Probably a little bit. A couple of times I just tried to get something out even though it sounded pretty stupid.

T2: Let's come back to what you said in a minute. Did your rational response turn out to be true? Were to able to think of *something* to say, even when you were the most anxious?

K: Yes. I came up with something. I guess it isn't that likely that I can't at least get something out.

T1: Exactly. Now I'm curious, which part did you think sounded stupid?

K: At the beginning when you asked me the question about what I was going to do this week, I said something about just staying home.

T1: As the person in the role play, it seemed reasonable to me. What did the rest of you think?

[Several group members concurred that none of her responses sounded stupid to them.]

T2: It sounds like the group has a more positive opinion of how you did than you do, Kathy. Let's remember that. Next time we'll come back to that thought about sounding stupid and see what kind of evidence you have for it. Now we'll let you off the hot seat. Congratulations on surviving your first exposure!

Kathy's homework for Session 3 was to initiate conversation with someone at work at least twice during the upcoming week. A conversation was defined as a greeting and two to three further exchanges. On her homework sheet Kathy was also reminded to sit down before going to work and develop rational responses for likely ATs, to use her rational responses as best she could during the conversations, and to repeat the cognitive procedures after the conversations had occurred. Review of the homework at the beginning of Session 4 revealed that she had completed the homework as assigned (two conversations), with moderate anxiety levels.

Session 5

Other group members were the target of exposures during the fifth session. Kathy served as an audience member for one public speaking exposure. She also contributed to the cognitive restructuring efforts of other group members. The latter, however, was only in response to direct questions. She made few spontaneous comments during the session. When the time came to assign homework for the upcoming week, Kathy indicated that she and her parents were going to New York City for a long weekend. Her homework was to initiate a conversation with someone who worked in the hotel and to practice her cognitive skills as described for the previous session. The next week Kathy reported great success with the behavioral portion of this assignment. She had taken several opportunities to speak with various people at the hotel, restaurants, and attractions they had visited. Although she reported moderate anxiety, she was pleased with her efforts. Other group members and the therapists offered positive support for her success. The therapists spent a few minutes helping her think about what she had learned about her anxiety from the experience.

Session 6

Because another group member's exposure ran longer than expected, Kathy did not complete an exposure during the sixth session. As during Session 5, the therapists encouraged her to participate in the cognitive work of other group members. Kathy reported that fall semester classes would start the following week. Since Kathy's primary concern involved improving socialization with peers, the therapists questioned her on any contact she would have with peers in the upcoming week. She indicated that she would probably spend at least a couple of hours standing in line buying books, paying fees, and so on. Typically, she took along a novel to read while standing in line to avoid having to interact with anyone. She agreed to initiate at least one conversation with someone standing near her for her homework assignment. The therapists emphasized the importance of using the cognitive restructuring procedures around this *in vivo* exposure. During Session 7, Kathy reported that she had spoken intermittently with the woman standing in line in front of her at the bookstore with only mild anxiety.

Session 7

Kathy was scheduled for an exposure in Session 7. Given that she had returned to school, the therapists chose a situation that involved speaking with a woman from one of her classes. Since she still appeared quite uncomfortable being the center of attention in group sessions and reported only modest changes outside of group, one of the therapists was selected as the role-play partner. Kathy reported the following ATs in anticipation of the exposure:

1. "I won't be able to keep the conversation going."
2. "I won't know what to say."
3. "She won't want to talk with me."
4. "I'll cry."

Again, it appeared that concern about keeping the conversation going was the first link in a chain that ended up with tears and, consequently, rejection. The therapists decided to explore the first thought.

T1: Kathy, what do you mean that you won't be able to keep the conversation going?

K: Well, it will just die. I won't know what to say.

T1: This sounds like what we talked about a couple of sessions ago—that you worry about coming up with something to say.

K: Yeah, I guess you are right.

T1: Does anyone remember the rational response we came up with for that thought last time?

K: There's a good chance I can think of something to say.

T1: Good. In the last couple of weeks have you had any evidence that that statement might be true? Have you been able to come up with things to say in the conversations you have had?

K: Well, I did this week talking with the woman in the bookstore. But that was easy because we were both there for the same reason.

T2: Hold on a second, does anyone hear a cognitive distortion in that statement? (*looking at M4*)

M4: That's disqualifying the positive, saying that the conversation didn't count for some reason. [This client had made the same cognitive error earlier in the session.]

T2: Right. Do you see that Kathy? (*she nods*) So, what kind of evidence do you have that your rational response might be true?

K: I came up with something to say in the bookstore.

T1: Um hmm. Anything else?

[The group members and therapists listed several homework assignments and the last exposure in which she was able to think of things to say.]

T2: It sounds to me like you worry about having things to say but it really doesn't come true.

K: I guess so. I just feel a lot of pressure to keep the conversation going.

T2: Maybe there's an automatic thought in there. What do you think, Kathy?

K: I don't know.

T1: Maybe a "should" statement?

K: I "should" keep the conversation going?

T2: That sounds like a thought that might be a problem. Let's add it to the list on the easel. You said before that you worry about saying something stupid. Is it that you feel like you have to say something, no matter what, because you have to keep the conversation moving along?

K: Yeah, that sounds right.

Since the cognitive distortion has already been identified as a "should" statement, the therapists moved on to questioning the anxiety-provoking thought. After several exchanges, Kathy was able to accept that it was illogical for her to be 100% responsible for a dyadic conversation. This led to the following rational response: "I'm only responsible for 50% of the conversation." The therapists then proceeded to stage the exposure in which Kathy would initiate an interaction with a woman from her sociology class while they were waiting for class to begin. They set the goal of initiating the conversation and continuing to interact for a minimum of 4 min.

Kathy's SUDS ratings started out at 80 for the 1st min then increased to 90. Almost immediately she became teary and after about 2½ min it became apparent she was unable to continue. The therapists interrupted the role play, gave her a moment to compose herself, and then began to explore what was making her so anxious that she had begun to cry. She explained that she was afraid that her anxiety was making her role-play partner uncomfortable. This, in turn, increased her anxiety in a vicious cycle. This concept was developed as another "should" statement ("I should make the other person feel comfortable"), which appeared to reflect an underlying belief that Kathy should be an excellent conversationalist who rapidly put others at ease with her sensitivity, wit, and charm. The therapists and group members helped Kathy challenge that belief by arguing that she was accountable only for carrying her half of the conversation without being rude or insensitive and the other person was responsible for his/her own feelings. Kathy agreed that this was a standard she could achieve and developed a rational response—"I don't have to make the other person feel comfortable"—to remind her of that fact.

Since Kathy had not yet achieved her goal of conversing for 4 min, the therapists recommenced the exposure. Although her anxiety was high (SUDS = 90, 90, 80, 80, 80 across 4 min), she was able to keep her tears mostly in check and carry on a moderately appropriate conversation. Postexposure processing was kept to a minimum to avoid lengthening her ordeal. The group members and therapists applauded her courage and moved on to the next task.

Since Session 7 is the beginning of the second half of treatment, group members are encouraged to begin engaging in *in vivo* exposure every day. Thus each client receives two homework assignments—one small daily assignment and another larger assignment similar to those of earlier sessions. Kathy's daily assignment was to say hello and one other thing to someone with whom she would not normally talk each day. At least one of the days, the target of her efforts had to be male. The other assignment consisted of initiating a greeting and three exchanges with someone from one of her classes. Her report the following week indicated that she had successfully completed her larger assignment. Although her anxiety had been moderately high in anticipation of the conversation, it quickly fell once she had said hello and the other person made a friendly response. She reported daily conversations for 6 of 7 days.

Session 8

Kathy was scheduled for an exposure in Session 8 and the therapists decided to continue the same theme, particularly given the difficulty she had experienced the previous week. They hoped that by repeating the same situation, her performance would improve such that the role-play partner would be able to enact a less helpful, more realistic level of participation. This time the situation involved having a conversation with a same-age coworker and the second therapist assumed the coworker role. Kathy's thoughts were nearly identical to those reported previously. Rational responses from earlier sessions were recalled and appeared adequate.

The therapists were concerned about her crying during role plays. They had never explored this AT because it seemed to be a consequence of other thoughts and their experience suggested that it might be a realistic fear. Although many clients fear displaying such visible symptoms, rarely are the symptoms as visible or disruptive as they fear. From Kathy's description of her interactions outside of the group, it seemed unlikely that her conversations were plagued with tears. In fact, the therapists had begun to suspect that crying had become functional in that the hint of tears would get her out of being the center of attention. This discussion proceeded as follows:

T1: Kathy, let's look at that thought "I'm going to cry." How often do you cry when you get anxious?

K: I almost always cry when I get really upset.

T1: How about actually crying in the kind of situations that are a problem for you? How often do you cry then?

K: Oh, I worry about it, but I have only actually cried in here.

T1: So, most of the time you don't cry. You always worry about it but it only happens in group.

K: Yes.

The therapists then treated "I'm going to cry" as an example of fortune telling and assisted Kathy in developing a rational response ("98% of the time I don't get teary and it doesn't matter if I do in group"). This strategy allowed them to encourage her to use her rational response when tears became evident but otherwise ignore the crying behavior in group.

The goal for the exposure was the same as last session (keep the conversation going for 4 min). Although Kathy had tears running down her cheeks most of the role play, she was able to actively participate in the conversation for 6 min with decreasing anxiety ratings (SUDS = 80, 70, 60, 50, 40, 40, 30). In fact, Kathy spontaneously offered an informal invitation to see a movie together. In the postexposure processing it was apparent that the discussion of the crying had reduced its significance. Attention was then turned to her SUDS pattern.

T1: Let's look at your SUDS. You started at 80 and then moved down steadily to 30. What was happening as you started to feel more comfortable?

K: As the conversation got going, it seemed like we had some common interests. I realized that we both had plenty to say.

T1: So you were each able to hold up your 50% of the conversation?

K: Um hmm.

T1: So things went OK, even though you didn't take full responsibility for the conversation or for her feeling comfortable?

K: Yeah, I guess so.

T1: What does that tell you about those automatic thoughts "I should carry the conversation" and "I should make her feel comfortable."

K: I guess I only have to be responsible for me.

Kathy's homework assignment for Session 8 was to continue the daily conversations (at least once a week make it a heterosocial conversation) and to explore possible ways to meet people. She was to investigate what activities she could join at the college and to explore the feasibility of joining a health club (something she had been considering for several months). It was hoped that she could expand her social network with involvement in a structured activity. The next week she reported initiating a conversation each day and finding a health club for which her parents had agreed to fund the membership. There appeared to be very little available at the college given that most students came to campus only to attend class.

Session 9

Kathy was not scheduled for an exposure in Session 9. For her homework assignment

she was asked to invite a female coworker to do something with her. It could be an activity such as having lunch together during the week or something outside of work. The daily assignment of initiating conversations was continued. In Session 10, Kathy reported success 6 out of 7 days on the daily assignment but she failed to offer the invitation to the coworker. She had initiated the conversation but she did not know what to invite her to do.

Session 10

All of Kathy's exposures to date had involved interactions with women. Given that the end of treatment was rapidly approaching and Kathy's more severe fears involved dating and other heterosocial interactions, her next exposure involved a conversation with a male student in one of her classes. Since both therapists were women and the other male group members experienced heterosocial anxiety themselves, another graduate research assistant was brought into group to enact the role of the classmate.

Before bringing the outside role player into the group, the therapists assured the group that confidentiality extended to the research assistant. Prior to the group, the therapists met with him to describe the upcoming role play and to clarify the role he was to enact. The therapists explained that Kathy often became teary during role plays and that he should ignore her tears and help keep the conversation on track. If she became too distressed, the therapists would stop the role play, conduct some cognitive restructuring, and, after Kathy had composed herself, continue the role play.

During cognitive restructuring, Kathy reported two new ATs—"I can't talk to guys" and "He'll think I'm weird." It appeared that the second thought was a derivative of the first—the guys would think she was weird because she was unable to carry on a conversation. The therapists decided to focus on the first thought since its absolute nature implied that it could be easily debunked by the role play and yet, this thought likely played an important role in her avoidance of heterosocial conversations. Kathy was able to identify the thought as all-or-nothing thinking (seeing things in black-and-white extremes without shades of gray).

With further discussion of what Kathy meant by "can't talk," it became apparent that she did believe she would be unable to say more than a word or two. Although the therapists hypothesized that she might make little contribution to the conversation because she was afraid of not being the perfect conversationalist, at this point they focused on simply speaking. When questioned about what evidence she had to support her belief that she would say only one or two words in a heterosocial interaction, Kathy was unable to recall a conversation with a same-age male in which she had done more than return a greeting or answer a brief question. Her fears of being unable to speak had resulted in her taking no opportunities to test her assumption. By focusing on the unlikelihood that she would be absolutely silent and her recent successes in same-gender conversations, Kathy was about to develop "I can probably think of *something* to say" as her rational response. The therapists also encouraged her to use her rational responses from previous sessions. Because the setup for the exposure is slightly different with an outside role player, that portion of the session is recapped.

T2: Kathy, as we mentioned earlier, we are going to have one of the research assistants come in to help us out with the role play tonight. I would like to remind everyone that all of the rules about confidentiality extend to him. He will not share anything he sees or hears here with anyone else. Before he comes in, let's work out the details of the role play. Kathy, is there someone in one of your classes that you can imagine having a conversation with?

K: Well, I don't know. I never talk to any of the guys.

T2: How about someone who sits near you or someone you've seen in other classes?

K: There is one guy in my economics class who asked to borrow my notes when he missed class one time. I have never talked with him though.

T2: Did you loan him your notes?

K: Yeah.

T2: So you must have talked with him a little about loaning your notes.

K: Well, yeah, just showing which pages he should copy.

T2: He sounds like a good person for the role play. Do you know anything about him that would help our role player make it more realistic?

K: Not much. He's about my age. I don't think he is an economics major because he doesn't seem too interested in the class.

T2: That's good. Anything else?

K: I heard him say something to someone else once about working in the library.

T2: Alright. When would you be mostly likely to have an opportunity to talk with him? Before class? After class?

K: Before class, I guess. We both usually arrive a few minutes early.

T2: Let's set up the conversation before class then. We need to set a goal. Do you have any ideas for a goal, Kathy? Group, you can help her out here.

The group went on to help Kathy set the same goal another client had used the previous week which was to say three things (statements or questions were acceptable). This goal fit well as a challenge to Kathy's AT that she would be unable to say anything at all. One of the therapists then stepped out of the room to get the research assistant.

T2: Doug, this is Kathy. Kathy, this is Doug. He's going to help us out tonight. Why don't you both sit on the couch there so you are side by side, like you would be in a classroom. Kathy, can you see your rational responses on the easel alright?

K: Yes.

T2: The situation is that the two of you have an economics class together. Doug, you are taking this class as an elective and aren't particularly invested in it. You major in something else, pick whatever you would like. Also, you are a work-study student at the library and you borrowed Kathy's notes once when you missed class due to illness.

D: OK, I can do that.

T2: Kathy, let's get an initial SUDS rating and read your rational responses. Then I would like you to start the conversation.

Kathy was quite anxious and teary-eyed throughout the conversation. Her minute-by-minute SUDS ratings were 90, 90, 80, 80, 80, 70, and the therapist counted five things she said that were not answers to direct questions. Kathy was generally able to respond to Doug's lead but he was forced to carry the bulk of the conversation. Thus, Kathy met her goal and demonstrated some habituation of her anxiety, even if she did not demonstrate perfectly skilled and relaxed performance. In the post–role-play discussion, Kathy clearly thought she had done better than she had expected to do. Doug gave her the feedback that she had seemed nice and that he was impressed that she was able to listen and respond appropriately to what he said despite her discomfort. Kathy was able to acknowledge that her AT of not being able to say *anything* had not been supported.

For homework, Kathy agreed to continue daily conversations, making at least two interactions per week with a man about her age. Since she had not completed the last week's assignment to invite a coworker to do something, that assignment was repeated. Kathy stated that the problem the previous week had been that she did not know what activity to select so the group brainstormed some possible ideas of things to do with either a coworker or someone from school (e.g., have coffee after class to discuss an upcoming exam). Kathy was instructed to call one of the therapists during the week if additional brainstorming was needed. At the next session she reported several conversations in excess of the one-per-day assignment, two of which had been with men. However, once again she had not offered an invitation to anyone.

Session 11

Kathy's final within-session exposure occurred during Session 11. Given the difficulty she was having completing her homework assignment, the therapists decided to use the final exposure to explore why she had difficulty offering invitations. Kathy indicated that the most difficult situation would be to ask a man out on a date. Typically, the therapists would have chosen a less threatening situation first, but since treatment was ending, they decided to attempt the invitation for a date. If Kathy were unable to complete the role play, the Session 12 schedule could be rearranged to give her another opportunity to succeed before treatment ended. This also allowed another opportunity for a heterosocial conversation that she needed.

The role play was set up similarly to the one the previous week. Another research assistant took on the role of the classmate. They were instructed to have a conversation until the therapist signaled Kathy that is was permissible to offer the invitation. Kathy could then do so whenever it felt appropriate. This strategy has three advantages. First, it prolongs the interaction and incorporates an exposure to having heterosocial conversations. Second, it prevents the client from avoiding his/her anxiety by blurting out the request immediately. Finally, it makes the situation more realistic because typically requests for a date are made in the context of an ongoing conversation. Social phobics are surprisingly ingenious at incorporating the invitation into the topic at hand, particularly in light of their inexperience in these situations. This prompts a positive response from other group members at how "smooth" or "sophisticated" the client appears. Although this positive image is foreign to social phobics' self-concept, it often matches their ideal image and thus can serve as a powerful reinforcer.

Kathy's primary ATs in anticipation of the exposure were: "If I ask, then I'll have to go out with him"; "He'll find out how weird I am on the date because I'll be anxious"; "I won't know what to say on the date"; and "He doesn't really want to go out with me." She acknowledged that the first thought had been what had prevented her from completing her homework. She was afraid to commit to a social event because she might be too anxious to follow through with it and it was more awkward to avoid something she had initiated. Kathy's worst fear was that he would agree to the date, as evidenced by her first three thoughts. The therapists and the group helped her break it down into one situation at a time. First, she should focus on the invitation and then, if he said yes, she could use her cognitive skills to prepare for the date itself. She was able to derive a rational response to summarize this strategy ("I can worry about the date later"). This capitalized on her competing AT that no one would want to go out with her. So it made little sense to worry about a date that would never happen.

The fourth AT incorporated the idea that his acceptance of the date did not indicate he wanted to go out with her. The therapists explored this issue with Kathy.

T2: Why would someone say yes if he didn't want to go out with you?

K: I don't know. Maybe he feels sorry for me or something.

T2: So he might feel sorry for you and agree to go out. Any other reason he might say yes and not mean it?

K: I don't know. I never really thought about it.

T2: How about the rest of the group? Any ideas why a guy would agree to a date he didn't want?

M4: Not in this kind of situation. If someone fixed you up or something, then he might be pressured into it. But in the situation you are talking about, it is easy for him to get out of it. Even if he doesn't say anything at the time you ask him, he could cancel later. I think if he actually goes, he wants to.

T2: What do you think about that, Kathy?

K: I don't know. Maybe.

T2: You don't sound convinced. What evidence could you have that someone was saying yes when they didn't mean it?

K: I don't know. I think I could just tell.

T2: Umm, it seems like there might be a cognitive distortion in there? What do you think, group?

M3: It seems like mind reading. She is guessing at what he is thinking.

T2: Do you think that fits, Kathy?

K: Yeah. I don't really have any evidence.

T2: So if you try and read his mind, you conclude that he doesn't want to go out with you?

K: Yes.

T2: What do you conclude if you just consider what you can see and hear, what he says and does?

K: Well, he is saying yes and he could actually go out with me.

T2: So when you read his mind he doesn't want to go out with you but if you look at his words and actions, he does. Which seems more reliable? If you were gambling and had to put your money on one of those, which would it make sense to bet on?

K: That if he says yes, he wants to go out with me.

T2: So which conclusion does it make sense to bet your dating life on?

K: The same one. He probably wouldn't say yes if he didn't want to go out with me.

T2: That sounds like an excellent rational response. Do you want to use that one?

For the exposure, three rational responses were written on the easel—one from the previous week ("I can probably think of *something* to say") and two from this week ("I can worry about the date later" and "he probably wouldn't say yes if he didn't want to go out with me"). The situation they enacted was similar to that of the previous week. The research assistant role-played a different student from one of her classes with whom she would have had several conversations as part of her daily exposures to conversations. Her goal for the exposure was to ask him out and make arrangements about day, time, and so on. Prior to bringing the research assistant into the room, he was instructed to respond enthusiastically to the invitation but to negotiate on one aspect of the arrangements.

Kathy's SUDS were slightly lower than the previous week (80, 80, 80, 80, 70, 70, 70, 70, 60), dropping 10 points after she had asked her interaction partner to a movie in the 4th min. The invitation was offered in the context of a discussion about movies. After he had indicated there was a particular one he would like to see, she suggested they see it together. When she suggested Friday night, he indicated that he was busy that night but suggested they go on Saturday. Kathy participated more in the conversation than she had during the previous exposure but became teary-eyed at several points. Although the group continued to be somewhat uncomfortable with her tears, they were genuinely enthusiastic about her performance, quickly challenging her when she attempted to disqualify the positive aspects of her behavior.

In addition to ongoing daily conversations, Kathy's homework assignment for Session 11 once again involved asking someone to do something. Given her previous lack of success, the assignment was made more specific and related to the role play. She agreed to invite one of her classmates, either male or female, to have coffee or a soft drink after class. The next week, Kathy reported that she had asked a woman to have coffee with her, but the woman declined because she did not have time. Since the request, not the activity, was the criterion, her homework was rated as a success. Kathy reported only moderate anxiety when completing the assignment and thought she would be able to do so again.

Session 12

As described above, approximately the first half of the final session is devoted to review of homework and one to two exposures. The last hour is devoted to a review of progress, identifying short-term goals for each client, scheduling a follow-up appointment, and saying good-bye. Kathy was not scheduled for an exposure during the last session. Although she had not made dramatic progress, it was possible to identify some positive steps such as increased casual conversations. The group was particularly positive about her courage in very difficult exposures. The therapists emphasized that, although she continued to become teary-eyed in group, she had never done so during an *in vivo* homework assignment. She set herself the short-term goal to continue to enter at least one situation each day that she would have avoided in the past, including casual conversations. The therapists emphasized the importance of continued use of cognitive restructuring skills and gave everyone new copies of the materials they had received previously to facilitate contin-

ued work. The session ended with about a half hour of social time over cake and soft drinks. In the individual follow-up appointment the next week with one of the therapists, it was agreed that Kathy would continue to attempt self-paced exposures using the cognitive restructuring skills she had gained in group. If she failed to make further progress, additional treatment would be considered.

Posttreatment Assessment

Kathy repeated the assessment battery she had completed prior to starting treatment. As shown in Table 3.6, the independent assessor rated her as only modestly improved and still in the range of clinical severity (CSR = 4 at posttest). The self-report questionnaires offered a more optimistic view of her progress with substantial improvements on the FNE, SADS, and FQ Social Phobia scale. Her depression, as measured by the BDI, improved dramatically from at 13 to a 3. Improvement on the fear and avoidance hierarchy ratings were consistent but also modest (see Table 3.5). Kathy's only change on the measures derived from the behavioral test was a slight increase in anticipatory anxiety that she associated with a concern that she would become tearful (see Figure 3.1). This picture was consistent with her therapists' view of her progress. She appeared to be more optimistic and was less likely to avoid feared situations as evidenced by her improvement on the FQ Social Phobia scale and SADS;

TABLE 3.6. Pretreatment, Posttreatment, and 6-Month Follow-up Assessment for Kathy

Measure	Pretest	Post-test	6-mo follow-up
CSR	5	4	2
BDI	13	3	0
SADS	21	13	6
FNE Scale	30	23	11
FQ Social Phobia scale	24	10	10
Behavioral test measures			
Peak anxiety	80	80	20
Performance quality	30	30	80

Note. BDI, Beck Depression Inventory; CSR, clinician's severity rating; FNE, Fear of Negative Evaluation; FQ, Fear Questionnaire.

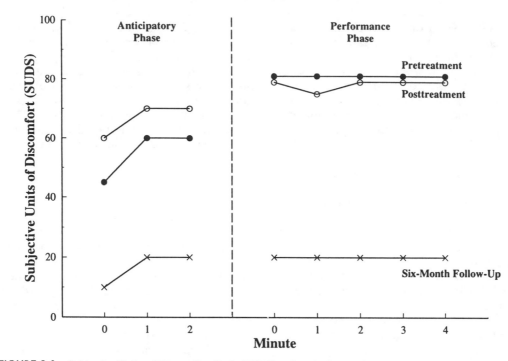

FIGURE 3.1. Subjective Units of Discomfort Scale (SUDS) ratings before and during the individualized behavioral test for Kathy at pretreatment, posttreatment, and 6-month follow-up.

however, she continued to experience significant levels of fear.

Six-Month Follow-up

Between posttest and 6-month follow-up, Kathy continued self-paced exposure including following through on joining a health club and becoming acquainted with her classmates. She had not sought further professional treatment. As is evident from the follow-up data presented in Tables 3.5 and 3.6 and Figure 3.1, Kathy had improved impressively during the intervening 6 months. The independent assessor gave her a CSR of 2, signifying that her social phobia was slightly distressing but resulted in no disability in role performance. All self-report questionnaire scores were within a standard deviation of the nonclinical mean. Although Kathy still reported significant anxiety in her most feared situation from her fear and avoidance hierarchy, it was relatively unlikely that she would avoid that situation or any of the others on the hierarchy. Kathy's most dramatic improvement, however, was in the behavioral test. For the first time she was able to converse with the role player

without tears or excessive dependence on him to carry the conversation. Her anxiety ratings were extremely low and probably not excessive for someone who is being videotaped and evaluated. For the first time, she gave herself a positive appraisal on the quality of her performance, improving 50 points on the 0–100 scale.

Approximately 1 year after the 6-month follow-up assessment, Kathy's mother reported that she was extremely pleased with the progress Kathy had made in treatment and described Kathy as "a new person." She said that Kathy had transferred to a college in another city where she did not know anyone and was making new friends and enjoying her independence.

Further Treatment Considerations

The case of Kathy presents a series of typical simulated exposures over the course of a treatment group. However, many times some creativity is required to create a situation that incorporates the individual's fears and has an adequate duration for effective exposure. Several examples of such situations and possible exposure scenarios are outlined below. (For further exposure ideas, see Hope, 1993, and Heimberg, 1991.)

Brief Situations

Occasionally social phobics fear brief situations such as asking directions, signing their name, and interrupting ongoing conversations. Any one occurrence is so brief that their anxiety immediately spikes, but the situation ends before habituation can occur or cognitive strategies can be employed. The solution is repeated exposures to the brief anxiety-provoking situation. This can be accomplished by having various group members and therapists positioned around the room. The target member then moves from one position to the next, staying long enough to complete the requisite behavior, then moving on before his/her anxiety decreases. For example, a recently treated client became anxious when he joined ongoing conversations at a party. Once he was participating in the conversation his anxiety diminished, but he frequently avoided parties because he spent much of the time standing alone. One of his role-played exposures consisted of approaching pairs of group members engaged in conversation, joining in the conversation, then moving to the next pair after he had made two or three contributions. In an 8-min exposure, he joined seven conversations with decreasing anxiety ratings at each encounter.

Another dimension that can be added to this type of exposure involves having the role-play partners vary their behavior to incorporate idiosyncratic fears. For example, one social phobic who avoided asking favors of friends and neighbors repeatedly approached the role players requesting to borrow small items, a ride to the airport, and so on. Because she feared being refused, role-play partners were sometimes signaled by the therapist to politely do just that. As she entered each situation she did not know whether the person would honor her request, as would be true in naturalistic encounters.

Physical Symptoms

Occasionally a social phobic's anxiety will be motivated by concern that a physical symptom, such as sweating, blushing, or a hand tremor, will be apparent to others. More often than not, their judgment of the severity and visibility of the symptom is exaggerated. In such cases, incorporating ratings of the symptom by other group members into the postexposure cognitive restructuring may be sufficient. Unfortunately, often these clients then state that although the feared outcome may be less likely than previously believed, if the symptom did become severe, others would evaluate them negatively and that would be disastrous. At this point it becomes important to create the symptom in group, and possibly for homework exposures also.

One common symptom that needs to be created in group is sweating. This can be done by have the target member drink hot liquids, stand in front of a space heater wearing warm clothing, or exercise vigorously just before the exposure. As in the case reported by Hope and Heimberg (in press), wearing certain shirts that are more likely to show perspiration may also be helpful.

Incorporating Unlikely Feared Outcomes

After one or two exposures in the group, it may become apparent that until the client experiences some particular circumstance, he/she will live in fear of its happening. Usually the probability of the feared event happening is extremely low, but not zero. Thus even if the individual stops avoiding anxiety-provoking situations, he/she is unlikely to encounter the central fear. Examples of this include a public speaking phobic who fears a hostile or jeering audience or dropping one's notes when approaching the lectern. Generalized social phobics with dating anxiety may have vivid images of a potential dating partner who laughs uproariously or insults them when they request a date. These are the types of situations in which the advantages of role-played exposure over *in vivo* exposure are most pronounced. All these circumstances can be created in the group by preparing audience members or interaction partners. Group members report that such creations are surprisingly real to them.

As a note of caution when attempting these types of exposures, therapists need to use the cognitive restructuring time before and after the exposure to prepare and debrief the target member adequately. The debriefing may happen automatically as the participants in the exposure spontaneously report being uncomfortable displaying a hostility they did not feel. Typically other group members quickly offer admiration at how well the target member performed under difficult circumstances. If these events do not happen spontaneously, therapists should elicit them.

Treatment Success and Failure

Predictors of Treatment Success

One important issue in understanding the efficacy of any treatment is to determine variables that predict a negative response to the intervention. Ideally, prospective clients could be screened for these variables and given another type of treatment. Unfortunately, the current state of knowledge is too unsophisticated to identify with precision who will and will not benefit from treatment. However, a few potential predictor variables have been identified.

Depression

As noted above, elevated depression, operationalized as high BDI scores, was associated with poor response to CBGT. High BDI subjects indicated more fear of negative evaluation and higher anxiety during the behavioral test than did low BDI subjects following treatment (Klosko et al., 1984). High BDI subjects were also more likely to withdraw early from treatment. In a similar vein, higher depression was associated with poorer treatment outcome in a sample of social phobics receiving a variety of group treatments including CBGT (Holt, Heimberg, & Hope, 1990).

Homework Compliance

Not surprisingly, homework compliance may also be related to treatment success. Hope, Herbert, and Bellack (1991) compared CBGT treatment responders and nonresponders on therapists' ratings of compliance with assigned homework. The groups differed significantly with the responders, on average, engaging in *in vivo* exposure that exceeded the therapists' assignment and nonresponders, on average,

engaging in somewhat less exposure than was assigned. This suggests that those who ultimately succeed in reducing their social phobia in CBGT begin to create opportunities to face their fears and/or take advantage of naturally occurring opportunities.

These data are too limited to determine the nature of the significant relationship between depression and homework compliance and treatment outcome. However, it may be that the demoralization and low energy that are characteristic of depression interfere with a client's ability to engage in self-initiated *in vivo* exposure. Issues such as these should be addressed in future research.

Alternative Strategies If Treatment Fails

At the end of the 12 sessions of treatment, the therapists and client must determine whether sufficient progress has been made in overcoming the client's social phobia. Rarely, are all social–evaluative fears eliminated in 3 brief months of treatment. More often, clients have stopped avoiding feared situations and believe they can use the skills gained in treatment to continue to work on their own. As in the case presentation, they are likely to continue to make progress in the coming months. On the other hand, it is sometimes painfully obvious to both the therapists and client that the treatment has been largely unsuccessful. This raises the question of what to do if CBGT fails.

The first step in selecting options for treatment failures is to assess why failure might have occurred. Fortunately, the time spent in treatment usually has yielded sufficient data to address this question. Sometimes, particularly with generalized social phobics, CBGT appears to be working but clients need more time in treatment to make further progress. Therefore continued CBGT in another group or adapted to an individual format would be recommended. If the data gathered in group reveal a serious deficit in social skill not apparent at the outset of treatment, social skills training that includes *in vivo* practice likely would be most appropriate.

Excessive physiological arousal represents another potential explanation for treatment failure. Some social phobics are so distracted by their bodily sensations that their ability to engage in effective social interaction is impaired. In fact, they may not be able to take full advantage of the cognitive coping skills. In this situation, an intervention to target the arousal, such as Ost's applied relaxation, could be used (Jerremalm, Jansson, & Ost, 1986).

Even the best diagnosticians make errors. Occasionally, it becomes apparent that social phobia may not have been the most appropriate diagnosis, or at least not the primary diagnosis. Consequently, a treatment for social fears may have little impact. Most often this confusion occurs with someone who presents with a complicated picture of panic attacks in social situations. These individuals may fear both social evaluation and their panic symptoms, the latter which are not evident until treatment has begun. If it appears that the client may have been misdiagnosed, then treatment invention appropriate for the diagnosis is the obvious solution.

In addition to the possibilities listed above, environmental factors such as secondary gains for continued avoidance behavior or an unsupportive family or spouse should be explored with the client. Logically such factors influence treatment outcome for certain cases. The extent to which environmental influences may play a role has not yet been researched, however.

If, after careful analysis, the clinician fails to find an obvious reason for treatment failure (and to develop an associated treatment plan), other empirically validated treatments should be considered. In addition to social skills training and applied relaxation, medication should be considered. There is growing evidence that monoamine oxidase inhibitors (MAOIs; e.g., Nardil [phenelzine]) effectively reduce the symptoms of social phobia, particularly more generalized social fears (Liebowitz et al., 1991, 1992). Unfortunately, MAOIs require dietary restrictions to avoid a hypertensive crisis. However, as the new reversible inhibitors of monamine oxidase that have fewer such restrictions become available in the United States, this treatment option will become more acceptable to clients and physicians (Liebowitz et al., 1991). Beta blockers such as atenolol have often been recommended for public speaking and performance anxiety and have the advantage that they may be needed only

as an acute treatment prior to encountering the feared situation (Liebowitz et al., 1985). More recent evidence, however, fails to support their efficacy for *clinically severe* social phobia (Liebowitz et al., 1992). Preliminary reports indicate that high-potency benzodiazepines (e.g., Klonopin [clonazepam]) may be effective for reducing social phobia (Davidson, Ford, Smith, & Potts, 1991). At this point, the efficacy of these drugs is not well established, particularly in comparison to MAOIs. Numerous drug trials are currently under way and it seems likely that several effective pharmacological interventions will be available in the near future.

Adaptation to Individual Treatment Format

Despite the many advantages of group treatment, including the flexibility for in-session exposures, the group format is not feasible in all settings for all social phobics. CBGT can be adapted to an individual format without great difficulty. As described by Hope (1993), office personnel and professional colleagues can supplement the therapist as role-play partners. Also, there is greater reliance on exposures completed as homework assignments. These should be discussed in more detail during the session than is possible in group treatment. Preparatory cognitive restructuring exercises are completed in the session and followed up with the postexposure processing in the subsequent session. Sometimes clients can enlist someone from their social support network to provide the type of feedback and encouragement typically given by the group. Thus, although a group format is recommended whenever possible, the therapeutic strategies outlined in this chapter may be used in individual treatment.

SUMMARY AND CONCLUSION

After decades of neglect, the volume of research on social phobia has grown dramatically in recent years. Current controversies, such as the most useful subtyping system, were unheard of only a decade ago. This research has also yielded several promising treatment strategies, including combined cognitive and exposure interventions such as CBGT. The purpose of this chapter was to provide a step-by-step analysis of the conduct of CBGT from initial screening of potential group members to following up on treatment response. Although the case presentation is not an ideal treatment case, it realistically highlights the ups and downs of a treatment group. Individuals like Kathy who make dramatic improvements in their life provide the impetus for continued research on the treatment of social phobia—a potentially debilitating disorder with an increasingly encouraging prognosis.

ACKNOWLEDGMENTS

Preparation of this chapter was supported in part by grants MH 48751 to the first author and MH 44119 to the second author from the National Institute of Mental Health.

REFERENCES

American Psychiatric Association. (1980). *Diagnostic and statistical manual of mental disorders* (3rd ed.). Washington, DC: Author.

American Psychiatric Association. (1987). *Diagnostic and statistical manual of mental disorders* (3rd ed., rev.). Washington, DC: Author.

American Psychiatric Association. (1993). *DSM-IV draft criteria as of 3/1/93*. Washington, DC: Author.

Arnkoff, D. B., & Glass, C. R. (1989). Cognitive assessment in social anxiety and social phobia. *Clinical Psychology Review, 9*, 61–74.

Bandura, A. (1977). Self-efficacy: Toward a unifying theory of behavioral change. *Psychological Review, 84*, 191–215.

Beck, A. T., & Emery, G. (1985). *Anxiety disorders and phobias: A cognitive perspective*. New York: Basic Books.

Beck, A. T., Ward, C. H., Mendelson, M., Mock, J., & Erbaugh, J. (1961). An inventory for measuring depression. *Archives of General Psychiatry, 4*, 561–571.

Bourdon, K. H., Boyd, J. H., Rae, D. S., Burns, B. J., Thompson, J. W., & Locke, B. Z. (1988). Gender differences in phobias: Results of the ECA Community Survey. *Journal of Anxiety Disorders, 2*, 227–241.

Bruch, M. A., Heimberg, R. G., & Hope, D. A. (1991). States of mind model and cognitive change in treated social phobics. *Cognitive Therapy and Research, 15*, 429–441.

Burns, D. D. (1980). *Feeling good: The new mood therapy*. New York: Morrow.

Butler, G. (1989). Issues in the application of cognitive and behavioral strategies to the treatment of social phobia. *Clinical Psychology Review, 9*, 91–186.

Butler, G., Cullington, A., Munby, M., Amies, P., & Gelder, M. (1984). Exposure and anxiety management in the treatment of social phobia. *Journal of Consulting and Clinical Psychology, 52*, 642–650.

Chambless, D. L., Cherney, J., Caputo, G. C., & Rheinstein, B. J. G. (1987). Anxiety disorders and alcoholism: A study with inpatient alcoholics. *Journal of Anxiety Disorders, 1*, 29–40.

Davidson, J. R. T., Ford, S. M., Smith, R. D., & Potts, N. L. S. (1991). Long-term treatment of social phobia with clonazepam. *Journal of Clinical Psychiatry, 52* (Suppl.), 16–20.

DiNardo, P. A. & Barlow, D. H. (1988). *The Anxiety Disorders Interview Schedule–Revised*. Albany, NY: Graywind Publications.

Elting, D. T., Hope, D. A., & Heimberg, R. G. (1992, November). *The factor structure of an assessment battery for social phobia*. Paper presented at the annual meeting of the Association for the Advancement of Behavior Therapy, Boston, MA.

Gelernter, C. S., Uhde, T. W., Cimbolic, P., Arnkoff, D. B., Vittone, B. J., Tancer, M. E., & Bartko, J. J. (1991). Cognitive-behavioral and pharmacological treatment of social phobia. *Archives of General Psychiatry, 48*, 938–945.

Glass, C. R., & Arnkoff, D. B. (1989). Behavioral assessment of social anxiety and social phobia. *Clinical Psychology Review, 9*, 75–90.

Heimberg, R. G. (1988). The Social Avoidance and Distress Scale and the Fear of Negative Evaluation Scale. In M. Hersen & A. S. Bellack (Eds.), *Dictionary of behavioral assessment techniques* (pp. 425–427). New York: Pergamon Press.

Heimberg, R. G. (1989). Cognitive and behavioral treatments for social phobia: A critical analysis. *Clinical Psychology Review, 9*, 107–128.

Heimberg, R. G. (1991). *A manual for conducting Cognitive-Behavioral Group Therapy for social phobia* (2nd ed.). Unpublished manuscript, State University of New York at Albany, Center for Stress and Anxiety Disorders, Albany, NY.

Heimberg, R. G., & Barlow, D. H. (1991). New developments in cognitive-behavioral treatment for social phobia. *Journal of Clinical Psychiatry, 52* (11, suppl.), 21–30.

Heimberg, R. G., Becker, R. E., Goldfinger, K., & Vermilyea, J. A. (1985). Treatment of social phobia by exposure, cognitive restructuring, and homework assignments. *Journal of Nervous and Mental Disease, 173*, 236–245.

Heimberg, R. G., Dodge, C. S., Hope, D. A., Kennedy, C. R., Zollo, L., & Becker, R. E. (1990). Cognitive-behavioral group treatment for social phobia: Comparison with a credible placebo control. *Cognitive Therapy and Research, 14*, 1–23.

Heimberg, R. G., Holt, C. S., Schneier, F. R., Spitzer, R. L., & Liebowitz, M. L. (in press). The issue of subtypes in the diagnosis of social phobia. *Journal of Anxiety Disorders*.

Heimberg, R. G., Hope, D. A., Dodge, C. S., & Becker, R. E. (1990). DSM-III-R subtypes of social phobia: Comparison of generalized social phobics and public speaking phobics. *Journal of Nervous and Mental Disease, 178*, 172–179.

Heimberg, R. G., Hope, D. A., Rapee, R. M., & Bruch, M. A. (1988). The validity of the Social Avoidance and Distress Scale and the Fear of Negative Evaluation Scale with social phobic patients. *Behaviour Research and Therapy, 26,* 407–410.

Heimberg, R. G., & Liebowitz, M. R. (1992, April). *A multi-center comparison of the efficacy of phenelzine and cognitive-behavioral group treatment for social phobia.* Paper presented at the 12th National Conference on Anxiety Disorders, Houston, TX.

Heimberg, R. G., Mueller, G. P., Holt, C. S., Hope, D. A., & Liebowitz, M. R. (1992). Assessment of anxiety in social interaction and being observed by others: The Social Interaction Anxiety Scale and the Social Phobia Scale. *Behavior Therapy, 23,* 53–73.

Heimberg, R. G., Salzman, D., Holt, C. S., & Blendell, K. (1993). Cognitive-behavioral group treatment for social phobia: Effectiveness at five-year follow-up. *Cognitive Therapy and Research, 17.*

Herbert, J. D., Hope, D. A., & Bellack, A. S. (1992). Validity of the distinction between generalized social phobia and avoidant personality disorder. *Journal of Abnormal Psychology, 101,* 332–339.

Holt, C. S., Heimberg, R. G., & Hope, D. A. (1989, November). *Baseline predictors of group psychotherapy outcome for the treatment of social phobia.* Paper presented at the annual meeting of the Association for Advancement of Behavior Therapy, Washington, DC.

Holt, C. S., Heimberg, R. G., & Hope, D. A. (1990, November). *Success from the outset: Predictors of cognitive-behavioral therapy outcome among social phobics.* Paper presented at the annual meeting of the Association for Advancement of Behavior Therapy, San Francisco, CA.

Holt, C. S., Heimberg, R. G., & Hope, D. A. (1992). Avoidant personality disorder and the generalized subtype of social phobia. *Journal of Abnormal Psychology, 101,* 318–325.

Holt, C. S., Heimberg, R. G., Hope, D. A., & Liebowitz, M. L. (1992). Situational domains of social phobia. *Journal of Anxiety Disorders, 6,* 63–77.

Hope, D. A. (1993). Conducting exposure-based treatments with social phobics. *Behavior Therapist, 16,* 7–12.

Hope, D. A., & Heimberg, R. G. (in press). Social phobia. In C. G. Last & M. Hersen (Eds.), *Adult behavior therapy casebook.* New York: Plenum Press.

Hope, D. A., Heimberg, R. G., & Bruch, M. A. (1990, March). *The importance of cognitive interventions in the treatment of social phobia.* Paper presented at the annual meeting of Phobia Society of America, Washington, DC.

Hope, D. A., Herbert, J. D., & Bellack, A. S. (1991, November). *Social phobia subtype, avoidant personality disorder and psychotherapy outcome.* Paper presented at the annual meeting of the Association for Advancement of Behavior Therapy, New York.

Hope, D. A., Holt, C. S., & Heimberg, R. G. (1993). Social phobia. In T. R. Giles (Ed.), *Handbook of effective psychotherapy* (pp. 227–251). New York: Plenum Press.

Hope, D. A., Rapee, R. M., Heimberg, R. G., & Dombeck, M. S. (1990). Representations of the self in social phobia: Vulnerability to social threat. *Cognitive Therapy and Research, 14,* 177–189.

Jerremalm, A., Jansson, L., & Ost, L-G. (1986). Cognitive and physiological reactivity and the effects of different behavioral methods in the treatment of social phobia. *Behaviour Research and Therapy, 24,* 171–180.

Klosko, J. S., Heimberg, R. G., Becker, R. E., Dodge, C. S., & Kennedy, C. R. (1984, November). *Depression, anxiety, and the outcome of treatment for social phobia.* Paper presented at the annual meeting of the Association for Advancement of Behavior Therapy, Philadelphia, PA.

Leary, M. R. (1983). A brief version of the Fear of Negative Evaluation Scale. *Personality and Social Psychology Bulletin, 9,* 371–375.

Leary, M. R. (1988). A comprehensive approach to the treatment of social anxieties: The self-presentational model. *Phobia Practice and Research Journal, 1,* 48–57.

Leary, M. R., Kowalski, R. M., & Campbell, C. D. (1988). Self-presentational concerns and social anxiety: The role of generalized impression expectancies. *Journal of Research in Personality, 22,* 308–321.

Levin, A. P., Schneier, F. R., & Liebowitz, M. R. (1989). Social phobia: Biology and pharmacology. *Clinical Psychology Review, 9,* 129–140.

Liebowitz, M. R., Gorman, J. M., Fyer, M. J., & Klein, D. F. (1985). Social phobia: Review of a neglected anxiety disorder. *Archives of General Psychiatry, 42,* 729–736.

Liebowitz, M. R., Schneier, F. R., Campeas, R., Hollander, E., Hatterer, J., Fyer, A., Gorman, J., Papp, L., Davies, S., Gully, R., & Klein, D. R. (1992). Phenelzine vs. atenolol in social phobia: A placebo-controlled comparison. *Archives of General Psychiatry, 49,* 290–300.

Liebowitz, M. R., Schneier, F. R., Hollander, E., Welkowitz, L. A., Saoud, J. B., Feerick, J., Campeas, R., Fallon, B. A., Street, L., & Gitow, A. (1991). Treatment of social phobia with drugs other than benzodiazepines. *Journal of Clinical Psychiatry, 52*(suppl.), 10–16.

Marks, I. M., & Mathews, A. M. (1979). Brief standard self-rating scale for phobic patients. *Behaviour Research and Therapy, 17,* 263–267.

Mattia, J. I., Heimberg, R. G., & Hope, D. A. (1993). The revised Stroop color-naming task in social phobics: Diagnostic and treatment outcome implications. *Behaviour Research and Therapy, 31,* 305–313.

Mattick, R. P., & Clarke, J. C. (1989). *Development and validation of measures of social phobia scrutiny fear and social interaction anxiety.* Unpublished manuscript.

Mattick, R. P., & Peters, L. (1988). Treatment of severe social phobia: Effects of guided exposure with and without cognitive restructuring. *Journal of Consulting and Clinical Psychology, 56,* 251–260.

Mattick, R. P., Peters, L., & Clarke, J. C. (1989). Exposure and cognitive restructuring for severe social phobia: A controlled study. *Behavior Therapy, 20,* 3–23.

Mullaney, J. A., & Trippett, C. J. (1979). Alcohol dependence and phobias: Clinical description and relevance. *British Journal of Psychiatry, 135,* 563–573.

Myers, J. K., Weissman, M. M., Tischler, G. L., Holzer, C. E., III, Leaf, P. J., Orvaschel, H., Anthony, J. D.,

Boyd, J. H., Burke, J. D., Jr., Kramer, M., & Stolzman, R. (1984). Six-month prevalence of psychiatric disorders in three communities. *Archives of General Psychiatry, 41,* 959–967.

Persons, J. B. (1989). *Cognitive therapy in practice: A case formulation approach.* New York: W. W. Norton.

Sanderson, W. C., DiNardo, P. A., Rapee, R. M., & Barlow, D. H. (1990). Syndrome comorbidity in patients diagnosed with a DSM-III-R anxiety disorder. *Journal of Abnormal Psychology, 99,* 308–312.

Sank, L. I., & Shaffer, C. S. (1984). *A therapist's manual for cognitive-behavior therapy in groups.* New York: Plenum Press.

Schlenker, B. R., & Leary, M. R. (1982). Social anxiety and self-presentation: A conceptualization and model. *Psychological Bulletin, 92,* 641–669.

Schneier, F. R., Spitzer, R. L., Gibbon, D., Fyer, A., & Liebowitz, M. R. (1991). The relationship of social phobia subtypes and avoidant personality disorder. *Comprehensive Psychiatry, 32,* 1–5.

Schwartz, R. M., & Garamoni, G. L. (1989). Cognitive balance and psychopathology: Evaluation of an information processing model of positive and negative states of mind. *Clinical Psychology Review, 9,* 271–294.

Smail, P., Stockwell, T., Canter, S., & Hodgson, R. (1984). Alcohol dependence and phobic anxiety states: I. A prevalence study. *British Journal of Psychiatry, 144,* 53–57.

Smith, T. W., Ingram, R. E., & Brehm, S. S. (1983). Social anxiety, anxious self-preoccupation, and recall of self-relevant information. *Journal of Personality and Social Psychology, 44,* 1276–1283.

Turner, S. M., Beidel, D. C., Borden, J. W., Stanley, M. A., & Jacob, R. G. (1991). Social phobia: Axis I and II Correlates. *Journal of Abnormal Psychology, 100,* 102–106.

Turner, S. M., Beidel, D. C., Dancu, C. V., & Keys, D. J. (1986). Psychopathology of social phobia and comparison to avoidant personality disorder. *Journal of Abnormal Psychology, 95,* 389–394.

Turner, S. M., Beidel, D. C., & Stanley, M. A. (1989). An empirically derived inventory to measure social fears and anxiety: The Social Phobia Anxiety Inventory. *Psychological Assessment, 1,* 35–40.

Turner, S. M., Beidel, D. C., & Townsley, R. M. (1992). Social phobia: A comparison of specific and generalized subtypes and avoidant personality disorder. *Journal of Abnormal Psychology, 101,* 326–331.

Turner, S. M., McCanna, M., & Beidel, D. C. (1987). Validity of the Social Avoidance and Distress and Fear of Negative Evaluation scales. *Behaviour Research and Therapy, 25,* 113–115.

Watson, D., & Friend, R. (1969). Measurement of social-evaluative anxiety. *Journal of Consulting and Clinical Psychology, 33,* 448–457.

Widiger, T. A. (1992). Generalized social phobia versus avoidant personality disorder: A commentary on three studies. *Journal of Abnormal Psychology, 101,* 340–343.

Wolpe, J., & Lazarus, A. A. (1966). *Behavior therapy techniques.* New York: Pergamon Press.

Chapter 4

GENERALIZED ANXIETY DISORDER

Timothy A. Brown
Tracy A. O'Leary
David H. Barlow
State University of New York at Albany

This chapter on generalized anxiety disorder is a new one for this volume. One might wonder why a disorder as central and ubiquitous as generalized anxiety disorder was not accorded a chapter in the last volume. Generalized anxiety disorder is, after all, the "basic" anxiety disorder in the sense that generalized anxiety is, by definition, a component of other anxiety disorders. But only recently have we begun to delve into the nature of generalized anxiety disorder. Only recently have we begun to evaluate effective psychological treatments for this problem, and only in the past several years has evidence begun to appear that we can, in fact, treat this problem successfully. This is no small feat since generalized anxiety disorder, although characterized by marked fluctuations, is chronic. Some have even considered that generalized anxiety disorder might be better conceptualized as a personality disorder since many individuals with this problem cannot report a definitive age of onset. Rather, they note that it has been with them all of their life. Drug treatments, although often tested, are surprisingly weak (Barlow, 1988). For this reason, further study of new treatment protocols is all the more pressing.

The protocol presented in this chapter, recently developed in our center, illustrates the relatively new procedures of "worry exposure" and "worry behavior prevention." These therapeutic procedures are derived from new theoretical conceptualizations of generalized anxiety disorder. In many ways these procedures depart radically from more traditional treatment approaches to generalized anxiety.—D. H. B.

OVERVIEW

Among the anxiety disorders, perhaps no diagnostic category has changed more over the past 12 years than has generalized anxiety disorder (GAD). With the publication of the third edition of the *Diagnostic and Statistical Manual of Mental Disorders* (DSM-III; American Psychiatric Association [APA], 1980), the subcategory of anxiety disorders that had been termed "anxiety neurosis" in DSM-II became "anxiety states (or anxiety neurosis)." This category contained two newly defined diagnoses: panic disorder and GAD (along with obsessive compulsive disorder [OCD]). Diagnostic criteria for GAD in DSM-III required the presence of generalized, persistent anxiety as manifested by symptoms from at least three of four categories: (1) motor tension (e.g., muscle aches and restlessness); (2) autonomic hyperactivity (e.g., sweating, dizziness, and accelerated heart rate); (3) apprehensive expectation (e.g., anxiety, worry, and fear); and (4) vigilance and scanning (e.g., concentration difficulties and irritability). Anxious mood, defined by the above symptoms, was required to be continuous for a period of at least 1 month. However, within the DSM-III diagnostic system, the diagnosis of GAD could not be assigned if patients met criteria for another mental disorder. In other words, GAD was a residual category that was very low in the hierarchy of possible anxiety disorder diagnoses if choices had to be made. For example, if a client presented with both generalized anxiety and social phobia, only the diagnosis of social phobia would be assigned.

At least partly the result of its status as a residual category, the diagnostic reliability (e.g., rates of agreement on the presence of the diagnoses between two independent interviewers) of DSM-III GAD was quite low (cf. Barlow & DiNardo, 1991). Moreover, the residual status of GAD had other deleterious effects, such as hindering research on patterns of comorbidity of GAD with other disorders. Also, because of the amorphous nature of GAD, little attention was paid to the development and evaluation of effective treatments.

Despite the hierarchical rules of DSM-III, clinical experience indicated that in addition to patients in whom generalized anxiety was their primary complaint, many others evidenced generalized anxiety that was independent of their principal disorder. The important diagnostic consideration in these comorbid cases was the differentiation of generalized anxiety from anticipatory anxiety, because the latter is virtually always present to some degree in the panic and phobic disorders. This differentiation was facilitated by determining whether the focus of apprehension (i.e., worry) was on the core feature of another disorder (e.g., panic or phobic situation) or on an area unrelated to another disorder (Barlow, Blanchard, Vermilyea, Vermilyea, & DiNardo, 1986; Barlow & DiNardo, 1991). For example, if a client presented with severe anxiety focused only on the next potential panic attack, only panic disorder would be assigned. However, if anxiety was *also* and *independently* focused pervasively on minor events of everyday life (e.g., finances or schedules), GAD would be assigned as well.

Accordingly, in the revised third edition of the *Diagnostic and Statistical Manual of Mental Disorders* (DSM-III-R; APA, 1987), the diagnostic criteria for GAD underwent considerable change. Along the lines of the clinical observations noted above, the apprehensive expectation cluster contained in the DSM-III criteria was restructured such that DSM-III-R GAD had its own key symptom: excessive and/or unrealistic worry in two or more areas unrelated to another Axis I disorder. In addition, the associated symptom criterion was revised to require the presence of at least 6 symptoms from a list of 18 forming the three clusters of Motor Tension, Autonomic Hyperactivity, and Vigilance and Scanning. Finally, based on clinical and empirical considerations (e.g., Breslau & Davis, 1985), the duration criterion was extended from 1 to 6 months. Among other reasons, the requirement of pervasive worry more days than not over a period of 6 months or greater was considered to facilitate the differentiation of GAD from transient reactions to negative life events (e.g., adjustment disorders).

In the fourth edition of the *Diagnostic and Statistical Manual of Mental Disorders* (DSM-IV; APA, 1993)* the criteria for GAD have been revised further to make them more user friendly and to emphasize the process of apprehensive expectation (worry). To this end, the requirement of two or more spheres of worry was eliminated. Nonetheless, DSM-IV specifies that the worry must be *excessive* (i.e., the intensity, duration, and frequency of the worry is out of proportion to the likelihood or impact of the feared event) and perceived by the individual as difficult to control. For reasons noted later, the 18 ratings comprising the associated symptom criterion have been reduced to 6, retaining symptoms from the Motor Tension and Vigilance and Scanning clusters and eliminating symptoms from the Autonomic Hyperactivity cluster. DSM-IV criteria for GAD are presented in Table 4.1.

Partly as a result of the reconceptual-

---

*The DSM-IV criteria cited in this chapter are those that were approved as final by the DSM-IV Anxiety Disorders Work Group and the Task Force on DSM-IV (APA, 1993). These criteria may be subject to minor editorial revisions before the publication of DSM-IV.

TABLE 4.1. Diagnostic Criteria for DSM-IV
Generalized Anxiety Disorder

A. Excessive anxiety and worry (apprehensive expectation) about a number of events or activities (such as work or school performance), occurring more days than not, for at least six months.

B. The person finds it difficult to control the worry.

C. The anxiety and worry are associated with at least three of the following six symptoms (with at least some symptoms present for more days than not for the past six months):
   (1) restlessness or feeling keyed up or on edge
   (2) being easily fatigued
   (3) difficulty concentrating or mind going blank
   (4) irritability
   (5) muscle tension
   (6) sleep disturbance (difficulty falling or staying asleep, or restless unsatisfying sleep)

D. The focus of the anxiety and worry is not confined to features of an Axis I disorder, e.g., the anxiety or worry is not about having a panic attack (as in Panic Disorder), being embarrassed in public (as in Social Phobia), being contaminated (as in Obsessive-Compulsive Disorder), being away from home or close relatives (as in Separation Anxiety Disorder), gaining weight (as in Anorexia Nervosa), or having a serious illness (as in Hypochondriasis), and is not part of Posttraumatic Stress Disorder.

E. The anxiety, worry, or physical symptoms significantly interfere with the person's normal routine or usual activities, or there is marked distress.

F. Not due to the direct effects of a substance or a general medical condition and does not occur exclusively during a Mood Disorder, Psychotic Disorder, or a Pervasive Developmental Disorder.

Note. From APA (1993). Copyright 1993 by the American Psychiatric Association. Reprinted by permission.

ization and restructuring of GAD in DSM-III-R, research on the nature of its defining features (i.e., chronic worry and persistent somatic symptoms) has burgeoned (cf. Rapee & Barlow, 1991). This increase in scientific inquiry into GAD is particularly important in light of the emergence of conceptual models of anxiety and anxiety disorders that posit that the core processes defining GAD, as the disorder is currently defined, represent the fundamental processes in all anxiety disorders (Barlow, 1988, 1991). Consequently, we have referred to GAD as the "basic" anxiety disorder (e.g.,

Barlow, 1988; Rapee, 1991), and have termed this fundamental process *anxious apprehension* (Barlow, 1988). Anxious apprehension is defined as a future-oriented mood state in which one becomes ready or prepared to attempt to cope with upcoming negative events. Anxious apprehension is associated with a state of high negative affect and chronic overarousal, a sense of uncontrollability, and an attentional focus on threat-related stimuli (e.g., high self-focused attention or self-preoccupation and hypervigilance). Whereas the process of anxious apprehension is considered to be present in all anxiety disorders, the content (focus) of anxious apprehension varies from disorder to disorder (e.g., anxiety over future panic attacks in panic disorder or anxiety over possible negative social evaluation in social phobia). We have suggested elsewhere (Barlow, 1988, 1991) that these processes (i.e., tension, vigilance, and a sense of uncontrollability) may emerge from early life experiences and may serve as vulnerability factors in the later development of a wide range of emotional disorders.

Consistent with this assertion, and important from a clinical perspective as well, is the observation that patients with GAD often present with a lifelong history of generalized anxiety. For example, several studies have found that a large proportion of patients with GAD cannot report a clear age of onset or report an onset dating back to childhood (e.g., Anderson, Noyes, & Crowe, 1984; Barlow et al., 1986; Butler, Fennell, Robson, & Gelder, 1991; Cameron, Thyer, Nesse, & Curtis, 1986; Noyes, Clarkson, Crowe, Yates, & McChesney, 1987; Noyes et al., 1992; Rapee, 1985; Sanderson & Barlow, 1990). Thus, in contrast to several other anxiety disorders, such as panic disorder, which tends to have a later onset and more acute presentation characterized by exacerbations and remissions, initial evidence suggests that GAD has a more characterological presentation (although fluctuations in the course of GAD are often noted corresponding to the presence or absence of life stressors). This observation is concordant with the aforementioned conceptualizations of GAD as the basic anxiety disorder because it exemplifies, most purely, the process of anxious apprehension (early onset and predispositional factor for the development of other disorders). Accordingly, studies examining rates and patterns of comorbidity have found GAD to be the most frequently assigned additional diagnosis in patients with a principal anxiety or mood disorder (e.g., Moras, DiNardo, Brown, & Barlow, 1992; Sanderson, Beck, & Beck, 1990). However, whereas some evidence points to generalized anxiety as a prodromal symptom of the development of other emotional disorders such as panic disorder (e.g., Garvey, Cook, & Noyes, 1988), the important empirical question concerning the temporal sequence of the emergence of GAD in relation to other comorbid disorders awaits future investigation. Nevertheless, in light of these findings, it is not surprising that GAD has begun to be conceptualized within the context of a personality disorder (Sanderson & Wetzler, 1991).

Since the arrival of DSM-III-R, research on the nature of worry has increased markedly, particularly within the area of delineating normal and pathological worry. Studies examining the nature of worry in GAD patients versus nonanxious controls have produced findings indicating that whereas these groups do not differ substantially on the content of worry, considerable differentiation exists on measures reflecting controllability of the worry process (e.g., percentage of day worried, frequency of unprecipitated worry, self-perceptions of controllability and realism of worry, number of worry spheres; cf. Borkovec, Shadick, & Hopkins, 1991; Craske, Rapee, Jackel, & Barlow, 1989; DiNardo, 1991). These findings, in part, have guided the revisions to the worry criterion in DSM-IV to emphasize the uncontrollable nature of worry as an essential feature of the disorder. Although data are limited, particularly with regard to between-group comparisons on controllability of the worry process, indices of this nature appear to differentiate GAD patients from other anxiety disorder groups. For example, Sanderson and Barlow (1990) found that a greater proportion of GAD patients than patients with other anxiety disorders (social phobia, panic disorder, simple phobia, or OCD) report worrying excessively over minor matters. In a similar analysis, DiNardo (1991) examined the discriminatory power of affirmative responses provided by GAD patients and non-GAD anxiety patients to

the question, "Do you worry excessively about minor matters?" an item in the GAD section of the Anxiety Disorders Interview Schedule—Revised (ADIS-R; DiNardo & Barlow, 1988). The positive predictive power (specificity) of this question was .36 (the probability of a GAD diagnosis, given an affirmative response); the negative predictive power (sensitivity) was .94 (the probability of not having a GAD diagnosis, given a negative response). These findings indicate that although an affirmative response to the question of excessive worry over minor matters cannot confirm the diagnosis, a negative response can rule out GAD with confidence.

Differences in responses to various ADIS-R items (i.e., "excessive worry over minor matters" and "percent day spent worried") have been replicated in a study comparing GAD patients to OCD patients only (Brown, Moras, Zinbarg, & Barlow, 1993). Moreover, in at least three studies, patients with GAD obtained significantly higher scores than did other anxiety disorder groups (including patients with OCD) and normal controls on the newly developed Penn State Worry Questionnaire (PSWQ), a psychometrically validated measure of the trait of worry (Brown, Antony, & Barlow, 1992; Brown et al., 1993; Meyer, Miller, Metzger, & Borkovec, 1990).

New evidence concerning the somatic component of GAD suggests that the symptoms most frequently associated with the disorder are those comprising the Motor Tension and Vigilance and Scanning clusters of the DSM-III-R associated symptom criterion. Indeed, in a multisite study examining the frequency and reliability of the 18 associated symptoms in a (combined) sample of 204 GAD patients, the most frequently endorsed symptoms were irritability, restlessness, muscle tension, easy fatigability, feeling keyed up, sleep difficulties, and concentration difficulties (Marten et al., in press). Interestingly, none of the symptoms from the Autonomic Hyperactivity cluster was endorsed with considerable frequency. The latter finding is concordant with laboratory data indicating that GAD patients respond to psychological stress with autonomic inflexibility; that is, relative to nonanxious controls, GAD patients show decreased variability in autonomic responses (e.g., heart rate and skin conductance) to laboratory-based psychological challenges (Hoehn-Saric & McLeod, 1988; Hoehn-Saric, McLeod, & Zimmerli, 1989; Lyonfields, 1991).

In addition to their high rate of endorsement by GAD patients (e.g., Marten et al., in press; Noyes et al., 1992), symptoms of motor or psychic tension may also be an important discriminating feature of GAD. For example, the one psychophysiological measure that has been found to differentiate GAD patients from normal controls at baseline and in response to psychological challenge is muscle tension (i.e., frontalis and gastrocnemius electromyogram; Hoehn-Saric et al., 1989). Moreover, scores on the Self-Analysis Questionnaire (SAQ) Tension scale (Lovibond, 1983) have been found to differentiate GAD patients from all other DSM-III-R anxiety disorder groups (except patients with OCD) and nonanxious controls (Brown, Antony, & Barlow, 1992). In this GAD sample, SAQ Tension scores were correlated more strongly with a measure of worry (PSWQ) than with all other measures examined (e.g., self-report and clinician ratings of anxiety and depression), suggesting a stronger convergence between worry and tension than between worry and other related symptomatology (e.g., autonomic arousal or depression).

TARGETS OF TREATMENT

On the basis of the evidence reviewed above, the two principal components that form the targets of a treatment intervention for GAD are excessive, uncontrollable worry and its accompanying persistent overarousal (primarily tension-related, central nervous system symptoms). As the literature review here will attest, these cognitive and somatic features have been most frequently addressed with cognitive therapy and some form of relaxation treatment, respectively. Moreover, following new conceptualizations of the nature of pathological worry (cf. Borkovec & Hu, 1990; Rapee & Barlow, 1991), the utility of targeting GAD worry via an exposure-based paradigm has recently emerged as a potentially effective treatment component for GAD (e.g., Craske, Barlow, & O'Leary, 1992; O'Leary, Brown, & Bar-

low, 1992). For instance, worry has been conceptualized as a negative reinforcer that serves to dampen physiological reactivity to emotional processing (Borkovec & Hu, 1990). In a sense, worry may serve to hinder complete processing of more disturbing thoughts or images. This is often evident during the process of decatastrophizing, a form of cognitive restructuring described later, where clients are reluctant to elaborate on the worst possible outcome of a feared negative event. Instead, clients may feel more comfortable ruminating over their anxious thoughts and then distracting from the catastrophic thought or image.

TREATMENT OUTCOME STUDIES

Perhaps due in part to the effects of some of the aforementioned characteristics of GAD (e.g., characterological nature and high rate of comorbidity), studies have noted only modest treatment gains following cognitive-behavioral or pharmacological interventions. This is particularly true in relation to the efficacy of these forms of treatments for other anxiety disorders (cf. Brown, Hertz, & Barlow, 1992). In addition, whereas most studies have found the treatments examined to be effective to some degree, comparative outcome studies have infrequently observed differential efficacy among active treatment conditions. Another factor that may have contributed to these modest treatment gains and lack of differential efficacy concerns the types of treatments that have been examined thus far. Given that GAD has only recently been reformulated to have a key diagnostic feature (i.e., excessive worry), the majority of outcome studies to date have examined the effectiveness of somewhat nonspecific interventions (e.g., relaxation training). This compares to extant treatments for other anxiety disorders that contain elements specifically tailored to address essential features of the disorder in question. For example, in panic-control treatment for panic disorder, components of breathing retraining and interoceptive exposure address hyperventilation and fear of physical sensations, respectively (cf. Craske & Barlow, Chapter 1, this volume). However, as will become evident later in this chapter, new treatments have appeared recently that target specifically the key feature of excessive, uncontrollable worry. Prior to delineating these treatments, we will provide an overview of the treatment literature on GAD.

Early treatment studies for GAD typically entailed the examination of the efficacy of relaxation-based treatments or biofeedback. Whereas the majority of these earlier studies used analog subjects (e.g., mildly anxious college students), the few studies utilizing clinical samples observed quite modest treatment effects when using these forms of treatment in isolation of other procedures. For instance, LeBoeuf and Lodge (1980) reported that only 4 of 26 patients showed more than marginal improvement in response to relaxation alone.

Only within the past 6 years have studies emerged that examined the efficacy of treatments for GAD using rigorous methodology (e.g., use of structured interviews to establish diagnoses, inclusion of control or comparison groups, and assessment of short- and long-term effects of treatment using multiple measures). The types of "active" treatments examined in these studies have typically involved cognitive therapy, relaxation training, anxiety management training, or some combination of these procedures. Most often, these treatments have been compared to nondirective treatments and/or wait-list control conditions. With regard to the use of wait-list comparison groups, these active treatments have been shown to produce greater improvement than no treatment (e.g., Barlow et al., 1984; Barlow, Rapee, & Brown, 1992; Blowers, Cobb, & Mathews, 1987; Butler, Cullington, Hibbert, Klimes, & Gelder, 1987; Lindsay, Gamsu, McLaughlin, Hood, & Espie, 1987). Moreover, studies reporting long-term outcome data (i.e., clinical functioning at 6 or more months posttreatment) have generally shown a maintenance of treatment gains (e.g., Barlow et al., 1992; Borkovec & Costello, in press; Borkovec & Mathews, 1988; Butler et al., 1987, 1991).

Another important finding observed in recent studies providing long-term outcome data is the substantial reduction in anxiolytic medication usage in treated subjects over the follow-up period (e.g., Barlow et al., 1992; Butler et al., 1991; White, Keenan, & Brooks, 1991). For instance, Barlow et al.

(1992) noted that, whereas many of their subjects were using benzodiazepines at pretreatment (33%–55%), virtually all subjects had discontinued medication usage by the 2-year follow-up. This finding is salient in light of the fact that benzodiazepines are particularly refractory to discontinuation (cf. Schweizer & Rickels, 1991) and may indicate that psychosocial treatments of the nature examined in Barlow et al. (1992) have utility as an approach to discontinuation of these types of medications.

However, as noted above, most studies have failed to observe clear evidence of differential efficacy when comparing two or more active treatments (e.g., Barlow et al., 1992; Borkovec & Mathews, 1988; Durham & Turvey, 1987; Lindsay et al., 1987), although there are a few exceptions to this general finding (e.g., Butler et al., 1991). Perhaps even more discouraging is the finding that shows no differences between cognitive-behavioral treatments and credible nondirective treatments (Blowers et al., 1987; Borkovec & Mathews, 1988; White et al., 1991). However, one study recently completed is a notable exception (Borkovec & Costello, in press). Despite the lack of evidence for differential efficacy in most of these studies, both the active and nondirective treatments produced significant (relative to wait-list control) and durable gains. Nevertheless, the collective findings indicating a lack of differential efficacy among active treatments or between active and nondirective treatments in most studies underscore the importance of continuing the search for effective mechanisms of action (cf. Butler & Booth, 1991).

Prior to outlining the application of specific techniques pertaining to the assessment and treatment of GAD, we review, in greater detail, a few noteworthy treatment outcome studies (i.e., studies producing evidence for differential efficacy among active treatments and/or observing quite encouraging treatment gains). For example, in the first of a series of studies, Butler et al. (1987) evaluated an anxiety management package for GAD that was loosely based on the early important work on anxiety management by Suinn and Richardson (1971). Treatment consisted of teaching patients to cope with various aspects of their anxiety via such methods as self-administered relaxation procedures and distraction procedures to deal with cognitive aspects of anxiety. The subtle types of avoidance of both somatic and situational cues often found in GAD patients were also addressed. Patients were encouraged to take control of their life by scheduling more pleasurable activities and noting areas in their life in which they were functioning well. Patients receiving this treatment were compared to a wait-list control group. Relative to wait-list controls ($n = 23$), patients receiving the anxiety management package ($n = 22$) evidenced greater improvement on all measures of anxiety (e.g., Hamilton rating scales, State–Trait Anxiety Inventory). At a 6-month follow-up, improvement on these measures was either maintained or increased further. For example, in the active treatment group, Hamilton Anxiety scale scores showed an average 59% reduction immediately following treatment (from a mean of 16 to a mean of 6.6) and a 69% reduction by the 6-month follow-up (to a mean of 5.0). As we have noted elsewhere, the latter figure exceeds the greatest benefit reported in any study evaluating the short-term effects of benzodiazepines on generalized anxiety (Barlow, 1988; Brown, Hertz, & Barlow, 1992). However, this observation should be tempered by the fact that direct comparisons to a medication group were not made and that the investigators only included patients who suffered substantial anxiety for 2 years or less, thereby eliminating any patients with "chronic" anxiety.

In their second study, Butler et al. (1991) evaluated the effects of a more extensive cognitive therapy based on the work of Beck and Emery (1985) with a version of their anxiety management treatment stripped of any cognitive therapy. The investigators opted to evaluate cognitive therapy in this manner since they hypothesized that this approach might have a more dramatic effect on the prominent symptom of worry in GAD. Subjects were individuals meeting DSM-III-R diagnostic criteria for GAD; no maximal duration criterion was used for selecting subjects, as was done in their first study. Treatment consisted of weekly sessions lasting up to 12 weeks. Booster sessions were also provided at 2, 4, and 6 weeks after treatment. At posttreatment, whereas both treatment groups evidenced

significant improvement relative to a wait-list control group ($n = 19$), patients receiving cognitive therapy ($n = 19$) were significantly better on most measures than were patients receiving the intervention without cognitive therapy ($n = 18$). At a 6-month follow-up, both treatment groups maintained their gains, with the cognitive therapy group continuing to show greater improvement than the behavioral therapy group on most measures. Consistent with the findings of Barlow et al. (1992), treatment had a substantial impact on medication usage in this sample. Whereas 40% of patients in the two treatment groups were taking anxiolytic and/or hypnotic medication at pretreatment, only 24% were still taking medication at posttreatment. Six months later, this had fallen to 15%, with every patient reducing his/her usual dosage.

Butler et al. (1991) attempted to determine the clinical significance of treatment gains via rather stringent criteria of end-state functioning (i.e., scoring within the "normal" range on three measures of anxiety—Hamilton Anxiety Scale, Beck Anxiety Inventory, Leeds Anxiety Scale). At posttreatment, the percentage of patients falling within the normal range on all three measures was 32% and 16% for the cognitive therapy and behavioral therapy groups, respectively; At the 6-month follow-up, this percentage had risen in the cognitive therapy group (42%), but fallen markedly in the behavioral therapy group (5%). These modest findings demonstrate once again that GAD can be a chronic and severe problem and that there is much room for improvements in our treatments. Moreover, whereas the Butler et al. (1991) study represents one of the few providing evidence of differential efficacy among active treatment conditions, as noted by Borkovec and Costello (in press), the behavioral therapy condition in this study produced the lowest amount of change among the extant treatment studies on GAD. Thus, regardless of the reasons for the limited efficacy of this condition, the negligible gains produced by behavioral therapy provided a liberal standard for detecting between-group differences with another active treatment condition (e.g., only 5% of subjects treated with behavioral therapy met high end-state functioning criteria at 6-month follow-up).

Borkovec and Costello (in press) have recently reported the findings of a very well done outcome study in which they examined the comparative efficacy of applied relaxation (AR), cognitive-behavioral therapy (CBT), and nondirective (ND) treatment in a sample of 55 patients carefully diagnosed as having DSM-III-R GAD. In view of the importance of this study, we describe it in some detail.

AR consisted of teaching patients progressive muscle relaxation (PMR) with slow breathing. PDMR initially entailed 16 muscle groups gradually reduced down to 4 groups, with the learning of cue-controlled relaxation and relaxation-by-recall to facilitate the deployment of relaxation procedures quickly and early in the process of anxiety activation. CBT included the elements of AR as well as the components of coping desensitization and cognitive therapy. Coping desensitization involved the generation of a hierarchy listing the clients' anxiety-provoking situations and their cognitive and somatic responses to these situations. After the clients were deeply relaxed, the therapist would present external and internal anxiety cues and instruct the clients to continue to imagine these cues while imagining themselves using their relaxation skills in that situation. Each scene in the hierarchy was repeated until it no longer elicited anxiety. The cognitive therapy component of CBT was modeled after the procedures outlined in Beck and Emery (1985), aimed at the generation of situation-specific cognitive coping responses.

Clients in the ND condition were told that the goals of treatment would be to enhance self-understanding and to discover, through their own efforts, things that they could do differently to affect how they feel. Therapists did not provide specific information about GAD, nor did they provide direct advice or coping methods for dealing with anxiety; instead, their role was to provide a time of self-reflection while assisting clients in clarifying or focusing on their feelings.

Results indicated that despite the lack of differences among conditions in credibility, expectancy, and client perception of the therapeutic relationship, at posttreatment, the AR and CBT conditions were clearly superior to ND. This was evidenced by between-group comparisons, within-group change, and the proportion of subjects meeting high end-state functioning criteria. Differences at posttreatment were particularly noteworthy because they indicated that elements of AR and CBT contained active ingredients independent of nonspecific factors. Whereas no clear evidence of differential efficacy was obtained for the AR and CBT conditions at posttreatment, 12-month follow-up results indicated that, in addition to maintenance of treatment gains across this follow-up period in both conditions, more clients treated with CBT met high end-state criteria (57.9%) than did those in the AR condition (37.5%). Conversely, 12-month follow-up results indicated losses in treatment gains in the ND condition (percentage meeting high end state = 26.7%); in fact, a significantly greater number of patients (61.1%) treated in this condition requested further treatment at the end of the active treatment phase than did subjects in the AR and CBT conditions (16.7% and 15.8%, respectively). Whereas Borkovec and Costello (in press) noted that the AR and CBT treatments in this study produced some of the largest treatment effect sizes noted in the GAD treatment literature to date, they acknowledged the fact that, because only one third and roughly one half of AR and CBT subjects, respectively, met high end-state functioning criteria at 12-month follow-up, the evolution of psychosocial treatments for GAD must continue.

Recently, we have developed a new treatment approach to GAD that addresses the worry component directly, taking advantage of the knowledge gained in the development of treatments for panic disorder in our setting. In an initial study (O'Leary et al., 1992), the efficacy of worry exposure in its pure form (i.e., without other treatment elements such as relaxation training or cognitive therapy) was evaluated using a multiple-baseline-across-subjects design. Three subjects, all of whom had received a DSM-III-R principal diagnosis of GAD, were seen in individual weekly sessions across 8 to 12 weeks. Worry exposure was completed via both intersession and intrasession exercises. Subjects self-monitored daily levels of mood and worry, and completed the following questionnaires weekly: PSWQ; Depression,

Anxiety, and Stress Scales (DASS); and Emotional Control Questionnaire (ECQ; Rapee, Craske, & Barlow, 1989).

Results indicated that two of the three subjects evidenced clinically significant decreases in daily levels of anxiety and depression along with dramatic declines in PSWQ scores. Although the third subject did not show as dramatic a decline in her levels of worry and anxiety, elevations in her ECQ scores over the course of treatment showed increased self-perceptions of control over worry and other emotional states. In addition, an examination of all subjects' anxiety ratings after generating the worst possible feared outcome (peak anxiety) and then after having generated alternatives to that outcome (post anxiety) revealed habituation effects: peak anxiety was consistently higher than post anxiety, suggesting that the intervention was indeed effective as a deconditioning strategy, as had been originally hypothesized.

The remainder of this chapter is devoted to a description of this treatment and to our approach to the assessment of GAD. A combined treatment protocol for GAD will be described involving worry exposure, as well as cognitive therapy, relaxation training, and other strategies (e.g., worry behavior prevention and problem solving).

CONTEXT OF THERAPY

Setting

To date, all of our assessment and treatment of clients with GAD has occurred within the Phobia and Anxiety Disorders Clinic of the Center for Stress and Anxiety Disorders. Presently at the Phobia and Anxiety Disorders Clinic, we have over 350 new admissions per year; roughly 10% of these patients ultimately receive a principal diagnosis of GAD. Principal means that although they might have several comorbid diagnoses, GAD is the most severe. Clients requesting assessment and/or treatment at our clinic first undergo a brief screening (usually conducted over the telephone) to ascertain their eligibility (i.e., appropriateness) for an evaluation. At this time, eligible clients are scheduled to undergo the standard intake evaluation (consisting of one or two ADIS–Rs, a

battery of questionnaires, and, in some cases, a psychophysiological assessment). Once a client has completed the general intake evaluation and has received a principal diagnosis (determined at a weekly staff meeting in which consensus diagnoses are established), the client is contacted by the clinic staff member who conducted the initial ADIS–R. At that time, he/she is given the results of the evaluation and a treatment referral. The majority of clients who receive a DSM-III-R anxiety disorder as their principal diagnosis are offered a referral to one of the ongoing treatment programs in our clinic. After acceptance in the program, clients typically complete some additional assessments specific to the treatment program and their presenting, principal disorder (e.g., pretreatment self-monitoring of anxiety and worry).

In the past, our treatment programs for GAD have been conducted in both an individual and a small-group (i.e., four to six clients) format. Whereas the GAD treatment protocol described in this chapter has been administered in both formats, at the present time we feel that it is best suited to be delivered in one-on-one hourly treatment sessions given some of the practical difficulties in implementing the "worry exposure" component in a small-group format. We have not found the integrity of the relaxation and cognitive restructuring components to be compromised substantially by the small-group format and, in fact, in some cases this format may hold certain advantages depending on the composition of the group (e.g., group assistance in cognitive restructuring). Nevertheless, the extent to which the format of treatment is associated with treatment outcome is an area that awaits future investigation.

Client Variables

The Overview section of this chapter indicates some of the characteristics of GAD clients that may have an impact on the treatment process. Beyond the features comprising the DSM-III-R criteria for the disorder, one characteristic that is particularly salient to the process of treatment is the high rate of comorbidity evident in clients with GAD. Although this is an area that has thus far received little empirical attention (cf. Brown & Barlow, 1992), the existence of coexisting psychological disorders must be considered by the therapist in treatment planning. For example, given the close boundary between generalized anxiety, worry, and depression (cf. Andrews & Borkovec, 1988; Zinbarg & Barlow, 1991), the extent to which the GAD client exhibits depression at either the symptom or syndrome level must be acknowledged, as depression has been associated with a poorer treatment response to cognitive-behavioral treatments for GAD (e.g., Barlow et al., 1992). Moreover, given that panic disorder and GAD often co-occur (cf. Moras et al., 1992), the presence of comorbid panic disorder should be acknowledged given its potential association with the problem of relaxation-induced anxiety.

Another characteristic that may be relevant to treatment outcome is the extent to which the client's worry is, for lack of a better term, *ego syntonic*. Adding some support for the conceptualization of GAD as a characterological disorder (e.g., Sanderson & Wetzler, 1991), we have observed that some of our clients with GAD evidence resistance in countering or attempting to reduce their worrying because they either view their worry as adaptive (e.g., worry is perceived as reducing the likelihood of the occurrence of some negative event) or they consider their worry as such an integral part of themselves that they express concern about how they will be when they no longer have anything to worry about. Typically, these clients present for treatment to receive help in reducing the somatic component of their disorder and may not even see worry as related to their symptoms of persistent tension and hyperarousal. This has only been a clinical observation on our part and no evidence exists attesting to the prevalence and salience of this characteristic in predicting treatment outcome.

Therapist Variables

Given that research on the efficacy of cognitive-behavioral treatments for GAD could be considered to be still in its infancy, to date no data exist regarding therapist variables associated with treatment outcome. Although little can said about the empirical basis of therapist qualities, we would certainly contend that therapists should possess a firm grounding in the use of cognitive-behavioral techniques in addition to a thorough understanding of current models of worry and GAD. Moreover, because cognitive therapy comprises one of the core components of our treatment for GAD, therapists should possess the ability to deliver the active components of this treatment (e.g., use of Socratic method, collaborative empiricism, and ability to assist the client in identifying and challenging automatic thoughts; cf. Beck & Emery, 1985; Young, Beck, & Weinberger, Chapter 6, this volume) and, ideally, should possess the "nonspecific" qualities considered to be evident in the most effective cognitive therapists (e.g., ability to communicate trust, accurate empathy, and warmth; ability to reason logically themselves; and ability to tailor the principles and techniques of cognitive therapy to the individual needs of the client).

Of the various components comprising our treatment of GAD, in our experience, clients have the most difficulty in learning and applying the cognitive techniques in a manner in which they are most effective. In addition, therapists who are training to learn our GAD treatment protocol are apt to require the most supervision and guidance in learning to deliver the cognitive therapy component. For both the client and the therapist-in-training, the most commonly occurring difficulty is that the methods of identifying and/or countering anxiogenic cognitions are not applied thoroughly (e.g., application of countering prior to identifying the most salient automatic thoughts and insufficient countering of automatic thoughts via the generation of incomplete or inappropriate counterarguments). We return to this issue in a later section.

As is also noted later in this chapter, a solid background in cognitive-behavioral theory and therapy is an asset when applying the exposure-based treatment component of our GAD treatment package. This knowledge will help ensure that the parameters of effective therapeutic exposure are delivered with integrity (e.g., recognition and prevention of client's distraction and provision of an ample exposure duration to promote habituation in clients' anxiety to images denoting their worry).

ASSESSMENT

Classification

Of the DSM-III-R anxiety disorders, GAD remains among the diagnoses most difficult to establish with high reliability (cf. DiNardo, Moras, Barlow, Rapee, & Brown, in press). Whereas the revisions in diagnostic criteria of GAD introduced in DSM-III-R have improved diagnostic agreement rates somewhat, in our recent study examining the reliability of the DSM-III-R anxiety disorder via the administration of two independent ADIS–R interviews, the κ for GAD when assigned as a principal diagnosis was only fair (κ = .57; DiNardo et al., in press). The consistent finding of lower diagnostic reliability of GAD relative to other anxiety disorders has led to the call by some investigators to mandate, as an inclusion criterion for studies examining GAD patients, the confirmation of the GAD diagnosis via two independent diagnostic interviews. Indeed, this methodological practice is beginning to appear in the literature (e.g., Borkovec & Costello, in press).

As we have articulated elsewhere (e.g., Brown et al., 1993; DiNardo et al., in press), many factors may be contributing to the lower rates of diagnostic agreement for GAD. For instance, some recent models noted earlier conceptualize GAD as the basic anxiety disorder because its defining features reflect fundamental processes of anxiety (cf. Barlow, 1988, 1991; Rapee, 1991). If these models are valid, one would expect the distinctiveness of the diagnosis to be mitigated by the fact that its features are present to some extent in all of the anxiety disorders, and possibly the mood disorders as well. Moreover, GAD is defined solely by features involving internal processes (i.e., excessive worry and persistent symptoms of tension or arousal). Thus, the lack of a clear "key feature" defining the disorder may also contribute to lower diagnostic reliability in contrast to the high rates of diagnostic agreement for disorders in which these features are often, or necessarily, present (e.g., compulsions in OCD, phobic avoidance in simple phobia; cf. DiNardo et al., in press).

Other aspects of the diagnostic criteria for GAD should also be considered in the exploration of potential factors contributing to lower its diagnostic reliability. For example, DSM-III-R specified that GAD should not be assigned when the symptoms defining the disturbance occur only during the course of a mood disorder or a psychotic disorder. This has been retained and expanded on in the DSM-IV criteria for GAD (see criterion F in Table 4.1). This diagnostic specification was incorporated, in part, to facilitate parsimony in the assignment of diagnoses (e.g., to prevent the assignment of both diagnosis A and diagnosis B when the features of diagnosis B can be subsumed as associated features of diagnosis A, the more debilitating disturbance of the two). However, particularly in the case of the mood disorders (e.g., major depression and dysthymia), many patients report a clinical history marked by a chronic course of alternating or overlapping episodes of depression and persistent anxiety (cf. Zinbarg & Barlow, 1991). Thus, the clinician may often be in the somewhat difficult position of relying on the client's retrospective report regarding the temporal sequence and duration of anxiety and depressive episodes to determine whether the diagnostic criteria for GAD have been met in the absence of a mood disorder.

Similar to DSM-III-R, DSM-IV criteria for GAD specify that "the focus of anxiety and worry is not confined to features of a single Axis I disorder" (see criterion D in Table 4.1). In many cases, the determination of whether the patient's worries represent areas of apprehension relating to another disorder can be relatively straightforward (e.g., in a patient with comorbid panic disorder, excluding worry over experiencing a future unexpected panic as a potential GAD worry). Nevertheless, particularly in light of the evidence for the high rate of comorbidity between GAD and other anxiety and mood disorders (e.g., Moras et al., 1992; Sanderson et al., 1990), occasionally these distinctions can be quite difficult (e.g., Is persistent worry about being late for appointments a manifestation of a fear-of-negative-evaluation characteristic of social phobia rather than a reflection of a general tendency to worry about a host of minor matters, which is often characteristic of GAD?; cf. Barlow & DiNardo, 1991). In addition, careful interviewing may be needed to clarify whether an area of worry that appears ostensibly to be a prototypical GAD worry is actually an area of worry that has arisen due to another disorder (e.g., Has concern about job performance and finances been a long-standing, frequent worry for the client or did these concerns arise only after the onset of unexpected panic attacks and now the client worries that the panics will occur at work, thereby interfering with his job performance or attendance?).

Under DSM-III-R, another potential source of diagnostic unreliability involved the requirement of the presence of two, distinct spheres of worry. In an attempt to discern sources of unreliability of the GAD diagnosis, DiNardo et al. (in press) noted that diagnosticians occasionally disagreed as to whether a topic of worry should be considered a single sphere as opposed to two, separate spheres (e.g., interviewer A deems the patient's worry about the health of his wife and the health and safety of his children a single sphere, "family concerns," whereas interviewer B views these as two, distinct spheres of worry). In DSM-IV, this issue may be no longer salient due to the fact that the criteria for DSM-IV GAD do not require the presence of two, separate spheres of worry (see criterion A in Table 4.1). However, under DSM-IV, clinical judgment is still required to determine what constitutes excessive worry about "a *number* of events or activities" (criterion A).

Finally, to achieve favorable diagnostic reliability of GAD, the criteria for the diagnosis should facilitate the distinction between "normal" and pathological worry. To aid in this distinction, the DSM-III-R worry criterion stated that the spheres of worry must be "excessive" and occur "for a period of 6 months or longer, during which the person has been bothered more days than not by these concerns" (APA, 1987, p. 252). These specifications (i.e., excessiveness, 6-month duration, marked distress/interference) have been retained and/or expanded on in DSM-IV. As noted earlier, the 6-month duration criterion was specified, in part, to differentiate GAD from transient reactions to psychosocial stressors that may be more aptly diagnosed as a form of adjustment disorder. We reviewed evidence previously attesting to the ability to distinguish normal

and pathological worry on such dimensions as amount of time spent worrying and perceived uncontrollability of the worry process (Borkovec et al., 1991; Craske et al., 1989; DiNardo, 1991). Despite this evidence, DiNardo et al. (in press) noted that confusion surrounding the excessive/unrealistic judgment requirements contributed to the occurrence of diagnostic disagreements in that study using DSM-III-R criteria. It is hoped that with the changes to the worry criteria in DSM-IV (criteria A and B), which emphasize and better operationalize the controllability and pervasiveness of worry rather than require the identification of specific spheres, this source of diagnostic confusion will be reduced considerably.

Collectively, the issues mentioned above suggest that the chances of reliably identifying GAD-related worries are quite slim. On the contrary, several studies have found that the content and presence of GAD-related worry can be reliably identified (Barlow & DiNardo, 1991; Borkovec et al., 1991; Craske et al., 1989; Sanderson & Barlow, 1990). Moreover, in the process of revising diagnostic criteria for DSM-IV, researchers noted a possible boundary problem between GAD and OCD (cf. Turner, Beidel, & Stanley, 1992). This concern was raised following the observation that the features of OCD may have the most overlap with the features of GAD (e.g., pervasive worry vs. obsessions and characterological presentation). In addition, the findings of Craske et al. (1989) indicate that many GAD patients' worries are associated with behavioral acts designed to reduce anxiety evoked by worry (e.g., checking the safety of one's child as he/she waits for the bus), thus introducing potential overlap with OCD compulsions. Nevertheless, results from Brown et al. (1993) indicate that the lower diagnostic reliability of GAD is not due to a boundary problem with OCD. Support for this contention was obtained by contrasting 46 patients with GAD and 31 patients with OCD on the basis of interview (ADIS–R) and questionnaire responses. For the 55% of subjects who received two independent ADIS–Rs, in no case did one interviewer assign a principal diagnosis of GAD and the other OCD, strongly suggesting that GAD versus OCD was not a problematic differential diagnostic decision. Moreover, examination of comorbidity patterns indicated that GAD and OCD rarely co-occurred (OCD with additional GAD = 6.5%; GAD with additional OCD = 2%). As noted earlier, scores on the PSWQ, a 16-item measure of the trait of worry (Meyer et al., 1990), successfully discriminated GAD patients from those with OCD in this study as well. However, despite the initial evidence that a variety of indices of worry can differentiate patients with GAD from patients with other DSM-III-R anxiety disorders (e.g., Brown, Antony, & Barlow, 1992; Brown et al., 1993; DiNardo, 1991; Meyer et al., 1990; Sanderson & Barlow, 1990), presently there is a paucity of data bearing on whether measures of worry discriminate GAD patients from patients with mood disorders such as dysthymia and major depression, diagnostic categories that may pose as great a boundary problem with GAD as with many of the anxiety disorders.

In DSM-IV, the associated symptom criterion has been revised considerably via the reduction in the number of symptoms in the list from 18 (in DSM-III-R) to 6 (of which the client must endorse at least 3; see criterion C in Table 4.1). Whereas initial evidence indicated difficulty in establishing the DSM-III-R symptom ratings reliably (e.g., Barlow & DiNardo, 1991; Fyer et al., 1989), more recent data indicate satisfactory reliability when simply calculating interrater agreement on the presence or absence of a symptom (which was required in DSM-III-R) rather than examining interrater concordance on symptom severity ratings (Marten et al., in press). However, as noted earlier, Marten et al. observed that the symptoms from the DSM-III-R associated symptom clusters of Vigilance and Scanning and Motor Tension were the most reliable and endorsed most frequently by patients with GAD. Accordingly, of the 6 symptoms retained in the DSM-IV associated symptom criterion, all were from these two clusters.

When establishing these ratings, careful interviewing is required to ascertain whether a symptom reported by the patient is associated with excessive worry or is due to a coexisting condition (e.g., Does the client often experience concentration difficulties when worrying about finances, or does this symptom only occur during her panic attacks?). Occasionally, this is no small task,

especially in light of the aforementioned evidence of high rates of comorbidity between GAD and the other anxiety and mood disorders (e.g., Moras et al., 1992). Data from Marten et al. (in press) indicate that these distinctions may be easier for establishing ratings for the symptoms retained in the DSM-IV associated symptom criterion; indeed, these symptoms may also have discriminant validity, at least in comparison to other DSM-III-R anxiety disorders (cf. Brown, Antony, & Barlow, 1992; Hoehn-Saric et al., 1989). However, as is the case with the symptom of excessive worry, data are lacking as to the extent to which these symptom ratings successfully discriminate GAD from the mood disorders (cf. Marten et al., in press).

Clinical Interview

The GAD section of the ADIS–R (DiNardo & Barlow, 1988) is shown in Figure 4.1. Given that the criteria for DSM-IV GAD were not finalized until the latter stages of the preparation of this chapter, the process of revising the ADIS–R to reflect changes in diagnostic criteria had not been completed. Nevertheless, virtually all of the diagnostic considerations presented below involving the use of the ADIS–R are relevant to the diagnosis of DSM-IV GAD.

The preceding section outlined several issues and potential difficulties that the clinician may encounter when attempting to decide whether to assign the GAD diagnosis. With regard to the worry criteria, these issues include whether (1) the worry is excessive; (2) the worry is pervasive (i.e., worry about "a number of events or activities"); (3) the worry is perceived by the individual as difficult to control; and (4) the focus of the worry is spheres unrelated to another Axis I condition. Item 1 of the ADIS–R (shown in Figure 4.1) assists in the identification of areas of worry by prompting the clinician to inquire about the things the client worries about (1a) and their duration (1b), and to include follow-up questions, if necessary, for guiding the client to identify areas of worry independent of concerns relating to another anxiety disorder (1a1). Item 2 inquires about the existence of worry about minor matters because this type

Questions in this section should be used to establish the presence of tension or anxiety with no apparent cause, or anxiety which is related to excessive worrying about family, job performance, finances, etc., and minor matters. This tension or anxiety is NOT part of, or anticipatory to, panics or phobic anxiety.

Ask Questions 1 and 2.

1.a. What kinds of things   Do you think you
do you worry about?   worry excessively?   Excessive/Unrealistic

_____

_____

If patient identifies anxiety or tension which is anticipatory to panics or exposures to phobic situations, e.g., "I worry about having an attack; I worry whenever I know I will have to cross a bridge," as a major source of anxiety:

Are there things other than _____ which make you feel tense, anxious, or worried?

Yes____   No____   If yes, What are they?

_____

_____

b. During the last six months, have you been bothered by these worries more days than not?
   Yes____   No____

2. Are you a worrier? Do you worry excessively about small things such as being late for an appointment, repairs to the house or car, etc.?
   Yes____   No____

> If there are 2 areas of excessive worry, or Yes to Question 2, continue:
> If No go to **HAMILTON SCALES** (optional) or **PTSD.**

3. On an average day over the last month, what percent (how much) of the day do you feel tense, anxious, worried?
   _____%

4. The last time you experienced an increase in tension, anxiety, or worry (aside from panics or phobic exposures), what was happening/what were you thinking?

   When _____

   Situation _____

   Thoughts _____

5. How long has the tension, anxiety, worry been a problem?

   From _____   to _____

   Duration in months _____

   NOTE: If patient responds "all my life," inquire further, e.g., **Can you remember feeling this way in school? What grade?**

_____

FIGURE 4.1. Generalized anxiety disorder section of the Anxiety Disorders Interview Schedule–Revised. From *Anxiety Disorders Interview Schedule–Revised* (pp. 8–10) by P. A. DiNardo and D. M. Barlow, 1988, Albany, NY: Graywind. Copyright 1988 by Graywind Publications. Reprinted by permission.

6. How much does this interfere with your life, work, social activities, family, etc.?

Rate interference

0	1	2	3	4
None	Mild	Moderate	Severe	Very severe/ grossly disabling

7. Generalized Anxiety Disorder Symptom Rating

Persistent symptoms (continuous for at least 6 months). Do *not* include symptoms present only during panic.

During the past 6 months, have you often been bothered by _____?

How severe is it

0	1	2	3	4
None	Mild	Moderate	Severe	Very severe/ grossly disabling

a. Motor Tension

_____ 1. Trembling, twitching, or feeling shaky

_____ 2. Muscle tension, aches, or soreness

_____ 3. Restlessness

_____ 4. Easy fatigability

b. Autonomic Hyperactivity

_____ 5. Shortness of breath or smothering sensations

_____ 6. Palpitations or accelerated heart rate

_____ 7. Sweating, or cold clammy hands

_____ 8. Dry mouth

_____ 9. Dizziness or lightheadedness

_____ 10. Nausea, diarrhea, or other abdominal distress

_____ 11. Flushes (hot flashes) or chills

_____ 12. Frequent urination

_____ 13. Trouble swallowing or lump in throat

c. Vigilance, Scanning

_____ 14. Feeling keyed up or on edge

_____ 15. Exaggerated startle response

_____ 16. Trouble falling or staying asleep

_____ 17. Difficulty concentrating or mind going blank because of anxiety

_____ 18. Irritablity

of worry may have potential in assisting in differential diagnosis in relation to other anxiety disorders (cf. Brown et al., 1993; DiNardo, 1991; Sanderson & Barlow, 1990).

Under the DSM-III-R, the lack of operationalization of what constituted unrealistic or excessive worry required considerable skill on the part of the clinician to make this determination. This often required going well beyond the open-ended questions contained in Item 1 of the ADIS–R. It should be noted that whereas one question in this item asks the client, "Do you think you worry excessively?" the distinction of whether the worry is excessive ultimately rested on the clinician's judgment. This point is particularly salient in light of the clinical observation that some clients may consider their worrying to be adaptive or productive, and thus not excessive at all even though it is associated with considerable tension and arousal (e.g., excessive concern over finances is perceived by the client as ensuring that money will always be available for paying bills or unexpected expenses).

Revisions to the criteria introduced in DSM-IV should facilitate this determination. For example, no longer must the clinician determine if the client's worry is "unrealistic," given findings that the parameters of uncontrollability and excessiveness possessed more discriminant validity (e.g., a "realistic" concern could be worried about in an excessive and uncontrollable fashion). Nevertheless, as was the case under DSM-III-R, several additional client queries may aid the diagnostician in judging whether the client's worries are excessive using DSM-IV criteria. Assuming a graduated funnel approach (cf. Nelson & Barlow, 1981), after asking in an open-ended fashion what things the client worries about (Item 1a of the ADIS–R), we have often followed with more detailed questions to ascertain the content, excessiveness, and pervasiveness of the worry. This may take the form of asking whether the client experiences worry over areas that are commonly reported by other GAD patients (e.g., family members' or friends' well-being, job or academic performance, finances, home management, health, or the future). However, a "prototypical" GAD patient may not require this prompting because GAD patients often reply that they worry about "everything" in response to the initial screening question about areas of worry.

In addition, several follow-up questions can be asked to help form the judgment about excessive and uncontrollable worry. For example:

1. Do you find it very difficult to stop worrying or, if you need to focus on something else, are you able to successfully put the worry out of your mind?
2. Do you find that, if you are attempting to focus on something like reading, working, or watching television, these worries often pop into your mind making it difficult to concentrate on these tasks?
3. Do you worry about things that you recognize that other people do not worry about?
4. When things are going well, do you still find things to be worried and anxious about?

5. Does your worry rarely result in your reaching a solution for the problem that you are worrying about?

Great care is often needed in distinguishing whether the worries identified by the patient represent areas that are independent of a coexisting condition or, in cases where no coexisting diagnosis is present, are more appropriately diagnosed as a disorder other than GAD. As mentioned earlier, some of the more common diagnostic decisions that arise involve distinguishing GAD worry from (1) apprehension over future panic attacks or the feared consequences of panic; (2) OCD obsessions; and (3) apprehension over negative social evaluation. Differentiating excessive worry about one's health or contracting a physical illness from hypochondriacal concerns can, at times, be a difficult task. Several follow-up questions to Item 1a1 of the ADIS–R were often required toward this end. Of course, the most important factor in correctly making these distinctions is the possession of a thorough knowledge of the diagnostic criteria for all disorders that may pose a boundary problem with GAD. Although sometimes difficult to establish reliably (especially when patients report a long-standing history of two or more disorders), ascertaining the temporal sequence of the onset of their symptomatology often can be helpful in determining whether areas of worry (as well as associated somatic symptomatology) have arisen in response to another disorder. Based on the aforementioned specifications in the diagnostic criteria for GAD, information pertaining to temporal sequence and duration is particularly important in the presence of signs of a coexisting mood disorder.

Item 7 of the GAD section of the ADIS–R assesses for the presence of the 18 associated symptoms. In the revision of the ADIS–R to correspond to DSM-IV criteria, these symptom ratings will be pared to six. The client must report that, over the past 6 months, three or more have been present more days than not associated with the client's worry. The task of acquiring these ratings during the clinical interview is usually straightforward. However, care should be taken to ensure that the symptoms endorsed are ones that (1) have occurred often over the past 6 months (i.e., persistent symptomatology) and (2) do not occur exclusively or predominantly as symptoms of another disorder (e.g., are not symptoms of a panic attack, generalized social anxiety, or substance use).

In many clinical settings, the administration of entire interview schedules, such as the ADIS–R, is impractical. Nevertheless, the clinician should comprehensively screen for additional diagnoses using, perhaps, portions of interview schedules such as the ADIS–R given that patients with GAD rarely present with this as their sole diagnosis. Furthermore, although data are sparse on this issue to date, the presence of comorbid conditions exert great influence on the patient's response to treatment (cf. Brown & Barlow, 1992). A brief medical history should be gathered as well, to determine whether current or past medical conditions (or medications) are contributing to, or even responsible for, symptoms comprising the client's clinical presentation (e.g., hyperthyroidism or temporomandibular joint syndrome). Often, clients should be encouraged to schedule a physical examination if over 2 years have elapsed since their last medical workup. Moreover, patterns of alcohol and drug use should be evaluated given that excessive use of, or withdrawal from, such substances may produce symptomatology quite similar to that of GAD and other anxiety disorders (Chambless, Cherney, Caputo, & Rheinstein, 1987).

Questionnaires

The administration of a variety of self-report questionnaires is a useful part of the clinical process, both in terms of aiding in the initial diagnostic process and for periodic assessment throughout the course of treatment to evaluate the extent of the client's progress. At our clinic, we routinely administer a battery of questionnaires as part of the intake evaluation; these measures were selected to assess the range of the key and associated features of the DSM-III-R anxiety and mood disorders (e.g., anxiety sensitivity, social anxiety, obsessions, compulsions, worry, phobic avoidance, and current levels of depression and anxiety). Although this

extensive intake battery is administered in part for research purposes at our clinic, a battery of questionnaires judiciously selected to assess several dimensions of the emotional disorders can be useful in purely clinical settings as well. For example, questionnaire results reflecting elevations in dimensions of anxiety or mood in addition to dimensions comprising the patient's principal complaint may have important ramifications in how the treatment program is delivered (cf. Brown & Barlow, 1992). This is particularly true for GAD, which most often co-occurs with other disorders such as panic disorder and social phobia (Moras et al., 1992).

A few measures that we have found to be particularly useful in the assessment of GAD are discussed here. We previously mentioned the PSWQ (Meyer et al., 1990) as a measure frequently used in our work with GAD patients. The PSWQ was developed by Borkovec and his colleagues at Penn State University to address the need for an easily administered, valid measure of the trait of worry. Indeed, at 16 items, the PSWQ can be administered to clients quite conveniently (range of possible scores equals 16 to 80). In their initial study introducing this measure, these researchers found the PSWQ to possess high internal consistency and temporal stability and favorable convergent and discriminant validity, and to be uncorrelated with social desirability (Meyer et al., 1990). In a study conducted at our clinic using a large sample of anxiety disorder patients ($n = 436$) and 32 nonanxious controls (Brown, Antony, & Barlow, 1992), we replicated the findings of Meyer et al. (1990) indicating the favorable psychometric properties of the PSWQ. Most encouraging was the finding in this study indicating that scores on the PSWQ distinguished GAD patients ($n = 50$) from each of the other anxiety disorder groups, including patients with OCD. The mean PSWQ score for GAD patients was 68.11 ($SD = 9.59$); means and standard deviations for selected other groups were as follows: panic disorder with agoraphobia, $M = 58.30$, $SD = 13.65$; social phobia, $M = 53.99$, $SD = 15.05$; OCD, $M = 60.84$, $SD = 14.55$; normal controls, $M = 34.90$, $SD = 10.98$.

Although perhaps less well-known than

other measures of its kind, another measure that has proven quite valuable in our work with GAD patients is the DASS (Lovibond & Lovibond, 1992). The DASS is the most recent iteration of the SAQ (Lovibond, 1983), which was mentioned earlier in our review of the GAD literature. The DASS is a 42–item measure that yields three psychometrically distinct subscales reflective of current (i.e., past week) symptomatology. Among the three subscales, the DASS Stress scale (Tension scale on the SAQ) has been particularly helpful in the assessment of GAD. For example, in the Brown, Antony, and Barlow (1992) study, the SAQ Tension scale differentiated GAD patients from all the other DSM-III-R anxiety disorder groups with the exception of patients with OCD. Of the variety of symptom measures (e.g., questionnaire and clinician ratings of anxiety, depression, stress/tension) in which correlations were calculated in this study, only SAQ Tension was significantly correlated with the PSWQ in the GAD sample. Noted earlier, this finding dovetails with other initial data suggesting that persistent symptoms of tension (vs. autonomic arousal) may have discriminant validity with regard to GAD.

Self-Monitoring

As will become evident later in the chapter, self-monitoring is an integral part of our treatment program for GAD. When the client is trained in proper use and completion of the self-monitoring forms, the data obtained from this mode of assessment can be among the most valuable information that the clinician has in the formulation and evaluation of the treatment program. Among the reasons for the importance of self-monitoring are the following: (1) to gauge the client's response to treatment by obtaining accurate information on relevant clinical variables (e.g., daily levels of anxiety, depression, positive affect, and amount of time spent worrying); (2) to assist in acquiring a functional analysis of the client's naturally occurring anxiety and worry episodes (e.g., situational factors or precipitants, nature of anxiogenic cognitions, and methods or behaviors engaged in to reduce worry or anxiety); and (3) to assess integrity and compliance with between-session homework as-

signments. An example of a form that we are apt to use in the treatment of GAD clients is shown in Figure 4.2.

Right from the start of therapy, self-monitoring is presented to the patient as an important part of the treatment process. In the spirit of collaborative empiricism (cf. Young, Beck, & Weinberger, Chapter 6, this volume), the client is told that both he/she and the therapist will be working together to first try to get a better understanding of the factors contributing to the client's naturally occurring anxiety, tension, and worry. Accordingly, self-monitoring is introduced as one of the best ways for obtaining the most accurate information about these processes, because, if the client and therapist were to rely solely on retrospective recall of the client's symptomatology, much important information could be lost or distorted.

These forms are introduced to the client by first defining the type of information that we are attempting to collect (e.g., helping the client to differentiate anxiety from depression). Once the form has been explained thoroughly, we often assist the client in generating a sample entry using the current day or a recent episode of anxiety/worry, depending on the type of form being introduced. This is to increase the probability that the client will use the forms properly between sessions. This step is critical when first introducing the self-monitoring forms, but it is also helpful to repeat it periodically throughout treatment to prevent drift.

OVERVIEW OF TREATMENT

Our treatment protocol for GAD typically averages 12 to 15 hour-long sessions held weekly, with the last two sessions held biweekly. For reasons noted earlier, although treatments for GAD have been delivered efficaciously in a small-group format (see section on Treatment Outcome Studies), at this stage in the development of our GAD treatment protocol, we prefer a format that is one on one.

As it currently stands (cf. Craske et al., 1992), our GAD protocol has several components that address each of the three systems of anxiety: (1) physiological—PMR training; (2) cognitive—cognitive restructur-

Name: *Claire T.*

Each evening before you go to bed, please make the following ratings, using the scale below:
1. Your AVERAGE level of anxiety (taking all things into consideration);
2. Your MAXIMUM level of anxiety which you experienced that day;
3. Your AVERAGE level of depression;
4. Your AVERAGE level of pleasantness;
5. The percentage of the day that you felt worried, using a 0–100% scale where 0 means no worry at all and 100 means worrried all the waking day.

Level of Anxiety/Depression/Pleasantness feelings

0	1	2	3	4	5	6	7	8
None		Slight		Moderate		A lot		As much as you can imagine

Date	Average anxiety	Maximum anxiety	Average depression	Average pleasantness	Percentage of day worried
9/17	4	6	4	2	60%
9/18	5	5	4	3	60%
9/19	4	5	3	3	65%
9/20	6	6	4	2	75%
9/21	6	8	5	1	80%
9/22	7	8	5	1	90%
9/23	5	7	4	2	75%

FIGURE 4.2. Weekly Record of Anxiety and Depression.

ing; and (3) behavioral—worry behavior prevention, problem solving, and time management. At the heart of our new treatment protocol for GAD is the element of worry exposure, in which clients are directed to spend a specified period of time daily (usually 1 hr) processing their worry content.

Whereas some evidence points to the possibility that multicomponent treatments may, in fact, result in lower efficacy due perhaps to dilution of their constituent treatment elements (cf. Barlow et al., 1992), we have retained a multicomponent protocol for a variety of reasons (e.g., early evidence reflecting the limited success of single component treatments and the DSM-IV conceptualization of GAD as a multidimensional disorder). Moreover, whereas a dilution effect may certainly account for the few findings noting diminished efficacy of multicomponent treatments, this factor may be of less concern when combined protocols are delivered in the clinical setting without the time and methodological constraints inherent in controlled treatment outcome studies.

PROCESS OF TREATMENT

Initial Sessions

Table 4.2 provides a general outline of a combined GAD treatment program. The initial sessions are most important because it is the time that the groundwork and rationale for what is to follow are delineated. Included in the first two sessions are the following elements: (1) delineation of client and therapist expectations; (2) description of the three components of anxiety (i.e., physiological, cognitive, behavioral) and

TABLE 4.2. Outline of GAD Treatment Protocol

Session 1
  Obtain client's description of anxiety and worry
  Introduce client to nature of anxiety and worry
  Describe three-systems model of anxiety
  Provide overview of treatment (e.g., importance of self-monitoring, homework, regular attendance)
  Provide treatment rationale
  Assign homework: self-monitoring

Session 2
  Review self-monitoring
  Review nature of anxiety, three-systems model
  Discuss physiology of anxiety
  Discuss maintaining factors in GAD
  Assign homework: self-monitoring

Session 3
  Review monitoring forms
  Rationale for 16-muscle-group PMR
  Do in-session PMR with audiotaping for home practices
  Assign homework: self-monitoring, PMR

Session 4
  Review monitoring forms, PMR practice
  Do 16-muscle-group PMR with discrimination training
  Introduce role of cognitions in persistent anxiety (e.g., nature of automatic thoughts, solicitation of examples
    from client)
  Describe and counter probability overestimation cognitions
  Introduce cognitive monitoring form
  Assign homework: self-monitoring (anxiety, cognitive monitoring, and countering), PMR

Session 5
  Review: self-monitoring, PMR, probability overestimation countering
  Do 8-muscle-group PMR with discrimination training
  Describe and counter catastrophic cognitions
  Assign homework: self-monitoring (anxiety, cognitive monitoring, and countering), PMR

Session 6
  Review: self-monitoring, PMR, cognitive countering (probability overestimation, decatastrophizing)
  Do 8-muscle-group PMR with discrimination training; introduce generalization practice
  Review types of anxiogenic cognitions and methods of countering
  Assign homework: self-monitoring (anxiety, cognitive monitoring, and countering), PMR

Session 7
  Review: self-monitoring, PMR, cognitive countering
  Do 4-muscle-group PMR
  Introduce worry exposure (e.g., imagery training, hierarchy of worry spheres, in-session worry exposure)
  Assign homework: self-monitoring (anxiety, cognitive monitoring, and countering), PMR, daily worry exposure

Session 8
  Review: self-monitoring, PMR, cognitive countering, worry exposure practices
  Introduce relaxation-by-recall
  Review rationale for worry exposure
  Do in-session worry exposure
  Assign homework: self-monitoring (anxiety, cognitive monitoring, and countering), worry exposure, relaxation-
    by-recall

Session 9
  Review: self-monitoring, cognitive countering, worry exposure, relaxation-by-recall
  Practice relaxation-by-recall
  Introduce worry behavior prevention (e.g., rationale, generation of list of worry behaviors, development of
    behavior prevention practices)
  Assign homework: self-monitoring (anxiety, cognitive monitoring, and countering), worry exposure, worry
    behavior prevention, relaxation-by-recall

(cont.)

TABLE 4.2. (*cont.*)

Session 10
  Review: self-monitoring, cognitive countering, worry exposure, worry behavior prevention, relaxation-by-recall
  Introduce cue-controlled relaxation
  Assign homework: self-monitoring (anxiety, cognitive monitoring, and countering), worry exposure, worry
    behavior prevention, cue-controlled relaxation

Session 11
  Review: self-monitoring, cognitive countering, worry exposure, worry behavior prevention, cue-controlled
    relaxation
  Practice cue-controlled relaxation
  Introduce time management or problem solving
  Assign homework: self-monitoring (anxiety, cognitive monitoring, and countering), worry exposure, worry
    behavior prevention, cue-controlled relaxation

Session 12
  Review: self-monitoring, cognitive countering, worry exposure, worry behavior prevention, cue-controlled
    relaxation
  Generalize relaxation techniques
  Practice time management or problem solving
  Assign homework: self-monitoring (anxiety, cognitive monitoring, and countering), worry exposure, worry
    behavior prevention, cue-controlled relaxation, time management/problem-solving practice

Session 13
  Review: self-monitoring, cognitive countering, worry exposure, worry behavior prevention, cue-controlled
    relaxation, time-management/problem-solving practice
  Practice cue-controlled relaxation
  Review skills and techniques
  Discuss methods of continued application of techniques covered in treatment

Note. Adapted from an unpublished protocol by Cote and Barlow (1992).

application of the three-system model to the client's symptomatology (e.g., discussion of the client's somatic symptoms of anxiety, content of worry, and worry behaviors); (3) discussion of the nature of anxiety (e.g., adaptive and maladaptive anxiety, "normalizing" the client's symptomatology); (4) rationale and description of the treatment components; and (5) instruction in the use of self-monitoring forms.

The importance of regular session attendance and completion of homework assignments is emphasized as crucial to treatment. Clients are given a general idea of what to expect in terms of their response to treatment in coming weeks (e.g., improvement is not immediate and initial increases in anxiety are possible due to the nature of therapy).

Cognitive Therapy

Cognitive therapy comprises an integral component of our treatment for GAD. The cognitive component of our treatment pro-

tocol, in many ways, is consistent with the procedures outlined by Beck and Emery (1985). Early in the treatment, the client is provided with an overview of the nature of anxiogenic cognitions (e.g., concept of automatic thoughts, situation-specific nature of anxious predictions, and reasons why inaccurate cognitions responsible for anxiety persist unchallenged over time). As part of this introduction to the tenets behind cognitive therapy, considerable care is taken to ensure that the client understands that in the case of inappropriate anxiety, it is a person's interpretations of situations, rather than the situations themselves, that are responsible for the negative affect experienced in response to the situation. Thus, through examples offered by the therapist, as well as client-generated examples solicited by the therapist, a most important first step in cognitive therapy is to assist clients in realizing that they must be able to identify the specific interpretations/predictions they are making in order to be in a position to challenge these cognitions effectively.

As do Beck and Emery (1985), we approach the task of automatic thought identification via a variety of techniques. Within the treatment session, these might include any or all of the following: therapist questioning (e.g., "What did you picture happening in that situation that made you tense up?"); imagery (asking the client to imagine the situation in detail as a means of providing additional cues for retrieving automatic thoughts occurring in that situation); and role playing. Beginning with the first session of cognitive therapy, clients are trained to use the Cognitive Monitoring Form (see Figure 4.3) to prospectively self-monitor and record their thoughts associated with anxiety. As noted earlier, a common problem with both clients and therapists-in-training is that the process of eliciting anxiogenic cognitions is done incompletely or superficially (e.g., discontinuing the process of questioning to uncover anxiogenic cognitions prematurely, prior to identifying the thought(s) principally responsible for the negative affect).

In addition, the therapist often needs to assist clients in identifying the appropriate times to make entries on the Cognitive Monitoring Form. For instance, one suggestion that we offer clients is to use any increase in their anxiety level as a cue to self-monitor (e.g., "My anxiety level just went from a two to a six. What was I thinking just then that may have contributed to this?"). (Shifts in the client's affect noted by the therapist in session are also good opportunities to assist the client in eliciting automatic thoughts.)

With regard to the problem of identifying the specific thought(s) that are chiefly responsible for a given episode of anxiety, we encourage clients to determine whether the thoughts they have identified would satisfy the criterion of producing the same emotion in anyone if they were to make the same interpretation of the situation. This is also an important guideline for therapists to adhere to when assisting the client to identify automatic thoughts in session.

After providing an overview of the nature of anxiogenic cognitions and methods of identifying them, the therapist defines two types of cognitive distortions involved in excessive anxiety: (1) probability overestimation and (2) catastrophic thinking. Cognitions involving probability overestimation are defined as those in which a person overestimates the likelihood of the occurrence of a negative event (that is actually unlikely to occur). For example, a client who is apprehensive over the possibility of job termination, despite a very good job record, would be committing this type of cognitive error in overpredicting the likelihood of losing his/her job. After defining and providing examples of probability overestimation thoughts, the therapist describes some reasons why these types of thoughts may persist over time, even despite repeated disconfirmation (e.g., the belief in having been "lucky" thus far, the belief that worry or its associated "worry behaviors" have prevented the negative outcome from occur-

Name: *Claire T.*

Trigger/ Event	Automatic thought	Anxiety (0–8)	Prob. (0–100%)	Countering (Alternatives, evidence)	Realistic prob. (0–100%)	Anxiety (0–8)
Son's football game today	*He'll get hurt or paralyzed.*	*6*	*75%*	*Only had sprained ankle. Never anything major. Might not get hurt. He's tough and a good player, like his dad. Maybe a minor injury*	*10%*	*3*

FIGURE 4.3. Cognitive Self-Monitoring Form (worry record).

ring, and the tendency to habitually focus on negative outcomes without examining other alternatives).

Catastrophic thinking is defined as the tendency to view an event as "intolerable," "unmanageable," and beyond one's ability to cope with successfully, when in actuality it is less "catastrophic" than it may appear on the face of it. In addition to catastrophic thoughts associated with perceptions of being unable to cope with negative events, regardless of their actual likelihood of occurrence (see dialogue below between therapist [T] and Chloe [C]), we would also put under the category of catastrophic thinking thoughts that involve drawing extreme conclusions/consequences to minor or unimportant events (e.g., "If my child fails an exam, it must mean that I have failed as a parent"). Cognitions reflecting a strong need for perfection or personal responsibility (and of drawing extreme negative conclusions of the consequences of not being perfect or responsible) would be apt to fall under this category as well.

Often, clients have some difficulty in making the distinction between probability overestimation thoughts and catastrophic thinking. The therapist should provide examples emphasizing their distinction on the basis of the dimensions of likelihood (probability overestimation) and perceived inability to cope or tendency to ascribe overly dire consequences to minor events (catastrophic thinking). Moreover, the therapist should note that the two types of thoughts are often associated with one another in the client's chain of worry.

T: You mentioned that two nights ago it was particularly difficult for you to get to sleep.

C: Well, it is always difficult, but that night I didn't fall asleep until 3:30.

T: Do you have an idea why that night was particularly difficult?

C: The phone rang at, I'd say, around 11:30 and, as you know by now, the damn phone is always a source of my anxiety. But, at that hour, I was worried that something was wrong. As it turned out, it was a wrong number, but by then . . .

T: What did you think the call might be about?

C: Well, you know, bad news of some sort, someone dying or something like that. After my visit home this summer, I have often worried that my father is getting up there in years, he turned 55 in July, and, well, since I moved to Albany I haven't seen my folks nearly as much as I would have liked to.

T: So, when the phone rang, were you worried that something may have happened with your father?

C: I don't think just then because I picked up the phone real fast, but the phone ringing kind of startled me. But after I hung up, I wondered why I was so anxious and I realized that I must have thought that something happened to him. Once I realized that, I was worried about him the rest of the night.

T: If I recall from what you said before, he's in pretty good health, isn't he?

C: Yeah, he had a mole removed a while ago. Since he's worked outside all of his life, I worry that all that sun will have caused him to get skin cancer some day.

T: What do you picture happening if your dad did pass away?

C: What do you mean? Do you mean what would I do? We shouldn't even talk about this unless you want to see me in a real state . . . you know, being an only child and all. . . .

T: Thinking about that really upsets you.

C: Well, I'm already anxious enough already. Something like that would really set me over the edge. I mean the fact that I'm this anxious as it is shows that I can't cope well with situations. I imagine that, if my dad died, I would really shut down and not be able to cope with anything. And not want to!

Although the therapist in this case example should go further to elucidate the nature of the client's catastrophic predictions associated with the loss of a parent, she would also be at good point to clarify the distinction between probability overestimation (e.g., overestimating the likelihood of the passing of a parent who is in good health and overestimating the risk associated with sun exposure) and catastrophic thinking (e.g., predicting that the parent's death would result a permanent breakdown in one's emotions and ability to cope) and how these two types of thoughts are interconnected in the client's "worry chain."

Whereas it would be appropriate at this point to provide an overview of the most common examples of probability overestimation and catastrophic thoughts reported by GAD clients, it should be noted that the few studies that have examined the nature of GAD clients' worries (e.g., Borkovec et al., 1991; Craske et al., 1989; Sanderson & Barlow, 1990) have found that the content of worries obtained using structured interviews (i.e., ADIS–R) has not fallen neatly into the *a priori* categories that have been used thus far (e.g., illness/health, family matters, work/school). Indeed, in each of the studies cited in the prior sentence, the category "miscellaneous" was among the top one or two most commonly categorized spheres of worry. Thus, unlike what has been found regarding the nature of the anxiogenic cognitions reported by panic disorder patients (cf. Craske & Barlow, Chapter 1, this volume), whereby the content of the majority of these patients' cognitions falls within relatively finite categories (e.g., fear of dying, going crazy, or losing control), no such evidence has been obtained pertaining to the content of GAD clients' worries thus far. Nevertheless, to reiterate findings reviewed earlier, the extant data bearing on this issue suggest that the nature of GAD worry reflects an excess of the same process (and content) found in nonclinical individuals; the parameter of uncontrollability of the worry process is the principal feature differentiating pathological and nonpathological worry (cf. Barlow, 1991; Borkovec et al., 1991).

As with the case of identifying anxiogenic cognitions, the therapist cannot underscore enough the importance of being thorough and systematic in countering these thoughts. The therapist does not introduce countering to replace negative thoughts with positive thoughts (e.g., "There is nothing to worry about, everything will be fine"). Instead, countering is introduced as part of the process of examining the validity of the interpretations/predictions the client is making and in order to replace inaccurate cognitions with realistic, evidence-based ones. The importance of repeated, system-

atic countering is emphasized by noting that whereas the thoughts responsible for excessive anxiety can be habit-like and hard to break, they indeed can be unlearned and replaced with more accurate cognitions via practice and repeated application of the techniques of countering.

In addition, the client is instructed that countering of anxiogenic cognitions involves the following guidelines: (1) considering thoughts as hypotheses (rather than facts) that can be either supported or negated by available evidence; (2) utilizing all available evidence, past and present, to examine the validity of the belief; and (3) exploring and generating all possible predictions or interpretations of an event or situation. In the case of countering probability overestimation thoughts, these guidelines are utilized to evaluate the realistic likelihood (i.e., real odds) of the future occurrence of the negative event.

To counter catastrophic thoughts, the therapist asks the client to imagine the worst possible feared outcome actually happening, and then to critically evaluate the severity of the impact of the event. This entails giving an estimation of the client's perceived ability to cope with the event if it were to occur. Additionally, in countering catastrophic thinking, it is extremely useful to have the client generate as many alternatives to the worst feared possible outcome as possible. The therapist may note difficulty on the client's part in generating alternatives, as clients with GAD typically manifest a negative attentional bias. The therapist should emphasize that decatastrophizing does not entail trying to get the client to view a negative event as positive or even neutral (e.g., "It would, indeed, be upsetting for most people if a parent passes on"). Rather, via critically evaluating the actual impact of the negative event, the client may come to view its effects as time-limited and manageable.

Worry Exposure

Guided by new conceptualizations of the nature of pathological worry reviewed earlier (cf. Borkovec & Hu, 1990; Rapee & Barlow, 1991), worry exposure (cf. Craske et al., 1992) entails the following procedures: (1) identifying and recording the client's two or three principal spheres of worry (ordered hierarchically beginning with the least distressing or anxiety-provoking worry); (2) practicing imagery training by imagining pleasant scenes; (3) practicing vividly evoking the first worry sphere on the hierarchy by having the client concentrate on his/her anxious thoughts while trying to imagine the worst possible feared outcome of that sphere of worry (e.g., for a client who worries when her husband is late from work, this might entail imagining her husband unconscious and slumped over the steering wheel of the car); (4) once the client is able evoke these images vividly, introducing the crux of the worry exposure technique, which entails reevoking these thoughts and images, holding them clearly in mind for at least 25–30 min; and (5) after 25–30 min have elapsed, having the client generate as many alternatives as he/she can to the worst possible outcome (e.g., if my husband is late, he may have gotten tied up at work, caught in traffic, or stopped at the store). As indicated on the Daily Record of Worry Exposure Form presented in Figure 4.4, at the end of the alternatives-generating phase of the exposure practice, clients record their levels of anxiety and imagery vividness for various points in the exposure (e.g., maximum anxiety during the 25–30 min of worry exposure or anxiety levels after generating alternatives to the worst outcome).

After 30 min or more have been spent processing the first sphere of worry according to the preceding procedures, clients are often instructed to repeat these steps for the second worry on the hierarchy. After the therapist is assured that the client is carrying out the worry exposure technique properly in session, the exercise is assigned as daily home practice. Clients are instructed that when the exposure exercise no longer evokes more than a mild level of anxiety (i.e., 2 or less on the 0–8 anxiety scale) despite several attempts of vividly imagining that worry, they should move on to the next sphere of worry on the hierarchy.

Of course, an important initial step in the application of the worry exposure technique is to prepare the client adequately by providing a thorough description of the rationale and purposes of the exercise. This should involve, at some level, a discussion of the concept of habituation and the reasons why habituation has not occurred naturally despite repeated exposures to these worries over time (e.g., the natural tendency to rapidly shift from one worry to the next in the worry chain). In addition, worry exposure should be introduced as providing additional opportunities to apply strategies learned thus far in the treatment protocol (i.e., cognitive restructuring and, perhaps, applied relaxation). Indeed, the therapist may wish to note that repeated exposure to the same worry thought or image may make it easier for the client to develop a more objective perspective on the worry, thus enhancing the client's facility in applying cognitive countering techniques.

Several possible difficulties may arise during the application of worry exposure. Theoretically (cf. Foa & Kozak, 1986), therapeutic exposure to feared thoughts, images, or situations should generally be reflected by the following patterns: (1) initial exposures elicit at least moderate anxiety levels; (2) protracted exposure to fear cues, in session, results in the reduction of the high levels of anxiety elicited at the onset of the exposure (i.e., within-session habituation); and (3) across several, separate exposure trials, maximum anxiety levels evoked by exposure decrease until the fear cues no longer elicit considerable anxiety (i.e., between-session habituation).

A potential problem is that the worry exposure will fail to elicit more than minimal anxiety during the initial exposures. A variety of reasons may contribute to this phenomenon, including the following: (1) images are insufficiently vivid; (2) images are too general, thereby hindering the client's focus on the worst outcome; (3) images are not salient to the client's sphere of worry, or the sphere itself does not contribute appreciably to the client's GAD symptomatology; (4) client is applying coping techniques (e.g., cognitive restructuring and cue-controlled relaxation) during the 25–30 min of worry exposure; and (5) client is covertly avoiding the processing of the most salient worry cues, perhaps via distraction to neutral thoughts or images.

Another potential difficulty that might arise is that the client evidences negligible within- or between-session habituation of

Name: *Claire T.*   **Date:** *11/15*
Time began: *3 am/pm*
Time ended: *5 am/pm*

Anxiety/Imagery (circle)	0	1	2	3	4	5	6	7	8
	None		Slight		Moderate		A lot		Extreme

Symptoms during exposure:

Trembling/shaky	_____	Nausea/abdominal distress	✓
Muscle tension	✓	Hot flashes/chills	_____
Restlessness	_____	Frequent urination	_____
Fatigue	✓	Trouble swallowing	_____
Shortness of breath	_____	Keyed up/on edge	✓
Pounding/racing heart	✓	Easily startled/jumpy	_____
Sweating/clammy hands	_____	Difficulty concentrating	_____
Dry mouth	_____	Trouble sleeping	_____
Dizzy/lightheaded	_____	Irritability	✓

Worry 1: Content   *Friend dropping by later—she'll see my messy house and be shocked. She'll laugh and think less of me.*

Worst possible feared outcome: *She'll call our friends to tell tell them—they'll also laugh, and not respect me.*

Anxiety (0–8): *7*   **Imagery (0–8):** *7*

Possible alternatives: *She won't even care—she's there to see me, not my house. She might not notice the floors. Even if she does, she might not think it so interesting to call everyone about it. She might be glad not to see me cleaning for a change.*

Anxiety (0–8): *2*   **Imagery (0–8):** *2*

FIGURE 4.4. Daily Record of Worry Exposure.

anxiety to the worry exposure cues, despite repeated exposure trials. Again, there may be several reasons for this problem, including (1) covert avoidance when high levels of anxiety are beginning to be experienced; (2) a failure to maintain the same image throughout the exposure (e.g., tendency to shift continually from one distressing image to another), thereby mitigating habituation to the image; and (3) insufficient exposure time (e.g., maintaining the worry image for less than 25 min, or, in some cases, 25–30 min does not provide ample exposure time for particularly distressing images).

As noted in the discussion of therapist variables that may contribute to treatment outcome, it is important that the therapist possess a thorough understanding of the theoretical parameters of therapeutic exposure. Accordingly, this underscores the importance of the systematic collection of clients' anxiety ratings during the worry exposures (both in session and during home practice) as these ratings will be useful indices of progress and potential problems.

Occasionally, clients evidence difficulties in generating alternatives to the worst feared outcome. This difficulty may be reflective of the client's limited facility in applying cognitive countering techniques (covered prior to worry exposure in our GAD protocol) or may indicate a relatively strong belief conviction associated with the sphere of worry in question. Related to this problem, therapists will sometimes observe that clients' anxiety ratings do not subside after alternatives to the worst feared outcome have been generated. When problems of this nature are noted, the therapist should question clients for their hypotheses about why anxiety reduction did not occur. In accordance with the common pitfalls of cognitive therapy (e.g., failure to challenge anxiogenic predictions thoroughly with evidence-based counterarguments), initially the therapist may need to assist the client in the generation of alternatives. In our experience, anxiety reduction will begin to occur with this feedback, in tandem with continued worry exposure (e.g., habituation to imaginal cues associated with the worst feared outcome may enhance the client's objectivity concerning the sphere of worry in question, thereby facilitating cognitive restructuring).

As noted above, distraction is an issue that should be routinely addressed in GAD treatment. Specifically, clients may try not to think of the worst possible feared outcome, or may allow their thoughts to wander during the procedure. The therapist needs to point out that although distraction from anxious thoughts or feelings may relieve anxiety in the short term, it is essentially an ineffective long-term strategy for anxiety management. In fact, distraction may reinforce the client's view that certain thoughts and images are to be avoided. Moreover, distraction will not allow for a proper appraisal of the client's anxiogenic cognitions and prohibits the rise in anxiety level necessary for adequate emotional processing of worry (cf. Foa & Kozak, 1986). Therefore, the therapist must be especially watchful for instances of client distraction, pointing out these instances to the client and offering reasons why this behavior is not beneficial to long-term anxiety reduction.

Relaxation Training

Relaxation training in our current combined treatment protocol for GAD does not differ appreciably from the manner in which we have administered this treatment com-

ponent in the past (e.g., Barlow, Craske, Cerny, & Klosko, 1989; Barlow et al., 1992). Our relaxation component is based on the procedures outlined by Bernstein and Borkovec (1973). The procedures begin with PMR (16 muscle groups) with discrimination training. Discrimination training entails teaching the client to discriminate sensations of tension and relaxation in each muscle group during the PMR exercise. The ultimate goal of discrimination training is to increase the client's ability to detect sources and early signs of muscle tension, thereby facilitating the rapid deployment of relaxation techniques to those areas. After working through each of the 16 muscle groups, relaxation deepening techniques are employed during the induction, including slow breathing (i.e., slow diaphragmatic breathing, repeating the word *relax* on the exhale).

Clients are given the rationale that relaxation is aimed at alleviating the symptoms associated with the physiological component of anxiety, partly via the interruption of the learned association between autonomic overarousal and worry. The 16-muscle-group PMR exercise averages 30 min in duration. Usually, the therapist conducts PMR, in session, while audiotaping the procedure so that the client may practice PMR twice daily at home using the tape. In addition to the practice of audiotaping, we adhere to all the typical guidelines of PMR administration (e.g., directives to the client to initially practice PMR in quiet, comfortable locations, but not immediately before going to bed).

After the client has had considerable practice with the 16-muscle-group exercise (typically over a span of 2 weeks), the number of muscle groups is gradually reduced from 16 to 8 and then to 4 (e.g., stomach, chest, shoulders, forehead). During the course of muscle-group reduction, the therapist should nonetheless be attuned to the specific body areas that the client reports to be problematic, consequently adapting the 4-group exercise to target those problem areas.

Of course, the rationale behind muscle-group reduction (i.e., 16 to 8 to 4) is to make the relaxation techniques more "portable," such that the client can rapidly deploy the technique at any time, when needed. Thus, after the client has practiced the 4-muscle-group exercise, relaxation-by-recall is introduced. Relaxation-by-recall consists of concentrating on each of the four muscle groups that have been targeted up to this point, and in turn, releasing tension in each muscle area via the recall of the feelings of relaxation achieved in past practices. It therefore does not involve tensing the muscles as in the prior methods, but simply recalling the experience of relaxing the muscles (e.g., "as you concentrate on your stomach, think of your stomach muscles letting go, and feel the warmth of relaxation as your stomach relaxes"). As with the full PMR exercise, clients are instructed to maintain a pattern of slow, regular breathing, covertly repeating the word *relax* with every exhalation. At this phase, clients are instructed to continue practicing the relaxation exercises daily in nondistracting environments, but are also encouraged to begin trying "mini-practices" in other situations (e.g., at the office).

After the client has mastered relaxation-by-recall, cue-controlled relaxation is introduced. This is essentially a "one-step relaxation" that entails taking a few slow breaths (about four or five) and repeating the word *relax* on the exhale. With the exhale, clients are instructed to release all the tension in their body, concentrating on the feelings of relaxation. Thus, cue-controlled relaxation is the most portable of the relaxation strategies covered in the protocol and clients are directed to employ the technique in a variety of situations, particularly those in which anxiety or tension is frequently experienced (e.g., work, home, waiting in line, talking on the telephone, and driving). In addition, we encourage our clients to continue periodically to go through the full 16-muscle-group PMR exercise for a variety of reasons (e.g., to rehearse discrimination training and to strengthen the association of the cue "relax" to feelings of relaxation).

Clients vary in the time it takes them to work through the various phases of relaxation training. When implemented in the clinical setting (i.e., without the confines of protocol treatment in controlled outcome studies), the therapist should not guide the client through the phases of the relaxation training too quickly (e.g., reduce from 16 to 8 to 4 too rapidly) as the clients' success with implementing subsequent techniques (e.g.,

relaxation-by-recall and cue-controlled relaxation) may depend largely on their mastery of earlier strategies (e.g., discrimination training during 16-muscle PMR).

In addition to several practical difficulties that may be associated with clients' relaxation training (e.g., noncompliance with homework due to not finding sufficient time to practice or problems in maintaining a sufficient attentional focus during practice), one problem noted in the research literature associated with these techniques has been referred to as relaxation-induced anxiety (RIA). Anxiety induced by the relaxation procedure itself appears to be associated with a heightened sensitivity to internal somatic cues (e.g., feelings of floating or subjective feelings of loss of control; cf. Borkovec et al., 1987; Heide & Borkovec, 1984). Attesting to the potential relevance of this phenomenon to clinical outcome, Borkovec et al. (1987), in a study comparing cognitive to ND therapy in patients who all received PMR as part of the treatment package, found RIA to be significantly and negatively associated with change on the Hamilton Anxiety and Depression scales.

Thus, the therapist should be watchful for signs of RIA, particularly in client's with comorbid panic disorder (cf. Cohen, Barlow, & Blanchard, 1985), a commonly occurring additional diagnosis in clients with a principal diagnosis of GAD (Moras et al., 1992). When RIA is observed, the therapist should reassure the client that it is most likely a temporary automatic response to a learned pattern of autonomic overarousal and that these feelings usually abate with repeated practice.

Worry Behavior Prevention

As noted earlier in the chapter, Craske et al. (1989) found that over half of GAD worries recorded by self-monitoring were associated with carrying through some corrective, preventive, or ritualistic behavior. Thus, as is the case with compulsions in OCD, these "worry behaviors" are negatively reinforcing to the client as they usually result in temporary anxiety reduction (cf. Brown et al., 1993). Examples of worry behaviors include frequent telephone calls to loved ones at work or at home, refusal to read obituaries or other negative events in the newspaper, and cleaning one's house daily in the event that someone drops by. As in the treatment of OCD (cf. Riggs & Foa, Chapter 5, this volume), a potentially useful intervention in the treatment of GAD is the systematic prevention of responses that are functionally related to worry.

Since clients may not see the contribution of these behaviors to the maintenance of their anxiety, it is useful for the therapist to approach this area as an opportunity to test out clients' beliefs that these behaviors actually prevent dire consequences from occurring (i.e., prediction testing). The procedure begins with the therapist assisting the client to generate a list of the client's common worry behaviors. Once these behaviors have been identified, we often have the client self-monitor and record the frequency with which each behavior occurs during the week. The next step is to instruct the client to refrain from engaging in the worry behavior, perhaps engaging in a competing response in its place (e.g., keeping the car radio on a news station during the entire commute home instead of turning it off to avoid hearing about reports of traffic accidents). Prior to performing the worry behavior prevention exercise, we record the client's predictions concerning the consequences of response prevention. After the worry behavior prevention exercise has been completed, the therapist assists the client in comparing the outcome of the exercise to the client's predictions (e.g., the frequency of engaging in worry behaviors is not correlated with the likelihood of the occurrence of future negative events). As is the case with the treatment of panic disorder (cf. Craske & Barlow, Chapter 1, this volume), prediction testing can be a useful adjunct to cognitive restructuring. An example of a completed Worry Behavior Prevention Form is presented in Figure 4.5.

Time Management

Many GAD clients report feeling overwhelmed by obligations and deadlines, in addition to everyday hassles and stressors. Because of the nature of GAD (e.g., anxious apprehension), these clients are apt to magnify these daily hassles, augmenting the impact of these minor stressors. Accordingly, basic skills in time management and goal setting are highly useful adjuncts to the treatment of GAD, partly because these techniques may assist clients to focus their efforts on the tasks at hand rather than worrying about accomplishing future tasks.

Our time-management strategies involve three basic components: delegating responsibility, assertiveness (e.g., saying "no"), and adhering to agendas. With regard to responsibility delegation, we often note to our clients that perfectionistic tendencies may prevent them from allowing others to take on the tasks that they typically assume themselves. Moreover, GAD clients may be reluctant to refuse unexpected or unrealistic demands placed on them by others, preventing them from completing planned activities (particularly likely in GAD clients with comorbid social phobia, a commonly occurring additional diagnosis). Usually, we target issues pertaining to responsibility delegation and assertiveness via the utilization of the worry behavior prevention and prediction testing exercises outlined above. For example, this might entail asking the client to delegate small tasks to coworkers to test the client's predictions associated with this activity (e.g., "the quality of work will suffer"; "it will take longer to explain it to someone than do it myself"; "I'll be perceived by other as shirking my responsibilities").

Agenda adherence should begin with the examination of the client's daily activities (generated by at least 1 week of client self-monitoring). Next, the therapist can assist the client in establishing an organized strategy for sticking to agendas and structuring daily activities such that the client's most important activities are accomplished. This objective can be facilitated via the generation of a "goal-setting list" in which the activities planned for the day are categorized as follows: A tasks—extremely important activities that need to be done that same day; B tasks—very important tasks that must get done soon, but not necessarily on that same day; and C tasks—important tasks that need to be done, but not very soon. Next, the therapist assists the client in allotting sufficient time to complete each activity (perhaps by allotting up to twice the amount of time expected to complete the task, if the

Name: *Claire T.*

Date	Practice task	Anxiety before task (0–8)	Anxiety after task (0–8)
11/27	*Ask husband to call only when leaving from work, not earlier*	4	3
11/28	" "	3	3
11/29	" "	3	2
11/30	" "	3	1
12/1	" "	2	2
12/2	" "	2	0
12/3	" "	1	0

FIGURE 4.5. Worry Behavior Prevention Form.

client evidences a tendency to rush through tasks or have unrealistic expectations regarding the length of time necessary to get things done).

After time estimates have been established for each task, the client is instructed to place the A-B-C tasks into time slots in their daily schedule. If their day is so erratic that this strategy is unfeasible, clients are instructed to make a three-header list of their A-B-C tasks and cross each off on completion. Although not evaluated in controlled treatment trials to date, our clinical experience suggests that these time-management strategies can be quite helpful in reducing clients' daily levels of stress while increasing their sense of mastery and control over their day-to-day life.

Problem Solving

A final component of our combined GAD treatment protocol is problem solving. As per Meichenbaum and Jaremko (1983), we present the technique to clients by noting that individuals often encounter two types of difficulties when problem solving: (1) viewing the problem in general, vague, and catastrophic ways and (2) failing to generate any possible solutions. The first difficulty is addressed by teaching the client to conceptualize problems in specific terms and to break the problem into smaller, more manageable segments (which will have already been addressed to some degree during cognitive therapy).

The second difficulty is addressed by teaching clients to brainstorm their way through the problem. For instance, clients may report trouble with incurring costly repairs to their car. The therapist can assist the client in generating as many possible solutions to the dilemma as possible, no matter how unreasonable they sound on the face of it (e.g., buying a used car, buying a new car, going to a different mechanic, or deliberately totaling the car and collecting the insurance money). After a host of potential solutions have been generated, each one is evaluated to determine which are the most practical, with the end goal of selecting and acting on the best possible solution (which may have not been realized prior to brainstorming). Clients are informed that with practice, brainstorming can be accomplished more efficiently (e.g., requiring less time and effort).

In addition to facilitating reaching a solution for the given problem, another potential benefit of this technique is that it fosters clients' ability to think differently about situations in their life and to focus on the realistic rather than the catastrophic. In this sense, the benefit of problem solving is similar to the mechanism of action presumed to be partly responsible for the efficacy of worry exposure.

CASE STUDY

The dialogue that follows between therapist (T) and "Claire" (C) is representative of our combined treatment protocol for GAD, covering a span of 13 individual, hourlong sessions. Because both clients and novice therapists may have the most difficulty applying the cognitive strategies, we have highlighted these techniques in the transcripts.

Session 1

The first session served as an introduction of the client to the therapist, as well as an overview of the treatment program.

T: This treatment program is geared toward helping you learn about generalized anxiety and develop skills that will help you cope with high anxiety. Because the program involves learning and applying skills, there will be some exercises that I will ask you to do both in our sessions and at home. We'll arrange to have 13 sessions, each usually lasting about one hour. In addition, we'll meet periodically through the next 12 months to monitor your progress. First, Claire, I'd like to get a sense from you about the kinds of problems you're experiencing that have brought you to the clinic.

C: I just feel anxious and tense all the time. It all started in high school. I was a straight-A student, and I worried constantly about my grades, whether the other kids and the teachers liked me, being prompt for classes—things like that. There was a lot of pressure from my parents to do well in school and to be a good role model for my younger sisters. I guess I just caved into all that pressure, because my stomach problems began in my sophomore year of high school. Since that time, I've had to be really careful about drinking caffeine and eating spicy meals. I notice that when I'm feeling worried or tense my stomach will flare up, and since I'm usually worried about something, I'm always nauseous. My husband thinks I'm neurotic. For example, I vacuum four times a week and clean the bathrooms every day. There have even been times when I've backed out of going out to dinner with my husband because the house needed to be cleaned. Generally, my husband is supportive, but it has caused a

strain on our marriage. I get so upset and irritated over minor things, and it'll blow up into an argument. I'm here because I'd like to live like normal people do, without all of this unending tension and anxiety.

T: You've mentioned, Claire, that you suffer from a number of physical symptoms, such as irritability, stomach problems, tension, and the like. In high school, you worried about your grades, whether others liked you, being on time, etcetera. What sorts of things do you worry excessively about now?

C: Oh, everything, really. I still worry about being on time to church and to appointments. Now I find I worry a lot about my husband. He's been doing a tremendous amount of traveling for his job, some of it by car, but most of it by plane. Because he works on the northeastern seaboard, and because he frequently has to travel in the winter, I worry that he'll be stuck in bad weather and get into an accident or, God forbid, a plane crash. It's just so scary. Oh, and I worry about my son. He just started playing on the varsity football team, so he's bound to get an injury sometime. It's so nerve-wracking to watch him play that I've stopped going to his games with my husband. I'm sure my son must be disappointed that I'm not watching him play, but it's simply too much for me to take.

T: Earlier you said that minor things get you upset. Give me some examples of those minor things.

C: When my son leaves his room a mess, or when my husband tracks dirt into the house. That annoys me so much! I pride myself on a neat and clean house, with floors so spotless that you could eat off them. It irritates me when they're not neat, and I let them know about it.

T: What you've been saying is quite typical of individuals who have generalized anxiety disorder. Let me first give you an overview of the nature of anxiety. Anxiety is one of the basic emotions that all species have, and thus it is a natural and necessary part of life. We as human beings experience anxiety in situations that might be dangerous, threatening, or challenging in some way. For instance, if you were walking in a jungle and heard a twig snap behind you, what would you think?

C: I suppose I'd imagine that a lion or tiger were behind me. I'd try to be still and listen.

T: Right. Physically, you'd probably feel your heart race, your breath get shorter and deeper, and some perspiration. Your body is in the process of preparing for fighting or fleeing the potential danger. Your heart races and pounds so that more blood will rapidly go toward your major muscle groups, like your upper thighs and arms. Your breath adjusts in the event that you'll need to exert yourself by running or fighting. Sweating helps you in that a predator will have a harder time grasping onto something slippery. That's where the term *fight or flight response* originates. By imagining the worst, you're in a better position to prepare for danger. How do you think you'd respond if instead of thinking that the snapped twig was due to a tiger or lion, thinking that it was due to a fallen branch?

C: I wouldn't be afraid at all.

T: So, you can see how important your thoughts are in determining your level of anxiety. Anxiety can be a productive and driving force in situations that are less dramatic. For instance, when you were in high school, how did you prepare for an exam?

C: I'd study like a madwoman the week beforehand, and review my notes over and over again until it was imprinted on my mind.

T: Why?

C: Fear of failure, I guess. Or more like fear of getting less than an "A."

T: How do you think you would have studied if you didn't have that anxiety?

C: Like most of my friends, who were perfectly content to study the night before and settle for a "B" or "C."

T: That's a good example of how anxiety can really help you to achieve goals and accomplish tasks. When anxiety is maladaptive or excessive is when it inter-

feres with your ability to relax when you want to, when it's too intense or too frequent for the situation at hand, or when there's no danger present. In this treatment we'll focus on removing that excessive anxiety, the anxiety that fuels your worries and those physical symptoms that you have.

We view anxiety as a reaction to a trigger that might be internal or external. Examples of triggers include your thoughts, physical sensations, certain events or situations, and so on. Because anxiety is a reaction, you can learn to control it through skills and exercises designed to help you manage your high anxiety episodes. Along with viewing anxiety as a reaction, we also break it apart into three distinct components: physical, cognitive, and behavioral. Before I explain each component, let me ask you if anyone's ever told you to just relax and stop worrying as a remedy for your anxiety.

C: Oh, yeah! That's my husband's favorite line.

T: Do you find it helpful for you?

C: Not at all. It doesn't tell me how to relax, or how to stop worrying.

T: Exactly. By looking at anxiety in a global way, it can be difficult to see how to control it. That's where examining your anxiety with the three-component model is useful, as we can break up your anxiety into specific parts and target each individually. The physical component of your anxiety is manifested in the bodily sensations that occur during anxiety and worry. In your case, it might be upset stomach, tension, irritability, etcetera. The second component, called the cognitive component, is shown in the thoughts you have during anxiety or worry. Finally, the behavioral component is manifested in the specific behaviors that occur during or as a consequence of anxiety. Some examples of these behaviors include leaving very early for appointments, pacing, foot or finger tapping, perfectionism, procrastination, cleaning, safety checks, and so on. As we continue in the sessions, it will be easier to identify some of those behaviors.

These behaviors tend to reduce anxiety in the short run, but may actually be maintaining your anxiety over the longer term. In many ways, those behaviors are similar to your anxious thoughts. Through time and repeated practice, they've become second nature, or automatic, for you.

Worry is a very interesting phenomenon. We as human beings worry so that we can prepare for future danger or threat. It helps us to problem-solve, in a sense, the things that we're afraid might happen in the future. By thinking things completely through, we can come up with a variety of solutions and occasionally alternatives to what we might be predicting in a situation. It's when we don't allow ourselves to think things through and to imagine our worst possible fears coming true that worry can spiral into increased worry and anxiety. You stated earlier, Claire, that you worried about being on time for classes in high school. Why was that?

C: The teachers were very strict, and would take points off each time you walked in the door late.

T: What was so bad about that?

C: It would come off your grade-point average for that class. I didn't want to be late so that I could avoid those points taken off, to preserve my 4.0 average.

T: What if you had arrived to class late a few times?

C: I wouldn't have graduated with a perfect GPA, and my parents would have been very disappointed in me.

T: And then what?

C: I'm not sure. Maybe they wouldn't have paid my college tuition bill or something. I couldn't have afforded college on my own, and would have missed the opportunity to go. That would have been terrible. I would never have met my husband, or gotten my present job, or been able to pay my bills.

T: I can see how being late was anxiety provoking for you, given those concerns. But, do you really think that your parents would not have paid for college if you hadn't graduated with a 4.0 GPA?

C: Looking back, probably not. My sisters just partied through school, and my parents footed the bill for them.

T: By *not* allowing yourself to think through the worst and *not* asking yourself the likelihood of the worst happening, you in effect reinforced your worry over being late to classes. As we continue with the sessions, we'll be examining your worries in a similar fashion and have you systematically experience your worry so that you can overcome this approach–avoidance mode for handling worries. You'll also learn to identify and challenge your anxious thoughts, learn how to physically relax your entire body, and learn to change some of your anxiety- and worry-related behaviors to ones that are more effective in the long run in decreasing your anxiety. Is that clear?

C: Yes, pretty much.

T: Good. Another important element in this program is self-monitoring and homework. Self-monitoring of your levels of anxiety and worry will allow you to be a more accurate observer of your experiences. Sometimes our clients tell us that they feel anxious continuously, but when they begin to self-monitor, we discover that some days of the week are better or worse than others. Another advantage of self-monitoring is its ability to give you a more objective understanding of your anxiety. You'll feel less like a victim and more like a scientist, trying to figure out and examine your anxiety. By monitoring your progress, we can evaluate the effectiveness of this treatment program for you and make any necessary adjustments along the way. Finally, because there will be regular homework assignments, you will learn the strategies much more rapidly if you consistently self-monitor. You may find a temporary increase in your anxiety when you first begin to self-monitor and attempt the homework, which is perfectly normal. This may happen because you're facing your anxiety, perhaps for the first time. It's a good sign that we're on the right track in identifying and targeting your anxiety.

[Client is instructed in the use of the Weekly Record of Anxiety and Depression and the Cognitive Monitoring Form.]

Session 2

In this session, the therapist began with a brief review of the week's self-monitoring and reiterated the treatment rationale provided in Session 1.

T: Let's start off today by reviewing your forms. It looks as though you had quite a bit of anxiety on the 20th through the 22nd; you gave average anxiety ratings of 6s and 7 on those days. [See Figure 4.2.]

C: Yes, those were tough days. My husband went away on business for a couple of days, and I was pretty worried about him while he was gone. You know, the same old thing of whether he's okay, if he's run into bad weather or has gotten into an accident. He came home in one piece, of course, but it's tough for me to see him go. I had him call when he arrived at the hotel and every night before he went to bed, so that made me feel somewhat better.

T: I'm glad that you mentioned that you had your husband call you several times during his trip. Does he call you from work regularly?

C: Yes, he does because he knows it makes me feel better. But I think sometimes it annoys him to have to keep "checking in" with me, as if I were his mother or something.

T: That's useful information to note, for we'll be on the lookout for those kinds of behaviors that you might do to relieve your anxiety in the short run.

To review items from our last session, we mentioned that the program will last a year. The first 13 sessions will take place over the next 15 weeks, with Sessions 12 and 13 occurring biweekly. It's vital that you regularly practice the strategies covered over the next several meetings in order to make them almost second nature, so that they'll eventually replace the anxious thoughts and behaviors that are fueling your high anxiety and worry. When you get a good checkup from the dentist, you wouldn't stop brushing, right? We use the same principle here: that complete consolidation of these skills takes time and daily practice.

As I mentioned last week, anxiety and worry are normal responses to danger or threat. As such, anxiety's main function is to protect and prepare the body for survival by initiating the fight or flight response. The physical component of anxiety is responsible for automatically activating certain sensations to prepare the body for action. This fight or flight response is part of the autonomic nervous system, composed of two distinct parts: the sympathetic nervous system and the parasympathetic nervous system. The sympathetic nervous system is activated in the face of danger and is responsible for sending impulses to the adrenal gland. The adrenal gland then releases the neurochemicals, adrenalin and noradrenalin, which send impulses to other parts of the body to signal the need to prepare for action. The parasympathetic nervous system, on the other hand, is the restoring branch of the autonomic nervous system and serves to return the body to its natural resting state. When you are anxious, the autonomic nervous system will propel various body systems, such as the cardiovascular, respiratory, and digestive systems. Your heart might race and pound, your might feel slightly short of breath, and your digestion might be disrupted, which results in feelings of nausea and upset.

The second component of the model of anxiety is the cognitive component. This refers to your specific thoughts and predictions occurring when the fight or flight response is initiated. Worrying is an attempt to problem-solve possible future danger or threat. If you are worried or anxious, your attentional focus will be diverted to those possible sources of threat, and it therefore will be difficult to concentrate on other things going on around you that do not pose an imminent threat. Because your concentration is affected, you might experience forgetfulness or a poor memory. This does not mean that you're losing your mind or your faculties. Rather, it indicates that your anxiety and worry are interfering with your ability to attend to sources of incoming information other than threat or danger. This inability to focus attention onto tasks is protective in the sense that when faced with real threat or danger, you need full attention onto what is going on around you.

Behaviorally, when you are anxious you may engage in certain behaviors designed to reduce or alleviate your anxiety. Moving around a lot by pacing, foot tapping, cleaning, etcetera, releases extra energy produced by anxiety and aids in distracting you from your thoughts at hand. Similarly, procrastinating on tasks is a common way people attempt to avoid feeling anxious about getting something completed. This can stem from a fear of failure or a fear of not doing something perfectly. You've mentioned before that you often feel irritable. This is another common behavioral manifestation of anxiety. Additionally, when we're anxious we might do other things to help reduce our anxiety and worry. For you, that might be having your husband phone you from work several times a day to make sure he's safe. Another example that you mentioned before, Claire, was that you've stopped going to your son's football games because of your anxiety while watching him play. Although you may feel temporarily better by not watching his games, you simultaneously are reinforcing your anxious belief that something dangerous will happen to your son on the football field.

C: You're right, but I couldn't bear seeing my son hurt or injured. It would really upset me, so it's much easier to avoid going to the games so that if he does get hurt, I won't have to see it.

T: You seem fairly convinced that your son will be seriously injured while playing football, but in fact the odds of his getting seriously injured are quite low. By not going to the games, you're really telling yourself that the odds of him

getting hurt are much higher than they really are. Also, you seem to be predicting that you wouldn't be able to bear seeing him hurt. Has there ever been a time in your life when you did see someone injured?

C: Umm, yes. My husband collided with another fielder during a softball game and had to get stitches in his forehead.

T: Were you able to tolerate seeing that?

C: Barely! I managed to get him to the hospital, but I was pretty shaky while I drove there.

T: The point is that although you were anxious in that situation, you did in fact cope with your husband's injury. We'll return to some of these concepts in a later session. I'd now like to describe how excessive worry and anxiety can develop.

C: That should be fairly easy to do in my case. Both of my parents were big worry warts who were always five minutes ahead in their thinking. I had to call home any time I went out, I had to keep my room immaculate, and I sometimes told white lies because I knew how little things would set them off, like the time I was pulled over for going ten miles over the speed limit when I first got my license. Even though I didn't get a ticket from the officer, I knew that if I told them that I got pulled over, my parents would be too worried and upset to ever let me drive on my own again. So I said I went to the library to drop off some books. It's funny, but to this day I never go over the speed limit, and I get this little rush of anxiety if I see a patrol car while I'm driving.

T: It sounds as though you grew up with parents who modeled anxious behaviors around you. In actuality, having anxious parents does not necessarily guarantee that an individual will be anxious as an adult. Several contributing factors interact to produce excessive anxiety and worry. These factors include a physical responsivity, or generalized overarousal to all kinds of events—both positive and negative. Are you moved to tears easily when watching a sad movie or being at a wedding?

C: Definitely.

T: We refer to that tendency as overarousal, or "being emotional." It appears that part of that overarousal may be inherited, while part of it may be learned from your environment. Other factors that may be responsible for excessive anxiety and worry are a tendency to view the world as a dangerous and threatening place, along with a tendency to feel a need to control things happening in your life.

Along with these factors, life experiences and stressors may trigger excessive anxiety and worry. In your case, Claire, the experiences of being in high school and stressors of grades and friends may have initially triggered your excessive worry. Of course, because those triggers are no longer in the picture, we will begin to identify current triggers and maintaining factors to your anxiety and worry.

There are several factors that maintain excessive worry. One is the tendency to try to resist worrying or to try to distract yourself from worrying without feeling as though you've resolved anything in your mind. Do you ever find yourself trying to think about something else when you start worrying?

C: Sure, all the time. I also try to keep busy, which sometimes helps me take my mind off what's bothering me.

T: Another factor is due to the interference in the ability to effectively problem-solve due to high emotional arousal. Because you're in a relatively frequent state of high anxiety and overarousal, you may be focusing exclusively on all the possible negative things, while not giving more realistic, less threat-laden alternatives proper attention. Also, worry can serve a superstitious function in that some individuals who worry excessively believe that worrying can avert negative outcomes, or that worrying is a sign of a conscientious person.

In the treatment program, we'll target the three components of anxiety using strategies specifically designed for each. First, you'll learn a technique called progressive muscle relaxation, involving tensing and releasing your muscles to reduce your physical anxiety. Next, you'll learn methods designed to counteract your negative predictions and to develop more realistic thoughts while anxious. You'll also learn to break the learned and automatic association between high arousal and specific images or thoughts fueling your worry. This will be accomplished by having you systematically experience your worry in a very controlled way. Finally, you'll develop the ability to engage in certain behaviors or activities that you may be avoiding, and changing the behaviors that reinforce your anxiety, so that you can test out some of your negative predictions if you do or don't carry the behaviors out.

For this week, it will be important to pay special attention to the kinds of thoughts you experience when anxious or worried, and the specific physical sensations and behaviors that accompany those anxious or worrisome thoughts.

Session 3

T: Today, we'll cover progressive muscle relaxation. First, tell me about your anxiety and worry this past week.

C: It was fairly high. A boy on my son's football team broke his leg in a scrimmage before the game. His leg was broken in two different places, and he'll be out for the rest of the season. That just threw me for a loop. My son was right next to the boy when this all happened. Then, to top it all off, my in-laws dropped by unexpectedly for the weekend, and I was a basket case trying to prepare good meals and make them feel welcome. Naturally, my husband was laid back about both events, saying that I got myself worked up for nothing. I was really worried for a good three days in a row, probably for about 75% of each day as I wrote down on the Weekly Record. You know, I was a bit leery about self-monitoring, because it would take time out of my schedule. But it's not so bad, and I do feel a little bit more in control of my anxiety. It's just sort of pathetic that I wasted my weekend worrying about stupid things like getting dinner on the table and whether my in-laws were comfortable in the guest room, like I wrote on the cognitions form.

T: It's great that you've been monitoring regularly. The amount of time that you invest in monitoring and practicing the skills is directly correlated with the amount of benefit you will gain from the treatment program.

Recall that general tension and over-arousal contributes to high anxiety and worry, and may result from excessive worry. By learning how to physically relax your body, you can stop your anxiety to spiral and can help yourself to feel better physically. Progressive muscle relaxation involves tensing and releasing your muscles, with fewer muscle groups being targeted as your skill in the technique increases. We'll first start with 16 muscle groups, then follow with 8 groups, and then down to 4. When you first begin this procedure, it will take about 30 minutes. Gradually, you will require less time to feel fully relaxed. Remember that because relaxation is a skill, it takes time and practice to become an expert in it. However, you should feel some effects almost immediately.

C: I know that I have to set aside time for homework, but 30 minutes sounds like a lot to me.

T: It may be that sense of time pressure that adds to your anxiety. Put it to yourself this way: by completing the relaxation every day, you're doing something that will help you physically and emotionally. All the other things that are going on in your life that "have to get done by such-and-such time" can wait. If you try to fit the relaxation in between several things on your daily agenda, you will most likely feel pressured to get it done and over with. So, you won't feel relaxed at all! Make sure that you do the relaxation exercise at a time when you won't feel rushed or pressured by other responsibilities.

The procedure entails tensing and then releasing or relaxing your muscles. By tensing, you can accentuate the feeling of release as well as discriminate when you might be unconsciously tensing your muscles during the day. Tensing your muscles shouldn't produce pain, but rather a sensation of tightness or pressure. You'll progress in sequence by tensing and releasing your lower and upper arms, lower and upper legs, abdomen, chest, shoulders, neck, face, eyes, and lower and upper forehead.

Be certain to practice in the beginning in quiet, nondistracting places. Concentration is a key element in learning how to relax, so you'll need to be in an environment where you can focus you attention completely on the sensations of tensing and releasing your muscles. This means no phone, TV, radio, or kids around during the exercise. It may help to lie on your bed during the exercise, but be sure not to fall asleep. Loosen or remove tight clothing, eyeglasses, contact lenses, shoes, belts, and the like. This exercise should be practiced twice a day, 30 minutes each time, for the following week.

Now I'll turn on the audiotape and record the relaxation procedure that I'll have you do to my voice in the session. You can use the audiotape at home for your practices. [The therapist then began the 16-muscle-group relaxation procedure and gave the tape to the client at the end of the session.]

T: (*After relaxation has been conducted*) How was that?

C: Wow. Great. I don't want to get up. At one point, I felt as though I were floating. It was a little scary, so I opened my eyes, and it went away.

T: That can happen when you first try relaxation. Sometimes people find the procedure frightening due to the feeling that they're not in control of their feelings, like floating or heaviness. The more you do the relaxation, the less that will occur. [Client was given the Relaxation Record, to self-monitor practices and to note any problems with concentration or relaxation.]

Session 4

Following a review of the client's week and the relaxation homework exercises, the 16-muscle-group relaxation was refined to involve discrimination training. After the therapist and client rehearsed this technique, the cognitive component of the treatment protocol was introduced.

T: I'd like to turn now to the cognitive component of anxiety. Remember that your thoughts are instrumental in determining emotions, like anxiety. Concerning excessive worry and anxious thoughts, the key question to ask yourself is whether your judgment of risk or danger is valid, that is, if it can be supported by existing and available evidence. In many cases, worry over the worst possible feared outcome is out of proportion. To challenge your worries and anxious thoughts, keep in mind several basic principles. First, challenging your thoughts does not mean positive thinking. Instead, when you challenge your anxious cognitions, you'll be thinking more realistically about situations. Second, because thinking is often an automatic process, it may be difficult at first to identify these thoughts when you're anxious. Think back to the very first time you learned how to drive. Was it easy?

C: Sort of. I enjoyed it, but I had to focus on my turning and braking when I first started to drive.

T: Do you think about those things now when you drive?

C: Not at all. I don't focus any attention on my driving. I'm usually thinking about how much time I have to get somewhere, and the shortest way to arrive at my destination.

T: That's because driving has become automatic for you. You are still thinking when you drive, but because you've driven so many times, your thoughts are more rapid and automatic when you're behind the wheel. The same idea applies to your anxious thoughts. Because you've lived with high anxiety for so long, you may have certain automatic thoughts associated with anxiety. A large part of the treatment will center on identifying and challenging these anxious thoughts in order to reduce your worry and anxiety. It is important to be as specific as possible from now on about the thoughts you have when you're anxious

or worried. Try to envision what it is that's making you anxious or nervous.

On one of your cognitive monitoring forms for this week, Claire, you wrote that you were afraid about your son playing in his football game. What specifically were you worried about?

C: That he'd get seriously hurt. His team was playing last year's state champions, so you know that those boys are big and strong. My son is good, but he hasn't been playing for years and years.

T: How specifically do you imagine your son getting hurt?

C: Getting a broken back or neck. Something that will result in paralysis or death. It happened to two NFL players this past year, remember?

T: What happened to your son when he played in the game?

C: Nothing, really. He came home that afternoon with a sore thumb, but that went away after a while. He said he scored a touchdown and had an interception. I guess he played really well.

T: So, what you're saying is that you had predicted that he would be injured during the game, but that didn't happen. When we're anxious, we tend to commit a common cognitive error, called probability overestimation. In other words, we overestimate the likelihood of an unlikely event. While you were feeling anxious and worried, what was the probability in your mind that your son would be hurt, from 0 to 100%?

C: About 75%.

T: And now what would you rate the probability of your son getting hurt in a future game?

C: Well, if you put it that way, I suppose around a 50% chance of him getting injured.

T: So that means that for every two times that your son plays football, he gets hurt once. Is that correct?

C: Umm, no, I don't think it's that high. Maybe about 30%.

T: That would be one out of every three times that your son gets hurt. To counter the tendency to overestimate the probability of negative future events, it's helpful to ask yourself what evidence from the past supports your anxious belief. What evidence can you provide from your son's playing history to account for your belief that he'll get hurt in one out of every three games?

C: Well, none. He had a sprained ankle during summer training, but that's it.

T: So, what you're saying is that you don't have very much evidence at all to prove that your son has a 30% chance of getting hurt in a game.

C: Gee, I never thought of it that way.

T: What are some alternatives to your son getting seriously hurt in a football game?

C: He might not get hurt at all. But I know he must have some pain, with all those bruises covering his arms and legs. He's a real stoic, just like his father.

T: What other alternatives can you think of instead of your son getting seriously hurt?

C: He could get a minor injury, like a sprained ankle or something of that nature.

T: Right. And what would be the probability of your son getting a minor versus a major injury?

C: Probably higher, like 60% or 70%.

T: To go back to your original worry, what would you rate the probability of your son getting seriously injured during a football game?

C: Low, about 10%.

T: So, one out of every ten times your son will get seriously hurt playing football. How many times has your son played football?

C: He just started varsity this year, and he's a junior. But he's been playing since he got to high school, about three years. All in all, about 25 games.

T: And how many times in those three years has he been seriously injured?

C: Not once. I see what you're doing. It's so foolish for me to think these irrational thoughts.

T: Well, it's understandable that your predictions about the future are biased toward negative possibilities. When we're in a state of high anxiety, we naturally focus on the more negative possibilities in order to prepare for them should they come true. Because you worry excessively, your thoughts will be more negative regarding future events. That's why it's essential that you regularly counter these probability overestimations every time you have a worry. On your cognitive monitoring form, you indicated that your anxiety was a 6 on the 0 to 8 scale while thinking about your son getting hurt. What would you rate your anxiety now, after having had gone through the countering?

C: Much lower. Around a 3 or so. But it could still happen to him, getting paralyzed. And by worrying over that possibility, no matter how small, I can somehow prepare myself emotionally if it were to really happen.

T: There's always that possibility, however minute. However, every time you tell yourself that "it could still happen," you're effectively throwing out all the evidence disconfirming that belief. You're also saying to yourself that your son's personal chances of paralysis from a football injury are much higher than everyone else's. To counter this tendency, remember that his chances of a serious injury remain the same as that of the rest of the team, every day.

Additionally, worrying about a future event does nothing to change its probability of occurring. What worrying will do, however, is make you feel even more anxious and distressed, along with giving you a false sense of control over the future.

Starting this week, record the countering of your worries on the Cognitive Monitoring Form [see Figure 4.3]. As before, you'll jot down every time you feel moderately anxious or worried about something. In the first column, identify the trigger or event that started the worry or anxiety. Then, write down your specific automatic thought and rate your anxiety, from 0 to 8. In the next column, rate from 0 to 100% the probability of that automatic thought occurring. However, from now on, counter that thought by asking yourself, "What's the evidence for my belief or prediction?

Are there other alternative possibilities that I can think of?" After countering the thought, rerate the probability of your automatic thought and then rate your anxiety. Ask yourself, what's the worst possible consequence of that automatic thought, and write it down. If you are still moderately anxious—(4 or above on the 0 to 8 scale)—go back to the first column and repeat the procedure, using the worst possible feared consequence that you wrote down in the column headed "trigger or event." Continue this until your anxiety is 3 or less [see Figure 4.3]. Next time, we'll talk about another cognitive strategy to target your worry and anxiety.

Session 5

Following a review of the client's week and the relaxation homework exercises, the 8-muscle-group relaxation was introduced in order to begin to make the relaxation strategies more readily applicable in naturalistic settings. When reducing the number of muscle areas, the therapist should instruct the client to continue to involve areas that are particularly salient (e.g., if the client reports considerable jaw tension or teeth clenching, the therapist should instruct the client to spend extra time focusing on the jaw and mouth when doing the exercise). After this exercise was rehearsed, probability overestimation was reviewed and decatastrophizing was introduced.

T: Last week, we went over the concept of probability overestimation. Tell me in your own words what is meant by probability overestimation.

C: If I remember correctly, it means that when I'm overly anxious I will predict some future negative event as more likely than it really is.

T: That's exactly right. Did you monitor any instances this week when you overestimated the probability of a negative event?

C: Of course. My husband had to take an unexpected overnight business trip be-

cause his coworker caught the flu. It was raining when he drove off, and naturally I assumed the worst, that he'd get into a car accident.

T: How did you rate the probability of that event?

C: I gave that an 80%, because it was coming down like cats and dogs. And other drivers aren't necessarily defensive drivers like my husband and I are.

T: Were you able to come up with any past evidence contrary to your belief that he'd get in an accident?

C: As a matter of fact, I realized that my husband has never been in a car accident before in his life. He's a great driver, very safe like I am, and he also never speeds. I remembered from a driver's ed class back in high school that most accidents are caused by speeding and drunk driving. That made me feel much better.

T: Could you think of any alternatives to your husband getting in an accident, Claire?

C: I wrote that maybe if he did get in an accident, it would be a little fender bender, like most accidents usually are. Or, he'd arrive at the hotel without any incident whatsoever. Or, if it were really dangerous to drive, he'd pull over until the storm passed. My husband has a good head on his shoulders. This exercise made me realize that I don't give him enough credit.

T: Given what you've just provided in the way of evidence and alternatives, what probability would you assign to your husband getting involved in an accident while driving?

C: Very low. I'd still give a slightly higher rating, like 10%, because of inclement weather. But really low.

T: What is your anxiety when you think about it that way?

C: Practically nothing, a 1 or 2.

T: Great. Along with probability overestimations, another common cognitive error associated with anxiety is called "catastrophizing." This refers to the tendency to blow things out of proportion, or to "make mountains out of molehills."

Using adjectives such as "intolerable," "awful," "terrible," "unbearable," and "horrible" to describe future negative events is one way to catastrophize. Another way to catastrophize is to jump to an extreme conclusion from an unimportant or irrelevant event. For instance, what do you think the nurse at the doctor's office thought of you when you were late a few weeks ago?

C: She probably thought I wasn't punctual or conscientious. I was a little concerned that she'd think I was irresponsible, and maybe because of that she wouldn't accept a personal check as a form of payment from me. I wouldn't be dependable in her eyes.

T: In order to *decatastrophize*, you must first imagine the worst possible outcome of what you're worried or anxious about, and then judge its realistic severity. Very often, when people are chronically anxious, they underestimate their ability to cope with future negative events. They also tend to believe that the event might continue forever, for example, that everyone would begin to think of you as undependable. It helps to keep in mind that events cannot continue forever. Even if a very negative event were to happen, like losing a loved one or facing a serious illness, we would still be able to cope with it, despite feeling like we couldn't. How you feel and what you do are two very different things. You might feel in your heart that you wouldn't be able to cope with a negative event, but the fact is that the hallmark of being a human being is having an extraordinary ability to adapt to our surroundings.

C: Sure, but how do I convince myself of that? I really don't believe that I could cope with losing my son or husband. It scares me so much that I dislike even talking about this.

T: Which is why we should probably discuss your fears, being that a majority of your worry centers on the safety of your husband and son. What would happen if you lost your son?

C: I'd be devastated. It really would be terrible. I'd never get over it. Maybe I'd have a breakdown and be placed in the psychiatric ward or something. I don't know, but it would be bad.

T: How do you know that it would be bad? What evidence can you provide to support your belief that you'd never get over your son's death?

C: Well, none, but children shouldn't die before their parents. I'm such a nervous wreck already that it would put me over the edge.

T: Again, you're using your anxious feelings as proof of your belief. We refer to that as "emotional reasoning." Tell me some alternatives to having a breakdown or being placed in a hospital.

C: I would cope, I guess, but I really can't fathom how I'd do that.

T: Has anyone in your life died?

C: Sure. When I was 17, my boyfriend was killed in a motorcycle accident. It was really hard on me. On a certain level I never really got over it. Sometimes I dream about him. He was a great guy, and his poor mother went through hell when he passed away. I never want to experience what she went through.

T: It must have been a very difficult time for you. An experience like that is unusual for a 17-year-old to have. It's pretty natural to have dreams about loved ones who have died, especially when the death was of a violent nature. Tell me some of the emotions you went through at the time.

C: I went through a whole range of feelings: anger, disbelief, anxiety, loneliness, pain. It was a tough time for me. He died the summer we graduated from high school, and we were supposed to go to college together.

T: Do you still feel those emotions?

C: Not at the same intensity. I sometimes feel anger when I see motorcycles on the road, and of course I get pretty anxious. But now, when I think of Todd, I try to think of the happy memories. He was a wonderful guy, and I was lucky to have known him for the time that I did. He's in heaven right now, I'm sure of it, and looking out for me, like he said he would before he died. I met my husband several months after Todd's death while I was in college, and felt like I met someone who could have been Todd's twin brother. Without Jim, I don't know how I would have ever gotten over Todd's death.

T: Despite having experienced the unexpected death of Todd, Claire, you did cope with your loss. You experienced the full range of emotions the people go through when they lose someone close, and you were still able to function. Is that right?

C: Yes, but it was a struggle to get up in the morning for a while there. I cried almost every day for a month or two.

T: What do you think would happen if you lost your husband or son?

C: Probably the same thing, maybe even more intense. But you're right. I would be able to cope. It would be a job and a half, but I would have to. Luckily, I have a very supportive and close-knit family who's always there for me.

T: Let's turn to another example of decatastrophizing. You mentioned that by coming in late, the nurse would think of you as being undependable, and that she wouldn't accept your personal check to pay for the visit. What would happen then?

C: I'd have to incur a balance, and I would pay it later.

T: Anything else?

C: No, other than embarrassment.

T: Why would that be bad?

C: I hate being embarrassed like that. People would think badly of me, and I'd lose the respect of others.

T: Then what?

C: Then I would lose friends and be lonely.

T: Then what?

C: Then I would feel sad and miserable, and lead a miserable little existence.

T: Tell me how able you would be to cope with that possibility, from 0 to 100%, where 0 equals completely unable to cope?

C: 5%.

T: Now try to think of some ways that you could cope with that possibility.

C: First of all, a true friend wouldn't lose respect for me because of something as mundane as not having a personal check accepted. And if I did lose friends over that, then what kinds of friends are they? Also, I could use a credit card, or go get a cash withdrawal from the bank if the doctor didn't accept credit cards.

T: Do you think you'd be miserable and sad for the rest of your life?

C: Oh, not at all. I'd feel bad for a little while, but it would eventually go away.

T: And how likely is it that all your friends would remember a minor event like that for years to come?

C: Not very likely at all.

T: Have you ever been embarrassed before?

C: Too many times to count!

T: How long, on average, does the embarrassment last?

C: A few minutes at the most. A day in rare instances, but usually not longer.

T: So, Claire, you see how these catastrophic images can add to your anxiety. To counter your catastrophic thoughts, write your anxious thoughts and worries down on the Cognitive Monitoring Form as you've been doing for probability overestimations. Then, ask yourself, "What's the worst possible consequence that could happen? If it happens, so what? Why would it be bad? How likely would it be to occur? How could I cope with it if it were to occur?" You should notice a substantial decline in your anxiety levels when you use your cognitive strategies regularly for each and every worry and anxious thought.

Session 6

Prior to the review of the types of anxiogenic cognitions (i.e., probability overestimation, catastrophic thinking) and corresponding methods of countering, eight-muscle-group relaxation was reviewed and refined to incorporate discrimination training. In addition, generalization practices were assigned.

T: By doing the relaxation as frequently as possible, you will enhance your skill in the technique and find it more and more helpful in dampening tension when it arises. So, now I'd like you to begin applying the relaxation procedure in more distracting and challenging situations. In this way, you'll be making the relaxation more portable. You can start applying the relaxation while you're in traffic, waiting in line, at home watching TV, and in the grocery store. Okay, why don't we review some of your records on the Cognitive Monitoring Form? You wrote down that you hadn't yet finished doing the laundry at 10:00 p.m. as one of your triggers, and that your automatic thought was that you'll have to stay up late to finish it all. You then rated your anxiety as a 6. Why was that so anxiety provoking for you?

C: I really need about 9 hours of sleep every night. If I don't get that amount, I feel dragged out and exhausted the next day, and find it difficult to get anything done at all because of my low energy level.

T: And what will happen if that takes place?

C: Well, I'll get behind in all the other things that need to be done in the house, and I won't be able to catch up on it all.

T: And then what?

C: It'll just pile up, and my family will be living in a pig sty. It's disgusting to think about it.

T: Then what will happen?

C: Then my husband will be embarrassed to bring people over the house, and get angry with me.

T: And then?

C: And maybe he'd want to leave me. Occasionally, we do some entertaining at our home, and so it is important that my husband and I make a good impression. If I can't have the house in presentable condition, then his colleagues and supervisors will think less of him and demote him, all because of my inability to do my job as a homemaker right.

T: Do you see how you chain these anxious thoughts together so that the end result is really quite negative? That's fairly typical of individuals who have generalized anxiety. It becomes crucial to identify these thoughts specifically so that you can target each one in your chain of worry and anxiety. Let's then begin with the first automatic thought; namely, that you would have to stay up later and lose some sleep, which would make it difficult to get things accomplished the next day. What is the probability of that happening, from 0 to 100%?

C: Oh, I suppose about 75%.

T: What evidence can you provide in support of your belief that there's a seventy-five percent chance that you won't get things accomplished the next day if you don't get 9 hours of sleep?

C: Once I had to stay up until 4 in the morning because one of the cakes I was making for our dinner party the following day was burned accidentally. I was so wiped out that I had to ask my husband to take care of setting the table and arranging to pick up the flowers from the florist that next day.

T: Does that necessarily translate into your not being able to do those things?

C: Well, no, but I felt I needed to take a nap if I wanted to be alert for the dinner conversation.

T: So, you could have gone to the florist and set the table if you had wanted to. Is that correct?

C: Yes.

T: How many times in the past have you had to stay up until 4 a.m.?

C: Really only that one time.

T: And how many times have you thrown dinner parties?

C: Oh, about 20 times so far.

T: That means that once out of 20 times have you not done something in preparation for a dinner party, and that due to your own choice. Correct?

C: If you put it that way, yes.

T: Now, back to the example at hand, how much later did you have to stay up to get your laundry done?

C: Until midnight.

T: And what happened the next day?

C: Nothing much. I felt a little sleepy, but I did manage to get up in time for my 9 a.m. hair appointment.

T: Did you fall behind on your other household responsibilities?

C: Not at all. In fact, yesterday I managed to have a very productive day. I was even able to fit in going to a movie in the evening with my husband, and write a letter to my mother later that evening.

T: So things didn't pile up. Do you think that your husband would be demoted if things did pile up?

C: You never know with his company! Oh, I just remembered something when we first got married. We were moving into our new apartment, and things still needed to be unpacked. We had some boxes in the corner, and I remember that we had some friends over at the time for the Super Bowl. Instead of commenting on the boxes, they said that they couldn't believe how quickly we settled into our new home. Wow, I really do focus on the negative, don't I?

T: Tell me some alternatives to your prediction that if things did in fact pile up in your house and his colleagues were over for a dinner party, that your husband would be demoted because of that.

C: Umm. Maybe they wouldn't notice, like our friends hadn't noticed in our first home. Or maybe they'd compliment us on the house, which is what they always do anyway. Or maybe they're just interested in having a good meal and a fun time and don't care either way. Perhaps they'd rib my husband a little bit at work about our house if it were messy, because they know how neat and clean we keep it, but that would be it. I guess it wouldn't be as bad as I think it would be.

T: And your final prediction, that your husband would leave you if he were demoted. Are there alternatives to that consequence?

C: That he wouldn't leave, that he loves me no matter what, that he would take an early retirement or find another job in a different field because he's been considering a job change, that he might actually be relieved that I wasn't spending tons of time cleaning the house.

T: Based on all the evidence and the alternatives that you've just generated, what would you rate the likelihood that if you don't get the laundry done and you have to stay up later in the night, that you wouldn't get things accomplished the next day and that all of these other consequences would follow? Recall that you originally assigned a probability of 75%.

C: Looking at it in the way you went through it, around 2%.

T: I think you can see the importance of being highly specific about your anxious thoughts, because more often than not, they are chained together in a larger sphere of worry. By breaking up that chain into its individual components— those thoughts and negative predictions—you can counter your worries more efficiently and effectively. How would you rate your anxiety now about not getting enough sleep?

C: Really low, a 2 or 1. I don't like feeling sleepy, because it makes me feel that I'm not on top of things in my life if I'm having to go to bed late, but I know that it's my anxiety and overly high standards that make me think that way.

T: Right. Sometimes it's helpful to consider the pros and cons of holding such high expectations and standards for yourself. It might be useful to write down the advantages and disadvantages of that belief, and then to ask yourself if you're being harder on yourself than other people are. To put it another way, would you think badly of a friend who didn't get everything done that she had wanted to do in a day, or who went to bed a little later one night and was tired the next day?

C: Oh, no, it's just in regard to myself. I have these standards that have been ingrained in me since childhood, so it's hard to break them, if you know what I mean. I would love to learn how to be less hard on myself.

T: Great. In a later session we'll discuss some exercises, called worry behavior prevention exercises, designed specifically for challenging some of your assumptions about your standards and what will or won't happen if you don't always abide by them.

Session 7

The main thrust of Session 7 was the introduction and rehearsal of worry exposure. However, this material was preceded by the 4-muscle-group relaxation (stomach, chest, shoulders, forehead). With this relaxation exercise, the therapist should remind the client that the refinement is to make the relaxation more portable, but that the client should continue to include any muscle groups that represent particular problem areas.

T: Today we will cover one of the most essential parts of the treatment program: systematic exposure to your worries. Recall that worrying is usually an attempt to problem-solve future threatening or dangerous situations. Often, excessive worry gets in the way of effective problem solving, and the individual focuses not on realistic solutions, but rather on anxiety-laden, negative predictions that only serve to increase anxiety. The method that I'll teach you will help you gain a sense of control over these worries and will also help you to manage them a bit more productively than you might be doing. The reason that these worries persist is because you might not be thinking about them completely, or may not be processing what you're thinking about completely. You might be trying to distract yourself when you experience these thoughts by saying things like, "Oh, I can't think about this now," or by doing some busy work to turn your attention away from the thoughts. You might also be saying, "I can't think about this at all," because the thoughts are so anxiety provoking. It's natural that you don't want to think about something that makes you upset. At the same time, though, if someone tells you not to think of pink elephants, probably the first thing you think about is pink elephants! That's why it's very difficult to successfully avoid the worries, because you're not allowing yourself to think about what it is that's frightening or scaring you. This technique is designed to help you overcome what we refer to as an "approach–avoidance" pattern. You'll learn to think about your fears and worries in

a different manner than the way you currently think about them. I'm going to ask you to think about a worry that we identify for at least 30 minutes a day. You'll do nothing but concentrate on worrying and thinking about this area of worry for 30 minutes. In this way, we're actually reducing the amount of time that you're worrying from 100% of the day, like you had first reported at the interview, to worrying for around 30 minutes a day. Generate the most feared possible outcomes to your worry that you can imagine, and then generate as many alternatives to that worst outcome that you can think of [see Figure 4.4].

Let's use an example from your Cognitive Monitoring Form to illustrate the process of worry exposure. Here you have that your friend called to say that she was dropping by in half an hour without having given you advance notice. What is the very worst image that you can envision when your friend comes over?

C: She'll have a look of shock on her face when she sees my dirty floors and unvacuumed rugs. She'll laugh at me and she'll go home and tell everyone that I'm not a good housekeeper or mother. I'll lose everyone's respect, and everyone will be laughing at me.

T: How vivid or clear is that image in your mind, from 0 to 8?

C: About a 5.

T: I want you to imagine that you're watching yourself in a movie. You can see very clearly the shock and then the hidden laughter on your friend's face as she comes into your apartment. You also see her dial the phone number of another mutual friend and tell that person in great detail how awful your house looked, and you see and hear her cruel laughter. How vivid is that image?

C: Very clear. About a 7.

T: Good. Now hold onto that image for at least another 5 or 10 minutes. Concentrate on what you're seeing and hearing in the situation. It is as though you can feel and touch what is happening around you. What is your anxiety level?

C: Umm, around a 7.

T: Continue to hold the image. (*waits until 5–10 min have elapsed*) What is your anxiety level now?

C: Still a 7.

T: Now continue to hold that image for a bit longer. (*waits another 5 min or so*) How is your anxiety?

C: Approximately a 5.

T: Very good. Now, Claire, I want you to begin to use your cognitive strategies to counter that catastrophic image in your mind. What are some alternatives to that image, first of all?

C: My friend won't care about the condition of my house. She's there to see me. Maybe she won't even notice that I haven't vacuumed the rugs or mopped the kitchen floor. She might notice, but not care and not think it so interesting to tell everyone we know that I keep a messy house. My house really isn't messy according to other people's standards. Compared to her place, my house is a temple anyway. She probably thinks that I'm too preoccupied with keeping the house neat and clean. Maybe she'd be glad or relieved to see that I wasn't cleaning for a change.

T: Great. How is your anxiety level now?

C: Wow, it went down to about a 2 or 1. But it feels uncomfortable to do this worry exposure. My stomach was doing little butterflies when you asked me to imagine the worst. I don't know if I can do this at home.

T: It is to be expected that you'll feel some emotional and physical discomfort, perhaps, while implementing the worry exposure. What you're doing in essence is facing and confronting the very thoughts that you avoid because of those same feelings and emotions that they evoke in you. Like anything else, becoming skilled in this procedure will take time and practice. If you're too anxious to continue the exposure while imagining the worst image, still try as best as you can to stick with the image. Your anxiety will come down, as you saw today. It is absolutely crucial that you allow 25 to 30 minutes at the very least for focusing on and envisioning the worst possible image of your worry. By giving yourself that much time, you're permitting the process of habituation to occur. Your anxiety will reach a peak and then decline to lower levels, once you acclimate to the image. Remember to use the cognitive strategies *after* you've imagined the worst. Additionally, you can use the relaxation after imagining the worst, if physically you're reactive to this procedure. Just make certain that during the exposure itself, you don't allow any sort of distraction from imagining the worst.

Session 8

In Session 8, worry exposure was reviewed and rehearsed and relaxation-by-recall was introduced.

T: You've been doing a tremendous job with the homework, especially with the worry exposure every day. It can be a lot of work, but keep in mind that it will all pay off in the long run, the more investment you make in the program.

C: Yes, I can see that. My anxiety has really dropped to lower levels compared to when I first came to the clinic. I feel more relaxed, and although I still worry a lot, it doesn't bother me as much as it used to.

T: Your efforts are to be commended. This is an intensive program that requires a good deal of motivation and desire to change your negative thought patterns and worry-related behaviors. How has the relaxation been going?

C: Very well. I do it every day, all through the day. Sometimes I'll do it in the shower, or when I'm driving, and I try to make a point of relaxing before I get up out of bed in the morning. I still have this scared feeling when I wake up, anticipating the day, I guess. But it's been getting less and less noticeable.

T: That's good to hear. Because you've seemed to master the relaxation exercise, I think you're ready now to start "relaxation-by-recall." This procedure entails recalling the feelings of relaxation. Instead of tensing the muscles before releasing them, you'll simply relax your muscles through the power of concentration and recall. You can concentrate on each of the four groups that you've been doing, and concentrate on releasing all the tension and pressure as you think back to how it feels to be relaxed in each part of your body. Maintain a regular pattern of fluid, smooth breathing with relaxation-by-recall, as you've been doing for the other forms of progressive muscle relaxation. Try to do this procedure in distracting, noisy, even stressful situations, so that the relaxation becomes a truly portable skill that can be used anywhere you are, in whatever circumstances that may be.

Session 9

In addition to a review of the skills introduced in the last two sessions (e.g., worry exposure and relaxation-by-recall), worry behavior prevention was introduced.

T: As I've mentioned several times in our earlier meetings together, part of the treatment program involves identifying certain behaviors and activities that you may either be doing or avoiding that serve to relieve your anxiety in the short term. What happens, however, is that those behaviors actually reinforce your worry and anxiety in the long term, so that they are counterproductive. Today, I'd like to generate a list of some of those behaviors that you might be doing, or activities that you may be avoiding, due to anxiety and worry. Some examples of such behaviors and activities include avoiding certain parts of the newspaper—like the health section or the obituaries—cleaning the house several times, being early for appointments, et cetera. Let's come up with some for you, Claire.

C: I think the most obvious behavior is my total avoidance of my son's football games. He's been begging me to go to the homecoming game, and I would really like to, because it's a big day for the team and there's a lot of pageantry about it. But it'll be tough to do, that I know for sure.

T: So that's one activity. What is your anxiety about going to the game, from 0 to 8?

C: Around a 7.

T: What other things can we put on the list? How about not cleaning for a few days?

C: Umm, that would also be around a 6 or 7.

T: How about not making your bed one morning?

C: Maybe a 4.

T: And cleaning the bathroom only once that day instead of your usual twice a day routine?

C: That would only be a 3. If I couldn't clean the bathroom at all one day, it would jump up to a 5.

T: And having your husband call you at work? What if he didn't call one day?

C: That might be a 6.

T: What if he didn't call until he left to come home?

C: Oh, so long as he calls at least once, it's not too bad. maybe about a 2.

T: We have a few things that can comprise the list. Here it is: Going to the homecoming game, 7. Not cleaning for a few days, 6 to 7. Not having husband call home at all, 6. Not cleaning bathroom at all one day, 5. Not making bed one morning, 4. Clean bathroom only once one day, 3. Husband calls only before leaving, 2.

For this week, you can begin the last item on the hierarchy, namely, having your husband call only when leaving work. Rate your anxiety during the day each week when you know he's not going to call until later, and then rate your anxiety after he calls. Let me know how this goes. If you find yourself worrying about him during the day, be sure to implement your cognitive strategies and the relaxation-by-recall to help you to control your worry and anxiety [see Figure 4.5].

Session 10

In Session 10, the therapist concentrated on reviewing the worry exposure and cognitive countering, relaxation-by-recall, and the worry behavior prevention exercises. He/ she should then assign the next higher item(s) on the worry behavior hierarchy that was composed in Session 9, depending on how well the client mastered the exercise and whether any problems were noted. In addition, cue-controlled relaxation was discussed.

Sessions 11 and 12

These sessions should be devoted to a review of all material thus covered, along with an inclusion of time-management and problem-solving principles and strategies. Because these techniques often overlap with some of the cognitive strategies previously covered, they are not covered in this section.

For example, if the client finds it difficult to fit everything in the day or has problems with meeting deadlines, the therapist should investigate overly high, unrealistic self-standards about performance and the perceived consequences of not getting everything done. Cognitive countering is usually the best intervention, along with teaching the client how to stick to a daily schedule and allocate ample time for tasks. Similarly, if the client reports difficulty making decisions due to fear of not making the right decision or choice, the therapist may wish to target the fear of making mistakes and the perceived consequences through decatastrophizing and probability estimations. Of course, introducing the concept of brainstorming, or generating as many alternatives as possible for a given problem situation, is very useful and should have already been fostered by regular practice of worry exposure exercises and cognitive monitoring forms.

Session 13

In addition to reviewing the skills covered over the prior 12 sessions and the progress that the client has made, a major objective of Session 13 was to provide an agenda for the client's continued application and consolidation of the treatment techniques.

T: Claire, we've covered a great deal of information about generalized anxiety and coping skills for it. As this is our last treatment session together before you go on your own for a while, it would be ideal for us to go over some of the skills

you've been faithfully practicing and to talk about the future.

C: That's reassuring to hear, because I've been feeling a little nervous about stopping therapy.

T: Why is that?

C: Well, I'm afraid that if I don't come regularly, that I'll lose all the gains that I've made and I'll be right back where I started: a nervous wreck who is miserable and unhappy with life. I don't want to go back to being that way.

T: Tell me some reasons why that might happen.

C: I won't be seeing you regularly, and maybe I'll forget the exercises and not know how to control my thoughts and feelings.

T: How can you be sure of that?

C: I can't. It's just a fear that I have. I guess I'm doing that "emotional reasoning" that you're always pointing out to me. I've been feeling so much better lately that I don't want it to end.

T: OK, but how have you accomplished that?

C: By doing the exercises and trying to change myself, which I think I've done to a big extent.

T: And where have you done most of the changing?

C: At home, and by myself! I see where you're getting. I'm not giving myself credit for the work I've done.

T: And you're discounting the fact that you are responsible for the change that you see. When we meet, our sessions are intended to introduce material and to review your homework, much like a teacher–student relationship. Except in our case, there's no grade given, just feedback on how you're doing and areas on which you could focus more attention. If you were to experience a resurgence in high anxiety and worry, Claire, what would you do? If you could write a letter to yourself in the future if that were to happen, what would you say?

C: I would say that I shouldn't let one minor setback color my whole view of myself, that I can always start doing the full hour of worry exposures and relaxation, and take out some of the cognitive monitoring forms, now that I know how to do them like the back of my hand. And I would tell myself, like you've told me, that it's OK and normal to feel anxious sometimes, that it doesn't necessarily mean that there's something wrong with me. It's so easy when I talk to you, but I struggle sometimes when I'm home trying to do these exercises and manage my worry. I am getting better, without a doubt, but it's been hard.

T: And that is to be expected, because what we're doing in essence is changing some ways of thinking, feeling, and acting when you're anxious that have been automatic reactions for you for some time. As you continue using the strategies, you've seen some changes in how you think about and act in anxiety-provoking situations. Is there any evidence you can provide to show that you won't see further changes so long as you regularly use these techniques?

C: No, of course not. It's just my fear getting the better of me. I know I can do it on my own.

T: Let's discuss briefly some of the strategies. First, you learned about the nature of anxiety and worry, and how it is maintained over time. Then, we went over relaxation, and now you're managing to relax your body in some highly stressful and distracting situations, like driving and while shopping. We spent a lot of time challenging your negative, anxious thoughts by identifying and countering probability overestimations and decatastrophizing. Next, we went over worry exposure, the daily hour of exposing yourself systematically to your worries and allowing yourself to fully visualize your anxious images and thoughts and then countering those. We followed this with worry behavior prevention exercises, when you gradually accomplished doing tasks that made you nervous or worried due to your negative predictions. You were even able to go to your son's homecoming game last week, right?

C: Yes! It wasn't bad at all. He played well, had some major running gains, and re-

ally impressed the coach who complimented him in front of the team after the game. I was so proud of myself. My anxiety was pretty high at first—about a 6—but it went down eventually, and I was doing the relaxation and the cognitive strategies all the while. It was actually a lot of fun for both my husband and I to go, because we sat with some close friends whose son is also on the team.

T: That's great. Then, we talked about time management and problem solving, with which you didn't have too many difficulties.

We'll be meeting again a month from now to monitor your progress and to troubleshoot any problems or difficulties you're experiencing. Then, we'll meet again several months later to discuss your progress to date. Certainly, if you're having any serious difficulties, you can give me a call. For now, concentrate on trying to use the techniques on your own. You've made tremendous progress, Claire, and there's no evidence to indicate that won't continue.

Claire's Progress

As is customary for clients who complete a treatment program at our clinic, whether or not it is a research protocol, Claire underwent posttreatment and follow-up assessments, each of which entailed administration of the ADIS–R and some self-report questionnaires. At posttreatment and across the follow-up period, Claire continued to experience decreasing levels of general anxiety and worry. When asked what components of the treatment she found especially useful for coping with her anxiety, Claire said that the daily worry exposure and cognitive monitoring/restructuring were particularly helpful and were strategies that she employed regularly. Additionally, Claire reported that most of her once-debilitating stomach problems had ceased to occur, and that she felt more in control of her worry and anxiety, both cognitively as well as physically. Claire maintained that although she still experienced some worry during the day, she felt more in control of it. Moreover, she stated that she noticed herself problem solving when she did worry, instead of distracting herself as she had for many years.

In comparison to her initial DSM-III-R diagnosis of GAD, with an ADIS–R clinical severity rating of 6, Claire received a posttreatment diagnosis of "GAD in partial remission," with a severity rating of 2, from an independent interviewer blind to her original diagnosis (0–8 scale). At 1-year follow-up, Claire was assigned a DSM-III-R diagnosis of "GAD in full remission."

CONCLUSION

Typically, we see clients a few more times on roughly a monthly basis in order to "fine tune" the client's application of treatment techniques or to assist in the handling of any setbacks. As noted in the review of the treatment literature, on the whole, clients who have completed a psychosocial treatment program for GAD evidence maintenance of their treatment gains. Moreover, in many instances, medication usage (e.g., anxiolytics) is reduced or eliminated (cf. Barlow et al., 1992). Nevertheless, a substantial number of patients undergoing these programs show no more than modest gains. This finding may in part be because it has been only recently that treatments have been tailored to address specifically the core component of GAD, namely, excessive and uncontrollable worry. Over the next few years, we should know whether these highly specialized treatments provide more substantial and lasting improvements in individuals with GAD.

REFERENCES

American Psychiatric Association. (1980). *Diagnostic and statistical manual of mental disorders* (3rd ed.). Washington, DC: Author.

American Psychiatric Association. (1987). *Diagnostic and statistical manual of mental disorders* (3rd ed., rev.). Washington, DC: Author.

American Psychiatric Association. (1993). *DSM-IV draft criteria as of 3/1/93.* Washington, DC: Author.

Anderson, D. J., Noyes, R., & Crowe, R. R. (1984). A comparison of panic disorder and generalized anxiety disorder. *American Journal of Psychiatry, 141,* 572–575.

Andrews, V. H., & Borkovec, T. D. (1988). The differential effects of inductions of worry, somatic anxiety, and depression on emotional experience. *Journal of Behavior Therapy and Experimental Psychiatry, 19,* 21–26.

Barlow, D. H. (1988). *Anxiety and its disorders: The nature and treatment of anxiety and panic.* New York: Guilford Press.

Barlow, D. H. (1991). The nature of anxiety: Anxiety, depression, and emotional disorders. In R. M. Rapee & D. H. Barlow (Eds.), *Chronic anxiety: Generalized anxiety disorder and mixed anxiety–depression* (pp. 1–28). New York: Guilford Press.

Barlow, D. H., Blanchard, E. B., Vermilyea, J. A., Vermilyea, B. B., & DiNardo, P. A. (1986). Generalized anxiety and generalized anxiety disorder: Description and reconceptualization. *American Journal of Psychiatry, 143,* 40–44.

Barlow, D. H., Cohen, A. S., Waddell, M., Vermilyea, J. A., Klosko, J. S., Blanchard, E. B., & DiNardo, P. A. (1984). Panic and generalized anxiety disorders: Nature and treatment. *Behavior Therapy, 15,* 431–449.

Barlow, D. H., Craske, M. G., Cerny, J. A., & Klosko, J. S. (1989). Behavioral treatment of panic disorder. *Behavior Therapy, 20,* 261–282.

Barlow, D. H., & DiNardo, P. A. (1991). The diagnosis of generalized anxiety disorder: Development, current status, and future directions. In R. M. Rapee & D. H. Barlow (Eds.), *Chronic anxiety: Generalized anxiety disorder and mixed anxiety–depression* (pp. 95–118). New York: Guilford Press.

Barlow, D. H., Rapee, R. M., & Brown, T. A. (1992). Behavioral treatment of generalized anxiety disorder. *Behavior Therapy, 23,* 551–570.

Beck, A. T., & Emery, G. (1985). *Anxiety disorders and phobias: A cognitive perspective.* New York: Basic Books.

Bernstein, D. A., & Borkovec, T. D. (1973). *Progressive relaxation training.* Champaign, IL: Research Press.

Blowers, C., Cobb, J., & Mathews, A. (1987). Generalized anxiety: A controlled treatment study. *Behaviour Research and Therapy, 25,* 493–502.

Borkovec, T. D., & Costello, E. (in press). Efficacy of applied relaxation and cognitive-behavioral therapy in the treatment of generalized anxiety disorder. *Journal of Consulting and Clinical Psychology.*

Borkovec, T. D., & Hu, S. (1990). The effect of worry on cardiovascular response to phobic imagery. *Behaviour Research and Therapy, 28,* 69–73.

Borkovec, T. D., & Mathews, A. M. (1988). Treatment of nonphobic anxiety disorders: A comparison of nondirective, cognitive, and coping desensitization therapy. *Journal of Consulting and Clinical Psychology, 56,* 877–884.

Borkovec, T. D., Mathews, A. M., Chambers, A., Ebrahimi, S., Lytle, R., & Nelson, R. (1987). The effects of relaxation training with cognitive therapy or nondirective therapy and the role of relaxation-induced anxiety in the treatment of generalized anxiety. *Journal of Consulting and Clinical Psychology, 55,* 883–888.

Borkovec, T. D., Shadick, R., & Hopkins, M. (1991). The nature of normal and pathological worry. In R. M. Rapee & D. H. Barlow (Eds.), *Chronic anxiety: Generalized anxiety disorder and mixed anxiety–depression* (pp. 29–51). New York: Guilford Press.

Breslau, N., & Davis, G. C. (1985). DSM-III generalized

anxiety disorder: An empirical investigation of more stringent criteria. *Psychiatry Research, 14,* 231-238.

Brown, T. A., Antony, M. M., & Barlow, D. H. (1992). Psychometric properties of the Penn State Worry Questionnaire in a clinical anxiety disorders sample. *Behaviour Research and Therapy, 30,* 33-37.

Brown, T. A., & Barlow, D. H. (1992). Comorbidity among anxiety disorders: Implications for treatment and DSM-IV. *Journal of Consulting and Clinical Psychology, 60,* 835-844.

Brown, T. A., Hertz, R. M., & Barlow, D. H. (1992). New developments in cognitive-behavioral treatment of anxiety disorders. In A. Tasman (Ed.), *American Psychiatric Press review of psychiatry* (Vol. 11, pp. 285-306). Washington, DC: American Psychiatric Press.

Brown, T. A., Moras, K., Zinbarg, R. E., & Barlow, D. H. (1993). Diagnostic and symptom distinguishability of generalized anxiety disorder and obsessive-compulsive disorder. *Behavior Therapy, 24,* 227-240.

Butler, G., & Booth, R. G. (1991). Developing psychological treatments for generalized anxiety disorder. In R. M. Rapee & D. H. Barlow (Eds.), *Chronic anxiety: Generalized anxiety disorder and mixed anxiety-depression* (pp. 187-209). New York: Guilford Press.

Butler, G., Cullington, A., Hibbert, G., Klimes, I., & Gelder, M. (1987). Anxiety management for persistent generalized anxiety. *British Journal of Psychiatry, 151,* 535-542.

Butler, G., Fennell, M., Robson, P., & Gelder, M. (1991). Comparison of behavior therapy and cognitive-behavior therapy in the treatment of generalized anxiety disorder. *Journal of Consulting and Clinical Psychology, 59,* 167-175.

Cameron, O. G., Thyer, B. A., Nesse, R. M., & Curtis, G. C. (1986). Symptom profiles of patients with DSM-III anxiety disorders. *American Journal of Psychiatry, 143,* 1132-1137.

Chambless, D. L., Cherney, J., Caputo, G. C., & Rheinstein, B. J. G. (1987). Anxiety disorders and alcoholism: A study with inpatient alcoholics. *Journal of Anxiety Disorders, 1,* 29-40.

Cohen, A. S., Barlow, D. H., & Blanchard, E. B. (1985). The psychophysiology of relaxation-associated panic attacks. *Journal of Abnormal Psychology, 94,* 96-101.

Craske, M. G., Barlow, D. H., & O'Leary, T. A. (1992). *Mastery of your anxiety and worry.* Albany, NY: Graywind Publications.

Craske, M. G., Rapee, R. M., Jackel, L., & Barlow, D. H. (1989). Qualitative dimensions of worry in DSM-III-R generalized anxiety disorder subjects and nonanxious controls. *Behaviour Research and Therapy, 27,* 189-198.

DiNardo, P. A. (1991). *MacArthur reanalysis of generalized anxiety disorder.* Unpublished manuscript.

DiNardo, P. A., & Barlow, D.H. (1988). *Anxiety Disorders Interview Schedule-Revised (ADIS-R).* Albany, NY: Graywind Publications.

DiNardo, P. A., Moras, K., Barlow, D. H., Rapee, R. M., & Brown, T. A. (in press). Reliability of the DSM-III-R anxiety disorder categories using the Anxiety Disorders Interview Schedule—Revised. *Archives of General Psychiatry.*

Durham, R. C., & Turvey, A. A. (1987). Cognitive therapy vs. behavior therapy in the treatment of chronic general anxiety. *Behaviour Research and Therapy, 25,* 229-234.

Foa, E. B., & Kozak, M. J. (1986). Emotional processing of fear: Exposure to corrective information. *Psychological Bulletin, 99,* 20-35.

Fyer, A. J., Mannuzza, S., Martin, L. Y., Gallops, M. S., Endicott, J., Schleyer, B., Gorman, J. ., Liebowitz, M. R., & Klein, D. F. (1989). Reliability of anxiety assessment: II. Symptom agreement. *Archives of General Psychiatry, 46,* 1102-1110.

Garvey, M. J., Cook, B., & Noyes, R. (1988). The occurrence of a prodrome of generalized anxiety in panic disorder. *Comprehensive Psychiatry, 29,* 445-449.

Heide, F. J., & Borkovec, T. D. (1984). Relaxation-induced anxiety: Mechanisms and theoretical implications. *Behaviour Research and Therapy, 22,* 1-12.

Hoehn-Saric, R., & McLeod, D. R. (1988). The peripheral sympathetic nervous system: Its role in normal and pathological anxiety. *Psychiatric Clinics of North America, 11,* 375-386.

Hoehn-Saric, R., McLeod, D. R., & Zimmerli, W. D. (1989). Somatic manifestations in women with generalized anxiety disorder: Psychophysiological responses to psychological stress. *Archives of General Psychiatry, 46,* 1113-1119.

LeBoeuf, A., & Lodge, J. (1980). A comparison of frontalis EMG feedback training and progressive relaxation in the treatment of chronic anxiety. *British Journal of Psychiatry, 137,* 279-284.

Lindsay, W. R., Gamsu, C. V., McLaughlin, E., Hood, E. M., & Espie, C. A. (1987). A controlled trial of treatments for generalized anxiety. *British Journal of Clinical Psychology, 26,* 3-15.

Lovibond, S. H. (1983, May). *The nature and measurement of anxiety, stress, and depression.* Paper presented at the meeting of the Australian Psychological Society, University of Western Australia.

Lovibond, S. H., & Lovibond, P. F. (1992). *Self-report scales (DASS) for the differentiation and measurement of depression, anxiety, and stress.* Unpublished manuscript.

Lyonfields, J. D. (1991, November). *An examination of image and thought processes in generalized anxiety.* Paper presented at the meeting of the Association for Advancement of Behavior Therapy, New York.

Marten, P. A., Brown, T. A., Barlow, D. H., Borkovec, T. D., Shear, M. K., & Lydiard, R. B. (in press). Evaluation of the ratings comprising the associated symptom criterion of DSM-III-R generalized anxiety disorder. *Journal of Nervous and Mental Disease.*

Meichenbaum, D. S., & Jaremko, M. E. (Eds.). (1983). *Stress reduction and prevention.* New York: Plenum Press.

Meyer, T. J., Miller, M. L., Metzger, R. L., & Borkovec, T. D. (1990). Development and validation of the Penn State Worry Questionnaire. *Behaviour Research and Therapy, 28,* 487-495.

Moras, K., DiNardo, P. A., Brown, T. A., & Barlow, D. H. (1992). *Comorbidity and depression among the DSM-III-R anxiety disorders.* Manuscript submitted for publication.

Nelson, R. O., & Barlow, D. H. (1981). Behavioral assessment: Basic strategies and initial procedures. In D. H. Barlow (Ed.), *Behavioral assessment of adult disorders* (pp. 13-43). New York: Guilford Press.

Noyes, R., Clarkson, C., Crowe, R. R., Yates, W. R., & McChesney, C. M. (1987). A family study of generalized anxiety disorder. *American Journal of Psychiatry, 144,* 1019–1024.

Noyes, R., Woodman, C., Garvey, M. J., Cook, B. L., Suelzer, M., Clancy, J., & Anderson, D. J. (1992). Generalized anxiety disorder vs. panic disorder: Distinguishing characteristics and patterns of comorbidity. *Journal of Nervous and Mental Disease, 180,* 369–379.

O'Leary, T. A., Brown, T. A., & Barlow, D. H. (1992, November). *The efficacy of worry control treatment in generalized anxiety disorder: A multiple baseline analysis.* Paper presented at the meeting of the Association for Advancement of Behavior Therapy, Boston, MA.

Rapee, R. M. (1985). The distinction between panic disorder and generalized anxiety disorder: Clinical presentation. *Australian and New Zealand Journal of Psychiatry, 19,* 227–232.

Rapee, R. M. (1991). Generalized anxiety disorder: A review of clinical features and theoretical concepts. *Clinical Psychology Review, 11,* 419–440.

Rapee, R. M., & Barlow, D. H. (Eds.). (1991). *Chronic anxiety: Generalized anxiety disorder and mixed anxiety-depression.* New York: Guilford Press.

Rapee, R. M., Craske, M. G., & Barlow, D. H. (1989, November). *The Emotional Control Questionnaire.* Paper presented at the meeting of the Association for Advancement of Behavior Therapy, Washington, DC.

Sanderson, W. C., & Barlow, D. H. (1990). A description of patients diagnosed with DSM-III-R generalized anxiety disorder. *Journal of Nervous and Mental Disease, 178,* 588–591.

Sanderson, W. C., Beck, A. T., & Beck, J. (1990). Syndrome comorbidity in patients with major depression or dysthymia: Prevalence and temporal relationships. *American Journal of Psychiatry, 147,* 1025–1028.

Sanderson, W. C., & Wetzler, S. (1991). Chronic anxiety and generalized anxiety disorder: Issues in comorbidity. In R. M. Rapee & D. H. Barlow (Eds.), *Chronic anxiety: Generalized anxiety disorder and mixed anxiety-depression* (pp. 119–135). New York: Guilford Press.

Schweizer, E., & Rickels, K. (1991). Pharmacotherapy of generalized anxiety disorder. In R. M. Rapee & D. H. Barlow (Eds.), *Chronic anxiety: Generalized anxiety disorder and mixed anxiety-depression* (pp. 172–186). New York: Guilford Press.

Suinn, R. M., & Richardson, F. (1971). Anxiety management training: A nonspecific behavior therapy program for anxiety control. *Behavior Therapy, 2,* 498–511.

Turner, S. M., Beidel, D. C., & Stanley, M. A. (1992). Are obsessional thoughts and worry different cognitive phenomena? *Clinical Psychology Review, 12,* 257–270.

White, J., Keenan, M., & Brooks, N. (1991). *Stress control: A controlled investigation of large group therapy for generalized anxiety disorder.* Unpublished manuscript.

Zinbarg, R. E., & Barlow, D. H. (1991). Mixed anxiety depression: A new diagnostic category? In R. M. Rapee & D. H. Barlow (Eds.), *Chronic anxiety: Generalized anxiety disorder and mixed anxiety-depression* (pp. 136–152). New York: Guilford Press.

Chapter 5

OBSESSIVE COMPULSIVE DISORDER

David S. Riggs
Edna B. Foa
Medical College of Pennsylvania/Eastern Pennsylvania Psychiatric Institute, Philadelphia

It will not take the reader long to see that successful therapy for obsessive compulsive disorder is markedly different both in structure and in content from the usual therapeutic approaches. For this reason, regrettably, few therapists feel self-efficacious enough to undertake this therapy. The information provided in this detailed chapter should be sufficient for any reasonably well-trained mental health professional to undertake these treatments, particularly if few other options are available. For the suffering involved with obsessive compulsive disorder can be extraordinary and even imperfect attempts at therapy can relieve much of this suffering. This chapter describes the detailed conduct of intensive daily sessions involving both imaginal and direct *in vivo* practice. Also noticeable is the ingenuity required by the therapists (e.g., Where do you find dead animals?). The importance of involving significant others continues a theme first described in Chapter 1 (Craske & Barlow, this volume) where spouses or other people close to the individual with the problem become an important and integral part of treatment. Finally, this chapter contains an up-to-date review of the current status of psychological and pharmacological approaches to obsessive compulsive disorder.—D. H. B.

INTRODUCTION

Obsessive-compulsive syndrome was first described by Esquirol in 1838, and for many years was considered one of the most intractable of mental illnesses. Advances in behavioral and pharmacological therapies in the last two decades have greatly improved the prognosis for these patients. In this chapter we first discuss diagnostic and theoretical issues of obsessive compulsive disorder (OCD) and review the available treatments. We then describe assessment procedures and illustrate in detail how to implement intensive behavioral treatment for OCD. Throughout the chapter, we use verbatim material representative of interactions that occur between therapist and patient in order to demonstrate the process that occurs during treatment.

DEFINITION

Over the years, the conceptualization of the obsessive compulsive syndrome has undergone significant changes. Early on, it was recognized the obsessive compulsives manifest both distressing intrusive ideas and repetitive behaviors that are unwanted but nevertheless are carried out compulsively. In both the first edition of the *Diagnostic and*

Statistical Manual of Mental Disorders (American Psychiatric Association [APA], 1952) and the second edition of the *Diagnostic and Statistical Manual of Mental Disorders* (APA, 1968), the definition of the syndrome was brief and nonspecific. The third edition of the *Diagnostic and Statistical Manual of Mental Disorders* (APA, 1980) and the revised third edition of the *Diagnostic and Statistical Manual of Mental Disorders* (DSM-III-R; APA, 1987) specified criteria for OCD. In these criteria, the two aspects of OCD, obsessions and compulsions, were defined separately and the relationship between them was explicated.

In the DSM-III-R criteria for OCD, obsessions were defined as follows:

[P]ersistent thoughts, impulses, or images that are experienced, at least initially, as intrusive and senseless. . . . The person attempts to ignore or suppress such thoughts or impulses or to neutralize them with some other thought or action. The person recognizes that the obsessions are the product of his or her own mind, and are not imposed from without. (p. 245)

Compulsions were defined as:

[R]epetitive, purposeful, and intentional behaviors that are performed in response to an obsession, according to certain rules, or in a stereotypic fashion. The behavior is designed to neutralize or to prevent discomfort or some dreaded event or situation. However, either the activity is not connected in a realistic way with what it is designed to neutralize, or it is clearly excessive. . . . The person recognizes that his or her behavior is excessive or unreasonable. (p. 245)

Foa and Kozak (1991) noted that the DSM-III-R definition reflects the influence of three traditional views of OCD: (1) obsessions are mental events and compulsions are behavioral events; (2) obsessions and compulsions may either be connected or occur independently of one another; and (3) individuals always recognize the senselessness of their obsessions and compulsions.

The view that obsessions and compulsions are functionally related has been advocated by Foa and Tillmanns (1980), who proposed that obsessions and compulsions be defined on the basis of their functional relationship to anxiety or distress rather than on the modality in which they are expressed (mental or behavioral). Accordingly, obsessions are defined as thoughts, images, or impulses that generate anxiety or distress, and compulsions are defined as overt (behavioral) or covert (mental) actions that are performed in an attempt to alleviate the distress brought on by the obsessions. Behavioral compulsions such as washing one's hands and checking the stove are equivalent (with respect to their functional relationship to obsessions) to mental actions such as silently repeating phrases or numbers and mentally reviewing one's nightly check. Both behavioral and mental compulsions may be performed in order to prevent harm, restore safety, or reduce distress. The functional model of obsessions and compulsions is reflected in the DSM-III-R criteria, and is supported by the results of a recently completed field study for the fourth edition of the *Diagnostic and Statistical Manual of Mental Disorders* (DSM-IV; APA, 1993)* indicating that 90% of compulsions are viewed by OCD individuals as functionally related to obsessions and only 10% are perceived as unrelated to obsessions (Foa & Kozak, in press).

The functional model of OCD implies that compulsions cannot exist without obsessions, but allows for obsessions to exist without compulsions (pure obsessionals). Data from the DSM-IV field study indicate that the vast majority (over 90%) of obsessive compulsives manifest both obsessions and behavioral compulsions. When mental compulsions are included, only 2% of the sample reported obsessions and no compulsions (Foa & Kozak, in press). Because pure obsessionals, although very uncommon, do exist, the DSM-IV retains the provision that a diagnosis of OCD can be assigned in the absence of compulsions.

The view represented in the DSM-III-R that individuals with OCD recognize obsessions as "senseless" and compulsions as "unreasonable" has been challenged. The DSM-III-R recognized the problem by labeling obsessive compulsives who do not view their symptoms as senseless as "overvalued

---

*The DSM-IV criteria cited in this chapter are those that were approved as final by the DSM-IV Anxiety Disorders Work Group and the Task Force on DSM-IV (APA, 1993). These criteria may be subject to minor editorial revisions before the publication of DSM-IV.

ideators" (i.e., having a strong belief that their obsessions or compulsions are sensible). Recent studies suggest that individuals with OCD vary greatly in the degree to which they recognize their symptoms as senseless or unreasonable (Insel & Akiskal, 1986; Lelliott, Noshirvani, Basoglu, Marks, & Monterio, 1988). Accordingly, a continuum of "insight" or "strength of belief" better represents the clinical picture than the idea that obsessive compulsives view their symptoms as sensible or senseless.

The DSM-III-R implied that overvalued ideas develop from obsessions that had originally been perceived as senseless. Indeed, the DSM-IV field study found that individuals who lacked insight at the time of assessment reported having had such insight at some earlier time. Moreover, clinical observations suggest that patients alternate between periods of insight and periods of strong belief. Such fluctuations may occur from moment to moment depending on the individual's mood and surrounding circumstances. Often obsessive compulsive individuals recognize that their symptoms are senseless when discussing them in the therapist's office, but lose this insight when confronted with a situation that elicits their obsessions. Therefore, the diagnostic criteria should allow for individuals without insight into the senselessness of their symptoms to be diagnosed as having OCD. The present requirement that individuals have such insight may result in misdiagnosis, which, in turn, may lead to inappropriate treatment.

The issues considered above have guided the proposed changes for the OCD diagnostic criteria in the DSM-IV. Accordingly, the diagnosis requires the presence of either obsessions or compulsions. Obsessions are defined as persistent thoughts, ideas, or impulses that are experienced as intrusive and inappropriate and cause marked anxiety or distress. To distinguish obsessions from worries, the DSM-IV specifies that the obsessions are not simply excessive worries about real-life problems. The person attempts to suppress or ignore the obsessions or to neutralize them with some other thought or action. To distinguish obsessions from psychotic processes, the criteria specify that the person recognize that the obsessions are a product of his/her own mind. Compulsions are defined in the DSM-IV

as repetitive behaviors (e.g., hand washing) or mental acts (e.g., praying silently) that the person feels driven to perform in response to an obsession or according to rigid rules. The compulsion is aimed at preventing or reducing distress or preventing some dreaded situation; however, the compulsions are either unrealistic or clearly excessive.

Criterion B of the DSM-IV diagnostic criteria for OCD addresses the issue of the person's recognition that his/her symptoms are senseless. This criterion states that "at some point during the course of the disorder, the person has recognized that the obsessions or compulsions are excessive or unreasonable. Note: this may not apply to children" (APA, 1993). To direct the attention of the clinician to the possible absence of insight in the current episode, there is a requirement in the DSM-IV to specify if, for most of the time during the current episode, the person is "with poor insight" (i.e., the person does not recognize that the obsessions and compulsions are excessive or unreasonable).

As in the DSM-III-R, there is a requirement that the obsessions or compulsions are severe enough to cause marked distress, are time-consuming, and interfere with daily functioning. If another Axis I disorder is present, the obsessions and compulsions cannot be restricted to the content of that disorder (e.g., preoccupation with food in the presence of eating disorders).

CLINICAL PICTURE

"Debbie" is a 36-year-old married woman with no children. At the time of presentation, she reported a 15-year history of obsessive fears and rituals. In the past, she had fears of making mistakes, forgetting things, and hurting people physically or emotionally, resulting in her spending time checking and mentally reviewing her activities. Debbie's fears at the time she presented for treatment centered around becoming contaminated with unspecified "germs" and passing this contamination to others who, as a result, would become ill and die, and that she would be held responsible for their deaths. These fears developed while she was working as a surgical nurse. She became concerned that during an operation she would contaminate the surgical field and

that this would result in serious consequences to the patient. She was no longer
able to work because of the OCD symptoms
and spent a good portion of her day washing and cleaning objects around her home.
She avoided contact with anything she
thought might contain germs, including
bathrooms, certain food products, and hospitals. In addition, she avoided most contact
with other people, particularly children, for
fear of passing on germs to them.

PREVALENCE AND COURSE OF OCD

Once thought to be a relatively rare disorder, the prevalence of OCD is now estimated to be about 2.5% (Karno, Golding,
Sorensen, & Burnam, 1988). Studies found
that slightly more than half of those suffering from OCD are female (Rasmussen &
Tsuang, 1986). The average age of onset of
the disorder ranges from early adolescence
to mid-20s, and it typically occurs earlier
in males (peak onset 13–15 years old) than
in females (peak onset 20–24 years old)
(Rasmussen & Eisen, 1990). The onset of
OCD is usually gradual, but acute onset has
been reported in some cases. The disorder
is mostly chronic, with symptoms waxing
and waning in severity. However, episodic
and deteriorating courses have been observed in about 10% of patients (Rasmussen
& Eisen, 1989).

Many individuals with OCD suffer for
years before seeking treatment. In one
study, individuals first presented for psychiatric treatment over 7 years after the onset
of significant symptoms (Rasmussen &
Tsuang, 1986). The disorder may cause severe impairment in functioning, resulting in
job loss and disruption of marital and other
interpersonal relationships. Marital distress
is reported by approximately 50% of married individuals seeking treatment for OCD
(Emmelkamp, de Haan, & Hoogduin, 1990;
Riggs, Hiss, & Foa, 1992).

ASSOCIATED DISORDERS

OCD commonly co-occurs with other symptoms and complaints such as depression,
anxiety, phobic avoidance, and excessive

worry (Tynes, White, & Steketee, 1990;
Karno et al., 1988; Rasmussen & Tsuang,
1986). Epidemiological studies found that
approximately 30% of individuals with OCD
also met criteria for a major depressive episode (Karno et al., 1988). Sleep disturbances
have been found in roughly 40% of people
with OCD. The presence of depression with
OCD is important in that some studies have
suggested that severe depression may impede
the efficacy of behavioral treatment of OCD
(Foa, 1979; Foa, Grayson, & Steketee, 1982).

The comorbidity of OCD with other anxiety disorders is also quite high. Rasmussen
and Tsuang (1986) reported that in a sample
of OCD patients, the lifetime incidence of
simple phobia was about 30%; for social
phobia, 20%; and for panic disorder, 15%.

A relationship of OCD with eating disorders has also been reported. About 10% of
women with OCD had a history of anorexia
nervosa (Kasvikis, Tsakiris, Marks, Basoglu,
& Noshirvani, 1986), and over 33% of
bulimics had a history of OCD (Hudson,
Pope, Yurgelun-Todd, Jonas, & Frankenburg, 1987; Laessle, Kittl, Fichter, Wittchen,
& Pirke, 1987).

Tic disorders such as Tourette's syndrome
and tics also appear related to OCD. Some
20% to 30% of individuals with OCD reported a current or past history of tics
(Pauls, 1989). Estimates of the comorbidity
of Tourette's and OCD range from 36% to
52% (Leckman & Chittenden, 1990; Pauls,
Towbin, Leckman, Zahner, & Cohen, 1986).
Also, 5% to 7% of OCD patients are thought
to suffer from Tourette's syndrome (Rasmussen & Eisen, 1989).

DIFFERENTIAL DIAGNOSIS

The high comorbidity of OCD with other
disorders sometimes renders differential
diagnosis difficult. The co-occurrence of
depression with OCD may call for a distinction between depressive rumination about
unpleasant life circumstances or problems
and true obsessions. Ruminations are common in depressed individuals and are considered congruent with depressed mood.
Unlike obsessive compulsives who invariably
attempt to ignore or suppress their obsessions, depressed individuals typically do not
try to suppress their depressive brooding.

The high rate of other anxiety disorders and anxiety symptoms among individuals with OCD complicates the diagnosis of OCD. For example, generalized anxiety disorder is characterized by excessive worry. Such worries are distinguished from obsessions in that worries typically represent excessive concerns about real-life circumstances and are experienced as appropriate. In contrast, the content of obsessions is more likely to be unrealistic, and the obsessions are experienced as inappropriate. In some cases, the content of the obsession reflects events that can realistically occur; however, in these cases, the individual greatly exaggerates the likelihood of such occurrences (e.g., the likelihood of developing cancer due to normal exposure to household chemicals).

Individuals with OCD frequently display phobic avoidance of situations that evoke the obsessions. For example, a person with obsessions about germs will avoid public rest rooms; a person with obsessions about hitting people with a car will avoid driving. In this way obsessive compulsives are similar to simple phobics. In severe cases, daily activities are so restricted that the individual becomes housebound and appears agoraphobic. However, OCD sufferers differ from simple phobics even when the feared object or situation is identical. First, the meaning of the threat is different. For example, both a dog phobic and an individual with OCD may fear a dog. However, the phobic is typically afraid of being bitten, whereas the obsessive compulsive usually fears that the dog may carry diseases such as rabies. Second, because of the nature of their fear (i.e., being bitten), simple phobics can successfully reduce their distress through avoidance or escape. In contrast, the threat perceived by the obsessive compulsive is not eliminated by the removal of the dog because the contamination remains. The failure of passive avoidance to reduce distress leads the OCD individual to actively ritualize when exposed to the feared situation (e.g., washing hands after contact with a dog). Thus, the obsessive compulsive, but not the simple phobic, will exhibit ritualistic behavior.

In hypochondriasis, the individual has the unfounded belief that he/she has a disease and repeatedly consults physicians for diagnoses and treatment. Hypochondriacal concerns are common in obsessive compulsives who manifest illness-related obsessions, and who exhibit somatic checking rituals and repeatedly visit physicians in search of reassurance (Rasmussen & Tsuang, 1986). Rasmussen and Eisen (1989) suggested that hypochondriacs who present with somatic obsessions and checking rituals should probably be diagnosed with OCD, but acknowledged that the differential diagnosis is often difficult. Perhaps the best way of differentiating the two disorders is by the presence or absence of compulsions. For example, the presence of obsessions about illness combined with rituals such as excessive hand washing would call for a diagnosis of OCD. If the symptoms consist only of preoccupation with one's own health and excessive information seeking about health and/or treatment, a diagnosis of hypochondriasis is most likely appropriate.

A similar diagnostic issue arises with body dysmorphic disorder (BDD). The essential feature of BDD is an obsessive preoccupation with an imagined physical defect in a person of essentially normal appearance. This preoccupation is sometimes coupled with compulsive checking behavior. Again, if other obsessions or compulsions are present in a person with BDD, a diagnosis of OCD may be indicated.

Stereotyped motor behaviors similar to compulsions are present in both Tourette's syndrome and tic disorder. These behaviors are distinguished from compulsions in that they are not aimed at neutralizing distress brought about by an obsession and they are generally involuntary and unintentional.

Individuals with OCD may present with obsessions that have delusional intensity and thus prompt the differential diagnosis of delusional disorder or schizophrenia. Delusional disorder is characterized by persistent nonbizarre delusions involving situations that occur in real life, such as having a disease. Because most people with OCD experience both obsessions and compulsions, obsessions of delusional intensity can best be distinguished from delusional disorder by the presence of associated compulsions.

Like some schizophrenic delusions, the content of obsessions in OCD may be extremely bizarre, such as the idea that the person might accidentally seal him/herself into an envelope and get deposited into a mailbox. Although obsessive compulsives may experience obsessions of delusional intensity or bizarre content, they typically do not show other symptoms of schizophrenia, such as marked loosening of associations, prominent hallucinations, flat or grossly inappropriate affect, thought insertion, or projection. In some cases, though, an individual may manifest sufficient symptoms of both OCD and schizophrenia to indicate a dual diagnosis.

THEORETICAL MODELS

Behavioral Models

Mowrer's (1939) two-stage theory for the acquisition and maintenance of fear and avoidance behavior has been commonly adopted to explain phobias and OCD. Further elaborated by Mowrer in 1960, this theory proposes that first a neutral event becomes associated with fear by being paired with a stimulus that by its nature provokes discomfort or anxiety. Through conditioning processes, objects as well as thoughts and images acquire the ability to produce discomfort. In the second stage of this process, escape or avoidance responses are developed to reduce the anxiety or discomfort evoked by the various conditioned stimuli and are maintained by their success in doing so. Dollard and Miller (1950) adopted Mowrer's two-stage theory to account for phobias and obsessive compulsive neurosis. As noted earlier, because of the intrusive nature of the obsessions, many of the situations that provoke obsessions cannot readily be avoided. Passive avoidance behaviors, such as those utilized by phobics, are ineffective in controlling the obsessional distress. Active avoidance patterns in the form of ritualistic behaviors are then developed and maintained by their success in alleviating this distress.

Support for Mowrer's conceptualization of fear acquisition is inadequate (e.g., Rachman & Wilson, 1980). In contrast, there is evidence to support the hypothesis regarding the maintenance of ritualistic behavior. Studies have demonstrated that obsessions give rise to anxiety/discomfort and compulsions reduce it. Obsessions were found to increase heart rate and deflect skin conductance more than do neutral thoughts (Boulougouris, Rabavilas, & Stefanis, 1977; Rabavilas & Boulougouris, 1974). Likewise, contact with contaminated objects resulted in increased heart rate and subjective anxiety (Hodgson & Rachman, 1972), as well as skin-conductance level (Hornsveld, Kraaimaat, & van Dam-Baggen, 1979). A series of experiments with washers and checkers revealed that in most instances anxiety decreased following the performance of a ritual after deliberate provocation of an urge to ritualize (Hodgson & Rachman, 1972; Hornsveld et al., 1979; Roper & Rachman, 1976; Roper, Rachman, & Hodgson, 1973).

Cognitive Models

Several cognitive explanations have been offered to account for OCD symptoms. Carr (1974) proposed that obsessive compulsives have unusually high expectations of negative outcome; they overevaluate the negative consequences for a variety of actions. He noted that obsessional content typically includes exaggerations of the concerns of normal individuals: health, death, welfare of others, sex, religion, and the like. This explanation views the sources of obsessive compulsive concerns as identical to those of generalized anxiety disorder, agoraphobia, and social phobia. In this way, Carr's explanation of OCD is similar to that offered by Beck (1976), which suggested that the content of obsessions is related to danger in the form of doubt or warning. Neither account makes a distinction between threat-related obsessions and threat-related thoughts in phobics.

In an attempt to address the psychopathology specific to OCD, McFall and Wollershein (1979) suggested that obsessive compulsives hold erroneous beliefs such as one must be completely competent in all endeavors to be worthwhile. Other erroneous ideas include the belief that failure to live up to perfectionistic ideals should be punished and that certain magical rituals can prevent catastrophes. Such mistaken beliefs, the authors suggested, lead to erroneous perceptions of threat, which in turn provoke anxiety. The obsessive compulsive's tendency to devalue his/her ability to deal adequately with such threats exacerbates the dysfunctional process. The resulting feelings of uncertainty, discomfort, and helplessness are reduced via magical rituals that the patient views as the only available method for coping with threat.

The most comprehensive cognitive analysis of OCD has been offered by Salkovskis (1985). The starting point of this analysis is that intrusive obsessional thoughts function as stimuli that may provoke certain types of negative automatic thoughts. Accordingly, an intrusive thought will lead to mood disturbances only if they trigger these negative automatic thoughts through interaction between the unacceptable intrusion and the individual's belief system (e.g., only bad people have sexual thoughts). Responsibility and self-blame are the central themes in the obsessive compulsive belief system. Neutralization, in the form of behavioral or cognitive compulsions, can be understood as an attempt to reduce this sense of responsibility and to prevent blame. In addition, frequently occurring thoughts regarding unacceptable actions may be perceived by the obsessive compulsive individual as representative of the actions themselves, so, for example, even if the person has not sinned, the thought of sinning is as bad as sinning itself.

Salkovskis (1985) proposed that five dysfunctional assumptions characterize obsessive compulsives and differentiate them from persons without OCD:

> 1) Having a thought about an action is like performing the action; 2) failing to prevent (or failing to try to prevent) harm to self or others is the same as having caused the harm in the first place; 3) responsibility is not attenuated by other factors (e.g., low probability of occurrence); 4) not neutralizing when an intrusion has occurred is similar or equivalent to seeking or wanting the harm involved in that intrusion to actually happen; 5) one should (and can) exercise control over one's thoughts. (p. 579)

Thus, while the obsession may be ego dystonic, the automatic thought that it elicits will be ego syntonic. This model implies that treatment of OCD should largely focus on identifying the erroneous assumptions and modifying the automatic thoughts.

The above explanations focus on the pathology in the content of OCD thoughts. In contrast, Reed (1985) proposed that the disorder reflects impairment not in the content, but in the organization and integration of experiences (i.e., in the form rather than the content of the thinking). According to Reed, the obsessional individual tries to compensate for this impairment by over-structuring his/her life, imposing strict categorical limits and time markers. While Reed (1985) suggested that this style is used consistently by the obsessive compulsive individual and impacts on all aspects of his/her life, he leaves open the possibility that the difficulties will be exacerbated when the task involves threatening content.

Foa and Kozak (1985) conceptualized anxiety disorders in general as specific impairments in emotional memory networks. Following Lang (1979), they view fear as an information network existing in memory that includes representation about fear stimuli, fear responses, and their meaning. With regard to the fear content, Foa and Kozak (1985) suggested that fear networks of anxiety-disordered individuals are characterized by the presence of erroneous estimates of threat, unusually high negative valence for the feared event, and excessive response elements (e.g., physiological reactivity) and are resistant to modification. This persistence may reflect failure to access the fear network, either because of active avoidance or because the content of the fear network precludes spontaneous encounters with situations that evoke anxiety in everyday life. Additionally, anxiety may persist because of some impairment in the mechanism of extinction. Cognitive defenses, excessive arousal with failure to habituate, faulty premises, and erroneous rules of inference are all impairments that would hinder the processing of information necessary for modifying the fear structure so as to reduce fear behavior.

Foa and Kozak (1985) suggested that several forms of fear occur in obsessive compulsives. The patient who fears contracting venereal disease from public bathrooms and washes to prevent such harm has a fear structure that includes excessive associations between the stimuli (e.g., bathroom) and the anxiety/distress responses as well as mistaken beliefs about the harm related to the stimulus. For other obsessive compulsives, fear responses are associated with mistaken meaning rather than with a particular stimulus. For example, some patients who are disturbed by perceived asymmetry and who reduce their distress by rearranging objects do not fear the objects themselves, nor do they anticipate disaster from the asymmetry. Rather, they are upset by their view that certain arrangements of stimuli are "improper."

Like Reed (1985), Foa and Kozak (1985) proposed that in addition to the pathological content of the obsessions, OCD is distinguished from other disorders by pathology in the mechanisms underlying information processing. Specifically, they suggested that OCD patients share an impairment in the interpretive rules for making inferences about harm. Obsessive-compulsives often conclude that a situation is dangerous based on the absence of evidence for safety and they often fail to make inductive leaps about safety from information about the absence of danger. Consequently, rituals that are performed to reduce the likelihood of harm can never really provide safety and must be repeated.

When observing obsessive compulsive checkers, one is impressed by what appears to be their difficulty in remembering whether they have performed their ritualistic actions. This observation has led researchers to hypothesize that obsessive compulsive checkers have specific memory defitics for actions (Sher, Frost, & Otto, 1983; Sher, Frost, Kushner, Crews, & Alexander, 1989). Alternatively, patients' doubts about having performed a ritual may not reflect a memory deficit but rather, as suggested by Foa and Kozak (1985), an impairment in the way that they infer danger. Regardless of whether the impairment lies in memory processes or in meaning transformation rules, it is unclear whether they are general, affecting the processing of all information, or specific, affecting only the processing of threat-related information.

To the extent that the pathology of OCD is related to the content of the fear network, treatment for this disorder should be similar to those for other anxiety disorders. However, if obsessive compulsives have deficits in information processing that are not shared by other anxiety disorders, specific treatment techniques that aim at correcting these deficits must be developed (e.g., training in identifying safety signals).

Biological Models

Neurochemical Factors

The most prevalent neurochemical hypothesis of OCD implicates the neurotransmitter serotonin as critical in the expression of OCD symptoms. Support for this hypothesis has come mainly from studies of the efficacy of serotonergic drugs such as clomipramine (CMI) as compared to nonserotonergic drugs. These studies indicate that CMI is more potent than placebo in reducing OCD symptoms and that other antidepressant medications such as imipramine, nortriptyline, and amitriptyline are ineffective (Zohar & Insel, 1987). Two studies found a significant correlation between the plasma levels of CMI and clinical improvement in OCD symptoms (Insel, Murphy, et al., 1983; Stern, Marks, Wright, & Luscombe, 1980).

Studies that directly investigated serotonin functioning in obsessive compulsives have not been conclusive (Joffe & Swinson, 1991). High correlations between improvement in OCD symptoms and a decrease in the serotonin metabolite 5-hydroxy indoleacetic acid (5-HIAA) were reported in two studies (Flament et al., 1985; Thoren, Asberg, Bertilsson et al., 1980). These results are consistent with the hypothesis that the antiobsessional effects of CMI are mediated by the serotonergic system. It is not clear, however, whether OCD individuals have an abnormality that involves serotonergic functioning. Studies of serotonin platelet uptake have not revealed any differences between obsessive compulsives and controls (Insel, Mueller, Alterman, Linnoila, & Murphy, 1985; Weizman et al., 1985). To examine directly the role of serotonin in mediating OCD symptoms, several studies have administered the serotonin agonist metachlorophenylpoprazine (mCPP) to obsessive compulsive patients. In two studies, Zohar and his colleagues (Zohar & Insel, 1987; Zohar, Mueller, Insel, Zohar-Kaduch, & Murphy, 1987) found an increase in obsessive compulsive symptoms following the oral administration of mCPP. Moreover, after treatment with CMI, the effect of mCPP was no longer observed. However, the administration of mCPP intravenously did not produce an increase in OCD symptoms (Charney et al., 1988). Why oral but not intravenous administration of mCPP exacerbates OCD symptoms is unclear.

Neuroanatomical Factors

Several studies suggest a neuroanatomical basis to OCD. Some studies indicated that many individuals with OCD have some deficits in frontal lobe functioning (e.g., Behar et al., 1984; Cox, Fedio, & Rapoport, 1989; Head, Bolton, & Hymas, 1989), but other studies failed to find such deficits (Insel, Donnelly, Lalakea, Alterman, & Murphy, 1983). Further support for the role of the frontal lobe in OCD comes from the therapeutic efficacy of psychosurgical techniques such as capsulotomy and cingulotomy (Ballantine, Bouckoms, Thomas, & Giriunas, 1987).

Additional evidence for neurobiological deficits in OCD comes from the relationship of this disorder to a variety of disorders with a known neurological basis in the basal ganglia. In particular, a high incidence of OCD has been noted following encephalitis lethargica (Schilder, 1938), Sydenham's chorea (Swedo et al., 1989), and Tourette's syndrome (Rapoport & Wise, 1988). Finally, the results of four studies using positron-emission tomography to assess metabolic activity in the brain suggested that obsessive compulsives show increased metabolic rates in the prefrontal cortex (Baxter et al., 1987; for a review, see Rapoport, 1991).

TREATMENTS

Traditionally, OCD was considered among the most intractable of psychological disorders. Psychodynamic psychotherapy and psychotropic medications have proven generally ineffective in ameliorating obsessive compulsive symptoms (Black, 1974; Perse, 1988). However, the advent of effective behavioral treatments and serotonergic medications has greatly improved the prognosis of this disorder.

Behavioral Treatments

Early Behavioral Treatments

Early behavioral treatments aimed at reducing the anxiety associated with OCD often used systematic desensitization. Despite initial claims that this approach was effective with OCD, case reports indicated that systematic desensitization reduced symptoms in only 30% of patients (Beech & Vaughn, 1978, Cooper, Gelder, & Marks, 1965). Treatment procedures designed to promote habituation of anxiety through prolonged exposure to feared cues (e.g., paradoxical intention, imaginal flooding, satiation, and aversion relief) also have been employed to treat OCD. The effectiveness of these procedures has not been impressive on the whole.

Behavioral treatments aimed at blocking or punishing obsessions and compulsions such as thought stopping, aversion therapy, and covert sensitization have also been applied to OCD. Thought stopping was found to be largely ineffective in several case studies and in one controlled study (Emmelkamp & Kwee, 1977; Stern, 1978; Stern, Lipsedge, & Marks, 1975). Aversion therapy using electrical shock, the snapping of a rubber band on the wrist, or covert sensitization have fared somewhat better (Kenny, Mowbray, & Lalani, 1978; Kenny, Solyom, & Solyom, 1973), but the long-term efficacy of these procedures has not been examined.

Exposure and Response Prevention

Employing prolonged exposure to obsessional cues and strict prevention of ritualistic behavior (response prevention), Meyer (1966) reported the successful treatment of two cases of OCD. Later reports indicated that this treatment program was highly successful in 10 of 15 cases and moderately effective in the others; only two patients relapsed after 5 to 6 years (Meyer & Levy, 1973; Meyer, Levy, & Schnurer, 1974). The results of numerous controlled and uncontrolled studies of exposure and response prevention have been remarkably consistent: approximately 65% to 75% of patients who were treated with this procedure were improved and stayed so at follow-up (for detailed reviews of these studies, see Foa, Steketee, & Ozarow, 1985; Rachman & Hodgson, 1980.)

A detailed description of the treatment program as it is conducted in our clinic is provided in Foa and Wilson (1991). Briefly, the program consists of repeated, prolonged (45 min to 2 hr) exposures of patients to situations that provoke discomfort and instructions to refrain from ritualizing throughout the treatment program regardless of the strength of the urges to do so. Exposures are usually graded so that stimuli that produce moderate distress are encountered prior to more upsetting ones, and treatment sessions typically include both imaginal and actual (*in vivo*) exposure exercises to threat-related cues. Patients are instructed to engage in additional exposure exercises between treatment sessions.

Exposure

The relative effects of exposure and response-prevention procedures were examined by Foa and her colleagues (Foa, Steketee, Grayson, Turner, & Latimer, 1984; Foa, Steketee, & Milby, 1980; Steketee, Foa, & Grayson, 1982). Obsessive-compulsive patients were treated with exposure only, response prevention only, or with a combination of the two techniques. At both posttreatment and follow-up, the combination treatment produced greater treatment gains than did the two individual components employed separately. A closer examination of the results suggested that the component treatments produced differential benefits; exposure affected primarily obsessional distress whereas response prevention impacted most on rituals.

Foa, Steketee, Turner, and Fischer (1980) compared the effects of combined *in vivo* and imaginal exposure versus *in vivo* exposure only. Both treatments included response-prevention instructions. Although no differences between the treatments emerged at the end of treatment, the combined exposure appeared superior in maintaining gains. However, examination of the outcome for individual patients indicated that some patients in the *in vivo* only treat-

ment relapsed, but others did not. It is possible that patients who are able to access all of the elements of their fear network (including feared consequences) during *in vivo* exposure do not need additional imaginal exposure, but individuals who tend to "cognitively avoid" confrontation with their feared catastrophes need the structure of imaginal exposure in addition to the *in vivo* exposure.

In most cases, it matters little whether anxiety-provoking stimuli are presented hierarchically beginning with the least distressing and proceeding to the most distressing or whether the most distressing stimulus is presented at the outset of treatment (Hodgson, Rachman, & Marks, 1972). However, clinical observations suggest that patients are more receptive to a treatment program in which they approach their most feared situation gradually. Therefore, we employ a five- or six-step hierarchy in our treatment program. This seems to strike an acceptable balance between the patients' desire for gradual exposure and the need for repeated exposures (about 10 sessions) to the most feared items.

On the whole, the therapist's modeling of exposure exercises does not appear to augment the efficacy of the exposure (Rachman, Marks, & Hodgson, 1973). However, individual patients often are more willing to engage in exposure exercises if the therapist models the behavior.

Two studies have compared therapist-aided exposure to self-exposures (Emmelkamp & van Krannen, 1977; Marks et al., 1988). Emmelkamp and van Kraanen compared a group of obsessive compulsives given 10 sessions of *in vivo* exposure conducted by a therapist to a group whose members performed exposures on their own. In both groups, the therapist developed a hierarchy of exposure items, but the patients determined the speed at which they worked through the hierarchy. No differences were found between the groups immediately after treatment. Marks et al. (1988) compared patients treated with CMI and self-guided exposure to those treated with CMI alone, self-guided exposure alone, and therapist-guided exposure. Therapist-guided exposure produced better outcome, but this advantage disappeared at the 1-year follow-up.

Long exposure periods have been found more effective than brief, interrupted exposures (Rabavilas, Boulougouris, & Stefanis, 1976). No research has been conducted on the optimal time for exposure. However, clinical observation suggests that an obsessive compulsive's discomfort during exposures begins to dissipate after about 30 min and continues for up to 90 min (Foa & Chambless, 1978; Rachman, DeSilva, & Roper, 1976). It is important that the exposure session not be terminated while the patient's distress level remains high, so exposure sessions should last at least 45 min.

Clearly exposure techniques are effective in ameliorating obsessive compulsive symptoms. When variants of exposure programs were compared to one another, no major differences were detected with the exception of the duration of the exposure: Long exposures produce outcome superior to that of short exposures. How frequently exposure sessions should be conducted with obsessive compulsives has not yet been addressed empirically. Clinical observation suggests that frequent (daily) sessions are preferable. However, with mild cases, especially those with few rituals, two to three sessions per week may be sufficient.

Response Prevention

Although deliberate exposure exercises reduce passive avoidance of obsessional stimuli, exposure does not automatically eliminate compulsive rituals. To reduce the urges to ritualize, patients are instructed to refrain from all ritualistic behavior during the treatment period. To this end, the therapist needs to teach patients to keep an accurate record of their main rituals and to enlist the aid of a support person. The role of the support person is to provide encouragement and to remind the patient of the rationale and instructions for response prevention. The support person should be available to help the patient resist the urge to ritualize, but it is important that the support person not attack the patient verbally or physically to prevent the patient from performing the rituals.

The strictness of response-prevention instructions has varied from study to study, ranging from normal washing without supervision to complete abstinence from washing for several days under continuous supervision. The level of supervision does not appear to significantly affect treatment outcome, but the data regarding the strictness of response-prevention instructions are less clear. Clinical observations suggest that patients are more able to comply with relatively strict instructions, perhaps because they are not required to decide if a particular wash is "normal" or ritualized. (Instructions for response prevention are presented later in the section on Treatment Period.)

Mental rituals are more difficult to treat than are overt rituals. This is most likely because there is relatively little time or distinction between the urge to perform mental rituals and their actual performance. Consequently, the patient has little control over their occurrence. In developing response-prevention instructions for mental rituals, the therapist must distinguish cognitions that comprise the ritual and aim at reducing distress related to obsessions. This distinction is important because the treatment of obsessive thoughts calls for prolonged exposure, whereas treatment of mental rituals calls for response prevention.

One form of ritualistic behavior that is often overlooked is repeated requests for reassurance. Although not all requests for information or reassurance are compulsions, when such requests become stereotyped and repetitive they serve the same function as do other compulsive rituals and should be addressed in treatment with response prevention. Patients often rely on specific people such as a spouse, parent, or close friend for reassurance. Response prevention for reassurance seeking consists of both instructing the patient not to request reassurance as well as instructing those who provided such reassurance in the past not to do so any longer. It is likely that refusals to offer reassurance will result in frustration as well as increased anxiety. Therefore, at the outset of treatment, the therapist should help the patient and the support person negotiate responses that will not provide reassurance but at the same time will not provoke potential conflicts. For example, a woman who was concerned with contaminated food had developed a ritual of asking her husband whether various products were spoiled. Prior to treatment, they agreed that should the woman slip and ask for reassurance, her husband's response would be, "I feel as though you are seeking reassurance again, and because I love you and want to help you get better, I'm not going to answer your question."

Cognitive Treatments

Recently, cognitive therapy has been employed with obsessive compulsives. Salkovskis and Warwick (1985) reported a case study in which cognitive therapy was used as an adjunct to exposure and response prevention with an obsessive compulsive with overvalued ideation. Initially, this woman had responded well to behavior therapy, but she relapsed following an episode of severe depression. Further exposure sessions failed to restore the initial gains. After 10 sessions of cognitive therapy combined with exposure and response prevention the patient improved significantly. Kearney and Silverman (1990) also found the combination of cognitive therapy with exposure and response prevention to be effective with an adolescent boy with OCD.

Emmelkamp and his colleagues (Emmelkamp & Beens, 1991; Emmelkamp, Visser, & Hoekstra, 1988) reported on two small studies comparing cognitive therapy, based on Ellis's (1962) A-B-C techniques, with self-controlled exposure and response prevention. Treatments consisted of six sessions held over a period of 4 weeks. Immediately posttreatment no differences between the two treatments emerged. Emmelkamp and Beens (1991) found that exposure and response prevention alone was as effective as the combination of cognitive therapy and exposure and response prevention. It appears, then, that cognitive techniques may be effective in reducing OCD symptom severity, particularly when employed in conjunction with exposure and response-prevention techniques. However, more studies are needed before clear conclusions about the efficacy of cognitive techniques may be drawn.

Serotonergic Medications

Recently, the use of serotonergic medications in the treatment of OCD has received a great deal of attention. Of the tricyclic antidepressants, CMI has been studied most extensively. In controlled trials of CMI versus placebo, CMI was found superior (DeVeaugh-Geiss, Landau, & Katz, 1989; Marks, Stern, Mawson, Cobb, & McDonald, 1980; Thoren, Asberg, Chronholm, Jornestedt, & Traskman, 1980; Zohar & Insel, 1987). Similar results have been obtained with fluvoxamine, another serotonin reuptake inhibitor (Goodman et al., 1989a, 1989b; Price, Goodman, Charney, & Heninger, 1987; Perse, Griest, Jefferson, Rosenfeld, & Dar, 1987). Yet another serotonin reuptake inhibitor, fluoxetine, also appears effective in reducing obsessive compulsive symptoms (Fontaine & Chouinard, 1985; Jenike, Buttolph, Baer, Ricciardi, & Holland, 1989).

These studies suggest that up to 60% of patients show some response to treatment with serotonin reuptake inhibitors; however, the average treatment gain is moderate at best (Greist, 1990; McCarthy & Foa, 1990). In addition, amelioration of obsessive compulsive symptoms is maintained only as long as the drug is continued (Thoren, Asberg, Chronholm et al., 1980). In a controlled double-blind discontinuation study, 90% of patients relapsed within a few weeks after being withdrawn from CMI (Pato, Zohar-Kadouch, Zohar, & Murphy, 1988).

Combined Behavioral and Pharmacological Treatments

Few studies have examined the effects of combining serotonin reuptake inhibitors with exposure and response prevention. Marks et al. (1980) studied the combination of CMI and behavioral therapy with 40 obsessive compulsive patients. A large effect of behavioral therapy and a small additive effect of the medication were found immediately posttreatment. However, because the drug-only period was short (4 weeks), the efficacy of drug therapy alone could not be adequately assessed. A subsequent study of 49 obsessive compulsives examined the relative contributions of CMI and exposure-based treatment (Marks et al., 1988). Medication had only a small and transitory (8 week) additive effect when combined with behavioral therapy. The authors concluded that systematic self-exposure is a relatively more potent intervention than CMI. The design of the study does not permit conclusions about the effects of behavioral therapy on relapse following drug discontinuation. A 6-year follow-up of 34 of the patients included in the above study revealed no drug effect. Superior long-term outcome was associated with better compliance with exposure instructions (O'Sullivan, Noshirvani, Marks, Monterio, & Lelliott, 1991).

One study compared the effects of fluvoxamine to those of exposure and response prevention (Cottraux et al., 1990). The results suggested that the two treatments were comparable in reducing OCD symptoms at the end of the 24-week treatment and at a 6-month follow-up. Immediately posttreatment, patients treated with the combination of the two active treatments fared slightly better than those treated with behavioral therapy combined with a placebo, but this effect was noted only on measures of depression, and as in the Marks et al. (1988) study, the effect was transient.

We have conducted an uncontrolled study of 62 OCD patients examining the long-term effects of intensive exposure and response prevention and serotonergic medication (Hembree, Cohen, Riggs, Kozak, & Foa, 1992). Patients had been treated with serotonergic medications (fluvoxamine or CMI), intensive behavioral therapy (exposure and response prevention), or intensive behavioral therapy with concurrent medication. All patients were contacted for a follow-up (mean 1½ years posttreatment) telephone interview. Among patients who were medication free at the time of the follow-up assessment ($n = 37$), those who had received behavioral therapy alone or behavioral therapy combined with medication reported less severe OCD symptoms than those who were treated with medication alone. Patients who were taking medications at follow-up ($n = 25$) did equally well regardless of whether they had received concurrent behavioral therapy and medication or medication alone. Thus, it appears that patients treated with behavioral therapy maintain their gains more than patients treated with serotonergic medication that was subsequently withdrawn. Medications produce long-term benefits equivalent to behavioral therapy, but they require that patients stay on the medication.

ASSESSMENT

Following a diagnostic interview to ascertain the presence of OCD, it is advisable to quantify the severity of the OCD symptoms using one or more of the instruments described below. Quantification of symptom severity will assist the therapist in evaluating how successful treatment was for a given patient. In our clinic, we use several assessment instruments.

Assessor Ratings

Assessors rate the patient on 8-point Likert-type rating scales in each of three areas: anxiety/distress, avoidance, and rituals. Based on information gathered in an initial interview, the assessor identifies three primary problems in each of the above areas and rates their severity. When rating the patient's anxiety/distress, the therapist should take into account how distressed the patient feels when confronted with the situation or object, how often he/she gets distressed, and how strongly he/she is convinced that the feared consequence will occur. For example, if a patient is concerned with contamination, the therapist should determine the three main contaminating stimuli (objects or situations) and rate each separately. Next, the therapist should assess the degree to which the patient avoids situations related to the stimuli identified as main distressing stimuli. For example, if the main contaminant is feces, the avoidance item selected for rating might be public rest rooms. Third, the therapist should rate the severity of the three main compulsive rituals. The severity of rituals is based on both the frequency and the duration of the ritualistic behavior. For example, the severity rating of a ritual that occurs 75 times a day and lasts only 30 sec each time would be based on the high frequency, whereas, the severity of a ritual that occurs only twice a day and takes 90 min to complete would be determined by the time spent on the ritual.

Although researchers have used these and similar ratings in treatment outcome studies of OCD (e.g., Emmelkamp & Beens, 1991; Foa et al., 1983b; Foa, Grayson, & Steketee, 1982; Marks et al., 1988; O'Sullivan et al., 1991), information about their psychometric properties is scarce. The scales appear to have adequate interrater agreement when completed by two independent assessors (Foa et al., 1983b), but there is less agreement between the ratings of therapists and patients (Foa, Steketee, Kozak, & Dugger, 1985). Support for the validity of these rating scales is derived mainly from their demonstrated sensitivity to therapeutic change.

The Yale–Brown Obsessive Compulsive Scale (Y-BOCS; Goodman et al., 1989a, 1989b) is a recently developed standardized rating scale that, like the scales described above, is completed by an interviewer. The Y-BOCS includes 10 items (5 assess obsessions and 5 compulsions) each of which is rated on a 5-point scale ranging from 0 (no symptoms) to 4 (severe symptoms). Assessors rate the time occupied by the obsessions and compulsions, the degree of interference with functioning, the level of distress, attempts to resist the symptoms, and level of control over the symptoms. The Y-BOCS has shown adequate interrater agreement, internal consistency, and validity (Goodman et al., 1989a, 1989b).

The Compulsive Activity Checklist (CAC), originally the Obsessive Compulsive Interview Checklist (Philpott, 1975), was developed as an assessor-rated measure of the extent to which OCD symptoms interfere with daily functioning. Originally the CAC included 62 items, but a shorter version containing 37 has been developed (Marks, Hallam, Connelly, & Philpott, 1977). A self-report version of the CAC which includes 38 items was developed by Freund, Steketee, and Foa (1985). This version was found to be reliable, valid, and sensitive to treatment change (for a review, see Freund, 1986).

A few self-report instruments for assessing OCD symptoms such as the Leyton Obsessional Inventory (Kazarian, Evans, & Lefave, 1977), the Lynfield Obsessional-Compulsive Questionnaire (Allen & Tune, 1975), and the Maudsley Obsessive Compulsive Inventory (Hodgson & Rachman, 1977) are available. These instruments are limited in that they assess only certain forms of obsessive compulsive behavior and/or they include items that are unrelated to OCD symptoms.

INITIAL INTERVIEW

After a diagnosis of OCD has been established, and before actually beginning treatment, the therapist should schedule 4 to 6 hr of appointments with the patient. In these sessions, the therapist needs to accomplish two important tasks. First, the sessions are used to collect information necessary to develop a treatment plan. Specifically, the therapist must identify specific cues that cause the patient distress (threat cues), avoidance, rituals, and feared consequences. Second, the therapist should develop good rapport with the patient. Because during intensive behavioral therapy the patient will engage in exposure exercises designed to elicit anxiety and distress, the lack of a good relationship between the therapist and the patient may render the treatment program less effective.

Threat cues may be either (1) tangible objects in the environment or (2) thoughts, images, or impulses that the person experiences (for lack of better terms, we have labeled them external cues and internal cues, respectively). Passive avoidance and ritualistic behavior (sometimes called active avoidance) both serve to reduce the distress associated with the threat cues. Rituals may be further divided into overt or covert (mental) forms.

External Fear Cues

Most obsessive compulsives experience fear in reaction to specific environmental cues (objects, persons, or situations), but each patient will have his/her own idiosyncratic threat cues. For example, individuals who fear contamination from toilets may differ as to whether all toilets are feared or only those open to the public. One patient may fear only the toilet itself, whereas another patient also fears bathroom floors, doorknobs, and faucets. Similarly, two individuals may experience distress at the prospect of a fire burning down their home, but one experiences the distress only when she is the last person to leave the house whereas the other experiences distress before going to bed at night when his children are present.

The therapist needs to gather specific information about cues that elicit the patient's distress in order to identify the basic sources of the fear. Identification of the basic source is important for planning the treatment program. Confronting the source of the fear is essential for successful behavioral treatment of OCD. Often, when such exposure does not take place during treatment, relapse will occur. For example, a patient who feared contamination by her hometown was treated with exposure and response prevention 3,000 miles away from the town. Because of the distances involved, exposure to the town was impossible, so treatment consisted of exposure to objects contaminated directly or indirectly by contact with the town. Although the patient habituated to the objects used in the exposure sessions, she continued to fear her hometown. Within 1 year after treatment, she had developed fears to new objects related to her hometown. It was not until she engaged in repeated exposures to the town itself that she experienced lasting improvement.

It is important that the therapist conduct a thorough investigation of objects, situations, and places that evoke obsessional distress for the patient at the time of presentation and at onset. Such information will help identify the source of the distress. To facilitate communication with the patient about situations that evoke distress, a subjective distress scale (Subjective Units of Discomfort [SUDs]) ranging from 0 to 100 is introduced. Patients are asked to rate each situation with respect to the level of distress that they expect to experience upon exposure. The source of the distress is expected to be 100. The following dialogue between therapist (T) and patient (P) illustrates the process of gathering information about distressing situations.

T: When do you get the urge to wash your hands?

P: In a lot of places. There are so many places.

T: Are there any places where the urges are particularly strong?

P: Well when I am sitting in my living room, particularly near the fireplace. Also in the laundry room. Which I never go to. Also, when I walk in the park.

T: Lets talk about your living room. How upset are you when you are sitting next to your fireplace?

P: That's bad. I guess about a 90.

T: Can you tell me what makes you so upset in your living room?

P: Well that is a long story . . . and I know it doesn't make sense.

T: Go on. Its important that we understand what makes you uncomfortable and fearful in your living room.

P: About two years ago, I got up in the morning and went into the living room and I saw a dead squirrel in the fireplace. I guess he got in through the chimney. So, I figured that if the squirrel was dead, he must have been sick. I know that a lot of squirrels have rabies, so I thought that if the squirrel died of rabies, then the germs are all over the chimney.

T: Have you tried to have the chimney and the fireplace cleaned?

P: Yes, we did have a company come in and clean the whole area, but I'm not sure that they can clean away all the germs.

T: I understand. How about the laundry room, how upsetting is it to be in the laundry room?

P: That would be a 100, that's why I don't go in there.

T: How did the laundry room become dangerous?

P: Oh, that's another story. Until a year ago, my children used to keep their guinea pigs in the laundry room. One day we found the female guinea pig dead. So, I thought that it probably died of rabies too.

T: Oh, I understand. So you are generally afraid that you will contract rabies if you come in contact with things that you think are contaminated with rabies germs. Is this true?

P: Exactly. That's why I don't like to walk in the woods or the park. You know those places have all kind of animals and you can never tell where the germs might be.

It is clear from the above conversation that it was not living rooms, laundry rooms, or parks per se that the patient feared. Rather, any situation or object that, in her mind, had some probability of being infested with rabies germs would become a source of contamination.

Internal Fear Cues

Anxiety and distress may also be generated by images, impulses, or abstract thoughts that the individual finds disturbing, shameful, or disgusting. Examples of such cues include impulses to stab one's child, thoughts of one's spouse injured in an accident, or images of religious figures engaged in sexual activity. Clearly, internal threat cues may be produced by external situations such as the sight of a knife triggering the impulse to stab one's child. Some patients may get distressed when experiencing certain bodily sensations, such as minor pains triggering the fear of having cancer.

In many cases, patients may be reluctant to express their obsessive thoughts, either because they are ashamed of them or because they fear that expressing them will make the consequence more likely to occur. In these cases, the therapist needs to encourage the expression of these thoughts through direct questioning and a matter-of-fact attitude. Sometimes it helps to tell the patient that many people with and without OCD have unwanted thoughts (as many as 85% of normal individuals) (Rachman & DeSilva, 1978). It may also be helpful to remind the patient that talking about the obsessions will be a part of therapy and the evaluation session provides an opportunity to begin this process.

T: So tell me, when is it that you feel the urge to count?

P: It seems like I'm always counting something, but its mostly when I think about certain things.

T: What kind of things?

P: I don't know. Bad things.

T: Can you give me some examples of bad thoughts that will make you want to count?

P: (*Brief silence*) I really prefer not to talk about them. It makes things worse.

T: You mean it makes the counting worse?

P: Yes.

T: All right, I know now that when you think or talk about certain bad things you have an urge to count, but I still don't know what those bad things are. How about you tell me so that I can help you with them.

P: I'd really rather not. Can't we talk about something else.

T: It is important that I know what the thoughts are in order to plan your treatment. I'll try to help you. Do the thoughts involve someone being hurt?

P: Yes.

T: Do the thoughts involve only certain people getting hurt or could it be anyone?

P: Mostly my family.

T: OK, what else can you tell me about the thoughts?

P: I really don't want to say anymore.

T: I know this is scary, but remember facing your fears is what this treatment is all about.

P: OK. It's not always thoughts. Sometimes I see pictures in my mind where my brother or my mom and dad are killed. I'm afraid when I talk about these thoughts and pictures that they really will die.

T: A lot of people have thoughts that they don't like to have. Even people without OCD. Just because you have these thoughts, or talk about them doesn't mean that bad things will actually happen or that you want them to come true.

It is important to reassure the patient that unpleasant thoughts occur often and to emphasize the distinction between thoughts and reality. Many obsessive compulsive patients have magical ideas in which the distinction between "thinking about" and "making things happen" is blurred. It is important to point out to the patient that thoughts are different from actions. Also, many patients think that if negative thoughts enter their mind, it means that they wish the bad thing will happen. The therapist should assure the patient that thinking about bad things does not mean that one wants them to happen.

Feared Consequences

Many obsessive compulsives are afraid that something terrible will happen if they fail to perform their rituals. Washers, for example, typically fear that they and/or someone else will become ill, become disabled, or die as a result of being contaminated. Many checkers fear that, because of their negligence, certain catastrophes will happen such as their home burning down or killing someone while driving. Some patients have only a vague notion of what these negative consequence might be (e.g., "I don't know exactly what will happen, but I feel that if I don't count to seven something bad will happen to my family"). Others do not fear catastrophes at all, but they cannot tolerate the emotional distress they experience if they do not perform rituals. Some fear that, unless they ritualize, anxiety will increase continually until they have a nervous breakdown.

It is important to identify the specific details of the patient's feared consequences in order to plan an effective exposure program. For example, the content of the imaginal exposure of a patient who checks while driving for fear of having hit a pedestrian and being sent to jail will differ from that of a patient who fears that hitting a pedestrian will result in being punished by God. Similarly, patients who ritualistically place objects in a specific order may differ with respect to their feared catastrophes. Some perform the ritual in order to magically prevent catastrophic consequences (e.g., death of parents) whereas others do so only to reduce distress elicited by disordered objects. The former would benefit from treatment that includes both imaginal and *in vivo* exposure, whereas the latter is likely to profit from *in vivo* exposure alone.

Strength of Belief

Clinical observations led Foa (1979) to suggest that obsessive compulsives who are overvalued ideators do not respond well to exposure and response prevention, although a later study failed to find a linear relationship between strength of belief in feared catastrophes and improvement following exposure and response prevention (Lelliott et al., 1988). Two issues need to be considered in evaluating these results. First, the reliability and validity of the measure of strength of belief used in the study are unknown. Second, the relationship between overvalued ideation and treatment outcome may not be linear. Clinical observation suggests that only patients who express *extreme* belief in their obsessional ideation show poor outcome. These patients appear delusional when discussing their feared catastrophes.

When assessing the strength of belief, it is important to remember that a patient's insight into the senselessness of his/her belief often fluctuates. Some patients readily acknowledge that their obsessional beliefs are irrational, but they still cause marked distress. A few individuals firmly believe that their obsessions and compulsions are rational. In most patients, though, the strength of belief fluctuates across situations, making it difficult to ascertain the degree to which they believe the obsessions are irrational. The following is an example of an inquiry into the strength of a patient's belief in her obsessional fear of contracting acquired immune deficiency syndrome (AIDS).

T: How likely is it that you will contract AIDS from using a public restroom?

P: I'm really terrified that I will get AIDS if I use a bathroom in a restaurant.

T: I know that you are afraid of getting AIDS, but if you think logically, how likely do you think you are to get AIDS by sitting on a public toilet?

P: I think I will get AIDS if I use a public toilet.

T: So do you mean to say that there is a 100% chance of you getting AIDS if you sat on a public toilet once?

P: Well, I don't know about once, but if I did it again and again I would.

T: What about other people, will they get AIDS if they use a public toilet?

P: I guess so. I'm not sure.

T: Since most people use public bathrooms, almost everyone should have AIDS by now. How do you explain the fact that there are a relatively small number of people with AIDS?

P: Maybe not everybody is as susceptible to AIDS as I am.

T: Do you think that you are more susceptible than other people?

P: I don't know for sure, maybe the likelihood of my getting AIDS is only 50%.

Based on the interaction described above, it was concluded that the patient was not an "overvalued ideator" and thus the prognosis for this patient is brighter than if she continued to strongly hold her original belief. Accordingly, the implementation of exposure and response prevention for this patient would follow the standard guidelines.

Avoidance and Rituals

In order to maximize treatment efficacy, all avoidance and ritualistic behaviors, even seemingly minor ones, should be prevented. Therefore, the therapist should gather complete information about all passive avoidance and rituals. When the therapist is in doubt as to whether a particular avoidance behavior is related to OCD he/she might suggest an "experiment" in which the patient is exposed to the avoided situation. If the patient experiences anxiety or distress, the avoidance behavior should be prevented as part of treatment. Similarly, if it is unclear whether a given action constitutes a ritual, a response-prevention "experiment" may be implemented. If refraining from performing the action evokes distress, the action would be identified as a ritual and should be addressed in therapy.

Obsessive compulsives, like phobics, often attempt to avoid anxiety-evoking situations. Most passive avoidance strategies are fairly obvious (e.g., not entering public rest rooms, not preparing meals, and not taking out the trash). However, the therapist also needs to be attentive to subtle forms of avoidance such as carrying money in one's pockets to avoid opening a wallet, wearing slip-on shoes to avoid touching laces, and using drinking straws to avoid contact with a glass or a can.

Active rituals, like passive avoidance, may be explicit (e.g., prolonged washing, repeated checks of the door, and ordering of objects) and/or subtle (e.g., wiping hands on pant legs, blinking, and thinking "good" thoughts). It is important that the therapist identify both explicit and subtle rituals so they all can be addressed during treatment.

Although compulsive rituals are intended to reduce the distress associated with obsessions, patients sometimes report that the performance of these rituals is aversive in itself. For example, Ms. S, who was obsessed with the orderliness of objects on her shelves, found reordering the shelves aversive because she was unable to find the "perfect" place for everything. Similarly, Mr. J, who felt contaminated by chemicals, found the act of decontaminating himself by repeated hand washing aversive because he was unable to decide when his hands were sufficiently clean and, therefore, he washed until his hands become raw. Another reason that rituals may become aversive is their intrusion into other aspects of the person's life. For example, Mr. J, who would take 2-hr-long showers in order to feel adequately clean, was reprimanded repeatedly by his supervisor for arriving late to work.

When certain compulsions become aversive, some patients decrease the time they spend performing the ritual by increasing avoidance behaviors or by substituting other less time-consuming rituals. For example, Ms. E was obsessed with fears of contamination by funeral-related objects (e.g., cemeteries and people returning from a funeral) to which she responded with hours of showering and hand washing. She eventually retreated into her bedroom and avoided all contact with the outside world. Mr. J, described above, avoided taking a shower for days at a time, but in between showers he would wipe his hands compulsively and avoid touching his wife.

In some cases, seemingly "new" rituals may develop during the course of treatment to fill the function of those previously identified and prevented. For example, Mr. F, who was concerned about his hands becoming contaminated, was successful in resisting the urge to wash his hands, but soon after response prevention was implemented, he started to rub his hands together vigorously in order to "decontaminate" them. When such a substitute ritual is identified, it too needs to be addressed in treatment with response prevention. Therapists must remain alert to such shifts in ritualistic behaviors.

History of Main Complaint

Many obsessive compulsives are unable to give a detailed account of the onset of their symptoms because the symptoms began subtly many years ago. Nevertheless, attempts should be made to collect as much information as possible about the onset and course of the disorder. Such information may provide clues about aspects of the threat network and variables associated with the maintenance of symptoms, and may help anticipate difficulties that could arise during treatment (e.g., old obsessions or rituals that may resurface as more prominent ones diminish).

Many obsessive compulsives have an extensive history of psychological and pharmacological treatments, and it is important to make a detailed inquiry about the outcome of previous treatments. If the patient has been treated with exposure and response prevention, the therapist should assess whether the treatment was implemented appropriately and whether the patient was compliant with treatment demands. Knowledge that a patient experienced difficulty complying with response-prevention instructions or that previous therapy failed to provide adequate exposure experiences or response-prevention instructions is important for designing the behavioral program. Other factors that may have prevented successful outcome or caused relapse such as job stress, death in the family, or pregnancy should be discussed.

Recently, we have seen a large number of obsessive compulsives who have been treated, or are currently being treated, with serotonergic medications. Some seek behavioral treatment in order to augment the partial gains they have achieved with the medication. Others wish to discontinue the medication because it was ineffective, because of side effects, or because they do not want to continue taking medicine indefinitely. Assessing the patient's treatment goals is necessary for planning his/her treatment program.

Social Functioning

Obsessive compulsive symptoms may severely disrupt the daily functioning of patients. Therapists should assess the impact of OCD symptoms on the various areas of functioning. Where appropriate, this information should be used to design suitable exposure exercises. For example, Ms. D experienced difficulties completing assignments at work because she repeatedly checked each task. Treatment included exposures to performing tasks at work without checking. Even if the client is not currently working, exposures simulating work situations may be necessary if symptoms created difficulties in previous jobs.

OCD clearly has a deleterious effect on the marital functioning of many patients. About half of married individuals seeking treatment for OCD experience marital distress (Emmelkamp et al., 1990; Riggs et al., 1992). Other family and social relationships may also suffer as a result of the OCD symptoms. The impairment in social functioning may arise either because social contact is perceived as threatening (e.g., "I may spread germs to other people") or because so much of the patient's time and energy is invested in performing rituals and planning ways to avoid distressing situations. Again, information about the relation of social dysfunction to OCD symptoms may lead the therapist to include specific exposures aimed at ameliorating these social difficulties.

The assessment of social functioning should also include an evaluation of what role, if any, other people play in the patient's compulsive rituals. If the patient relies on others for reassurance or compliance with rituals (e.g., family members must remove their shoes before entering the house), the therapist should instruct the family in how to respond appropriately when they are asked to participate in the patient's rituals. A careful analysis of the relationship is called for before specific instructions are given to significant others.

Mood State

Although some patients with serious depression and OCD may benefit from behavioral therapy for OCD (Foa, Kozak, Steketee, & McCarthy, 1992), research has suggested that severe depression may limit the extent to which the OCD symptoms are reduced and the maintenance of those gains (Foa et al., 1982; Foa, Grayson, Steketee, & Doppelt, 1983a; Marks, 1977; Rachman & Hodgson, 1980). Therefore, it is important to assess the mood state of the patient prior to beginning behavioral therapy. Patients with severe depression should be treated with antidepressant medication or cognitive therapy to reduce the depressive symptoms prior to implementing behavioral therapy for the OCD. Treatment with antidepressants such as CMI or fluvoxamine are likely to reduce OCD symptoms as well as depression. Since the effects of such medications on OCD symptoms may not be evidenced until 3 months after treatment begins, the therapist needs to use his/her clinical judgment to decide whether to begin behavioral therapy when the depression decreases or to wait until the effects of the medication on OCD symptoms can be assessed.

TREATMENT

How should a therapist determine what is the most suitable treatment for a given patient? As discussed earlier, exposure and response prevention as well as serotonergic medications have demonstrated efficacy for OCD. The therapist and patient are faced with the choice of behavioral therapy, pharmacotherapy, or a combination of the two. Neither treatment is effective with all patients and no predictors of who will benefit most from which treatment modality have been identified. Therefore, unless the patient has been particularly successful or unsuccessful with some previous course of treatment, the decision should be based on factors such as availability of treatment, amount of time the patient is able or will-

ing to invest in treatment, his/her motivation, and the patient's willingness to tolerate side effects.

The intensive behavioral treatment requires a considerable investment of time over a period of several weeks. Many patients are unable or unwilling to devote 4 to 5 hr a day to treatment. These patients should be advised to try pharmacological treatment because it does not require the same extensive time commitment. Some patients may be unwilling (sometimes expressed as "I can't do that") to experience the temporary discomfort caused by exposure and response prevention. These patients, too, may be advised to try medications.

Some patients are concerned about the potential (or already experienced) side effects of medications or their unknown long-term effects. These patients often prefer behavioral therapy. Other patients are concerned with the prospect of entering an "endless" treatment since, according to present knowledge, relapse occurs when medication is withdrawn (Pato et al., 1988; Thoren, Asberg, Chronholm, et al., 1980). This concern is particularly relevant for women who plan to bear children in the future and would need to withdraw from the medication during pregnancy. Behavioral therapy should be recommended to these patients because its effects are more enduring.

The long-term effects of combining behavioral therapy and medication are unclear; therefore, it is premature to recommend treatment programs that combine the two therapies. However, some patients who present for behavioral treatment are already on antidepressant medication. Because these medications were not found to interfere with the effectiveness of behavioral therapy, it is recommended that patients continue to take the medication if they have experienced some improvement in either obsessive compulsive symptoms or depression. However, if the patient has not experienced improvement with medication, withdrawal of the medication before or during behavioral therapy should be considered. Special consideration should be given to patients with severe depression concurrent with their OCD. It is recommended that these patients be treated with antidepressants or with cognitive therapy for the depression prior to entering intensive behavioral therapy for the OCD.

Intensive Exposure and Response Prevention

The intensive treatment program consists of four phases: (1) information gathering, (2) intensive exposure and response prevention, (3) a home visit, and (4) a maintenance and relapse-prevention phase.

Information Gathering and Treatment Planning

The first stage of information gathering consists of a thorough diagnostic evaluation to ascertain that the patient's main psychopathology is OCD. The second step is to assess whether the patient is appropriate for behavioral treatment. We recommend that individuals who are abusing drugs or alcohol should be treated for the substance abuse prior to intensive treatment for OCD. Patients who have clear delusions and hallucinations are also poor candidates for intensive treatment. Individuals with severe major depressive disorder should be treated for depression before beginning treatment for OCD. Third, the patient's motivation to comply with the demands of intensive treatment should be carefully evaluated. It is important to describe the treatment program in enough detail so that the patient is not surprised when treatment begins. If the patient does not express strong motivation and commitment to treatment, it might be preferable to delay the implementation of intensive treatment or to offer alternative treatments such as medication or a trial of less intensive behavioral treatment.

Once a patient is judged to be appropriate for intensive treatment, information gathering for treatment planning begins. This phase typically consists of 4 to 6 hr of contact with the patient conducted over a period of 2 to 3 days. During this phase, the therapist collects information about the patient's obsessive compulsive symptoms, general history, and the history of treatment for OCD as described above. During these sessions, the rationale for treatment is discussed, the program is described in detail, patients are taught to monitor their rituals, and a treatment plan is developed.

It is very important to discuss the rationale for treatment and to describe the treatment program in detail. The program requires that the patient abandon his/her OCD habits and, therefore, temporarily experience substantial discomfort. If patients do not understand why they are asked to suffer this short-term distress or are not convinced that treatment will work, they will be unlikely to comply with treatment instructions. The treatment rationale is explained as follows:

"You have a set of habits which, as you know, are called obsessive compulsive symptoms. These are habits of thinking, feeling, and acting which are extremely unpleasant, wasteful, and difficult to get rid of on your own. Usually, these habits involve thoughts, images, or impulses which habitually come to your mind even though you don't want them. Along with these thoughts you have unwanted feelings of extreme distress or anxiety and strong urges to do something to reduce the distress. To try to get rid of the anxiety, people get into the habit of engaging in various special thoughts or actions, which we call rituals.

"Unfortunately, as you know, the rituals do not work all that well, and the distress goes down for a short time only and comes back again. Eventually, you may find yourself doing more and more ritualizing to try to reduce anxiety, but even then, the relief is temporary and you have to do the ritual all over again. Gradually, you find yourself spending so much time and energy ritualizing—which does not work that well anyway—and other areas of your life get seriously disrupted.

"The treatment we are about to begin is called exposure and response prevention. It is designed to break two types of associations. The first one is the association between sensations of anxiety and the objects, situations, or thoughts that produce this distress. [*Use* information you have collected as examples, for example, 'Every time you touch anything associated with urine you feel anxious, distressed, or contaminated.'] The second association we want to break is the one between carrying out ritualistic behavior and the feeling of less anxiety or less distress. In other words, after you carry out [*specify* the identified rituals], you temporarily feel less distress. Therefore, you continue to engage in this behavior frequently. The treatment we offer will break the automatic bond between the feelings of discomfort/anxiety/contamination of [*specify* the obsession] and your rituals. It will also train you not to ritualize when you are anxious."

After presenting the treatment rationale, the therapist should begin to collect information about the patient's OCD symptoms. The rationale for information gathering and a description of the treatment is presented as follows:

"In the next two sessions, I will ask you specific questions about the various situations and thoughts that generate discomfort or anxiety in you. We will order them according to the degree of distress they generate in you on a scale from 0 to 100, where 0 means no anxiety and 100 means maximum anxiety or panic. The exposure treatment program involves confronting you with situations and thoughts which you avoid because they generate anxiety and urges to carry out ritualistic behavior. Why do we want to expose you to places and objects that will make you uncomfortable, situations that you have attempted to avoid even at much cost? We know that when people are exposed to situations which they fear, anxiety gradually declines. Through exposure, then, the association between anxiety and [*specify* obsessions] will weaken because you will be repeatedly exposed to these situations so that the previously evoked anxiety decreases with time.

"For many obsessive compulsives the obsessions occur within their imagination and rarely take place in reality. This makes it impossible to practice exposure by actually confronting those situations for prolonged periods. For example, if a person fears that her home will burn down, we certainly do not wish to have her house catch on fire in order to practice exposure. Similarly, someone who fears that he has run over a person who is now lying in the road cannot be exposed in reality to such a situation.

"If confrontation with the feared situation is necessary to reduce obsessions, how can you improve without directly confronting the situation? You can confront these fears through imagery, in which you visualize the circumstances that you fear will happen. In *imagery practice*, you create in your mind detailed pictures of the terrible consequences that you are afraid will occur if you do not engage in their ritualistic behavior. During prolonged exposure to these images, the distress level associated with them gradually decreases.

"When obsessive compulsives encounter their feared situations or their obsessional thoughts, they become anxious or distressed and feel compelled to perform the ritualistic behavior as a way to reduce their distress. Exposure practices can cause this same distress and urge to ritualize. Usually, performing rituals strengthens the pattern of distress and rituals. Therefore in treatment, ritual prevention is practiced to break the habit of ritualizing. This requires that you stop ritualizing, even though you are still having urges to do so. By facing your fears without resorting to compulsions, you will gradually become less anxious. Behavior therapists call this process habituation. Therefore, during the three weeks of intensive exposure, the association between relief from anxiety and carrying out [*specify* patient's rituals] will become weaker because you will not be allowed to engage in such behaviors and therefore you will find out that anxiety decreases even without resorting to these activities."

The initial information-gathering session is also used to begin training the patient to accurately monitor his/her rituals. Accurate reports of the frequency and duration of ritualistic behavior are important for evaluating the progress of treatment and for demonstrating the reality of changes to the patient. In some cases, the monitoring also serves an active role in treatment. Patients begin to recognize that rituals do not truly occur "all day long" and the act of monitoring the rituals may decrease their frequency and duration.

A copy of the monitoring form that we use is included in Figure 5.1. Guidelines for

Name:_____   Date: _____

Ritual A: _____   Ritual B: _____

In the second column of the table below, please describe the activity or thought that evokes a ritual. In the third column record the anxiety/discomfort level (0–100). In the fourth column write the number of minutes you spend in performing rituals during the time stated in Column 1. Record SUDs for each homework assignment, when treatment is in progress.

Time of day	Activity or thought that evokes the ritual (brief description)	Discomfort (0–100)	Number of minutes spent on rituals	
			A	B
6:00–6:30 a.m.				
6:30–7:00				
7:00–7:30				
7:30–8:00				
8:00–8:30				
8:30–9:00				
9:00–9:30				
9:30–10:00				
10:00–10:30				
10:30–11:00				
11:00–11:30				
11:30–12:00 p.m.				
12:00–12:30				
12:30–1:00				
1:00–1:30				
1:30–2:00				
2:00–2:30				
2:30–3:00				
3:00–3:30				
3:30–4:00				
4:00–4:30				
4:30–5:00				
5:00–5:30				
5:30–6:00				
6:00–6:30				
6:30–7:00				
7:00–7:30				
7:30–8:00				
8:00–8:30				
8:30–9:00				
9:00–9:30				
9:30–10:00				
10:00–10:30				
10:30–11:00				
11:00–6:00 a.m.				

FIGURE 5.1. Self-Monitoring of Rituals.

instructing the patient in self-monitoring are presented below.

"It is very important for the treatment program that we have an accurate picture of the extent to which you engage in obsessive thinking and compulsive behavior. Having a clear picture of how much of your time is taken up by your problem would help you and me to monitor your progress and adjust the treatment program accordingly. Therefore, during this week while I am still collecting information in order to form a treatment program, I would like you to record your symptoms every day. It is not easy to report accurately on how much you engage in your obsessive compulsive behavior and therefore we will spend some time now and in the next session going over some rules for how to record your symptoms. Here are some monitoring forms on which you will record your thoughts and rituals."

The therapist should specify which ritual(s) the patient is to record, go over the instructions carefully with the patient, and practice with the patient by filling out the form together using an "imaginary day" of his/her life. The following rules can be helpful in monitoring rituals:

1. Use your watch to monitor the time you spend on your rituals.
2. Do not guess the time of ritualizing, be exact.
3. Write the time immediately on your monitoring form.
4. Do not save the recording to the end of the day or the beginning of the next day.
5. Write a *short* sentence to describe the trigger for ritualizing.

Prior to beginning treatment, the patient should identify an individual (e.g., parent, spouse, or close friend) who can serve as a support person during the intensive treatment program. The patient is instructed to rely on this person for support during exposures and the support person is asked to help monitor compliance with response-prevention instructions. If the patient experiences difficulty resisting the urge to ritualize, the support person should be contacted to offer support. Because the support person will be involved in the therapy, the therapist should allocate time during the information-gathering phase to describe the treatment and discuss its rationale with the support person.

The therapist should make an effort to ensure that the support person and the patient find a mutually agreed-on way for the support person to offer constructive criticism and observations. In making these suggestions, one should be sensitive to any difficulties that have arisen in the past. For example, Mr. B, who served as his wife's primary source of reassurance, also criticized her severely when he "caught" her performing her hand washing ritual. To prevent these responses from hampering treatment, the therapist spent time with the couple negotiating appropriate responses to requests for reassurance and a means for the husband to help supervise his wife's response prevention without being critical.

The support person should be in regular (at least twice weekly) contact with the therapist in order to be informed about the specific homework exposures that the patient has to accomplish and to relay his/her observations about the patient's behavior outside the therapy session. In addition, the support person should, with the consent of the patient, contact the therapist if major treatment violations occur (e.g., refusal to do homework or engaging in ritualistic behavior).

Second Information-Gathering Session

At the beginning of the second information-gathering session, the therapist should devote time to examining the patient's self-monitoring form. This includes examining the descriptions of situations that trigger ritualistic behavior and offering constructive comments when necessary. The patient should be reminded to use short phrases or sentences to describe the trigger situations. The therapist should assess the accuracy of the patient's time estimates and remind him/her of the need for accurate measurements.

Generating Treatment Plan

The bulk of the second information-gathering session is allotted to gathering detailed information about the patient's symptoms and, based on what is learned about the patient's symptoms, developing a treatment program with the patient. The following are guidelines for designing a treatment plan.

Guidelines for selecting exposure situations are presented below.

- Items for exposure (i.e., objects, situations or thoughts evoking discomfort and urges to ritualize) are selected according to patients' self-report about their discomfort-evoking capacity.
- These items are arranged hierarchically according to their SUDs levels and are presented in ascending order beginning at the approximate midpoint. That is, if the top item evokes 100 SUDs, a 50 SUDs item is presented first.
- Exposure to the most disturbing item should be introduced no later than the sixth session of treatment.
- Sessions 7 through 15 are repetitions of Session 6 with minor variations, focusing on aspects of the situation that provoke the most discomfort.
- If some items have been inadvertently omitted, they should be incorporated in the remaining sessions.
- Exposure to an item may be omitted if it evokes minimal or no discomfort for 2 successive days.

Guidelines for imaginal exposure are as follows.

- Several scenes of gradually increasing anxiety-evoking potential are prepared in advance of treatment. Each script should create a vivid imaginal picture for the patient with more severe concerns and feared consequences being included in later images. Generally, the greater the detail of these images, the more effective they are in evoking the desired result. Equal emphasis should be placed on including descriptions of external situations and thoughts, images, and physiological responses in the feared scene. An abbreviated example of a typical imaginal exposure scene is described here.

"I want you to imagine the following scene as vividly as you can, as if it is actually happening, and to experience the feelings as you imagine. I want you to imagine that you are sitting here in the chair, and I am with you. The door opens and your mother comes in. She enters the room, she sees you, and she says, 'Hello, it has been a long time.' She comes to you and she touches you. She wants to hug you. Your mother is astonished that you let her hug you, and she says, 'I am allowed to hug my daughter again.' Now you feel the contamination spreading all over you. You can feel her hands on your back. You begin to feel that it will never go away. It can never be washed. You would like your mother to leave and you want to take a shower or a bath so you can feel clean again. You can't say anything. You just let her hold your hand and let her hug you. You can't move, you are overwhelmed by the feeling of being contaminated. Your mother is standing beside you, and she is holding your hand and you can feel how she becomes even more contaminating. You would like her to take her hand off. And she is asking you, 'Are you afraid of me?' and you would like to explain to her how much afraid of her you are, but you don't say anything. You just let her hold your hand and let her hug you. You let her sit beside you, real close, and she is contaminating you. You can feel the contamination all over your body. You wish you could run out and scream and never come in contact with her again. But you stay here, you stay beside her as she contaminates you more and more. You feel that you will never be clean again. You realize that your mother is contaminating you. You feel the contamination on your skin. You feel the burning spots on your back and hands. It is the feeling of contamination, creeping up your arms, creeping up your face, it's all over your body. You try to keep your hand close to your body to make sure that the parts that are not contaminated now will remain clean. But it is spreading over your whole body. And your mother is still beside you, still contaminating you. She is contaminating you more and more. She is telling you something but you can't really listen to her. You are so upset, your heart is beating, you can feel your heart beating really fast. You feel as though you are going to faint. But something forces you to stay and listen to her. You would like to run to the next room, but you realize that you have to face the fact that you can't avoid your mother any longer. You feel trapped. She will never go away, she will go on contaminating you forever, more and more. You will never feel free again. You have the urge to leave the room and to forget everything about your mother. But her touch is everywhere on your body. How are you feeling now?"

Describing Homework

At the end of the second information-gathering session, the therapist should describe the homework assignments that will be included in the treatment program. The homework usually requires 2 to 3 hr in addition to the 2–hr treatment session. Homework consists of additional exposure exercises to be done between treatment sessions at the patient's home or elsewhere (e.g., shopping malls or a relative's home). We suggest that the patient monitor his/her SUDs level every 10 min during the homework exposures. In some cases, it will be impossible for the patient to maintain an exposure for 45–60 min. In these cases, the therapist should work with the patent to develop a plan that will allow the exposure to be prolonged. For example, instead of asking the patient to spend 45 min sitting in the rest room of a local restaurant, one might suggest that he/she contaminate a handkerchief on the toilet seat and carry this "contamination rag" in a pocket.

Treatment Period

The treatment program at our center typically consists of 15 2-hr-long treatment sessions conducted daily for 3 weeks. Clinical observations suggest that massed sessions produce better results than do sessions spread out over time; therefore, we recommend a minimum of three sessions per week. Each session begins with a 10- to 15-min discussion of homework assignments and ritual monitoring of the previous day. The next 90 min are divided into 45 min of imaginal exposure and 45 min of *in vivo* exposure. The final 15 min are spent discussing the homework assignment for the following day. This format should be adjusted when necessary. For example, if an *in vivo* exposure requires that the therapist and patient travel to a local shopping mall

to contaminate children's clothing, the entire session will be devoted to this activity. Some patients have difficulty engaging emotionally in imaginal exposures (i.e., the images fail to elicit distress). In these cases, treatment should focus exclusively on *in vivo* exercises.

In the beginning of the session it is recommended that the therapist discuss the plan for that session with the patient. During imaginal exposure the patient is seated in a comfortable chair and is given the following instructions:

"Today you will be imagining [*describe* scene]. I'll ask you to close your eyes so that you won't be distracted. Please try to picture this scene as fully and vividly as possible, not like your being told a story, but as if you were experiencing it now, right here. Every few minutes I will ask you to rate your anxiety level on a scale from 0 to 100. Please answer quickly and try not to leave the image."

The imaginal exposure sessions are audio-taped and the patient is asked to repeat the exposure by listening to the tape as part of that day's homework.

The situations that are included in *in vivo* exposure vary greatly from patient to patient (particularly with checkers). Below are some examples of instructions that might be offered to patients during *in vivo* exposure exercises.

For washers:

"Today, you will be touching [*specify* item(s)]. This means that I will ask you to touch it with your whole hand, not just the fingers and then to touch it to your face and hair and clothing, all over yourself so you feel that no part of you has avoided contamination. Then I'll ask you to sit and hold it and repeatedly touch it to your face, hair, and clothes during the rest of the session. I know that this is likely to make you upset but remember the anxiety will eventually decrease. I also want you to go ahead and let yourself worry about the harm you are afraid will happen—for example, disease—since you won't be washing or cleaning after this exposure. I am sorry that this treatment has to be difficult and cause so much discomfort, but I'm sure you can do it. You'll find it gets easier as time goes on. OK, here it is, go ahead and touch it."

The therapist should give the patient the object to hold [or ask him/her to touch it] and then ask the patient to touch the object or the "contaminated" hands directly to the face, hair, and clothing. Every 10 min the patient should be asked, "What is your level of anxiety or discomfort from zero to one hundred right now as you focus on what you're touching?" [This can be shortened to "What is your SUDs?" once patient understands the question.]

For checkers:

"Now, I'd like you to [e.g., write out your checks to pay your monthly bills without looking at them after you've finished; just put them in the envelope and then we will mail them right away without checking even once after you've done it]. Then we will go on and do [e.g., drive on a bumpy road without looking in the rearview mirror] in the same way. While doing this, I would like you to worry about what harm might happen because you aren't check-

ing your actions, but don't let the thoughts interfere with actually doing those activities."

Patients should be reminded of the specific instructions for *response prevention* on the first day of treatment and periodically during treatment. We have found that giving a printed copy of the rules for response prevention outlined in Figure 5.2 patients can help them to understand and remember the rules. If the rules outlined for the patient do not adequately cover the type of ritual(s) the patient exhibits, the therapist should provide them with a written set of instructions modeled after these forms.

During the last few sessions of treatment, the patient should be introduced to rules of "normal" washing, cleaning, or checking. Guidelines for such "normal behavior" are presented in Figure 5.3. Response-prevention requirements should be relaxed to enable the patient to return to what would be considered a normal routine. For washers

---

Rules for response prevention for washers are as follows:

During the intensive treatment, patients are not permitted to use water on their body; that is, no hand washing, no rinsing, no wet towels or washcloths are permitted. The use of creams and other toiletry articles (bath powder, deodorant, etc.) is permitted except where use of these items reduces contamination. Shaving is to be done using an electric shaver. Water can be drunk or used to brush teeth, with care not to get any on the face or hands. Supervised showers lasting no more than 10 min are permitted every 3 days. Ritualistic washing of specific areas of the body (e.g., genitals or hair) is prohibited, and the patient must recontaminate immediately after the shower.

At home, response prevention is supervised by predesignated relatives or friends who are instructed to be available to the patient should he/she have difficulty controlling a strong urge to wash. The patient is to report any such concern to the support person, who will remain with the patient until the urge decreases to a manageable level. Observed violations of response prevention should be reported to the therapist. The support person is to attempt to stop such violations through firm verbal insistence, but physical force should not be used and arguments should be avoided. Faucets can be turned off by the support person if the patient gives prior consent to such a plan. Showers are timed by the support person but no direct observation of showering behavior is made.

Exceptions to these rules should be allowed under unusual circumstances (e.g., medical conditions necessitating cleansing), but all efforts should be made to ensure that washing serves only to cleanse and not to "decontaminate." We have found that if patients must shower, it is important to have them recontaminate themselves immediately after the shower.

Rules for response prevention for checkers are as follows:

Beginning with the first session of exposure and response prevention, the patient should not engage in any ritualistic behavior. Only normal checking is permitted (e.g., one check of door locks). Checking of items ordinarily *not* checked is prohibited.

At home, response prevention is conducted under the supervision of previously designated relatives or friends who have been instructed by the therapist to be available to help the patient. Support persons should be available at the patient's request whenever an urge to check is difficult to resist. They are to stay with the patient until the urge decreases to a manageable level. Again physical force should not be used, but any violations are to be reported to the therapist.

FIGURE 5.2. Response prevention guidelines for washers and for checkers.

Washing

1. Do not exceed one 10-min shower daily.
2. Do not exceed five hand washings per day, 30 sec each.
3. Restrict hand washing to when hands are visibly dirty or sticky.
4. Continue to expose yourself deliberately on a weekly basis to objects or situations that used to disturb you.
5. If objects or situations are still somewhat disturbing, expose yourself twice weekly to them.
6. Do not avoid situations that cause discomfort. If you detect a tendency to avoid a situation, confront it deliberately at least twice a week.

Checking

1. Do not check more than *once* any objects or situations that used to trigger an urge to check.
2. Do not check even once in situations that your therapist has advised you do not require checking.
3. Do not avoid situations that trigger an urge to check. If you detect a tendency to avoid, confront these situations deliberately twice a week and exercise control by refraining from checking.
4. Do not assign responsibility for checking to friends or family members in order to avoid checking.

Other rules: _____

FIGURE 5.3. Guidelines for "normal behavior."

this would include one 10-min shower daily and hand washing only after handling dirty, greasy, or sticky objects. Initially, any washing should be followed immediately by reexposure to contaminants. Also, the therapist may wish to continue some restrictions, particularly when strong urges to wash are still present. For example, patients whose obsessions were focused on bathroom germs may be asked refrain from washing after bathroom use for several months after completion of intensive treatment.

The final treatment session follows the same format as previous sessions except that homework instructions for specific exposure and response prevention are not given. Instead, the therapist should instruct the patient in a self-exposure maintenance regimen to ensure periodic contact with previously avoided situations and to prevent a return to former avoidance patterns. For example, the therapist could suggest to a patient with an obsessive fear of "leukemia germs" that she engage routinely in activities she had previously avoided, such as

touching all doorknobs, using public rest rooms and waiting areas, eating at restaurants, and so on. Additionally, we could ask her to visit the waiting area of a cancer hospital, first weekly and then biweekly until her discomfort was minimal and urges to wash were under control.

Home Visit

It is important to ensure that the patient's gains from the treatment program generalize to the home environment. Usually, homework assignments function to produce this generalization, but we have found that visits made by the therapist to the patient's home can be quite helpful, especially in cases where the patient is not able to return home daily during the intensive treatment phase (e.g., patients from out of town or hospitalized patients). The home visit also offers an opportunity for the therapist and patient to discuss guidelines for "normal" behavior. The therapist should discuss the plans for these visits with the patient and his/her family before the treatment ends.

Typically, the home visit consists of 4-hr sessions held on each of 2 days at the end of the treatment program. The bulk of the time in these sessions is used for conducting additional exposures to obsessive stimuli in and around the patient's home or workplace. For example, the therapist might accompany the patient as he/she contaminates objects around the house or at the local grocery store. Similarly, the patient might be asked to turn the stove on and off without checking and leave the house with the therapist. Most patients, particularly those patients who were able to return home during treatment, will report little or no discomfort when doing these exposures because they represent repetitions of homework assignments. In some cases, though, the therapist will discover some areas that the patient has not contaminated or some areas at home that continue to generate distress despite previous exposures. The home visit should focus on exposure to situations or objects that remain problematic.

Maintenance Period

In addition to prescribing continued self-exposure tasks to help the patient maintain therapy gains, the therapist may wish to schedule regular maintenance sessions. These sessions may be used to plan additional exposures, refine guidelines for normal behavior, and address issues that arise as the patient adjusts to life without OCD.

There is some evidence that patients benefit from continued contact with the therapist following the intensive therapy sessions. In one study, 12 weekly supportive therapy sessions (no exposure exercises) appeared to reduce the number of relapses in a sample of obsessive compulsives treated with 3 weeks of intensive exposure and response prevention (Foa et al., 1992). In another study, following the intensive treatment with 1 week of daily cognitive-behavioral sessions followed by eight brief (10 min) weekly telephone contacts resulted in better long-term outcome than following intensive treatment with 1 week of treatment with free association (Hiss, Foa, & Kozak, 1992).

Therapeutic Setting

It is advisable for patients to remain in their normal environments during intensive treatment. This is particularly important for patients whose fears are cued mainly by stimuli in their home environment. The hospital may be an artificially protected setting, particularly for checkers who may not feel responsible for their surroundings and hence will not experience their usual urges to check. If patients live too far away to commute for daily sessions, we recommend that they rent an apartment or hotel room near the clinic. When this is not possible, hospitalization should be considered. Hospitalization is recommended for patients deemed to be at risk for suicide or psychotic breakdown and those who need close supervision but lack a support system sufficient to aid them during treatment.

If a patient is employed, and his/her OCD symptoms are work related, the patient should be encouraged to continue working so that relevant exposures can be included in treatment. However, since treatment requires 5 to 6 hr per day, the patient may opt to work half days during the intensive treatment.

In cases where the patient's symptoms are unrelated to work, the patient may decide not to continue working during intensive treatment. Because of the time-consuming nature of the treatment, we often suggest that patients take some time off from work. If it is not possible for the patient to take 3 full weeks away from work, the therapist might suggest that the patient work half days or take time off from work during the 1st and 2nd weeks of the treatment program.

Therapist Variables

Intensive treatment with exposure to feared situations and response prevention of ritualistic behavior provokes considerable stress for patients. Their willingness to undergo such "torture" attests to their strong motivation to rid themselves of the OCD symptoms. The intensive treatment regimen requires that the therapist maintain a delicate balance between pressuring the patient to engage in the treatment and empathizing with his/her distress. Clinical observations and findings from a study by Rabavilas, Boulougouris, and Perissaki (1979) suggest that a respectful, understanding, encouraging, explicit, and challenging therapist will be more likely to achieve a successful outcome than a permissive, tolerant therapist.

During treatment, patients' behavior may range from being extremely cooperative and willing to participate in exposures to being blatantly manipulative and refusing to follow the therapist's instructions. An individual patient may fluctuate depending on what exposure is conducted during a particular session. To a great extent, the "art" of conducting behavioral therapy for OCD involves knowing when to push, when to confront, and when to be more flexible. Such decisions require that the therapist carefully observe the patient's reactions and make a judgment based on his/her experience. As much as possible, the therapist should display an attitude that counteracts the harshness of the treatment program while holding to the rules for therapy established at the beginning of the program.

Patient Variables

A primary factor that influences a patient's potential for benefiting from intensive behavioral treatment is the level of his/her motivation. Because exposure and response prevention causes high distress, patients need to be highly motivated to undertake the treatment. Often the level of motivation is related to the severity of the patient's symptoms. When symptoms are sufficiently intolerable, patients are more likely to tolerate considerable discomfort for a short period in order to gain relief from their symptoms in the long run.

Sometimes individuals are pressured into entering therapy by their family, and they agree to participate in treatment only to appease a spouse or a parent. These patients are unlikely to follow the therapist's instructions strictly, and therefore, they are less likely to make lasting gains in therapy.

It is important that the therapist clearly explain to the patient that 1 month of therapy, albeit intensive, is unlikely to eliminate all OCD symptoms. Rather, patients should expect that their anxiety and the urges to ritualize will diminish and become more manageable. An expectation of becoming symptom free at the end of treatment may lead to disappointment and can potentiate relapse because maintenance of treatment gains usually requires continued effort over time following the intensive treatment.

It is also important to explain to patients that exposure and response-prevention treatment is not a panacea for all of their psychological and interpersonal problems. This treatment is specifically aimed at reducing the patient's obsessions and urges to ritualize. Problems that existed prior to treatment (e.g., marital discord or depression) are likely to remain, although they may be somewhat alleviated after treatment.

As mentioned earlier, patients with severe depression and/or an extremely strong belief in the reality of the obsessive fear may not benefit from behavioral therapy for OCD. An additional factor that has been identified as a potential hindrance to the behavioral and pharmacological treatment of OCD is concurrent schizotypal personality disorder (Jenike, Baer, Minichiello, Schwartz, & Carey, 1986; Minichiello, Baer, & Jenike, 1987). Although some questions have been raised about the method used to diagnose schizotypy (see Stanley, Turner, & Borden, 1990), therapists should be alerted to the probability that schizotypal patients may respond poorly to treatment for OCD.

CASE STUDY

In this section we demonstrate through verbatim material the process of gathering information relevant to treatment, planning the treatment program, and conducting exposure sessions.

Case Description

"June," a 26–year-old married woman who had just completed her bachelor's degree in nursing, sought treatment for a severe washing and cleaning problem. She was extremely agitated in the first interview and described herself as "crying a whole lot" during the previous 6 weeks. She arrived in the company of her husband of 6 months and her sister-in-law, whom she considered a good friend. Previous treatment by systematic desensitization, antidepressants, tranquilizers, and cognitive restructuring had proven ineffective. June had been unable to seek employment as a nurse due to her symptoms.

The above information was collected at June's initial evaluation for participation in treatment by exposure and response prevention. After ascertaining the absence of psychosis, drug and alcohol abuse, and organic disorders, June was assigned a therapist.

Information Gathering

Current Symptomatology

First, the therapist (T) sought information from June (J) about the obsessional content, including external and internal fear cues, beliefs about consequences, and information about passive avoidance patterns and types of rituals. Because *rituals* are the most concrete symptom, it is often convenient to begin the inquiry by asking for a description of this behavior.

T: I understand from Dr. F that you are having a lot of difficulty with washing and cleaning. Can you tell me more about the problem?

J: I can't seem to control it at all recently. I wash too much. My showers are taking a long time, and my husband is very upset with me. He and my sister-in-law are trying to help, but I can't stop it. I'm upset all the time and I've been crying a whole lot lately. (*on the verge of tears*) Nothing seems to help.

T: I see. You look upset right now. Please try to explain what your washing has been like in the past few days so I can understand. How much washing have you been doing?

J: Much too much. My showers use up all the hot water. And I have to wash my hands, it seems like all the time. I never feel clean enough.

T: About how long does a shower take? How many minutes or hours would you say?

J: About 45 minutes I guess. I try to get out sooner. Sometimes I ask Kenny to make me stop.

T: And how often do you take one?

J: Usually only twice, once in the morning and once at night before bed, but sometimes if I'm really upset about something I could take an extra one.

T: And what about washing your hands? How much time does that take?

J: You mean how many times do I wash?

T: How long does it take each time you wash your hands and how often do you wash your hands in a day?

J: Umm, maybe 20 times a day. It probably takes me five minutes each time, maybe more sometimes. I always have the feeling they're not really clean, like maybe I touched them to the side of the sink after I rinsed and then I think they're dirty again.

The therapist now had some basic information about the most prominent rituals. Some further questioning clarified whether *other compulsions* were also in evidence.

T: Do you do anything else to make yourself feel clean?

J: Yes, I alcohol things. I wipe with alcohol, like the car seat before I sit down.

T: Do you wipe yourself with alcohol?

J: No, only things that I think are dirty.

T: Can you tell me how much you do that?

J: I use about a bottle of alcohol a week.

Here the therapist had to choose whether to inquire about what objects June cleans or to ask about possible *additional rituals*. The therapist chose to continue the inquiry about ritualistic actions, and to turn to the subject of "contaminants" as soon as the inquiry was completed.

T: OK, can you think of any other things that you do to clean yourself or other things around you that you feel are dirty?

J: That's all I can think of right now.

T: What about other kinds of what we call "compulsive" type of activities? Do you have to check or repeat things over and over?

J: No, except when I wash if I don't feel it's enough. Then I wash again.

T: No other repetitive actions besides washing?

J: Nope.

Since this patient did not appear to have multiple types of ritualistic behaviors, the therapist turned to the *obsessional content*. *External cues* are usually solicited first.

T: What are the things that make you feel you want to wash. For instance, why do you wipe the car seat with alcohol.

J: I think that maybe I got dog dirt on it when I got in from before, or Kenny might have.

T: From your shoes?

J: Yes, I also worry about the hem of my dress touching the seat. I've been worrying that my shoe could kick my skirt hem or when I step up a step like to go in a building, the dress could touch the step.

T: A dress like this? [June was wearing a dress that came to just below her knee. The likelihood that it could have touched a curb or sole of her shoe was very slim.]

J: Yes.

T: Has your skirt ever had dog dirt on it?

J: I don't think so, but in my mind I think that maybe it could have gotten some on it. I suppose it would be hard for that to happen, wouldn't it?

Thoughts that highly improbable events might have occurred are common in OCD. Such distortions may be the result of intense anxiety. Doubts about "safety" often lead to requests for reassurance or to rituals. Reassuring June that her dress is unlikely to be soiled would have been countertherapeutic since it perpetuates the neurotic fears. Rather, the therapist proceeded to inquire further about the obsessional content.

T: Is dog "dirt" the most upsetting thing that you worry about?

J: Probably. Yes, I think so, but bathroom germs are pretty bad too.

T: What sort of germs?

J: From toilets. You know, when you go to the bathroom.

T: Urine and feces?

J: Yes, urine doesn't bother me as much as the other.

T: Why?

J: Because I learned in nursing school that it's almost sterile. I had a hard time in the course about microbiology because it upset me to try to learn about bacteria and microorganisms. They make it sound like there are all kinds of germs everywhere that are real dangerous. I didn't learn it very well; I tried to avoid thinking about it.

June's concerns with both dog "dirt" and bathroom germs suggested that her fear structure includes apprehension about potential illness. The therapist questioned her to better understand the nature of the feared consequences of contamination.

T: Are you afraid of diseases that could come from feces?

J: Yes, I guess so. The thing of it is, though, I know other people don't worry about it like I do. To them, you know, they just go to the bathroom and wash their hands and don't even think about it. But I can't get it out of my head that maybe I didn't get clean enough.

T: If you didn't wash enough, would you get sick or would you cause someone else to get sick?

J: Mostly I worry that I'll get sick, but sometimes I worry about Kenny too.

T: Do you worry about a particular kind of disease?

J: I'm not sure. Some kind of illness.

It is not uncommon for patients who fear harm that may ensue from not ritualizing to be unable to identify a specific feared consequence. Checkers often fear they will forget or throw out something important, but they do not always know exactly what this will be. Repeaters may fear that something bad will happen to a loved one but often cannot specify what particular disaster will befall them. However, many obsessive compulsives do fear specific consequences (e.g., blindness or leukemia). At this point, the therapist may either choose to complete the inquiry about external threat cues or pursue the investigation about the feared consequences and the belief that such harm is indeed likely to occur. The latter course was selected here.

T: Let's say that you did actually touch dog feces or human feces and you weren't aware of it, so you didn't wash to remove it. What is the likelihood that you or Kenny would really get seriously ill?

J: Well, I feel like it really could happen.

T: I understand that when it happens and you become very distressed, it feels like you will actually become sick, but if I ask you to judge objectively, right now how likely is it that you will get sick from touching feces and not washing? For example, if you were to touch feces 10 times, how many times would you get sick?

J: Oh, I know it's pretty unlikely, but sometimes it seems so real.

T: Can you put a number on it? What's the percent chance that if you touched a small amount of feces and didn't wash that you'd get sick?

J: I'd say low, less than 25%.

T: That means that one time in every four, you'd get sick.

J: No, that's not right. I guess it's really less than 1%.

From the above dialogue it is clear that June did not strongly believe that her feared disasters would actually occur, although her initial estimate of the likelihood was high. A person with poor insight regarding the senselessness of his/her OCD symptoms would have assigned higher probabilities (usually over 80%) and would insist on the accuracy of his/her estimate even in the face of persistent questioning.

T: OK. Now, besides disease, what else could happen if you got feces on you?

J: I suppose I'm also afraid of what other people might think if I got dog feces on my shoe or on my dress. Somebody would see it or smell it and think it was really disgusting and I was a dirty person. I think I'm afraid they would think I'm not a good person.

The therapist then questioned June further about this feared consequence, inquiring about the possibility of others evaluating her character negatively because she had feces on her dress. The material regarding feared consequences was collected for later inclusion in the imaginal exposure scenes. To conclude the inquiry about the nature of the obsessions, the external feared stimuli were further elucidated.

T: Besides dog and human feces and toilets, what else can "contaminate" you? Is it OK if I use the word *contaminated* to describe how you feel if you handle these things?

J: Yes, it's like I can feel it on my skin, even if I can't see it. Umm, I also get upset if I see bird "doo" on my car.

T: Bird droppings? The whitish spots?

J: Yeah, I have to hold my skirt close to me when I get in or out of the car so it doesn't touch the outside of the car.

Here the patient also provided information about avoidance behaviors associated with her contaminants. The therapist noted

this and returned later to ask about additional avoidance patterns.

T: OK, bird "doo," what else?

J: Dead animals, like on the roadside. I feel like the germs, or whatever it is, get on the tires from the pavement and get on the car. Even if I don't run over it. Like it's spread around the street near it.

T: What do you do if you see a dead animal?

J: I swerve wide around it. Once I parked the car and as I got out, I saw this dead cat right behind the car. I had to wash all my clothes and take a shower right away. It was really a mess that day.

T: It sounds like that was very difficult for you.... Is there anything else besides dead animals that contaminates you?

J: I can't think of any. There are lots of places I avoid now but that's because of what we just talked about.

The therapist should question the patient further about other items that are likely to be contaminated because of their potential relationship to the ones she has already noted.

T: What about trash or garbage?

J: Yeah, that bothers me. And I also avoid gutters on the street.

T: What's in the gutter that upsets you?

J: Dead animals, I guess. And then the rain spreads the germs down the street. Also rotten garbage. It's really dirty. Sometimes the gutters are really disgusting.

T: Um hmm. Are you afraid you could get sick from dead animals and garbage?

J: Yes, it's like the toilets or dog dirt.

In order to prepare for an exposure program in which objects are presented hierarchically with respect to their ability to provoke discomfort, the patient was asked to rank her major contaminants.

T: Now, let's make a list of the main things that upset you. I'm going to ask you how distressed you would be on a 0–100 scale if you touched the thing I'll name. Zero indicates no distress at all and 100 means you'd be extremely upset, the most you've ever felt.

J: OK.

T: What if you touched dog dirt?

J: And I could wash as much as I wanted?

T: No, let's say you couldn't wash for a while.

J: 100.

T: A dead animal.

J: Also 100.

T: Bird doo on your car.

J: That depends on whether it is wet or dry.

T: Tell me for both.

J: 100 wet and 95 dry.

T: Street gutter.

J: 95.

T: Garbage in your sink at home.

J: Not too bad. Only 50. But, the trash can outdoors would be 90.

T: Why the difference?

J: Because the inside of the trash can is dirty from lots of old garbage.

T: I see. What about a public toilet seat?

J: That's bad. 95.

T: Car tires?

J: Usually 90. But if I just passed a dead animal they'd be 99.

T: What about a doorknob to a public bathroom?

J: The outside knob is low, like 40. But the inside knob is 80 because people touch it right after they've used the bathroom and I've seen that some don't wash their hands.

T: I understand. How about grass in a park where dogs are around?

J: If I did walk in the grass, it would be about 80 or 85, but I don't usually do it. I also have a lot of trouble on sidewalks. You know, the brown spots on the concrete. I guess most of it is just rust or other dirt, but I think maybe it could be dog dirt.

T: How much does that bother you?

J: To step on a brown spot? About 90. I always walk around them.

The therapist should continue in this manner until a list of 10 to 20 items is formed. More items may be necessary for patients with multiple obsessional fears or rituals. The items will be ordered from low to high in preparation for treatment by exposure. Items equivalent with regard to their disturbance are grouped together.

Considerable information about *avoidance patterns and rituals* emerged from the above interview about external threat cues. More details can be obtained by asking the patient to provide a step-by-step description of a typical day's activities from the time he/she wakes up until bedtime. For June we were particularly concerned with bathroom routines, her shower, use of the toilet, handling of towels and dirty clothes, and dressing and putting on shoes. Additional information about avoidance patterns can be ascertained by inquiring about other routine activities such as shopping, eating out, house cleaning, preparing meals, working, and so on. The following dialogue exemplifies the degree of detail desired.

T: June, in order for us to plan your treatment carefully, I need to know what you avoid in your daily routine. Why don't you start by describing what you do first when you wake up.

J: I go to use the bathroom first.

T: Nightgown on or off?

J: I take off my nightgown because I don't want it to touch the toilet. That way it's clean at night after I shower.

T: Go on.

J: I go to the toilet. I suppose I use a lot of toilet paper because I don't want to get anything on my hand. Then I have to shower after a bowel movement.

T: How do you get ready to shower?

J: I have to put a new towel on the rod near the shower. I don't like it to touch anything before I use it. Oh, and I put my slippers facing the door, near the shower so I can put them on without stepping on the bathroom floor when I get out of the shower. Then I get into the shower.

T: You said you shower for 45 minutes. Why does it take so long?

J: I have to wash myself in a special order and I count how many times I wash each part. Like I wash my arm four times. That's why it takes so long.

T: What is the order you use?

J: First I wash my hands, then my face and hair and then I go from the top down.

T: What about the genital and anal area? [This area should disturb this patient most since she feels contamination from fecal "germs."]

J: Oh yes, those are last, after my feet.

Such a detailed description helps the therapist to anticipate possible avoidance by the patient during treatment and to plan specific exposure instructions. Supervision of normal washing behavior at the end of treatment will address June's tendency to count and to order her washing. During the initial session of information gathering, June was instructed to self-monitor the frequency and duration of her compulsions.

T: Between now and our next session, I'd like you to record all the washing and cleaning that you do, including wiping things with alcohol. You can use this form [see Figure 5.1]. Please write down every time you wash, how long you washed, what made you wash, and how anxious you were before you washed. This kind of record will help us identify any sources of contamination you've forgotten to mention, and we can also use it to measure your progress during treatment.

J: Do you want me to write in each space for each half hour?

T: No, only when you wash or use alcohol.

J: OK.

History of Symptoms

After assessing the patient's current symptoms, the therapist sought information about the onset of the problem with particular reference to the presence of specific stressors at the time and whether these stressors are still present.

T: How long have you been washing like this?

J: It started about 2 years ago in my first year of nursing school. It wasn't real bad right away. It started with the city. I had to go into the city to classes and the city seemed real dirty.

T: Did nursing have something to do with it?

J: Maybe. I was under a lot of tension. I had to quit working as a secretary and it was pretty hard without an income and a lot of school bills. My mother and dad weren't much help. And then we started to learn all the sterilizing techniques and I already told you about the course in microbiology.

T: Did it gradually get worse?

J: Mostly, but I did notice that it was a lot worse after a rotation on surgery where I was really worried about germs contaminating the instruments. That's when I started to wash more than usual.

T: Did you seek help at that time?

J: I was already seeing Dr. W at the university, and he tried to help.

T: You were already in treatment with him? For what reason?

J: He was helping me with an eating problem. I had anorexia. I'd been seeing him for about a year when the washing started.

T: Anorexia? did treatment help?

J: Yes, I was down to 85 pounds and I'm up around 105 now. He mostly asked me to increase my weight every week and he did "cognitive therapy" I think its called.

T: I see. What about the washing problem?

J: He tried the same type of therapy, but it didn't work for that. That's why I'm here. My sister-in-law heard about it and Dr. W said I should come.

T: What about drugs? Were you ever given medication for this problem?

J: Yes, I tried Anafranil [clomipramine] for a while, it helped a little, but it made me dizzy and sleepy so I decided to stop taking it. Also, I heard that you can't take the medication when you are pregnant and Kenny and I want to have a baby soon. Before that, I took Xanax [alprazolam], it calmed me down, but didn't stop the washing.

T: Have you tried any other treatments?

J: Only for the anorexia. I went to another counseling center at the university for about a year, but that didn't really help at all.

June's history was unusual only in the relatively recent onset of her symptoms. Typically, patients in our clinic present a much longer duration of symptoms with the mean around 8 years. Other centers in England and Holland report similar figures. June's treatment history of trying various psychotherapeutic and pharmacological treatments prior to seeking behavior therapy was quite typical. Since previous failure with nonbehavioral treatments has not been found to influence outcome with exposure and response prevention, the clinician should not be discouraged by such a history. However, because of a possible skeptical attitude about the value of treatment, the therapist should provide the patient with a clear rationale for exposure and response-prevention treatment along the lines discussed earlier and demonstrated below.

T: Before I continue to collect more information about your problem, let me tell you about our treatment.

J: Well, Dr. F told me something about it, but I'm still not sure what this treatment is going to be like.

T: The treatment is called exposure and response prevention. I'll be asking you to confront situations and things that frighten you or make you feel contaminated. We will do this gradually, working up to the hardest things. For example, we may begin with the outside door handles of bathrooms and work our way up to toilet seats and bird doo. We'll do this together, and I'll be there to help you. The sessions will last an hour and a half or 2 hours and we'll meet every weekday. In addition, I'll assign you homework to do similar things between the therapy sessions.

J: You mean I have to touch them, even dog dirt?

T: Yes, in order to get over these kind of fears, people must learn to confront what they're afraid of and stay with it until the discomfort decreases.

J: Even if I did, it would probably take me a year to get used to it.

T: Remember, you didn't always feel like this about dog dirt. When you were younger, did you ever step in dog dirt and just wipe it off on the grass and go on playing.

J: Yeah, I forget that. It seems such a long time ago. I used to not think twice about this stuff.

T: To get you back to how you used to feel, we need to expose you directly to what you're afraid of. Now, there's a second part to treatment. I'm also going to ask you not to wash for 3 days at a stretch. No hand washing or showering for 3 days. Then you can take a shower, but you will have to limit it to 10 minutes. After the shower, you will have to contaminate yourself again and then wait another 3 days for your next shower.

J: I can't believe it! I'll never be able to do that. If I could, I wouldn't be here. How can I not wash? Every day I resolve to stop, but I always give in. You mean I wouldn't be able to wash after I use the bathroom or before I eat? Other people wash after they use the toilet. Why can't I just wash less, like normal people do?

T: Other people don't have OCD. Remember for you, washing makes you feel less "contaminated" and less anxious. Right?

J: Yes.

T: If you wash, even briefly whenever you feel "contaminated," you never get a chance to learn that the feeling of contamination would go away by itself without washing. If you are really very anxious, it might take a while, even several hours, before you feel better, but it will eventually happen. On the other hand, if you wash, even briefly every few hours, it will reinforce your idea that you have to wash to feel better.

J: But why 3 days? Couldn't I shower once a day like other people?

T: For the same reason. You'd still feel relief even if you waited 24 hours between washings. And that would strengthen your belief that you need to "decontaminate" by washing yourself. You must learn to use soap and water to feel clean and fresh, but not to "decontaminate" yourself.

J: I think I understand. I know I shower now to get the things I'm afraid of off my body. I used to shower just to get sweat and dirt off and feel nice. I'm still not sure I could stand it though, not washing for that long.

T: The treatment is very demanding. Before we start the treatment program you will need to make a commitment to yourself that even though you will feel very uncomfortable and even quite upset at times, you won't wash. I'll try to help you as much as I can by planning the treatment so you know what to expect each day and by supporting you whenever you need it. Someone will have to be available to help supervise and support you any time you need it. Between sessions you can always call me here or at home if a problem comes up. I know the treatment won't be easy for you, but I'm sure you can do it if you make up your mind.

At this point, a firm commitment should not be requested. Rather, the patient should be made aware of what will be required of him/her so that he/she can adjust to these expectations and plan activities during the treatment period accordingly. The patient should make the arrangements necessary for attending daily treatment sessions for 3 to 4 weeks. As we discussed earlier, three sessions per week may be sufficient for patients with less severe symptoms. It is important that the therapist not minimize the difficulty of the treatment regimen, so the patient is prepared to struggle and enters treatment with a readiness to mobilize inner resources.

The history of the patient is usually taken in the first session. Since collecting histories of obsessive compulsives does not differ from collecting histories of other psychiatric patients, details are not provided here.

Treatment Planning

The therapist began the second session by briefly reviewing the patient's self-monitoring of rituals. The remainder of the session was devoted to developing a treatment plan.

T: OK, now. I want to discuss our plan for each day during the first week of therapy. We need to expose you both in imagination and in reality to the things that bother you, which we talked about in our first sessions. As I said already we'll also limit your washing. The scenes you will imagine will focus on the harm that you fear will happen if you do not wash. The actual exposures will focus on confronting the things that contaminate you. Restricting your washing will teach you how to live without rituals. In imagination you will picture yourself touching something you're afraid of, like toilet seats, and not washing and then becoming ill. We can have you imagine going to a doctor who can't figure out what's wrong and can't fix it. That's the sort of fear that you have, right?

J: Yes, that and Kenny getting sick and it being my fault.

T: OK, so in some scenes you'll be sick and in others Kenny will get sick. Should I add that other people blame you for not being careful? Is this what you're afraid of?

J: Yes, especially my mother.

T: OK. We'll have her criticize you for not being careful enough. Can you think of anything else we should add to the image?

J: No, that's about it.

T: We can compose the scenes in detail after we plan the actual exposures. Let's review the list of things you avoid or are afraid to touch to make sure that we have listed them in the right order. Then we'll decide what to work on each day. OK?

J: OK. [June went over the list, which included such items as trash cans, kitchen floor, bathroom floor, public hallway carpet, plant dirt, puddles, car tires, dried dog "dirt," and bird "doo." Changes were made as needed.]

T: Good. Now let's plan the treatment. On the first day we should start with things that you rated below a 60. That would include touching this carpet, doorknobs that are not inside bathrooms, books on my shelves, light switches, and stair railings. On the second day, we'll do the 60- to 70-level items, like faucets, bare floors, dirty laundry, and the things on Ken's desk. [The therapist continued to detail Sessions 3 to 5 as above, increasing the level of difficulty each day.] In the second week we will repeat the worse situations like gutters, tires, public toilets, bird doo, and dog dirt, and we'll also find a dead animal to walk near and touch the street next to it.

On rare occasions, direct confrontation with a feared object (e.g., pesticides or other chemicals) may have some likelihood of producing harm. In such cases, judgment should be exercised to find a middle ground between total avoidance and endangerment. With chemicals, for example, patients are exposed to small quantities that are objectively nonharmful. In June's case the therapist decided that direct contact with a dead animal was not called for and that stepping on the animal's fur with her shoe and then touching the shoe sole constituted sufficient exposure.

T: How does this plan sound?

J: The first week is OK, but I'm really scared about the second week. I'm not sure I'll be ready to do the bathrooms and dog dirt by then.

T: Many people feel this way at the beginning, but by the end of the first week, you won't be as frightened as you are now about touching tires or public toilets. Remember, I will be here to help you because it will probably be difficult in the beginning.

J: Yes, I know it. I feel like I don't really have a choice anyhow. This washing is crazy and I'm disgusted with myself. I suppose I'm as ready as I'll ever be.

T: Good. Now remember, I'll ask you to keep working on these things for 2 to 3 hours at home after each session, but you will already have done it with me so I don't think it will be too hard. I take it that you talked to Kenny about assisting us with supervising, since I saw him out in the waiting room.

J: Yes, he said that that's fine. He wanted to know what he should do.

T: Let's call him in. Did you talk to your sister-in-law about being available when Kenny is at work during the day?

J: Yes, she was really good about it but she couldn't come today because of the kids.

T: If it's difficult for her to come, I could talk to her on the phone. Why don't you go get Kenny now.

Treatment

June was seen for 15 treatment sessions, which were held every weekday for a period of 3 weeks. During the 4th week the therapist visited her twice for 4 hours each time at her home. During these visits June, under the therapist's supervision, contaminated her entire house and exposed herself to objects that provoked distress at home and in her neighborhood. Thereafter, once-weekly follow-up sessions were instituted to ensure maintenance of gains and to address any other issues of concern to her.

As discussed earlier, treatment begins with exposure to moderately difficult items on the hierarchy and progresses to the most disturbing ones by the beginning of the 2nd week. The major distressing items are repeated during the remainder of the 2nd and 3rd week. The following sequence, which occurred on the 6th day of treatment, exemplifies of this process.

T: How was your weekend?

J: Not that great. I suppose it was as good as I could expect. I took my shower Sunday night and I was so nervous about finishing in time I don't even know if I washed right.

T: Most people feel the same way. Remember though, you aren't supposed to wash "right," just to wash. Did Ken time it?

J: Yes, he called out the minutes like you said, "5, 7, 9," and then "stop."

T: You stopped when he said to.

J: Yes, but it still wasn't easy.

T: I know. I'm really pleased that you were careful to follow the rules.

J: I have pretty much decided that this is my chance to get better so I'm trying my best.

T: Good. I am glad you feel so positive. How was the homework?

J: I touched the floor and the soles of my shoes and the cement. It is all written on the daily sheet there. On Saturday, I went to my sister's so I could play with the kids like we said. They stepped on me when I lay on the floor and I tried to touch their bottoms when I held them. On Sunday, Kenny and I went to the park. I didn't sit in the grass but I did walk around and touched my shoes afterward.

T: The soles?

J: Yeah. We also went downtown and I threw some things in the trash cans and pushed them down and tried to touch the sides. It's sort of hard because I felt conspicuous but I did it anyway.

T: That sounds really good. I'm glad to hear it. How about your doormat and going into the garden?

J: I did the doormat and I stood in the garden, but I couldn't touch the dirt. The neighbor's dog always runs all over. I know I should have touched it but I just couldn't get up the courage.

T: Well, you did do many other things. Let's plan to go outside today and do it together so it will be easier for you to walk in the garden when you go home.

J: OK.

June was very compliant with the treatment regimen. Some patients occasionally lapse on response prevention, particularly during the 1st week of the treatment program. The therapist should reinforce the patient for partial compliance but emphasize the need to fully comply with treatment instructions. With regard to exposure homework, it is not uncommon that patients will neglect to complete some assignments. Again, they should be reinforced for what they have achieved and encouraged to complete all of the assignments.

T: How are you and Kenny doing?

J: He got mad on Sunday night after the shower because I started to ask him how he showered and if I was clean enough. I think I nagged him too much so he lost his temper. We just watched TV, and after a while we talked a bit and he sort of apologized for getting mad. But I understand; I ask too many questions. Otherwise the rest of the weekend was OK.

T: Well, it's unfortunate that Ken got mad, but it's good that he didn't answer your questions. He's not supposed to reassure you about cleanliness.

J: I think he has a hard time knowing when to answer me and when not to. I am not real sure either, so if you could talk to him before Wednesday when I shower again.

T: That's a good idea. I'll call him after we're done with today's session. Now, today we'll start with the scene about you driving your car to an appointment with me and you get a flat tire and have to change it. The cars splash the puddle near you and it lands on the car and on you. Then you notice a dead animal when you walk behind the car and it's right behind you. You really feel contaminated. You walk to the gas station nearby to see if they can fix the tire and you have to urinate so badly that you have to use their rest room. They agree to fix the tire if you remove it and bring it to them because otherwise they are too busy. Of course, that means you will have to handle the tire which is contaminated by the dead animal. We'll add some bird doo on the street and on the sidewalk too. Then, later you start to feel sick and you feel like it's from the dead animal. Sound awful enough?

J: Yeah. Ugh. That one is really bad. Do I have to? Never mind, I know the answer.

T: OK. I want you to close your eyes now and imagine that you are driving your car on West Avenue.

Note that the therapist checked the patient's assignment from the previous day to verify that she completed it and did not engage in avoidance and rituals. This provided an opportunity to reinforce efforts at self-exposure. It is important to keep track of completion of homework, since patients do not always volunteer information about omissions. They will, however, admit failure to comply if directly asked and are likely to carry out the next assignment if reinforced adequately.

With regard to the conflict between June and Kenny, it is our experience that, like Kenny, most family members are quite willing to help. Difficulty may, however, arise when they are unable to help without becoming upset, thereby increasing the patient's tension. Providing them with an opportunity to ventilate their frustration by contacting the therapist, who also may coach them in alternative reactions, may reduce familial tension.

Since the imaginal scene had already been planned with the patient, it posed no surprises for her. It is presented for up to 1 hour, or until a substantial decrease in anxiety is evident. Next, the patient is confronted *in vivo* with situations like those included in the fantasized scene.

T: It's time to do the real thing now. I looked for a dead animal by the side of the road yesterday and I found one about a mile away. I think we should go there.

J: Yuck, that's terrific. Just for me you had to find it.

T: Today's our lucky day. You knew we were going to have to find one today anyhow. At least it's close.

J: Great.

Humor is encouraged and can be quite helpful if the patient is capable of responding to it. It is important that the therapist not laugh *at* but rather *with* the patient.

T: [Outside the office.] There it is, behind the car. Let's go and touch the curb and street next to it. I won't insist that you touch it directly because it's a bit smelly, but I want you to step next to it and touch the sole of your shoe.

J: Yuck! It's really dead. It's gross!

T: Yeah, it is a bit gross, but it's also just a dead cat if you think about it plainly. What harm can it cause?

J: I don't know. Suppose I got germs on my hand?

T: What sort of germs?

J: Dead cat germs.

T: What kind are they?

J: I don't know. Just germs.

T: Like the bathroom germs that we've already handled?

J: Sort of. People don't go around touching dead cats.

T: They also don't go running home to shower or alcohol the inside of their car. It's time to get over this. Now, come on over and I'll do it first. (*patient follows*) OK. Touch the curb and the street, here's a stone you can carry with you and a piece of paper from under its tail. Go ahead, take it.

J: (*Looking quite uncomfortable*) Ugh!

T: We'll both hold them. Now, touch it to your front and your skirt and your face and hair. Like this. That's good. What's your anxiety level?

J: Ugh! 99. I'd say 100 but it's just short of panic. If you weren't here, it'd be 100.

T: You know from past experience that this will be much easier in a while. Just stay with it and we'll wait here. You're doing fine.

J: (*A few minutes pass in which she looks very upset*) Would you do this if it wasn't for me?

T: Yes, if this were my car and I dropped my keys here, I'd just pick them up and go on.

J: You wouldn't have to wash them?

T: No. Dead animals aren't delightful but they're part of the world we live in. What are the odds that we'll get ill from this.

J: Very small I guess . . . I feel a little bit better than at first. It's about 90 now.

T: Good! Just stay with it now.

The session continued for another 45 min or until anxiety decreased substantially. During this period conversation focused generally on the feared situations and the patient's reaction to them. The therapist inquired about June's anxiety level approximately every 10 min.

T: How do you feel now?

J: Well, it is easier, but I sure don't feel great.

T: Can you put a number on it?

J: About 55 or 60 I'd say.

T: You worked hard today. You must be tired. Let's stop now. I want you to take this stick and pebble with you so that you continue to be contaminated. You can keep them in your pocket and touch them frequently during the day. I want you to contaminate your office at work and your apartment with them. Touch them to everything around, including everything in the kitchen, chairs, your bed, and the clothes in your dresser. Oh, also, I'd like you to drive your car past this spot on your way to and from work. Can you do that?

J: I suppose so. The trouble is going home with all this dirt.

T: Why don't you call Ken and plan to get home after he does so he can be around to help you. Remember, you can always call me if you have trouble.

J: Yeah. That's a good idea. I'll just leave work after he does. See you tomorrow.

This scenario illustrates the process of *in vivo* exposure. The therapist answered clearly the questions raised without detouring from the essential purpose of the session, exposure to the feared contaminant. After the initial increase the anxiety may begin to drop relatively quickly for some patients and may require longer for others. As noted previously, it is advisable to continue the exposure until the patient appears visibly more at ease and reports a substantial decrease in anxiety (40% or 50%).

After 10 to 15 sessions, the patient's reported anxiety level is expected to decrease considerably. At the 15th session, June reported a maximum discomfort of 70 SUDs (still somewhat high although reduced from 99 SUDs), which lasted for a few minutes. Her minimal anxiety was 35 SUDs. Her average anxiety level during this session was 45 SUDs. Ideally, by the end of treatment the highest level should not exceed 50 SUDs and should drop below 20 SUDs at the end of the session. In June's case more follow-up sessions were required because anxiety was still quite high.

To facilitate a transition to normal washing and cleaning behavior, the therapist instituted a normal washing regimen during the 3rd week of treatment. The patient was allowed one 10-min shower daily and no more than five 30-sec hand washes when there was visible dirt on her hands or when they were sticky.

When the therapist arrived for a home treatment session the next week, the following conversation ensued:

T: How did it go over the weekend?

J: Not too bad. But I got sort of upset Saturday. We went to a picnic and there were several piles of dog dirt around. I had on my flip-flops and I wanted to play volleyball. You can't in flip-flops so I went barefoot.

T: That's great! I'm glad to hear it.

J: Yeah, but then I got really upset about going home and carrying it into the apartment. I did it, I walked all over barefoot and with the flip-flops but I worried about it for another whole day, till I talked to Kenny about my thoughts on Sunday around noon. I felt better when he said he wouldn't worry about it. It seems like I feel guilty or something, like the house isn't clean enough. But lately if he says it is, I've been able to take his word for it.

T: Well, in time you'll be able to make this kind of judgment yourself. How about your washing and cleaning?

J: It was all right. I washed for half a minute before I ate because I was dusty from playing volleyball. I deliberately didn't wash when I got home because I felt bad and I knew if I did, it would be to "decontaminate" myself. I showered Saturday night and I did feel relieved but I knew I should go and walk around barefoot and touch the floors I'd walked on. So I did that.

T: That's great! It sounds like you handled it fine. I'm really pleased. You avoided washing when it would mean reducing feelings of contamination and you exposed yourself when you felt concerned about germs. That's excellent. Now, let's go over the problem situations that still need work here at home. What things still disturb you?

J: The basement. I haven't done much with the kitty litter box and old shoes that I threw down there a year ago because they got contaminated. The closet still has some contaminated clothes. And I still worry about the backyard some. Also the porch. Pigeons have been perching on the roof and there are droppings on the railing now so I thought I'd wait until you came to do that.

T: OK. Let's start low and work up. Which is easiest?

J: The basement and closets.

T: Fine, down we go.

Exposure to contaminants during the home visit is conducted in the same manner as during treatment sessions. Typically, home sessions last longer, from 2 to 4 hr until all "dirty" items are touched and "clean" places are contaminated. These visits should be repeated if the patient expresses considerable concern about his/her ability to adopt a permanent regimen of nonavoidance.

Follow-up Sessions

June was seen weekly for 3 months until she experienced a setback following the development of a new obsession. She became concerned about hitting a pedestrian while driving. Thoughts that she "might have hit someone" intruded, particularly after turning a corner or glancing in the mirror to change lanes. Once evoked, they persisted for several hours. To overcome this new problem, the therapist directed her to increase her driving and refrain from retracing her path or looking in the mirror to check for casualties. June was told that she could stop her car only if she knew for certain that she hit someone. Thoughts that it "might" have occurred were to be ignored. To reduce June's anxiety about having obsessions (e.g., "Oh, my God, here it is again, this is terrible"), she was advised to expect occasional recurrences of obsessive thoughts. The frequency of obsessions about hitting someone decreased from several each day to once weekly after 3 weeks of self-exposure; the associated anxiety diminished from 95 to 50 SUDs or less.

Of June's germ-related obsessions, only that of dog feces partially recurred. Fears of public bathrooms and dead animals remained low. The therapist felt that the fear of dog feces had received insufficient attention during treatment. To address this return of fear, June was seen three times a week for 1-hour exposure sessions in which she touched brown spots on the sidewalk and walked near and eventually stepped on dog feces. Homework consisted of going to parks, walking on sidewalks without looking, stepping on dog feces, and stepping on the grass where she thought dogs had been. This treatment continued for 4 weeks and was reduced to twice a week for an additional 3 weeks. Thereafter, June came once weekly for another 6 weeks during which self-exposure was assigned and everyday concerns were dealt with. News media coverage of herpes led to a brief concern about public toilets, but this dissipated within a few days.

In the dialogue below, the therapist reviewed with June her progress at a 9-month follow-up.

T: I'd like to know how you feel compared to when you first came here 9 months ago.

J: I'm definitely a lot better. But, I still have some bad days when I worry a lot about something, and I get down on myself. But when I remember how upset I was last summer and all that washing I did, it's really a whole lot better. Maybe about 80% better. I'm not ready to be a floor nurse yet, but the job I got after treatment is pretty good for now. Kenny and I are doing fine except he's real sensitive if I bring up one of my fears. I wish he'd just listen and say "OK" or something instead of looking worried about me. It's like he's afraid I'm going to get upset again. It makes it hard to talk freely but sometimes he does handle it fine. I really can't complain, he's been through a lot too when I was really a mess last year and before that.

T: I'm glad to hear you feel so much better. You look a lot more at ease. You laugh more now. I don't know if you recall, but you never did in the beginning.

J: I remember.

T: What's left now, the other 20%.

J: Obsessions I guess. I can still worry about driving over someone. Mostly it lasts less than 15 minutes, but now and then it hangs on through an evening.

T: How often?

J: Once every week or two I think. And I still have an urge to avoid walking on the grass in parks. Like I'm hyper alert. I do it pretty often, but I'm self-conscious.

T: You mean you have to remind yourself not to avoid dog feces?

J: Yeah. And I tend to see things in black and white, all good or all bad. I catch myself feeling guilty for dumb things like eating dessert after a full meal. I can stop but it's like I'm out to punish myself or think badly about what I did. I have to watch out for it. Still, the thoughts are nothing like they used to be. I can have fun now. And work is pretty absorbing, so I can go whole days without getting down on myself for something. Will I always do that?

T: Maybe to some extent. We know that you have a tendency to obsess. Most people who have had an obsessive compulsive problem say that the rituals and urges to do them decrease more quickly than the obsessive ideas. You might have disturbing thoughts for a while, but you can expect them to become less frequent if you're careful not to attempt to control them through rituals or by avoiding things. Can you handle that?

J: I suppose so. They're not a lot of fun, but I feel like I'm living a normal life again. I suppose everyone has some problems to deal with.

Rarely do patients report complete remission of all obsessions. It is unrealistic to lead a patient to expect that 4 weeks of treatment will result in a total absence of obsessions and rituals. Patients should expect some continued struggle with obsessions and urges to ritualize. Strategies for coping with such occasional difficulties should be rehearsed.

COMPLICATIONS DURING BEHAVIORAL TREATMENT

Obviously, difficulties may arise during implementation of exposure and response-prevention treatment for OCD. Several of these are described below and possible solutions are discussed.

Noncompliance with Response Prevention Instructions

Obsessive compulsives often report engaging in a ritual despite the response-prevention instructions. In most cases these represent brief "slips" and the therapist should address them by reiterating the rational for the treatment regimen and the need to follow the response-prevention instructions strictly. The therapist also may offer ways in which the ritual might be "undone" (e.g., recontaminating or turning the stove on and off again).

Sometimes the supervisor will report violations of response prevention to the therapist. These should be discussed with the patient and the fact that continued failure to comply with the response-prevention instructions will result in treatment failure should be emphasized. The following is an example of how violations of response prevention can be presented to the patient.

"I understand from your father that on three occasions this weekend he saw you checking the front-door lock five or six times before you left the house. As we agreed in the first session, he called to inform me about your checking. I am sure you remember that we had an agreement that you would check the doors only once, and that if you had a problem, you would discuss it with me or your father right away so we could help you overcome your urge to ritualize. Will you explain to me what happened?"

If the patient acknowledges the slip and responds with a renewed agreement to follow instructions, the therapist need not pursue the issue further. However, if a second significant infraction of the response-prevention instructions occurs, the therapist should again remind the patient of the therapy rules and the rationale for these rules, and discuss the possibility of discontinuing treatment if the patient is not ready to comply.

"It seems that right now you aren't able to stop ritualizing. For treatment to be successful, it is essential that you completely stop your rituals. Every time you relieve your discomfort by ritualizing, you prevent yourself from learning that anxiety would have declined eventually without rituals and you don't permit your obsessional fears to be disconnected from distress and anxiety. Exposing you to feared situations without stopping your rituals won't be helpful. If you cannot follow the no-rituals rule quite strictly, then we ought to stop treatment now and wait until you are really prepared to follow through with all the requirements. It is very hard for people to resist the urge to ritualize and it may be that you are just not ready yet and will feel more able to do so in the future. It is much better for us to stop treatment now than to continue under conditions where you are unlikely to benefit from treatment. That would only leave you feeling more hopeless about future prospects for improvement."

As discussed above, patients sometimes replace identified rituals with less obvious avoidance patterns. For example, a patient may use hand lotion to "decontaminate" the hands instead of the excessive washing that was done originally. If this occurs, the therapist should immediately instruct the patient to stop the new ritual. Other examples of replacement washing rituals include brushing off one's hands or blowing off "germs"; extensive checks are often replaced with quick glances. Direct questioning of the patient to solicit such information should proceed as follows:

"Now that you've stopped your washing rituals, do you find yourself doing other things to relieve your anxiety? For example, some people start to wipe their hands with paper towels or tissues as a substitute for washing with soap and water. Are you doing anything like this?"

If the answer is positive, the therapist should identify these new behaviors as rituals and instruct the patient to resist engaging in these new behaviors in the same manner as he/she resists other compulsions.

Continued Passive Avoidance

Some individuals who carry out the required exposure without ritualizing may continue to engage in unreported and sometimes unnoticed passive avoidance behaviors. For example, a patient may put "contaminated" clothing back in the closet as instructed, but in doing so he/she may ensure that the contaminated clothes do not touch clean garments. Such avoidance reflects an ambivalent attitude toward treatment and hinders habituation of anxiety to feared situations. Because it predicts failure, continued avoidance behavior calls for the therapist (T) and patient (P) to reevaluate whether the patient should continue treatment.

T: Jim, let's make sure that you are doing your homework the right way. I know that you had a problem putting your dirty underwear in with your other dirty clothes. How are you doing with it now?

P: Well, I was afraid you might ask that. I still haven't mixed them up. I was too scared to do it.

T: We discussed this several days ago and you were instructed to have done it that night. It would have been better had you told me the next day that you weren't able to. What I'd like you to do for tomorrow is to bring in some dirty clothes. Bring in the underwear and the other clothes in separate bags, and we will mix them here in the office. Are there any other things that you have been avoiding that you haven't told me about.

P: I don't think so.

T: I want you to pay careful attention to things that you are doing, or not doing, and make a list of anything you are avoiding, particularly things that you are supposed to do for therapy. It is very important that you don't protect yourself by avoiding distressing situations since if you don't face these situations, your obsessive compulsive symptoms won't get better. Let's give it another try, but if you can't bring yourself to confront these problematic situations without these little avoidances, perhaps you would be better off delaying your treatment to a later time when you will be more ready to comply with the treatment program.

Arguments

It is quite tempting to get involved in arguments with patients over what they will or will not do during treatment. In order to avoid this, it is important for the therapist and the patient to agree on some ground rules before the intensive program begins. Patients must agree to follow the treatment plan that they developed in conjunction with the therapist, and to expose themselves to the distressing situations without argument. If new feared situations are discovered, they should be discussed and a new exposure program should be developed and agreed to before exposures to the new situations are carried out. If a patient balks at a planned exposure or attempts to alter the exposure, the therapist should acknowledge and empathize with the patient's the discomfort, inquire about the reasons for the hesitation, and encourage the patient to proceed in the following manner:

> "I'm sorry to see that you are having so much trouble sitting on the floor. I know it's difficult and that you're frightened, but it won't do you any good if we delay the exposure for another day or let you skip it all together. You really need to touch the floor, so let's go ahead and do it now. We have agreed that today is the 'floor' day, and I wouldn't be doing you a favor if I allowed you to avoid it. Remember, though, I am here to support you as much as I can when you become upset."

In some instances, difficulties can be overcome by first exposing the patient to similar items that generate a lower level of distress. For example, if a patient is refusing to touch a toilet seat, the therapist may ask him/her to first touch the bathroom floor or the door to the bathroom stall. Thereafter, the patient might touch the walls of the stall and the toilet handle before proceeding to the toilet seat itself.

Emotional Overload

Occasionally during treatment a patient will become overwhelmed by fear or another emotion that is not directly related to his/her OCD symptoms. For example, a patient may be upset by a recent event (e.g., the death of a relative), or by fears of facing future plans (such as living on one's own or getting a job). When the patient is ex-

tremely upset, implementing exposure exercises is inadvisable because it is unlikely that the patient will adequately attend to the exposure stimulus and, therefore, anxiety is unlikely to habituate. Instead, the therapist should discuss the distressing situation with the patient and proceed with exposure only when the patient is calmer. On rare occasions, exposure may be postponed altogether until the next day's session. If this becomes a repetitive pattern, it may be advisable to interrupt treatment until the crisis is over.

Nonanxious Reactions to Exposures

Sometimes patients will respond to exposures with emotions other than anxiety or distress, such as anger or depression. Clinical observations suggest that anger often serves as a means for the patient to avoid the distress or anxiety that is the target of exposure. If this happens, the anger should be viewed as an avoidance. The therapist should refocus the patient on the anxiety-evoking aspects of the situation and point out to the patient that anger will only stand in the way of progress.

Sometimes, when patients are exposed during imaginal exposure to the feared consequences of their behaviors, they become depressed. Like anger, depression reduces the efficacy of treatment and therapists need to help the patient to focus on the anxiety-evoking cues. This may be done by directing the content of the imaginal exposure away from the feared consequences and toward the external threat cues. In some cases, such redirection does not resolve the problem and the patient continues to display a depressive reaction to the exposure. When this happens, alternative scenarios that do not elicit depression should be developed.

Emergent Fears and Rituals

As mentioned earlier, sometimes patients develop "new" fears or rituals during treatment. Often, the content of these new symptoms are closely related to the original fears and may be treated by extending to these fears the exposure and response-prevention instructions given earlier in treatment. For example, following the successful implementation of response prevention for his compulsive hand washing, Mr. F began to rub his hands together to decontaminate them. His therapist identified this as another ritual and instructed him to resist the urge to rub his hands together. Next, Mr F began subtly to rub his fingers against the palms of his hands to cleanse his hands and reduce anxiety. He was asked to stop this ritual as he had the others and was again successful.

Some emergent fears may not be as clearly connected to the patient's original fears. For example, the fear that June developed of hitting someone while driving was not obviously related to her fears of contamination. Further assessment often results in the discovery of a conceptual link between the two reported fears. In June's case, her fear of being blamed for causing someone to become ill or die, and her concern about being thought of as a "bad person" because she killed someone or because she smelled of dog feces, may have been the connection between her two identified fears. In cases such as these, it is important for the therapist to develop exposures that include cues for this more general fear. June's therapist might conduct imaginal exposures that include images of people criticizing her or blaming her for causing someone to die.

Family Reactions

Because family members have typically experienced years of frustration with the patient's symptoms, it is not surprising that some are impatient, expecting treatment to progress smoothly and to result in total symptom remission. It is not uncommon for family members to become disappointed or angry when they perceive that the symptoms are not subsiding quickly enough. In such cases, the therapist should assure family members that occasional strong anxiety reactions are to be expected and do not reflect failure. The family should be encouraged to respond calmly and be supportive should the patient experience a burst of anxiety.

Often, families have developed patterns of behavior designed to reduce the OCD patient's distress. Some family members may continue these patterns either to try to protect the patient from upsetting situations or because it is difficult to break habits established over years of accommodating the patient's requests. For example, Mr. P, who was accustomed to entering his home through the basement, immediately removing his clothes, and showering for his wife's sake, was instructed to enter through the front door and toss his overcoat on the couch. Similarly, family members may find themselves continuing to perform a variety of household activities that they have come to regard as their responsibility because of the patient's wishes to avoid the distress that the activity caused. For instance, Mr. P was responsible for preparing all the family meals because his wife was distressed by the possibility that she might inadvertently contaminate the food. Because such familiar patterns may hinder progress in treatment, the therapist should inquire about such habits from both the patient and family members and prescribe appropriate alternative behaviors that maximize the patient's exposure and minimizes avoidance.

Functioning Without Symptoms

At the end of treatment, many obsessive compulsives find themselves left with a considerable void in their daily routines. The fact that they no longer need to allocate a large portion of their day to performing rituals leaves them wondering what to do. The therapist should be sensitive to these issues and aid in planning new social or occupational goals to be achieved following therapy. If needed, the therapist should conduct additional sessions or refer the patient to another therapist who will focus on adjustment-related issues.

Because they have spent years performing their rituals, patients may be unsure about what constitutes normal behavior. The therapist should offer guidelines for what constitutes appropriate washing, checking, repeating, or ordering. If rituals are still present, the therapist needs to give instructions to continue the response prevention of some behaviors in order to help ensure maintenance of treatment gains. Patients may also develop a fear that the OCD symptoms will return. The therapist should reassure the patient that a single washing of his/her hands does not signal the beginning of a relapse.

CONCLUSION

The treatment program described in this chapter produces marked improvement in most obsessive compulsive patients. Over 90% of patients show clinically significant improvement immediately after treatment and about 75% show long-term improvement in their obsessive compulsive symptoms. Follow-up programs that include minimal contact with the therapist, in person or by telephone, aid maintenance of gains and therefore should be implemented whenever possible. The illustration of how intensive behavioral therapy is conducted utilized the case of a washer, largely because the washer's treatment program is more straightforward than the treatment program for checkers. The results with checkers are not less favorable. However, planing a therapy program for them requires some ingenuity. For example, a patient who feared shaming her husband by mistakenly writing that he was a homosexual was requested to write "Jerry Smith is a homosexual" on blank checks and pieces of scrap paper that were strewn about in public places. An example of response prevention for a checker is provided by a patient who checked his food for sharp objects (e.g., glass) that could harm him. In this case blindfolded eating was instituted.

In this chapter we have described what we consider to be the optimal treatment for obsessive compulsives: intensive treatment for a short period followed by 8 to 10 weekly sessions when needed. The concentrated efforts required during the intensive treatment phase may not be feasible for the therapist in clinical practice. Perhaps three sessions each week would be sufficient to achieve satisfactory results; our clinical experience suggests that once-weekly sessions are not adequate. The clinician for whom the allocation of even 6 hours each week is not feasible may enlist assistance from paraprofessionals for *in vivo* exposure exercises. Alternatively, two therapists may share the intensive phase of treatment, with one assuming the coordinating role.

Although most patients show immediate improvement after exposure and response prevention, about 20% relapse. Data from our studies suggest that patients at greatest risk for relapse are those who were only moderately improved at the end of treatment (Foa et al., 1983a). It seems, then, that the therapist should aspire to produce maximal improvement in the patient's symptoms. When a pattern of slow but consistent gains is evident, additional intensive treatment should be considered for patients with minimal improvement. On the other hand, if a patient does not show further improvement with additional sessions, intensive treatment should be terminated.

A variable that seems associated with relapse is the absence of adequate follow-up treatment. Such follow-up can be provided to patients in the form of occasional contact with the therapist who conducted the intensive treatment, attending a support group, or referral to another therapist who is familiar with behavioral treatment for OCD. Follow-up treatment should focus on both systematic reinforcement of a nonritualistic life-style and helping the patient overcome obstacles to normal functioning.

Although intensive behavioral treatment is quite effective in ameliorating OCD symptoms, it should be noted that 25% of patients who have approached us refuse to participate in this program, and an additional 10% fail to benefit. Therefore, complacency with these techniques is not justified. Methods for increasing motivation and for improving the existing treatment are needed.

REFERENCES

Allen, J. J., & Tune, G. S. (1975). The Lynfield Obsessional-Compulsive questionnaire. *Scottish Medical Journal, 20,* 21–24.

American Psychiatric Association. (1952). *Diagnostic and statistical manual of mental disorders* (1st ed.). Washington, DC: Author.

American Psychiatric Association. (1968). *Diagnostic and statistical manual of mental disorders* (2nd ed.). Washington, DC: Author.

American Psychiatric Association. (1980). *Diagnostic and statistical manual of mental disorders* (3rd ed.). Washington, DC: Author.

American Psychiatric Association. (1987). *Diagnostic and*

statistical manual of mental disorders (3rd ed., rev.). Washington, DC: Author.

American Psychiatric Association. (1993). *DSM-IV draft criteria as of 3/1/93.* Washington, DC: Author.

Ballentine, H. T., Bouckoms, H. A., Thomas, E. K., & Giriunas, I. E. (1987). Treatment of psychiatric illness by stereotactic singulotomy. *Biological Psychiatry, 22,* 807–809.

Baxter, L. R., Phelps, M. E., Maziotta, J. C., Guze, B. H., Schwartz, J. M., & Selin, C. E. (1987). Local cerebral glucose metabolic rates in obsessive and compulsive disorder: A comparison with rates in unipolar depression and normal controls. *Archives of General Psychiatry, 44,* 211–218.

Beck, A. T. (1976). *Cognitive therapy and the emotional disorders.* New York: International Universities Press.

Beech, H. R., & Vaughn, M. (1978). *Behavioral treatment of obsessive states.* New York: Wiley.

Behar, D., Rapoport, J. L., Berg, C. J., Denckla, M., Mann, L., Cox, C., Fedio, P., Zahn, T., & Wolfman, H. (1984). Computerized tomography and neuropsychological test measures in adolescents with obsessive-compulsive disorder. *American Journal of Psychiatry, 141,* 363–369.

Black, A. (1974). The natural history of obsessional neurosis. In H. R. Beech (Ed.), *Obsessional states.* London: Methuen.

Boulougouris, J. C., Rabavilas, A. D., & Stefanis, C. (1977). Psycho-physiological responses in obsessive-compulsive patients. *Behaviour Research and Therapy, 15,* 221–230.

Carr, A. T. (1974). Compulsive neurosis: A review of the literature. *Psychological Bulletin, 81,* 311–318.

Charney, D. S., Goodman, W. K., Price, L. H., Woods, S. W., Rasmussen, S. A., & Heninger, G. R. (1988). Serotonin function in obsessive-compulsive disorder: A comparison of the effects of tryptophan and m-chlorophenylpiperazine in patients and healthy subjects. *Archives of General Psychiatry, 45,* 177–185.

Cooper, J. E., Gelder, M. G., & Marks, I. M. (1965). Results of behaviour therapy in 77 psychiatric patients. *British Medical Journal, 1,* 1222–1225.

Cottraux, J., Mollard, E., Bouvard, M., Marks, I., Sluys, M., Nury, A. M., Douge, R., & Ciadella, P. (1990). A controlled study of fluvoxamine and exposure in obsessive-compulsive disorder. *International Clinical Psychopharmacology, 5,* 17–30.

Cox, C. S., Fedio, P., & Rapoport, J. L. (1989). Neuropsychological testing of obsessive-compulsive adolescents. In J. L. Rapoport (Ed.), *Obsessive-compulsive disorder in children and adolescents.* Washington, DC: American Psychiatric Press.

DeVeaugh-Geiss, J., Landau, P., & Katz, R. (1989). Treatment of OCD with clomipramine. *Psychiatric Annals, 19,* 97–101.

Dollard, J., & Miller, N. E. (1950). *Personality and psychotherapy: An analysis in terms of learning, thinking and culture.* New York: McGraw-Hill.

Ellis, A. (1962). *Reason and emotion in psychotherapy.* New York: Lyle Stuart.

Emmelkamp, P. M. G., & Beens, H. (1991). Cognitive therapy with obsessive-compulsive disorder: A comparative evaluation. *Behaviour Research and Therapy, 29,* 293–300.

Emmelkamp, P. M. G., de Ha⸓⸓, E., & Hoogduin,

C. A. L. (1990). Marital adjustment and obsessive-compulsive disorder. *British Journal of Psychiatry, 156,* 55–60.

Emmelkamp, P. M. G., & Kwee, K. G. (1977). Obsessional ruminations: A comparison between thought-stopping and prolonged exposure in imagination. *Behaviour Research and Therapy, 15,* 441–444.

Emmelkamp, P. M. G., & van Kraanen, J. (1977). Therapist-controlled exposure *in vivo:* A comparison with obsessive-compulsive patients. *Behaviour Research and Therapy, 15,* 491–495.

Emmelkamp, P. M. G., Visser, S., & Hoekstra, R. J. (1988). Cognitive therapy vs. exposure *in vivo* in the treatment of obsessive-compulsives. *Cognitive Therapy and Research, 12,* 103–114.

Esquirol, J. E. D. (1838). *Des maladies mentales* (Vol. 2). Paris: Bailliere.

Flament, M. F., Rapoport, J. L., Berg, C. J., Sceery, W., Kilts, C., Mellstram, B., & Linnoila, M. (1985). Clomipramine treatment of childhood obsessive-compulsive disorder: A double-blind controlled study. *Archives of General Psychiatry, 42,* 977–983.

Foa, E. B. (1979). Failure in treating obsessive-compulsives. *Behaviour Research and Therapy, 16,* 391–399.

Foa, E. B., & Chambless, D. L. (1978). Habituation of subjective anxiety during flooding in imagery. *Behaviour Research and Therapy, 16,* 391–399.

Foa, E. B., Grayson, J. B., & Steketee, G. (1982). Depression, habituation and treatment outcome in obsessive-compulsives. In J. C. Boulougouris (Ed.), *Practical applications of learning theories in psychiatry.* New York: Wiley.

Foa, E. B., Grayson, J. B., Steketee, G., & Doppelt, H. G. (1983a). Treatment of obsessive-compulsives: When do we fail? In E. B. Foa & P. M. G. Emmelkamp (Eds.), *Failures in behavior therapy.* New York: Wiley.

Foa, E. B., Grayson, J. B., Steketee, G. S., Doppelt, H. G., Turner, R. M., & Latimer, P. R. (1983b). Success and failure in the behavioral treatment of obsessive-compulsives. *Journal of Consulting and Clinical Psychology, 51,* 287–297.

Foa, E. B., & Kozak, M. J. (1985). Treatment of anxiety disorders: Implications for psychopathology. In A. H. Tuma & J. D. Maser (Eds.), *Anxiety and the anxiety disorders.* Hillsdale, NJ: Erlbaum.

Foa, E. B., & Kozak, M. J. (in press). Report on the DSM-IV field trial for obsessive-compulsive disorder. In *DSM-IV source book.* Washington, DC: American Psychiatric Association.

Foa, E. B., & Kozak, M. J. (1991). DSM-IV in progress: Diagnostic criteria for obsessive-compulsive disorder. *Hospital and Community Psychiatry, 42,* 679–684.

Foa, E. B., Kozak, M. J., Steketee, G., & McCarthy, P. R. (1992). Treatment of depressive and obsessive-compulsive symptoms in OCD by imipramine and behavior therapy. *British Journal of Clinical Psychology, 31,* 279–292.

Foa, E. B., Steketee, G., Grayson, J. B., Turner, R. M., & Latimer, P. (1984). Deliberate exposure and blocking of obsessive-compulsive rituals: Immediate and long-term effects. *Behavior Therapy, 15,* 450–472.

Foa, E. B., Steketee, G. S., Kozak, M. J., & Dugger, D. (1985). *Effects of imipramine on depression and on obsessive-compulsive symptoms.* Paper presented at the

European Association for Behavior Therapy, Munich, Federal Republic of Germany.

Foa, E. B., Steketee, G. S., & Milby, J. B. (1980). Differential effects of exposure and response prevention in obsessive-compulsive washers. *Journal of Consulting and Clinical Psychology, 48,* 71–79.

Foa, E. B., Steketee, G. S., & Ozarow, B. (1985). Behavior therapy with obsessive-compulsives: From theory to treatment. In M. Mavissakalian (Ed.), *Obsessive-compulsive disorder: Psychological and pharmacological treatment.* New York: Plenum Press.

Foa, E. B., Steketee, G., Turner, R. M., & Fischer, S. C. (1980). Effects of imaginal exposure to feared disasters in obsessive-compulsive checkers. *Behaviour Research and Therapy, 18,* 449–455.

Foa, E. B., & Tillmanns, A. (1980). The treatment of obsessive-compulsive neurosis. In A. Goldstein & E. B. Foa (Eds.), *Handbook of behavioral interventions: A clinical guide.* New York: Wiley.

Foa, E. B., & Wilson, R. (1991). *Stop obsessing: How to overcome your obsessions and compulsions.* New York: Bantam.

Fontaine, R., & Chouinard, G. (1985). Fluoxetine in the treatment of obsessive-compulsive disorder. *Progress in Neuropsychopharmacology and Biological Psychiatry, 9,* 605–608.

Freund, B. (1986). *Comparison of measures of obsessive-compulsive symptomatology: Rating scales of symptomatology and standardized assessor- and self-rated.* Unpublished doctoral dissertation, Southern Illinois University, Carbondale.

Freund, B., Steketee, G., & Foa, E. B. (1985). *Comparison of obsessive-compulsive symptomatology measures: Standardized versus global rating scales, assessor- versus self-rated.* Unpublished manuscript.

Goodman, W. K., Price, L. H., Rasmussen, S. A., Mazure, C., Fleischmann, R. L., Hill, C. L., Heninger, G. R., & Charney, D. S. (1989a). The Yale–Brown Obsessive-Compulsive Scale. I. Development, use, and reliability. *Archives of General Psychiatry, 46,* 1006–1011.

Goodman, W. K., Price, L. H., Rasmussen, S. A., Mazure, C., Delgado, P., Heninger, G. R., & Charney, D. S. (1989b). The Yale–Brown Obsessive-Compulsive Scale. II. Validity. *Archives of General Psychiatry, 46,* 1012–1016.

Greist, J. H. (1990). Treatment of obsessive-compulsive disorder: Psychotherapies, drugs, and other somatic treatments. *Journal of Clinical Psychiatry, 51,* 44–50.

Head, D., Bolton, D., & Hymas, N. (1989). Deficit in cognitive shifting in patients with obsessive-compulsive disorder. *Biological Psychiatry, 25,* 929–937.

Hembree, E. A., Cohen, A., Riggs, D. S., Kozak, M. J., & Foa, E. B. (1992). *The long-term efficacy of behavior therapy and serotonergic medications in the treatment of obsessive-compulsive ritualizers.* Unpublished manuscript.

Hiss H., Foa, E. B., & Kozak, M. J. (1992). *A relapse prevention program for treatment of obsessive-compulsive disorder.* Unpublished manuscript.

Hodgson, R. J., & Rachman, S. (1972). The effects of contamination and washing in obsessional patients. *Behaviour Research and Therapy, 10,* 111–117.

Hodgson, R. J., & Rachman, S. (1977). Obsessional-compulsive complaints. *Behavior Research and Therapy, 15,* 389–395.

Hodgson, R. J., Rachman, S., & Marks, I. M. (1972). The treatment of chronic obsessive-compulsive neurosis: Follow-up and further findings. *Behaviour Research and Therapy, 10,* 181–189.

Hornsveld, R. H. J., Kraaimaat, F. W., & van Dam-Baggen, R. M. J. (1979). Anxiety/discomfort and handwashing in obsessive-compulsive and psychiatric control patients. *Behaviour Research and Therapy, 17,* 223–228.

Hudson, J. I., Pope, H. G., Yurgelun-Todd, D., Jonas, J. M., & Frankenburg, F. R. (1987). A controlled study of anorexia nervosa and obsessive nervosa. *British Journal of Psychiatry, 27,* 57–60.

Insel, T. R., & Akiskal, H. (1986). Obsessive-compulsive disorder with psychotic features: A phenomenologic analysis. *American Journal of Psychiatry, 12,* 1527–1533.

Insel, T. R., Donnelly, E. F., Lalakea, M. L., Alterman, I. S., & Murphy, D. L. (1983). Neurological and neuropsychological studies of patients with obsessive-compulsive disorder. *Biological Psychiatry, 18,* 741–751.

Insel, T. R., Mueller, E. A., Alterman, I. S., Linnoila, M., & Murphy, D. L. (1985). Obsessive-compulsive disorder and serotonin: Is there a connection? *Biological Psychiatry, 20,* 1174–1188.

Insel, T. R., Murphy, D. L., Cohen, R. M., Alterman, I. S., Kilts, C., & Linnoila, M. (1983). Obsessive-compulsive disorder: A double-blind trial of clomipramine and clorgyline. *Archives of General Psychiatry, 40,* 605–612.

Jenike, M., Baer, L., Minichiello, W., Schwartz, C., & Carey, R. (1986). Concomitant obsessive-compulsive disorder and schizotypal personality disorder. *American Journal of Psychiatry, 143,* 530–532.

Jenike, M. A., Buttolph, L., Baer, L., Ricciardi, J., & Holland, A. (1989). Open trial of fluoxetine in obsessive-compulsive disorder. *American Journal of Psychiatry, 146,* 909–911.

Joffe, R. T., & Swinson, R. P. (1991). *Biological aspects of obsessive-compulsive disorder.* Paper prepared for the DSM-IV committee on obsessive-compulsive disorder.

Karno, M. G., Golding, J. M., Sorensen, S. B., & Burnam, A. (1988). The epidemiology of OCD in five U.S. communities. *Archives of General Psychiatry, 45,* 1094–1099.

Kasvikis, Y. G., Tsakiris, F., Marks, I. M., Basoglu, M., & Noshirvani, H. F. (1986). Past history of anorexia nervosa in women with obsessive-compulsive disorder. *International Journal of Eating Disorders, 5,* 1069–1075.

Kazarian, S. S., Evans, D. R., & Lefave, K. (1977). Modification and factorial analysis of the Leyton Obsessional Inventory. *Journal of Clinical Psychology, 33,* 422–425.

Kearney, C. A., & Silverman, W. K. (1990). Treatment of an adolescent with obsessive-compulsive disorder by alternating response prevention and cognitive therapy: An empirical analysis. *Journal of Behavior Therapy and Experimental Psychiatry, 21,* 39–47.

Kenny, F. T., Mowbray, R. M., & Lalani, S. (1978). Faradic disruption of obsessive ideation in the treatment of obsessive neurosis: A controlled study. *Behavior Therapy, 9,* 209–221.

Kenny, F. T., Solyom, L., & Solyom, C. (1973). Faradic disruption of obsessive ideation in the treatment of obsessive neurosis. *Behavior Therapy, 4,* 448–451.

Laessle, R. G., Kittl, S., Fichter M. M., Wittchen, H., & Pirke, K. M. (1987). Major affective disorder in anorexia nervosa and bulimia: A descriptive diagnostic study. *British Journal of Psychiatry, 151*, 785–789.

Lang, P. J. (1979). A bio-informational theory of emotional imagery. *Psychophysiology, 6*, 495–511.

Leckman, J. F., & Chittenden, E. H. (1990). Gilles de la Tourette's syndrome and some forms of obsessive-compulsive disorder may share a common genetic diathesis. *L'Encephale, XVI*, 321–323.

Lelliott, P. T., Noshirvani, H. F., Basoglu, M., Marks, I. M., & Monterio, W. O. (1988). Obsessive-compulsive beliefs and treatment outcome. *Psychological Medicine, 18*, 697–702.

Marks, I. M. (1977). Recent results of behavioral treatments of phobias and obsessions. *Journal of Internal Medicine Research, 5*, 16–21.

Marks, I. M., Hallam, R. S., Connelly, J., & Philpott, R. (1977). *Nursing in behavioral psychotherapy*. London: Royal College of Nursing of the United Kingdom.

Marks, I. M., Lelliott, P., Basoglu, M., Noshirvami, H., Monteiro, W., Cohen, D., & Kasvikis, Y. (1988). Clomipramine self-exposure, and therapist-aided exposure for obsessive-compulsive rituals. *British Journal of Psychiatry, 152*, 522–534.

Marks, I. M., Stern, R. S., Mawson, D., Cobb, J., & McDonald, R. (1980). Clomipramine and exposure for obsessive-compulsive rituals–I. *British Journal of Psychiatry, 136*, 1–25.

McCarthy, P., & Foa, E. B. (1990). Treatment interventions for obsessive-compulsive disorder. In M. Thase, B. Edelstein, & M. Hersen (Eds.), *Handbook of outpatient treatment of adults*. New York: Plenum Press.

McFall, M. E., & Wollersheim, J. P. (1979). Obsessive-compulsive neurosis: A cognitive-behavioral formulation and approach to treatment. *Cognitive Therapy and Research, 3*, 333–348.

Meyer, V. (1966). Modification of expectations in cases with obsessional rituals. *Behaviour Research and Therapy, 4*, 273–280.

Meyer, V., & Levy, R. (1973). Modification of behavior in obsessive-compulsive disorders. In H. E. Adams & P. Unikel (Eds.), *Issues and trends in behavior therapy*. Springfield, IL: C. C. Thomas.

Meyer, V., Levy, R., & Schnurer, A. (1974). A behavioral treatment of obsessive-compulsive disorders. In H. R. Beech (Ed.), *Obsessional states*. London: Methuen.

Minichiello, W. E., Baer, L., & Jenike, M. A. (1987). Schizotypal personality disorder: A poor prognostic indicator for behavior therapy in the treatment of obsessive-compulsive disorder. *Journal of Anxiety Disorders, 1*, 273–276.

Mowrer, O. A. (1939). A stimulus-response analysis of anxiety and its role as a reinforcing agent. *Psychological Review, 46*, 553–565.

Mowrer, O. A. (1960). *Learning theory and behavior*. New York: Wiley.

O'Sullivan, G., Noshirvani, H., Marks, I., Monteiro, W., & Lelliott, P. (1991). Six-year follow-up after exposure and clomipramine therapy for obsessive-compulsive disorder. *Journal of Clinical Psychiatry, 52*, 150–155.

Pato, M. T., Zohar-Kadouch, R., Zohar, J., & Murphy, D. L. (1988). Return of symptoms after discontinuation of clomipramine in patients with obsessive-compulsive disorder. *American Journal of Psychiatry, 145*, 1521–1525.

Pauls, D. L. (1989). *The inheritance and expression of obsessive-compulsive behaviors*. Proceedings of the American Psychiatric Association, San Francisco, CA.

Pauls, D. L., Towbin, K. E., Leckman, J. F., Zahner, G. E., & Cohen, D. J. (1986). Gilles de la Tourette's Syndrome and obsessive-compulsive disorder. *Archives of General Psychiatry, 43*, 1180–1182.

Perse, T. (1988). Obsessive-compulsive disorder: A treatment review. *Journal of Clinical Psychiatry, 49*, 48–55.

Perse, T., Griest, J. H., Jefferson, J. W., Rosenfeld, R., & Dar, R. (1987). Fluvoxamine treatment of obsessive-compulsive disorder. *American Journal of Psychiatry, 144*, 1543–1548.

Philpott, R. (1975). Recent advances in the behavioral measurement of obsessional illness: Difficulties common to these and other instruments. *Scottish Medical Journal, 20*, 33–40.

Price, L. H., Goodman, W. K., Charney, D. S., & Heninger, G. R. (1987). Treatment of severe obsessive-compulsive disorder with fluvoxamine. *American Journal of Psychiatry, 144*, 1059–1061.

Rabavilas, A. D., & Boulougouris, J. C. (1974). Physiological accompaniments of ruminations, flooding and thought-stopping in obsessive patients. *Behaviour Research and Therapy, 12*, 239–243.

Rabavilas, A. D., Boulougouris, J. C., & Perissaki, C. (1979). Therapist qualities related to outcome with exposure *in vivo* in neurotic patients. *Journal of Behavior Therapy and Experimental Psychiatry, 10*, 293–299.

Rabavilas, A. D., Boulougouris, J. C., & Stefanis, C. (1976). Duration of flooding sessions in the treatment of obsessive-compulsive patients. *Behaviour Research and Therapy, 14*, 349–355.

Rachman, S., & DeSilva, P. (1978). Abnormal and normal obsessions. *Behaviour Research and Therapy, 16*, 233–248.

Rachman, S., DeSilva, P., & Roper, G. (1976). The spontaneous decay of compulsive urges. *Behaviour Research and Therapy, 14*, 445–453.

Rachman, S., & Hodgson, R. (1980). *Obsessions and compulsions*. Englewood Cliffs, NJ: Prentice-Hall.

Rachman, S., Marks, I. M., & Hodgson, R. (1973). The treatment of obsessive-compulsive neurotics by modelling. *Behaviour Research and Therapy, 8*, 383–392.

Rachman, S., & Wilson, G. T. (1980). *The effects of psychological therapy*. Oxford, England: Pergamon Press.

Rapoport, J. L. (1991). Recent advances in obsessive-compulsive disorder. *Neuropsychopharmacology, 5*, 1–10.

Rapoport, J. L., & Wise, S. P. (1988). Obsessive-compulsive disorder: Evidence for basal ganglia dysfunction. *Psychopharmacology Bulletin, 24*, 380–384.

Rasmussen, S. A., & Eisen, J. L. (1989). Clinical features and phenomenology of obsessive-compulsive disorder. *Psychiatric Annals, 19*, 67–73.

Rasmussen, S. A., & Eisen, J. L. (1990). Epidemiology of obsessive-compulsive disorder. *Journal of Clinical Psychiatry, 51*, 10–14.

Rasmussen, S. A., & Tsuang, M. T. (1986). Clinical characteristics and family history in DSM-III obsessive-compulsive disorder. *American Journal of Psychiatry, 1943*, 317–382.

Reed, G. E. (1985). *Obsessional experience and compulsive behavior: A cognitive structural approach*. Orlando, FL: Academic Press.

Riggs, D. S., Hiss, H., & Foa, E. B. (1992). Marital distress and the treatment of obsessive-compulsive disorder. *Behavior Therapy, 23*, 585–597.

Roper, G., & Rachman, S. (1976). Obsessional-compulsive checking: Experimental replication and development. *Behaviour Research and Therapy, 14*, 25–32.

Roper, G., Rachman, S., & Hodgson, R. (1973). An experiment on obsessional checking. *Behaviour Research and Therapy, 11*, 271–277.

Salkovskis, P. M. (1985). Obsessional compulsive problems: A cognitive-behavioral analysis. *Behaviour Research and Therapy, 23*, 571–583.

Salkovskis, P. M., & Warwick, H. M. C. (1985). Cognitive therapy of obsessive-compulsive disorder: Treating treatment failures. *Behavioral Psychotherapy, 13*, 243–255.

Schilder, P. (1938). The organic background of obsessions and compulsions. *American Journal of Psychiatry, 94*, 1397.

Sher, K. J., Frost, R. O., Kushner, M., Crews, T. M., & Alexander, J. E. (1989). Memory deficits in compulsive checkers: A replication and extension in a clinical sample. *Behaviour Research and Therapy, 27*, 65–69.

Sher, K. J., Frost, R. O., & Otto, R. (1983). Cognitive deficits in compulsive checkers: An exploratory study. *Behaviour Research and Therapy, 21*, 357–364.

Stanley, M. A., Turner, S. M., & Borden, J. W. (1990). Schizotypal features in obsessive-compulsive disorder. *Comprehensive Psychiatry, 31*, 511–518.

Steketee, G. S., Foa, E. B., & Grayson, J. B. (1982). Recent advances in the treatment of obsessive-compulsives. *Archives of General Psychiatry, 39*, 1365–1371.

Stern, R. S. (1978). Obsessive thoughts: The problem of therapy. *British Journal of Psychiatry, 132*, 200–205.

Stern, R. S., Lipsedge, M. S., & Marks, I. M. (1975). Obsessive ruminations: A controlled trial of thought-stopping technique. *Behaviour Research and Therapy, 11*, 650–662.

Stern, R. S., Marks, I. M., Wright, J., & Luscombe, D. K. (1980). Clomipramine: Plasma levels, side effects and outcome in obsessive-compulsive neurosis. *Postgraduate Medical Journal, 56*, 134–139.

Swedo, S. E., Rapoport, J. L., Cheslow, D. L., Leonard, H. L., Ayoub, E. M., Hosier, D. M., & Wald, E. R. (1989). High prevalence of obsessive-compulsive symptoms in patients with Sydenham's chorea. *American Journal of Psychiatry, 146*, 246–249.

Thoren, P., Asberg, M., Bertilsson, L., Mellstrom, B., Sjoqvist, F., & Traskman, L. (1980). Clomipramine treatment of obsessive-compulsive disorder. II. Biochemical aspects. *Archives of General Psychiatry, 37*, 1289–1294.

Thoren, P., Asberg, M., Chronholm, B., Jornestedt, L., & Traskman, L. (1980). Clomipramine treatment of obsessive-compulsive disorder. I. A controlled clinical trial. *Archives of General Psychiatry, 37*, 1281–1285.

Tynes, L. L., White, K., & Steketee, G. S. (1990). Toward a new nosology of obsessive-compulsive disorder. *Comprehensive Psychiatry, 31*, 465–480.

Weizman, A., Carmi, M., Hermesh, H., Shahar, A., Apter, A., Tyano, S., & Rehavi, M. (1985). *High-affinity imipramine binding and serotonin up-take platelets of adolescent and adult obsessive-compulsive patients*. Paper presented at the 4th International Congress of Biological Psychiatry, Philadelphia, PA. (From abstract)

Zohar, J., & Insel, T. (1987). Obsessive-compulsive disorder: Psychobiological approach to diagnoses treatment and pathophysiology. *Biological Psychiatry, 22*, 667–687.

Zohar, J., Mueller, E. A., Insel, T. R., Zohar-Kadouch, R., & Murphy, D. L. (1987). Serotonergic responsivity in obsessive-compulsive disorder: Comparison of patients and healthy controls. *Archives of General Psychiatry, 44*, 946–951.

Chapter 6

DEPRESSION

Jeffrey E. Young
Columbia University

Aaron T. Beck
University of Pennsylvania, Philadelphia

Arthur Weinberger
Wall Street Center for Cognitive Therapy, New York

Oₙₑ of the most important developments in psychosocial approaches to emotional problems has been the success of cognitive therapy for depression. The promise of this approach has increased since the first edition of this book, with evidence accumulating on successful long-term outcome. Employing a variety of well-specified cognitive and behavioral techniques, cognitive therapy is also distinguished by the detailed structure of each session with its specific agendas and the very deliberate and obviously effective therapeutic style of interacting with the patient through a series of questions. The authors also underscore very clearly the importance of the collaborative relationship between the therapist and the patient and outline specific techniques to achieve that collaborative state so that the patient and therapist become an investigative team.

But cognitive therapy for depression has not stood still during the past 5 years. In this chapter the authors present a second important phase of treatment not described in the first edition of this book. This phase, called the "schema-focused phase of treatment," concentrates on identifying and modifying early maladaptive or "core" schemas that developed during childhood. These schemas may make the patient vulnerable to relapse. Detailed explication of this second phase of treatment will be invaluable to experienced cognitive therapists as well as to those becoming acquainted with cognitive therapy for depression for the first time.—D. H. B.

OVERVIEW

Depression is one of the most common presenting problems encountered by mental health professionals. A variety of approaches have been applied to the treatment of depression, with growing emphasis on short-term psychotherapies: Short-term approaches that have received considerable attention in outcome research include behavioral therapy, interpersonal psychotherapy, brief psychodynamic therapy, and cognitive therapy (Bergin & Lambert, 1978; Rehm, 1990; McDermott & Wright, 1992). Of all the cognitive-behavioral approaches to depression, cognitive therapy has received the most empirical attention (Rehm, 1990).

Despite the tremendous advances in psychotherapy for depression, pharmacotherapy remains the standard against which other treatments are compared. Initial research suggested that cognitive-behavioral therapy is at least as effective as tricyclic antidepressants in the treatment of non-bipolar, depressed outpatients (Rush, Beck, Kovacs, & Hollon, 1977; Beck, Rush, Shaw, & Emery, 1979; Blackburn & Bishop, 1979, 1980; McLean & Hakstian, 1979). More recent studies continue to support these early findings: An exhaustive review of studies reported between 1976 and 1987 indicated that cognitive therapy "is more effective than nothing at all, behavior therapy or pharmacotherapy in the treatment of clinical depression" (Dobson, 1989, p. 417). Although some continue to question the efficacy of cognitive therapy as a viable alternative to antidepressant medication based on the existing literature, their reservations are based largely on methodological and experimental issues (Hollon, Shelton, & Loosen, 1991). The efficacy of the cognitive-behavioral approach with depression is especially striking in light of a number of studies in the past showing that traditional psychotherapies are only slightly more effective than pill placebos in reducing depressive symptomatology (Hollon & Beck, 1978).

COGNITIVE MODEL OF DEPRESSION

The cognitive model assumes that cognition, behavior, and biochemistry are all important components of depressive disorders. We do not view them as competing theories of depression but rather as different levels of analysis. Each treatment approach has its own "focus of convenience." The pharmacotherapist intervenes at the biochemical level; the cognitive therapist intervenes at the cognitive, affective, and behavioral levels. Our experience suggests that when we change depressive cognitions, we simultaneously change the characteristic mood, behavior, and (we presume) biochemistry of depression. The exact mechanism of change, however, remains a target of considerable investigation and debate (Barber & DeRubeis, 1989; DeRubeis et al., 1990; DeRubeis & Feeley, 1990; Sullivan & Conway, 1991).

Our focus in this chapter is on the cognitive disturbances in depression. Cognitive science research emphasizes the importance of information processing in depressive symptomatology (Ingram & Holle, 1992). According to these theories, negatively biased cognition is a core process in depression. This process is reflected in the "cognitive triad of depression": Depressed patients typically have a negative view of themselves, their environment, and the future. They view themselves as worthless, inadequate, unlovable, and deficient. Depressed patients view the environment as overwhelming, as presenting insuperable obstacles that cannot be overcome, and as continually resulting in failure or loss. Moreover, they view the future as hopeless; they believe that their own efforts will be insufficient to change the unsatisfying course of their life. This negative view of the future often leads to suicidal ideation and actual attempts.

Depressed patients consistently distort their interpretations of events so that they maintain negative views of themselves, the environment, and the future. These distortions represent deviations from the logical processes of thinking used typically by people. For example, a depressed woman whose husband comes home late one night may conclude that he is having an affair with another woman, even though there is no other evidence supporting this conclusion. This example illustrates an "arbitrary inference"—the patient has reached a conclusion that is not justified by the available evidence. Other distortions include all-or-nothing thinking, overgeneralization, selective abstraction, and magnification (Beck et al., 1979).

According to recent developments within the cognitive model, an important predisposing factor for many patients with depression is the presence of early schemas (Beck, Freeman, & Associates, 1990; Young, 1990; Stein & Young, 1992). Beck (1967) emphasized the importance of schemas in depression and provided the following definition:

> A schema is a (cognitive) structure for screening, coding, and evaluating the stimuli that impinge on the organism. . . . On the basis of this matrix of schemas, the individual is able to orient himself in relation to time and space and to categorize and interpret experiences in a meaningful way. (p. 283)

More recently, Beck et al. (1990) have noted:

In the field of psychopathology, the term "schema" has been applied to structures with a highly personalized idiosyncratic content that are activated during disorders such as depression, anxiety, panic attacks, and obsessions, and become prepotent. . . . Thus, in clinical depression, for example, the negative schemas are in ascendancy, resulting in a systematic negative bias in the interpretation and recall of experiences as well as in short-term and long-term predictions, whereas the positive schemas become less accessible. It is easy for depressed patients to see the negative aspects of an event, but difficult to see the positive. They can recall negative events much more readily than positive ones. They weigh the probabilities of undesirable outcomes more heavily than positive outcomes. (p. 32)

Through clinical observation, Young has identified a subset of schemas (the deepest level of cognition), which he calls early maladaptive schemas: "Early Maladaptive Schemas refer to extremely stable and enduring themes that develop during childhood and are elaborated upon throughout the individual's lifetime" (Young, 1990, p. 9). Young has identified 16 of these early maladaptive schemas in six different domains (see Figure 6.1).

According to Young's schema approach, the child learns to construct reality through his/her early experiences with the environment, especially with significant others. Sometimes these early experiences lead children to accept attitudes and beliefs that will later prove maladaptive. For example, a child may develop the schema that no matter what he/she does, his/her performance will never be good enough. These schemas are usually out of awareness, and may remain dormant until a life event (such as being fired from a job) stimulates the schema. Once the schema is activated, the patient categorizes, selects, and encodes information in such a way that the failure schema is maintained. Early maladaptive schemas, therefore, predispose depressed patients to distort events in a characteristic fashion, leading to a negative view of themselves, the environment, and the future.

Early maladaptive schemas have several defining characteristics. They are experienced as (1) a priori truths about oneself and/or the environment; (2) self-perpetuating and resistant to change; (3) dysfunctional; (4) often triggered by some environmental change (e.g., loss of a job or mate); (5) tied to high levels of affect when activated; and (6) usually result from an interaction of the child's innate temperament with dysfunctional developmental experiences with family members or caretakers (Young, 1990).

The focus of cognitive therapy is on changing depressive thinking. These changes may be brought about in a variety of ways: through behavioral experiments, logical discourse, examination of evidence, problem solving, role playing, and imagery restructuring, to name just a few.

CHARACTERISTICS OF THERAPY

Cognitive therapy with adult depressed outpatients is usually undertaken in the therapist's office. It has most frequently been applied in a one-to-one setting, with just the patient and the therapist. However, group cognitive therapy has also been tried and shown to be successful with many depressed outpatients (Beutler et al., 1987; Jarrett & Nelson, 1987), although it may not be as effective as individual treatment (Wierzbicki & Bartlett, 1987). It is not unusual to involve spouses, parents, and other family members during treatment. They might be used, for example, to provide information that will help patients test the validity of their thinking regarding how others in the family view them. Moreover, "couples therapy" based on the cognitive model is often very effective in relieving depression related to chronic interpersonal problems (Beck, 1988; O'Leary & Beach, 1990).

In our clinical experience, a number of therapist characteristics contribute to effective cognitive therapy. First, cognitive therapists should ideally demonstrate the "nonspecific" therapy skills identified by other writers (e.g., Truax & Mitchell, 1971). They should be able to communicate warmth, genuineness, sincerity, and openness. Second, the most effective cognitive therapists seem to be especially skilled at seeing events through the patient's perspective (accurate empathy). They are able to suspend their

INSTABILITY & DISCONNECTION

(Expectation that one's needs for security, safety, stability, nurturance, and empathy will not be met in a predictable manner within the context of intimate or family relationships. Typical family origin is detached, explosive, unpredictable, or abusive.)

1. ABANDONMENT / INSTABILITY

The perceived *instability* or *unreliability* of those available for support and connection.

Involves the sense that significant others will not be able to continue providing emotional support, connection, strength, or practical protection because they are emotionally unstable, unpredictable, unreliable, or erratically present; because they will die imminently; or because they will abandon the patient in favor of someone better.

2. MISTRUST / ABUSE

The expectation that others will hurt, abuse, humiliate, cheat, lie, manipulate, take advantage, or explode with violence or anger . Usually involves the perception that the harm is intentional or the result of unjustified and extreme negligence. May include the sense that one always ends up being cheated relative to others or "getting the short end of the stick."

3. EMOTIONAL DEPRIVATION

Expectation that one's desire for a normal degree of emotional support will not be adequately met by others.

A. *Deprivation of Nurturance*: Absence of attention, affection, warmth, or companionship.

B. *Deprivation of Protection*: Absence of strength, direction, or guidance from others.

C. *Deprivation of Empathy*: Absence of understanding, listening, self-disclosure, or mutual sharing of feelings from others.

IMPAIRED AUTONOMY

(Expectations about oneself and the environment that interfere with one's perceived ability to separate, survive, and function independently. Typical family origin is enmeshed, undermining of child's judgment, or overprotective.)

4. FUNCTIONAL DEPENDENCE/ INCOMPETENCE

Belief that one is unable to handle one's everyday responsibilities in a competent manner, without considerable help from others (e.g., take care of oneself, solve daily problems, exercise good judgment, tackle new tasks, make good decisions). Often presents as a pervasive passivity.

5. VULNERABILITY TO HARM AND ILLNESS

Exaggerated fear that disaster is about to strike at any time (natural, criminal, medical, or financial), and that one is unable to protect oneself. May include unrealistic fears that one will have a heart attack, get AIDS, go crazy, go broke, be mugged, crash, etc.

6. ENMESHMENT / UNDEVELOPED SELF

Excessive emotional involvement and closeness with one or more significant others (often parents), at the expense of full individuation or normal social development. Often involves the belief that at least one of the enmeshed individuals cannot survive or be happy without the constant support of the other. May also include feelings of being smothered by, or fused with, others. OR Insufficient individual identity or inner direction. Often experienced as a feeling of emptiness or of floundering.

UNDESIRABILITY

(The expectation that one will not be desirable to -- or is different from -- other people, in terms of any of the following: physical attractiveness, social skills, inner worth, moral integrity, interesting personality, career accomplishment, values, interests, masculinity/femininity, socio-economic background, etc. Typical origin is criticalness or rejection from family or peer group.)

7. DEFECTIVENESS/ SHAME

The feeling that one is *inwardly* defective, flawed, or invalid; that one would be fundamentally unlovable to significant others if exposed; or a sense of shame regarding one's perceived internal inadequacies. Often involves excessive self-criticism, self-punishment, comparisons with others, and exaggerated expectations of rejection and blame -- within *intimate* relationships.

8. SOCIAL UNDESIRABILITY / ALIENATION

The belief that one is *outwardly* undesirable to others (e.g., ugly; sexually undesirable; low in status; poor in conversational skills; dull) OR the feeling that one is isolated from the rest of the world, different from other people, and/or not part of any group or community. Often involves self-consciousness, alienation, comparisons with others, and insecurity within *social* situations.

9. FAILURE TO ACHIEVE

The belief that one will inevitably fail, or is fundamentally inadequate relative to one's peers, in areas of achievement (school, career, sports, etc.). Often involves the belief that one is stupid, inept, untalented, ignorant, etc.

(cont.)

FIGURE 6.1. Early maladaptive schemas in six domains. Copyright 1993 by Jeffrey Young, PhD. Reprinted by permission.

RESTRICTED SELF-EXPRESSION

(Inordinate restriction, suppression, or ignoring of one's emotions or daily preferences. Typical family origin is suppression of feelings and domination by adults.)

10. SUBJUGATION

Excessive surrendering of control over one's own decisions and preferences--usually to avoid anger, retaliation, or abandonment. Involves the perception that one's own desires are not valid or important to others. Often leads to anger at the subjugator. Frequently presents as excessive compliance and eagerness to please.

11. EMOTIONAL INHIBITION

Excessive difficulty expressing or discussing feelings (anger, hurt, sadness, joy, etc.), because one expects their expression to result in loss of esteem, harm to others, embarrassment, retaliation, or abandonment.

RESTRICTED GRATIFICATION

(Excessive emphasis on work, status, duty, standards, responsibility to others, or the negative aspects of life - - at the expense of happiness, natural inclinations, pleasure, health, optimism, or creativity. Typical family origin is grim: pain, performance, sacrifice, self-control, and negativity predominate over pleasure, playfulness, and optimism.)

12. SELF-SACRIFICE / OVERRESPONSIBILITY

Excessive focus on meeting the needs of others, at the expense of one's own gratification. The most common reasons are: to prevent causing pain to others; to avoid guilt; to gain in esteem; to maintain the connection with others perceived as needy . Often results from an acute sensitivity to the pain of others. Often involves an exaggerated sense of duty and responsibility to others. Usually leads to a sense that one's own needs are not being adequately met and sometimes to resentment of those who are taken care of.

13. UNRELENTING/ UNBALANCED STANDARDS

The relentless striving to meet high or unbalanced expectations of oneself or others, at the expense of happiness, pleasure, relaxation, spontaneity, playfulness, health, sense of accomplishment, or satisfying relationships. Usually involves undue emphasis on any of six broad areas: (1) achievement or competition; (2) money, physical appearance, or social status; (3) self-control or discipline; (4) perfectionism, order, or attention to detail; (5) control and mastery of the environment ; or (6) moral, ethical, or religious precepts (other than self-sacrifice).

14. NEGATIVITY / PESSIMISM

A pervasive, lifelong focus on the negative aspects of life (pain, death, loss, disappointment, conflict, guilt, resentment, unsolved problems, potential mistakes, betrayal, things that could go wrong, etc.) while minimizing or neglecting the positive or optimistic aspects. May include feelings of helplessness or uncontrollability, based on the expectation that one cannot prevent negative outcomes in life.

IMPAIRED LIMITS

(Deficiency in internal limits, leading to difficulty respecting the rights of others or meeting one's own personal goals. Typical family origin is permissiveness and indulgence.)

15. ENTITLEMENT/ SELF-CENTEREDNESS

Insistence that one should be able to have whatever one wants, regardless of what others consider reasonable or the cost to others. Often involves excessive control over others, demandingness, and lack of empathy for others' needs.

16. INSUFFICIENT SELF-CONTROL/ SELF-DISCIPLINE

Pervasive difficulty exercising sufficient self-control and frustration tolerance to achieve one's personal goals, or to restrain the excessive expression of one's emotions and impulses.

own personal assumptions and biases while they are listening to depressed patients describe their reactions and interpretations. Third, skilled cognitive therapists can reason logically and plan strategies. They are not "fuzzy" thinkers. In this respect they resemble good trial lawyers, who can spot the sometimes subtle flaws in another individual's reasoning and skillfully elicit a more convincing interpretation of the same events. Cognitive therapists plan strategies several steps ahead, anticipating the desired outcome. Fourth, the best practitioners of this approach are active. They have to be comfortable taking the lead, providing structure and direction to the therapy process.

Although patient characteristics have received some empirical attention (Shea et al.,

1990; Persons, Burns, & Perloff, 1988), we do not yet adequately know which patient characteristics are related to success in cognitive therapy. Our experience suggests that patients with major depressive disorder (single episode or recurrent)[1] and dysthymic disorder (with or without major depressive disorder) respond well to the cognitive therapy approach described in this chapter. The relapse-prevention phase has proven particularly valuable in reducing the frequency of relapse with these patients. To the extent that the patient is diagnosed with Axis II personality disorders, the schema-focused phase of treatment may be significantly longer in duration and may become more crucial in obtaining a positive response to treatment.

We have observed clinically that cognitive therapy can be an important adjunct to pharmacotherapy with bipolar I and bipolar II disorders, and in patients with severe endogenous depression, especially with melancholia. With such patients, cognitive therapy techniques are often useful in reducing the frequency of relapse or cycling, once the acute symptomatology has been reduced.

Several subtypes of depressives seem less amenable to short-term cognitive therapy. These include patients with hallucinations or delusions, schizoaffective disorders, and impaired memory functioning (e.g., organic brain syndromes). For these patients, cognitive therapy may be helpful over a longer period in preventing relapse, often in combination with pharmacotherapy, milieu treatment, or extra support from the environment.

In our experience, certain patient characteristics are predictive of a more rapid response. Patients who are appropriately introspective; can reason abstractly; are well organized and good planners; are conscientious about carrying out responsibilities; are employed; are not excessively angry, either at themselves or at other people; are less dogmatic and rigid in their thinking; can identify a clear precipitating event for the depressive episode; and have close relationships with others often show faster improvement in depressive symptoms through cognitive therapy. Recent findings indicate that age is not an obstacle, as older adults seem to benefit as much as do younger adults from cognitive therapy (Beutler et al., 1987; Gallagher-Thompson, Hanley-Peterson, & Thompson, 1990).

COLLABORATION

Basic to cognitive therapy is a collaborative relationship between patient and therapist. When the therapist and patient work together, the learning experience is enhanced for both and a cooperative spirit is developed that contributes greatly to the therapeutic process. Equally important, the collaborative approach helps to ensure compatible goals for treatment and to prevent misunderstandings and misinterpretations between patient and therapist. Because of the importance of the collaborative relationship, we place great emphasis on the interpersonal skills of the therapist, the process of joint selection of problems to be worked on, regular feedback, and the investigative process we call collaborative empiricism.

Interpersonal Qualities

Since collaboration requires that the patient trust the therapist, we emphasize those interpersonal qualities that contribute to trust. Warmth, accurate empathy, and genuineness are desirable personal qualities for the cognitive therapist, as for all psychotherapists. It is important that the cognitive therapist not seem to be playing the *role* of therapist. The therapist should be able to communicate, verbally and nonverbally, that he/she is sincere, open, concerned, and direct. It is also important that the therapist not seem to be withholding impressions or information, or evading questions. The therapist should be careful not to seem critical or disapproving of the patient's perspective.

Rapport between patient and therapist is crucial in the treatment of depressed patients. When rapport is optimal, patients perceive the therapist as someone who is tuned in to their feelings and attitudes, someone who is sympathetic and understanding, and someone with whom they can communicate without having to articulate feelings in detail or qualify statements. When the rapport is good, both patient and therapist feel comfortable and secure.

A confident, professional manner is also important in cognitive therapy. Therapists should convey relaxed confidence in their ability to help the depressed patient. Such confidence can help counteract the patient's initial hopelessness about the future. Since the cognitive therapist must sometimes be directive and impose structure, especially in the early stages of treatment, it is helpful to maintain a clear sense of professionalism.

Joint Determination of Goals for Therapy

In the collaborative relationship, the patient and therapist work together to set therapeutic goals, determine priorities among them, and set an agenda for each session. Problems to be addressed over the course of therapy include specific depressive symptoms (e.g., hopelessness, crying, and difficulty concentrating) and external problems (e.g., marital difficulties, career issues, and child-rearing concerns). Priorities are then jointly determined in accordance with the amount of distress generated by a particular problem and how amenable to change the particular problem is. During the agenda-setting portion of each therapy session (discussed in detail in the next section), therapist and patient together determine the items to be covered in that session. Through this collaborative process, target problems are selected on a weekly basis.

The process of problem selection often presents difficulties for the new cognitive therapist. These include failure to reach agreement on specific problems on which to focus, selection of peripheral concerns, and the tendency to move from problem to problem instead of persistently seeking a satisfactory solution to only one problem at a time. Because the problem-selection process entails both structuring and collaboration on the part of the therapist, considerable skill is necessary.

Regular Feedback

Feedback is especially important in therapy with depressed patients; it is a crucial ingredient in developing and maintaining the collaborative therapeutic relationship. The cognitive therapist initiates the feedback component early in therapy by eliciting the patient's thoughts and feelings about many aspects of the therapy, such as the handling of a particular problem, the therapist's manner, and homework assignments. Since many patients misconstrue therapists' statements and questions, it is only through regular feedback that the therapist can ascertain whether he/she and the patient are on the same "wavelength." The therapist must also be alert for verbal and nonverbal clues to covert negative reactions.

As part of the regular feedback process, the cognitive therapist shares the rationale for each intervention mode. This helps to demystify the therapy process and facilitates the patient's questioning the validity of a particular approach. In addition, when patients understand the connection between a technique or assignment the therapist uses and the solution of a problem, they are more likely to participate conscientiously.

The third element of the feedback process is for the therapist to check regularly to determine whether the patient understands the therapist's formulations. Patients sometimes agree with a formulation simply out of compliance, and depressed patients frequently exhibit both compliance and reluctance to "talk straight" with the therapist for fear of being rejected, criticized, or making a mistake. The therapist must therefore make an extra effort to elicit feelings or wishes relevant to compliance (e.g., anxiety about rejection and wish to please) from the patient and must be alert for verbal and nonverbal clues that the patient may not indeed understand the explanations.

As a regular part of the feedback process, at the close of each session the cognitive therapist provides a concise summary of what has taken place and asks the patient to abstract and write down the main points from the session. The patient keeps this summary for review during the week. In practice, the therapist uses capsule summaries at least three times during a standard therapeutic interview: in preparing the agenda, in a midpoint recapitulation of the material covered up to that point, and in the final summary of the main points of the interview. Patients generally respond favorably to the elicitation of feedback and presentation of capsule summaries. We have observed that the development of empathy and rapport is facilitated by these techniques.

Collaborative Empiricism

When the collaborative therapeutic relationship has been successfully formed, the patient and therapist act as an investigative team. Though we elaborate on the investigative process later, it is appropriate to introduce it in the context of the collaborative relationship. As a team, patient and therapist approach the patient's automatic thoughts and schemas in the manner that scientists approach questions: Each thought or schema becomes a hypothesis to be tested and evidence is gathered that supports or refutes the hypothesis. Events in the past, circumstances in the present, and possibilities in the future are the data that constitute evidence, and the conclusion to accept or reject the hypothesis is jointly reached by subjecting the evidence to logical analysis. Experiments may also be devised to test the validity of particular cognitions. The cognitive therapist need not persuade patients of illogicality or inconsistency with reality since patients "discover" their own inconsistencies. This guided discovery process is a widely accepted educational method and is one of the vital components of cognitive therapy.

PROCESS OF COGNITIVE THERAPY

Here we attempt to convey a sense of how cognitive therapy sessions are structured and a sense of the course of treatment. A detailed discussion of particular techniques follows this section.

Initial Sessions

A main therapeutic goal of the first interview is to produce some symptom relief. Relief of symptoms serves the patient's needs by reducing suffering and also helps to increase rapport, collaboration, and confidence in the therapeutic process. Symptom relief should be based on more than rapport, sympathy, and implied promise of "cure," however, so the cognitive therapist seeks to provide a rational basis for reassurance by attempting to define a set of problems and demonstrating some strategies for dealing with them.

Problem definition continues to be a goal in the early stages of therapy. The therapist works with the patient to define specific problems to focus on during therapy sessions. The cognitive therapist does this by obtaining as complete a picture as possible of the patient's psychological and life situation difficulties. The therapist also seeks details concerning the depth of depression and particular symptomatology. Cognitive therapists are especially concerned with how patients see their problems.

Once the specific problems have been defined, the patient and the therapist establish priorities among them. Decisions are made on the basis of amenability to therapeutic change and centrality of the life problem or cognition to the patient's emotional distress. In order to help establish priorities effectively, the therapist must see the relationships among particular thoughts, particular life situations, and particular distressing emotions.

Another goal of the initial session is to illustrate the close relationship between cognition and emotion. When the therapist is able to observe the patient's mood change (e.g., crying), he/she points out the alteration in affect and asks for the patient's thoughts just before the mood shift. The therapist then labels the negative thought and points out its relationship to the change in mood. The therapist initially gears homework assignments toward helping the patient see the intimate connection between cognition and emotion.

A frequent requirement in the early stage of therapy is to socialize the patient to cognitive therapy. Particularly if they have previously undertaken analytically oriented or Rogerian therapies, many patients begin cognitive therapy expecting a more insight-oriented, nondirective therapeutic approach. The cognitive therapist can facilitate the transition to a more active and structured one by maintaining a problem-oriented stance, which often entails gently interrupting patients who tend to speculate about the sources of their problems and seek interpretations from the therapist.

Finally, the therapist must communicate the importance of self-help homework assignments during the initial session. Therapists can do this by stressing that doing the homework is actually more important than the therapy session itself. The therapist can also provide incentive by explaining that patients who complete assignments generally improve more quickly. The nature and implementation of self-help homework assignments are considered in further detail in a later section of this chapter.

Progress of Typical Therapy Session

Each session begins with the establishment of an agenda for the session. This ensures optimal use of time in a relatively short-term, problem-solving therapeutic approach. The agenda generally begins with a short synopsis of the patient's experiences since the last session, including discussion of the homework assignment. The therapist then asks the patient what he/she wants to work on during the session and often offers topics to be included.

When a short list of problems and topics has been completed, the patient and therapist determine the order in which to cover them and, if necessary, the time to be allotted to each topic. There are several issues to be considered in establishing priorities, including stage of therapy, severity of depression, likelihood of making progress in solving the problem, and potential pervasiveness of the effect of a particular theme or topic. The cognitive therapist is sensitive to patients' occasional desires to talk about something that seems important to them at the moment, even if such discussion seems not to be productive in terms of other goals. This kind of flexibility characterizes the collaborative therapeutic relationship.

After these preliminary matters have been covered, the patient and therapist move on to the one or two problems to be considered during the session. The therapist begins the discussion of a problem by asking the patient a series of questions designed to clarify the nature of the patient's difficulty. In doing so, the therapist seeks to determine whether early maladaptive schemas, misinterpretations of events, or unrealistic expectations are involved. The therapist also

seeks to discover whether the patient had unrealistic expectations, whether the patient's behavior was appropriate, and whether all possible solutions to the problem were considered. The patient's responses will suggest to the therapist a cognitive-behavioral conceptualization of why the patient is having difficulty in the area concerned. The therapist will now have discerned the one or two significant thoughts, schemas, images, or behaviors to be worked on. When this target problem has been selected, the therapist chooses the cognitive or behavioral techniques to apply and shares their rationale with the patient. The specific techniques used in cognitive therapy are explained in the following sections of this chapter.

At the close of the session, the therapist asks the patient for a summary, often in writing, of the major conclusions drawn during the session. The therapist asks for the patient's reactions to the session in order to ascertain whether anything disturbing was said and in order to forestall any delayed negative reactions following the interview. Finally, the therapist gives a homework assignment designed to assist the patient in applying the particular skills and concepts from the session to the problem during the following week.

Progression of Session Content Over Time

Although the structure of cognitive therapy sessions does not change during the course of treatment, the content often changes significantly. The first phase of treatment, symptom reduction, focuses on overcoming hopelessness, identifying problems, setting priorities, socializing the patient to cognitive therapy, establishing the collaborative relationship, demonstrating the relationship between cognition and emotion, labeling errors in thinking, and making rapid progress on a target problem. Therapy is initially centered on the patient's symptoms, with attention given to behavioral and motivational difficulties. Once the patient shows some significant changes in these areas, the emphasis shifts to the content and pattern of the patient's thinking.

In contrast to the first phase, the second, or schema-focused, phase emphasizes relapse prevention. Once the patient is feeling less depressed, the therapist and patient turn from specific thoughts about particular problems to core schemas about self and life, because they often underlie many of the patient's problems. Once identified, schemas reveal rules and formulas by which developing individuals learned to "make sense" of the world, and the schemas continue to determine how they organized perceptions into cognitions, set goals, evaluated and modified behavior, and understood events in their life. Cognitive therapy aims at counteracting the effects of schemas and replacing dysfunctional techniques and methods with new approaches. If the schemas themselves can be changed, we believe that the patient will become less vulnerable to future depressions.

Rehm (1990) has noted:

> The negative schemata may be replaced in use by more realistic schemata under usual life circumstances, but they remain intact as "latent" schemata with the potential of reactivation under circumstances of loss. With time and the improvement of circumstances, these schemata may again become latent unless they are modified by some form of intervention. (p. 80)

In this second phase, the patient assumes increased responsibility for identifying problems, coming up with solutions, and implementing the solutions through homework assignments. The therapist increasingly assumes the role of adviser or consultant as the patient learns to implement therapeutic techniques without constant support. As the patient becomes a more effective problem solver, the frequency of sessions is reduced, and eventually therapy is discontinued.

The remainder of this chapter is devoted to a detailed description of the two phases of treatment.

PHASE ONE: SYMPTOM REDUCTION

Cognitive Techniques

The specific cognitive techniques provide points of entry into the patient's cognitive organization. The cognitive therapist uses techniques for eliciting automatic thoughts, testing automatic thoughts, and identifying schemas to help both therapist and patient understand the patient's construction of reality. In applying specific cognitive techniques in therapy, it is important that the therapist work within the framework of the cognitive model of depression. Each set of techniques is discussed in turn.

Eliciting Automatic Thoughts

Automatic thoughts are those thoughts that intervene between outside events and the individual's emotional reactions to them. They often go unnoticed because they are part of a repetitive pattern of thinking and because they occur so often and so quickly. We rarely stop to assess their validity because they are so believable, familiar, and habitual. The patient in cognitive therapy must learn to recognize these automatic thoughts for therapy to proceed effectively. The cognitive therapist and the patient make a joint effort to discover the particular thoughts that precede such emotions as anger, sadness, and anxiety. Therapists use questioning, imagery, and role playing to elicit automatic thoughts.

The simplest method to uncover automatic thoughts is for the therapist to ask patients what thoughts went through their mind in response to particular events. This questioning provides patients with a model for introspective exploration that they can use on their own when the therapist is not present and after completing of treatment.

Alternatively, when the patient is able to identify those external events and situations that evoke a particular emotional response, the therapist may use imagery by asking the patient to picture the situation in detail. The patient is often able to identify the automatic thoughts connected with actual situations when the image evoked is clear. In this technique, the therapist asks patients to relax, close their eyes, and imagine themselves in the distressing situation. Patients describe in detail what is happening as they relive the event.

If the distressing event is an interpersonal one, cognitive therapists can utilize role playing. The therapist plays the role of the other person in the encounter, while patients play themselves. The automatic thoughts can usually be elicited when patients become sufficiently engaged in the role play.

In attempting to elicit automatic thoughts, the therapist is careful to notice and point out any mood changes that occur during the session and to ask the patient's thoughts just before the shift in mood. Mood changes include any emotional reaction, such as tears or anger. This technique can be especially useful when the patient is first learning to identify automatic thoughts.

Once patients become familiar with the techniques for identifying automatic thoughts, they are asked to keep a Daily Record of Dysfunctional Thoughts (Beck et al., 1979; see Figure 6.2), in which they record the emotions and automatic thoughts that occur in upsetting situations between therapy sessions. In later sessions they are taught to develop rational responses to their dysfunctional automatic thoughts and to record them in the appropriate column. The therapist and patient generally review the daily record from the preceding week near the beginning of the next therapy session.

Eliciting automatic thoughts should be distinguished from the interpretation process of other psychotherapies. In general, the cognitive therapist works only with those automatic thoughts mentioned by patients. Suggesting thoughts to patients may undermine collaboration and might inhibit patients from learning to continue the process on their own. As a last resort, however, when nondirective strategies fail, the cognitive therapist may offer several possible automatic thoughts, asking the patient whether any of the choices fit.

Even when many efforts to elicit automatic thoughts have been made by the therapist, the thoughts sometimes remain unavailable. When this is the case, the cognitive therapist tries to ascertain the particular meaning of the event that evoked the emotional reaction. For example, one patient began to cry whenever she had an argument with her roommate and friend. Efforts to elicit automatic thoughts proved unsuccessful. Only after the therapist asked a series of questions to determine the meaning of the event did it become clear that the patient connected having an argument or fight with the end of a relationship. Through this process, the therapist and

DATE	SITUATION Describe: 1. Actual event leading to unpleasant emotion, or 2. Stream of thoughts, daydream, or recollection, leading to unpleasant emotion.	EMOTION(S) 1. Specify sad/ anxious/ angry, etc. 2. Rate degree of emotion, 1-100.	AUTOMATIC THOUGHT(S) 1. Write automatic thought(s) that preceded emotion(s). 2. Rate belief in automatic thought(s), 0-100%.	RATIONAL RESPONSE 1. Write rational response to automatic thought(s). 2. Rate belief in rational response, 0-100%.	OUTCOME 1. Rerate belief in automatic thought(s), 0-100%. 2. Specify and rate subsequent emotions, 0-100.

Explanation: When you experience an unpleasant emotion, note the situation that seemed to stimulate the emotion. (If the emotion occurred while you were thinking, daydreaming, etc., please note this.) Then note the automatic thought associated with the emotion. Record the degree to which you believe this thought: 0% = not at all; 100% = completely. In rating degree of emotion: 1 = a trace; 100 = the most intense possible.

FIGURE 6.2. Daily Record of Dysfunctional Thoughts.

patient were able to see the meaning that triggered the crying.

Testing Automatic Thoughts

When the therapist and patient have managed to isolate a key automatic thought, they approach the thought as a testable hypothesis. This "scientific" approach is fundamental to cognitive therapy, where the patient learns to think in a way that resembles the investigative process. Through the procedures of gathering data, evaluating evidence, and drawing conclusions, the patient learns firsthand that one's view of reality can be quite different from what actually takes place. By designing experiments that subject their automatic thoughts to objective analysis, patients learn how to modify their thinking because they learn the *process* of rational thinking. Patients who learn to think this way during treatment will be better able to continue the empirical approach after the end of formal therapy.

The cognitive therapist approaches the testing of automatic thoughts by asking patients to list evidence from their experience for and against the hypothesis. Sometimes, after considering the evidence, patients will immediately reject the automatic thought, recognizing that it is either distorted or actually false.

When previous experience is not sufficient or appropriate to test a hypothesis, the therapist asks the patient to design an experiment for that purpose. The patient then makes a prediction and proceeds to gather data. When the data contradict the prediction, the patient can reject the automatic thought. The outcome of the experiment may, of course, confirm the patient's prediction. It is therefore very important that the therapist not assume that the patient's automatic thought is distorted.

There are some automatic thoughts that do not lend themselves to hypothesis testing through the examination of evidence. In these cases, there are two options available: The therapist may produce evidence from his/her experience and offer it in the form of a question that reveals the contradiction, or the therapist can ask a question designed to uncover a logical error inherent in the patient's beliefs. The therapist might say, for

example, to a patient who is sure he cannot survive without a close personal relationship, "You were alone last year and you got along fine, what makes you think you can't make it now?"

In testing automatic thoughts, it is sometimes necessary to refine the patient's use of a word. This is particularly true for global labels such as "bad," "stupid," or "selfish." What is needed in this case is an operational definition of the word. To illustrate, a patient at our clinic had the recurring automatic thought, "I'm a failure in math." The therapist and patient had to narrow down the meaning of the word before they could test the thought. They operationalized "failure" in math as being unable to achieve a grade of "C" after investing as much time studying as the average class member. Now they could examine past evidence and test the validity of the hypothesis. This process can help patients to see the all-inclusiveness of their negative self-assessments and the idiosyncratic nature of many automatic thoughts.

Reattribution is another useful technique for helping the patient reject an inappropriate, self-blaming thought. It is a common cognitive pattern in depression to ascribe blame or responsibility for adverse events to oneself. Reattribution can be used when the patient unrealistically attributes adverse occurrences to a personal deficiency such as lack of ability or effort. The therapist and patient review the relevant events and apply logic to the available information to make a more realistic assignment of responsibility. The aim of reattribution is not to absolve the patient of all responsibility but to examine the many factors that help contribute to adverse events. Through this process, patients gain objectivity, relieve themselves of the burden of self-reproach, and can then search for ways to solve realistic problems or prevent a recurrence.

Another strategy involving reattribution is for the therapist to demonstrate to patients that they use stricter criteria for assigning responsibility to their own unsatisfactory behavior than they use in evaluating the behavior of others. Cognitive therapists also use reattribution to show patients that some of their thinking or behavioral problems can be symptoms of depression (e.g., loss of concentration) and not signs of physical decay.

When the patient is accurate in identifying a realistic life problem or skill deficit, the cognitive therapist can use the technique of generating alternatives, in which therapist and patient actively search for alternative solutions. Because the depressed person's reasoning often becomes restricted, an effort to reconceptualize the problem can result in the patient's seeing a viable solution that may previously have been rejected.

It should be noted that the cognitive techniques outlined above all entail the use of questions by the therapist. A common error we observe in new cognitive therapists is an exhortative style. We have found that therapists help patients to change their thinking more effectively by using carefully formed questions. If patients are prompted to work their own way through problems and reach their own conclusions, they will learn an effective problem-solving process. We elaborate on the use of questioning in cognitive therapy later in the chapter.

Behavioral Techniques

Behavioral techniques are used throughout the course of cognitive therapy but are generally concentrated in the earlier stages of treatment. Behavioral techniques are especially necessary for those more severely depressed patients who are passive, anhedonic, socially withdrawn, and unable to concentrate for extended periods of time. By engaging the patient's attention and interest, the cognitive therapist tries to induce the patient to counteract withdrawal and become more involved in constructive activity.

From a variety of behavioral techniques, the therapist selects those that will help the patient cope more effectively with situational and interpersonal problems. Through homework assignments, patients implement specific procedures for dealing with concrete situations or for using time more adaptively.

The cognitive therapist uses behavioral techniques with the goal of modifying automatic thoughts. For example, a patient who believes "I can't stay with anything anymore" can modify this thought after completing a series of graded tasks designed to increase mastery. The severely depressed patient is caught in a vicious cycle in which a reduced activity level leads to negative self-label, which, in turn, results in even further discouragement and consequent inactivity. Intervention with behavioral techniques can enter and change this self-destructive pattern.

The most commonly used behavioral techniques include scheduling activities that include both mastery and pleasure exercises, cognitive rehearsal, self-reliance training, role playing, and diversion techniques. The scheduling of activities is frequently used in the early stages of cognitive therapy to counteract loss of motivation, hopelessness, and excessive rumination. The therapist uses an activity schedule for planning activities hour by hour, day by day (see Figure 6.3). Patients maintain an hourly record of the activities that they engaged in. Activity scheduling also helps patients obtain more pleasure and a greater sense of accomplishment from activities on a daily basis. The patients rate each completed activity (using a 0–10 scale) for both mastery and pleasure. The ratings usually contradict patients' beliefs that they cannot accomplish or enjoy anything anymore. In order to assist some patients in initiating mastery and pleasure activities, the therapist sometimes finds it necessary to subdivide an activity into segments ranging from the simplest to the most difficult and complex aspects of the activity. We call this the "graded task" approach. The subdivision enables depressed patients to undertake tasks that were initially impossible and thus provides proof of success.

Cognitive rehearsal entails asking the patient to picture or imagine each step involved in the accomplishment of a particular task. This technique can be especially helpful with those patients who have difficulty carrying out a task that requires successive steps for its completion. Sometimes impairment in the ability to concentrate creates difficulties for the patient in focusing attention on the specific task. The imagery evoked by the cognitive rehearsal technique helps the patient to focus and helps the therapist to identify obstacles that make the assignment difficult for the particular patient.

Some depressed patients rely on others to take care of most of their daily needs. With self-reliance training, patients learn to as-

Note: Grade activities *M* for mastery and *P* for pleasure 0–10.

		Mon.	Tues.	Wed.	Thurs.	Fri.	Sat..	Sun.
Morning	6–7							
	7–8							
	8–9							
	9–10							
	10–11							
	11–12							
	12–1							
Afternoon	1–2							
	2–3							
	3–4							
	4–5							
	5–6							
	6–7							
	7–8							
	8–9							
Evening	9–10							
	10–11							
	11–12							
	12–6							

Remarks:

FIGURE 6.3. Weekly Activity Schedule.

sume increased responsibility for routine activities such as showering, making their bed, cleaning the house, cooking their own meals, and shopping. Self-reliance involves gathering increased control over emotional reactions.

Role playing has many uses in cognitive therapy. It may be used to bring out automatic thoughts through the enactment of particular interpersonal situations, such as an encounter with a supervisor at work. Role playing may also be used, through homework assignments, to guide the patient in practicing and attending to new cognitive responses in problematic social encounters. A third use of role playing is to rehearse new behaviors. Thus, role playing may be used as part of assertiveness training and is often accompanied by modeling and coaching.

Role reversal, a variation of role playing, can be very effective in helping patients test how other people might view their behavior. This is well illustrated by a patient who had a "humiliating experience" while buying some clothes in a store. After playing the role of the clerk, the patient had to conclude that she had insufficient data for her previous conclusion that she appeared clumsy and inept. Through role reversal, patients begin to view themselves less harshly as "self-sympathy" responses are elicited.

Finally, the therapist may introduce various diversion techniques to assist the patient in learning to reduce the intensity of painful affects. The patient learns to divert negative thinking through physical activity, social contact, work, play, and visual imagery. Practice with diversion techniques also helps the patient gain further control over emotional reactivity.

Questioning

As we have stressed throughout this chapter, questioning is a major therapeutic device in cognitive therapy. A majority of the therapist's comments during the therapy session are questions. Single questions can serve several purposes at one time, while a carefully designed series of questions can help the patient consider a particular issue, decision, or opinion. Through questioning the cognitive therapist seeks to elicit what patients are thinking; the therapist tries to avoid telling patients what he/she believes they are thinking.

In the beginning of therapy, questions are employed to obtain a full and detailed picture of the patient's particular difficulties. They are used to obtain background and diagnostic data; to evaluate the patient's stress tolerance, capacity for introspection, coping methods, and so on; to obtain information about the patient's external situation and interpersonal context; and to modify vague complaints by working with the patient to arrive at specific target problems to work on.

As therapy progresses, the therapist uses questioning to explore approaches to problems, to help the patient to weigh advantages and disadvantages of possible solutions, to examine the consequences of staying with particular maladaptive behaviors, to elicit automatic thoughts, and to demonstrate early maladaptive schemas and their consequences. In short, the therapist uses questioning in most cognitive therapeutic techniques.

While questioning is itself a powerful means of identifying and changing automatic thoughts and schemas, it is important that the questions be carefully and skillfully posed. If questions are used to "trap" patients into contradicting themselves, patients may come to feel that they are being attacked by the therapist or manipulated. Too many open-ended questions can leave patients wondering what the therapist expects of them. Therapists must carefully time and phrase questions to help patients recognize their thoughts and schemas and to weigh issues objectively.

Self-Help Homework Assignments

Rationale

Regular homework assignments are very important in cognitive therapy. When patients systematically apply what they have learned during therapy sessions to their outside life, they are more likely to make significant progress in therapy and to be able to maintain their gains after termination of treatment. Homework assignments are often the means through which patients gather data, test hypotheses, and thus begin to modify their thoughts and schemas. In addition, the data provided through homework assignments help to shift the focus of therapy from the subjective and abstract to more concrete and objective concerns. When the patient and therapist review the previous week's activities during the agenda-setting portion of the interview, they may do so quickly, and the therapist can draw relationships between what takes place in the session and specific tasks, thereby avoiding tangents and side issues. Homework assignments further the patient's self-reliance and provide methods for the patient to continue working on problems after the end of treatment. Cognitive therapists emphasize the importance of homework by sharing with patients their rationale for assigning homework in therapy. They are also careful to explain the particular benefits to be derived from each individual assignment.

Assigning and Reviewing Homework

The cognitive therapist designs each assignment for the particular patient. The assignment should be directly related to the content of the therapy session so that the patient understands its purpose and importance. Each task should be clearly articulated and very specific in nature. Near the end of each session, the assignment is written in duplicate, with one copy going to the therapist and one to the patient.

Some typical homework assignments include reading a book or an article about a specific problem, practicing diversion or relaxation techniques, counting automatic thoughts on a wrist counter, rating activities for pleasure and mastery on the activities schedule, maintaining a Daily Record of Dysfunctional Thoughts, and listening to a tape of the therapy session.

During the therapy session, therapists ask for patients' reactions to homework assignments. They ask, for example, whether the assignment is clear and manageable. In order to determine potential impediments, the therapist may ask the patient to imagine taking the steps involved in the assignment. This technique can be especially helpful during the earlier stages of therapy. The patient assumes greater responsibility for developing homework assignments as therapy progresses through the middle and later stages.

It is essential that the patient and therapist review the previous week's homework during the therapy session itself. If they do not, the patient may conclude that the homework assignments are not important. During the first part of the therapy sessions, the therapist and patient discuss the last week's assignment and the therapist summarizes the results.

Difficulties in Completing Homework

When patients do not complete their homework assignments, or do them without conviction, cognitive therapists elicit automatic thoughts, schemas, or behavioral problems that may help both therapist and patient understand where the difficulty resides. The therapist does not presuppose that the patient is being resistant or passive–aggressive. When the difficulties have been successfully identified, the therapist and patient work collaboratively to surmount them. It is, of course, common for patients to have difficulties in completing homework, and we will

consider some of the typical problems and ways to counteract them.

When patients do not understand the assignment completely, the therapist should explain it more fully, specifying his/her expectations in detail. Sometimes using the behavioral technique of cognitive rehearsal (described above) can be helpful in such situations.

Some patients believe that they are naturally disorganized and cannot maintain records and follow through on detailed assignments. The therapist can usually help invalidate such general beliefs by asking patients about other circumstances in which they make lists (e.g., when planning a vacation or shopping trip). The therapist can also ask these patients whether they could complete the assignment if there were a substantial reward entailed. This kind of question helps make the patient recognize that self-control is not the problem; rather, the patient does not believe that the reward is great enough. When the patient comes to see that the problem is an attitudinal one, the therapist and patient can proceed to enumerate the advantages of completing the assignment.

More severely depressed patients may need assistance to structure their time so that homework becomes a regular activity. This can generally be accomplished by setting a specific time each day for the homework assignment. If necessary, the patient and therapist can set up a reward or punishment system to make sure the homework gets done. For example, patients can reward themselves for doing the assignment with a special purchase or punish themselves for not doing it by not watching a favorite television program.

Some patients are afraid of failing the assignments or doing them inadequately. In these cases, the therapist can explain that self-help assignments cannot be failed: Doing an assignment partially is more helpful than not doing it at all, and mistakes provide valuable information about problems that still need to be worked on. In addition, since performance is not evaluated, patients cannot lose if they view the activity from a more adaptive perspective.

Sometimes patients believe their problems are too deeply embedded and complex to be resolved through homework assignments. The therapist can explain to these patients that even the most complex undertakings begin with and consist of small concrete steps. Some writers, for example, resolve their "writer's blocks" by taking the attitude, "If I can't write a book, I can at least write a paragraph." When enough paragraphs have been written, the result is a book. The therapist and patient can consider the advantages and disadvantages of the patient's believing that problems cannot be solved by doing homework. Or the therapist can ask the patient to experiment before reaching such a conclusion. In those instances in which the patient believes that he/she has not made enough progress, and therefore that the homework is not helpful, the therapist can detail the progress the patient has made or can help the patient see that it may take more time before substantial change can be perceived.

When patients seem to resent being given assignments, the therapist can encourage them to develop their own assignments. The therapist might also offer the patient alternative assignments from which to choose, making one of the alternatives noncompliance with homework assignments. If patients choose noncompliance, the therapist can help to examine the consequences of that choice. Still another strategy is to present patients with a consumer model of therapy: Patients have a certain goal (overcoming depression) and the therapist has a means of achievement to offer; patients are free to use or reject the tools, just as they are free to buy or not buy in the marketplace.

When patients believe that improvement can be made just as readily without homework, therapists have two options. They can offer their own clinical experience that most patients who held that opinion were proven wrong and progressed more slowly in therapy. The other option is to set up an experiment for a given period, during which patients do not have to complete assignments. At the end of the predetermined period, the therapist and patient can evaluate the patient's progress during that time interval. Once again, it is important that the cognitive therapist keep an open mind: some patients do indeed effect significant change without formally completing homework assignments.

Special Problems

The novice cognitive therapist often makes the error of staying with the standard method outlined above even if it is not working very well. The cognitive therapist should be flexible enough to adapt to the needs of patients and to the several special problems that commonly arise in therapy. We have grouped these special problems into two categories: difficulties in the therapist–patient relationship and problems in which the therapy itself seems not to be working.

Therapist-Patient Relationship Difficulties

The first set of problems concerns the therapist–patient relationship itself. When the therapist first perceives a patient to be dissatisfied, angry, or hostile, it is imperative that the therapist present the patient with these observations. The therapist can then ask about the accuracy of the observations, the patient's feelings, and thoughts the patient has about the therapist. It is essential that therapists be aware that many interventions can be misinterpreted by depressed patients in a negative way.

With problems of misinterpretation, therapists approach the thought in the same way that they approach other thoughts: They work with the patient to gather data and search for alternative accounts of the evidence. Difficulties in the therapist–patient relationship can generally be resolved through dialogue. There are times when therapists may need to tailor behavior to the particular needs of the individual patient. For instance, therapists may become freer with self-disclosure and personal reactions to meet the needs of patients who persist in seeing the therapist as impersonal. Similarly, therapists can make a point of checking formulations of the patients' thoughts more frequently to meet the needs of patients who continue to believe the therapist does not understand them.

It is imperative in situations like these that the therapist not assume that the patient is being stubbornly resistant or irrational. Cognitive therapists collaborate with patients to achieve a better understanding of patients' responses. The reactions themselves often provide data regarding the kinds of distortions patients make in their other social and personal relationships. The patients' responses therefore give the therapist the opportunity to work with patients on their maladaptive interpretations in relationships.

Unsatisfactory Progress

A second set of problems occurs when the therapy appears not to be working even when patients conscientiously complete homework assignments and the collaborative relationship seems successful. Sometimes problems stem from inappropriate expectations on the part of the patient—or unrealistic expectations on the part of the therapist—regarding the rapidity and consistency of change. When therapy seems not to be progressing as quickly as it "should," both patient and therapist must remember that ups and downs are to be anticipated in the course of treatment. It is important for therapists to keep in mind that some patients simply progress more slowly than others. The therapist or patient, or both, may be minimizing small changes that have indeed been taking place. In this case the therapist can emphasize the small gains that have been made and remind the patient that large goals are attained through small steps toward them.

At times, patients' hopelessness can lead them to invalidate their gains. Therapists should seek to uncover the thoughts and maladaptive assumptions that contribute to the pervasive hopelessness. In these cases, therapists must work to correct mistaken notions about the process of change and about the nature of depression before further progress in therapy can occur.

In some cases in which therapy seems not to be working successfully, it may be that some of the therapeutic techniques have not been correctly used. Problems often arise when patients do not really believe the rational responses or are not able to remember them in times of emotional distress. It is important that the therapist determine the amount of belief the patient has in the rational responses and help the patient use the new responses as closely as possible to the moment when the automatic thought occurs. To the patient who does not fully believe a rational response, the therapist can

suggest an experimental stance, to take the new belief and "try it on for size." The patient who cannot think of answers because of emotional upset should be told that states of emotional distress make reasoning more difficult and that thoughts such as "if this doesn't work, nothing will" can only aggravate the problem. Patients should be assured that they will be able to think of rational responses more readily with practice.

Another problem deriving from the misapplication of cognitive therapy techniques occurs when the therapist uses a particular technique inflexibly. It is often necessary for the therapist to try out several behavioral or cognitive techniques before finding an approach to which the patient responds well. The cognitive therapist must stay with a particular technique for a while to see if it works, but he/she must also be willing to try an alternative technique when it becomes apparent that the patient is not improving. To give a specific example, behavioral homework assignments are sometimes more helpful with particular patients, even though the therapist has every reason to predict in advance that cognitive assignments will be more effective.

In some instances in which it appears that little progress is being made in therapy, it turns out that the therapist has selected a tangential problem. The cognitive therapist should be alert to this possibility, especially during the early stages of therapy. When there appears to be little or no significant change in depression level, even when the patient seems to have made considerable progress in a problem area, the therapist should consider the possibility that the most distressing problem has not yet been uncovered. A typical example of this kind of difficulty is the patient who presents difficulty at work as the major problem when it turns out that marital problems are contributing significantly to the work difficulties. The real issue may be withheld by the patient because it seems too threatening.

Finally, cognitive therapy is not for everyone. If the therapist has tried all available approaches to the problem and has consulted with other cognitive therapists, it may be best to refer the patient to another therapist, either with the same or a different orientation.

Regardless of why therapy is not progressing satisfactorily, cognitive therapists should attend to their own cognitions. They must maintain a problem-solving stance and not allow themselves to be influenced by their patient's despair or to see themselves as incompetent. Hopelessness in patient or therapist is an obstacle to problem solving. If therapists can effectively counteract their own negative self-assessments and other dysfunctional thoughts, they will be better able to concentrate on helping patients find solutions to their problems.

Symptom-Reduction Phase
Case Study: Irene

In the case study that follows, we describe the course of treatment for a depressed woman seen at our clinic. Through the case study we illustrate many of the concepts described earlier in this chapter, including eliciting automatic thoughts, the cognitive triad of depression, collaborative empiricism, structuring a session, and feedback.

Assessment and Presenting Problems

The patient, whom we will call Irene, phoned the center for help because she had heard about cognitive therapy on a local radio show. Irene recognized that she was experiencing many of the symptoms of depression described on the program.

She went through the typical assessment procedure at the center, which consists of 1½ hr of a standard clinical interview and an additional 1½ hr of paper-and-pencil testing.

The intake interviewer reported that Irene was a 29-year-old Caucasian woman, living with her husband and two young children. She was a high school graduate who had stopped work after marrying. Irene described her major problems as depression (for the past few years), difficulty coping with her children, marital conflict, and a sense of "being kept back" by her husband. In terms of her marriage, Irene said she felt stigmatized because her husband had just been released from a drug abuse center. Furthermore, her husband had just been laid off from work and was thus unemployed. He refused to participate in marital counseling with her.

Irene said she had been socially isolated since her marriage, although she reported having had normal friendships as a child and a teenager. One factor that she felt made it difficult for her to socialize with other women in the neighborhood was her belief that they looked down on her because she had such poor control over her children and because of her husband's drug record.

The interviewer diagnosed the patient as having major depression, recurrent, on Axis I and dependent personality disorder on Axis II. Her test scores verified the diagnosis of depression. Irene's Beck Depression Inventory (BDI) score was 29, placing her in the moderate-to-severe range of depression. Her most prominent depressive symptoms included guilt, self-blame, loss of pleasure, irritability, social withdrawal, inability to make decisions, fatigue, difficulty motivating herself to perform daily functions, and loss of libido. Her Young Loneliness Inventory score (Young, 1982) was 30, indicating an extremely high degree of loneliness. We use this scale because we have observed clinically that depression is often related to lack of satisfaction with interpersonal relationships. The Young Loneliness Inventory is similar in format to the Beck Depression Inventory and assesses the extent to which patients are distressed by the absence of various types of friendships and intimate ties.

Session 1

Irene was treated initially by the second author (A.T.B.). Since an intake interview had already been completed by another therapist, this therapist did not spend time reviewing symptoms in detail or taking a history. The session began with Irene describing the "sad states" she was having. The therapist (T) almost immediately started to elicit Irene's (I) automatic thoughts during these periods:

T: What kind of thoughts were you having during these four days when you said your thoughts kept coming over and over again?

I: Well, they were just—mostly, "Why is this happening again"—because, you know, this isn't the first time he's been out of work. You know, "What am I going to do"—like I have all different thoughts. They are all in different things like being mad at him, being mad at myself for being in this position all the time. Like I want to leave him or if I could do anything to make him straighten out and not depend so much on him. There's a lot of thoughts in there.

T: Now can we go back a little bit to the sad states that you have. Do you still have that sad state?

I: Yeah.

T: You have it right now?

I: Yeah, sort of. They were sad thoughts about—I don't know—I get bad thoughts, like a lot of what I'm thinking is bad things. Like not—there is like, uh, it isn't going to get any better, it will stay that way. I don't know. Lots of things go wrong, you know, that's how I think.

T: So one of the thoughts is that it's not going to get any better?

I: Yeah.

T: And sometimes you believe that completely?

I: Yeah, I believe it, sometimes.

T: Right now do you believe it?

I: I believe—yeah, yeah.

T: Right now you believe that things are not going to get better?

I: Well, there is a glimmer of hope but it's mostly . . .

T: What do you kind of look forward to in terms of your own life from here on?

I: Well, what I look forward to—I can tell you but I don't want to tell you. (*giggles*) Umm, I don't see too much.

T: You don't want to tell me?

I: No, I'll tell you but it's not sweet and great what I think. I just see me continuing on the way I am, the way I don't want to be, like not doing anything, just being there, like sort of with no use, that like my husband will still be there and he will, you know, he'll go in and out of drugs or whatever he is going to do, and I'll just still be there, just in the same place.

By inquiring about Irene's automatic thoughts, the therapist began to understand her perspective—that she would go on forever, trapped, with her husband in and out of drug centers. This illustrates the hopelessness about the future that is characteristic of most depressed patients. A second advantage to this line of inquiry is that the therapist introduced Irene to the idea of looking at her own thoughts, which is central to cognitive therapy.

As the session continued, the therapist probed the patient's perspective regarding her marital problems. The therapist then made a decision not to focus on the marriage as the first therapeutic target, since it would probably require too much time before providing symptom relief. Instead, the therapist chose to focus on Irene's inactivity and withdrawal. This is frequently the first therapeutic goal in working with a severely depressed patient.

In the sequence that follows, the therapist guided Irene to examine the advantages and disadvantages of staying in bed all day:

I: Usually I don't want to get out of bed. I want to stay there and just keep the covers up to my head and stay there, you know. I don't want to do anything. I just want to be left alone and just keep everything out, keep everything away from me.

T: Now, do you feel better when you get under the covers and try to shut everything out?

I: Yeah.

T: You do feel better?

I: Yeah, I feel better that way.

T: And so how much time do you spend doing that?

I: Now, lately? I don't get to do it too much because I have two kids. I don't ever get to do it all that much. I would love to do it more. It would help. I mean I feel safe, sort of secure, like they are over on the other side of the wall and they are not near me.

T: Now after you have spent some time in the covers, how do you feel about yourself?

I: If I'm laying there, I don't know.

T: Let's say afterwards?

I: Afterwards? I don't usually have any bad feeling about—oh yeah. I do, I feel like, Oh Christ, you've been laying there doing nothing, you should have been doing this, you should have been doing that, you should have got up and done something, whatever it is I was supposed to do. You know, even when I'm there, I'm not making any solutions to any problems, I'm just there.

T: On the one hand you seem to enjoy and on the other hand afterwards you're a little bit critical of yourself?

Note that the therapist did not try to debate or exhort Irene to get out of bed. Rather, through questioning, he encouraged her to examine more closely her assumption that she is really better off in bed. This is the process we call collaborative empiricism. By the second session, Irene had reexamined her hypothesis about remaining in bed:

I: About staying in bed versus getting up, I thought about that the other day. I thought when I told you—like I said something about like keeping the bad things away from me. Like when I was under the covers or just staying in bed they weren't really kept away from me. Like I always felt like I was always beating them down, I always had to ward them off. I don't know. I thought I told you it made me feel better to stay there, but I don't know if it really did. I don't think it did now that I am thinking about it.

T: It is funny then that when you talked about it your recollection was that it actually was comforting, but that sometimes happens with people. It happens to me too. I think that something is really good that's not so hot when I actually check it out.

Returning to the first session, after some probing by the therapist, Irene mentioned that cognitive therapy "is like my last hope." The therapist used this as an opportunity to explore her hopelessness and suicidal thinking:

T: What was going through your mind when you said, "This is my last hope"? Did you have some kind of vision in your mind?

I: Yeah, that if it doesn't work out that I don't think that I could take living like this the rest of my life.

T: If it doesn't work out, then what?

I: Then I wouldn't really care what happened to me.

T: Did you have something more concrete in mind?

I: Well, right this minute I don't think I could commit suicide but maybe if afterwards I thought there was nothing left, I could. I don't know though, I thought about suicide before but I have never been able to bring myself to do it. I've come close but I've never been able to succeed. I know certain things stop me like my kids, I don't think—even though I sometimes think I'm not as good a mother as I could be—I think they would be a lot worse off with my husband. I think it would destroy some other people, like my mother if I did something like that, you know. That is what I think mainly stops me, my children and my mother. Just that they would—I guess I'm afraid that if I did something like that, maybe my mother would feel that she failed somewhere, which is not true, I don't think, and just about my kids. I couldn't trust my husband with my kids. I think it would really—even though I'm messed up—I think that he would mess them up more.

T: Now these are some of the reasons for not committing suicide, now what are some of the reasons why you wanted to, do you think?

I: Because sometimes it is just hopeless, there are no solutions, there's no—it continues constantly the same way, all the time.

The therapist wanted the patient to feel as free as possible to discuss suicidal thoughts; thus, he tried hard to understand both the reasons for her hopelessness and the deterrents. After determining that she had no imminent plans to make an attempt (although she had made an attempt a couple of years earlier), the therapist said he would work with her to solve the problems in her life now and also "work things out inside your own head." He then asked her to select a small problem that they could work on together.:

T: Now are there any other smaller decisions that you could make that would affect your life right away?

I: I don't know. Well, I guess just trying—like for a long time I have been wanting to go out and do other things, like I don't know, join something, feel like I'm a part of something, you know, and I haven't been able to do it. I don't know if it's financial why I haven't been able to do it. I mean that is the excuse I come up with but I think sometimes it is not financial, sometimes it's just I don't get up and do it.

T: Well is there some specific group that you have in mind you could join?

I: I don't know. (*giggles*) I guess that is another decision I can't make. I think like everything interests me and nothing interests me.

T: Why don't we make a list and see what happens—a mental list? What are some of the things you would be interested in doing?

I: Tennis, I have been wanting to do that for a long time.

T: Now does this involve joining a tennis team?

I: Yeah, well that is what I would want to do.

T: Well, do you know people who belong to it?

I: No, I know other people but they don't belong to it in Philadelphia. Well, they do but I guess . . .

T: How would you go about finding out about a tennis team?

I: You would only have to go down to the nearest tennis court and that's it.

T: What would happen when you went down there?

I: I don't know. I have never been on one.

T: Well, what do you think you could do when you got there?

I: I guess you just—I don't know how many people are in one group. I don't know if you have to have a whole group go down with you and say OK we want to be a team, but I guess there are some people who are short of the whole group and then you could get on that team. You know, I guess.

T: Well, how could you get that information?

I: I guess if I went down there.

T: Do you think you could get the information if you went down there?

I: Yeah.

T: You could find out then whether you join as individuals or groups of how many, if they need somebody to fill in?

I: Yeah, um hmm.

T: How do you feel about doing that?

I: Kind of stupid. (*giggles*)

T: Does it seem so trivial?

I: Yeah, it seems like well why didn't I just do it before.

T: Well, you probably had good reasons for not doing it before. Probably you were just so caught up in the hopelessness.

I: Right, right.

T: When you are hopeless you tend to deny, as it were, or cut off possible solutions. Remember when your husband lost his job, you said that you refused to accept the fact that he would get compensation?

I: Right.

T: When you get caught up in hopelessness then there is nothing you can do, is that what you think?

I: Yeah.

T: So then rather than be down on yourself because you haven't gone over before, why don't we carry you right through?

This excerpt illustrates the process of graded tasks that is so important in the early stages of therapy with a depressed patient. The therapist asked the patient a series of questions to break down the process of joining a tennis league into smaller steps. Irene realized that she had known all along what to do but, as the therapist pointed out, her hopelessness prevented her from seeing possible solutions:

I: First steps are really hard for me.

T: First steps are harder for everybody, but that's why there is an old expression "A journey of a thousand miles starts with the first step."

I: That's very true.

T: Because that step—it's very important to take the first step, and second step, and third step, and so on. So all you have to do is take one and you don't have to take giant steps.

I: Well, yeah, I can see that now. I don't think I'd seen it before. I think before I was thinking every step was just as hard as the first step and maybe it's not that way at all, maybe it's easier.

In the second session, Irene reported success:

I: I called about the tennis and they said just to come in and give them your name. That's all you had to do, just come in and give them your name, which was really easy to do. It would have been a first step. I was surprised that it was so easy. I guess I thought it was going to be a lot harder, but it wasn't.

At the end of the first session, the therapist helped Irene write out an activity schedule for the coming week. The activities were quite simple, such as taking the children out, visiting her mother, reading a book, going shopping, and checking out the tennis team. Finally, the therapist asked her for feedback about the session and about her hopelessness:

T: Do you have any reactions?

I: I know I went through stages from happy to sad to happy to sad to happy to sad.

T: Where are you at now?

I: Where am I at now? Half decent.

T: Half sad/half happy?

I: No, a little more happier than I am sadder.

T: Now it may be that when you leave you'd

be thinking that we haven't really worked on the big problems, and you have to have a way to answer that.

I: I guess I'll just say it will take a little more time.

Session 2

In Session 2, the therapist began by collaborating with Irene to set an agenda. Irene wanted to discuss an argument she had with her husband and to deal with her feelings of inferiority; the therapist added the issue of activity versus inactivity to the agenda. They then reviewed the previous homework. Irene had carried out all the scheduled activities and had also listed some of her negative thoughts in between sessions. Her BDI score had dropped somewhat. (Patients routinely fill out the BDI before each session so that both the patient and the therapist can monitor the progress of treatment.)

Irene then shared her list of negative thoughts with the therapist. One concern was that she had cried during the first session:

I: Well, I know you are a professional but I felt like I was changed from one mood so easily to another. Like that sort of—when I interpreted it to myself, I felt like I could be manipulated and that was like—I don't know, I don't want to be easily led.

T: Well, that's good. You had the thought then that I was manipulating you, that I was somehow pushing the buttons and turning the knobs?

I: Well, yeah.

The therapist offered Irene an alternative perspective:

T: I would say just that I wasn't intending to manipulate you, that you yourself are not so gullible that you were easily manipulated. It is just that the way we were going through the interview, we were hitting some points that were sensitive and other points that were not so sensitive and when we talked about the negatives, you felt worse and when we talked about some positive things, then you felt better or perhaps when you were able to work through some particular problem, get on top of it, made you feel better. Then we go on to another problem, you feel worse. So it was just the nature of the interview rather than having anything to do with you being weak and me being overpowering, manipulative. But that was very good, and going through this explanation again not only to give you the information but to show you how to cope with the negative thoughts.

This is an illustration of how a cognitive therapist can utilize events during the session to teach patients to identify their automatic thoughts and to consider alternative interpretations.

Irene next discussed her argument with her husband, and specifically her thought that maybe she should leave him. She and the therapist agreed that it might be better to wait until her depression lifted a little before trying to make such a major decision. We often recommend that depressed patients postpone major decisions until they are able to regain a realistic perspective on their lives.

The therapist provided a summary of the two key themes he had identified from listening to Irene's automatic thoughts about her husband and about therapy. The first theme was her fear of being controlled by other people, including the therapist (subjugation schema); the second was that other people did not care about her (emotional deprivation schema). Cognitive therapists often identify and begin to correct early maladaptive schemas during the first phase of treatment. They work more intensively on changing these schemas during the second phase when the patient is less depressed, as we will elaborate in the next section of this chapter. In the segment that follows, the therapist explained how he arrived at the conclusion that the emotional deprivation schema is important for Irene:

T: Like for instance, when you say the way your husband treats you, it sounded as though you were really bothered about his lack of concern for your feelings and wishes.

I: Yeah, yeah.

T: I don't want to make too much out of this at the moment, but you also said that after your second baby was born you had the feeling that nobody cared for you, namely, your family.

I: Well, I don't know what happened, I can't remember the circumstances of what happened.

T: But whatever it was, this was the upshot.

I: Yeah.

T: So one of the things that seizes you, can really grab hold and make you feel terrible, is this notion that nobody cares, and that even that you are so sensitive in that one area that you thought that we were just using you as a guinea pig here and they were just interested in seeing how I work and not interested in you, the clinic wasn't interested in you, and I wasn't interested in you. So again it seems to be this notion of people who are important not caring. Is that correct?

I: Yeah, in most instances, yeah.

T: In all the instances I have mentioned.

I: Yeah.

T: Well, what this tells us is that you have to be alert to the sense that they don't care because this can really make you feel bad. It may not even be correct. If you found out, for instance, that your mother does care, so that you are wrong in thinking that but still the thought came through very strongly and your current thought is that we don't care, or it was.

About halfway through the session, the therapist asked the patient for feedback thus far:

T: Now at this point, is there anything that we have discussed today that bothered you?

I: That bothered me?

T: Yeah.

I: Uh, I'm feeling stupider and stupider as we go along.

T: That is important, OK. Can you . . .

I: Well, I'm trying not to but I don't know.

T: Well, if you are, you are. Why don't you just let yourself feel stupid and tell me about it.

I: Well, I just feel that I should be recognizing all these things, too.

This comment led to identification of a third theme, the incompetence schema: Irene had been viewing herself as increasingly dumb for the past few years. By this point, however, the patient was beginning to catch on to the idea of answering her thoughts more rationally. After the therapist pointed out the negative thought in the excerpt above, the patient volunteered:

I: I know what to do with the thought, "I'm stupid for not recognizing these things myself."

T: What are you going to do with it right this minute?

I: I am going to say—"Well, you are the professional, you are supposed to see these things."

T: Right, you'd fire me if I didn't see them. Right?

I: I didn't think of that but (*laughs*) . . . no, I wouldn't fire you. I wouldn't fire anybody.

T: So what you are saying is that since I am professionally trained I can see certain things. The other thing is that other people are objective and can often see things in us much more readily than we can in ourselves. It just happens to be a fact of human nature.

I: Yeah.

The same automatic thoughts arose again later in the session, when Irene felt stupid for not knowing the answer to one of the therapist's questions. In the extended excerpt below, the therapist helped Irene set up an experiment to test the thought, "I look dumb":

T: OK, now let's just do an experiment and see if you yourself can respond to the automatic thought and let's see what happens to your feeling. See if responding rationally makes you feel worse or makes you feel better.

I: OK.

T: OK, why didn't I answer that question right? I look dumb. What is the rational answer to that? A realistic answer?

I: Why didn't I answer that question? Because I thought for a second that was what I was supposed to say, and then when I heard the question over again, then I realized that was not what I heard. I didn't hear the question right, that's why I didn't answer it right.

T: OK, so that is the fact situation. And so is the fact situation that you look dumb or you just didn't hear the question right?

I: I didn't hear the question right.

T: Or is it possible that I didn't say the question in such a way that it was clear.

I: Possible.

T: Very possible. I'm not perfect so it's very possible that I didn't express the question properly.

I: But instead of saying you made a mistake, I would still say I made a mistake.

T: We'll have to watch the video and see. Whichever. Does it mean if I didn't express the question, if I made a mistake, does it make me dumb?

I: No.

T: And if you made the mistake, does it make you dumb?

I: No, not really.

T: But you felt dumb?

I: But I did, yeah.

T: Do you feel dumb still?

I: No.

The preceding exchange demonstrates the use of reattribution. At first, the patient attributed her difficulty in answering the therapist as evidence that she was stupid. As a result of the guided discovery approach, she reattributed the problem to one of two factors: Either she didn't hear the question right or the therapist did not ask the question clearly enough. At the end of the experiment, Irene expressed satisfaction that she was finally recognizing this tendency to distort her appraisals:

I: Right now I feel glad. I'm feeling a little better that at least somebody is pointing all these things out to me because I have never seen this before. I never knew that I thought that I was that dumb.

T: So you feel good that you have made this observation about yourself?

I: Right.

After summarizing the main points of the second session, the therapist assigned homework for the coming week: to fill out the Daily Record of Dysfunctional Thoughts (see Figure 6.2) and the Weekly Activity Schedule (with mastery and pleasure ratings) (see Figure 6.3).

Session 3

By the beginning of Session 3, Irene's mood had visibly improved. She had joined a tennis league with her sister, and had begun to respond more rationally to her automatic thoughts about being dumb. In fact, she was practicing her cognitive therapy skills by helping a friend with a similar problem of self-blame. The primary agenda item Irene chose to work on was "how I back away from other people," an aspect of her subjugation schema. She described an incident in which a neighbor was taking advantage of her but she could not assert herself. In discussing her thoughts, Irene expressed the ambivalence that is characteristic of the subjugation schema, and that interfered with her behaving assertively:

I: I want to be a nice person. I don't want to cause a lot of trouble. I don't want to be fighting with everybody constantly. But I don't like myself when I give in too much too.

T: Well, is it possible to be a nice person without giving in all the time?

I: I guess.

The therapist continued probing to understand why the patient believed that a nice person cannot get angry or be assertive. As the discussion progressed, it became obvious that, while in the abstract the patient could see that she was not necessarily bad because she got angry, in real-life situations Irene nevertheless felt she was wrong. The therapist's task next was to help the patient bring her rational thinking to bear on her distorted thinking in the context of a concrete event. At the therapist's request, Irene then described an argument in which she yelled at a neighbor with good justification yet felt she was bad. The therapist helped her use logic to evaluate her maladaptive schema:

T: You had the thought, "I was wrong to get mad at her, to yell at her." It seems likely that you believe that thought and that the thought was right and that you were wrong. And since you thought that thought was right, you then had to wish to withdraw behind your hat, as it were.

I: Right.

T: Now, let's look at it. Do you think that thought is correct?

I: No. I don't see how it could have been correct.

T: So according to your own values, you don't think that it is wrong to stick up for your rights?

I: Right.

T: And do you think that you were sticking up for yourself when she called the cops for a car that is blocking her car?

I: Well, the car shouldn't have been blocking her car . . .

T: That wasn't—the question was, should she have called the cops?

I: No. I didn't call the cops when she put her car in the middle of both driveways.

T: Right. So, do you think that it is natural for anybody to get mad at someone who calls the cops over something like that?

I: Wait, what was that?

T: Let me put it again. Do you think it was natural for you to get mad in that situation?

I: Yeah.

T: OK, so you don't see anything wrong in getting mad?

I: No.

T: No. And yet you have the thought right after that that it was wrong to get mad and yell at her?

I: Yeah, I did have that thought.

T: OK, now this is one of the problems. If you want to get over this sense of giving in all the time, one of the things that you can do is look for this thought—I was wrong to do such and such a thing—and refer back to this conversation that we are having now and decide for yourself whether, indeed, you were wrong. Now if every time you asserted yourself in that particular way, you think—I was wrong to do that—you are going to feel bad and then you are not going to want to assert yourself again. Is that clear?

I: Um hmm.

T: So we have to decide here and now, do you indeed think that you were wrong to assert yourself with her?

I: No.

T: Now the next time you get the thought—I was wrong, I shouldn't have said that, I shouldn't have stood up for my rights—how are you going to answer that thought?

I: If I was wrong? I wasn't wrong and I should stick up for my rights.

T: Now are you saying that because that is the answer or because you really believe it?

I: No, I believe it. I did the right thing there, I think. I did the right thing there. I did the right thing.

The therapist followed this discussion with a technique called "Point–Counterpoint" to help Irene practice rational responses to her automatic thoughts even more intensively. In this excerpt the therapist expressed the patient's own negative thinking, while she tried to defend herself more rationally:

T: Now I am going to be like the prosecuting attorney and I'll say, "Now I understand you were yelling at your neighbor because she called the cops. Is that true?"

I: Yeah.

T: Now it seems to me that that was a very bad thing for you to do.

I: No, it wasn't.

T: You don't think it was?

I: No, I should have hit her.

T: Well, you can sit there and say you should have hit her. I thought you said before that you wanted to be a nice person.

I: I was a nice person when I didn't call the cops when she blocked the driveway.

T: I know, but now you are saying that you are going to go out and hit her.

I: No, I wouldn't hit her. I wouldn't hit her unless she hit me.

T: Well, but still you yelled at her.

I: I yelled at her, yeah.

T: It doesn't seem to me that nice people yell at other people.

I: Well, I am still a nice person, but she did something wrong and I had to do something wrong.

T: Well, how can you still be a nice person if you yell at people?

I: How can you still be a nice person? You just are. You are a nice person. It is just that a nice person gets mad too.

T: You say a nice person gets mad too?

I: When somebody does something wrong to them.

T: Where did you ever get that idea nice people get mad when they are wrong?

I: When the other person is wrong? Where did I get that idea? It's true.

T: You really believe that's true?

I: Yeah, nice people are the same as everybody else.

T: So, nice people can get mad?

I: Um hmm.

Finally, the therapist returned to the schema and asked the patient how much she believed the new perspective:

T: If you get mad, you are not a nice person. Now do you believe that?

I: No.

T: Do you believe it partially?

I: Umm, no. Well, they don't get mad for nothing. They get mad when there is a reason.

T: OK, so right now would you say that you believe—now what about the belief—let's put it the other way, the belief that you can get mad and still be a nice person. How much do you believe that?

I: 100.

T: 100%?

I: Yeah.

T: You are sure 100%, not 90% or 80%?

I: No, I think 100%.

For the remainder of Session 3, Irene and the therapist reviewed other instances of nonassertiveness to reinforce the main point of the session: that nice people can behave assertively and sometimes even get mad. The session ended with a summary of the main issues raised in the first three sessions.

Summary of Initial Sessions

In the first three sessions, the therapist laid the groundwork for the remainder of treatment. He began immediately by teaching Irene to identify her negative automatic thoughts. By doing that the therapist began to understand her feelings of hopelessness and explored her suicidal ideation. By identifying her thoughts in a variety of specific situations, he was able to deduce several key schemas that later proved central to Irene's thinking: the belief that other people did not care about her, that she could be easily controlled by others, that she was dumb, and that she would not be a nice person if she asserted herself. The therapist made especially skillful use of the patient's thoughts during the therapy session to help Irene see that she was distorting evidence about the therapeutic interaction and coming to the inaccurate conclusion that she was easily manipulated and dumb.

Beyond identifying thoughts and distortions, the therapist guided Irene to take concrete steps to overcome her inactivity and withdrawal: He asked her to weigh the advantages and disadvantages of staying in bed; broke down the task of joining a tennis group into small, manageable steps; and worked with her to develop an activity schedule to follow during the week.

Finally, the therapist employed a variety of strategies to demonstrate to Irene that she could test the validity of her thoughts, develop rational responses, and feel better. For example, during the course of the three sessions, the therapist set up an experiment, used reattribution, offered alternative perspectives, and practiced the Point–Counterpoint technique.

One final point we want to emphasize is that the primary therapeutic mode was questioning. Most of the therapist's comments were in the form of questions. This helped Irene to evaluate her own thoughts outside of the session and prevented her from feeling attacked by the therapist.

By the end of these initial sessions, Irene reported being more optimistic that her life could change. She was then transferred to another cognitive therapist, Dr. Judith Eidelson, for the remainder of treatment. (This transfer had been explained to the patient before she saw the first therapist [A.T.B.].)

Later Sessions

The first issue that the second therapist dealt with was Irene's belief that she was stupid. The patient began to fill out the Daily Record of Dysfunctional Thoughts and gathered evidence that she was not as stupid as she believed. In fact, Irene brought up the possibility of taking a college course.

There were several obstacles: (1) her husband had never given her keys to either their car or their house; (2) she did not have enough money to take the course; and (3) she worried that her husband would try to punish her if she tried to become more independent.

The therapist set up several experiments with Irene to test a series of beliefs: that her husband would punish her, that she would fail at a job even if she could get one, and that she would fail a college-level course.

Through graded tasks, Irene asked her husband about obtaining keys, joined the tennis league, and began socializing with friends. Although her husband felt rejected and accused Irene of being stupid, he never took any active steps to stop her, despite her predictions. Irene then got a job as a waitress and again, contrary to her expectations, she was very successful and received a great deal of positive feedback on the job. Soon after getting the job, Irene enrolled in a sociology course and received a grade of "A." At each step in the sequence, Irene identified her automatic thoughts and responded to them before taking the next step toward independence.

During the final sessions of therapy, the patient raised the issue of leaving her husband. The therapist worked with Irene to evaluate several thoughts: (1) "somehow he'll change and the marriage will work"; (2) "marriage is a lifetime commitment"; (3) "I can't manage on my own"; and (4) "leaving him would represent a failure to me." Irene eventually discarded each of these beliefs as invalid or unlikely and decided to end the marriage. Shortly thereafter, Irene terminated therapy. She felt confident about herself and her decision, and her BDI score was in the normal range. The symptom-reduction phase of treatment was successfully completed in 20 sessions.

The next section describes and illustrates the relapse-prevention phase of cognitive therapy.

PHASE TWO: SCHEMA-FOCUSED TREATMENT FOR RELAPSE PREVENTION

Even after patients feel better, they nevertheless remain vulnerable to further depression unless their early maladaptive schemas have been identified and modified. Consequently, relapse prevention is an important component of the treatment of depression. Even though relapse appears less frequently among patients treated with cognitive therapy than with some other forms of therapy (Beck et al., 1979; Hollon et al., 1991; Whisman, Miller, Norman, & Keitner, 1991), it nevertheless remains a matter of significant concern to clinicians. As a result, an additional phase of treatment has been developed to deal with this deeper, predisposing psychological structure. This new phase is termed the *schema-focused phase* of treatment, so-called because of the emphasis on identifying and changing the patient's underlying schemas. Young and Klosko (1993) have recently published a self-help book for patients to guide them through this phase.

Beck et al. (1990) have noted:

[S]chemas are difficult to alter. They are held firmly in place by behavioral, cognitive, and affective elements. The therapeutic approach must take a tripartite approach. To take a strictly cognitive approach and try to argue patients out of their distortions will not work. Having the patients abreact within the session to fantasies or recollections will not be successful by itself. A therapeutic program that

addresses all three areas is essential. A patient's cognitive distortions serve as signposts that point to the schema. (p. 10)

As a result, the schema-focused phase of treatment is significantly different from the earlier phase in that it places more emphasis on early developmental patterns and origins, long-term interpersonal difficulties, the patient–therapist relationship, and emotive or experiential exercises.

Relapse-Prevention Phase
Case Study: Michelle

The second case study[2] demonstrates the importance of treating schemas in depressive episodes by highlighting the schema-focused phase of treatment.

History and Presenting Problems

The patient, "Michelle," read about cognitive therapy in a number of magazines, thought it could help her, and called the center for an appointment. The intake interviewer reported that Michelle was a 30–year-old Jewish woman married for the past 6 years to Jim, a Catholic who worked on Wall Street in investment banking. Neither of them had been married before. She reported being "happily married until about 6 to 8 months ago." Up to that time she maintained a successful career selling real estate.

Her immediate impetus to enter treatment was her reaction to a visit to her gynecologist: Upon hearing that she was not pregnant, Michelle broke out crying uncontrollably, and was prevailed upon to seek psychological assistance.

She scored 28 on the BDI, placing her in the moderate-to-severe range of depression. She also completed the Multimodal Life History Inventory (Lazarus & Lazarus, 1991), a 15–page assessment tool covering a wide range of issues dealing with feelings, thoughts, behaviors, and a variety of other psychotherapeutic issues. On her Multimodal Life History Inventory, she reported her main problems as depression, unhappy with self, and feeling unloved and unappreciated. She also listed the following behaviors as applicable to her: procrastination, withdrawal, concentration difficulties, sleep disturbance, crying, and outbursts of temper. She further indicated that she often felt angry, sad, depressed, conflicted, unhappy, hopeless, and lonely. She endorsed the following statements: "I am worthless. Life is empty, a waste. There is nothing to look forward to."

At the time she came in for her first interview, Michelle was no longer working, hardly left the house, except to go shopping, and spent most of her time in bed or watching television. Based on all the intake data, the interviewer diagnosed the patient as having major depression, single episode. She was referred to the third author (A.W.) for treatment.

The therapist (T) followed the same general approach described earlier in this chapter for Irene: He identified and challenged dysfunctional thoughts, kept thought records, and constructed and followed agendas and activity schedules until Michelle's (M) depression lifted. The schema-focused phase of treatment usually begins after patients start to feel better and resume more effective functioning. After 18 sessions Michelle's BDI score was 17, and the therapist then shifted into the schema-focused phase, with an explanation for the transition:

T: Well, what I thought we could work on now, Michelle—now that you're not so depressed and you're able to get out of bed and you're able to function during the day—is the issue that's going on with you and your husband.

M: Well, yes, I was afraid we were going to have to deal with that.

T: And when we start looking at relationship problems and these kinds of issues, we try to look at what we call schemas, and schemas are like lifelong patterns, lifelong themes in our lives that we sort of repeat over and over again. They're like buttons that get pushed and when they get pushed we react very emotionally to them.

M: Well I think he certainly knows how to push my buttons.

T: Yes, and what I think we could do now in this part of the therapy is try to find out exactly what those buttons are that

he pushes in you and help you to learn how to work better with those buttons.

In this phase, the therapist focuses on longer-term patterns, problems, and themes that might predispose the patient to future episodes of depression. In Michelle's case, the therapist focused on the following life problems:

1. Her inability to express herself and ask for things, especially from her husband. She readily acknowledged, "I know I need to demand more but just can't." Specifically, this included wanting a child but believing that "it would spoil things for Jim."
2. Recurrent thoughts about her marriage dissolving because "he always makes me feel as if he has one foot out the door."
3. Low self-esteem, feeling undesirable and unlovable because "I'm 12–15 pounds overweight."

Assessment Component

The schema-focused phase can be divided into two distinct components: an assessment component and a change or treatment component. The assessment itself consists of three unique but interrelated parts: a focused review of the patient's history, in an attempt to link past experiences to current problems; the use of the Schema Questionnaire (SQ), an instrument designed to identify schemas; and an experiential part to activate, or trigger, schemas.

The therapist initiated the focused life review by probing into the patient's childhood and the onset and course of her emotional difficulties. Michelle's recollection of her early family life was sketchy. She remembered her father as very bright and a good provider who was "hardly ever around." Her mother she recalled as gentle but seemingly passive. While growing up she could not confide in either of them for fear of engendering anger, ridicule, or "worse," especially on the part of her father. A sister, 2 years her junior, was favored by her parents and "she has remained their darling even up to now."

Michelle reported no "real" depressive episodes until she started dating and began experiencing feelings of "being terribly lonely and discarded" whenever her relationships suffered. Further questions about her past and her previous experience with psychotherapy revealed several minor episodes of depression, and at least one major depressive episode. Perceived or actual fluctuations in her relationship with Jim, her husband, seemed to have triggered many of her depressive reactions, during their marriage as well as during their courtship. Her previous major depression was triggered by Jim's announcement, after months of dating, that he was breaking up with her. She became listless and unmotivated to continue her studies, and was on the verge of dropping out of school. Her family advised her to seek help and she entered treatment with a counselor in college. Although therapy was "somewhat helpful," she recovered fully only after she and Jim were securely reunited and treatment was discontinued.

Based on this focused review of her history, which revealed themes of emotional isolation, an "absentee" father, fear of self-expression, and devaluation, the therapist hypothesized that Michelle's current difficulties—inability to express her needs to her husband and feelings of insecurity about her marriage—were linked to specific Early Maladaptive Schemas and fell in the Disconnection and Undesirability domains. According to the schema approach, disconnection themes revolve around the expectation that one's need for safe, stable, and secure relationships will not be met in a predictable way. Undesirability refers to the belief that one will not be desirable to others (see Figure 6.1).

To explore this hypothesis further, the therapist proceeded to the next step in the assessment process and asked Michelle to complete the SQ as homework. The SQ, consisting of 205 items, is used to assess the 16 underlying schemas listed in Figure 6.1. Patients are asked to rate each statement according to how accurately they feel it represents them. The therapist then reviews the responses in detail with the patient, asking for additional information or clarification during the process. Michelle scored highest on items tapping abandonment (the perceived instability or unreliability of those available for support and connection), defectiveness (the belief that one is fundamentally unlovable, defective, flawed, or invalid),

and subjugation (excessive surrendering of one's decisions and preferences to others, usually to avoid anger, retaliation, or abandonment) schemas. She strongly endorsed such items as: "I find myself clinging to people I'm close to because I'm afraid they'll leave me"; "No one I desire would want to stay close to me if he/she knew the real me"; and "I let other people have their way because I fear the consequences." She also endorsed a number of items dealing with emotional deprivation, but to a lesser extent. The SQ is a useful tool in hypothesis building. With this additional information, the therapist was able to identify four different schemas. This strengthened the hypothesis that part of Michelle's current problem was schema driven.

Up to this point the assessment is essentially historical and "rational." In the final component of the assessment, the therapist investigates and triggers schemas experientially in order to further test relevant assumptions, explore the schema origins, and find out how they may be related to the presenting problems. A clear indication that a schema has been triggered is the presence of a high degree of affect. As Beck et al. (1990) have noted: "The arousal of a strong feeling suggests not only that a core schema has been exposed, but also that the dysfunctional thinking is more accessible to modification" (p. 82). An additional rationale for triggering schemas is to have the patient experience directly both the content and the intensity of the schema.

In the following excerpt, the therapist helped Michelle identify and reexperience the origins of her abandonment schema:

T: Michelle, why don't you close your eyes now and see if you can get a visual image of anything that comes into your mind. Just tell me what you see.

M: Do I have to see it?

T: Yes, it's not thoughts but pictures that we want. It could be a picture of a person, of a place, anything at all; almost as if you were looking at a movie in your head.

M: What is the point of all this again?

T: Well the point is to try to discover feelings and themes, buttons if you like, that are getting pushed, but that you're not aware of right now, like, right now you told me you're feeling butterflies but you don't know why. We often find that when people close their eyes, they get pictures that tell them why they're feeling those butterflies, why they're nervous, so it's a way of sort of getting to deeper issues without directly talking about them, but rather through picturing them.

M: Well, nothing's coming.

T: Just continue to relax, because sometimes it takes a while and you have to let it happen. So don't worry, just keep your eyes closed and eventually something will come.

M: What if nothing comes?

T: Well, that's alright. If nothing comes we can always come back and try this again later.

M: I'm seeing something. I see my father leaving the house. He doesn't want to come in and be with me.

T: You're actually picturing him leaving the house?

M: Yeah, he's outside the house now leaving, and he knows I'm inside, he knows I want to be with him, but he just doesn't care to be with me. (*cries*)

T: OK, he's leaving the house. Where is he going?

M: I don't know, he just wants to get away from me.

T: And does he know that you want to see him?

M: Yes, he knows. But he makes believe as if I don't exist, that I'm not worth being with. That's the way he always made me feel.

This emotive strategy poignantly revealed Michelle's unhealthy childhood experiences with her father, as it epitomized her feelings of abandonment and defectiveness. The therapist then guided the imagery to assess whether there was a link between these early childhood experiences with her father and her current problems with her husband:

T: Now Michelle, please keep your eyes closed and see if you can get an image of Jim and tell me what you see.

M: Well, as you said that, what I saw Jim doing was just walking out the door and just slamming the door. He had his suitcase packed and with him, and he just walked out the door and there I was in the house all alone by myself.

T: Just like you were with your father, the same feeling that you had there?

M: Yeah, it feels exactly the same.

Based on these types of links, the therapist was able to conjecture that as a result of her maladaptive experiences with her father, she was now struggling with similar feelings in her relationship with her husband. By continuing to believe her marriage unstable and that she might be left alone once again, especially if she expressed her needs and feelings, she continued to reinforce her link with her past and her abandonment schema.

In the following session, the patient remembered through imagery that when she was 6 years old, she broke into tears in a supermarket when she couldn't find her father, thinking that he had left her. Taken together, the results of the different phases of the assessment corroborated one another, allowing the therapist to form a comprehensive conceptualization of the origins of the patient's schemas, how they interrelate, and how they contribute to her present problems. The therapist then shared this formulation with Michelle and asked her for feedback:

T: Why don't we begin by summarizing where we are right now in terms of understanding some of the schemas that we've been discussing and how they are affecting your life. The three we have identified through reviewing your early life history, Schema Questionnaire, imagery, and other work we did are abandonment, subjugation, and defectiveness.

Subjugation, you may recall, is the belief that you can't express what you want for fear of retaliation, which in your case means somebody getting angry at you and ultimately leaving you. That you can't ask for what you want without Jim, or your father, getting annoyed at you, withdrawing or actually leaving you.

Underneath your subjugation is the abandonment schema, the sense that people are going to leave you, that you can't count on them to stay. This is why you become so frightened and terrified, as a child with your father, and now in your life with Jim.

The explanation that you came up with to explain why you would be abandoned was that somehow you are defective: the sense that there is something bad about you, that you are worthless, that you could be discarded easily, that somehow, by asking for what you want, you're a nuisance or a bad person. This serves to explain, in your head, why Jim would want to leave you, why when you disagree you already see him as being out the door. And the way you've dealt with your fear of being abandoned up till now is through subjugating your needs.

Does this explanation feel as if we're on the right track? Does it sound right to you? Are these the three buttons or schemas that are being triggered by the situation with Jim?

Michelle agreed with the therapist's formulation, yet she continued to insist that, "If I ask for things he *will* leave me. He's happy to stay with me as long as I ask for nothing."

Change Component

In order to prepare Michelle for the change component of schema treatment, the therapist started educating her about the nature of early schemas and the process of schema change. Although Michelle had been given some explanation about the significance and search for schemas when she was asked to complete the SQ, the therapist now provided a more thorough description.

In addition to suggesting that she read a client handout about schemas, he now gave her a fuller description of how schemas originate, why they are such strong beliefs, and how they come to be supported by a lifetime of attitudes and behaviors. To further prepare her for the change phase, the therapist also advised her to expect a great deal of resistance on the part of her schemas, and that her fears of abandonment

and defectiveness would be triggered whenever she would attempt to express herself and overcome her subjugation schema.

The interventions, strategies, and techniques used during the treatment or change phase vary from patient to patient. The particular methods employed depend on the nature of the specific schemas involved and how they interrelate (Bricker, Young, & Flanagan, 1993). Nevertheless, we have selected four representative strategies—cognitive, experiential, interpersonal, and behavioral—to illustrate this segment of the treatment.

Though there is a tendency to select partners who retrigger underlying schemas as a way of maintaining them, patients with abandonment issues can and do overestimate the extent to which their partners are indeed abandoning. Consequently, the therapist began the change phase with a cognitive strategy: examining the evidence for Michelle's insecurity about her marriage and her husband's willingness to leave her should she divulge her needs to him.

T: Is it possible, based on some of these schemas that we talked about, some of the feelings of being defective or that people will leave you, that you have tended to exaggerate how little Jim is attracted to you?

M: That would be wonderful if it were true, but I don't think so.

T: Well, let's look. What could you point to as evidence that he is attached and committed to you?

M: He says he loves me. Often he's happy to see me, to be around me. . . . He compliments me at times when we go out so I know he's attracted to me. He buys me very nice gifts—rings, jewelry, pocketbooks—and he takes me out on weekends. He asks me where I want us to go on vacation. I guess he does think of me.

T: Is there any evidence about his leaving you? Has he ever left you or threatened to leave you?

M: When we dated he left several times.

T: And since you've been married?

M: No, not since we've been married. He's never left.

T: Did he ever say anything about wanting to leave?

M: No.

Because the therapeutic effects of these cognitive interventions tend to dissipate over time when patients' beliefs are schema driven, they have to be repeated again and again until the patient can challenge the schema more consistently. A follow-up cognitive technique that we have found extremely effective is the use of flashcards. A flashcard is a simple index card containing a summary of the schema and a cognitive antidote or counter. The card that Michelle was instructed to read regularly was constructed, with her collaboration, so as to combat her schemas in a way that directly addressed her presenting problems as they related to subjugation, defectiveness, and abandonment:

Right now I believe that I must give up on the idea of a baby or else Jim will certainly leave me. I feel this way, though, because of my Subjugation, Abandonment, and Defectiveness schemas. I developed these beliefs as a result of my father's lack of attention, and his frustration with me whenever I wanted to be with him. The reality is that Jim has never threatened to leave me since we were married, and even when we were dating, he came back every time he actually left me.

I have much evidence that Jim is very attached to me, loves me, and would not leave. The evidence is that he says he loves me; he's stayed with me for ten years; he buys me expensive gifts; takes me out on weekends; never wants to take separate vacations; worries about me if I go away; and his family approves of me. The one time that I really insisted on what I wanted regarding moving to the suburbs, he put up a fight but gave in and did not leave me. Therefore I can tell Jim what I want and trust that he probably will not leave me.

The first part of this cognitive strategy revealed how Michelle misperceived her husband. She underestimated Jim's commitment and overestimated his willingness to leave her. She recognized the discrepancy between her feelings and expectations and her actual experiences with Jim; a review of the facts showed him to be responsive to her when she really asked for something. And even when he disagreed with her, he did not voice or demonstrate any inclination to leave her. The therapist explained to Michelle that by not expressing herself and by continuing to suppress her needs, she actually maintained and reinforced her schemas. The second part of the strategy, involving the use of a flashcard, provided her with an effective tool that she could use to fight her schemas outside sessions.

It is relevant to note here that had Jim turned out to be truly uncaring and prone to abandoning Michelle, the therapist then would have pursued a different therapeutic route, including couples therapy or possibly leaving the marriage.

The therapist then went on to apply experiential exercises to help Michelle loosen her schemas still further. This entailed, in part, getting into a dialogue with her father and expressing her anger at him for making her feel abandoned and defective. She also needed to learn to "feel" that her father's neglect of her was not her fault:

T: Can you now get an image of your father walking away from you and you asking him to come back to spend some time with you?

M: Daddy, daddy, daddy, I want you to come back and play with me.

T: What does he say?

M: He pretends he doesn't hear me and continues to walk away.

T: And now see if you can say out loud what he's thinking.

M: (*As father*) "There she goes whining again, wanting me to be with her. She just expects too much. There must be something wrong with her to be so demanding."

T: And what do you want to tell your father, as an adult, now that you've overheard his thoughts?

M: (*To father*) "I'm very angry at you, how could you feel that way about me?"

T: Good, continue to tell him how you feel right now and what you think.

M: OK. (*to father*) "I'm your daughter. I'm not a pest. I just want to be with you because I love you and I feel good being next to you. I'm your daughter, you're supposed to love me and want to be with me. You're a bad father for not feeling the same way."

The dialogue with her father allowed Michelle to ventilate her feelings toward her father in a constructive fashion, and thus feel empowered to assert her needs and rights.

Throughout the schema-focused phase of treatment, close attention is paid to schemas that are activated between patient and therapist within the sessions. This provides patients with additional knowledge about how they play out their schemas even in situations that are neutral or supportive. In the following vignette, the therapist helped Michelle see how her defectiveness schema became activated during a session in which he explained the concept of schema maintenance:

T: The upsetting thing about schemas is that they perpetuate themselves even though they make the person unhappy. It's like it's more comfortable to stay with a belief that's familiar even if it's painful than to change to a belief that's different, even though it would make the person happier.

M: I must be very stupid for doing that to myself, then. It just makes me feel so terrible to think that I would be doing this to myself.

T: Terrible meaning like you're blaming yourself, or terrible like it's sad that you're doing this?

M: Both. And that now you, too, see my stupidity.

T: Well, see if you could try to step out of yourself for a second and be more objective. If every patient who comes in to see me has schemas and they all repeat patterns over and over again like you're doing, do you think I view them as stupid for having these problems?

M: No, I'm sure you don't. But I just feel so convinced that that's how you see me.

T: Well, I'm wondering then if you're not using this defectiveness schema against yourself as proof that there is something wrong with you again. Is that what you are doing right now?

M: Yeah, yeah.

T: So here is another example of how here in the therapy, and in other situations, you can take what is really an expression of concern and empathy for what you're going through and interpret it as a put-down, or that somehow you are inadequate. And maybe we can keep trying to watch for situations here in the therapy and outside where you feel that you're stupid or that someone's thinking you're stupid and keep getting yourself to question it and to say, wait, maybe this is my schema operating, maybe that's not really what Arthur means or that's not really what Jim means.

As this exchange indicates, the therapy relationship itself can be a useful vehicle for identifying, discussing, and subsequently modifying schemas. By paying close attention to Michelle's moods, responses, and behaviors *in vivo*, the therapist demonstrated to her additional and very convincing instances of how she continued to misinterpret some of her experiences based on her schemas.

The therapist then targeted specific schemas for change within the therapeutic relationship. For Michelle, this included not subjugating herself, not even to the directions of her therapist. Otherwise, going along with the therapist's formulations, homework assignments, and suggestions when she genuinely opposed them could easily have prolonged the pattern of her schema maintenance or even sabotaged her progress. In order to prevent this, the therapist routinely asked her for feedback, as a way of ensuring that she was not merely "yessing" him to avoid triggering her schemas. An essential part of Michelle's therapy focused on her becoming increasingly aware of her own needs and expressing them, initially to her therapist and later on to her husband.

The next and final step to be illustrated is the changing of schema-driven behaviors. This entails getting patients to modify long-term behavior patterns that have been used to reinforce the schema for the better part of a lifetime. To act against the dictates of these beliefs is no doubt the hardest and most difficult part of the therapeutic process. To achieve success, the therapist needs to push patients to act contrary to years of dysfunctional patterns of behavior. For Michelle this meant expressing her needs to her husband and not feeling defective for it, or feeling that she would be abandoned as a result. Keeping in mind her subjugation schema, the therapist asked Michelle to set her own agenda:

T: Is there something that you would like to do with or around Jim that you're avoiding, that you're fearful of pursuing?

M: I'm sure there are many things but what I would really like is to make love more frequently. But I'm scared of asking him, I'm afraid of approaching him.

T: Can you think of a way that you could present it to him so that you'd be more likely to get a positive or at least a neutral answer so that you wouldn't buy into your schemas the way you used to?

M: Yes, I could snuggle up to him and kiss him and not actually ask him for it outright, but indicate to him in a way that I do want to make love with him, that I want to be close. So I would try kissing him, stroking him, seducing him, you know.

T: Good. Then how would you feel about making that your homework assignment, to snuggle up to him and to initiate love making?

M: Wonderful. I think that's the best homework assignment you've given me.

After the patient followed up on her homework and reported success, she was subsequently encouraged, through more flashcards and other techniques, to speak directly to her husband not only about her sexual needs but also about her desire to have a baby and to raise a family. She soon was sufficiently improved, and felt confident enough to stop treatment. At the present time, she has been out of treatment for over 3 years. Through a patient she recently referred to us, we heard that Michelle had a

baby, that her marriage seems much happier, and that she has not had any relapses of depression.

CONCLUSION

There is mounting evidence that cognitive therapy is an effective, short-term treatment for adult outpatients with nonbipolar depressions. Cognitive therapy teaches patients to elicit their automatic thoughts and early maladaptive schemas. These cognitions are then "put to the test" by examining evidence, setting up *in vivo* experiments, weighing advantages and disadvantages, trying graded tasks, and employing other intervention strategies. Through this process, patients begin to view themselves and their problems more realistically, feel better, change their maladaptive behavioral patterns, and take steps to solve real- life difficulties. These changes take place as a direct result of carefully planned, self-help assignments at home.

Throughout the treatment, cognitive therapists maintain a collaborative alliance with their patients. They are very active in structuring the session, yet go to considerable lengths to help patients reach conclusions on their own. The therapist serves as a guide, helping the patient maneuver through a labyrinth of dysfunctional cognitions, including early maladaptive schemas, that need to be reevaluated.

NOTES

1. In this chapter, diagnoses are generally based on the system approved as final by the DSM-IV Mood Disorders Work Group and the Task Force on DSM-IV (American Psychiatric Association [APA], 1993). However, diagnoses for patients described in the case materials are based on the revised third edition of the *Diagnostic and Statistical Manual of Mental Disorders* (APA, 1987), the system in effect at the time of assessment.

2. At the time Irene was in treatment, the schema-focused phase of treatment had not yet been fully developed. She terminated once her symptoms were relieved, as many patients do. We are therefore using a different case, that of Michelle, to illustrate the second phase of therapy.

REFERENCES

American Psychiatric Association. (1987). *Diagnostic and statistical manual of mental disorders* (3rd ed., rev.). Washington, DC: Author.

American Psychiatric Association. (1993). *DSM-IV draft criteria as of 3/1/93*. Washington, DC: Author.

Barber, J. P., & DeRubeis, R. J. (1989). On second thought: Where the action is in cognitive therapy for depression. *Cognitive Therapy and Research, 13*(5), 441–457.

Beck, A. T. (1967). *Depression: Causes and treatment*. Philadelphia: University of Pennsylvania Press.

Beck, A. T. (1988). *Love is never enough*. New York: Harper & Row.

Beck, A. T., Freeman, A., & Associates. (1990). *Cognitive therapy of personality disorders*. New York: Guilford Press.

Beck, A. T., Rush, A. J., Shaw, B. F., & Emery, G. (1979). *Cognitive therapy of depression*. New York: Guilford Press.

Bergin, A. E., & Lambert, M. J. (1978). The evaluation of therapeutic outcomes. In S. L. Garfield & A. E. Bergin (Eds.), *Handbook of psychotherapy and behavior change: An empirical analysis* (2nd ed.) (pp. 139–190). New York: Wiley.

Beutler, L. E., Scogin, F., Kirkish, P., Schretlen, D., Corbishley, A., Hamblin, D., Meredith, K., Potter, R., Bamford, C. R., & Levenson, A. I. (1987). Group cognitive therapy and Alprazolam in the treatment of depression in older adults. *Journal of Consulting and Clinical Psychology, 55*(4), 550–556.

Blackburn, I., & Bishop, S. (1979, July). *A comparison of cognitive therapy, pharmacotherapy, and their combination in depressed outpatients*. Paper presented at the annual meeting of the Society for Psychotherapy Research, Oxford, England.

Blackburn, I., & Bishop, S. (1980, July). *Pharmacotherapy and cognitive therapy in the treatment of depression: Competitors or allies?* Paper presented at First World Congress on Behavior Therapy, Jerusalem, Israel.

Bricker, D., Young, J. E., & Flanagan, C. (1993). Schema-focused cognitive therapy: A comprehensive framework for characterological problems. In K. T. Kuehlwein & H. Rosen (Eds.), *Cognitive therapies in action: Evolving innovative practice* (pp. 88–125). San Francisco: Jossey-Bass.

DeRubeis, R. J., & Feeley, M. (1990). Determinants of change in cognitive therapy for depression. *Cognitive Therapy and Research, 14*(5), 469–482.

DeRubeis, R. J., Hollon, S. D., Grove, W. M., Evans, M. D., Garvey, M. J., & Tuason, V. B. (1990). How does cognitive therapy work? Cognitive change and symptom change in cognitive therapy and pharmacotherapy for depression. *Journal of Consulting and Clinical Psychology, 58*(6), 862– 869.

Dobson, K. S. (1989). A meta-analysis of the efficacy of cognitive therapy for depression. *Journal of Consulting and Clinical Psychology, 57*(3), 414–419.

Gallagher-Thompson, D., Hanley-Peterson, P., & Thompson, L. W. (1990). Maintenance of gains versus relapse following brief psychotherapy for depression. *Journal of Consulting and Clinical Psychology, 58*(3), 371–374.

Hollon, S. D., & Beck, A. T. (1978). Psychotherapy and drug therapy: Comparison and combinations. In S. L. Garfield & A. E. Bergin (Eds.), *Handbook of psychotherapy and behavior change: An empirical analysis* (2nd ed.) (pp. 437–490). New York: Wiley.

Hollon, S. D., Shelton, R. C., & Loosen, P. T. (1991). Cognitive therapy and pharmacotherapy for depression. *Journal of Consulting and Clinical Psychology, 59*(1), 88–99.

Ingram, R. E., & Holle, C. (1992). Cognitive science of depression. In D. J. Stein & J. E. Young (Eds.), *Cognitive science and clinical disorders* (pp. 187–209). San Diego: Academic Press.

Jarrett, R. B., & Nelson, R. O. (1987). Mechanisms of change in cognitive therapy of depression. *Behavior Therapy, 18*, 227–241.

Lazarus, A. A., & Lazarus, C. N. (1991). *Multimodal Life History Inventory* (2nd ed.). Champaign, IL: Research Press.

McDermott, S. P., & Wright, F. D. (1992). Cognitive therapy: Long-term outlook for a short-term psychotherapy. In J. S. Rutan (Ed.), *Psychotherapy for the 1990s* (pp. 61–99). New York: Guilford Press.

McLean, P. D., & Hakstian, A. R. (1979). Clinical depression: Comparative efficacy of outpatient treatments. *Journal of Consulting and Clinical Psychology, 47*, 818–836.

O'Leary, K. D., & Beach, S. R. H. (1990). Marital therapy: A viable treatment for depression and marital discord. *American Journal of Psychiatry, 147*(2), 183–186.

Persons, J. B., Burns, D. D., & Perloff, J. M. (1988). Predictors of dropout and outcome in cognitive therapy for depression in a private practice setting. *Cognitive Therapy and Research, 12*(6), 557–575.

Rehm, L. P. (1990). Cognitive and behavioral theories. In Wolman, B. B., & Stricker, G. (Eds.), *Depressive disorders: Facts, theories, and treatment methods* (pp. 64–91). New York: Wiley.

Rush, A. J., Beck, A. T., Kovacs, M., & Hollon, S. (1977). Comparative efficacy of cognitive therapy and imipramine in the treatment of depressed outpatients. *Cognitive Therapy and Research, 1*, 17–37.

Shea, M. T., Pilkonis, P. A., Beckham, E., Collins, J. F., Elkin, I., Sotsky, S. M., & Docherty, J. P. (1990). Personality disorders and treatment outcome in the NIMH treatment of depression collaborative research program. *American Journal of Psychiatry, 147*(6), 711–718.

Stein, D. J., & Young, J. E. (1992). Schema approach to personality disorders. In D. J. Stein & J. E. Young (Eds.), *Cognitive science and clinical disorders* (pp. 271–288). San Diego: Academic Press.

Sullivan, M. J. L., & Conway, M. (1991). Dysphoria and valence of attributions for others' behavior. *Cognitive Therapy and Research, 15*(4), 273–282.

Truax, C. B., & Mitchell, K. M. (1971). Research on certain therapist interpersonal skills in relation to process and outcome. In A. E. Bergin & S. L. Garfield (Eds.), *Handbook of psychotherapy and behavior change: An empirical analysis* (pp. 299–344). New York: Wiley.

Weissman, A., & Beck, A. T. (1978). *Development and validation of the Dysfunctional Attitude Scale*. Paper presented at the annual meeting of the American Association of Behavior Therapists, Chicago. (Available from Center for Cognitive Therapy, Room 602, 133 South 36th St., Philadelphia, PA 19104)

Whisman, M. A., Miller, I. W., Norman, W. H., & Keitner, G. I. (1991). Cognitive therapy with depressed inpatients: Specific effects on dysfunctional cognitions. *Journal of Consulting and Clinical Psychology, 59*(2), 282–288.

Wierzbicki, M., & Bartlett, T. S. (1987). The efficacy of group and individual cognitive therapy for mild depression. *Cognitive Therapy and Research, 11*(3), 337–342.

Young, J. E. (1982). *Loneliness: A sourcebook of current theory, research, and therapy* (pp. 388–389). New York: Wiley.

Young, J. E. (1990). *Cognitive therapy for personality disorders: A schema-focused approach.* Sarasota, FL: Professional Resource Exchange.

Young, J. E., & Klosko, J. S. (1993). *Reinventing your life: How to break free of negative life patterns.* New York: Dutton.

Chapter 7

EATING DISORDERS

G. Terence Wilson
Rutgers University

Kathleen M. Pike
Columbia University

The fourth edition of the *Diagnostic and Statistical Manual of Mental Disorders* (DSM-IV; American Psychiatric Association [APA], in press) will more clearly define and separate anorexia nervosa and bulimia nervosa and describe for the first time a new eating disorder termed *binge eating disorder*. This chapter, written by authors involved in the creation of the DSM-IV eating disorder categories and also among the originators of the most successful treatment yet devised for these disorders, describes their state-of-the-art treatment for bulimia nervosa. Although concentrating on bulimia nervosa, the disorder we know the most about, the authors point out that the treatment protocol has wide applicability to anorexia nervosa and binge eating disorder. In what may be a surprising departure to some readers, the authors note that the central problem requiring intervention is not necessarily bingeing or purging, but rather the culturally driven abnormal attitudes and beliefs regarding shape and weight. This chapter contains one of the most detailed examples of cognitive therapy applied to eating disorders yet encountered. It should be extraordinarily useful to clinicians working with these difficult problems.—D. H. B.

INTRODUCTION

Classification and Diagnosis

The two most well-established eating disorders are anorexia nervosa and bulimia nervosa. Three features define anorexia nervosa. The first is the presence of an abnormally low body weight of 15% below that expected. The second, in females, in whom the disorder predominantly occurs, is amenorrhea (i.e., the absence of three consecutive menstrual cycles). The third is disturbance in the way body weight or shape is experienced, such as the denial of the seriousness of abnormally low weight or the undue influence of body weight and shape on self-evaluation (DaCosta & Halmi, 1992). Two subtypes of anorexia nervosa are distinguished in DSM-IV: (1) restrictors, or individuals who neither binge nor purge; and (2) those who regularly engage in either binge eating or purging (APA, 1993).* The prevalence in young women is roughly 0.5% to 1%.

Bulimia nervosa is also characterized by three major clinical features: (1) binge eating (i.e., the uncontrolled consumption of large amounts of food); (2) the regular re-

---

*The DSM-IV criteria cited in this chapter are those that were approved as final by the DSM-IV Eating Disorders Work Group and the Task Force on DSM-IV (APA, 1993). These criteria may be subject to minor editorial revisions before the publication of DSM-IV.

sort to methods designed to influence weight and shape, such as purging (self-induced vomiting or laxative abuse), fasting, or vigorous exercise; and (3) self-evaluation, which is unduly influenced by body shape and weight. The diagnostic criteria for bulimia nervosa in DSM-IV are somewhat different from those in the revised third edition of the *Diagnostic and Statistical Manual of Mental Disorders* (DSM-III-R; APA, 1987) and are listed in Table 7.1. In contrast to DSM-III-R, the diagnosis of bulimia nervosa excludes patients who currently meet diagnostic criteria for anorexia nervosa. Most patients with bulimia nervosa are within the normal weight range. An important reason for allowing the diagnosis of

anorexia nervosa to prevail over that of bulimia nervosa is the prognostic significance of the former. There is an urgent need for weight gain in these patients, whose dangerously low weight can be life threatening. Furthermore, clinical experience has shown that patients with anorexia nervosa pose much greater problems for clinical management because they actively resist attempts to change their eating behavior and weight. They typically fare far more poorly in treatment than do patients with bulimia nervosa. The prevalence of bulimia nervosa among young women is estimated to be roughly 1% to 3%, but it rarely occurs in males (Fairburn & Beglin, 1990; Hsu, 1990). This eating disorder is frequently associated with other forms of psychopathology (e.g., major depression, anxiety disorders, and substance abuse) both in patients themselves and in their family members (Kassett et al., 1989; Laessle et al., 1989; Schwalberg, Barlow, Alger, & Howard, 1992; Wilson, 1993d).

A third category of eating disorder is included in DSM-IV as "eating disorders not otherwise specified" (EDNOS). This imprecise category embraces individuals who have an eating disorder of clinical severity but do not meet formal diagnostic criteria for either anorexia nervosa or bulimia nervosa. For example, there are individuals with all of the features of bulimia nervosa but the frequency of binge eating is too low to meet diagnostic criteria. Although rarely the focus of research, patients in this category are well-known to clinical practitioners who treat the full range of eating disorders. An example of the EDNOS category, and one that has attracted intense recent interest, is identified in DSM-IV as "binge eating disorder" (BED). Patients with this diagnosis regularly engage in binge eating but do not show either the extreme compensatory behavior such as purging, which is designed to influence body weight and or shape, or the attitudinal disturbance required for the diagnosis of bulimia nervosa (Spitzer et al., 1992).

The present chapter focuses on the cognitive-behavioral treatment (CBT) of patients with bulimia nervosa, the most intensively researched of all the eating disorders. The therapeutic strategies described here are also relevant to the other disorders, however. Patients with anorexia nervosa, especially those who binge or purge, can be

TABLE 7.1. Proposed DSM-IV Diagnostic Criteria for Bulimia Nervosa

Bulimia Nervosa

A. Recurrent episodes of binge eating. An episode of binge eating is characterized by both of the following:
   (1) eating in a discrete period of time (e.g., within any two hour period), an amount of food that is definitely larger than most people would eat in a similar period of time in similar circumstances; and,
   (2) a sense of lack of control over eating during the episode (e.g., a feeling that one cannot stop eating or control what or how much one is eating).

B. Recurrent inappropriate compensatory behavior in order to prevent weight gain, such as: self-induced vomiting, misuse of laxatives, diuretics or other medications; fasting; or excessive exercise.

C. The binge eating and inappropriate compensatory behaviors both occur, on average, at least twice a week for three months.

D. Self-evaluation is unduly influenced by body shape and weight.

E. The disturbance does not occur exclusively during episodes of Anorexia Nervosa.

Specify type:
Purging type: The person regularly engages in self-induced vomiting or the misuse of laxatives or diuretics.
Nonpurging type: The person uses other inappropriate compensatory behaviors, such as fasting or excessive exercise, but does not regularly engage in self-induced vomiting or the misuse of laxatives or diuretics.

Note: From APA, 1993. Copyright 1993 by the American Psychiatric Association. Reprinted by permission.

treated with CBT, although the clinical literature on these applications is sparse (Garner, 1993; Garner & Bemis, 1985). Obese patients with binge eating or BED are increasingly being treated with an adaptation of CBT (Marcus, 1993; Telch, Agras, Rossiter, Wilfley, & Kenardy, 1990; Wilfley et al., 1993; see Brownell & O'Neil, Chapter 8, this volume).

Review of Treatments

A wide range of psychological therapies have been used to treat patients with binge eating and bulimia nervosa, including CBT, behavior therapy, psychodynamic therapy, family therapy, experiential therapy, and the 12-Step approach based on an addiction model of the disorder (Fairburn & Wilson, 1993; Garner & Garfinkel, 1985). In addition, a variety of pharmacological treatments have been used, including antidepressants, anticonvulsants, and opiate antagonists (Mitchell & de Zwaan, 1993).

Pharmacological Treatment

The two most thoroughly studied and best documented treatments have been antidepressant medication on the one hand and CBT on the other. Several controlled studies have shown that different classes of antidepressant drugs, including tricyclics (e.g., imipramine and desipramine), monoamine oxidase inhibitors (e.g., phenelzine), and serotonin uptake blockers (e.g., fluoxetine), are more effective than a pill placebo in reducing binge eating and purging at the end of treatment. For example, in their review of eight studies, Craighead and Agras (1991) reported a mean reduction in the rate of purging of 82% (range = 64% to 91%), with an average remission rate of 45%. Interpretation of box-score statistics of this sort must be done cautiously, however. These studies varied greatly in methodological quality. Also, this review did not include the findings from the largest study of tricyclic antidepressant drug (desipramine) treatment (Walsh, Hadigan, Devlin, Gladis, & Roose, 1991). In this double-blind, placebo-controlled study of 80 patients, the mean reduction was 47% in binge eating, with a remission rate of only 12.5%. The results with fluoxetine are roughly comparable,

with an average decrease in frequency of binge eating of 65% and a 27% remission rate (Walsh, 1991).

The maintenance of drug-induced treatment effects has been largely ignored. What data exist are discouraging. Most patients relapse rapidly when antidepressant medication is withdrawn, and even those who continue on active medication during post-treatment maintenance phases relapse or drop out (Pyle et al., 1990; Walsh et al., 1991). The absence of evidence of longer-term effects, taken in conjunction with a relatively high dropout rate (Craighead & Agras, 1991) and a general reluctance on the part of patients to accept medication as the sole form of treatment (Leitenberg et al., 1992), underscores the importance of effective psychological treatment for this disorder.

Cognitive-Behavioral Treatment

The best controlled studies of CBT show a mean percentage reduction in binge eating ranging from 93% to 73%; the comparable figures for purging range from 94% to 77%. Mean remission rates for binge eating range from 51% to 71%, and for purging from 36% to 56% (Agras, Schneider, Arnow, Raeburn, & Telch, 1989; Agras et al., 1992; Fairburn et al., 1991; Garner et al., 1991; Mitchell, Pyle, Eckert, Hatsukami, Pomeroy, & Zimmerman, 1990). Aside from clinically significant reductions in binge eating and purging, studies have consistently shown that dietary restraint is reduced (Fairburn et al., 1991; Garner et al., 1993; Wilson, Eldredge, Smith, & Niles, 1991), with an increase in the amount of food eaten between bulimic episodes (Rossiter, Agras, Losch, & Telch, 1988). Attitudes to shape and weight, a key psychopathological feature and one that is central to the cognitive view on the disorder, also improve (Fairburn et al., 1991; Garner et al., 1993; Wilson et al., 1991).

As a whole, studies of CBT have shown reasonably good maintenance of change at both 6-month and 1-year follow-ups. The most impressive findings are those from the most rigorously conducted follow-up evaluations by Fairburn and his colleagues at Oxford (Fairburn, Jones, Peveler, Hope, & O'Connor, 1993). At 1 year, both binge eating and purging had declined by over 90%. Thirty-six percent of patients had ceased all binge eating and purging.

Another reliable finding is the broad effect that CBT has on associated psychopathology. Most studies have shown striking improvements in depression, self-esteem, social functioning, and measures of personality disorder (e.g., Fairburn, Kirk, O'Connor, & Cooper, 1986; Fairburn, Peveler, Jones, Hope, & Doll, in press; Garner et al., 1993).

Studies of bulimia nervosa have shown that CBT is consistently superior to wait-list control groups (Fairburn, Agras, & Wilson, 1992). CBT has been shown to be more effective than antidepressant drug treatment and alternative psychological interventions (Fairburn et al., 1992; Wilson, 1993a). The latter include supportive psychotherapy (Kirkley, Schneider, Agras, & Bachman, 1985) and supportive–expressive psychotherapy (Garner et al., 1993). Although superior to interpersonal psychotherapy (IPT) in the short term (Fairburn et al., 1991), CBT and IPT appear to be equally effective in the long term (Fairburn, Jones, et al., 1993). The combination of antidepressant drug treatment with CBT appears to be no more effective than CBT alone on most measures (Agras et al., 1992; Leitenberg et al., 1992; Mitchell et al., 1990).

How CBT works is unclear. It is a multifaceted treatment approach comprising both cognitive and behavioral procedures that are tailored to the individual patient's needs. It is therefore possible that it helps different patients through different mechanisms. Possible mechanisms of action are discussed elsewhere (Wilson & Fairburn, 1993). It does appear, however, that CBT has specific therapeutic effects rather than operating through so-called nonspecific effects common to all credible psychological treatments. First, CBT has been shown to be significantly more effective than some alternative treatments that would have had comparable nonspecific effect. Second, the therapeutic effects of CBT show a different time course from alternative treatments. For example, in the comparative study by Fairburn et al. (1991), CBT produced greater changes than IPT at posttreatment on most outcome measures even though IPT eventually matched these effects by the 1-year follow-up. This discriminative pattern of results is consistent with Hollon, DeRubeis, and Evans's (1987) distinction between causal specificity and consequential nonspecificity, namely, that separate mediating mechanisms may operate in different treatments even if they produce the same ultimate outcome.

A COGNITIVE-BEHAVIORAL MODEL

The etiology of bulimia nervosa and the other eating disorders remains unclear. Nevertheless, there is agreement on some of the important elements that are responsible for the development and maintenance of bulimia nervosa. Perhaps the most striking feature of both bulimia nervosa and anorexia nervosa is that they occur almost exclusively in women. Furthermore, bulimia nervosa was largely unknown prior to the late 1970s, strongly indicating the role of current cultural context in its genesis.

Psychosocial Context

The current cultural milieu defines the ideal female body shape as slim and lithe, and women experience considerable pressure to conform to this physical ideal (Striegel-Moore, Silberstein, & Rodin, 1986). As a result, the majority of young women in the United States diet to influence body weight and shape. It is no coincidence that bulimia nervosa is most common among that segment of the population—predominantly white women from middle and upper-middle socioeconomic class—who diet most to meet cultural expectations. There is an overall correlation between cultural pressure to be thin and prevalence of eating disorders, both across and within different ethnic groups (Hsu, 1990).

Dieting

Clinical experience and epidemiological data strongly suggest that dieting is closely linked to the onset of bulimia nervosa (Hsu, 1990; Polivy & Herman, 1993). The vast majority of patients with bulimia nervosa report the occurrence of binge eating following a severe diet. Still more persuasive, a prospective study of 1,010 high school girls in London showed that dieters were significantly more likely than nondieters to develop an eating disorder 1 year later (Patton, Johnson-Sabine, Wood, Mann, & Wakeling, 1990). Although the precise relationship between dieting and the onset of bulimia nervosa remains to be determined, dieting can have a variety of biological, cognitive, and affective consequences that predispose to binge eating (for further details, see Booth, Lewis, & Blair, 1990; Polivy & Herman, 1993; Wilson, 1993b). The occurrence of binge eating is soon followed by extreme weight-control behaviors, such as purging, which are designed to compensate for what the person perceives to be excessive food intake.

CBT was designed to modify these extreme attitudes about body weight and shape and the unhealthy dieting they drive. Fairburn (1985) described what he termed the cognitive model of bulimia nervosa as follows:

> [T]he extreme dieting, vomiting, and laxative abuse, the preoccupation with food and eating, the sensitivity to changes in shape and weight, and the frequent weighing or total avoidance of weighing are all comprehensible, once it has been appreciated that these patients believe that their shape and weight are of fundamental importance and that both must be kept under strict control. Even the apparently paradoxical binge eating can be understood in cognitive terms, since it seems that it may represent a secondary response to extreme dietary restraint. . . . Thus, rather than being simply symptomatic of bulimia, these beliefs and values appear to be of primary importance in the maintenance of the condition. (pp. 160–191)

It follows from this model that modification of abnormal attitudes about the personal significance of body shape and weight and replacement of dysfunctional dietary restraint with more normal eating patterns should be a central focus of treatment. As we illustrate in the remainder of this chapter, this has been the mainstay of CBT for bulimia nervosa.

Etiology of Bulimia Nervosa

Despite the diverse evidence indicting dieting in the development and maintenance of binge eating, it may not be a necessary causal condition (Blundell, 1990) and is not a sufficient one (Wilson, 1993b). On the one hand, binge eating can develop in the absence of dieting. Although relatively rare, clinicians are familiar with cases of bulimia nervosa in which dieting did not appear to precede the development of binge eating (Striegel-Moore, 1993). This pattern is far more common in obese bingers (Marcus, 1993; Wilson, Nonas, & Rosenblum, 1993). On the other hand, dieting alone does not cause bulimia nervosa. Whereas a majority of young women in the United States diet, only a small minority develop an eating disorder. Some other factor or set of factors must interact with diet-induced mechanisms to cause the eating disorder. The possibilities range from genetic predisposition (Kendler et al., 1991) through personality and individual psychopathology (Hsu, 1990) to familial influences (Attie & Brooks-Gunn, 1989; Humphrey, 1987, 1988; Pike & Rodin, 1991).

Recognition of the role of factors other than dieting in the etiology and maintenance of bulimia nervosa has been implicit in the CBT programs that have derived from Fairburn's (1985) cognitive model. The focus on modifying abnormal attitudes and dietary restraint has been embedded in a more general cognitive-behavioral framework which, among other features discussed below, includes an emphasis on developing cognitive and behavioral skills for coping with intra- and interpersonal triggers for binge eating and purging, enhancing self-control skills for regulating eating behavior, and training in relapse-prevention strategies. This amalgam of diverse cognitive and behavioral interventions arguably addresses aspects of psychopathology, such as affective instability, that are commonly believed to interact with dieting in causing the eating disorder.

CONTEXT OF THERAPY

Setting

CBT for bulimia nervosa is typically conducted on an outpatient basis. Individual treatment is probably the most common clinical practice, although several studies have administered CBT in a group setting.

The relative effectiveness of individual versus group treatment has never been evaluated, and at present there are no empirical grounds for favoring one or the other approach. Treatment studies that have used group CBT have included relatively homogeneous samples of patients meeting formal diagnostic criteria for bulimia nervosa. More traditional group psychotherapy for more heterogeneous groups, which include patients with different eating disorders, is not uncommon in clinical practice. In our clinical experience, however, the often marked differences between patients with anorexia nervosa and bulimia nervosa in clinical management and response to treatment outweigh the commonalities and create more problems than therapeutic opportunities in such mixed groups. Group CBT is more appropriately conducted with diagnostically homogeneous patients.

There are few reasons to hospitalize patients with bulimia nervosa. One exception is if the patient is too depressed to be treated as an outpatient, or if there is a risk of suicide. A second exception is the presence of a compelling medical problem, such as severe electrolyte disturbance. Such complications are relatively rare in normal-weight patients with bulimia nervosa, and can be managed as part of outpatient treatment. It is not unusual even for hospital-based treatment programs to forgo routine screening for electrolyte abnormalities. However, a more conservative view, and our recommendation, favors routine screening. The third reason to hospitalize a patient is if intensive outpatient treatment fails. A tightly supervised hospital setting can be useful in directly modifying refractory eating habits.

Patient Variables

Most patients with bulimia nervosa and anorexia nervosa are women, as we have noted earlier. In patients with obese binge eating or BED, women also appear to be in the majority. In contrast to bulimia nervosa and anorexia nervosa, however, there is a much higher proportion of men (Spitzer et al., 1992). Relatively little is known about the small number of male patients with bulimia nervosa. There appears to be a higher than expected prevalence of homosexuality among men with bulimia nervosa which has been attributed to greater disturbances in psychosexual development than in their female counterparts (Fichter & Hoffman, 1990). Nevertheless, our clinical experience is consistent with the sparse literature on this subject in indicating that male and female patients with bulimia nervosa are more alike than dissimilar. They show the same core eating disorder psychopathology and response to treatment (Andersen, 1990).

Most patients with bulimia nervosa seek treatment in late adolescence or early adulthood (Hsu, 1990). Patients with anorexia nervosa are often younger, whereas those with BED are typically older. The average age of BED patients in the different samples of Spitzer et al.'s (1992) field trial was in the 40s.

Clinical cases of anorexia nervosa and bulimia nervosa are characterized by a wide range of co-occurring psychiatric disorders. Depression and anxiety disorders are particularly prevalent in patients with these eating disorders (Laessle et al., 1991), and high rates of psychoactive substance abuse and personality disorders have also been reported (Johnson, Tobin, & Enright, 1989; Wilson, 1993d). Similarly, some studies have revealed high rates of depression and substance abuse in the first-degree family members of patients with anorexia and bulimia nervosa (Kassett et al., 1989).

These findings have led some investigators to suggest that underlying both eating disorders and depression is a common biological cause. Despite the co-occurrence of depression and eating disorder, however, the consensus is that neither anorexia nor bulimia nervosa is a form of an underlying depressive disorder. For example, therapy outcome studies with bulimic patients consistently show that co-occurring psychiatric disorders typically disappear following successful treatment of the eating disorder, suggesting that they are secondary consequences of the eating disorder. Another popular view is that eating disorders are expressions of an underlying addictive disorder. Although high rates of substance abuse have been reported in patients with eating disorders, and in their family members, there is as yet no convincing evidence of any significant co-occurrence between these problems in unselected community sample. It could be that patients with eating disorders who seek treatment are those with more than one type of disorder. Moreover, the rates of co-occurring depression and anxiety disorders in patients with bulimia nervosa are much higher than psychoactive substance abuse disorder. It must be emphasized that bulimia nervosa and anorexia nervosa are primary psychiatric disorders in their own right and cannot be reduced to an expression of some other underlying disorder.

The comorbidity of psychoactive substance abuse and other forms of "impulsivity" in patients with bulimia nervosa varies widely across different treatment centers. It is a serious mistake to stereotype "the bulimic patient" as someone who lies, impulsively abuses psychoactive substances, steals, and engages in promiscuous sexual behavior. Although a small minority of patients might fit this bill, the majority do not. Furthermore, bulimia nervosa occurs in patients with different personalities. There is no such entity as the "bulimic personality." Perpetuating misleading stereotypes of this sort does a great disservice to the patients who struggle with this disorder.

Normal-weight bulimia nervosa seldom causes major physical complications. Purging can produce an electrolyte imbalance which may have serious consequences, such as cardiac arrhythmias. Vomiting may also lead to dental erosion. Although they have been noted in the literature, problems such as gastric ruptures are extremely rare.

Therapist Variables

As in all cognitive-behavioral therapy, it is imperative that the therapist and patient form an effective therapeutic relationship (O'Leary & Wilson, 1987). The therapist must earn the patient's trust and respect. The success of CBT depends in large part on the willingness of the patient to play an active role in treatment and follow through on homework assignments. In CBT for bulimia nervosa, patients are asked to do things that can be very threatening and run contrary to their deeply held beliefs about eating and regulation of body weight. For example, they are urged to resume eating three balanced meals a day instead of skipping meals and severely restricting food intake. The majority of patients understandably fear that this will cause weight gain, the very outcome that they dread. Patients will not take what for them is the major psychological risk of altering their eating habits unless they have confidence in their therapist and are persuaded that his/her approach is credible.

Patients with eating disorders often feel ashamed of their behavior and are very sensitive to cues of disapproval and rejection. Accordingly, therapists must convey their acceptance of the patient and their understanding of her problem. It is not uncommon to encounter patients with eating disorders who have previously received unsympathetic treatment from professionals—male and female alike—not experienced with these disorders. A patient recently recounted the following interaction with her female psychiatrist. During the course of her clinical interview, the patient referred to a discussion she had had with her boyfriend about her eating disorder. Her therapist promptly made the following comment: "You mean he will still go out with you even though he knows about the disgusting things you do?"

There is no evidence that the gender of the therapist affects treatment outcome. As in the CBT of other disorders, whether the therapist is female or male is much less important than considerations of caring, interpersonal effectiveness, and technical competence. Therapists must be knowledgeable about the nature of eating disorders and have specific training in their treatment. The optimal combination from a CBT viewpoint is a therapist who has a strong background in the CBT of clinical problems in general, with specific training in the application of these principles and procedures to eating disorders.

Therapists should ideally be specialists in the treatment of eating disorders, rather than generalists who adopt the same basic approach with virtually all patients irrespective of diagnosis. They must be informed about the biological disturbances associated with the disorder so that they can intervene or make referrals where appropriate. They must also know about weight regulation and the processes governing dieting, binge eating, and purging. Finally, they must have sufficient clinical experience and acumen to identify—and if necessary treat—associated psychopathology such as depression and psychoactive substance abuse. Clinical psychologists and psychiatrists with the requisite training are the professionals who are most likely to provide this level of expertise.

ASSESSMENT

Clinical Interview

Some sort of clinical interview has been among the most widely used means of assessing binge eating in patients. These interviews vary widely in how structured they are and whether they are respondent or investigator based. The best-known clinical interview for assessing the specific psychopathology of eating disorders is the Eating Disorder Examination (EDE) (Fairburn & Cooper, 1993). The EDE is widely used in clinical and epidemiological research in North America, Europe, and Australia, and has been translated into several different languages.

The EDE offers the practitioner several advantages (for further details, see Rosen, Vara, Wendt, & Leitenberg, 1990; Wilson, 1993c). First, it has excellent reliability and validity. Second, it directly assesses the diagnostic criteria of all eating disorders. Third, it provides both depth and breadth of assessment of the core features of bulimia nervosa and other eating disorders that no other interview or questionnaire equals.

Recurrent binge eating is a diagnostic criterion not only for bulimia nervosa, but also for anorexia nervosa, binge eating/ purging subtype, and BED (APA, 1993). Yet it has been poorly defined, and what patients and individuals in the community mean by "binge" is frequently at variance with the DSM-IV definition (Beglin & Fairburn, 1992). The EDE has the most detailed and comprehensive scheme for classifying different forms of overeating. The EDE defines four different forms of overeating depending on whether the amount of food consumed is genuinely large (objective overeating), and whether the person experienced a sense of loss of control (bulimic episodes). These different patterns of actual and perceived overeating are not mutually exclusive, and the data indicate that both patients with bulimia nervosa and those who are obese binge eaters engage in both objective and subjective bulimic episodes.

In contrast to most self-report questionnaires, the EDE defines binge eating and ensures that both therapist and patient share the same meaning of key concepts. A "large amount" is defined by the interviewer as what other people would regard as an unusually large amount under the specific circumstances. The interviewer asks a number of probe questions to make this judgment. "Loss of control" is defined as the inability to resist an episode of overeating, or to stop eating once started. Uncontrolled consumption of an objectively large amount of food defines binge eating in DSM-IV. Given the absence of any compelling evidence bearing on the fundamentally important issues of whether differences in the size of "binges" are of diagnostic or prognostic significance (Garner, Shafer, & Rosen, 1992; Rossiter & Agras, 1990), clinicians and researchers should assess all forms of overeating. Only in this way can the large versus small controversy be resolved on empirical grounds.

Self-induced vomiting and laxative abuse are relatively unambiguous and straightforward to assess. Severe dieting, however, is difficult to assess. Although DSM-IV, unlike DSM-III-R, no longer includes dieting as an inappropriate compensatory behavior for binge eating, it is important to assess in order to obtain a full clinical picture of the patient's eating and her attitudes regarding it. This is of particular clinical relevance in CBT, given the importance attributed to dieting in the cognitive-behavioral model of bulimia nervosa. The EDE provides a detailed analysis of dietary restraint, including skipping meals, avoiding particular foods, adhering to caloric limits, reactions to breaking self-imposed dietary rules, and preoccupation with food and its caloric content. The effect of mood on eating is also probed.

Attitudinal disturbance about body weight and shape is one of the diagnostic criteria for bulimia nervosa and anorexia nervosa. As discussed above, it is also the seminal element in the cognitive-behavioral model of these disorders, and the degree of treatment-induced change in these attitudes has been shown to predict relapse (Fairburn et al., in press). Yet it is rarely defined or assessed systematically. The EDE provides detailed information on attitudes about weight and shape. A "weight concern" subscale consists of five items (importance of weight, reaction to prescribed weighing, preoccupation with shape or weight, dissatisfaction with weight, pursuit of weight loss); a "shape concern" subscale consists of eight items (importance of shape, preoccupation with shape or weight, dissatisfaction with shape, fear of fatness, discomfort seeing body, avoidance of exposure, feelings of fatness, desire for a flat stomach). Figure 7.1 describes the item "importance of shape."

The major disadvantage of the EDE is that it requires specific training in its administration and can take up to 1 hour or more to administer. Nevertheless, the rich detail it provides, coupled with the intensive interaction with the patient that it entails, can greatly help the therapist in understanding the patient and details of her eating disorder.

Self-Report Questionnaires

A number of different questionnaires can be used to assess the overall psychopathology of patients with eating disorders. Two of the more commonly used instruments are the Eating Disorder Inventory (EDI-2; Garner, 1991) and the Binge Eating Scale (BES; Gormally, Black, Daston, & Rardin, 1982). The EDI-2 provides a psychometrically sound, broad-gauge assessment of the psychopathology of anorexia and bulimia nervosa. The BES has been widely used to assess binge eating in obese patients (Marcus, 1993).

These questionnaires provide a general gauge of the overall severity of the symptoms of an eating disorder and therefore have proved useful in assessing therapeutic change. They are economical and efficient ways of assessing problems, which can be used with large numbers of subjects when a time-consuming clinical interview is impractical. However, they have significant limitations for clinical practice. One disadvantage in assessing binge eating is that the terms *binge* and *binge eating* typically are not defined, a serious problem in view of the evidence that there is no generally agreed-on definition of binge eating. Furthermore, the questionnaires do not assess binge eating directly. Instead of providing a clear-cut measure of the specific behavior of overeating, they yield some sort of composite index of eating habits and the attitudes and feelings associated with overeating. They do

---

*Over the past four weeks has your shape been important in influencing how you feel about (judge, think, evaluate) yourself as a person?

... *If you imagine the things which influence how you feel about (judge, think, evaluate) yourself—such as your performance at work, being a parent, your marriage, how you get on with other people—and put these things in order of importance, where does your shape fit in?

If, over the past four weeks, your shape had changed in any way, would this have affected how you feel about yourself? Is it important to you that your shape does not change?

[Rate the degree of importance the subject has placed on body shape and its position in his or her scheme for self-evaluation. To make this rating, comparisons need to be made with other aspects of the subject's life which are of importance in his or her scheme for self-evaluation, e.g., quality of relationships, being a parent, performance at work or in leisure activities. Do not prompt with the terms "some," "moderate," or "supreme." If the subject has regarded both shape and weight as being of equivalent supreme importance, rate 6 on this item and on "Importance of weight."]

0 – No importance

1 –

2 – Some importance (definitely an aspect of self-evaluation)

3 –

4 – Moderate importance (definitely one of the main aspects of self-evaluation)

5 –

6 – Supreme importance (nothing is more important in the subject's scheme for evaluation)   [ ]

[Ask about preceding 2 months.]

[Rate preceding 2 months. Rate 9 if not asked.]
                                          Month 2   [ ]
                                          Month 3   [ ]

FIGURE 7.1. Importance of Shape item from the Eating Disorder Examination (12th ed.). Questions with an asterisk *must* be asked. From Fairburn and Cooper, 1993, p. 351. Copyright 1993 by Christopher G. Fairburn and Zafra Cooper. Reprinted with permission.

not provide the detailed information or a specific count of the frequency of binge eating, which is needed for diagnosis, planning therapeutic interventions, or monitoring treatment progress and outcome (Wilson, 1993c).

A number of questionnaires assess dietary restraint. Perhaps the most useful for the clinician is Stunkard and Messick's (1985) three-factor Eating Questionnaire, a 51-item questionnaire that has three subscales derived by factor analysis of the scale as a whole: cognitive restraint, disinhibition of eating, and perceived hunger. Attitudes to body shape and weight can be assessed using the EDI Drive for Thinness and Body Dissatisfaction scales and the Body Shape Questionnaire (BSQ; Cooper, Taylor, Cooper, & Fairburn, 1987). The EDI measure lacks the discriminant validity of the EDE interview (Wilson & Smith, 1989). The BSQ is strongly correlated with the EDE measure of attitudinal disturbance (Loeb, Walsh, & Pike, 1992) and has been recommended as a self-report alternative to the EDE interview (Rosen et al., 1990). Cooper and Fairburn (1993), however, have argued that the EDE and BSQ assess different features of the psychopathology of bulimia nervosa. They contend that the EDE assesses abnormal attitudes or what they call overvalued ideas about shape and weight, which is a necessary diagnostic feature, whereas the BSQ measures body dissatisfaction, which does not have diagnostic significance and primarily a function of current mood. Consistent with this proposed distinction, Cooper and Fairburn (1993) have reported data showing that the EDE measure of attitude toward shape and weight was linked to changes in self-esteem, whereas the BSQ was closely associated with change in mood.

Self-Monitoring

Self-monitoring is an indispensable assessment method in cognitive-behavioral therapy in general, and is invaluable in CBT treatment of bulimia nervosa. It typically consists of patients recording in eating diaries or on special monitoring forms their entire daily food and liquid intake, usually over a 1-week period. Patients should also be asked to record food intake as soon as possible after eating to maximize accuracy. Patients need to be given an explanation of its purpose and its importance to assessment and treatment. Potential obstacles to completing self-monitoring should be anticipated and suggestions made for overcoming them.

Self-monitoring provides the therapist with an ongoing, daily account of binge eating and purging and the circumstances under which they occur. The proximal antecedents or triggers of binge eating are identified primarily by asking patients to record the circumstances in which episodes occurred. Self-monitoring provides the information that allows the therapist to determine when and where the episode took place; what the patient was thinking, feeling, and doing at the time; and the nature of the interpersonal context. This information is essential in CBT for selecting and implementing cognitive and behavioral change strategies (for a more detailed analysis of the use of self-monitoring as an assessment tool, see Wilson, 1993c).

PROCESS OF TREATMENT

The now widespread use of CBT in North America, Europe, and Australia derives directly from Fairburn's first formulation of this approach in the early 1980s. The publication of a detailed treatment manual greatly facilitated the dissemination of CBT and controlled research on its effectiveness (Fairburn, 1985).

As described by Fairburn (1985), CBT consists of 19 sessions of individual treatment spanning roughly 20 weeks. Treatment is problem oriented and focused primarily on the present and future. The treatment has three stages. The first stage involves education about bulimia nervosa and orientation to its treatment with CBT. The cognitive view of the maintenance and modification of the disorder is explained, and its relevance to the patient's current problems is made clear. The structure and goals of treatment are discussed. Information about nutrition and weight regulation, and how they are critical to eliminating eating disorders, is detailed. Core behavioral techniques are introduced. Self-monitoring is initiated for tracking eating habits and for assessing situations that trigger binge eating and purging. Other self-regulatory strategies for reducing the frequency of binge eating and normalizing eating patterns, such as stimulus control, are also used. The goal at this stage is to return the patient to eating three meals a day with the provision for healthy snacks.

Although the emphasis during this early stage tends to be on behavioral change, the therapist repeatedly relates the cognitive view of bulimia nervosa to the patient's particular problems. For example:

> [I]f an episode of overeating is precipitated by the breaking of a dietary rule, for instance eating chocolate, this may be used to illustrate the important point that the presence of rigid dietary rules promotes intermittent overeating. The aim is to help the patient gain an understanding of the mechanisms which perpetuate the eating problem and to appreciate the need for both behaviour and cognitive change. (Fairburn, 1989, pp. 287–288).

Stage 2 has an increasingly cognitive focus. The techniques from Stage 1 are supplemented with a variety of procedures for reducing dietary restraint and developing cognitive and behavioral coping skills for resisting binge eating. This cognitive approach is modeled after Beck's (1976) cognitive therapy for depression. Patients are taught to identify and alter the dysfunctional thoughts and attitudes regarding shape, weight, and eating. Cognitive change is achieved by prompting patients to engage in behavioral experiments designed to challenge their dysfunctional assumptions.

In Stage 3, the focus is on the use of relapse-prevention strategies to ensure the maintenance of change following treatment (Marlatt & Gordon, 1885). Other than under exceptional circumstances (e.g., a suicidal patient), CBT is conducted on an outpatient basis. CBT can be applied to hospital patients, but treatment must be continued following discharge to help patients learn to regulate their eating and cope with specific high-risk situations for binge eating and purging that cannot be adequately addressed during inpatient therapy.

There are differences in the ways in which this approach is implemented across treatment settings. For example, adaptations of Fairburn's (1985) treatment program have been described by Agras et al. (1989) and Wilson et al. (1991). Nevertheless, a common set of treatment goals and techniques defines CBT for the treatment of bulimia nervosa. Fairburn's (1985) manual for bulimia nervosa has also been adapted for the treatment of recurrent binge eating in obese patients (Fairburn, Marcus, & Wilson, 1993). The case study we describe next illustrates the treatment of a patient with bulimia nervosa using a treatment manual adapted from Fairburn (1985) for a controlled treatment trial (Wilson, 1989). The case is drawn from a 20-session outpatient treatment program for bulimia nervosa at the New York Psychiatric Institute, Columbia University.

CASE STUDY

This is the case of "Claire," a 26-year-old woman who had suffered from bulimia nervosa for 8 years at the time she presented for treatment. Some details of the case have been changed to conceal the patient's identity and to illustrate some of the issues that arise in treatment of this sort.

Assessment

Because treatment is provided in the context of programatic clinical research at our Eating Disorders Clinic, the assessment procedures are quite extensive. To begin, when an individual contacts our clinic for treatment, she is briefly screened on the phone to determine whether she appears to meet the necessary diagnostic criteria to be eligible for the clinical trial. If so, the treatment program is described to her and, if she is interested in participating, a two-part evaluation is scheduled. The evaluation consists of an extensive clinical assessment to confirm the diagnosis of bulimia nervosa and to assess the course of development as well as the current presentation of the disorder. In addition, associated psychopathology, substance abuse, and family, social, and medical histories are assessed. Finally, a complete physical exam is conducted, including blood tests, a pregnancy test, and a drug screen. Particular attention is given to electrolyte abnormalities. Active drug abuse renders someone ineligible for the treatment study. Also, because some of the patients are randomly assigned to active drug treatment, pregnancy renders someone ineligible for the current treatment study. The assessment evaluation also includes extensive self-report questionnaires.

The evaluation is conducted in part by a clinical assessor trained in the administration of structured interviews. The physical exam is conducted by one of the attending psychiatrists. Thus, the clinician begins "Session 1" with much more information than would be the case in private practice. Although it is unlikely that such formal procedures are necessary in private practice, a thorough evaluation is nonetheless essential before starting treatment.

Specific Psychopathology

At the time of presentation for treatment, Claire reported binge eating approximately 10 to 15 times per week. Five of these overeating episodes constituted binges as defined by DSM-IV (i.e., uncontrolled consumption of what others would regard as a large amount of food), and 5 to 10 were what the EDE labels subjective bulimic episodes (i.e., episodes that did not constitute an unusually large amount of food but were subjectively experienced as out of control). The subjective binges usually occurred in the evening during the week. She purged approximately 10 to 15 times per week, after every binge episode. If she thought that she had eaten especially "bad foods" she vomited once after binge eating, drank a lot of water and vomited again to "clean [herself] out."

Claire commuted by train to arrive at work by 7:30 a.m. She ate breakfast, which consisted of half a dry bagel and coffee, at work at approximately 8:30 a.m. Approximately once every 2 weeks someone in the office brought in donuts or cookies for breakfast. Claire usually ate either a donut or five or six cookies and purged afterwards. Claire frequently skipped lunch, but when she did eat a midday meal it typically consisted of salad, pizza, or Chinese food. Approximately one third of the times that she did eat lunch, she purged. Claire did not eat snacks during the day unless there was a special occasion in the office during which she "always took a piece of cake and purged afterwards."After work, Claire typically went straight home to binge and purge. During the week, these overeating episodes were typically not very large. Most often they consisted of a salty snack food such as Doritos and potato chips or cereal with milk, sugar, raisins, four slices of bread, and three diet sodas. Claire always purged after these episodes.

On the weekend, Claire started the day about 11 a.m. with a binge. A typical binge at this time was three or four slices of toast with cheese or jam, cereal with milk and sugar, one to three donuts, a bagel with cream cheese, and anything else that she could get her hands on. She then purged and took a shower. "Then I'm good for a few hours. I feel like I'm clean, like I wasn't bad for a few hours." On the weekend, Claire would usually eat a sandwich for lunch sometime between 2 p.m. and 3 p.m. She would binge and purge again about 1 hr after lunch on "whatever was in the refrigerator." Dinner would typically begin as a normal, social meal with her husband and possibly other relatives who would be visiting for the evening. However, at least half the time these meals would turn into binges, which were followed by purging after the guests left and her husband went to sleep.

A typical large weekend binge for Claire consisted of four cups of pasta with sauce and cheese, three pieces of garlic bread, one bowl of cereal with a half cup of chocolate chips with milk, ice cream, and three to four 8-oz glasses of diet soda. These binges usually occurred during the middle of the day while her husband was out doing errands. However, Claire reported that these binges sometimes occurred while her husband was home or while she was visiting at her mom's house "if I just couldn't help myself. . . . My family knows but it's embarrassing for me, I wouldn't want to binge in front of them . . . we don't talk about it, my mom thinks it's like taboo . . . unless she's angry, then she'll call me a freak. My husband wants everything to be okay, so even when he asks me if I'm still doing it, I just say no."

While binge eating, Claire claimed that she felt out of control: "I feel like I'm in a different state, like I don't really know what I'm doing. There's really no emotion there. I go numb. It's just something I do." She described her experience of purging as follows: "I feel better to get the food out, but I feel kind of like a freak, I feel alone . . . bad. I wonder how I could do something like this over and over again." Although Claire had abused laxatives for approximately 6 months, 2 years before presenting for treatment, she stopped using them when she became frightened after experiencing dizziness and heart palpitations. She also tried using diuretics once.

Claire exercised "in spurts" and was not exercising at the time that she presented for treatment. During the brief periods when she would exercise, she awoke at 3:30 a.m. to do a 1½-hr aerobic workout prior to going to work. She was excessively concerned about her weight and expressed significant dissatisfaction with her body despite the fact that her weight was well within the normal range. She avoided buying new clothes because she never thought that she looked good in anything.

Claire had begun binge eating and purging at age 18 after she overheard two girls at college discussing another girl who had bulimia nervosa. She thought the binge eating and purging sounded repulsive but not long after, she gave it a try. The first year that she binged, she either dieted severely or vomited. She vomited less frequently then because it was harder to do. When it became easier to vomit spontaneously, she started using vomiting to purge more frequently. This increased rate of vomiting led to significant weight loss; Claire lost approximately 15 lb, became amenorrheic during this period and was also exercising 1 to 2 hr per day. For approximately three quarters of her 20th year, Claire had met the diagnostic criteria for anorexia nervosa. Claire did not present with any other significant associated psychopathology.

Family/Social History

Claire grew up with her parents, an older sister, and an older brother in a large, suburban neighborhood. When Claire was 12 years old her parents got divorced. She described their divorce as "probably the single most traumatic experience of my whole life. . . . I feel like I wouldn't be the way I am if it weren't for that . . . I was always Daddy's girl and after they divorced I hardly

ever saw him again." After the divorce, her mother was forced to assume responsibility for the majority of the family expenses which resulted in her working more hours. Claire reported that during this time she would frequently spend the afternoons alone and depressed. There was no significant family history for obesity, eating disorders, or any other psychiatric disorder.

At age 23, Claire married a man whom she dated during college. At the time that Claire presented for treatment, she was living with her husband of 3 years in a one-bedroom apartment in the same town as Claire's mother. She described their relationship as good but described feeling that they had grown apart in the recent years. Her husband worked many long days and was required to travel frequently for work. As a result, she had a lot of time at home alone and reported that many times when she binged she would be feeling bad about her relationship with him but she was not able to articulate any details. She and her husband had no children.

Course of Treatment

Many patients have had previous treatment, usually based on a psychodynamic model that is less structured and directive than CBT. It is important for the therapist to clarify some of the major distinctions between CBT and this more traditional supportive psychotherapy. In particular, the therapist should emphasize that the primary focus of CBT is placed on identifying the patterns of binge eating and purging, together with the factors or conditions that trigger and maintain these patterns. Once these patterns and proximal triggers are identified, the focus of the work is on identifying the thoughts and feelings associated with these episodes and developing alternative strategies for dealing with high-risk situations. It should be emphasized that CBT works in the here and now and that more emphasis is placed on the current constellation of problems than on the historical concerns regarding the development of the eating disorder.

An essential component of CBT is homework between therapy sessions. It should be emphasized to the patient that completing the homework between sessions is a critical part of therapy. The therapist should clarify that the homework will provide important material for understanding and treating the patient's particular problems. The effort the patient expends on her homework is tied closely to the attention it receives from her therapist. Most sessions should begin with a review of the homework. It is helpful to give a patient a folder or large envelope to keep forms in during the course of treatment. This will help the patient keep track of her homework and handouts and will allow the therapist and patient to refer back to various homework assignments throughout the course of the treatment. Patients are weighed on a weekly basis by the therapist at the beginning of each therapy session.

Finally, it is important to clarify for the patient the length of the therapy sessions (which in our clinic is 45 min) and the length of the treatment program (which in our clinic is 20 sessions occurring over the course of approximately 5 months). Some patients are concerned that this will not be enough time to treat their eating disorder. It is important to emphasize to the patient that she should expect that just as the development of her eating disorder was gradual, so, too, the reestablishment of personal control and normal eating will take time. It should be explained to the patient that through the course of treatment she will be learning many of the skills necessary to become her own therapist and therefore should be encouraged to expect improvement to continue beyond the end of treatment. However, it should also be emphasized that if the patient does need further treatment at the end of the 20 sessions appropriate referrals will be offered.

Session 1

Objectives

1. Establish rapport.
2. Outline treatment program and goals:
   a. Identify patterns of binge eating.
   b. Identify environmental, cognitive, and emotional triggers.
   c. Normalize and stabilize eating patterns.
   d. Learn to become own therapist (stress collaborative effort of treatment).
3. Emphasize importance of homework.
4. Introduce high-risk hierarchies.

Selective Transcript

Therapist: I know you have met with several people prior to our appointment today, how are you feeling about finaling getting started?

Claire: Well, I'm really glad. I know I shouldn't feel this way, I mean I know you're only trying to help but I was pretty frustrated about having those other appointments and then having to wait a week before seeing you.

T: Shouldn't feel this way?

C: Well, you know . . . I shouldn't get angry.

T: Actually, I appreciate your telling me that you are feeling frustrated, angry. I can imagine that it's difficult to have to go through the evaluation process which requires your meeting with several people, answering lots of questions, sometimes more than once, and then waiting a week for treatment to really begin.

Let's begin by my reviewing with you the structure and rationale of this treatment intervention. We will meet for 20 sessions. The first eight sessions will be on a twice-per-week basis and thereafter we will meet weekly. Our primary focus will be on understanding your current eating problems. We will focus on both your binge eating and your eating outside of the binges. In our experience it is not only during the binge-eating episode that someone with bulimia nervosa has difficulty with food. We are going to pay particular attention to the situations that are most difficult for you to manage in terms of your eating. We call these "high-risk situations." After identifying these high-risk situations, we will try to figure out what it is about these situations that make them particularly difficult for you. In other words, why is it that you binge in one situation and not another? We will focus on how you are feeling and what you are thinking at these times. The goal is to link your thoughts, feelings, and behavior in a meaningful way so that we can understand what is currently maintaining your bulimia nervosa and make changes so that you can function more adaptively.

Before we get started on that, I also want to mention to you that I will be weighing you weekly at the beginning of the session. Do you weigh yourself now?

C: Oh, yes. I must weigh myself five times a day . . . before I get into the shower in the morning, after I get out, and all the time before and after I binge and purge.

T: What happens when you weigh yourself?

C: Well, if my weight is up, I feel fat and sometimes that sets off a binge. I know this sounds crazy but sometimes if my weight is down that sets off a binge, too, because I feel like I can afford the calories without getting fat—it's like a reward.

T: You think you can afford the calories without getting fat.

C: Yeah. I don't know. . . . Pretty much no matter what it isn't pleasant for me.

T: That's precisely why I want to encourage you to put your scale away for now. You see, the way we think about weight is that it is an end product that is influenced by many variables—where you are in your menstrual cycle, what time of day it is, whether you ate a lot of salty foods yesterday, how much exercise you are getting, and so on. As a result, your weight is bound to fluctuate a few pounds up and down. That's normal and healthy, but for you it's alarming. One of the goals of our treatment is for you to grow more comfortable with your weight and the fluctuations that are inevitable. As we begin to make some changes in your eating, I want to weigh you here so that we can keep track of what is happening with your weight and discuss it. As your eating normalizes, and as you grow more comfortable with your eating and your weight we will gradually move that job back into your court at home. So do you think you can put the scale away for now?

C: I'll give it a try.

T: OK. So to go back to the first point—we now know that weighing yourself is a high-risk situation for you in terms of triggering a binge.

C: Yeah, I guess that's right.

T: Here's a form that we will begin to complete together now and that I will ask you to complete for homework for your next session [see Figure 7.2]. What we want to do here is list the situations in which you find it impossible to resist the temptation to binge, where you always resist the temptation to binge, and the situations that can go either way. When you weigh yourself for example, how often does that trigger a binge?

C: Oh, probably half the time.

T: Okay so that would go here: 50/50. Now what about last week, what were the situations that triggered your binge episodes?

C: Well, I almost always binge when I get home from work, before my husband gets home.

T: Almost always—is that 75% of the time, more, less?

C: About three out of the five nights.

T: Okay so that would go here. And how about a situation that always sets off a binge.

C: If I have a fight with my husband and then he leaves the house.

T: So that goes here. And how about a situation that never triggers a binge.

C: I never binge when I am out a restaurant with other people—mostly because I know I won't be able to purge.

T: OK, so we have a few examples here. What I want you to do for homework is complete this form. Include about three or four situations in each column and do it both for binge eating and purging. When we meet next time we'll go over it together.

In addition to identifying high-risk situations, I would like you to indicate the frequency that you binge eat and purge each day by using this diary of binge–purge episodes. This daily self-monitoring is important because it will help us keep track of how frequently you are binge eating and purging as we proceed with treatment. Initially, this will be especially useful in terms of marking these episodes so that we can discuss

Binge eating:

| Always can resist temptation | 50/50 chance | Never can resist temptation |

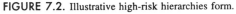

Vomiting:

| Always can resist temptation | 50/50 chance | Never can resist temptation |

FIGURE 7.2. Illustrative high-risk hierarchies form.

what is happening around the times that you are binge eating and purging and thereby identify patterns and high-risk situations. As we attempt to make changes in your eating, it will be important for us to monitor what is happening with your binge eating and purging because this will enable us to know what interventions are working and where the problems continue.

Now is a good time for me to emphasize to you the importance of homework. Between sessions, you will have homework to do that will provide us with important information about your problems with binge eating and purging. Sometimes it will entail writing things down. Sometimes it will entail experimenting with some new behavior. It's really important that you do the homework—some tasks may be difficult but I want you to do the best you can and we'll discuss any problems that you have along the way.

The last thing I want to do today is give you two handouts that I would like you to read. One is about vomiting and laxative abuse and the other is about eating a range of foods including fats and carbohydrates in your diet. When we meet next time we'll discuss them.

Homework

1. Complete the high-risk hierarchies form.
2. Read the handouts.
3. Complete a daily diary of binge–purge episodes.

Session 2

Objectives

1. Review homework:
   a. Provide positive feedback.
   b. Question patient about patterns or reactions to the self-monitoring.
   c. Reiterate importance of homework if necessary
2. Review high-risk hierarchies form for binge eating and purging.
3. Explore patient's reaction to her weight. Emphasize the importance of limiting the number of times the patient weighs herself.

Selective Transcript

T: So you weigh 136 today. [The patient's weight was 136, up 1 lb.] What do you think, how do you feel about that?

C: Terrible. I should weigh at least 10 pounds less. That's just what makes me feel better.

T: Makes you feel better?

C: Yeah, when I weigh this much, I feel fat and I just feel like a failure.

T: You *think* you're fat, and you *think* you are a failure for weighing 136 and it looks like that leaves you *feeling* pretty frustrated, maybe angry, maybe sad. As we work on these issues, I'm going to try to help you begin to be clearer about whether we are talking about thoughts or feelings. Surely they are very closely linked but as we try to figure out what is going on with your eating we want to know whether the problems lie in your thoughts, emotions, or both.

As difficult as it is, I want to encourage you to hold judgment on your weight until you have your eating under control. Until then it is impossible for us to know where your weight will settle down. Also, as I mentioned last week, everyone's weight fluctuates some. I want to encourage you to think of your weight as a window of about 5 pounds rather than as one specific number. In other words, instead of thinking that you weigh 136, think of your weight as 134 to 139. Anything in that window doesn't really constitute a significant weight change.

C: That's going to be really hard for me. I'm afraid I'm just going to keep on gaining weight.

T: I know this is difficult but let's remember that gaining 1 pound is not the same as gaining 25 pounds—we call it "magnification" when we give more importance to something than it really deserves.

C: I know what you mean but it's hard for me to remember that all the time.

T: Well, this would be a good time for us to talk about the handouts on vomiting and laxative abuse and the one on fats and carbohydrates. My guess is that the driving force for purging is that you are unhappy with your weight and that you are trying to counteract the binge. What did you think of the handout on this?

The handout describes the deleterious consequences of vomiting and laxative abuse and explains how these compensatory behaviors really fail to help individuals manage their weight effectively. The cycle that is outlined states that for many people vomiting is employed because they want to counteract the binge and lose weight but that just the opposite happens: When individuals vomit or use laxatives regularly they tend to eat more because of the erroneous belief that they are able to rid themselves of all the calories. As a result, it is argued that individuals wind up consuming more calories than they would if they did not vomit or use laxatives.

C: Well, it makes sense even though I have a hard time believing that I'm not going to gain weight if I stop.

T: I'm sure. You have been binge eating and purging for 8 years. We are going to try to make gradual changes in your eating, at a pace that you can manage so you can find out for yourself what the truth is. I just want to assure you that we are going to go slowly, and we will continue to closely monitor your weight and your eating so that as you make changes you will have your own data.

Let's look at the high-risk hierarchies form that you completed for homework now to get a better sense of what your current eating habits are like—what are the eating habits associated with this weight.

Session 2 picks up where Session 1 left off with the high-risk hierarchies. The therapist and patient should go over each of the situations listed with the goal of deciphering what factors differentiate when the patient does binge–purge and when she doesn't. One of the primary goals of this intervention is to loosen the patient's self-labeling as bulimic by pointing out that she is not continually binge eating or purging.

T: So one of the things that we can see is that you are not "always" out of control—there are numerous situations that are not associated with binge eating and purging for you. This is important because for many women who label themselves "bulimic," they think that all their eating is out of control. These are problems with labeling and all-or-nothing thinking. In other words, many times we find that the way someone thinks about things can actually contribute to the problem.

In your lists here you have identified several kinds of situations that are linked to binge eating and vomiting for you. What are some of the emotional triggers for you?

C: Umm . . . well a lot of times when I'm frustrated or angry I wind up holding it in and then binge and purge when I'm alone. Like a lot of times that's what happens with my husband. He does something that drives me crazy but I don't say anything.

T: That reminds me of last session when you told me you shouldn't be angry or frustrated about all the hoops you had to jump before starting treatment. Is that what happens with other people—you hold it in because you shouldn't be angry, or you shouldn't feel a certain way.

C: Yeah that happens all the time. I guess my mom always told me that I shouldn't be angry that my parents got divorced, I shouldn't be angry about anything because it won't do me any good . . . that I should just be happy for all that I have.

T: So what you are describing is how you came to believe that you shouldn't have certain feelings, anger in particular. This is a perfect example of how our past experiences shape the way we think about things in our current life. Rather than focus extensively on how you learned to think about things in a particular way, we are going to ask the question whether a given way of thinking about things is supported by your current experiences and whether it is adaptive for you now.

You have the idea that you shouldn't express your anger because it won't do you any good but look at what happens when you don't express your anger, does that do you any good?

C: I guess not but I'm really not sure how to change that now.

T: Well, we'll get to that but first what I'd like you to do for the next session is add to this list of high-risk hierarchies some emotional states—what are the emotional states that are most and least associated with triggering binge eating and purging for you. And with the situations that you have already listed, describe how you typically feel in these situations.

The last thing that I would like to do with you today is begin filling out what we call the decision analysis form [see Figure 7.3]. This will help us understand why you want to change as well as highlight for us what some of the issues are that interfere with your being able to end the bulimia nervosa on your own.

In the first column, you should list the positive, short-term consequences of stopping binge eating, in the next column list the negative, short-term consequences, in the third column list the positive long-term consequences, and in the fourth column list the negative, long-term consequences. Then flip it around and list the consequences of continuing to binge eat and purge. Do the best you can and we'll go over it next time.

Homework

1. Expand on the high-risk hierarchies form.
2. Complete the decision analysis form.
3. Complete daily diary.

	Immediate consequences		Delayed consequences	
	Positive	Negative	Positive	Negative
If I stop bingeing and purging				
If I continue to binge and purge				

FIGURE 7.3. Decision analysis form. From "Relapse Prevention: Theoretical Rationale and Overview of the Model" by G. A. Marlatt, 1985, in Relapse Prevention: Maintenance Strategies in the Treatment of Addictive Behaviors, G. A. Marlatt and J. R. Gordon, Eds., p. 58. New York: Guilford Press. Copyright 1985 by The Guilford Press. Adapted by permission.

Session 3

Objectives

1. Review homework.
2. Introduce dysfunctional thoughts:
   a. Link thoughts, emotions, and behaviors as highlighted by the 50/50 situations on the high-risk hierarchies form.
   b. Identify specific dysfunctional cognitions. The patient is given a list of types of dysfunctional cognitions and asked to provide an example of selected cognitions, preferably from the past week.
   c. Clarify concept of dysfunctional and functional thinking styles verses "irrational" or "crazy" thinking (i.e., Do these thoughts work for you or against you?).

Selective Transcript

C: The past few days have been really tough. I started binge eating on Thursday when I got home and it only ended because I fell asleep. My husband has been away for business all week. I have a big problem being home alone like that, especially when I'm upset about work.

T: So that's another high-risk situation.

C: Yeah, I was feeling really bad about work. My boss was disappointed with me because I didn't get this report to her in time. I knew she was right. I mean, I spent half the day before the report was due binge eating and purging at work. I was so anxious about getting it done right that I wound up getting it done a day late.

T: Okay, so we know that feeling anxious is another emotional state that sets you up for a binge.

C: Oh, yeah. That's a big one.

T: Let's look at your high-risk hierarchies form for a moment to go over the other feelings that you link with these episodes and then we'll see which ones apply to this most recent binge. OK, so you have here that when you are feeling angry and depressed that there is a very high risk that you will binge and purge. And you wrote that when you are calm and happy that you never binge and purge.

You also wrote that when you feel that your husband should be home more that it could go either way. "Feeling that your husband should be home more" is really a thought, you *think* that your husband should be home more and when he is not you feel . . .

C: Lonely and neglected. I mean if he really loved me he would make more of an effort. I don't know, he says he is doing this for us, we are trying to save money to buy a house and all, but a lot of times I think he would rather be at work than with me.

T: Is that part of what precipitated this last binge?

C: Yeah, I think that if it were just work or just him I might have been able to handle it but I couldn't deal with both at the same time.

T: OK, well let's look at the situation and identify how you were thinking about everything and try to begin to understand how your thinking may contribute to creating the difficult situation.

In terms of work you said you felt so anxious about getting the job done right that you wound up binge eating and purging. What's that about?

C: Well, I guess I'm a perfectionist. I have to do something perfectly or else I think it's no good at all. And this report for my boss . . . well I didn't have all the information I needed to do it exactly right so I kept putting it off until the day before it was due and then I wound up binge eating and purging—I was there until the middle of the night trying to get that thing done.

T: So there were really two binge episodes, one before you handed in the report and one the night you got home after handing it in, right?

C: Yeah.

T: What else were you thinking about when you had the binge episode at work?

C: I felt like a complete failure because I couldn't get anything right.

T: You *thought* you were a complete failure. What do you mean you couldn't get *anything* right?

C: Well you know, with the report.

T: You said you didn't have all the information but did you have enough information to do some of the report?

C: Oh yeah, there were four parts to the report. It was for the third part that I was missing information.

T: So in fact you had most of the information you needed to do the report but because you were missing some of the information for part 3 you thought you wouldn't be able to do a good job and felt inadequate.

C: Yeah.

T: As you describe that situation to me, I notice that there are certain ways that you are thinking about the situation that seemed to make the whole situation more difficult for you. We all have rules that govern the way we think about the world, ourselves, and our experiences in the world. Some of these rules or ideas are so automatic that we don't even realize that we have them or that they are having an effect on us. Part of the work that we will be doing together is figuring out what the automatic thoughts are that you have that contribute to your problems with bulimia. We call these thoughts "dysfunctional thoughts" or "cognitive distortions."

There are lots of automatic thoughts that are healthy, adaptive, and essential to our daily functioning. Take, for example, learning how to ride a bike. When you are first learning how to ride a bike you have to think about every detail: where to hold the handle bars, how to brake, how to balance, where to keep your eyes, and so on. Once you have learned to ride you don't think about these things, they just come naturally. You could be thinking about the friend you are on your way to visit, get on the bike and start pedaling without paying much attention to the logistics of riding the bike. This kind of automatic thinking is very adaptive. It allows you to learn something and then move on to learning and doing other things.

Sometimes, however, the automatic thoughts are not so functional—these are the dysfunctional thoughts or cognitive distortions. We're not going to focus so much on how you got to thinking about things in a particular way but what the impact of these dysfunctional thoughts are on your current life. We have got to evaluate these thoughts and consider how much support they have in your current life and whether there are more adaptive ways to think about yourself and the situations you find yourself in.

It's important to keep in mind as we go through this that when we talk about dysfunctional thoughts and cognitive distortions [see Table 7.2] we are not calling someone irrational or crazy. Although it is sometimes difficult for people to trace the history of how they got to thinking about something in a particular way, many times people know immediately why they think in certain ways. Typically, people have had certain experiences that they interpreted in a particular way or were told certain things growing up that led them to think about the world in a one way or another. You are not crazy for having certain thoughts. The issue is, do they work for you today? Of all the automatic thoughts that govern and influence your behavior, which ones are accurate, helpful, and adaptive and which ones are dysfunctional in the sense that they have no support in your current reality and only contribute to making situations more difficult.

To go back to the binge that you had at work, you said that you have to do things perfectly or not at all. This is an example of all-or-nothing thinking. It's got to be 100% perfect or it's not worth doing.

You also called yourself a "complete failure." That's another example of all-or-nothing thinking. It's also an example of labeling.

Let's read through each of these ten cognitive distortions together. These are the ten most problematic thought patterns that we see with individuals with bulimia nervosa. You may recognize some of these thought patterns in yourself right away. Others may not seem to describe you at all. What we're going to do for the next few weeks is work on identifying which ones are most charac-

TABLE 7.2. Examples of Dysfunctional Cognitions Targeted by Cognitive-Behavioral Therapy

1. *Dichotomous (all-or-nothing) thinking:* the tendency to interpret events in black or white terms. There is no moderation, no shades of gray. The patient is either in total control or out of control: food is "good" or "bad."

2. *Arbitrary inference:* the tendency to reach a conclusion in the absence of supportive evidence, or when the evidence is unsupportive.

3. *Overgeneralization:* the tendency to draw a general conclusion from an isolated event and apply it inappropriately to unrelated situations.

4. *Magnification or minimization:* the tendency to evaluate erroneously the significance of things. A patient typically exaggerates another woman's beauty and downgrades her *own* physical attractiveness.

5. *Personalization:* the tendency to blame oneself for negative external events when there is no basis for such an attribution.

6. *Selective abstraction:* the tendency to focus exclusively on a single detail while ignoring more accurate and important information.

Note. From Beck, Rush, Shaw, and Emery (1979, p. 14). Copyright 1979 by Aaron T. Beck, A. John Rush, Brian F. Shaw, and Gary Emery. Adapted by permission.

teristic of you and what that means for your bulimia nervosa.

With time our goal is to begin to challenge the dysfunctional thoughts that you identify and try to establish more adaptive ways of thinking about things. Your problems with bulimia did not happen overnight, you did not learn to think in certain dysfunctional ways all at once. Similarly, identifying and overcoming the dysfunctional thoughts will be a gradual process of unlearning or retraining the thoughts, feelings, and behaviors that led to and maintain the bulimia. Between now and our next session, I want you to try to think of at least one example of each of the first five cognitive distortions on the list. Also, when you think about the binge–purge episodes that you have had in the past week, I want you to pay special attention to what you were thinking before you started the episode. See if you can identify from this list some dysfunctional thoughts that contributed to triggering the episode. After thinking about these

past episodes, try to identify the dysfunctional thoughts that occur prior to potential binge–purge episodes between now and the next time we meet. We'll go over it together next time.

Homework

1. Bring in at least one example of each of the first three dysfunctional thoughts.
2. Try to identify dysfunctional thoughts linked to binge–purge episodes from the past week and from the current week.
3. Complete food diary of binge–purge episodes.

Session 4

Objectives

1. Review homework:
   a. Provide positive feedback.
   b. Discuss examples of first three dysfunctional thoughts
2. Define, and provide examples for, additional dysfunctional cognitions from the past week.

3. Introduce challenges to dysfunctional thoughts:
   a. Examine process of identifying and labeling thought and reality test: Is it true? What is my evidence for this thought? Formulate functional or adaptive challenge in response to the dysfunctional thoughts.

In Session 3, the therapist did not have time to review the decision analysis form with the patient. It is important to do this within one of the next sessions both for the intrinsic worth of the information gained from the form and to support and respect the patient's efforts in completing the homework. When the therapist does not have sufficient time to review all the homework in the session for which it was prepared, it is useful to acknowledge this to the patient and assure her that he/she will focus on it soon.

Selective Transcript

The patient was weighed on the way down to the therapist's office prior to Session 4. She weighed 135 lb.

T: What do you think of your weight today?

C: I still think that I'm really fat. I hate looking at myself in the mirror or even when I take a shower I'm totally grossed out.

T: Totally grossed out . . .

C: Yeah, I mean, I see all these beautiful women walking up and down the street and I just don't compare. I mean look at me. My husband says he likes my body, he likes me just the way I am but I don't believe him. I mean there are a lot of women that he works with who are younger and more attractive than I am, how could he possibly find me attractive? I would feel so much better about myself if I could just lose 10 pounds, but no matter how hard I try to diet it seems I always wind up blowing it within a few days.

T: What do you mean blowing it, how does that happen?

C: Well you know, I'll start dieting. I'll be really good. I'll eat really good, healthy foods. Usually, I'll have fruit for breakfast, one of those fiber bars for lunch, and some nonfattening type of dinner like fish

or chinese vegetables. I feel really good when I stick to this but it doesn't last very long. There's always a party or business dinner or something. I wind up eating cake or too much bread and then it turns into a full-blown binge.

T: So the idea is that when you are dieting you have to be perfect. And being perfect means sticking to a very strict diet, no exceptions. No cake. No bread. If you eat any of these foods then you have blown your diet, you've failed.

C: Yeah.

T: Sounds pretty harsh to me.

C: Well how else am I going to lose this weight? I know myself. I can't eat just a little bit of these foods . . . if I have even a small bite I want more. It's better for me not to have any.

T: I'm not so sure about that. Look what happens when you try to avoid these foods completely. You severely restrict your diet, you wind up feeling deprived, and you wind up binge eating and purging if you eat the "wrong" thing. Also, take a look at your weight. Over the past 8 years, it has steadily increased to where you are now.

C: All I know is that if I eat those foods I am going to get fat.

T: I think just the opposite. As long as those foods are forbidden, you are going to have problems with eating and weight. We're not ready to do this just yet but down the road I am going to encourage you and will work with you to challenge some of these automatic thoughts about food and weight.

Before we get there let's go back for a few minutes to the high-risk hierarchies and decision analysis forms. What we know so far is that there are certain interpersonal situations and emotional states that you find difficult to manage which are frequently associated with triggering a binge. What we also know from today is that there are certain ideas that you have about your body and food as well as certain ways that you manage your eating that put you at risk for binge eating and purging.

Now, let's go back to the decision analysis form and figure out how well the bulimia is doing in terms of solving these problems and let's figure out what problems it creates. In other words, the binge eating and purging does something for you or else you wouldn't be doing it. So here on the decision analysis form what did you put in the columns for the negative short- and long-term consequences of stopping the binge–purge episodes? What would you lose, what would be more difficult if you didn't binge and purge? [Review responses.]

C: (*Going through the list*) Well, one thing for sure, I wrote it here, is that I am afraid I will gain weight. I'm afraid I'll never be able to eat my favorite foods again. Another thing is that I'll have to deal with some of the problems that I'm avoiding in my relationships.

T: OK, so you think you will gain weight if you stop binge eating and purging. That's a thought: If I stop binge eating or more importantly if I stop purging, I'm going to be fat. That makes you feel anxious and scared but the truth is you really don't know what will happen. For the past eight years you've been doing things in a certain way because of these thoughts and assumptions but you really don't know what would happen if you stopped binge eating and purging. That's called the "fortune teller's error." [Therapist and patient should go through each entry identified in the negative consequences columns in a similar fashion.]

T: OK, now what problems are created by the bulimia, or at least not helped by it? In other words, what would you gain by giving up the binge eating and purging? What would be the positive short- and long-term consequences of not binge eating and purging any more? [Review responses.]

C: I'll be able to do more things socially because I won't be so afraid of losing control.

T: You'll be able to do more social activities. Does it happen now that you avoid certain situations because you are afraid that you will binge or purge?

C: Oh yeah, all the time. Or else I wind up canceling things because I'm in the middle of a binge or have just finished purging and am exhausted.

One of the other things I listed here is that I think my relationship with my husband would be better. I mean now it's one of those unspoken secrets.

T: So eliminating the binge eating and purging would potentially help your relationships but as you noted in the other column, that means dealing with some of the problems that you've been avoiding. Giving up the bulimia isn't going to take care of these problems automatically but it does make it possible for you to take care of them rather than continuing to avoid them.

The therapist and patient should review the decision analysis form thoroughly by going over each item. In addition to accurate appraisals of the consequences of eliminating the bulimia, frequently there are cognitive distortions in the responses that will interfere with treatment if they are not explicitly addressed.

T: As we've gone through the decision analysis form, we've been able to clarify why it is that you want help and some of what it is that interferes with making changes. We've identified some of the distortions in your thinking about your bulimia.

Let's start going through some of these distortions and begin challenging them. We can start with the distortions that you have already identified for homework today. We'll work together on developing some functional or rational challenges and you can continue the rest for homework.

The therapist should review the list of cognitive distortions that the patient has identified and select one or two examples to challenge with the patient in order to model the process.

T: Let's take this example . . . "My boss was angry that I didn't get the report in on time. I am not a good employee. I am a failure." Let's take it one statement at a time. Your boss was angry. How do you know that?

C: She said she was.

T: What did she say?

C: She said she wished I had told her that I would be late with the report and in the future to keep her posted on delays.

T: OK, so she didn't like the way you handled the delay and was able to tell you so. Does that make you "not a good employee"?

C: Well, I guess not but that's how I feel.

T: What kind of cognitive distortion is that?

C: Emotional reasoning?

T: That's right. You think you're a failure so you are. Now how would you challenge that.

C: I don't know. I guess I'm not such a bad employee.

T: How do you know that?

C: Well, I've been there 5 years now.

T: And what kind of feedback have you gotten, have you had any promotions, raises?

C: Oh yeah, people tell me that they like working with me—both my superiors and the people who work for me.

T: So the challenge to the idea that you are a bad employee is that just because you think you are a failure at a given moment does not make you a failure. You have received a lot of feedback that would support just the opposite idea— that you are a valued employee. Now part of this distortion is that when you get the slightest bit of negative feedback, you think you are a failure. This is what kind of distortion?

C: Magnification. Labeling and all-or-nothing thinking, too.

T: That's right. Try to challenge that. Begin here with your homework and continue through the list of dysfunctional thoughts that you have listed here as well as the ones that we have identified as we went through the decision analysis form. I want you to write down the dysfunctional thoughts, identify the distortions, and try to challenge the distortions. Have a discussion with yourself or imagine that a friend is telling you the cognitive distortion. How can you challenge the distortion, how can you begin to think about things differently?

Homework

1. Provide examples of numbers 6 through 10 on the cognitive distortion sheet.
2. Identify dysfunctional thoughts and challenges.
3. Complete binge–purge diary.

Session 5

Objectives

1. Review homework:
   a. Discuss examples of numbers 6 through 10 of dysfunctional thoughts and discuss challenges.
2. Introduce Daily Record of Dysfunctional Thoughts (see Figure 7.4).

The session began with a review of the homework, focusing on the identified dysfunctional thoughts and challenges. As is the case with many patients, Claire found it very difficult to provide cogent and persuasive challenges to diffuse the negative feelings associated with her dysfunctional thoughts. It is extremely important for the therapist to help the patient generate challenges to the cognitive distortions that do not pale in comparison. It typically requires numerous repetitions before the patient is able to generate strong and convincing challenges. This is a major part of the core work of cognitive restructuring in CBT for bulimia nervosa.

Once the patient is able to identify cognitive distortions and is able to generate challenges, the next step is to help her link these distortions to the high-risk situations that she associates with binge eating and purging. One of the primary instruments that is used to facilitate this work is the dysfunctional thought record (DTR). The following segment from Session 5 illustrates how to introduce the DTR and begin working with it.

Selective Transcript

T: OK, so, we've been able to identify some examples of the cognitive distortions that seem to be most common and most problematic for you. What we need to do now is link these distortions to specific situations, particularly to the times that you binge and purge. Let's take a

DATE	SITUATION Describe: 1. Actual event leading to unpleasant emotion, or 2. Stream of thoughts, daydream, or recollection, leading to unpleasant emotion.	EMOTION(S) 1. Specify sad/ anxious/ angry, etc. 2. Rate degree of emotion, 1-100.	AUTOMATIC THOUGHT(S) 1. Write automatic thought(s) that preceded emotion(s). 2. Rate belief in automatic thought(s), 0-100%.	RATIONAL RESPONSE 1. Write rational response to automatic thought(s). 2. Rate belief in rational response, 0-100%.	OUTCOME 1. Rerate belief in automatic thought(s), 0-100%. 2. Specify and rate sub-sequent emotions, 0-100.
12/1	My boyfriend and I started discussing what we think is attractive in men and women. I then started feeling fat and as if he couldn't possibly be attracted to me even though he says he is.	Sad, angry 100%	I'm fat and he'll never look at me like I'm attractive. He'd be much happier and satisfied with another person. 100%	1. Of course he's attracted to me—we've been going out for a long time. I also admire things in other men, that doesn't mean I don't love him or find him attractive. 2. No one is perfectly satisfied with how they look. 3. Bingeing and vomiting won't make me lose weight.	20% 30%

Explanation: When you experience an unpleasant emotion, note the situation that seemed to stimulate the emotion. (If the emotion occurred while you were thinking, daydreaming, etc., please note this.) Then note the automatic thought associated with the emotion. Record the degree to which you believe this thought: 0% = not at all; 100% = completely. In rating degree of emotion: 1 = a trace; 100 = the most intense possible.

FIGURE 7.4. Daily Record of Dysfunctional Thoughts. From *Cognitive Therapy of Depression* (p. 403) by A. T. Beck, A. J. Rush, B. F. Shaw, and G. Emery, 1979, New York: Guilford Press. Copyright 1979 by Aaron T. Beck, A. John Rush, Brian F. Shaw, and Gary Emery. Adapted by permission.

look at your diary. You have indicated here that you binged and purged yesterday after you got home from work. Let's look at this situation in more detail using what we call the dysfunctional thought record or DTR. We'll use this form to help us better understand the situations that precipitate binge and purge episodes for you, focusing on the thoughts and feelings that you have right before you binge or purge. What was the situation yesterday?

C: Well it was 8 p.m and I had just gotten home. I was feeling down because Tom was not going to be home—he's in California until tomorrow.

T: Okay. So the situation is that you are home alone after a long day at work. We write that in column 1 here. In column 2 we write down how you are feeling. You said you were feeling down, what else?

C: I was feeling bad that Tom didn't call me at work . . . usually he calls me when he's on the road.

T: Feeling "bad," what do you mean exactly?

C: Oh, I guess I was feeling depressed and I guess a little angry, too.

T: Okay, so we have depressed and angry in column 2. What else?

C: Kind of anxious, too.

T: Anxious?

C: Yeah, I had handed in a report to my boss that day and I wasn't sure what she thought of it.

T: We have depressed, angry and anxious. Let's connect up the thoughts associated with each of these feelings. You were feeling depressed because . . .

The goal here is to connect the feeling states with the underlying cognitive distortions. The cognitive distortions will generally not be apparent in the patient's first thought. It is essential that the therapist help the patient follow a particular thought as far as possible because usually the distortion is several steps from the surface thought. If the therapist stops too early in this exploration, the distortions will remain intact and undiscovered. One of the most effective ways of getting to these underlying distortions is by using open-ended statements that the patient can complete.

C: Tom didn't call.

T: And that makes you feel depressed because . . .

C: I feel like he doesn't care about me.

T: You think he doesn't care about you and that makes you feel depressed. You think he doesn't care about you because he didn't call.

C: I know. I'm being stupid and needy.

T: Stupid and needy?

C: Yeah, I mean I know it's stupid for me to get myself so worked up here but when he goes away I feel so rejected.

T: Rejected? (*adding this to the list in column 2*)

C: Yeah, I mean sometimes I think that he likes traveling more than he likes being home with me.

T: OK. So you were feeling depressed because Tom didn't call and since he didn't call you think that he doesn't care about you. You feel rejected and think that he likes traveling more than being home with you. Let's look at the distortions here. Your thoughts were that Tom doesn't care about you because he didn't call. What kind of distortion is that? (*handing Claire the list of cognitive distortions*)?

C: Well, magnification?

T: Magnifying the importance of this single event, right. You also said that you feel rejected and think he likes traveling more than being home with you even though he says that he doesn't. What kind of distortion is that?

C: I guess it's emotional reasoning.

T: Right . . . assuming that your negative emotions necessarily reflect the way things are—"I feel it, therefore it must be true." Have you ever checked this out with him?

C: No.

T: So in a way it's also an example of "mind reading."

C: Yeah, I guess I should find out rather than assuming the worst.

T: In addition to feeling depressed you also said that you were feeling angry. You were angry because . . .

C: Well, sort of for the same reasons. If he really cares about me he should call.

T: That's a "should statement."

C: I know, but he should call.

T: Would it be more accurate to say that you *want* him to call and when he doesn't you feel sad and put out?

C: Yeah.

T: Okay, so the first step here is recognizing the should statement. The challenge to the should statement is . . ?

C: There are lots of ways that he shows he cares about me, even when he is away so it's not that he should always call or that he has to call in order for me to know he cares, it's just that I like it when he calls.

T: OK, so when you put it that way how sad and angry do you feel?

C: Not as much. Maybe just a little sad still because I miss him.

T: So the next step then is figuring out how to manage these feelings more effectively. In other words, even after working through the distortions you are left with some feelings that are difficult for you to manage or tolerate. Right now what you do is binge. We need to work on some alternative strategies to binge eating at times like this. Before we do this let's look at your anxiety.

C: Oh, that had to do with my boss. I always get anxious when I hand things in to her.

T: You handed in a report to your boss and that makes you feel anxious because . . .

C: Well, I know there were parts of it that could have been stronger. I wish that I had spent more time on it so that it would have been better.

T: There were parts of it that could have been stronger and that makes you feel anxious because . . .

C: Well, because my boss is going to send it back for corrections.

T: And that makes you feel anxious because . . .

C: Because that means it wasn't perfect.

T: And since it's not perfect that makes you anxious because . . .

C: My boss will think that I'm not a very good employee.

T: Okay, so you hand in a report; that makes you anxious because parts of it could have been stronger—it's not perfect; the fact that it's not perfect makes you anxious because then your boss is going to think you're not a good employee. What are the distortions here?

C: Well I guess that's "mental filter." I mean most of the report was pretty good.

T: So as you see you're dwelling on the small negative details to the exclusion of the overall report which was pretty good.

C: Yeah, I guess it's a problem with perfectionism, too. I have to do things perfectly or else I think I'm a total failure.

T: So that's a form of all-or-nothing thinking. Now, what are the challenges?

C: It was a big report. Most of it was really good. I need to remember that most of the report was in great shape and the parts that need work are things that need my boss's input anyway. She doesn't expect it to be perfect so why should I?

T: So how do you feel now?

C: Better. If only I could stop to think these things through when I'm in the situation. I mean it all happens so fast.

T: That's what we're going to work on for now—helping you slow down enough so that you can think more clearly about how you're feeling and what you're thinking in situations like this. Right now it's as if you're on automatic pilot. A difficult situation arises and you wind up binge eating and purging—you go right from here (*pointing to column 1 of the DTR*) to here (*pointing to the line between columns 3 and 4*). I call this the "binge–purge line." We're going to work on slowing you down so that you can focus on your thoughts and feelings—

columns 2 and 3. And we're also going to try to get you over this hump, past this binge–purge line, without binge eating and purging by working on the challenges and by developing alternative coping strategies.

Homework

1. Complete the first four columns of the DTR during a high-risk situation.
2. Complete food diary of binge–purge episodes.

Session 6

Objectives

1. Review homework.
2. Complete DTR for a binge–purge episode that occurred last week.
3. Introduce three meals per day.
4. Plan some possible meals.

Most frequently when the DTR is first introduced and given to patients to complete for homework, patients do not fill out the form before they binge and purge. Sometimes patients will complete it after they binge and purge or not complete it at all. Usually they describe not even thinking of using the DTR until they are already deep into their binge or until they have completed the entire episode. It usually takes several repetitions with the therapist of completing the DTR retrospectively before the patient starts using the tool effectively on her own. Each session the therapist should continue to encourage the patient to use the DTR and help her think retrospectively about what would facilitate her completing the DTR before the binge. An example of this work is described in Session 6.

Selected Transcript

T: On your diary you have indicated that you had five binge–purge episodes last week. Let's look at the DTR that you filled out for one of them.

C: Well, on Saturday and Sunday I didn't even remember about the DTR. I did it on Tuesday but it was after the whole thing was over.

T: What do you think happened?

C: I don't know. It happens so fast, it's like my brain turns off. I finally remembered the DTR on Tuesday but that was after the whole thing was over.

T: It's not unusual for it to take some time before you get into the practice of using the DTR. Let's look at what you were able to complete on Tuesday. The situation was that you were at work and ate a piece of birthday cake that was for one of your coworkers. You felt guilty, depressed and fat. The thoughts you have here are, "cake is a binge food"; "I shouldn't eat such fattening food"; and "I'm going to get fat."

Let's start with feeling guilty. Whenever you feel guilty look for the "should statement." What you say here is that you shouldn't eat such fattening foods because you are going to get fat. What are the distortions?

C: Like you said, that's a should statement.

T: What else?

C: Overgeneralization. I mean one piece of cake is not going to make me fat.

T: So that's the distortion and the challenge. Part of that distortion is also the fortune teller's error don't you think?

C: Yeah. But even though I "know" that one piece of cake is not going to make me fat, I don't really believe it yet.

T: Well you probably won't fully believe it until you find out for yourself that it's true. Soon we'll try some mini-experiments so that you can find out for yourself what does happen if you eat an occasional piece of cake.

One of the other distortions that we see here is the labeling of certain foods as forbidden. Labeling is an extreme example of all-or-nothing thinking. Either a food is "good" or "bad."

C: That's definitely the case for me. I've got a long list of bad foods.

T: The way we think about food is that there are no good or bad foods. No single food is going to make you fat. Your eating habits are important. Your pattern of eating from day to day is what

we need to work on rather than eliminating individual food items from your diet. Although that sounds pretty scary, we see here that you are eating these so-called forbidden foods already but you are not enjoying them very much. We're going to work on bringing them into your regular meals so that eating is more satisfying for you.

So what are the challenges to the distortions that you've identified?

C: Well, no single food is going to make me fat. It's OK if I eat cake every once in a while.

T: Do you really believe that?

C: Well sort of. I think it's true for everyone else but I really am afraid that if I have one bite I'll wind up having a binge.

T: If you have one bite you'll wind up having a binge because . . .

C: Because I feel like a failure and that I shouldn't have any because it will make me fat.

T: We've challenged the idea that one piece of cake will make you fat. What's the distortion and challenge to the idea that you are a failure.

C: Well, I feel in control if I don't eat and I feel totally out of control when I do eat that stuff.

T: So that's an example of . . .

C: All-or-nothing thinking.

T: And the problem is that when you're not eating, are you really in control? It seems to me that not eating any of the foods that you like is really just the flip side of the binge. Also, it sets you up to binge. No one can go on indefinitely forbidding themselves the foods that they really like. The way I think about it, you'll really be in control when you are able to eat some of these foods in moderation during your regular meals.

Next time you think you are about to binge, I want you to go back to this DTR and review the distortions and challenges. Also, I want you to fill out a new DTR. After you complete the list of feelings, thoughts, distortions and challenges, I want you to come up with five alternatives to binge eating and implement at least one.

The other thing I want to work on is your eating outside of binge episodes. Our goal is for you to eat three meals per day. This is the surest way for you to eat a wide range of foods and enough calories so that you can avoid feeling physically starved and psychologically deprived. Right now you're skipping lots of meals. This is one of the things that sets you up for binge eating because by the end of the day you feel deprived and, in fact, excessively hungry. Thus, in addition to the other triggers, by the end of the day you are especially vulnerable. In fact, this is one the most difficult times of the day for you in terms of your binge eating and purging, isn't it?

C: Yeah, but I'm afraid if I start eating in the morning, I'll wind up eating all day and that will just trigger a binge.

T: How would that trigger a binge?

C: Well, I'll be thinking that I'm eating too much and that I'm going to get fat. . . . So, I'll figure that I have to vomit up what I've eaten, and if I'm going to vomit, I might as well eat all the foods that I otherwise forbid myself.

T: I know it's difficult for you to believe that you are not going to get fat if you eat three meals a day. That's the way you have been thinking about your eating for a long time now. What I want to encourage you to consider is that you are actually consuming more calories than you've counted in the past because you've always dismissed all the calories that you consumed while binge eating because you thought you got rid of all of them when you purged. Now you know that isn't the case. So, as difficult as it is, I want to encourage you to experiment with bringing some of these calories into your regular eating, ease up on your restraint during the day, so that you don't put yourself at risk at the end of the day because you are so starved and deprived. Let's plan for three meals for the next few days and see how it goes.

C: OK.

The therapist should go through complete meal planning with the patient for the days between this and the next session. Typically the patient will want to plan for excessively restrictive meals. It is the therapist's job to ensure that the meals are sufficiently caloric and appealing.

Homework

1. Complete the DTR during a high-risk situation.
2. Complete eating diary—planned and actual consumption.
3. Complete food diary of binge–purge episodes.

Session 7

Objectives

1. Review homework.
2. Complete DTR for any problem episodes since last session.
3. Discuss alternatives to binge eating and purging and delay strategies.
4. Review success of three meals per day.

This session focused on the patient's experience of trying to eat three meals per day. On the days that she did eat three meals, she did not binge or purge. However, after eating three meals per day for 2 days she was "feeling fat" and "anxious" so she decided to skip dinner that day and wound up binge eating and purging late that night. This experience offered sufficient support for the link between binge and non-binge eating that the patient was then able to state for herself that the best way to avoid a binge episode is to plan to eat. Nonetheless, she had significant anxiety about gaining weight as transcribed below.

Selective Transcript

C: I feel a lot better that I ate some regular meals but I know that I can't keep this up or I am going to blow up.

T: Let's review again some of the thoughts you have about managing your weight. Right now you are afraid to eat three meals per day because you're afraid you'll gain weight. I understand that it's difficult for you to believe otherwise until you experiment with this new behavior for a while but I want to emphasize a couple of points that may help you as you try to continue eating three meals per day.

First, remember the handout I gave you on vomiting and laxative abuse? Go over that periodically as you begin experimenting with three meals per day. Remember, contrary to popular belief, purging is not a very effective means of either avoiding weight gain or losing weight. Your body absorbs more calories than you think. And laxative abuse is ineffective and dangerous. Eighty percent of the calories consumed are absorbed by the body almost immediately, and hence the only real effect of purging is depletion of fluids. Similarly, weight loss due to laxatives is also a consequence of water loss. Taking laxatives has the added danger, however, of causing rebound water retention once the laxatives have been discontinued.

Another big danger of vomiting or abusing laxatives is that is sets you up to have even larger binges because you figure you are going to get rid of it all anyway and that probably also deters you from eating regular meals at other times of the day. If you binge and vomit in the afternoon chances are that you will be feeling bad and wind up not eating dinner either because you are too exhausted or because you feel guilty for the binge or . . .

C: Oh yeah, if I binge at work, I never eat dinner.

T: And if you skip dinner what happens later?

C: Well either I go right to sleep or late in the evening I feel hungry and then chances are I'll wind up binge eating at midnight.

T: So the cycle continues. . . . We need to continue to work on breaking the cycle both by managing the high-risk situations without binge eating and vomiting and by working on establishing healthier eating habits during non-binge times. So as difficult as it is, I want you to continue to plan on three meals per day. In terms of managing the potential binge episodes, I want you to continue filling out the DTR at high-risk times with the addition of coming up with at least five alternatives to binge eating and purging for each situation.

What are some things that you think you could do instead of binge eating or purging?

C: That's hard to imagine . . . when I get to the point of binge eating or purging I feel like there are no alternatives.

T: That would be an example of what kind of thinking?

C: All or nothing.

T: It's easy to see that you would think this way since this is the way that you've managed your eating for so long but let's work together to try to come up with some alternatives. The other day for example, when you binged after you got home, what could you have done instead?

C: Well, I could have cleaned my apartment when I got home . . . it's an absolute mess. I really should do that anyway.

T: The alternatives should be engaging and pleasurable. Maybe it's true that your apartment needed to be cleaned but did you really want to clean when you were feeling like binge eating? Let's try to come up with some more pleasurable activities that might really work.

C: I could have stop by a friend's house on my way home and planned to have dinner with her since my husband was away.

T: Good. What else? What could you do this week if you get home one evening and feel like binge eating?

C: I could read for a while.

T: Will that be sufficiently engaging for you to avoid a binge?

C: Well, I'm reading a really good book right now so maybe.

T: OK, let's start there. If you try that and still feel like binge eating what could you do?

C: I could plan to eat a regular meal and then go out for a walk immediately so that it doesn't turn into a binge.

T: Good. It's important that you eat dinner even when you feel the urge to binge so that may be a safe way to eat dinner without it's becoming trouble. What else?

C: I guess I could call a friend. If I manage to eat alone I could just talk to my friend until I don't feel anxious anymore . . . I could also call one of my best friends who lives nearby and visit her or have her come over for dinner if I'm going to be home alone all night.

T: This is a great start. What I want you to do for next time is come up with a list of alternatives that will help you delay or completely avoid binge eating and purging. When you are feeling like you want to binge or purge I want you to have a variety of activities listed that are engaging *and* pleasurable so you can refer to it to help you get through the most difficult time right before you start binge eating or purging.

Homework

1. Complete the DTR during a high-risk situation with alternatives.
2. Complete eating diary—planned and actual consumption.
3. Complete food diary of binge–purge episodes.
4. List alternatives and delay strategies.

Sessions 8 and 9

Objectives

1. Review homework:
   a. Focus on continuing high-risk situations.
   b. Go over alternative strategies to binge eating.
   c. Assess any continuing difficulties with DTR.
2. Review three meals per day.
3. Identify forbidden foods.

At this stage in the therapy many new concepts, tools, strategies, and behavioral changes have been introduced. Therefore, much of the work during this phase entails working on the areas in which the patient has the most difficulty, which will vary from individual to individual. In Claire's case, she continued to have significant problems with eating dinner during the week. Also, if she did eat, even if she did not have a true binge, she would feel the urge to vomit. The

focus of our work during Sessions 8 and 9 centered on eating dinner and the cognitive distortions that she maintained about the effects of eating dinner. This led to the introduction of the concept of forbidden foods as transcribed below.

Selective Transcript

C: . . . well, I ate dinner almost every night last week but I wound up vomiting after dinner a couple of times, too.

T: So was it the same pattern each evening that you vomited?

C: Yeah, I got home, planned to eat dinner, started nibbling while I was getting dinner ready, wound up eating more than I planned and felt so fat that I decided to vomit.

T: OK, so let's go through the DTR for the last time that happened.

C: Last night. I got home. I planned to make pasta, salad, and bread. I wound up eating two slices of bread with butter before dinner and took a second helping of pasta during dinner. I was stuffed and had to get rid of it.

T: Feelings, thoughts?

C: Anxious. If I keep eating like this I'm going to get fat. I ate butter, and that's not allowed.

T: Distortions?

C: Fortune teller's error, magnification, all-or-nothing thinking—I mean as soon as I tasted the butter I decided I had to vomit because butter is fattening and if I eat it I'll get fat.

At this point, Claire was well versed in the procedure of using the DTR so the therapeutic task is to get to the remaining issues without spending a lot of time focusing on the parts that she is managing successfully on her own. She was able to challenge the idea that feeling full is the same thing as being fat but she was stuck with regard to having eaten the butter.

T: Now is the time for us to work more aggressively on the list of forbidden foods that you have in your head. By having such a list, we can see that you are setting yourself up to vomit at times. Our goal is to gradually bring these foods into your eating so that you can enjoy the times that you do eat them and not have them set off binges or vomiting episodes.

Also, in some ways it seems like the whole experience of eating dinner is forbidden in your mind. Whether or not you have a real binge, you think you have to counteract your eating by vomiting. What we need to work on at times like this is not changing your eating so much as changing the way you are thinking about your eating. Our goal is for you to be able to eat the dinner that you describe without vomiting rather than changing your eating behavior as we would want to do in the case of an objective binge.

What I would like you to do for the next session is continue working on eating three meals per day with special attention to having dinner. Also, I want you to write down all the forbidden foods you can think of so that we can begin working on bringing these foods into your diet.

Sessions 10 through 15

Objectives

1. Continue working on identifying high-risk situations and using the DTR to work on developing more adaptive functioning.
2. Address the issues of body shape concern and weight as the patient's eating behavior normalizes
3. Incorporate a wider range of foods in the patient's diet, including former forbidden foods.

During this middle phase of treatment, Claire was able to establish healthier eating habits, which included eating three meals per day and incorporating her forbidden foods into her diet. She also made regular use of the DTR to manage difficult situations, employed delay strategies and alternatives, and was able to avert binge eating and purging episodes almost always. The work of the sessions focused on the times

that she was not able to avert the binge–purge episodes and on building a wider range of alternative behaviors to binge eating and purging. As is typical, one of the issues that arose during this phase of the treatment was Claire's continuing dissatisfaction with her weight and body shape. A segment addressing some of these issues is included below.

Selective Transcript

C: . . . I don't know, I just feel so fat that at times I want to go back on a diet. If I could just lose 15 pounds . . .

T: What would that do for you?

C: Well, I would feel better about myself. I think I would look better. Clothes would look better on me. I look better when I weigh 120.

T: What has happened to your weight during the course of therapy?

C: It's basically stayed the same. I think I've lost 2 pounds according to the last time I weighed myself.

T: And how are you feeling about having your eating under control?

C: Great. I am so much more productive at work and it's helped me deal more effectively with my relationships but I just wish I weighed a little less.

T: What's the magic of 120 lbs?

C: I don't know. I just think that I would be happier. I need some new clothes and I have been putting off shopping because I know I'm going to look like a moose.

T: Like a moose?

C: OK, so I'm exaggerating. I guess there's some all-or-nothing thinking about my weight. If I weigh 120 pounds that's great and anything else is unacceptable.

T: It would be useful for you to try to start thinking about an acceptable weight range rather than striving for a specific ideal weight. In this vein it would be useful for you to go shopping and try on some clothes that fit you well now. Don't buy something that is two sizes too small. Get something that is flattering now. You may find out that, in fact, you can look good at your current weight.

C: I doubt that but I'll try.

T: For next session, why don't you go shopping and try to find something that you can take with you on your upcoming vacation.

Sessions 16 through 19

Objectives

1. Continue to identify underlying assumptions about weight, body image, etc., using examples brought in as homework.
2. Work on relapse prevention:
   a. "Avoid what ifs"—I binged, purged, gained weight, etc.?
   b. Redefine "I blew it" as a "slip" and a learning opportunity.
   c. Adopt a problem-solving attitude.
3. Identify potential high-risk situations after termination of treatment.

The goal of this phase of treatment is for the patient to learn to reframe inevitable future "slips" as less than disastrous. The patient should be made aware that for a while, there may be rough situations in which she may experience and possibly even succumb to the urge to binge and/or purge. It should be explained to the patient that until she has fully normalized her eating habits and become more comfortable with her body weight and shape that food and weight issues will be her "soft spot" or "Achille's heel," that the true test of therapy will be her ability to utilize a problem-solving attitude with respect to "getting on track" rather than panicking and giving up.

Selective Transcript

C: No binge or purge episodes again!

T: That's great. And how are meals going?

C: Pretty well. Usually I am able to eat three meals a day. Sometimes I still wind up skipping a meal here or there but for the most part I've been sticking with regular meals. I even ate dessert when I went out to dinner with Tom last night.

T: That's great progress. Is there anything left on your forbidden food list that you haven't tried yet?

C: Nope. I don't eat that stuff all the time but when I want something sweet I let myself have it now and I don't feel like I have to have a full-blown binge just because I've had an ice cream cone.

T: You've made a lot of progress. One of the things that we should discuss at this stage is what you are going to do when therapy is over and you have some rough times. We know it's still difficult for you when Tom travels, and you also are under a lot of pressure at work. It's important for us to think ahead to times that may be difficult for you to manage so that you can work on preventing any big trouble.

One of the images that may be useful is for you to think back to when you first started in treatment. You were stuck in a pretty destructive cycle and had dug yourself into a hole by the repetitions of binge eating and purging. At this point, you've climbed out and have started on a new path. There will be times that you will feel that you are not exactly on course but that doesn't mean that you are back in the pit. At those difficult times remember that you are well on your way down this new path, just a little off course. What you want to do is remain sensitive to the cues that will tell you when you are on track and when you have fallen off course so that you can get back on track without a major relapse.

C: Yeah, in a way I hate to think about that but I guess you're right. I'm feeling so good now, I don't want to jinx myself.

T: I know it's scary but by planning ahead you'll increase your chances of staying on course not reduce them. Can you think of any potential high-risk situations?

C: Oh yeah. One that's coming up soon is my sister's wedding. There are going to be so many people and I'm her maid of honor so I have to look good in my dress and everything. I'm really proud of myself though. When we were fitted for dresses I resisted the urge to tell the dressmaker to make the dress smaller so that I would have to diet to fit into it and, you know, it looks OK on me now!

T: Good, that's real progress. Anything else?

C: Well, I'm worried about work, with a new boss and everything.

T: What can you do to avoid setting yourself up for more binge–purge episodes?

C: Well, I think I'm handling the pressure much better. But even when I don't feel like binge eating or purging if I'm having a bad day I fill out one of those DTRs. It just helps me figure out what's going on.

The therapist and patient should go through the list of potential high risk situations as the examples above indicate. The therapist should continue to reinforce the use of the cognitive–behavioral strategies in the whole range of situations that the patient describes as difficult even if the patient does not feel the urge to binge or purge.

Session 20

Objectives

1. Review homework.
2. Review treatment gains.
3. Discuss maintenance phase of treatment.
4. Encourage patient to continue using the skills she has gained when the formal treatment is over—concept of becoming your own therapist.

The bulk of this session is devoted to a review of progress that has been made and, more important, how that progress was made. Attention should be paid to the specific factors that were most important to the patient in the recovery of normal eating patterns, and the necessity for the patient to continue to implement the strategies that have brought her so far.

Selective Transcript

T: This is our last session. How are you feeling?

C: Great. I am going to miss you and I don't know what I'm going to do on Monday evenings now but I feel great about my eating. I haven't binged or purged in over two months. I'm a little worried about falling back, but to tell you the truth, I really don't think I will. I have the DTR form in my head now and I find that I'm using the steps all the time. The other day I was in a meeting that was going badly and I found myself saying to myself, "Now what is the situation? How am I feeling, what do I think?" I almost started laughing out loud when I realized what I was doing. It just comes so naturally to me now.

T: So the DTR has helped a lot. Do you catch yourself with the list of cognitive distortions?

C: The other day I told Tom that what he said was an example of all-or-nothing thinking! It's amazing. Now that I am listening for the distortions, I hear them and am able to address the problems that I'm having much better. I really think that has helped me a lot in dealing with my boss and with Tom.

T: And how about your meals?

C: Pretty good. I know I have to eat. Sometimes when I think about skipping a meal I hear your voice saying, "The best way to manage your weight is to eat." I also think of what you said, "Full doesn't mean fat." That's a big one that I have to remember.

T: And how about your weight?

C: Well, I still wouldn't mind if I lost a few pounds but I realize it's not going to solve all my problems and I definitely know that dieting is not the way for me to do it. I'm thinking about joining an aerobics class in the fall.

T: That may be a good idea. Just remember to check yourself on how important you make your weight. Try to keep that in check. But certainly a moderate exercise program is good for most everyone as long as you don't get carried away or have unrealistic expectations.

You've made a lot of progress. It took a lot of hard work and you can be proud of how well you're doing. I think you have integrated the ideas and made real changes in your behavior that will help you stay on track in the future. Just remember that even there, it's not all or nothing. Some days will be better than others. The key is for you to continue to check in with yourself on a regular basis and use the skills that you have learned when the going gets rough.

I expect that things will continue to go well for you but please feel free to be in touch if you feel that you need some help down the road.

C: Thanks for all your help.

T: I wish you all the best.

Manual-Based Treatment and Clinical Practice

The treatment we have described was based on a specific manual. It was, therefore, highly structured and time limited. Treatment of this sort is quite unlike everyday clinical practice in which cognitive-behavioral therapists can freely draw from a wider range of treatment techniques, often over a longer period of time. The latter, it can be argued, should be more effective than the necessarily truncated form of manual-based CBT. In unrestricted clinical practice treatment can more freely be tailored to the individual patient's particular needs.

Whether unrestricted clinical practice is more effective than the standard treatment prescribed in manuals of the sort illustrated in this chapter is unknown. With the increasing use of manuals not only in treatment studies but also in clinical practice, there is a general need to compare manual-based treatment with more conventional, "no holds barred" clinical practice within the same time frame. In the meantime, there are good reasons for adhering to manual-based treatment even in everyday clinical practice given that the clinical effectiveness of the treatment has been repeatedly demonstrated (Fairburn, Agras, & Wilson, 1992). A second advantage is that the highly structured and time-limited nature of this treatment focuses the attention of both therapist and patient in working hard to make well-defined changes (Fairburn, Marcus, & Wilson, 1993). Finally, adding additional elements to the treatment requires either replacing some aspects or making it longer. Both options have disadvantages. It is unclear whether extending treatment has any advantages. In the treatment we describe an explicit message is that patients are being helped to be their own therapists so that they can continue to make progress following the termination of formal treatment.

PREDICTORS OF THERAPEUTIC SUCCESS AND FAILURE

There is no consensus on reliable predictors of treatment outcome. To a large extent, this is probably attributable to the use of what have been small samples of patients in outcome studies that have examined this issue, and hence lack of statistical power for identifying treatment × patient interactions.

There is evidence that self-esteem is a pretreatment predictor of outcome in bulimia nervosa (Fairburn, Kirk, O'Connor, Anastasiades, & Cooper, 1987; Fairburn et al., in press). Patients with low scores on the Rosenberg (1965) self-esteem scale (a brief, 14–item measure) respond least well to psychological treatment. Attitudinal disturbance at pretreatment has also been found to predict response to psychological treatment, but in a counterintuitive way—patients with the most extreme attitudinal disturbance fared best in response to CBT and IPT (Fairburn et al., in press). It is difficult to explain this finding, which needs replication in a larger patient sample. Nonetheless, it is consistent with Walsh et al.'s (1991) finding that patients who responded to treatment with desipramine had higher scores on the BSQ than did nonresponders.

No other variable has yielded unequivocal results. It has become clinical lore that the co-occurrence of personality disorders, particularly borderline personality, identifies a subgroup of patients who are difficult to treat and who do not respond to CBT (Johnson, Tobin, & Dennis, 1990). A sizable minority of bulimia nervosa patients are often diagnosed with a personality disorder, and data from a recent Stanford study suggest that patients with personality disorders, particularly cluster B characteristics, fare relatively poorly with CBT (Rossiter, Agras, Telch, & Schneider, 1993). Consistent with these data is Fairburn et al.'s (in press) finding from their 1-year follow-up that patients who dropped out had higher scores on the Personality Diagnostic Questionnaire (Hyler, Rieder, Spitzer, & Williams, 1978) than did patients who continued in the treatment trial.

In contrast to these results, however, Ames-Frankel et al. (1992) have reported a positive correlation between cluster B scores and therapeutic improvement in the treatment of bulimia nervosa patients with desipramine. A problem in assessing the role of personality disorders in the treatment of bulimia nervosa is the consistent finding that they often disappear following the successful treatment of the eating disorder (Ames-Frankel et al., 1992; Garner et al., 1990). The state–trait influence of measures of personality disorder remains to be resolved.

A prior history of anorexia nervosa was a strong negative prognostic factor in Garner et al.'s (1993) study, but neither Fairburn et al. (1991) nor Walsh et al. (1991) replicated this finding in their studies of psychological and pharmacological treatment respectively. There are also mixed findings on frequency of binge eating at pretreatment, with one study (Garner et al., 1990) showing positive results, and others (Fairburn et al., 1991; Wilson & Eldredge, 1991) negative results. Three other variables that might have been assumed to predict outcome have failed to do so, namely, duration of the disorder (Fairburn et al., in press), degree of depression at pretreatment (Agras, Dorian, Kirkley, Artnow, & Bachman, 1987; Walsh et al., 1988), and a prior history of psychoactive substance abuse (Mitchell, Pyle, Eckert, Hatsukami, & Soll, 1990; Strasser, Pike, & Walsh, 1992). It is not uncommon to find coexisting psychoactive substance abuse in patients with eating disorders. Controlled treatment trials have excluded these patients. In clinical practice, the therapist must decide whether to treat both disorders simultaneously or to sequence treatments (see Wilson, 1993d). We recommend that if the psychoactive substance abuse is severe, it should be treated first.

Even less is known about predictors of relapse following successful treatment. A major prediction of the cognitive–behavioral model of bulimia nervosa is that maintenance of treatment-induced change is a function of the degree of attitudinal disturbance concerning body shape and weight at the end of treatment. An initial test has confirmed that prediction, and underscored the importance of modifying abnormal attitudes about shape and weight (Fairburn et al., in press).

CONCLUSION AND RECOMMENDATIONS

Bulimia nervosa and binge eating in obese patients can be effectively treated. Taking into account the available evidence from controlled outcome studies as a whole, CBT appears to be the most effective form of treatment. Nevertheless, it is often insufficient. CBT is ineffective with some patients, and produces only limited improvement in still others. No more than 50% of bulimia nervosa patients treated with CBT achieve full remission of their symptoms. Bulimia nervosa is probably a heterogeneous disorder for which no single treatment will suffice. Unfortunately, we are not yet at the point where we can match treatments to identifiable subgroups of patients because there are no data on treatment-specific predictors of outcome. Thus, while there is evidence indicating that CBT is less effective in patients with personality disorders, it does not follow that alternative forms of psychotherapy are any more effective as has been suggested by Johnson et al. (1990).

We recommend CBT as the treatment of choice for bulimia nervosa for three reasons: (1) it has been shown to be as effective, if not more so, as any psychological or pharmacological therapy with which it has been compared; (2) it is a relatively brief, and therefore efficient, treatment; and (3) it has been described in detailed manuals which makes it widely available to clinicians even if they have not had specific training in cognitive-behavior therapy.

Given the limitations of CBT, alternative methods for treating nonresponders need to be developed. IPT is a promising approach which warrants additional study. Not only does it appear to equal CBT in longer-term effectiveness with bulimia nervosa (Fairburn, Jones, et al., 1993) and obese binge eaters (Wilfley et al., 1993), but it has also produced improvement in diabetic patients with bulimia nervosa who had failed to respond to CBT (Peveler & Fairburn, 1992). It does not seem likely that antidepressant drugs will succeed where CBT has failed. However, drugs such as fluoxetine would be recommended to treat associated psychopathology, such as depression, which might be impeding progress in modifying the eating disorder. A final option if outpatient CBT treatment fails is to recommend a day hospital program, or full hospitalization, for more direct and intensive treatment of the patient's disordered eating habits. Food intake can be better regulated, and binge eating and purging prevented, in such a structured setting. Day hosptial treatment is preferred because it is less expensive and does not completely remove the patient from the psychosocial situations that are associated with binge eating and purging (Piran & Kaplan, 1990).

Finally, it should be noted that an intensive form of psychological treatment such as CBT (or IPT) is not always necessary. Some individuals with bulimia nervosa respond favorably to a structured, educational approach conducted in a group setting (Olmsted et al., 1991). This type of cost-efficient program seems well suited to high-functioning individuals with no complicating psychopathology. Ideally, a treatment center might offer a stepped-care approach in which patients would initially receive the most cost-effective treatment, followed by more a intensive program should they fail to respond (Fairburn et al., 1992).

REFERENCES

Agras, W. S., Dorian, B., Kirkley, B. G., Artnow, B., & Bachman, J. (1987). Imipramine in the treatment of bulimia: A double-blind controlled study. *International Journal of Eating Disorders, 6,* 29–38.

Agras, W. S., Schneider, J. A., Arnow, B., Raeburn, S. D., & Telch, C. F. (1989). Cognitive-behavioral treatment with and without exposure plus response prevention in the treatment of bulimia nervosa: A reply to Leitenberg and Rosen. *Journal of Consulting and Clinical Psychology, 57,* 778–779.

Agras, W. S., Rossiter, E. M., Arnow, B., Schneider, J. A., Telch, C. F., Raeburn, S. D., Bruce, B., Perl, M., & Koran, L. M. (1992). Pharmacologic and cognitive-behavioral treatment for bulimia nervosa: A controlled comparison. *American Journal of Psychiatry, 149,* 82–87.

American Psychiatric Association. (1987). *Diagnostic and statistical manual of mental disorders* (3rd ed., rev.). Washington, DC: Author.

American Psychiatric Association. (1993). *DSM-IV draft criteria as of 3/1/93.* Washington, DC: Author.

Ames-Frankel, J., Devlin, M. J., Walsh, B. T., Strasser, T. J., Sadik, C., Oldham, J., & Roose, S. P. (1992). Personality disorder diagnoses in patients with bulimia nervosa: Clinical correlates and changes with treatment. *Journal of Clinical Psychiatry, 53,* 90–96.

Andersen, A. (Ed.). (1990). *Males with eating disorders.* New York: Brunner/Mazel.

Attie, I., & Brooks-Gunn, J. (1989). Development of eating problems in adolescent girls: A longitudinal study. *Developmental Psychology, 25,* 70–79.

Beck, A. T. (1976). *Cognitive therapy and the emotional disorders.* New York: International Universities Press.

Beck, A. T., Rush, A. J., Shaw, B. F., & Emery, G. (1979). *Cognitive therapy of depression.* New York: Guilford Press.

Beglin, S. J., & Fairburn, C. G. (1992). What is meant by the term "binge"? *American Journal of Psychiatry, 149,* 123–124.

Blundell, J. E. (1990). How culture undermines the biopsychological system of appetite control. *Appetite, 14,* 113–115.

Booth, D. A., Lewis, V. J., & Blair, A. J. (1990). Dietary restraint and binge eating: pseudo-quantitative anthropology for a medicalized problem habit? *Appetite, 14,* 116–119.

Cooper, P. J., & Fairburn, C. G. (1993). Confusion over the "core psychopathology" of bulimia nervosa. *International Journal of Eating Disorders, 13,* 385–390.

Cooper, P. J., Taylor, M. J., Cooper, Z., & Fairburn, C. G. (1987). The development and validation of the Body Shape Questionnaire. *International Journal of Eating Disorders, 6,* 485–494.

Craighead, L. W., & Agras, W. S. (1991). Mechanisms of action in cognitive-behavioral and pharmacological interventions for obesity and bulimia nervosa. *Journal of Consulting and Clinical Psychology, 59,* 115–125.

DaCosta, M., & Halmi, K. A. (1992). Classification of anorexia nervosa: Question of subtypes. *International Journal of Eating Disorders, 11,* 305–314.

Fairburn, C. G. (1985). Cognitive-behavioral treatment for bulimia. In D. M. Garner & P. E. Garfinkel (Eds.), *Handbook of psychotherapy for anorexia nervosa and bulimia* (pp. 160–192). New York: Guilford Press.

Fairburn, C. G., Agras, W. S., & Wilson, G. T. (1992). The research on the treatment of bulimia nervosa: Practical and theoretical implications. In G. H. Anderson & S. H. Kennedy (Eds.), *The biology of feast and famine: Relevance to eating disorders* (pp. 318–340). New York: Academic Press.

Fairburn, C. G., & Beglin, S. J. (1990). Studies of the epidemiology of bulimia nervosa. *American Journal of Psychiatry, 147,* 401–408.

Fairburn, C. G., & Cooper, Z. (1993). The Eating Disorder Examination (12th edition). In C. G. Fairburn & G. T. Wilson (Eds.), *Binge eating: Nature, assessment, and treatment* (pp. 317–360). New York: Guilford Press.

Fairburn, C. G., Jones, R., Peveler, R. C., Carr, S., Solomon, R., O'Connor, M. E., & Hope, R. A. (1991). Three psychological treatments for bulimia nervosa: A comparative trial. *Archives of General Psychiatry, 48,* 463–469.

Fairburn, C. G., Jones, R., Peveler, R. C., Hope, R. A., & O'Connor, M. E. (1993). Psychotherapy and bulimia nervosa: The long-term effects of interpersonal psychotherapy, behavior therapy and cognitive behavior therapy for bulimia nervosa. *Archives of General Psychiatry, 50,* 419–428.

Fairburn, C. G., Kirk, J., O'Connor, M., Anastasiades, P., & Cooper, P. J. (1987). Prognostic factors in bulimia nervosa. *British Journal of Clinical Psychology, 26,* 223–224.

Fairburn, C. G., Kirk, J., O'Connor, M., & Cooper, P. J. (1986). A comparison of two psychological treatments for bulimia nervosa. *Behaviour Research and Therapy, 24,* 629–643.

Fairburn, C. G., Marcus, M. D., & Wilson, G. T. (1993). Cognitive-behavioural therapy for binge eating and bulimia nervosa: A comprehensive treatment manual. In C. G. Fairburn & G. T. Wilson (Eds.), *Binge eating: Nature, assessment, and treatment* (pp. 361–404). New York: Guilford Press.

Fairburn, C. G., Peveler, R. C., Jones, R., Hope, R. A., & Doll, H. (in press). Predictors of 12–month outcome in bulimia nervosa and the influence of attitudes to shape and weight. *Journal of Consulting and Clinical Psychology.*

Fairburn, C. G., & Wilson, G. T. (Eds.). (1993). *Binge eating: Nature, assessment, and treatment.* New York: Guilford Press.

Fichter, M. M., & Hoffman, R. (1990). Bulimia (nervosa) in the male. In M. M. Fichter (Ed.), *Bulimia nervosa: Basic research, diagnosis and therapy* (pp. 99–111). Chichester, England: Wiley.

Garner, D. M. (1993). Binge eating in anorexia nervosa. In C. G. Fairburn & G. T. Wilson (Eds.), *Binge eating: Nature, assessment, and treatment* (pp. 50–76). New York: Guilford Press.

Garner, D. M. (1991). *Eating Disorders Inventory-2.* Odessa, FL: Psychological Assessment Resources.

Garner, D. M., & Bemis, K. M. (1985). Cognitive therapy for anorexia nervosa. In D. M. Garner & P. E. Garfinkel (Eds.), *Handbook of psychotherapy for anorexia nervosa and bulimia* (pp. 107–146). New York: Guilford Press.

Garner, D. M., & Garfinkel, P. E. (Eds.). (1985). *Handbook of psychotherapy for anorexia nervosa and bluimia.* New York: Guilford Press.

Garner, D. M., Olmsted, M. P., Davis, R., Rockert, W., Goldbloom, D., & Eagle, M. (1990). The association between bulimic symptoms and reported psychopathology. *International Journal of Eating Disorders, 9,* 1–15.

Garner, D. M., Rockert, W., Davis, R., Garner, M. V., Oldsted, M. P., & Eagle, M. (1993). A comparison between cognitive-behavioral and supportive-expressive therapy for bulimia nervosa. *American Journal of Psychiatry, 150,* 37–46.

Garner, D. M., Shafer, C. L., Rosen, L. W. (1992). Critical appraisal of the DSM-III-R diagnostic criteria for eating disorders. In S. R. Hooper, G. W. Hynd, & R. E. Mattison (Eds.), *Child psychopathology, diagnostic criteria and clinical assessment* (pp. 261–302). Hillsdale, NJ: Erlbaum.

Gormally, J., Black, S., Daston, S., & Rardin, D. (1982). The assessment of binge eating severity among obese persons. *Addictive Behaviors, 7,* 47–55.

Hollon, S. D., DeRubeis, R. J., & Evans, M. D. (1987). Causal mediation of change in treatment for depression: Discriminating between nonspecificity and noncausality. *Psychological Bulletin, 102,* 139–149.

Hsu, L. K. G. (1990). *Eating disorders.* New York: Guilford Press.

Humphrey, L. L. (1987). A comparison of bulimic-anorexic and non-distressed families using structural analysis of social behavior. *Journal of the American Academy of Child and Adolescent Psychiatry, 26,* 248–255.

Humphrey, L. L. (1988). Relationships within subtypes of anorexic, bulimic, and normal families. *Journal of the American Academy of Child and Adolescent Psychiatry, 27,* 544–551.

Hyler, S. E., Rieder, R. O., Spitzer, R. L., & Williams, J. B. W. (1978). *Personality Diagnostic Questionnaire (PDQ).* New York: New York State Psychiatric Institute.

Johnson, C., Tobin, D. L., & Enright, A. (1989). Prevalence and clinical characteristics of borderline patients in an eating-disordered population. *Journal of Clinical Psychiatry, 50,* 9–15.

Johnson, C., Tobin, D. L., & Dennis, A. (1990). Differences in treatment outcome between borderline and nonborderline bulimics at one-year follow-up. *International Journal of Eating Disorders, 9,* 617–627.

Kassett, J. A., Gershon, E. S., Maxwell, M. E., Guroff, J. J., Kazuba, D. M., Smith, A. L., Brandt, H. A., & Jimerson, D. C. (1989). Psychiatric disorders in the first-degree relatives of probands with bulimia nervosa. *American Journal of Psychiatry, 146,* 1468–1471.

Kendler, K. S., MacLean, C., Neale, M., Kessler, R., Heath, A., & Eaves, L. (1991). The genetic epidemiology of bulimia nervosa. *American Journal of Psychiatry, 148,* 1627–37.

Kirkley, B. G., Schneider, J. A., Agras, W. S., & Bachman, J. A. (1985). Comparison of two group treatments for bulimia. *Journal of Consulting and Clinical Psychology, 53,* 43–48.

Laessle, R. G., Beumont, P. J. V., Butow, P., Lenneris, W., O'Connor, M., Pirke, K. M., Touyz, S. W., & Waadi, S. (1991). A comparison of nutritional management and stress management in the treatment of bulimia nervosa. *British Journal of Psychiatry, 159,* 250–261.

Laessle, R. G., Wittchen, H. U. Fichter, M. M., & Pirke, K. M. (1989). The significance of subgroups of bulimia and anorexia nervosa: Lifetime frequency of psychiatric disorders. *International Journal of Eating Disorders, 8,* 569–574.

Leitenberg, H., Rosen, J. C., Wolf, J., Vara, L. S., Detzer, M. J., & Srebnik, D. (1992). Comparison of cognitive-behavior therapy and desipramine in the treatment of bulimia nervosa. Unpublished manuscript, University of Vermont.

Loeb, K., Walsh, T. B., & Pike, K. M. (1992, April 24). The assessment of bulimia nervosa. Paper presented at the Fifth International Conference on Eating Disorder, New York.

Marcus, M. D. (1993). Binge eating in obesity. In C. G. Fairburn & G. T. Wilson (Eds.), *Binge eating: Nature, assessment, and treatment* (pp. 77–96). New York: Guilford Press.

Marcus, M. D., Smith, D., Santelli, R., & Kaye, W. (1992). Characterization of eating-disordered behavior in obese binge eaters. *International Journal of Eating Disorders, 12,* 249–256.

Marlatt, G. A., & Gordon, J. (1985). *Relapse prevention.* New York: Guilford Press.

Mitchell, J. E., & de Zwaan, M. (1993). Pharmacological treatments of binge eating. In C. G. Fairburn &

G. T. Wilson (Eds.), *Binge eating: Nature, assessment, and treatment* (pp. 250–269). New York: Guilford Press.

Mitchell, J. E., Pyle, R. L., Eckert, E. D., Hatsukami, D., Pomeroy, C., & Zimmerman, R. (1990). A comparison study of antidepressants and structured intensive group psychotherapy in the treatment of bulimia nervosa. *Archives of General Psychiatry, 47,* 149–157.

Mitchell, J. E., Pyle, R., Eckert, E. D., Hatsukami, D., & Soll, E. (1990). The influence of prior alcohol and abuse problems on bulimia nervosa treatment outcome. *Addictive Behaviors, 15,* 169–173.

O'Leary, K. D., & Wilson, G. T. (1987). *Behavior therapy: Application and outcome* (2nd ed.). Englewood Cliffs, NJ: Prentice-Hall.

Olmsted, M. P., Davis, R., Garner, D. M., Eagle, M., Rockert, W., & Irvine, M. J. (1991). Efficacy of a brief group psychoeducational intervention for bulimia nervosa. *Behaviour Research and Therapy, 29,* 71–84.

Patton, G. C., Johnson-Sabine, E., Wood, K., Mann, A. H., Wakeling, A. (1990). Abnormal eating attitudes in London schoolgirls—a prospective epidemiological study: Outcome at twelve month follow-up. *Psychological Medicine, 20,* 383–394.

Peveler, R. C., & Fairburn, C. G. (1992). The treatment of bulimia nervosa in patients with diabetes mellitus. *International Journal of Eating Disorders, 11,* 45–54.

Pike, K. M., & Rodin, J. (1991). Mothers, daughters, and disordered eating. *Journal of Abnormal Psychology, 100,* 198–204.

Piran, N., & Kaplan, A. S. (1990). *A day hospital group treatment program for anorexia nervosa and bulimia nervosa.* New York: Brunner/Mazel.

Polivy, J. M., & Herman, C. P. (1993). Etiology of binge eating: Psychological mechanisms. In C.G. Fairburn & G.T. Wilson (Eds.), *Binge eating: Nature, assessment, and treatment* (pp. 173–205). New York: Guilford Press.

Pyle, R. L., Mitchell, J. E., Eckert, E. D., Hatsukami, D., Pomeroy, C., & Zimmerman, R. (1990). Maintenance treatment and 6-month outcome for bulimic patients who respond to initial treatment. *American Journal of Psychiatry, 147,* 871–875.

Rosen, J. C., Vara, L., Wendt, S., & Leitenberg, H. (1990). Validity studies of the Eating Disorder Examination. *Behavior Therapy, 9,* 519–528.

Rosenberg, M. (1965). *Society and the adolescent self-image.* Princeton, NJ: Princeton University Press.

Rossiter, E. M., & Agras, W. S. (1990). An empirical test of DSM-III-R definition of binge. *International Journal of Eating Disorders, 9,* 513–518.

Rossiter, E. M., Agras, W. S., Losch, M., & Telch, C. F. (1988). Dietary restraint of bulimic subjects following cognitive-behavioral or pharmacological treatment. *Behaviour Research and Therapy, 26,* 495–498.

Rossiter, E. M., Agras, W. S., Telch, E. F., & Schneider, J. A. (1993). Cluster-B personality disorder characteristics predict outcome in the treatment of bulimia nervosa. *International Journal of Eating Disorders, 13,* 349–358.

Schwalberg, M. D., Barlow, D. H., Alger, S. A., & Howard, L. J. (1992). A comparison of bulimics, obese binge eaters, social phobics, and individuals with panic disorder on comorbidity across DSM-III-R anxiety disorders. *Journal of Abnormal Psychology, 101,* 675–681.

Spitzer, R. L., Devlin, M. J., Walsh, B. T., Hasin, D., Wing, R., Marcus, M. D., Stunkard, A. J., Wadden, T., Yanovski, S., Agras, W. S., Mitchell, J., & Nonas, C. (1992). Binge eating disorder: To be or not to be in DSM-IV? *International Journal of Eating Disorders, 10,* 627–630.

Strasser, T. J., Pike, K. M., & Walsh, B. T. (1992). The impact of prior substance abuse on treatment outcome for bulimia nervosa. *Addictive Behaviors, 17,* 387–393.

Striegel-Moore, R. H. (1993). Etiology of binge eating: A developmental perspective. In C. G. Fairburn & G. T. Wilson (Eds.), *Binge eating: Nature, assessment, and treatment* (pp. 144–172). New York: Guilford Press.

Striegel-Moore, R. H., Silberstein, L. R., & Rodin, J. (1986). Toward an understanding of risk factors for bulimia. *American Psychologist, 41,* 146–163.

Stunkard, A. J., & Messick, S. (1985). The Three Factor Eating Questionnaire to measure dietary restraint, disinhibition and hunger. *Journal of Psychosomatic Research, 29,* 71–83.

Telch, C. F., Agras, W. S., Rossiter, E. M., Wilfley, D., & Kenardy, J. (1990). Group cognitive-behavioral treatment for the non-purging bulimic: An initial evaluation. *Journal of Consulting and Clinical Psychology, 58,* 629–635.

Walsh, B. T. (1991). Fluoxetine treatment of bulimia nervosa. *Journal of Psychosomatic Research, 35,* 471–475.

Walsh, B. T., Gladis, M., Roose, S. P., Stewart, J. W., Stetner, F., & Glassman, A. H. (1988). Phenelzine vs placebo in 50 patients with bulimia. *Archives of General Psychiatry, 45,* 471–475.

Walsh, B. T., Hadigan, C. M., Devlin, M. J., Gladis, M., & Roose, S. P. (1991). Long-term outcome of antidepressant treatment for bulimia nervosa. *Archives of General Psychiatry, 148,* 1206–1212.

Wilfley, D. E., Agras, W. S., Telch, C. F., Rossiter, E. M., Schneider, J. A., Cole, A. G., Sifford, L., & Raeburn, S. D. (1993). Group CBT and group interpersonal psychotherapy for non-bingeing bulimics: A controlled comparison. *Journal of Consulting and Clinical psychology, 61,* 296–305.

Wilson, G. T. (1989). A manual for cognitive-behavioral treatment of bulimia nervosa. Unpublished manuscript, Rutgers University.

Wilson, G. T. (1993a). Psychological and pharmacological treatment of bulimia nervosa: A research update. *Applied and Preventive Psychology: Current Scientific Perspectives, 2,* 35–42.

Wilson, G. T. (1993b). Short-term psychological benefits and adverse effects of weight loss. *Annals of Internal Medicine.*

Wilson, G. T. (1993c). Assessment of binge eating. In C. G. Fairburn & G. T. Wilson (Eds.), *Binge eating: Nature, assessment, and treatment* (pp. 227–249). New York: Guilford Press.

Wilson, G. T. (1993d). Binge eating and addictive behaviors. In C. G. Fairburn & G. T. Wilson (Eds.), *Binge eating: Nature, assessment, and treatment* (pp. 97–120). New York: Guilford Press.

Wilson, G. T., & Eldredge, K. L. (1991). Frequency of binge eating in bulimic patients: Diagnostic validity. *International Journal of Eating Disorders, 10,* 557–561.

Wilson, G. T., Eldredge, K. L., Smith, D., & Niles, B. (1991). Cognitive-behavioral treatment with and without response prevention for bulimia. *Behaviour Research and Therapy, 29,* 575–583.

Wilson, G. T., & Fairburn, C. G. (1993). Cognitive treat-
ments for eating disorders. *Journal of Consulting and Clinical Psychology, 61,* 261–269.

Wilson, G. T., Nonas, K. A., & Rosenblum, G. D. (1993). Assessment of binge eating in obese patients. *International Journal of Eating Disorders, 13,* 25–39.

Wilson, G. T., & Smith, D. (1989). Assessment of bulimia nervosa: An evaluation of the Eating Disorder Examination. *International Journal of Eating Disorders, 8,* 173–179.

Chapter 8

OBESITY

Kelly D. Brownell
Yale University
Patrick Mahlen O'Neil
Medical University of South Carolina, Charleston

Despite rapid advances in our knowledge, few areas have witnessed a more dramatic change in our thinking than obesity. Of course, obesity, severe enough to be associated with substantial cardiovascular risk factors, is one of the more common problems confronting professionals in this country. Often overlooked, however, are the even more substantial psychological problems that develop as a consequence of obesity. Two of the leading experts in the world provide the latest scientific findings on this very difficult problem and include answers to the all-important question, Who is it that suffers from obesity? In the context of a state-of-the-art discussion of the etiology of obesity and the value of dieting, Brownell and O'Neil provide a conceptual model for assessment and treatment that illustrates the complementary roles of the many resources available to deal with obesity in our society. The authors also provide invaluable information on the relative worth of such resources as self-help groups, commercial weight-loss programs, and more dramatic medical procedures (e.g., surgery). In the midst of the crass commercialism that dominates this field, the authors present a detailed outline of one approach with a good chance of producing long-term success. That approach involves a network of techniques and procedures that includes setting realistic goals and changing behavior and attitudes to result in a substantial and long-lasting alteration of life-style. The creativity involved in accomplishing these difficult goals is illustrated with numerous useful examples and transcripts.—D. H. B.

OVERVIEW

From both a public health perspective and for the individuals affected, obesity is a major problem (Brownell & Wadden, 1992). Using the criterion of 20% overweight, the point at which health risk is increased, 24% of men and 27% of women in the United States are obese. The prevalence of obesity has doubled since 1900 and has increased even in recent years.

Hidden within these figures are especially high rates of obesity in some segments of the population. The prevalence of obesity increases with age, especially in females, and is high in minority and economically disadvantaged groups. Van Itallie (1985) notes that when these factors come together, as in the case of black women ages 45 to 75, the rates rise to 60%.

Obesity carries substantial risk for serious disease. In overweight individuals, risk is elevated for hypertension, diabetes, cardiovascular disease, and some cancers (Pi-

Sunyer, 1991). Some studies even suggest that risk begins to increase with as little as 5% overweight (Manson et al., 1990), but there is little doubt that an individual 20%–30% overweight or greater joins a high-risk group. The location of body fat is also important. Fat distributed in the upper body, especially fat stored in the intraabdominal cavity, brings greater risk than does fat stored in the lower body (Sjostrom, 1992).

Weight Cycling

Work on weight cycling began with the hypothesis that the body protects itself against threats to its energy stores by slowing weight loss and promoting regain with successive diets (Brownell, Greenwood, Stellar, & Shrager, 1986). Research on the topic is now divided between studies showing this cycling effect and others showing no effect (Brownell & Rodin, 1993; Wing, 1992). It is not possible to say, with current knowledge, that weight cycling does or does not affect subsequent weight loss.

Recent work has investigated whether weight cycling is associated with negative health consequences. Several studies have shown strong links in both men and women between body weight variability and risk for all-cause mortality and mortality from coronary heart disease (Blair, Shaten, Brownell, Collins, & Lissner, in press; Lissner et al., 1991). These data underscore the importance of weight maintenance.

MEANING OF EXCESS WEIGHT IN MODERN CULTURE

The pressure to be thin in our culture is intense and unrelenting. Individuals are reminded repeatedly through television, magazines, billboards, and general discussion that the ideal body shape is extremely thin. Children internalize this, and at a very early age recognize that being overweight is undesirable. Some begin to see their body as a source of embarrassment and shame.

The case of "Catherine" illustrates this point. Catherine is a 36-year-old white secretary, 180 pounds and 5'6". She is quite attractive and dresses fashionably; several staff members were surprised that her weight was as high as the scale indicated. Catherine recently began treatment. During a group discussion with the therapist (T) of feelings about being overweight, Catherine (C) became uncharacteristically quiet.

T: Catherine, have you had any of these experiences of feeling embarrassed by your weight?

C: I try not to let myself get into situations where I'll feel that way.

T: Do you mean you avoid doing things where your weight would be more apparent?

C: If you mean things like going to the beach, of course, I won't do that, I haven't been since I hit 130.

T: What about other places?

C: I really don't like to go out anywhere I don't have to when I'm this fat. My husband's always complaining about that.

T: Can you give us some recent examples?

C: Last week, we had an argument because I wouldn't go with him to our son's soccer game. And he gripes about having to go to parties by himself.

T: You won't go to parties?

C: The last one I went to, about four years ago, I was mortified the whole time, knowing how fat I was and that everyone else could see how fat I'd gotten. It's worse for people who knew me before I gained so much weight.

T: Did these people make comments about your weight?

C: No, people are much too polite to do that. They actually told me how nice I looked. But you know how people say one thing and mean another. After that night of having my fat on display, I decided to stay home as much as I could until I lose my weight.

T: Avoiding social situations like that, has it caused problems?

C: Like I said, my husband has run out of patience with me. And last week, I . . . *(tears)* . . . I found out my father has cancer. He's just about 200 miles away, but I haven't been to see him in three years, because I didn't want him to see me this way, and now I just keep thinking, if I hadn't gained all this weight, I wouldn't have lost those years with him.

Were the culture to view differences in body weight as a natural biological variation, as is the case with hair color and height, discrepancies between the ideal and the actual would not be the basis of such distress. This is not the case with body weight, and discrepancies can be troubling indeed. The reason is that society bestows extraordinary meaning on body weight and shape. As the following discussion between therapist (T) and clients (C1 and C2) within a group indicated, many clients feel that obesity has had an indelible impact on their life.

T: Someone mentioned how troubling it is to be fat. How do you think it compares with other problems?

C1: Sometimes I think it isn't so bad, but then other times I think I would rather have any other problem. I have one friend who is depressed but I get just as depressed about my weight.

C2: I would rather be alcoholic or a drug addict than be fat. I think about it all the time and I hate myself for getting this way.

T: Is that true Sally, that you would rather be alcoholic than fat? That is a serious statement.

C2: It seems at times that I cannot put up with another minute of hating myself. I would do anything to be rid of this fat body.

The pressure to be thin, although seemingly ubiquitous, falls disproportionately into several demographic groups. For example, women exhibit greater dissatisfaction with their weight than do men (Fallon & Rozin, 1985). In addition, body dissatisfaction does not mirror the prevalence of obesity. Despite higher rates of obesity in black women than in white women, black women are less likely to think of themselves as overweight (Kumanyika, 1987).

Seeking or attaining the "perfect body" symbolizes important attributes in our society (Barsky, 1988; Brownell, 1991; Glassner, 1988; Rodin, 1992). It signifies control over impulses, delay of gratification, concern with one's appearance and health, and other personal qualities considered important. To have an imperfect body offers a visible statement to others of weak will, lack of restraint, lazy and slovenly behavior, and absence of control. Given these cultural values, it is logical to believe that society will react negatively to those who fail to meet prevailing standards and that individuals will suffer from this reaction at both social and psychological levels.

SOCIAL AND PSYCHOLOGICAL SUFFERING

Numerous studies have shown bias toward and stereotyping of obese persons. Individuals rating pictures or descriptions of obese and lean persons ascribe negative characteristics to the obese persons, using descriptors such a lazy, sloppy, and lacking control. This is true even when young children are making the ratings. These children rate people with physical handicaps and facial disfigurements as more likable than an obese child.

Although it is not as well documented, it appears that negative attitudes create bias, which in turn can affect such factors as hiring decisions. For example, an employer who considers appearance to be important may reject an obese job applicant despite his/her qualifications. Teenagers have been refused participation in marching bands and cheerleading squads because of weight standards. Numerous lawsuits have been filed by obese persons who claim they were not hired, were forced to leave a job, or were refused participation in an activity because of their weight. A number of such cases have been settled in favor of the complainants.

Society's attitudes regarding obesity are reflected in the attitudes of overweight individuals themselves. In a clinical setting, one hears disparaging self-statements from individuals in severe distress, with a damaged self-concept, who feel despair that is inescapable for a day or even for a few hours. The intensity and overpowering nature of this despair are described in writings such those by Millman (1980) and Jasper (1992).

An interesting paradox exists in the obesity field pertaining to the psychological correlates of obesity; clinical impression and the literature are in conflict. Most studies that examine psychological factors compare obese and nonobese groups. The inconsistent findings across studies have led most authors to conclude that obesity does not increase risk for psychological problems (Leon & Roth, 1977; O'Neil & Jarrell, 1992; Stunkard & Wadden, 1992; Wadden & Stunkard, 1985).

Friedman and Brownell (1992) have approached the topic in a different way. They suggest that inconsistent findings in the comparative studies of obese and nonobese groups are an expected, if not inevitable, outcome of the approach used; most studies use small samples, do not represent the general obese population, and typically employ a single measure of only one aspect of psychopathology. These studies are helpful as a first generation of research in the area, and they point to considerable heterogeneity within the obese population.

Friedman and Brownell (1992) argue for a different approach in which a second and third generation of studies occur. In the second generation of studies, the question whether obese individuals as a group display psychological problems will yield to the question, Who will suffer from their obesity? The basis of this approach is a risk-factor model, which attempts to specify factors that might place an individual at risk. Possible factors might be age at onset of obesity, social class, gender, and binge eating. These studies would provide correlational findings, which would then be examined in the longitudinal studies that would constitute the third generation.

We have covered the social and psychological correlates of obesity in some detail because of the implications for treatment. Psychotherapy for overweight individuals should include assessment of the social and psychological ramifications of obesity for the individual. There is a social reality of bias and discrimination that influences psychological functioning. Understanding this social reality is helpful in acquiring a clear picture of the individual's life.

The notion that the blame for excess weight rests with the individual is understandable given cultural assumptions about weight and shape. Clients who feel this way blame themselves and feel that they can attain a slender body if they only try hard enough. This can lead to unrealistic goals

and to self-defeating reactions to setbacks in a program. Therefore, a clinician should be sensitive to the cultural context in which excess weight occurs.

ETIOLOGY OF OBESITY

Significant historical shifts have occurred in conceptualizations of the etiology of obesity. In the 1950s, obesity was considered a psychological problem. Because Freudian concepts dominated psychology and psychiatry at the time, obesity was thought to reflect an underlying personality disturbance, the conflicts of which were acted out in excessive eating. Beginning in the 1960s, behavior therapists entered the scene and obesity was conceptualized as a result of maladaptive eating habits.

The 1980s were the biological decade in which genetics, metabolism, and biology in general were considered paramount. Several studies published in the 1980s highlight this point. Stunkard et al. (1986), using the Danish Adoption Register, found a clear genetic contribution to obesity. Ravussin et al. (1988) found that energy expenditure could be used to predict weight gain in a prospective fashion.

Convergence of Risk Factors

In the 1990s, there has been general recognition that multiple factors contribute to obesity (Bjorntorp & Brodoff, 1992; Brownell & Wadden, 1992). Genetics, culture, personal behavior, and other factors are influential, and probably act in different combinations across individuals. Therefore, two people who weigh the same might have very different reasons for the excess weight. Table 8.1 shows different levels of risk factors thought to be important (Brownell & Wadden, 1992).

The levels of risk factors outlined in Table 8.1 are comprehensive to the extent that they capture what is known from research. The fact that some individuals gain weight because they eat a high-fat diet and fail to exercise does not explain *why* individuals behave as they do, with the exception of the biological and cultural factors noted in the table. What is missing is life circumstance.

TABLE 8.1. Risk Factors Likely to Contribute to the Genesis of Obesity

Risk to the population
  Availability of high-fat foods
  High levels of dietary fat
  Decreasing levels of physical activity
  Food intake patterns which promote obesity

Risks to individuals: Biological factors
  Genetics
  Low resting metabolic rate
  Elevated fat cell number

Risks to individuals: Behavioral factors
  High energy intake
  Specific eating patterns (e.g., binge eating)
  Lack of exercise

Note. Assembled from information provided in Brownell and Wadden (1992).

The issue has received very little attention from researchers; hence its absence from a table of risk factors. It is clear from clinical experience that psychological reactions to life events can feature prominently in the weight history of certain individuals.

Occasionally a person can date the onset or worsening of a weight problem to specific interpersonal pressures. "Martha" is a 60-year-old black school administrator. Although she has been obese most of her adult life, this is her first weight-loss program, joined at her physician's urging because of her diabetes and hypertension. Here Martha (M) with therapist (T) recalls the distressing circumstances of her first serious weight gain.

M: When I was a very young woman, I had to watch my weight but I was successful at it. I really ate carefully to try to keep my figure. In fact, not to brag, but I was considered very attractive.

I had just married, very young and naive, and we had moved to this small black community. It was a closed kind of place; we were probably the first new people to move there in ten years. A lot of the other women, most of them overweight, were jealous of my looks. It was clear from how they acted, and I heard about it from my one good friend. It got so bad, some of them were spreading all kinds of rumors about me, claiming that I was cheating on my husband. Some of those stories got back to him.

T: How did he react?

M: He'd always had a mean streak, and sometimes he'd break things.

T: Did he abuse you?

M: He didn't hit me, but this one time he did something that felt worse. We didn't have much money, but we didn't have any children then, so if I made some extra money I could sometimes buy a present for myself. Well, all my life I'd wanted a fur coat, and I decided, if I have to live in this mean town, I'm at least going to get that fur coat. So I took an extra job, and saved my money, and I bought myself a fur coat. It was a cheap little thing, looking back, but I felt like a movie star in it.

One night not long after I got the coat, my husband went into a rage over some stories he'd heard about me from the town gossips. I went out to take a ride until he could cool off. When I got back, he was in the backyard staring at a small fire on the ground. He'd poured gasoline on my fur coat and was watching it burn. He said, "If you don't want to wind up like your damned coat, you'd better stop your running around."

Right then and there, I decided I'd had it with being trim and good-looking.

T: Is that when you started to gain weight?

M: I almost looked forward to being fat, and it didn't take me long to get fat. And you know, for a couple of years I felt like I was happier for it. The women in town acted nicer to me, and for a while my husband treated me better, but it didn't last.

We divorced, and I moved away and got my degree and remarried. Obviously, I knew by then that the troubles I'd had were caused by my ex-husband and jealous women, not by being trim. But every time I'd start to lose weight, I'd remember how it felt to walk down the street in that nasty little town with those mean women cutting their eyes at me, and I'd see that coat burning. And that would be it for the diet.

Different theoretical approaches to etiology, of course, argue for very different treatments. Intensive psychotherapy would be needed to resolve unconscious conflicts, skills training would be needed to unlearn destructive habits, interpersonal psychotherapy might be helpful in coping with difficult life circumstances, and pharmacological, surgical, or nutritional interventions would be needed to overcome biology. No clear solution to the obesity problem has emerged from any of these approaches.

The modern-day conceptualization of etiology as multifactorial should now influence the way the profession develops treatments. Making a fresh start based on theory and what is known about etiology is likely to lead in beneficial directions. Just as there are different etiological paths to obesity, different treatments are likely to be helpful. Thus, an issue discussed in detail here is a philosophy of matching individuals to treatments.

IS DIETING GOOD OR BAD?

A fiery controversy has erupted recently. Previously, dieting was considered a worthwhile, if not often successful, enterprise. There were signs much earlier than 1991 and 1992 that some scientists questioned the wisdom of this approach (Bennett & Gurin, 1982; Polivy & Herman, 1983; Wooley & Wooley, 1984; Wooley, Wooley, & Dyrenforth, 1979). It was in 1991 and 1992, however, that an anti-dieting movement gained momentum and was heard by health professionals and the public alike.

A small number of scholarly articles have challenged dieting on different grounds (Garner & Wooley, 1991; Goodrick & Foreyt, 1991; Polivy & Herman, 1985; Wooley & Garner, 1991). Collectively, these articles make a number of key points:

1. The health risks of obesity are overstated.
2. Weight loss has never been shown to lower rates of morbidity and mortality.
3. Diets are universally ineffective.
4. Dieting leads to disordered eating (binge eating, bulimia nervosa, or anorexia nervosa).

A number of books and articles have now been published that condemn dieting in varying degrees and propose programs in which food restriction is discarded and body acceptance is emphasized (Bennett & Gurin, 1982; Ciliska, 1990; Foreyt & Goodrick, 1992; Polivy & Herman, 1983). A few empirical evaluations have been done on such programs, with positive effects on such psychological outcomes as self-concept (Lewis, Blair, & Booth, 1992; Polivy & Herman, 1992; Roughan, Seddon, & Vernon-Roberts, 1990). Weight loss is not the focus of these programs and does not occur.

Brownell and Rodin (1992), in response to the categorical question whether dieting is good or bad, addressed each of the points raised in the anti-dieting arguments and attempted to present a balanced view. Their conclusions are as follows:

1. The health hazards of obesity are clear and are serious.

2. Weight loss has not been shown to reduce morbidity and mortality because the issue has not been studied. Studies with risk factors such as blood pressure and metabolic control in diabetics generally show beneficial changes with weight loss.

3. All information on the effectiveness of weight-loss programs comes from clinical settings where the average person is heavier, is more likely to be a binge eater, and displays more psychopathology than do overweight individuals in general. These are negative prognostic factors. It may not be possible to generalize from the small number of people enrolled in university-based research programs to the millions engaged in commercial and self-help programs, and to the individuals who try to lose weight on their own.

   In support of this point, a 1992 telephone survey administered to a national probability sample of U.S. women found that of overweight women who had tried to lose at least 15 lb, fewer than 20% used the methods tested in most treatment outcome studies, namely professional-directed programs or prescription weight-loss medications. Further, the average weight loss reported for all weight-loss attempts was about 11% of initial body weight, enough to improve health risk factors (O'Neil, Dansky, Kilpatrick, & Brewerton, 1992).

4. Dieting, combined with other psychological factors, does have the potential to create disordered eating. In persons near ideal weight, this risk is not justified by the questionable payoff from dieting. In individuals with excess weight, dieting has not

yet been isolated as a risk factor for eating disturbances, and if such risk does exist, it must be balanced against a compelling need for weight loss.

A number of issues must be addressed to understand the role dieting should assume in the health and well-being of our society. It is clear that excess weight increases health risk. It is not clear whether weight loss reduces risk, and in turn lowers morbidity and mortality, partly because the appropriate studies have not been done. Contemporary methods for weight control, while effective at producing short-term weight losses, fall short of offering reliable means for sustaining weight loss. Dieting clearly has costs, and for some, has the potential for benefit. The primary challenges are: a) to identify individuals who will be helped or harmed by dieting; b) to reduce the extraordinary rates of dieting in those who do not need to lose weight; c) to better understand the physiological and psychological reasons why some people can lose and others cannot; and d) to develop safe and effective means for weight loss and its maintenance and target these methods to individuals who stand to benefit medically. The current debate on whether dieting is good or bad, which is having a polarizing effect, threatens to divert attention from important issues such as who *should* lose weight, who *can* lose weight, the conditions under which dieting should occur, how much an individual should aspire to lose, and how weight can best be lost and maintained." (Brownell & Rodin, 1992, p. 4; italics in original)

We believe this debate over dieting is of considerable clinical importance. Whether for biological, cultural, psychological, or behavioral reasons, some individuals seem destined to fight a battle they cannot win. The process of fighting can produce preoccupation with eating and weight, self-condemnation and depression, and repeated bouts of losing weight and regaining. In these cases, a program of compassion, acceptance of the excess weight, and a focus on healthy eating and exercise habits may be indicated. The challenge lies in identifying such people and knowing with some degree of certainty that the individual will not lose weight.

Clients often inquire about this issue, sometimes in a direct way, by asking whether they should diet at all, or in an indirect way by questioning whether the program is effective, whether they will become a yo-yo dieter, and so forth. It is helpful to discuss these issues in detail and to explain that there are alternatives to dieting. Each individual must decide whether dieting is the right choice for him/her, and if so, which program or approach is likely to be most helpful.

CONCEPTUAL MODEL FOR ASSESSMENT AND TREATMENT

Unlike the topics of the other chapters in this book, obesity is not a psychological disorder. The fourth edition of the *Diagnostic and Statistical Manual of Mental Disorders* (DSM-IV; American Psychiatric Association, 1993) does not include obesity as a psychiatric disorder, and obesity in and of itself does not signify the presence of accompanying psychological distress.*

Neither is obesity a behavior. However, behavior change is an absolute necessity if the condition of obesity is to be managed. Simply put, the obese person attempting to lower his/her weight must instigate and maintain changes in the behaviors that influence nutrient intake and caloric expenditure. These behavior patterns and their determinants are surprisingly complex and individualistic.

Although the early behavioral approaches to weight loss were characterized by short-term, curriculum-driven group interventions usually targeting the terminal behaviors affecting energy balance (eating and exercise), subsequent interventions have become increasingly more sophisticated, complex, and multidisciplinary (Brownell & Wadden, 1992). Further, it is now recognized that the goal of treatment is management rather than cure, and that this goal requires long-term intervention (Perri, Nezu, & Viegener, 1992).

Intervention requires tailoring treatment to individual client characteristics and circumstances. Stuart's (1967) early paper describing the application of behavioral principles to the goal of weight loss spawned scores of reports of short-term rather simplistic group treatments. It is rarely acknowl-

---

*The DSM-IV criteria cited in this chapter are those that were approved as final by the DSM-IV Eating Disorders Work Group and the Task Force on DSM-IV (APA, 1993). These criteria may be subject to minor editorial revisions before the publication of DSM-IV.

edged that Stuart's paper actually described individual treatment delivered over 1 year.

Focus on Life-Style Change

We advocate that behavioral management of obesity be construed by both client and therapist as an effort to effect *life-style change*, that is, to develop long-standing, routine patterns of behavior that will support attainment and maintenance of a lower weight in the face of genetic, interpersonal, and environmental influences to the contrary. In some ways, this could be considered a "behavioral prosthesis." This approach is different in important ways from *dieting*. It makes explicit the necessity of long-term change, moves emphasis from weight *loss* to weight *maintenance*, and shifts the client's attention from the unpredictability of *weight* change to the more controllable target of *behavior* change.

In the long run, it is usually an excellent use of session time to explain this concept to the client, in as many ways as possible, to overcome the years of contrary messages from weight-loss ads and the client's own quick attempts at weight loss. This approach can also help to spare the client unnecessary guilt and impaired self-esteem over past weight-control failures.

There are several ways to present this life-style approach to the client. One author (K.D.B.) has used the acronym LEARN (Lifestyle, Exercise, Attitudes, Relationships, and Nutrition; Brownell, 1992). LEARN also communicates that in addition to behavioral change, one of the goals of treatment is education. Another mnemonic, used by the other author (P.M.O.), is ABCD'S (Activity increase, Behavioral change, Cognitive restructuring, Dietary modification, Social support). Either approach provides a means of organizing information around the essential elements of a program. The client should be given an easily recalled and adopted way of viewing constructively the enterprise on which he/she is about to embark.

Matching Individuals to Treatments

Historically, the field has made advances in treating obesity by conducting controlled studies with random assignment, parametric statistics, and a search for treatments that provide an increment in weight loss beyond the prevailing standard. Pharmacological agents have been tested against placebos and other drugs in randomized, double-blind studies. Behavioral treatments and very-low-calorie diets (VLCDs) have been evaluated in trials where treatments or combinations of treatments are applied to groups of individuals who are then compared to other groups of individuals exposed to different approaches.

Embedded in this approach is the assumption that the population being tested is homogeneous, so that random assignment is effective in establishing equivalent groups, and that a treatment found superior to another should be embraced while the alternative is discarded. To use a hypothetical example, a behavioral approach might be more effective in a controlled study than is general psychotherapy. The typical interpretation would be that behavior therapy is superior, perhaps even the "treatment of choice," and that general psychotherapy is not useful for obesity. Masked by this interpretation is the reality that general psychotherapy may have been successful for some individuals, and ultimately, may be more successful than behavior therapy for selected persons.

Brownell and Wadden (1991, 1992) have argued that obesity is a heterogeneous disorder and that it is likely that different treatments will be effective for different individuals.

> The time has come to abandon the mentality that a single approach can be used with all individuals and that one program stands above others. After eliminating approaches that are dangerous or fraudulent, many programs for obesity remain. Each will provide a "best fit" for at least some individuals. The challenge is no longer to conduct only parametric studies to determine if one approach is superior to another, but to develop criteria to match the needs of individuals. (Brownell & Wadden, 1992, p. 510)

Matching Scheme

Many possible approaches are available for matching individuals to treatments, yet none has been validated by experimental studies.

In the natural environment, intuition often prevails because the overweight individual may choose the approach he/she feels will be most helpful. In clinical settings, a single program is likely to be offered, so no matching occurs. When different approaches are available, an individual's degree of obesity is usually the determining factor, with the most aggressive programs used for the most severely overweight.

A scheme proposed by Brownell and Wadden (1992) is shown in Figure 8.1. This is a conceptual approach in which three possible matching processes are integrated into a scheme in which a classification decision is made first, followed by a stepped-care decision and then a matching decision. The classification decision is based on percentage overweight and helps narrow the range of approaches that would be relevant to the individual. For instance, a person who is massively overweight would not likely respond to a self-directed program and might need something more intensive. Conversely, a person who is mildly overweight would not be appropriate for surgery.

The second level is based on a stepped-care approach. After a range of approaches has been established by the classification decision, approaches or programs may be ranked according to cost, intrusiveness, side effects (in the case of medication), risk, and other factors used to make a cost-effectiveness judgment. As with the stepped-care treatment of hypertension, the least expensive and least distressing treatments are the first level of intervention.

The third step is a matching decision

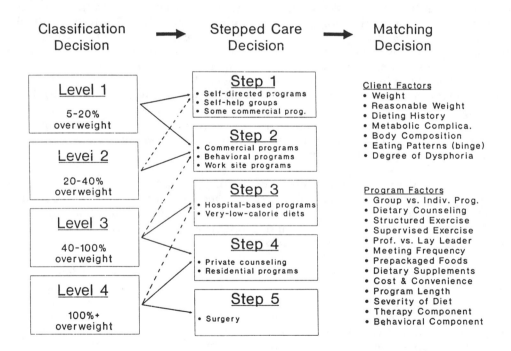

FIGURE 8.1. A conceptual scheme showing the three-stage process in selecting a treatment for an individual. The first step, the classification decision, divides individuals according to percentage overweight into four levels. This level dictates which of the five steps would be reasonable in the second stage, the stepped-care decision. This indicates that the least intensive, costly, and risky approach will be used from among alternative treatments. The third stage, the matching decision, is used to make the final selection of a program, and is based on a combination of client and program variables. The dashed lines with arrows between the classification and stepped-care stages show the lowest level of treatment that may be beneficial, but more intensive treatment is usually necessary for people at the specified weight level. From "The Heterogeneity of Obesity: Fitting Treatments to Individuals" by K. D. Brownell and T. A. Wadden, 1991, *Behavior Therapy*, 22, p. 162. Copyright 1991 by the Association for Advancement of Behavior Therapy. Reprinted by permission.

based on the personal needs of the individual. Issues such as probable response to group versus individual treatments, the need for supervised exercise, and the degree to which the diet needs to be structured may be considered. Possible matching factors are listed in Figure 8.1.

Brownell and Wadden (1992) note that this matching scheme has not been tested, and steps may be added or deleted, but for now, clinical judgment and the intuition of the individual will be the most helpful means of matching. The scheme's value from a conceptual perspective might be heuristic. From a clinical perspective, the scheme embodies a message that is central to our chapter. One of the most useful services a professional (P) might offer is to discuss this matching concept with the client (C) and to serve not only as a source of a particular treatment but to remain open to referring clients elsewhere.

P: Please tell me why you chose our program.

C: It has a good reputation and I have read things about it in the newspaper. A neighbor was in your program and had nice things to say about it.

P: One of my first responsibilities is to discuss our program with you, as well as other programs or approaches that might be helpful for you. As you know, there are many approaches to weight loss. You have probably tried some before now. Tell me about them.

C: I have been to Weight Watchers several times and I tried a fasting program at Saint Mary's Hospital.

P: How did these work?

C: The first time at Weight Watchers I lost weight pretty fast. I regained it all and then went back about two years later but didn't lose much. I tried the fasting program about a year ago. I loved it while I was losing weight but was scared to death about what would happen when they stopped giving me the packets of supplement. I was OK for a while, but then I let down and the weight came right back.

P: This is valuable information. We can speak about these past diets in detail to see what went right and what went wrong. This will help us formulate a picture about you and about what type of program will work best for you.

C: I think this program will work best for me. That's why I am here.

P: Your intuition may very well be right, but don't forget your intuition told you that the past programs you tried would be the best. I would like to keep an open mind, and if working with us is the most sensible approach, we will be happy to help you.

At this point, the professional would discuss the factors that he/she and the client felt were most important. These factors vary from person to person. For instance, one person might need an aggressive, structured diet, while for another, exercise is the key. One individual might care a great deal about whether a program takes place in groups or in individual sessions, but another might not. Once the relevant factors have been identified, the range of options available in the community can be discussed. The classification and stepped-care decision processes can be helpful in narrowing the range of programs that may be suited to the client.

Primer on Available Programs

We recommend that both professionals and clients become thoroughly educated about programs available in the community. The professional can do this by inquiring about other programs when interviewing clients, visiting other programs, obtaining written materials from the programs, or meeting with program directors. The staff in other programs are typically forthcoming if a sense of partnership is displayed and it is clear that referrals are likely to occur. In some clinics, a guide can be typed and copied for clients which lists the names and addresses of local programs, along with information about cost, program content, and so forth. Table 8.2 is an example of such information assembled for different approaches to weight loss.

Clients can become better educated about local resources by visiting programs and by speaking with as many people as possible

TABLE 8.2. Information About Various Resources for Weight Loss

	Nutrition counseling	Behavior counseling	Activity plan	Food plan	Adult calorie levels
REGISTERED DIETITIANS					
Registered Dietitians in private practice, hospital-based programs, public health clinics or other outpatient settings.	Individual or group counseling.	Individual or group counseling depending on the individual's needs. Variety of counseling strategies utilized.	Individual guidance and support provided.	Based on individual eating plan. Takes into consideration ethnic, social, and financial situation.	Dependent on weight loss goals and medical condition. Calorie range varies from low to moderate intake with increased activity.
FORMAL WEIGHT-LOSS PROGRAMS Community-based, multicenter program					
Diet Center Inc. 921 Penn Ave. Pittsburgh, PA 15222 412-338-8700	Individual counseling.	Individual and group classes.	Individualized exercise goals developed by counselor with use of computerized program.	Emphasizes real food available in grocery stores. Foods that meet Diet Center nutritional criteria are sold in centers.	Men—1300 base Women—945 base Additional caliories at the counselor's discretion. Some centers customize calorie intake based on body composition analysis.
Jenny Craig, Inc. 445 Marine View Dr. Suite 300 Del Mar, CA 92014 619-259-7000	Individual counseling.	Group class discussions assisted by videotapes. Audiotapes available at additional cost.	Personal Exercise Plan booklet; walking-program booklet with 2 videotapes and 2 audiotapes.	Proprietary food line with weekly pre-planned menus plus fresh fruits, vegetables, grains, and milk products.	Men—1200–1700 Women—1000–1500
Nutri/System, Inc. 380 Sentry Pkwy. Blue Bell, PA 19422 215-940-3000	Individual counseling.	Small-group classes tailored to the individual through use of a behavioral profile.	3-part personalized activity plan for daily activities, walking, low-intensity stretching and aerobics. 2 videotapes of graduated aerobic activity in conjunction with the Aerobic and Fitness Association of America.	Proprietary food line providing individual client selection from nearly 100 items. Fresh fruits, vegetables, and nonfat milk from grocery.	Men—1200–1500 or higher depending on individual needs Women-100–1500 or higher depending on individual needs [Canada—1200 calories]
Weight Watchers International Inc. Jericho Atrium 500 N. Broadway Jericho, NY 11753-2196 516-939-0400	Group meetings (25–30 average) providing: specific instructions on how to follow the program; support for meeting weight loss challenges; motivation to encourage program adherence, and leader who has successfully completed program as "role model."		Individualized, multi-level exercise plan emphasizing low-intensity, long-duration aerobic activities. Includes guidelines for toning and stretching.	Food plan based on set number of selections from each of 6 food lists using foods sold in grocery stores.	Men—1200–1600 Women—1000–1450

(Regional programs in this category also may be available.)

Note. This chart is compiled from information provided by corporate headquarters of each company in July 1991. Because programs are constantly changing, it is important to update information periodically. There is variability in how programs are staffed and administered locally. Physicians and patients should be encouraged to check with their local centers for staff credentials. Program characteristics may differ in Canada.

Listing of resources does not imply endorsement by the Editorial Board of Health Learning Systems or by any sponsoring, accrediting, or cooperating groups. This is not intended as a complete list, but rather a sampling of the variety of options available.

From Health Learning Systems, 1991, pp. 2–5. Copyright 1991 by Health Learning Systems, Inc. Reprinted by permission.

(cont.)

TABLE 8.2. (*cont.*)

Diet composition						
Pro.	Fat	Cho.	Contact frequency	Maintenance	Cost	Staff Training
Individualized			Based on need and goals. Direct contact and phone follow-up included. Varies: once per week to bi-monthly, then quarterly and bi-yearly. Intensive intervention initially. Medical visits and labortory tests as required.	Considered critical component of plan. Yearly plan available	Varies with services needed.	Strong science and nutrition background with a minimum of bachelor's degree and advanced training. Must meet continuing education requirements to maintain registration. In addition to or as part of private practice, may be associated with physicians, psychologists or exercise physiologists.
16–27% [nutrient levels depend upon program phase]	20–28%	52–62%	Recommended daily during reducing phase; throughout stabilization phase 2–3d/wk; maintenance 1×/wk for 1 year.	1-year plan.	Average full-service program for 30lb weight loss and maintenance $600. Cost varies by location and center.	Certification training at corporate office and continuous seminars in the field. 1,500 centers in US and Canada.
20%	20%	60%	2×/wk: (1)20-minute individual consultation and (1)40-minute class.	1-year plan. 50% refund with maintenance of reduced weight for 1 year.	Average full-service program for all the weight one wants to lose including maintenance $178. Food costs $10/d.	40-hour training program with 8-hour follow-up and individual training in center. 520 centers in US and Canada.
22–23%	15–16%	62%	1×/wk for 1 hour and Care Calls by phone. Clients may visit center additional times if desired.	1-year personalized plan. 50% refund with maintenance of reduced weight for 1 year.	Average full-service program for 30lb weight loss and maintenance $300–$400. Food costs $9.50/d.	Nutri/System formal classroom and in-center training and certification for nutrition and behavior counselors. Counselors continue to receive individual training after certification. Approximately 1,800 centers in US and Canada.
26%	Canada 18%	56%				
12–20%	<30%	50–60%	1×/wk for up to 1 hour	Individualized maintenance plans plus lifetime membership available at no cost if reduced weight is maintained.	Registration fee (avg. $17) and weekly group meeting charges (avg. $10/wk). Approx. $175 for 30lb weight loss based on a maximum of 1–2lb/wk. Discounts available for prepayment.	Company-trained "graduates" formerly on program, must maintain weight. Initial: 30 hours classroom plus exam; 30 hours "in meeting" coaching. Ongoing: 2 hours every 6 weeks; annual assessment of skills and program knowledge. 20,000 meetings in 5,000 locations in US and Canada.

(*cont.*)

TABLE 8.2. (cont.)

	Nutrition counseling	Behavior counseling	Activity plan	Food plan	Adult calorie levels
VERY LOW CALORIE DIET PLANS Medically supervised hospital or office- based program					
Optifast Sandoz Nutr. Corp. 5320 W. 23nd St. P.O. Box 370 Minneapolis, MN 55440 612-925-2100	Medically supervised, hospital-based program utilizing a very low calorie diet. Behavior modification, psychological group support, nutrition education, exercise, and medical monitoring (physician visits, laboratory testing) weekly for 26 weeks.			*Very low calroie diet (VLCD) phase (12 weeks)*—patients consume liquid supplement (OPTIFAST 70 or 800) 5 times daily, providing approximately 420–800 calories. *Refeeding phase (6 weeks)*—reintroduction of solid foods, with gradual increase in calories. *Stabilization phase (7 weeks)*—approximately 1200–1500 calorie stabilization diet, supplement discontinued.	

(Other national, hospital-based programs such as New Direction (Ross Laboratories) and Health Management Resources are similar approaches.)

	Nutrition counseling	Behavior counseling	Activity plan	Food plan	Adult calorie levels
Medifast Jason Pharmaceuticals, Inc. P.O. Box 370 Owings Mills, MD 21117 301-581-8042	Education component of Medifast is the LifeStyles Program. Set up as group sessions or individual counseling. Patient material is a 16-chapter guide. Group leader's manual has corresponding lesson plan. The 16 chapters cover areas in nutrition, behavior changes, and exercise.			16-week fasting phase; 4–6 week refeeding phase; and optional 12-week stabilization phase. High-protein, low-carbohydrate formula. 3 formulas, 2 protocols. Medifast 55 or 70 intake is 5 packets/day (440–480 calories), no food. Alternate plan adds minimeal (600–650 calories). Medifast Plus is 880 calorie daily intake: 4 packets (375 calories) and a defined meal (505 calories).	

(Other physical office-based programs use similar approaches. Look for completeness of nutirtion, exercise and behavior components.)

	Nutrition counseling	Behavior counseling	Activity plan	Food plan	Adult calorie levels
SELF-HELP GROUPS Support Group					
Overeaters Anonymous World Service Office P.O. Box 92870 Los Angeles, CA 90009 213-542-8363	Nonprofit support group. Members participate in weekly meetings, retreats, and annual conventions. Follows Alcoholics Anonymous 12-step program to correct behavior. No food plans, nutrition counseling or exercise component. Encourages members who seek such counseling to consult qualified professionals.	None		None	–
TOPS Club, Inc. **(Take Off pounds** **Sensibly)** P.O. Box 07360 Milwaukee, WI 53207 800-932-8677	Members referred to their private physicians for diets and counseling.	None	None	Exchange food lists.	1200–1800 Specific food plan

	Nutrition counseling	Behavior counseling	Activity plan	Food plan	Adult calorie levels
LIQUID MEAL REPLACEMENTS Product					
Ultra Slim-Fast **& Slim-Fast** Slim-Fast Foods Co. 919 Third Ave. New York, NY 10022 212-688-4420	Self-motivated, self-monitored program. Consumer brochures on meal planning, shopping and dining out available.		Product insert suggests 30 min. of brisk walking 3×/wk at minimum.	Ultra Slim-Fast shakes for breakfast and lunch; 2–3 snacks up to 250 cal and 600 cal dinner of solid food.	200/serving
DynaTrim Lederle Consumer Health Products American Cyanamid Co. Wayne, NJ 07470 201-821-200	Self-motivated, self-monitored program. Consumer brochure available		Product literature suggests exercise, particularly walking, also provides tips for behavior modification.	DynaTrim shake or mousse for breakfast, lunch and snack; solid food meal for dinner.	220/serving

(Use of liquid meal replacements for self-devised very low calorie diet plans is not recommended.)

(cont.)

TABLE 8.2. (*cont.*)

| Diet composition | | | | | Cost (as of 7/91; | |
Pro.	Fat	Cho.	Contact frequency	Maintenance	varies by region)	Staff training
35–67%	4–15%	29–50%	1×/wk clinic visits with behaviorist and dietitian. Weekly MD visit during VLCD phase; bi-weekly thereafter.	Stabilization phase plus 26-week ENCORE! Program, a behaviorally based maintenance program including exercise, nutrition education and group, with the physician available as needed.	Varies among centers; approximately $3,000 for 26-week program. ENCORE! maintenance program approximately $500.	Registered dietitians and Nurses, physicians, exercise specialists and psychologists. 1-week intensive training offered at least 6×/year, 3-day annual post-graduate advanced training, 12-volume program manual.
43–53%	2–25%	28–35%	1×/wk for medical check and counseling. Physician visit required 2×/mo.	LifeStyles II is a 24-week group program. Group Leader's Manual gives lesson plans, patient activity sheets and handout copies.	Varies with location and extent of program. Average cost is $65–$75/wk for office visit and supplement. 16-week program $1,040–$1,200. LifeStyles II 24-week maintenance program $192–$288.	3-volume program manuals supplied to associate physicians. 1-day training course covering program and patient management. 24 training sessions offered nationwide for physicians and staff. Annual 2-day obesity education seminar.
			1×/wk meetings.		No membership fees.	Members (nonprofessional) conduct activities; no training required. 11,000 groups worldwide.
20–22% recommended but not required.	35–38%	40–44%	1×/wk in local chapters	Members graduate to KOPS (Keep Off Pounds Sensibly) an inner honor society that further motivates then to maintain new weights.	$16/yr.	Volunteer chapter leaders receive guidance from area TOPS coordinators. 11,650 chapters worldwide.
31% (with 8oz. skim milk)	6%	63%	Not applicable (self-monitored pogram).	Ultra Slim-Fast shake for breakfast; low-fat meals for lunch and dinner. Regular exercise recommended.	Powdered shake mix: <$1.00/serving when mixed with milk. Cost of solid food meal additional.	Not applicable.
31% (with 8oz. 1% fat milk)	13%	56%	Not applicable (self-monitored program).	DynaTrim once or twice daily to replace a meal or as a snack; low-calorie meals. Menu guide with examples of balanced lunches and dinners provided.	Powdered shake mix: $.75/serving when mixed with milk. Cost of solid food meal additional.	Not applicable.

who have been in various programs. If clients are referred to a program other than ours, we suggest that this is the first step in becoming an educated and critical consumer of weight-loss programs. Even when clients remain in our program, we recommend that they remember this matching process if they enroll in other programs subsequently.

One often assumes that clients and professionals working with them have extensive knowledge of available programs. Most clients have tried many programs before they seek treatment in specialty centers such as ours, but not always. Men, who are less likely to join formal programs, and women whose weight problem is recent may have little experience with weight loss. Using the stepped-care approach described above, such clients may benefit from advice on realistic expectations, general nutritional and exercise guidance, and recommendations about self-monitoring. Special problems uncovered by assessment, such as binge eating (discussed later), may suggest other interventions.

Clients who have not succeeded on their own after a fair trial may consider no-fee self-help groups, commercial programs or hospital-based programs, if they have not already tried these venues. There are two major self-help groups. Take Off Pounds Sensibly (TOPS) chapters provide social support and generally good, although not necessarily sophisticated, advice. Clients in TOPS should be monitored to ensure that they do not overemphasize weight loss at the expense of behavioral change.

Overeaters Anonymous (OA) follows a 12-step approach modeled after Alcoholics Anonymous. Like its forebear, OA encourages a "lack of control" philosophy that may be antithetical to other aims of therapy; its emphasis on spirituality is at once a very meaningful context for some clients and a barrier to others. Some OA chapters feature strong nutritional prohibitions unsupported by experimental evidence. Nonetheless, certain people who have failed at other methods report success at OA. Clients interested in OA should be encouraged to sample meetings of several chapters and then to attend several meetings of the chapter at which they feel most comfortable or least uncomfortable, to ensure that rejection of the format is not grounded in denial of problems.

Traditionally, "commercial programs" encompassed free-standing, for-profit weight-loss enterprises ranging from fly-by-night curbside operations to such generally reputable storefront standbys as Weight Watchers. All have the common denominators of being staffed by persons who are not health professionals and of following a standardized "treatment" regimen, which in some cases includes generally sound behavioral techniques. Although these programs often rely on testimonial advertisements, and their published "success" figures are often rendered meaningless by high attrition rates, many customers appear to be successful. Clients should be warned against overreliance on packaged foods and claims of special diets. At the time this chapter was written, considerable federal regulatory attention was being paid to these providers.

Clients should be advised to ask appropriate questions when evaluating commercial programs. The first attempt to help clients in this regard was undertaken in 1991 by the New York City Commissioner of Consumer Affairs. Table 8.3 presents these standards.

In an age of increasingly competitive, revenue-conscious health care, and encouraged by the recent popularity of corporate-related medically monitored VLCDs, many hospitals have entered the weight-control arena and may be considered "commercial."

TABLE 8.3. Weight Loss Consumer Bill of Rights

1. You have the right to ask questions about the potential health risks of this program, its nutritional content, and its psychological-support and educational components.
2. You have a right to know the actual cost of treatment including extra products, services, supplements, and laboratory tests.
3. You have a right to inspect the qualifications of program personnel.
4. You have a right to inspect the program's client dropout rate for moderately and severely overweight clients.
5. You have a right to be told the program duration that is being recommended for you.
6. You have a right to confidentiality and privacy.

Note. From New York City Commissioner of Consumer Affairs, 1991.

Recently, there has been a considerable shakedown in this part of the health care industry, and these programs, like the ones mentioned just above, have become the subject of intense regulatory scrutiny. Unlike the free-standing franchise programs, however, hospital-based programs are usually staffed by health professionals. Nonetheless, clients should be advised to ask the same questions.

To summarize, many resources are available to most overweight individuals. Health professionals often adopt an antagonistic attitude toward commercial and self-help programs, but we feel these can be valuable allies in the search for long-term weight loss. It is important that both provider and client learn about local resources and approach the decision of *how* to lose weight in an educated, unbiased fashion.

CENTRAL ROLE OF ASSESSMENT

Broad Initial Assessment

As with any problem, thorough assessment is a necessary first step in formulating a treatment plan for obesity. Obesity is especially complex because of its multiple etiologies, behavioral correlates, psychosocial effects, and medical consequences. Based on the matching concept presented earlier, detailed information must be collected to help select the best treatment for an individual, to rule out medical complications, to understand the social environment, and to identify the pathology of eating or of psychological functioning, among other reasons. A comprehensive list of assessment factors is presented in Table 8.4.

Consideration of the medical risk presented by the client's obesity is necessary to determine whether the individual should lose weight, and if so, to what extent and with what urgency. Information from the client's personal physician, if he/she has one, is useful here, and clients who have not had a recent medical examination should be encouraged to do so. Some measures collected in a medical assessment can sometimes show rapid improvement with weight loss and can be strong sources of reinforcement for clients. Resting heart rate and body circumferences are among these. In other cases, medical complications of obesity such as blood pressure and diabetes can improve with weight loss and need to be monitored by a physician.

An appraisal of the psychosocial sequelae of obesity can also underscore the need for treatment and, in addition, can determine whether particular psychological or social factors in the person's life are causing sufficient distress to warrant special attention. Some of this information will surface when a detailed weight history is undertaken.

Evaluation of the biomedical factors affecting weight, a thorough weight history, and an assessment of the client's expectations help the professional develop a picture of physical limitations to weight loss and of psychological factors such as unrealistic notions of how rapidly weight loss will occur. The issue of treatment goals is discussed in detail below in the sections on Ideal versus Reasonable Weight and Goals and Expectations as Barriers to Weight Change.

Current eating patterns are best assessed via self-monitoring. A number of formats are available to facilitate this (see Figure 8.2. Several considerations are important if valid information is to be obtained. First, the effort required to self-monitor accurately should be acknowledged while putting it in perspective; the nuisance of this exercise is indisputable, but the actual time required is minimal. Second, some means of objectively determining quantities should be agreed on. Third, the reactive effects of self-monitoring notwithstanding, the client should be encouraged to eat as he/she usually does. Self-monitoring can be aided by assuring the client that the forms are not a means of being "graded" but rather simply a way of bringing his/her customary eating patterns into the therapist's office. It should be made clear that the therapist will not condemn the client on the basis of these data (or anything else for that matter). Fourth, this is an ideal time to begin to change perfectionistic expectations: the client should be assured that while complete records are desirable, partial records are usable. Finally, when turned in, the records should be reviewed with the client to clarify them, for example, to allow the client to indicate any eating episodes considered "binges" and to elaborate on related precipitants of loss of control. Additional informa-

TABLE 8.4. Factors to Be Included in Initial Assessment

I. Medical severity of the weight problem
   A. Current medical problems associated with obesity
   B. Family history of obesity-related medical problems
   C. Body mass index or percentage overweight
   D. Body composition
   E. Body fat distribution (upper body vs. lower body)

II. Psychosocial sequelae of the weight problem
   A. Discrimination encountered at work and socially
   B. Pressure from others to lose weight
   C. Physical limitations on occupational and recreational activities
   D. Dependence of self-esteem on body weight
   E. Overattribution of problems to weight

III. Biomedical factors affecting weight
   A. Family history of obesity
   B. Medications
   C. Resting metabolic rate (when available)
   D. [For women] Menopausal status and parity
   E. Recent medical exam

IV. Weight history
   A. Age at onset
   B. Lifetime adult high and low weights
   C. Previous weight-loss attempts (methods, initial losses, amount and duration of maintenance)
   D. Precipitants of previous relapses

V. Expectations
   A. Weight goal
   B. Rate of weight loss
   C. Ease of weight loss
   D. Requirements for weight loss
   E. Consequences of weight loss
      1. Reality of desired positive effects
      2. Awareness of possible negative effects

VI. Current eating patterns
   A. Nutritional selections
      1. Daily caloric intake
      2. Macronutrient selection
      3. Balance among food groups
      4. Fiber intake
      5. Sodium intake
   B. Eating topography
      1. Number of daily meals and snacks
      2. Eating rate (meal duration)
   C. Behavioral factors influencing eating
      1. Cues for overeating and unplanned eating (time of day, location, concomitant activities, time since last meal, persons, food-cue salience, etc.)
      2. Perceived reinforcers for overeating
   D. Binge eating
      1. Amount eaten
      2. Frequency
      3. Indicators of loss of control

VII. Cognitive factors
   A. Self-efficacy for weight loss, maintenance, and program requirements
   B. Self-evaluative style (dichotomous, all-or-none approach vs. continuous, matter-of-degree approach)
   C. Attributional style for success and failure

(cont.)

TABLE 8.4. (*cont.*)

VIII. Activity patterns
    A. Current exercise program
        1. Type
        2. Frequency
        3. Intensity
        4. Duration
    B. Previous exercise programs
        1. Type, etc. (as above)
        2. Reasons for discontinuation
    C. Current impediments to exercise
    D. Patient preferences about type of exercise
    E. Leisure activities
    F. Extent of physical activity in daily routine

IX. Social support
    A. Persons who can influence patient's success (spouse, family, friends, coworkers, etc.)
    B. Patient's plans to use social support
    C. Reactions of others to previous weight loss and weight-loss attempts

---

tion on encouraging client compliance with the self-monitoring task is provided later in the discussion of intervention.

Once eating records are obtained and reviewed, knowledgeable appraisal of their nutritional meaning is important, as is assessment of their behavioral messages. This is another of several instances in which the expertise of other professionals is desirable. Whenever possible, a registered dietitian should be consulted to provide feedback and recommended changes on nutritional issues.

Information on cognitive factors is obtained both from explicit questioning and from attention to how the client relates other data. There are no norms for self-efficacy, yet much can be learned from asking the client to provide ratings on a 10-point scale of his/her confidence in coping with different diet-related situations and in accomplishing the various behavioral changes that will be required. Client ratings of self-efficacy of weight-related goals have been found to predict subsequent weight loss (Stotland & Zuroff, 1991). At the same time, an attentive ear may provide much information regarding how the client evaluates his/her efforts and whether successes and failures are attributed to self or to external factors.

Accurate assessment of activity patterns requires insistence on actual accounts of behavior and on specificity. The client who says, "I usually walk a few times a week," may reveal on more careful questioning that 3 months have passed since the last walk. "Exercise" may mean anything from 45 grueling min of step aerobics to a round of golf while riding a motorized cart. Further, undeniable physical and life-style impediments to exercise must be identified if they are to be considered in devising a realistic program of exercise that has a chance of success. If a capable exercise physiologist (with an appreciation of the difficulty of exercise for obese persons) is available, consultation is advisable.

Social support should also be appraised specifically and realistically. The client's desired means of support from each significant other should be determined. A client may wish applause and curious interest from a close friend while preferring that her husband limit his involvement to watching their son while she takes her walks. Possible ways that the client can reinforce these people for the desired type of support should be considered. The reactions of others to previous weight losses suggest how they will react to the next loss; if these reactions are unsupportive, the client should be prepared to modify or deflect them.

In some settings, some aspects of assessment listed in Table 8.4 will not be feasible because of cost or lack of equipment. Body composition and resting metabolic rate are examples. The core information about weight history, eating and exercise patterns, and various psychosocial factors can be obtained by traditional self-report and interview methods. More detailed information about specific assessment approaches is available from several sources (Brownell, 1980; Brownell & Wadden, 1991; Wadden, 1985).

Diet Readiness

Losing weight and sustaining the requisite behavioral changes over the long term can be a challenge under any circumstances. For a person who is not highly committed and motivated, or who has significant life circumstances likely to interfere, the challenge is even more daunting. With this in mind, Brownell (1990) developed a Dieting Readiness Test, which is a 23-item self-report instrument used to assess the degree to which

an individual is prepared and motivated to begin a program. The test is presented in Figure 8.3.

This readiness assessment is divided into six sections. The respondent can add points for the questions in each section and compare these to the criteria provided as part of the test. The focus of each section is clear from the titles shown in Figure 8.3.

It is important to recognize that the Dieting Readiness Test was designed as a clinical tool that could serve as a means for stimulating discussion of important issues between therapist and client. The psychometric properties and the predictive utility of the test were being examined at the time this chapter was being written. Therefore, it is important for both professional and client to avoid using the test as the sole means for deciding whether and how a person should begin a weight-loss program. Rather,

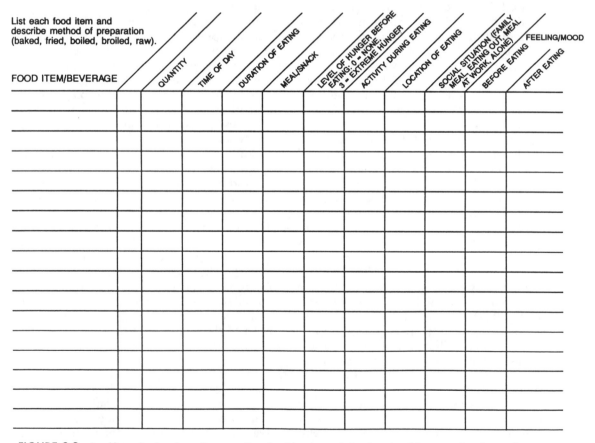

FIGURE 8.2. A self-monitoring form for recording food intake and the situational factors related to eating.

Answer the questions below to see how well your attitudes equip you for a weight-loss program. For each question, circle the answer that best describes your attitude. As you complete each of the six sections, add the numbers of your answers and compare them with the scoring guide at the end of each section.

Section 1: Goals and Attitudes

1. Compared to previous attempts, how motivated to lose weight are you this time?

1	2	3	4	5
Not At All Motivated	Slightly Motivated	Somewhat Motivated	Quite Motivated	Extremely Motivated

2. How certain are you that you will stay committed to a weight loss program for the time it will take to reach your goal?

1	2	3	4	5
Not At All Certain	Slightly Certain	Somewhat Certain	Quite Certain	Extremely Certain

3. Consider all outside factors at this time in your life (the stress you're feeling at work, your family obligations, etc.). To what extent can you tolerate the effort required to stick to a diet?

1	2	3	4	5
Cannot Tolerate	Can Tolerate Somewhat	Uncertain	Can Tolerate Well	Can Tolerate Easily

4. Think honestly about how much weight you hope to lose and how quickly you hope to lose it. Figuring a weight loss of 1 to 2 pounds per week, how realistic is your expectation?

1	2	3	4	5
Very Unrealistic	Somewhat Unrealistic	Moderately Unrealistic	Somewhat Realistic	Very Realistic

5. While dieting, do you fantasize about eating a lot of your favorite foods?

1	2	3	4	5
Always	Frequently	Occasionally	Rarely	Never

6. While dieting, do you feel deprived, angry and/or upset?

1	2	3	4	5
Always	Frequently	Occasionally	Rarely	Never

Section 1 - TOTAL Score_____

If you scored:

6 to 16: This may not be a good time for you to start a weight loss program. Inadequate motivation and commitment together with unrealistic goals could block your progress. Think about those things that contribute to this, and consider changing them before undertaking a diet program.

17 to 23: You may be close to being ready to begin a program but should think about ways to boost your preparedness before you begin.

24 to 30: The path is clear with respect to goals and attitudes.

Section 2: Hunger and Eating Cues

7. When food comes up in conversation or in something you read, do you want to eat even if you are not hungry?

1	2	3	4	5
Never	Rarely	Occasionally	Frequently	Always

8. How often do you eat because of **physical hunger?**

1	2	3	4	5
Always	Frequently	Occasionally	Rarely	Never

9. Do you have trouble controlling your eating when your favorite foods are around the house?

1	2	3	4	5
Never	Rarely	Occasionally	Frequently	Always

Section 2 - TOTAL Score_____

If you scored:

3 to 6: You might occasionally eat more than you would like, but it does not appear to be a result of high responsiveness to environmental cues. Controlling the attitudes that make you eat may be especially helpful.

(continued)

FIGURE 8.3. The Dieting Readiness Test. This test assesses the degree to which an individual is prepared to begin a weight loss program. From "Dieting Readiness" by K. D. Brownell, 1990, *Weight Control Digest, 1*, pp. 6–8. Copyright 1990 by American Health Publishing Co. Reprinted by permission.

7 to 9:   You may have a moderate tendency to eat just because food is available. Dieting may be easier for you if you try to resist external cues and eat only when you are physically hungry.

10 to 15:   Some or most of your eating may be in response to thinking about food or exposing yourself to temptations to eat. Think of ways to minimize your exposure to temptations, so that you eat only in response to physical hunger.

Section 3: Control Over Eating

If the following situations occurred while you were on a diet, would you be likely to eat **more** or **less** immediately afterward and for the rest of the day?

10. Although you planned on skipping lunch, a friend talks you into going out for a midday meal.

1	2	3	4	5
Would Eat Much Less	Would Eat Somewhat Less	Would Make No Difference	Would Eat Somewhat More	Would Eat Much More

11. You "break" your diet by eating a fattening, "forbidden" food.

1	2	3	4	5
Would Eat Much Less	Would Eat Somewhat Less	Would Make No Difference	Would Eat Somewhat More	Would Eat Much More

12. You have been following your diet faithfully and decide to test yourself by eating something you consider a treat.

1	2	3	4	5
Would Eat Much Less	Would Eat Somewhat Less	Would Make No Difference	Would Eat Somewhat More	Would Eat Much More

Section 3 - TOTAL Score_____

If you scored:

3 to 7:   You recover rapidly from mistakes. However, if you frequently alternate between eating out of control and dieting very strictly, you may have a serious eating problem and should get professional help.

8 to 11:   You do not seem to let unplanned eating disrupt your program. This is a flexible, balanced approach.

12 to 15:   You may be prone to overeat after an event breaks your control or throws you off the track. Your reaction to these problem-causing eating events can be improved.

Section 4: Binge Eating and Purging

13. Aside from holiday feasts, have you ever eaten a large amount of food rapidly and felt afterward that this eating incident was excessive and out of control?

2	0
Yes	No

14. If you answered yes to #13 above, how often have you engaged in this behavior during the last year?

1	2	3	4	5	6
Less Than Once A Month	About Once A Month	A Few Times A Month	About Once A Week	About Three Times A Week	Daily

15. Have you ever purged (used laxatives, diuretics or induced vomiting) to control your weight?

5	0
Yes	No

16. If you answered yes to #15 above, how often have you engaged in this behavior during the last year?

1	2	3	4	5	6
Less Than Once A Month	About Once A Month	A Few Times A Month	About Once A Week	About Three Times A Week	Daily

Section 4 - TOTAL Score_____

If you scored:

0 to 1:   It appears that binge eating and purging is not a problem for you.

2 to 11:   Pay attention to these eating patterns. Should they arise more frequently, get professional help.

12 to 19:   You show signs of having a potentially serious eating problem. See a counselor experienced in evaluating eating disorders right away.

(continued)

Section 5: Emotional Eating

17. Do you eat more than you would like to when you have negative feelings such as anxiety, depression, anger or loneliness?

1	2	3	4	5
Never	Rarely	Occasionally	Frequently	Always

18. Do you have trouble controlling your eating when you have positive feelings - do you celebrate feeling good by eating?

1	2	3	4	5
Never	Rarely	Occasionally	Frequently	Always

19. When you have unpleasant interactions with others in your life, or after a difficult day at work, do you eat more than you'd like?

1	2	3	4	5
Never	Rarely	Occasionally	Frequently	Always

Section 5 - TOTAL Score_____

If you scored:

3 to 8:   You do not appear to let your emotions affect your eating.

9 to 11:   You sometimes eat in response to emotional highs and lows. Monitor this behavior to learn when and why it occurs and be prepared to find alternate activities.

12 to 15:   Emotional ups and downs can stimulate your eating. Try to deal with the feelings that trigger the eating and find other ways to express them.

Section 6: Exercise Patterns and Attitudes

20. How often do you exercise?

1	2	3	4	5
Never	Rarely	Occasionally	Somewhat	Frequently

21. How confident are you that you can exercise regularly?

1	2	3	4	5
Not At All Confident	Slightly Confident	Somewhat Confident	Highly Confident	Completely Confident

22. When you think about exercise, do you develop a positive or negative picture in your mind?

1	2	3	4	5
Completely Negative	Somewhat Negative	Neutral	Somewhat Positive	Completely Positive

23. How certain are you that you can work regular exercise into your daily schedule?

1	2	3	4	5
Not At All Certain	Slightly Certain	Somewhat Certain	Quite Certain	Extremely Certain

Section 6 - TOTAL Score_____

If you scored:

4 to 10:   You're probably not exercising as regularly as you should. Determine whether your attitudes about exercise are blocking your way, then change what you must and put on those walking shoes.

11 to 16:   You need to feel more positive about exercise so you can do it more often. Think of ways to be more active that are fun and fit your lifestyle.

17 to 20:   It looks like the path is clear for you to be active. Now think of ways to get motivated.

After scoring yourself in each section of this questionnaire, you should be able to better judge your dieting strengths and weaknesses. Remember that the first step in changing eating behavior is to understand the conditions that influence your eating habits. □

it can be a useful method for identifying factors that may be problematic and require further discussion.

Clinical Sensitivity During Assessment

There are many opportunities to learn about a client, even when asking routine questions. For example, obtaining a weight history is of obvious importance. In some programs, a weight history is obtained by paper-and-pencil questions asking individuals to list their weight at certain ages and/or to list their weight loss in previous programs. In addition to these measures, however, we interview each client to learn as much as possible about the onset of weight problems, precipitants of relapse, experiences with maintenance, and so forth. In the scenario that follows, such an interview uncovered important weight-related psychological factors.

"Serena" (S) is a 32-year-old single respiratory therapist who is 195 pounds and 5'7". Her first statement to the therapist (T) at her initial visit was, "I'm sick and tired of the roller coaster. I hate regaining even more than I hate dieting. I want to learn how to keep it off this time."

T: When did your weight problem begin?

S: I've always been a little chunky, but it really got serious my senior year in high school.

T: What was the weight change then?

S: I went from about 130 to 155, but what made it worse, all my friends were losing weight to get ready for college.

T: Can you remember what might have contributed to your weight gain?

S: Not really. I guess I just started snacking more, eating more at parties, that sort of thing.

T: What's your weight been like since then?

S: Up and down, but always more up than down.

T: What are the least and most you've weighed as an adult?

S: This is my highest. My lowest was 140, right before I graduated from college.

T: When did you first try to lose weight?

S: Near the end of my senior year in high school, not long after I gained all that weight. My mother took me to Weight Watchers. I lost about 12 pounds.

T: Was that what you wanted to lose?

S: Of course not, I wanted to lose a lot more. But I was the only young person there, and I just kind of lost interest in the program.

T: How long did you keep it off?

S: Not long. I started college, and you know about the "freshman 15," except in my case it was the "freshman 30."

T: So you gained up to, let's see, 175.

S: Something like that.

T: When did you next try to lose?

S: I was always going on some kind of diet or another in college, but they never amounted to much. I had some diet pills for a while, but they just made me nervous. I got serious my last year in college, I knew I'd have a better chance of getting a job if I wasn't so heavy, so I just started eating one meal a day and exercising a lot. By graduation, I'd lost I guess about 35 or 40 pounds, I don't remember, but I do remember that my low weight then was 142.

T: What did you do to try to keep that weight off?

S: (*Laughs*) Not much. I moved to take my first job, and gained about 40 or 45 pounds the next two years.

T: What happened?

S: I guess it was a bunch of things. New job, working nights, new people. I don't really remember.

T: Have you had other major weight losses?

S: Two main ones. When I was about 25, I went to Nutri/System, and lost about 30 pounds, down to about 155.

T: How long did you maintain that?

S: Maybe a half year or so. I had taken a moonlighting job, and I guess I just didn't have much time to eat. I think I started to regain as soon as I gave up the second job. I even tried to exercise at first, but it got to be too much of a hassle.

The other time, was not long before

I turned 30. (*laughs*) I guess I was nervous about it. I drank a lot of Slim-Fast, and bought an exercise bike and put a lot of miles on it.

T: How much did you lose?

S: I don't remember what I weighed when I started, I wouldn't go near a scale, but it was less than now because I was one or two dress sizes smaller. I got down as low as 145. I didn't keep it off long.

T: Long enough to turn 30?

S: (*Laughs*) Yeah, but not much longer. In fact, you could say I started gaining the night of my birthday. Some friends threw a party for me, and even invited some eligible guys, they were always trying to fix me up, and I started going out with one of them. We went out to eat a lot, and I guess I just started eating more all of the time.

T: What happened to the guy?

S: He stopped coming around after a while, not that I could blame him, as big as I was getting.

T: What have your other relationships been like?

S: I haven't had very many. Sometimes when I lose weight, I'll go out with someone for a while, you know how it is, you get a lot more attention. I guess they lose interest when I gain weight.

T: So what you're saying is that when you're heavy, you don't have much of a dating life, and when you lose weight, you start dating more, and then you gain weight.

S: I never thought of it that way. Are you saying men are fattening? (*laughs*) And all this time I've been trying to cut out chocolates.

T: Some people find relationships a little scary when they get more serious, and some of these people might kind of back off, retreat from the relationship and return to overeating. It's a familiar comfort if nothing else. And you're right that for a woman, being overweight lowers the odds of beginning a new relationship. In that respect, it's kind of safe.

S: But I hate being single. (*pauses*) But I guess there is less to have to think about when you're alone than when you're going with someone.

T: This is obviously a complicated area, but it might be very important to you, and for a lot more reasons than keeping your weight off. Would you be willing to explore this issue, either with me or with another therapist, to try to figure it out and perhaps break out of a self-defeating cycle?

S: I never thought *I'd* have to be in therapy, but if you think it might help, yeah, I'll try it.

STRUCTURE AND CONTENT OF INTERVENTION

The therapist assisting a client with weight loss may find it useful to conceptualize the most elemental goal of treatment as helping the client adopt appropriate behavioral and cognitive strategies that will facilitate adherence to a prescribed regimen of nutrition and exercise. In this regard, it may be helpful to distinguish between, on the one hand, the nutritional and exercise changes to be accomplished, and on the other hand, the methods of effecting these changes. It follows that the dietary and exercise plans, although representing goals that may not be immediately attainable, should be constructed early in treatment. Both will be based in large part on the assessment, and both may require consultation with professionals from the appropriate disciplines.

Diet and Exercise Prescriptions

Dietary Plan

Although it is not always necessary to specify a precise level of caloric intake, a general range, at a minimum, should be established based on the client's estimated energy needs, the desired rate of weight loss, the client's ability to restrict intake without precipitating disinhibited binge eating, and the extent to which there will be concurrent medical monitoring. VLCDs are defined as diets providing 800 or fewer calories per day. VLCDs should be restricted to persons who are at least 30% overweight and must not be used without careful medical screening and monitoring. In the absence of monitoring, weight-loss diets should generally provide at least 1,200 calories per day. Clients should be advised that the reinforcing rapid weight loss that accompanies highly restrictive, calorically deficient diets is accomplished in part by loss of water and lean body mass.

The concept of limiting fat intake rather than caloric intake has achieved some popularity in lay publications. Although fat represents the greatest source of excess calories in the diet of the average American, attention to fat grams only may be inadvisable. It is still possible to consume a substantial number of excess calories while keeping fat intake at a minimum, especially as more low-fat and fat-free food items are produced, many with caloric content nearly as high as the original versions.

Attention to fat or calories only may lead to a diet unbalanced in macronutrients (carbohydrates, protein, and fat), vitamins, minerals, and fiber. A sound dietary plan should include foods from all food groups. Recently, the United States Department of Agriculture issued revised recommendations for a balanced diet, the "Food Pyramid," which can be used as a guide for food selection. Diet plans based on an exchange system also have the advantage of nutritional balance.

Most veteran dieters have a history of declaring certain foods to be taboo, leading to restrictions that cannot be followed for more than a short time. This sets the stage for lapses which may trigger further dietary deterioration. It is usually advisable to disabuse clients of the idea that foods are either "good" or "bad." Rather, foods should be described according to how frequently they are consumed. This can reduce the dichotomous "all-or-none" cognitive set that often dooms weight-loss attempts.

Many obese adults have medical conditions that require more specialized dietary prescriptions. Clients with such conditions should be referred to a registered dietitian who can provide a diet in consultation with the client's physician. For example, diabetes may necessitate greater attention to carbohydrate content and spacing of meals and snacks, and hypercholesterolemia may demand a larger reduction in saturated fat and cholesterol intake.

Exercise Plan

Exercise has increasingly been recognized as crucial to long-term weight management. However, many clients have unrealistic expectations about the short-term results of exercise (see following exchange between client [C] and therapist [T]); when these expectations are not met, the client may become frustrated and discouraged and give up attempts to establish regular exercise.

The exact nature of the role of exercise in weight control has not yet been determined. Perhaps surprisingly, studies of the effect of including exercise during weight loss are inconsistent in showing an increased rate of loss, except when the exercise is very frequent and long. Results are slightly more consistent in suggesting that exercise may help to preserve lean body mass during weight loss on moderate caloric restriction. However, most studies of the correlates of long-term outcome show that a regular program of moderate aerobic exercise is a critical factor in weight maintenance.

C: I told you that exercise doesn't work for me. This week proves it. I went out and walked four times this week, and I only lost a half pound. I did better than that the last 2 weeks when I didn't walk at all.

T: How did you think the walking would affect your loss?

C: I should have lost at least 2 more pounds. I was really working up a sweat and breathing hard when I was walking.

T: I know exercise has been a difficult part of this for you, and it would be good to see the results on the scale after you have a good week of exercise. But let's review some of the mathematics of weight loss that we've discussed before. Remember that each pound of body fat contains about 3,500 calories, as a rough estimate. So to lose a pound of fat, you'd need to burn about 3,500 more calories than you take in. Now, how far did you walk?

C: I mapped out a 1-mile route, and did it on 4 days, twice the last time.

T: So you walked 5 miles this week. That's a real achievement. But let's see if maybe you were expecting a little too much to come of it. How many extra calories do you think you burned by walking those 5 miles?

C: I don't know, maybe 1000 per mile?

T: Actually, a lot less. A really rough estimate is that you burn about 100 extra calories per mile.

C: So I'd have to walk that much for 7 weeks to lose 1 extra pound? Forget it. I lost that much each day on the Atkins diet, and never exercised once.

T: Not so fast. Remember, you said that this time you're trying for long-term success. Let's continue the math for a bit. If you walked the same amount every week for a year, that would be a little over 7 pounds. That may not seem like much, but I believe you said that you gained about 70 pounds over the last 10 years, that's an average of 7 pounds a year. In the next ten years, that 500 calories per week from walking might let you maintain your loss instead of gaining another 70 pounds.

C: But that doesn't help me now.

T: Then we'll need to think of some ways to reward yourself for walking, each week or even each day, to keep you motivated until your walking program gets to be routine and even enjoyable. Even if the walking meant a bigger loss each week, you wouldn't see it because of how your water weight shifts. Let's work on finding some rewards that you control.

Aerobic exercise is usually recommended during weight loss because of the added cumulative calorie burn, the body's increased use of body fat stores during moderate aerobic exercise, and the well-known effects on cardiovascular fitness, blood glucose control, and cholesterol fractions. Aerobic exercises include brisk walking, running, stationary or regular cycling, rowing, aerobic dance and exercise classes, swimming, and stepping.

The relevant parameters of aerobic exercise can be remembered as "FIT": Frequency (per week), Intensity (measured as heart rate or ratings of perceived exertion), and Time (duration of the exercise session). In shaping an exercise program, it is probably best to start at a relatively low inten-

sity and time and increase the frequency until the client is exercising four or five times per week. This establishes the priority and habit of exercise. Once a suitable frequency is established, the client can begin to increase the time and later the intensity.

Recently there has been interest in the value of (nonaerobic) resistance training for weight loss. Muscle is the metabolically active tissue. It is supposed that resistance exercise helps to preserve muscle mass during weight loss and therefore protects resting metabolic rate. Although this matter has not been clarified experimentally, resistance training may be included with aerobic exercise as a weight-control regimen, especially for clients undergoing a VLCD.

The therapist should be cognizant of the difficulty of exercise for many obese people. Excess weight represents an extra load to be supported and carried. Joint problems may limit the types of exercise that are advisable. Finally, many obese people are self-conscious about exercising in public; indeed, many clients report stories of jeers and insults they have received from strangers. The therapist should inquire about these issues.

It should be remembered that obese adults represent a medically high-risk group. Clients should be cleared for unsupervised exercise by a physician. A fitness assessment by an exercise physiologist can provide a useful baseline measure against which later improvements can be judged; this measure can give the client a motivational outcome, besides weight change, to use in assessing the personal benefits of exercise. For clients with physical conditions that affect their capacity for exercise, consultation may be advisable with an exercise physiologist who understands the difficulty of exercise for obese people.

Strategies to Promote Dietary and Exercise Changes

In the initial phase of weight management, the key roles of the behavior therapist are to directly help the client to accomplish the dietary and exercise changes that are recommended and to lay the groundwork for the behavioral patterns that will promote maintenance. This includes self-monitoring, goal setting and self-reinforcement, eating-behavior changes and stimulus control, adoption of cognitive-behavioral strategies, and mobilization of social support.

Self-Monitoring

Self-monitoring is important not only during initial assessment but throughout and after treatment. The reactive effects of self-monitoring can be used to advantage after initial assessment. During treatment, it is a means of tracking success and identifying problem areas; self-monitoring gives the therapist ready access to more precise information about the fate of the client's efforts in the natural environment. Self-monitoring is also a valuable self-management tool during maintenance (for a sample self-monitoring form, see Figure 8.2).

Food intake is a natural target of self-monitoring. Once treatment has commenced, it is usually not necessary to elicit the detailed information desired during initial assessment. Food types and quantities, method of preparation, and time of consumption are ordinarily adequate. These data should be examined and commented on so as to reward the act of recording no matter how much or how little the reported intake conforms to recommendations.

In some cases, clients may resist completing the records. Besides the common complaint that too much effort is involved, many people have used food records as part of other programs and may find the endeavor repetitive and boring. Others may be embarrassed or feel that the exercise is childish. We insist that the records be kept because of the valuable information they provide both to us and to the client. An example of a rationale that might be used to encourage higher rates of return on the monitoring forms is shown in Figure 8.4.

Exercise should also be self-monitored, as much for reinforcement effects as for information. Similarly, application of recommended eating-behavior changes is a useful subject of self-monitoring, as are stimuli that accompany unplanned eating episodes.

The extent to which body weight is self-monitored varies according to phase of treatment and client characteristics. It is essential that the client be prepared to engage in some form of self-monitoring of weight indefinitely after treatment, so that recovery plans may be triggered when weight rises above a selected point.

Self-monitoring of weight during weight loss must be prescribed and explained in a way that will not encourage overreliance on weight change as the only measure of progress. Some individuals who are preoccupied with weight change, often to the point of weighing several times a day, may do better if they are discouraged from self-directed weighings at first. However, it should be remembered that if weight loss is the goal of treatment, weights will have to be obtained on some occasions, and the client's reactions cannot be avoided. The therapist should never assume that de-emphasizing weight changes in therapy sessions eliminates the client's focus on them.

An argument can be made that daily recording of weight is desirable for some clients. From the perspective of habit acquisition, daily practice, especially when done at the same time each day, is likely to be more effective than is weekly practice. Given that fluctuations in body water overshadow changes in fat stores in the short run, daily weighing can allow the client to learn both the randomness and the patterns in these shifts. For the client who is emotionally hyperreactive to weight changes, exposure while in treatment to daily body weight variation can allow some measure of desensitization to the capriciousness of these day-to-day changes. Weight graphs with many data points may indicate overall patterns better than do graphs with few data points. Further, the client can derive solace from the fact that if a disappointing weight is obtained, the next "verdict" is only 24 hr away, rather than, for example, 7 days away. For other clients who do not tolerate the daily fluctuation, weighing less frequently is indicated.

Behavioral Goals and Rewards

An important element in short- and long-term efforts to manage obesity is the proper use of goal-setting and self-reinforcement techniques. The client should be helped to acquire this skill early on to allow modeling and practice throughout treatment and to avoid the frustrations caused by unrealistic client goals whether set overtly or covertly.

The first, and perhaps most important, lifestyle behavior you will learn is to keep records. You will be keeping records of your eating, exercise, and weight. You will have more records than an accountant! Don't worry, there is a good reason for it.

Awareness is a key step in changing habits. You may already know a great deal about your habits and your weight patterns, particularly if you have kept records for an earlier diet. You will be surprised by how much more there is to learn.

The awareness you gain from record keeping has several benefits. These will become clear within a few weeks.

You learn about calories. There are calories lurking where you least suspect. Do you think yogurt is a good diet food? One cup of fruit yogurt has more calories than an ice cream cone. Ten innocent potato chips contain 110 calories, more than 5 cups of plain popcorn. Becoming a calorie expert insures that you won't be derailed by calorie surprises.

You are aware of what you eat. You might be thinking, "Of course I know what I eat." However, one does not always recall the exact number of Doritos consumed at happy hour or the ounces of milk poured into the bowl of Wheaties. These are "forgotten" calories, sometimes because we like to forget them!

You increase control over eating. Knowing exactly where you stand with the day's calorie count permits you to judge whether you can afford certain foods. You may have the calories "banked" to have that snack you are considering. Knowing where you stand makes the choice easier.

Eating patterns become clear. You may discover that most of your eating is done between dinner and bedtime. Another person might eat throughout the day. Some people eat when they have certain feelings (anger, anxiety, etc.), and others find they eat when doing something else (watching TV). Knowing your patterns is a big help in changing habits.

The records help you "bank" calories. Your body is like a bank account in which you make calorie deposits and withdrawals. If you keep your calories down, you have some calories to bank for a special occasion. If you have a party to attend on the weekend, you can cut back during the week, and can afford to indulge with some special dessert. Calorie records give you the information to make such a decision.

The weight change record prevents despair. There may be one or more weeks when you fail to lose weight, or even worse, you gain weight! There are many reasons for this, as I will discuss later. Such a discouraging bout with the scale can make life difficult. This despair can be prevented by reviewing your change in weight over many weeks. A slight gain is easier to tolerate when you are reminded by your records that you have been losing weight in a steady manner.

FIGURE 8.4. Rationale to encourage clients' completion of monitoring forms. From *The LEARN Program for Weight Control* (p. 8) by K. D. Brownell, 1992, Dallas, TX: American Health. Copyright 1992 by American Health Publishing Co. Reprinted by permission.

An important distinction should be drawn between long-term goals (actually, objectives, such as ultimate target weight) and short-term goals (the means to the long-term ends, e.g., following an exercise plan for a week). Useful short-term goals focus on behaviors, which are within the control of the client, rather than body weight, which will fluctuate significantly in the short run because of factors outside the client's control.

Effective goals are specific and quantifiable. They should require a reasonable effort but at the same time should be attainable and realistic. They should also be somewhat "forgiving" (i.e., they should not require perfection). Over time, the therapist (T) should help the client (C) to shape the pattern of setting and following up on goals that meet these criteria.

T: It would be helpful for you to focus on one or two goals to really work on this week. Any ideas?

C: I want to work on exercising more.

T: Let's try to get a little more specific about the exercise.

C: OK, I'm going to walk this week.

T: So the exercise will be walking. How much and how often will you walk?

C: Let's say 5 miles, every day.

T: How much are you walking presently?

C: Well, I haven't been getting out much lately.

T: So it's been a while since you exercised regularly?

C: Yeah, actually I haven't done anything consistently in about 5 or 6 years.

T: Maybe 5 miles is expecting a little too much, too soon. You might injure yourself if you start up too quickly.

C: I could say 1 mile a day, but that won't help me lose much weight.

T: You're right, you won't be able to tell when you get on the scale here next week, but we're trying to develop some habits that will make a big difference in your weight over the long haul.

C: Okay, I'll walk a mile every day.

T: If you get tied up at work or we have bad weather one day, you might not achieve that "every day" goal. How about 4 days? That would be 4 more days than you're doing now, and the success you'd enjoy might help you to reach your next goal.

C: You mean success breeds success? Alright, I'll give it a try. I'll walk a mile on 4 days this week.

Most behavioral goals involve behaviors that may have short-term cost (e.g., difficulty) and only long-term rewards. As illustrated in the transcript of the disappointed walker, it is often necessary to help a client develop a reinforcement system to provide short-term rewards for behavior changes until naturally occurring reinforcers take hold.

There are several criteria for an effective reward. First, the reward should be something that the client finds reinforcing. This is not always as obvious as it seems; occasionally a client groping for a reward will include things that on questioning are found to have little reinforcement value. Second, the reward should be attainable shortly after the goal is met. Third, it should be something that the client will forgo unless the goal is met. Finally, it should not be food.

In our experience, selecting effective rewards can be a difficult task for clients. A history of relying on food for reward is often revealed. Some clients resist the idea of "bribing myself to do what I ought to do on my own." Others assert that they do not deny themselves anything they can afford, leaving nothing for additional rewards. Many clients are simply unable to generate ideas for potential rewards.

Clients may be given a homework assignment to list possible rewards, using catalogues and advertisements to suggest tangible rewards. If the client can only think of items too expensive to use for short-term goals, one such item can be designated to be bought only with money earned through meeting behavioral goals; for example, a client who desires a necklace might agree to put aside money for it at the rate of $10 for each weekly exercise goal that she meets.

Clients should not consider only tangible items. Desirable activities might be used as rewards, for example, a day at the beach, at the lake, or in the mountains, or attendance at a certain movie or concert. Even when not used as rewards, clients should be encouraged to engage in more frequent enjoyable activities as a way of compensating for their restriction of an important pleasurable activity, eating. The concept of "time off for good behavior" is also useful. For clients with demanding schedules, an afternoon off, to do as one chooses, can be a valuable reward. Sometimes family members can be enlisted to take over some of the client's home responsibilities to allow the client to enjoy this type of reward.

Eating Behavior Changes and Stimulus Control Techniques

The earliest proposed application of behavior modification to the problem of obesity was based on methods of modifying the terminal behaviors of eating and restricting the cues associated with eating. Despite the flawed assumptions that these behaviors were exhibited differently by obese and nonobese people, programs based on effecting these changes facilitated weight loss. Consequently, behavioral approaches to weight loss include such efforts. These techniques are best presented as ways to make it easier to control eating, and best applied when assessment information indicates that these corrections are necessary.

A major goal of many changes in eating behavior is to slow the rate of food consumption. There is ample reason to believe that this is useful. The manifold satiety cues following eating take 15 to 20 min to develop. Further, Spiegel, Wadden, and Foster (1991) have shown that weight-loss clients who slow their eating the most lose the most weight. Unfortunately, this same study showed that this slowdown decays over time (i.e., a faster eating rate returns). Clients can be encouraged to slow their eating rate by various means: self-monitoring meal durations, putting down their fork between bites, and building in pauses in their meals. This is especially important for clients whose self-monitoring records reveal a pattern of rapid eating. Clients should be reminded that this is one change that does not entail feelings of deprivation and in fact may reduce such feelings.

Stimulus control techniques can be helpful in restricting the client's exposure to eating cues. As the simplest example, food in the home should be limited to as few locations as possible and kept out of view. Similarly, clients should do what they can to reduce the prominence and availability of food in the workplace. Family meals should be served buffet style rather than from serving bowls located prominently and conveniently on the table. A single eating location should be chosen and all eating, whether "legal" or not, should occur only in that place. This can extinguish associations between other activities or areas of the house and eating, for example, snacking while watching television in the den.

Stimulus control techniques can also be used in helping the client cope with certain high-risk situations. A client who has a long-standing habit of snacking on returning home from work may be helped by entering the house through a different door. Declaring the car off limits for eating can, over time, reduce the desire for snacking on trips.

Cognitive-Behavioral Strategies

Attention to the cognitive domain is essential if the client is to adhere to the recommended dietary and exercise changes, cope with cravings and setbacks, and develop maintenance skills. Additionally, the client's self-efficacy may be impaired by a history of failures at weight control. Exercises in generating and using efficacy-enhancing self-statements and in identifying and countering maladaptive attributions for success and failure are appropriate interventions.

Cravings should be expected. The client can be instructed in such strategies as thought stopping, imagery, and delaying the decision about eating, as well as using self-statements concerning the transient nature of cravings. Similarly, rationalizations should be detected and countered with appropriate self-statements.

Long-term maintenance requires the ability to recover from lapses (Brownell, Marlatt, Lichtenstein, & Wilson, 1986; Marlatt & Gordon, 1985; Perri et al., 1992). A major cause of failure to recover from such lapses is a dichotomous, all-or-none style of evaluating one's success. Clients with this style consider anything less than perfection to be a complete failure. When the inevitable setback occurs, the client overgeneralizes and may consider the entire weight-control attempt doomed, often attributing this failure to personal flaws rather than to situational factors. Clients who exhibit this evaluative style should be helped to detect implicit all-or-none assumptions in their reactions to lapses during treatment and to rehearse alternative self-statements that embody a continuous, matter-of-degree approach to measuring success.

The case of "Peter" is a good example. He is a 44-year-old postal supervisor, 5'11" and 205 lb after a loss of 30 lb. Peter (P) slumped dejectedly into his chair after learning that he had gained 1 lb.

P: I started not to bother coming in today.

T: Why is that?

P: I had a terrible week. I didn't do anything I was supposed to do, and I pigged out at the father–son dinner at my son's school yesterday.

T: Does that mean you didn't meet your exercise goal?

P: I did that, but I didn't do anything else.

T: Like keeping your eating diary?

P: Oh, I did that, it's all here for you to see.

T: So you kept your diary, and you met your exercise goal. What made it such a terrible week besides the father–son dinner?

P: Wasn't that enough? I knew I wouldn't be able to stick to my diet there, I never can, I just don't have any willpower.

T: What do you think gave you trouble?

P: We had an urgent meeting at work at noon, and I didn't get to eat lunch, so I was ready to eat anything when I got to the dinner.

T: It's not surprising you overate at the dinner if you missed lunch. By the way, my mail carrier delivered one of my magazines to the neighbors yesterday.

P: What's that got to do with anything? We handle thousands of pieces of mail each day. What about all the mail that was delivered correctly? You can't expect people to never make a mistake.

T: Unless we're talking about you and your weight-loss program.

P: (*Pauses*) I guess I get your point. Even though I blow it one day, it doesn't mean that the whole week's a failure.

T: That's right. It might help to remember my magazine the next time you fall a little short on one of your goals.

Mobilization of Social Support

Body size is always a public matter. Weight-loss attempts are rarely private struggles that are independent of the client's interpersonal milieu. Changes by the client in dietary and exercise patterns frequently affect the family and close friends. In addition, these significant persons can influence the client's chances of success. Friends may support or sabotage; the spouse may cheer or complain (see the example of Martha, her husband, and the fur coat presented earlier).

The client is not a passive participant in these weight-related interactions. He/she can influence, within limits, the amount of support provided by important others. As noted in the assessment section, the client should decide how each person can best help and, when appropriate, should ask for that help. At the same time, the client can foster mutuality by asking how to reinforce these people for providing the desired support. It is not uncommon for a client who is dissatisfied with others' reactions to reveal

on questioning that the preferred type of support has never been communicated.

"Mary Agnes" is a 38-year-old shipyard worker who entered a VLCD program at 220 lb at 5'8". She had lost 40 lb. The scenario is between Mary Agnes (M), therapist (T), and other group members (GM) who are discussing reactions of significant other people to their weight loss.

M: My husband hasn't said word one about my loss.

T: Are you saying he's ignored all your efforts to lose weight?

M: Yeah. I might as well have skipped the whole thing, as much as he cares.

T: When you lost weight previously, did he react the same way, ignoring it?

M: The last time I lost weight, he drove me crazy by making too much of it of it every time I lost a few pounds.

T: Did you let him know that?

M: Not in so many words, but he got the message.

T: So up until now he's always made a big deal over your losses?

M: No. Earlier on, he used to act like a cop, always asking me if what I was eating was allowed. After a while, he got the message on that too.

T: You told him to back off.

M: He figured it out.

T: So he's tried acting like your conscience, and he's tried praising you, but you didn't want either of those. What would you like him to do?

M: What anybody would want their husband to do, show a little understanding.

T: You know what you mean by showing understanding, but it's different for each person. I wonder if the reason he's not saying anything this time might be that he figures whatever he does will be wrong.

M: Do you mean I have to tell him what to do? If I have to draw him a picture, it won't mean anything.

GM: Maybe he wants to help you. Maybe he doesn't. But you won't be able to tell unless you let him know how to help. I used to get furious with my husband because every time I came home from group, he'd ask how much I'd lost. When I finally told him it felt like bringing home a report card, he said he was just trying to show that he wanted me to succeed. Once I told how to do that, he was great, most of the time.

Assertiveness skills are important in a variety of situations. Most clients have at least one "food pusher" in their lives; food refusal responses can be rehearsed in therapy sessions. It is often desirable to have clients anticipate events where they will be encouraged to overeat; when appropriate, they can notify in advance the relevant people (e.g., hosts) that they are restricting their intake, to avoid awkward encounters.

Compliments about weight loss require assertiveness skills for some clients who feel uncomfortable in such situations. Assertive responses are also sometimes needed when requesting modifications to menu items in restaurants.

Weight may play a critical, complicated role in marriage and other intimate relationships. In such cases, it is usually the woman who is the obese partner. In some dysfunctional marriages, the husband may use the wife's weight as an excuse for emotional withdrawal and avoidance of sex. In others, weight loss by the wife may incite feelings of jealousy and insecurity (not always unwarranted) on the part of the husband; physical abuse is sometimes noted in these cases. There are also instances in which the wife's obesity functions as a means of avoiding intimacy with a husband who is no longer desired or loved and, sometimes, as a guard against extramarital affairs. The intricacies of these issues are described in a book by Stuart and Jacobson (1987), and are illustrated by the dialogue that follows between "Nora" (N) and therapist (T).

Nora is a 40-year-old married small business owner, mother of two, who had lost 40 lb. She returned to the clinic after an unannounced 3-week absence and a 10-lb weight gain.

T: Looks like you've had a few rough weeks.

N: It's just not fair. . . . (*tears*)

T: What's not fair?

N: When you're a fat woman, you're just fat, not a woman. You're asexual.

T: And when you lose weight?

N: All of a sudden, men notice you, even though they've known you for years, the bastards. I'm the same person I was 60 pounds ago, but now they're all grins, acting like I'm the best thing they've seen. It's not just "buddies" anymore.

T: Someone came on to you?

N: One of my husband's best friends.

T: Sounds like that made you mad.

N: Yeah, but that's not the problem.

T: What is?

N: I was really tempted. You know, I've been unhappy at home for years, but as long as I was fat, I didn't have to think about it. Now I have to decide, and I'm not sure I can decide to say no. It scares the hell out of me. It was simpler being fat.

Treatment Providers and Treatment Settings

It is tempting to say that the ideal setting in which to work with overweight individuals is a clinic where staff are available with backgrounds in psychology, nutrition, exercise physiology, and medicine. Such a clinic would have state-of-the-art equipment and technical expertise to undertake assessment of metabolic rate, fat cell size and number, body fat distribution, and the like.

Aside from being impractical and not available to most overweight persons, such intensive, costly treatment is probably not necessary or desirable for many individuals. Here again, the concept of matching individuals to treatments is important (Figure 8.1). Clients differ in which setting works best, in the level of expertise needed in a program leader, and in the background of the provider with whom they are best suited to work. As long as the program delivered is sound, who provides the program and where it is provided becomes a matter of meeting the needs of the client. Looking back to the stepped-care model presented in Figure 8.1, the most intensive treatments should be reserved for individuals who are unlikely to succeed with less.

Professionals and even nonprofessionals from many backgrounds have been involved in assisting overweight individuals. To assume that advanced professional training and a multidisciplinary staff are necessary is to ignore the success stories from commercial and self-help programs, from clients treated by professionals working alone, or from those who have lost weight on their own.

Among the professionals we have found capable of providing weight-loss treatment are psychologists, nurses, dietitians, exercise specialists, and physicians. Beyond a basic knowledge of nutrition, exercise, and cognitive-behavioral approaches, the particular background and training of the individual appear less important than personal skills such as empathy, dedication, warmth, and ability to motivate clients week after week.

We hasten to add that the potential effectiveness of different professionals does not imply that *any* approach delivered by *any* professional will be valuable. There is much exploitation and useless treatment being delivered by individuals who claim miracle results. Nearly every week, for example, one can find newspaper advertisements from "hypnotherapists" who guarantee staggering weight losses. Hence, some standards must be employed, and clients should be educated according to the guidelines discussed earlier about legitimate approaches to weight control.

PREPARING THE INDIVIDUAL FOR LONG-TERM MAINTENANCE

Although we have presented here a separate discussion of some issues concerning maintenance of weight loss, it is not advisable in treatment to isolate maintenance strategies from weight-loss interventions. This may communicate to the client that implementation of these strategies is optional or postponable. It is preferable to imbue the entire span of treatment with an emphasis on long-term change and with institution of the cognitive and behavioral methods that will be required to maintain a weight loss over the years. While it is true that the skills most important for weight loss are often differ-

ent from those most important for maintenance, they are rarely incompatible; early initiation of maintenance behaviors will allow the client to practice them while under a longer period of supervision by the therapist.

In the first book specifically devoted to maintenance of weight loss, Perri et al. (1992) argue for a continuous-care model of treatment which calls for contact with a health care professional over an extended period. Perri et al. (1992) stress the importance of communicating to the client that obesity is a chronic condition that is controlled through active self-management efforts.

> Thus, clinicians must convey to obese patients an appropriate awareness of the long-term implications regarding the management of obesity. Obese individuals need to know that, similar to patients who are diabetic or hypertensive, they may never be "cured" of their "disease." (p. 103)

Relapse-prevention skills are essential to long-term success. These include identification of high-risk situations, development of strategies to avoid or cope with high-risk situations, and acquisition of cognitive and behavioral responses to regain control after lapses. Lengthier discussions of relapse-prevention techniques are available elsewhere (Brownell et al., 1986; Marlatt & Gordon, 1985). The client should be instructed in these techniques throughout treatment.

Relapse-prevention techniques are grounded in problem-solving and coping-skills philosophies. Individuals are taught to identify specific eating problems in their life, to plan both cognitive-behavioral and emotion-based strategies for preventing lapses, and to react constructively when lapses do occur. Anticipating possible problems and developing a set of responses to be used when the problems are encountered can greatly strengthen a client's self-efficacy and the resulting ability to cope with the day-to-day threats encountered during both weight loss and maintenance. Some additional suggestions for enhancing maintenance have been proposed by Brownell and Jeffery (1987) and are presented in Table 8.5.

The specific interventions necessary during long-term work with the post-weight-loss

TABLE 8.5. Suggested Methods for Improving the Maintenance of Weight Loss

1. Consider other treatments for our patients.

2. Develop criteria to match patients to treatments.

3. Develop criteria for screening patients to determine if there would be a better time to diet or a better program to join.

4. Increase initial weight losses.

5. Increase the length of treatment.

6. Be more aggressive about attaining goal weight. Consider the "initial treatment phase" as the period necessary to reach goal weight. "Maintenance" should not be considered until there is a substantial weight loss to maintain.

7. Increase the emphasis on exercise. Structured, supervised exercise programs need to be tested against current programs in which patients are given only verbal or written advice about exercise.

8. Exploit the social environment as a means to improve long-term adherence. More research is necessary to define the factors in the family, work site, community, etc., that can be used to facilitate weight loss.

9. Financial incentives, which have been effective in producing some of the best losses in behavioral studies, need to be extended for use in the long term.

10. Combine behavioral programs with other treatments, such as commercial and self-help programs, aggressive diets, or surgery.

11. Evaluate the cognitive factors that are included in most programs by consensus, but which have not been studied in detail.

12. Possibly extend stimulus control methods into the dieter's daily life by considering different mechanisms for food delivery and for supervised exercise.

13. Study the use and timing of relapse-prevention methods in more detail.

Note. From Brownell and Jeffery (1987, p. 370). Copyright 1987 by Association for Advancement of Behavior Therapy. Reprinted by permission.

client will depend on the needs and circumstances of the client, which vary over time. At any given point, a client may require assistance with stress management, marital counseling, assertiveness training, body-image remediation, dating skills, exercise compliance, or dealing with commitment and intimacy issues. Obviously, one therapist may not be proficient in all these areas.

However, the overall role of the therapist in this long-term endeavor may be described rather consistently over time and across clients. Perri et al. (1992) propose that "the health-care professional's role is to serve as an *active problem solver* who systematically and continuously aids the client in identifying effective strategies to sustain the behavioral changes needed for long-term success" (p. 103, italics added). To that we add that the role also incorporates the important elements of social support, empathy, and a source of reality testing for client expectations.

The importance of encouraging the client to use the therapist in these ways over an extended period cannot be overemphasized. The idea of a continuous-care approach to obesity is novel to most obese people. Many clients feel that continued reliance on professional help is a sign of weakness. Further, many clients are most reluctant to attend treatment when they most need it: when they are gaining weight. Thus, from the outset, the therapist should use any means available to help the client to accept and act on a long-term model of care.

Program Structure

There is some variability across programs in the length of intervention, the use of group and individual treatment, the presence and frequency of follow-up meetings after the initial program ends, staffing patterns, and other factors. These factors have not been evaluated systematically in controlled research, so it is not possible to say with certainty that one structure is better than another.

Perhaps the most frequently used format for cognitive-behavioral approaches is to provide treatment for 16–20 weekly sessions in groups of 10–15 clients. The sessions are 60–90 min in length and involve a mixture of didactic material aimed at building skills and group discussion aimed at maximizing social support. Having subsequent meetings, sometimes called booster sessions, is the norm, but the frequency and total duration of this phase are highly variable. One such schedule is to hold biweekly meetings for 2 months, meetings every 3 weeks for the next 3 months, and then monthly meetings extending for at least 7 months. However, such a tapering schedule may require aggressive efforts by the therapist to prevent absences from leading to premature termination.

In many programs, written materials are provided to clients as an adjunct to the information provided by group leaders. These materials have been organized into books and manuals, an example of which is the LEARN manual discussed earlier (Brownell, 1992). This manual is a step-by-step guide written for the general public which emphasizes life-style change, exercise, attitude change, social support, and nutrition. No studies have been done comparing programs with and without manuals, but our impression is that such a manual can be helpful for several reasons:

1. A manual can provide a fundamental education in the key areas of weight control (e.g., nutrition and safe exercise). Few professionals are expert in all the relevant areas, so a manual permits professionals with various backgrounds and levels of expertise to deliver services.
2. Often clients do not remember all the information presented in a session. This occurs because a client is preoccupied with something else, there is insufficient time in a session to adequately convey important material, the information may not be pertinent to a client at the time it is presented, or for other reasons. Having the information available between sessions, and accessible when it is relevant to the needs of the individual, increases the likelihood that it will be accessed and used.
3. In some sessions, issues arise that lead the professional and clients away from the educational material to be presented. For example, information on exercise may be the topic of discussion, but a client might disclose troubling information about sabotage by a spouse. Knowing the intended material is covered in a manual permits both professional and client to be more flexible in the use of session time.
4. Many clients will use a treatment manual after the program has ended as a self-help refresher course and source of motivation.

5. Family members and friends often seek to read such a manual or may be asked to do so by the client. Given the potentially positive influence of social support, this education of significant others can be helpful.

It is our belief that written materials that accompany a program should be considered more than reference materials and should be used as a workbook. Important points can be underlined or highlighted, notes may be made in the margins, and signs of wear can be symbolic of motivation and interest in developing new skills. Clients who work though such a program are developing individualized, tailored programs based on their specific situations and needs.

SPECIAL CLINICAL ISSUES

Importance of Binge Eating

An important development in the field occurred when a distinct subgroup of the obese population was defined. These are individuals who engage in binge eating. Stunkard (1959) first described the pattern, and although the issue was noted in his later writings (Stunkard, 1976), the field was slow to recognize the importance of the issue until the late 1980s. At that point, the study of binge eating in obese persons began in earnest, so currently, a great deal is known about the problem.

Various definitions have been proposed and assessment devices used in the study of binge eating (see also Wilson & Pike, Chapter 7, this volume). The most extensive work on diagnosis has been done by Spitzer et al. (1992). These investigators conducted a large, multisite field trial with more than 1,900 subjects, and used the data to propose diagnostic criteria for a new disorder called binge eating disorder (BED). These criteria are shown in Table 8.6.

Spitzer et al. (1992) argued that BED be included as a diagnostic category in DSM-IV. The decision of the DSM-IV task force was to include binge eating in the appendix as an area in need of further study. In any case, these criteria are helpful in identifying individuals with binge eating problems.

TABLE 8.6. Proposed Diagnostic Criteria for Binge Eating Disorder

A. Recurrent episodes of binge eating. An episode of binge eating is characterized by both of the following:
   1. Eating, in a discrete period of time (e.g., within any 2-hr period), an amount of food that is definitely larger than most people would eat in a similar period of time under similar circumstances.
   2. A sense of lack of control over eating during the episode (e.g., a feeling that one cannot stop eating or control what or how much one is eating).

B. The binge-eating episodes are associated with at least three of the following:
   1. Eating much more rapidly than normal.
   2. Eating until feeling uncomfortably full.
   3. Eating large amounts of food when not feeling physically hungry.
   4. Eating alone because of being embarrassed by how much one is eating.
   5. Feeling disgusted with oneself, depressed, or very guilty after overeating.

C. Marked distress regarding binge eating.

D. The binge eating occurs, on average, at least twice a week for 6 months.

E. Does not occur exclusively during the course of anorexia nervosa or bulimia nervosa.

Note. Criteria for binge eating disorder were first proposed by Spitzer et al., 1992. From APA (1993). Copyright 1993 by the American Psychiatric Association. Reprinted by permission.

The key features of BED are eating large amounts of food and feeling out of control. Previous criteria have used subjective reports of a binge, but some people would eat small amounts of a "forbidden food" and consider the act a binge. The DSM-IV criteria judge the eating episode in the context of whether the respondent believes that the amount eaten is larger than most people would eat. Recognizing that the judgment on the part of the respondent is still subjective, the therapist should attempt to obtain an estimate of the actual quantity consumed in a binge episode. This determination can indicate whether the primary eating problem is the amount consumed or the perception that eating is out of control. The cognitive feature of eating out of control is important and is likely the genesis of at least part of the distress individuals experience.

These diagnostic criteria for BED are helpful in bringing attention to a key clinical problem. From a clinical perspective, however, it would be a mistake to assume that each criterion has been validated or will be helpful in developing treatment methods. For instance, a person might not meet criteria for BED because of binges that occur less than twice a week, or have been occurring for less than 6 months. Such a person might still have an important problem and might require the same intervention that would be provided to a person who has been bingeing more frequently and for a longer period.

Binge eating is common in obese persons seeking treatment, so to the extent these individuals require special treatment, the issue must be taken seriously. Among those in clinical treatment programs for obesity, 25%–50% are binge eaters (Marcus, Wing, & Lamparski, 1985; Spitzer et al., 1992). The rate of binge eating increases with increasing weight (Telch, Agras, & Rossiter, 1988). The prevalence of binge eating in obese persons in the general community is approximately 2% (Bruce & Agras, 1992; Spitzer et al., 1992). In a national probability sample of U.S. women, the lifetime prevalence of BED, across all weight categories, was estimated to be 1.6% (Brewerton, Dansky, O'Neil, & Kilpatrick, 1993).

Comparisons of obese persons who are or are not binge eaters began only recently, but data thus far suggest key differences. For example, in laboratory test meals, obese women who meet BED criteria ate more calories than did non-BED obese women, whether instructed to avoid bingeing (2,343 vs. 1,640 kcal) or to binge (2,963 vs. 2,017 kcal). When bingeing only, BED subjects, relative to non-BED subjects, chose a greater percentage of calories as fat (38.9% vs. 33.5%) and a smaller percentage of calories as protein (11.4% vs. 15.4%; Yanovski et al., 1992). In spite of these differences in eating variables, another study found no differences between BED and non-BED subjects on metabolic variables such as blood glucose, blood lipids, and resting metabolic rate, after controlling for body mass index and age (O'Neil, Jarrell, et al., 1992).

Body image correlates of binge eating are not entirely clear. Within a clinical sample of obese women, bingers did not differ from

nonbingers on a silhouette selection procedure used to obtain measures of current
body size estimation or ideal (desired) body
size (Davis, Williamson, Goreczny, & Bennett, 1989). However, on measures of affective components of body image among a
nonclinical survey sample, bingeing obese
men and women, relative to nonbingeing
obese subjects, reported greater body dissatisfaction, evaluated their appearance more
negatively, and were more occupied with
their appearance and weight (Cash, 1991).

Obese binge eaters and non-binge eaters
differ in two additional ways that must now
be considered in designing treatment programs. First, obese binge eaters presenting
for weight loss treatment have higher levels
of psychopathology than do non-binge-eat-
ing obese persons also seeking treatment
(LaPorte, 1992; Marcus, Wing, & Hopkins,
1988). Second, binge eating in obese persons appears to be associated with poor
response to treatment (Keefe, Wyshogrod,
Weinberger, & Agras, 1984; Marcus et al.,
1988), although there is a report of no differences between binge eaters and non-
binge-eaters (Jarrell, 1991).

It is our belief that binge eating in obese
persons represents an eating disorder super-
imposed on obesity. It is not yet clear
whether the binge eating precedes or follows from obesity. Establishing the causal
relationship will be important to designing
treatments for the subset of obese persons
who are binge eaters. In the meantime, it
is clear that binge eaters have high levels of
psychological disturbance, may do less well
in treatment, and have a very troubling pattern of eating. In some cases, enrolling these
individuals in conventional weight-loss programs without addressing the disordered
eating may lead to disappointing results.

It is our clinical impression that some
binge eaters may require treatment for their
disordered eating prior to or during a
weight-loss program. However, no studies
have tested this assumption. One fruitful
area for research would be to examine the
progress of obese binge eaters in conventional weight-loss treatment compared to
others in a program dealing with binge eating first and weight subsequently.

Several promising treatments for binge
eating have been derived from work on
bulimia nervosa, namely cognitive-behavior

therapy and interpersonal psychotherapy
(Fairburn et al., 1991; Wilfley et al., 1993,
Wilson & Pike, Chapter 7, this volume).
Cognitive-behavioral approaches target dysfunctional attitudes about weight and shape
and aim to create more structured eating
from the chaos of binges. Interpersonal psychotherapy does not deal with the core
symptoms of the eating disorder per se, but
rather focuses on key relationships in the
client's life.

Essentially equivalent results have been
produced by these two fundamentally different approaches, for both bulimia nervosa
(Fairburn et al., 1991) and binge eating in
obese persons (Wilfley et al., 1993). This
raises several important possibilities. First,
eating-disorder symptoms may arise from
different causes. Second, binge eating
per se, among some persons, may be a reflection of other pathology, perhaps as a
"secondary symptom." Third, matching individuals to treatments may prove to be part
of treating obese binge eaters. Research is
now under way to examine matching factors, but criteria for matching are not yet
available. One might speculate that individuals with serious relationship disturbances,
which would include those with one of the
personality disorders, might require interpersonal psychotherapy, whereas the symp-
tom-focused cognitive-behavioral approach
might be preferable with others. We underscore the speculative nature of this notion.

More detailed coverage of the binge-
eating issue is not possible within the scope
of this chapter. We refer the reader to a
comprehensive volume on binge eating and
its treatment (Fairburn & Wilson, 1993).

Weight Loss Goals and Expectations as Barriers to Weight Change

Goals

Previously we discussed the importance of
emphasizing behavioral goals so that
changes on the scale are not the only criteria against which clients judge their behavior. One cannot deny the power of the
scale, however, and clinicians must recognize that clients generally begin treatment
with a weight-loss goal. Clients who fix on
this number can become extremely frustrated.

This concept of "goal weight" is foremost in the minds of most individuals who attempt to lose weight. The criteria used to establish a goal weight can be highly idiosyncratic and may change with time. Many people aspire to a weight they recall from a landmark point in their life. Examples are high school or college graduation, a wedding, military service, lowest adult weight, or weight after participation in a weight-loss program. In some cases, individuals have a goal weight based on a health referent, usually "ideal" weights derived from height–weight tables. In commercial programs, a goal weight is typically established from a mixture of what the individual wishes to weigh and figures from the tables of ideal weights.

The goal weight represents an individual's long-range aspirations and could take months or even years to reach. At the very least, the goal is distant and represents the ultimate product of many changes in attitudes, affect, and behavior. It is our experience that clients may feel that the goal is remote and in some cases unreachable, even when satisfactory progress is occurring. The goal weight can be a significant obstacle rather than a source of motivation and encouragement. This is especially true of people with significant excess weight. It is easy to envision a person who begins a program 60 lb from a goal weight feeling worse about 40 lb yet to lose than 20 lb already lost, even though the 20-lb loss might have taken 4 months and considerable effort.

Inherent in this concept of goal weight is the notion that the individual can, in fact, reach that weight. This ignores the possibility that the goal weight might be an impossible weight for some individuals. Biological factors such as fat cell number, resting energy expenditure, or other factors influenced by genetics may impose barriers to weight loss. For others, the degree of food restriction and physical activity necessary to lose to and maintain the goal weight may be untenable.

Ideal Versus Reasonable Weight

One possible means of avoiding the problems created by goal weights is to abandon the concept of ideal weight in favor of a "reasonable weight" (Brownell & Rodin, 1990; Brownell & Wadden, 1991, 1992). The weight would be determined by a number of factors and would represent the weight a person can achieve and maintain by making reasonable changes in life-style.

This concept runs counter to the stance that elevated weight brings elevated risk, and that all excess weight should be lost. While theoretically correct, we feel this approach is counterproductive. Because the distant goal is likely to discourage people, the goal weight could set the stage for relapse (Brownell et al., 1986). In addition, impressive changes in risk factors can occur with relatively small weight losses (Blackburn & Kanders, 1987; Goldstein, 1992). Blood pressure reduction and improved metabolic control in diabetics are among the changes. The overriding point may be that smaller but better maintained losses will be more beneficial than larger losses followed by relapse (Brownell & Wadden, 1992).

How, then, can a reasonable weight be established? Again, we must rely on clinical judgment and the intuition of the clients. Table 8.7 presents five questions that may be helpful in negotiating a reasonable weight with a client. Research has yet to be done to validate these or any other criteria, but we have found them helpful in providing the basis for a client to settle on a reasonable goal.

Clients may be unaccustomed to the concept of reasonable weight, so it must be presented with a strong rationale as illustrated during the following session between therapist (T) and client (C).

T: Let's talk about goal weight. What do you think when you hear this?

C: I want to weigh 120 pounds.

T: Why 120 pounds?

C: The nurse at my doctor's office said I should weigh 125 from the tables, but I weighed 120 when I got married and I looked great.

T: Is this the goal you have set before when you joined other programs?

C: Sure. This is what I want to weigh.

T: How long do you figure it will take to get there?

C: Well, I weigh 182 now, so I figure it will take 3 or 4 months.

TABLE 8.7. Questions Used as Clinical Criteria to Help Establish a "Reasonable Weight" for an Individual Client

1. Is there a history of excess weight in your parents or grandparents?

2. What is the lowest weight you have maintained as an adult for at least 1 year?

3. What is the largest size of clothes that you feel comfortable in, at the point you say, "I look pretty good considering where I have been"? At what weight would you wear these clothes?

4. Think of a friend or family member (with your age and body frame) who looks "normal" to you. What does the person weigh?

5. At what weight do you believe you can live with the required changes in eating and/or exercise?

Note. These questions are based in part on criteria proposed by Brownell and Rodin, 1990, and represent clinical impression. Research-based criteria have not been established. From Brownell and Wadden, 1992), p. 509. Copyright 1992 by the American Psychological Association. Reprinted by permission.

T: We will talk about this later, because how *fast* you expect to lose is tied up in how *much* you expect to lose. For now, let's go back to your weight loss goal. If 120 is your goal, it is easy to see how you might get discouraged during a program. Can you see how this might happen?

C: Well, I haven't been successful doing this before, so I might feel afraid that I won't make it.

T: True. The fear you feel might be realistic given the circumstances. You want to avoid setting a trap for yourself. What do you think of setting a goal of 120, when you have not been able to reach 120 before?

C: It might inspire me, but I might also never reach it.

T: Would it make sense to set a different goal—one that you are more likely to reach?

C: How would I do this?

T: This is a good time to talk about a *reasonable* weight for you. Reasonable weight is the weight you feel you can reach with hard work and persistence. It would be a weight at which you can live with the changes you have made. It is a weight you could maintain.

C: How do I know what weight this would be?

T: Let me ask you several questions. These should help us close in on a reasonable weight. Were your parents or grandparents overweight?

C: My mother was overweight, and so was my grandfather. My grandmother was stocky, but not really heavy.

T: I cannot say for certain, but the history of overweight in your family raises the possibility of an inherited predisposition to gain weight.

C: Does this mean I can't lose weight?

T: No. You may not have such a genetic tendency at all, and even if you do, it should still be possible for you to lose weight. Let's move on to the second question and see how the information begins to fit together.

C: OK.

T: What is the lowest weight you have been able to maintain as an adult for at least one year?

C: That's hard to say. I guess I got down to about 140 when I went on the liquid fast.

T: Were you able to stay at 140 for a year or longer?

C: I bounced between 140 and 150 for about a year.

T: The third question. Think about the largest size of clothes you would feel comfortable in—where you would feel you look pretty good. What would you weigh to be able to wear these clothes?

C: Well, I want to say 120 because I'd like to look like I did when I got married.

T: Remember now that we are talking about a *reasonable* weight.

C: I think I could wear clothes that would make me look much better than I do now at say 140 or 150. When I lost weight with the fast, I looked a lot better and my friends said lots of nice things.

T: Then I will ask the fourth question. Think of a friend or family member, with about the same height and frame size as you, who you feel looks "normal." What does the person weigh?

C: My sister-in-law Sally is about my size. She is chunky, but doesn't look real heavy. I'd say she weighs about 135.

T: The final question. At what weight do you think you can live with the changes you would have to make in your eating and exercise? Remember back on diets in the past and think about what you were doing to maintain the lower weights. What did it take, and can you live like that?

C: After the fast, I was eating regular meals. They were small, but I felt good being able to eat normally. I was walking with my friend three times a week or so. I felt great being in better shape.

T: Do you think you could live like this permanently?

C: I guess so. I did it for a year, but then things got crazy at work and my schedule went nuts with the kids.

T: If you could develop some way of handling stress, or perhaps keeping your life on a more even keel, do you think you could live with the eating and exercise habits you were practicing then?

C: I think so.

T: Good. Let's put all this together. You may be susceptible to weight gain because of the family history you described, so getting down to 120 may or may not be possible. You were able to stay between 140 and 150 after the liquid diet program and did so for a year. You think you looked a lot better then. Your sister-in-law looks reasonable to you and you figure she weighs about 135. Finally, you said you might be able to live with the changes you made after the liquid diet when you were down to 140 to 150. Do these suggest any number to you to consider as a reasonable weight?

C: 140 to 150?

T: This sounds like the right range to me. The 140 might be low, however, because this is at the bottom of the range from 140 to 150. Let's play it safe and pick a weight you think is *truly* reasonable.

C: I guess 150 sounds about right.

T: How do you think this would work for you?

C: I understand what you are saying, but it will be hard to get the 120 pounds out of my mind.

T: The 120 has been part of your thinking for so long, that what you say does not surprise me. If you catch yourself each time you think of the 120 and say something like the following, the 120 will fade and the new weight can take its place. "The 120 sounds good but it may just discourage me. I will be making great progress if I lose to 150, then I can worry about losing more."

Expectations as Barriers

Often clients enter treatment with expectations that can be realistic and constructive or unrealistic and problematic. Having a weight goal that is based on faulty assumptions is one version of this. Others might involve expecting weight loss to be more rapid than is feasible, for the task to be easier than is possible, or for life to improve in a dramatic fashion once weight loss occurs. We will discuss the last of these in some detail below. The rate of weight loss is a common issue where expectations often exceed reality. The following exchange highlighted one approach to confronting this issue with the client mentioned above.

T: Before you mentioned that it would take you 3 or 4 months to reach your goal. Would you explain more about where this number comes from?

C: I didn't think about it very much, but this seems like a long time.

T: Let's do some arithmetic and see what we get. How much do you figure you might lose each week?

C: Maybe 3 pounds.

T: That would be a rapid weight loss. You may lose this much in the first week or two, but in a program like ours, where you are making reasonable life-style changes, you can count on losing 1 to 2 pounds per week. Just to be on the safe side, let's say 1 pound a week will be your loss. You wanted to lose from 182 to 150, which is a 32-pound loss. How long then, should it take to reach the 150?

C: Let's see. About 32 weeks?

T: Right. This is 8 months, which is double your guess.

C: This is horrible. I can't imagine being on a diet for 8 months.

T: This may be one of the problems that got in your way in the past. It is very common for people to be losing weight at a fine pace, but feel discouraged. The discouragement comes not from lack of progress, but from the way the progress looks when stacked against unrealistic expectations.

C: So what do I do?

T: Many people I work with find it helpful to plot a graph with expected weight losses, so they know what they might expect to weigh at given points in time. Since it is February 1st and you are beginning, you might project a 6-pound loss, to 176 pounds, when your children have their March vacation from school. By tax day, on April 15, you might have lost 10 or 12 pounds, let's say down to 170 pounds. On your birthday in June, you might be down to 160, and by July 4th down to 155. You can work out your own landmark dates and the exact rate of weight loss, but this will give you some idea of how to approach it.

C: This doesn't sound like very exciting weight loss.

T: True, but it is *realistic* weight loss. What can be different about this time is that you may lose more slowly than you like, but if you make the right changes, you can maintain.

Using Principles of Shaping to Establish Short-Term Goals

The discussion of reasonable weight provides an excellent opportunity to introduce the concept of shaping and to help clients accept the notion that short-term goals must be identified as treatment begins.

T: Now that you have established a reasonable weight, let's talk about what your very first goal in the program might be.

C: My top goal is to get to the 150 pounds we discussed.

T: This is your ultimate goal, but I am talking about your first goal. Let me explain an interesting principle called shaping. Any guess about what this refers to?

C: That we shape better goals?

T: In a way, yes. It means taking long-range goals and breaking them into short-term goals which are more manageable.

C: What difference does it make? I'll either lose or won't lose. Why does this goal business matter when the bottom line is my willpower?

T: If you shoot for only the big goal, you only feel fulfilled after reaching it. By making goals over the short term, you create more opportunities to feel good and to reward yourself. These can keep you going over the months it will take you to lose weight.

C: How do I do this?

T: If you want to lose from 182 to 150, perhaps we can set a 2-pound loss as your first goal, and then go in 5-pound blocks from that point on. You would focus on the 2 pounds or 5, with these being your *only* goals at the time.

C: But how do I not think about how much I want to lose altogether?

T: What I am about to say may sound trite, but give it a try. You know how people say they are going to take it a day at a time? Coaches are always saying they are thinking ahead only one game when reporters ask them about games far in the future. In both cases, individuals are saying they will be distracted or discouraged if they think too far ahead, and if they concentrate on the immediate goal, they will do better. This will be true for you. If you can keep focused on the smaller goal, you will be drawn toward something more attainable. This makes you feel proud and increases your self-confidence, which in the long-run may be your greatest asset.

SUMMARY

Obesity is a complex disorder with multiple etiologies, medical and psychological effects, and avenues for treatment. The putative solution—dieting—is a widespread activity that occurs now at record rates. The high rates of dieting are due in part to the high rates of obesity, but much dieting occurs because individuals aspire to unrealistically lean body shapes. Such unrealistic aspirations, combined with recent recognition that dieting may have negative consequences, suggests that any individual should make an informed decision about whether to embark on a weight-loss program before deciding how to lose weight.

Many approaches are available for the person attempting to lose weight. After ruling out the unsafe and unsound approaches, there are still many choices among the commercial and self-help programs, counseling available from a number of health professionals, and countless plans for losing weight "on your own." Professionals can consider these approaches and programs as allies and resources, so that referral to other programs, combining approaches, or using different approaches in sequence can now be part of service delivery for overweight persons. This is in keeping with the philosophy that obesity is a chronic problem that requires long-term management.

Fundamental to any program are alterations in food intake and physical activity. This is to be distinguished from the means chosen to accomplish these alterations. Thus several conceptual factors are important. The first is a life-style change philosophy in which reasonable changes in eating and exercise are encouraged, and where the emphasis is on weaving these changes into day-to-day patterns of living. The second involves setting reasonable goals and working toward large changes by making small, incremental, and manageable changes. The third is a focus on the maintenance of behavior change. Losing weight and then regaining is far too common, but there are methods, mainly derived from theories of behavior change, that can increase a person's likelihood of success.

ACKNOWLEDGMENTS

The authors acknowledge the assistance of Susan Franks, Ph.D., Catherine R. Jones, B.A., and Karen L. Pellegrin, Ph.D., in assembling case example material.

REFERENCES

American Psychiatric Association. (1993). *DSM-IV draft criteria as of 3/1/93*. Washington, DC: Author.

Barsky, A. J. (1988). *Worried sick: Our troubled quest for wellness*. Boston: Little Brown.

Bennett, W., & Gurin, J. (1982). *The dieter's dilemma: Eating less and weighing more*. New York: Basic Books.

Bjorntorp, P., & Brodoff, B. (Eds.). (1992). *Obesity*. Philadelphia, PA: Lippincott.

Blackburn, G. L., & Kanders, B. S. (1987). Medical evaluation and treatment of the obese patient with cardiovascular disease. *American Journal of Cardiology, 60*, 55g–58g.

Blair, S. N., Shaten, J., Brownell, K. D., Collins, G., & Lissner, L. (in press). Body weight change, all-cause and cause-specific mortality in the Multiple Risk Factor Intervention Trial. *Annals of Internal Medicine*.

Brewerton, T. D., Dansky, B. S., O'Neil, P. M., & Kilpatrick, D. (1993). *The prevalence of Binge Eating Disorder in a national sample of women*. Paper presented at the meeting of the American Psychiatric Association, San Francisco, CA.

Brownell, K. D. (1980). Assessment of eating disorders. In D. H. Barlow (Ed.), *Behavioral assessment of adult disorders* (pp. 329–404). New York: Guilford Press.

Brownell, K. D. (1990). Dieting readiness. *Weight Control Digest, 1*, 1–10.

Brownell, K. D. (1991). Dieting and the search for the perfect body: Where physiology and culture collide. *Behavior Therapy, 22*, 1–12.

Brownell, K. D. (1992). *The LEARN program for weight control*. Dallas, TX: American Health Publishing.

Brownell, K. D., Greenwood, M. R. C., Stellar, E., & Shrager, E. E. (1986). The effects of repeated cycles of weight loss and regain in rats. *Physiology and Behavior, 38*, 459–464.

Brownell, K. D., & Jeffery, R. W. (1987). Improving long-term weight loss: Pushing the limits of treatment. *Behavior Therapy, 18*, 353–374.

Brownell, K. D., Marlatt, G. A., Lichtenstein, E., & Wilson, G. T. (1986). Understanding and preventing relapse. *American Psychologist, 41*, 765–782.

Brownell, K. D., & Rodin, J. (1990). *The weight maintenance survival guide*. Dallas, TX: American Health Publishing.

Brownell, K. D., & Rodin, J. (1992). *The dieting maelstrom: Is it possible and advisable to lose weight?* Manuscript submitted for publication.

Brownell, K. D., & Rodin, J. (1993). *Medical, metabolic, and psychological effects of weight cycling*. Manuscript submitted for publication.

Brownell, K. D., & Wadden, T. A. (1991). The heterogeneity of obesity: Fitting treatments to individuals. *Behavior Therapy, 22*, 153–177.

Brownell, K. D., & Wadden, T. A. (1992). Etiology and treatment of obesity: Understanding a serious, prevalent, and refractory disorder. *Journal of Consulting and Clinical Psychology, 60*, 505–517.

Bruce, B., & Agras, W. S. (1992). Binge eating in females: A population-based investigation. *International Journal of Eating Disorders, 12*, 365–374.

Cash, T. F. (1991). Binge eating and body images among the obese: A further evaluation. *Journal of Social Behavior and Personality, 6*, 367–376.

Ciliska, D. (1990). *Beyond dieting: Psychoeducational interventions for chronically obese women, a non-dieting approach*. New York: Brunner/Mazel.

Davis, C. J., Williamson, D. A., Goreczny, A. J., & Bennett, S. M. (1989). Body-image disturbances and bulimia nervosa: An empirical analysis of recent revisions of the DSM-III. *Journal of Psychopathology and Behavioral Assessment, 11*, 61-69.

Fairburn, C. G., Jones, R., Peveler, R. C., Carr, S. J., Solomon, R. A., O'Connor, M. E., Burton, J., & Hope, R. A. (1991). Three psychological treatments for bulimia nervosa. *Archives of General Psychiatry, 48*, 463-469.

Fairburn, C. G., & Wilson, G. T. (Eds.). (1993). *Binge eating: Nature, assessment, and treatment*. New York: Guilford Press.

Fallon, A., & Rozin, P. (1985). Sex differences in perception of desirable body size. *Journal of Abnormal Psychology, 94*, 102-105.

Foreyt, J. P., & Goodrick, G. K. (1992). *Living without dieting*. Houston, TX: Harrison.

Friedman, M., & Brownell, K. D. (1992). *Psychological correlates of obesity: A risk factor model to explain who will suffer*. Manuscript submitted for publication.

Garner, D. M., & Wooley, S. C. (1991). Confronting the failure of behavioral and dietary treatments for obesity. *Clinical Psychology Review, 11*, 729-780.

Glassner, B. (1988). *Bodies: Why we look the way we do and how we feel about it*. New York: Putnam.

Goldstein, D. J. (1992). Beneficial health effects of modest weight loss. *International Journal of Obesity, 6*, 397-416.

Goodrick, G. K., & Foreyt, J. P. (1991). Why treatments for obesity don't last. *Journal of the American Dietetic Association, 91*, 1243-1247.

Health Learning Systems. (1991, Fall). Weight management resources. *Contemporary Management of the Overweight Patient* (3), 2-5.

Jarrell, M. P. (1991). Obese binge eaters: Psychological characteristics and response to treatment. *International Journal of Obesity, 15*(Suppl. 3), 19 (abstract).

Jasper, J. (1992). The challenge of weight control: A personal view. In T. A. Wadden & T. B. VanItallie (Eds.), *Treatment of the seriously obese patient* (pp. 411-434). New York: Guilford Press.

Keefe, P. H., Wyshogrod, D., & Weinberger, E., & Agras, W. S. (1984). Binge eating and outcome of behavioral treatment of obesity: A preliminary report. *Behaviour Research and Therapy, 22*, 319-321.

Kumanyika, S. (1987) Obesity in black women. *Epidemiologic Reviews, 9*, 31-50.

LaPorte, D. J. (1992). Treatment response in obese binge eaters: Preliminary results using a very-low-calorie diet (VLCD) and behavior therapy. *Addictive Behaviors, 17*, 247-257.

Leon, G. R., & Roth, L. (1977). Obesity: Psychological causes, correlations, and speculations. *Psychological Bulletin, 84*, 117-139.

Lewis, V. J., Blair, A. J., & Booth, D. A. (1992). Outcome of group therapy for body-image emotionality and weight control self-efficacy. *Behavioural Psychotherapy, 20*, 155-165.

Lissner, L., Odell, P. M., D'Agostino, R. B., Stokes, J., Kreger, B. E., Belanger, A. J., & Brownell, K. D. (1991). Variability of body weight and health outcomes in the Framingham population. *New England Journal of Medicine, 324*, 1839-1844.

Marlatt, G. A., & Gordon, J. R. (Eds.). (1985). *Relapse prevention: Maintenance strategies in the treatment of addictive behaviors*. New York: Guilford Press.

Manson, J. E., Colditz, G. A., Stampfer, M. J., Willett, W. C., Rosner, B., Monson, R. R., Speizer, F. E., & Hennekens, C. H. (1990). A prospective study of obesity and risk of coronary heart disease in women. *New England Journal of Medicine, 322*, 882-889.

Marcus, M. D., Wing, R. R., & Hopkins, J. (1988). Obese binge eaters: Affect, cognitions, and response to behavioral weight control. *Journal of Consulting and Clinical Psychology, 56*, 433-439.

Marcus, M. D., Wing, R. R., & Lamparski, D. M. (1985). Binge eating and dietary restraint in obese patients. *Addictive Behaviors, 10*, 163-168.

Millman, M. (1980). *Such a pretty face: Being fat in America*. New York: Norton.

O'Neil, P. M., Dansky, B. S., Kilpatrick, D. G., & Brewerton, T. D. (1992). *Methods and results of dieting by U.S. women: Preliminary findings from the National Women's Study*. Paper presented at the meeting of the North American Association for the Study of Obesity, Atlanta, GA.

O'Neil, P. M., & Jarrell, M. P. (1992). Psychological aspects of obesity and dieting. In T. A. Wadden & T. B. VanItallie (Eds.), *Treatment of the seriously obese patient* (pp. 252-270). New York: Guilford Press.

O'Neil, P. M., Jarrell, M. P., Hedden, C. E., Cochrane, C., Sexauer, J., & Brewerton, T. D. (1992). *Metabolic correlates of binge eating in obesity*. Paper presented at the meeting of the North American Association for the Study of Obesity, Atlanta, GA.

Perri, M. G., Nezu, A. M., & Viegener, B. J. (1992). *Improving the long-term management of obesity: Theory, research, and clinical guidelines*. New York: Wiley.

Pi-Sunyer, F. X. (1991). Health implications of obesity. *American Journal of Clinical Nutrition, 53*, 1595S-1603S.

Polivy, J., & Herman, C. P. (1983). *Breaking the diet habit: The natural weight alternative*. New York: Basic Books.

Polivy, J., & Herman, C. P. (1985). Dieting and binging: a causal analysis. *American Psychologist, 40*, 193-201.

Polivy, J., & Herman, C. P. (1992). Undieting: A program to help people stop dieting. *International Journal of Eating Disorders, 11*, 261-268.

Ravussin, E., Lillioja, S., Knowler, W. C., Christin, L., Freymond, D., Abbott, W. G. H., Boyce, V., Howard, B. V., & Bogardus, C. (1988). Reduced rate of energy expenditure as a risk factor for body-weight gain. *New England Journal of Medicine, 318*, 462-472.

Rodin, J. (1992). *Body traps*. New York: Morrow.

Roughan, P., Seddon, E., & Vernon-Roberts, J. (1990). Long-term effects of a psychologically based group programme for women preoccupied with body weight and eating behavior. *International Journal of Obesity, 14*, 135-147.

Sjostrom, L. (1992). Morbidity and mortality of severely obese subjects. *American Journal of Clinical Nutrition, 55*(Suppl.), 508S-515S.

Spiegel, T. A., Wadden, T. A., & Foster, G. D. (1991). Objective measurement of eating rate during behavioral treatment of obesity. *Behavior Therapy, 22*, 61-67.

Spitzer, R. L., Devlin, M., Walsh, B. T., Hasin, D., Wing, R. R., Marcus, M., Stunkard, A., Wadden, T., Yanovski, S., Agras, S., Mitchell, J., & Nonas, C.

(1992). Binge eating disorder: A multisite field trial of the diagnostic criteria. *International Journal of Eating Disorders, 11,* 191–203.

Stotland, S., & Zuroff, D. D. (1991) Relations between multiple measures of dieting self-efficacy and weight change in a behavioral weight change program. *Behavior Therapy, 22,* 47–59.

Stuart, R. B. (1967). Behavioral control of overeating. *Behaviour Research and Therapy, 5,* 357–365.

Stuart, R., & Jacobson, B. (1987). *Weight, sex, and marriage: A delicate balance.* New York: Norton.

Stunkard, A. J., Sorenson, T. I. A., Hanis, C., Teasdale, T. W., Chakraborty, R., Schull, W. J., & Schlusinger, F. (1986). An adoption study of human obesity. *New England Journal of Medicine, 314,* 193–198.

Stunkard, A. J., & Wadden, T. A. (1992). Psychological aspects of severe obesity. *American Journal of Clinical Nutrition, 55*(Suppl.), 524S–532S.

Telch, C. F., Agras, W. S., & Rossiter, E. M. R. (1988). Binge eating increases with increasing adiposity. *International Journal of Eating Disorders, 7,* 115–119.

Wadden, T. A. (1985). Treatment of obesity in adults: A clinical perspective. In P. A. Keller & L. G. Ritt (Eds.), *Innovations in clinical practice: A source book, IV* (pp. 127–152). Sarasota, FL: Professional Resource Exchange.

Wadden, T. A., & Stunkard, A. J. (1985). Social and psychological consequences of obesity. *Annals of Internal Medicine, 103,* 1062–1067.

VanItallie, T. B. (1985). Health implications of overweight and obesity in the United States. *Annals of Internal Medicine, 103,* 983–988.

Wilfley, D. E., Agras, W. S., Telch, C. F., Rossiter, E. M., Schneider, J. A., Cole, A. G., Sifford, L., & Raeburn, S. D. (1993). Group cognitive-behavioral therapy and group interpersonal psychotherapy for the nonpurging bulimic: A controlled comparison. *Journal of Consulting and Clinical Psychology, 61,* 296–305.

Wing, R. R. (1992). Weight cycling in humans: A review of the literature. *Annals of Behavioral Medicine, 14,* 113–119.

Wooley, S. C., & Garner, D. M. (1991). Obesity treatment: The high cost of false hope. *Journal of the American Dietetic Association, 91,* 1248–1251.

Wooley, S. C., & Wooley, O. W. (1984). Should obesity be treated at all? In A. J. Stunkard & E. Stellar (Eds.), *Eating and its disorders* (pp. 185–192). New York: Raven Press.

Wooley, S. C., Wooley, O. W., & Dyrenforth, S. R. (1979). Theoretical, practical and social issues in behavioral treatment of obesity. *Journal of Applied Behavior Analysis, 12,* 3–25.

Yanovski, S. Z., Leet, M., Yanovski, J. A., Flood, M., Gold, P. W., Kissileff, H. R., & Walsh, B. T. (1992). Food selection and intake of obese women with binge eating disorder. *American Journal of Clinical Nutrition, 56,* 975–980.

Chapter 9

ALCOHOLISM

Barbara S. McCrady
Rutgers University

Clinicians working with alcoholics or other substance abusers, as well as clinicians-in-training, may find this chapter one of the more unique resources available in guiding their treatment approaches. The author begins by describing how recent societal trends and legislative initiatives have altered the nature of the clientele who come for treatment with drinking problems. After briefly reviewing the available empirical evidence on treatment approaches ranging from Alcoholics Anonymous to intensive brief inpatient treatment, the author describes the myriad factors that every clinician must consider in choosing and carrying out appropriate interventions for problem drinkers. In a manner that emphasizes the humanity of the couple and makes them come to life, the case study in this chapter illustrates the all-too-frequent tragic consequences of excessive drinking. In the context of this case description, the author describes in great detail what clinicians will not find in books that simply lay out various treatment procedures: that is, the thrusts and parries of a superb and an experienced clinician in overcoming the roadblocks that inevitably emerge during treatment.—D. H. B.

INTRODUCTION

The societal context in which clinical treatment is offered to alcoholics has changed dramatically. These changes have resulted in changes in the clinical populations presenting for treatment, and require clinicians to incorporate new concepts into their practice. The 1980s ushered in the era of the war on drugs, with its "Just say no" campaigns, police pursuit of drug users and dealers, increased prison sentences, and a shifting societal attitude toward drug use. New drugs became popular, such as "crack" cocaine, and "designer drugs." Drug use patterns have gradually shifted in American society, becoming increasingly concentrated among the economically disadvantaged.

Societal attitudes toward alcohol use have shifted as well. The legal drinking age, low-ered to 18 during the Vietnam War era, has now been returned to 21 in virtually all states, primarily in response to increased drinking/driving death rates among young people. Stricter drunk driving laws have been enacted in response to the work of advocacy groups such as Mothers Against Drunk Driving, and loss of one's driver's license for a first offense is common. Society has also become more concerned with enforcing drinking laws, and prominent figures in the field have suggested that the concept of "responsible drinking" cannot apply to any person under the age of 21 because underage drinking is illegal and therefore never responsible. Some have argued that we are witnessing a "new prohibition" in the United States.

Complementing these heavily prescriptive and punitive perspectives on drinking and drug use have been efforts to take a rehabilitative approach to psychoactive substance use. Employee assistance programs have proliferated, as have pretrial intervention programs for drug users and educational and treatment programs for drunk drivers. These programs are based on the belief that many people who are functioning poorly (on the job, in their driving, or in their adherence to the law) are doing so because of alcohol or drug use. Offering treatment rather than punishment is believed to maximize a person's chances of returning to productive functioning (on the job, behind the wheel, or as a member of society). These various programs identify persons who have problems as a result of drinking or drug use, require that they seek treatment as an alternative to punishment, and usually monitor their functioning after treatment. A substantial number of clients now enter treatment through a mandated program.

One result of these societal shifts is a changing treatment population. Although many people continue to seek treatment voluntarily, the network of societal programs for the "early" detection of alcohol and drug problems has resulted in mixed clinical populations who have problems in multiple life areas, are resentful of being in treatment, and do not recognize their drinking or drug use as problematic. Their presence in treatment programs and individual clinical practice presents special challenges to the clinician.

In contrast to these reluctant clients, a second trend in the 1980s was the burgeoning of an enormous self-help movement. Drawing originally on the popularity of Alcoholics Anonymous (AA) and its sister organization, Al-Anon, other self-help groups such as Narcotics Anonymous, Cocaine Anonymous, and Potsmokers Anonymous became popular. The 1980s also saw the popularization of concern for persons who grew up in alcoholic families, resulting in the Adult Children of Alcoholics movement. All these programs are grounded in disease models of addiction and have extended their nets in ever-widening circles. The result is a large and diverse "recovery" movement (e.g., Room, 1993), and a large population of people seeking treatment for problems that may be related to psychoactive substance use in some way.

The clinician functioning in the 1990s must provide treatment within this rather complex and contradictory network, having tools to work with involuntary and voluntary clients, those who adhere passionately to a recovery perspective, and those who are offended by it. Clinical decision making is further complicated by insurance regulations and reimbursement policies that seem to shift almost daily.

Given this complex picture, and given the alcoholic's notorious reputation for being difficult and frustrating to treat, many clinicians might ask, Why bother? The answer to this question must, on one level, be as individual as each clinician's motives for doing therapy. This chapter, however, assumes that the clinician who has a set of useful and effective tools for working with people with drinking problems, and who has had a bit of success with this population, will find positive reasons to continue. People with drinking problems *are* treatable, are challenging to treat, and are rewarding to treat, and, when someone changes successfully, the clinician has had the rare opportunity to help that person make major and satisfying changes in his/her life.

This chapter begins with a discussion of approaches to the diagnosis and definitions of alcohol problems and provides models for conceptualizing drinking problems and planning treatment. Following the theoretical presentation is an overview of the types of treatment options available to the clinician. The next section of the chapter, using the case of Carl and Maria,[1] illustrates clinical techniques.

DIAGNOSIS AND DEFINITIONS OF ALCOHOL PROBLEMS

Diagnosis

Contemporary approaches to the diagnosis of alcohol problems are based on a hypothetical construct, the alcohol dependence syndrome (ADS; Edwards & Gross, 1976). The ADS is a constellation of behavioral patterns and problems resulting from drinking that are hypothesized to constitute a syndrome. The diagnosis of alcohol problems in the revised third edition of the

Diagnostic and Statistical Manual of Mental Disorders (DSM-III-R; American Psychiatric Association [APA], 1987) is based on the ADS. Two primary alcohol diagnoses are included (separate from organically based alcohol-related problems): alcohol dependence and alcohol abuse. To be diagnosed as alcohol dependent, an individual must meet at least three of nine criteria that relate to loss of control, physical tolerance and withdrawal, interference of alcohol with functioning, and use of alcohol in dangerous or hazardous ways. Alcohol dependence is classified as mild, moderate, or severe and can be classified as in partial or full remission. Alcohol abuse is diagnosed based on problem use, including drinking repeatedly in a manner that creates the potential for harm (such as drinking and driving), or continuing to drink despite known negative consequences of drinking. Although diagnostic criteria of the fourth edition of the *Diagnostic and Statistical Manual of Mental Disorders* (DSM-IV; APA, 1993) have not been finalized, it is likely that the distinction between alcohol abuse and dependence will remain, as will severity and remission modifiers. Additional diagnostic criteria for alcohol dependence will probably focus on recurrent legal or interpersonal problems and continued use despite knowledge of problems that are caused or exacerbated by drinking. The diagnosis will also include a judgment of the presence or absence of physiological dependence. The severity modifier may be more exactly defined (specifying the number of symptoms for each level of severity), and the remission criterion may be modified to define "early" and "sustained" remission. The alcohol abuse diagnosis may be modified to emphasize symptoms that relate to inability to fulfill role obligations, experience of legal or interpersonal problems, reduction of important activities due to drinking, and recurrent use in physically hazardous situations.

Alternative Definitions

In contrast to the formal psychiatric diagnosis of alcohol abuse or dependence, behavioral researchers and clinicians have suggested that alcohol problems represent one part of a continuum of alcohol use, ranging from abstinence to nonproblem use to different types and degrees of problem use. From this perspective, problems may be exhibited in a variety of forms, some of which are consistent with a formal diagnosis, and some of which are milder or more intermittent. By using an alcohol-problems perspective, the clinician's attention is focused more clearly on the pattern of drinking, the kinds of negative consequences that the individual presenting for treatment has accumulated, the client's behavioral excesses and deficits across various areas of life functioning, and the client's particular strengths. A deemphasis on diagnosis forces the clinician to consider clients from a more individual perspective. Therefore, although formal diagnosis is useful for identifying and defining the severity of a client's problems, and is clearly necessary for formal record keeping, the approach to clinical assessment emphasized in this chapter attends less to diagnostic issues per se and more to problem identification.

This chapter views alcohol use problems as a multivariate set of problems, with alcohol consumption as a common characteristic. These problems vary in their severity, from severe alcohol dependence to mild and circumscribed problems. For some, alcohol consumption itself is a major presenting problem, while for others the consequences of alcohol use, such as disruption of a relationship, occupational problems, or health problems are the major reason for seeking treatment. In viewing alcohol problems as multivariate, we also assume multiple etiologies for these problems, with genetic, psychological, and environmental determinants contributing in differing degrees for different clients.

Complicating Problems

Drinking problems are complicated by a variety of concomitant problems. Of significance is the comorbidity of alcohol use disorders with other psychiatric diagnoses. Research has shown that a high percentage of those who can be diagnosed as alcohol abusers or alcohol dependent also experience other psychological problems, which occur concurrently with, antecedent to, or resulting from their drinking (e.g., Hasin, Grant, & Endicott, 1988; Hesselbrock, Meyer, & Keener, 1985; Ross, Glaser, & Germanson, 1988). The most common Axis I disorders are other psychoactive substance use disorders, depression, and anxiety disorders, occurring in up to 60% of males in treatment. The most common Axis II disorder comorbid with alcoholism in males is antisocial personality disorder (ASP), with ASP diagnosis rates ranging from 20% to 50% of all male alcoholics. Females more often present with depressive disorders than with Axis II disorders.

Alcohol problems are also complicated by other problems with cognition, physical health, interpersonal relationships, the criminal justice system, the employment setting, and the environment. Many alcoholics have subtle cognitive deficits, particularly in the areas of abstract reasoning, memory, and problem solving (for a review of this literature, see Parsons, Butters, & Nathan, 1987). Since verbal functioning is usually unimpaired, these cognitive problems are not immediately apparent. Heavy drinking also causes a variety of medical problems and can affect any organ system in the body. Such conditions as cardiomyopathy, liver disease, gastritis, ulcers, pancreatitis, and peripheral neuropathies may all be caused by heavy drinking. Even when obvious medical conditions are not present, the effects of heavy drinking can be insidious and debilitating. Many people eat poorly when drinking, resulting in nutritional deficits, poor energy, or vague and diffuse physical discomfort.

Interpersonal relationships may also be disrupted in the alcoholic client. The rates of separation and divorce in this population range up to seven times that of the general population (Paolino, McCrady, & Diamond, 1978), spousal violence is higher among alcoholics, and emotional and behavioral problems are more common among the spouse and children of alcoholics (Moos & Billings, 1982; Moos, Finney, & Gamble, 1982).

Persons presenting for treatment of a drinking problem may be involved with the legal system because of charges related to driving while intoxicated (DWI), other alcohol-related offenses such as assault, or involvement with the child welfare system. Drug-related charges may also bring a client to treatment.

Clients also may vary substantially in the degree to which they recognize that drinking is creating problems, and in the degree of motivation to change their drinking patterns.

In conclusion, the client presenting for treatment may be drinking in a manner that creates concern, may be formally diagnosed as alcohol dependent or an alcohol abuser, and may also meet criteria for one or more Axis I or Axis II disorders. The person may also have other major life problems in terms of cognitive impairment, physical health problems, interpersonal or occupational problems, or legal problems. Problem recognition and motivation to change may also vary substantially among clients. How does the clinician develop a rational approach to conceptualizing and treating this complicated clinical picture?

THEORETICAL MODEL

My model for treatment planning considers three major dimensions: extent and severity of problems, motivation, and an analysis of factors maintaining the current drinking pattern. Each of these dimensions must be considered in developing a rational treatment plan.

Problem Severity

The preceding section on diagnosis and definitions considered the extent and severity of problems in some detail. This dimension is relatively atheoretical and is most important in decision making about the types of treatments to be offered, the intensity of the treatment, and the initial treatment setting. Additionally, some data suggest that patients who have characteristics of antisocial personality, and those with different levels of severity of psychiatric problems, will respond differently to different types of treatment approaches (Kadden, Cooney, Getter, & Litt, 1989). These findings also should be taken into account in the selection of treatments.

Motivation

Clients vary in the degree to which they recognize their drinking as problematic and in their personal readiness to change. Prochaska and DiClemente (1982) have proposed a continuum of stages of readiness for change. The continuum ranges from the stage of precontemplation, in which a person does not recognize a behavior as problematic, to contemplation, where the person begins to consider that a behavioral pattern might be problematic, to the action stage, in which a person is ready to change his/her behavior to deal with a problem. Following action is the maintenance stage, if the behavior change is successful, or the relapse stage, if the person returns to the problem behavior. Miller (1985) has suggested that several factors influence a person's readiness to change, including awareness of problem severity, awareness of positive consequences for changing the behavior, and perception of choices in making changes. Clients' apparent stage of change and their self-perception of their problems should guide a clinician's initial approach to treatment and treatment planning. Specific treatments to enhance motivation have been developed and evaluated (for a summary of this literature, see Miller & Rollnick, 1991).

Factors Maintaining Current Drinking Pattern

A third aspect of case conceptualization focuses on factors that maintain the problematic drinking pattern. The treatment model assumes that drinking can best be treated by examining current factors that maintain drinking, rather than historical factors. Factors that maintain drinking may be individual or related to environmental circumstances or interpersonal relationships. The model assumes external antecedents to drinking that have a lawful relationship to drinking, through repeated pairings with positive or negative reinforcement or through the anticipation of reinforcement. The model assumes that cognitions and affective states mediate the relationship between external antecedents and drinking behavior, and that expectancies about the reinforcing value of alcohol play an impor-

tant role in determining subsequent drinking behavior. Finally, it is assumed that drinking is maintained by its consequences, and that these consequences may be physiological, psychological, or interpersonal in their origins.

The SORC model is used to integrate these assumptions into a model that conceptualizes drinking. Environmental *stimuli* (S), which occur antecedent to drinking, elicit cognitive, affective, and physiological *organismic* (O) reactions. The drinking *response* (R) follows, and is believed to be maintained by the positive *consequences* (C) of drinking.

A variety of individual, familial, and other interpersonal factors may be associated with drinking. At the individual level, environmental antecedents may be associated with specific drinking situations, times of the day, or the mere sight or smell of alcohol. Organismic variables may include craving for alcohol; withdrawal symptoms; negative affects such as anger, anxiety, or depression; negative self-evaluations or irrational beliefs; or positive expectancies about the effects of alcohol in particular situations. Individual reinforcers may include decreased craving or withdrawal symptoms, decreases in negative affect or increases in positive affect, decreased negative self-evaluations, or being able to forget problems.

At the familial level, a variety of antecedents to drinking occur. Alcohol may be a usual part of family celebrations or daily rituals. Family members may attempt to influence the drinker's behavior, by nagging him/her to stop, or attempting to control the drinking through control of finances or liquor supply. These actions may become antecedents to further drinking. Families in which a member is drinking heavily may also develop poor communication and problem-solving skills and/or marital, sexual, financial, and child-rearing problems which then cue further drinking. The drinker may have a variety of reactions to these familial antecedents, experiencing negative affect, low self-efficacy for coping with problems, or retaliatory thoughts.

Positive consequences of drinking may also come from the family. The family may shield the drinker from the negative consequences of drinking by caretaking the person when intoxicated or assuming his/her responsibilities. A number of investigators have observed positive changes in marital interactions associated with drinking, suggesting that drinking may be reinforced by its positive marital consequences (e.g., Frankenstein, Hay, & Nathan, 1985).

Other interpersonal antecedents to drinking also occur. These may revolve around social pressures to drink, work-related drinking situations, friendships in which alcohol consumption plays a major role, or interpersonal conflicts with work associates, friends, or acquaintances. The drinker may react to interpersonal antecedents to drinking with craving, positive expectancies for alcohol use, social discomfort, or negative self-evaluations for not drinking. Positive interpersonal consequences of drinking may include decreased craving or social anxiety or increased social comfort or assertiveness. Marlatt (in Marlatt & Gordon, 1985) has classified antecedents to drinking as intrapersonal or interpersonal. Intrapersonal antecedents include negative and positive emotional states, negative physical states, testing personal control, and urges and temptations. Interpersonal antecedents include social conflict, social pressure to drink, and positive emotional states.

CLINICAL APPLICATION OF THEORETICAL MODEL

The three-dimensional model for conceptualizing drinking problems, described above, has direct implications for the planning and delivery of treatment. Initially, the clinician must make decisions about the most appropriate setting in which to provide treatment and then select the therapeutic modalities most appropriate to the client. Then, therapeutic techniques for use within the treatment modalities must be tailored to the client's needs. The therapist must also consider the social context in which drinking occurs, as well as the social context in which change occurs. The therapist must be cognizant of the subtle and nonspecific aspects of providing treatment to this population, both from the client's perspective and the therapist's point of view. Finally, the therapist must be knowledgeable about issues related to therapeutic goals, particularly around the selection of drinking goals.

Treatment Settings

There are a number of settings available for the treatment of alcoholism. These include inpatient or residential settings, partial hospitals, outpatient clinics, and halfway houses. Self-help groups are also widely available. The research literature provides little information to guide clinical decision making about the level of care appropriate for an individual client. A number of studies have reported no difference in outcome among inpatient treatments of differing lengths, and no differences when inpatient and partial hospital treatment have been compared (reviewed in Miller & Hester, 1986). Less intensive treatments result in substantial cost savings (McCrady et al., 1986), but there is some concern that attrition may be higher in less intensive settings (Hayashida et al., 1989).

The American Society of Addictive Medicine (ASAM) has suggested criteria for the selection of level of care (ASAM, 1991). Although the ASAM criteria have some logical appeal, they are as yet untested. The clinician must make a decision with each individual client about what setting is most appropriate for the initiation of treatment. This decision should be based partially on medically oriented criteria such as need for detoxification and medical status, but should also consider psychosocial variables such as past treatment history, results of previous attempts to stop drinking, social supports and personal resources, the seriousness of other psychological problems, the client's initial attitudes about treatment, practical concerns, and the client's personal preference for the initial treatment setting.

Detoxification

If a client is physically dependent on alcohol, he/she will experience alcohol withdrawal symptoms when decreasing or stopping drinking. There are a number of signs that a client may be physically dependent on alcohol (Femino & Lewis, 1980). Daily drinking, drinking regularly or intermittently throughout the day, and morning drinking all suggest physical dependence. Awaking during the night with fears, trembling, or nausea, or experiencing such symptoms on first awakening, is also suggestive of dependence. Further, in a physically dependent client, cessation of or a substantial decrease in drinking will result in the appearance of minor withdrawal symptoms, such as tremulousness, nausea, vomiting, difficulty sleeping, irritability, anxiety, and elevations in pulse, blood pressure, and temperature. Such symptoms usually begin within 5–12 hr of the cessation of drinking. More severe withdrawal symptoms, such as seizures, delirium, or hallucinations, may also occur, usually within 24–72 hr of the cessation of drinking.

If the client has not consumed alcohol for several days prior to initial clinical contact, concerns about alcohol withdrawal are not relevant. If the client has stopped drinking within the last 3 days, the clinician needs to inquire about and observe for signs of withdrawal. If the client is currently drinking, the clinician must rely on drinking history, pattern, and the results of previous attempts to stop drinking to determine whether detoxification will be necessary.

If the client needs detoxification, four alternatives are available: inpatient medical detoxification, partial hospital medical detoxification, inpatient nonmedical detoxification, or outpatient medical detoxification. Inpatient medically assisted detoxification is essential if the client has a history of disorientation, delirium, hallucinations, or seizures during alcohol withdrawal or is showing current signs of disorientation, delirium, or hallucinations. If the client does not believe that he/she can stop drinking without being physically removed from alcohol but does not show any major withdrawal signs, is in good health, and does not abuse other drugs, a social setting detoxification might be appropriate. If the client has some social supports, detoxification could be initiated on a partial hospital or outpatient basis. The choice between the latter two settings is determined by how much support the individual will need during withdrawal and whether a structured program will be needed after detoxification. If the client needs a fairly structured program, the partial hospital is the preferred setting for detoxification.

Medical Problems

As noted, when considering the best setting for detoxification, the presence of other medical problems should be considered. A cautious approach dictates that every client should have a thorough physical examination and blood and urine studies at the beginning of treatment. The clinician should *routinely* include questions about physical health in the first contact with an alcoholic client, and if significant physical complaints are noted, the client should receive quick medical attention. Some clients have medical problems that require hospitalization, and, if so, the hospital should initiate the treatment.

Treatment History

After physical health issues have been considered, the clinician should look at the client's previous treatment history. Questions to consider are:

1. Has the client attempted outpatient treatment in the past and been able to stop or decrease drinking successfully? If so, another attempt at outpatient treatment might be indicated.
2. Has the client dropped out of outpatient treatment in the past? If so, and there is no indication that any variables have changed in the interim, a more intensive partial hospital or inpatient program should be considered.
3. Has the client dropped out of or drunk repeatedly while in a partial hospital program? If so, inpatient treatment might be indicated.
4. Did the client relapse immediately after discharge from an inpatient program? If so, a partial hospital or outpatient setting might be appropriate, as the relapse may have been associated with problems in generalization from the inpatient to the natural environment. Alternatively, a halfway house might be considered to provide longer-term, structured treatment.

Previous Quit Attempts

Many clients have successfully decreased or stopped drinking on their own at some time. It is important to determine whether a client has engaged in such attempts in the past, and the results. Outpatient treatment is more likely to be successful for the client who has a history of stopping successfully on his/her own than for a client without any history of successful change.

Social Support Systems

Social support systems are a critical variable to consider in determining the appropriate setting for initial treatment. If a client has supports, such as a spouse, an older child, a parent, close friends, a concerned employer, an AA sponsor, or some other person who is readily available, *and* that person is perceived as an important source of support and reinforcement, *and* the person is willing to provide support and reinforcement, the client is a good candidate for some form of ambulatory treatment. If the client is lacking in social supports, or is in an environment that supports heavy drinking, inpatient or partial hospital treatment might be advisable. Alternatively, a half-way house might provide a good setting for treatment for persons who do not have current social supports, and have not been successful at developing them in the past, even during periods of abstinence.

Personal Resources

The next area to consider encompasses the client's personal psychological resources. Has the client been successful in other areas of life in setting goals, changing behavior, and completing tasks? If so, outpatient treatment is more feasible. Another aspect of personal resources is cognitive functioning. If the client shows significant cognitive deficits in memory, attention, abstraction or problem solving, a higher level of care might be considered. Otherwise, the client may have difficulty with retaining information presented in treatment, and may have difficulty in generating successful ways to avoid drinking.

Other Psychological Problems

As noted earlier in the chapter, persons with drinking problems often have other significant psychological problems. The clinician must assess these problems, and also determine level of care based on the appropriate setting for treatment of these other problems. If a client presents with serious depression, suicidality must be assessed and appropriate precautions taken.

Attitudes About Treatment

Although attitudes are a difficult area to assess, the client's commitment to treatment and desire to change are important factors in selecting level of care (as well as selecting initial treatment approach). The client who is ambivalent but willing to come to treatment might respond better to a more intensive program that can provide a higher density of reinforcement for attending treatment and making changes. However, sometimes the client's ambivalence makes it impossible to provide treatment in a more intensive setting because the client is unwilling to disrupt his/her life to the extent required for such a program.

Practical Concerns

There are a number of practical concerns that the clinician must consider. Although certain therapeutic approaches might consider these issues evidence of client "denial," we prefer to view them as real barriers to treatment and to work with the client to overcome these barriers. Some practical barriers revolve around employment: whether the client can get time off from work, if the job is in jeopardy, if the employer is willing to support treatment, or whether missing any more work would result in termination of employment. If the client's job is in jeopardy, pushing for inpatient treatment is likely to result in the loss of the client.

A second concern is the client's financial condition. Can the client afford to take time off from work and experience a reduction in income while he/she collects temporary disability (if sick time is not available)? If not, outpatient treatment or a partial hospital program that allows the person to work would be appropriate. Another financial concern is the client's ability to pay for treatment. If health insurance covers inpatient treatment but not partial hospitalization, the former setting might be necessary.

Other practical concerns revolve around transportation and child care. Can the client get to outpatient appointments? Does the client have a driver's license, and if not, is other transportation available? Is child care available if the person has to be hospitalized? If not, a day treatment setting might be preferred.

There are a whole host of other, idiosyncratic practical concerns to which the clinician must be sensitive. Research has long shown that alcoholics are more likely to become involved with and remain in treatment if their immediate needs are recognized (e.g., Chafetz et al., 1962), so this becomes an important concern when initiating treatment.

Personal Preference

Finally, the client's own preferences for treatment must be carefully considered. If the client feels strongly about wanting to be in a hospital or residential treatment program, the clinician should listen carefully to this request even if the initial assessment suggests that outpatient treatment is feasible. Similarly, if the client wants outpatient treatment, it should be attempted even if the clinician believes that a more intensive treatment is preferable.

General Considerations

In general, the selection of the initial treatment setting must be seen as a tentative decision. Often, an initial contract must be established that includes the client's preferred setting, but with specification of the circumstances that would dictate a different level of care. For example, if the clinician believes that the client will find it extremely difficult to discontinue drinking on an outpatient basis, but this is the client's desire, the initial contract should involve a plan for reducing and stopping drinking, teaching skills to support that plan, and a time limit. If the person were unsuccessful within the specified time frame, the contract would be reviewed and alternative settings considered. Thus, while the initial setting decision is important, continuing to consider and discuss other treatment settings is an important early step in the treatment process. Table 9.1 summarizes some of the indicators for treatment settings.

Treatment Modalities

Six major treatment modalities are available for the treatment of alcoholism. These include self-help groups, individual therapy, group therapy, couple therapy, family therapy, and intensive treatment programs.

Self-Help Groups

AA is the most commonly utilized self-help group. With groups in all 50 states, as well as more than 100 countries throughout the world, AA is widely available. AA offers a specific approach to recovery, rooted in the view that alcoholism is a physical, emotional, and spiritual disease and that there is no cure for alcoholism but the disease can be arrested. Recovery is viewed as a lifelong process that involves working the 12 steps of AA and abstaining from the use of alcohol (for a detailed description of AA, see McCrady & Irvine, 1989). The only requirement for membership in AA is a desire to stop drinking; members do not have to pay dues or formally join the organization. Persons who become involved with AA usually attend different meetings, have a relationship with an AA sponsor who helps them with their recovery, and become involved with other AA-related activities ranging from making the coffee before meetings to going on "commitments," where members of one AA group speak to another group. More active involvement is correlated with more successful change (Emrick, Tonigan, Montgomery, & Little, 1993).

Research suggests that the people most likely to affiliate with AA have a history of using social supports as a way to cope with problems, describe loss of control over their drinking, drink more per occasion than people who do not affiliate, experience more anxiety about their drinking, believe that alcohol enhances their mental functioning, and are more religious or spiritual (Emrick et al., 1993).

Alternative self-help groups have developed in recent years. Rational recovery (RR; Trimpey, 1989) is a self-help approach based largely on the precepts of rational–emotive therapy. RR offers several steps to recovery, emphasizing awareness of irrational beliefs, self-perceptions, and expectancies as core to successful change. RR suggests abstinence as a preferred drinking goal but emphasizes personal choice. The Secular Organization for Sobriety (SOS) was developed largely in response to the spiritual aspects of AA and does not invoke a higher power as a part

TABLE 9.1. Guidelines for Selection of Treatment Setting

Level of care	Indicators
Medical hospitalization	Acute medical problems Seizures Delirium
Inpatient, medical detoxification	Physical dependence History of/current major withdrawal History of seizures Serious medical problems Serious psychiatric problems Patient does not think can stop drinking without supervision
Social setting detoxification	Physical dependence No acute health problems No history of seizures, major withdrawal Patient does not think can stop drinking without supervision
Outpatient detoxification	Physical dependence No complicating conditions Patient does not want to be hospitalized Social supports for stopping
Inpatient treatment	History of dropping out of outpatient treatment History of dropping out of or drinking during partial hospital treatment Poor social supports Social support for drinking, not change Cognitive deficits Other acute psychiatric problems Suicidal Lack of insurance or resources for ambulatory treatment Lack of transportation Strong personal preference
Partial hospital/day treatment	History of dropping out of outpatient treatment History of immediate relapse after inpatient treatment Fair to good social supports Ambivalence about treatment or change Lack of child care Unable to get time off of work Strong personal preference
Outpatient treatment	History of successful use of outpatient treatment Successful previous quit attempts on own Good social supports History of successful change Lack of resources for more intensive treatment Lack of child care Unable to get time off of work Strong personal preference
Halfway house	History of relapse after inpatient treatment Lack of social supports

of the change process. Women for Sobriety is a self-help approach for women that emphasizes women's issues such as assertiveness, self-confidence, and autonomy as a part of the change process. All three of these alternative approaches are more compatible with behavioral approaches than is AA, but none is as widely available to clients.

Individual Treatment

Individual therapy is widely offered on an outpatient basis. Few data are available to guide the choice of individual versus group therapy. The literature on women alcoholics is replete with suggestions that women respond better to individual than to group therapy, although empirical support for that assertion is lacking (e.g., McCrady & Raytek, in press). Similar assertions apply to the treatment of elderly alcoholics, although data are lacking about this population as well (e.g., Gomberg, 1980).

Group Therapy

There is a strong belief in the alcohol field that group therapy is preferable to individual therapy (however, see above in regard to women and the elderly). Group therapy is clearly more economical to provide, and the interaction among group members provides opportunities for modeling, feedback, and behavioral rehearsal that are less available in the individual setting. Behavioral models for providing group therapy to individuals (Monti, Abrams, Kadden, & Cooney, 1989) and to alcoholics and their spouses (O'Farrell & Cutter, 1984) are well documented. Clients who are able to function in a group setting and who do not require intensive individual attention because of other psychological problems can be assigned to group therapy.

Couple Therapy

A number of studies have suggested that involving the spouse in alcoholism treatment will increase the probability of a positive treatment outcome (reviewed in McCrady, 1990). Despite the empirical evidence, traditional alcoholism counselors prefer individual or group therapy over couple therapy, emphasizing the importance of a focus on personal change before relationship change. Models for treatments that integrate individual and relationship treatment are available (McCrady & Epstein, in press), and a couple therapy case is the focus of the second half of the chapter. Couple therapy is most appropriate for clients who have a stable relationship in which the partner is willing to be involved in treatment and can function in a supportive manner in the early phases of treatment. Couples who have a history of domestic violence, or in which one partner's commitment to the relationship is highly ambivalent, are less appropriate for couple therapy.

Techniques have also been developed to provide treatment to partners of alcoholics separate from treatment for the drinker. Behavioral groups that emphasize personal decision making, communication, and limit setting around drinking are effective in motivating the drinker to seek treatment or decrease drinking (Sisson & Azrin, 1986; Thomas, Santa, Bronson, & Oyserman, 1987). Alanon offers a self-help approach to partners and other family members of alcoholics.

Family Therapy

Despite a strong interest in alcoholism in the family therapy field, models for working with whole families in which alcoholism is present are scarce. The models that are available draw from family systems therapy (e.g., Kaufman, 1984) and are completely untested. Within the self-help area, Alateen is available for teens affected by a family member's alcoholism and Alatot is available for younger family members.

Intensive Treatment Programs

Although technically a treatment setting rather than a modality, intensive treatment programs have such a specific and defined role in alcoholism treatment that they should be considered. The "Minnesota model of treatment" (Cook, 1988a, 1988b) is an intensive treatment approach that includes group therapy, education, self-help group involvement, and some individual counseling. Programs based on the Minnesota model emphasize confrontation of denial, acceptance that one is an alcoholic who is powerless over alcohol, and commitment to AA involvement. Over time, Minnesota model programs have incorporated many behavioral strategies and techniques, including social skills and relaxation training and relapse-prevention techniques (although these draw more from the popular work of Gorski & Miller, 1986, than from the original scientific and theoretical work of Marlatt & Gordon, 1985).

Minnesota model programs have been marketed as the most appropriate approach to alcoholism treatment, but data are lacking to support these claims. Most research on these programs has involved the evaluation of a single treatment program, and all the evaluations have been of private treatment centers. The evaluations suggest substantial levels of abstinence among persons receiving treatment (e.g., Alford, 1980; Filstead, 1991; Wallace, McNeill, Gilfallan, MacLean, & Fanella, 1988), but the subjects in these studies tend to be patients with a good prognosis, and without appropriate controls no inferences can be drawn about the relative efficacy of these treatments compared to other approaches. However, the wide visibility of the Minnesota model programs has made them the apparent choice of many alcoholics and their families.

Treatment Techniques

A wide range of treatment techniques are available to the clinician. A complete description of techniques is beyond the scope of this chapter, and the reader is referred to Hester and Miller (1989) for a practitioner-oriented description of techniques with the best empirical support for their effectiveness.

Broadly speaking, behavioral treatment techniques include stimulus-control procedures, consequence-control procedures, cognitive restructuring techniques, behavioral skills training, and behavioral marital therapy techniques. Additionally, behavioral therapists have integrated antidipsotropic medications with behavioral contracting procedures (Antabuse [disulfiram] in the United States, as well as calcium carbamide in Canada). Techniques have been integrated into comprehensive treatment approaches through relapse-prevention training (Marlatt & Gordon, 1985) and broad-spectrum behavioral therapy.

Social Context of Treatment

As noted above, the literature on the treatment of alcoholism suggests that involvement of some significant social system is associated with positive treatment results. Because of these findings, the clinician should first try to involve the spouse or some significant other in the treatment. There are a number of types of involvement of significant others, including information, differential reinforcement for abstinence, emotional or practical support, relationship-focused treatment, treatment of significant others, and/or helping the client access new social systems.

Information

Folklore in the alcohol field suggests that alcoholics minimize or lie about their drinking and its consequences. The empirical literature suggests that alcoholics provide relatively accurate data when sober and when there are no strong negative consequences for telling the truth (reviewed in Babor, Stephens, & Marlatt, 1987). Despite these results, there are a number of clinical considerations that suggest that obtaining information from a family member may be useful in the assessment phase of treatment. First, clients who are referred to or coerced into treatment are often reluctant to provide full information about their drinking. Collecting data from the referring agent, with the client present and involved, helps both the client and the clinician understand the reasons for the referral.

Even with more motivated clients, a significant other can provide information that may be unavailable to the drinker because of problems with memory or recall. Finally, an intimate significant other has usually observed the drinker over a long period, in multiple environments, and may have valuable observations to contribute to the conceptualization of antecedents to drinking.

Responses to Drinking and Abstinence

A different type of social system involvement is the establishment of a network that will provide differential reinforcement contingent upon abstinence, and that will facilitate the immediate application of negative consequences contingent upon drinking. Such reinforcement can be relatively simple, such as positive comments and encouragement from friends and family, or can involve the negotiation of detailed contracts that specify the consequences of drinking and abstinence. The community-reinforcement approach (CRA) (Azrin, 1976; Azrin, Sisson, Meyers, & Godley, 1982; Hunt & Azrin, 1973) helps clients access potential reinforcers (jobs, families, social clubs), teaches clients and partners behavioral coping skills, and develops contingency contracts to make access to reinforcers contingent upon sobriety. Additionally, clients take Antabuse, and compliance is monitored by a significant other. Results of the CRA suggest that clients are significantly more successful than controls in not drinking, maintaining employment, avoiding hospitalizations or jail, and maintaining a stable residence.

In addition to formal treatments that focus on manipulation of environmental contingencies, treatments may also focus on teaching spouses and other family members how to allow the drinker to experience the naturally occurring negative consequences of drinking. Many spouses protect their partner from these consequences by covering for the person at work, doing his/her chores, lying to friends and family about the drinking, and so on (Orford et al., 1975). Treatment interventions can teach the family member to allow naturally occurring consequences to be experienced by the drinker. Experience of these negative consequences can increase the drinker's awareness of the extent and severity of his/her drinking problem and provide further motivation for change.

Decreasing Cues for Drinking

Significant others can also engage in a number of behaviors that actually cue drinking. For example, a wife may want her husband to stop drinking and may nag him repeatedly about the problems his drinking is causing, hoping that her concerns will motivate him to change. Or, a husband may try to get his wife to stop drinking by trying to control her behavior through limiting her access to alcohol or tightly controlling their money. Such behaviors often have a contrary effect, however, eliciting anger or defensiveness from the drinker and resulting in further drinking. Helping spouses to identify such behaviors, recognize the results of these actions, and learn alternatives to discussing concerns about drinking can be helpful in decreasing drinking.

Support for Not Drinking

Significant others can provide a variety of supports to a drinker. Support may involve helping the client to implement behavioral change, discussing urges to drink, supporting a client's plan to avoid high-risk situations for drinking, or, on the request of the client, assisting in the implementation of other cognitive or behavioral skills that support sobriety.

Relationship Change

For many clients, interactions with their spouse, children, parents or close friends cue drinking. Thus, treatment that focuses on changing those interpersonal relationships is another way that significant others can become involved in treatment. The interventions can be marital or family therapy or parent skills training. Some data (McCrady, Stout, Noel, Abrams, & Nelson, 1991) suggest that a focus on changing the marital relationship during conjoint alcoholism treatment results in more stability of drinking outcomes, less marital separations, and more marital satisfaction.

Accessing New Social Systems

For some clients, there are no social systems available to modify. For such clients, it is important to develop ways to access new systems that can provide differential reinforcement for drinking or abstinence, or that will be incompatible with drinking. The self-help groups described above are one potential source of such support. Many religious groups are against the use of alcohol, and serious involvement in such a group can also support abstinence.

Many group activities are also incompatible with drinking. Running, hiking, or bicycling groups are examples. Unfortunately, alcohol can be involved in almost any activity, and the therapist and client need to look carefully at activity groups to determine whether the group norm includes drinking.

In summary, decisions about the social context of alcoholism treatment are complicated. The initial assessment should involve at least one significant other. The results of the assessment should reveal who is most available for treatment and who are potential sources of support and reinforcement. Some clients have no readily accessible supports, and thus need to develop new support systems.

Therapist Variables

As with any form of therapy, the therapist's relationship with the client and the therapeutic stance assumed by the therapist are important. Empathy, active listening, instillation of hope, and establishing a sense that the therapist and client are working toward mutually agreed-on goals are essential (Miller, 1985). Miller and Rollnick (1991) have described a complete approach to treatment, "motivational interviewing," which defines a therapeutic relationship built on empathy and positive regard at the same time that the clinician helps create a sense of dissonance between the client's current situation and personal goals to enhance motivation to change.

Working with an alcoholic client is often difficult, both because of the drinker's behavior during treatment and because of the history of drinking-related behaviors that the therapist may find repugnant or upsetting. The client also may lie or minimize drinking during treatment. If the spouse is also involved in the treatment, the therapeutic relationship becomes even more complicated. By treating a client with a drinking problem, along with a spouse who wants that client to stop or decrease drinking, the therapist is allied de facto with the nonalcoholic partner. That partner may attempt to enhance his/her alliance with the therapist by echoing the therapist's comments, expressing anger at the client's behavior, being confrontational, or, alternatively, being submissive and allowing the alcoholic partner to be verbally aggressive or dominant.

Certain therapist attitudes and behaviors appear to be conducive to successful treatment. First is a sense of empathy with the client. The therapist must develop some understanding of the client's subjective experience of entering therapy and admitting to behaviors that are personally embarrassing and often not socially sanctioned. Additionally, the therapist needs to have some appreciation of the incredible difficulties involved with long-term change in drinking behavior. The therapist may develop this appreciation by attempting to change an addictive behavior of his/her own, by attending meetings of some self-help group (AA, RR, SOS), and by listening carefully to the client.

A second important therapist skill is the ability to discriminate between the individual and the drinking-related behavior. The therapist needs to be able to allow the client to describe drinking-related actions without feeling that the therapist is repulsed, but also without feeling that the therapist condones or accepts such behaviors. This is a delicate balance to achieve, especially when a client describes drinking episodes in a joking manner that may hide embarrassment or disgust with the drinking. The therapist needs to encourage the client to discuss the actions, and experience the negative feelings associated with the actions, as a part of enhancing the client's motivation to change. At the same time, the therapist needs to communicate to the client a sense of hope, by anticipating positive changes associated with changes in drinking, and emphasizing that it is possible for the client to develop skills to change his/her drinking and eliminate the most unacceptable behaviors. Thus, the implied message to the client is, "You have done many things when drinking that are distressing to you and to the people around you. The fact that you are in treatment is a statement that you want to change some of these. It is important to talk about things you have done when drinking, because by being aware of them, you will have a strong incentive to stop drinking and stop doing these things. Making changes will take time and a lot of work on your part, but I believe that you will be successful if you stick with treatment." Such a message is positive about change but negative about drinking-related behavior.

A third important therapist quality is honesty. Because of their discomfort and their reinforcement history, it is difficult for some clients to be honest, especially about reporting drinking episodes, failed homework assignments, or their feelings and attitudes about being in treatment. The therapist can acknowledge how difficult it is for the client to be honest, as lying was probably adaptive in the past, but that part of therapy involves learning how to be honest. The therapist also must provide a positive model of honesty. The therapist should not ignore the smell of alcohol on a client's breath and should review homework assigned each week. Attending to the client's behavior teaches the client the importance of following through on commitments and increases the chances that the therapist and client will be able to identify problems and blocks to progress in treatment.

The therapist also must be able to set clear expectations about the client's responsibilities to the therapy, as well as set appropriate limits: The client is expected to come to scheduled sessions on time, call if unable to attend, pay the bill for therapy, come in sober, and complete assigned homework. The therapist should also establish his/her own commitment to therapy by being at sessions on time, being reasonably available by telephone, providing coverage when away, and providing treatments with the best empirical support for their effectiveness. Being clear about expectations for the client's behavior during therapy emphasizes the therapist's commitment to therapy as a serious process.

Client Variables

The clinician must be aware of and sensitive to a number of issues that people with drinking problems bring to treatment. While some of the comments in this section are based on empirical research, many are derived from clinical observation and require further research to validate or disconfirm. The client's emotional experience, beliefs and attitudes, and physical state, and the social context of drinking (described in preceding sections) are all important aspects of the therapeutic plan.

An individual has a variety of reactions to the initial realization that his/her drinking is causing problems. Most commonly, as negative consequences accumulate, the individual begins to feel out of control and ashamed of the behavior. The individual's actions may be unacceptable to his/her self-definition. Thus, financial or work irresponsibility, neglecting family, engaging in physical violence, and verbal abuse may all be actions about which the individual feels intense guilt and self-blame. The prospect of admitting these actions to a stranger is frightening and embarrassing, making it

difficult for clients to discuss drinking-associated problems. Because many clients ascribe their problems to weakness or lack of will power, and believe that if they were only "stronger" these events would not occur, they blame themselves. Thus, clients are reluctant to be honest and are unusually sensitive to implied criticisms from the therapist. The therapist can attenuate this difficulty by making empathic comments while asking questions, by letting clients know that many of their actions are common among heavy drinkers, and by listening to clients' descriptions of drinking-related actions in an accepting manner.

Clients also hold a number of beliefs and attitudes about alcohol and their ability to change that make change difficult. Alcoholics have positive expectancies about the effects of alcohol on feelings and behavior, and they hold these more strongly than do nonalcoholics. They also may attribute their drinking to reasons external to themselves and do not believe that they are personally responsible for drinking or not drinking. They may have low self-efficacy about their ability to change their drinking or to handle alcohol-related situations without drinking, or may have unrealistically high self-efficacy that is not grounded in actuality. Finally, if alcoholics stop drinking and then consume alcohol again, cognitive dissonance may occur, and they may experience an "abstinence violation effect" (Marlatt & Gordon, 1985), characterized by an excessively negative reaction to initial alcohol consumption and a self-perception that they have "blown" their abstinence and will inevitably relapse to their previous drinking pattern.

Drinking Goals

The final major area to consider in treatment planning is the selection of drinking goals. Traditional approaches to alcoholism treatment view abstinence as the only appropriate drinking goal, because traditional treatments view alcoholism as a progressive disease that can only be arrested with abstinence. Behavioral clinicians have examined alternatives to abstinence and have developed a number of strategies to teach clients how to drink moderately. Moderation training continues to be a controversial treatment approach, and the clinician who elects to provide such treatment may be vulnerable to severe criticism from the mainstream alcoholism treatment community.

A number of studies suggest that the long-term outcomes of alcoholism include reduced drinking as one outcome (e.g., Helzer et al., 1985; Peele, 1992; Vaillant, 1983), but data about the success of moderation training are mixed. Two European studies, however, have found that giving clients the opportunity to *select* treatment goals increases compliance with treatment and may improve treatment outcome (Orford & Keddie, 1986; Ojehegan & Berglund, 1989).

I have argued strongly for abstinence as a preferred treatment goal (e.g., McCrady, 1992; Nathan & McCrady, 1987), and I continue to view it as the preferred treatment goal. Abstinence is clearly defined and is in accord with usual clinical practice and societal norms for the goals of alcoholism treatment in the United States. Agreeing to a controlled drinking goal may reinforce a client's distorted view of alcohol as an overvalued substance, a view that I believe is irrational. However, under certain circumstances, the use of a reduced drinking goal may be appropriate.

Moderation may be used as a provisional goal to engage a client in treatment; may be used when the client will not agree to abstinence but does want assistance to change; or may be used when the client shows few signs of alcohol dependence, does not have medical problems that would be exacerbated by continued drinking, is younger, and does not have a family history of alcoholism. If the clinician and client do select a moderation goal, a period of initial abstinence usually makes it easier for the client to drink moderately. In selecting a moderation goal, the clinician should help the client to recognize the current and potential negative consequences of excessive drinking and to make an informed, thoughtful choice of a treatment goal. The clinician should also view any initial drinking goal as tentative, to be reevaluated as therapy progresses.

CASE STUDY

The couple in the case presented here was seen as part of a research project evaluating different approaches to the maintenance of change following conjoint behavioral alcoholism treatment. Couples in the study had to be married or cohabitating for at least 6 months, neither could be a primary drug abuser or show evidence of gross organic brain syndrome or psychosis, and the spouse could not show evidence of alcohol abuse or dependence. All couples were seen by a therapist for 15 to 17 sessions of weekly outpatient treatment and agreed to a baseline assessment and 18 months of post-treatment follow-up.

"Carl" and "Maria" are a married couple, both 32 years of age, who came to treatment because of Carl's drinking. Maria was of average height, had long, black, wavy hair, and was quite heavy. Carl was also of average height, had blond hair, and was slim but showed the beginnings of a "beer belly." They were both neat and attractive.

The couple had been married for 5 years and had known each other for 12 years. Their two children were boys, ages 2 and 3. Both came from intact families, although Carl's father had died a number of years previously. Carl's family was primarily Polish; Maria's was Italian.

At the time of treatment, Carl and Maria had been separated from each other for 5 months. He was living with his mother in her home while Maria was renting a one-bedroom apartment in a poor community, where she lived with the two boys. Maria was a trained hairdresser; Carl was a carpenter who worked out of the union hall. Carl was not working because he did not want to establish a pattern of support for Maria or the children in case she filed for divorce. Additionally, if he did not work for a certain period of time he would be able to withdraw his money from the union's pension plan, and he thought that that would be an easy way to obtain money. Maria was not working because she had decided that Carl would have to babysit while she worked, and she did not feel that he would be reliable about coming to her apartment to care for the children. She was supported by welfare; he worked odd jobs "under the table." Both were high school graduates.

The couple came to treatment at Maria's urging. She had seen a notice in a local newspaper advertising our research couples treatment clinic and convinced Carl to come. She was very concerned about Carl's drinking and cited it as the primary reason for their marital separation.

Behavioral Assessment and Case Conceptualization

Carl and Maria were assessed using a variety of approaches. Their assessment was somewhat more extensive than is usual in clinical practice because of their involvement with the treatment research project. However, the main elements of the assessment are applicable to clinical practice as well.

Drinking Assessment

To assess Carl's drinking, a clinical interview was used to ask him about his drinking history and perceptions of his current drinking. A hand-held breathalyzer was used at the beginning of each session to assess his current blood alcohol level (BAL). In addition, two structured interviews, the Timeline Followback Interview (TLFB; Sobell, Maisto, Sobell, Cooper, & Saunders, 1980) and the alcohol section of the Composite International Diagnostic Interview–Substance Abuse Module (CIDI–SAM; Robins et al., 1988), and two self-report measures, the Michigan Alcoholism Screening Test (Selzer, 1971) and the Alcohol Dependence Scale (ADS; Skinner & Allen, 1982) were used to obtain a more complete picture of his drinking. Maria was present for all interviews and contributed additional information.

The TLFB inquires about drinking behavior on each day in a set window of time before treatment. For this study, we asked about drinking in the prior 6 months, cuing clients' recall of drinking by noting other salient events in their life such as social events, medical appointments, holidays, and other celebrations. The TLFB revealed that Carl had drunk alcohol virtually every day of the previous 6 months. His only abstinent day came when he and some friends were arrested for breaking and entering (they were intoxicated, decided they needed better carpentry tools, and thought that breaking into a store would be a good way to obtain them). His preferred beverages were

beer and vodka, and he reported that the most he drank on any one day was about 32 drinks. His usual consumption was in the range of 10–12 drinks daily.

The alcohol section of the CIDI–SAM asks about a variety of behaviors associated with the criteria necessary to establish a DSM-III-R diagnosis of alcohol abuse or dependence. Carl clearly met criteria for a DSM-III-R diagnosis of alcohol dependence and would meet proposed DSM-IV criteria as well. Carl had been drinking since high school, and he reported his first problems as a result of alcohol at the age of 25. He reported a variety of problem consequences of his use: three arrests for DWI, with two of these arrests in the same month of the year he sought treatment, one arrest for breaking and entering, warnings from job supervisors for intoxication on the job, problems in his relationship with his wife, and feeling that he had neglected his responsibilities to his wife and sons. He had experienced numerous blackouts, and (on the ADS) reported many signs of physical dependence, including morning drinking, a sense of "panic" when he thought he would not be able to obtain a drink when he wanted one, and drinking throughout the day. However, he said that he had never experienced any of the physical symptoms of alcohol withdrawal. He also reported no health or emotional problems associated with his drinking. When asked about his goals for treatment, he indicated that his preference was to cut down and drink moderately, but that his wife insisted on abstinence and he was willing to work toward that goal.

Two assessment techniques were used to identify antecedents to Carl's drinking. A self-report questionnaire, the Drinking Patterns Questionnaire (DPQ; Zitter & McCrady, 1979) contains lists of potential environmental, cognitive, affective, interpersonal, and intrapersonal antecedents to drinking or drinking urges. Carl completed the DPQ by checking off all antecedents that applied to his drinking in the previous 6 months, and Maria completed the measure as well to indicate her views of Carl's drinking. They also were asked to rate the most influential antecedents from their own perspective. They both perceived environmental influences as being most important to Carl's drinking, citing drinking settings such as bars and his home, afternoons when he was not working, any celebratory occasions, and being around others who were drinking as most salient. The second most important set of drinking cues related to their relationship, with Carl citing arguments, feeling angry, feeling nagged, or having a good time together as antecedents. The third area of concern, which they both cited, was physiological antecedents, primarily restlessness and fatigue. Although we use the DPQ in our clinical research, an alternative questionnaire that assesses drinking antecedents is the Inventory of Drinking Situations (Annis, 1982), a shorter measure that assesses situations in which a client drinks heavily.

Carl also used daily self-recording cards throughout the treatment to record drinks and drinking urges. By reviewing the information he recorded and discussing events associated with drinking or drinking urges, it was apparent that being with close friends who were also heavy drinkers was an important component of his drinking. The self-recording cards also clarified factors associated with his feelings of "restlessness." When he and Maria were together, the children were active and he wanted to leave or go somewhere; he would get restless and irritable and would want to drink to "take the edge off." Finally, it was apparent from discussing drinking episodes noted on the self-recording cards that Carl felt like drinking when Maria reminded Carl of a commitment that he had made (even something simple such as bringing over a book that he had at home) or tried to get him to make a commitment to any responsible course of action, or when he felt "trapped," even if Maria had not said anything explicit.

Questionnaires and self-recording cards were also used to assess how Maria coped with Carl's drinking. She recorded her perceptions of his drinking each day on a Likert scale (none, light, moderate, or heavy), as well as her daily marital satisfaction. Her responses antecedent to and consequent to drinking episodes were discussed in the therapy sessions. Additionally, both partners completed a modified version of the Spouse Behavior Questionnaire (SBQ; Orford et al., 1975). On the SBQ, they indicated how frequently Maria had engaged in a variety of behaviors related to drinking. These included behaviors that might be construed as antecedents to drinking, positive consequences of drinking, negative consequences of drinking, positive consequences of sobriety, and positive or self-protective behaviors. Data from these assessment sources made it apparent that Maria often questioned Carl about his actions, threatened him, or pleaded with him not to drink. She had reacted to his drinking in a number of negative ways, by separating from him, calling the police, and refusing sex. At the same time, she had made serious efforts to support him and encourage him toward abstinence by doing nice things for him or talking about positive experiences they could enjoy together if he did not drink.

Marital Relationship

In addition to assessing Carl's drinking problem, we also looked closely at the couple's relationship. The couple's relationship was assessed by using the Areas of Change Questionnaire (Margolin, Talovic, & Weinstein, 1983) and the Dyadic Adjustment Scale (Spanier, 1976), and by viewing a videotape of the couple discussing a problem in their relationship. Maria had a number of major concerns about their relationship, as evidenced by her seeking the marital separation. In addition to Carl's drinking, she was concerned about his apparent lack of "responsibility," citing his unwillingness to work, care for the children, or be independent of his mother. In general, Maria felt that Carl could not be relied on for concrete or emotional support. A second concern that she expressed was their role definitions. She felt that Carl dictated her role to her, and that she allowed him to do so. She often felt angry and resentful as a result. Finally, Maria cited Carl's mother as a problem; she said that his mother was an "enabler" who rescued him from his problems and made no demands on him. Maria reported that when she and Carl first dated they liked to drink, stay out late, ride motorcycles, and have a good time, but that she felt that it was time to "move forward" with their lives and "get somewhere."

Carl had fewer marital concerns. He disliked Maria's "nagging" him about or discussing his drinking, stating at one point during therapy: "If I had a different wife I wouldn't have a drinking problem." He also disliked her "persistence" in wanting to discuss topics at length, and disliked her "attitude change" when he drank.

In viewing a videotape of their interactions, it was clear that the couple had a number of communication problems. They interrupted each other frequently and did not listen to the other's comments. They made frequent, sarcastic, and biting comments about the other, but usually with a smile and a funny comment. Maria complained about her excessive responsibilities; Carl criticized her for not fulfilling her responsibilities but refused to acknowledge any responsibilities of his own.

Despite their considerable marital problems, the couple clearly enjoyed each other's company, shared many activities and pleasures (such as fishing, and going to parks with the children), and had a very positive sexual relationship. Maria said of their relationship: "We get along great when I don't demand anything."

Behavioral Formulation

Carl's drinking appeared to have developed in a social context, with virtually all his drinking occurring within social groups with similar drinking patterns. Clearly the pattern was reinforced by these positive social interactions, both with friends and, early in their relationship, with Maria. He had developed significant tolerance for alcohol, so that he could consume increasingly larger amounts, resulting in a pattern of daily drinking with some signs of alcohol dependence. For Carl, alcohol provided a number of positive consequences—he enjoyed the tastes and sensations associated with drinking, he enjoyed the social context of drinking, and he liked the feelings of relaxation that drinking engendered. Although he had accumulated a number of significant negative consequences of drinking, none had impacted upon his internal perceptions of himself or of alcohol. From his perspective, negative consequences were imposed on him by others—the police, job supervisors, and his wife. In addition, Carl had been able to avoid responsibility for his actions in many areas of his life. When he did not work, he was able to live with his mother, who shielded

him from the negative consequences of not working by providing shelter and food for him. When his wife made demands on him that he experienced as aversive, he avoided or ignored her. To some degree, his problems with alcohol were accentuated by the different developmental stages of Carl and Maria. She was ready to move to a more adult stage of life, with increased responsibilities and long-term goals. Carl, in contrast, wanted to maintain the lifestyle and behavioral patterns of his early 20s.

Despite Carl's externalizing attributions for his problems and his ability to avoid negative consequences and responsibility, his wife and children were important to him, and he did not want them out of his life. Therefore, he came to treatment to maintain these desired reinforcers, but not necessarily to make the behavioral changes his wife saw as necessary for them to have a successful long-term marriage. As treatment progressed, Carl engaged in a variety of maneuvers to maintain the relationship but avoid behavioral change, and his wife, and, at times, the therapist, reinforced these behaviors.

Maria had a limited repertoire of effective ways to obtain positive reinforcers for herself. She appeared to expect most positive feelings to come from outside herself and knew only nagging and criticizing as verbal behaviors to use to try to get what she wanted. Maria reinforced Carl's drinking by continuing to have contact with him and have positive interactions, but she engaged in aversive negative verbal behavior at the same time. She placed responsibility for her happiness with Carl, stating that she could not work (something she enjoyed a great deal) until he stopped drinking and was more responsible and that she could not lose weight until he stopped drinking and she was less upset.

As a couple, Carl and Maria lacked the verbal skills to discuss these major problems. Aversive control, avoidance of responsibility, and lack of empathic communication characterized their interactions.

Preparing Client for Change

Carl and Maria were seen together for all phases of the evaluation. In the initial evaluation, both were asked to describe their perceptions of Carl's drinking, their relationship, and how each had attempted to cope with Carl's drinking. By seeing the couple together, I began to communicate my view that the drinking was intimately connected to their relationship, and that both would need to examine their own behavior to effect positive changes. At the end of the evaluation, I provided them with feedback about the main difficulties that I perceived (as summarized above), and oriented them to the plan for treatment. In discussing the treatment plan, I covered the following[2]:

"We have asked you to come to treatment as a couple. This is because, as you know, drinking affects other areas of your life, including your marriage and your family. I know from what you have said, Maria, that you have tried many different ways to cope with Carl's drinking, and that you have been angry and frustrated at times. It is clear that you have tried to help, but it seems, Carl, that you mostly have resented it when Maria has said anything about your drinking. In the treatment, we will look at your drinking, how you have tried to cope with it, and how the two of you are getting along as a couple. Right now the two of you are separated, and you have a lot of concerns about your relationship. As we go along in the therapy, I will give you feedback about how to improve your communication, and I will ask you to try new ways to spend time together and discuss problems.

"Overall, the therapy will focus on three main topics—your drinking, how you [Maria] have coped with it and how to cope in ways that work better for both of you, and your relationship with each other."

In addition to this overall orientation, which both Carl and Maria felt captured their goals for the treatment, we discussed Carl's drinking goals in more detail and plans for how to achieve those goals. As indicated earlier, Carl's preferred drinking goal was moderate drinking. However, Maria felt strongly that she wanted him to abstain, and he had agreed to that goal prior to coming to treatment. Since he had been drinking daily and showed evidence of

tolerance to alcohol, I was concerned that he would not be able to stop drinking without assistance. I therefore discussed with him the possibility of being detoxified under medical supervision:

"I am concerned, Carl, that it will be difficult for you to stop drinking on your own. You drink every day, and have been drinking a lot. On the questionnaires, you indicated that you 'panic' if you think that you will not be able to get any alcohol, and you typically drink throughout the day. All of these things suggest to me that you may be 'hooked' on alcohol, and that your body will have a strong reaction to going without any alcohol at all. The easiest way to get through the first few days without drinking is to check into a hospital detoxification program, and I would like you to consider it."

Carl had a very negative reaction to the thought of being hospitalized. He was afraid of being "locked up" and said, "I know that I would go crazy. I can't stand being confined. After 24 hours I would just have to leave. It's not a good idea."

In behavioral treatment, I am most interested in engaging the client and working to develop mutually agreed-on goals, so I thought it inappropriate to try to force Carl to enter a detoxification center. I was certain that if I made a brief hospitalization a prerequisite to further treatment, Carl would leave treatment completely. Therefore, we developed a plan to achieve abstinence. The plan had two major components: (1) Carl was to come to therapy sessions sober, and his BAL would be verified by a breathalyzer reading, and (2) Carl would set goals to gradually reduce his drinking, with a target date for abstinence 6 weeks hence. If he was not able to achieve either goal, we would reevaluate the need for supervised detoxification. Carl was amenable to this agreement, as was Maria.

Process of Treatment

The course of treatment is described sequentially, to provide the reader with the clearest picture of the progress and pitfalls of a fairly typical therapy case. The treatment covered several major areas, including

(1) procedures to facilitate Carl's reducing his drinking and then stopping; (2) techniques to teach Carl skills to assist him in maintaining abstinence; (3) techniques to enhance Carl's perception of his drinking as problematic; (4) techniques to teach Maria more constructive coping strategies; (5) procedures to teach the couple how to engage in positive interactions; and (6) procedures to teach the couple mutual problem-solving techniques. Additionally, as treatment progressed, we focused on some other areas of individual behavioral change for Maria.

Intake and Sessions 1-2

At the initial intake session, Carl had a BAL greater than 400mg%. Although he did not show signs of gross intoxication, he was belligerent, and the clinician doing the intake did not feel that he could conduct a reasonable intake interview. He suggested that Carl receive medical attention because his BAL was so high, but Carl refused and the clinician rescheduled the intake. At the rescheduled appointment, Carl was sober and was able to provide information, give informed consent for the research aspects of the program, and schedule the baseline data collection session, at which he arrived sober.

At the first treatment session, however, Carl again had an elevated BAL (0.12). He acknowledged only having "a couple of beers," and insisted that he was fine. We had some discussion about Carl and Maria's concerns and goals, but I suggested that we would not be able to have a very productive session with Carl's BAL so high. (My general policy is to set a limit of no treatment session if the client's BAL is greater than 0.05.) Carl agreed to come to the next session sober and to have no more than four drinks per day. I gave Carl and Maria self-recording cards on which I asked them to record drinks, drinking urges, and marital satisfaction on a daily basis. Carl was given one card for each day, and I asked him to record each drink he actually consumed, to note urges to drink not followed by drinking, and to note on the back of the card the situations in which he drank or had urges to drink. A sample self-recording card is shown in Figure 9.1.

Name _____

Date _____

Urges to drink		Drinks		
Time	How strong (1–7)	Time	Type	How much

Comments:

Marital satisfaction (1–7):

FIGURE 9.1. Sample client self-recording card.

Rate drinking: None, Low, Medium, or High. Rate urge intensity: 0 (none) through 7 (greatest ever). Rate marriage satisfaction: 1 (very low) through 7 (greatest ever).

Day	Date	Drinking	Urge intensity	Marriage satisfaction
		No L M H	0 1 2 3 4 5 6 7	0 1 2 3 4 5 6 7
		No L M H	0 1 2 3 4 5 6 7	0 1 2 3 4 5 6 7
		No L M H	0 1 2 3 4 5 6 7	0 1 2 3 4 5 6 7
		No L M H	0 1 2 3 4 5 6 7	0 1 2 3 4 5 6 7
		No L M H	0 1 2 3 4 5 6 7	0 1 2 3 4 5 6 7
		No L M H	0 1 2 3 4 5 6 7	0 1 2 3 4 5 6 7
		No L M H	0 1 2 3 4 5 6 7	0 1 2 3 4 5 6 7

FIGURE 9.2. Sample spouse self-recording card.

Maria received one card to use for the entire week. On the card I asked her to make a daily estimate of Carl's drinking as none, light, moderate, or heavy, and also to record her estimate of the strength of his urges to drink that day. She also made a daily rating of her marital satisfaction. A sample spouse self-recording card is shown in Figure 9.2.

When Carl and Maria came to the second session, his BAL was again elevated, at 0.06. He reported drinking about four beers during the day. We continued the discussion of detoxification presented earlier, and Carl said that he felt he was "addicted" to alcohol. He suggested that he would consider detoxification, and we scheduled a telephone conversation to discuss detoxification further. After speaking twice by phone, Carl decided again that he did not want to be hospitalized. Carl did not use the self-recording cards during these first 2 weeks, although Maria completed his cards for him while they drove to the treatment session. Therefore, I did not feel that I had a clear picture of Carl's drinking, but it was clear that he was continuing to drink daily.

Sessions 3–5

Carl came to the third session with a BAL of zero. He again reiterated his desire to stop without hospitalization, and we worked out the details of the contract described in the previous section (abstinent at treatment sessions, complete abstinence within 6

weeks of the beginning of treatment). In addition to setting drinking goals, we began to discuss a behavior-analytic view of drinking. To introduce the couple to a behavioral way of thinking about their drinking, I discussed the following:

"Together we are going to carefully observe and analyze all the factors that seem to be part of your drinking. I think that we can look at your drinking and figure out what kinds of situations lead you to feel like drinking. If we can figure this out, then we can work together to come up with *alternatives* for these situations. We will be using these sheets, called 'triggers sheets' to analyze your drinking. Let's go through one of these together."

I then asked Carl to identify a recent drinking situation. He indicated that he liked to drink when he went fishing, so we used fishing as an example. I explained to him that in looking at any drinking situation, we would look at the actual situation and then at how he reacted to the situation. As we spoke, I completed the boxes on the "triggers sheet," which is illustrated in Figure 9.3. (Some clinicians, such as Marlatt and Gordon, 1985, refer to high-risk situations rather than triggers. A high-risk situation is one in which the client is at high risk to drink. Carl did not believe that he was at any "risk" to drink—he thought that he could avoid drinking any time he wanted to, but he rarely wanted to. Therefore, I chose to talk about triggers as situations in which

Analyzing drinking

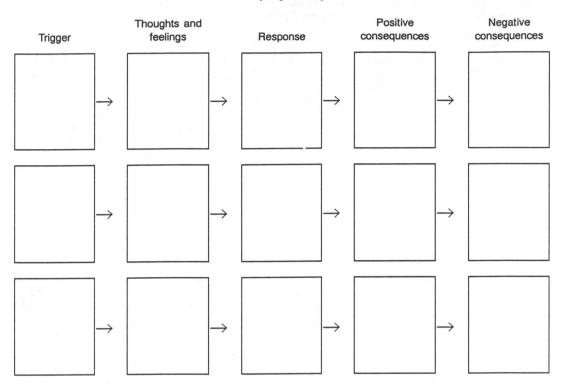

FIGURE 9.3. Sample triggers sheet.

he was likely to drink.) Carl had a fairly unpsychological view of his drinking. He described his thoughts related to alcohol and fishing as "I want to get some beer," and his feelings as "happy." He viewed drinking in that situation as having clear positive consequences—"I have a blast." He felt that the only negative consequences came from Maria, who would be angry when he came home.

Carl and Maria grasped the behavioral analysis quickly and found it a comfortable way to conceptualize his drinking. As homework, I asked then each to complete the DPQ and to bring it to the next treatment session. I gave Carl and Maria additional self-recording cards to use for the week.

Carl also came to the fourth session sober, but reported heavy drinking over the weekend. The graph of his weekly alcohol consumption during treatment is plotted in Figure 9.4. Carl's and Maria's average weekly marital satisfaction ratings are shown in Figure 9.5.

Carl expressed no concern about his continued heavy drinking and showed no evidence that he was trying to cut down. I indicated:

"I am glad that you have come to the last two sessions sober—I know that that's not easy for you, and it does show that you want treatment to succeed. However, I am concerned that you have not cut down at all between sessions. If anything, your drinking seems a bit heavier. It's not clear to me if you don't really want to cut down, or if you just don't know how to."

Carl said that it was hard to cut down, but that he was committed to stopping drinking because he wanted to have Maria and the boys back again. We then discussed a number of potential strategies to help him avoid drinking, such as sleeping (his suggestion), having alternative beverages available in the house (my suggestion), or going back to work (Maria's suggestion). He was quite reluctant to commit to any plans, and Maria challenged whether he was really willing to stop drinking. At that point, Carl said:

"In some ways, I think if I had a different wife I wouldn't have to stop drinking. Before, Maria and I could drink together and have a good time, but now that she doesn't drink she's on me all the time. I know I have to stop if I want to get her back, but I don't know. . . ."

To respond to Carl's ambivalence, I suggested that we examine consequences of his drinking other than Maria's disapproval and the arguments that they had about his drinking. Carl was unable to think of any other adverse consequences. I asked Carl about his legal problems from the DWIs and the arrest for breaking and entering, but Carl said that he did not believe that alcohol had anything to do with the latter charge, and that the DWI laws were "ridiculous." He also indicated that he was still driving even though he did not have a driver's license, and that he would continue to drive even if his license was revoked for 10 years (a real possibility since he had had three DWIs in less than 10 years, with two in the same month). Carl expressed a similar lack of concern about any other aspects of his drinking, but reiterated that he was willing to stop because of his commitment to the marriage and his children. I made a list of the negative consequences that he or Maria had reported at various points in the intake and initial treatment sessions, and asked him to review the list at least twice daily and to

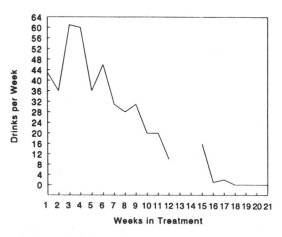

FIGURE 9.4. Carl's weekly alcohol consumption.

FIGURE 9.5. Carl's and Maria's weekly marital satisfaction.

think about which of these consequences were of concern to him. He reported looking at the list "once or twice" between sessions but was relatively indifferent to the content.

Despite my concern about Carl's relative lack of motivation to change, I decided to proceed with a behavioral analysis of his drinking. I thought that if we could identify a discrete set of antecedents to drinking, and if he could be successful at avoiding drinking in some of these situations some of the time, his motivation to change might increase as his self-efficacy about coping without alcohol increased. We discussed two other drinking situations in the session and, as homework, I had him complete two behavioral chains at home. A complete summary of the behavioral analysis of his drinking is included in Table 9.2.

Carl came to the next treatment session with a BAL of 0.118, and he reported heavy drinking for the last several days prior to the treatment session. After a lengthy discussion, he agreed to go for detoxification. Carl was afraid of the hospitalization and also indicated that he was concerned that he would not be able to be abstinent after detoxification. I tried to emphasize that the detoxification was only the first step in treatment, and that we would be working together to help him learn ways to cope with the triggers without drinking. Carl also expressed his belief that life would not be fun if he did not drink. Maria vacillated between encouraging Carl to get detoxified and tell-

TABLE 9.2. Sample Behavioral Analysis of Carl's Drinking

Triggers[a]	Thoughts and feelings	Response	Positive consequences	Negative consequences
Going fishing	"Get some beer" "Happy time"	Drink beer and fish	Have a blast	Come home to Maria, have an argument
Argument with Maria	"She's angry because I had a drink" Angry "I've got to get away"	Leave house Drink	None	Feel like "shit"
Steve comes over, asks me to go out	"Sounds good, I'll go"	Stop at a bar and drink	Have a blast	Get home late Maria's upset
Scott comes over with 12-pack; no one else is home	Glad to see him—like to talk to him Like to see beer "It'll be fun to sit and rap"	Sit on patio Drink and talk Listen to radio	Feels good to talk— get things off my chest Relaxed, takes the edge off Excited about plans (such as fishing)	Maria comes home and gets mad Scott leaves I feel like shit No sex Argument Home disrupted
Get up at Maria's— kids get up, lots of action	Edgy "A beer will take the edge off"	Have a morning beer	Takes the edge off	Maria unhappy Keeps the addiction going

[a]Other triggers Carl reported included: noontime at work; going out for pizza; kids acting up and I don't like how Maria's handling them—I yell and nothing happens; unscheduled time; Maria asks/reminds me about a responsibility; Maria makes critical remarks about my drinking; passing a bar with a friend; other people drinking, social situation; holidays with my family.

ing me that Carl was only agreeing to the detoxification to get out of my office. Because Carl was so concerned, I had him call the detoxification center from my office to ask any questions he had. He did so and scheduled himself for admission the next day.

Sessions 6–8

Carl had not admitted himself for detoxification and said again that he could not face being locked up. He was still drinking daily and was making minimal efforts to decrease his drinking. I suggested outpatient detoxification and gave Carl the phone number of a physician colleague who supervises

outpatient detoxification, but I did not expect that Carl would follow through with that referral either. Carl continued to express willingness to be in treatment and to change his drinking, and I decided to continue, despite doubts about whether he had sufficient incentive to change. During Session 6, we completed the behavioral analysis of Carl's drinking and identified several aspects of Maria's actions that served as antecedents to his drinking. These included her reminding him about responsibilities, her slow-moving pace when they had an appointment and there was a lot to do to get themselves and their children ready to go out, and her commenting on his drinking.

At one point during Session 6, Carl said, "You know, Maria has a real temper. You should ask her what she did to me at the beach." Maria responded immediately by saying, "Show Barbara your arms." Carl rolled up his sleeves, revealing a number of scratches and bruises covering both of his lower forearms. Maria then explained that she had experienced intense frustration with Carl because of his drinking and often grabbed him, scratched him, or tried to hit him in the chest or abdomen when angry. The behavior had started in the last 4 months, and she found it very upsetting. She then stated that she was concerned that she might become abusive to her children, and that she sometimes used physical punishment when she was angry at them. Although Maria's anger and frustration were not surprising, and are common reactions among partners of alcoholics, the physical expression of this anger, particularly in the absence of any physical abuse from Carl, was unusual. We discussed her behavior toward the children in great detail, as I was concerned about whether there was any evidence of child abuse. She reported, and Carl confirmed, that she had never bruised, cut, or injured the children in any way, and that they had never had to take either of the children to a physician or emergency room because of her discipline. They both reported that they believed that physical punishment, in the form of "swats on the bum" or physically removing the child from a dangerous situation, were appropriate forms of discipline. Maria, however, felt that she did not always discipline the children rationally and that she occasionally was hitting them on the arm or pulling too hard when removing them from a situation. From Carl and Maria's reports, I did not believe that Maria was abusing the children in any way but felt that it was important to address her concerns in the therapy. I instructed her to use the self-recording cards to write down any time that she felt she was reacting too strongly to the children, or when she was physically aggressive toward Carl.

Over the next two sessions, Carl began to decrease his drinking substantially and was abstinent for each treatment session. Carl and Maria began to spend more time together and reported that their time together was more positive. They had a family bar-becue and went fishing at the beach with the children.

Maria had been faithful in recording her reactions to her children, noting two times each week when she either slapped one of the children on the arm or felt that she had grabbed him too hard. We discussed the antecedents to these incidents and identified several salient aspects—she was tired, the child was tired, and she attempted to tell him to do something when she could not enforce it (she was across the room or had her hands full). In each situation, she repeated her verbal instructions to the boy several times, to no avail, and then felt angry and stomped across the room and grabbed him. We discussed alternative strategies, and I emphasized the importance of being able to follow through on a verbal instruction immediately rather than allowing herself to get frustrated. She quickly picked up on my suggestions and also expressed relief at being able to discuss her concerns. After 2 weeks, she reported no further instance of excessive physical reaction to the boys and reported feeling more in control of herself as a parent again. Carl's observations confirmed Maria's reports.

At that same time that we discussed Maria's problems with disciplining the children, we began to implement some self-management planning techniques for Carl. I suggested to Carl that it would be easier not to drink if he had some clear ideas about how to handle certain triggers without alcohol. He could avoid situations, or rearrange them to minimize the importance of alcohol in the situation. On the sheet Carl listed environmental antecedents to drinking and several ideas for coping with each antecedent. He also wrote down positive and negative consequences associated with each of his coping plans, to help him decide which would be most feasible to implement.

We selected fishing as a topic for self-management planning because it was a high-frequency, high-drinking activity for Carl. Carl had a number of ideas about how to fish without alcohol. These included taking his older son, taking his wife, or inviting an older friend who was an excellent fisherman and did not drink at all. Additionally, Carl thought that if he bought soft drinks the night before he went fishing, and filled his cooler with the sodas before he left the house, he would be less tempted to stop at the liquor store at the end of his block. For homework, I asked Carl to implement this plan and to develop another self-management plan for getting together with a friend without drinking.

Carl successfully implemented the fishing plan. He also developed a plan to get together with his friend Scott. He planned to ask Scott to play tennis and then go to a fast-food restaurant to eat, because alcohol would not be available there. Although Carl saw no obstacles to implementing this plan, he never used it but could provide no reasons why. He did, however, tell Scott that he was trying not to drink, and his friend reacted positively and supportively.

The other major topic of these sessions was reinforcement for changes in drinking. Because Carl was so ambivalent about changing his drinking, I thought it particularly important that he experience some positive consequences for decreased drinking and for abstinence. I also wanted to provide Maria with some positive rather than coercive ways to interact around Carl's drinking. In introducing this topic, I suggested that they both think about ways to make abstinence and reduced drinking more positive. I first suggested that Maria might give Carl positive feedback when he was not drinking, but Carl reacted quite negatively to this suggestion, saying "I would just think it was another one of her sneaky ways to try to pressure me to stop. I don't want her to say anything." I asked if there was anything that Maria could do that would make not drinking worthwhile to him. Carl suggested that she could refrain from talking about alcohol and spend time with him without being "picky." They decided on several mutually enjoyable activities when he was not drinking, such as sharing a shrimp dinner, and Maria's telling Carl when she was enjoying their time together. They were able to implement these plans successfully, and although Carl drank while they were together, the amount was substantially less on these occasions.

Sessions 9–11

By this point in the treatment, Carl had reduced his drinking to three to six drinks per day but had not yet abstained from drinking. His reports of urges to drink had also begun to decrease. Maria reported high marital satisfaction almost every day (ratings of 7 on a 1–7 scale), and they were spending most of their free time either at her apartment or at Carl's mother's home. However, in the therapy sessions they began to argue more frequently. Their conflict revolved around two major topics: Maria's desire to move to North Carolina, and Maria's feeling that Carl was not emotionally supportive of her. I began to implement some structured communication training with them, teaching them skills to allow the other to finish before speaking, reflective listening, and making specific positive requests. These sessions were supplemented with handouts about communication. After reading the first handout, which covered basic topics such as the value of being polite and respectful of your spouse, and some of the sources of bad communication, they came into the session absolutely surprised at the notion that calling each other names (such as idiot, asshole, or shithead) could have any negative impact on their relationship. They had begun to use positive rather than negative communication at home and were pleased with the impact it had on their conversations.

Although we were making some positive progress in the treatment, I was concerned that Carl was continuing his pattern of daily drinking and reflected this concern to him. Carl said that he believed that he could now stop, and he contracted to be abstinent for 2 days in the following week. The 1st week that he developed this contract he did not want to discuss strategies for abstinence, and he was unsuccessful. The 2nd week we discussed very specific plans for how he would abstain. He planned to be with Maria and the children for part of each day and decided not to buy more beer to have in his mother's house on those days. Additionally, he would stock up on soft drinks and plan on going to bed early. I also suggested that Carl might use Maria as a support in his attempts to abstain. I often encourage clients to find someone with whom to discuss urges, and the partner is often a good source of support. (Some clients find this support through members of AA.) Carl again was resistant to involving Maria, saying, "I wouldn't tell her that I wanted to drink—all I'd get is a lecture." I suggested that he usually disliked her comments because they were unsolicited, but in this situation he would be in charge, because he would be the person concerned about his drinking. He responded positively to this reframing. I then asked Carl if there was anything Maria could say that would be helpful to him, and he suggested that Maria tell him it was his choice. Maria indicated that it would be difficult for her not to lecture but agreed to a role play. They imagined that they were driving to the beach, and Carl said, "I want to stop to pick up a six-pack on the way down." Maria answered, "It's your choice if you want to, but we could stop to get some sodas instead if you want." Carl was amazed at how much he liked her response, and although Maria acknowledged that it was very difficult to be that neutral, she liked not feeling that it was her responsibility to prevent his drinking. They agreed to try out such a discussion once during the coming week.

Carl was not successful in maintaining any abstinent days, although he did implement most of the rest of the plans and drank only one beer on each of the 2 target days. However, he did not tell Maria about any of his urges to drink. He expressed little concern at not meeting his goals. During the session, Carl and Maria announced that they were going to North Carolina for a 2-week trip. Carl knew a contractor who had offered him work there, and Maria was intrigued with the possibility of moving to an area with a lower cost of living and a more rural environment in which to raise the children. She said that she would not move while Carl was still drinking, but they both decided that a trip to explore the possibilities was attractive to them.

Sessions 12–15

Carl and Maria returned from their 2-week trip very enthusiastic about North Carolina. They believed that work was available and the cost of living was clearly lower, and they liked the area they had visited. Maria said again that she would not move unless Carl had been abstinent for a considerable length of time, as she did not want to leave her family if she could not depend on Carl. He again said that he would stop drinking.

I had taken advantage of the break in the therapy to review all of my progress notes and to think about the couple with a bit more detachment. It was clear to me that Carl had agreed to abstinence because of Maria's pressure but really wanted to reduce his drinking. However, he had dealt with this conflict by providing verbal reassurances that his behavior would change without the accompanying behavioral changes. Carl had implemented only a few of the behavioral plans that we had developed, and I did not think that the lack of implementation reflected a skills deficit. I had decided to confront Carl with his behavioral inconsistencies at this treatment session.

I told the couple that I wanted to discuss their progress so far. I emphasized the positive changes that they had made so far—Carl had decreased his drinking substantially, he had developed some skills to assist him in drinking less, their communication had begun to improve, they were spending time together that was mutually enjoyable, and they had begun to consider possible long-term plans together. I noted, however, that Carl had made a series of promises about his drinking on which he had not followed through. I read them several passages from my progress notes, emphasizing the target date for abstinence that Carl had initially agreed to, his broken agreement about detoxification, and his broken agreements about abstinent days. I suggested two alternative explanations to them—that Carl did not want to stop drinking completely but felt that he had to agree to abstinence to keep Maria happy, or that he really could not stop drinking and needed further assistance to do so. By framing my explanations this way, I tried to avoid labeling Carl dishonest or unmotivated to change. I also suggested that Maria had helped Carl to keep drinking by reporting high marital satisfaction even though he was still drinking, and that perhaps reduced drinking was really acceptable to her as well.

Both reacted quite strongly to my feedback. Carl said, "At first I didn't want to stop, but now it doesn't seem that bad. I'm not drinking enough now for it to mean anything, so I'll just quit. It's no big deal, and I don't want to disappoint you." Maria said:

"I always feel like Carl is just saying whatever he has to get me off his back or get you off his back. But I have been so much happier since he cut down that I kind of lost sight of that fact that he's still drinking. I am afraid to move anywhere with him while he's still drinking at all—it was so bad before, I don't want to go back to that."

After this conversation, Carl denied that he preferred moderate drinking, and announced that he was going to "quit for good."

Over the next 2 weeks, Carl had 1 drinking day each week—one beer the 1st week and two beers the 2nd week. Although we discussed a variety of behavioral coping strategies, such as developing behavioral alternatives for drinking situations, rehearsing strategies for refusing drinks, and using various strategies for coping with urges, Carl deemphasized their importance. Instead, he focused on cognitive coping strategies—when he had urges to drink he would think about reasons not to drink—"It's not worth it—Maria and the kids are more important." Or, he would use delay tactics, "I won't have anything right now—if I still feel like drinking at 5:00 [or some other, later time during the day], then I'll have a beer." Or, he would deemphasize the positive aspects of alcohol, thinking, "One or two beers won't do anything for me, and I don't want to get blasted."

Carl and Maria also began to discuss their long-term goals together. I asked each to write down how they would like their life to be in 5 years—separately or together. Carl wrote down the following[3]:

> Comfortable place to live for Maria and the kids. Good schools, backyard. Get finances in order; save money, consolidate bills, improve credit. Maintane stable income ie. steady construction work or other. Obtain a loving relationship with Maria.
> Self improvement: manage money better, listen to Maria more objectivly, secure steadier employment.
> Maria: better self discipline, controll temper, improve self confidence, weight loss, less pestimistic in dialy matters. ie. scared of bugs, traffic, mishaps, ect.

Maria wrote down remarkably similar 5-year goals:

> Five years from now—1996–39 years old; Jonathan 8 years, Marc 7 years. We are living in North Carolina in a rented House. I'm working, Carls working the boys are in school. We have two cars. Carl is 5 yrs sober. I'm 4 years thin. We are two yrs away from getting credit back from filing bankruptcy in 1991. Some nights we will be together as a family to relax or to go to a baseball or soccer game of Jonathan's or Marc's. Other nights I will be out to socialize or run errands. Other nights Carl will do the same. We will be somewhat financialy comfortable.
> Three things I want out of:

Maria	Carl
calmness	motivation
thinness	sobriety
contentness	responsability
to feel secure	
a car	
money	
independence	
control over my life	

Because Carl's and Maria's goals were so similar, I asked them if I could read them aloud. Both were amenable to this suggestion, and I did so. Both reacted quite positively and felt encouraged, since their long-term goals were so similar, that they could work together in therapy to achieve these goals. I began to teach them skills related to assertiveness and problem solving, discussing ways to implement these skills both in their relationship and in other interpersonal situations.

Sessions 16–18

Carl abstained from drinking from Session 15 to the end of the treatment. He reported a few urges to drink, but these soon decreased. However, he discussed very strong reactions to not drinking. He felt sad, saying that he missed drinking, and felt that he had lost something important to him. He also said that it was frustrating, because he always had been able to drink when he felt bad, but now he could not do so. I tried to reframe Carl's feelings for him, noting that his ability to recognize that he missed alcohol was an important step toward being able to reorganize his life without it, and that his reaction suggested that he was quite serious about his intentions not to drink. He seemed to find the reframing helpful but continued to find abstinence uncomfortable.

As Carl remained abstinent, his marital satisfaction ratings decreased. Previously, Carl had reported fairly high marital satisfaction, but as he stopped drinking he became more unhappy. When I asked him about his ratings, he said that he felt they were "going nowhere" in terms of reconciling. We had begun assertion and problem-solving training, and I suggested that Carl could use these skills to express his feelings to Maria more directly. They had a fairly positive discussion during the session of Carl's feelings about wanting to reconcile and Maria's concerns about how difficult that would be, with each using some of the positive skills we had worked on. Both agreed that they now wanted to live together again, but it would be difficult to develop a plan to do so. We used structured problem-solving techniques over two treatment sessions to develop a plan.

The major impediment to reconciliation was financial. Maria was receiving welfare, but if either she or Carl began to work they would receive less public assistance. However, to be able to live together, they would have to save sufficient money for a security deposit and the 1st month's rent. They finally decided that Maria would begin to work a few hours a week as a hairdresser, "under the table," and that Carl would care for the children while she worked. If that worked well, Carl would begin to look for work again, and once they were both working, they would move in with his mother for a limited period to save money for the deposits and rent, and would then either obtain an apartment together in New Jersey or find a trailer to rent in North Carolina and move. They also used problem-solving techniques to develop a plan to deal with their other debts.

Termination

Because Carl and Maria were part of a clinical research study, we had to terminate treatment after 18 sessions (including the sessions when Carl was intoxicated). They had made significant progress during treatment—Carl had been abstinent for more than a month, Maria had learned more effective ways to discipline the children and no longer reported concerns about being overly punitive toward them, the couple's relationship was significantly improved, and they had a constructive plan for reconciliation. I was concerned that Carl still was uncomfortable with abstinence, and I thought that he had acquired only a few effective coping strategies to deal with triggers for drinking. We had not worked directly on Carl's responsibility-avoidance style, except by following through on his commitment to abstinence and through long-term goal setting. Whether Carl would implement his part of these agreements was relatively untested. The couple was fairly comfortable with termination but asked about possible follow-up treatment, inquiring specifically about AA or other support groups that were more focused on couples or on behavioral approaches to change. I referred them to RR, and to a couples AA meeting that devotes most of its discussion to relationship issues rather than AA-oriented recovery issues. If they had been in one of the other experimental groups for the study, I would have scheduled several clinical follow-up sessions with them over the course of the next year, and that is my usual clinical practice with clients with drinking problems. The constraints of the clinical research protocol precluded such clinical follow-ups.

Comment

Carl and Maria were a fairly typical couple. Carl's ambivalence about change, his entry into treatment solely because of an external agent, and his resistance to many behavioral interventions are fairly representative. I believe that he began to engage in treatment when he stopped feeling that he was the sole focus of the treatment, after Maria began to discuss her aggressive behavior and feelings. The second critical point in treatment was the confrontation of his continued drinking. I was willing to allow them to renegotiate for a goal of moderate drinking but did not think it therapeutic for Carl to feel that he could make a verbal agreement (to abstinence) and then avoid the agreement. Confronting his behavior forced him either to be assertive and renegotiate treatment goals or to follow through on his commitment.

The role of behavioral skills training in facilitating Carl's abstinence was somewhat more limited than with some clients. Carl tried various skills introduced during the treatment but relied primarily on cognitive coping strategies. However, the role of reinforcement was probably more important in understanding Carl's changed drinking behavior. His marital relationship was important to him at the beginning of treatment, and focusing on ways to improve that relationship increased its reinforcement value to him. Maria's consistency in saying that they could only reconcile if Carl were abstinent, discussing long-term goals for the relationship, and seeing the possible positive life they could live in North Carolina all contributed.

Finally, my relationship with the couple probably contributed to the positive changes that they made. I found them a likable, appealing couple, despite their difficulties. At times I would tease or cajole Carl into compliance, and he commented at the end of the treatment, "At first I didn't know if I liked you or not, but then I decided you were kind of cute, and then I realized that you weren't going to let up on me, so I decided that I'd give it a try." With Maria, I tried to reinforce her ability to take care of herself, and I suspect that she saw me as a role model in some sense. She often asked me personal questions (was I married, how old was my son), and gave me a desk calendar as a thank-you gift at termination. Our research has suggested that our more experienced therapists are more successful at keeping clients in treatment (Epstein, McCrady, Miller, & Steinberg, 1992), and I suspect that being able to deal with these complex relationships is one skill that our more experienced therapists had more fully acquired.

Typical Problems

The problems presented in this case are fairly typical—coming to treatment sessions intoxicated, continued drinking during treatment, ambivalence about change, noncompliance with assignments, and discovering new and major problems as the therapy progresses. Lying and failing to come to scheduled treatment sessions are other typical behaviors that problem drinking clients sometimes present. By working with Carl and Maria together I was able to minimize these particular problems, as Maria was highly motivated for treatment and very responsible about keeping scheduled appointments. Also, by having them both record Carl's drinking and drinking urges I had a clearer picture of his drinking and was able to maintain a clear idea of our progress (or lack thereof).

CLINICAL PREDICTORS OF SUCCESS OR FAILURE

A number of factors predict the success of failure of therapy. However, before addressing these factors, it is important to discuss definitions of "success." In any treatment, a minority of clients will successfully stop drinking or substantially decrease and then maintain abstinence or a nonproblem drinking pattern for extended periods (i.e., several years) (Helzer et al., 1985; Pettinati, Sugerman, DiDonato, & Maurer, 1982). The proportion varies with the demographic characteristics of the population, and individuals who are married, have stable employment, a stable residence, and no comorbid psychopathology have the best treatment outcomes. Additionally, a person's posttreatment environment plays an important role (Moos, Finney, & Cronkite, 1990) in determining long-term outcomes.

Observations of the long-term instability of drinking outcomes have led many to consider alcoholism as a chronic, relapsing disorder, and to reconceptualize success as a process rather than a static outcome. That is, the client who learns effective skills to avoid drinking or heavy drinking, but who also learns ways to cope with relapses by minimizing their length and severity, would also be considered successful (e.g., Marlatt & Gordon, 1985). In treatment outcome studies, investigators look at percentage of abstinent or moderate drinking days and length of periods of abstinence compared to periods of heavy drinking as ways to assess relative rather than absolute success.

From the individual clinician's perspective, certain client characteristics and behaviors bode well for the course of treatment. The client who has important incentives to change (either internal or external), and who has some recognition of a relationship between his/her drinking and life problems is easier to treat. Compliance with early homework assignments, coming to sessions sober, and honesty about behavior outside treatment are also positive indicators.

However, clinician behavior is also an important predictor of success. Various studies have pointed to different aspects of clinician behavior—empathy, specific goal setting and treatment planning, developing drinking goals with the client rather than imposing goals, and providing the client with options for treatment—as associated with better compliance with treatment.

CONCLUSION

Providing treatment to individuals with drinking problems is a complex and continuously fascinating process. The clinician is faced with complex decisions about matching each client to the appropriate level of care, setting for treatment, treatment modalities, and techniques. Diagnostic skills to identify concomitant medical, psychological, psychiatric, and cognitive problems are challenged by each client. Therapy requires knowledge of a range of behavioral treatment techniques, an ability to be able to form a positive therapeutic relationship with sometimes frustrating and difficult clients, and the ability to "think on your feet." From the briefest, one-session treatments to motivate heavy drinkers to reduce their drinking to the complex and longer treatment provided to the chronic alcoholic, treatment is never dull or routine. The clinician has a large body of empirical literature to guide the selection of treatments, and a significant clinical literature as well that illustrates clinical techniques and problems. And, while many people with drinking problems do change successfully on their own or with minimal assistance (e.g., Miller & Rollnick, 1991; Sobell, Sobell, & Toneatto, in press) treatment can provide an effective means for people to successfully change a major life problem.

ACKNOWLEDGMENTS

Preparation of this chapter was supported by Grants AA07070 and P50 AA08747.

NOTES

1. Carl and Maria are an actual couple, but identifying information and some aspects of the course of therapy are altered to protect their privacy.
2. All dialogue is paraphrasing of actual therapist or client comments.
3. These are verbatim transcripts, and include client spelling of all words.

REFERENCES

Alford, G. (1980). Alcoholics Anonymous: An empirical outcome study. *Addictive Behaviors, 5,* 359–370.

American Psychiatric Association. (1987). *Diagnostic and statistical manual of mental disorders* (3rd ed., rev.). Washington, DC: Author.

American Psychiatric Association. (1993). *DSM-IV draft criteria as of 3/1/93.* Washington, DC: Author.

American Society of Addictive Medicine. (1991). *Patient placement criteria for the treatment of psychoactive substance use disorders.* Washington, DC: Author.

Annis, H. M. (1982). *Inventory of Drinking Situations (IDS-100).* Toronto, Canada: Addiction Research Foundation of Toronto.

Azrin, N. H. (1976). Improvements in the community-reinforcement approach to alcoholism. *Behaviour Research and Therapy, 14,* 339–348.

Azrin, N. H., Sisson, R. W., Meyers, R., & Godley, M. (1982). Alcoholism treatment by disulfiram and community reinforcement therapy. *Journal of Behavior Therapy and Experimental Psychiatry, 13,* 105–112.

Babor, T. F., Stephens, R. S., & Marlatt, G. A. (1987). Verbal report methods in clinical research on alcoholism: response bias and its minimization. *Journal of Studies on Alcohol, 48,* 410–424.

Chafetz, M. E., Blane, H. T., Abram, H. S., Golner, J., Lacy, E., McCourt, W. F., Clark, E., & Meyers, W. (1962). Establishing treatment relations with alcoholics. *Journal of Nervous and Mental Diseases, 134,* 395–409.

Cook, C. C. H. (1988a). The Minnesota Model in the management of drug and alcohol dependency: Miracle, method or myth? Part I. The philosophy and the programme. *British Journal of Addiction, 83,* 625–634.

Cook, C. C. H. (1988b). The Minnesota Model in the management of drug and alcohol dependency: Miracle, method or myth? Part II. Evidence and conclusions. *British Journal of Addiction, 83,* 735–748.

Edwards, G., & Gross, M. M. (1976). Alcohol dependence; provisional description of a clinical syndrome. *British Medical Journal, 1,* 1058–1061.

Emrick, C., Tonigan, J. S., Montgomery, H., & Little, L. (1993). Alcoholics Anonymous: What is currently known? In B. S. McCrady & W. R. Miller (Eds.), *Research on Alcoholics Anonymous: Opportunities and alternatives.* New Brunswick, NJ: Alcohol Research Documentation.

Epstein, E. E., McCrady, B. S., Miller, K., & Steinberg, M. (1992, June). *Attrition from conjoint alcoholism treatment: Do dropouts differ from completers?* Paper presented at the Annual Meeting of the Research Society on Alcoholism, San Diego, CA.

Femino, J., & Lewis, D. C. (1980). *Clinical pharmacology and therapeutics of the alcohol withdrawal syndrome.* Brown University Program in Alcoholism and Drug Abuse, Medical Monograph No. 1.

Filstead, W. (1991). *Two-year treatment outcome. An evaluation of substance abuse services for adults and youths.* Park Ridge, IL: Parkside Medical Services.

Frankenstein, W., Hay, W. M., & Nathan, P. E. (1985). Effects of intoxication on alcoholics' marital communication and problem solving. *Journal of Studies on Alcohol, 46,* 1-6.

Gomberg, E. L. (1980). *Drinking and problem drinking among the elderly.* Ann Arbor, MI: University of Michigan Institute of Gerontology.

Gorski, T., & Miller, M. (1986). *Staying sober: A guide for relapse prevention.* Independence, MO: Independence Press.

Hasin, D. S., Grant, B. F., & Endicott, J. (1988). Lifetime psychiatric comorbidity in hospitalized alcoholics: Subject and family correlates. *International Journal of the Addictions, 23,* 827-850.

Hayashida, M., Alterman, A. I., McLellan, A. T., O'Brien, C. P., Purtill, J. J., Volpicelli, J., Raphaelson, A. H., & Hall, C. P. (1989). Comparative effectiveness and costs of inpatient and outpatient detoxification of patients with mild-to-moderate alcohol withdrawal. *New England Journal of Medicine, 320,* 358-365.

Helzer, J. E., Robins, L. N., Taylor, J. R., Carey, K., Miller, R. H., Combs-Orme, T., & Farmer, A. (1985). The extent of long-term moderate drinking among alcoholics discharged from medical and psychiatric treatment facilities. *New England Journal of Medicine, 312,* 1678-1682.

Hesselbrock, M., Meyer, R., & Keener, J. J. (1985). Psychopathology in hospitalized alcoholics. *Archives of General Psychiatry, 42,* 1050-1055.

Hester, R., & Miller, W. R. (1989). *Handbook of alcoholism treatment approaches.* New York; Pergamon Press.

Hunt, G. M., & Azrin, N. H. (1973). A community-reinforcement approach to alcoholism. *Behaviour Research and Therapy, 11,* 91-104.

Kadden, R. M., Cooney, N. L., Getter, H., & Litt, M. D. (1989). Matching alcoholics to coping skills or interactional therapies: Posttreatment results. *Journal of Consulting and Clinical Psychology, 57,* 698-704.

Kaufman, E. (1984). *Power to change. Family case studies in the treatment of alcoholism.* New York: Gardner Press.

Margolin, G., Talovic, S., & Weinstein, C. D. (1983). Areas of Change Questionnaire: A practical approach to marital assessment. *Journal of Consulting and Clinical Psychology, 51,* 921-931.

Marlatt, G. A., & Gordon, J. R. (Eds.). (1985). *Relapse prevention: Maintenance strategies in the treatment of addictive behaviors.* New York: Guilford Press.

McCrady, B. S. (1990). The marital relationship and alcoholism treatment. In R. L. Collins, K. E. Leonard, B. A. Miller, & J. S. Searles (Eds.), *Alcohol and the family: Research and clinical perspectives* (pp. 338-355). New York: Guilford Press.

McCrady, B. S. (1992). A reply to Peele: Is this how you treat your friends? *Addictive Behaviors, 17,* 67-72.

McCrady, B. S., & Epstein, E. E. (in press). Marital therapy in the treatment of alcohol problems. In N. Jacobson & A. Gurman (Eds.), *Clinical handbook of marital therapy* (2nd ed.). New York: Guilford Press.

McCrady, B. S., & Irvine, S. (1989). Self-help groups in the treatment of alcoholism. In R. Hester & W. R. Miller (Eds.), *Handbook of alcoholism treatment approaches.* New York: Pergamon Press.

McCrady, B. S., Longabaugh, R. L., Fink, E., Stout, R., Beattie, M., Ruggieri-Authelet, A., & McNeill, D. (1986). Cost effectiveness of alcoholism treatment in partial hospital versus inpatient settings after brief inpatient treatment: Twelve-month outcomes. *Journal of Consulting and Clinical Psychology, 54,* 708-713.

McCrady, B. S., & Raytek, H. (in press). Women and substance abuse: Treatment modalities and outcome. In E. Gomberg & T. D. Nirenberg (Eds.), *Women and substance abuse.* Ablex Press.

McCrady, B. S., Stout, R., Noel, N., Abrams, D., & Nelson, H. F. (1991). Effectiveness of three types of spouse-involved behavioral alcoholism treatment. *British Journal of Addiction, 86,* 1415-1424.

Miller, W. R. (1985). Motivation for treatment: A review with special emphasis on alcoholism. *Psychological Bulletin, 98,* 84-107.

Miller, W. R., & Hester, R. (1986). Inpatient alcoholism treatment: Who benefits? *American Psychologist, 41,* 794-805.

Miller, W. R., & Rollnick, S. (1991). *Motivational interviewing: Preparing people to change addictive behavior.* New York: Guilford Press.

Monti, P. M., Abrams, D. B., Kadden, R. M., & Cooney, N. L. (1989). *Treating alcohol dependence. A coping skills training guide.* New York: Guilford Press.

Moos, R., & Billings, A. (1982). Children of alcoholics during the recovery process: Alcoholic and matched control families. *Addictive Behaviors, 7,* 155-163.

Moos, R., Finney, J., & Cronkite, R. (1990). *Alcoholism treatment: Context, process, and outcome.* New York: Oxford University Press.

Moos, R., Finney, J. W., & Gamble, W. (1982). The process of recovery from alcoholism. II. Comparing spouses of alcoholic patients and matched community controls. *Journal of Studies on Alcohol, 43,* 888-909.

Nathan, P. E., & McCrady, B. S. (1987). Bases for the use of abstinence as a goal in the behavioral treatment of alcohol abusers. *Drugs and Society, 1,* 109-132.

O'Farrell, T. J., & Cutter, H. S. G. (1984). Behavioral marital therapy couples groups for male alcoholics and their wives. *Journal of Substance Abuse Treatment, 1,* 191-204.

Ojehegan, A., & Berglund, M. (1989). Changes in drinking goals in a two-year outpatient alcoholic treatment program. *Addictive Behaviors, 14,* 1-10.

Orford, J., Guthrie, S., Nicholls, P., Oppenheimer, E., Egert, S., & Hensman, C. (1975). Self-reported coping behavior of wives of alcoholics and its association with drinking outcome. *Journal of Studies on Alcohol, 36,* 1254-1267.

Orford, J., & Keddie, A. (1986). Abstinence or controlled drinking in clinical practice: A test of the dependence and persuasion hypotheses. *British Journal of Addiction, 81,* 495-504.

Paolino, T. J., Jr., McCrady, B. S., & Diamond, S. (1978). Some alcoholic marriage statistics: An overview. *International Journal of Addictions, 13*, 1252–1257.

Parsons, O. A., Butters, N., & Nathan, P. E. (Eds.). (1987). *Neuropsychology of alcoholism: Implications for diagnosis and treatment.* New York: Guilford Press.

Peele, S. (1992). Alcoholism, politics, and bureaucracy: The consensus against controlled-drinking therapy in America. *Addictive Behaviors, 17*, 49–62.

Pettinati, H. M., Sugerman, A. A., DiDonato, N., & Maurer, H. S. (1982). The natural history of alcoholism over four years after treatment. *Journal of Studies on Alcohol, 43*, 201–215.

Prochaska, J. O., & DiClemente, C. C. (1982). Transtheoretical therapy: Toward a more integrative model of change. *Psychotherapy: Theory, Research and Practice, 19*, 276–288.

Robins, L. N., Wing, J., Wittchen, H. U., Helzer, J. E., Babor, T. F., Burke, J., Farmer, A., Jablenski, A., Pickens, R., Regier, D. A., Sartorius, N., & Towle, L. H. (1988). The prevalence of psychiatric disorders in patients with alcohol and other drug problems. *Archives of General Psychiatry, 45*, 1023–1031.

Room, R. (1993). Alcoholics Anonymous as a social movement. In B. S. McCrady & W. R. Miller (Eds.), *Research on Alcoholics Anonymous: Opportunities and alternatives.* New Brunswick, NJ: Alcohol Research Documentation.

Ross, H. E., Glaser, F. B., & Germanson, T. (1988). The prevalence of psychiatric disorders in patients with alcohol and other drug problems. *Archives of General Psychiatry, 45*, 1023–1031.

Selzer, M. L. (1971). The Michigan Alcoholism Screening Test: The quest for a new diagnostic instrument. *American Journal of Psychiatry, 127*, 1653–1658.

Sisson, R. W., & Azrin, N. (1986). Family-member involvement to initiate and promote treatment of problem drinkers. *Journal of Behaviour Therapy and Experimental Psychiatry, 17*, 15–21.

Skinner, H., & Allen, B. A. (1982). Alcohol dependence syndrome: Measurement and validation. *Journal of Abnormal Psychology, 91*, 199–209.

Sobell, M. B., Maisto, S. A., Sobell, L. C., Cooper, T., & Saunders, B. (1980). Developing a prototype for evaluating alcohol treatment effectiveness. In L. C. Sobell, M. B. Sobell, & E. Ward (Eds.), *Evaluating alcohol treatment effectiveness: Recent advances.* New York: Pergamon Press.

Sobell, L. C., Sobell, M. B., & Toneatto, T. (in press). Recovery from alcohol problems without treatment. In N. Heather, W. R. Miller, & J. Greeley (Eds.), *Self-control and addictive behaviors.* New York: Pergamon Press.

Spanier, G. (1976). Measuring dyadic adjustment: New scales for assessing the quality of marriage and similar dyads. *Journal of Marriage and the Family, 38*, 15–28.

Thomas, E. J., Santa, C., Bronson, D., & Oyserman, D. (1987). Unilateral family therapy with the spouses of alcoholics. *Journal of Social Service Research, 10*, 145–162.

Trimpey, J. (1989). *The small book.* New York: Delacorte Press.

Vaillant, G. (1983). *The natural history of alcoholism.* Cambridge, MA: Harvard University Press.

Wallace, J., McNeill, D., Gilfallan, D., MacLean, K., & Fanella, F. (1988). I. Six-month treatment outcomes in socially stable alcoholics: Abstinence rates. *Journal of Substance Abuse Treatment, 5*, 247–252.

Zitter, R. E., & McCrady, B. S. (1979). *The Drinking Patterns Questionnaire.* Unpublished manuscript.

Chapter 10

BORDERLINE PERSONALITY DISORDER

Marsha M. Linehan
Constance A. Kehrer
University of Washington, Seattle

This chapter presents one of the more remarkable developments in all of psychotherapy. Few therapists are willing to undertake the overwhelmingly difficult and wrenching task of treating "borderline" individuals and yet these people are among the neediest encountered in any therapeutic setting. They also impose an enormous burden on the health care system. Over the past decade, Linehan and her colleagues have developed a psychological treatment for individuals with borderline personality. More important, data now indicate that this treatment is effective when compared to alternative interventions. If this result holds up in future clinical trials, treatment will constitute one of the most substantial contributions to the armamentarium of the psychotherapist in recent times. What is even more interesting is that this approach blends psychodynamic, interpersonal systems and cognitive-behavioral approaches into a coherent whole. To this mix, Linehan adds her personal experience with Eastern philosophies and religions. Among the more intriguing strategies incorporated into this approach are "entering the paradox" and "extending," borrowed from *aikido*, a Japanese form of self-defense. And yet, the authors remain true to the empirical foundations of their approach. The fascinating case study presented in the context of this chapter illustrates Linehan's therapeutic expertise and strategic timing in a way that will be invaluable to all therapists who deal with personality disorders. The surprising and tragic outcome illustrates the enormous burden of clinical responsibility inherent in any treatment setting as well as the practical issues that arise when treatment ultimately fails.—D. H. B.

INTRODUCTION

Clinicians generally agree that clients with a diagnosis of borderline personality disorder (BPD) are challenging and difficult to treat. Indeed, the treatment of borderline individuals is something that many practitioners approach with trepidation and concern. Several of the behavioral patterns that define the condition are particularly problematic and are among the most stressful that therapists encounter (Shearin & Linehan, 1989). Perhaps of greatest concern is the generally high incidence of suicidal behavior among this population. From 70% to 75% of borderline clients have a history of at least one parasuicidal act (Clarkin, Widiger, Frances, Hurt, & Gilmore, 1983; Cowdry, Pickar, & Davies, 1985), defined as any intentional, acute, self-injurious behavior with or without suicidal intent, including both suicide attempts and self-mutilative behaviors. Suicide threats and crises are frequent even among those who never engage in any parasuicidal behaviors. Although much of this behavior is without lethal consequence, 5%–10% eventually suicide (Stone, Stone, & Hart, 1987; Paris, Brown, & Nowlis, 1987; Frances, Fyer, & Clarkin, 1986). Borderline individuals also have difficulties with anger and anger expression. Not infrequently, intense anger is directed at the therapist. The frequent coexistence of BPD with both Axis I conditions such as affective or anxiety disorders and other personality disorders clearly complicates treatment further.

The criteria for BPD, as currently defined within the fourth edition of the *Diagnostic and Statistical Manual of Mental Disorders* (DSM-IV; American Psychiatric Association [APA], 1993)* and the Diagnostic Interview for Borderlines (Gunderson & Kolb, 1978; Gunderson, Kolb, & Austin, 1981; Zanarini, Gunderson, Frankenburg, & Chauncey, 1989), the most commonly used research assessment instrument, reflect a pervasive pattern of instability and dysregulation across emotional, behavioral, cognitive, and interpersonal domains. Reorganizing somewhat and summarizing criteria within each domain (see Linehan, 1993a), borderline individuals have the following characteristics. First, they generally experience emotional dysregulation and instability. Emotional responses are reactive, and the individual generally has difficulties with episodic depression, anxiety, and irritability as well as problems with anger and anger expression. Second, borderline individuals have patterns of behavioral dysregulation, as evidenced by extreme and problematic impulsive behavior. As noted above, an important characteristic of borderline individuals is their tendency to direct apparently destructive behaviors toward themselves. Attempts to injure, mutilate, or kill themselves, as well as actual suicide, occur frequently in this population. Third, borderline individuals are sometimes cognitively dysregulated. Brief, nonpsychotic thought and sensory dysregulation, including depersonalization, dissociation, and delusions, including delu-

sions about the self, are at times brought on by stressful situations and usually cease when the stress is ameliorated. Dysregulation of the sense of self is common. Borderline individuals frequently report that they have no sense of a self at all, feel empty, and do not "know" who they are. Fourth, borderline individuals often experience interpersonal dysregulation. Their relationships may be chaotic, intense, and marked with difficulties. Even though their relationships are so difficult, borderline individuals often find it extremely hard to relinquish relationships. Instead, they may engage in intense and frantic efforts to prevent significant individuals from leaving them. The polythetic format of the DSM-IV definition allows for considerable heterogeneity in diagnosis, and clinical experience with borderline clients confirms that this diagnostic category comprises a heterogeneous group.

In the last decade there has been a virtual explosion in the clinical literature on BPD; a recent literature review indicated that over 40% of all journal articles addressing personality disorders were exclusively devoted to research on BPD (Widiger & Frances, 1989). Today, BPD has a reputation as the most widely researched personality disorder. Despite this widespread interest, empirically based treatment research on BPD is lacking. Given the myriad difficulties in conducting psychotherapy with borderline individuals, even in clinical settings without the added complexity of a research study, the paucity of carefully controlled treatment outcome studies is perhaps understandable. Consequently, treatment efficacy of the many therapeutic modalities currently applied in treating the borderline client has not been empirically demonstrated. Presently, there is no treatment of choice for BPD.

METHODS OF TREATMENT

A variety of approaches have been applied to the treatment of BPD. Although it is not our purpose to present a scholarly review of the many treatments for BPD, we believe it

---

*The DSM-IV criteria cited in this chapter are those that were approved as final by the DSM-IV Personality Disorders Work Group and the Task Force on DSM-IV (APA, 1993). These criteria may be subject to minor editorial revisions before the publication of DSM-IV.

helpful to briefly review the status of current treatments before presenting in detail dialectical behavior therapy. (For an in-depth review of comparative treatments, the interested reader is referred to Tutek & Linehan, 1993.)

Psychodynamic

Psychodynamic approaches that have received the greatest attention include the work of Kernberg (Kernberg, 1975, 1984; Kernberg, Selzer, Koenigsberg, Carr, & Appelbaum, 1989), Masterson (1976, 1981), Rinsley (1982), Adler and Buie (Adler, 1981, 1985; Adler & Buie, 1979; Buie & Adler, 1982), and Gunderson (1984). Among these, Kernberg's contributions are clearly prominent. His object-relations model is comprehensive as to theory and technique and has had considerable influence on the psychoanalytic literature. His expressive psychotherapy for borderline clients emphasizes three primary factors: interpretation, the maintenance of technical neutrality, and transference analysis. The focus of the therapy is exposure and resolution of intrapsychic conflict. Treatment goals include increased impulse control and anxiety tolerance, ability to modulate affect, and the development of stable interpersonal relationships.

Kernberg has also distinguished a "supportive" psychotherapy for more severely disturbed borderline clients. Like expressive psychotherapy, supportive psychotherapy also places great emphasis on the importance of the transference; however, interpretations are less likely to be made early in treatment and only the negative transference is explored. Both expressive and supportive psychotherapy are expected to last several years, with primary foci on suicidal behaviors and therapy-interfering behaviors.

In terms of treatment efficacy, it is difficult to evaluate any of the major models of psychodynamic psychotherapy. As previously noted, clients with BPD constitute an extremely heterogeneous group and are often lumped together with individuals not meeting stringent BPD criterion. Second, there are at present no controlled treatment outcome studies of any of the psychoanalytically oriented treatments for BPD. Furthermore, naturalistic studies cast doubt on the feasibility of long-term psychodynamic treatment; many if not most clients fail to complete even 6 months of therapy (Kernberg et al., 1972; Stone et al., 1987; Waldinger & Gunderson, 1984).

In addition to psychodynamically oriented individualized treatments, Marziali and Munroe-Blum (1987; Munroe-Blum & Marziali, 1987) have developed a psychodynamic group approach to treating BPD, relationship management psychotherapy (RMP). Differentiating RMP from traditional psychodynamic approaches is its emphasis on a client orientation phase as well as therapist accessibility outside the group format. Within the group setting, clients are engaged individually and encouraged to express internalized conflicts around self-attributes, with feedback provided by other group members. In addition, the group format helps dilute the intensity of the transference relationship across clients and cotherapists and aids limit setting for members with poor impulse control. Preliminary results of a controlled clinical trial comparing RMP to individual treatment as usual in the community reported no differences in treatment outcome at the 6–month follow-up (Munroe-Blum & Marziali, 1987, 1989; Clarkin, Marziali, & Munroe-Blum, 1991). However, clients who remained in either group or individual therapy had significantly more improvement on behavioral indicators than did clients who dropped out of therapy. These preliminary results warrant caution in interpreting the treatment efficacy of RMP.

Interpersonal

Interpersonal approaches to the conceptualization and treatment of personality disorders are relatively recent. Among these, Benjamin's (1974, 1979, 1993) Structural Analysis of Social Behavior (SASB) has received much attention. Based on interpersonal behavior classification system parameters, this nosological system presents a testable theory for understanding how personality disorders are, to a large extent, created and maintained by an individual's social learning experiences. Benjamin's SASB attempts to measure both interpersonal and intrapsychic behavior along three dimensions: the focus of the behavior (either "self" or "other"), interdependence, and affiliation. According to Benjamin, the SASB analysis holds promise in terms of improving the reliability and clinical usefulness of the DSM-IV descriptions of personality disorders, and can also be used to make predictions about the sequences of behavior during didactic interaction and for planning interventions based on these predictions (Benjamin, 1993). The SASB–Reconstructive Learning (SASB–RCL) approach stresses six phases of treatment: (1) developing a collaborative relationship between client and therapist; (2) providing insight into and understanding of the client's past and present interactive patterns; (3) strengthening the client's will to give up destructive wishes and fears; (4) grieving following the client's decision to give up prior patterns of interacting; (5) panicking following this decision to change; and (6) emerging as a new self. Benjamin's interpersonal approach is relatively recent, and as yet, no data exist as to treatment efficacy.

Cognitive

Treatment of BPD has received increasing attention from cognitive theorists. Beck's approach (Beck, Freeman, & Associates, 1990) views cognitive distortions or errors in thinking as primarily responsible for the behavioral and emotional problems of borderlines. Three assumptions are believed typical of borderline clients: "The world is dangerous and malevolent"; "I am powerless and vulnerable"; "I am inherently unacceptable." Dichotomous thinking ("all-or-nothing," "black-or-white" thinking) is seen as central to the extreme behaviors characteristic of BPD and becomes the initial focus of therapy following the establishment of a trusting and collaborative relationship. Beck's overall approach is one of "guided discovery," where therapist and client collaborate in obtaining new data. Additional emphasis is placed on the development of concrete behavioral goals, improving emotional and impulse control, and strengthening the client's sense of identity.

The cognitive-behavioral therapies of Turner (1984; Turner & Hersen, 1981), Young (1983, 1990; Young & Swift, 1988), and Pretzer (1990) attempt to address some of the difficulties experienced with traditional cognitive approaches to the treatment of borderline clients. Turner hypothesizes that maladaptive schemas are reinforced over time to produce the difficulties characteristic of BPD. His structured, multimodal treatment consists of pharmacotherapy combined with concurrent individual and psychoeducational group therapy in which specific strategies target interpersonal and anxiety-management skill deficits. Similarly, Young postulates that stable patterns of thinking (early maladaptive schemas) can develop during childhood and result in maladaptive behavior, which reinforces the schemas. His schema-focused cognitive therapy includes a variety of interventions aimed at challenging and changing these early schemas. Pretzer's approach emphasizes modifying standard cognitive therapy to address difficulties often encountered in treating borderline clients, such as establishing a collaborative relationship between therapist and client, maintaining a directed treatment, and improving homework compliance. At present, Pretzer and Young have published little about their treatments and outcome data do not exist. However, Turner has reported case study data on four clients and has recently completed a randomized controlled trial of his treatment (Turner, 1989, 1992). Results indicate promising outcomes, with gradual reductions reported in problematic cognitions and behaviors, anxiety, and depression.

Psychopharmacological

Psychopharmacological research on BPD has tended to focus on three distinct areas of behavioral patterns commonly observed in these clients: affective instability, transient psychotic phenomena, and impulsive–aggressive behavior. The effects of a variety of drugs have been studied, including neuroleptics (Cowdry & Gardner, 1988; Soloff et al., 1989), antidepressants (Cowdry & Gardner, 1988; Parsons et al., 1989; Soloff et al., 1989), minor tranquilizers (Faltus, 1984; Gardner & Cowdry, 1986), anticonvulsant medications (Cowdry & Gardner, 1988), and lithium carbonate (Links, Steiner, Boiago, & Irwin, 1990).

In general, results indicate that several agents may be useful for improving measures of global functioning, depression, schizotypal symptoms, and impulsive–aggressive behavior (for an excellent review, see Gardner & Cowdry, 1989). Nevertheless, caution is in order when considering pharmacotherapy for this particular client population. Therapists must be cognizant of the potential for contraindicated effects, problems with compliance, drug abuse, and suicide attempts. With these caveats in mind, carefully monitored pharmacotherapy may be a useful and important adjunct to psychotherapy in the treatment of BPD.

DIALECTICAL BEHAVIOR THERAPY

Dialectical behavior therapy (DBT) evolved from standard cognitive-behavioral therapy as a treatment for BPD, particularly the chronically suicidal, severely dysfunctional individual. The theoretical orientation to treatment blends behavioral and crises intervention theories with an emphasis on acceptance and tolerance drawn both from Western contemplative and Eastern meditation practice. Balancing this emphasis on acceptance with a corresponding emphasis on change is accomplished within the framework of a dialectical position. Although dialectics was first adopted as a description of this emphasis on balance, dialectics soon took on the status of guiding principles that have advanced the therapy in directions not originally anticipated. DBT is based within a consistent theoretical position. However, the actual procedures and strategies overlap considerably with those of various alternative therapy orientations, including psychodynamic, client-centered, strategic, and cognitive therapies. The philosophy and theory underlying DBT as well as the treatment protocol follow.

Dialectics

The term *dialectics* as applied to behavioral therapy refers both to a fundamental nature of reality and to a method of persuasive dialogue and relationship (for documentation of a shift toward dialectical approaches across all the sciences during the last 150 years, see Wells, cited in Kegan, 1982). As a world view or philosophical position, dialectics guides the clinician in developing theoretical hypotheses relevant to the client's problems and to the treatment. Alternately, as dialogue and relationship, dialectics refers to the treatment approach or strategies used by the therapist to effect change. Thus, central to DBT are a number of therapeutic dialectical strategies. These are described later in this chapter.

Dialectics as a World View

A dialectical world view emphasizes wholeness, interrelatedness, and process (change) as fundamental characteristics of reality. Similar to contextual and systems theories, a dialectical view argues that analysis of parts of any system are of limited value unless the analysis clearly relates the part to the whole. Although dialectics focuses on the whole, it also emphasizes the complexity of any whole. Thus, dialectics asserts that reality is nonreducible, that is, within each one thing or system, no matter how small, there is polarity. In dialectics, the polar forces are called the thesis and antithesis, the state of change that results is the synthesis of these forces. It is the transactional tension between these forces within each system, positive and negative, good and bad, children and parents, client and therapist, person and environment, and so on, that produces change. The new state, following change, however, also comprises polar forces and, thus, change is continuous and constitutes the essential nature of life. A very important dialectical idea is that all propositions contain within them their own oppositions. Or as Goldberg (1980) put it:

> I assume that truth is paradoxical, that each article of wisdom contains within it its own contradictions, that truths stand side by side. Contradictory truths do not necessarily cancel each other out or dominate each other, but stand side by side, inviting participation and experimentation. (pp. 295–296)

Dialectical Persuasion

From the point of view of dialogue and relationship, dialectics refers to change by persuasion and by making use of the oppositions inherent in the therapeutic relationship, rather than by formal impersonal logic. Through the therapeutic opposition of contradictory positions, both client and therapist can arrive at new meanings within old meanings, moving closer to the essence of the subject under consideration. The spirit of a dialectic point of view is never to accept a final truth or an undisputable fact. Thus, the question addressed by both client and therapist is: "What is being left out of our understanding?" Dialectics as persuasion is represented in the specific dialectical strategies described later in the chapter.

As demonstrated when we discuss case management strategies, dialectical dialogue is also very important in therapist consultation meetings. Perhaps more than any other factor, attention to dialectics can reduce the chances of staff splitting in treating borderline clients. Splitting among staff is often due to one or more factions within the staff deciding that they (and sometimes they alone) hold the truth about a particular client or clinical problem.

Dialectical Case Conceptualization

Dialectical assmptions influence case conceptualization in DBT in a number of ways. First, dialectics suggests that psychological disorders are best conceptualized as systemic dysfunctions. Systemic dysfunction is characterized by (1) defining disorder with respect to normal functioning, (2) assuming continuity between health and disorder, and (3) assuming that disorder results from multiple rather than single causes (Hollandsworth, 1990). Similarly, the biosocial theory of BPD presented here assumes that BPD represents a breakdown in normal functioning, and that this disorder is best conceptualized as a systemic dysfunction of the emotion regulation system. The theory proposes that the pathogenesis of BPD results from numerous factors, some constitutional predispositions that create individual differences in susceptibility to emotion dysregulation, others resulting from the individual's interaction with the environment. Assuming a systemic view has the advantage of compelling the theorist to integrate work from a variety of fields and disciplines.

A second dialectical assumption that underlies Linehan's (1987b, 1993a) biosocial theory of BPD is that the relationship between the individual and the environment is a process of reciprocal influence, the outcome at any given moment is due to the transaction between the person and the environment. Within social learning theory this is the principle of reciprocal determinism. Besides focusing on reciprocal influence, a transactional view also highlights the constant state of flux and change of the individual–environmental system. Millon (1987) has made much the same point in discussing the etiology of BPD and the futility of locating the "cause" of the disorder in any single event or time period.

Both transactional and interactive models, such as the diathesis–stress model of psychopathology, call attention to the role of dysfunctional environments in bringing about disorder in the vulnerable individual. A transactional model, however, highlights a number of points that are easy to overlook in an interactive, diathesis–stress model. For example, person A might act in a manner stressful to person B only because of the stress person B is putting on person A. Take the child who, due to an accident, requires most of the parents' free time just to meet survival needs. Or the client who, due to the need for constant suicide precautions, uses up much of the inpatient nursing resources. Both of these environments are stretched in their ability to respond well to further stress. Both may invalidate or temporarily blame the victim if any further demand on the system is made. Although the system (e.g., the family or the therapeutic milieu) may have been predisposed to respond dysfunctionally in any case, such responses may have been avoided in the absence of exposure to the stress of that particular individual. A transactional, or dialectical, account of psychopathology may allow greater compassion because it is incompatible with the assignment of blame. This is particularly relevant with a label as stigmatized among mental health professionals as borderline (for examples of the misuse of the diagnosis, see Reiser & Levenson, 1984).

A final assumption in our discussion regards the definition of behavior and the implications of defining behavior broadly. Linehan's theory (1993a), and behaviorists in general, takes behavior to mean "anything an organism does involving action and responding to stimulation" (Webster, 1983, p. 100). Conventionally, behaviorists categorize behavior as motor, cognitive–verbal, and physiological, all of which may be either public or private. There are several points to make here. First, the division of behavior into these three categories is arbitrary and made for conceptual clarity rather than in response to evidence that these response modes actually are functionally separate systems. This point is especially relevant to understanding emotion regulation, given that basic research on emotions demonstrates that these response systems are sometimes overlapping, somewhat independent, but definitely not wholly independent. A related point here is that in contrast to biological and cognitive theories of BPD, biosocial theory suggests that there is no a priori reason for favoring explanations that emphasize one mode of behavior as intrinsically more important or compelling than others. Rather, from a biosocial perspective, the crucial issue is under what conditions a given behavior–behavior relationship or response system–response system relationship does hold and under what conditions these relationships enter causal pathways for the etiology and maintenance of BPD.

BIOSOCIAL THEORY

Emotion Dysregulation

Linehan's (1987a, 1993a) theory suggests that BPD is primarily a dysfunction of the emotion regulation system. Borderline behavioral patterns are functionally related to or are unavoidable consequences of this fundamental dysregulation across several, perhaps all, emotions, including both positive and negative emotions. This emotional dysfunction is the core pathology and, thus, is neither simply symptomatic or definitional. This systemic dysregulation is a product of the combination of emotional vulnerability and difficulties modulating emotional reactions. Emotional vulnerability is conceptualized as high sensitivity to emotional stimuli, intense emotional responses, and a slow return to emotional baseline. Deficits

in emotion modulation may be due to difficulties in (1) inhibiting mood-dependent dysfunctional behaviors, (2) organizing behavior in the service of goals independent of current mood, (3) increasing or decreasing physiological arousal as needed, (4) distracting attention from emotionally evocative stimuli, and/or (5) experiencing emotion without either immediately withdrawing or producing an extreme secondary negative emotion (for a further discussion, see Gottman & Katz, 1990). While the mechanisms of the initial dysregulation remain unclear, it is likely that biological factors play a primary role. These contributions may range from genetic influences, to prenatal factors, to traumatic childhood events affecting development of the brain and nervous system.

Invalidating Environments

Most individuals with an initial temperamental vulnerability to emotion dysregulation do not develop BPD. Thus, the theory suggests further that particular developmental environments are necessary. The crucial developmental circumstance in Linehan's (Linehan, 1987a, 1987b, 1989, 1993a) theory is the invalidating environment. An invalidating environment is defined by the tendency to negate and/or respond erratically and inappropriately to private experience and, in particular, to private experiences not accompanied by easily interpreted public accompaniments (e.g., high temperature when feeling sick). Private experience, and especially emotional experiences and interpretations of events, are often taken as invalid responses to events; are punished, trivialized, dismissed, or disregarded; and/or are attributed to socially unacceptable characteristics such as overreactivity, inability to see things realistically, lack of motivation, motivation to harm or manipulate, lack of discipline, failure to adopt a positive (or, conversely, discriminating) attitude, and their verbal description is often viewed as an inaccurate description of private experience (e.g., "you are so angry but won't admit it"). These families emphasize controlling emotional expressiveness, oversimplify the ease of solving one's problems, and are intolerant of displays of negative affect. Emotional pain is attributed to lack of motivation, lack of discipline, or not trying hard enough. Individuals in an invalidating environment also tend to use punishment in their efforts to control behavior. Such a scenario exacerbates the emotional vulnerability and dysregulation of the borderline individual, whose behavioral responses reciprocally influence the invalidating environment. The high incidence of childhood sexual abuse within this population (Bryer, Nelson, Miller, & Kroll, 1987; Herman, 1986; Herman, Perry, & van der Kolk, 1989; Wagner, Linehan, & Wasson, 1989) suggests that sexual abuse may be the prototypical invalidating experience for children.

The overall result of this transactional pattern is the emotional dysregulation and behavioral patterns exhibited by the borderline adult. Such an individual has never learned how to label and regulate emotional arousal, how to tolerate emotional distress, or when to trust his/her own emotional responses as reflections of valid interpretations of events (Linehan, 1993a). In more optimal environments, public validation of one's private, internal experiences results in the development of a stable identity. In the borderline's family, however, private experiences are responded to erratically and with insensitivity. The individual thus learns to mistrust his/her internal states and instead scans the environment for cues about how to act, think, or feel. This general reliance on others results in the borderline individual's failure to develop a coherent sense of self. Emotion dysfunction also interferes with the development and maintenance of stable interpersonal relationships, which depend on both a stable sense of self and a capacity to self-regulate emotions. The invalidating family's tendency to trivialize or ignore the expression of negative emotion also shapes an expressive style later seen in the borderline adult; a style that vacillates between inhibition and suppression of emotional experience and extreme behavioral displays. Behaviors such as overdosing, cutting, and burning have important affect-regulating properties and are additionally quite effective in eliciting helping behaviors from an environment that otherwise ignores efforts to ameliorate intense emo-

tional pain. From this perspective, the dysfunctional behaviors characteristic of BPD can be viewed as maladaptive solutions to overwhelming, intensely painful negative affect.

STAGES OF THERAPY AND TREATMENT GOALS

Progress toward DBT treatment targets can be grouped in four stages, as outlined in Table 10.1. The pretreatment stage prepares the client for therapy and elicits a commitment to work toward the various treatment goals. Orientation to specific goals and treatment strategies and commitment to work toward goals addressed during this stage are likely to be important throughout all stages of treatment. Following pretreatment orientation, the first stage of therapy concentrates on attaining basic capacities and stability by focusing on suicidal behaviors, therapy-interfering behaviors, quality-of-life interfering behaviors, and behavioral skills. The second stage of therapy directly addresses post-traumatic stress syndrome and may include "uncovering" and reexperiencing prior traumatic or emotionally impor-

TABLE 10.1. The Hierarchy of Primary Therapy and Treatment Targets in DBT

Pretreatment targets (commitment):
   Orientation to treatment and agreement on goals

First-stage targets (stability, connection, and safety):
   1. Decreasing suicidal behaviors
   2. Decreasing therapy-interfering behaviors
   3. Decreasing quality-of-life-interfering behaviors
   4. Increasing behavioral skills
      A. Core mindfulness skills
      B. Interpersonal effectiveness
      C. Emotion regulation
      D. Distress tolerance
      E. Self-management

Second-stage targets (exposure and emotionally processing the past):
   5. Decreasing post-traumatic stress

Third-stage targets (synthesis):
   6. Increasing respect for self
   7. Achieving individual goals

Note. Linehan (1993a, p. 167). Copyright 1993 by the Guilford Press.

tant events. Overlapping with the previous two stages, the third and final stage of therapy targets goals of independent self-respect, generalization of behavioral skills, integration, and termination.

Pretreatment: Orienting and Commitment

Specific tasks of orientation are twofold. First, both client and therapist must arrive at a mutually informed decision to work together. Typically, Sessions 1 to 3 are presented to the client as opportunities for client and therapist to explore this possibility. Diagnostic interviewing, history taking, and formal behavioral analyses of priority targeted behaviors can be woven into initial therapy sessions or conducted separately. Second, both client and therapist must negotiate a common set of expectancies to guide the initial steps of therapy. A specific outline of what client and therapist can expect from each other is discussed and agreed to. When necessary, the therapist attempts to modify dysfunctional beliefs of the client regarding the process of therapy. Issues addressed include the rate and magnitude of change that can reasonably be expected, the goals of treatment and general treatment procedures, and various myths the client may have about the process of therapy in general. The dialectical/biosocial view of BPD is also presented.

Orientation covers several additional points. First, DBT is presented as a supportive therapy requiring a strong collaborative relationship between client and therapist. DBT is not a suicide-prevention program but a life-enhancement program in which client and therapist function as a team to create a life worth living. Second, DBT is described as a cognitive-behavioral therapy with a primary emphasis on analyzing and replacing problematic behaviors with skillful behaviors, and on changing ineffective beliefs and rigid thinking patterns. Third, the client is told that DBT is a skill-oriented therapy, with special emphasis on behavioral skills training. The commitment and orienting strategies, balanced by validation strategies, described later are the most important strategies during this phase of treatment.

Stage I: Attaining Basic Capacities

The primary focus of the first stage of therapy is on attaining a life pattern that is reasonably functional and stable. Specific targets in order of importance are to reduce suicidal behaviors, therapy-interfering behaviors, and quality-of-life interfering behaviors and to increase behavioral skills. These targets are approached hierarchically and recursively as higher-priority behaviors reappear. With severely dysfunctional and suicidal clients, significant progress on Stage I targets can usually be expected to take up to 1 year or more.

In addition to the above therapy targets, the goal of increasing dialectical behaviors is universal to all modes of treatment. Unlike other therapy targets, however, the dialectical focus is on the qualitative rather than the topographical aspects of behavior. Dialectical thinking encourages clients to see reality as complex and multifaceted, to hold contradictory thoughts simultaneously and learn to integrate them, and to be comfortable with inconsistency and contradictions. Dialectical behavior encourages clients to seek the middle path and avoid the extremes. The therapist advocates balance in behavior and openness of thought. For borderline individuals who are extreme, rigid, and dichotomous in their thinking and behavior, this is a formidable task indeed.

A dialectical emphasis applies equally to client patterns of behavior, as the client is encouraged to integrate and balance emotional and overt behavioral responses. In particular, dialectical tensions arise in the areas of skill enhancement versus self-acceptance, problem solving versus problem acceptance, and affect regulation versus affect tolerance. Behavioral extremes, whether emotional, cognitive, or overt responses, are constantly confronted while more balanced responses are taught.

Suicidal Behaviors

Keeping a client alive must, of course, be the first priority in any psychotherapy. Thus, reducing suicide crises behaviors (any behaviors that place the client at high and imminent risk for suicide or threaten to do so, including credible suicide threats, planning, preparations, obtaining lethal means, and high suicide intent) is the highest priority in DBT. The target and its priority are explicit in DBT (rather than implicit as in many other therapy manuals) simply because suicidal behavior and the risk of suicide are of paramount concern with BPD clients. Similarly, any acute, intentional self-injurious behaviors (i.e., all instances of parasuicidal behaviors) share the top priority. The priority here is due both to the risk of parasuicidal behavior (parasuicidal behavior being the single best predictor of subsequent suicide) and to the inherent conflict between ignoring self-injurious behavior and a collaborative self-help pursuit such as psychotherapy. Similarly, DBT also targets suicide ideation and client expectations about the value and long-term consequences of suicidal behavior, although these behaviors would not necessarily be targeted directly. (As in other treatments, however, keeping a client from taking the life of or seriously injuring another is an implicit first priority in DBT.)

Therapy-Interfering Behaviors

Keeping clients and therapists working together collaboratively is the second priority in DBT. Once again, this is likely an implicit second priority in most psychotherapies. However, the chronic nature of most borderline clients' problems, clients' high tendency to end therapy prematurely, and the likelihood of therapist burnout and iatrogenic behaviors when treating BPD require explicit attention with this population. Both client and therapist behaviors that threaten the relationship or therapeutic progress are addressed in a direct manner immediately, consistently, constantly, and, most important, before, rather than after, either the therapist or the client no longer wants to continue. Interfering behaviors of the client, such as those that interfere with actually receiving the therapy or with other clients benefiting from therapy (in group or milieu settings) and that burn out or cross the personal limits of the therapist, are treated within therapy sessions. Those of the therapist, including any that are iatrogenic as well as behaviors that unnecessarily cause the client distress or make progress difficult, are

dealt with within therapy sessions if brought up by the client but are also dealt with during the consultation/supervision meeting.

Quality-of-Life-Interfering Behaviors

The third target of Stage I is the reduction of behavioral patterns that seriously interfere with any chance of having a reasonable quality of life. Typical behaviors in this category include serious substance abuse, severe eating disorders, high risk and out-of-control sexual behaviors, extreme financial difficulties (uncontrollable spending or gambling, inability to handle finances), criminal behaviors that are likely to lead to incarceration, employment or school-related dysfunctional behaviors (a pattern of quitting jobs or school prematurely, getting fired or failing in school, not engaging in any productive activities), housing-related dysfunctional behaviors (living with abusive people, not finding stable housing), mental health-related patterns (going in and out of hospitals, failing to take or abusing necessary medications), and health-related problems (failing to treat serious medical disorders). The goal here is to achieve a stable life-style that meets reasonable standards for safety and adequate functioning.

Behavioral Skills

The fourth goal of Stage I is to achieve a reasonable capacity for skillful behaviors in the areas of distress tolerance, emotion regulation, interpersonal effectiveness, self-management, and the capacity to respond with awareness without being judgmental (mindfulness skills). In our outpatient program, the primary responsibility for skills training lies with the weekly DBT skills group. The individual therapist monitors the acquisition of skills and their use over time and aids the client in applying skills to specific problem situations.

Mindfulness skills are viewed as central in DBT and are thus labeled the "core" skills. These skills represent a behavioral translation of meditation (including Zen) practice and include observing, describing, spontaneous participating, a nonjudgmental stance, focused awareness (one-mindfulness), and focusing on effectiveness. Unlike standard behavioral and cognitive therapies, which ordinarily focus on changing distressing emotions and events, a major emphasis of DBT is on learning to bear pain skillfully. Representing a natural progression from mindfulness skills, distress tolerance skills represent the ability to experience and observe one's thoughts, emotions, and behaviors without evaluation and without attempting to change or control them. Emotion regulation skills target the reduction of this emotional distress through exposure to the primary emotion in a nonjudgmental atmosphere. Emotion regulation skills include affect identification and labeling, mindfulness to (i.e., experiencing nonjudgmentally) the current emotion, identifying obstacles to changing emotions, increasing positive emotional events, and behavioral expressiveness opposite to the emotion. Interpersonal skills training develops effectiveness for deciding on objectives within conflict situations and the priority of those objectives vis-à-vis maintaining a positive relationship and one's self-respect and teaches strategies that maximize the chances of obtaining those objectives without harming the relationship or sacrificing self-respect. Taught in conjunction with the other behavioral skills, self-management skills include knowledge of the fundamental principles of learning and behavioral change, the ability to set realistic goals, the ability to conduct one's own behavioral analysis, and the ability to implement contingency management plans. (For a more extensive discussion of the DBT behavioral skills, see Linehan, 1993b.)

Stage II: Post-Traumatic Stress Reduction

Stage I of DBT takes a very here-and-now approach to managing dysfunctional behavioral and emotional patterns. Although the connection between current behavior and previous traumatic events, including those from childhood, may be explored and noted, the focus of the treatment is distinctly on analyzing the relationship among current thoughts, feelings, and behaviors and accepting and changing current patterns. The second stage of therapy, in contrast, specifically targets the emotional processing of previous traumatic events via reexposure to associated cues within the therapy setting.

Thus, the primary aim of Stage II is to reduce post-traumatic stress. In the language of psychodynamic therapy, Stage I is the containment phase and Stage II is the uncovering phase. Four targets are particularly important: remembering and accepting the facts of earlier traumatic events, reducing stigmatization and self-blame commonly associated with some types of trauma, reducing the oscillating denial and intrusive response syndromes common among individuals who have suffered severe trauma, and resolving dialectical tensions regarding who to blame for the trauma.

Movement to the second stage only occurs when previous target behaviors are clearly under control. Similar to most experts in the treatment of both post-traumatic stress disorder and adult sequalae of childhood abuse, DBT does not encourage the systematic exposure to traumatic stress cues (or step-by-step "uncovering") before the client has successfully negotiated Stage I. Clients must first be able to resist urges to suicide and/or parasuicide, refrain from severely dysfunctional behaviors such as substance abuse or out-of-control sexual behavior or spending, maintain a somewhat stable life-style, including having a place to live and productive daily activities, have at least rudimentary interpersonal, emotion regulation, and distress tolerance skills, and be secure within a collaborative therapeutic relationship. That is, clients must be able to cope with the emotions associated with the therapeutic exposure to trauma-related cues.

Stage III: Respect for Self

The final stage of DBT targets the client's independent self-respect, as the client is helped to value, believe in, trust, and validate him/herself. The targets here are the abilities to evaluate one's own behavior nondefensively, trust one's own responses, and hold on to self-evaluations independent of the opinions of others. Ultimately, the therapist must pull back and persistently reinforce the client's independent attempts at self-validation, self-care, and problem solving. While the goal is not for clients to become independent of all people, it is important that they achieve sufficient self-reliance so that they can relate to and depend on others without self-invalidating.

CONTEXT OF THERAPY

Modes of Treatment: Who Does What and When

Responsibility for working on the specific target goals is spread across the various modes of treatment, with focus and attention varying depending on the mode of therapy. The individual therapist, who is the primary therapist in DBT, attends to one order of targets and the skills training therapists another, and when doing telephone therapy, yet another hierarchy takes precedence. In the consultation/supervision mode, therapists' behaviors are the targets. Therapists engaging in more than one mode of therapy (e.g., individual, group, and telephone therapy) must stay cognizant of the order of targets specific to each mode and switch smoothly from one hierarchy to another as the modes of treatment change.

Individual Therapy

DBT assumes that effective treatment must attend both to capability and behavioral skills deficits and to motivational and behavioral performance issues that interfere with use of skillful responses. Although there are many ways to effect these principles (referred to as standard DBT), in our clinic the individual therapist is responsible for the assessment and problem solving of skill deficits and motivational problems, and for organizing other modes to address problems in each area. Individual outpatient therapy sessions are usually scheduled on a once-a-week basis for 50–90 min, although biweekly sessions may be held during crisis periods or at the beginning of therapy.

The priority of specific targets within individual therapy is the same as the overall priorities of DBT discussed above. Therapeutic focus within individual therapy sessions is determined by the highest-priority treatment target relevant at the moment. This ordering does not change over the course of therapy; however, the relevance of a target does change. Relevance is determined either by the client's most recent day-to-day behavior (since the last session) or by current behavior during the therapy session; problems not currently in evidence are not considered relevant. If satisfactory progress on one target goal has been achieved, has never been a problem, or is currently not evident, the therapist shifts attention to the immediately following treatment target.

The consequence of this priority allocation is that when high-risk suicidal behaviors or parasuicide, therapy-interfering, or serious quality-of-life interfering behaviors are occurring, at least part of the session agenda must be devoted to these topics. If these behaviors are not occurring at the moment, the topics to be discussed during Stages I and III are set by the client. The therapeutic focus (within any topic area discussed) depends on the stage of treatment, the skills targeted for improvement, and any secondary targets. During Stage I, for example, any problem or topic area can be conceptualized in terms of interpersonal issues and skills needed, opportunities for emotion regulation, and/or a necessity for distress tolerance. During Stage III, regardless of the topic, the therapist focuses on helping the client achieve independent self-respect, self-validation, and self-acceptance both within the session and within his/her everyday life. (These are, of course, targets throughout the treatment, but during Stage III, the therapist pulls back further and does less work for the client than during the two preceding stages.) During Stage II, the major focus is on structured exposure to traumatic cues.

For highly dysfunctional clients, it is likely that early treatment will necessarily focus on the upper part of the hierarchy. For example, if parasuicidal behavior has occurred during the previous week, attention to it would take precedence over attention to therapy-interfering behavior. In turn, focusing on therapy-interfering behaviors would take precedence over working on quality-of-life interfering behaviors. Although it is often possible to work on more than one target (including those generated by the client) in a given session, higher-priority targets always take precedence. Determining the relevance of targeted behaviors is assisted by the use of diary cards. These cards are filled out during at least the first two stages of therapy and brought to weekly sessions. Failure to complete or bring in the card would be considered a therapy-interfering behavior. Diary cards record daily instances of parasuicidal behavior, suicidal ideation, urges to parasuicide, "misery," use of substances, licit and illicit, and use of behavioral skills. Other targeted behaviors, such as bulimic episodes, daily productive activities, flashbacks, and so on, may also be recorded on the blank area of the card. The therapist doing DBT must develop the pattern of routinely reviewing the card at the beginning of each session. If the card indicates that a parasuicidal act has occurred, it is noted and discussed. If high suicide ideation is recorded, it is assessed to determine whether the client is at risk for suicide. If a pattern of substance abuse or dependence appears, it is treated as a quality-of-life interfering behavior.

Work on targeted behaviors involves a coordinated array of treatment strategies described later in this chapter. Essentially, each session is a balance between structured as well as unstructured problem solving (including simple interpretive activities by the therapist) and unstructured validation. The amount of the therapist's time allocated to each—problem solving and validating—depends on the urgency of the behaviors needing change or problems to be solved and the urgency of the client's needs for validation, understanding, and acceptance without any intimation of change being needed.

Skills Training

The necessity of crises intervention and attention to other issues makes skills acquisition within individual psychotherapy very difficult. Thus, a separate component of treatment directly targets the acquisition of behavioral skills. In our clinic, this has taken the form of separate weekly, 2- to 2½-hr group skills training sessions which clients must attend for the 1st year of treatment. After this period, remaining in skills training is a matter of personal preference and need.

Skills training in DBT follows a psychoeducational format. In contrast to individual therapy, where the agenda is determined primarily by the problem to be solved, in skills training the agenda is set by the skill to be taught. Thus, the fundamental priority here is skills acquisition and strengthening. Although stopping client behaviors that seriously threaten life (e.g., potential suicide or homicide) or continuation of therapy (e.g., not coming or attacking others in group skills training) would still be a first priority, less severe therapy-interfering behaviors (e.g., refusing to talk in a group setting, restless pacing in the middle of sessions, and attacking the therapist and/or the therapy) are not given the attention in skills training that they are given in the individual psychotherapy mode. If such behaviors were a primary focus, there would never be time for teaching behavioral skills. Generally, therapy-interfering behaviors are put on an extinction schedule while the client is "dragged" through skills training and simultaneously soothed. In DBT, all skills training clients are required to be in concurrent psychotherapy. Throughout, the client is urged to address other problematic behaviors with the primary therapist; if a serious risk of suicide develops, the skills training therapist (if different than the primary therapist) refers the problem to the primary therapist.

Although all the strategies described below are used in both individual psychotherapy and skills training, the mix is decidedly different. Skills acquisition, strengthening, and generalization strategies are the predominant change strategies in skills training. In addition, skills training is highly structured, much more so than the psychotherapy component. Half of each session is devoted to reviewing homework practice of the skills currently being taught and the other half is devoted to presenting new skills. Except when interpersonal process issues seriously threaten progress, the agenda and topics for discussion in skills training are usually set by the therapist.

Telephone Consultation

Telephone calls between sessions (or other extratherapeutic contact when DBT is conducted in other settings, such as inpatient units) are an integral part of DBT. They have three important functions: (1) to provide coaching in skills and to promote skill generalization, (2) to provide emergency crises intervention and simultaneously to break the link between suicidal behaviors and therapist attention, and (3) to provide a context for repairing the therapeutic relationship without requiring the client to wait until the next session. With respect to calls for help, the focus of a telephone session varies depending on the complexity and severity of the problem to be solved and the amount of time the therapist is willing to spend on the telephone. In clear situations where what the client can or should do is reasonably easy to determine, the focus is on helping the client use behavioral skills (rather than dysfunctional behaviors) to address the problem. When problems are complex or too severe for the client to resolve soon, the focus is on ameliorating and tolerating distress and inhibiting dysfunctional problem-solving behaviors until the next therapy session. In the latter case, resolving the problem that is setting off the crisis is not the target of telephone sessions.

With the exception of taking necessary steps to protect the client's life when suicide is threatened, all calls for help are handled as much alike as possible. This is to break the contingency between suicidal behaviors (ideation, parasuicide, and crises behaviors) and increased telephone contact. To do this, one can do one of two things: refuse to accept any calls, including suicidal crises calls, or insist that the client who calls during suicidal crises also call during other crises and problem situations. As Linehan (1993a) notes, experts on suicidal behaviors uniformly say that therapist availability is necessary with suicidal clients. Thus, DBT chooses the latter course and encourages (and at times insists on) calls during nonsuicidal crises periods. In DBT, calling the therapist too infrequently, as well as too frequently, is considered therapy-interfering behavior.

The final priority for telephone calls to individual therapists is relationship repair. Borderline clients often experience delayed emotional reactions to interactions that have occurred during therapy sessions. From a DBT perspective, it is not reasonable to require clients to wait up to a whole week before dealing with these emotions, and it is appropriate for clients to call for a brief "heart-to-heart" talk. In these situations, the role of the therapist is to soothe and reassure. In-depth analyses should wait until the next session.

Skills therapists use telephone calls for only one reason, to keep the client in the therapy (including, of course, keeping the client alive when necessary). All other problems are handled by the primary therapist and suicidal crises are turned over to the primary therapist as soon as possible.

Consultation/Supervision Team

DBT assumes that effective treatment of BPD must pay as much attention to the therapist's behavior and experience in therapy as it does to the client's. Treating borderline clients is enormously stressful, and staying within the DBT therapeutic frame can be tremendously difficult. Thus, an integral part of the therapy is the treatment of the therapist. All therapists are required to be in a consultation or supervision relationship, either with one other person or with a group. DBT consultation meetings are held weekly and are attended by therapists currently utilizing DBT with borderline clients. The role of consultation/supervision is to hold the therapist within the therapeutic frame and to address problems that arise in the course of treatment delivery.

Setting

DBT has been adapted to a variety of settings, including outpatient community mental health settings, long-term inpatient units, day treatment, and acute hospitalization. Individual circumstances dictate adapting the treatment to the needs of both the client and the therapist as well as to the resources available. Consequently, the division of labor will change depending on the particular situation. For example, while the standard setting for skills training in our clinic has been group therapy, a private practice setting or small clinic may not have the resources or clients to organize a separate group. In such cases the individual therapist might elect to see the client twice weekly, once for individual therapy and once for skills training. Alternatives include an extended weekly session with approximately half of the period devoted to skills training or having a second therapist or behavioral technician do individual skills training with the client.

In our clinic, individual therapy has been delivered in the therapist's clinical practice office with separate group skills training conducted in a clinic classroom. Occasionally, temporary treatment requirements may necessitate a move to different settings. For example, clients undergoing surgical or other medical procedures have been seen in the hospital or in their home following hospital release. For some adolescent clients who are highly ambivalent regarding therapy, out-of-office sessions in places such as coffee shops, bowling alleys, and cars can be helpful in continuing contact through difficult phases.

Client Variables

There are a number of requisite client characteristics for DBT. Of these, voluntary participation and a commitment to a specified time period (usually 6 months to 1 year) are critical. The effective application of DBT requires a strong interpersonal relationship between therapist and client. The therapist must work to become a major reinforcer in the life of the client and then use the relationship to promote change in the client. Continuing the relationship can only be used as a positive contingency when clients want to be in treatment; contingency management is thus seriously compromised with involuntary clients. Court-ordered treatment is acceptable if clients will agree to remain in therapy even if the order is rescinded. To be accepted into treatment, clients must also agree to work on both decreasing suicidal and therapy-interfering behaviors and increasing behavioral skills. It has also been our experience that a local residence is desirable. Clients who do not live in the immediate area or who must move to the area for therapy are more likely to terminate early. A client characteristic necessary for group therapy is the ability to control hostile behavior toward others.

DBT was developed and evaluated with perhaps the most extremely disturbed portion of the borderline population: All clients accepted into treatment had a history of multiple parasuicidal behaviors. However, the treatment has been designed flexibly and is likely to be effective with less severely disturbed individuals. It should also be noted that to date, all clients in the outcome studies have been women between the ages of 18 and 45. While it is likely that the treatment may be equally applied to male clients, this application has not been submitted to rigorous empirical analysis.

Therapist Variables

In comparison to other aspects of therapy, therapist characteristics that facilitate DBT have received comparatively little attention. However, recent evidence supports the assumption that effective therapy with borderline clients requires the proficient balancing of acceptance and change strategies (Shearin & Linehan, 1992). This research also found that therapists' nonpejorative perceptions of clients were also associated with less suicidal behavior.

Linehan (1993a) describes requisite therapist characteristics in terms of three bipolar dimensions that must be balanced in the conduct of therapy. The first dimension represents the balance of an orientation of acceptance versus the orientation of change. The therapist must be able to inhibit judgmental attitudes, often under very trying circumstances, and to practice acceptance of the client, of him/herself, and the therapeutic relationship and process exactly as it is in the current moment. Nevertheless, the therapist remains cognizant that the therapeutic relationship originated in the necessity of change and assumes responsibility for directing the therapeutic influence.

Second, the therapist must balance unwavering centeredness with compassionate flexibility. Unwavering centeredness is the quality of believing in one's self, the therapy, and the client. Compassionate flexibility is the ability to take in relevant information about the client and modify one's position accordingly. Perhaps most important, flexibility represents an overall willingness to admit and repair one's inevitable therapeutic mistakes.

Finally, the DBT therapist must be able to balance a high degree of nurturing with benevolent demanding. Nurturing refers to teaching, coaching, assisting, and strengthening the client, while benevolent demanding requires the therapist to recognize existing capabilities, reinforce adaptive behavior, and refuse to "do" for the clients when they can "do" for themselves. Above all, the ability to demand requires a concomitant willingness to believe in the client's ability to change; the effective DBT therapist must see his/her client as empowered.

TREATMENT STRATEGIES

Treatment strategies in DBT refer to both the role and focus of the therapist as well as a coordinated set of procedures that function to achieve specific treatment goals. Although DBT strategies usually consist of a number of steps, use of a strategy does not necessarily require the application of every step. It is considerably more important that the therapist apply the intent of the strategy rather than inflexibly leading the client through a series of prescribed maneuvers.

DBT employes five sets of treatment strategies to achieve the previously described behavioral targets: (1) dialectical strategies, (2) core strategies, (3) stylistic strategies, (4) case management strategies, and (5) integrated strategies. DBT strategies are illustrated in Figure 10.1. Within an individual session and with a given client, certain strategies may be used more than others and not all strategies may be necessary or appropriate. An abbreviated discussion of the DBT treatment strategies follows. For greater detail, the reader is referred to the treatment manual (Linehan, 1993a).

Dialectical Strategies

Dialectical strategies permeate the entire therapy and their use provides the rationale for adding the term *dialectics* to the title of the therapy. There are three types of strategies—those that have to do with how the therapist structures interactions, those that have to do with how the therapist defines skillful behaviors, and certain specific strategies used during the conduct of treatment.

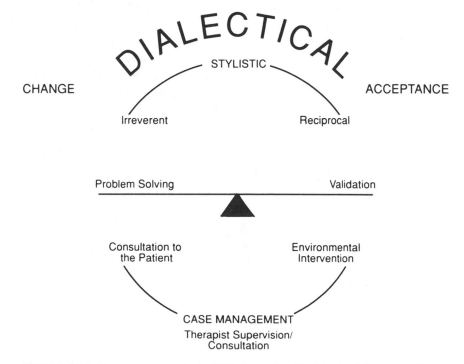

FIGURE 10.1. Treatment strategies in DBT. From *Cognitive-Behavioral Treatment of Borderline Personality Disorder* (p. 200) by M. M. Linehan, 1993, New York: Guilford Press. Copyright 1993 by The Guilford Press.

Dialectics of the Relationship: Balancing Treatment Strategies

Dialectical strategies in the most general sense of the word have to do with how the therapist balances the dialectical tensions within the therapeutic relationship. As noted above, the fundamental dialectic within any psychotherapy, including that with BPD clients, is that between acceptance of what is and efforts to change what is. A dialectical therapeutic position is one of constant attention to combining acceptance with change, flexibility with stability, nurturing with challenging, and a focus on capabilities with a focus on limitations and deficits. The goal is to bring out the opposites, both in therapy and in the client's life, and to provide conditions for syntheses. The presumption is that change may be facilitated by emphasizing acceptance, and acceptance by emphasizing change. The emphasis on opposites sometimes takes place over time (i.e., over the whole of an interaction) rather than simultaneously or in each part of an interaction. Although many, if not all, psychotherapies, including cognitive and behavioral treatment, attend to these issues of balance, placing the concept of balance at the center of the treatment assures that the therapist remains attentive to their importance.

Strategies emphasizing acceptance are very similar to (or in some cases identical to) strategies used in client-centered therapy and to case management outreach strategies emphasized in community psychiatry. Those emphasizing change are drawn primarily from cognitive and behavioral therapies, although the particular rendition in DBT overlaps considerably with both strategic and psychodynamic therapies. The categorization is artificial since in many ways every strategy comprises both acceptance and change. Indeed, the best strategies are those that combine acceptance and change in one move. The overall emphasis on balance (both within and outside of therapy) is similar to gestalt and to systems therapies.

Teaching Dialectical Behavior

Behavioral extremes and rigidity, whether cognitive, emotional, or overt, are signals that synthesis has not been achieved and, thus, can be considered nondialectical. Instead, a middle path, similar to that advocated in Buddhism, is advocated and modeled. "The important thing in following the path to Enlightenment is to avoid being caught and entangled in any extreme, that is, always to follow the Middle Way" (Kyokai, 1966). This emphasis on balance is similar to the approach advocated in relapse-prevention models proposed by Marlatt and Gordon (1985) for treating addictive behaviors. Thus, the therapist helps the client move from "either–or" to "both–and." The key here is to not invalidate the first idea or polarity when asserting the second.

Specific Dialectical Strategies

There are eight specific dialectical treatment strategies: (1) entering and using paradox, (2) using metaphor, (3) playing the devil's advocate, (4) extending, (5) activating the client's "wise mind," (6) making lemonade out of lemons (turning negatives into positives), (7) allowing natural change (and inconsistencies even within the therapeutic milieu), and (8) assessing dialectically by always asking the question, "What is being left out here?" Due to space limitations, a selection of these strategies will be addressed in the following section. For a complete review, the interested reader is referred to the DBT treatment manual (Linehan, 1993a).

Entering the Paradox

Entering the paradox is a powerful technique because it contains the element of surprise. The therapist presents the paradox without explaining it and highlights the paradoxical contradictions within the behavior, the therapeutic process, and reality in general. The essence of the strategy is the therapist's refusal to step in with rational explanation; client attempts at logic are met with silence, a question, or a story designed to shed a small amount of light on the puzzle to be solved. The client is pushed to achieve understanding, move toward synthesis of the polarities, and resolve the dilemma him/herself.

Linehan (1993a) has highlighted a number of typical paradoxes and their corresponding dialectical tensions encountered over the course of therapy. Clients are free to choose their own behavior, but they cannot stay in therapy if they do not work at changing their behavior. Clients are taught to achieve greater independence by becoming more skilled at asking for help from others. Clients have a right to kill themselves, but if they ever convince the therapist that suicide is imminent they may be locked up. Clients are not responsible for being the way they are, but they are responsible for what they become. In highlighting these paradoxical realities, both client and therapist struggle with confronting and letting go of rigid patterns of thought, emotion, and behavior so that more spontaneous and flexible patterns may emerge.

Metaphor: Parable, Myth, Analogy, and Story Telling

The use of metaphor, stories, parables, and myth is extremely important in DBT and provides an alternate means of teaching dialectical thinking. Stories are usually more interesting, are easier to remember, and encourage the search for alternative meanings of events under scrutiny. In general, the idea of the metaphor is to take something the client does understand and compare it by way of analogy to something the client does not understand. Used creatively, metaphors can aid understanding, suggest solutions to problems, and reframe the problems of both clients and the therapeutic process.

Devil's Advocate

The devil's advocate technique is quite similar to the argumentative approach used in rational–emotive and cognitive restructuring therapies as a method of addressing a client's dysfunctional beliefs or problematic rules. With this strategy, the therapist presents a propositional statement that is an extreme version of one of the client's own dysfunctional beliefs and then plays the role of devil's advocate to counter client attempts to disprove the extreme statement or rule. For example, a client may state, "Because I'm overweight, I'd be better off dead." The therapist argues in favor of the dysfunctional belief, perhaps by suggesting that since this is true for the client, it must

be true for others as well; hence, all overweight people would be better off dead. The therapist might continue along these lines with, "And since the definition of what constitutes being overweight varies so much among individuals, there must be an awful lot of people who would be considered overweight by someone. That must mean they'd all be better off dead!" And, "Gosh, I'm about 5 pounds overweight, I guess that means I'd be better off dead too." Any reservations the client proposes can be countered by further exaggeration until the self-defeating nature of the belief becomes apparent.

Devil's advocate is often used in the first several sessions to elicit a strong commitment from the client. Used in this manner, the therapist argues that since the therapy will be painful and difficult, it is not clear how making such a commitment (and, therefore, being accepted into treatment) could possibly be a good idea. This usually has the effect of moving the client to take the opposite position in favor of therapeutic change. To successfully employ this technique, it is important that the therapist's argument seem reasonable enough to invite counterargument by the client, and that the delivery be made with a straight face, in a naive but offbeat manner.

Extending

The term *extending* has been borrowed from *aikido*, a Japanese form of self-defense. In that context, extending is when the *aikido* practitioner waits for a challenger's movements to reach their natural completion and then extends his/her end point slightly further than what would naturally occur, leaving the challenger vulnerable and off balance. In DBT, extending is when the therapist takes the severity or gravity of what the client is communicating more seriously than the client intends. This strategy is the emotional equivalent of the devil's advocate strategy. It is particularly effective when the client is threatening dire consequences of an event or problem. Take the interaction with a client who threatens suicide if an extra appointment time for the next day is not scheduled. The following interchange between therapist (T) and client (C) occurs after attempts to find a mutually acceptable time have failed.

C: I've got to see you tomorrow or I'm sure I will end up killing myself. I just can't keep it together by myself any longer.

T: Hmm, I didn't realize you were so upset! We've got to do something immediately if you are so distressed that you might kill yourself. What about hospitalization? Maybe that is needed.

C: I'm *not* going to the hospital! Why won't you just give me an appointment?

T: How can we discuss such a mundane topic as session scheduling when your life is in danger! How are you planning to kill yourself?

C: You know how. Why can't you cancel someone or move an appointment around. You could put an appointment with one of your students off until another time. I *can't stand it anymore.*

T: I'm really concerned about you. Do you think I should call an aid car?

The aspect of the communication that the therapist takes seriously (suicide as a possible consequence of not getting an appointment) is not the aspect (needing an extra appointment the next day) that the client wants taken seriously. The therapist takes the consequences seriously and extends the seriousness even further. The client wants the problem taken seriously, and indeed is extending the seriousness of the problem.

Making Lemonade out of Lemons

Making lemonade out of lemons is similar to the notion in psychodynamic therapy of utilizing a client's resistances; therapeutic problems are seen as opportunities for the therapist to help the client. The strategy involves taking something that is apparently problematic and turning it into an asset; problems become opportunities to practice skills; suffering allows others to express empathy; weaknesses become one's strengths. The danger in using this strategy is that it is easily confused with the invalidating refrain, repeatedly heard by borderline clients. The therapist should avoid the tendency to oversimplify clients' problems and refrain from implying that the lemons in their life are really lemonade already.

While recognizing that the cloud is indeed black, the therapist assists the client in finding the positive characteristics of a situation and thus the silver lining.

Core Strategies

Validation and problem-solving strategies, together with dialectical strategies, make up the core of DBT and form the heart of the treatment. DBT core strategies are listed in Figure 10.2. Validation strategies are the most obvious acceptance strategies, while problem-solving strategies are the most obvious change strategies. Both validation and problem-solving strategies are used in every interaction with the client, although the relative frequency of each depends on the particular client and the current situation and vulnerabilities of that client. Many treatment impasses are due to an imbalance of one strategy over the other.

Validation

Borderline clients present themselves clinically as individuals in extreme emotional pain. They plead, and at times demand, that the therapist do something to change this state of affairs. It is very tempting to focus the energy of therapy on changing the client by modifying irrational thoughts, assumptions, or schemas, critiquing interpersonal behaviors or motives contributing to interpersonal problems, giving medication to change abnormal biology, reducing emotional overreactivity and intensity, and so on. In many respects, this focus recapitulates the invalidating environment by confirming the client's worst fears: The client is the problem, and the client indeed cannot trust his/her own reactions to events. Mistrust and invalidation of how one responds to events, however, are extremely aversive and can elicit intense fear, anger, shame, or a combination of all three. Thus, the entire focus of change-based therapy can be aversive since by necessity the focus contributes to and elicits self-invalidation.

The first two steps of validation are common to all psychotherapies, consisting of eliciting and accurately reflecting the client's feelings, thoughts, and assumptions and providing accurate feedback about the

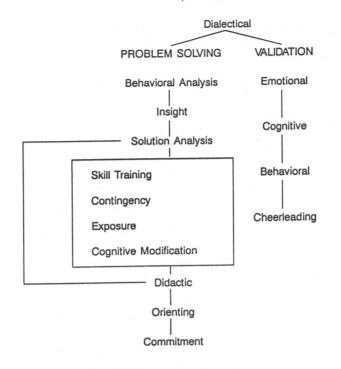

FIGURE 10.2. DBT Core Strategies.

client's patterns of behavior. "Reading the client's mind," or knowing just how the client feels or figuring out what the client did or is doing without being told directly, can be quite helpful during early stages of treatment. A considerable portion of therapy with borderline clients involves the active sorting out of complex emotional responses first to events and secondarily to the client's responses to his/her initial reactions. This somewhat unstructured "making sense" of response patterns is an essential part of validation. The third step of validation is the crucial defining feature. The therapist must look for that part of the client's response that is wise and/or valid and reflect that validity or understandability. The therapist is not blinded by the dysfunctionality of the response but finds the stimuli in the current environment that support the client's behavior. When validating, the therapist communicates in a nonambiguous way that the client's current and past behavior, thoughts, or emotions make sense and are understandable within the context in which they occur. Suggesting that current dysfunctional

responses make sense only in terms of previous events (but not in terms of current events) is not validating. Thus, validation of apparently dysfunctional behaviors, including emotional responses and perceptions/interpretations of events, may require the therapist to search for the nugget of gold buried in a sandy river bed.

Cheerleading strategies are another form of validation, and are the principal strategies for combatting the borderline client's active–passive behavior and tendencies to hopelessness. In cheerleading, the therapist communicates the belief that clients are doing their best and validates clients' ability to eventually overcome their difficulties (a type of validation that, if not handled carefully, can simultaneously invalidate clients' perceptions of their helplessness). In addition, the therapist expresses a belief in the therapy relationship, offers reassurance, and highlights any evidence of improvement. Within DBT, cheerleading is used in every therapeutic interaction. While active cheerleading by the therapist should be reduced as clients learn to trust and validate themselves, cheerleading strategies always remain an essential ingredient of a strong therapeutic alliance.

Problem Solving

We have previously discussed how therapies with a primary focus on client change are typically experienced as invalidating by the borderline client. However, therapies that focus exclusively on validation can prove equally problematic. Exhortations to accept one's current situation offer little solace to the individual who experiences life as painfully unendurable. Within DBT, problem-solving strategies are the core change strategies, designed to foster an active problem-solving style. With borderline clients, however, the application of these strategies is fraught with difficulties. The therapist must keep in mind that the process will be more difficult with borderline clients than with many other client populations. When working with borderline clients, the need for sympathetic understanding and interventions aimed at enhancing current positive mood can be extremely important. The validation strategies just described as well as the irreverent communication strategy that follows can be tremendously useful here.

Within DBT, problem solving is a two-stage process that concentrates first on understanding and accepting a selected problem and then on generating alternative solutions. The first stage employs (1) behavioral analysis, (2) insight into recurrent behavioral-context patterns, and (3) giving didactic information about principles of behaviors, norms, and so on. The second stage specifically targets change by (4) employing analyses of possible solutions to problems, (5) orienting the client to therapeutic procedures likely to bring about desired changes, and (6) selecting strategies designed to elicit and strengthen commitment to these procedures. The following sections specifically address behavioral and solution analyses.

Behavioral Analysis

Behavioral analysis is one of the most important strategies in DBT. It is also the most difficult. The purpose of a behavioral analysis is to select a problem and empirically determine what is causing it, what is preventing its resolution, and what aids are available for solving it. Behavioral analysis addresses four primary issues:

1. Are ineffective behaviors being reinforced, are effective behaviors followed by aversive outcomes, or are rewarding outcomes delayed?
2. Does the client have the requisite behavioral skills to regulate his/her emotions, respond skillfully to conflict, manage his/her own behavior?
3. Are there patterns of avoidance, or are effective behaviors inhibited by unwarranted fears or guilt?
4. Is the client unaware of the contingencies operating in his/her environment, or are effective behaviors inhibited by faulty beliefs or assumptions?

Answers to these questions will guide the therapist in the selection of appropriate treatment procedures, such as contingency management, behavioral skills training, exposure, or cognitive modification. Thus, the value of an analysis is in helping the therapist assess and understand a problem fully in order to guide effective therapeutic response.

The first step in conducting a behavioral analysis is to help the client identify the problem to be analyzed and describe it in behavioral terms. Problem definition usually evolves from a discussion of the previous week's events, often in the context of reviewing diary cards. The assumption of facts not in evidence is perhaps the most common mistake at this point. Defining the problem is followed by conducting a chain analysis—an exhaustive, blow-by-blow description of the chain of events leading up to and following the behavior.

In a chain analysis, the therapist constructs a general road map of how the client arrives at dysfunctional responses, including where the road actually starts, notated with possible alternative adaptive pathways or junctions along the way. Additional goals are to identify events that automatically elicit maladaptive behavior, behavioral deficits that are instrumental in maintaining problematic responses, and environmental and behavioral events that may be interfering with more appropriate behaviors. The overall goal is to determine the function of the behavior or, from another perspective, what problem the behavior was instrumental in solving.

Chain analysis always begins with a specific environmental event. Pinpointing such an event may be difficult, as clients are frequently unable to identify anything in the environment that set off the problematic response. Nevertheless, it is important to obtain a description of the events co-occurring with the onset of the problem. The therapist then attempts to identify both environmental and behavioral events for each subsequent link in the chain. Here, the therapist must play the part of a keen observer, thinking in terms of very small chunks of behavior. The therapist asks the client, "What happened next?" or "How did you get from there to there?" Although from the client's point of view such links may be self-evident, the therapist must be careful not to make assumptions. For example, a client who once attempted suicide reported that she decided to kill herself because her life was too painful to live any longer. From the client's point of view, this was an adequate explanation for her suicide attempt. For the therapist, however, taking one's life because life is too painful was only one solution. One could decide that life was too painful and then decide to change one's life. Or, one could believe that death might be even more painful and decide to tolerate life despite its pain. In this instance, careful questioning revealed that the client actually assumed she would be happier dead than alive. Challenging this assumption then became a key to ending her persistent suicide attempts.

It is equally important to pinpoint exactly what consequences are maintaining the problematic response. Similarly, the therapist should also search for consequences that weaken the problem behavior. As with antecedent events, the therapist probes for both environmental and behavioral consequences, obtaining detailed descriptions of emotions, somatic sensations, actions, thoughts, and assumptions. A rudimentary knowledge of the rules of learning and principles of reinforcement is crucial.

The final step in behavioral analysis is to construct and test hypotheses about events that are relevant to generating and maintaining the problem behavior. The biosocial theory of BPD suggests several factors of primary importance. For example, DBT focuses most closely on intense or aversive emotional states; the amelioration of negative affect is always suspected as among the primary motivational variables in borderline dysfunctional behavior. The theory also suggests typical behavioral patterns, such as deficits in dialectical thinking or behavioral skills, which are likely instrumental in producing and maintaining problematic responses.

Once the problem has been identified and analyzed, problem solving proceeds with an active attempt at finding and identifying alternative solutions. At times, solutions will be suggested during the conduct of the behavioral analysis and pointing to these alternative solutions may be all that is required. At other times, a more complete solution analysis will be necessary. Here, the task is to "brainstorm" or generate as many alternative solutions as possible. Solutions should then be evaluated in terms of the various outcomes expected. The final step in solution analysis is choosing a solution that will somehow be effective. Throughout the evaluation, the therapist guides the client in choosing a particular behavioral solution. Here, it is preferable that the therapist pay particular attention to long-term gain over short-term gain, and that solutions be chosen that render maximum benefit to the client rather than benefit to others.

Problem-Solving Procedures

DBT employs four problem-solving procedures taken directly from the cognitive and behavioral treatment literature. These four—skills training, contingency procedures, cognitive modification, and exposure—are viewed as primary vehicles of change since they influence the direction that client changes take. Although discussed as distinct procedures by Linehan (1993a), it is not clear that they can in fact be differentiated in every case in clinical practice. The same therapeutic sequence may be effective because it teaches the client new skills (skills training), provides a consequence that influences the probability of preceding client behaviors occurring again (contingency procedures), changes the client's dysfunctional assumptions or schematic processing of events (cognitive modification), or provides nonreinforced exposure to cues associated previously but not currently with threat (exposure procedures). In contrast to many cognitive and behavioral treatment programs in the literature, these procedures, with some exceptions noted below, are employed in an unstructured manner, interwoven throughout all therapeutic dialogue. Thus, although the therapist must be well aware of the principles governing the effectiveness of each procedure, the use of each is usually an immediate response to events unfolding in a particular session. The exceptions are in skills training, where skills training procedures predominate, and Stage II, where exposure procedures predominate.

Skills Training. An emphasis on skill building is pervasive throughout DBT. In both individual and group therapy, the therapist insists at every opportunity that the client actively engage in the acquisition and practice of behavioral skills. The term *skill* is used synonymously with *ability*, and includes in its broadest sense cognitive, emotional, and overt behavioral skills as well as their integration, which is necessary for effective performance. Skills training is called for when a solution requires skills not currently in the individual's behavioral repertoire, or when the individual has the component behaviors but cannot integrate and use them effectively. Skills training in DBT incorporates three types of procedures: (1) skill acquisition (modeling, instructing, and advising), (2) skill strengthening (encouraging *in vivo* and within-session practice, role playing, and feedback) and (3) skill generalization (telephone calls to work on applying skills, taping therapy sessions to listen to between sessions, and homework assignments).

Contingency Procedures. Every response within an interpersonal interaction is potentially a reinforcement, a punishment, or a withholding or removal of reinforcement. Contingency management requires therapists to organize their own behavior so that behaviors that represent client progress are reinforced while unskillful or maladaptive

behaviors are extinguished or lead to aversive consequences. The most important contingency with most borderline clients is the therapist's interpersonal behavior with the client. The ability of the therapist to influence the client's behavior is directly tied to the strength of the relationship between the two. Thus, contingency procedures are less useful in the very beginning stages of treatment. A first requirement for effective contingency management is that therapists attend to the client's behavior and reinforce those behaviors that represent progress toward DBT targets. Equally important is that therapists take care not to reinforce behaviors targeted for extinction. In theory this may seem obvious, but in practice it can be quite difficult. The problematic behaviors of borderline clients are often quite effective in obtaining reinforcing outcomes or in stopping painful events. Indeed, the very behaviors targeted for extinction have been intermittently reinforced by mental health professionals, family members, and friends.

Contingency management at times requires the use of aversive consequences, similar to "setting limits" in other treatment modalities. Three guidelines are important here. First, the punishment should "fit the crime," and the client should have some way of terminating its application. For example, in DBT a detailed behavioral analysis follows a parasuicidal act, an aversive procedure for most clients. Once it has been completed, however, the client's ability to pursue other topics is restored. Second, it is crucial that therapists use punishment with great care, in low doses, and very briefly, and that a positive interpersonal atmosphere be restored following any client improvement. Third, punishment should be just strong enough to work. While the ultimate punishment is termination of therapy, a preferable fallback strategy is putting clients on "vacations from therapy." This approach is considered when all other contingencies have failed, or when the situation is so serious that the therapist's therapeutic or personal limits have been crossed. When utilizing this strategy, the therapist clearly identifies what behaviors must be changed and clarifies that once the conditions have been met, the client can return. The therapist maintains intermittent contact by telephone or letter and provides a referral or backup while the client is on vacation. (In the colloquial, the therapist kicks the client out and then pines for his/her return.)

Observing limits constitutes a special case of contingency management involving the application of problem-solving strategies to client behaviors that threaten or cross a therapist's personal limits. Such behaviors interfere with the therapist's ability or willingness to conduct the therapy and thus constitute a special type of therapy-interfering behavior. Therapists must take responsibility for monitoring their own personal limits and clearly communicate to the client which behaviors are tolerable and which are not. Therapists who do not do this will eventually burn out, terminate therapy, or otherwise harm the client.

DBT favors natural over arbitrary limits. Thus, limits vary between therapists and with the same therapist over time and circumstance. Limits should also be presented as for the good of the therapist, not for the good of the client. The effect of this is that while clients may argue about what is in their own best interest, they do not have ultimate say over what is good for the therapist.

Cognitive Modification. The fundamental message given to clients in DBT is that cognitive distortions are just as likely to be caused by emotional arousal as to be the cause of the arousal in the first place. The overall message is that, for the most part, the source of the client's distress is the extremely stressful events of his/her life rather than a distortion of events that are actually benign. Although direct cognitive restructuring procedures, such as those advocated by Beck (Beck, Rush, Shaw, & Emery, 1979; Beck et al., 1990) and Ellis (1962, 1973), are used, they do not hold a dominant place in DBT. In contrast, contingency clarification strategies are used relentlessly, highlighting contingent relationships operating in the here and now. Emphasis is placed on the immediate and long-term effects of the client's behavior, both on the client and on others, clarifying the effects of certain situations on the client's own responses and examining future contingencies the client is likely to encounter. An example here is orienting the client to DBT as a whole and to treatment procedures as they are implemented.

Exposure. Therapeutic exposure procedures are used informally throughout the whole of therapy and formally during Stage II, where the client is systematically exposed to cues of previous traumatic events. In reality, exposure to emotion-eliciting cues cannot be avoided in psychotherapy. In DBT, efforts are made to provide titrated exposure to cues that elicit problematic emotions to facilitate effective emotion regulation. Four principles developed by researchers in exposure techniques (see Foa & Kozak, 1986; Foa, Steketee, & Grayson, 1985) are important. First, because context is crucial, it is important that the exposure situation mimic the problem situation. Second, exposure to situations eliciting maladaptive emotions should be arranged such that the client receives corrective information (i.e., the emotional responses to be reduced should not be reinforced further). Clients excessively afraid of disclosing information out of fear of therapeutic disapproval will not be helped by an overly critical therapist. Third, client and therapist must block emotional action or expressive tendencies and escape responses associated with the problem emotion. A collaborative effort here is necessary. A fourth and crucial step of exposure procedures is that clients be taught how to control the event. It is critical that clients have some means of titrating or ending exposure when emotions become unendurable. The therapist and client should collaborate in developing positive, adaptive ways for the client to end exposure voluntarily, preferably after some reduction in the problem emotion has occurred.

Stylistic Strategies

DBT balances two quite different styles of communication. The first, reciprocal communication, is similar to the communication style advocated in client-centered therapy. The second, irreverent communication, is quite similar to the style advocated by Whitaker (Whitaker, 1975) in his writings on strategic therapy. Reciprocal communication strategies are designed to reduce a perceived power differential by making the therapist more vulnerable to the client. In addition, they serve as a model for appropriate but equal interactions within an important interpersonal relationship. Irreverent communication is usually riskier than reciprocal communication. However, it can facilitate problem solving or produce a breakthrough after long periods when the pace of progress has been glacial. To be used effectively, irreverent communication must balance reciprocal communication, and the two must be woven into a single stylistic fabric. Without such balancing, neither strategy represents DBT.

Reciprocal Communication

Responsiveness, self-disclosure, and genuineness are the basic guidelines of reciprocal communication. Responsiveness requires the therapist to take the client's agenda and wishes seriously. It is a friendly, affectionate style reflecting warmth and engagement in the therapeutic interaction. Both self-involvement and personal self-disclosure, used in the interest of the client, are encouraged. Disclosure of immediate, personal reactions to the client and his/her behavior is frequent. For example, a therapist whose client complained about his coolness said, "When you demand warmth from me, it pushes me away and makes it harder to be warm." Similarly, when a client repeatedly failed to fill out diary cards but nevertheless pleaded with her therapist to help her, the therapist responded, "You keep asking me for help but you won't do the things I believe are necessary to help you. I feel frustrated because I want to help you but feel you won't let me." Such statements serve to both validate and challenge. They are instances of both contingency management, because the client typically experiences the therapist's statements as either reinforcing or punishing, and contingency clarification, because the client's attention is directed to the consequences of his/her interpersonal behavior. Self-disclosure of professional or personal information is used to validate and model coping and normative responses.

Irreverent Communication

Irreverent communication is used to push the client "off balance," get the client's attention, present an alternative viewpoint, or shift affective response. It is a highly useful strategy when the client is immovable or when therapist and client are "stuck." It has an "offbeat" flavor and uses logic to weave a web the client cannot unravel. Although it is responsive to the client, irreverent communication is almost never the response the client expects. The therapist highlights some unintended aspect of the client's communication, or "reframes" it in an unorthodox manner. For example, if the client says, "I am going to kill myself," the therapist might say, "I thought you agreed not to drop out of therapy." Irreverent communication has a matter-of-fact, almost deadpan style, which is in sharp contrast to the warm responsiveness of reciprocal communication. Humor, a certain naiveté, and guilelessness are also characteristics of this style. A confrontational tone can also be irreverent, communicating disbelief about responses that are not the targeted adaptive response. For example, the therapist might say, "Are you out of your mind?" or "You weren't for a minute actually believing I would think that was a good idea, were you?" The irreverent therapist also calls the client's bluff. For the client who says, "I'm quitting therapy," the therapist might respond, "Would you like a referral?" The trick here is to carefully time your bluff with the simultaneous provision of a safety net; it is important to leave the client a way out.

Case Management Strategies

When there are problems in the client's environment that interfere with the client's functioning or progress, the therapist moves to case management strategies. Although not new, case management strategies direct the application of core strategies around case management problems. There are three strategy groups, the consultant strategy, environmental intervention, and the consultation/supervision team meeting.

Consultant-to-the-Client Strategy

The consultant-to-the-client-strategy is deceptively simple in theory and extremely difficult in practice. In essence, the strategy requires the therapist to be a consultant to the client rather than to the client's network. The overriding implication is that, in general, DBT therapists do not intervene to adjust environments for the sake of the client, nor do they consult with other professionals about how to treat the client unless the client is present. According to this philosophy, the client, not the therapist, is the intermediary between the therapist and other professionals. The therapist's job is to consult with the client on how to effectively interact with his/her environment, rather than consult with the environment on how to interact effectively with the client. The consultant strategy is the preferred case management strategy and perhaps the most innovative aspect of DBT.

The consultant strategy was chosen with three objectives in mind. First, clients must learn how to manage their own life and care for themselves by interacting effectively with other individuals in the environment, including health professionals. The consultant strategy believes in clients' capacities and targets their ability to take care of themselves. Second, the consultant strategy was designed to decrease instances of "splitting" between DBT therapists and other individuals interacting with the client. Splitting occurs when different individuals in the person's network hold differing opinions on how to treat the client. By remaining in the role of a consultant to the client, the therapist stays out of such arguments. Finally, the consultant-to-the-client strategy promotes respect for clients by imparting the message that they are credible and capable of performing interventions on their own behalf.

Traditionally, health care professionals routinely exchange information helpful to the professional who is currently treating the client. Thus, routine use of the consultant strategy will ordinarily require attention to orienting professionals in one's own community to the strategy. Although consultation between professionals is actually encouraged, not discouraged, the requirement that clients be present (and, preferably, arrange the consultation) is almost always going to be different and require the expenditure of some extra time. In our experience, however, once the community is oriented, the strategy works well and actually can save time in the long run.

Environmental Intervention

As outlined above, the bias in DBT is for teaching clients how to effectively interact with their environment. The consultant strategy is thus the dominant case management strategy and is used whenever possible. There are times, however, when intervention by the therapist is needed. In general, the environmental intervention strategy is used over the consultant-to-the-client strategy when substantial harm may befall the client if the therapist does not intervene. The general rule for environmental intervention is that when clients lack abilities that they need to learn, are impossible to obtain, or are not reasonable or necessary, the therapist may intervene.

Consultation/Supervision Meeting

Consultation/supervision with therapists is integral, rather than ancillary, to DBT. The consultant-to-the-therapist treatment strategy balances the consultant-to-the-client strategy discussed above. DBT, from this perspective, is defined as a treatment system in which (1) therapists apply DBT to the clients, and (2) the consultation team and/or supervisor apply DBT to the therapists. The consultation team and/or supervisor provide a dialectical balance for therapists in their interactions with clients.

There are three primary functions of consultation to the therapist in DBT. First, the consultation team or supervisor helps to keep each individual therapist in the therapeutic relationship. The role here is to cheerlead and support the therapist. Second, the consultation team or supervisor balances the therapist in his/her interactions with the client. In providing balance, consultants may move close to the therapist, helping him/her maintain a strong position. Or consultants may move back from the therapist, requiring the therapist to move closer to the client to maintain balance. Third, within programmatic applications of DBT, the team provides the context for the treatment. At its purest, DBT is a transactional relationship between and among a community of borderline clients and a community of mental health professionals.

CASE STUDY

Background

At the time of referral, "Cindy" was a 30-year-old, white, married woman with no children living in a middle-class urban area with her husband. She has a college education and successfully completed almost 2 years of medical school. Cindy was referred to the first author by her psychiatrist of 1½ years who was unwilling to provide more than pharmacotherapy following a recent hospitalization for a near-lethal suicide attempt. In the 2 years prior to referral, Cindy had been hospitalized at least 10 times (one lasting 6 months) for psychiatric treatment of suicidal ideation, had engaged in numerous instances of parasuicidal behavior, including at least 10 instances of drinking Clorox bleach, multiple cuts and burns, and three medically severe or nearly lethal episodes, one of which was a suicide attempt. At the time of referral, Cindy met criteria for BPD, from the revised third edition of the *Diagnostic and Statistical Manual of Mental Illness* (DSM-III-R; APA, 1987) as well as from Gunderson (1984). She was also taking a variety of psychotropic drugs.

Until age 27, Cindy was able to function well in work and school settings. When Cindy was in the 2nd year of medical school, a classmate she knew only slightly committed suicide. Cindy reported that when she heard about the suicide, she immediately decided to kill herself also, but had very little insight into what about the situation actually elicited the inclination to kill herself. Within weeks she left medical school and became severely depressed and actively suicidal. Further questioning revealed a history of severe anorexia, bulimia, and alcohol and prescription medication abuse, originating at the age of 14 years. Indeed, Cindy met her husband at an Alcoholics Anonymous (AA) meeting while attending Yale. Nevertheless, until the student's suicide in medical school, Cindy had been successful at maintaining an overall appearance of relative competence.

Treatment

At the initial meeting, Cindy was accompanied by her husband, who stated that he and Cindy's family considered Cindy too lethal to be out of a hospital setting. Consequently, he and her family were seriously contemplating the viability of finding long-term inpatient care. However, Cindy stated a strong preference for outpatient treatment, although no therapist other than the first author (M.M.L.) appeared willing to take her into outpatient treatment. The therapist agreed to accept Cindy into therapy contingent on the client's stated commitment to work toward behavioral change and stay in treatment at least 1 year. (It was later pointed out repeatedly that this also meant that the client had agreed not to suicide.) Thus, the therapist began the crucial first step of establishing a strong therapeutic alliance by agreeing to accept the client despite the fact that no one else was willing to do so. The therapist pointed out, however, that acceptance into therapy did not come without a cost. In this manner, the therapist communicated acceptance of the client, exactly as she was in the current moment, while concomitantly making clear that the client's commitment toward change was the foundation of the therapeutic alliance.

At the fourth therapy session, Cindy reported that she felt she could no longer keep herself alive. When reminded of her previous commitment to stay alive for 1 year of therapy, Cindy replied that things had changed and she could not help herself. Subsequent to this session, almost every individual session for the next 6 months revolved around the topic of whether (and how) to stay alive versus committing suicide. Cindy began coming to sessions wearing mirrored sunglasses and would slump in her chair or ask to sit on the floor. Questions from the therapist were often met with a minimal comment or long silences. In response to the therapist's attempts to discuss prior parasuicidal behavior, Cindy would become angry and withdraw (slowing down the pace of therapy considerably). The client also presented with marked dissociative reactions, which often occurred during therapy sessions. During these reactions, Cindy appeared unable to concentrate on or hear much of what was being said. When queried by the therapist, Cindy described her experience as feeling "spacy" and distant. The client reported that she felt she could no longer engage in many activities, such as drive, work, or attend school. Overall, Cindy viewed herself as incompetent in all areas.

The use of diary cards, which Cindy filled

out weekly (or filled out at the beginning of the session if she forgot), assisted the therapist in carefully monitoring Cindy's daily experiencing of suicidal ideation, misery, and urges to self-harm as well as actual parasuicidal acts. Behavioral analyses that attempted to identify the sequence of events leading up to and following Cindy's parasuicidal behavior soon became an important focus of therapy. At every point the therapist presented parasuicidal behavior as to be expected given the strength of the behavior (but ultimately beatable), and pointed out repeatedly that if the client suicided therapy would be over, so they had better work really hard now while she was alive.

Over the course of several months the behavioral analyses began to identify a frequently recurring behavioral pattern that preceded parasuicide. For Cindy, the chain of events would often begin with an interpersonal encounter, often with her husband, which culminated in her feeling threatened, criticized, or unloved. These feelings would often be followed by urges either to self-mutilate or to kill herself, depending somewhat on the covarying levels of hopelessness, anger, and sadness. Decisions to self-mutilate and/or to attempt suicide were often accompanied by the thought, "I'll show you." At other times, hopelessness and a desire to end the pain permanently seemed predominant. Following the conscious decision to self-mutilate or suicide, Cindy would immediately dissociate and at some later point cut or burn herself, usually while in a state of "automatic pilot." Consequently, Cindy often had difficulty remembering specifics of the actual act. At one point, Cindy burned her leg so badly (and then injected it with dirt to convince the doctor that he should give her more attention) that reconstructive surgery was required. Behavioral analyses also revealed that dissociation during sessions usually occurred following Cindy's perception of therapist disapproval or invalidation, especially when the therapist appeared to suggest that change was possible. In-session dissociation was targeted by the therapist's immediately addressing it as it was occurring.

By several months into therapy, an apparently long-standing pattern of suicidal behaviors leading to inpatient admission was apparent. The client would report intense suicidal ideation, express doubts that she could resist the urge to kill herself, and request admission to her preferred hospital, or without warning she would cut or burn herself severely and require hospitalization for medical treatment. Attempts to induce Cindy to stay out of the hospital or to leave before she felt she was ready typically resulted in an escalation of suicidality followed by her pharmacotherapist (a psychiatrist) insisting on her admission or the hospital agreeing to extend her stay. Observation of this behavioral pattern led the therapist to hypothesize that the hospitalization itself was reinforcing suicidal behavior, and consequently she made an effort to change the contingencies for suicidal behaviors. Using didactic and contingency clarification strategies, the therapist attempted to help Cindy understand how hospitalization might be strengthening the very behavior they were working to eliminate.

This issue became a focal point of disagreement within the therapy, with the client viewing the therapist's position as unsympathetic and nonunderstanding of the client's phenomenal experience. In Cindy's opinion, the intensity of her emotional pain rendered the probability of suicide so high that hospitalization was necessary in order to guarantee her safety. Cindy would buttress her position by citing frequently her difficulties with dissociative reactions, which she reported as extremely aversive and which, in her opinion, made her unable to function much of the time. From the therapist's perspective, the deleterious long-term risk of suicide created by repeated hospitalization in response to suicidal behavior was higher than the short-term risk of suicide if hospitalization stays were reduced.

These differences in opinion led to frequent disagreements within sessions. It gradually became clear that the client viewed any explanations of her behavior as influenced by reinforcement as a direct attack, implying that if hospitalization was reinforcing suicidal behavior, the therapist must believe that she was always suicidal in order to get into the hospital. This was obviously not the case (at least some of the time), but all attempts to explain reinforcement theory in any other terms failed. The therapist compensated somewhat for insisting on the possibility that she (the therapist) was correct by doing three things. First, she repeatedly validated the client's experience of almost unendurable pain. Second, she was certain to address the client's dissociative behavior repeatedly, explaining it as an automatic reaction to intensely painful affect (or the threat of it). Third, she frequently addressed the quality of the relationship between them so as to strengthen the relationship and maintain the client in therapy even though it was a source of even more emotional pain.

By the 5th month, the therapist became concerned that the current treatment regime was going to have the unintended consequence of killing the client (via suicide). At this point, the therapist's limits for effective treatment were crossed and she therefore decided to employ the consultant strategy to address Cindy's hospitalizations. The first-choice strategy would have been to get Cindy to negotiate a new treatment plan with her preferred hospital and admitting psychiatrist. Cindy refused to go along, however, because she disagreed with the wisdom of changing her current unlimited access to the inpatient unit. The therapist was able to get her to agree to a consultation meeting with all her treatment providers and, with some tenacity, the therapist actually got Cindy to make all the calls to set up the meeting (including inviting her insurance monitor who was coordinating payment for treatment).

At the case conference the therapist presented her hypothesis that contingent hospitalization was reinforcing Cindy's suicidal behavior. She also assisted Cindy in making her case that the therapist was wrong. Using reciprocal communication and contingency management, the therapist stated that she simply could not conduct a therapy she thought might kill the client (and she had to go along with what she thought was best even if she were wrong—"to do otherwise would be unethical"). The therapist requested that a new system of contingencies designed to disrupt the functional relationship between suicidal behavior and hospitalization be agreed on. A plan was therefore developed wherein the client was not required to be suicidal in order to gain hospital admittance. Under this new set of contingencies, Cindy could elect, at will, to

enter the hospital for a stay of up to 3 days, at the end of which time she would always be discharged. If she convinced people that she was too suicidal for discharge, she would be transferred to a least preferred hospital for safety. Parasuicidal behavior would no longer be grounds for admission except to a medical unit when required. Although there was some disagreement as to the functional relationship between suicidal behavior and hospitalization, this system was agreed on.

Following this meeting, Cindy's husband announced that he was no longer able to live with or tolerate his wife's suicidal behavior, and that the constant threat of finding her dead had led to his decision to file for divorce. The focus of therapy then shifted to helping Cindy grieve this event and find a suitable living arrangement. Cindy alternated between fury that her husband would desert her in her hour of need (or illness as she put it) and despair that she could ever cope alone. She decided that "getting her feelings out" was the only useful therapy. This led to many tearful sessions, with the therapist simultaneously validating the pain, focusing on experiencing the affect in the moment without escalating or blocking it, and cheerleading the client's ability to manage without going back into the hospital. Due to Cindy's high level of dysfunctionality, both Cindy and her therapist decided that she would enter a residential treatment facility for a 3-month period. At the end of that period, it was arranged that Cindy would return to her own home with a roommate.

Over the course of treatment, a number of strategies were used to treat parasuicidal and therapy-interfering behaviors. In-depth behavioral chain and solution analysis helped the therapist (and sometimes the client) gain insight into the factors influencing current suicidal behavior. For Cindy, as is true for most clients, performing these analyses was quite difficult, as the process usually generated intense feelings of shame, guilt, or anger. Thus, behavioral analysis also functioned as an exposure strategy, encouraging the client to observe and experience painful affect. It additionally served as a cognitive strategy in helping change Cindy's expectancies concerning the advantages and disadvantages of suicidal behavior, especially as the therapist repeatedly made statements such as "How do you think you would feel if I got angry at you and then threatened suicide if you didn't change?" Finally, behavioral analysis served as contingency management in that the client's ability to pursue topics of interest in therapy sessions was made contingent upon the successful completion of chain and solution analysis.

Cindy presented early in therapy with exceedingly strong perceptions as to her needs and desires, with a concomitant willingness to engage in extremely lethal parasuicidal behavior. As previously mentioned, several of these acts were serious attempts to end her life, while others functioned as attempts to gain attention and care from significant others. This client additionally presented with an extreme sensitivity to any attempts at obvious change procedures, which typically were interpreted as communicating to the client a message of incompetence and unworthiness. Although initially committed to attending weekly group skills training for the 1st year of therapy, Cindy's attendance at group meetings was quite erratic, and she generally tended to either miss entire sessions (but never more than three in a row) or else leave during the break. Therapist attempts at addressing this issue were met by the client's stating that she could not drive at night due to night blindness. Although considered a therapy-interfering behavior and frequently addressed over the course of therapy, missing skills training was not made a major focus of treatment due to the continuing presence of higher-priority suicidal behavior. Therapist efforts to engage the client in active skills acquisition during individual therapy sessions were somewhat limited and were always preceded by obtaining a verbal commitment to problem solving. The stylistic strategy of irreverent communication was also of value to the therapeutic process. Therapist irreverence often served to "shake up" the client, resulting in a loosening of dichotomous thinking and maladaptive cognitions. The result was an increased willingness to explore new and adaptive behavioral solutions. Finally, relationship strategies were heavily employed as a tool to strengthen the therapeutic alliance and to keep it uncontingent on suicidal and/or dissociative behaviors. Included here were between-session therapist-initiated telephone calls to

see how Cindy was doing, routine giving out of telephone numbers when traveling, and sending the client postcards when the therapist was out of town.

Cindy continues in therapy. After 12 months, her parasuicidal behavior as well as urges to parasuicide have receded. In addition, her hospital stays have been reduced, with none in the last 4 months. Currently, Cindy maintains a residence at home with a roommate and has returned to school. Her therapy continues to focus on changing the contingencies of suicidal behavior, reducing both emotional pain and inhibition, and tolerating distress. In addition, therapy is now focusing on maintaining sobriety and reasonable food intake. During the first months of living in her home without her husband, Cindy had several alcoholic binges and her food intake dropped precipitously. These became immediate targets. The therapist's strong attention to these behaviors also communicated to Cindy that the therapist would take her problems seriously even if she was not suicidal. Therapy is also focused on maintaining Cindy in school and expanding her social network. As with suicidal behaviors, attention to these targets serves as a pathway to treating associated problems. As crises situations reduce in frequency, much greater attention is being paid to analyzing family patterns, including experiences of neglect and invalidation, that might have led up to Cindy's current problems. Cindy does not report a history of sexual or physical abuse. Thus, the explicit goal of Stage II (which is being cautiously entered into as an overlap to Stage I) is to understand her history and its relationship to her current problems.[1]

In other cases, especially when there has been sexual and/or physical abuse in childhood, movement to Stage II before Stage I targets have been mastered is likely to result in retrogression to previously problematic behaviors. For example, another client treated by the first author (M.M.L.), Terry, had been quite seriously abused physically by her mother throughout childhood and sexually abused by her father beginning at age 5. Previously nonviolent, the sexual advances became physically abusive at approximately age 12. Prior to this therapy, Terry had not disclosed incidents of the abuse to anyone. After successful negotiation of Stage I targets, the therapist preceded to expose Terry to trauma-related cues by simply having Terry begin to disclose details of the abuse. These exposure sessions were intertwined with work on other current problems in Terry's life. Following one exposure session focused on the sexual abuse, Terry reverted to some of her previously problematic behaviors, evidenced by withdrawal and silence in sessions, suicidal ideation, and medication noncompliance. The appearance of such behavior marked the necessity of stopping Stage II discussions of previous sexual abuse in order to recursively address Stage I targets. Three sessions were devoted to behavioral analyses of her current suicidal, therapy-interfering, and life-interfering behaviors which were eventually linked both to fears about how the therapist would view her childhood emotional responses to her father and to holiday visits with her father precipitating conflicts over how she should be feeling about him in the present. This two-steps-forward-one-step-back approach is common to therapy with borderline clients, and in particular may mark the transition between Stage I and Stage II.

As previously mentioned, Stage III targets the client's self-respect, independent of the opinions of others. Betty, also in treatment with the first author (M.M.L.), has successfully negotiated Stages I and II and now is a highly competent nurse with training and supervision responsibilities. Currently, therapy with Betty focuses on maintaining her self-esteem in the face of very powerful significant others (e.g., her supervisor) who constantly invalidate her. Components to the treatment include the therapist's noting and highlighting for the client her tendency to modify her self-opinion in accordance with that of others, persistent attempts to extract from Betty self-validation and self-soothing, and imagery exercises wherein the client imagines and verbalizes herself standing up to powerful others. Much of the therapy focus is on the interpersonal behavior of the client within the therapy session with attention to relating this behavior to her interactions with other important people. Thus, the treatment at this point is very similar to the functional analytical psychotherapy regime developed by Kohlenberg and Tsai (1991). Overall, this Stage III

therapy involves the movement to a more egalitarian relationship between the client and the therapist, where the emphasis is placed on the client's standing up for her own opinions and defending her own actions. This requires that the therapist both reinforce the client's assertions and also step back and refrain from validating and nurturing the client in the manner characteristic of Stages I and II. In addition, therapy sessions have been reduced to every other week and issues surrounding eventual termination are periodically discussed.

TRANSCRIPTS

The following (composite) transcripts represent actual examples of the process of therapy occurring over several sessions with different clients. These particular dialogues between therapist (T) and client (C) have been chosen to provide the reader with comprehensive examples of the application of a wide range of DBT treatment strategies.

The session targets in the following transcript were orienting and commitment. The strategies used were validation, problem solving (insight, orienting, and commitment), dialectical (devil's advocate), and integrated (relationship enhancement).

Obtaining the client's commitment is a crucial first step in beginning therapy with borderline clients. As illustrated here, the dialectical technique of devil's advocate can be highly effective when used as a commitment strategy. In this first therapy session, the therapist's ultimate goal was to obtain the client's commitment to therapy as well as a commitment to eliminate suicidal behavior. She began by orienting the client to the purpose of this initial session.

T: So, are you a little nervous about me?

C: Yeah, I guess I am.

T: Well, that's understandable. For the next 50 minutes or so we have this opportunity to get to know each other and see if we want to work together. So what I'd like to do is talk a little bit about the program and how you got here. So tell me, what do you want out of therapy with me and what are you doing here?

C: I want to get better.

T: Well, what's wrong with you?

C: I'm a mess. (*laughs*)

T: How so?

C: Um, I don't know, I just can't even cope with everyday life right now. And I can't even . . . I'm just a mess. I don't know how to deal with anything.

T: So, what does that mean exactly?

C: Um, well, everything I try these days just seems overwhelming. I couldn't keep up on my job and now I'm on medical leave. Plus everyone's sick of me being in the hospital so much. And I think my psychiatrist wants to send me away because of all my self-harming.

T: How often do you self-harm?

C: Maybe once or twice a month. I use my lighter or cigarettes, sometimes a razor blade.

T: Do you have scars all over?

C: (*Client nods yes.*)

T: Your psychiatrist tells me you've also drunk Clorox. Why didn't you mention that?

C: I guess it didn't enter my mind.

T: Do things just not enter your mind very often?

C: I don't really know. Maybe.

T: So maybe with you I'm going to have to be a very good guesser.

C: Hmm.

T: Unfortunately, though, I'm not the greatest guesser. So we'll have to teach you how to have things come to mind. So what is it exactly that you want out of therapy with me? To quit harming yourself, quit trying to kill yourself, or both?

C: Both. I'm sick of it.

T: And is there anything else you want help with?

C: Um, well, I don't know how to handle money and I don't know how to handle relationships. I don't have friends, they don't connect with me very often. I'm a former alcoholic and a recovering anorexic/bulimic. I still have a tendency toward that.

T: Do you think maybe some of what is going on with you is that you've replaced your alcoholic and anorexic behaviors with self-harm behaviors?

C: I don't know. I haven't thought about it that way. I just feel that I don't know how to handle myself, by all means, and you know, and I guess work through stuff, and that is obviously getting to me because if it wasn't I wouldn't be trying to kill myself.

T: So, from your perspective one problem is that you don't know how to do things. A lot of things.

C: Yeah, and a lot of it is I do know how but for some reason I don't do it anyway.

T: Um hmm.

C: You know, I mean I know I need to save money and I know that I need to budget myself and I do every single month but every single month I get in debt. But, um, you know, it's really hard for me, you know, it's like sometimes I know it, or I know I shouldn't eat something and I do it anyway.

T: So it sounds like part of the problem is you actually know how to do things, you just don't know how to get yourself to do the things you know how to do.

C: Exactly.

T: Does it seem like maybe your emotions are in control, that you are a person who does things when you're in the mood?

C: Yes. Everything's done by the mood.

T: So you're a moody person.

C: Yes. I won't clean the house for 2 months and then I'll get in the mood to clean and then I'll clean it immaculately and keep it that way for 3 weeks, I mean just immaculate, and then when I'm in the mood I go back to being a mess again.

T: So one of the tasks for you and me would be to figure out a way to get your behavior and what you do less hooked up with how you feel.

C: Right.

The therapist used insight to highlight for the client the observed interrelationship between the client's emotions and her behavior. She then begins the process of shaping a commitment through the dialectical strategy of devil's advocate.

T: That of course is going to be hell to do, don't you think? Why would you want to do that? It sounds so painful.

C: Well, I want to do it because it's so inconsistent. It's worse, you know, because when I'm, I know that, like with budgeting money, or whatever, I know I need to do it and then when I don't do it it makes me even more upset.

T: Why would you ever want to do something you're not in the mood for?

C: Because I've got to. Because I can't survive that way if I don't.

T: Sounds like a pretty easy life to me.

C: Yeah, but I can't afford to live if I just spend my money on fun and stupid frivolous things that I . . .

T: Well, I guess maybe you should have some limits and not be too off the wall, but in general, I mean, why clean the house if you're not in the mood?

C: Because it pisses me off when it's a mess. And I can't find things, like I've lost bills before and then I end up not paying them. And now I've got collection agencies on my back. I can't deal with all this, and I end up self-harming and going into the hospital. And then I just want to end it all. But it still doesn't seem to matter because if I'm not in the mood to clean it, I won't.

T: So, the fact that it makes horrible things happen in your life so far hasn't been enough of a motivation to get you to do things against your mood, right?

C: Well, obviously not (laughs), because it's not happening.

T: Doesn't that tell you though, this is going to be a big problem, don't you think? This isn't going to be something simple. It's not like you're going to walk in here and I'm going to say, "OK, magic wand," and then all of a sudden you're going to want to do things that you're not in the mood for.

C: Yeah.

T: Yeah, so it seems to me that if you're not in the mood for things, if you're kind of mood dependent, that's a very tough thing to crack. As a matter of fact, I think it's one of the hardest problems there is to deal with.

C: Yeah, great. (eyes downcast and voice low)

T: I think we could deal with it but I think it's going to be hell. The real question is whether you're willing to go through hell to get where you want to get or not. Now I figure that's the question.

C: Well, if it's going to make me happier, yeah.

T: Are you sure?

C: Yeah, I've been going through this since I was 11 years old. I'm sick of this shit. I mean, excuse my language, but I really am, and I'm backed up against the wall. Either I need to do this or I need to die. Those are my two choices.

T: Well, why not die?

C: Well, if it comes down to it I will.

T: Um hmm, but why not now?

C: Because, this is my last hope. Because if I've got one last hope left, why not take it?

T: So, in other words, all things being equal, you'd rather live than die, if you can pull this off.

C: If I can pull it off, yeah.

T: OK, that's good, that's going to be your strength. We're going to play to that. You're going to have to remember that when it gets tough. But now I want to tell you about this program and how I feel about you harming yourself and then we'll see if you still want to do this.

As illustrated by the foregoing segment, the therapist's relentless use of devil's advocate successfully achieved "the foot in the door" and an initial client commitment. The therapist then "ups the ante" with a brief explanation of the program and its goals.

T: Now, the most important thing to understand is that we are not a suicide-prevention program, that's not our job. But we are a life-enhancement program. The way we look at it, living a miserable life is no achievement. If we decide to work together I'm going to help you try to improve your life so that it's so good that you don't want to die or hurt yourself. You should also know that I look at suicidal behavior, including drinking Clorox, as problem-solving behavior. I think of alcoholism the same way. The only difference is that cutting, burning, unfortunately, it works. If it didn't work, nobody would do it more than once. But it only works in the short term, not the long term. So quitting cutting, trying to hurt yourself, is going to be exactly like quitting alcohol. Do you think this is going to be hard?

C: Stopping drinking wasn't all that hard.

T: Well, in my experience, giving up self-harm behavior is usually very hard. It will require both of us working, but you will have to work harder. And like I told you when we talked briefly, if you commit to this it's for 1 year. Individual therapy with me once a week, and group skills training once a week. So, the question is, are you willing to commit for 1 year?

C: I said I'm sick of this stuff. That's why I'm here.

T: So you've agreed to not drop out of therapy for a year, right?

C: Right.

T: And you do realize that if you don't drop out for a year, that really does, if you think about it, rule out suicide for a year?

C: Logically, yeah.

T: So, we need to be absolutely clear about this, because this therapy won't work if you knock yourself off. The most fundamental mood-related goal we have to work on is that, no matter what your mood is, you won't kill yourself, or try to.

C: Alright.

T: So that's what I see as our number one priority, not our only one but our number one, that we will work on that. And getting you to agree, meaningfully of course, and actually following through on staying alive and not harming yourself and not attempting suicide no mat-

ter what your mood is. Now the question is, whether you agree to that.

C: Yes, I agree to that.

The therapist successfully obtained the client's commitment to work on suicidal behavior. To reinforce the strength of the commitment, she again employs the strategy of devil's advocate.

T: Why would you agree to that?

C: I don't know. (*laughs*)

T: I mean, wouldn't you rather be in a therapy where if you wanted to kill yourself, you could?

C: I don't know. I mean, I never really thought about it that way.

T: Hmm.

C: I don't want to . . . I want to be able to get to the point where I could feel like I'm not being forced into living.

T: So are you agreeing with me because you're feeling forced into agreeing?

C: You keep asking me all these questions.

T: What do you think?

C: I don't know what I think right now, honestly.

A necessary and important skill for the therapist conducting DBT is the ability to sense when the client has been pushed to her limits, as well as the concomitant skill of being willing and able to step back and at least temporarily refrain from further pressuring. In these instances, continued pressure from the therapist is likely to boomerang and have the opposite effect of what the therapist intends. Here, the client's confusion was noticed by the therapist, who sensed that further pushing was likely to result in the client's falling back on the strength of her commitment. Consequently, the therapist steps back and moves in with validation.

T: So you're feeling pushed up against the wall a little bit, by me?

C: No, not really. (*client starts to cry*)

T: What just happened just now?

C: (*Pause*) I don't know. I mean, I don't think I really want to kill myself. I think

I just feel like I have to. I don't think it's really even a mood thing. I just think it's when I feel like there's no other choice. I just say, "Well, you know there's no other choice, so do it." You know. And so, right now I don't see any ray of hope. I'm going to therapy, which I guess is good. I mean I know it's good, but I don't see anything any better than it was the day I tried to kill myself.

T: Well, that's probably true. Maybe it isn't any better. I mean, trying to kill yourself doesn't usually solve problems. Although, it actually did do one thing for you.

C: It got me in therapy.

T: Yeah. So my asking you all these questions makes you start to cry. You look like you must be feeling pretty bad.

C: Just overwhelmed, I guess the word is.

T: That's part of the reason we're having this conversation, to try to structure our relationship so that it's very clear for both of us. And that way, at least, we'll try to cut down on how much you get overwhelmed by not knowing what's going on with me. OK?

C: Um hmm.

T: And so, I just want to be clear on what our number one goal is, and how hard this is because if you want to back out, now's the time. Because I'm going to take you seriously if you say, "Yes, I want to do it."

C: I don't want to back out.

T: OK. Good. Now, I just want to say that this seems like a good idea right now. You're in kind of an energized mood today, getting started, a new program. But in 5 hours, it might not seem like such a good idea. It's kind of like it's easy to commit to a diet after a big meal, but much harder when you're hungry. But we're going to work on how to make it keep sounding like a good idea. It'll be hell, but I have confidence, I think we can be successful working together.

Note how the therapist ended the session by preparing the client for the difficulties she is likely to experience in keeping her commitment and working in therapy. Cheerleading and relationship enhancement laid the foundation for a strong therapeutic alliance.

The following session occurred approximately 4 months into therapy. The session target was suicidal behavior. The strategies used were validation, problem solving (contingency clarification, didactic, behavioral and solution analysis), stylistic (irreverent communication), dialectical (metaphor, making lemonade out of lemons), and skills training (distress tolerance). The therapist reviewed the client's diary card and noted a recent parasuicide in which the client opened up a previously self-inflicted wound following her physician's refusal to provide pain medication. The therapist began by proceeding with a behavioral analysis.

T: OK. Now. You were in here last week telling me you were never going to hurt yourself again because this was so ridiculous, you couldn't stand it, you couldn't hurt yourself any more. So let's figure out how that broke down on Sunday so we can learn something from it. OK. So when did you start having urges to hurt yourself?

C: My foot began to hurt on Wednesday. I started to have a lot of pain.

T: It hadn't hurt before that?

C: No.

T: So the nerves were dead before that or something, huh? So you started having a lot of pain. Now, when did you start having the pain and when did the urge to harm yourself come?

C: At the same time.

T: They just came at the identical moment?

C: Just about.

The specification of an initial prompting environmental event is always the first step in conducting a behavioral chain analysis. Here, the therapist begins by directly inquiring when the urges to parasuicide began. Note also the therapist's use of irreverent communication early in the session.

T: So how is it that feeling pain sets off an urge to parasuicide? Do you know how that goes? How you get from one to the other?

C: I don't know, maybe it wasn't till Thursday but I asked my nurse. I go, look, I'm in a lot of pain you know. I'm throwing up my food because the pain is so bad. And the nurse tried. She called the doctor and told him I was in a lot of pain, and asked if he'd give me some pain killers. But no! So I kept asking, and the answer kept being no, and I got madder and madder and madder. So I felt like I had to show somebody that it hurts because they didn't believe me.

T: So let's figure this out. So is it that you're assuming that if someone believed it hurt as bad as you said it does, they would actually give you the pain killers?

C: Yes.

T: OK. That's where the faulty thinking is. That's the problem. You see, it's entirely possible that people know how bad the pain is, but still aren't giving you medication.

C: I believe firmly, and I even wrote it in my journal, that if I'd gotten pain medication when I really needed it I wouldn't have even thought of self-harming.

The therapist proceeded by beginning to obtain a description of the events co-occurring with the onset of the problem. Here, it became apparent that maladaptive thinking was instrumental in the client's decision to self-harm. In the following segment the therapist uses the dialectical strategy of metaphor to highlight for the client her cognitive error.

T: Now. Let me ask you something. You've got to imagine this, OK? Let's imagine that you and I are on a raft together out in the middle of the ocean. Our boat has sunk and we're on the raft. And when the boat sunk your leg got cut really badly. And together we've wrapped it up as well as we can. But we don't have any pain medicine. And we're on this raft together and your leg really hurts and you ask me for pain medicine and I say no. Do you think you would then have

an urge to hurt yourself and make it worse?

C: No, it would be a different situation.

T: OK, but if I did have the pain medication and I said no because we have to save it, what do you think?

C: If that were logical to me I'd go along with it and wouldn't want to hurt myself.

T: What if I said no, because I didn't want you to be a drug addict?

C: I'd want to hurt myself.

T: OK. So we've got this clear. The pain is not what's setting off the desire to self-harm. It's someone not giving you something to help, when you feel they could if they wanted to.

C: Yes.

The therapist used contingency clarification to point out to the client the effects of other's responses on the client's own behavior. In the following segment, the therapist again employs contingency clarification in a continued effort to highlight for the client the communication function of parasuicide.

T: OK, so in other words, hurting yourself is communication behavior, OK? So what we have to do is figure out a way for the communication behavior to quit working.

C: Why?

T: Because you're not going to stop doing it until it quits working. It's like trying to talk to someone; if there's no one in the room you eventually quit trying to talk to them. It's like when a phone goes dead, you quit talking.

C: I tried three nights in a row in a perfectly assertive way and just clearly stated I was in a lot of pain.

T: You know, I think I'll switch chairs with you. You're not hearing what I'm saying.

C: And they kept saying, "No," and then some little light came on in my head.

T: I'm considering switching chairs with you.

C: And it was like, "Here, now can you tell that it hurts a lot?"

T: I'm thinking of switching chairs with you.

C: Why?

T: Because if you were sitting over here I think you would see that no matter how bad the pain is, hurting yourself to get pain medication is not an appropriate response. The hospital staff may not have been appropriate either. It may be that they should have given you pain medicine. But we don't have to say they were right in order to say that hurting yourself was not the appropriate response.

C: No, I don't think it was the appropriate response.

T: Good. So what we've got to do is figure out a way to get it so that the response doesn't come in, even if you don't get pain medicine. So far it has worked very effectively as communication. And the only way to stop it is to get it to not work any more. And of course it would be good to get other things to work. What you're arguing is "Well, OK, if I'm not going to get it this way then I should be able to get it another way."

C: I tried this time!

T: Yes, I know you did, I know you did.

C: A lady down the hallway from me was getting treatment for her diabetes and it got real bad and they gave her pain medication.

T: Now, we're not on the same wavelength in this conversation.

C: Yes we are. What wavelength are you on?

T: I'm on the wavelength that it may have been reasonable for you to get pain medicine, and I certainly understand your wanting it. But I'm also saying that no matter what's going on, hurting yourself is something we don't want to happen. You're functioning like if I agreed with you that you should get pain medication I would think this was OK.

C: Hmm?

T: You're talking about whether they should have given you pain medication or not. I'm not talking about that. Even if they should have, we've got to figure out how you could have gotten through without hurting yourself.

As illustrated by the foregoing exchange, borderline clients often want to remain focused on the crisis at hand. This poses a formidable challenge for the therapist, who must necessarily engage in a back-and-forth dance between validating the client's pain and pushing for behavioral change. This segment also illustrates how validation does not necessarily imply agreement. Although the therapist validated the client's perception that the refusal to provide pain medication may have been unreasonable, she remained steadfast in maintaining the inappropriateness of the client's response.

C: I tried some of those distress tolerance things and they didn't work.

T: OK. Don't worry, we'll figure out a way. I want to know everything you tried. But first I want to be sure I have the picture clear. Did the urges start building after Wednesday and get worse over time?

C: Yeah. They started growing with the pain.

T: With the pain. OK. But also they started growing with their continued refusal to give you pain medicine. So you were thinking that if you hurt yourself they would somehow give you pain medicine?

C: Yeah. Cause if they wouldn't listen to me then I could show them.

T: OK, so you were thinking, "If they won't listen to me I'll show them." And when did that idea first hit? Was that on Wednesday?

C: Yeah.

T: OK. Well, we've got to figure out a way to tolerate bad things without harming yourself. So let's figure out all the things you tried, and then we have to figure out some other things because those didn't work. So what was the first thing you tried?

At this juncture the behavioral analysis remains incomplete, and it would normally be premature to move to the stage of solution analysis. However, in the therapist's judgment it was more critical at this point to reinforce the client's attempts at distress tolerance by responding to the client's communication that she attempted behavioral skills.

C: I thought that if I just continued to be assertive about it that the appropriate measures would be taken.

T: OK, but that didn't work. So why didn't you harm yourself right then?

C: I didn't want to.

T: Why didn't you want to?

C: I didn't want to make it worse.

T: So you were thinking about pros and cons, that if I make it worse I'll feel worse?

C: Yeah.

One aspect of DBT behavioral skills training stresses the usefulness of evaluating the pros and cons of tolerating distress as a crisis survival strategy. Here, the therapist employed the dialectical strategy of making lemonade out of lemons by highlighting for the client how she did, in fact, use behavioral skills. Note in the following response how the therapist immediately reinforced the client's efforts with praise.

T: That's good thinking. That's when you're thinking about the advantages and disadvantages of doing it. OK, so at that point the advantages of making it worse were outweighed by the disadvantages. OK. So you keep up the good fight here. Now what else did you try?

C: I tried talking about it with other patients.

T: And what did they have to say?

C: They said I should get pain medication.

T: Right. But did they say you should cut yourself or hurt yourself if you didn't get it?

C: No. And I tried to get my mind off my pain by playing music and using mindfulness. I tried to read and do crossword puzzles.

T: Um hmm. Did you ever try radical acceptance?

C: What's that?

T: It's where you sort of let go and accept the fact that you're not going to get the pain medication. And you just give yourself up to that situation. You just accept that it ain't going to happen, that you're going to have to cope in some other way.

C: Which I did yesterday. I needed a little Ativan [lorazepam] to get me there but I got there.

T: Yesterday?

C: Yeah. I took a nap. When I woke up I basically said, "Hey, they're not going to change, so you've just got to deal with this the best that you can."

T: And did that acceptance help some?

C: I'm still quite angry about what I believe is discrimination against borderline personalities. I'm still very angry about that.

T: OK. That's fine. Did it help though, to accept?

C: Um hmm.

T: That's good. That's great. That's a great skill, a great thing to practice. When push comes to shove, when you're really at the limit, when it's the worst it can be, radical acceptance is the skill to practice.

C: That's AA.

During a solution analysis it is often necessary that therapists facilitate the process by helping the client "brainstorm" or by making direct suggestions for handling future crises. Here, the therapist suggested a solution that is also taught in the DBT skills training module on distress tolerance. The notion of radical acceptance stresses the idea that acceptance of one's pain is a necessary prerequisite for ending emotional suffering.

T: OK. Now let's go back to how did you give in to the urge. Because you really managed to battle all the way till then, right? OK. Usually with you we can assume that something else happened. So let's figure out Sunday and see if there wasn't an interpersonal situation on that day that made you feel criticized, unloved or unacceptable.

C: Well on Saturday I was so pissed off and I went to an AA meeting. And it got on my brain how alcohol would steal away my pain. I went looking all around the neighborhood for an open store. I was going to go get drunk. That's how much my pain was influencing me. But I couldn't find a store that was open so I went back to the hospital.

T: So you got the idea of getting alcohol to cure it, and you couldn't find any so you went back to the hospital, you were in a lot of pain, and then what happened?

C: I told the nurse I've been sober almost 10 years and this is the first urge I've had to drink, that's how bad my pain is. And that wasn't listened to.

T: So you figured that should have done it?

C: Yeah.

T: Yeah. Cause that's a high-level communication, that's like a suicide threat. Very good though. I want you to know, that's better than a suicide threat because that means you had moved your threats down.

The above response was very irreverent in that most clients would not expect their therapist to view making a threat as a sign of therapeutic progress. The therapeutic utility of irreverence is often in its "shock" value, which may temporarily loosen a client's maladaptive beliefs and assumptions and open clients up to the possibility of other response solutions.

C: And I just told her how I was feeling about it, and I thought that would do it. And the doctor still wouldn't budge.

T: So what did she do? Did she say she would call?

C: She called.

T: OK. And then what happened?

C: She came back, she was really sweet and she just said, "I'm really sorry but the doctor said no."

T: Then did you feel anger?

C: I don't know if I was really angry but I was hurt.

T: Oh really? Oh, that's pretty interesting. OK. So you were hurt . . .

C: Because I ended up hugging my teddy bear and just crying for a while.

T: Before or after you decided to hurt yourself?

C: Before.

T: OK. So you didn't decide right away to hurt yourself. You were thinking about it. But when did you decide to do it?

C: Later on Saturday.

T: When?

C: After I got sick of crying.

T: So you layed in bed and cried, feeling uncared about and hurt, abandoned probably, and unlovable, like you weren't worth helping?

C: Yes.

T: That's a really adaptive response. That's what I'm going to try to teach you. Except that you've already done it without my teaching it to you. So how did you get from crying, feeling unloved and not cared about and you cry and sob, how did you get from there to deciding to hurt yourself, instead of like going to sleep . . .

C: Because then I got angry. And I said, "Fuck this shit, I'll show him."

T: Now did you quit crying before you got angry, or did getting angry make you stop crying?

C: I think getting angry made me stop crying.

T: So you kind of got more energized. So you must have been ruminating while you were lying there, thinking. What were you thinking about?

C: For a long time I was just wanting somebody to come care about me.

T: Um hmm. Perfectly reasonable feelings. Makes complete sense. Now maybe there you could have done something different. What would have happened if you had asked the nurse to come in and talk to you, hold your hand?

An overall goal of behavioral analysis is the construction of a general road map of how the client arrives at dysfunctional responses, notated with possible alternative pathways. Here, the therapist was searching for junctures in the map where possible alternative responses were available to the client.

C: They don't have time to do that.

T: They don't? Do you think that would have helped?

C: I don't know. She couldn't help me.

T: She could have made you feel cared

about. That would have been a caring thing to do.

C: Yeah, but I don't think it would have helped.

T: What would have helped?

C: Getting pain medication.

T: I thought you'd say that. You have a one-track mind. Now listen, we've got to figure out something else to help you because it can't be that nothing else can help. That can't be the way the world works for you. There's got to be more than one way to get everywhere, because we all run into boulders on the path. Life is like walking on a path, you know, and we all run into boulders. It's got to be that there are other paths to places. And for you, it really isn't the pain in your ankle that's the problem, it's the feeling of not being cared about. And probably, a feeling that has something to do with anger, or a feeling that other people don't respect you, a feeling of being invalidated.

C: Yes.

T: So I think it's not actually the pain in your ankle that's the problem. Because if you were out on that raft with me you would have been able to handle the pain if I hadn't had any medicine, right? So it's really not the pain, it's the sense of being invalidated and the sense of not being cared about. That's my guess. Do you think that's correct?

C: Yes.

T: See, the question is, is there any other way for you to feel validated and cared about other than them giving it to you?

C: No.

T: Now is this a definite, like, "I'm not going to let there be any other way," or is it more open like, "I can't think of another way but I'm open to the possibility?"

C: I don't think there's another way.

T: Does that mean you're not even open to learning another way?

C: Like what?

T: I don't know. We have to figure it out. See what I think's happening is that when you're in a lot of pain and you feel either not cared about or not taken seriously, invalidated, that's what sets you up to hurt yourself, and also want to die. The problem that we have to solve is how to be in a situation that you feel is unjust without having to harm yourself to solve it. Are you open to that?

C: Yeah.

As illustrated above, behavioral analysis is often an excruciating and laborious process for client and therapist alike. Therapists often feel demoralized and tempted to abandon the effort. With repeated analyses, however, clients learn that their therapist will not "back down." Such persistence on the part of the therapist will eventually extinguish a client's refusal to attempt new and adaptive problem-solving behaviors. As clients increasingly acquire new behavioral skills, more adaptive attempts at problem resolution eventually become discernible.

In the following session (approximately 10 months into therapy) the client arrived wearing mirrored sunglasses (again) and was angry because collection agencies were persistent in pressuring her for payment on delinquent accounts. In addition, her therapist had been out of town for a week. The session targets were emotion regulation and interpersonal effectiveness. The strategies used were dialectical (metaphor), validation (cheerleading), problem solving (contingency clarification, contingency management), stylistic (reciprocal communication, irreverent communication), and integrated (relationship enhancement). In this first segment the therapist used cheerleading, contingency clarification, and the contingency management strategy of shaping to get the client to remove her sunglasses and to work on expressing her anger.

T: It's not a catastrophe that the collector did this to you and it's not a catastrophe to be mad at the collector. It's made your life a lot harder but you can handle this, you can cope with this, this is not more than you can cope with. You're a really strong woman, you've got it inside you. But you've got to do it, you've got to use it. I'm willing to help you but I can't do it alone, you have to work with me.

C: How?

T: Well, by taking off your sunglasses, for starters.

The therapist began the exchange by attempting to normalize the issue ("It's not a catastrophe . . ."), validating the client ("It's made your life a lot harder . . ."), and cheerleading ("you can handle this, you can cope . . . you're a really strong woman . . . "). The therapist then moved to contingency clarification by pointing out that provision of the therapist's assistance is contingent on the client's willingness to work. The therapist immediately followed this by requesting a response well within the client's behavioral repertoire.

C: I knew you'd say that.

T: And I knew you knew I'd say that.

C: Sunglasses are your biggest bitch, I think.

T: Well, how would you like to look at yourself talking to someone else? (*long pause*) They make it difficult for me. And I figure they make it harder for you, I think you do better when you're not wearing those sunglasses. It's like a step, you always do better when you go forward. And when you do, you feel better. I've noticed that. (*long pause*) So that's what you should do, you should take off your sunglasses and then we should problem solve on how to cope when you can't get angry. There's nothing freakish about that. Something has happened in your life that has made it so that you're afraid to be angry and we just have to deal with that, you and me. It's just a problem to be solved, it's not a catastrophe, it's not the worst thing any one ever did. It's just a problem that you have and that's what you and I do, we solve problems, we're a problem-solving team. (*pause*)

C: (*Removes sunglasses*) Alright.

T: Thank you. That's a big step, I know, for you.

The therapist's use of reciprocal communication informed the client of her feelings regarding the sunglasses. Note the matter-of-fact attitude taken by the therapist and the therapist's continued attempt to normalize the issue (i.e., "There's nothing freakish about that . . . it's not the worst thing any one ever did"). Also note the framing of the issue as a problem to be solved as well as the therapist's use of the relationship strategy to enhance the therapeutic alliance. The therapist also made a point of validating the client by letting her know that she realized this was difficult.

T: Now c'mon, I want you to find it inside yourself, I know you've got it, I know you can do it. You can't give up, you can't let your feet slip. Keep going, just express directly to me how you feel. That you're angry at yourself, that you're angry at the collection agency and that you're damn angry with me. (*long pause*)

C: (*Barely audible*) I'm angry at you, at myself, and the collection agency.

The therapist still relied on cheerleading and praise as she continued the shaping process in an attempt to bring the client to directly express her anger.

T: Good, that kill you? (*long pause*) That's great. Is that hard? (*long pause*) It was, wasn't it? Now, say it with a little vigor. Can't you say it with a little energy?

C: (*Shakes her head, no*)

T: Yes, you can. I know you've got it in you. I have a good feel for what your strengths are. I don't know how I've got this good feel, but I do. And I know you can do it and you need to do it, and you need to say it with some energy. Express how angry you are, you don't have to yell and scream or throw things. Just say it aloud—"I'm angry!" (*long pause*) You can scream of course if you want, you can say, "I'm angry! . . ."

C: That's it. That's all I can do.

T: Listen, you have to take the risk. You're not going to get past this or through this. You have to take the risk. You are like a person mountain climbing and we've come to this crevasse and it's very deep, but we can't go back because there's an avalanche and the only way to go forward is for you to jump over this crevasse. You've got to do it. Tell me how mad you are, in a way that I can understand how you really feel.

C: (*Long pause*) I can't do any of it.

T: That is bullshit.

C: You want me to get angry at you, don't you?

T: I don't care who you get angry at. I think you already are angry. I just want you to express it. I'm not going to ask you to do anything more today, by the way. I figure the only thing today you have to do is say "I'm angry," in a voice that sounds angry and I figure you're capable of that. And I might be angry if you don't do it, I don't think I will be, but I might. That's okay, I can be angry, you can be angry, we can be angry sometimes and it isn't going to kill either one of us.

Cheerleading and metaphor were unsuccessful in moving the client to express her anger more forcefully. Consequently, the therapist switched to irreverent communication in an attempt to get the client to "jump track." Also note how the therapist communicated to the client the potential negative consequences of her continued refusal to express her anger (i.e., "I might be angry . . ."). In this manner, the therapist used the relationship as a contingency in order to promote change in the client.

T: OK, so how angry are you? On a scale of 1 to 100, how angry would you say you are, 100 is you're ready to kill, you're so enraged, you'd go to war if you could.

C: (*Barely audible*) Maybe 100.

T: Really?

C: They know my situation.

T: Um hmm.

C: They're persistent.

T: Um hmm. (*pause*) Who's the safest to be angry at? Yourself, me, or the collection agency?

C: Collection agency.

T: OK, then, tell me how angry you are. You don't have to make it sound like a 100, try to make it sound like a 50.

C: They really pissed me off! (*uses a loud, angry voice*)

T: Well, damn right. Piss me off too. (*slams the table with her fist*)

As illustrated by the foregoing exchange, a primary difficulty in working with borderline clients is their not-uncommon tendency to refuse to engage in behavioral work. Thus, it is absolutely necessary that therapists maintain persistence and not give up in the face of their clients' "I can't" statements. In situations like these, the use of irreverent communication often succeeds in producing a breakthrough and gaining client compliance.

RESEARCH DATA

Although it is commonly assumed, even by biologically oriented therapists, that psychosocial intervention of some sort is necessary to treat BPD, to date almost no outcome studies have been conducted testing the effectiveness of psychotherapy for this population. Other than the studies on DBT, the exceptions are the as-yet-unpublished treatment trials conducted by Turner (1992) indicating efficacy of his blended dynamic-cognitive-behavioral therapy and the emerging studies of Marziali and Munroe-Blum (Munroe-Blum & Marziali, 1989; Clarkin, Marziali, & Munroe-Blum, 1991) indicating superior treatment retention for their psychodynamic group therapy versus individual treatment as usual in the community.

Linehan, Armstrong, Suarez, Allmon, and Heard (1991) have recently reported results of a randomized clinical trial of DBT, compared with treatment as usual, for 44 severely dysfunctional, parasuicidal women meeting DSM-III-R and Gunderson's (1984) criteria for BPD. The treatment lasted 1 year, with assessment every 4 months. At most assessment points and over the entire year, DBT subjects had fewer incidences of parasuicide and less medically severe parasuicides, had a much lower attrition rate (16.7%), and had fewer inpatient psychiatric days, compared to subjects assigned to treatment as usual. The study was conducted in two waves with approximately equal numbers of subjects in each. Analyses of the second wave (Linehan, Tutek, & Heard, 1992), where a number of additional outcome measures were added to the assessment battery, indicated that subjects assigned to DBT, as compared to those assigned to treatment as usual, also reported significantly less anger, greater social adjustment, better work performance, and less anxious rumination, and were rated by the interviewer as more socially adjusted and as less severely disturbed on the Global Assessment Scale (Endicott, Spitzer, Fleiss, & Cohen, 1976). The superiority of DBT compared to treatment as usual was generally maintained at the 6-month and 12-month follow-ups (Linehan, Heard, & Armstrong, 1992). Overall, the results suggest DBT to be an effective and promising treatment for chronically parasuicidal borderline clients, particularly in terms of reducing parasuicidal behavior and maintaining clients in treatment.

ACKNOWLEDGMENT

Writing of this chapter was supported by a National Institute of Mental Health, Bethesda, Maryland, Grant MH34486 given to the first author. Parts of this chapter are drawn from Linehan (1993a), Linehan and Koerner (1992), and Koerner and Linehan (1992).

NOTE

1. Between the writing of this case history and its publication, at 14 months into therapy, Cindy died of a prescription drug overdose plus alcohol. The immediate precipitant was a call to her estranged husband, during which she discovered that another woman was living with him. As she told her therapist during a phone call the next morning, her unverbalized hope that they might someday get back together, or at least be close friends, had been shattered. She phoned again that evening, in tears, stating that she had just drank half of a fifth of liquor. Such drinking incidents had occurred several times before and the phone call was spent "remoralizing" her; offering hope; problem solving how she could, indeed, live without her husband; and using crises intervention techniques to get her through the evening until her appointment the following day. Her roommate was home and she agreed to talk with her, watch a TV movie together, and go to bed (plans she did follow through on). She stated that although she felt suicidal, she would stop drinking and would not do anything self-destructive until her appointment. She was instructed to call the therapist

back later that evening if she wanted to talk again. The next day, when Cindy was not at her appointment, the therapist called her home just as her roommate discovered her dead, still in bed from the night before.

At this point, the therapist was faced with a number of tasks. The therapist called other therapists who had been treating the client to inform them and spoke with a legal consultant to review the limits of confidentiality when a client has died. Once the family (parents and husband) were alerted, the therapist called each to offer her condolences. The next day the therapist (who was the senior therapist and supervisor on the treatment team) called a meeting of the treatment team to discuss and process the suicide. It was especially important to notify individual therapists of the remaining three members of Cindy's skills-training group. Group members were notified of the suicide by their individual psychotherapists. Within minutes of the beginning of the next group session, however, two members became seriously suicidal and one had to be briefly hospitalized. (By the third week following the suicide, however, both had regained their forward momentum.) A third group member took this occasion to quit DBT and switch to another therapy, saying that this proved the treatment did not work. In the days and weeks following the suicide, the therapist attended the funeral and met with Cindy's roommate and with her parents.

What can we learn from this suicide? First, it is important to note that even when a treatment protocol is followed almost to the letter, it might not save the client. Even an effective treatment can fail in the end. In this case DBT failed. That does not mean that the progress made was unimportant or not real. Had this "slippery spot over the abyss" been negotiated safely, perhaps the client would have been able to develop, finally, a life of quality. Risk is not eliminated, however, just because the individual makes substantial progress. In this case, the therapist did not believe during the last phone call that the client was at a higher than ordinary risk for imminent suicide. In contrast to many previous phone calls and therapy sessions in which the client cried that she might not be able to hold on, during the last call the client made plans for the evening, agreed to stop drinking and not to do anything suicidal or self-destructive, and seemed to the therapist (and the roommate) to be in better spirits following the phone call. Her roommate was home and available. Thus, the therapist did not take extraordinary measures that evening to prevent suicide. Indeed, the problem behavior focused on during the call was the drinking. The topic of suicide was brought up by the therapist in the course of conducting a risk assessment. Could the therapist have known? Only (perhaps) if the therapist had paid more attention to the precipitant and less to the affect expressed at the end of the phone call. In reviewing notes about the client, the therapist saw that each previous near-lethal attempt was a result of the client believing that the relationship with her husband had irrevocably ended. Although the client could tolerate losing her husband, she could not tolerate losing all hope for a reconciliation at some point, even many years hence. Had the therapist linked these two ideas (complete loss of hope and suicide attempt), she might have been able to work out a better plan with the client for a reemergence of the crisis later in the evening. The value of both conducting thorough behavioral assessments and organizing them into a coherent pattern is highlighted in this case.

Second, when all is said and done, the borderline individual must ultimately be able and willing to tolerate the almost unimaginable pain of his/her life until therapy has a chance to make a permanent difference. Ultimately the therapist cannot save the client; only the client can do that. Even if mistakes are made, the client must nonetheless persevere. In this case, the DBT protocol of "no lethal drugs for lethal people" was violated, even though the client had a past history of near lethal overdoses. Why was the protocol not enforced? Primarily, for two reasons: (1) The client came into therapy with a strong belief that the host of medications she was on were essential to her survival. Any attempt on the therapist's part to manage her medications would have been met by very strong resistance. Although dispensed in small doses, the only safe alternative would have been to have the person living with her (her husband, at first, and then her roommate) manage her medications, which the client also resisted. In addition, the "no lethal drug" protocol of DBT is regularly criticized by some mental health professionals who believe that psychoactive medications are a treatment of choice for suicidal individuals. In the face of professional and client resistance to the policy, in this case the therapist relented. (2) The lethal behavior of the client during therapy consisted of cutting and slashing; thus her using drugs to suicide did not seem likely, and the therapist allowed herself a false sense of safety with respect to them.

Third, a member's suicide is extraordinarily stressful for borderline clients in group therapy. Although it is easy to believe that alliances are not strong in a group psychoeducational behavioral-skills group, this has universally not been our experience. The suicide of one member is a catastrophic event and can lead to contagious parasuicide, suicide, and therapy dropouts. Thus,

extreme care is needed in conducting group meetings for some time following a suicide. Similar care is needed with the treatment team, where the thread of hope that maintains therapists in the face of a daunting task is also strained. It is important that personal reactions of therapists as well as a period of mourning and grieving be shared and accepted. Fears of legal responsibility, never far from the surface, must be confronted directly; legal counsel sought as necessary; and, in time, a careful review of the case and the therapy must be conducted, if only to improve treatment in the future.

REFERENCES

Adler, G. (1981). The borderline–narcissistic personality disorder continuum. *American Journal of Psychiatry, 138,* 46–50.

Adler, G. (1985). *Borderline psychopathology and its treatment.* New York: Aronson.

Adler, G., & Buie, D. H. (1979). Aloneness and borderline psychopathology: The possible relevance of child development issues. *International Journal of Psychoanalytic Psychotherapy, 60,* 83–96.

American Psychiatric Association. (1987). *Diagnostic and statistical manual of mental disorders* (3rd ed., rev.). Washington, DC: Author.

American Psychiatric Association. (1993). *DSM-IV draft criteria as of 3/1/93.* Washington, DC: Author.

Beck, A. T., Freeman, A., & Associates. (1990). *Cognitive therapy of personality disorders.* New York: Guilford Press.

Beck, A. T., Rush, A. J., Shaw, B. F., & Emery, G. (1979). *Cognitive therapy of depression.* New York: Guilford Press.

Benjamin, L. S. (1974). Structural analysis of social behavior. *Psychological Review, 81,* 392–425.

Benjamin, L. S. (1979). Structural analysis of differentiation failure. *Psychiatry, 42,* 1–23.

Benjamin, L. S. (1993). *Interpersonal diagnosis and treatment of personality disorders.* New York: Guilford Press.

Bryer, J. B., Nelson, B. A., Miller, J. B., & Kroll, P. A. (1987). Childhood sexual and physical abuse as factors in adult psychiatric illness. *American Journal of Psychiatry, 144,* 1426–1430.

Buie, D. H., & Adler, G. (1982). Definitive treatment of the borderline personality. *International Journal of Psychoanalytic Psychotherapy, 9,* 51–87.

Clarkin, J. F., Marziali, E., & Munroe-Blum, H. (1991). Group and family treatments for borderline personality disorder. *Hospital and Community Psychiatry, 42,* 1038–1043.

Clarkin, J. F., Widiger, T. A., Frances, A. J., Hurt, S. W., & Gilmore, M. (1983). Prototypic typology and the borderline personality disorder. *Journal of Abnormal Psychology, 92,* 263–275.

Cowdry, R. W., & Gardner, D. L. (1988). Pharmacotherapy of borderline personality disorder: Alprazolam, carbamazepine, trifluoperazine, and tranylcypromine. *Archives of General Psychiatry, 45,* 111–119.

Cowdry, R. W., Pickar, D., & Davies, R. (1985). Symptoms and EEG findings in the borderline syndrome. *International Journal of Psychiatry and Medicine, 15,* 202–211.

Ellis, A. (1962). *Reason and emotion in psychotherapy.* New York: Lyle Stuart.

Ellis, A. (1973). *Humanistic psychotherapy: The rational-emotive approach.* New York: Julian Press.

Endicott, J., Spitzer, R. L., Fleiss, J. L., & Cohen, J. (1976). The global assessment scale: A procedure for measuring overall severity of psychiatric disturbance. *Archives of General Psychiatry, 33,* 766–771.

Faltus, F. (1984). The positive effect of alprazolam in the treatment of three patients with borderline personality disorder. *American Journal of Psychiatry, 141,* 802–803.

Foa, E. B., & Kozak, M. J. (1986). Emotional processing of fear: Exposure to corrective information. *Psychological Bulletin, 99,* 20–35.

Foa, E. B., Steketee, G., & Grayson, J. B. (1985). Imaginal and in vivo exposure: A comparison with obsessive-compulsive checkers. *Behavior Therapy, 16,* 292–302.

Frances, A., Fyer, M., & Clarkin, J. F. (1986). Personality and suicide. *Annals of the New York Academy of Sciences, 487,* 281–293.

Gardner, D. L., & Cowdry, R. W. (1986). Alprazolam-induced dyscontrol in borderline personality disorder. *American Journal of Psychiatry, 143,* 519–522.

Gardner, D. L., & Cowdry, R. W. (1989). Pharmacotherapy of borderline personality disorder: A review. *Psychopharmacology Bulletin, 25,* 515–523.

Goldberg, C. (1980). The utilization and limitations of paradoxical intervention in group psychotherapy. *International Journal of Group Psychotherapy, 30,* 287–297.

Gottman, J. M., & Katz, L. F. (1990). Effects of marital discord on young children's peer interaction and health. *Developmental Psychology, 25,* 373–381.

Gunderson, J. G. (1984). *Borderline personality disorder.* Washington, DC: American Psychiatric Press.

Gunderson, J. G., & Kolb, J. E. (1978). Discriminating features of borderline patients. *American Journal of Psychiatry, 135,* 792–796.

Gunderson, J. G., Kolb, J. E., & Austin, V. (1981). The diagnostic interview for borderlines. *American Journal of Psychiatry, 138,* 896–903.

Herman, J. L. (1986). Histories of violence in an outpatient population. *American Journal of Orthopsychiatry, 56,* 137–141.

Herman, J. L., Perry, J. C., van der Kolk, B. A. (1989). Childhood trauma in borderline personality disorder. *American Journal of Psychiatry, 146,* 490–495.

Hollandsworth, J. G., Jr. (1990). *The physiology of psychological disorders.* New York: Plenum Press.

Kegan, R. (1982). *The evolving self: Problem and process in human development.* Cambridge, MA: Harvard University Press.

Kernberg, O. F. (1975). *Borderline conditions and pathological narcissism.* New York: Aronson.

Kernberg, O. F. (1984). *Severe personality disorders.* New Haven, CT: Yale University Press.

Kernberg, O. F., Burstein, E., Coyne, L., Appelbaum, A., Horwitz, L., & Voth, H. (1972). Psychotherapy and psychoanalysis: Final report of the Menninger Foundation's Psychotherapy Research Project. *Bulletin of the Menninger Clinic, 36,* 1–275.

Kernberg, O. F., Selzer, M. A., Koenigsberg, H. W., Carr, A. C., & Appelbaum, A. H. (1989). *Psychodynamic psychotherapy of borderline patients.* New York: Basic Books.

Koerner, K., & Linehan, M. (1992). Integrative therapy for borderline personality disorder: Dialectical behavior therapy. In J. C. Norcross, & M. R. Goldfried, (Eds.), *Handbook of psychotherapy integration* (pp. 433–459). New York: Basic Books.

Kohlenberg, R. J., & Tsai, Mavis (1991). *Functional analytic psychotherapy.* New York: Plenum Press.

Kyokai, B. D. (1966). *The teachings of buddha.* Tokyo, Japan: Author.

Linehan, M. M. (1987a). Dialectical behavior therapy: A cognitive-behavioral approach to parasuicide. *Journal of Personality Disorders, 1,* 328–333.

Linehan, M. M. (1987b). Dialectical behavior therapy for borderline personality disorder: Theory and method. *Bulletin of the Menninger Clinic, 51,* 261–276.

Linehan, M. M. (1989). Cognitive and behavior therapy for borderline personality disorder. In A. Tasman, R. E. Hales, & A. J. Frances (Eds.), *Review of psychiatry* (pp. 84–102). Washington, DC: American Psychiatric Press.

Linehan, M. M. (1993a). *Cognitive-behavioral treatment of borderline personality disorder.* New York: Guilford Press.

Linehan, M. M. (1993b). *Skills training manual for treating borderline personality disorder.* New York: Guilford Press.

Linehan, M. M, Armstrong, H. E., Suarez, A., Allmon, D., & Heard, H. L. (1991). Cognitive-behavioral treatment of chronically parasuicidal borderline patients. *Archives of General Psychiatry, 48,* 1060–1064.

Linehan, M. M., Heard, H. L., & Armstrong, H. E. (1992). *Naturalistic follow-up of a behavioral treatment for chronically parasuicidal borderline patients.* Unpublished manuscript, University of Washington, Seattle, WA.

Linehan, M. M., & Koerner, K. (1992). A behavioral theory of borderline personality disorder. In J. Paris (Ed.), *Borderline personality disorder: Etiology and Treatment* (pp. 103–121). Washington, DC: American Psychiatric Association.

Linehan, M. M., Tutek, D., & Heard, H. L. (1992, November). *Interpersonal and social treatment outcomes for borderline personality disorder.* Poster presented at the annual meeting of the Association for the Advancement of Behavior Therapy, Boston, MA.

Links, P. S., Steiner, M., Boiago, I., & Irwin, D. (1990). Lithium therapy for borderline patients: Preliminary findings. *Journal of Personality Disorders, 4,* 173–181.

Marlatt, G. A., & Gordon, J. R. (Eds.). (1985). *Relapse prevention: Maintenance strategies in the treatment of addictive behaviors.* New York: Guilford Press.

Marziali, E. A., & Munroe-Blum, H. (1987). A group approach: the management of projective identification in group treatment of self-destructive borderline patients. *Journal of Personality Disorders, 1,* 340–343.

Masterson, J. (1976). *Psychotherapy of the borderline adult.* New York: Brunner/Mazel.

Masterson, J. (1981). *The narcissistic and borderline disorders*. New York: Brunner/Mazel.

Millon, T. (1987). On the genesis and prevalence of the borderline personality disorder: A social learning thesis. *Journal of Personality Disorders, 1,* 354–372.

Munroe-Blum, H., & Marziali, E. (1987). *Randomized clinical trial of relationship management time-limited group treatment of borderline personality disorder*. Unpublished manuscript, Ontario Mental Health Foundation, Hamilton, Ontario.

Munroe-Blum, H., & Marziali, E. (1989). *Continuation of a randomized control trial of group treatment for borderline personality disorder*. Unpublished manuscript, Canadian Department of Health and Human Services, Hamilton, Ontario.

Paris, J., Brown, R., & Nowlis, D. (1987). Long term follow-up of borderline patients in a general hospital. *Comprehensive Psychiatry, 28,* 530–535.

Parsons, B., Quitkin, F. M., McGrath, P. J., Stewart, J. W., Tricamo, E., Ocepek-Welikson, K., Harrison, W., Rabkin, J. G., Wager, S. G., & Nunes, E. (1989). Phenelzine, imipramine, and placebo in borderline patients meeting criteria for atypical depression. *Psychopharmacology Bulletin, 25,* 524–534.

Pretzer, J. (1990). Borderline personality disorder. In A. Freeman, J. Pretzer, B. Fleming, & K. M. Simon, *Clinical applications of cognitive therapy* (pp. 181–202). New York: Plenum Press.

Reiser, D. E., & Levenson, H. (1984). Abuses of the borderline diagnosis: A clinical problem with teaching opportunities. *American Journal of Psychiatry, 141,* 1528–1532.

Rinsley, D. (1982). *Borderline and other self disorders*. New York: Aronson.

Shearin, E. N., & Linehan, M. M. (1989). Dialectics and behavior therapy: A meta-paradoxical approach to the treatment of borderline personality disorder. In L. M. Ascher (Ed.), *The therapeutic paradox* (pp. 255–288). New York: Guilford.

Shearin, E. N., & Linehan, M. M. (1992). Patient–therapist ratings and relationship to progress in dialectical behavior therapy for borderline personality disorder. *Behavior Therapy.*

Soloff, P. H., George, A., Nathan, R. S., Schulz, P. M., Cornelius, J. R., Herring, J., & Perel, J. M. (1989). Amitriptyline versus haloperidol in borderlines: Final outcomes and predictors of response. *Journal of Clinical Psychopharmacology, 9,* 238–246.

Stone, M. H., Stone, D. K., & Hurt, S. W. (1987). Natural history of borderline patients treated by intensive hospitalization. *Psychiatric Clinics of North America, 10,* 185–206.

Turner, R. M. (1984, November). *Assessment and treatment of borderline personality disorders*. Paper presented at the meeting of the Association for Advancement of Behavior Therapy, Philadelphia, PA.

Turner, R. M. (1989). Case study evaluations of a biocognitive-behavioral approach for the treatment of borderline personality disorder. *Behavior Therapy, 20,* 477–489.

Turner, R. M. (1992). *An empirical investigation of the utility of psychodynamic techniques in the practice of cognitive behavior therapy*. Paper presented at the annual meeting of the Association for the Advancement of Behavior Therapy, Boston, MA.

Turner, R. M., & Hersen, M. (1981). Disorders of social behavior: A behavioral approach to personality disorders. In S. M. Turner, K. S. Calhoun, & H. E. Adams (Eds.), *Handbook of clinical behavior therapy* (pp. 103–123). New York: Wiley.

Tutek, D. A., & Linehan, M. M. (1993). Comparative treatments for borderline personality disorder: Theory and research. In T. R. Giles (Ed.), *Handbook of effective psychotherapy* (pp. 355–378). New York: Plenum Press.

Wagner, A. W., Linehan, M. M., & Wasson, E. J. (1989, November). *Parasuicide: Characteristics and relationship to childhood sexual abuse*. Poster presented at the meeting of the Association for Advancement of Behavior Therapy, Washington, DC.

Waldinger, R. J., & Gunderson, J. G. (1984). Completed psychotherapies with borderline patients. *American Journal of Psychotherapy, 38,* 1, 90–201.

Webster, M. (1983). *New universal unabridged dictionary*. Cleveland, OH: Ohio: Dorset and Baber.

Whitaker, C. A. (1975). Psychotherapy of the absurd: With special emphasis on the psychotherapy of aggression. *Family Process, 14,* 1–16.

Widiger, T. A., & Frances, A. J. (1989). Epidemiology, diagnosis, and comorbidity of borderline personality disorder. In A. Tasman, R. E. Hales, & A. J. Frances (Eds.), *American psychiatric press review of psychiatry* (Vol. 8, pp. 8–24). Washington, DC: American Psychiatric Press.

Young, J. (1983, August). *Borderline personality: Cognitive theory and treatment*. Paper presented at the annual meeting of the American Psychological Association, Anaheim, CA.

Young, J. E. (1990). *Cognitive therapy for personality disorders: A schema-focused approach*. Sarasota, FL: Professional Resources Exchange.

Young, J., & Swift, W. (1988). Schema-focused cognitive therapy for personality disorders: Part I. *International Cognitive Therapy Newsletter, 4,* 13–14.

Zanarini, M. C., Gunderson, J. G., Frankenburg, F. R., & Chauncey, D. L. (1989). The revised diagnostic interview for borderlines: Discriminating BPD from other axis II disorders. *Journal of Personality Disorders, 3,* 10–18.

Chapter 11

SEXUAL DYSFUNCTION: MALE ERECTILE DISORDER

Michael P. Carey
Syracuse University

John P. Wincze
Brown University

Andrew W. Meisler
Yale University

The authors are among the leading sex therapists and researchers in the country. In this chapter they describe their own approach to treating problems with male sexual arousal, which is easily the most common problem confronting therapists who deal with sexual dysfunction.

After presenting a state-of-the-art biopsychosocial model of sexual dysfunction that covers biology as expertly as psychology, the authors point out that the organic-psychogenic distinction is no longer particularly useful in the assessment of these problems. The six essential components of modern-day sex therapy are then described with the notation that some of the traditional components (sensate focus) may not be the most important in many cases.

The authors present a seemingly straightforward case of psychologically based erectile dysfunction in a male. But the reader may be struck by the twists and turns that the authors, as therapists, take with this case and the particular therapeutic strategies required. For example, the therapists point out that they are not necessarily attempting to increase erectile firmness.

In sex therapy we see one of the best integrations of cognitive-behavioral and systems approaches, and the importance of that integration is readily apparent in the case study presented here.—D. H. B.

INTRODUCTION

For many men, there is no more threatening experience than failing to achieve an erection at will. It is common for a man with erectile difficulties to describe his problem by saying that he has "lost his manhood" or that "he is no longer a man." Thus, erectile difficulties are often associated with loss of self-esteem, depression, and despair. To make matters worse, men who are not in a relationship often avoid social contact with potential partners, fearing the humiliation and embarrassment of "not being able to perform." Similarly, men who already have a partner may avoid all physical contact with their partner; when asked why they do not kiss, hug, and caress their partner any longer, such men respond rhetorically: "What's the use in starting something I cannot finish?" Their avoidance robs them of any opportunity to obtain social support, comfort, and psychological intimacy.

In this chapter we discuss the problem of

male erectile disorder. First we provide a working definition of the problem, discuss its prevalence, and give an overview of the conceptual model that guides our intervention. We then discuss the context of our clinical work, present our approach to assessment and treatment, and illustrate this approach with a recent clinical case.

Definition of Male Erectile Disorder

According to the fourth edition of the *Diagnostic and Statistical Manual of Mental Disorders* (DSM-IV; American Psychiatric Association, 1993), male erectile disorder is the "persistent or recurrent inability to attain or maintain an adequate erection until completion of the sexual activity."* This diagnosis requires that the erectile problem causes "marked distress or interpersonal difficulty." Male erectile disorder would not be diagnosed if the erectile problems were the result of another psychological disorder (e.g., major depression) and/or substance abuse.

In previous writing and discussion, male erectile disorder has also been referred to as erectile dysfunction, erectile incompetence, and impotence. The latter two terms have been abandoned by many therapists because they have pejorative connotations. Note, however, that the term *impotence* is still used by most physicians and the general public.

According to the DSM-IV, male erectile disorder can be further classified as lifelong (occurs during the person's entire sexual life, also referred to by some authors as "primary") or acquired (also known as "secondary"), and as generalized (i.e., the disorder occurs across all partners, sexual activities, and situations) versus situational (i.e., limited to certain partners, sexual practices, or situations). In our experience, acquired male erectile disorder is much more common than lifelong male erectile disorder; however, when the disorder is characterized as lifelong, it is likely to be more serious and difficult to treat.

Some men with erectile disorder may report that they are completely unable to obtain an erection; however, men with such complete disorder are unlikely to seek services from a mental health professional such as a psychologist or a psychiatrist. That is, such men usually go directly to a physician, typically their primary care doctor or a urologist, for help. It is more common for psychologists to see men who report that (1) they are able to obtain a partial erection but this erection is too soft to achieve penetration, (2) they can achieve a full erection but are unable to maintain their erection long enough to permit penetration and intravaginal ejaculation, or (3) they can achieve an erection with one partner but not another. Some of these men report that full erections are possible during masturbation or when they awake from sleeping. Finally, some men who are able to obtain usable erections remain dissatisfied with the quality of their erections.

As noted above, men who experience erectile problems are embarrassed, discouraged, depressed, and even suicidal as a result of their erectile difficulties. Many have tried self-help remedies such as medication (e.g., alcohol, aphrodisiacs, or other drugs), viewing erotica, or becoming involved in an affair. These "remedies" usually fail because men often approach affairs or masturbation with a self-defeating and maladaptive attitude, for example, with a demand to "perform." That is, they focus on the outcome of achieving an erection rather than the process of enjoying sexual excitement and arousal. Thus, the man may masturbate to "see if it works" and he may not approach masturbation in a relaxed, erotic way. When such self-help approaches do not work, they can result in additional frustration and even despair. Additional marital or relationship discord (or increased social isolation in single men) may also result. Thus, by the time the man and his partner reach the office of a sex therapist, it is likely that the problem is overwhelming and has had secondary side effects.

Prevalence

It is probably safe to say that almost all men will experience occasional difficulties

*The DSM-IV criteria cited in this chapter are those that were approved as final by the DSM-IV Sexual Disorders Work Group and the Task Force on DSM-IV (APA, 1993). These criteria may be subject to minor editorial revisions before the publication of DSM-IV.

in obtaining or maintaining an erection at some time during their life. Consider the following example: A man who works hard all week goes to a party on Friday night. He is literally exhausted, but he looks forward to the change of pace and excitement. While at the party, he and his partner have several drinks and stay up late. They return home in a playful, erotic mood, but the man is too tired and inebriated to obtain an erection.

For some men, this difficulty represents a transitory problem of little consequence; for others, however, this experience is more persistent and will lead to troublesome concerns. Accurate estimates of the latter group have been difficult to obtain. Kaplan (1974) has estimated that as many as 50% of all men experience such erectile difficulties. Indirect support for her estimate comes from many sources: (1) the number of self-help organizations for men with erectile problems (e.g., Impotents Anonymous), (2) the numerous advertisements that appear in the so-called men's magazines offering magical "cures" of one type or another, and (3) an active and flourishing commercial interest in medical treatments (e.g., self-injections of papaverine, hormonal treatments, vacuum-aided erections, penile implants). Unfortunately, there are no well-controlled, community-based epidemiological studies of sexual health. Conservative estimates suggest that male erectile disorder may affect between 4% and 9% of the adult male population (Frank, Anderson, & Rubinstein, 1978; Nettelbladt & Uddenberg, 1979). Interestingly, Kinsey, Pomeroy, and Martin (1948) found that erectile disorder occurs in less than 1% of the male population before age 19, increasing to 25% by age 75.

Additional estimates of the prevalence of erectile disorder, however, can be culled from the clinical treatment literature. Spector and Carey (1990) reviewed the literature and found that erectile disorder was the most common presenting complaint at sex therapy clinics. For example, Masters and Johnson (1970) reported that 50% of men requesting treatment at their institute in St. Louis complained of secondary (i.e., acquired) erectile disorder, and 8% complained of primary (i.e., lifelong) erectile disorder. Frank, Anderson, and Kupfer (1976) and Bancroft and Coles (1976) found that 36% and 40% of males presenting for

sex therapy had erectile disorder as their primary complaint. Hawton (1982) replicated the Bancroft and Coles (1976) study (in the same clinic, several years later) and observed that male erectile disorder accounted for 53% of the presenting problems at this clinic. More recently, Renshaw (1988), at her clinic in Chicago, reported that 3.5% of her clients complained of lifelong erectile disorder, and 48% complained of acquired disorder. It should be noted that the figures cited above are from psychosocially oriented sex therapy clinics. It is likely that an even larger number of men present initially to clinics located in departments of urology and medicine. Unfortunately, systematic data are not yet available from these settings.

BIOPSYCHOSOCIAL MODEL

Traditionally, efforts to understand the cause of male erectile disorder have been dualistic; that is, etiological formulations, diagnostic procedures, and therapeutic interventions reflected the view that the problem was *either* organic (i.e., biologically caused) *or* functional (i.e., psychologically caused). We now understand that most sexual problems involve a complex interaction among biological, psychological, and social risk factors. Several recent studies have demonstrated that at least two "causes" (i.e., risk factors) have been found in two thirds (or more) of all cases (cf. Buvat, Buvat-Herbaut, Lemaire, Marcolin, & Quittelier, 1990). Assessment and treatment may require input from multiple disciplines and therapeutic strategies in order to address the multiple causes of the disorder. Here we describe briefly some of the many possible risk factors for erectile impairment and discuss our understanding of their interaction. This understanding serves as the model that guides our clinical work.

Biological Risk Factors for Male Erectile Disorder

At the biological level of analysis, penile tumescence requires an intact and functioning physiological network; traditionally, the endocrine, vascular, and neurological systems have been viewed as most important for erectile functioning.

Endocrine deficiencies have long been suspected as a leading cause of erectile difficulties; among the leading culprits have been abnormally low levels of testosterone and abnormally high levels of prolactin.

Empirical research has provided only mixed support for the hypothesis that reduced testosterone levels are responsible for erectile disorder (Jones, 1985). Several scientific reports document the fact that men with prepubertal levels of serum testosterone can continue to obtain adequate erections (e.g., Davidson, Camargo, Smith, & Kwan, 1983). Other investigators (e.g., Salmimies, Kockott, Pirke, Vogt, & Schill, 1982) have reported that providing testosterone replacement therapy to hypogonadal men leads to increases in the frequency of spontaneous erections. Subsequent, more fine-grained analysis suggests that testosterone may be more important to fantasy-based arousal and sexual desire than it is to externally stimulated erections (Bancroft & Wu, 1983).

Other hormonal problems typically do not impair erectile capacity. Although severe hyperprolactinemia (which is rare) is probably associated with erectile disorder, mild hyperprolactinemia probably does not cause erectile difficulties (Buvat et al., 1985). In summary, most experts agree that hormonal factors are rarely the sole or primary cause of most cases of erectile disorder (e.g., Jones, 1985; Schover & Jensen, 1988).

Vascular diseases and difficulties, on the other hand, represent a much more serious threat to erectile functioning (Papadopoulos, 1989). Because erection is primarily a vascular phenomenon (i.e., erection is achieved by a threefold increase in penile blood flow), malfunctions in either the arterial (i.e., inflow) or venous (i.e., outflow) systems are likely to result in erectile difficulties. Arterial inflow may be insufficient as a result of any pathological condition that limits the amount of blood reaching the penis; diseases affecting the central pelvic arteries (supplying the legs) and/or the finer arteries (supplying the penis directly) can be implicated. Arteriosclerosis (i.e., thickening, hardening, and loss of elasticity of the walls of the arteries) may be the most common cause of arterial insufficiency (Wagner &

Metz, 1981). Ruzbarsky and Michal (1977) completed postmortem investigations of 30 men ages 19 to 85 and reported that all men over 38 years of age began to show signs of vascular disease in the penile arteries. The adequacy of the arterial inflow can be assessed with Doppler studies (Jevtich, 1980), and surgical revascularization interventions are available if a specific obstruction exists in the penile artery. (Note, however, that revascularizations are usually not viable if there is systemic arterial disease.)

The role of the venous system in erectile disorder has subsequently received considerable research attention (e.g., Lewis, 1991; Lue, Hricak, Schmidt, & Tanagho, 1986). The basic problem here is "venous leakage"; that is, arterial inflow of blood is adequate to produce an erection but the venous outflow occurs so rapidly that the erection cannot be maintained. Assessment of venous leakage problems is possible by inducing an artificial erection with papaverine and studying the escape pattern of the blood from the penis (i.e., cavernosography). Moreover, treatment by surgical revascularization can successfully treat some cases, providing indirect support for this etiological mechanism (e.g., Williams, Mulcahy, Hartnell, & Kiely, 1988). It should be noted, however, that venous leakage problems probably account for only a small percentage of erectile disorder cases, and they may be the most difficult to repair with surgery (Lewis, 1991).

Neurological disease can also contribute to erectile difficulties. Potential etiological contributors include diseases of the cerebral hemispheres (e.g., epilepsy), diseases of the hypothalamic–pituitary axis (e.g., pituitary lesions), diseases of the spinal cord (e.g., multiple sclerosis), diseases involving the peripheral nervous system (e.g., diabetes and renal disease), and trauma (e.g., spinal cord injury). Among the most common neurologically related causes is diabetes, which places men at high risk for neuropathy and subsequent erectile disorder. Overall, the evidence suggests that neurological factors are often implicated in diabetic erectile disorder (Meisler, Carey, Lantinga, & Krauss, 1989).

Impairments in endocrine, vascular, and nervous systems can arise from a number of chronic medical conditions. In addition, chronic alcohol consumption is also associated with increased risk for erectile disorder, perhaps by instigating premature neuropathy (Schover & Jensen, 1988). The effects of other substances of abuse on erectile functioning are less well studied (Buffum, 1982, 1986). However, it has been suggested that the frequency of erectile disorder among heroin users is 28%–43%, and 40%–50% among methadone users (Segraves, Madsen, Carter, & Davis, 1985)— both estimates are considerably higher than is found in the general population. Reliable estimates are not available for other commonly abused substances (e.g., amphetamines, marijuana, and cocaine). Psychiatric medications (including the antipsychotics, tricyclic antidepressants, lithium, and the minor tranquilizers) can also adversely affect erectile functioning (Segraves, 1989; Segraves & Segraves, 1992).

It is widely believed that antihypertensive medications impair erectile functioning (Papadopoulos, 1989). It is important to point out, however, that not all antihypertensive drugs have this effect, and that even where erectile difficulties do occur, these difficulties may be the result of the disease (i.e., hypertension), its treatment (i.e., the medications), and/or the patient's reaction to the disease–treatment (Bansal, 1988). For example, estimates suggest that 8% to 10% of untreated hypertensives have erectile problems prior to treatment (Oaks & Moyer, 1972), and this is probably an underestimate. Nevertheless, some types of antihypertensive medications do appear to be particularly troublesome, including diuretics (e.g., hydrochlorothiazide, chlorthalidone, and spironolactone), central antiadrenergic agents (e.g., methyldopa, clonidine, and reserpine), some beta blockers (e.g., propranolol), and some calcium channel blockers (e.g., verapamil; Segraves & Segraves, 1992). Finally, it is noteworthy that few studies have provided convincing evidence regarding dose–response relationships, and considerable individual variation (based on age, underlying pathology, relationship factors, etc.) in response is the norm; as a result, it has been difficult—even for experts—to draw well-supported conclusions regarding the antihypertensive–male erectile dysfunction relationship (cf. Papadopoulos, 1989; Segraves & Segraves, 1992).

Overall, then, there are many physiological factors that can impair erectile functioning. It is necessary to determine whether hormonal, vascular, pharmacological, or neurological problems are operating prior to beginning an intensive psychologically based assessment and treatment. There are at least two ways to accomplish this: (1) determine during a screening interview that the client can obtain and maintain a usable erection on at least some of his attempts (it is wise to obtain confirmation of this from the partner), or (2) determine by psychophysiological monitoring of penile tumescence that the man can achieve an erection. If both of these preliminary evaluations do not provide evidence that the man can achieve an erection, it would be wise to require the man to obtain a comprehensive medical examination from a urological specialist. (Further information regarding the detection of organic contributions to male erectile disorder can be found in Buvat et al., 1990.)

The rest of this chapter is based on the assumption that the client is currently able, under some circumstances (e.g., during masturbation, nocturnally, or during some erotic activities), to obtain a "usable" erection (i.e., an erection that will allow him to achieve vaginal or anal penetration and intercourse). This erection need not be 100% of the man's previous capability; however, if the man wishes to resume intercourse (as most do), the potential for a 50%–75% erection must be present. If a man does not appear to have the potential to achieve such an erection and he still wishes to have vaginal or anal intercourse, he may require a medical intervention (e.g., a penile prosthesis). In this case, the client may still profit from the principles outlined here, but additional medical treatment and follow-up will be necessary (cf. Schover, 1989). In either case, the goal of our approach is to identify psychosocial factors that set further limits on erectile capacity and overall sexual satisfaction.

Psychosocial Risk Factors for Male Erectile Disorder

Numerous psychosocial factors have been proposed as causal agents in the etiology of male erectile disorder. We can classify the more proximal psychosocial causes of male erectile disorder into two broad categories: individual factors and relationship factors.

Individual Risk Factors

Many potential individual factors can impair a man's erectile capacity. Some of these factors reflect serious acute or chronic conditions associated with global impairments of psychological and social functioning. We have already suggested that long-term substance abuse can impair the physiological systems needed for erection. Short-term substance abuse may also impair erections directly (by acting as a central nervous system depressant) or indirectly (e.g., by lowering self-esteem or increasing relationship discord). Similarly, psychological conditions such as dysthymic disorder, major depressive disorder, bipolar disorder, schizophrenia, and some personality disorders can impair an individual's psychic integrity to the extent that sexual functioning is nearly impossible. Therefore, when such psychological disorders co-occur with male erectile disorder, sex therapy should be postponed until the more pervasive psychological condition has been treated.

Erectile functioning can also be impaired by a variety of less serious psychological factors. For ease of discussion, we can divide these into affective and cognitive factors.

Negative affect has been suggested as an etiological factor by several theorists. The emotion most often identified is anxiety. For example, Kaplan (1974) has stated that performance anxiety "almost invariably contributes to impotence" (p. 129). Similarly, Masters and Johnson (1970) highlighted the "profound role played by fears of performance" (p. 84). Performance-related fears and anxieties usually occur secondarily to an initial episode of erectile disorder. That is, a man may be unable to achieve an erection on one occasion (for any of a variety of reasons); then, during subsequent opportunities, the man begins to experience anticipatory apprehension, which may, in turn, distract him from focusing on erotic cues, fantasies, his partner, and so on.

Relatedly, nonsexual sources of anxiety can impair erections. In this case, a man may be preoccupied with financial difficulties, work-related stressors, child-rearing concerns, and so forth. Preoccupation with these perceived threats to well-being can undermine the man's ability to relax, to play, and to enjoy the luxury of sexuality. Such background stress and associated anxiety need not be overwhelming or even apparent to the man or his partner. That is, the influence of such stress may be subtle. However, when such stress is coupled with other risk factors, male erectile disorder might result. In support of this point, a recent study by Morokoff, Baum, McKinnon, and Gillilland (1987) is relevant. These authors evaluated the interactive effects of chronic stress (i.e., actual or threatened unemployment) and acute stress (i.e., giving a speech about their sexual behaviors). Their results suggested that erectile impairment occurs as a result of a combination of chronic and acute stress.

In addition to anxiety, Meisler and Carey (1991, 1992) have recently reported that acute depressed affect—less severe than the clinical syndrome of major depression—can also reduce subjective arousal. Similarly, Barlow (1986, 1988) has recognized the potential effect of depressed affect on male arousal. In his research, men who experience erectile disorder often display negative affect in the presence of erotic stimulation.

Anger is a third emotion that has been linked with male erectile disorder. For example, in an early experiment investigating the impact of affect on sexual arousal, Wolchik et al. (1980) found that erotically stimulated sexual arousal was decreased by preexposure to a film that produced feelings of depression and anger. This is consistent with what we see clinically; couples presenting with sexual problems frequently report (and often display) anger toward one another. In some cases, such anger seems to stem from sexual difficulties. In others, however, a man's anger toward his partner is a clear predisposing factor. One of us (J. P. W.) recently saw a client who harbored anger toward his wife for an affair she had 12 years prior. In addition to this anger's remaining unresolved, resentment and ill feelings were actively maintained; the man complained bitterly that his wife made no effort to "help him" get an erection, and he contended that she continued to do things to sabotage their sexual relationship.

Closely linked with (and perhaps inseparable from) the negative affect that can impair male erectile disorder are cognitions that may lead to male erectile disorder. We have already mentioned that performance concerns and anxious apprehension can lead to interfering thoughts and distraction from erotic cues. The work of Barlow and his colleagues (e.g., Barlow, Sakheim, & Beck, 1983; Beck, Barlow, & Sakheim 1983; Sakheim, Barlow, Beck, & Abrahamson, 1984) has been especially instrumental in delineating cognitive factors related to erectile disorder. They have compared men experiencing erectile disorder to men not experiencing any erectile problems and have found the following: (1) men who experience erectile disorder tend to underestimate the amount of erectile response they are actually achieving, while functional men are more accurate in their estimation of arousal; (2) men who experience erectile disorder tend to increase their erectile response when they focus on nonerotic stimuli during erotic stimulation, while men who experience no erectile disorder tend to decrease their erectile response when they focus on nonerotic stimuli; and (3) men who experience erectile disorder tend to decrease their erectile response when demands to get aroused are made, whereas functional men experience the opposite. In addition to the negative cognitions (e.g., anxious apprehension and performance concerns) associated with erectile dysfunction, recent evidence suggests that dysfunctionals also experience fewer positive cognitions during exposure to erotic material (Meisler & Carey, 1992). That is, dysfunctionals focus less on the positive or arousing aspects of the situation.

Another cognitive contributor to erectile difficulties is ignorance, particularly about sexual psychophysiology. For example, some of our older clients have expectations that they should be able to obtain an erection just by thinking sexy thoughts or by seeing an attractive person. Because this was their experience as young men, they expect this hypersensitivity/hyperresponsivity to continue forever. However, many men require increased direct stimulation to obtain an erection as they age. If this stimulation is not forthcoming, an erection is unlikely to occur.

Male erectile disorder can also occur secondarily to other sexual dysfunctions, such as premature ejaculation and low desire. Because a discussion of the etiology, assessment, and treatment of these disorders is beyond the scope of this chapter, we refer the interested reader to the recent book by Wincze and Carey (1991).

Relationship Risk Factors

Just as physiological and psychological integrity facilitate erections, so does relationship integrity. It is not surprising, then, that several relationship characteristics have been linked with male erectile disorder (Leiblum & Rosen, 1991, 1992).

Relationships in which trust has not developed or in which it has been eroded are particularly fertile ground for male erectile disorder. Some relationships were not built on a foundation of mutual respect and trust. During early stages of the relationship, this deficit was overridden by a robust attraction and a healthy vasculature. However, as these strengths diminish over time, the lack of trust becomes more apparent. Trust that had been well established may also be weakened or dissolved by infidelities or other relationship mishaps.

Men who are no longer attracted to their partner may experience erectile problems. It is not uncommon for clients to report that they love their wife, but they are no longer physically attracted to her. In some cases, the man may never have found his wife attractive (and married her for her other qualities) but was able to compensate for this.

Partners can also differ in their sexual scripts (Gagnon, 1990; Gagnon, Rosen, & Leiblum, 1982; Leiblum & Rosen, 1992). *Scripts* is a term drawn from sociology and social psychology which is used to describe the sexual activities that are acceptable as well as when and how these activities should occur. Scripts serve as a rough plan, or guideline, of what to do when "being sexual." Scripts differ between partners, of course, but what is critical is whether partners resolve their differences in a mutually acceptable and sexually satisfying manner. Couples who do not negotiate a mutually compatible sexual script are prone to sexual difficulties, including male erectile disorder (Leiblum & Rosen, 1992).

If partners are to effectively negotiate their sexual scripts, they must be able to communicate (e.g., Metts & Cupach, 1989). Communication difficulties often play some role in male erectile disorder, as noted by Masters and Johnson (1970): "[T]he failure of communication in the bedroom extends rapidly to every other phase of the marriage. When there is no security or mutual representation in sexual exchange, there rarely is freedom of other forms of marital communication" (p. 15). Whether communication difficulties begin in the bedroom is debatable, but there is little disagreement that when partners fail to communicate, they are at risk for sexual problems.

Unfortunately, there is little research evaluating the effects of relationship factors on male erectile disorder. Thus, we have relied on our clinical experiences to guide our discussion. We are convinced of the importance of these factors, but welcome empirical data to inform our work.

Model Guiding Our Work

We hypothesize that biological, psychological, and social forces can contribute—separately and in combination—to causing male erectile disorder (Meisler & Carey, 1990; Wincze & Carey, 1991). In some instances, a single causal agent may be strong enough to prevent erections. Such cases are relatively easy to recognize, assess, and (sometimes) treat. More often, however, a combination exists of subtle forces that work together to impair erectile capacity. In explaining this kind of model to clients, the metaphors of weights, anchoring down an erect penis, can be used. A single weight (representing, for example, lack of effective communication) may not be sufficient to pull down an erect penis in a young, healthy man in an otherwise healthy relationship. However, the combined effects of several factors (e.g., atherosclerosis, depressed affect, and mismatched scripts) might be sufficient to impair erections in a middle-aged man.

We also hypothesize that the "final" effect of several risk factors may be "negatively" synergistic (rather than just additive); expressed differently, when multiple risk factors are present, the net effect may be more than just the sum of the individual factors. For example, Leiblum and Rosen (1991) reviewed literature that suggests that lowered social status (resulting from failure experiences) may actually reduce circulating levels of testosterone. The corollary of this hypothesis is that treatment may have a greater effect than originally anticipated (i.e., based on an analysis of the likely direct effects of the intervention) because of a kind of "positive" synergism. Thus, the problem and the intervention might be thought of as biopsychosocial patterns going in different directions (one toward sexual dysfunction and the other toward sexual satisfaction).

Finally, a biopsychosocial model such as this allows for multiple pathways to the clinical end point of male erectile disorder. Erectile problems can result from a plethora of combinations of risk factors. The model also helps to explain how narrowly trained clinicians looking for a causal agent from within their unique perspective, discipline, or paradigm might actually find it—but treatment fails because it has addressed only one of several causal factors. A model such as this requires a multimodal assessment and treatment strategy.

CONTEXT OF ASSESSMENT AND THERAPY

As is the case for many psychological disorders, it is likely that only a minority of men will seek psychosocial assessment and treatment directly from a mental health professional. Many men first confide in a physician—an internist, a family doctor, or a urologist. Physicians are likely to refer some of these men, particularly younger men or men with no obvious pathophysiology, to a sex therapist for a psychosocial evaluation and, if indicated, therapy. However, not all of these men will find their way a sex therapist. In a thought-provoking study, Segraves, Schoenberg, Zarins, Knopf, and Camic (1982) reported that only 62% of the men referred to them from a urology clinic (in the same hospital) made an appointment. Of those who were seen and for whom sex therapy was recommended, only 32% accepted this recommendation. Finally, of those who became involved in treatment, only 43% did not terminate prematurely. And these are not isolated findings: Catalan, Hawton, and Day (1990) reported that only 60% of the men offered sex therapy through a sexual dysfunction service setting in the United Kingdom took up the offer. Of these, only two thirds completed treatment (Hawton, Catalan, & Fagg, 1992). Tiefer and Melman (1987) also reported that the majority of men evaluated for male erectile disorder had not followed through (2 to 3 years later) on the treatment recommendations that were made to them.

What do these findings imply? An obvious interpretation is that most men prefer a medical solution to their problem. Less obvious is that erectile functioning may improve "spontaneously" (i.e., without professional treatment). Segraves and his colleagues have reported that 14% to 30% of all men who experience male erectile disorder experience improvement without any therapeutic intervention (Segraves, Camic, & Ivanoff, 1985; Segraves, Knopf, & Camic, 1982). Of course, it is important to keep in mind that compliance with medical treatment recommendations in general, and especially those involving a referral to another health care provider, is notoriously poor in many areas of medicine and psychology (Tiefer & Melman, 1987).

Setting

Assessment and treatment of erectile problems occur in a number of different settings. As a practical matter, we believe that the optimal environment is a medical center with its ready access to other health care professionals. In this environment, a sex therapist is more visible to referring physicians, and his/her clients will find it easier to obtain a medical examination (if needed). In addition, the medical center environment can serve to allay some clients' concerns about the legitimacy of their problem. However, we have also seen clients in university-based clinics and private offices. (Please note: If your practice is located outside of a medical center, you should be prepared to work harder to secure referrals. We have found it helpful to participate in the local medical school urology grand rounds and case conference programs. It is even better if you can participate directly in clinical teaching and research, and obtain an adjunct appointment in the local department of urology or family medicine.)

Several process-related issues involving "setting" (broadly defined) may be important during assessment and treatment. Factors such as the therapist's appearance, the appearance of his/her office, and the therapist's educational credentials may be important to a client. Being responsive to client requests for information and returning telephone calls promptly also facilitate positive rapport. These factors are present in any professional interaction and are not the special domain of sex therapy.

For the assessment and treatment approach presented in this chapter, we assume that a comprehensive medical evaluation has already occurred. Further, we assume that physiological factors cannot provide a complete explanation for the cause of the male erectile disorder. Thus, we are assuming a mixed (i.e., both biological and psychosocial factors contributing) or primarily psychosocial etiology.

To do a complete psychosocial and psychophysiological assessment requires two types of rooms. For the former, a private interview room that will accommodate a couple and the therapist is necessary. For the latter, a two-room arrangement is ideal. The smaller room (preferably nested within the larger room) needs to be private, sound attenuated and temperature controlled; it is used to seat the client, to present erotic stimuli, and to measure penile tumescence. The larger room houses the physiological recording equipment and audiovisual equipment. (For more information regarding how to establish a sexual psychophysiological assessment practice, see Laws, 1989.)

Spacing of Sessions and Length of Therapy

Our general approach to male erectile disorder is to conduct assessment and treatment sessions at weekly intervals. Although Masters and Johnson (1970) originally advocated daily sessions, this turns out to be impractical for most clients; moreover, recent empirical evidence (i.e., Heiman & LoPiccolo, 1983) suggests that men with male erectile disorder respond better to weekly, rather than daily, treatment. If we have reason to believe that more frequent sessions would be helpful (especially early during assessment), we see clients at a more accelerated pace. In our experience, however, weekly sessions allow for homework practice without losing continuity. Of course, the spacing of sessions should be reevaluated regularly to determine whether a different schedule will better serve the couple, for whatever reason, without disrupting the flow of therapy. If a couple or an individual follows therapy instructions carefully, spacing sessions every 2, 3, or even 4 weeks is possible once progress has been established. When the interval between sessions is lengthened, instructions should be given that would allow telephone contact and even emergency sessions if needed. Most of our clients have been able to successfully reach therapy goals within 15 sessions.

A second difference between the original Masters and Johnson approach and ours is that we typically do not use a dual-sex therapy team. Although such an approach has value, it adds to the expense of therapy for the clients. Because we often train graduate students and interns, we are sometimes afforded this luxury, but it is not necessary.

Social Factors

When we work with men who are already in a relationship, we emphasize the importance of working with the couple rather than just the man. Thus, we strongly recommend that both partners attend assessment and treatment sessions. During the initial visit with the couple, the therapist should communicate the philosophy that overcoming sexual difficulties requires the cooperative efforts of both partners. It is necessary to make this explicit because many clients believe that (1) one person is to blame for the problems, and (2) it is the role of the therapist to "cure" the "guilty/sick" one.

Although it is important to see the couple together, it is also important to interview each person separately following the introduction. The purpose of the individual meeting is to gather accurate information that is unencumbered by a partner's presence. Time can be wasted if the partners are always seen together. For many individuals, there are hidden details (e.g., affairs or homosexual interest) that might not be revealed in the presence of their partner. However, this information is vital for developing a case formulation and planning the therapy program.

In some of our cases, the client enters therapy without the full cooperation of his partner. Some of these men have a partner who is reported to be shy but cooperative; in a minority of cases the partner believes that the problem is the client's and refuses to participate. Reluctance to involve partners is often given as a reason for declining psychosocial approaches. This always presents a difficult situation and one in which the therapist can never be sure if he/she has all the pertinent facts. To help an uncooperative partner become engaged in therapy, the therapist can suggest talking to the partner by telephone. If the partner still refuses, the therapist can suggest reading material for the partner that is pertinent to the problem.

Crucial components of therapeutic change (e.g., sensate focus and effective communication) can almost never be achieved when one partner refuses to participate. This is especially true when the uncooperative partner is purported to be angry and blaming. The therapist can, of course, offer some therapeutic benefit to the participant client by providing etiological explanations and information, clearing up misunderstandings, putting the problem in perspective, and outlining strategies for change. However, the therapist must also describe the limitations of therapy and try not to shift blame or fuel anger toward the absent partner. The end result of the therapy is often a client who has improved his understanding of the problem and feels better about himself but still has a dysfunctional relationship with his partner.

A final issue involves the nonmonogamous man. On some occasions we have had married clients who wanted to bring in a lover rather than their marriage partner. This presents obvious legal and ethical concerns that are in the therapist's best interest to avoid. We counsel such clients on the pros and cons of legal separation and divorce. If the client chooses to take no action, the limitations and value of therapy must be fully discussed with him.

Not all men are currently in a relationship, of course. In fact, approximately 42% of adult males are single, separated, divorced, or widowed (Reynolds, 1991). Single clients such as these often require a few special considerations by the therapist; in general, however, most of what is discussed here is applicable to these clients. It is common for a single client to enter therapy after having experienced a "sexual failure" with low self-esteem, sexual insecurities, and avoidance of social interactions. The therapist must be sensitive to these likely areas of concern and spend more time in identifying barriers that may impede social interactions.

Some single clients offer to bring in a casual partner to help with the therapy process. Our general approach is to allow a partner to participate only if there is a genuine commitment. The reason for this is to protect the client, since assessment and therapy require the revelation and open discussion of vulnerabilities and intimacies that the client may later regret having discussed.

Client Variables

LoPiccolo (1992) has recently outlined several client characteristics that may be good prognostic markers. He suggests that sex therapy is more likely to be effective if (1) the man is not receiving adequate sexual stimulation prior to therapy, (2) the partner's sexual pleasure is currently dependent on the man's obtaining an erection, (3) the couple has a poor understanding of age-related changes in sexual functioning, and (4) the man and/or his partner hold beliefs that place unrealistic demands on the man for sexual performance. Generally speaking, these characteristics represent behavioral deficits or cognitive distortions and misinformation rather than serious relationship discord or pervasive individual psychopathology.

Unfortunately, however, there is very limited empirical evidence to document the specific client characteristics that promote greater success. In one of the few studies, Hawton et al. (1992) reported that positive treatment outcomes were associated with better pretreatment communication and general sexual adjustment (especially the female partner's interest and enjoyment of sex), absence of psychiatric problems in the female partner, higher socioeconomic status, and a couple's early engagement in treatment. Outcome was not associated with age or general relationship status.

Consistent with Hawton et al. (1992), we have found that couples characterized by poor communication are less likely to profit from sex therapy approaches unless the marital concerns are addressed first (cf. Meisler, Carey, Krauss, & Lantinga, 1988). Our clinical experience also suggests that men who are very rigidly "macho" (cf. Mosher, 1991) in their characteristic style of relating to the world find psychosocial approaches challenging. Finally, it may be that individuals with a limited educational background or those who hold orthodox religious views are less likely to profit (cf. LoPiccolo, 1992; Masters & Johnson, 1970). These generalizations should be used not as a rationale to exclude such clients from therapy but just to acknowledge the additional challenge they may provide.

Therapist Variables

There is no empirical evidence to suggest that specific therapist characteristics promote greater success (Mohr & Beutler, 1990). We believe, however, that certain qualities are likely to facilitate the process of assessment and therapy. It has been our experience that therapists who possess a direct yet supportive posture are well received by clients. We believe that it is helpful to speak candidly and comfortably about sexual matters. It is inappropriate to joke about sexual matters and to appear offended by a client's behavior, fantasies, or values.

ASSESSMENT

In this section we address the goals of assessment, process issues that may arise during the assessment, and specific methods of assessment. We conclude with a brief discussion regarding the integration of data accrued across methods. The approach presented here draws on our previous discussions of these topics (e.g., Wincze & Carey, 1991).

Goals of Assessment

Clients are eager to see change and improvement—after all, they came to us for treatment. Because of this, it can be tempting to jump right in and intervene. However, we believe that it is worthwhile to use a minimum of two or three sessions to conduct a careful assessment before intervening.

A primary goal of the assessment process is to determine the diagnosis for the presenting complaint, that is, to name and describe the problem: Is the problem truly male erectile disorder, or is it premature ejaculation, Peyronie's disease, retrograde ejaculation, or low desire? (Readers unfamiliar with these conditions can consult Wincze & Carey, 1991, for further details.) How often does the problem occur? Under what conditions does it occur? The assessment procedure necessary for accurate diagnosis of sexual disorder has become more complex in recent years. We now understand that most sexual problems present with an interplay of medical and psychosocial factors and demand a wide range of expert diagnostic input.

A second goal of the assessment process is to formulate the cause(s) of the presenting complaint (Carey, Flasher, Maisto, & Turkat, 1984). This formulation should occur across levels of analysis (i.e., biological, psychological, and social levels) and time (i.e., predisposing, precipitating, and maintaining factors). The formulation should be thought of as a working hypothesis that will be refined over time (cf. Carey et al., 1984).

A third goal is to provide some feedback to the client. In this sense, assessment can be therapeutic. Therapists can communicate to the client that his problem is understood and that they have a target for the therapeutic plan. A fourth goal is to establish a baseline level from which to evaluate the efficacy of treatment.

A comprehensive assessment cannot be separated from therapy. Within the assessment process, a client's attitudes are often challenged, new information is learned, and misunderstandings are corrected. By asking the client about various factors that influence his sexual response, the therapist is helping the client to view the sexual problem as a state rather than an unchangeable trait. This conceptualization is important to help to restore optimism in the client and his partner. Similarly therapeutic is the reduction or removal of blame for the sexual problem. Assessment solicits information from each partner and thus helps redirect blame and guilt and focuses the couple's energies on solving problems. Assessment also facilitates the breakdown of barriers to communication. This process is begun during the assessment as the client is asked to discuss details of his own sexual behavior and details of his partner's sexual behavior. Clients observe the therapist discussing sexual matters in an open and nonthreatening manner and this models effective communication.

Thus, through the assessment process, couples are exposed to an appropriate communication style. They are encouraged to approach, not avoid, and to discuss sexual matters in a constructive rather than a destructive manner. It is not surprising that many couples report positive change during the assessment procedures.

Process Issues

"Process" can be used to describe the interaction between the client and the therapist; this interaction can either facilitate or inhibit assessment and therapy. It is clear that many clinicians feel uncomfortable in dealing with sexual problems. Personal feelings of shock and embarrassment often show through attempts to be empathic and accepting. Mismanagement of these negative feelings could be divisive and create a barrier to effective therapy. If a therapist's feelings cannot be managed appropriately, he/she should not be dealing with sexual problems. Clients readily discern embarrassment or incompetence.

Additional examples of process factors that can sabotage assessment (and subsequent therapy as well) include differences between the therapist and clients in terms of age, gender, and/or ethnicity and erotic attractions or interpersonal repulsion between therapist and client or client and therapist.

In conducting assessments, we have found it useful to adopt some "default assumptions," that is, hypotheses about our clients (cf. Wincze & Carey, 1991). These assumptions reflect the preferred direction of error. Thus, for example, we assume a low level of verbal understanding on the part of the client so that language is directed to the client in a clear and concrete manner. Obviously, as we learn more about our client, we modify these assumptions accordingly. Other default assumptions that we adopt in our work include the following:

- Clients will be embarrassed and have difficulty discussing sexual matters. We have already mentioned that erectile difficulties can be very threatening for many men. This embarrassment may cause them to present limited information, to miss sessions, and to generally avoid discussing their concerns.
- Clients will not understand medically correct terminology. Most men do not use the same terms we do when describing sexual functioning. They may have heard of terms such as *erection, ejaculation, intromission, foreplay,* and *coitus,* and they may even use these terms —but that is no guarantee that they know what the terms mean.
- Clients will be misinformed about sexual functioning. One client of ours assumed, for example, that erectile problems meant that he was homosexual— even though he had never had a homosexual contact and he had no sexual interest in men. Many do not know that there is a refractory period for men following an orgasm, that early morning erections have nothing to do with dream content, and that older men usually require additional physical stimulation to achieve an erection.
- Clients will be in crisis and may be suicidal. It is important to be sensitive to a client's level of desperation and depression. Although a client's problem may seem straightforward or interesting to the therapist, it may well be the triggering event in a vulnerable man. Probing to learn the meaning of the disorder, as well as the man's expecta-

tions for the future, is worthwhile. Until the therapist has these data, it is wise to err on the conservative side.

We also assume that partners have not been open with each other and do not freely discuss sexual matters. We assume that when they discuss sexual problems with us it may be the first time they have ever done so; also, they may not discuss this material between sessions. Finally, we assume that the couple will have avoided sex because of fear and discomfort.

No doubt each sex therapist will develop additional default assumptions that are worthwhile to keep in mind.

Assessment Methods

The psychosocial assessment of male erectile disorder may involve information gathered from three sources: a clinical interview, self-report questionnaires, and psychophysiological procedures.

Clinical Interview

The interview serves as the cornerstone of the assessment process (Wincze & Carey, 1991); for many practitioners, this will be the sole source of data they obtain. Interviewing about sexual matters can be especially challenging because most people in our culture are uncomfortable discussing their sexuality. Furthermore, many individuals have religious and cultural beliefs about what sexual conduct is acceptable or unacceptable, and they may be offended if a therapist's views do not agree with their own.

An interview best serves the needs of the client if the therapist obtains important information in a sensitive but time-efficient manner. Therefore, we recommend following an organized outline during the interview. We have found that three sessions devoted to obtaining the history is usually adequate. The first two sessions are devoted (largely) to conducting separate interviews with each partner; the third session involves both partners.

Assessment should always begin with an appropriate introduction for the client(s). During this time, the assessment structure and content should be outlined. We prefer to do this while both partners are present. For illustrative purposes, consider a fictitious couple:

> "Today in this first interview I would like to obtain same background information. Then I would like to get an understanding of what issues brought you here today. I'd like to spend three meetings gathering information. My previous experience suggests that it is most helpful if I interview each of you, separately, for one session each. So, I'd like to begin, today, by interviewing you, Bob. While I do this, I'd like to ask Mary to complete some questionnaires that my secretary has for you. Next week when we meet, I'd like to interview Mary alone, and ask Bob to complete the questionnaires. Then, at our third session, I'd like to see the both of you, together. At the end of the third session, I will be able to provide you with my clinical impression and outline a therapy program for you, if this is indicated."

After the introductory remarks, the couple should be invited to ask any questions they might have. The remainder of the first session is then spent interviewing one of the partners alone.

The goals of this first session include establishing rapport with the client, obtaining a general description of the erectile problem, obtaining a thorough psychosocial history, and obtaining a description of other life concerns, current stressors, and so on, to determine whether sex therapy is appropriate for the client/couple at this time.

With regard to the latter goal, there are no specific guidelines for making this determination. Thus, the therapist should determine, on a case-by-case basis, whether working on a sexual problem will benefit the client/couple. Certainly, if either partner is depressed and/or overly anxious, or if there is a great deal of anger between partners, it is more appropriate to address nonsexual issues first. In some cases, sexual reparation may be secondary to other, more pressing problems. Furthermore, effective assessment and therapy require a collaborative attitude among both partners and the therapist, which is compromised in the presence of such hostility. Similarly, there may be dysfunctional communication between partners which must be addressed before sexual issues can be effectively addressed.

We believe that it is to the client's benefit for a therapist to get to the heart of the client's concerns. Thus, spending several sessions "breaking the ice" or "establishing a relationship" is not warranted in most cases. However, it is useful to get a general sense of the client's history, especially as it relates to his sexual adjustment.

We do not advise following a rigid order of questions for all clients. Instead, the structure and content of the interview should reflect the needs of the client. There are frequently crisis issues that must be attended to before sexual matters can be addressed. Or, it may be important to allow a client to digress beyond the usual structure, but only if the digression contributes ultimately to a better understanding of the client or the client's problem.

While recognizing the need to individualize the interview structure and content to each client, we can nevertheless suggest an order that might be useful as a template or "default" structure.

First, it may be helpful to start with nonthreatening demographics (e.g., age, marital status, who lives in household, current employment, educational background, address, and telephone number) and then continue with open-ended questions: "What brings you here today?" "How can I be of help?" Notice how freely and comfortably the client discusses his sexual matters and his particular difficulty. Use probes and directive comments to keep the client on target. Once the therapist has formed a general impression concerning the scope of the erectile problem, he/she can move on to the detailed chronological history.

It is usually helpful to obtain a psychosexual and psychosocial history. Regarding the client's childhood, the therapist may wish to ask about family structure and experiences. In addition, it may be useful to ask about social status, abuse or neglect, first sexual experience (upsetting–pleasant), parents' relationship, alcohol and substance use, messages about sex, and any other information that is potentially relevant. Adolescence is often rich with information. The therapist should probably inquire about relationships with peers, self-esteem and body image, dating, sexual experiences (both homosexual and heterosexual), success–failure in school, substance use, and any other potentially relevant information.

More recent information from the adult years is likely to be most important. The therapist should do the following:

- Ask about significant relationships and events after age 20;
- Try to address self-esteem, marriage/relationship history, sexual experiences, etc.;
- Inquire about any unusual sexual experiences, psychiatric history, or treatment; and
- Acquire details regarding the current sexual situation, including sexual and nonsexual experiences in the current relationship, recent changes in sexual functioning and/or satisfaction, flexibility in sexual attitudes and behaviors, extramarital affairs, strengths and weaknesses of partner, likes and dislikes of partner's sexual behavior, and so on.

Even if the client has had a recent medical evaluation, it is helpful to obtain a brief medical history. The therapist should ask about significant childhood/teenage diseases, surgery, medical care, congenital disorders, and so forth. He/she should inquire about how the client experienced secondary sex changes. The therapist must also pay particular attention to the client's medical history after age 20, asking about any significant diseases, surgery, medical care, etc. The therapist must be sure to ask whether the client has had regular medical care (if not, refer for medical workup), is currently taking prescribed medication, or is currently being treated for any medical problems.

Throughout the history, the therapist should be sensitive to potential covert issues. He/she should ask whether there are any issues that the client does not want to discuss in front of his partner. We believe strongly in creating an interview environment in which each partner can be assured of confidentiality. Without separate and confidential interviews, crucial information might remain hidden.

All couples are told that it is more helpful and efficient to undergo initial interviews separately, even though the overall therapeu-tic emphasis will be on the couple's interaction and communication. Furthermore, couples are told that at times it may be helpful to deal with either person alone in order to work through specific issues. By making these statements at the outset, the therapist can establish conditions that allow for working through problems that present later during therapy.

Provide the client with a second opportunity to reveal anything he thinks may be relevant. In this regard, LoPiccolo and Heiman (1978) recommend ending the interview with the following question: "Is there anything else that you would like to tell me about your background that you feel bears on your sexual life?"

The second session is used to interview the partner. We ask this partner if anything has changed since the first interview and if the other partner discussed the first interview with him/her. The answers to these queries will yield information about a couple's interaction pattern, openness in communication, and ability to schedule time for important issues. It is also important to ask the other partner whether there are any issues or questions that he/she would like addressed before the interview begins. This open-ended approach allows a discussion of process issues (e.g., a client's doubt about a therapist's qualifications) as well as important personal issues that may impact on the therapy (e.g., a client's affair or a death in the family).

Once the open-ended issues are dealt with, the therapist can move on to the interview proper, which should follow the outline that was used for the first interview (with modifications as necessary).

The third assessment session normally includes both partners. An exception to this might occur if one individual's needs were so overwhelming that individual therapy was indicated prior to couple therapy. The session with both partners should begin in an open-ended manner to determine what changes and conversations may have occurred since the last session. A couple's response to this approach is important diagnostically because it gives the therapist an understanding of how a couple approaches and discusses important problematic topics. The therapist can observe which partner takes responsibility for what, and how effectively each person communicates his/her needs. Consider, also, that a couple may be overwhelmed with recently occurring problems or stress. Obviously, it is important to acknowledge issues that may preoccupy the couple and distract them from the current focus of the assessment. The therapist should spend the remainder of the third session relating his/her assessment, identifying treatment goals (sexual and nonsexual), outlining therapy plans, and explaining details regarding the initial stages of therapy. To further facilitate rapport and maximize therapy compliance, the therapist should ask each partner how he/she feels about the plan and what problems each anticipates as barriers to progress.

For some clients, further assessment information is needed, such as psychological testing, psychophysiological assessment, and/or medical evaluation. If this is the case, therapy instructions may have to be postponed until the assessment picture is completed. It is very important to explain the need for further assessment so that the client does not get discouraged or frustrated.

Self-Report Questionnaires

Self-report questionnaires are generally standardized paper-and-pencil measures that can be easily administered and scored by the therapist and completed quickly by clients; these measures can help to provide a picture of the client's condition at any point in time and/or over repeated administrations. Such questionnaires have many potential advantages: They provide extensive information to the therapist at little cost; they allow a client to organize his/her thoughts in a reflective, considered way that is not always possible within the time constraints of an interview; they permit clients to disclose sensitive information that they might not reveal during a "live" interaction, or that they might find difficult to verbalize; they allow the therapist to compare a client's progress over time, making treatment evaluation more precise and less prone to therapist-related biases; they allow the therapist to compare his/her client to other individuals (with the help of established norms); they can serve as an additional stimulus that encourages a client to think through aspects of his/her sexuality; and they can serve as

screening devices that help an interviewer to be more efficient in getting to the heart of the presenting complaint.

We use questionnaires in two (perhaps novel) ways. First, we sometimes use a brief battery of measures that we send out in advance of the first session (along with directions to our office, parking suggestions, information on fees, etc.). We encourage clients to complete this battery before the first session in order to prepare them for the session as well as to provide some initial clinical material to guide the interview.

Second, we have tried the paired-reports method (cf. Ross, Clifford, & Eisenman, 1987) for couples whom we suspect have communication difficulties, mismatched sexual scripts, and so on. With this method, the same questionnaire is completed twice by each partner: first for themselves, and a second time as they believe that their partner would complete it. This allows us to examine the agreement between partners as well as the amount of understanding that they have for each other's preferences and views. Use of this paired-reports method can be diagnostic of and therapeutic for dyadic problems.

There are a number of useful questionnaires. Following are a few that we have found helpful. For more information on questionnaires specific to sexuality, consult Davis, Yarber, and Davis (1988) and Talmadge and Talmadge (1990).

The Index of Sexual Satisfaction (ISS; Hudson, Harrison, & Crosscup, 1981) contains 25 items designed to measure the degree of sexual satisfaction and dissatisfaction in the relationship. It can be used for both homosexual and heterosexual couples and is based on common clinical complaints presented by clients (e.g., "I feel that my sex life is lacking in quality"; "It is not easy for me to get sexually excited by my partner"; "My partner is too rough or brutal when we have sex"). The focus of the ISS is on the relationship rather than on specific erection items. Research supports the reliability and validity of the ISS (Hudson et al., 1981).

The Derogatis Sexual Functioning Inventory (DSFI; Derogatis, 1975, 1978) is a 258-item questionnaire that can be scored to provide an evaluation of the following 10 areas: information, experience, drive, attitudes, psychological symptoms, affects, gender-role definition, fantasy, body image, and satisfaction. Evidence (reviewed by Conte, 1983) suggests that the DSFI is reliable and valid, and normative data are available. The primary drawback of the DSFI is its length; however, we often use only those subtests that are most relevant for a particular client.

The Dyadic Adjustment Scale (DAS; Spanier, 1976) is particularly valuable for assessing problem areas within a couple's interaction outside the sexual domain. This measure consists of 32 items designed to assess the quality of the relationship as perceived by married or cohabiting couples. Scoring yields four subscales and a total score; however, we tend to use only the total score in our work. It provides a general measure of marital/cohabiting satisfaction. Because the wording of the DAS is at the eighth-grade reading level (Jensen, Witcher, & Upton, 1987), it is possible to use the DAS with most clients. Research suggests that the DAS is valid and reliable (see Spanier, 1976; Carey, Spector, Lantinga, & Krauss, in press). Most people can complete the DAS in 15 min, and it can be scored in about 5 min.

The Sexual Opinion Survey (SOS; Fisher, 1988; Fisher, Byrne, White, & Kelley, 1988) consists of 21 items intended to assess "affective and evaluative responses to a range of sexual stimuli (autoerotic, heterosexual, and homosexual behavior; sexual fantasy; visual sexual stimuli)" (Fisher, 1988, p. 34). Each of these 21 items describes a sexual situation and a negative or positive affective response; clients then indicate the extent to which they agree (or disagree) with the response. We use the SOS to aid our understanding of the individual. Research suggests that the SOS is valid and reliable, and norms are available (see Fisher et al., 1988). Most people can complete the SOS in 10 min, and it can be scored in about half that time.

The Sexual Self-Efficacy Scale–Erectile Functioning (SSES–E; Libman, Rothernberg, Fichten, & Amsel, 1985) is a measure specifically designed for use in the context of male erectile disorder. It contains 25 desirable male sexual performance tasks (e.g., "get an erection sufficient for intercourse within a reasonable period of time"; "regain an erection if it is lost during foreplay"), and respondents are asked to indicate those that they could perform and to rate their confidence on a 10-point scale

ranging from 10 ("quite uncertain") to 100 ("quite certain"). The SSES–E has been found to be reliable and valid in previous research (e.g., Libman et al., 1985).

Sometimes it is helpful to use questionnaires to obtain information about another clinical domain, or to screen for psychopathology. Although questionnaires should not be the sole source of such information, they can be a helpful adjunct. We have found the Symptom Check List (Derogatis, 1983) and the Beck Depression Inventory (Beck, Ward, Mendelson, Mock, & Erbaugh, 1961) helpful for general psychopathology and depression, respectively. We sometimes use the brief version of the Michigan Alcohol Screening Test (Pokorny, Miller, & Kaplan, 1972) and the Drug Abuse Screening Test (Skinner, 1982) for substance abuse screening. A good general source of other brief questionnaires is Corcoran and Fischer (1987).

Psychophysiological Assessment

Psychophysiological assessment can be a powerful tool in one's assessment armamentarium. This approach tends to be less susceptible to the distortions and biases that can occur with interviews and questionnaires. In addition, psychophysiological measures allow one to better understand the physiological underpinnings, and sometimes the actual mechanisms, of the disorder.

In practice, however, psychophysiological methods are used infrequently because they require a significant amount of technical skill, and psychophysiological recording apparatus and supplies are expensive. Regarding the latter, it is likely that a basic unit will cost $1,000 or more; a state-of-the-art assessment laboratory will cost $10,000 or more.

If the skills and the cost are not a problem, two approaches are worthy of attention. The first approach is the physiological recording of nocturnal penile tumescence (NPT) during sleep. This is usually done in a full sleep laboratory. Briefly, the rationale for this procedure is as follows: If a man can obtain an erection during sleep (which most men do on two to five occasions per night) but cannot obtain an erection during partner stimulation, it is assumed that the source of the erectile disorder is primarily psychosocial. In contrast, if a man cannot obtain an erection at night, it has been assumed that his disorder is a product of primarily biological factors (although psychological overlay is to be expected).

Despite the promise of NPT, there are several important challenges to its use and interpretation. We will discuss two here (for an extended discussion of these challenges elsewhere, see Meisler & Carey, 1990). First, from a purely technical viewpoint, recent data indicate that NPT may be influenced by sleep problems (e.g., apnea, hypopnea, or periodic leg movements) not routinely assessed in the typical NPT evaluation. These sleep parameters may produce artifacts that can interfere with interpretation of NPT tracings. Second, from a practical perspective, NPT monitoring is very costly. The typical procedure requires expensive equipment, is labor intensive, and necessitates that a client spend two or three nights in a sleep center. As a result, this assessment procedure is well beyond the financial means of most clients.

Recently, there has been a proliferation of home-based NPT monitors. These devices provide a more cost-effective method of NPT evaluation. For example, we have used the Rigi-Scan to assist in clinical decision making. Similar devices can also provide a useful adjunct to the assessment procedure, but they are also expensive and can provide misleading data if not carefully supervised. We (Gordon & Carey, in press) are also experimenting with the use of monitoring tumescence during daytime naps. Initial results are promising but additional research is needed before this procedure will be ready for clinical adoption.

A second approach is the physiological recording of penile tumescence in response to erotic stimulation; indeed, it is the lack of such a response that is often reported as the problem in erectile disorder. Such daytime-arousal studies or visual-sexual-stimulation studies, as they have been called, have provided valuable information in the assessment process. For example, Wincze et al. (1988) found that exposing some dysfunctional men to erotic stimulation resulted in full erectile responses even though those men reported an inability to obtain an erection. Such data can be critically helpful in formulating a case.

In sum, psychophysiological procedures are technically challenging and expensive but can be valuable. Readers interested in establishing this capability are referred to Laws (1989) for detailed instructions.

Integration of Data Across Methods

As mentioned earlier, one of the goals of the assessment is to develop a coherent case formulation (i.e., a working hypothesis of the etiology of the problem). This formulation should relate all aspects of the client's complaints to one another and explain why the individual developed these difficulties (Carey et al., 1984). One purpose of this formulation is to aid the therapist in the development of a treatment plan. A second purpose is to communicate to clients that (1) their problem is an understandable one, given their physiology, medical history, life experiences, and so on (i.e., they are not crazy); (2) there is reason for hope and optimism; and (3) there is a conceptual "road map" and rationale on which to build a therapeutic plan. Finally, developing a case formulation allows the therapist to check with the client to see if he/she has obtained all the necessary information and that the information is correct.

One of the more challenging aspects of sex therapy is integrating multiple levels of influence (i.e., biological, psychological, dyadic, and cultural) into a coherent case formulation. Despite its difficulty, a biopsychosocial case formulation captures the richness of sexual function and dysfunction. A client is more likely to agree to try a psychosocial approach if the therapist recognizes that biological causes are not irrelevant but might be overridden or compensated for if he/she inquires about and recognizes specific dyadic and sociocultural influences. It is important to be sensitive to specific rituals and traditions that a couple has established as well as ethnic, cultural, or religious issues.

The case formulation should include biological, psychological, and social areas even if the therapist believes that one of the areas is not contributing to the problem at the moment. It is always hard to predict the future, and the groundwork should be laid in case additional information becomes available and/or future developments occur. Moreover, this comprehensive approach to case formulation will give the client confidence that the therapist has considered all possibilities. Indirectly, the therapist communicates to the client that he should also think about his problem in a multifaceted, biopsychosocial framework.

THERAPY

In this section we discuss our view of the appropriate goals for therapy and process concerns that often arise. In addition, we provide information regarding a number of useful therapy methods and discuss the importance of developing a comprehensive approach to therapy.

Goals of Therapy

In our view, the primary goal of therapy should be to create or restore mutual sexual comfort and satisfaction (cf. Wincze & Carey, 1991). This view is consistent with the "new" male sexuality discussed by Zilbergeld (1992). This new model of sex is "one that emphasizes pleasure, closeness, and self- and partner-enhancement rather than performance and scoring" (p. 4). Along with Zilbergeld (and other sex therapists), we believe that it is misguided to focus on increasing erectile firmness for two reasons. First, this is likely to increase performance anxiety, which will probably exacerbate the problem, especially if performance anxiety has been inhibiting the response. Second, the goal of increasing erectile firmness buys into the myth that the only true sex is intercourse. We believe that even if a man cannot achieve an erection, he should be able to enjoy other forms of sexual expression.

Two implications of this position warrant discussion. First, it is often the case that erections improve when the therapy is focused on nonperformance goals. In such cases, these performance-related outcomes should be looked on as pleasant side effects secondary to achievement of the goal of increasing mutual pleasure.

Second, the question arises: Who should set treatment goals—the client(s) or the therapist? We have found that clients often enter therapy with very specific but inappropriate goals. For example, a couple with severe communication problems may enter therapy with the goal of having the male partner experience improved erections. This goal, established by the couple, is not likely to be reached as long as angry conflict exists between the partners. It is the task of the therapist to help the couple to understand the factors that contribute to satisfactory arousal and sexual enjoyment; in so doing, new goals are established. These new goals must be presented by the therapist to the couple in such a way that the couple understands that, in order to reach their goals, they must first work on preliminary goals. Moreover, it is important for the couple to understand that achieving these preliminary goals will require a change in their established routine and may even cause discomfort. We encourage clients to conceptualize these preliminary goals as "stepping stones."

Process Issues

Default Assumptions

As in the case of assessment, it is helpful to begin therapy with a set of default assumptions (Wincze & Carey, 1991). These assumptions are advised in order to facilitate efficient and effective progress. Some common assumptions include:

1. The client has a narrow definition of sex and he will focus on performance as a marker of success;
2. The client has stereotyped views of masculine and feminine sex roles which will interfere with the assimilation of new information;
3. The client does not understand the ingredients conducive to sexual arousal (e.g., favorable times to have sex and interfering factors);
4. The client has a pattern of avoidance of sexual interactions and, as a result, he may unintentionally sabotage therapy; and
5. The client is uninformed about sexually transmitted diseases and is not using safer sex practices.

By making these assumptions—a priori—the therapist will be prepared for potential pitfalls in the therapeutic process, which will increase the likelihood of success. Of course, if the assumptions are inaccurate, the therapist can alter his/her approach. In every case, an inaccurate assumption indicates a therapeutic gain.

Challenges to Therapy

Sex therapy brings its own set of challenges. First, the typical client initially expects and prefers a medical solution to his problem. We have already cited the study by Segraves, Schoenberg, et al. (1982) in which the vast majority of men who sought treatment through a department of urology failed to follow through with recommendations that involved psychosocial assessment and/or treatment. Even though a conservative urologist may recommend a trial of sex therapy prior to penile prosthesis surgery, the client may prefer the seemingly simpler solution of surgery (better yet, a pill). The therapist's task is to earn the trust of the client.

Second, the discussion of sensitive and potentially embarrassing material requires special sensitivity. It is common for a client to say, "I have never told this to anyone else before." The therapist's reaction to such information is crucial and can either encourage or discourage further discussion. The therapist can encourage further discussion by acknowledging that the client may find it difficult to discuss sexual topics, by reassuring the client of his/her experience in dealing with sexual problems, and by remaining poised.

Third, a therapist working alone with couples *must* avoid the appearance of taking sides. Clients often assume that the therapist is aligned with the same-gender client. This issue should be discussed at the beginning of therapy, and throughout therapy as needed, to counteract such assumptions. Similarly, a therapist working alone with a single client of the opposite gender must reassure the client that he/she is experienced in dealing with other-gender sexual problems. In both client situations (couple or single), clients may make false assumptions about the therapist's knowledge or biases based solely on the therapist's gender.

Fourth, the therapist may encounter a client whose religious or cultural beliefs clash with a healthy approach to sex. For example, sensate focus may be contrary to some religious viewpoints. The therapist should, of course, always be sensitive to the possibility of such issues and never proceed with therapy until religious and culturally based beliefs related to sexual practice are thoroughly explored. We have found at times that a misinterpretation of a religious belief has been standing in the way of therapy. In such cases it is helpful to refer the client to an appropriate pastoral counselor who can interpret the belief system and work in consultation with the therapist.

Fifth, a wealth of data indicate that alcohol and drug abuse can adversely effect erectile functioning (Segraves & Segraves, 1992). The psychological and interpersonal effects of substance use can also be adverse. We have found it futile to work on sexual problems when there is an ongoing substance abuse problem. The substance abuse problem in almost all cases must be treated first and under control before a consistent program for sexual disorder can be implemented.

Sixth, we know from published accounts (e.g., Catalan et al., 1990; Segraves, Schoenberg, et al., 1982) that many clients terminate therapy prematurely. Knowing this in advance can help the therapist prevent it in some cases. We have found it useful to encourage our clients to discuss their reservations with us openly, and to join them in their skepticism: "I can understand why you are reluctant about this approach, I would be too if I were in your shoes. Why don't we give it a try for six weeks; then we can reevaluate the usefulness of this kind of approach for you. Is this plan acceptable to you?"

Treatment Methods

There are many ways to initiate healthy change. We are most comfortable with methods traditionally described as cognitive-behavioral, methods that have been researched more than other approaches in this domain. We have also been influenced by alternative paradigms and these influences are apparent. In this section we outline six general strategies that serve as the core of our therapeutic armamentarium.

Sensate Focus/Sexual Skills Training

Sensate focus was developed by Masters and Johnson (1970). Several key principles guide our use of this approach. The first and most important principle of sensate focus involves helping the client or couple to develop a heightened awareness of, and focus on, sensations rather than performance—hence, *sensate focus*. By doing this, a person or couple reduces anxiety by striving toward something that is immediately achievable (i.e., emotional comfort and physical pleasure) rather than simply trying to get an erection. The latter may not be achievable and may increase the risk of "failure" and embarrassment.

Second, sensate focus involves a structured but flexible approach to therapy. Sensate focus is structured in that clients are given explicit instructions for intimacy; if these instructions are followed, the client/couple gradually regains confidence in themselves and in their relationship. Thus, couples know what is expected of them; however, sensate focus is very flexible in that it can be accommodated to any couple's unique circumstances. It is critical that the therapist not forget to accommodate the procedures to the specific needs of his/her clients.

Third, sensate focus is a gradual approach to change. It is anticipated that change will take time, and there is no effort to rush ahead. One example of this principle is that clients discontinue intercourse early in therapy so that they can relearn the "basics" of being affectionate, receiving pleasure, and so on. For some clients, intercourse will not be reintroduced into their sexual repertoire for weeks or even months. The gradual approach can be distressing to some because it seems slow, so special care is needed in explaining the importance of this approach to clients. Failure to prepare clients for gradual change may lead to premature termination of the therapy.

Fourth, sensate focus therapy and home exercises need to be conducted in a shared and nonthreatening environment. The therapist needs to attend to both partners in a

couple to be sure that the exercises are proceeding at a nonthreatening pace.

There are also specific procedures guiding the sensate focus approach. The procedures outlined here, and in other sources, are not intended to be followed in a cookbook-type fashion. Rather, they are proffered as a guide and should only be followed as long as they are consistent with the spirit of the principles just outlined.

The procedures of sensate focus involve encouraging a couple to approach intimate physical and emotional involvement with each other in a gradual, nonthreatening manner. The general operating procedure involves homework, which encourages the couple to engage in sexually related exercises, and ongoing therapy sessions, which are used to discuss the exercises, emotions triggered by these exercises, problems, and so on.

Homework involves explicit instructions that the therapist has provided to the client; these instructions require practice of some exercise outside the therapeutic sessions. Both therapist and client understand that the homework will be reviewed and modified (as necessary) at each session. The homework exercises can be broken down into four "steps"; these steps are typically followed in a sequential fashion, but there are no absolutes here. Whether each step should be included, and the amount of time devoted to each, involve clinical judgments that the therapist will have to make.

The first step of sensate focus typically includes nongenital touching (i.e., pleasuring) while both partners are dressed in comfortable clothing. The least threatening behaviors may include back rubs or holding hands. Variations in the amount of clothing worn, the length of sessions, who initiates, the types of behaviors participated in, and the frequency of sessions should all be discussed in the therapy sessions before a couple goes home to practice. The couple should begin their physical involvement at a level that is acceptable to both participants.

Because many couples find this behavior to be somewhat slow, the therapist must emphasize right from the start that they are going through a necessary process in order to address their long-term goal, but that the short-term goal is to focus on sensations and not on performance. Discuss with the couple the mechanics of the approach. Be sure to discuss the value of structured versus unstructured practice and the frequency of the practice, as well as potentially interfering factors and potential problems.

Even if the therapist gives a clear explanation of the nonperformance aspects of sensate focus, some clients may miss the point. So, we try to be particularly explicit and often tell clients: "The next time you have a therapy session, I will *not* ask you about erections or orgasms; what I will ask you about is your ability to concentrate on receiving and giving pleasure, and on your ability to enjoy what you are doing." We repeat this message with couples because most couples are performance oriented (i.e., they focus on erection and orgasm) and, unless the therapist disabuses them of this notion, they retain performance criteria during the exercises. At this point, the therapist might also discuss with the client or couple the concept of performance anxiety. This should include exposing all-or-none thinking (e.g., sex equals intercourse) and other factors that interfere with enjoyable sex. The application of sensate focus cannot proceed unless the couple understands this concept, acknowledges that it applies to them, and appreciates the need for a different approach in thinking and behavior.

The second step, typically, involves genital pleasuring. During this phase of therapy, partners are encouraged to extend gentle touching to the genital and breast regions. Partners are encouraged to caress each other, in turn, in a way that is pleasurable. As before, the couple should be discouraged from focusing on performance-related goals (e.g., erection and orgasm). As the therapist progresses through sensate focus, he/she should review factors that facilitate or inhibit goals. By discussing these factors with the couple in a nonjudgmental way, they can become more in control of their own progress and feel less like pupils in a classroom.

Once a couple becomes comfortable with genital touching and is ready to resume sexual intercourse, we find it necessary to emphasize that even sexual intercourse can be broken down into several behaviors. Thus, we might encourage some couples to engage in "containment without thrusting." That is, the receptive partner permits penetration and controls all aspects of this exercise. For example, the depth of penetration and the amount of time spent on penetration can be varied. Again, we encourage flexibility and variation in order to remove pressure associated with a couple's tendency to think in all-or-none terms.

A common problem with this stage of sensate focus is that therapists rigidly adhere to the proscription on intercourse (Lipsius, 1987). Under some circumstances, proscription of intercourse can lead to loss of erotic feelings, loss of spontaneity, unnecessary frustration, and increase in resistance. Our approach to the proscription issue is to discuss with the couple all of the potential benefits and liabilities of proscription and point out that the couple is working on a process that will build for the future. Pressure from the therapist to ensure that a couple adheres to a proscription depends on clinical judgment.

In our view, a proscriptive approach may help a couple resume physical contact under certain circumstances. Three such circumstances include: (1) if a couple is very stressed by "sexual performance," (2) when there are a lot of interfering performance-oriented thoughts, and/or (3) if the couple has previously avoided all physical contact. On the other hand, couples who have not approached sexual relations so rigidly or with such intense emotional reactions may benefit from a general understanding of the purpose of sensate focus but with a more relaxed attitude toward proscription.

The final step of sensate focus proper includes thrusting and intercourse. Again, it is usually a good idea to encourage the receptive partner to initiate the movement, and for movements to be slow and gradual. As always, the couple is encouraged to focus on the sensations association with intercourse and not to be concerned about orgasm. The couple might try experimenting with different positions, not only assuming the same position(s) they used prior to therapy.

These are the general procedures that constitute sensate focus. Several authorities have elaborated the basics provided here (e.g., Kaplan, 1974; Masters & Johnson, 1970); the therapist may find it helpful to consult these references once he/she has worked comfortably with the procedures outlined above. At this point, however, we want to identify some of the potential problems that the therapist is likely to encounter.

It is relatively simple to use the sensate focus procedures, but sometimes the procedures are misunderstood and misapplied. For example, we have had couples enter therapy and report that they tried to avoid sex during a previous therapy but it did not work. Recently, a couple enrolled in therapy for the purpose of dealing with erectile difficulties. The husband explained that they had previously participated in sex therapy and had tried sensate focus. The approach used was to abstain from sex for a 2-week period. The couple had no understanding of the purpose of the procedure or the guidelines for their behavior. They left their previous therapy very dissatisfied.

McCarthy (1985) pointed out a number of the common mistakes in the use of sensate focus homework assignments. The most common mistake that therapists make is not explaining the details of the procedure and not engaging the couple in the decision-making process of the application. This often results in noncompliance. A second common mistake is a therapist's demand for performance as part of the procedure: "The next step in the procedure is to stimulate your partner in the genital area to the point of orgasm." This type of a statement may increase performance anxiety, especially in a vulnerable person. It would be preferable to state, "You have done well so far in concentrating on your sensations and feelings as you and your partner stimulate each other. Thus far you have included genital caressing. What do you feel the next step should be?" This approach allows a variety of responses without the anticipation of sexual failure or pressure. One additional mistake some therapists make involves premature termination of the sensate focus approach when a couple is noncompliant or encounters difficulties. Premature termination only reinforces avoidance. Difficulties should be discussed at length and barriers to progress should be identified and removed. Generally, we allow 3 weeks of noncompliance before changing procedures.

Another potential difficulty can emerge when therapy moves into the arena of homework procedures. At this time, a po-tential conflict exists between being natural and unstructured versus planned and structured. Most couples and individuals prefer to approach homework assignments in a "natural, unstructured" manner. With this approach the therapist describes the procedures involved and the principles behind the procedures but leaves it up to the couple to schedule other details such as the frequency and times for "practice." Although intuitively this may be the preferred strategy, couples often return to therapy without having carried out the assignment. Perhaps the reason is that all too often, there is a strong history of sexual avoidance; therefore, the individual or couple cannot get started without raising anxiety levels unacceptably high.

Thus, we usually explain the pluses and minuses of structured versus unstructured strategies before providing homework exercises. The client can then choose a strategy while being fully aware of the potential for noncompliance. At times, a client may "try out" a certain strategy and, upon failure, adopt a different approach. In addition to the issue of structured versus unstructured practice, the therapist should explore other potential obstacles in the face of carrying out therapy procedures (e.g., relatives living in the house, work schedules, medical concerns, and travel plans). Once these potential obstacles are identified and solutions are generated, the rationale and details of homework can begin.

Many benefits may result from the sensate focus procedure. New behaviors may be learned, along with new approaches to sexual interactions. We have dealt with couples who have had very narrow approaches to sex. It is not unusual, for example, for a couple to report that they engage in no touching behavior at all. They may kiss once and then have intercourse. We have even encountered couples who view foreplay as "something that kids do." For such a couple, sensate focus offers a structured opportunity to challenge established habits that may be restricting pleasure and causing sex problems.

Sensate focus may also help to change a person's perception of his/her partner. A common problem is approaching sexual intimacy with intercourse as the only goal. In a heterosexual couple, the female partner may begin to see herself as an object of her partner's pleasure and not as a companion who is loved. The sensate focus procedure can help a couple to focus on each other with mutual affection rather than as objects of arousal. Sensate focus can also be quite diagnostic. Difficulties that emerge often carry important information about other problems that a couple is having. These other problems often cannot be addressed through sensate focus itself.

Sensate focus should be viewed as one part of a total treatment approach; it is *not* a complete therapy in itself. Thus, communication issues, faulty attitudes that interfere with sexual enjoyment, and nonsexual marital conflicts are examples of therapy concerns that may be dealt with concomitantly with sensate focus.

Education

Providing information may be the most common component of sex therapy. Information can help to correct myths and to reverse misunderstandings that impair sexual functioning. For example, the belief that foreplay is for kids or that intercourse is the only true form of sex can be devastating to a middle-aged or elderly male and his partner. Similarly, the belief that the erection must appear first (i.e., *before* sexual activity) in order to signal sexual interest and desire can limit a man's sexual opportunities. The net effect of these beliefs is that a male who does not obtain an erection prior to a sexual interaction will not participate in sex. We have known many men who avoided sexual interactions for years partly because they adhered to these beliefs.

Zilbergeld (1992) lists a dozen of the more common myths that men (and women) believe:

1. We're liberated folks who are very comfortable with sex;
2. A real man isn't into sissy stuff like feelings and communicating;
3. All touching is sexual or should lead to sex;
4. A man is always interested in and always ready for sex;
5. A real man performs in sex;
6. Sex is centered on a hard penis and what's done with it;

7. Sex equals intercourse;
8. A man should be able to make the earth move for his partner, or at the very least knock her socks off;
9. Good sex requires orgasm;
10. Men don't have to listen to women in sex;
11. Good sex is spontaneous, with no planning and no talking; and
12. Real men don't have sex problems.

The trouble with these and similar myths is that they create expectations that cannot be fulfilled (most of the time) and inevitably lead to disappointment, guilt, and blame. A surprisingly valuable service is providing accurate information and debunking such myths. For example, informing a couple or individual that biological factors may play a role in erectile disorder can relieve guilt or blame. It is also helpful to provide correct information about anatomy and physiology, as well as normative sexual behavior. (Education about sexually transmitted diseases, including human immunodeficiency virus and acquired immunodeficiency syndrome, and safer sex practices can be lifesaving and should be offered routinely.)

Education can be provided in a number of ways. For example, some clients request reading suggestions. Fortunately, there are many excellent books available (see, e.g., Schover, 1984; Spark, 1991; Zilbergeld, 1992). A therapist may want to develop his/her own reading list as new books become available and others go out of print. The therapist may also find it useful to purchase several copies of his/her favorite guides and have them available to loan out. Alternatively, a therapist might identify one or two local bookstores and ply them with purchasing suggestions. In any event, we advise therapists to read any book they recommend to a client and be prepared to discuss its contents during the sessions. Other clients prefer to ask questions during therapy. Still others are reluctant to ask for information directly; for these clients, the therapist needs to take advantage of naturally occurring opportunities to give impromptu lectures.

Stimulus Control

We know that awkward circumstances are not conducive to relaxed, enjoyable sexual relations. When taken to an extreme, such circumstances can contribute to erectile disorder. Consider the following example: A client complained of loss of erection with his very sensuous and eager girlfriend and wanted to know why. During the assessment interview he was asked about the circumstances under which sex occurred. He reported that the first time he attempted sexual intercourse with his girlfriend, he was in the back seat of a Volkswagen in a church parking lot. With horrified churchgoing onlookers walking by, it is easy *for us* to understand why he lost his erection. However, our client had not identified his circumstances as a source of interference.

The moral of the story is that you should never assume that a couple is approaching sexual relations in a manner that is conducive to arousal. On many occasions we have encountered clients who never kiss, touch, fondle, stroke, or hug prior to attempting intercourse; yet these clients expect an erection to emerge once they attempt intromission. Inquire about the details of the foreplay, as well as the erotic environment. Ask whether each partner is satisfied with what has been occurring.

Stimulus control refers to efforts to establish a pleasant, relaxing environment that is conducive to sexual expression, thereby minimizing interfering circumstances. Even simple suggestions such as arranging for a baby sitter, cleaning up the bedroom, or putting on relaxing music can be helpful. Surprisingly, these suggestions are not obvious to some clients. Clients sometimes need to be reminded of the efforts they made during courtship to "set the mood." Once ensconced in a relationship, many forget these preparations, or think that they are unimportant.

Relatedly, many couples do not set aside a time for sexual expression. Commonly, couples attempt sex under the pressure of "the first free moment during a busy week." They expect good sex to be spontaneous and unplanned. Again, many will have forgotten all the planning that went into "spontaneous" sexual expression during courtship. We often encourage clients to schedule a time for sex, and to plan for it with as much effort as they might for any other special event in their life. We remind them that anticipation fuels desire.

Cognitive Restructuring

Two forms of cognitive restructuring can be helpful: challenging negative attitudes and reducing interfering thoughts. Exposing and helping a client to change negative attitudes is a complex therapeutic task. One of the differences between a myth (or misunderstanding) and a negative attitude is that the latter is held onto tenaciously despite compelling data to the contrary. For example, a man may feel very negatively toward women and believe that women cannot be trusted. This attitude may be the result of a previous relationship in which the man's partner was unfaithful. In this man's current relationship, he may interpret his partner's lack of passion as evidence of being unfaithful. Assuming that the partner's low desire is due to other factors (e.g., fatigue), it may take considerable therapeutic effort to address his general negative and untrusting attitude toward women.

A second example of a negative attitude involves men who become very upset with themselves because of their erectile problems and fear ridicule from their partner. Also not uncommon in heterosexual males are fears of homosexuality; that is, heterosexual men often interpret difficulty in obtaining or maintaining an erection as a sign that they are gay. In both homosexual and heterosexual males, erectile difficulties raise fears regarding masculinity. In all cases, these negative attitudes should be approached with caution—a client may be very defensive and have a great deal invested in holding on to a negative belief. Therapists may have to deal with such issues in individual therapy before couple therapy can proceed.

Regardless of the precipitating factors, most cases of erectile disorder are *exacerbated* and *maintained* by interfering thoughts that precede and occur during sexual relations. As we explain to clients, these interfering thoughts are not erotic or sexy thoughts; moreover, they decrease arousal and inhibit erection. In non-dysfunctional men, thoughts preceding and occurring during sexual relations usually focus on their partner's or their own body parts, seductive behaviors, and anticipation of arousal and pleasure. In contrast, the dysfunctional male is preoccupied with worries regarding the firmness of his erection; images of one's partner being disappointed, angry, or ridiculing; and distinct feelings of anxiety and depression.

To deal with interfering thoughts, the therapist must first help the client to identify the presence of such thoughts. Once such thoughts are identified and it is agreed that they do occur in association with sexual behavior, the therapist must help the client reduce the occurrence of such thoughts. It is often helpful to give the client alternative thoughts on which to focus during sexual activity. For example, focusing on body parts or a sequence of sexual activities is usually more conducive to arousal. However, the therapist should be prepared for such suggestions to lead to discussions about whether it is "normal" or "healthy" to fantasize about sex (or about sex with another partner) during actual sexual activity. Some clients feel strongly that fantasizing is tantamount to cheating on their partner. Obviously, such discussions have to be approached with a great deal of care and sensitivity. We also find it helpful to have clients read the chapter on sexual fantasies in McCarthy (1988) or the material in Zilbergeld (1992, pp. 125–133).

Another strategy to help the client focus his thinking on more positive thoughts is to have him recall his thought content during past satisfying sexual experiences. This usually sensitizes the client to the types of thoughts on which he should concentrate. If the client has difficulty remembering positive sexual thoughts, the therapist may wish to supply "typical" helpful thoughts. Here exposure to erotic literature or videotapes may be helpful.

It is always intriguing that despite the obvious presence of interfering thoughts, many clients ignore or dismiss such thoughts as contributors to sexual difficulties; instead they focus on the perception of their own, or their partner's, inadequacy.

It may also be helpful to a client to suggest compartmentalizing thoughts. Specific times during the day should be set aside to focus on worry and problem solving; other times should be set aside for pleasant thoughts and sexual thoughts. Putting such categories of thoughts on schedule may help a client to eliminate negative thinking during sexual time.

When a partner is involved in treatment, it is important also to consider that partner's cognitions around the disorder. Just as the man with erectile disorder harbors negative associations around this problem, so, too, the partner can be expected to have negative cognitions. Typical partner responses may include the following: "I'm no longer attractive"; "he doesn't love me anymore"; "he must be having an affair with someone else"; "he isn't trying; he doesn't want to have sex with me."

We always ask the partner what he/she thinks is the cause of the erectile problem. It is very important to help clear up possible misunderstandings before proceeding to an intervention. If potential misunderstandings are not addressed, it is likely they will arise again and sabotage treatment progress.

Negative beliefs and interfering thoughts can present impediments to sexual expression and enjoyment. In some cases, it is possible to address these cognitive difficulties as a part of the sex therapy itself. In other cases, however, more intensive cognitive restructuring may be needed, usually in the context of individual therapy. Because cognitive therapy techniques and process can be quite involved and quite useful, we recommend that the therapist familiarize him/herself with more detailed accounts of these methods (e.g., Beck, 1976; see also Young, Beck, & Weinberger, Chapter 6, this volume).

Communication Training

Communication problems are frequently encountered when dealing with male erectile disorder. In our practice, we have developed a handout to clients that serves as both an assessment tool and a therapeutic guide. The handout is a 10-page pamphlet which describes common couple communication problems and suggests how to overcome these problems. The typical problems in communication include:

1. *Off beam.* Starting to discuss one problem and drifting into another.
2. *Mind reading.* Guessing the meaning of your partner's statement because you think you know your partner so well.
3. *Kitchen sinking.* Starting to discuss one problem and bringing in every other problem.

4. *Yes butting.* Each partner listening but continuing to think that the other is wrong.
5. *Cross complaining.* Each response containing a new complaint.
6. *Standoff.* Tending to repeat the same argument over and over without progress or resolution.

We have found it both time saving and effective to hand out the communication pamphlet to couples at the first sign of communication problems. We typically instruct clients to read the handout independently (we give one to each partner), and to check off those problems that seem to apply to their relationship. We then discuss the various areas of communication difficulties, often with examples from the couple's own experiences. It is very important for the therapist to establish, from the beginning, that the review of the examples is designed to look at the process of communication and not to illustrate or determine who was right or wrong.

Tannen (1990) has also proven to be a helpful adjunct for some heterosexual couples. Tannen skillfully identifies common problems in women's and men's attempts to communicate with each other. She traces these problems to our culture and, in so doing, avoids blaming either gender. Her writing is entertaining and informative, and many clients will profit from it.

Another way to work on communication involves the paired-reports assessment methodology described previously. Recall that the partners complete a questionnaire (e.g., a list of statements about sexual preferences) for themselves and then as they think their partner would. We study the level of agreement and understanding in these paired reports. It can be therapeutic to discover partners' views and false perceptions of one another. Of course, this approach can also be threatening to some, so caution is advised.

The therapist should serve as a model of good communication style during all sessions. This is achieved by active listening, a display of empathy, asking clients to express themselves clearly, and other such social and communication skills. In addition, the therapist should continually look for improvements in communication skills and point

these out to a couple when they occur. It is helpful to inform the couple that, throughout the therapy, communication skills will be continually monitored and addressed when appropriate. By stating this at the outset, clients will not feel picked on when a communication issue is raised.

In many cases, the erectile problem cannot be addressed until communication improves. In such cases, we often point out that sexual expression is a form of communication and that it will be enhanced by focusing on communication training.

Health Promotion Strategies

It is unlikely that yogurt and bean sprouts will cure erectile problems. However, there is evidence that men with erectile problems are more likely to smoke cigarettes as well as drink coffee and alcohol (Cranston-Cuebas & Barlow, 1989). Moreover, there is now evidence that regular exercise (3 days per week) results in enhanced sexual health, including frequency of intimate activities, improved erections, and higher percentage of satisfying orgasms (White, Case, McWhirter, & Mattison, 1990). The amount of enhancement is correlated with the degree of an individual's improvement in fitness.

Based on findings such as these, some surgeons (e.g., Lewis, 1991) require patients who smoke or chew tobacco to cease prior to consideration for revascularization surgery. Similarly, we encourage men who are inactive to become active, smokers to reduce or quit, drinkers to exercise moderation, and carnivores to be more selective about their diet. We do not lead clients to expect large improvements in their sexual functioning, but such suggestions can help. Clients who are seriously motivated to improve their erectile functioning may initiate such lifestyle changes independently, whereas others may require the therapist's guidance.

Developing a Comprehensive Therapy Approach

In most instances, clients present with a variety of concerns that require a multifaceted therapy plan. We have found it useful to include clients in setting priorities, and, since all presenting concerns are not equally urgent, in deciding which ones should be addressed first. It is often the case that higher-order concerns (e.g., marital distress) need attention prior to the erectile disorder. It is most helpful when clients can recognize this for themselves. Even though one may target a nonsexual problem as being a higher priority, sometimes there is positive transfer from one target domain to another; in these cases, progress seems to occur simultaneously, as if yoked on parallel tracks. In other cases, it will be necessary to proceed sequentially, addressing one part of the client's problem portfolio at a time. It is important to share this view of therapy with one's client.

Because other authors in this book have presented detailed information about related problems (e.g., depression and marital distress), we have not addressed these concerns in detail. Nevertheless, this does not suggest that such concerns will recede if the sexual problem is addressed. Rather, it may be necessary to consult these chapters (Young, Beck, & Weinberger, Chapter 6, this volume; Cordova & Jacobson, Chapter 12, this volume) for guidance when developing a comprehensive therapy plan for one's client.

CASE STUDY

Background

"Fred" was referred for sex therapy by a urologist who had examined him for a complaint of male erectile disorder. The urologist's examination was negative for any complicating diseases and the medical report included the following information:

"On physical examination, he is a well-developed, well-virilized male. He has a normal, circumcised phallus. His testes are both descended and normal in size. He has normal cremasteric reflexes and normal perinal sensations. His prostrate is small and benign. His Testosterone is 49l. He has a normal CBC [complete blood count] and his Prolactin is 5. He has penile Doppler studies done at City Hospital using papaverine pre- and post-study and he has perfectly normal blood flow. NPT [nocturnal penile tumescence

monitoring] studies indicate full erection."

Based on the urologist's report, it was almost certain that Fred's erectile disorder was unlikely to be the result of biological risk factors. Thus, our assessment was designed to evaluate the role of psychosocial risk factors. As will be evident, much of the clinical data implicated dyadic concerns caused primarily by psychosocial factors.

Clinical Interview

Fred (F) and his wife, Emily (E), both attended the first session. Following introductory remarks, the session with therapist (T) began:

T: Fred, as you know, you were referred by Dr. Russell and he has sent me your medical evaluation. He could find no medical explanation for your sexual difficulties and referred you to me to help evaluate the nonmedical factors that may be affecting you. My usual procedure is to meet with each partner alone in order to gather information from each person's perspective. Before I meet with each of you individually, I would like to give you an opportunity to ask me about my background or therapy procedures. Also, I need to ask you some background information for my records.

At this point, there was an exchange of questions and answers and background information was obtained.

Fred was a 42-year-old prominent educator in the state and the president of a large professional organization. This was his second marriage; his first marriage lasted 7 years and he had retained custody of his daughter, Donna, who was now 20 yeas old. Fred's first marriage had ended in a divorce after he discovered that his wife was having an affair. He had been married to Emily, his second wife, for 8 years. Donna was away at college; he and Emily had no children together.

Emily was a 39-year-old social worker. This was her first marriage. She worked as a homemaker and mother for the first 6 years of the marriage. When Donna left home for college, Emily returned to her social work position full time. Although this was her first marriage, Emily had had a number of long-term relationships and was very comfortable with her sexuality.

Both Fred and Emily described the problem as difficulty attaining an erection, compounded by a lack of interest in sex (i.e., low sexual desire). They had avoided all sexual relations for about 3 months and both agreed that it was "Fred's problem," although Emily reported low desire also since "it's been so long without sex that I don't even want it anymore."

Following the initial questions and answers, Fred chose to be the first to be interviewed alone. Both Fred and Emily were given the DSFI; they were instructed to complete it, without consulting each other, and to return the questionnaire by mail before the next session.

Session 1

T: [With Fred alone.] Fred, in this time alone, I would like to learn from your point of view details of your relationship with Emily with particular emphasis on your sexual concerns. I want you to know that everything you tell me is strictly confidential and will only be shared with Emily if you give me permission to do so. Perhaps, you can begin by giving me a chronology of your relationship with Emily starting with when you met her.

F: Well, I met Emily about two years before we were married. A friend introduced us and we seemed to hit it off right away. She had a good personality and seemed to be a very stable person but . . . I don't want you to tell her this but . . . umm . . . I was never strongly sexually attracted to her.

T: Did you find her unattractive?

F: No, nothing like that. I mean, she's very clean and she takes very good care of herself. But it's just that she's not really . . . sexy, I guess.

T: What do you find "sexy"?

F: Well, umm, that's hard . . . I guess someone who is more . . . risqué . . .

or wilder. But, then again, it is hard for me to see myself with that kind of person. I like stable, conservative kind of people. I know I am talking out of both sides of my mouth, right?

T: Well, it does seem like you are attracted by personal characteristics that may conflict.

F: Don't get me wrong. I was attracted to her but sex just wasn't that strong of a drive for me when it came to our relationship.

T: Did you ever have any sexual problems with Emily at the beginning of your relationship.

F: Oh . . . no. No problems, but probably not all that frequent for a new relationship. Compared to other women, not that I have been involved in that many relationships, Emily just wasn't that . . . umm . . . sexually arousing to me.

T: What did you find attractive about Emily?

F: Emily is a very stable person; she's caring and reliable, and I needed a good mother for my daughter. I wanted companionship and Emily was a good companion. She's very well rounded. But, as I said, sex was not a big part of our relationship. We got along well and she was someone I could count on. My daughter, Donna, liked Emily and Emily liked Donna. I was able to do my work and we got along fine.

T: Was sex ever a problem or a concern at the beginning of your relationship?

F: Not really. I think Emily might have questioned why we didn't have sex more often but I really didn't give it much thought. We never really fought about it . . . we . . . I . . . just kind of, well, avoided it, I guess.

T: What were things like once you got married? Did anything change?

F: Not really. Everything was fine for the first few years. I became more and more involved in my professional organization; eventually, I became the president— I'm very proud of that. Emily didn't complain about my involvement, at first, maybe because she was so busy with my daughter—they were very close and did everything together. Plus, she knew it was good for my career.

T: When did sexual problems start to develop between you and Emily?

F: I guess everything started after my daughter went to college. This was a real loss to Emily and she seemed to be very stressed out. She started complaining more and more about the time I was spending in the organization and about the lack of sex.

T: Did you begin to experience difficulty getting an erection at that time?

F: Yes. And, Emily would ask me, "What's wrong?" She would say, "How come you're not hard?" And, she would cry. God, this made me feel awful and I didn't want to hurt her so I just avoided it more and more.

T: What did you think was causing the problem at the time?

F: I don't know. It was hard for me to find the time and I was tired a lot. I also thought that something was physically wrong.

T: Why would you think there was something physically wrong?

F: Well . . . because my father had a heart attack when he was young . . . and he and my mother were never sexually . . . compatible, I'd guess you'd say. I think he had erection problems.

T: How did you know about your parents' sex life?

F: I would hear remarks my mother made and they fought about it once in a while. Sometimes I overheard their arguments . . . they didn't know I could hear them . . . but I've always thought maybe the same thing was going to happen to me because of the heart problem.

T: Do you have any history of cardiac problems?

F: No, and I've been checked out by the best in town, Dr. Hilgard [a well-regarded cardiologist]. My cholesterol is 220, which, hey, ain't bad for a guy my age, and my blood pressure is normal. As you can see I'm a little overweight but I like to eat.

T: What about diabetes?

F: No, no one in my family . . . no, I don't think so.

T: Any other diseases that might cause you sex problems?

F: No.

T: Are you taking any medications currently?

F: Just an occasional aspirin for a headache. Oh, and allergy pills, antihistamines, in the spring.

T: OK, as Dr. Russell suggested, you appear to have few medical risk factors, but it is understandable for you to think there might be a medical problem behind your erection difficulties. Many men suspect this, and for good reason. But, fortunately, you have been given a clean bill of health as Dr. Russell found no significant medical problems.

F: I know its foolish to think there were medical problems, especially since I do get erections at times.

T: When do you get erections?

F: During the night and in the morning before I go to the bathroom.

T: Do you often awaken with an erection?

F: Yes, nearly every day, I think.

T: It is very normal for men to masturbate throughout their life. Some men might use masturbation to make sure everything works OK. What is your experience? [Note that the question was framed in a sensitive way because some men are uncomfortable with masturbation. We try to avoid asking: "Do you masturbate?"]

F: Oh yeah. It works OK during masturbation. I'm not ashamed. I know it's normal to masturbate.

T: Can you get an erection if Emily stimulates you manually?

F: Sometimes, especially if I don't expect it and I am relaxed, like on the weekends when we sleep in . . . sometimes, before, she would surprise me, so to speak. I like that . . . (*voice trails off*)

T: Have you, on some occasions, been able to have sexual intercourse with Emily with a full erection?

F: Yes. At times, but I can't predict when.

T: What is your relationship with Emily like right now?

F: It's ... very tense. I feel somewhat pressured ... like get up or get out. We haven't had sex for several months now and Emily is very upset. I've been so busy, I can't seem to find the time. I'm out every night of the week with my organization. I feel I have an obligation since I am president. I can't let people down.

The remainder of the first interview focused on Fred's relationship with Emily and on his past marriage. He reported that he loved Emily and he did not wish to end his marriage. He also revealed that when he is able to get an erection, everything about sex is enjoyable. He had no complaints about Emily's sexual functioning and saw the problem as his.

He reported that his first wife had an affair behind his back and later told him it was because he was never around. Toward the end of the interview he was asked: "Is there anything, that we haven't discussed, that Emily would complain about?" Fred answered by saying that Emily would complain that he drank too much but he didn't consider this a problem. He told the therapist that he could share everything with Emily except the part about not being sexually attracted to her at first.

Session 2

T: [With Emily alone.] Emily, in this time alone, I would like to learn from your point of view details of your relationship with Fred with particular emphasis on your sexual concerns. As I mentioned to Fred, everything we discuss will be kept confidential unless you tell me it is OK to share it.

E: Fine, good. I understand this. I tell my [social work] clients the same thing. I'm glad you do it this way although I have no secrets. I tell Fred what I think.

T: Did Fred discuss anything about my session with him?

E: No, nothing. You see ... he doesn't volunteer much these days, and he isn't

much for discussions about our sexuality ... or about our relationship. He avoids it actually.

T: Has anything changed since I last met with you.

E: No, everything is basically the same but we haven't had any fights this week. I've kind of backed off ... I'm taking a "wait-and-see" approach. I want to see if this [therapy] can help.

T: Emily, would you please tell me about your relationship with Fred? For example, How did it begin? What attracted you to him? What was sex like at the beginning?

E: Everything was fine at the beginning. I thought he was charming and sophisticated. He *is* ... but back then, he used to talk to me all the time. We were very close. I got along well with his daughter, Donna, and we were a happy family. We didn't have the usual problems that step mothers and daughters have.

T: What was sex like at the beginning?

E: Sex was OK, but I don't think we had it often enough.

T: Did you think this was a problem?

E: Yes. I think I even mentioned it to him but he would say he was too tired, or too busy. He worked an awful lot, and put in a lot of time on the extracurricular stuff. But you know about that.

T: When did he start having erection problems?

E: Several years ago. At first I figured that it was temporary—maybe stress or fatigue worsened by his drinking. Then, when it persisted, I told him he should get help. You know he became president of [the organization] and it seemed that ended our relationship. I've asked him over and over again to quit but it is too important to him. More important than me. (*teary*)

T: Do you feel he chooses work over you?

E: I know he does. I told him that and he admits it. You know, he also drinks too much and I think he is an alcoholic. He won't accept it. My father was an alcoholic and I'm very sensitive to this problem. Fred drinks every day. He chooses to drink with his business friends every day after work rather than coming home. He says it—the socializing and the drinking—is an important part of his work since his position is political. He comes home really drunk sometimes. He has an addictive personality, but won't admit it. Even when he is home, he is always on the phone with business associates.

T: Has he ever been confronted on his drinking?

E: Hundreds of times, but I've given up. I've even said if you love me you would stop. My father was an alcoholic and I hate it. But, he goes right on drinking.

T: If Fred isn't drinking and he had been attentive to you and he is able to get an erection, what is sex like then?

E: Actually, sex has been quite good . . . when we've had it. Fred is a good lover and he seems to enjoy it. I know I do. I need the closeness, it's important to a relationship—it's important to me. It is just . . . well . . . that he is never interested . . . and he chooses his work over me.

T: Do you feel things have gone too far between you two? Is there too much water over the dam?

E: (*After long pause*) Yes. I don't see any hope. (*tearful*)

T: I get the impression though that if Fred was more sensitive to your needs you would be happy. You don't seem to hate him but rather you seem hopeless to make him change.

E: You're right. I don't hate him. He is a good man.

T: You mentioned before that your father drank a lot. What was your childhood like?

E: My father was a doctor and I had two brothers and two sisters. My father was a drunk and one of my brothers and one of my sisters are alcoholics. My mother was a good woman but she was weak and overwhelmed by all of us children and couldn't really care for us. We were left on our own a lot and I was taken care of by my older sisters.

The remainder of the session focused on Emily's childhood, psychosexual development, and current health status. She was never sexually abused and had a healthy attitude toward sex but had somewhat low self-esteem in spite of her academic and professional achievements. She was in excellent health; she did not drink or smoke, and walked 2 miles a day.

Summary of Assessment

On the basis of the medical and clinical interview data and the DSFI it was clear that there were some significant psychosocial risk factors present for the erection concerns. The DSFI suggested that both Emily and Fred had a good fund of basic sexual knowledge. Moreover, the DSFI confirmed the lack of sexual activity but suggested that Fred did have a level of sexual desire that was within normal limits. Emily reported a lack of confidence in her body image, which was a reflection of her more generalized, low self-esteem.

The following areas were targeted as worthy of therapeutic attention:

1. Fred's alcohol use;
2. Fred's commitment to his work and placement of Emily (and their relationship) as secondary;
3. The couple's inability to schedule time together;
4. Fred's low desire for Emily since the beginning of the relationship;
5. Emily's low self-esteem;
6. Emily pressuring Fred for sex and negative comments about his erection disorder; and
7. Fred's performance anxiety.

Since both Fred and Emily seemed to like and respect each other, there seemed to be some hope of working on the problem in spite of Emily's statement that there was too much "water over the dam." Both also recognized that Fred had too much of a commitment to his work and his presidency position; thus, it seemed logical to address this issue first in order to establish quality time to work on other marital and sexual issues.

Session 3

T: [With Fred and Emily together.] Before we begin, I was wondering if there have been any changes or new issues which we should discuss?

E: Things are a little less tense but nothing has really changed.

F: I would agree. I think since we started coming here there has been less pressure.

T: Well, in reviewing all of the information from both of you, I think both of you would agree that the amount of time you spend together is very limited. I also think you would both agree that Fred's commitment to his presidency position is very time-consuming and seems to interfere with you two getting together. I think this is the first important area we have to look at. So, before we can successfully address the sexual issues, we need to work together to do two things: First, we need to increase the amount of quality time you two spend together. And, second, we need to enhance your ability to communicate effectively. Both of you seem to want to work on the relationship—that's a big plus from my point of view—and both seem to be able to point to many positive attributes in one another—another plus. You two may disagree, however, on the problem of drinking and this is something that we will also have to address. Basically, I am suggesting that we address the issue of time commitment and priorities in your lives; once this is settled, we will be able to address the alcohol and sexual issues. [Note that additional information obtained from interviewing (not transcribed here) and questionnaire data revealed that Fred's drinking difficulties were not serious enough to postpone the sexual and marital therapy.] How do you feel about what I have been saying?

E: I agree. I don't see how we can have sex if Fred is never home.

F: I agree too but I don't see how I can give up the presidency. People elected me and they are counting on me.

T: Let me allay your concern Fred: You are not being asked to give up your presi-

dency. However, you will be asked to look at all of your time commitments in order to see which are discretionary and which are absolutely essential in your view. I am encouraged by your commitment to coming to see me and you have already shown considerable flexibility in this regard. Let me emphasize, though, that if you can't schedule quality time together that is satisfactory to both of you, then we won't get very far in addressing your sexual concerns.

E: (Addressing Fred) You don't have to stay and drink with the board members every Friday.

F: (Defensively) It's not all social. A lot gets accomplished during that social time. My position is very political—you know that—and many important decisions are made on Friday afternoons.

T: Fred, I'm sure you are in the best position to judge what is important about your job. On the other hand, can you understand how your work-related time commitment affects Emily and your relationship together?

F: I'm sure it makes her very upset but I don't know what I can do. People are counting on me. Besides, I'm afraid that if I start giving up my time, Emily will just want more and more.

E: That's not true. Fred always gets his way about everything. He does what's good for Fred. I feel so unimportant.

T: This is an issue which undoubtedly deserves a lot of discussion. Therapy isn't designed to determine who is right or wrong, and relationships—by definition—require compromises. So we will use the therapy to look at the process of decision making. We can use examples, such as Fred's socializing with his board on Fridays, but only to illustrate a problem which you two have to make decisions about and which you have to communicate about. You'll have to work together on this, like a team, toward a goal.

The remainder of the session focused on how therapy should proceed. It was decided that therapy should begin with Fred alone since he agreed that he was responsible for most of the critical issues. The pros and cons of this strategy were discussed. In addition, Fred and Emily discussed what each wanted out of the relationship. It was clear from this discussion that Fred did not have very well-developed expectations for his marriage. He was asked to think about this for the next meeting.

Session 4

T: [With Fred alone.] Fred, I would like to begin this session by getting an update from you since our session last week. I would like to know if you have given any thought to what expectations you had for your marriage and also, whether you have given any thought to your time commitments?

F: I've given it a little thought although I have been very busy. Basically, when I married Emily, I was looking for someone who could take care of my daughter and someone whom I could get along with. I wasn't really thinking of love or long-term commitment. I guess I had a problem with commitment after my first marriage. I'm afraid that if I'm committed to someone, it will restrict my freedom and I'm also afraid that it will be painful if the relationship breaks up.

T: Can you understand how Emily might feel like this: Because Fred is putting almost all of his time into his profession, he is choosing his professional life over his personal life?

F: I have kind of resigned myself to the fact that my marriage will fail and there is nothing I can do about it.

T: It seemed to me that Emily wants the relationship to work. She also wants to feel that you care. I think that if you really wanted to work on the relationship you could build a good relationship.

The remainder of the session was spent on exploring and challenging the cognitions Fred held concerning commitment to Emily. He was able to challenge the idea that Emily would want "more and more" and that she would reject him at some point. He was challenged to think more about his re-

lationship with the understanding that therapy would not address couple-related issues until he made some personal decisions.

Session 5

F: [With Fred alone.] (*Begins talking before being addressed*) I think I've made a lot of progress. I thought a lot about our last session and I have made some real efforts to change. I've set aside time and I've spent three nights with Emily. It was like dating again. I even felt . . . horny. (*nervous laugh*) I also met an old friend of mine and he told me how miserable he is in his marriage. His wife is terrible —it helped me to realize what I have. I feel different . . . hopeful. (*smiling*)

T: You certainly sound enthusiastic. What thoughts have you given to some of the problematic issues we had previously discussed such as your drinking and commitment?

F: As far as the drinking goes, I don't think I can give it up but I guess I'll have to try. I know it is important to Emily but I really don't think it is as bad as she thinks. You see, Emily is very . . . touchy on this subject because of her father. She is quick to call someone an alcoholic . . . it's almost if you drink at all, in her eyes, you're an alcoholic. I don't think a couple of drinks makes you a drunk. You know, I'm a member of a wine tasting club and I approach this very intellectually. I enjoy it.

The remainder of the session focused on the possibility of a controlled drinking approach, which Fred thought was a good compromise. He was going to discuss this with Emily. He also mentioned that both he and Emily were being tested for sexually transmitted diseases (STDs) since each had genital infections. Both had failed to mention this in the initial separate interviews when asked about their medical history because of embarrassment.

This session seemed to be a real turning point in the therapy. Fred had evaluated the thinking behind his behavior and concluded that he wanted to work on and improve his marriage. He had a renewed sense of hope, which allowed him to consider his priorities regarding work and his relationship. He considered ways to spend more time with Emily. This session also revealed that Fred's fear of STDs was a strong but previously latent concern that had been affecting his sexual desire and comfort with sexual intercourse.

Sessions 6–10

Progress in therapy continued rapidly once the couple was given a clean bill of health concerning the possibility of STDs. Sexual intercourse resumed without erectile disorder and both Emily and Fred reported increased sexual desire. Fred had rearranged his work schedule and cut down his outside commitments to a level that was acceptable to both him and Emily. The couple set aside priority time for each other and each shared responsibility for planning time together.

Excessive drinking may have contributed to low desire and erectile difficulties. When Fred was drinking, Emily was angry and not the least bit interested in sex; she had many negative associations because of her family history. Moreover, when he was drinking, it was more difficult for Fred to obtain an erection. Fred and Emily were able to work out a satisfactory controlled drinking agreement as follows: Fred would drink only in connection with his wine tasting club or when Emily was with him.

Prior to therapy, both his drinking and his commitment to his job were viewed by Fred as black-and-white issues. Indeed, the couple had argued about both issues in an all-or-none fashion and had not been able to negotiate a compromise solution. The more flexible approach to both of these issues discussed in therapy, along with Fred's willingness to work on the problems, helped to promote constructive change.

Emily attended the final two sessions and corroborated all the gains reported by Fred. One final aspect of therapy was relapse prevention (see McCrady, Chapter 8, this volume). Working with the therapist, Fred conceptualized himself as a "risk taker, addictive personality and as someone who likes to burn the candle at both ends." Accepting this conceptualization helped Fred to set up a program to "protect himself from himself." He agreed not to take on any additional responsibilities without first discussing them with Emily.

Based on the assessment information, it seemed likely that a comprehensive therapy plan for this couple would have included all six core components. The data that suggested a need for each of the core components appear in Table 11.1.

Therapy moved along very rapidly once Fred took stock of his situation, made significant changes in his time commitment to Emily, and reduced his drinking. These changes had an almost immediate and very positive effect on Emily; as a result, communication between the partners improved with only minimal therapist guidance. In relatively few sessions, the therapist was able to address the educational issues, stimulus-control issues, and cognitive restructuring. The couple resumed enjoyable sexual relations without the introduction of sensate focus procedures. As it turned out, the positive feelings that were triggered, the lack of alcohol use during sexual activity, and the reassurance that neither partner had an STD combined to contribute to the improvement in sexual satisfaction. In our experience, it appears that couples like Emily and Fred, who at one time in their relationship enjoyed satisfying sexual relations, are much more likely to overcome sexual difficulties than are couples who have never enjoyed a satisfactory sexual relationship.

CONCLUDING COMMENTS

In this chapter we have tried to provide basic information regarding the definition, prevalence, and etiology of male erectile disorder. Although our overview on these topics has been necessarily brief, we hope that it has been heuristic. We have provided more details about the context, principles, and procedures of assessment and treatment. We believe that awareness of the special concerns that can arise in association with the assessment and treatment of sexual problems is important. At the same time, and despite the increased specialization that is occurring in our field, we continue to see many common themes in the assessment

TABLE 11.1. Core Components for Therapeutic Change and Related Assessment Information for "Fred" and "Emily"

Core component	Assessment information
1. Sensate focus	Fred's stated performance anxiety was related to erectile failure.
2. Education	Although the couple had good sex knowledge (based on the DSFI and interview), they did not understand the impact of various factors on their sexual relationship and there was some misattribution of what was causing the sexual problem.
3. Stimulus control	The couple did not have a romantic ambience; very little time was spent together and the presence of alcohol triggered repulsion in Emily.
4. Cognitive restructuring	Fred believed that if he gave in to Emily she would want more and more; Fred also believed that by not commiting to Emily he would avoid pain and not be restricted in his freedom.
5. Communication training	It appeared that both Emily and Fred made important decisions with minimal or no communication with each other; also, there seemed to be little ability to compromise on important decisions.
6. Health promotion	Fred's drinking behavior was potentially adversely affecting his desire and arousal; it was also having a negative effect on Emily.

and treatment of many of the disorders discussed in this book. The case presented here illustrates how understanding anxiety and depression as well as alcohol and marital concerns can be useful in the treatment of male erectile disorder.

Finally, we wish to note that working with men and their partners to treat male erectile disorder can be a very rewarding professional experience. As we have noted elsewhere (Wincze & Carey, 1991), we have enjoyed the grateful responses of our clients. Many report that they are expressing their sexual concerns, fears, and secrets for the first time. They also tell us that this opportunity to discuss sexual matters openly and without shame can be very liberating. It is indeed gratifying when, working together with our clients, we can help them to reestablish sexual functioning and enhance their sexual satisfaction.

REFERENCES

American Psychiatric Association. (1993). *DSM-IV draft criteria as of 3/1/93.* Washington, DC: Author.

Bancroft, J., & Coles, L. (1976). Three years' experience in a sexual problems clinic. *British Medical Journal,* i, 1575–1577.

Bancroft, J., & Wu, F. (1983). Changes in erectile responsiveness during androgen replacement therapy. *Archives of Sexual Behavior, 12,* 59–66.

Bansal, S. (1988). Sexual dysfunction in hypertensive men: A critical review of the literature. *Hypertension, 12,* 1–10.

Barlow, D. H. (1986). Causes of sexual dysfunction: The role of anxiety and cognitive interference. *Journal of Consulting and Clinical Psychology, 54,* 140–148.

Barlow, D. H. (1988). *Anxiety and its disorders: The nature and treatment of anxiety and panic.* New York: Guilford Press.

Barlow, D. H., Sakheim, D., & Beck, J. G. (1983). Anxiety increases sexual arousal. *Journal of Abnormal Psychology, 92,* 49–54.

Beck, A. T. (1976). *Cognitive therapy and the emotional disorders.* New York: International Universities Press.

Beck, A. T., Ward, C., Mendelson, M., Mock, J., & Erbaugh, J. (1961). An inventory for measuring depression. *Archives of General Psychiatry, 4,* 561–571.

Beck, J. G., Barlow, D. H., & Sakheim, D. (1983). The effects of attentional focus and partner arousal on sexual responding in functional and dysfunctional men. *Behaviour Research and Therapy, 21,* 1–8.

Buffum, J. (1982). Pharmacosexology: The effects of drugs on sexual function—A review. *Journal of Psychoactive Drugs, 14,* 5–44.

Buffum, J. (1986). Pharmacosexology update: Prescription drugs and sexual function. *Journal of Psychoactive Drugs, 18,* 97–106.

Buvat, J., Buvat-Herbaut, M., Lemaire, A., Marcolin, G., & Quittelier, E. (1990). Recent developments in the clinical assessment and diagnosis of erectile dysfunction. *Annual Review of Sex Research, 1,* 265–308.

Buvat, J., Lemaire, A., Buvat-Herbaut, M., Fourlinnie, J. C., Racadot, A., & Fossati, P. (1985). Hyperprolactinemia and sexual function in men. *Hormone Research, 22,* 196–203.

Carey, M. P., Flasher, L. V., Maisto, S. A., & Turkat, I. D. (1984). The a priori approach to psychological assessment. *Professional Psychology: Research and Practice, 15,* 515–527.

Carey, M. P., Spector, I. P., Lantinga, L. J., & Krauss, D. J. (in press). Reliability of the Dyadic Adjustment Scale. *Psychological Assessment*.

Catalan, J., Hawton, K., & Day, A. (1990). Couples referred to a sexual dysfunction clinic: Psychological and physical morbidity. *British Journal of Psychiatry*, *156*, 61–67.

Conte, H. R. (1983). Development and use of self-report techniques for assessing sexual functioning: A review and critique. *Archives of Sexual Behavior*, *12*, 555–576.

Corcoran, K., & Fischer, J. (1987). *Measures for clinical practice: A sourcebook*. New York: Free Press.

Cranston-Cuebas, M. A., & Barlow, D. H. (1989). *A comparison of sexual history, alcohol, and nicotine use in sexually functional and dysfunctional males*. Poster presented at the Annual Meeting of the Association for Advancement of Behavior Therapy.

Davidson, J. M., Camargo, C. A., Smith, E. R., & Kwan, M. (1983). Maintenance of sexual function in a castrated man treated with ovarian steroids. *Archives of Sexual Behavior*, *12*, 263–274.

Davis, C. M., Yarber, W. L., & Davis, S. L. (Eds.). (1988). *Sexuality-related measures: A compendium*. Lake Mills, IA: Graphic Publishing.

Derogatis, L. R. (1975). *Derogatis Sexual Functioning Inventory*. Baltimore, MD: Clinical Psychometrics Research.

Derogatis, L. R. (1978). *Derogatis Sexual Functioning Inventory* (rev. ed.). Baltimore, MD: Clinical Psychometrics Research.

Derogatis, L. R. (1983). *SCL-90-R: Administration, scoring and procedures manual—II*. Baltimore, MD: Clinical Psychometric Research.

Fisher, W. A. (1988). The Sexual Opinion Survey. In C. M. Davis, W. L. Yarber, & S. L. Davis (Eds.), *Sexuality-related measures: A compendium* (pp. 34–37). Lake Mills, IA: Graphic Publishing.

Fisher, W. A., Byrne, D., White, L. A., & Kelley, K. (1988). Erotophobia–erotophilia as a dimension of personality. *Journal of Sex Research*, *25*, 123–151.

Frank, E., Anderson, C., & Kupfer, D. J. (1976). Profiles of couples seeking sex therapy and marital therapy. *American Journal of Psychiatry*, *133*, 559–562.

Frank, E., Anderson, C., & Rubinstein, D. (1978). Frequency of sexual dysfunction in "normal" couples. *New England Journal of Medicine*, *299*, 111–115.

Gagnon, J. H. (1990). The explicit and implicit use of the scripting perspective in sex research. *Annual Review of Sex Research*, *1*, 1–43.

Gagnon, J. H., Rosen, R. C., & Leiblum, S. R. (1982). Cognitive and social aspects of sexual dysfunction: Sexual scripts in sex therapy. *Journal of Sex and Marital Therapy*, *8*, 44–56.

Gordon, C. M., & Carey, M. P. (in press). Penile tumescence monitoring during morning naps: A pilot investigation of a cost-effective alternative to full night sleep studies in the assessment of male erectile disorder. *Behaviour Research and Therapy*.

Hawton, K. (1982). The behavioural treatment of sexual dysfunction. *British Journal of Psychiatry*, *140*, 94–101.

Hawton, K., Catalan, J., & Fagg, J. (1992). Sex therapy for erectile dysfunction: Characteristics of couples, treatment outcome, and prognostic factors. *Archives of Sexual Behavior*, *21*, 161–175.

Heiman, J. R., & LoPiccolo, J. (1983). Clinical outcome of sex therapy. *Archives of General Psychiatry*, *40*, 443–449.

Hudson, W. W., Harrison, D. F., & Crosscup, P. C. (1981). A short-form scale to measure sexual discord in dyadic relationships. *Journal of Sex Research*, *17*, 157–174.

Jensen, B. J., Witcher, D. B., & Upton, L. R. (1987). Readability assessment of questionnaires frequently used in sex and marital therapy. *Journal of Sex and Marital Therapy*, *13*, 137–141.

Jevtich, M. J. (1980). Importance of penile arterial pulse sound examination in impotence. *Journal of Urology*, *124*, 820–824.

Jones, T. M. (1985). Hormonal considerations in the evaluation and treatment of erectile dysfunction. In R. T. Segraves & H. W. Schoenberg (Eds.), *Diagnosis and treatment of erectile disturbances: A guide for the clinician* (pp. 115–158). New York: Plenum Press.

Kaplan, H. S. (1974). *The new sex therapy*. New York: Brunner/Mazel.

Kinsey, A. C., Pomeroy, W. B., & Martin, C. E. (1948). *Sexual behavior in the human male*. Philadelphia, PA: Saunders.

Laws, D. R. (Ed.). (1989). *Relapse prevention with sex offenders*. New York: Guilford Press.

Leiblum, S. R., & Rosen, R. C. (1991). Couples therapy for erectile disorders: Conceptual and clinical considerations. *Journal of Sex and Marital Therapy*, *17*, 147–159.

Leiblum, S. R., & Rosen, R. C. (1992). Couples therapy for erectile disorders: Observations, obstacles, and outcomes. In R. C. Rosen & S. R. Leiblum (Eds.), *Erectile disorders: Assessment and treatment* (pp. 226–254). New York: Guilford Press.

Lewis, R. W. (1991). Results of surgery for veno-occlusive disease. *Journal of Sex and Marital Therapy*, *17*, 129–135.

Libman, E., Rothernberg, I., Fichten, C. S., & Amsel, R. (1985). The SSES–E: A measure of sexual self-efficacy in erectile functioning. *Journal of Sex and Marital Therapy*, *11*, 233–244.

Lipsius, S. H. (1987). Prescribing sensate focus without proscribing intercourse. *Journal of Sex and Marital Therapy*, *11*, 185–191.

LoPiccolo, J. (1992). Postmodern sex therapy for erectile failure. In R. C. Rosen & S. R. Leiblum (Eds.), *Erectile disorders: Assessment and treatment* (pp. 171–197). New York: Guilford Press.

LoPiccolo, J., & Heiman, J. R. (1978). Sexual assessment and history interview. In J. LoPiccolo & L. LoPiccolo (Eds.), *Handbook of sex therapy* (pp. 103–112). New York: Plenum Press.

Lue, T. F., Hricak, H., Schmidt, A., & Tanagho, E. A. (1986). Functional evaluation of penile veins by cavernosography and cavernosometry in papaverine induced erections. *Journal of Urology*, *135*, 479–482.

Masters, W. H., & Johnson, V. E. (1970). *Human sexual inadequacy*. Boston: Little, Brown.

McCarthy, B. W. (1985). Uses and misuses of behavioral homework exercises in sex therapy. *Journal of Sex and Marital Therapy*, *11*, 185–191.

McCarthy, B. W. (1988). *Male sexual awareness*. New York: Caroll & Graf.

Meisler, A. W., & Carey, M. P. (1990). A critical reevaluation of nocturnal penile tumescence monitoring in the diagnosis of erectile dysfunction. *Journal of Nervous and Mental Disease, 178,* 78–89.

Meisler, A. W., & Carey, M. P. (1991). Depressed affect and male sexual arousal. *Archives of Sexual Behavior, 20,* 541–554.

Meisler, A. W., & Carey, M. P. (1992). *Mood and sexual arousal: The role of affect and cognitions in erectile dysfunction.* Unpublished manuscript, Syracuse University, Syracuse, NY.

Meisler, A. W., Carey, M. P., Krauss, D. J., & Lantinga, L. J. (1988). Success and failure in penile prosthesis surgery: Two cases highlighting the importance of psychosocial factors. *Journal of Sex and Marital Therapy, 14,* 108–119.

Meisler, A. W., Carey, M. P., Lantinga, L. J., & Krauss, D. J. (1989). Erectile dysfunction in diabetes mellitus: A biopsychosocial approach to etiology and assessment. *Annals of Behavioral Medicine, 11,* 18–27.

Metts, S., & Cupach, W. R. (1989). The role of communication in human sexuality. In K. McKinney & S. Sprecher (Eds.), *Human sexuality: The societal and interpersonal context* (pp. 139–161). Norwood, NJ: Ablex.

Mohr, D., & Beutler, L. (1990). Erectile dysfunction: A review of diagnostic and treatment procedures. *Clinical Psychology Review, 10,* 123–150.

Morokoff, P. J., Baum, A., McKinnon, W. R., & Gilliland, R. (1987). Effects of chronic unemployment and acute psychological stress on sexual arousal in men. *Health Psychology, 6,* 545–560.

Mosher, D. L. (1991). Macho men, machismo, and sexuality. *Annual Review of Sex Research, 2,* 199–247.

Nettelbladt, P., & Uddenberg, N. (1979). Sexual dysfunction and sexual satisfaction in 58 married Swedish men. *Journal of Psychosomatic Medicine, 23,* 141–147.

Oaks, W. W., & Moyer, J. H. (1972). Sex and hypertension. *Medical Aspects of Human Sexuality, 61,* 128–137.

Papadopoulos, C. (1989). *Sexual aspects of cardiovascular disease.* New York: Praeger.

Pokorny, M. D., Miller, B. A., & Kaplan, H. B. (1972). The brief MAST: A shortened version of the Michigan Alcohol Screening Test. *American Journal of Psychiatry, 129,* 343–345.

Renshaw, D. C. (1988). Profiles of 2376 patients treated at Loyola Sex Clinic between 1972 and 1987. *Sexual and Marital Therapy, 3,* 111–117.

Reynolds, B. (1991). Psychological treatment of erectile dysfunction in men without partners. *Journal of Sex and Marital Therapy, 17,* 136–146.

Rosen, R. C., & Leiblum, S. R. (Eds.). (1992). *Erectile disorders: Assessment and treatment.* New York: Guilford Press.

Ross, J. L., Clifford, R. E., & Eisenman, R. (1987). Communication of sexual preferences in married couples. *Bulletin of the Psychonomic Society, 25,* 58–60.

Ruzbarsky, V., & Michal, V. (1977). Morphologic changes in the arterial bed of the penis with aging: Relationship to the pathogenesis of impotence. *Investigative Urology, 15,* 194–199.

Sakheim, D., Barlow, D. H., Beck, J. G., & Abrahamson, D. (1984). The effect of an increased awareness of erectile cues on sexual arousal. *Behaviour Research and Therapy, 22,* 151–158.

Salmimies, P., Kockott, G., Pirke, K. M., Vogt, H. J., & Schill, W. B. (1982). Effects of testosterone replacement on sexual behavior in hypogonadal men. *Archives of Sexual Behavior, 11,* 345–353.

Schover, L. R. (1984). *Prime time: Sexual health for men over fifty.* New York: Holt, Rinehart, & Winston.

Schover, L. R. (1989). Sex therapy for the penile prosthesis recipient. *Urologic Clinics of North America, 16,* 91–98.

Schover, L. R., & Jensen, S. B. (1988). *Sexuality and chronic illness: A comprehensive approach.* New York: Guilford Press.

Segraves, R. T. (1989). Effects of psychotropic drugs on human erection and ejaculation. *Archives of General Psychiatry, 46,* 275–284.

Segraves, R. T., Camic, P., & Ivanoff, J. (1985). Spontaneous remission in erectile dysfunction: A partial replication. *Behaviour Research and Therapy, 23,* 203–204.

Segraves, R. T., Knopf, J., & Camic, P. (1982). Spontaneous remission in erectile impotence. *Behaviour Research and Therapy, 20,* 89–91.

Segraves, R. T., Madsen, R., Carter, C. S., & Davis, J. M. (1985). Erectile dysfunction associated with pharmacological agents. In R. T. Segraves & H. W. Schoenberg (Eds.), *Diagnosis and treatment of erectile disturbances: A guide for clinicians* (pp. 23–63). New York: Plenum Press.

Segraves, R. T., Schoenberg, H. W., Zarins, C. K., Knopf, J., & Camic, P. (1982). Referral of impotent patients to a sexual dysfunction clinic. *Archives of Sexual Behavior, 11,* 521–528.

Segraves, R. T., & Segraves, K. B. (1992). Aging and drug effects on male sexuality. In R. C. Rosen & S. R. Leiblum (Eds.), *Erectile disorders: Assessment and treatment* (pp. 96–140). New York: Guilford Press.

Skinner, H. A. (1982). The drug abuse screening test. *Addictive Behaviors, 7,* 363–371.

Spanier, G. B. (1976). Measuring dyadic adjustment: New scales for assessing the quality of marriage and similar dyads. *Journal of Marriage and the Family, 38,* 15–28.

Spark, R. F. (1991). *Male sexual health: A couple's guide.* Mount Vernon, NY: Consumer Reports Books.

Spector, I. P., & Carey, M. P. (1990). Incidence and prevalence of the sexual dysfunctions: A critical review of the literature. *Archives of Sexual Behavior, 19,* 389–408.

Talmadge, L. D., & Talmadge, W. C. (1990). Sexuality assessment measures for clinical use: A review. *American Journal of Family Therapy, 18,* 80–105.

Tannen, D. (1990). *You just don't understand: Women and men in conversation.* New York: William Morrow.

Tiefer, L., & Melman, A. (1987). Adherence to recommendations and improvement over time in men with erectile dysfunction. *Archives of Sexual Behavior, 16,* 301–309.

Wagner, F., & Metz, P. (1981). Arteriosclerosis and erectile failure. In G. Wagner & R. Green (Eds.), *Impotence: Physiological, psychological, surgical diagnosis and treatment* (pp. 63–72). New York: Plenum.

White, J. R., Case, D. A., McWhirter, D., & Mattison, A. M. (1990). Enhanced sexual behavior in exercising men. *Archives of Sexual Behavior, 19,* 193–209.

Williams, G., Mulcahy, M. J., Hartnell, G., & Kiely, E.

(1988). Diagnosis and treatment of venous leakage: A curable cause of impotence. *British Journal of Urology, 61,* 151–155.

Wincze, J. P., Bansal, S., Malhotra, C. M., Balko, A., Susset, J. G., & Malamud, M. A. (1988). A comparison of nocturnal penile tumescence and penile response to erotic stimulation during waking states in comprehensively diagnosed groups of males experiencing erectile difficulties. *Archives of Sexual Behavior, 17,* 333–348.

Wincze, J. P., & Carey, M. P. (1991). *Sexual dysfunction: A guide for assessment and treatment.* New York: Guilford Press.

Wolchik, S. A., Beggs, V. E., Wincze, J. P., Sakheim, D. K., Barlow, D. H., & Mavissakalian, M. (1980). The effect of emotional arousal on subsequent sexual arousal in men. *Journal of Abnormal Psychology, 89,* 595–598.

Zilbergeld, B. (1992). *The new male sexuality: A guide to sexual fulfillment.* New York: Bantam.

Chapter 12

COUPLE DISTRESS

James V. Cordova
Neil S. Jacobson
University of Washington, Seattle

The last edition of this book presented an up-to-date and engaging account of behavioral marital therapy. But few areas in psychotherapy have seen as dramatic a change as the treatment of distressed interpersonal relationships. This change has occurred not only at the level of technique, but also in conceptions underlying the approach to couple distress. These changes in technique and conceptualization are profound enough to warrant a new name for this approach, integrative behavioral couple therapy. The value of this chapter to the clinician is far more than a description of the latest and most up-to-date technology for treating couple distress. More important are detailed descriptions of the process and the art of implementing these procedures in the context of numerous transcripts with a variety of different and interesting cases. Since couple therapy requires considerable clinical talent, beginning therapists in particular should learn much from the interchanges and strategies presented in this engaging chapter.–D. H. B.

INTRODUCTION

As practicing clinicians, we have all seen the profound suffering that can be caused by distressed relationships. Poor communication and destructive quarreling often lead two people who may be deeply in love to bring each other more sorrow than joy. In addition to considerable emotional pain, there is mounting evidence that people in distressed relationships become more susceptible to a host of both physical and psychological disorders. Initial efforts to help troubled couples led to the development of behavioral couple therapy (BCT), a treatment consistently demonstrated to be one of the most effective available (Baucom & Hoffman, 1986; Gurman, Kniskern, & Pinsof, 1986; Jacobson, 1978; Jacobson, 1984). Despite its proven efficacy, BCT continues to evolve. In the spirit of this continuing evolution, we present in this chapter a reformulation of BCT recently developed by Jacobson and Christensen (Christensen, Jacobson, & Babcock, in press; Jacobson, 1992; Jacobson & Christensen, in press). This reformulation is based on the integration of new strategies for promoting emotional acceptance with the more traditional strategies promoting change. We refer to this revised approach as integrative behavioral couple therapy (IBCT). The term *integrative* is used to denote the mixture of the traditional focus on promoting change with the newer focus on promoting acceptance. "Couple therapy" has replaced "marital therapy" to emphasize the utility of this approach for gay and lesbian as well as heterosexual couples regardless of their marital status.

The evolution of IBCT from BCT resulted from our research findings and clinical experience with couples for whom BCT was not effective. Although research showed that BCT effectively improved relationship quality for approximately two thirds of couples presenting for therapy (Jacobson, Schmaling, & Holtzworth-Munroe, 1987), we remained concerned about those couples who were not improving. Such couples could have been written off as "difficult," or simply labeled treatment failures. However, continued exposure to these couples led to the conclusion that the exclusive emphasis of BCT on change was not the best strategy in all cases. The most consistent predictors of treatment response showed us that (1) severely distressed couples are less likely to respond favorably than are less severely distressed couples (Baucom & Hoffman, 1986), (2) younger couples are more likely to respond favorably than are older couples (Baucom & Hoffman, 1986), (3) the more emotionally disengaged couples are, the harder they are to treat (Hahlweg, Schindler, Revenstorf, & Brengelmann, 1984), and (4) the more incompatible a couple, or the more polarized on basic issues, the harder they are to treat (Jacobson, Follette, & Pagel, 1986). It became apparent that each of these factors was in some way related to the couple's amenability to accommodation and compromise. Severely distressed couples, older couples who have engaged in their destructive patterns for years, couples who are emotionally disengaged, and couples who are incompatible are the very couples who find it the most difficult to be collaborative and compromising. The change strategies of BCT, however, are highly dependent on a couple's ability to collaborate. For couples for whom collaboration and compromise are more difficult, the traditional approach is simply not as effective. For these couples, many of the behavioral patterns that we were instructing them to change were simply, for all practical purposes, unchangeable. Therefore, if our goal was to try to strengthen the relationship, we had to help these couples accept their differences and "give up the struggle" to change them.

Oftentimes it appeared that our efforts to change these couples were simply making things worse, as each partner became increasingly more entrenched in his/her position. We found that with some couples we were better off using their problems as vehicles for intimacy, rather than trying to help get rid of them. IBCT evolved from this shift in emphasis, and throughout the rest of the chapter we discuss the resulting integration of acceptance and change strategies. We begin with a discussion of the theoretical rationale supporting this shift in emphasis. Following that, we describe in detail the standard course of treatment from assessment through strategies for promoting both acceptance and change.

BEHAVIORAL ROOTS

In discussing the theory underlying the evolution of IBCT from BCT, we attempt to answer two important questions.

1. What does it mean to say that an approach to couple therapy is behavioral?
2. What is different theoretically between the current approach and formulations that we presented in the past?

First it must be pointed out that there are many different approaches to behaviorism, not all of them entirely compatible. Although we will not go into a long treatise detailing the differences, we do want to emphasize that we are basing our approach on a very specific definition of behaviorism that should not be confused with the common conception of the term. At a theoretical level, IBCT represents a return to the basic philosophy of modern behaviorism. First and foremost, this means that our approach is contextual. We believe that the behavior of each individual, and therefore each individual couple, is shaped and maintained by unique environmental events. Therefore, we believe that the behavior of individuals can only be understood when considered from within their unique personal contexts. In other words, within a particular couple, each member has learned how to behave in an intimate relationship through a lifetime of different experiences, including their continuing experiences within the current relationship. How each member of the couple behaves within that relationship can therefore only be understood by taking all those unique experiences into account. Adequate understanding is essential to the effectiveness of therapy.

Our behavioral approach to couple therapy adheres to the assumption that change only occurs within the present moment. Therefore, therapy focuses on changing the current contingencies and context within which ongoing relationship problems occur. Although discussion of an individual's or couple's past often occurs within IBCT, those discussions are used exclusively for altering the context supporting current dysfunctional interactions. Adherence to focusing on current contexts is based firmly on pragmatics. The primary focus is on what works to promote change and change only occurs in the present.

As will become apparent, the discrimination of naturally occurring contingencies is of tantamount importance when conducting IBCT: that discrimination is only possible through functional analyses at an idiographic level. Behaviorists have long been advocates of an idiographic approach to studying human behavior; as therapists dealing with the complexities of individual couples, we have found an idiographic approach to treatment most effective. In contrast, the principles of BCT were originally developed from the nomothetic study of distressed versus nondistressed couples. Behaviors that discriminated between groups of distressed and nondistressed couples became the targets of therapeutic intervention. However, what is most effective about a behavioral approach to couple therapy is that an idiographic analysis allows the therapist to take into account the unique learning history of each individual within a couple. The importance of this becomes obvious when one realizes that what may be an effective intervention for one couple may not necessarily be effective for a couple with a different history. IBCT is much more flexible than BCT in determining the proper course of treatment for each couple. In essence, IBCT tailors the treatment to meet the unique needs and capacities of each couple as determined by their unique learning histories.

In terms of tailoring treatment to the needs and capacities of individual couples, functional analyses of a couple's interactions are essential. An emphasis on the *function* behaviors serve rather than their *topography* is at the very heart of our behavioral approach to couple therapy. This is because behaviors that appear similar topographically across couples may very easily serve different functions for individual couples. For example, leaving the house may be seen topographically as a distancing behavior, and in some couples it may very well serve that function. However, in other couples, leaving the house may precipitate pursuit and thus may function as an approach behavior. Leaving the house may result in pursuit and reconciliation for some, whereas for others, leaving the house may simply create distance for "cooling off." Without conducting an idiographic functional analysis, a couple therapist cannot make this distinction and, as a result, misses a great deal of useful information.

Furthermore, attending to the function behaviors serve allows the therapist to take advantage of what may be called functional equivalence classes. These are groups of behaviors that may be topographically different but that all serve a similar function. Jacobson (1992) gives the example of a husband who engaged in several topographically different behaviors that all served to create distance between himself and his partner (e.g., ignoring, walking away, and keeping busy). After the therapist promoted a dialogue between husband and wife in which the husband was reinforced for talking about his difficulty in being close, the husband began to distance himself less in the natural environment. This was because talking about being close was in a functionally equivalent class to behaviors the husband was avoiding at home, and thus decreasing the aversiveness of talking about being close affected the entire equivalence class.

The theory underlying IBCT differs from that presented in previous formulations primarily in its focus on several critical distinctions made by radical behaviorists. These include distinctions between arbitrary and natural reinforcement, between contingency-shaped and rule-governed behavior, and between public and private events. We discuss each of these distinctions in order.

All principles of behaviorism can be derived from the basic supposition that behavior is shaped and maintained by its consequences, given genetic constraints and predispositions. Unfortunately, this postulate has often been misunderstood as meaning that all behavior is responsive to the reinforcing qualities of a big bag of M&Ms. Behaviorists, however, make an important distinction between arbitrary and natural reinforcement (Ferster, 1967). Arbitrary reinforcement is defined as the utilization of a reinforcing event that is not available in the organism's natural environment or does not stem naturally from the transaction between the individual and the environment. Within traditional BCT, instructing couples to exchange sex for conversation is a good example of the use of arbitrary reinforcement since conversation per se is not necessarily a setting event for wanting to make love. Natural reinforcement, on the other hand, is defined as utilization of a reinforcing event that is naturally available in the organism's environment and that does stem naturally from the transaction between organism and environment. Studies have shown that children who are paid for working puzzles will not play with those puzzles in their free time, whereas children who are simply allowed to work puzzles, and therefore to make contact with the naturally reinforcing events inherent to the task, will continue to play with those puzzles in their free time. Therefore, the distinction between arbitrary and natural reinforcers is important not because arbitrary reinforcers do not work as reinforcers (they do increase the frequency of behavior) but because behavior that is arbitrarily reinforced is not as likely to generalize outside of the laboratory and, more important, is not as likely to be maintained once therapy ends. BCT has often been guilty of utilizing arbitrary reinforcers, whereas IBCT strongly urges therapists to pay strict attention to the distinction and to make use of natural reinforcers whenever possible. If a goal of therapy is to increase the couple's satisfaction with the relationship through increasing the frequency with which they have interesting or intimate conversations, these *naturally* occurring reinforcers should be the focus of any effective intervention.

Within behaviorism, a similar distinction is also made between contingency-shaped behavior and rule-governed behavior. Rule-governed behavior is defined in the broad sense to mean behavior determined by verbal contingencies. Contingency-shaped behavior, on the other hand, refers to behavior determined by specifically nonverbal contingencies. Because we are verbal organisms, many of the contingencies with which we make contact are verbal. One of the primary effects of verbal contingencies is to allow for the shaping of effective behavior without direct contact with the natural contingencies. For example, we can avoid becoming involved with more than one partner through contact with verbal stimuli equating such behavior with ill health, without ever having to make contact with the direct consequences of becoming involved with more than one partner. Although in many instances this distancing from the naturally occurring contingencies works in our favor, it also has its downside. In many cases, failure to contact direct contingencies precludes the shaping of effective and durable behavior. The behavior-analytic literature suggests that behavior under instructional control will only prove to be generalizable and durable to the extent that it eventually comes to be controlled by natural (nonverbal) contingencies (Skinner, 1974; Hayes, 1989). For example, within therapy couples may be taught to paraphrase whatever their partner says during a conversation. If a couple engages in paraphrasing only because the therapist has asked them to (a verbal rule), they aren't likely to paraphrase when the therapist is not around. However, if the couple can be led to make direct contact with the benefits of paraphrasing (e.g., avoiding destructive misunderstandings and feeling more completely understood), they are more likely to continue to paraphrase regardless of whether the therapist is present. The implication for couple therapy is that the communication skills shaped by the structured training of traditional BCT may never come to be controlled by naturally occurring contingencies. Therefore, they may not generalize outside therapy and they may be susceptible to quick extinction once therapy is over. The shaping of true intimacy, in fact, may be made more difficult by these ritualized tasks because of the lack of direct contact with naturally occurring contingencies. IBCT, however, attempts to promote direct contact with natural (nonverbal) contingencies in order to increase the likelihood that treatment gains will generalize outside therapy and that they will be maintained after therapy is over. Many of the acceptance strategies described later facilitate exposure to naturally occurring contingencies to a greater extent than did traditional change strategies.

The last, and possibly the most important, principle of behaviorism with implications for how we conduct IBCT is the distinction between private and public behavior and the different effects that verbal contingencies have on each. The distinction between public and private behavior is important to make specifically because of the different effects that verbal behavior has on each. For example, we can tell a person to stop eating a banana, and if the person is trying to do what we say, he/she will stop. However, we cannot tell a person to stop *thinking* about a banana and expect the same kind of result, because (1) the verbal stimuli specify the stimuli to be avoided and thus "help create the very private event the person is trying to avoid" (Hayes, 1987, p. 341), and (2) the community/environment cannot shape control of private behavior as effectively as it shapes control of public behavior. A couple therapist can make a verbal contract with an individual to do the dishes more often or to stop verbally criticizing and expect that contract to have the desired effect most of the time. However, a therapist cannot make the same kind of contract with an individual to feel closer to his/her partner or to feel more love or less anger. We would argue, based on the principles of behaviorism, that direct verbal instruction has different effects on private and public behavior because of the process through which one learns how to respond to verbal stimuli.

Human beings may be born with a genetic capacity to learn verbal behavior, but it is only through contact with a verbal culture that a nonverbal child learns to be verbal. Skinner (1974) observed that verbal training is most effective when the culture (primary caretakers) can make direct contact with the appropriate contingencies and can therefore commend and correct accordingly. Therefore, it is easier to teach the appropriate verbal responses to public stimuli than to private stimuli. For example, teaching a child the appropriate response to the verbal stimulus "stop" requires that the teacher make direct contact with whatever it is that he/she wants stopped. A child can be taught to stop throwing food, to stop running with scissors, and to stop smacking her little brother, because all these behaviors are available publicly and can be finely controlled. However, a child cannot as easily be taught to stop feeling angry or sad or to stop thinking about monsters in the closet, because these behaviors are not available publicly and, therefore, are not available for commendation or correction. In teaching a child how to respond to private stimuli, the verbal culture relies on public accompaniments. Thus, when a child is observed to be crying, he is taught to say he is sad. When a child is seen to be injured, she is taught to say it hurts. A person can be taught to describe or control private stimuli only because they are associated with public events. Unfortunately, this training can never be very precise, because the behavior in question is private and thus unavailable to the teacher.

This is not to say that a therapist cannot affect a client's private behavior, but that he/she does so in ways very different from how he/she affects a client's public behavior. The therapist can take advantage of the precise verbal control that can be exerted over public behavior, but must engage in very different behavior in order to affect a person's private experience. Traditional BCT, with its emphasis on directly observable change, either ignored whether effects were occurring privately or simply hoped that they would dutifully follow from changes in directly observable behavior. IBCT, in contrast, has developed a large collection of interventions designed specifically to have an effect on private events. The distinction we make between change and acceptance is primarily the distinction between the effects of verbal behavior on private versus public behavior. Interventions designed to promote "acceptance" are, for the most part, interventions designed to have an effect on a person's private experience. On the other hand, interventions promoting "change" are interventions designed to have an effect on behavior that is publicly observable.

Affecting private behavior is exceedingly important, particularly when affecting public behavior is unlikely. As stated previously, many of the behavioral patterns that we were instructing couples to change in BCT were for all practical purposes simply unchangeable. However, strategies designed to affect an individual's private experience within the context of publicly unchangeable events are proving very effective in terms of promoting a couple's satisfaction.

Furthermore, attempting to handle private experiences as though they were directly amenable to techniques designed to affect public behavior often compounds the problem. As stated earlier, in many applications the verbal stimuli specify the stimuli to be avoided and thus "help create the very private event the person is trying to avoid" (Hayes, 1987, p. 341). In other applications, the failure of direct verbal demands to have an effect on private behavior leads to feelings of failure on the part of one partner and resentment on the part of the other. Distressed couples have often been attempting just such interventions on their own for years prior to therapy, resulting in nothing but extreme frustration and resentment. Acceptance techniques aimed at helping couples give up the struggle often ameliorate the negative effects of attempting to control private behavior directly through verbal demands.

Finally, private events often have a profound effect on what types of stimuli function as reinforcers. What is reinforcing to someone when he/she is feeling loving and close is quite different from what is reinforcing when he/she is feeling angry and resentful. When someone is angry, behavior that is hurtful to the other person is what is reinforced, not demonstrations of love and affection. This is why partners find it particularly hard to be nice to one another when they are angry, even if their therapist has instructed them to do so. If, however, the therapist can affect the private experience of anger by making it more probable that the person will feel sympathy, entire classes of reinforcers are changed. This is particularly important when the therapist is relying on the partners' collaboration for the success of an intervention.

In closing this section, it is important to state that the discussion of behavioral principles in no way does justice to the philosophy as a whole, but simply presents those aspects most relevant to IBCT. Having said that, we shift from our discussion of theory to our description of the therapy, starting with assessment and working through the various strategies for acceptance and change.

ASSESSMENT

The first stage of IBCT is the assessment phase. This phase is primarily designed to provide a thorough overview of the couple's complaints in order to determine whether IBCT is an appropriate treatment, and if so, the proper emphasis to place on change versus acceptance. The necessity of an idiographic focus here is obvious in that not only does each couple have their own unique blend of problems, but those problems themselves differ for each couple according to whether they are more amenable to change or to acceptance.

The assessment phase covers the first two to three sessions, and within those sessions the following six areas are assessed:

1. How distressed is this couple?
2. How committed is this couple to the relationship?
3. What are the issues that divide them?
4. How do these issues manifest themselves within the relationship?
5. What are the strengths holding them together?
6. What can treatment do to help them?

These questions are addressed during an initial conjoint interview as well as during subsequent individual interviews. The conjoint interview provides the therapist with an opportunity to see how the couple is currently getting along, as well as how open the couple is to discussing their problems with the therapist. The individual interviews, in addition, allow the therapist to assess problems that each member may feel unable to openly discuss in front of the other.

How Distressed Is This Couple?

The first area to be assessed is the couple's level of distress. This determines the initial course of therapy, as well as indicating whether initially to emphasize change or acceptance. Less distress indicates that the couple may be more amenable to change strategies early in therapy. Severely distressed couples are likely to derive greater benefits from an early emphasis on acceptance. Some severely distressed couples, however, may require immediate intervention (e.g., spousal abuse, child abuse, suicidality, or psychosis).

The clinician assesses level of distress during the initial conjoint interview through direct questions about what brought the couple into therapy. Each partner is given an opportunity to answer these questions without interruption by the other. This allows the therapist to observe the style and manner in which each spouse presents his/ her side of the story. Generally the more anger, resentment, blaming, and hopelessness expressed, the more distressed the couple is likely to be. Level of distress can also be assessed using questionnaires such as the Dyadic Adjustment Scale (DAS; Spanier, 1976) or the Marital Satisfaction Inventory (Snyder, 1979). Packets of such relevant questionnaires prove most valuable if administered prior to the first meeting with the couple. The therapist then has time to look over the questionnaires and provide preliminary answers to assessment questions.

Regardless of level of distress, all couples are assessed for the presence of violence. This is done during the individual interviews, where each partner usually feels more comfortable discussing such issues. Marital violence may also be assessed through the use of questionnaires such as the Conflict Tactics Scale (Straus, 1979). Often, IBCT is not the most appropriate treatment for couples with a long history of domestic violence, or for couples where the violence is at all severe. In such cases, we recommend some alternate treatment to stop the violence before beginning marital therapy. If, however, the violence is relatively mild, and of recent origin, and if the wife's level of fear is low, IBCT may be pursued contingent upon there being no further violent incidents. These conditions are stated in no uncertain terms, and verbal or written contracts are often utilized. Within the individual interview, issues of safety should be discussed, and if there are any concerns, appropriate steps should be taken immediately.

How Committed Is This Couple to the Relationship?

The question of commitment to the relationship has implications for how hard the therapist can expect the couple to work during therapy and between sessions. Furthermore, level of commitment to the relationship has a profound effect on whether the therapist will begin the couple's treatment by emphasizing change or acceptance. A couple that is no longer committed to maintaining the relationship simply lacks the motivation necessary to profit from change strategies initially. Since feeling committed to a relationship is a private event, emphasizing emotional acceptance promises to be a more effective approach than emphasizing change. Lack of commitment to the relationship may indicate that things have simply gone too far for any intervention aimed at keeping the couple together; however, beginning therapy with an emphasis on emotional acceptance strategies is more likely to have a positive effect on commitment than would emphasizing instrumental change.

Level of commitment to the relationship is assessed separately from level of distress, because at times even severely distressed couples may be highly committed to the relationship. The DAS (Spanier, 1976) includes a question assessing each person's desire for the relationship to succeed. The answers range from feeling that the relationship can never succeed and is beyond help to wanting desperately for the relationship to succeed at any cost. The Marital Status Inventory (Weiss & Cerreto, 1980) assesses the various steps the couple has taken toward divorce and is a good indicator of how committed the couple is to the relationship. However, the best indicators of how committed each member is to the relationship come from the individual interviews. Couples feel more comfortable talking to the therapist about feelings of hopelessness, or long-harbored doubts about the viability of the relationship, without the other partner present. Individual interviews also provide a format for disclosure of issues such as past or current affairs that may interfere with the person's level of commitment to the relationship.

Related to both distress and commitment is the collaborative set (Jacobson & Margolin, 1979). This refers to the couple's willingness to cooperate with each other in the attempt to improve their relationship. As with both commitment and distress, willingness to collaborate affects whether acceptance or change strategies are more appropriate during the initial phases of therapy. For couples that are highly collaborative, change strategies may be implemented immediately. The less collaborative a couple, however, the more likely that acceptance strategies will prove most effective early on, because they are more likely to have a positive impact on the couple's willingness to collaborate. As noted above, this is because promoting acceptance has a profound effect on what types of stimuli function as reinforcers. If lack of commitment is fostered by anger, resentment, or hurt feelings, each member of the couple is more likely to be reinforced by behavior that is hurtful to the other and less likely to cooperate to improve the relationship. If the therapist can increase the probability that each member of the couple will feel either sympathy or tenderness, the reinforcement value of those behaviors involved in collaboration increases.

What Are the Issues That Divide Them?

Assessment of the major issues that are currently dividing the couple occurs during the conjoint interview. The issues themselves are discussed, and each partner is given an opportunity to express his/her point of view on each issue. It is important that the therapist fully understand each partner's position in order to assess how much emphasis to place on change versus acceptance for each theme as well as to identify the understandable human reactions motivating each partner. Issues dividing the couple that seem unlikely to change or that are centered around private experiences (e.g., different desires for closeness) should be treated using pri-

marily acceptance strategies. Issues concerning more instrumental/public behaviors (e.g., how to manage family income) call for a greater emphasis on change strategies. However, even for instrumental behaviors, acceptance work is most likely still necessary to deal with the emotional fallout surrounding such sensitive issues.

The issues that divide can also be assessed using, for example, the Areas of Change Questionnaire (Weiss & Birchler, 1975). Questionnaires such as this are useful for assessing issues that the couple might feel uncomfortable discussing during the first interview, such as the couple's sexual relationship.

How Do These Issues Manifest Themselves Within the Relationship?

Understanding how couples attempt to grapple with their problems is of particular importance to the course of IBCT, because it is often not the issues themselves but how the couple deals with these issues that determines their current level of distress. The IBCT therapist tries to identify the common patterns of interaction that occur around the couple's particular issues by asking the couple to describe several recent negative events. Identification of such patterns, or themes, is important, because they form the basis for much of the following acceptance work. The themes identified by the therapist are often unique to a particular couple; however, one common theme is termed *pursuer–distancer*. This theme usually takes the form of one member of the couple pursuing while the other withdraws either physically or emotionally. Patterns and themes such as this are discussed in order to help the couple develop a nonblaming way of understanding conflict.

What Are the Strengths Holding Them Together?

The strengths currently holding the couple together are the foundation from which the therapist works to improve their relationship. Therefore, it is crucial to get a clear picture of what those strengths are, as well as what is motivating each partner to work toward improving the relationship. Asking what initially attracted each partner to the other is often one of the best questions for assessing their strengths. Answering is usually fun for the couple, and often generates pleasant memories and positive feelings. We usually ask this question at the end of the first session in order to provide some perspective for the couple on their problems and to conclude on a positive note.

Each partner is asked separately about how they first met, and what initially attracted them to each other. While they each answer, the IBCT therapist attends to which characteristics are still strong and positive in the relationship and which characteristics might now be manifesting themselves as problems. Often something that was initially attractive has developed into a point of contention. For example, orderliness and a sense of responsibility that were at first considered wonderful might now be seen as compulsive and demanding. The IBCT therapist makes note of these possibilities so they may be used later to promote acceptance. If the therapist can help the couple begin to see the connection between a current complaint and what they have identified as a past strength, their experience of those events may shift from primarily negative to positive through their reassociation with positively valenced memories.

Knowledge of a couple's strengths serves as an excellent indicator of how well a couple will do in therapy. If a couple cannot generate positive memories of how they first met, the success of therapy is somewhat doubtful. It is sometimes the case that relationships form out of convenience or necessity, and when such couples hit rocky times they are often difficult to treat. However, if it is easy for the couple to generate positive memories of how they first met, the prognosis is often somewhat better. In general, although something of a truism, the more strengths a couple has, the easier it is to help them.

What Can Treatment Do to Help Them?

Following the assessment phase, the IBCT therapist is in a good position to determine what therapy can do for the couple. Assessment information is converted into an out-

line of a treatment plan. The IBCT therapist considers the various themes that have made themselves apparent so far, and considers which of the various change strategies might be of most value. The plan for the course of treatment is generally some combination of change and acceptance, with the emphasis on each depending on the particular needs of that couple. Each partner must be considered separately to determine his/her capacity for both change and acceptance. Generally, the more collaborative the couple, the more change can be expected initially; the more their problems seem irreconcilable, the more the therapist is going to want to start therapy by promoting emotional acceptance. Research has shown that capacity for change is negatively associated with severity of distress, proximity to divorce, total or near cessation of the sexual relationship, and traditional sex roles.

FEEDBACK SESSION

The IBCT therapist's answers to the six assessment questions are subsequently presented to the couple at the feedback session along with a proposed treatment plan. Each question is answered in a way that helps set the stage for the rest of therapy. For example, when discussing the couple's level of distress, what the therapist says depends on whether the couple is moderately or more severely distressed. When a couple is severely distressed, the therapist uses this information to underscore the seriousness of the situation and to prepare the couple for the hard work of therapy. In contrast, if the couple is only mildly distressed, the feedback session provides a good opportunity for the clinician to help the couple normalize their situation and alleviate some of the distress that may be associated with thinking that their problems are irreconcilable.

Discussion of the couple's level of distress is often related to their level of commitment in that more distressed couples are often less committed and vice versa. If the couple is committed to each other, and to trying to work things out, the prognosis for the success of therapy is good. This can be shared with the couple as another way of helping to normalize their situation and provide positive expectancies for the outcome of therapy. If, however, the couple is feeling hopeless and that things between them may be irreconcilable, discussion of these feelings is essential to the acceptance work with which therapy will begin.

Discussing the issues that divide the couple begins the process of promoting acceptance. The issues are presented in such a manner that both partners are shown to be behaving in a reasonable and understandable way. Emphasis is placed on the soft emotions underlying each partner's actions, and on the understandable reactions that have led them to their current dichotomized, and unsatisfying, positions. Presenting the issues that divide the couple in this way helps lead them away from blaming each other and toward mutual acceptance. This begins the process of teaching the couple how to relinquish the struggle and the perpetual defensiveness that have been interfering with their ability to be intimate up to this point.

The feedback session also addresses any dysfunctional strategies used to deal with the divisive issues. The various manifestations of the couple's problems are generally presented in the form of a theme, or pattern, that is played out in most, if not all, of their negative interactions. Many times one theme, such as demand–withdraw, can be used to characterize most of the couple issues; however, with some couples, discussion of more than one theme is necessary in order to capture the majority of their issues.

Couples are given plenty of opportunity to respond to the validity and appropriateness of the thematic formulations. The couple is asked often if the formulation sounds right to them, and if they have anything to add to it. Generally we have found that if the themes are presented in more of a lecture format, couples have the tendency to tune out, and the therapist is left with little opportunity to check whether the formulation is going to be effective.

The thematic formulation itself focuses on the general patterning of responses, as well as the contributions of each partner to the overall theme. Explicit emphasis is placed on the understandable human motives behind each partner's behavior in order to begin promoting emotional accep-

tance right away. Much use is made of the couple's previously assessed recent negative incidents as examples of the ways in which the couple's themes manifest themselves. This begins the process of making each of the couple's issues an "it" that they can recognize and accept, rather than the explicit fault of one or the other's maliciousness.

The following transcript is an example from the feedback session between therapist (T), Richard (R), and Jill (J) of the first presentation of the couple's main theme.

T: What I want to focus on tonight is what I see as a theme, or a pattern, that underlies your different areas of disagreement. This is an important way to think about your relationship and it's important that I understand it clearly, and that I can convey it to you clearly. So if I'm not making sense, feel free to let me know. OK?

R & J: OK.

T: First, I want to present the pattern I see from each of your perspectives, starting with you. (to Richard) It seems to me, based on what we've talked about, that you want to feel important to Jill, and loved by her, and feel secure in the relationship with her; and that sometimes when something is bothering you in the relationship, and you ask her to change, her refusal leads to your feeling unimportant, and you conclude that she doesn't care about you. If she doesn't do it, you feel that you aren't important to her. How does that sound to you?

R: Yeah. And then I tell her that, in any relationship, you need to make changes, and you need to be compromising, and be willing to do things for the other person that you wouldn't ordinarily do by yourself.

T: OK, now I want to describe this pattern from [Jill's] perspective. It seems that what is important to you is to feel loved and accepted for who you are, which is a very reasonable thing to want in a relationship. So when Richard repeatedly asks you to change something, it feels like he doesn't accept you as you are. That makes you feel bad, and then you are less likely to make the change that he wants. How does that fit for you?

J: See that's what I can't get across to him. There are certain things I'm not willing to change and that's just the way I feel about them. When I put my foot down, he says he feels that I don't love him.

T: And that is the bind. You (*to Richard*) want to feel cared about. And you (*to Jill*) want to feel accepted as you are. Yet, what each of you is doing actually results in the opposite of what you want.

Notice in this transcript that the therapist placed a great deal of emphasis on the soft emotions underlying each partner's behavior. This helped mitigate feelings that the other was simply acting maliciously. As can be seen from this brief transcript, however, these soft emotions may need to be emphasized often before they begin to have the desired effect.

The most important aspect of acceptance work is the formulation. All formulations have at least three components. The first is the difference between the partners. Most couples enter therapy insisting that the difference *is* the problem. Our perspective is that differences are inevitable, and that they only become problems to the extent that they are dealt with ineffectively. Thus, the second aspect of a formulation includes the well-intentioned but self-defeating ways that partners have of coping with these differences. The third aspect of the formulation is the mutual trap: This refers to each partner's experience of being trapped in a self-defeating strategy, which seems to be the best possible course given the situation. The trap occurs because both partners do what they think is best to deal with the difference, but the more they do, the deeper the hole that they get themselves into.

Following discussion of the couple's issues and themes, the clinician provides feedback about what treatment can do to help. The various goals of treatment are discussed, as well as the procedures that will be used to achieve these goals. The goals are usually presented as a combination of both acceptance and change. The process of therapy is described as involving in-session discussions about the couple's themes, instruction and practice in the use of appropriate change strategies, and the assignment of homework outside the session. The clinical

purpose of describing the treatment is to give the couple an accurate understanding of the process of therapy and to orient them toward the goals of accommodation and acceptance.

The feedback session generally includes an emphasis on the couple's strengths. Their strengths are presented as valuable assets, and as providing the foundation for confidence in the outcome of therapy. Discussion of the couple's strengths ends the session on a positive note and provides balance to the session, given that most of the feedback has focused on the couple's problems.

STRUCTURE OF THERAPY

Deciding how to structure a couple's therapy depends on the formulation of their problems provided by the assessment phase of therapy. The initial treatment plan varies depending on whether the therapist decides to begin treatment with an emphasis on change or on acceptance. For the most part, the treatment plan usually consists of some combination of both acceptance and change strategies. In terms of deciding whether to begin therapy with an emphasis on change or on acceptance, it is best to keep in mind that change strategies are often greatly facilitated when partners first experience a certain amount of acceptance. If partners see each other's positions as understandable and reasonable, and accept that no matter how much change occurs problems and conflict are simply part of being in a relationship, attempts to change are more likely to succeed. This is particularly true for couples who are severely distressed, seriously considering divorce, emotionally disengaged, or highly incompatible.

In some cases, particularly those in which the couple is highly collaborative and only mildly or moderately distressed, beginning treatment with an emphasis on change strategies is recommended. However, even in cases where the therapist decides to begin with change strategies, acceptance strategies should be integrated into the process of therapy. Durable change is more likely, and the amount of change more profound, if emotional acceptance is included as part of any attempt at change.

It is also possible to structure therapy in such a way that both change and acceptance strategies are introduced and utilized concurrently. Depending on the needs of the particular couple, the therapist may decide to give change and acceptance equal time, perhaps emphasizing acceptance for part of a session and change for the remainder, or alternating from session to session. One would choose this type of strategy when indicators do not point decisively to either change or acceptance.

For the clinician deciding how to integrate change and acceptance in a particular case, the most helpful indicators are the couple's level of distress, commitment, emotional engagement, compatibility, and collaboration. If these indicators tend toward the positive, an emphasis on change is suggested. If they tend toward the negative, it is usually best to begin therapy with an emphasis on acceptance. Finally, as noted above, if these indicators are mixed, a more concurrent integration of change and acceptance strategies should be considered. In any case, often the most powerful determinants of the therapy structure are the wishes of the particular couple being seen. It is not uncommon for a couple to express a strong preference for one type of strategy over another. In those cases, unless the therapist has powerful reasons for disagreeing with the couple, it is usually best to adhere to the couple's wishes.

Because of the wide assortment of both couples and couple's problems, the responsibility for determining how long the couple should remain in treatment depends on the particulars of each individual case. The average length of treatment is generally about 20 sessions; however, depending on the couple and their problems, individual cases may be resolved in one session or may require quite lengthy and extensive therapy.

Throughout the remainder of the chapter, we present both types of strategies in detail. We begin by discussing the promotion of emotional acceptance and then discuss strategies for the promotion of behavioral change. We present 10 of the new acceptance strategies and 2 of the most common and effective change strategies. The acceptance strategies include (1) empathic joining around the problem, (2) making the problem an "it," (3) exploring a couple's themes, (4) the context for promoting acceptance, (5) promoting emotional acceptance through tolerance building, (6) positive reemphasis, (7) emphasizing complementary differences, (8) preparing for backsliding, (9) faking bad, and (10) emotional acceptance through greater self-care. The two change strategies are, (1) behavior exchange, and (2) communication and problem-solving training.

STRUCTURE OF THERAPEUTIC SESSION

Providing a consistent structure for each session ensures that the goals of therapy remain in focus and that the couple remains on task. In collaboration with the couple, each session starts with setting an agenda that outlines the goals for that session. This agenda usually includes reviewing any homework that may have been assigned as well as discussing any further developments stemming from the previous week's session (i.e., further thoughts, feelings, or implementations of any decisions). Following this, the session moves on to new business. Usually the IBCT therapist allows the individual couple to determine which problem to focus on each week. This flexibility is important because couples are often more motivated to work on issues that are causing problems currently. In any case, couples must learn how to deal with problems while they are still "hot." Furthermore, most of a couple's conflicts represent one or another of their main themes, and thus generally, the problem they choose allows the therapist to continue promoting emotional acceptance. In order to assure that valuable therapy time is not spent discussing a trivial issue, however, the therapist generally restricts the problem selection to those relating to a major difficulty in the relationship. Each session generally ends with a summary of what has been discussed and the assignment of further homework if appropriate.

STRATEGIES FOR PROMOTING EMOTIONAL ACCEPTANCE

Oftentimes when couples present for marital therapy, each member in some way blames the other for the problems they are having: Somehow if the other person would just change and quit being such a jerk, the relationship would be just fine. Each finds it easier to blame the other than to see what part he/she plays in perpetuating the pain that they are in. The relationship has problems because the partner is selfish, hateful, deceitful, controlling, or frigid. Each member often believes that if he/she could somehow change the partner, his/her own life would dramatically improve. However, it is rarely the case that a couple's problems are the result of the actions or characteristics of one partner independent of the actions and characteristics of the other. The job of the IBCT therapist in the context of this kind of cross-blaming is to help the couple reformulate their problems as arising out of the common and understandable reactions they are having to equally common and understandable differences between them.

Empathic Joining Around the Problem

Empathic joining around the problem means emphasizing pain without accusation. IBCT therapists encourage each member of the couple to express the soft emotions underlying the expression of hard emotions. Hard emotions are characterized by statements that put one partner in the role of the accuser, or of the wronged party who is rightfully seeking redress for some unjustified transgression by the other. The expression of hard emotions presents that partner as on the offense, dominant, and invulnerable. The natural reaction of the listener is to become defensive and to counterattack with examples of the other's misbehavior or imperfections. Soft emotions, on the other hand, express such feelings as hurt, loneliness, insecurity, fear, desire, and love. The expression of these emotions reveals the partner's vulnerability within the relationship, and the listener is therefore less likely to be defensive and more likely to hear what his/her partner is saying and to empathize. However, by the time a couple seeks therapy, blaming and accusations have usually become so deeply ingrained within their style of interacting that learning how to identify and respond with the expression of soft emotions is rarely an easy accomplish-

ment. At first the IBCT therapist usually has to take primary responsibility for helping the couple identify the softer emotions behind the hard emotions that are typically more easily expressed. Soft emotions identified by the therapist are thoroughly checked out with the partner to whom they are being attributed, and the other partner, in turn, is asked what effect hearing these softer emotions has had on him/her.

It is important to note at this point that we are not advocating a particular *style* of communication. Each couple is going to have their own unique style and the IBCT therapist does not try to force that style into a preconceived model of "good" communication. The therapist, in promoting empathic joining around the problem, works with the couple's own way of communicating to help each partner express his/her soft emotions and understand the soft emotions of the other. It is important to keep in mind that what works for one couple may not necessarily work for another. Rule-governed adherence to a particular conception of good communication may interfere with the primary goal of these strategies, which is to help each member of the couple understand the pain generated for both of them by their disagreements.

The following scenario demonstrates the process of promoting empathic joining around the problem. The husband (H) and wife (W) were focusing on the issue of housework, and the therapist (T) used this discussion to reveal the softer emotions underlying their negative feelings.

T: (*To wife*) So, he tends to compliment you when things are neat around the house, but something about that doesn't feel good to you. Is that right?

W: Sometimes it just irritates me, because I'd like for him to appreciate me as I am and not . . .

H: I think she's just disappointed that it's so easy to please me.

W: No, no.

H: All you've got to do is keep the house clean.

T: (*To wife*) So it's not necessarily good news that it pleases him as much as it does.

H: I've definitely had that reaction from you, that I'll be really tickled with something, and you'll feel put down.

W: Well sometimes when he's so impressed that I've done something, it feels patronizing.

H: And the feeling I get is that I don't know how the hell to please her. I really don't.

W: I think the thing that irritated me most recently was on Monday. I had a meeting and I had to take my child because John had to work late. I didn't get home until 9:30, and the house was a mess, and he was irritated, because the house didn't look in perfect shape.

T: Um hmm.

W: He didn't have any idea what my day was like, but he was irritated with me, because the house wasn't the way he thought it should be. That to me is insulting. It's saying, "This house is more important than our relationship." He doesn't assume that there's some reason why things don't look exactly perfect. He just assumes that I did this to him. That's kind of how it feels, he takes what the house looks like as a personal affront to him.

T: Um hmm. I guess what really strikes me about what you just said is that you end up feeling taken for granted.

W: Yeah.

T: (*To husband*) To you it probably seems inconsequential that you get viscerally irritated about neatness. It may not be obvious that she feels taken for granted when you express that irritation, but I think it's important that you know that's how she feels. Did you already know that?

H: Yeah, I think I did, because I've known, for instance, that she doesn't like it that I'm quite so happy about it when the house is clean, you know.

T: Do you understand how she gets from you complimenting her about it, or being irritated by it, to feeling put down? Or are there still some missing pieces?

H: No, I think I understand it.

T: What's your reaction to it?

H: Well I don't feel like there's anything I can do to make her feel better about that.

T: I don't know. (*To wife*) What do you think? Do you think that's true? Do you think there's anything he can do?

W: I think I would feel better about it if he came into the house and said, "gosh you must have had a hell of a day," or "it looks like things got a little out of hand," rather than being mad at me.

T: I don't know exactly how to pursue it, but the thing I keep coming back to is the struggle that you undergo in this relationship to feel OK.

W: Um hmm.

W: To feel like he thinks you're OK.

H: I think that's true.

T: (*To husband*) I'm wondering how aware you are of it on a day-to-day basis, that seemingly inconsequential things that you might do or say have an impact beyond the obvious pragmatics of the moment.

H: I don't know why I don't want to answer that question, but I want to say I just don't know how to make her feel better. I don't know how to get through. I don't think it would be flattering to not complain about the house.

T: Yeah, I think I agree with that. Do you feel like she's right about your sometimes being insensitive to how difficult things are at home?

H: Sure, yes. I don't like doing it. I mean I don't like being at home at all.

T: Do you sometimes take it for granted that she does it?

H: Sure, yeah, I'm absolutely guilty about that, because when I do stay at home and do a day of that, you know, I find it exhausting.

T: (*To wife*) How do you react when you hear him talking about what a mystery it is to him how to make you feel better? Does it surprise you that he's so perplexed about how to do it? Do you think he should know, or is it understandable to you that he finds it such a mystery?

W: Well, no, I'm not surprised at that.

H: In fact when therapy started one of my firmest feelings about "gotta get help," is that nothing pleased her. You know, as an individual I think that's my feeling toward you, is that I don't know how to please you.

In this example, note that the therapist attempted to draw the husband's attention to his partner's feelings of invalidation, and away from focusing exclusively on her anger. In this way, the therapist hoped to begin to soften the husband's typical response to a less than pristine house by helping him make more contact with how hurtful that response can be to his wife. In the same vein, the therapist also attempted to draw the wife's attention to her husband's feeling of being stuck and feeling incapable of responding in a way that would be pleasing to her. Again, the therapist hoped this would help the wife to experience her partner as less of a hateful, invalidating, neatnik, and more as a man feeling caught between liking a neat house and not knowing how to validate his wife. Helping the couple to see those aspects of each other that were masked by the expression of hard emotions is expected to lead them away from feelings of resentment and toward greater intimacy within the relationship.

A major area of controversy within IBCT is whether acceptance can only be fostered by communication changes or whether the formulation can suffice in the absence of actual changes in communication. For example, when the therapist identifies a destructive pattern of dealing with a difference, does the couple have to improve the way they communicate, or does the therapist's pronouncement have the capacity to produce acceptance in and of itself? Our position is that the formulation, as verbalized by the therapist, is a powerful acceptance-inducing tactic, independent of whether the partners actually begin to talk about the problem in a way consistent with the therapist's formulation. The formulation changes the context in which their interaction occurs, and serves as a setting event for their old patterns. This means that the formulation can alter the function of the old patterns so that they do not have the destructive impact they once did. The formulation becomes part of the couple's revision-

ist relationship history, and it begins to impact their levels of marital satisfaction, even if their communication remains unchanged subsequent to the formulation.

Making the Problem an "It"

Although a couple may come to experience the soft emotions underlying a common area of disagreement between them, that experiencing often does not change the typical pattern of their disagreement. They may continue to disagree on that issue for the duration of their relationship. Oftentimes when it appears that this may be the case, the IBCT therapist attempts to help the couple reformulate their problem as an "it" rather than as something that each is maliciously doing to the other. Essentially, this means helping the couple to give up the struggle to change either their own or their partner's reactions to a particular issue. It also means providing for them a shared perspective from which to deal with these disagreements. The therapist helps the couple see the interaction in its entirety as a natural series of valid reactions. Through reformulating the problem as an "it," each partner is expected to become increasingly able to tolerate this difference between them without feeling either personally guilty or blaming of his/her partner. It also provides a perspective from which the couple can share the problem, and commiserate about it, without blaming each other for its existence. The pattern of the couple in the above transcript was set in motion by a messy house, to which the husband responded by being irritated. The wife responded to his irritation by becoming hurt and defensive and the husband responded in kind by also becoming hurt and defensive. If this couple can be led to see this sequence of events as an "it," although it may continue to happen in their relationship, it will happen within an entirely new context. Each partner will be in a better position to recognize that he/she is engaging in a familiar pattern that is not necessarily the fault of either of them. Thus, through acceptance of these differences between them, each is better able to tolerate the occurrence of this particular interaction and it is therefore much less likely to have a dramatic impact on their overall happiness and satisfaction with the relationship. Furthermore, seeing the problem as an "it" gives them a perspective from which they can actually form a closer relationship through dealing with this problem together. Finally, despite the continuation of this pattern between them, it is hoped that the positive aspects of the couple's relationship will far outweigh the existence of these differences.

Exploring a Couple's Themes

As implied previously, a large part of promoting acceptance takes the form of discussing the themes and patterns that characterize the couple's negative interactions. Although a particular couple's themes are often unique, there are some common themes that we tend to see again and again. One of the most frequently occurring themes is referred to as demand–withdraw. This theme is characterized by one partner's nagging and demanding while the other becomes silent, refuses to talk about it, or actually physically leaves. Emotional–logical is another common theme characterized by one partner's expressing feelings while the other partner offers reasons and solutions. Other common themes include criticize–defend (one partner criticizes while the other defends him/herself), mutual avoidance, mutual blame, mutual threat, and pressure–resist (one partner pressures the other for change, while the other resists).

As noted in the section Making the Problem an "It," identification of such themes allows the couple in essence to "see the forest for the trees." In seeing individual sequences of events as representative of common themes, the couple is provided a perspective from which to relinquish what may be an unwinnable struggle to change either themselves or their partner. Thus, all the pain and effort that go into trying to win these debates is avoided, and the couple is left with the less intense pain associated with the simple fact that they disagree. Furthermore, the common perspective provided by identification of common themes creates a context in which intimacy can actually be fostered despite the perpetuation of common problems. The couple is provided with a means of talking about these problematic interactions without cross-blaming or feeling victimized and is able to commiserate and sympathize with each other over their common problem. This in itself is expected to lead to quicker recovery from these arguments and thus also to spare the couple the pain associated with having such arguments drag out for hours or actually threaten the stability of the relationship.

Context for Promoting Acceptance

Identifying themes, turning the problem into an "it," and promoting empathic joining around the problem all occur during discussions of three different types of events. These include recent negative events, upcoming events that may be problematic, and recent events that were potentially negative but went well. In discussing the structure of therapy, we noted that for the most part the couple is allowed to decide which issue to discuss during any particular session. Most frequently couples choose to discuss a recent negative incident and these discussions are golden opportunities to promote acceptance. Initially discussions of recent negative events are used to identify the couple's common themes. After the couple's themes have been identified, future discussions of recent events can be used to illustrate the recurrence of these themes.

Recent events also provide the material from which individual problems are reformulated into an "it." Discussion of recent negative events sometimes reveals that the couple is having trouble dealing with problems such as chronic physical illness, depression, or work schedule conflicts. These types of problems may not present themselves as themes, and thus reformulating the problem as an "it" is often the most appropriate intervention.

Discussions of recent negative events are also useful in terms of promoting the expression of soft emotions. Each step in a recent negative interaction can be probed for the soft emotions that may have been hidden at the time of the actual argument. Eventually, through such work, the entire interaction can be seen as the result of natural and understandable reactions eliciting sympathy and caring rather than anger and defensiveness.

Upcoming events that the couple anticipates will go poorly provide ideal material for discussing a couple's themes as well as problems they have reformulated into an "it." Discussion of such events prior to their actual occurrence helps the couple avoid being caught off guard by those events and may in some cases facilitate the introduction of new responses to the situation. Furthermore, being able to anticipate and plan for the recurrence of common problems generally ameliorates feelings of helplessness and resentment. This provides the couple with enough distance from the particulars of the event to enable them to commiserate about its occurrence.

Discussion of anticipated negative events can also be used to promote the expression of soft emotions. In some cases, the expression of soft emotions is enough to actually change the outcome of the event from negative to positive. However, even if the actual structure of the scenario doesn't change, each partner's increased understanding of the other's reactions often mitigates feelings of resentment, anger, and victimization.

It is also the case that not every potentially problematic incident goes badly. IBCT therapists are vigilant for incidents in which problems might have occurred but were avoided. These incidents are discussed in some detail, focusing specifically on the point at which things could have gone badly but didn't, or the point where things took a dramatic turn for the better. The points at which common themes broke down are of particular interest and these are thoroughly explored in hopes of uncovering strategies the couple may use in the future. Soft emotions that occurred during the incident are also explored to clarify for the couple what was different about this interaction in the way each responded emotionally.

However, given that acceptance work of this sort is generally done on problems that are chronic and recurrent, often the best strategy when things have gone well for the couple is to begin to prepare them for possible slip-ups. During the stage in therapy in which the couple begins to feel more and more positive about the relationship, they become particularly vulnerable to the devastating effects of backsliding. A couple's outlook may become overly rosy following a period of positive interactions and any slip-up may leave both partners feeling hopeless and defeated. Therefore, at times like these it is essential that the IBCT therapist discuss with the couple the likelihood of slip-ups. These events should be anticipated and normalized, and the responses of each partner should be thoroughly discussed. It may seem counterproductive to burst the couple's bubble in this way, but experience has shown us that this is often much less destructive than allowing the couple to be blind-sided by the recurrence of a problem that could have been easily anticipated.

Promoting Emotional Acceptance Through Tolerance Building

Many of the couples that we see are heavily engaged in the process of trying to change things about one another. Each has identified certain things about the other that he/she is convinced cause all of the relationship's problems. Once these things have been identified, the struggle then begins to change them. Usually the partner is told that the behavior he/she is currently engaging in is wrong, or illogical, in the hopes that simply pointing this out to the partner will help to change things. When these accusations lead instead to anger and defensiveness, it is taken as further evidence that the partner is obstinate or uncaring. The conclusion is often drawn that if the partner really loved him/her, the partner would gladly accept his/her criticisms and promptly change. Unfortunately, this strategy leads more frequently to fights, and greater polarization between partners, than it does to any kind of reconciliation. Each becomes hopelessly entangled in the struggle to change the other or to resist changing, and this state of hopeless entanglement is often the one the couple brings with them into therapy. Usually when the couple arrives in the therapist's office, each is hoping that the therapist will take his/her side and help convince the other partner of the error of his/her ways.

Rather than taking sides, however, the IBCT therapist focuses on helping the couple give up the struggle to change one another. The couple is helped to see that much, if not all, of the pain that is being generated is a direct result of their engaging in an unwinnable struggle, and that simply giving up the struggle promises to alleviate much of that pain. This is often much easier said than done given that the couple has had a great deal of practice at engaging in these particular struggles. The struggle becomes so much a defining part of the relationship that it is often difficult to get the couple to step far enough back from it to see it in full relief. Building tolerance necessitates giving up the struggle; furthermore, giving up the struggle is often sufficient by itself to generate tolerance.

One strategy for helping the couple give up the struggle is to short-circuit their motivation for engaging in it. Often the motivation behind trying to change a particular behavior in the partner lies in a perception of that behavior as an attack, a demonstration of uncaring, or a lack of acceptance. For example, in the case of Mike and Susan, Mike was heavily invested in trying to get Susan to come home on time from work, something she rarely did. His attempts at trying to get her to stop coming home late ranged from complaining about it or sulking to accusing her of not loving him and threatening to leave her. This type of escalation is often the result of a struggle for change that has been going on for some time. Susan, on the other hand, took Mike's attempts at trying to get her to come home on time as an attack on her independence. Given this, she was not about to capitulate to his demands and strongly resisted his attempts to get her to come home earlier.

Emotional acceptance through tolerance building was promoted in several ways at this point with Mike and Susan. One way was to provide for them a more complete picture of the variables controlling both Susan's coming home late and Mike's attempts to get her to come home early. As it stood, each partner was focusing solely on the negative aspects of the other's behavior. Each saw what the other was doing as deliberately intended to be hurtful, and nothing else. The IBCT therapist helped illuminate the more reasonable and understandable factors that were leading to the behaviors each found objectionable about the other.

Mike wanted Susan to come home on time because he believed that coming home

late meant that she didn't love him and would rather be at work than spend any more time with him than she absolutely had to. Therapy focused on bringing to light Mike's feelings of insecurity in the marriage and his uncertainty about whether Susan truly loved him. Mike's complaints about coming home late became more tolerable to Susan as she began to see that they resulted from a need for reassurance rather than from a desire to stifle her independence.

Susan often stayed late at work because her job provided her with feelings of accomplishment and purpose. It was a source of both joy and a sense of meaning for her, and her dedication to her job in no way reflected on how deeply she loved Mike, or how much she enjoyed the time they spent together. Over the course of therapy, it became clear to Mike that Susan's dedication to her job didn't result from her wanting to be away from him but rather from the enrichment and joy it brought her. Susan's coming home late thus became more tolerable for him, particularly as other means of reassurance about the quality of the relationship became available.

Couples in distress, much like depressives, have the tendency to focus almost exclusively on the negative aspects of their partner's behavior. Each insensitive remark or unthoughtful action becomes another demonstration of all the things that are wrong with their relationship. Motivations are usually inferred, rather than confirmed, and they are often inferred to be selfish or intentionally hurtful. The IBCT therapist in this case works to provide a more complete picture of the variables controlling each partner's behavior. Since the partners themselves are unable to see beyond the inferred negative motivations of the other, the IBCT therapist helps to point out other sources of motivation present that are less negative and more understandable. It is often simply not the case that the sole motivation behind the partner's behavior is to be hurtful or malicious. His/her negative behavior might primarily be under the control of hurt feelings, feelings of insecurity, or simple ignorance of the behavior's effects on the partner. When these other sources of motivation are pointed out, and woven into one of the couple's general themes, those behaviors that were seen before as unbearable become more tolerable. Again, it is important to point out that this is not necessarily because the form of the behaviors themselves has changed, but because the context in which they now occur has changed. If this particular intervention has been successful, the occurrence of these negative behaviors is more likely to be seen as a demonstration of some more understandable theme, rather than a demonstration of all that is wrong with the relationship. Therefore, the changes that are seen are much more likely to be at a thematic level rather than at the level of the particular negative behaviors themselves.

Positive Reemphasis

Another strategy for increasing tolerance is to point out the positive features of negative behavior. This works to increase tolerance by decreasing the saliency of the negative aspects of the behavior in favor of the more positive. For example, what one partner is currently seeing as an overinvolvement with friends may be the gregariousness that he initially found very attractive. Or what the other partner sees as stodginess may be the stability that initially attracted her. The task of the IBCT therapist is to emphasize these initially attractive elements, thus helping the couple to appreciate the positive facets of what are now being considered purely negative behaviors. The main differences between this technique and the more traditional strategic use of reframing are that (1) rather than labeling a negative behavior as entirely positive, the IBCT therapist continues to acknowledge the negative aspects while illuminating the positive, and (2) the IBCT therapist emphasizes only positive features that actually exist for the couple. The attempt is not to alter the partner's perceptions of the problem from completely negative to completely positive, but instead to provide a more integrated picture that includes positive as well as negative aspects.

Complementary Differences

Differences often create balance. One person's gregariousness may balance the other

person's stability. One person's attention to detail may balance the other's impulsivity. It is often possible to present these differences as part of what makes the relationship viable. If this particular balance were to be lacking, it could lead to more trouble than it is currently causing. Those differences can become a positive aspect of the couple's relationship and can be something for them to be proud of, and to feel close about, rather than something that threatens to destroy them.

The following transcript is an example of attempting to build tolerance by focusing on the complementary nature of the couple's differences. In this case the therapist (T) had been working with Robert (R) and Melissa (M) on problem-solving strategies, but because of the nature of the couple's issues, the therapist shifted to promoting emotional acceptance.

T: Let me ask you both a question. Is one of the problems here that you prioritize things differently? For example, (*to Robert*) you might value getting tasks done more than she does.

R: Definitely.

T: (*To Melissa*) And you might value spending time together with no goal in particular more than he does.

M: Definitely.

R: I think we don't prioritize. I think that's our major problem. In other words, right now we are trying to sell a house. How big a priority is getting out of here, and getting to someplace else? If that is a very high priority, then we need to define a goal, to work together, and to plan the tasks, whether they are farmed out or done ourselves, whatever, but we need to plan the tasks that we have to get accomplished to sell the house. Now if that is the most important thing then we must weigh those tasks that have to be completed to achieve a goal. Many times she'll say, "Forget about that task. It's a nice day. Let's go do something else," but this goal is still hanging out here, and now we're ignoring it. What is the most important thing we need to focus on today? Now if we have an understanding that every sunny day we are going to go enjoy ourselves, or whatever. If every sunny day we are going to go and enjoy ourselves, and that's more important than selling the house and moving out of here, then that's fine. Now we've prioritized, and now that's more important than selling the house. But if selling the house is the most important thing, then we've got to remember that that is the most important thing and prioritize things so that we move forward and accomplish our objectives. Just like some day you are going to retire. You've got to prioritize, or you may not buy this, or you may not do that; so that some day you will arrive at the objective.

M: I feel like I just heard a sermon.

T: Well, if I were to hazard a guess, you (*to Melissa*) probably have some difficulty with the concept of prioritizing because, to you, it implies a restriction of one's freedom to act spontaneously.

M: Yeah, I don't like it.

T: So if you (*to Melissa*) were writing the script for how the two of you would spend your life, you might say, "OK, selling our house is the top priority. We really want to sell it, but if there is a sunny day, I want to stop everything and enjoy it."

M: Because it is so rare, yes.

T: And that might be a difference between the two of you that's quite *interesting*. Would it be fair to say that you (*to Robert*) are the kind of guy who, if there is a goal that is out front there, and number one on your list, that you are not going to let anything interfere with that until it gets accomplished?

R: I wouldn't say anything but I . . .

T: But you're more in that direction than she is.

R: Well, yeah.

T: Your value is that you list your priorities, and then you go about your business trying to accomplish them, and you basically don't let anything get in the way. (*To Melissa*) Your values are different. Your values are, yeah you have goals, but you are sort of loosey goosey about them, and if it's a nice day, you'd rather do the nice day. You wish that he

were more like you, more loosey goosey.

And you (*to Robert*) wish she were more like you. But although this is a source of conflict now, one could look at it as a very interesting difference between the two of you that you could enjoy, rather than complain about. For example, (*to Melissa*) having Robert in your life in a way allows you to be more loosey goosey, because he is going to make sure that things get done. And (*to Robert*) having Melissa in your life is a check against you becoming too regimented, because if she has a say in the matter, there is going to be some spontaneity in your lives. So you could see these differences between you as a source of strength, as well as a source of conflict. It doesn't have to destroy your marriage. It can be a boon. It can be a nice thing.

(*To Robert*) You might live longer, because you've got her around to drag you out from underneath the car, and take you to a picnic. That might be good for you in the long run, and you (*to Melissa*) might have some money left when you retire, because of him. So it's a nice marriage in that sense.

R: That's one of the things I like about her. That she'll drag me out from underneath the car.

Notice that the result of this type of intervention was that each partner was shown something valuable about what they had seen as primarily negative about the other. In addition, each partner was allowed to feel good about some part of him/her that until now had been nothing but a source of conflict. This intervention will not necessarily lead to a change in either Robert's goal directedness or Melissa's spontaneity, but it created an atmosphere in which each was more able to tolerate that aspect of the other.

Preparation for Backsliding

Even successful therapy is characterized by uneven progress and occasional slip-ups. Given the virtual inevitability of slip-ups, and the potentially devastating effect these may have on the relationship, it is particularly important that the therapist prepare the couple for these instances. This is especially important during the initial period of change when couples may be fooled into thinking that the changes are impervious to relapse. During this stage of therapy, couples often come to the session exuberant over the progress that they have been making, particularly if they have just had a good week. Generally this is the time that the IBCT therapist focuses on preparing the couple for slip-ups. The couple is congratulated for the progress they are making in therapy and then warned that backsliding is still a likely occurrence. They are asked to consider the various circumstances in which backsliding might occur, and to work out their responses to such a backslide in advance. Working out how to deal with backsliding while the couple is doing well helps to build tolerance to such events. This strategy falls under the rubric of tolerance building, because couples are, in a sense, being inoculated against the recurrence of negative patterns. If their tolerance for backsliding is not increased, slip-ups can lead to hopelessness and frustration.

Faking Bad

An additional strategy for building tolerance involves instructing the couple to "fake" negative behavior at home. Each partner is instructed to engage in a specified negative behavior sometime over the course of the next week when he/she is *not* feeling like it. These instructions are given in front of the partner, so that each partner knows that some negative behavior in the future might be faked. Faking introduces an element of ambiguity into future negative incidents that may interfere with the couple's typical responses, as well as give them some perspective on their stereotypical patterns. Furthermore, faking gives each partner an opportunity to observe the effects of their negative behavior at a time when they are more capable of being sympathetic. The faker is instructed to let the partner know about the fake soon after it has been initiated in order to prevent escalation and to allow the couple to discuss their reactions.

The following example demonstrates how this assignment is presented to a couple. The issue being discussed by this couple revolved around Anne's (A) frequent complaints about the Seattle weather and Will's (W) tendency to respond by pointing out places where the weather is even worse.

T: The point is that, to be realistic, I think that no matter how hard you work, this chain is so automatic, and happens so quickly, that we have to accept the fact that it's going to happen. You are probably not going to be able to eliminate these interchanges, although you might be able to decrease their frequency. The question is that, given that these are inevitable, what can you do to minimize the harm that they do to the relationship? And one of the things that I would like you to do (*to Anne*) is at some point during the week when you don't feel badly about the weather, complain about it. I want you to observe the impact that that has on him at a time when you are not really feeling bad, so you can more objectively see his pain.

W: Any time this weekend would probably be fine.

T: It would be more credible if you did it at a time when the weather wasn't beautiful. That is, if the weather is beautiful then you (*to Will*) are probably going to recognize that she's just play acting.

A: You know, it's deeper than all that though. It's deeper, and goes beyond my making a comment and him reacting to it. It's so bad that he reacts defensively even when I haven't said anything. I mean he'll watch a weather report on CNN in Tokyo and talk to me about how it was cruddy on the East Coast, and nice here; or how it's, you know, we could have had rain for 45 straight days and never seen the sun for two months here and it could be raining in Denver, and he couldn't wait to get home and tell me that it rained in Denver or LA. I mean it's that bad. He's defensive without me even saying anything.

T: Right, that's going to be part of the assignment too. But what I'm hoping will happen is that at some point during the week, when he's not expecting it, make some derogatory comment about the Seattle weather at a time when you are not feeling bad about the weather.

A: OK.

T: I'm assuming that he's going to have the same defensive reaction he always does, but you won't be upset, and so you will be able to see his defensiveness. What I'm hoping is that it will be more sympathetic to you, because you're not going to be upset. That is, you will be able to more objectively observe his reaction, and maybe empathize more with the bind that he's in when you react that way. Now, shortly after he reacts defensively, I think you should say to him, "I'm just kidding. It was the assignment." So it doesn't turn into an argument. And if possible you (to Will) should just put what we are saying out of your mind so that you're not walking around expecting her to say something. What I'm trying to do is put her in a situation where she can see your response, because it makes good sense to me, at a time when she's not upset, and thereby able to be more empathic with the bind that you're in when she makes those type of responses. What I've written down is that Anne will complain about the weather at a time when she's not upset about the weather, and observe Will's reaction. After a few minutes, she will tell him she is faking.

W: (To Anne) You have to use the word "faking" so I know it's the assignment. It's not "just kidding," which you use a lot.

T: Right, OK. Now here's your side of it. At some point during the week, I'd like you to tell her how bad the weather is. Take a weather map and point out all the places where the weather is worse than it is in Seattle.

A: He did that this morning.

T: OK, but do that at a time when you are not really feeling an impulse to show her anything about the weather. Fake it. That is, this will be at a time when you are not feeling defensive. You are doing it because it is the assignment. And I want you to observe the impact on Anne.

A: I usually just ignore it.

T: Yeah, but your body language is very expressive.

W: I did that this morning.

A: And I just ignored it.

W: I couldn't believe it. It's so warm, record highs on the West Coast and in the upper great lakes. They are saying 4 to 5 inches of snow tomorrow. And I'm sitting there going, "holy smokes, talk about an extreme." And I was just trying to point out to her the extremes, and she got very cold and . . .

A: Oh, I did not.

W: Oh, you bristled right down the back of your . . .

A: I could have cared less. I just thought it was . . .

W: But next time I'll remember to say I was faking.

T: OK, so (to Will) will you point out all the places in the world or just in the United States?

W: Let's just go with the United States.

T: All the places in the United States.

This transcript demonstrates all the important elements of presenting this assignment. The therapist specified the negative behavior to be faked and also informed the couple of the rationale for the assignment. Furthermore, the assignment was written down to aid the couple in remembering exactly what it was that they were supposed to do. Note that although the therapist told the husband not to pay attention to the assignment that the wife was given, the husband could not help but be affected by hearing it. As noted above, this was expected to introduce an element of doubt into this type of negative interaction and therefore interfere with the husband's stereotypical response to his wife's complaints about the weather. For this couple, the perspective provided by the assignment did work to disrupt their typical responses to each other. As a result, complaints about the weather no longer led to the long drawn-out negative interactions that they had led to before.

There are three ways in which tolerance-promoting interventions can improve a relationship. First, they can promote acceptance in the way that the rationale for these interventions suggests. Second, they can change the form and/or the function of the old patterns, so that even though they continue to occur, their impact changes. Third, they can result in a termination of the patterns (i.e., change). Once the functions of the old patterns have been removed, the behaviors themselves may drop out. The power of tolerance promotion is that there are so many different ways that change or acceptance can be promoted.

Emotional Acceptance Through Greater Self-Care

The promotion of greater self-care is the last acceptance strategy covered in this chapter. Self-care is promoted in IBCT by encouraging each partner to take personal responsibility for his/her own needs. Unfortunately, it is almost never the case that all a person's needs can be met at all times by one person within any one relationship. By encouraging both partners to take personal responsibility for their own needs, the IBCT therapist changes the usual response to dissatisfaction. Both are more likely to respond by strongly addressing their own needs and less likely to passively fume over their partner's inadequacies. Even for needs that must be met within the context of the relationship (e.g., sexual needs), this shift in responsibility encourages each partner to take an active role in the pursuit of those needs. As a result, partners are less likely to blame each other for their own discontent and are more likely to get their needs met. It should be emphasized, however, that taking responsibility for their own needs does not relieve partners of responsibility for doing what they can to make the relationship successful.

The shift in responsibility, from partner to self, is also exceptionally useful in the context of negative interactions. By taking responsibility for their own self-care, both partners are able to assertively intervene in their own best interest during negative interactions. This self-care may take the form of leaving a negative interaction for a set amount of time or assertively altering the form or direction of a negative situation. Given our previous discussion of couple themes, greater self-care might also involve

redefining a negative interaction as a temporary slip-up or as an instance of a familiar pattern. Redefined in this way, the partner may more easily ride out the instance, without becoming hopelessly entangled in it.

STRATEGIES FOR PROMOTING CHANGE

Behavior Exchange

Behavior exchange (BE) was typically the first strategy to be implemented within BCT, and for couples who are only moderately distressed, BE remains an excellent way to begin therapy. However, the success of BE depends a great deal on the degree of collaboration that can be expected between partners; therefore, in cases where the couple's distress level is high and/or their commitment to the relationship is low, it is now considered best to start therapy with an emphasis on promoting acceptance. If partners are angry and resentful, there will be little motivation to engage in the kind of positive interactions that are at the heart of BE. Therefore, within IBCT, BE is most often implemented later in therapy, after a good deal of acceptance has already taken place. Furthermore, within IBCT, less is riding on the immediate success of BE than would be the case in BCT. In those cases where BE interventions are unsuccessful in increasing the frequency of positive interactions between partners, BE often serves as a diagnostic for areas requiring more emotional acceptance work.

The primary goal of BE is to increase the proportion of positive interactions occurring within the couple's day-to-day relationship. Couples have often become so polarized by the time they enter therapy that they no longer do even simple things for each other that could increase their overall satisfaction with the relationship. Generally, BE refers to procedures that help couples begin to take advantage of their remaining capacity to increase each other's relationship satisfaction through simple positive actions. Increasing positive interactions helps alleviate the distressed couple's tendency to attend only to the negative aspects of their relationship. In addition, although the reduction of negative behavior is not addressed specifically in BE, increases in positive behaviors have been shown to be associated with decreases in negative behaviors.

BE procedures are designed to have a short-term but immediate effect. Rapid increases in the amount of positive interactions are often imperative in couples that have become too focused on the negative aspects of their relationship. This often provides needed encouragement to the couple and helps foster the belief that they can improve the quality of their relationship. BE generally consists of two common steps. The first is to identify those things that each partner can do to increase the other's relationship satisfaction without requiring personal changes that might be considered too costly. The second is to attempt to increase the frequency of those behaviors in the day-to-day life of the couple. The assignment initially is for each member of the couple to independently generate a list of things he/she can do to increase his/her partner's satisfaction with the relationship. This is generally given as a homework assignment and the partners are instructed not to discuss their lists with each other until the following session. Partners are discouraged from discussing the content of each other's list in order to alleviate any threat of the other's criticism and to ensure that each partner remains focused on his/her own list. During the following therapy session, each partner goes over his/her list with the therapist in order to ensure that each item is behaviorally specific and that the list is comprehensive.

After each partner's list has been discussed in session, they are given the assignment of doing at least one of the things on their list sometime over the course of the next week. During the following therapy session the partners are asked to evaluate how they did during the week and whether what they did had the desired affect on their partner. Items on the list that do not seem to be having the desired effect are discussed and either reworked or temporarily abandoned. Again, partners are discouraged from criticizing each other's performance in order to maintain the emphasis on their own behavior. Later in therapy, once BE has begun to have an effect, feedback can be solicited in order to optimize the effects of those items remaining on the lists. It is important for the therapist to assure that this feedback is both constructive and noncritical in order to maintain the positive focus of the intervention.

Over the years, we have radically changed the context in which we deliver BE directives. Traditionally, each partner was asked what he/she would like more of, and the directives were designed to help each giver provide more of what the recipient wants. Now, we begin with a focus on the giver, and ask him/her to change him/herself in order to improve the relationship. This mode of beginning BE is considerably more effective than the traditional mode. We believe that there are two reasons for the advantage of our more contemporary version: (1) it is more consistent with the notion of "collaborative set" (cf. Jacobson & Margolin, 1979); (2) it increases the likelihood that subsequent changes will be well received by the recipients.

BE does not always proceed smoothly, however, and there are some common ways in which it can be derailed. The most common is probably noncompliance with the assignment by either one or both partners. If this happens, it is important for the therapist to help the couple figure out what has been interfering. Often the answer is that either one or both of the partners feel that the other simply does not deserve any of the positive things on their list. At this point it is usually best to shift to doing acceptance work on any incidents that are representative of what has derailed BE, and to come back to BE after the couple is once again in a position to engage in positive exchanges. As noted above, even if BE fails to work with a couple, it often provides direction for further acceptance work. It is important, in doing this type of couple therapy, not to push a couple toward more change than they are ready for at the time. Although this kind of enforced change may work in the short run, it is less likely to result in long-term gains for the couple.

The following transcript demonstrates the initial presentation of BE early in therapy. Rather than having the couple generate the entire list on their own, the therapist (T) in this example helped Bill (B) and Nancy (N) come up with the first few items.

T: What are some small things that each of you could do that would make the other person's life easier, or more fun, or more enjoyable, or get more of whatever it is you're here to get. I just want to hear what your sense is of what you each could do to make a difference for the other.

N: Well, let Bill say something first. I've been doing all the talking so far, so let him say something.

B: Well, I'm looking for a small thing. And the way I state it might not sound small. I think a good starting place would be to stop collecting things.

T: No, no, no. Things that you can do for Nancy.

B: Oh, that I can do for her. Not that she's gonna do for me.

T: That's right.

B: Oh, I see.

T: We'll let Nancy worry about what she could do for you. What are you aware of that would help support Nancy.

B: Help around the house.

T: Specifically, when you say help around the house, what do you mean?

B: Whatever she thinks is necessary.

T: What would your guess be as to what she might see as useful?

B: Well, perhaps, prepare some meals. Perhaps help clean up the house.

T: Do you have a different sense of what a clean house is than Nancy? When you say clean up around the house, do you think you'd be able to agree on what cleaning up means?

B: No.

T: OK. So what would Nancy's version of cleaning up mean?

B: I'll vacuum. I'll do dishes, perhaps do the kitchen floor. I can't stop there though, because part of our disagreement is that I refuse to vacuum when I can't find the center of the floor. If some of that stuff was removed, I mean removed permanently, not moved to another spot, then I'd be glad to vacuum.

T: The thing that I want you to focus on at the moment is what would help Nancy. And it may be we need to talk about what vacuuming means. That sounds like it's still not too clear. We need to find a way of talking about it so that despite your not liking it or wanting to do it, you at least know what she would appreciate. Just so you know what it is. At the moment I just want to be clear about that so you don't get into an argument before you even get started. So, there's some stuff you could do around the house like doing dishes or vacuuming. Is there anything else? Remember that your not necessarily committing to doing any of these things, I'm just curious about what you could hypothetically do.

B: Be cooperative in doing what I can to help her with her job like forms, filing, or whatever's necessary.

T: And that means putting the forms in order, or in filing cabinets, or something like that?

B: Right.

T: What else?

B: At this point, I don't know. It seems like that's her major complaint.

T: OK. Well, I think that's a good start and it sounds like you're not sure what else. There may in fact be some other things but at the moment you're just not quite sure what they could be. Let's try the other side of this for a moment. What are you (*to Nancy*) aware of that you could do that would be caring, or supportive, or whatever Bill is looking for?

N: Well, I think he hit the nail on the head. If he would help with some of that, then I could do some of the other stuff that he wants.

T: Tell me what the other stuff is.

N: He wants me to be ready to go out with his friends, whether it's go to dinner, or play chess, or go out for a ride.

T: What else?

N: I'm sure he'd like to get the clothes put away where they're supposed to be and I haven't gotten to that.

T: OK. So right now what I have is going out with friends to dinner, or to play chess, or whatever; and the other item is getting the clothes put away. Can you think of anything else?

N: Well, if we got rid of some of the filing and stuff, that would eliminate a lot of clutter around the floors. A lot of my stuff is in boxes and not in the files, because I haven't had time to put it all in the files.

T: OK. One thing that you think Bill might appreciate is to have some of the files put away so it's in cabinets, rather than on the floors. Is that right?

N: Um hmm.

As you can see, the therapist spent a good deal of time during this session keeping the couple on task. It is usually much easier for a couple to talk about what they want the other person to do, or to stop doing, than to talk about what they themselves might do for their partner. If it seems like this might be the case with a particular couple, it is usually best to help them generate at least the first few items in session, in order to ensure that the purpose of the assignment is understood.

COMMUNICATION AND PROBLEM-SOLVING TRAINING

Many problems are exacerbated, if not outright caused, by how the two partners communicate about an issue, rather than by something inherent to the issue itself. Effective communication is a skill, and although most couples communicate well without any formal training, for distressed couples poor communication is often one of the primary reasons for their unhappiness. Poor communication is particularly destructive when couples are trying to negotiate some kind of change within their relationship.

Often when one partner wants some type of change from the other, his/her first response to any resistance is to resort to coercion. This may take the form of inducing guilt, crying, threatening, withholding affection, or even verbal and physical aggression. Usually the partner trying to get

change engages in one of these techniques until the other eventually capitulates. Unfortunately, coercion is very effective in that one partner is reinforced for being coercive by the compliance of the partner, and the other is reinforced for complying by no longer being subjected to the coercive behavior. The use of coercion within a relationship, however, almost always leads to the escalation of conflict, because more and more extreme forms of coercion become necessary to achieve a similar result (Patterson & Hops, 1972). It is through just such destructive patterns that two people who were initially in love can become as polarized as opposing armies.

Communication and problem-solving training (CPT) is designed to help couples learn the skills necessary for discussing important issues and negotiating changes in their relationship without resorting to modes of communication that are likely to destroy their relationship. Unlike BE, CPT is not designed to promote immediate change within the relationship, but to provide couples with the necessary skills to deal with relationship problems on their own after therapy has concluded. In other words, in conjunction with emotional acceptance work, CPT teaches couples how to function as their own therapist. Furthermore, the couple is taught how to negotiate positive change in the relationship effectively without resorting to destructive coercion techniques. The focus in CPT is not so much on the content of the couple's communication as on the process through which they attempt to express their needs. Through improving this process, CPT works to prevent deterioration of the relationship in the future and to promote positive growth following the termination of therapy. Initially CPT is taught in relation to the couple's current problems; however, the goal is to teach the couple effective skills that they can use throughout the future course of their relationship. Nevertheless, it is important to restate that although change is promoted wherever it may be possible, partners in a relationship will never be able to change completely in accordance with each other's wishes. Therefore, it remains essential to the overall success of therapy that CPT take place within the context of promoting acceptance.

Communication Training

Communication training (CT) is presented to the couple as a means of learning more effective ways of talking about conflict. It is explained that with the proper skills in place, they will be able to communicate more openly and consistently about their relationship. They are told that this will serve not only to decrease the likelihood that issues will sit and stew into major blow-ups, but to increase the level of intimacy within the relationship in general.

Initial training takes place in session, under the watchful eye of the therapist. Most couples are being taught to communicate in a way that is far different from what they are used to, and they are prone to slip into old patterns. The first step in CT involves instructing the couple in the general type of communication that the therapist is advocating. The destructive consequences of blaming and criticizing are discussed and the couple is taught how to keep the focus of what they say on themselves without blaming or criticizing their partner. Furthermore, in order to continue promoting acceptance, the couple is instructed to talk about the soft emotions underlying whatever issue is currently troubling them and to refrain from criticizing each other for characteristic emotional reactions.

Double-checking, or paraphrasing, is taught as a means of ensuring that neither partner is misread during important conversations. Often one of the main communication mistakes that couples make is mind reading, or jumping to conclusions about what their partner "really meant" by what he/she said. Paraphrasing functions to slow down the couple's interaction and to lessen the potential for unintended miscommunication.

The second step in CT involves having the couple engage in practice conversations. Focusing on the self, avoiding blaming and criticizing, expressing soft emotions, and paraphrasing are presented as the "rules" for these practice conversations. After initial instruction and some demonstration of these skills, a recent negative interaction is chosen for the couple to talk about in session. The couple is instructed to discuss how they each experienced the incident and how they each currently feel about it. Trying to follow all the rules of CT may seem artificial to the couple at first; therefore, the IBCT therapist should discuss this potential awkwardness prior to the first practice, explaining that the rules of CT will become more natural with continued use. During the first few practice conversations, the clinician usually has to interrupt quite often in order to either remind the couple to paraphrase or stop them from blaming or criticizing.

The third step in CT is to provide feedback. After each practice conversation, the exercise should be thoroughly debriefed with the couple, attending to the effects of focusing on oneself, not blaming, paraphrasing, and sharing softer emotions. Feedback is given as to the areas in which the couple is doing well, as well as on what they might do to improve even more. These exercises may continue for several sessions depending on the needs of the individual couple. When the therapist is confident in the couple's skills, practicing communication can be assigned as homework.

Problem-Solving Training

It is often the little, everyday difficulties that can do the most damage to a couple's relationship. Issues around doing the household chores, whether and how to discipline the children, or whose parents to spend which holidays with can lead to feelings of resentment and anger that eventually permeate the entire relationship. Arguments around these daily hassles often grow to enormous proportions, and at times even result in a couple's separation. More often than not, what does the most damage is not the issue itself but rather how the couple attempts to resolve the issue. Often such arguments start out with one partner blaming, accusing, or somehow berating the character of the other, while simultaneously avoiding any responsibility him/herself. The partner, in turn, becomes defensive and angry and usually engages in counterblaming, and character assault. Soon an issue as simple as cleaning off the dinner table has become an argument between a "lazy, irresponsible monster" and a "selfish, unloving shrew."

Problem-solving training (PT) teaches couples concrete strategies for dealing with the types of instrumental problems that invariably crop up over the course of a relationship. Problem-solving strategies are designed specifically to promote change and are used only in those circumstances where change is believed to be possible through skilled negotiation. Problem solving is not recommended for conflicts over issues involving attitudes, feeling, desires, or predilections. These types of problems are not usually solvable through the use of simple negotiation strategies and are instead treated using emotional acceptance strategies. For example, issues such as one partner's wanting the other to like his/her parents or to enjoy going out more are not readily resolved through negotiation. One cannot simply agree to like or enjoy something. Such feelings must be accepted, and the couple must decide whether their relationship can withstand these things not changing.

However, with the couple's more instrumental, although often equally destructive, problems, PT is typically the most effective strategy. PT teaches couples a series of formal steps to follow when negotiating a solution to a problem. First, couples are taught to make a distinction between problem definition and problem solution. During problem definition, the goal is simply to arrive at a clear, specific statement of the situation. The couple is instructed to proceed to the problem solution phase only after a clear definition of the problem has been agreed on. Couples are directed during this phase to stick with the problem as it has been defined and not to return to the problem definition phase. The goal of the problem solution phase is for the couple to arrive at a decision about how best to deal with the problem at hand. The clear distinction between problem definition and problem solution is emphasized because couples often try to solve problems that are vague and ambiguous. Without a clear conception of the problem, clear solutions are rarely possible. A distinct problem definition phase fosters clear communication and ensures that the problem is clearly understood by both partners.

General Guidelines

There are four primary guidelines facilitating the success of PT. First, couples should discuss only one problem at a time. During arguments, couples are prone to bring up several grievances in rapid succession, virtually precluding the effective resolution of any of them. During problem solving, however, couples are taught to focus on one specific problem at a time, fully resolving that problem before moving on to any other. Through such guidelines couples are taught to differentiate between simple arguing and effective problem solving.

Second, couples are encouraged to paraphrase their partner's statements in order to ensure that what he/she has said was properly understood. This helps avoid the damaging effects that often result from negative mind reading and protracted miscommunication. Furthermore, it increases the likelihood that both partners will spend at least some time considering each other's position.

Third, couples are asked to avoid inferring malevolent intentions from their partner's behavior. Such assumptions require the partner to defend him/herself, and thus generally lead to arguing rather than effective problem solving. The focus of PT should stay on public, instrumental behavior, because this is behavior that can more easily be changed through negotiation. Motivations, intentions, and other such private behavior are simply not within the domain of PT and should be dealt with instead using more acceptance-oriented techniques.

Finally, couples are instructed to avoid engaging in aversive verbal and nonverbal exchanges during problem-solving sessions. If partners are angry with each other, and thus not sufficiently collaborative, the focus of therapy should return to emotional acceptance. PT can be reinstituted once the couple has achieved the necessary degree of collaboration.

Problem Definition

Distressed couples usually bring up problems in the form of complaints directed at the other partner. PT teaches couples a series of specific steps to follow when defining a problem. First, partners are taught to express appreciation, affection, and understanding for their partner before presenting the problem itself. This expression helps lessen the likelihood that the other person will become defensive, and reminds both partners of some positive aspect of their relationship. For example, rather than saying "Where the hell were you," a partner is taught to start off by saying something such as "I know that you work hard, and sometimes need to stay late, but I miss you when you stay late so often." Distressed couples are particularly prone to tracking the negative, and ignoring the positive, aspects of their relationship. By beginning the problem-solving session with an expression of appreciation, couples are more likely to maintain a spirit of collaboration.

Following the expression of appreciation, the next step involves defining the problem as specifically as possible. Vague problem formulations hinder effective problem solving. Rather than state the situation in general terms, the couple is taught to specify the distinct behavior and circumstances that define the problem. For example, rather than stating that the partner never cleans up around the house, the problem could be defined as wanting the partner to help out more with the evening meals. Specifically defined problems are usually easier to solve and avoid miscommunication between partners.

In the spirit of continued fostering of emotional acceptance, partners are instructed to express their feelings, paying particular attention to their softer emotions. If one partner can say that spending so much time at work makes him feel lonely and unloved, the other is less likely to feel attacked and more likely to sympathize with his feelings. It is often hard for partners to talk about even simple problems in their relationship without feeling accused or being critical. Fully understanding each other's feelings helps prevent the discussion from becoming a full-blown clash of wills, with each partner merely trying to avoid being controlled by the other.

The final step in problem definition is for both partners to acknowledge their respective role in perpetuating the problem. This is usually hard for couples practiced in avoiding blame. However, acknowledging the part each plays in the problem is important both for the person presenting the problem and for the person hearing it. For the partner stating the problem, considering how he/she might be contributing to

the problem alleviates feelings of victimization and lessens the tendency to consider the partner's position unreasonable. The partner hearing about the problem is less likely to feel blamed, and more likely to compromise, if the partner presenting the problem does not avoid all responsibility for it. For the partner hearing the problem, admitting that he/she does, or doesn't do, the specific thing the partner is upset about intercepts a natural tendency to justify his/her behavior, rather than simply accepting that the partner has a complaint. However, it should be emphasized that accepting the partner's complaint does not commit the receiver to changing his/her behavior. The only issue at this point should be clearly defining the problem.

Problem Solution

Once the problem has been defined, and as much as possible has been done to foster collaboration, steps are laid out for arriving at a workable solution. The first of these steps is called brainstorming, and the goal is to come up with as many different solutions to the problem as possible. Brainstorming can often be quite playful, and toward this end the couple is told that all solutions, even impossible or silly ones, should be suggested. They are also told that there will be plenty of time later to work out which solutions are more viable than others. No evaluative comments are allowed at this stage so that each partner feels as free as possible to offer every solution he/she can think of. All suggestions are written down for later consideration.

The following transcript is an example of how brainstorming usually proceeds. Steve, the husband in this couple, traveled a great deal as part of his job, and Steve (S) and Jean (J) and therapist (T) were brainstorming solutions for how best to balance household chores and recreation when he is home.

T: OK, so the idea is that when you brainstorm, you just mention as many possible solutions as you can think of without evaluating them in any way. The idea is to generate ideas, and not censor yourselves. Even if an idea seems completely absurd, you should throw it in.

And at the end of brainstorming you'll have a list of possible solutions, and then you go through them, and eliminate the ones that don't make sense, and keep the ones that do. I'll write them down. Can I participate as well?

S: Sure.

T: Actually, you (*to Steve*) already suggested one, which was sit down and prioritize how to spend time.

S: The other obvious one is to quit my job and become independently wealthy.

T: Quit job.

J: This is supposed to be serious.

T: Oh no. It doesn't have to be.

J: We should get rid of the computer then.

T: OK, get rid of computer.

S: We could get rid of the kids too.

T: OK, get rid of kids.

J: No, be serious. I have a real serious one. Have the oil changed in the car at Jiffy Lube, instead of Steve trying to do it, and for me to remember to do that when he's gone.

S: (*Laughs*)

T: It seems to me that one way of phrasing that, that would make it more general, is to farm out things to other people.

J: Oh, but I think we have to itemize each one, otherwise it doesn't . . .

T: For the purposes of brainstorming, I think we can just get the concept down on paper. Then when we go to the agreement phase, if you'd like, you can itemize. But if you're talking about preserving time, farming out things to experts would apply not only to the car, but to other things as well. We aren't evaluating these ideas at this point. We're just writing them down.

S: We could have a meeting when I get home, or weekly, to define and prioritize projects around the house. They can involve kids, or changing the oil, or whatever.

T: So in other words, either after you get back from a trip, or on some regular basis, you'd sit down, and you'd look at the time you have left until the next trip, and then sort of block it out.

S: Block it out. Say, well, you need to paint the rail on the deck, and mow the lawn.

J: I think another thing would be for me to try to take over things like the insurance stuff, and do as much of that kind of thing as possible while he's gone.

T: Do some of the . . . do we call this scut work?

J: Insurance work.

S: High-level pain-in-the-ass work.

T: OK, let's call it pain-in-the-ass work. Jean will do some of the pain in the ass work while Steve is away.

J: And that Steve try when he's sitting in a hotel room, to take stuff that he could do while he's just sitting there.

T: Steve take pain-in-the-ass work with him on trips. OK, you know there are some creative possibilities in here, but let's hear from you (*to Steve*) a little bit too. I want you to be part of the brainstorming.

S: I like everything she said. I would like to prioritize . . .

J: (*Laughs*) Back to that again.

As you can see, brainstorming can be a fairly lighthearted exercise as well as being productive. As in this example, one partner sometimes comes up with more suggestions than the other; therefore it is important for the therapist to make sure that both partners contribute all they can to the list.

Following brainstorming, the next step is for the couple to go over the list marking out those solutions that are obviously just silly, or that do not adequately address the problem. Both partners have to agree before an item is marked out. If either partner thinks an item might be a good solution, it is kept on the list for later negotiation.

Deriving a Change Agreement

During this stage the pruning of the list continues. Each item is reviewed one at a time, and each partner is given an opportunity to discuss the item's pros and cons. Couples are encouraged to reflect what their partner has said about an item, in order to ensure that each understands the position of the other in as sympathetic a light as possible.

During the last passage through the list, a final decision is made about each of the remaining items. An item can be marked out if it is agreed to be too costly, or it can be modified or reworked as long as both partners agree to the changes. Items can also be skipped for later consideration, or accepted as a whole or in part.

The Change Agreement

Any solutions that are still questionable at this point are considered again until some compromise is worked out or the item is eliminated. The remaining items on the list are used to formulate a viable solution to the problem. This agreement is then written down, and both partners are asked to sign it. The final step is to discuss any foreseeable problems that might interfere with the agreement, and to work out strategies for dealing with each of them. The couple is then encouraged to post the agreement where they can both see it, and a date is agreed on for its review. During each of the next few sessions the therapist checks to see how the agreement is working out and encourages the couple to bring it in for renegotiation if either spouse feels dissatisfied.

The first few attempts to use these problem-solving techniques occur in session, under the close supervision of the therapist. It is often very hard for couples to adhere to the rules of PT, and the therapist must spend a good deal of time with the couple teaching them the proper techniques. Problem solving may at first seem too artificial to the couple, but with time and practice, they will come to see it as a more useful and less destructive way of dealing with their instrumental problems. Again, it is expected that once the couple learns these skills they will be able to implement them on their own in the future.

CONCLUSION

In this chapter we have attempted to present the latest developments in the area of BCT. These developments have been a product of both concern for those couples whom tra-

ditional BCT was unable to help, as well as a return to the theoretical roots of radical behaviorism. A shift in emphasis from form to function, as well as an emphasis on the broader contextual factors within which couples' relationships evolve, has led to the development of an approach to couple therapy free from the constraints of traditional definitions of change. This has, in turn, allowed us to promote change not only of overt behavior but of the emotional contexts that underlie and influence a couple's relationship. The integration of strategies designed to promote the kind of change we call acceptance with the more traditional strategies of BCT, we believe, is a considerable step forward in the evolution of couple therapy.

The strategies proposed in this chapter show excellent promise as powerful interventions for distressed couples seeking therapy. At this point, we are only beginning rigorous empirical investigation of the newer strategies; however, pilot work to date is very encouraging. It is certain that the development of these techniques is not the final answer to all the problems of couple therapy; however, it is equally certain that IBCT will continue to evolve, through both research and practice, toward increasingly better methods for the treatment of couple's distress.

REFERENCES

Baucom, D. H., & Hoffman, J. A. (1986). The effectiveness of marital therapy: Current status and applications to the clinical setting. In N. S. Jacobson & A. S. Gurman (Eds.), *Clinical handbook of marital therapy* (pp. 597–620). New York: Guilford Press.

Christensen, A., Jacobson, N. S., & Babcock, J. C. (in press). Integrative behavioral couples therapy. In N. S. Jacobson & A. S. Gurman (Eds.), *Clinical handbook of marital therapy* (2nd ed.). New York: Guilford Press.

Ferster, C. B. (1967). Arbitrary and natural reinforcement. *Psychological Record, 22,* 1–16.

Gurman, A. S., Kniskern, D. P., & Pinsof, W. M. (1986). Research on the process and outcome of marital and family therapy. In S. L. Garfield & A. E. Bergin (Eds.), *Handbook of psychotherapy and behavior change* (3rd ed.) (pp. 565–624). New York: Wiley.

Hahlweg, K., Schindler, L., Revenstorf, D., & Brengelmann, J. C. (1984). The Munich marital therapy study. In K. Hahlweg & N. S. Jacobson (Eds.), *Marital interaction: Analysis and modification* (pp. 3–26). New York: Guilford Press.

Hayes, S. C. (1987). A contextual approach to therapeutic change. In N. S. Jacobson (Ed.), *Psychotherapists in clinical practice: Cognitive and behavioral perspectives* (pp. 327–387). New York: Guilford Press.

Hayes, S. C. (1989). *Rule-governed behavior: Cognition, contingencies, and instructional control.* New York: Plenum Press.

Jacobson, N. S. (1978). A review of the research on the effectiveness of marital therapy. In T. J. Paolino & B. S. McCrady (Eds.), *Marriage and marital therapy: Psychoanalytic, behavioral, and systems theory perspectives* (pp. 395–444). New York: Brunner/Mazel.

Jacobson, N. S. (1984). A component analysis of behavioral marital therapy: The relative effectiveness of behavior exchange and problem solving training. *Journal of Consulting and Clinical Psychology, 52,* 295–305.

Jacobson, N. S. (1992). Behavioral couple therapy: A new beginning. *Behavior Therapy, 23,* 493–506.

Jacobson, N. S., & Christensen, A. (in press). *Couple therapy: An integrative approach.* New York: Norton.

Jacobson, N. S., Follette, W. C., & Pagel, M. (1986). Predicting who will benefit from behavioral marital therapy. *Journal of Consulting and Clinical Psychology, 54,* 518–522.

Jacobson, N. S., Schmaling, K. B., Holtzworth-Munroe, A. (1987). Component analysis of behavioral marital therapy: Two-year follow-up and prediction of relapse. *Journal of Marital and Family Therapy, 13,* 187–195.

Patterson, G. R., & Hops H. (1972). Coercion, a game for two: Intervention techniques for marital conflict. In R. E. Ulrich & P. Mounjoy (Eds.), *The experimental analysis of social behavior* (pp. 424–440). New York: Appleton.

Skinner, B. F. (1974). *About behaviorism.* New York: Knopf.

Snyder, D. K. (1979). Multidimensional assessment of marital satisfaction. *Journal of Marriage and the Family, 41,* 813–823.

Spanier, G. B. (1976). Measuring dyadic adjustment: New scales for assessing the quality of marriage and similar dyads. *Journal of Marriage and the Family, 38,* 15–28.

Straus, M. A. (1979). Measuring intrafamily conflict and violence: The conflict tactics (CT) scales. *Journal of Marriage and the Family, 41,* 75–88.

Weiss, R. L., & Birchler, G. R. (1975). *Areas of change.* Unpublished manuscript, University of Oregon, Eugene.

Weiss, R. L., & Cerreto, M. C. (1980). The marital status inventory: Development of a measure of dissolution potential. *American Journal of Family Therapy, 8,* 80–85.

AUTHOR INDEX

SUBJECT INDEX